FOUNDATIONS
OF BUSINESS

3E

W9-BPL-437

William M. Pride
Texas A&M University

Robert J. Hughes
Dallas County Community Colleges

Jack R. Kapoor
College of DuPage

SOUTH-WESTERN
CENGAGE Learning

Australia • Brazil • Japan • Korea • Mexico • Singapore • Spain • United Kingdom • United States

SOUTH-WESTERN
CENGAGE Learning

Foundations of Business, Third edition
William M. Pride, Robert J. Hughes, Jack R. Kapoor

Vice President of Editorial, Business: Jack W. Calhoun

Publisher: Erin Joyner

Acquisitions Editor: Jason Fremder

Managing Developmental Editor: Joanne Dauksewicz

Editorial Assistant: Meghan Fischer

Marketing Manager: Michelle Lockard

Content Project Manager: Darrell Frye

Media Editor: Kristin Meere

Manufacturing Planner: Ron Montgomery

Sr. Marketing Communications Manager: Sarah Greber

Production Service: MPS Limited, a Macmillan Company

Sr. Art Director: Stacy Jenkins Shirley

Internal and Cover Designer: KeDesign

Cover Image: ©Artic-Images/Getty

Rights Acquisitions Specialist (text): Sam A. Marshall

Rights Acquisitions Specialist (image): Deanna Ettinger

Library of Congress Control Number: 2011939830

ISBN-13: 978-1-111-58015-5

ISBN-10: 1-111-58015-4

South-Western
5191 Natorp Boulevard
Mason, OH 45040
USA

Cengage Learning products are represented in Canada by Nelson Education, Ltd.

For your course and learning solutions, visit **www.cengage.com**

Purchase any of our products at your local college store or at our preferred online store **www.cengagebrain.com**

Printed in the United States of America
1 2 3 4 5 6 7 15 14 13 12 11

To Nancy, Allen, Mike, Ashley, and Charlie Pride
To my wife Peggy and to my mother Barbara Hughes
To my wife Theresa; my children Karen, Kathryn, and Dave; and in memory of my parents
Ram and Sheela Kapoor

BRIEF CONTENTS

PART 1 THE ENVIRONMENT OF BUSINESS 1

Chapter 1 Exploring the World of Business and Economics 2
Chapter 2 Being Ethical and Socially Responsible 34
Chapter 3 Exploring Global Business 67

PART 2 BUSINESS OWNERSHIP AND ENTREPRENEURSHIP 102

Chapter 4 Choosing a Form of Business Ownership 103
Chapter 5 Small Business, Entrepreneurship, and Franchises 131

PART 3 MANAGEMENT AND ORGANIZATION 162

Chapter 6 Understanding the Management Process 163
Chapter 7 Creating a Flexible Organization 188
Chapter 8 Producing Quality Goods and Services 210

PART 4 HUMAN RESOURCES 240

Chapter 9 Attracting and Retaining the Best Employees 241
Chapter 10 Motivating and Satisfying Employees and Teams 270

PART 5 MARKETING 302

Chapter 11 Building Customer Relationships Through Effective Marketing 303
Chapter 12 Creating and Pricing Products that Satisfy Customers 330
Chapter 13 Distributing and Promoting Products 366

PART 6 MANAGING INFORMATION, ACCOUNTING, AND FINANCE 405

Chapter 14 Understanding Information and e-Business 406
Chapter 15 Using Accounting Information 439
Chapter 16 Mastering Financial Management 468

Notes N-1
Answer Key AK-1
Glossary G-1
Name Index NI-1
Subject Index SI-1

The following appendices appear on the companion site www.cengagebrain.com

Appendix A: Understanding Personal Finances and Investments A-1
Appendix B: Careers in Business B-1
Appendix C: Enhancing Union-Management Relations C-1
Appendix D: Risk Management and Insurance D-1
Appendix E: Business Law, Regulation, and Taxation E-1

© Laurent davoust/iStockphoto 12228983

CONTENTS

PART 1 THE ENVIRONMENT OF BUSINESS 1

CHAPTER 1: EXPLORING THE WORLD OF BUSINESS AND ECONOMICS 2

→ *Inside Business:* The Walt Disney Company's Script for Blockbuster Business Results 3

Your Future in the Changing World of Business 4
Why Study Business?, 5

Career Success: Clicking Your Career into High Gear 6

Spotlight: How Important Are Employee Benefits? 7
Special Note to Students, 8

Business: A Definition 10
The Organized Effort of Individuals, 10 • Satisfying Needs, 10 • Business Profit, 11

Types of Economic Systems 12
Capitalism, 13 • Capitalism in the United States, 14 • Command Economies, 16

Measuring Economic Performance 17
The Importance of Productivity in the Global Marketplace, 17 • Important Economic Indicators that Measure a Nation's Economy, 18

The Business Cycle 20

Types of Competition 21
Perfect Competition, 21 • Monopolistic Competition, 23 • Oligopoly, 23 • Monopoly, 24

American Business Today 24
Early Business Development, 24 • Business Development in the 1900s, 25 • A New Century: 2000 and Beyond, 26

Entrepreneurial Success: Meet Scott Heiferman, Meetup Entrepreneur 26
The Current Business Environment, 27

Sustain the Planet: Avon Says: "Hello Green Tomorrow" 27
The Challenges Ahead, 28

Summary 29
Key Terms 30
Discussion Questions 30
Test Yourself 31
Video Case: Entertainment Means Profits for Nederlander Concerts 32
Building Skills for Career Success 33

CHAPTER 2: BEING ETHICAL AND SOCIALLY RESPONSIBLE 34

→ *Inside Business:* Eco-Friendly Cars Become Big Business 35

Business Ethics Defined 36

Ethical Issues 36
Fairness and Honesty, 37 • Organizational Relationships, 37 • Conflict of Interest, 38 • Communications, 38

Factors Affecting Ethical Behavior 38
Individual Factors Affecting Ethics, 38 • Social Factors Affecting Ethics, 39

Ethical Challenges & Successful Solutions: Green or Greenwashing? 39
"Opportunity" as a Factor Affecting Ethics 40

Encouraging Ethical Behavior 40
Government's Role in Encouraging Ethics, 40 • Trade Associations' Role in Encouraging Ethics, 41 • Individual Companies' Role in Encouraging Ethics, 41

Social Responsibility 44

Going for Success: American Express "Crowdsources" Philanthropy 46

The Evolution of Social Responsibility in Business 47
Historical Evolution of Business Social Responsibility, 47

Two Views of Social Responsibility 49
The Economic Model, 49 • The Socioeconomic Model, 49 • The Pros and Cons of Social Responsibility, 49

Sustain the Planet: Sustainability 50

Consumerism 51
The Six Basic Rights of Consumers, 51 • Major Consumerism Forces, 52

Employment Practices 54
Affirmative Action Programs, 54 • Training Programs for the Hard-Core Unemployed, 55

Concern for the Environment 56
Effects of Environmental Legislation, 57

Spotlight: Recession and Responsibility 58
Who Should Pay for a Clean Environment?, 60

Implementing a Program of Social Responsibility 60
Developing a Program of Social Responsibility, 60 • Funding the Program, 61

Summary 62
Key Terms 63
Discussion Questions 63
Test Yourself 63
Video Case: Scholfield Honda—Going Green with Honda 65
Building Skills for Career Success 65

CHAPTER 3: EXPLORING GLOBAL BUSINESS 67

→ *Inside Business:* PepsiCo Gobbles Up Growth in Global Markets 68

The Basis for International Business 69
 Absolute and Comparative Advantage, 69 • Exporting and Importing, 70

Restrictions to International Business 71
 Types of Trade Restrictions, 72 • Reasons for Trade Restrictions, 74 • Reasons Against Trade Restrictions, 75

The Extent of International Business 75
 The World Economic Outlook for Trade, 76

Career Success: Today's Global Career Path 78

International Trade Agreements 79
 The General Agreement on Tariffs and Trade and the World Trade Organization, 79

Spotlight: Leading Exporters in World Merchandise Trade, 2009 79

 World Trade and Global Economic Crisis, 81 • International Economic Organizations Working to Foster Trade, 81

Methods of Entering International Business 84
 Licensing, 84 • Exporting, 85

Going for Success: LEGO Builds on Licensing for Global Growth 85
 Joint Ventures, 87 • Totally Owned Facilities, 87 • Strategic Alliances, 87 • Trading Companies, 88 • Countertrade, 88 • Multinational Firms, 88

Sources of Export Assistance 90

Financing International Business 90
 The Export-Import Bank of the United States, 91 • Multilateral Development Banks, 91

Sustain the Planet: Selling Eco-Friendly Goods, Services, and Technologies 91
 The International Monetary Fund, 92

Summary 92
Key Terms 93
Discussion Questions 93
Test Yourself 94
Video Case: Evo: Creatively Exceeding Customer Expectations Here and Abroad 95
Building Skills for Career Success 96
 Running a Business: Part 1: Let's Go Get a Graeter's! 97
 Building a Business Plan: Part 1 99

PART 2 BUSINESS OWNERSHIP AND ENTREPRENEURSHIP 102

CHAPTER 4: CHOOSING A FORM OF BUSINESS OWNERSHIP 103

→ *Inside Business:* Raising Cane's Serves Up Small Business Success 104

Sole Proprietorships 105
 Advantages of Sole Proprietorships, 105 • Disadvantages of Sole Proprietorships, 107

Entrepreneurial Success: Student Business Incubators 108
 Beyond the Sole Proprietorship, 108

Partnerships 108
 Types of Partners, 109

Social Media: Going Social with SCORE 109
 The Partnership Agreement, 110 • Advantages of Partnerships, 111 • Disadvantages of Partnerships, 112 • Beyond the Partnership, 112

Corporations 113
 Corporate Ownership, 113 • Forming a Corporation, 114 • Corporate Structure, 116 • Advantages of Corporations, 116 • Disadvantages of Corporations, 117

Spotlight: Business Profits 117

Special Types of Business Ownership 119
 S-Corporations, 119 • Limited-Liability Companies, 119 • Not-for-Profit Corporations, 120

Going for Success: Growth through Global Joint Ventures 121

Joint Ventures and Syndicates 121
 Joint Ventures, 121 • Syndicates, 122

Corporate Growth 122
 Growth from Within, 122 • Growth Through Mergers and Acquisitions, 122 • Merger and Acquisition Trends During an Economic Crisis, 124

Summary 125
Key Terms 126
Discussion Questions 126
Test Yourself 127
Video Case: Annie's Homegrown: A Corporation with Entrepreneurial Spirit 128
Building Skills for Career Success 129

CHAPTER 5: SMALL BUSINESS, ENTREPRENEURSHIP, AND FRANCHISES 131

→ *Inside Business:* Small Businesses Get Boost from Big Business 132

Small Business: A Profile 133
 The Small-Business Sector, 133 • Industries that Attract Small Businesses, 134

The People in Small Businesses: The Entrepreneurs 135
 Characteristics of Entrepreneurs, 135 • Other Personal Factors, 136 • Motivation, 136 • Women as Small-Business Owners, 136

Career Success: Looking for an Internship? Think Small 137
 Teenagers as Small-Business Owners, 137 • Why Some Entrepreneurs and Small Businesses Fail, 138

The Importance of Small Businesses in Our Economy 139

Providing Technical Innovation, 139 • Providing Employment, 140 • Providing Competition, 141 • Filling Needs of Society and Other Businesses, 141

The Pros and Cons of Smallness 141
Advantages of Small Business, 141

Sustain the Planet: Tips from the Environmental Protection Agency 142
Disadvantages of Small Business, 142 • Developing a Business Plan, 142 • Components of a Business Plan, 143

Entrepreneurial Success: Prep Your Elevator Pitch 144

The Small Business Administration 145
SBA Management Assistance, 145 • Help for Minority-Owned Small Businesses, 146 • SBA Financial Assistance, 148 • State of Small Business During the Recession, 149

Franchising 149
What Is Franchising?, 150 • Types of Franchising, 150

The Growth of Franchising 151
Are Franchises Successful?, 152 • Advantages of Franchising, 152 • Disadvantages of Franchising, 153 • Global Perspectives in Small Business, 154

Spotlight: SUBWAY's Foreign Franchising Around the World 154

Summary 155
Key Terms 156
Discussion Questions 156
Test Yourself 157
Video Case: Murray's Cheese: More Cheese Please 158
Building Skills for Career Success 159

Running a Business: Part 2: Graeter's: A Fourth-Generation Family Business 160
Building a Business Plan: Part 2 161

PART 3 MANAGEMENT AND ORGANIZATION 162

CHAPTER 6: UNDERSTANDING THE MANAGEMENT PROCESS 163

→ **Inside Business:** How H.J. Heinz Manages for a Healthy Company, People, and Planet 164

What Is Management? 165

Basic Management Functions 166
Planning, 167

Going for Success: Be Prepared with a Contingency Plan 170
Organizing the Enterprise, 170 • Leading and Motivating, 171 • Controlling Ongoing Activities, 171

Kinds of Managers 172
Levels of Management, 172 • Areas of Management Specialization, 173

Key Skills of Successful Managers 174
Conceptual Skills, 174

Career Success: First-time Manager? Avoid These Rookie Mistakes! 175
Analytic Skills, 175 • Interpersonal Skills, 175 • Technical Skills, 176 • Communication Skills, 176

Leadership 176
Formal and Informal Leadership, 177 • Styles of Leadership, 177

Spotlight: Executives Rank Men and Women Differently on Workplace Characteristics 177
Which Leadership Style Is the Best?, 178

Managerial Decision Making 178
Identifying the Problem or Opportunity, 179 • Generating Alternatives, 179

Social Media: Through Social Media, Do Workers Create Problems for Their Employers? 180
Selecting an Alternative, 180 • Implementing and Evaluating the Solution, 180

Managing Total Quality 181
Summary 182
Key Terms 183
Discussion Questions 183
Test Yourself 184

Video Case: L.L. Bean Relies on Its Core Values and Effective Leadership 185
Building Skills for Career Success 186

CHAPTER 7: CREATING A FLEXIBLE ORGANIZATION 188

→ **Inside Business:** Why Nokia Needed a New Structure 189

What Is an Organization? 190
Developing Organization Charts, 191 • Major Considerations for Organizing a Business, 192

Job Design 192
Job Specialization, 192 • The Rationale for Specialization, 192 • Alternatives to Job Specialization, 193

Departmentalization 193
By Function, 193 • By Product, 193 • By Location, 194 • By Customer, 194 • Combinations of Bases, 194

Delegation, Decentralization, and Centralization 195
Delegation of Authority, 195

Career Success: Your Green Career Path? 196
Decentralization of Authority, 196

The Span of Management 197
Wide and Narrow Spans of Management, 197 • Organizational Height, 197

Forms of Organizational Structure 198
The Line Structure, 198 • The Line-and-Staff Structure, 198

Sustain the Planet: Green Citizenship at General Electric 199
The Matrix Structure, 200 • The Network Structure, 201

Spotlight: Top-Ranked Barriers to Women in the Workplace 201

Corporate Culture 201

Entrepreneurial Success: Building Innovation and Involvement into the Corporate Culture 203

Committees and Task Forces 203

The Informal Organization and the Grapevine 204

Summary 205
Key Terms 206
Discussion Questions 206
Test Yourself 206

Video Case : At Numi Organic Tea, Teams and Organizational Culture Are Critical 208
Building Skills for Career Success 208

CHAPTER 8: PRODUCING QUALITY GOODS AND SERVICES 210

→ *Inside Business:* Unilever's Bold Plans for New Products, Greener Production 211

What Is Production? 212
How American Manufacturers Compete in the Global Marketplace, 212 • Careers in Operations Management, 213

The Conversion Process 214
Manufacturing Using a Conversion Process, 214

Ethical Challenges & Successful Solutions: The Ethics of Ecotourism Services 216

The Increasing Importance of Services 216
Planning Quality Services, 217 • Evaluating the Quality of a Firm's Services, 217

Sustain the Planet: Sustainable Manufacturing Initiative 217

Where Do New Products and Services Come From? 218
Research and Development, 218 • Product Extension and Refinement, 219

How Do Managers Plan Production? 219
Design Planning, 219 • Site Selection and Facilities Planning, 221 • Operational Planning, 223

Operations Control 224
Purchasing, 224 • Inventory Control, 225 • Scheduling, 226 • Quality Control, 226

Going for Success: Measuring Reliability by the Nines 228
Production Planning: A Summary, 229

Improving Productivity with Technology 229
Productivity Trends, 229 • Improving Productivity Growth Rates, 230

Spotlight: Productivity Growth Rates 230
The Impact of Computers and Robotics on Productivity, 231

Summary 233
Key Terms 234
Discussion Questions 234
Test Yourself 235
Video Case: Burton Snowboards' High-Quality Standards 236
Building Skills for Career Success 237

Running a Business: Part 3: Graeter's Leadership and Management Efforts Enhance Performance 238

Building a Business Plan: Part 3 239

PART 4 HUMAN RESOURCES 240

CHAPTER 9: ATTRACTING AND RETAINING THE BEST EMPLOYEES 241

→ *Inside Business:* Good Employees Keep Southwest Airlines on Growth Course 242

Human Resources Management: An Overview 243
HRM Activities, 243 • Responsibility for HRM, 243

Human Resources Planning 244
Forecasting Human Resources Demand, 244 • Forecasting Human Resources Supply, 244 • Matching Supply with Demand, 245

Cultural Diversity in Human Resources 245

Job Analysis 247

Recruiting, Selection, and Orientation 248
Recruiting, 248

Social Media: Salesforce.com's Social Recruiting Strategy 249
Selection, 249

Career Success: What Can a Career Coach Do for You? 250

Ethical Challenges & Successful Solutions: Tough Questions, Honest Answers 252
Orientation, 253

Compensation and Benefits 253

Spotlight: When Should Compensation and Benefits be Discussed with Job Applicants? 254
Compensation Decisions, 254 • Comparable Worth, 255 • Types of Compensation, 255 • Employee Benefits, 256

Training and Development 257
Analysis of Training Needs, 258 • Training and Development Methods, 258 • Evaluation of Training and Development, 258

Performance Appraisal 258
Common Evaluation Techniques, 259 • Performance Feedback, 260

The Legal Environment of HRM 261
National Labor Relations Act and Labor–Management Relations Act, 261 • Fair Labor Standards Act, 262 • Equal Pay Act, 262 • Civil Rights Acts, 263 • Age Discrimination in Employment Act, 263 • Occupational Safety and Health Act, 263 • Employee Retirement Income Security Act, 263 • Affirmative Action, 263 • Americans with Disabilities Act, 264

Summary 264
Key Terms 265
Discussion Questions 266
Test Yourself 266
Video Case: Whirlpool's Award-Winning Diversity Program Is Facilitated Through Employee Network 268
Building Skills for Career Success 268

CHAPTER 10: MOTIVATING AND SATISFYING EMPLOYEES AND TEAMS 270

→ *Inside Business:* How Google, Now Teenaged, Drives Employee Motivation 271

What Is Motivation? 272

Historical Perspectives on Motivation 272
Scientific Management, 272 • The Hawthorne Studies, 274 • Maslow's Hierarchy of Needs, 274 • Herzberg's Motivation–Hygiene Theory, 276 • Theory X and Theory Y, 277 • Theory Z, 278 • Reinforcement Theory, 278

Contemporary Views on Motivation 280
Equity Theory, 280 • Expectancy Theory, 280 • Goal-Setting Theory, 281

Key Motivation Techniques 282
Management by Objectives, 282 • Job Enrichment, 284

Entrepreneurial Success: Motivation Gives Bonobos a Competitive Edge 285
Behavior Modification, 285 • Flextime, 286 • Part-Time Work and Job Sharing, 286 • Telecommuting, 287

Spotlight: Motivation Factors 287

Career Success: Get Ready to Telecommute 288
Employee Empowerment, 288 • Employee Ownership, 289

Teams and Teamwork 289

Sustain the Planet: Good Green Fun 290
What Is a Team?, 290 • Types of Teams, 290 • Developing and Using Effective Teams, 292 • Roles Within a Team, 293 • Team Cohesiveness, 293 • Team Conflict and How to Resolve It, 293 • Benefits and Limitations of Teams, 294

Summary 294

Key Terms 295
Discussion Questions 296
Test Yourself 296
Video Case: At L.L. Bean, Everyone Is Family 298
Building Skills for Career Success 298

Running a Business: Part 4: Graeter's: Where Tenure Is "a Proud Number" 300

Building a Business Plan: Part 4 301

PART 5 MARKETING 302

CHAPTER 11: BUILDING CUSTOMER RELATIONSHIPS THROUGH EFFECTIVE MARKETING 303

→ *Inside Business:* Domino's Pizza Cooks Up Marketing Turnaround 304

Managing Customer Relationships 305

Utility: The Value Added by Marketing 306

The Marketing Concept 307
Evolution of the Marketing Concept, 307 • Implementing the Marketing Concept, 309

Career Success: Marketing Yourself via Webcam 309

Markets and Their Classification 310

Developing Marketing Strategies 310
Target Market Selection and Evaluation, 311 • Creating a Marketing Mix, 314 • Marketing Strategy and the Marketing Environment 315

Social Media: Online Videos Add Vitality to Marketing Mix 316

Developing a Marketing Plan 316

Market Measurement and Sales Forecasting 317

Spotlight: Most Promising Growth Opportunities in the Technology Industry 318

Marketing Information 318
Marketing Information Systems, 318 • Marketing Research, 318

Ethical Challenges & Successful Solutions: Limits to Online Privacy? 320
Using Technology to Gather and Analyze Marketing Information, 320

Types of Buying Behavior 322
Consumer Buying Behavior, 322 • Business Buying Behavior, 324

Summary 324
Key Terms 326
Discussion Questions 326
Test Yourself 326
Video Case: E*Trade Focuses on Building Long-Term Customer Relationships, Even from the Crib 328
Building Skills for Career Success 328

CHAPTER 12: CREATING AND PRICING PRODUCTS THAT SATISFY CUSTOMERS 330

→ *Inside Business:* E-Book Readers Battle On 331

Classification of Products 332

Consumer Product Classifications, 332 • Business Product Classifications, 333

The Product Life-Cycle 333
Stages of the Product Life-Cycle, 334 • Using the Product Life-Cycle, 336

Product Line and Product Mix 336

Managing the Product Mix 337
Managing Existing Products, 337 • Deleting Products, 338 • Developing New Products, 339 • Why Do Products Fail?, 341

Going for Success: Where Do Big Companies Get New Product Ideas? 341

Branding, Packaging, and Labeling 342
What Is a Brand?, 342 • Types of Brands, 342 • Benefits of Branding, 343

Social Media: Local Businesses Use Social Media to Build Brand Loyalty 344
Choosing and Protecting a Brand, 344 • Branding Strategies, 345 • Brand Extensions, 345 • Packaging, 346 • Labeling, 347

Pricing Products 348
The Meaning and Use of Price, 348 • Supply and Demand Affects Prices, 348 • Price and Non-Price Competition, 349 • Buyers' Perceptions of Price, 350

Pricing Objectives 350
Survival, 350 • Profit Maximization, 350 • Target Return on Investment, 351 • Market-Share Goals, 351 • Status-Quo Pricing, 351

Pricing Methods 351
Cost-Based Pricing, 351 • Demand-Based Pricing, 353 • Competition-Based Pricing, 353

Pricing Strategies 353
New-Product Pricing, 354 • Differential Pricing, 354

Entrepreneurial Success: New Day, New Deal 355
Psychological Pricing, 356 • Product-Line Pricing, 357 • Promotional Pricing, 358

Spotlight: Which Online Content Are People Willing to Pay for? 358

Pricing Business Products 358
Geographic Pricing, 359 • Transfer Pricing, 359 • Discounting, 359

Summary 360
Key Terms 361
Discussion Questions 362
Test Yourself 362
Video Case: From Artistic Roots, Blu Dot Styles Marketing Strategy 363
Building Skills for Career Success 364

CHAPTER 13: DISTRIBUTING AND PROMOTING PRODUCTS 366

→ *Inside Business:* Macy's Blends the Best of National and Local Marketing 367

Distribution Channels and Market Coverage 368
Commonly Used Distribution Channels, 368

Entrepreneurial Success: Furniture Store? That Used to Be Our Roller-Skating Rink! 369
Level of Market Coverage, 370

Partnering Through Supply-Chain Management 371

Marketing Intermediaries: Wholesalers 371
Wholesalers Provide Services to Retailers and Manufacturers, 372 ● Types of Wholesalers, 372

Marketing Intermediaries: Retailers 373
Types of Retail Stores, 373

Social Media: Nonstore Selling Gets Facebook Friendly 376
Types of Nonstore Selling, 376 ● Types of Shopping Centers, 378

Physical Distribution 379
Inventory Management, 379 ● Order Processing, 379 ● Warehousing, 380 ● Materials Handling, 380 ● Transportation, 380

What Is Integrated Marketing Communications? 382

The Promotion Mix: An Overview 383

Advertising 384

Types of Advertising by Purpose, 384 ● Major Steps in Developing an Advertising Campaign, 385

Spotlight: Internet Advertising on the Rise 385

Career Success: Marketing and Media Jobs Beyond *Mad Men* 388
Advertising Agencies, 388 ● Social and Legal Considerations in Advertising, 389

Personal Selling 389
Kinds of Salespersons, 389 ● The Personal-Selling Process, 390 ● Major Sales Management Tasks, 391

Sales Promotion 392
Sales Promotion Objectives, 392 ● Sales Promotion Methods, 392 ● Selection of Sales Promotion Methods, 392

Public Relations 394
Types of Public-Relations Tools, 394 ● Uses of Public Relations, 395

Summary 395
Key Terms 397
Discussion Questions 398
Test Yourself 398
Video Case: L.L.Bean Employs a Variety of Promotion Methods to Communicate with Customers 400
Building Skills for Career Success 400

Running a Business: Part 5: Graeter's Is "Synonymous with Ice Cream" 402

Building a Business Plan: Part 5 404

PART 6 MANAGING INFORMATION, ACCOUNTING, AND FINANCE 405

CHAPTER 14: UNDERSTANDING INFORMATION AND E-BUSINESS 406

→ *Inside Business:* How Mars Built My M&M's into a Sweet e-Business 407

How Can Information Reduce Risk When Making a Decision? 408
Information and Risk, 408 ● Information Rules, 409 ● The Difference Between Data and Information, 409 ● Knowledge Management, 410

What Is a Management Information System? 410
A Firm's Information Requirements, 410 ● Size and Complexity of the System, 412

How Do Employees Use a Management Information System? 412
Step 1: Collecting Data, 412 ● Step 2: Storing Data, 413 ● Step 3: Updating Data, 413 ● Step 4: Processing Data, 414 ● Step 5: Presenting Information, 414

Improving Productivity with the Help of Computers and Technology 415
Making Smart Decisions, 416 ● Helping Employees Communicate, 416 ● Assisting the Firm's Sales Force, 417

Entrepreneurial Success: Apps Become Big Business 418
Recruiting and Training Employees, 418 ● Telecommuting, Virtual Offices, and Technology, 418 ● Business Applications Software, 419

Sustain the Planet: The Green Grid 420

Using Computers and the Internet to Obtain Information 420
Computers, Software, the Internet, and Networks, 420

Spotlight: Top Two U.S. Web Sites 421
Accessing the Internet, 421 ● Creating Web Sites, 421

Defining e-Business 422
Organizing e-Business Resources, 422 ● Satisfying Needs Online, 422 ● Creating e-Business Profit, 424

Fundamental Models of e-Business 426
Business-to-Business (B2B) Model, 427 ● Business-to-Consumer (B2C) Model, 427

The Future of Computer Technology, the Internet, and e-Business 428
Internet Growth Potential, 428 ● Social Media, 429 ● Ethical and Legal Concerns, 429 ● Future Challenges for Computer Technology and e-Business, 430

Ethical Challenges & Successful Solutions: How Green Is Cloud Computing? 431

Summary 432
Key Terms 434
Discussion Questions 434
Test Yourself 435
Video Case: E*Trade Provides Information to Its e-Business Customers 436
Building Skills For Career Success 437

CHAPTER 15: USING ACCOUNTING INFORMATION 439

→ *Inside Business:* KPMG Helps Keep Businesses Running Smoothly 440

Why Accounting Information Is Important 441
Recent Accounting Scandals, 441 ● Why Audited Financial Statements Are Important, 442

Ethical Challenges & Successful Solutions: Who Audits Overseas Auditors? 443
Reform: The Sarbanes-Oxley Act of 2002, 443

Who Uses Accounting Information 444
The People Who Use Accounting Information, 444 ● Different Types of Accounting, 444 ● Careers in Accounting, 445

Spotlight: Accounting Careers Are Attracting More Students! 446

Career Success: More Accountants and Auditors Needed! 447

The Accounting Process 447
Steps in the Accounting Cycle, 447 ● The Accounting Equation, 448

The Balance Sheet 449
Assets, 450 ● Liabilities and Owners' Equity, 451

The Income Statement 452
Revenues, 452 ● Cost of Goods Sold, 453 ● Operating Expenses, 454 ● Net Income, 455

The Statement of Cash Flows 455

Evaluating Financial Statements 457
Using Accounting Information to Evaluate a Potential Investment, 457 ● Comparing Data with Other Firms' Data, 458 ● Profitability Ratios, 458 ● Short-Term Financial Ratios, 459

Social Media: The Big Four Go Social 459
Activity Ratios, 460 ● Debt-to-Owners'-Equity Ratio, 461 ● Northeast's Financial Ratios: A Summary, 461

Summary 462
Key Terms 464
Discussion Questions 464
Test Yourself 464
Video Case: Accounting Information Helps Level the Playing Field for the Little Guys 466
Building Skills for Career Success 467

CHAPTER 16: MASTERING FINANCIAL MANAGEMENT 468

→ ***Inside Business:*** General Motors Goes Public—Again 469

What Is Financial Management? 470
The Need for Financing, 470 ● The Need for Financial Management, 472 ● Careers in Finance, 473

Planning—The Basis of Sound Financial Management 474
Developing the Financial Plan, 474 ● Monitoring and Evaluating Financial Performance, 476

Financial Services Provided by Banks and Other Financial Institutions 477

Traditional Banking Services for Business Clients, 477 ● Why Has the Use of Credit Transactions Increased?, 478 ● Electronic Banking Services, 478

Social Media: Outsmart the Scam Artists 478
International Banking Services, 479

Sources of Short-Term Debt Financing 480
Sources of Unsecured Short-Term Financing, 480 ● Sources of Secured Short-Term Financing, 482 ● Factoring Accounts Receivable, 482 ● Cost Comparisons, 483

Sources of Equity Financing 483
Selling Stock, 483

Spotlight: The Roller Coaster Ride for IPOs 484

Going for Success: Who's Getting Venture Capital? 486
Retained Earnings, 486 ● Venture Capital and Private Placements, 487

Sources of Long-Term Debt Financing 487

Ethical Challenges & Successful Solutions: Banks as Eco-Cops? 488
Long-Term Loans, 489 ● Corporate Bonds, 489 ● Cost Comparisons, 491

Summary 492
Key Terms 493
Discussion Questions 493
Test Yourself 494
Video Case: Financial Planning Equals Profits for Nederlander Concerts 495
Building Skills for Career Success 496

Running a Business: Part 6: Graeter's Adds MIS and Financing to the Recipe 497

Building a Business Plan: Part 6 499

Notes N-1
Answer Key AK-1
Glossary G-1
Name Index NI-1
Subject Index SI-1

The following appendices appear on the companion site www.cengagebrain.com

Appendix A: Understanding Personal Finances and Investments A-1
Appendix B: Careers in Business B-1
Appendix C: Enhancing Union-Management Relations C-1
Appendix D: Risk Management and Insurance D-1
Appendix E: Business Law, Regulation, and Taxation E-1

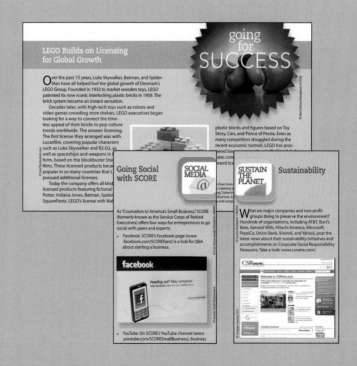

TAKE PRIDE IN YOUR
SUCCESS...
WITH NEW ENGAGING CONTENT

entrepreneurial SUCCESS

Student Business Incubators

Whether you're starting a new venture or expanding an existing company, you may be able to get expert help, office space, and even some funding without leaving your campus, if your school has a student business incubator. A growing number of colleges and universities are setting up incubators to help student entrepreneurs choose an appropriate form of business ownership and proceed to develop, test, implement, and refine their business ideas in a supportive environment.

The incubator at the University of Northern Iowa, for instance, invites student entrepreneurs to apply for a semester of on-campus assistance, including legal and accounting services, management training, and access to seed funds. Carlos Arguello was the first student entrepreneur to "graduate" from this incubator, working with his mother to successfully launch the Spanish-language newspaper *La Prensa* in northern Iowa.

At the University of Wisconsin-Madison, student entrepreneurs compete for six spaces in the on-campus incubator by submitting a written application and making a presentation to the Student Business Incubator Board. At the University of Michigan, the TechArb incubator houses up to 12 student-owned high-tech businesses at a time. One recent tenant was Mobil33t, which designed the iPhone app DoGood to encourage people to do a good deed every day. Can an incubator set you on the path toward entrepreneurial success?

Sources: Melissa Domsic, "East Lansing's The Hatch Gets Its First Student Tenant," *Lansing State Journal*, December 29, 2010, www.lansingstatejournal.com; Nathan Bomey, "University of Michigan Strikes Deal to Establish Permanent Student Business Incubator," AnnArbor.com, November 5, 2009, www.annarbor.com/business-review/university-of-michigan-strikes-deal-to-establish-permanent-student-business-incubator/; University of Wisconsin-Madison Student Business Incubator, www.asm.wisc.edu/sbi.html; University of Northern Iowa Student Business Incubator, www.bcs.uni.edu/jpec/sbi.htm.

« **NEW!** Each chapter contains **two new box features** reinforcing the text's success theme, including Career Success, Ethical Challenges and Successful Solutions, Entrepreneurial Success, and Going for Success.

NEW! All-new opening cases about real **business organizations** drive home the relevance of the chapter concepts.

NEW! A **Personal Applications feature** provides special student-centered examples and explanations that help you immediately grasp and retain the material. »

a shop's location, open a new store, or close an old one. Suppose that the sole proprietor of an appliance store finds that many customers now prefer to shop on Sunday afternoons. He or she can make an immediate change in business hours to take advantage of this information (provided that state laws allow such stores to open on Sunday). The manager of a store in a large corporate chain such as Best Buy Company may have to seek the approval of numerous managers and com-

Personal App Do you dream of being your own boss? If you become a sole proprietor, you'll have all the flexibility that comes with making your own decisions. But remember: Although you'll have the final say, you'll also be responsible if something goes wrong.

Disadvantages of Sole Proprietorships

The disadvantages of a sole proprietorship stem from the fact that these businesses are owned and often managed by one person. Some capable sole proprietors ex-

...with a dream. As a homebuilder, Shelley Reynolds, ...resident of Reynolds Signature Homes, has faced ...ges since the downturn in home sales that began ...go. In most areas of the United States, there are fewer homeowners that can qualify for home mortgages, which makes it hard for business owners like Reynolds to construct upscale homes and sell them for a profit.

SUSTAIN THE PLANET
Sustainability

What are major companies and non-profit groups doing to preserve the environment? Hundreds of organizations, including AT&T, Burt's Bees, General Mills, Hitachi America, Microsoft, PepsiCo, Union Bank, Vivendi, and Yahoo!, post the latest news about their sustainability initiatives and accomplishments on Corporate Social Responsibility Newswire. Take a look: www.csrwire.com/.

« **NEW! Sustain the Planet and Social Media mini-boxes** highlight the green movement and social media's impact on today's business world.

CSRwire

July 30, 2010

Welcome to CSRwire.com

TAKE PRIDE IN YOUR

SUCCESS...

WITH RELEVANT BUSINESS FEATURES

Whether it's the latest business developments or traditional strengths, **everywhere you look in Pride's _Foundations of Business_, 3e, you'll find SUCCESS,** with features such as:

« **_Why Should You Care?_** features begin each chapter to help you grasp the relevance of business in your life and guide you in your studies.

Why should you care?
There's a good chance that during your lifetime you will work for a business or

LEARNING OBJECTIVE
1 Understand what is meant by _business ethics._

Learning Objectives
What you will be able to do once you complete this chapter:

1 Understand what is meant by _business ethics._

2 Identify the types of ethical concerns that arise in the business world.

3 Discuss the factors that affect the level of ethical behavior in organizations.

4 Explain how ethical decision making can be encouraged.

5 Describe how our current views on the social responsibility of business have evolved.

6 Explain the two views on the social responsibility of business and understand

the arguments f
social responsib

7 Discuss the factor
consumer moven
results.

8 Analyze how present employment practices are being used to counteract past abuses.

9 Describe the major types of pollution, their causes, and their cures.

10 Identify the steps a business must take to implement a program of social responsibility.

34   Get Flashcards, Quizzes, Games, Crosswords, and more @ www.cengagebrain.com

BUSINESS ETHICS DEFINED

Ethics is the study of right and wrong and of the morality of the choices individuals make. An ethical decision or action is one that is "right" according to some standard of behavior. **Business ethics** is the application of moral standards to business situations. Recent court cases involving unethical behavior have helped to make business ethics a matter of public concern. In one such case, Copley Pharmaceutical, Inc., pled guilty to federal criminal charges (and paid a $10.65 million fine) for falsifying drug manufacturers' reports to the Food and Drug Administration. In another much-publicized case, lawsuits against tobacco companies have led to $246 billion in settlements, although there has been only one class-action lawsuit filed on behalf of all smokers. The case, _Engle v. R. J. Reynolds_, could cost tobacco companies an

« **_Learning Objectives_** throughout each chapter remind you of the core concepts under discussion.

Concept Checks at the end of each major **»** topic help you self-check your understanding of each important concept.

* Concept Check

☐ Explain the difference between an open corporation and a closed corporation.

☐ How is a domestic corporation different from a foreign corporation and an alien corporation?

☐ Outline the incorporation process, and describe the basic corporate structure.

☐ What rights do stockholders have?

Corpo
The org
a sole p
to grow
officers

BOARD
through
director
ers. In t
corpora
director
  Boa
Note: F
you can

TAKE PRIDE IN YOUR
SUCCESS...
WITH RELEVANT BUSINESS FEATURES

TEST YOURSELF

Matching Questions

1. _____ It is an association of two or more business owners.
2. _____ A distribution of earnings to the stockholders of a corporation.
3. _____ This type of ownership is the simplest type of business to start.
4. _____ A person who invests only money in a partnership.
5. _____ The concept of being personally responsible for all debts of a business.
6. _____ A business entity or artificial being with most of the legal rights of a person.
7. _____ A legal document that describes the purpose of the corporation.
8. _____ An offer to purchase the stock of a firm targeted for acquisition.
9. _____ A temporary association of individuals or firms organized to perform a specific task.
10. _____ A company chartered in a foreign country doing business in the United States.

a. alien corporation
b. articles of incorporation
c. syndicate
d. tender offer
e. vertical venture
f. limited partner
g. voluntary association
h. corpor...
i. divide...
j. partne...
k. sole p...
l. unlimi...

> « **Test Yourself** quizzes at the end of each chapter help you prepare for exams and gauge your mastery of key concepts and terminology.

The **Building a Business Plan** feature at » the end of each part walks you step-by-step through the preparation of a real business plan. It also coordinates with the Interactive Business Plan product, which is available as an online learning tool.

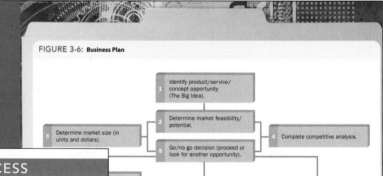

Building a Business Plan: Part 1

A *business plan* is a carefully constructed guide for a person starting a business. The purpose of a well-prepared business plan is to show how practical and attainable the entrepreneur's goals are. It also serves as a concise document that potential investors can examine to see if they would like to invest or assist in financing a new venture. A business plan should include the following 12 components:

- Introduction

business plan if you really want to open this type of business.

Now that you have decided on a specific type of business, it is time to begin the planning process. The goal for this part is to complete the introduction and benefits-to-the-community components of your business plan.

Before you begin, it is important to note that the business plan is not a document that is written and then set aside. It is a living document that an entrepreneur should

FIGURE 3-6: Business Plan

1. Identify product/service/concept opportunity (The Big Idea).
2. Determine market feasibility/potential.
3. Determine market size (in units and dollars).
4. Complete competitive analysis.
5. Go/no go decision (proceed or look for another opportunity).

BUILDING SKILLS FOR CAREER SUCCESS

1. Exploring the Internet

Arguments about mergers and acquisitions often come down to an evaluation of who benefits and by how much. Sometimes the benefits include access to new products, talented management, new customers, or new sources of capital. Often, the debate is complicated by the involvement of firms based in different countries.

The Internet is a fertile environment for information and discussion about mergers. The firms involved will provide their view about who will benefit and why it is either a good thing or not. Journalists will report facts and offer commentary as to how they see the future result of any merger, and of course, chat rooms located on the Web sites of many journals promote discussion about the issues.

Assignment

1. Using an Internet search engine such as Google or Yahoo!, locate two or three sites providing information about a recent merger (use a keyword such as *merger* or *acquisition*).

2. After examining these sites and reading journal articles, report information about the merger, such as the dollar value, the reasons behind the merger, and so forth.

3. Based on your assessment of the information you have read, do you think the merger is a good idea or not for the firms involved, the employees, the investors, the industry, and society as a whole? Explain your reasoning.

2. Building Team Skills

Suppose that you have decided to quit your job as an insurance adjuster and open a bakery. Your business is now growing, and you have decided to add a full line of catering services. This means more work and responsibility. You will need someone to help you, but you are undecided about what to do. Should you hire an employee or find a partner? If you add a partner, what type of decisions should be made to create a partnership agreement?

> « **Building Skills for Career Success** exercises focus on three important areas: Exploring the Internet, Building Team Skills, and Researching Different Careers.

TAKE PRIDE IN YOUR
SUCCESS...
WITH CONNECTIONS TO REAL WORLD CONTENT

VIDEO CASE
Scholfield Honda—Going Green with Honda

Signs of green marketing can be found everywhere today: reusable shopping bags are the rule rather than the exception, organic and natural products fill grocers' shelves, and socially responsible companies are increasing their efforts to reduce pollution, conserve water and energy, and recycle waste paper, plastic, and other reusable materials.

Of course, some companies have always been ahead of the curve. Since the early 1970s, Honda has been producing the low-emissions, fuel-efficient Civic model, and the company has never strayed from its roots. Today's Honda line consists of four classes of vehicles: Good, Better, Best, and Ultimate. Its regular gas cars are Good, with about 30 mpg; hybrids are Better at about 45 mpg; and its Best solution is a natural gas-powered Civic GX, which gets about 220 miles to a tank. Honda also has Ultimate solutions in the works, such as the new Honda FCX Clarity—a hydrogen fuel cell car that uses hydrogen and oxygen to create electricity. Although the Civic GX and Clarity models are available to consumers, neither vehicle is practical for the average driver as fueling stations are scarce.

In May 2007, a devastating tornado hit the nearby town of Greensburg, Kansas, leveling the area. Once again Lee Lindquist approached his boss. This time, he proposed donating both a Honda Civic GX and a natural-gas fueling station to Greensburg as a way of helping the town rebuild. Upon careful reflection, Roger realized that Lee's idea would benefit his dealership through good publicity and higher awareness of alternative fuel vehicles. Scholfield made the Civic model and fuel station available to Greensburg residents free of charge, [...] green bandwagon ev [...]

Although there ar [...] ing, Roger Scholfield [...] more interested in al [...] nated the Civic GX. In [...] plenty of goodwill in [...] Scholfield Honda has [...] commitment to the e [...] burg, even opening a [...]

> « **All-new Videos, Video Cases, and fresh Chapter Cases** feature memorable organizations impacting business today.

These **new dynamic videos** focus on **successful businesses**, such as E*Trade, L.L. Bean, Whirlpool, Nederlander Concerts, Burton Snowboards, Annie's Homegrown, BlueDot Furniture, and Numi Organic Tea, illustrating key concepts from each chapter. »

David DaPonte
MGR, product research & testing

Running a Business: Part 1

Let's Go Get a Graeter's!

Only a tiny fraction of family-owned businesses are still viable four generations after their founding, but happily for lovers of premium-quality ice cream, Graeter's is one of them.

Graeter's, now a $20 million firm, was founded in Cincinnati in 1870 by a young couple named Charlie and Regina Graeter, who made ice cream and chocolate candies in the back room of their shop, sold them in the front room, and lived upstairs. Refrigeration was unknown at the time, and ice cream was a novelty. Regina carried on the

Another success factor is the use of simple, fresh ingredients. Fresh eggs, high-grade chocolate, pure cane sugar, and the choicest raspberries, strawberries, and other fruits in season are among the basic ingredients, and the company gets its milk and cream only from local farmers who guarantee their cows are not fed artificial growth hormones. (These hormones are believed to have environmental effects and health effects on humans.) "We use a really great grade of chocolate," says Bob Graeter, vice president of manufacturing. "We don't cut corners on that. . . . Specially selected great black raspberries, strawberries, blueberries, cherries, go into our ice cream because we feel that we want to provide flavor

> « The **new ongoing Video Case at the end of each part features Cincinnati specialty ice cream retailer, Graeter's.** You get an insider's perspective as these engaging video cases look into **day-to-day business operations.** And, you gain a better understanding of the real challenges today's business owners face as they analyze problems, develop solutions, and take action.

TAKE PRIDE IN YOUR
SUCCESS...
WITH THE LATEST & MOST INNOVATIVE TECHNOLOGY

CourseMate

This unique website makes course concepts come alive with interactive learning, study, and exam preparation tools supporting the printed text. CourseMate delivers what you need, including an interactive eBook, an interactive glossary, quizzes, videos, KnowNOW blogs, Career Transitions, and more!

- **Media Quizzing Activities** allow you to relate the real-world events and issues shown in the chapter videos to specific in-text concepts.

- **Interactive decision-making scenarios** reinforce the text with memorable business scenarios and concise decision-making simulations that encourage you to see how business decisions lead to actionable business outcomes.

- **Career Transitions** is an interactive tool that provides activities designed to help you understand what career paths interest you, as well as practical tools and guidance to help you set and obtain your employment goals.

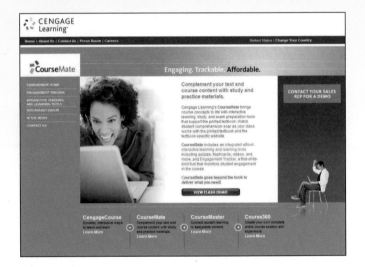

TAKE PRIDE IN YOUR
SUCCESS...
WITH THE LATEST & MOST INNOVATIVE TECHNOLOGY

Ensure You Are Getting It

CengageNOW™ is an integrated, online learning system that provides more control in less time and delivers more student success. This innovative, intuitive tool combines the best of current technology to save you time in studying and preparing for your class and exams.

- **A diagnostic Personalized Study Plan** identifies troublesome concepts and creates individualized study plans for better class preparations and grades.

- With CengageNOW you also get PowerPoint slides, videos, digital flash cards, games, an Integrated eBook, full access to the Business and Company Resource Center, and more! These make studying Business more effective and convenient.

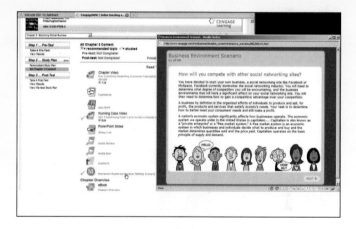

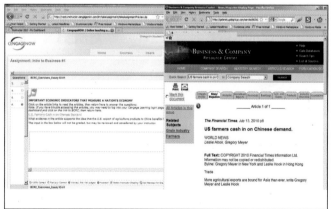

ABOUT THE AUTHORS

SUCCESS No.2

WILLIAM M. PRIDE Texas A&M University

William M. Pride is professor of marketing, Mays Business School at Texas A&M University. He received his PhD from Louisiana State University. He is the author of Cengage Learning's *Marketing*, 15th edition, and a market leader. Dr. Pride's research interests are in advertising, promotion, and distribution channels. Dr. Pride's research articles have appeared in major journals in the fields of advertising and marketing, such as *Journal of Marketing, Journal of Marketing Research, Journal of the Academy of Marketing Science*, and *Journal of Advertising*. Dr. Pride is a member of the American Marketing Association, Academy of Marketing Science, Association of Collegiate Marketing Educators, Society for Marketing Advances, and the Marketing Management Association. Dr. Pride has taught principles of marketing and other marketing courses for more than 30 years at both the undergraduate and graduate levels.

ROBERT J. HUGHES Richland College, Dallas County Community Colleges

Robert J. Hughes (PhD, University of North Texas) specializes in business administration and college instruction. He has taught Introduction to Business for more than 35 years both on campus and online for Richland College—one of seven campuses that are part of the Dallas County Community College District. In addition to *Business* and *Foundations of Business*, published by Cengage Learning, he has authored college textbooks in personal finance and business mathematics; served as a content consultant for two popular national television series, *It's Strictly Business* and *Dollars & Sense: Personal Finance for the 21st Century*; and is the lead author for a business math project utilizing computer-assisted instruction funded by the ALEKS Corporation. He is also active in many academic and professional organizations and has served as a consultant and investment advisor to individuals, businesses, and charitable organizations. Dr. Hughes is the recipient of three different Teaching in Excellence Awards at Richland College. According to Dr. Hughes, after 35 years of teaching Introduction to Business, the course is still exciting: "There's nothing quite like the thrill of seeing students succeed, especially in a course like Introduction to Business, which provides the foundation for not only academic courses, but also life in the real world."

JACK R. KAPOOR College of DuPage

Jack R. Kapoor (EdD, Northern Illinois University) is professor of business and economics in the Business and Technology Division at the College of DuPage, where he has taught Introduction to Business, Marketing, Management, Economics, and Personal Finance since 1969. He previously taught at Illinois Institute of Technology's Stuart School of Management, San Francisco State University's School of World Business, and other colleges. Professor Kapoor was awarded the Business and Services Division's Outstanding Professor Award for 1999–2000. He served as an Assistant National Bank Examiner for the U.S. Treasury Department and as an international trade consultant to Bolting Manufacturing Co., Ltd., Mumbai, India.

Dr. Kapoor is known internationally as a coauthor of several textbooks, including *Foundations of Business*, 2nd edition (Cengage Learning), has served as a content consultant for the popular national television series *The Business File: An Introduction to Business*, and developed two full-length audio courses in business and personal finance. He has been quoted in many national newspapers and magazines, including *USA Today, U.S. News & World Report*, the *Chicago Sun-Times, Crain's Small Business*, the *Chicago Tribune*, and other publications.

Dr. Kapoor has traveled around the world and has studied business practices in capitalist, socialist, and communist countries.

A SPECIAL
THANKS

SUCCESS No.2

The quality of this book and its supplements program has been helped immensely by the insightful and rich comments of a special set of instructors. Their thoughtful and helpful comments had real impact in shaping the final product. In particular, we wish to thank our Advisory Board:

Michael Bento
Owens Community College

Patricia Bernson
County College of Morris

Brennan Carr
Long Beach City College

Paul Coakley
The Community College of Baltimore County

Donna K. Fisher
Georgia Southern University

Charles R. Foley
Columbus State Community College

Connie Golden
Lakeland Community College

John Guess
Delgado Community College

Frank Harber
Indian River State College

Anita Kelley
Harold Washington College

Mary Beth Klinger
College of Southern Maryland

Pamela G. McElligott
St. Louis Community College Meramec

Mark Nagel
Normandale Community College

Angela J. Rabatin
Prince George's Community College

Anthony Racka
Oakland Community College—Auburn Hills Campus

Carol Rowey
Community College of Rhode Island

Christy Shell
Houston Community College

Cindy Simerly
Lakeland Community College

Yolanda I. Smith
Northern Virginia Community College

Gail South
Montgomery College

Rieann Spence-Gale
Northern Virginia Comm. College—Alexandria Campus

Kurt Stanberry
University of Houston, Downtown

John Striebich
Monroe Community College

Keith Taylor
Lansing Community College

Tricia Troyer
Waubonsee Community College

We are also grateful to the following additional reviewers:

John Adams
San Diego Mesa College

Ken Anglin
Minnesota State University, Mankato

Ellen A. Benowitz
Mercer County Community College

Harvey Bronstein
Oakland Community College - Orchard Ridge

Laura Bulas
Central Community College, NE

Jean Condon
Mid-Plains Community College

Mary Cooke
Surry Community College

Dean Danielson
San Joaquin Delta College

John Donnellan
Holyoke Community College

Gary Donnelly
Casper College

Karen Edwards
Chemeketa Community College

Mark Fox
Indiana University South Bend

Karen Gore
Ivy Tech Community College - Evansville

Carol Gottuso
Metropolitan Community College

Linda Hefferin
Elgin Community College

Tom Hendricks
Oakland Community College

Eileen Kearney
Montgomery Community College
Natasha Lindsey
University of North Alabama
Robert Lupton
Central Washington University
John Mago
Anoka Ramsey Community College
Rebecca J. Mahr
Western Illinois University
Myke McMullen
Long Beach City College

Carol Miller
Community College of Denver
Jadeip Motwani
Grand Valley State
Dyan Pease
Sacramento City College
Jeffrey D. Penley
Catawba Valley Community College
Dwight Riley
Richland College
Kim Rocha
Barton College

Gail South
Montgomery College - Gemantown
Leo Trudel
University of Maine - Fort Kent
Randy Waterman
Richland College
Leslie Wiletzky
Pierce College - Ft. Steilacoom
Anne Williams
Gateway Community College

We thank Carmen Powers of Monroe Community College and Kenneth Jones of Ivy Tech Community College—Central Indiana for their contributions to the Instructor Manual, as well as Larry Flick of Three Rivers Community College for his work on the PowerPoint slides and eLecture program. For their help in developing the Test Bank, CNow quiz materials and homework problems, CourseMate decision scenarios and online quizzing, Business & Company Resource Center (BCRC) exercises, video guide, and interactive video exercises, we thank Amit Shah, Frostburg State University; Christy Shell, Houston Community College; and Linda M. Hoffman and Colette Wolfson of Ivy Tech Community College. Finally, we thank the following people for their professional and technical assistance: Marian Wood, Elisa Adams, Theresa Kapoor, Dave Kapoor, Kathryn Thumme, Karen Tucker, Courtney Bohannon, Whitney Pearce, Clarissa Means, and Laurie Marshall.

Many talented professionals at Cengage Learning have contributed to the development of *Foundations of Business,* Third Edition. We are especially grateful to Jack Calhoun, Erin Joyner, Jason Fremder, Michelle Lockard, Joanne Dauksewicz, Darrell Frye, Stacy Shirley, Sarah Greber, Kristen Meere, Renee Yocum, Jana Lewis, and Megan Fischer. Their inspiration, patience, support, and friendship are invaluable.

W. M. P.
R. J. H
J. R. K

PART ONE
THE ENVIRONMENT OF BUSINESS

© Neil Sullivan/iStockphoto.com

In Part 1 of *Business*, we begin with an examination of the world of business and how the economy affects our life. Next, we discuss ethical and social responsibility issues that affect business firms and our society. Then we explore the increasing importance of international business.

Chapter 1   Exploring the World of Business and Economics
Chapter 2   Being Ethical and Socially Responsible
Chapter 3   Exploring Global Business

1

CHAPTER 1 EXPLORING THE WORLD OF BUSINESS AND ECONOMICS

© Songquan Deng/Shutterstock

Why should you care?

Studying business will help you to choose a career, become a successful employee or manager, start your own business, and become a more informed consumer and better investor.

Learning Objectives

What you will be able to do once you complete this chapter:

1 Discuss what you must do to be successful in the world of business.

2 Define *business* and identify potential risks and rewards.

3 Define *economics* and describe the two types of economic systems: capitalism and command economy.

4 Identify the ways to measure economic performance.

5 Examine the four different phases in the typical business cycle.

6 Outline the four types of competition.

7 Summarize the factors that affect the business environment and the challenges that American businesses will encounter in the future.

Get Flashcards, Quizzes, Games, Crosswords, and more @ www.cengagebrain.com

The Walt Disney Company's Script for Blockbuster Business Results

The Disney name has been connected with entertainment magic since 1923, when Walt and Roy Disney created a partnership to make short animated movies. The company scored its earliest successes with hand-drawn Mickey Mouse cartoons. Today, the Walt Disney Company uses advanced animation technology and clever story-telling to enchant audiences and earn big box-office profits from mega hits such as *Tangled, Up,* and *Toy Story 3.*

Over the years, Disney has expanded well beyond animation to become a global entertainment giant, with $38 billion in annual revenue and 149,000 employees. The company's studio division makes films for movie-goers of all ages, produces big-budget Broadway musicals, and distributes recorded music. Its parks and resort division operates theme parks in the United States, Japan, France, and Hong Kong, as well as family resorts and cruise ships. Disney's consumer products division puts the company's well-known brand and characters on everything from toys and T-shirts to books and beverages. The company's media holdings include the ABC television network, the ESPN sports network, and the Disney Interactive Media Group, which offers online, mobile, and video games.

One key to Disney's continued success is its acquisition of businesses with strengths that complement its own. The company bought Pixar in 2006 and Marvel Entertainment in 2009, bringing such beloved characters as Buzz Lightyear and Spider-Man under the Disney umbrella. Seeing the huge influence of the Internet, it bought the popular children's Web site Club Penguin in 2007 and has introduced new activities year after year to keep the site fresh and exciting for loyal visitors.

Another key to success is Disney's legendary focus on excellence in critical areas such as innovation and employee satisfaction. In fact, other businesses pay to send their executives to Disney Institute courses so they can learn exactly what's in Disney's script for blockbuster business results.

For a company approaching its 90th birthday, Disney really knows how to think young. The company is planning a glitzy new theme park, Shanghai Disneyland, to bring its special brand of magic to children of all ages in China.[1]

Did you know?

Disney is a global entertainment giant, with $38 billion in annual revenue and 149,000 employees worldwide.

Wow! What a challenging world we live in. Just for a moment, think about the economic problems listed here and how they affect not only businesses but also individuals.

- Unemployment rates hovering around 10 percent
- Increased government spending to stimulate a troubled economy
- Reduced consumer spending
- Increased cost of government programs that created the largest national debt in the nation's history
- A record number of home foreclosures
- A volatile stock market and concerns about banks and financial institutions
- Troubling concerns about the economic health of the nation and how economic problems affect the average American

In fact, just about every person around the globe was affected in some way by the economic crisis that began in late 2007. Despite the efforts of the U.S. government and other world governments to provide the economic stimulus needed to stabilize the economy, it took nearly two years before the economy began to improve. Hopefully, by the time you read this material, the nation's economy will be much stronger. Still, it is important to remember the old adage, "History is a great teacher." Both the nation and individuals should take a look at what went wrong to avoid making the same mistakes in the future.

Our economic system provides an amazing amount of freedom that allows businesses that range in size from the small corner grocer to The Walt Disney Company—the company profiled in the Inside Business opening case for this chapter—to adapt to changing business environments. Within certain limits, imposed mainly to ensure public safety, the owners of a business can produce any legal good or service they choose and attempt to sell it at the price they set. This system of business, in which individuals decide what to produce, how to produce it, and at what price to sell it, is called **free enterprise**. Our free-enterprise system ensures, for example, that Disney can create feature-length movies, produce and distribute television programs, and operate hotels, cruise ships, and theme parks. Our system gives Disney's owners and stockholders the right to make a profit from the company's success. It gives Disney's management the right to compete with entertainment rival Time Warner and other cruise lines including Carnival and Royal Caribbean.

In this chapter, we look briefly at what business is and how it became that way. First, we discuss what you must do to be successful in the world of business and explore some important reasons for studying business. Then we define *business*, noting how business organizations satisfy their customers' needs and earn profits. Next, we examine how capitalism and command economies answer four basic economic questions. Then our focus shifts to how the nations of the world measure economic performance, the phases in a typical business cycle, and the four types of competitive situations. Next, we look at the events that helped shape today's business system, the current business environment, and the challenges that businesses face.

LEARNING OBJECTIVE

1 Discuss what you must do to be successful in the world of business.

YOUR FUTURE IN THE CHANGING WORLD OF BUSINESS

The key word in this heading is *changing*. When faced with both economic problems and increasing competition not only from firms in the United States but also from international firms located in other parts of the world, employees and managers began to ask the question: What do we do now? Although this is a fair question, it is difficult to answer. Certainly, for a college student taking business courses or an employee just starting a career, the question is even more difficult to answer. Yet there are still opportunities out there for people who are willing to work hard, continue to learn, and possess the ability to adapt to change. Let's begin our discussion in this section with three basic concepts.

- What do you want?
- Why do you want it?
- Write it down!

During a segment on *The Oprah Winfrey Show*, Joe Dudley, one of the world's most successful black business owners, gave the preceding advice to anyone who wanted to succeed in business. His advice can help you achieve success. What is so amazing about Dudley's success is that he started a manufacturing business in his own kitchen, with his wife and children serving as the new firm's only employees. He went on to develop his own line of more than 400 hair-care and cosmetic products sold directly to cosmetologists, barbers, and beauty schools. Today, Mr. Dudley has built a multimillion-dollar empire—one of the most successful minority-owned companies in the nation. He is not only a successful business owner but also a winner

free enterprise the system of business in which individuals are free to decide what to produce, how to produce it, and at what price to sell it

of the Horatio Alger Award—an award given to outstanding individuals who have succeeded in the face of adversity.[2] Although many people would say that Joe Dudley was just lucky or happened to be in the right place at the right time, the truth is that he became a success because he had a dream and worked hard to turn his dream into a reality. Today, Dudley's vision is to see people succeed—to realize "The American Dream." He would be the first to tell you that you have the same opportunities that he had. According to Mr. Dudley, "Success is a journey, not just a destination."[3]

Whether you want to obtain part-time employment to pay college and living expenses, begin your career as a full-time employee, or start a business, you must *bring* something to the table that makes you different from the next person. Employers and our economic system are more demanding than ever before. Ask yourself: What can I do that will make employers want to pay me a salary? What skills do I have that employers need? With these two questions in mind, we begin the next section with another basic question: Why study business?

Why Study Business?

The potential benefits of higher education are enormous. To begin with, there are economic benefits. Over their lifetimes, college graduates on average earn much more than high school graduates. Although lifetime earnings are substantially higher for college graduates, so are annual income amounts (see Figure 1-1). In addition to increased income, there are at least five compelling reasons for studying business.

FOR HELP IN CHOOSING A CAREER What do you want to do with the rest of your life? At some time in your life, someone probably has asked you this same question. Like many people, you may find it a difficult question to answer. This business course will introduce you to a wide array of employment opportunities. In private enterprise, these range from small, local businesses owned by one individual to large companies such as American Express and Marriott International that are owned by thousands of stockholders. There are also employment opportunities with federal, state, county, and local governments and with not-for-profit organizations such as the Red Cross and Save the Children. For help in deciding which career might be right for you, read Appendix B: Careers in Business, which appears on the textbook Web site at www.cengagebrain.com.

In addition to career information in Appendix B, a number of additional Web sites provide information about career development. For more information, visit the following sites:

- Career Builder at www.careerbuilder.com
- Career One Stop at www.careeronestop.org
- Monster at www.monster.com

FIGURE 1-1: **Who Makes the Most Money**

Education makes a difference. Dollar amounts represent the average salary for full-time workers.

High school graduate	$39,962
Some college, no degree	$50,323
Associate's degree	$59,163
Bachelor's degree or more	$85,127

Source: The 2011 Statistical Abstract of the U.S. Web site at www.census.gov (accessed January 11, 2011). Salary amounts were obtained from Table 691.

Clicking Your Career into High Gear

In today's competitive business world, you should be networking online if you want to click your career into high gear. You can use Facebook, Twitter, LinkedIn, and other networking Web sites to locate job openings, help prospective employers to find you, and make a good impression on current and future bosses.

For example, David Gallant posted his résumé on job-search Web sites and followed up on leads from tech industry sources even before he graduated from the University of New Hampshire. He also set up his own blog to showcase his skills and hobbies and started conversing with other tech enthusiasts via Twitter posts. When he noticed a tweet about a job opening in his field, he applied immediately. Before interviewing Gallant, company managers checked his blog page and Twitter posts—and they liked what they saw. Gallant's job search ended successfully: He was hired within two weeks of graduation.

How can you make the most of online networking? First, identify and join sites where you can connect with potential employers, former classmates, and others who may have, or may hear of, job openings. Second, be sure your online profiles, photographs, and posts communicate your abilities and interests without being offensive or overly revealing. Finally, be ready to click quickly when you spot a job opening.

Sources: David Willis and Tehani Schneider, "Social Networking Tools You Can Use to Find Work," *The Daily Record*, January 17, 2011, www.dailyrecord.com, James Limbach, "Social Networking Explodes as Job-Search Tool," *ConsumerAffairs.com*, November 23, 2009, www.consumeraffairs.com/news04/2009/11/social_networking_jobs.html; Sarah E. Needleman, "A New Job Just a Tweet Away," *Wall Street Journal*, September 8, 2009, http://online.wsj.com/article/SB1000142405297020458440457 4393102737256542.html; Barbara Kiviat, "Using Twitter and Facebook to Find a Job," *Time*, June 8, 2009, www.time.com/time/business/article/0,8599,1903083,00.html; Glenda Kwek, "Twitter: The New Way to Find a Job," *Sydney Morning Herald*, March 27, 2009, www.smh.com.au/articles/2009/03/27/1237657117773.html; "UNH Grad Finds a Job Using Twitter," *University of New Hampshire Information Technology Pipeline*, March 27, 2009, http://pipeline.unh.edu/tag/twitter/.

One thing to remember as you think about what your ideal career might be is that a person's choice of a career ultimately is just a reflection of what he or she values and holds most important. What will give one individual personal satisfaction may not satisfy another. For example, one person may dream of a career as a corporate executive and becoming a millionaire before the age of 30. Another may choose a career that has more modest monetary rewards but that provides the opportunity to help others. What you choose to do with your life will be based on what you feel is most important. And *you* are a very important part of that decision.

TO BE A SUCCESSFUL EMPLOYEE

Personal App Whether you're co-captain of your softball team or looking to move up the career ladder, you won't succeed unless you can think beyond today, reason things out, get along with people, do a good job, and make yourself understood. These are business skills you can start to develop right now.

Deciding on the type of career you want is only the first step. To get a job in your chosen field and to be successful at it, you will have to develop a plan, or a road map, that ensures that you have the skills and knowledge the job requires. You will also be expected to have the ability to work well with many types of people in a culturally diverse workforce. **Cultural (or workplace) diversity** refers to the differences among people in a workforce owing to race, ethnicity, and gender. These skills, together with a working knowledge of the American business system and an appreciation for a culturally diverse workplace, can give you an inside edge when you are interviewing with a prospective employer.

cultural (or workplace) diversity differences among people in a workforce owing to race, ethnicity, and gender

This course, your instructor, and all the resources available at your college or university can help you to acquire the skills and knowledge you will need for a successful career. But do not underestimate your part in making your dream a reality. In addition to job-related skills and knowledge you need to be successful in a specific job, employers will also look for the following characteristics when hiring a new employee or promoting an existing employee:

- Honesty and integrity
- Willingness to work hard
- Dependability
- Time management skills
- Self-confidence
- Motivation
- Willingness to learn
- Communication skills
- Professionalism

Employers will also be interested in any work experience you may have had in cooperative work/school programs, during summer vacations, or in part-time jobs during the school year. These things can make a difference when it is time to apply for the job you really want.

How Important Are Employee Benefits?

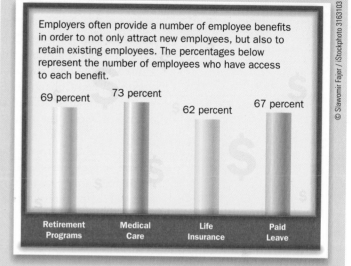

Employers often provide a number of employee benefits in order to not only attract new employees, but also to retain existing employees. The percentages below represent the number of employees who have access to each benefit.

| 69 percent | 73 percent | 62 percent | 67 percent |

| Retirement Programs | Medical Care | Life Insurance | Paid Leave |

Source: "Employee Benefits in the United States," The Bureau of Labor Statistics Web site at www.bls.gov, accessed July 27, 2010.

TO IMPROVE YOUR MANAGEMENT SKILLS

Often, employees become managers or supervisors. In fact, many employees want to become managers because managers often receive higher salaries. Although management obviously can be a rewarding career, what is not so obvious is the amount of time and hard work needed to achieve the higher salaries. For starters, employers expect more from managers and supervisors than ever before. Typically, the heavy workload requires that managers work long hours, and most do not get paid overtime. They also face increased problems created by the economic crisis, increased competition, employee downsizing, the quest for improved quality, and the need for efficient use of the firm's resources.

To be an effective manager, managers must be able to perform four basic management functions: planning, organizing, leading and motivating, and controlling—all topics discussed in Chapter 6, Understanding the Management Process. To successfully perform these management functions, managers must possess three very important skills.

- *Interpersonal skills*—The ability to deal effectively with individual employees, other managers within the firm, and people outside the firm.
- *Technical skills*—The skill required to accomplish a specific kind of work being done in an organization. Although managers may not actually perform the technical tasks, they should be able to train employees and answer technical questions.
- *Conceptual skills*—The ability to think in abstract terms in order to see the "big picture." Conceptual skills help managers understand how the various parts of an organization or idea can fit together.

Putting moms to work. Dixie McDaniel de Andrade used her interpersonal, technical, and conceptual skills to build a successful (and profitable) business. Her business, Mom Corps of Miami, matches moms that want to work with employers who need employees that appreciate a flexible work schedule.

In addition to the three skills just described, a successful manager will need many of the same skills that an employee needs to be successful.

TO START YOUR OWN BUSINESS Some people prefer to work for themselves, and they open their own businesses. To be successful, business owners must possess many of the same skills that successful employees and managers have, and they must be willing to work hard and put in long hours.

It also helps if your small business can provide a product or service that customers want. For example, Mark Cuban started a small Internet company called Broadcast.com that provided hundreds of live and on-demand audio and video programs ranging from rap music to sporting events to business events over the Internet. Because Cuban's company met the needs of his customers, Broadcast.com was very successful. When Cuban sold Broadcast.com to Yahoo! Inc., he became a billionaire.[4]

Unfortunately, many small-business firms fail; approximately 70 percent of them fail within the first seven years. Typical reasons for business failures include undercapitalization (not enough money), poor business location, poor customer service, unqualified or untrained employees, fraud, lack of a proper business plan, and failure to seek outside professional help. The material in Chapter 5, Small Business, Entrepreneurship, and Franchises, and selected topics and examples throughout this text will help you to decide whether you want to open your own business. This material will also help you to overcome many of these problems.

TO BECOME A BETTER INFORMED CONSUMER AND INVESTOR The world of business surrounds us. You cannot buy a home, a new Ford Fusion Hybrid from the local Ford dealer, a pair of jeans at Gap Inc., or a hot dog from a street vendor without entering a business transaction. Because you no doubt will engage in business transactions almost every day of your life, one very good reason for studying business is to become a more fully informed consumer. Many people also rely on a basic understanding of business to help them to invest for the future. According to Julie Stav, Hispanic stockbroker-turned-author/radio personality, "Take $25, add to it drive plus determination and then watch it multiply into an empire."[5] The author of *Get Your Share* believes that it is important to learn the basics about the economy and business, stocks, mutual funds, and other alternatives before investing your money. She also believes that it is never too early to start investing. Although this is an obvious conclusion, just dreaming of being rich does not make it happen. In fact, like many facets of life, it takes planning and determination to establish the type of investment program that will help you to accomplish your financial goals.

Special Note to Students

It is important to begin reading this text with one thing in mind: *This business course does not have to be difficult.* We have done everything possible to eliminate the problems that students encounter in a typical class. All the features in each chapter have been evaluated and recommended by instructors with years of teaching experience. In addition, business students were asked to critique each chapter component. Based on this feedback, the text includes the following features:

- *Learning objectives* appear at the beginning of each chapter.
- *Inside Business* is a chapter-opening case that highlights how successful companies do business on a day-to-day basis.
- *Margin notes* are used throughout the text to reinforce both learning objectives and key terms.
- *Boxed features* highlight how both employees and entrepreneurs can be ethical and successful.
- *Spotlight* features highlight interesting facts about business and society and often provide a real-world example of an important concept within a chapter.
- *Sustaining the Planet* features provide information about companies working to protect the environment.

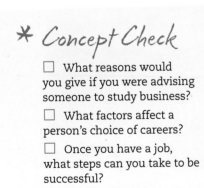

✱ Concept Check

☐ What reasons would you give if you were advising someone to study business?

☐ What factors affect a person's choice of careers?

☐ Once you have a job, what steps can you take to be successful?

- *Social Networking* features discuss how you can use the Internet and social networking Web sites to obtain employment or advance your career.
- *Concept Checks* at the end of each major section within a chapter help you test your understanding of the major issues just discussed.
- *End-of-chapter materials* provide a chapter summary, a list of key terms, discussion questions, a "Test Yourself" Quiz, and a video case about a successful, real-world company. The last section of every chapter is entitled Building Skills for Career Success and includes exercises devoted to exploring the Internet, building team skills, and researching different careers.
- *End-of-part materials* provide a continuing video case about Graeter's Ice Cream, a company that operates a chain of retail outlets in the Cincinnati, Ohio, area and sells to more than 760 Kroger Stores throughout the country. Also, at the end of each major part in the text is an exercise designed to help you to develop the components that are included in a typical business plan.

In addition to the text, a number of student supplements will help you to explore the world of business. We are especially proud of the Web site that accompanies this edition. There, you will find online study aids, such as key terms and definitions, crossword puzzles, interactive quizzes, student PowerPoint slides, and links to the videos for each chapter. If you want to take a look at the Internet support materials available for this edition of *Foundations of Business*,

1. Make an Internet connection and go to www.cengagebrain.com.
2. At the CengageBrain.com home page, search for the ISBN of your title (from the back cover of your book) using the search box at the top of the page. This will take you to the product page where free companion resources can be found.

As authors, we want you to be successful. We know that your time is valuable and that your schedule is crowded with many different activities. We also appreciate the fact that textbooks are expensive. Therefore, we want you to use this text and get the most out of your investment. To help you get off to a good start, a number of suggestions for developing effective study skills and using this text are provided in Table 1-1. Why not take a look at these suggestions and use them to help you succeed in this course and earn a higher grade. Remember what Joe Dudley said, "Success is a journey, not just a destination."

TABLE 1-1: **Seven Ways to Use this Text and Its Resources**

1. Prepare before you go to class.	Early preparation is the key to success in many of life's activities. Certainly, early preparation can help you to participate in class, ask questions, and improve your performance on examinations.
2. Read the chapter.	Although it may seem like an obvious suggestion, many students never take the time to really read the material. Find a quiet space where there are no distractions, and invest enough time to become a "content expert."
3. Underline or highlight important concepts.	Make this text yours. Do not be afraid to write on the pages of your text or highlight important material. It is much easier to review material if you have identified important concepts.
4. Take notes.	While reading, take the time to jot down important points and summarize concepts in your own words. Also, take notes in class.
5. Apply the concepts.	Learning is always easier if you can apply the content to your real-life situation. Think about how you could use the material either now or in the future.
6. Practice critical thinking.	Test the material in the text. Do the concepts make sense? To build critical-thinking skills, answer the questions that accompany the cases at the end of each chapter. Also, many of the exercises in the Building Skills for Career Success require critical thinking.
7. Prepare for the examinations.	Allow enough time to review the material before the examinations. Check out the summary and discussion questions at the end of the chapter. Then use the resources on the text Web site.

Because a text should always be evaluated by the students and instructors who use it, we would welcome and sincerely appreciate your comments and suggestions. Please feel free to contact us by using one of the following e-mail addresses:

Bill Pride: **w-pride@tamu.edu**
Bob Hughes: **bhughes@dcccd.edu**
Jack Kapoor: **kapoorj@cod.edu**

BUSINESS: A DEFINITION

LEARNING OBJECTIVE

2 Define *business* and identify potential risks and rewards.

Business is the organized effort of individuals to produce and sell, for a profit, the goods and services that satisfy society's needs. The general term *business* refers to all such efforts within a society (as in "American business"). However, *a business* is a particular organization, such as Kraft Foods, Inc., or Cracker Barrel Old Country Stores. To be successful, a business must perform three activities. It must be organized, it must satisfy needs, and it must earn a profit.

The Organized Effort of Individuals

For a business to be organized, it must combine four kinds of resources: material, human, financial, and informational. *Material* resources include the raw materials used in manufacturing processes as well as buildings and machinery. For example, Sara Lee Corporation needs flour, sugar, butter, eggs, and other raw materials to produce the food products it sells worldwide. In addition, this Illinois-based company needs human, financial, and informational resources. *Human* resources are the people who furnish their labor to the business in return for wages. The *financial* resource is the money required to pay employees, purchase materials, and generally keep the business operating. *Information* is the resource that tells the managers of the business how effectively the other three resources are being combined and used (see Figure 1-2).

Today, businesses are usually organized as one of three specific types. *Manufacturing businesses* process various materials into tangible goods, such as delivery trucks, towels, or computers. Intel, for example, produces computer chips that, in turn, are sold to companies that manufacture computers. *Service businesses* produce services, such as haircuts, legal advice, or tax preparation. Some firms called *marketing intermediaries* buy products from manufacturers and then resell them. Sony Corporation is a manufacturer that produces stereo equipment, among other things. These products may be sold to a marketing intermediary such as Best Buy, which then resells the manufactured goods to consumers in their retail stores.

business the organized effort of individuals to produce and sell, for a profit, the goods and services that satisfy society's needs

Organization when it counts. Imagine what would happen if the medical professionals in a hospital operating room weren't organized—especially if you were the patient. Like a surgical operating room, a business must be organized in order to meet the needs of its customers and earn a profit.

Satisfying Needs

The ultimate objective of every firm must be to satisfy the needs of its customers. People generally do not buy goods and services simply to own them; they buy products and services to satisfy particular needs. Some of us may feel that the need for transportation is best satisfied by an air-conditioned BMW with navigation system, stereo system, heated and cooled seats, automatic transmission, power windows, and remote-control side mirrors. Others may believe that a Chevrolet Aveo with a stick shift will do just fine. Both products are available to those who want them, along with a wide variety of other products that satisfy the need for transportation.

FIGURE 1-2: Combining Resources

A business must combine all four resources effectively to be successful.

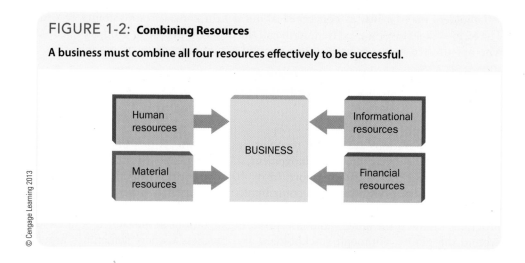

When firms lose sight of their customers' needs, they are likely to find the going rough. However, when businesses understand their customers' needs and work to satisfy those needs, they are usually successful. Back in 1962, Sam Walton opened his first discount store in Rogers, Arkansas. Although the original store was quite different from the Walmart Superstores you see today, the basic ideas of providing customer service and offering goods that satisfied needs at low prices are part of the reason why this firm has grown to become the largest retailer in the world. Although Walmart has over 8,900 retail stores in the United States and 14 other countries, this highly successful discount-store organization continues to open new stores to meet the needs of its customers around the globe.[6]

Business Profit

A business receives money (sales revenue) from its customers in exchange for goods or services. It must also pay out money to cover the expenses involved in doing business. If the firm's sales revenues are greater than its expenses, it has earned a profit. More specifically, as shown in Figure 1-3, **profit** is what remains after all business expenses have been deducted from sales revenue.

A negative profit, which results when a firm's expenses are greater than its sales revenue, is called a *loss*. A business cannot continue to operate at a loss for an indefinite period of time. Management and employees must find some way to increase sales revenues and reduce expenses to return to profitability. If some specific actions are not taken to eliminate losses, a firm may be forced to close its doors or file for bankruptcy protection.

Although many people—especially stockholders and business owners—believe that profit is literally the bottom line or most important goal for a business, many

FIGURE 1-3: The Relationship Between Sales Revenue and Profit

Profit is what remains after all business expenses have been deducted from sales revenue.

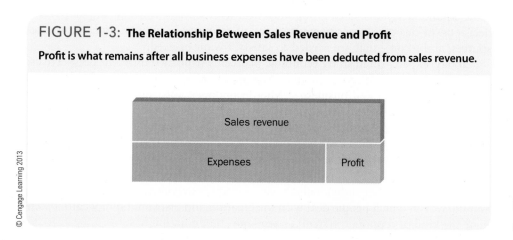

profit what remains after all business expenses have been deducted from sales revenue

stakeholders may be just as concerned about a firm's social responsibility record. The term **stakeholders** is used to describe all the different people or groups of people who are affected by the policies, decisions, and activities made by an organization.

Personal App In your daily life, you're a customer of many businesses, a resident of your town or city, and a student at your school. And that means you're a stakeholder, because the actions of all these organizations can affect you to some degree.

Many corporations are careful to point out their efforts to sustain the planet, participate in the green ecological movement, and help people to live better lives in an annual social responsibility report. In its 100-page social responsibility report, General Mills describes how it has contributed approximately 5 percent of its pre-tax profits each year since 2000 to a wide variety of causes, including support for programs that feed the hungry and non-profit organizations in the United States and around the globe.[7] Although stockholders and business owners sometimes argue that the money that a business contributes to charitable causes could have been used to pay larger dividends to stockholders or increase the return on the owners' investment, the fact is that most socially responsible business firms feel social responsibility is the right thing to do and is good for business.

The profit earned by a business becomes the property of its owners. Thus, in one sense, profit is the reward business owners receive for producing goods and services that consumers want. Profit is also the payment that business owners receive for assuming the considerable risks of business ownership. One of these is the risk of not being paid. Everyone else—employees, suppliers, and lenders—must be paid before the owners.

A second risk that owners undertake is the risk of losing whatever they have invested into the business. A business that cannot earn a profit is very likely to fail, in which case the owners lose whatever money, effort, and time they have invested.

To satisfy society's needs and make a profit, a business must operate within the parameters of a nation's economic system. In the next section, we define economics and describe two different types of economic systems.

TYPES OF ECONOMIC SYSTEMS

Economics is the study of how wealth is created and distributed. By *wealth*, we mean "anything of value," including the products produced and sold by business. *How wealth is distributed* simply means "who gets what." Experts often use economics to explain the choices we make and how these choices change as we cope with the demands of everyday life. In simple terms, individuals, businesses, governments, and society must make decisions that reflect what is important to each group at a particular time. For example, suppose you want to take a weekend trip to some exotic vacation spot, and you also want to begin an investment program. Because of your financial resources, though, you cannot do both, so you must decide what is most important. Business firms, governments, and to some extent society face the same types of decisions. Each group must deal with scarcity when making important decisions. In this case, *scarcity* means "lack of resources"—money, time, natural resources, and so on—that are needed to satisfy a want or need.

Today, experts often study economic problems from two different perspectives: microeconomics and macroeconomics. **Microeconomics** is the study of the decisions made by individuals and businesses. Microeconomics, for example, examines how the prices of homes affect the number of homes individuals will buy. On the other hand, **macroeconomics** is the study of the national economy and the global economy. Macroeconomics examines the economic effect of national income, unemployment, inflation, taxes, government spending, interest rates, and similar factors on a nation and society.

The decisions that individuals, business firms, government, and society make, and the way in which people deal with the creation and distribution of wealth determine the kind of economic system, or **economy**, that a nation has.

* Concept Check

☐ Describe the four resources that must be combined to organize and operate a business.

☐ What is the difference between a manufacturing business, a service business, and a marketing intermediary?

☐ Explain the relationship among profit, business risk, and the satisfaction of customers' needs.

LEARNING OBJECTIVE

3 Define *economics* and describe the two types of economic systems: capitalism and command economy.

stakeholders all the different people or groups of people who are affected by the policies and decisions made by an organization

economics the study of how wealth is created and distributed

microeconomics the study of the decisions made by individuals and businesses

macroeconomics the study of the national economy and the global economy

economy the way in which people deal with the creation and distribution of wealth

Over the years, the economic systems of the world have differed in essentially two ways: (1) the ownership of the factors of production and (2) how they answer four basic economic questions that direct a nation's economic activity.

Factors of production are the resources used to produce goods and services. There are four such factors:

- *Land and natural resources*—elements that can be used in the production process to make appliances, automobiles, and other products. Typical examples include crude oil, forests, minerals, land, water, and even air.
- *Labor*—the time and effort that we use to produce goods and services. It includes human resources such as managers and employees.
- *Capital*—the money, facilities, equipment, and machines used in the operation of organizations. Although most people think of capital as just money, it can also be the manufacturing equipment in a Pepperidge Farm production facility or a computer used in the corporate offices of McDonald's.
- *Entrepreneurship*—the activity that organizes land and natural resources, labor, and capital. It is the willingness to take risks and the knowledge and ability to use the other factors of production efficiently. An **entrepreneur** is a person who risks his or her time, effort, and money to start and operate a business.

New energy from an old source: the wind To protect the environment, as well as to reduce our dependence on oil from foreign nations, many utility companies are developing alternative energy sources such as wind power. Once developed, wind energy may actually be cheaper than using foreign oil.

© morguefile.com/iStockphoto.com

Personal App Think about a few entrepreneurs you know or have heard about. Did they worry about losing money? Did they work long hours to get their businesses off to a good start? Did their risk pay off in the end?

A nation's economic system significantly affects all the economic activities of its citizens and organizations. This far-reaching impact becomes more apparent when we consider that a country's economic system determines how the factors of production are used to meet the needs of society. Today, two different economic systems exist: capitalism and command economies. The way each system answers the four basic economic questions listed here determines a nation's economy.

1. What goods and services—and how much of each—will be produced?
2. How will these goods and services be produced?
3. For whom will these goods and services be produced?
4. Who owns and who controls the major factors of production?

Capitalism

Capitalism is an economic system in which individuals own and operate the majority of businesses that provide goods and services. Capitalism stems from the theories of the 18th-century Scottish economist Adam Smith. In his book *Wealth of Nations*, published in 1776, Smith argued that a society's interests are best served when the individuals within that society are allowed to pursue their own self-interest. According to Smith, when individuals act to improve their own fortunes, they indirectly promote the good of their community and the people in that community. Smith went on to call this concept the "invisible hand." The **invisible hand** is a term created by Adam Smith to describe how an individual's own personal gain benefits others and a nation's economy. For example, the only way a small-business owner who produces shoes can increase personal wealth is to sell shoes to customers. To become even more prosperous, the small-business owner must hire workers to produce even more shoes. According to the invisible hand, people in the small-business owner's community not only would have shoes but also would have jobs working for the

factors of production resources used to produce goods and services

entrepreneur a person who risks time, effort, and money to start and operate a business

capitalism an economic system in which individuals own and operate the majority of businesses that provide goods and services

invisible hand a term created by Adam Smith to describe how an individual's personal gain benefits others and a nation's economy

© Cengage Learning 2013

FIGURE 1-4: **Basic Assumptions for Adam Smith's Laissez-Faire Capitalism**

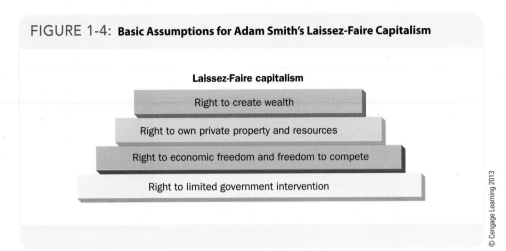

Laissez-Faire capitalism

Right to create wealth

Right to own private property and resources

Right to economic freedom and freedom to compete

Right to limited government intervention

shoemaker. Thus, the success of people in the community and, to some extent, the nation's economy is tied indirectly to the success of the small-business owner.

Adam Smith's capitalism is based on the four fundamental issues illustrated in Figure 1-4.

market economy an economic system in which businesses and individuals decide what to produce and buy, and the market determines quantities sold and prices

mixed economy an economy that exhibits elements of both capitalism and socialism

1. The creation of wealth is properly the concern of private individuals, not the government.
2. Private individuals must own private property and the resources used to create wealth.
3. Economic freedom ensures the existence of competitive markets that allow both sellers and buyers to enter and exit the market as they choose.
4. The role of government should be limited to providing defense against foreign enemies, ensuring internal order, and furnishing public works and education.

One factor that Smith felt was extremely important was the role of government. He believed that government should act only as rule maker and umpire. The French term *laissez faire* describes Smith's capitalistic system and implies that there should be no government interference in the economy. Loosely translated, this term means "let them do" (as they see fit).

Adam Smith's Laissez-Faire capitalism is also based on the concept of a market economy. A **market economy** (sometimes referred to as a *free-market economy*) is an economic system in which businesses and individuals decide what to produce and buy, and the market determines prices and quantities sold. The owners of resources should be free to determine how these resources are used and also to enjoy the income, profits, and other benefits derived from ownership of these resources.

An apple a day . . . Regarded as one of the most successful and profitable businesses in the very competitive technology industry, Apple has a history of introducing state-of-the-art consumer products like the iPhone and iPad. Although there are many ways to obtain Apple products, one way to "try out" the latest products is to visit one of their retail stores.

Capitalism in the United States

Our economic system is rooted in the Laissez-Faire capitalism of Adam Smith. However, our real-world economy is not as Laissez-Faire as Smith would have liked. Our economy is, in fact, a **mixed economy**, one that exhibits elements of both capitalism and socialism.

In a mixed economy, the four basic economic questions discussed at the beginning of this section (what,

FIGURE 1-5: The Circular Flow in Our Mixed Economy

Our economic system is guided by the interaction of buyers and sellers, with the role of government being taken into account.

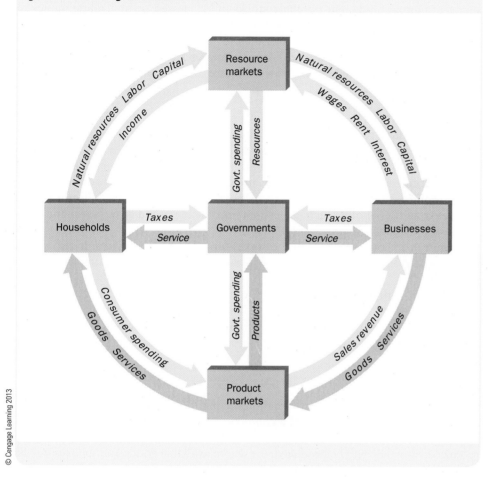

© Cengage Learning 2013

how, for whom, and who) are answered through the interaction of households, businesses, and governments. The interactions among these three groups are shown in Figure 1-5.

HOUSEHOLDS Households, made up of individuals, are the consumers of goods and services as well as owners of some of the factors of production. As *resource owners*, the members of households provide businesses with labor, capital, and other resources. In return, businesses pay wages, rent, and dividends and interest, which households receive as income.

As *consumers*, household members use their income to purchase the goods and services produced by business. Today, approximately 70 percent of our nation's total production consists of **consumer products**—goods and services purchased by individuals for personal consumption.[8] This means that consumers, as a group, are the biggest customers of American business.

BUSINESSES Like households, businesses are engaged in two different exchanges. They exchange money for natural resources, labor, and capital and use these resources to produce goods and services. Then they exchange their goods and services for sales revenue. This sales revenue, in turn, is exchanged for additional resources, which are used to produce and sell more goods and services.

Along the way, of course, business owners would like to remove something from the circular flow in the form of profits. When business profits are distributed to business owners, these profits become household income. (Business owners are,

consumer products goods and services purchased by individuals for personal consumption

after all, members of households.) Households try to retain some income as savings. But are profits and savings really removed from the flow? Usually not! When the economy is running smoothly, households are willing to invest their savings in businesses. They can do so directly by buying stocks in businesses, by purchasing shares in mutual funds that purchase stocks in businesses, or by lending money to businesses. They can also invest indirectly by placing their savings in bank accounts. Banks and other financial institutions then invest or lend these savings as part of their normal business operations. Thus, business profits, too, are retained in the business system, and the circular flow in Figure 1-5 is complete. How, then, does government fit in?

GOVERNMENTS The Preamble to the Constitution sets forth the responsibility of the government to protect and promote public welfare. The numerous government services are important but they (1) would either not be produced by private business firms or (2) would be produced only for those who could afford them. Typical services include national defense, police, fire protection, education, and construction of roads and highways. To pay for all these services, governments collect a variety of taxes from households (such as personal income taxes and sales taxes) and from businesses (corporate income taxes).

Figure 1-5 shows this exchange of taxes for government services. It also shows government spending of tax dollars for resources and products required to provide these services.

Actually, with government included, our circular flow looks more like a combination of several flows. In reality, it is. The important point is that together the various flows make up a single unit—a complete economic system that effectively provides answers to the basic economic questions. Simply put, the system works.

Command Economies

Before we discuss how to measure a nation's economic performance, we look quickly at another economic system called a *command economy*. A **command economy** is an economic system in which the government decides what goods and services will be produced, how they will be produced, for whom available goods and services will be produced, and who owns and controls the major factors of production. The answers to all four basic economic questions are determined, at least to some degree, through centralized government planning. Today, two types of economic systems—*socialism* and *communism*—serve as examples of command economies.

SOCIALISM In a socialist economy, the key industries are owned and controlled by the government. Such industries usually include transportation, utilities, communications, banking, and industries producing important materials such as steel. Land, buildings, and raw materials may also be the property of the state in a socialist economy. Depending on the country, private ownership of smaller businesses is permitted to varying degrees. Usually, people may choose their own occupations, although many work in state-owned industries.

What to produce and how to produce it are determined in accordance with national goals, which are based on projected needs and the availability of resources. The distribution of goods and services—who gets what—is also controlled by the state to the extent that it controls taxes, rents, and wages. Among the professed aims of socialist countries are the equitable distribution of income, the elimination of poverty, and the distribution of social services (such as medical care) to all who need them. The disadvantages of socialism include increased taxation and loss of incentive and motivation for both individuals and business owners.

Today, many of the nations that have been labeled as socialist nations traditionally, including France, Sweden, and India, are transitioning to a free-market economy. Currently, many countries that were once thought of as communist countries are now often referred to as socialist countries. Examples of former communist countries often referred to as socialists (or even capitalists) include most of the

command economy an economic system in which the government decides what goods and services will be produced, how they will be produced, for whom available goods and services will be produced, and who owns and controls the major factors of production

nations that were formerly part of the Union of Soviet Socialist Republics, China, and Vietnam.

COMMUNISM If Adam Smith was the father of capitalism, Karl Marx was the father of communism. In his writings during the mid-19th century, Marx advocated a classless society whose citizens together owned all economic resources. All workers would then contribute to this *communist* society according to their ability and would receive benefits according to their need.

Since the breakup of the Soviet Union and economic reforms in China and most of the Eastern European countries, the best remaining examples of communism are North Korea and Cuba. Today these so-called communist economies seem to practice a strictly controlled kind of socialism. The basic four economic questions are answered through centralized government plans. Emphasis is placed on the production of goods the government needs rather than on the products that consumers might want. Workers have little choice of jobs, but special skills or talents seem to be rewarded with special privileges.

Concept Check ✱

☐ What are the four basic economic questions? How are they answered in a capitalist economy?

☐ Describe the four basic assumptions required for a *laissez-faire* capitalist economy.

☐ Why is the American economy called a mixed economy?

☐ How does capitalism differ from socialism and communism?

MEASURING ECONOMIC PERFORMANCE

LEARNING OBJECTIVE

4 Identify the ways to measure economic performance.

Today, it is hard to turn on the radio, watch the news on television, use the Internet, or read the newspaper without hearing or seeing something about the economy. Consider for just a moment the following questions:

- Are U.S. workers as productive as workers in other countries?
- Is the gross domestic product for the United States increasing or decreasing?
- Why is the unemployment rate important?

The information needed to answer these questions, along with the answers to similar questions, is easily obtainable from many sources. More important, the answers to these and other questions can be used to gauge the economic health of a nation. For individuals, the health of the economy can affect your ability to get a job, the financing you need to continue your education, or the amount of interest you pay for homes, automobiles, and credit card purchases.

The Importance of Productivity in the Global Marketplace

One way to measure a nation's economic performance is to assess its productivity. **Productivity** is the average level of output per worker per hour. An increase in productivity results in economic growth because a larger number of goods and services are produced by a given labor force. To see how productivity affects you and the economy, consider the following three questions:

Question: *How does productivity growth affect the economy?*

Answer: Because of productivity growth, it now takes fewer workers to produce more products and services. As a result, employers have reduced costs, earned more profits, and sold their products for less. Finally, productivity growth helps American business to compete more effectively with other nations in a competitive world.

productivity the average level of output per worker per hour

Question: *How does a nation improve productivity?*

Answer: Reducing costs and enabling employees to work more efficiently are at the core of all attempts to improve productivity. For example, productivity in the United States is expected to improve dramatically as more economic activity is transferred onto the Internet, reducing costs for servicing customers and handling

© Peter zijlstra/Shutterstock

routine ordering functions between businesses. Other methods that can be used to increase productivity are discussed in detail in Chapter 8.

Question: *Is productivity growth always good?*

Answer: Fewer workers producing more goods and services can lead to higher unemployment rates. In this case, increased productivity is good for employers but not good for unemployed workers seeking jobs in a very competitive work environment. For example, employers were reluctant to hire new employees in the midst of the recent economic crisis. Because they had been able to produce more goods and services with fewer employees, these same employers did not want to increase the firm's salary expense by hiring new employees after the economy began to improve.

Important Economic Indicators that Measure a Nation's Economy

In addition to productivity, a measure called *gross domestic product* can be used to measure the economic well-being of a nation. **Gross domestic product (GDP)** is the total dollar value of all goods and services produced by all people within the boundaries of a country during a one-year period. For example, the values of automobiles produced by employees in an American-owned Ford plant and a Japanese-owned Toyota plant in the United States are both included in the GDP for the United States. The U.S. GDP was $14.7 trillion in 2010.[9]

The GDP figure facilitates comparisons between the United States and other countries because it is the standard used in international guidelines for economic accounting. It is also possible to compare the GDP for one nation over several different time periods. This comparison allows observers to determine the extent to which a nation is experiencing economic growth. For example, government experts project that GDP will grow to $21.8 trillion by the year 2018.[10]

To make accurate comparisons of the GDP for different years, we must adjust the dollar amounts for inflation. **Inflation** is a general rise in the level of prices. (The opposite of inflation is deflation.) **Deflation** is a general decrease in the level of prices.

> **Personal App** Inflation isn't just an economic indicator—it means that you'll pay more for many goods and services. If you're saving to buy a car or a home, the money you put aside won't go as far when prices are on the rise.

By using inflation-adjusted figures, we are able to measure the real GDP for a nation. In effect, it is now possible to compare the products and services produced by a nation in constant dollars—dollars that will purchase the same amount of goods and services. Figure 1-6 depicts the GDP of the United States in current dollars and the real GDP in inflation-adjusted dollars. Note that between 1990 and 2010, America's real GDP grew from $8 trillion to $13 trillion.[11]

In addition to GDP and real GDP, other economic measures exist that can be used to evaluate a nation's economy. Because of the recent economic crisis, one very important statistic that is in the news on a regular basis is the unemployment rate. The **unemployment rate** is the percentage of a nation's labor force unemployed at any time. According to the Bureau of Labor Statistics, when workers are unemployed, they, their families, and the country as a whole lose. Workers and their families lose wages, and the country loses the goods or services that could have been produced. In addition, the purchasing power of these workers is lost, which can lead to unemployment for yet other workers.[12] Despite both federal and state programs to reduce the unemployment rate for the United States, it was hovering around 10 percent at the time of publication. This is an especially important statistic—especially if you are unemployed.

The **consumer price index (CPI)** is a monthly index that measures the changes in prices of a fixed basket of goods purchased by a typical consumer in an urban area.

gross domestic product (GDP) the total dollar value of all goods and services produced by all people within the boundaries of a country during a one-year period

inflation a general rise in the level of prices

deflation a general decrease in the level of prices

unemployment rate the percentage of a nation's labor force unemployed at any time

consumer price index (CPI) a monthly index that measures the changes in prices of a fixed basket of goods purchased by a typical consumer in an urban area

FIGURE 1-6: GDP in Current Dollars and in Inflation-Adjusted Dollars

The change in GDP and real GDP for the United States from one year to another year can be used to measure economic growth.

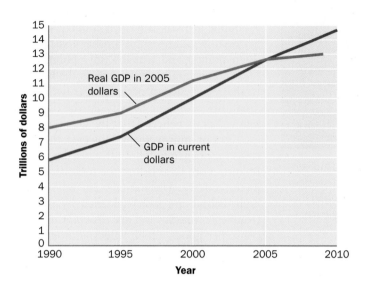

Source: U.S. Bureau of Economic Analysis Web site at www.bea.gov (accessed January 10, 2011).

producer price index (PPI) an index that measures prices that producers receive for their finished goods

Goods listed in the CPI include food and beverages, transportation, housing, clothing, medical care, recreation, education, communication, and other goods and services. Economists often use the CPI to determine the effect of inflation on not only the nation's economy but also individual consumers. Another monthly index is the producer price index. The **producer price index (PPI)** measures prices that producers receive for their finished goods. Because changes in the PPI reflect price increases or decreases at the wholesale level, the PPI is an accurate predictor of both changes in the CPI and prices that consumers will pay for many everyday necessities.

Some additional economic measures are described in Table 1-2. Like the measures for GDP, these measures can be used to compare one economic statistic over different periods of time.

Concept Check ✱

☐ How does an increase in productivity affect business?

☐ Define gross domestic product. Why is this economic measure significant?

☐ How does inflation affect the prices you pay for goods and services?

☐ How is the producer price index related to the consumer price index?

TABLE 1-2: Common Measures Used to Evaluate a Nation's Economic Health

Economic Measure	Description
1. Balance of trade	The total value of a nation's exports minus the total value of its imports over a specific period of time.
2. Bank credit	A statistic that measures the lending activity of commercial financial institutions.
3. Corporate profits	The total amount of profits made by corporations over selected time periods.
4. Inflation rate	An economic statistic that tracks the increase in prices of goods and services over a period of time. This measure is usually calculated on a monthly or an annual basis.
5. National income	The total income earned by various segments of the population, including employees, self-employed individuals, corporations, and other types of income.
6. New housing starts	The total number of new homes started during a specific time period.
7. Prime interest rate	The lowest interest rate that banks charge their most credit-worthy customers.

© Scott Olson/Getty Images

A sign of the times! Very few consumers will spend money on clothing and nonessential items if they are worried about losing their paycheck. To attract more customers during the recent economic crisis, this retailer offered a money-back guarantee—if customers lose their jobs.

5 Examine the four different phases in the typical business cycle.

business cycle the recurrence of periods of growth and recession in a nation's economic activity

recession two or more consecutive three-month periods of decline in a country's GDP

depression a severe recession that lasts longer than a typical recession

monetary policies Federal Reserve decisions that determine the size of the supply of money in the nation and the level of interest rates

fiscal policy government influence on the amount of savings and expenditures; accomplished by altering the tax structure and by changing the levels of government spending

THE BUSINESS CYCLE

All industrialized nations of the world seek economic growth, full employment, and price stability. However, a nation's economy fluctuates rather than grows at a steady pace every year. In fact, if you were to graph the economic growth rate for a country such as the United States, it would resemble a roller coaster ride with peaks (high points) and troughs (low points). These fluctuations are generally referred to as the **business cycle**, that is, the recurrence of periods of growth and recession in a nation's economic activity. At the time of publication, many experts believed that the U.S. economy was showing signs of improvement. However, the recent economic crisis that began in fall 2007 caused a recession that will require more time before the nation experiences a complete recovery. The nation's unemployment rate is still high. People are still frightened by the prospects of a troubled economy and are reluctant to spend money on consumer goods. Stock values, although improving, are still below the record values experienced a few years ago. Although the federal government has enacted a number of stimulus plans designed to help unemployed workers, to shore up the nation's banks and Wall Street firms, to reduce the number of home foreclosures, and to free up credit for both individuals and businesses, many experts still believe that we have serious financial problems. For one, the size of the national debt—a topic described later in this section—is a concern. To make matters worse, the recent economic crisis did not affect just the U.S. economy but also the economies of countries around the world.

The changes that result from either economic growth or economic downturn affect the amount of products and services that consumers are willing to purchase and, as a result, the amount of products and services produced by business firms. Generally, the business cycle consists of four phases: the peak (sometimes called prosperity), recession, the trough, and recovery (sometimes called expansion).

During the *peak period*, the economy is at its highest point and unemployment is low. Total income is relatively high. As long as the economic outlook remains prosperous, consumers are willing to buy products and services. In fact, businesses often expand and offer new products and services during the peak period to take advantage of consumers' increased buying power.

Generally, economists define a **recession** as two or more consecutive three-month periods of decline in a country's GDP. Because unemployment rises during a recession, total buying power declines. The pessimism that accompanies a recession often stifles both consumer and business spending. As buying power decreases, consumers tend to become more value conscious and reluctant to purchase frivolous or nonessential items. In response to a recession, many businesses focus on producing the products and services that provide the most value to their customers. Economists define a **depression** as a severe recession that lasts longer than a typical recession. A depression is characterized by extremely high unemployment rates, low wages, reduced purchasing power, lack of confidence in the economy, lower stock values, and a general decrease in business activity.

Economists refer to the third phase of the business cycle as the *trough*. The trough of a recession or depression is the turning point when a nation's output and employment bottom out and reach their lowest levels. To offset the effects of recession and depression, the federal government uses both monetary and fiscal policies. **Monetary policies** are the Federal Reserve's decisions that determine the size of the supply of money in the nation and the level of interest rates. Through **fiscal policy**, the government can influence the amount of savings and expenditures by altering the tax structure and changing the levels of government spending.

Although the federal government collects approximately $2.0 trillion in annual revenues, the government often spends more than it receives, resulting in a **federal deficit**. For example, the government had a federal deficit for each year between 2002 and 2010. The total of all federal deficits is called the **national debt**. Today, the U.S. national debt is over $14.0 trillion or approximately $45,000 for every man, woman, and child in the United States.[13]

Since World War II, business cycles have lasted from three to five years from one peak period to the next peak period. During the same time period, the average length of recessions has been 11 months.[14] Some experts believe that effective use of monetary and fiscal policies can speed up recovery and reduce the amount of time the economy is in recession. *Recovery* (or *expansion*) is movement of the economy from recession or depression to prosperity. During recovery, high unemployment rates decline, income increases, and both the ability and the willingness to buy rise.

At the time of publication, many business leaders and politicians were debating whether the U.S. economy was showing signs of improvement. Unfortunately, many of the problems that caused the recent economic crisis are still there, and they will take years to correct and resolve.

TYPES OF COMPETITION

Our capitalist system ensures that individuals and businesses make the decisions about what to produce, how to produce it, and what price to charge for the product. Mattel, Inc., for example, can introduce new versions of its famous Barbie doll, license the Barbie name, change the doll's price and method of distribution, and attempt to produce and market Barbie in other countries or over the Internet at www .mattel.com. Our system also allows customers the right to choose between Mattel's products and those produced by competitors.

Competition like that between Mattel and other toy manufacturers is a necessary and extremely important by-product of capitalism. Business **competition** is essentially a rivalry among businesses for sales to potential customers. In a capitalistic economy, competition also ensures that a firm will survive only if it serves its customers well by providing products and services that meet needs. Economists recognize four different degrees of competition ranging from ideal, complete competition to no competition at all. These are perfect competition, monopolistic competition, oligopoly, and monopoly. For a quick overview of the different types of competition, including numbers of firms and examples for each type, look at Table 1-3.

Perfect Competition

Perfect (or pure) competition is the market situation in which there are many buyers and sellers of a product, and no single buyer or seller is powerful enough to affect the price of that product. Note that this definition includes several important ideas. First, we are discussing the market for a single product, such as bushels of wheat. Second,

Concept Check *

☐ What are the four phases in the typical business cycle?

☐ At the time you are studying the material in this chapter, which phase of the business cycle do you think the U.S. economy is in? Justify your answer.

☐ How has the government used monetary policy and fiscal policy to reduce the effects of the economic crisis?

LEARNING OBJECTIVE

6 Outline the four types of competition.

federal deficit a shortfall created when the federal government spends more in a fiscal year than it receives

national debt the total of all federal deficits

competition rivalry among businesses for sales to potential customers

perfect (or pure) competition the market situation in which there are many buyers and sellers of a product, and no single buyer or seller is powerful enough to affect the price of that product

TABLE 1-3: **Four Different Types of Competition**

The number of firms determines the degree of competition within an industry.

Type of Competition	Number of Business Firms or Suppliers	Real-World Examples
1. Perfect	Many	Corn, wheat, peanuts
2. Monopolistic	Many	Clothing, shoes
3. Oligopoly	Few	Automobiles, cereals
4. Monopoly	One	Software protected by copyright, many local public utilities

© Cengage Learning 2013

there are no restrictions on firms entering the industry. Third, all sellers offer essentially the same product for sale. Fourth, all buyers and sellers know everything there is to know about the market (including, in our example, the prices that all sellers are asking for their wheat). And fifth, the overall market is not affected by the actions of any one buyer or seller.

When perfect competition exists, every seller should ask the same price that every other seller is asking. Why? Because if one seller wanted 50 cents more per bushel of wheat than all the others, that seller would not be able to sell a single bushel. Buyers could—and would—do better by purchasing wheat from the competition. On the other hand, a firm willing to sell below the going price would sell all its wheat quickly. However, that seller would lose sales revenue (and profit) because buyers are actually willing to pay more.

In perfect competition, then, sellers—and buyers as well—must accept the going price. The price of each product is determined by the actions of all buyers and all sellers together through the forces of supply and demand.

THE BASICS OF SUPPLY AND DEMAND The **supply** of a particular product is the quantity of the product that producers are willing to sell at each of various prices. Producers are rational people, so we would expect them to offer more of a product for sale at higher prices and to offer less of the product at lower prices, as illustrated by the supply curve in Figure 1-7.

The **demand** for a particular product is the quantity that buyers are willing to purchase at each of various prices. Buyers, too, are usually rational, so we would expect them—as a group—to buy more of a product when its price is low and to buy less of the product when its price is high, as depicted by the demand curve in Figure 1-7.

FIGURE 1-7: **Supply Curve and Demand Curve**

The intersection of a supply curve and a demand curve is called the *equilibrium*, or *market, price*. This intersection indicates a single price and quantity at which suppliers will sell products and buyers will purchase them.

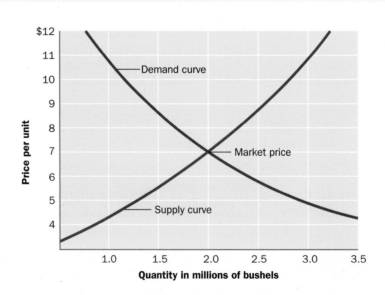

supply the quantity of a product that producers are willing to sell at each of various prices

demand the quantity of a product that buyers are willing to purchase at each of various prices

THE EQUILIBRIUM, OR MARKET, PRICE There is always one certain price at which the demanded quantity of a product is exactly equal to the quantity of that product produced. Suppose that producers are willing to *supply* two million bushels of wheat at a price of $7 per bushel and that buyers are willing to *purchase* two million bushels at a price of $7 per bushel. In other words, supply and demand are in balance, or in equilibrium, at the price of $7. Economists call this price the *market price*. The **market price** of any product is the price at which the quantity demanded is exactly equal to the quantity supplied.

In theory and in the real world, market prices are affected by anything that affects supply and demand. The *demand* for wheat, for example, might change if researchers suddenly discovered that it offered a previously unknown health benefit. Then buyers would demand more wheat at every price. Or the *supply* of wheat might change if new technology permitted the production of greater quantities of wheat from the same amount of acreage. Other changes that can affect competitive prices are shifts in buyer tastes, the development of new products, fluctuations in income owing to inflation or recession, or even changes in the weather that affect the production of wheat.

Perfect competition is quite rare in today's world. Many real markets, however, are examples of monopolistic competition.

Monopolistic Competition

Monopolistic competition is a market situation in which there are many buyers along with a relatively large number of sellers. The various products available in a monopolistically competitive market are very similar in nature, and they are all intended to satisfy the same need. However, each seller attempts to make its product different from the others by providing unique product features, an attention-getting brand name, unique packaging, or services such as free delivery or a lifetime warranty.

Product differentiation is the process of developing and promoting differences between one's products and all competitive products. It is a fact of life for the producers of many consumer goods, from soaps to clothing to furniture to shoes. A furniture manufacturer such as Thomasville sees what looks like a mob of competitors, all trying to chip away at its share of the market. By differentiating each of its products from all similar products produced by competitors, Thomasville obtains some limited control over the market price of its product.

Personal App Next time you go to the supermarket or drug store, notice all the products competing for your dollars. No two shampoos or candies are exactly alike. Thanks to product differentiation, you have a lot of choices when you shop.

Oligopoly

An **oligopoly** is a market (or industry) situation in which there are few sellers. Generally, these sellers are quite large, and sizable investments are required to enter into their market. Examples of oligopolies are the automobile, airline, car rental, cereal, and farm implement industries.

Because there are few sellers in an oligopoly, the market actions of each seller can have a strong effect on competitors' sales and prices. If General Motors, for example, reduces its automobile prices, Ford, Honda, Toyota, and Nissan usually do the same to retain their market shares. In the absence of much price competition, product differentiation becomes the major competitive weapon; this is very evident in the advertising of the major automobile manufacturers. For instance, when Toyota was faced with declining sales as a result of quality and safety issues, it began offering buyer incentives to attract new-car buyers. Quickly, both Ford and General Motors began offering similar incentives and for the same reason—to attract new-car buyers.

market price the price at which the quantity demanded is exactly equal to the quantity supplied

monopolistic competition a market situation in which there are many buyers along with a relatively large number of sellers who differentiate their products from the products of competitors

product differentiation the process of developing and promoting differences between one's products and all similar products

oligopoly a market (or industry) in which there are few sellers

Monopoly

A **monopoly** is a market (or industry) with only one seller, and there are barriers to keep other firms from entering the industry. In a monopoly, there is no close substitute for the product or service. Because only one firm is the supplier of a product, it would seem that it has complete control over price. However, no firm can set its price at some astronomical figure just because there is no competition; the firm would soon find that it has no customers or sales revenue either. Instead, the firm in a monopoly position must consider the demand for its product and set the price at the most profitable level.

Classic examples of monopolies in the United States are public utilities, including companies that provide local gas, water, or electricity. Each utility firm operates in a **natural monopoly**, an industry that requires a huge investment in capital and within which any duplication of facilities would be wasteful. Natural monopolies are permitted to exist because the public interest is best served by their existence, but they operate under the scrutiny and control of various state and federal agencies. Although many public utilities are still classified as natural monopolies, there is increased competition in many industries. For example, there have been increased demands for consumer choice when selecting a company that provides electrical service to both homes and businesses.

A legal monopoly—sometimes referred to as a *limited monopoly*—is created when a government entity issues a franchise, license, copyright, patent, or trademark. For example, a copyright exists for a specific period of time and can be used to protect the owners of written materials from unauthorized use by competitors that have not shared in the time, effort, and expense required for their development. Because Microsoft owns the copyright on its popular Windows software, it enjoys a legal-monopoly position. Except for natural monopolies and legal monopolies, federal antitrust laws prohibit both monopolies and attempts to form monopolies.

AMERICAN BUSINESS TODAY

Although our economic system is far from perfect, it provides Americans with a high standard of living compared with people in other countries throughout the world. **Standard of living** is a loose, subjective measure of how well off an individual or a society is, mainly in terms of want satisfaction through goods and services. Also, our economic system offers solutions to many of the problems that plague society and provides opportunities for people who are willing to work and to continue learning.

To understand the current business environment and the challenges ahead, it helps to understand how business developed.

Early Business Development

Our American business system has its roots in the knowledge, skills, and values that the earliest settlers brought to this country. The first settlers in the United States were concerned mainly with providing themselves with basic necessities—food, clothing, and shelter. Almost all families lived on farms, and the entire family worked at the business of surviving. They used their surplus for trading, mainly by barter, among themselves and with the English trading ships that called at the colonies. **Barter** is a system of exchange in which goods or services are traded directly for other goods or services without using money. As this trade increased, small-scale business enterprises began to appear. Some settlers were able to use their skills and their excess time to work under the domestic system of production. The **domestic system** was a method of manufacturing in which an entrepreneur distributed raw materials to various homes, where families would process them into finished goods. The merchant entrepreneur then offered the goods for sale.

LEARNING OBJECTIVE

7 Summarize the factors that affect the business environment and the challenges that American businesses will encounter in the future.

monopoly a market (or industry) with only one seller, and there are barriers to keep other firms from entering the industry

natural monopoly an industry requiring huge investments in capital and within which any duplication of facilities would be wasteful and thus not in the public interest

standard of living a loose, subjective measure of how well off an individual or a society is, mainly in terms of want satisfaction through goods and services

barter a system of exchange in which goods or services are traded directly for other goods or services without using money

domestic system a method of manufacturing in which an entrepreneur distributes raw materials to various homes, where families process them into finished goods to be offered for sale by the merchant entrepreneur

Then, in 1793, Samuel Slater set up a textile factory in Pawtucket, Rhode Island, to spin raw cotton into thread. Slater's ingenuity resulted in America's first use of the **factory system** of manufacturing, in which all the materials, machinery, and workers required to manufacture a product are assembled in one place. The Industrial Revolution in America was born. A manufacturing technique called *specialization* was used to improve productivity. **Specialization** is the separation of a manufacturing process into distinct tasks and the assignment of the different tasks to different individuals.

The years from 1820 to 1900 were the golden age of invention and innovation in machinery. At the same time, new means of transportation greatly expanded the domestic markets for American products. Certainly, many basic characteristics of our modern business system took form during this time period.

The Great Depression—could it happen again? While economists still debate the answer to this question, most Americans were frightened by the recent economic crisis that some experts described as the worst the nation has experienced since the Great Depression. In this Depression era photo, unemployed workers line up to get free soup, coffee, and donuts.

© Getty Images

Business Development in the 1900s

Industrial growth and prosperity continued well into the 20th century. Henry Ford's moving automotive assembly line, which brought the work to the worker, refined the concept of specialization and helped spur on the mass production of consumer goods. Fundamental changes occurred in business ownership and management as well. No longer were the largest businesses owned by one individual; instead, ownership was in the hands of thousands of corporate shareholders who were willing to invest in—but not to operate—a business.

The Roaring Twenties ended with the sudden crash of the stock market in 1929 and the near collapse of the economy. The Great Depression that followed in the 1930s was a time of misery and human suffering. People lost their faith in business and its ability to satisfy the needs of society without government involvement. After Franklin D. Roosevelt became president in 1933, the federal government devised a number of programs to get the economy moving again. In implementing these programs, the government got deeply involved in business for the first time.

To understand the major events that shaped the United States during the remainder of the 20th century, it helps to remember that the economy was compared to a roller coaster ride earlier in this chapter—periods of economic growth followed by periods of economic slowdown. Major events that shaped the nation's economy occurred during the period from 1940 to 2000 include:

- World War II, the Korean War, and the Vietnam War
- Rapid economic growth and higher standard of living during the 1950s and 1960s
- The social responsibility movement during the 1960s
- A shortage of crude oil and higher prices for most goods in the mid-1970s
- High inflation, high interest rates, and reduced business profits during the early 1980s
- Sustained economic growth in the 1990s

During the last part of the 20th century, the Internet became a major force in the economy. e-Business—a topic we will continue to explore throughout this text—became an accepted method of conducting business. **e-Business** is the organized effort of individuals to produce and sell *through the Internet,* for a profit, the products and services that satisfy society's needs.

factory system a system of manufacturing in which all the materials, machinery, and workers required to manufacture a product are assembled in one place

specialization the separation of a manufacturing process into distinct tasks and the assignment of the different tasks to different individuals

e-business the organized effort of individuals to produce and sell *through the Internet,* for a profit, the products and services that satisfy society's needs

entrepreneurial SUCCESS

© Jon Schulte / iStockphoto 6184858

Meet Scott Heiferman, Meetup Entrepreneur

By the time he was 30, Scott Heiferman had founded and sold a profitable Internet advertising agency (i-traffic, now owned by Agency.com). He then co-founded and sold a thriving social media site for photo bloggers (Fotolog.com, now owned by Hi-Media Group).

Heiferman was also co-founder (and remains CEO of) Meetup.com, an Internet-based global business for the 21st century. Meetup provides online space and interactive tools to help its 7 million members organize and coordinate in-person meetings in 45,000 cities worldwide. This fast-growing company rings up more than $12 million in annual revenue and employs 77 people.

Although he didn't set out to start one business after another, Heiferman has an enviable record of entrepreneurial success. He offers five tips for startup success:

- *Stay focused.* Think of a startup as a puzzle to be solved one piece at a time, and don't try to put all the pieces into place simultaneously.

- *Be ready for surprises.* Heiferman was surprised when people began using Meetup in political campaigns. That's when he learned that entrepreneurs should leave room for surprises in a new business.

- *Work on what you find fascinating.* If you're interested in something and it doesn't exist, use your interest as an entrepreneurial opportunity.

- *Throw yourself into your product.* Know your customers so you can create and deliver the best product you can offer.

- *Recruit the right people.* "You need a team that's going to care about this thing as much as you do," Heiferman says. His advice: Choose talented, dedicated people who share your goals for the new venture.

Sources: Teri Evans, "Reaping Success Through Stranger 'Meetups,'" *Wall Street Journal*, November 21, 2010, www.wsj.com; Radhika Marya, "5 Tips for Startup Success from the CEO of Meetup," *Mashable*, October 28, 2010, www.mashable.com/2010/10/28/startup-tips-meetup/; Doree Shafrir, "Tweet Tweet Boom Boom," *New York Magazine*, April 18, 2010, http://nymag.com/news/media/65494/.

Unfortunately, by the last part of the 20th century, a larger number of business failures and declining stock values were initial signs that larger economic problems were on the way.

A New Century: 2000 and Beyond

According to many economic experts, the first part of the 21st century might be characterized as the best of times and the worst of times rolled into one package. On the plus side, technology became available at an affordable price. Both individuals and businesses could now access information with the click of a button. They also could buy and sell merchandise online.

In addition to information technology, the growth of service businesses also changed the way American firms do business in the 21st century. Because service businesses employ approximately 85 percent of the nation's workforce, we now have a service economy.[15] A **service economy** is an economy in which more effort is devoted to the production of services than to the production of goods. Typical service businesses include restaurants, laundries and dry cleaners, real estate, movie theaters, repair companies, and other services that we often take for granted.

Personal App If you've ever worked in a restaurant or a store, you've been part of the service economy. Your career possibilities in the service economy are expanding every day, especially with the rapid growth of Internet-related businesses.

service economy an economy in which more effort is devoted to the production of services than to the production of goods

More information about how service businesses affect the economy is provided in Chapter 8, Producing Quality Goods and Services.

On the negative side, it is hard to watch television, surf the Web, listen to the radio, or read the newspaper without hearing some news about the economy. Because many of the economic indicators described in Table 1-2 on page 19 indicate troubling economic problems, there is still a certain amount of pessimism surrounding the economy.

The Current Business Environment

Before reading on, answer the following question:

In today's competitive business world, which of the following environments affects business?

a. The competitive environment
b. The global environment
c. The technological environment
d. The economic environment
e. All of the above

The correct answer is "e." All the environments listed affect business today. For example, businesses operate in a *competitive environment*. As noted earlier in this chapter, competition is a basic component of capitalism. Every day, business owners must figure out what makes their businesses successful and how their businesses are different from the competition. Often, the answer is contained in the basic definition of business provided on page 10.

In the definition of business, note the phrase *satisfy society's needs*. These three words say a lot about how well a successful firm competes with competitors. If you meet customer needs, then any business or entrepreneur has a better chance at success.

Related to the competitive environment is the *global environment*. Not only do American businesses have to compete with other American businesses, but they also must compete with businesses from all over the globe. According to global experts, China is one of the fastest-growing economies in the world. And China is not alone. Other countries around the globe also compete with U.S. firms. According to Richard Haass, president of the Council on Foreign Relations, "There will be winners and losers from globalization. We win every time we go shopping because prices are lower. Choice is greater because of globalization. But there are losers. There are people who will lose their jobs either to foreign competition or [to] technological innovation."[16]

Although both increased competition and technological innovation have changed the way we do business, the *technology environment* for U.S. businesses has never been more challenging. Changes in manufacturing equipment, communication with customers, and distribution of products are all examples of how technology has changed everyday business practices. New technology will require businesses to spend additional money to keep abreast of an ever-changing technology environment and even more money to train employees to use the new technology.

In addition to the competitive, global, and technology environments, the *economic environment* must always be considered when making business decisions. This fact is especially important when the nation's economy takes a nosedive or an individual firm's sales revenue and profits are declining. For example, both small and large business firms reduced both spending and hiring new employees over the last three years because of economic concerns related to the depressed housing, automotive, banking, and financial industries.

In addition to economic pressures, today's socially responsible managers and business owners must be concerned about the concept of sustainability. According to the U.S. Environmental Protection Agency, **sustainability** means meeting the

Avon Says: "Hello Green Tomorrow"

Avon Products, an $8 billion beauty company, is slashing water and power usage to save natural resources and boost long-term profits. To preserve forests, it will be printing all its catalogs on recycled paper by 2020. Now it's inviting the public to help make tomorrow greener. Take a look: www.hellogreentomorrow.com.

sustainability meeting the needs of the present without compromising the ability of future generations to meet their own needs

needs of the present without compromising the ability of future generations to meet their own needs.[17] Although the word *green* used to mean a simple color in a box of crayons, today green means a new way of doing business. As a result, a combination of forces, including economic factors, growth in population, increased energy use, and concerns for the environment, is changing the way individuals live and businesses operate.

When you look back at the original question we asked at the beginning of this section, clearly, each different type of environment—competitive, global, technological, and economic—affects the way a business does *business*. As a result, there are always opportunities for improvement and challenges that must be considered.

The Challenges Ahead

There it is—the American business system in brief.

When it works well, it provides jobs for those who are willing to work, a standard of living that few countries can match, and many opportunities for personal advancement. However, like every other system devised by humans, it is not perfect. Our business system may give us prosperity, but it also gave us the Great Depression of the 1930s, the economic problems of the 1970s and the early 1980s, and the economic crisis that began in the fall of 2007.

Obviously, the system can be improved. Certainly, there are plenty of people who are willing to tell us exactly what they think the American economy needs. However, these people often provide conflicting opinions. Who is right and who is wrong? Even the experts cannot agree.

The experts do agree, however, that several key issues will challenge our economic system (and our nation) over the next decade. Some of the questions to be resolved include:

- How can we create a more stable economy and create new jobs for the unemployed?
- How can we regulate banks, savings and loan associations, credit unions, and other financial institutions to prevent the type of abuses that led to the banking crisis?
- How do we reduce the national debt and still maintain a healthy economy and stimulate business growth?
- How can we make American workers more productive and American firms more competitive in the global marketplace?
- How can we preserve the benefits of competition and small business in our American economic system?
- How can we encourage economic growth and at the same time continue to conserve natural resources and sustain our environment?
- How can we meet the needs of two-income families, single parents, older Americans, and the less fortunate who need health care and social programs to exist?
- How can we defeat terrorism and resolve conflict with Iran, North Korea, and other countries throughout the world?

The answers to these questions are anything but simple. In the past, Americans have always been able to solve their economic problems through ingenuity and creativity. Now, as we continue the journey through the 21st century, we need that same ingenuity and creativity not only to solve our current problems but also to compete in the global marketplace and build a nation and economy for future generations.

The American business system is not perfect by any means, but it does work reasonably well. We discuss some of its problems in Chapter 2 as we examine the topics of social responsibility and business ethics.

* ## Concept Check

☐ How does your standard of living affect the products or services you buy?

☐ What is the difference between the domestic system and the factory system?

☐ Choose one of the environments that affect business and explain how it affects a small electronics manufacturer located in Portland, Oregon.

☐ What do you consider the most important challenge that will face people in the United States in the years ahead?

Get Flashcards, Quizzes, Games, Crosswords, and more @ **www.cengagebrain.com**

SUMMARY

1 Discuss what you must do to be successful in the world of business.

For many years, people in business—both employees and managers—assumed that prosperity would continue. When faced with both economic problems and increased competition, a large number of these people began to ask the question: What do we do now? Although this is a fair question, it is difficult to answer. Certainly, for a college student taking business courses or an employee just starting a career, the question is even more difficult to answer. And yet there are still opportunities out there for people who are willing to work hard, continue to learn, and possess the ability to adapt to change. The kind of career you choose ultimately will depend on your own values and what you feel is most important in life. By studying business, you may also decide to start your own business and become a better consumer and investor.

2 Define *business* and identify potential risks and rewards.

Business is the organized effort of individuals to produce and sell, for a profit, the goods and services that satisfy society's needs. Four kinds of resources—material, human, financial, and informational—must be combined to start and operate a business. The three general types of businesses are manufacturers, service businesses, and marketing intermediaries. Profit is what remains after all business expenses are deducted from sales revenue. It is the payment that owners receive for assuming the risks of business—primarily the risks of not receiving payment and of losing whatever has been invested in the firm.

3 Define *economics* and describe the two types of economic systems: capitalism and command economy.

Economics is the study of how wealth is created and distributed. An economic system must answer four questions: What goods and services will be produced? How will they be produced? For whom will they be produced? Who owns and who controls the major factors of production? Capitalism (on which our economic system is based) is an economic system in which individuals own and operate the majority of businesses that provide goods and services.

Our economic system today is a mixed economy. In the circular flow that characterizes our business system (see Figure 1-5), households and businesses exchange resources for goods and services, using money as the medium of exchange. In a similar manner, the government collects taxes from businesses and households and purchases products and resources with which to provide services.

In a command economy, government, rather than individuals, owns many of the factors of production and provides the answers to the three other economic questions. Socialist and communist economies are—at least in theory—command economies.

4 Identify the ways to measure economic performance.

One way to evaluate the performance of an economic system is to assess changes in productivity, which is the average level of output per worker per hour. Gross domestic product (GDP) can also be used to measure a nation's economic well-being and is the total dollar value of all goods and services produced by all people within the boundaries of a country during a one-year period. In addition to GDP, other economic indicators include a nation's balance of trade, bank credit, corporate profits, consumer price index (CPI), inflation rate, national income, new housing starts, prime interest rate, producer price index (PPI), and unemployment rate.

5 Examine the four different phases in the typical business cycle.

Generally, the business cycle consists of four states: the peak (sometimes called prosperity) recession, the trough, and recovery (sometimes called expansion). Some experts believe that effective use of monetary policy (the Federal Reserve's decisions that determine the size of the supply of money and the level of interest rates) and fiscal policy (the government's influence on the amount of savings and expenditures) can speed up recovery.

A federal deficit occurs when the government spends more than it receives in taxes and other revenues. Today, the national debt is over $14 trillion or approximately $45,000 for every man, woman, and child in the United States.

6 Outline the four types of competition.

Competition is essentially a rivalry among businesses for sales to potential customers. In a capitalist economy, competition works to ensure the efficient and effective operation of business. Competition also ensures that a firm will survive only if it serves its customers well by providing products and services that meet their needs. Economists recognize four degrees of competition. Ranging from most to least competitive, the four degrees are perfect competition, monopolistic competition, oligopoly, and monopoly. The factors of supply and demand generally influence the price that customers pay producers for goods and services.

7 Summarize the factors that affect the business environment and the challenges that American businesses will encounter in the future.

From the beginning of the Industrial Revolution to the phenomenal expansion of American industry in the 19th and early 20th centuries, our government maintained an essentially Laissez-Faire attitude toward business. However, during the Great Depression of the 1930s, the federal government began to provide a number of social services to its citizens. The government's role in business has expanded considerably since then.

To understand the major events that shaped the United States during the remainder of the 20th century, it helps to remember that the economy was compared to a roller coaster ride earlier in this chapter—periods of economic growth followed by periods of economic slowdown. Events including wars, rapid economic growth, the social responsibility movement, a shortage of crude oil, high inflation, high interest rates, and reduced business profits all have affected business and the economy.

Now more than ever before, the way a business operates is affected by the competitive environment, global environment, technological environment, and economic environment. As a result, business has a number challenges for the future.

KEY TERMS

You should now be able to define and give an example relevant to each of the following terms:

free enterprise (4)
cultural (or workplace) diversity (6)
business (10)
profit (11)
stakeholders (12)
economics (12)
microeconomics (12)
macroeconomics (12)
economy (12)
factors of production (13)
entrepreneur (13)
capitalism (13)
invisible hand (13)

market economy (14)
mixed economy (14)
consumer products (15)
command economy (16)
productivity (17)
gross domestic product (GDP) (18)
inflation (18)
deflation (18)
unemployment rate (18)
consumer price index (CPI) (18)
producer price index (PPI) (19)

business cycle (20)
recession (20)
depression (20)
monetary policies (20)
fiscal policy (20)
federal deficit (21)
national debt (21)
competition (21)
perfect (or pure) competition (21)
supply (22)
demand (22)
market price (23)

monopolistic competition (23)
product differentiation (23)
oligopoly (23)
monopoly (24)
natural monopoly (24)
standard of living (24)
barter (24)
domestic system (24)
factory system (25)
specialization (25)
e-business (25)
service economy (26)
sustainability (27)

DISCUSSION QUESTIONS

1. In what ways have the problems caused by the recent economic crisis affected business firms? In what ways have these problems affected employees and individuals?
2. What factors caused American business to develop into a mixed economic system rather than some other type of economic system?
3. Does an individual consumer really have a voice in answering the four basic economic questions?
4. Is gross domestic product a reliable indicator of a nation's economic health? What might be a better indicator?
5. Discuss this statement: "Business competition encourages efficiency of production and leads to improved product quality."
6. In our business system, how is government involved in answering the four basic economic questions? Does government participate in the system or interfere with it?
7. Choose one of the challenges listed on page 28 and describe possible ways in which business and society could help to solve or eliminate the problem in the future.

TEST YOURSELF

Matching Questions

1. _____ Materials, machinery, and workers are assembled in one place.

2. _____ The government spends more than it receives.

3. _____ System of exchange.

4. _____ The process of distinguishing Colgate from Crest toothpaste.

5. _____ The average level of output per worker per hour.

6. _____ A study of how wealth is created and distributed.

7. _____ An organized effort to produce and sell goods and services for a profit.

8. _____ A system where individuals own and operate the majority of businesses.

9. _____ A person who takes the risk and invests in a business.

10. _____ Value of all goods and services produced within a country during a one-year period.

    a. capitalism
    b. economics
    c. federal deficit
    d. productivity
    e. product differentiation
    f. business
    g. factory system
    h. entrepreneur
    i. gross domestic product
    j. barter

True False Questions

11. **T F** The majority of small business firms are successful during the first seven years.

12. **T F** For a business to be organized, it must combine four types of resources: workers, natural resources, capital, and ownership.

13. **T F** The equilibrium price means that the supply and demand for a product are in balance.

14. **T F** Under communism, individual consumers determine what will be produced.

15. **T F** Hewlett-Packard Corporation and Dell Computer use product differentiation in the marketplace.

16. **T F** If a firm's sales revenues exceed its expenses, the firm has earned a profit.

17. **T F** Fiscal policy determines the level of interest rates.

18. **T F** The main objective of business firms should be to satisfy the needs of their customers.

19. **T F** Adam Smith is the father of communism and advocated a classless society.

20. **T F** A business cycle consists of four states: peak, recession, trough, and recovery.

Multiple-Choice Questions

21. _____ Demand is a
    a. relationship between prices and the quantities purchased by buyers.
    b. relationship between prices and the quantities offered by producers.
    c. quantity of goods available for purchase.
    d. price the consumer is willing to pay.
    e. by-product of communism.

22. _____ The process of separating work into distinct tasks is called
    a. bartering.
    b. networking.
    c. specialization.
    d. a factory system.
    e. a domestic system.

23. _____ What term implies that there shall be no government interference in the economy?
    a. market economy
    b. free-market economy
    c. command economy
    d. *laissez-faire*
    e. socialism

24. _____ When the level of prices in an economy rise, it's called
    a. prosperity.
    b. recession.
    c. depression.
    d. recovery.
    e. inflation.

25. _____ The total of all federal deficits is called
    a. depression.
    b. fiscal policy.
    c. gross domestic product.
    d. national debt.
    e. business cycle.

26. _____ The ability to work well with many types of people in the workplace is referred to as
   a. workplace differentiation.
   b. cultural diversity.
   c. economic stability.
   d. career unity.
   e. employee magnification.

27. _____ Best Buy and Wal-Mart are both examples of
   a. production intermediaries.
   b. manufacturing businesses.
   c. service businesses.
   d. marketing intermediaries.
   e. small businesses.

28. _____ The study of the national economy and the global economy is referred to as
   a. factors of the economy.
   b. microeconomics.
   c. macroeconomics.
   d. *laissez-faire* capitalism.
   e. a command economy.

29. _____ How well off an individual or a society is, mainly in terms of want-satisfaction through goods and services is referred to as
   a. microeconomics.
   b. national satisfaction index.
   c. economic standard.
   d. standard of living.
   e. global comparison measure.

30. _____ A monthly index that measures changes in prices that consumers pay for goods is referred to as the
   a. prosperity index.
   b. producer's price index.
   c. prosperity price predictor.
   d. inflation rate index.
   e. consumer price index.

Answers to the Test Yourself questions appear at the end of the book on page TY-1.

VIDEO CASE
Entertainment Means Profits for Nederlander Concerts

Nederlander Concerts is based in Los Angeles, one of the two biggest markets in the U.S. concert industry (New York is the other). The company specializes in booking and promoting musical artists like the Goo Goo Dolls, Maroon 5, and Cyndi Lauper in small- to mid-sized venues across the western United States. It owns some of the theaters, amphitheaters, and arenas, including the Greek Theatre in Los Angeles, the Santa Barbara Bowl, the San Jose Civic Theater, and the Grove in Anaheim, and it rents space for concerts and events in other third-party venues along the West Coast. Nederlander Concerts also partners with some of California's major cities such as Santa Monica and San Jose to manage or operate their civic theaters and present events there.

Since Nederlander Concerts deliberately focuses on small- to mid-sized venues, it can offer a unique concert experience that brings audiences and performers closer together. It can therefore sell that high-quality experience at a higher price than seats in a bigger theater yield, and it can more often count on selling out the house, which helps the company and the artists to profit. The concert company's chief operating officer says, "The key areas or departments of the company include talent-buying and marketing, operations, finance, and business development... I have a talent-buying team, I have a marketing team, we have a general manager of the building, we have a substantial team of people who take care of the fans, take care of the artist, and look after the shows that we buy. We're in a competitive market, and it's pretty interesting what we do."

Although it might seem odd that the concert business is a competitive one, in fact Nederlander Concerts competes with other promoters (like Live Nation) not just for audiences at its events but for bookings by popular artists. Therefore, it counts as its clients or customers musicians as well as music lovers, and the performers need to be happy with the financial deal they are getting. As Nederlander's chief operating officer explains, "It's not always easy to get the show; there is competition.... We have a great reputation with the artist. But also there's one other factor, and that's making the deal. That's making your best offer. That's trying to think about whether the agent is ... telling you that your competition is paying more, willing to go more. You have to get your own 'I won't go above' number and stop bidding (for the act), or you have to say, 'Okay, I'll pay a little bit more and try to get the show.' So there's a real gamesmanship between agent and buyer ... the art of the deal is something we live with every day."

Given the talent, how does Nederlander find the audience? Says its vice president of marketing, "It's learning about the market, and picking up every newspaper you can find, listening to every radio station you can find, watching all of the TV, all the news programming ... it still comes back to, who is the artist, and who is their audience? And how do you find them? ... The number one reason why people don't go to a show, so they say, is that they don't know about it. Which is infuriating. But we just try to make that percentage of people ... smaller, and smaller, and smaller."

When everything is going well, the company profits. "Where we like to do most of our business, and in fact is where we probably do 90 percent of our business, is in the venues that we own or operate, so that the risk profile of those shows goes down ... we have more revenues coming in to ensure that we're able to cover the cost, including the cost of talent, and then walk away with a greater profit."[18]

Questions

1. Nederlander Concerts competes for audiences and with other concert arenas and promoters. Do you think it also competes for those audiences with TV, movies, CDs, DVDs, streaming video, and sports events? Why or why not? If yes, what implications does this type of competition have for Nederlander's business?

2. How many different groups can you think of whose needs Nederlander Concerts must satisfy to remain a successful business?

3. Give an example showing how Nederlander Concerts uses each of the four factors of production.

BUILDING SKILLS FOR CAREER SUCCESS

1. Exploring the Internet

The Internet is a global network of computers that can be accessed by anyone in the world. For example, your school or firm is most likely connected to the Web. And today more people have high-speed Internet connections at home than ever before.

To familiarize yourself with the wealth of information available through the Internet and its usefulness to business students, this exercise focuses on information services available from a few popular search engines used to explore the Web.

To use one of these search engines, enter its Internet address in your Web browser. The addresses of some popular search engines are

www.ask.com
www.google.com
www.msn.com
www.yahoo.com

Assignment

1. Examine the ways in which two search engines present categories of information on their opening screens. Which search engine was better to use in your opinion? Why?

2. Think of a business topic that you would like to know more about; for example, careers, gross domestic product, national debt, or another concept introduced in this chapter. Using your preferred search engine, explore a few articles and reports provided on your topic. Briefly summarize your findings.

2. Building Team Skills

Over the past few years, employees have been expected to function as productive team members instead of working alone. People often believe that they can work effectively in teams, but many people find working with a group of people to be a challenge. Being an effective team member requires skills that encourage other members to participate in the team endeavor.

College classes that function as teams are more interesting and more fun to attend, and students generally learn more about the topics in the course. If your class is to function as a team, it is important to begin building the team early in the semester. One way to begin creating a team is to learn something about each student in the class. This helps team members to feel comfortable with each other and fosters a sense of trust.

Assignment

1. Find a partner, preferably someone you do not know.

2. Each partner has two to three minutes to answer the following questions:
   a. What is your name, and where do you work?
   b. What interesting or unusual thing have you done in your life? (Do not talk about work or college; rather, focus on such things as hobbies, travel, family, and sports.)
   c. Why are you taking this course, and what do you expect to learn? (Satisfying a degree requirement is not an acceptable answer.)

3. Introduce your partner to the class. Use one to two minutes, depending on the size of the class.

3. Researching Different Careers

In this chapter, *entrepreneurship* is defined as the willingness to take risks and the knowledge and ability to use the other factors of production efficiently. An *entrepreneur* is a person who risks his or her time, effort, and money to start and operate a business. Often, people believe that these terms apply only to small business. However, employees with entrepreneurial attitudes have recently advanced more rapidly in large companies as well.

Assignment

1. Go to the local library or use the Internet to research how large firms, especially corporations, are rewarding employees who have entrepreneurial skills.

2. Find answers to the following questions:
   a. Why is an entrepreneurial attitude important in corporations today?
   b. What makes an entrepreneurial employee different from other employees?
   c. How are these employees being rewarded, and are the rewards worth the effort?

3. Write a two-page report that summarizes your findings.

CHAPTER 2 BEING ETHICAL AND SOCIALLY RESPONSIBLE

© PR Newswire/7-Eleven, Inc.

Why should you care?

Business ethics and social responsibility issues have become extremely relevant in today's business world. Business schools teach business ethics to prepare managers to be more responsible. Corporations are developing ethics and social responsibility programs to help meet these needs in the work place.

Learning Objectives

What you will be able to do once you complete this chapter:

1 Understand what is meant by *business ethics*.

2 Identify the types of ethical concerns that arise in the business world.

3 Discuss the factors that affect the level of ethical behavior in organizations.

4 Explain how ethical decision making can be encouraged.

5 Describe how our current views on the social responsibility of business have evolved.

6 Explain the two views on the social responsibility of business and understand the arguments for and against increased social responsibility.

7 Discuss the factors that led to the consumer movement and list some of its results.

8 Analyze how present employment practices are being used to counteract past abuses.

9 Describe the major types of pollution, their causes, and their cures.

10 Identify the steps a business must take to implement a program of social responsibility.

Eco-Friendly Cars Become Big Business

Although early eco-friendly cars were regarded as curiosities, today many major auto man-ufacturers are racing to get ahead in this fast-growing business. Japan's Toyota leads the pack: When it launched its Prius hybrid electric-gasoline car in 1997, sales started out sluggish. Still, Toyota stuck to its vision of building long-term profits by designing, manufacturing, and marketing cars that are "greener" than traditional gas-powered vehicles. That vision finally paid off: Toyota's fuel-efficient Prius has become the world's best-selling hybrid, with more than 450,000 driven out of car showrooms every year.

U.S. automakers are also steering in an eco-friendly direction. General Motors, for exam-ple, invested hundreds of millions of dollars to develop the Chevrolet Volt, an electric car that gets more than 90 miles per gallon when running on battery power. The company will sell the Volt under the Opel brand in Europe, as well. Ford, meanwhile, has attracted the attention of SUV lovers with a hybrid Escape SUV. In addition, it offers an all-electric version of its popular Focus compact car. Start-up Tesla Motors is selling an upscale, all-electric roadster and supply-ing Toyota with batteries and control systems for its new electric RAV4 SUV.

Other automakers are also racing to market with greener cars. Honda, for example, is doing well with hybrids. Nissan, avoiding the hybrid route, has chosen to focus its eco-friendly efforts on all-electric cars. Its first entry, the full-sized Leaf sedan, is powered by a lithium-ion battery that requires a special plug to be recharged at home. Hyundai has several hybrid electric-gasoline vehicles on the market and is testing a hydrogen fuel cell electric car. Daimler and BMW are working on a compact all-electric car, and Mitsubishi has partnered with Peu-geot to develop a green car for future release.

Despite the clear environmental benefits, eco-friendly cars can be a tough sell. First, they're generally priced higher than traditional gas-powered vehicles. Second, all-electric cars have a limited driving range, and many require special plugs or high-speed recharging sta-tions. As these bumps in the road get smoothed out, automakers believe their green vehicles will continue to attract buyers who care about the environment and are weary of high gas prices.[1]

Did You Know?

Toyota, a pioneer in eco-friendly cars, launched its hybrid electric-gasoline Prius in 1997; today, the Prius is by far the world's best-selling hybrid.

Obviously, organizations like Toyota and General Motors want to be recognized as responsible corporate citizens. Such companies recognize the need to harmonize their operations with environmental demands and other vital social concerns. Not all firms, however, have taken steps to encourage a consideration of social responsi-bility and ethics in their decisions and day-to-day activities. Some managers still re-gard such business practices as a poor investment, in which the cost is not worth the return. Other managers—indeed, most managers—view the cost of these practices as a necessary business expense, similar to wages or rent.

Most managers today, like those at Toyota and General Motors, are finding ways to balance a growing agenda of socially responsible activities with the drive to generate profits. This also happens to be a good way for a company to demonstrate its values and to attract like-minded employees, customers, and stockholders. In a highly competitive business environment, an increasing number of companies are, like Toyota and General Motors, seeking to set themselves apart by developing a reputation for ethical and socially responsible behavior.

We begin this chapter by defining *business ethics* and examining ethical issues. Next, we look at the standards of behavior in organizations and how ethical behavior can be encouraged. We then turn to the topic of social responsibility. We compare and contrast two present-day models of social responsibility and present arguments for and against increasing the social responsibility of business. We then examine the major elements of the consumer movement. We discuss how social responsibility in business has affected employment practices and environmental concerns. Finally, we consider the commitment, planning, and funding that go into a firm's program of social responsibility.

BUSINESS ETHICS DEFINED

LEARNING OBJECTIVE

1 Understand what is meant by *business ethics*.

Ethics is the study of right and wrong and of the morality of the choices individuals make. An ethical decision or action is one that is "right" according to some standard of behavior. **Business ethics** is the application of moral standards to business situations. Recent court cases involving unethical behavior have helped to make business ethics a matter of public concern. In one such case, Copley Pharmaceutical, Inc., pled guilty to federal criminal charges (and paid a $10.65 million fine) for falsifying drug manufacturers' reports to the Food and Drug Administration. In another much-publicized case, lawsuits against tobacco companies have led to $246 billion in settlements, although there has been only one class-action lawsuit filed on behalf of all smokers. The case, *Engle v. R. J. Reynolds*, could cost tobacco companies an estimated $500 billion. In yet another case, Adelphia Communications Corp., the nation's fifth-largest cable television company, agreed to pay $715 million to settle federal investigations stemming from rampant earnings manipulation by its founder John J. Rigas, and his son, Timothy J. Rigas. Prosecutors and government regulators charged that both father and son had misappropriated Adelphia funds for their own use and had failed to pay the corporation for securities they controlled. John Rigas and Timothy Rigas are serving 12 years and 17 years in prison, respectively. John Rigas applied for a presidential pardon in January 2009, but George W. Bush left office without making a decision on Rigas' request. Mr. Rigas is scheduled to be released from federal prison in 2018.[2]

Personal App Business ethics apply to customers as well as to managers and employees. In some buying situations, the "right" thing to do isn't always clear, is it? For example, should you buy from a retail store that has been found to be unfair to its employees? Read on for tips about recognizing and resolving ethical issues.

ETHICAL ISSUES

LEARNING OBJECTIVE

2 Identify the types of ethical concerns that arise in the business world.

Ethical issues often arise out of a business's relationship with its stakeholders: investors, customers, employees, creditors, or competitors. Each of these groups has specific concerns and usually exerts pressure on the organization's managers. For example, investors want management to make sensible financial decisions that will boost sales, profits, and returns on their investments. Customers expect a firm's products to be safe, reliable, and reasonably priced. Employees demand to be treated fairly in hiring, promotion, and compensation decisions. Creditors require accounts to be paid on time and the accounting information furnished by the firm to be accurate. Competitors expect the firm's competitive practices to be fair and honest. Consider TAP Pharmaceutical Products, Inc., whose sales representatives offered every urologist in the United States a big-screen TV, computers, fax machines, and golf vacations if the doctors prescribed TAP's new prostate cancer drug Lupron. Moreover, the sales representatives sold Lupron at cut-rate prices or gratis while defrauding Medicare. Recently, the federal government won an $875 million judgment against TAP when a former TAP vice president of sales, Douglas Durand, and Dr. Joseph Gerstein blew the whistle. Now, TAP is a wholly-owned subsidiary of Takeda Pharmaceutical Company, Limited of Japan.[3]

ethics the study of right and wrong and of the morality of the choices individuals make

business ethics the application of moral standards to business situations

In late 2006, Hewlett-Packard Co.'s chairman, Patricia Dunn, and general counsel, Ann Baskins, resigned amid allegations that the company used intrusive tactics in observing the personal lives of journalists and the company's directors, thus tarnishing Hewlett-Packard's reputation for integrity. According to Congressman John Dingell of Michigan, "We have before us witnesses from Hewlett-Packard to discuss a plunderers' operation that would make (former president) Richard Nixon blush were he still alive." Alternatively, consider Bernard Madoff, former stockbroker, financial advisor, and chairman of the NASDAQ stock exchange. In 2009, he was convicted of securities and other frauds including a Ponzi scheme that defrauded clients of $65 billion.

Businesspeople face ethical issues every day, and some of these issues can be difficult to assess. Although some types of issues arise infrequently, others occur regularly. Let's take a closer look at several ethical issues.

Fairness and Honesty

Fairness and honesty in business are two important ethical concerns. Besides obeying all laws and regulations, businesspeople are expected to refrain from knowingly deceiving, misrepresenting, or intimidating others. The consequences of failing to do so can be expensive. Recently, for example, Keith E. Anderson and Wayne Anderson, the leaders of an international tax shelter scheme known as Anderson's Ark and Associates, were sentenced to as many as 20 years in prison. The Andersons; Richard Marks, their chief accounting officer; and Karolyn Grosnickle, the chief administrative officer, were ordered to pay more than $200 million in fines and restitution.[4] In yet another case, the accounting firm PricewaterhouseCoopers LLP agreed to pay the U.S. government $42 million to resolve allegations that it made false claims in connection with travel reimbursements it collected for several federal agencies.[5]

Many years ago, Deere & Company developed and implemented Business Conduct Guidelines which provide specific guidelines to all employees. The company requires each employee to deal fairly with its customers, suppliers, competitors, and employees. "No employee should take unfair advantage of anyone through manipulation, concealment, abuse of privileged information, misrepresentation of material facts or any other unfair dealing practice." Employees are encouraged to report possible violations of company ethics policies using a 24-hour hotline or anonymous e-mails.[6]

Organizational Relationships

A businessperson may be tempted to place his or her personal welfare above the welfare of others or the welfare of the organization. For example, in late 2002, former CEO of Tyco International, Ltd, Leo Dennis Kozlowski, was indicted for misappropriating $43 million in corporate funds to make philanthropic contributions in his own name, including $5 million to Seton Hall University, which named its new business-school building Kozlowski Hall. Furthermore, according to Tyco, the former CEO took $61.7 million in interest-free relocation loans without the board's permission. He allegedly used the money to finance many personal luxuries, including a $15 million yacht and a $3.9 million Renoir painting, and to throw a $2 million party for his wife's birthday. Mr. Kozlowski, currently serving up to 25 years in prison, paid $134 million in restitution to Tyco and criminal fines of $70 million. In 2009, the U.S. Supreme Court denied his petition for a judicial review. His $26 million giant mansion in New Hampshire was up for auction in 2011.[7]

Violating ethics can be humiliating and costly. Former Cuyahoga County Sheriff Gerald McFaul listens to his attorney after McFaul pleaded guilty to theft in office and ethics violation.

Relationships with customers and co-workers often create ethical problems. Unethical behavior in these areas includes taking credit for others' ideas or work, not meeting one's commitments in a mutual agreement, and pressuring others to behave unethically.

Conflict of Interest

Conflict of interest results when a businessperson takes advantage of a situation for his or her own personal interest rather than for the employer's interest. Such conflict may occur when payments and gifts make their way into business deals. A wise rule to remember is that anything given to a person that might unfairly influence that person's business decision is a bribe, and all bribes are unethical.

For example, Nortel Networks Corporation does not permit its employees, officers, and directors to accept any gifts or to serve as directors or officers of any organization that might supply goods or services to Nortel Networks. However, Nortel employees may work part-time with firms that are not competitors, suppliers, or customers. At AT&T, employees are instructed to discuss with their supervisors any investments that may seem improper. Verizon Communications forbids its employees and executives from holding a "significant" financial stake in vendors, suppliers, or customers.

At Procter & Gamble Company (P&G), all employees are obligated to act at all times solely in the best interests of the company. A conflict of interest arises when an employee has a personal relationship or financial or other interest that could interfere with this obligation, or when an employee uses his or her position with the company for personal gain. P&G requires employees to disclose all potential conflicts of interest and to take prompt actions to eliminate a conflict when the company asks them to do so. Generally, it is not acceptable to receive gifts, entertainment, or other gratuities from people with whom P&G does business because doing so could imply an obligation on the part of the company and potentially pose a conflict of interest.

Communications

Business communications, especially advertising, can present ethical questions. False and misleading advertising is illegal and unethical, and it can infuriate customers. Sponsors of advertisements aimed at children must be especially careful to avoid misleading messages. Advertisers of health-related products also must take precautions to guard against deception when using such descriptive terms as *low fat*, *fat free*, and *light*. In fact, the Federal Trade Commission has issued guidelines on the use of these labels.

FACTORS AFFECTING ETHICAL BEHAVIOR

Is it possible for an individual with strong moral values to make ethically questionable decisions in a business setting? What factors affect a person's inclination to make either ethical or unethical decisions in a business organization? Although the answers to these questions are not entirely clear, three general sets of factors do appear to influence the standards of behavior in an organization. As shown in Figure 2-1, the sets consist of individual factors, social factors, and opportunities.

Individual Factors Affecting Ethics

Several individual factors influence the level of ethical behavior in an organization.

- *Individual knowledge of an issue.* How much an individual knows about an issue is one factor. A decision maker with a greater amount of knowledge regarding a situation may take steps to avoid ethical problems, whereas a less-informed person may take action unknowingly that leads to an ethical quagmire.

✳ Concept Check

☐ What is meant by business ethics?

☐ What are the different types of ethical concerns that may arise in the business world?

☐ Explain and give an example of how advertising can present ethical questions.

LEARNING OBJECTIVE

3 Discuss the factors that affect the level of ethical behavior in organizations.

ETHICAL challenges & successful SOLUTIONS

Green or Greenwashing?

Is it ethical for a company to say its product is "green" if even the tiniest aspect is not eco-friendly? Many customers seek out goods and services that are considered green because they are made in sustainable ways, for example, or are recyclable. But is a product truly green if it is delivered by a jet that burns fossil fuel? What if one or more parts are not biodegradable or the manufacturing operation consumes lots of energy?

The Federal Trade Commission enforces advertising guidelines to ensure that firms do not make misleading environmental claims. Yet, consumers may believe a company is not doing enough to make its products green or, at the other extreme, is in some way exaggerating—*greenwashing*—its environmental claims.

To earn and retain the trust of their customers, companies must therefore be as transparent as possible about how green their products and processes really are. The outdoor clothing company Patagonia is a leader here, disclosing the carbon footprint of many of its products and labeling items that contain non-ecofriendly materials. Apple, once a Greenpeace target because some products contained environmentally questionable chemicals, is forcing suppliers to replace those materials. The company is polishing its green credentials by publicly reporting its total annual company-wide carbon footprint.

Sources: "Facts Should Match 'Green' Image," *MMR*, November 16, 2009, 8; Weston Kosova, "It Ain't Easy Being Green," *Newsweek*, September 21, 2009, www.newsweek.com/id/215886; "FTC Cites Kmart, Tender, Dyna-E for False Green Claims," *Environmental Leader*, June 10, 2009, www.environmentalleader.com; Peter Burrows, "Finally, a Big Green Apple?" *BusinessWeek*, October 5, 2009, 68–69.

- *Personal values*. An individual's moral values and central, value-related attitudes also clearly influence his or her business behavior. Most people join organizations to accomplish personal goals.
- *Personal goals*. The types of personal goals an individual aspires to and the manner in which these goals are pursued have a significant impact on that individual's behavior in an organization. The actions of specific individuals in scandal-plagued companies, such as Adelphia, Arthur Andersen, Enron, Halliburton, Qwest, and WorldCom, often raise questions about individuals' personal character and integrity.

Social Factors Affecting Ethics

- *Cultural norms*. A person's behavior in the workplace, to some degree, is determined by cultural norms, and these social factors vary from one culture to another. For example, in some countries it is acceptable and ethical for customs agents to receive gratuities for performing ordinary, legal tasks that are a part of their jobs, whereas in other countries these practices would be viewed as unethical and perhaps illegal.

FIGURE 2-1: **Factors that Affect the Level of Ethical Behavior in an Organization**

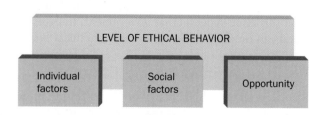

Source: Based on O. C. Ferrell and Larry Gresham, "A Contingency Framework for Understanding Ethical Decision Making in Marketing," *Journal of Marketing* (Summer 1985), 89.

- *Co-workers.* The actions and decisions of co-workers constitute another social factor believed to shape a person's sense of business ethics. For example, if your co-workers make long-distance telephone calls on company time and at company expense, you might view that behavior as acceptable and ethical because everyone does it.
- *Significant others.* The moral values and attitudes of "significant others"—spouses, friends, and relatives, for instance—also can affect an employee's perception of what is ethical and unethical behavior in the workplace.
- *Use of the Internet.* Even the Internet presents new challenges for firms whose employees enjoy easy access to sites through convenient high-speed connections at work. An employee's behavior online can be viewed as offensive to co-workers and possibly lead to lawsuits against the firm if employees engage in unethical behavior on controversial Web sites not related to their job. Interestingly, one recent survey of employees found that most workers assume that their use of technology at work will be monitored. A large majority of employees approved of most monitoring methods such as monitoring faxes and e-mail, tracking Web use, and even recording telephone calls.

"Opportunity" as a Factor Affecting Ethics

- *Presence of opportunity.* *Opportunity* refers to the amount of freedom an organization gives an employee to behave unethically if he or she makes that choice. In some organizations, certain company policies and procedures reduce the opportunity to be unethical. For example, at some fast-food restaurants, one employee takes your order and receives your payment, and another fills the order. This procedure reduces the opportunity to be unethical because the person handling the money is not dispensing the product, and the person giving out the product is not handling the money.
- *Ethical codes.* The existence of an ethical code and the importance management places on this code are other determinants of opportunity (codes of ethics are discussed in more detail in the next section).
- *Enforcement.* The degree of enforcement of company policies, procedures, and ethical codes is a major force affecting opportunity. When violations are dealt with consistently and firmly, the opportunity to be unethical is reduced.

Do you make personal telephone calls on company time? Many individuals do. Although most employees limit personal calls to a few minutes, some make personal calls in excess of 30 minutes. Whether you use company time and equipment to make personal calls is an example of a personal ethical decision.

Now that we have considered some of the factors believed to influence the level of ethical behavior in the workplace, let us explore what can be done to encourage ethical behavior and to discourage unethical behavior.

ENCOURAGING ETHICAL BEHAVIOR

Most authorities agree that there is room for improvement in business ethics. A more problematic question is: Can business be made more ethical in the real world? The majority opinion on this issue suggests that government, trade associations, and individual firms indeed can establish acceptable levels of ethical behavior.

Government's Role in Encouraging Ethics

The government can encourage ethical behavior by legislating more stringent regulations. For example, the landmark **Sarbanes-Oxley Act of 2002** provides sweeping new legal protection for those who report corporate misconduct. At the signing ceremony, President George W. Bush stated, "The act adopts tough new provisions to deter and punish corporate and accounting fraud and corruption, ensure justice for

* Concept Check

☐ Describe several individual factors that influence the level of ethical behavior in an organization.

☐ Explain several social factors that affect ethics in an organization.

☐ How does "opportunity" influence the level of ethical behavior in the workplace?

LEARNING OBJECTIVE

4 Explain how ethical decision making can be encouraged.

Sarbanes-Oxley Act of 2002 provides sweeping new legal protection for employees who report corporate misconduct

wrongdoers, and protect the interests of workers and shareholders." Among other things, the law deals with corporate responsibility, conflicts of interest, and corporate accountability. However, rules require enforcement, and the unethical businessperson frequently seems to "slip something by" without getting caught. Increased regulation may help, but it surely cannot solve the entire ethics problem.

Trade Associations' Role in Encouraging Ethics

Trade associations can and often do provide ethical guidelines for their members. These organizations, which operate within particular industries, are in an excellent position to exert pressure on members who stoop to questionable business practices. For example, recently, a pharmaceutical trade group adopted a new set of guidelines to halt the extravagant dinners and other gifts sales representatives often give to physicians. However, enforcement and authority vary from association to association. Because trade associations exist for the benefit of their members, harsh measures may be self-defeating.

Individual Companies' Role in Encouraging Ethics

Codes of ethics that companies provide to their employees are perhaps the most effective way to encourage ethical behavior. A **code of ethics** is a written guide to acceptable and ethical behavior as defined by an organization; it outlines uniform policies, standards, and punishments for violations. Because employees know what is expected of them and what will happen if they violate the rules, a code of ethics goes a long way toward encouraging ethical behavior. However, codes cannot possibly cover every situation. Companies also must create an environment in which employees recognize the importance of complying with the written code. Managers must provide direction by fostering communication, actively modeling and encouraging ethical decision making, and training employees to make ethical decisions.

Personal App Think about the kinds of behaviors that seem ethical to you and the behaviors that seem unethical. If you were writing a code of ethics for the company where you work or for your own small business, what would you include?

During the 1980s, an increasing number of organizations created and implemented ethics codes. In a recent survey of *Fortune* 1,000 firms, 93 percent of the companies that responded reported having a formal code of ethics. Some companies are now even taking steps to strengthen their codes. For example, to strengthen its accountability, the Healthcare Financial Management Association recently revised its code to designate contact persons who handle reports of ethics violations, to clarify how its board of directors should deal with violations of business ethics, and to guarantee a fair hearing process. S. C. Johnson & Son, makers of Pledge, Drano, Windex, and many other household products, is another firm that recognizes that it must behave in ways the public perceives as ethical; its code includes expectations for employees and its commitment to consumers, the community, and society in general. As shown in Figure 2-2, the ethics code of electronics giant Texas Instruments (TI) includes issues relating to policies and procedures; laws and regulations; relationships with customers, suppliers, and competitors; conflicts of interest; handling of proprietary information; and code enforcement.

Assigning an ethics officer who coordinates ethical conduct gives employees someone to consult if they are not sure of the right thing to do. An ethics officer meets with employees and top management to provide ethical advice, establishes and maintains an anonymous confidential service to answer questions about ethical issues, and takes action on ethics code violations.

Sometimes even employees who want to act ethically may find it difficult to do so. Unethical practices can become ingrained in an organization. Employees with high personal ethics may then take a controversial step called *whistle-blowing*.

code of ethics a guide to acceptable and ethical behavior as defined by the organization

FIGURE 2-2: Defining Acceptable Behavior: Texas Instruments' Code of Ethics

Texas Instruments encourages ethical behavior through an extensive training program and a written code of ethics and shared values.

TEXAS INSTRUMENTS CODE OF ETHICS

"Integrity is the foundation on which TI is built. There is no other characteristic more essential to a TIer's makeup. It has to be present at all levels. Integrity is expected of managers and individuals when they make commitments. They are expected to stand by their commitments to the best of their ability.

One of TI's greatest strengths is its values and ethics. We had some early leaders who set those values as the standard for how they lived their lives. And it is important that TI grew that way. It's something that we don't want to lose. At the same time, we must move more rapidly. But we don't want to confuse that with the fact that we're ethical and we're moral. We're very responsible, and we live up to what we say."

Tom Engibous, President and CEO
Texas Instruments, 1997

We Respect and Value People By:

Treating others as we want to be treated.

- Exercising the basic virtues of respect, dignity, kindness, courtesy and manners in all work relationships.
- Recognizing and avoiding behaviors that others may find offensive, including the manner in which we speak and relate to one another and the materials we bring into the workplace, both printed and electronically.
- Respecting the right and obligation of every TIer to resolve concerns relating to ethics questions in the course of our duties without retribution and retaliation.
- Giving all TIers the same opportunity to have their questions, issues and situations fairly considered while understanding that being treated fairly does not always mean that we will all be treated the same.
- Trusting one another to use sound judgment in our use of TI business and information systems.
- Understanding that even though TI has the obligation to monitor its business information systems activity, we will respect privacy by prohibiting random searches of individual TIers' communications.
- Recognizing that conduct socially and professionally acceptable in one culture and country may be viewed differently in another.

We Are Honest By:

Representing ourselves and our intentions truthfully.

- Offering full disclosure and withdrawing ourselves from discussions and decisions when our business judgment appears to be in conflict with a personal interest.
- Respecting the rights and property of others, including their intellectual property. Accepting confidential or trade secret information only after we clearly understand our obligations as defined in a nondisclosure agreement.
- Competing fairly without collusion or collaboration with competitors to divide markets, set prices, restrict production, allocate customers or otherwise restrain competition.
- Assuring that no payments or favors are offered to influence others to do something wrong.
- Keeping records that are accurate and include all payments and receipts.
- Exercising good judgment in the exchange of business courtesies, meals and entertainment by avoiding activities that could create even the appearance that our decisions could be compromised.
- Refusing to speculate in TI stock through frequent buying and selling or through other forms of speculative trading.

Source: Courtesy of Texas Instruments, www.ti.com/corp/docs/csr/corpgov/conduct.shtml#top, (accessed March 5, 2011).

Whistle-blowing is informing the press or government officials about unethical practices within one's organization.

The year 2002 was labeled as the "Year of the Whistle-blower." Consider Joe Speaker, a 40-year-old acting chief financial officer (CFO) at Rite Aid Corp. in 1999. He discovered that inventories at Rite Aid had been overvalued and that millions in expenses had not been reported properly. Further digging into Rite Aid's books revealed that $541 million in earnings over the previous two years was really $1.6 billion in losses. Mr. Speaker was a main government witness when former Rite Aid Corp. Chairman and CEO Martin L. Grass went on trial. (Today, the company has a special code of ethics for the CEO and senior financial officers.) Mr. Speaker is among dozens of corporate managers who have blown the whistle. Enron's Sherron S. Watkins and WorldCom's Cynthia Cooper are now well-known whistle-blowers and *Time* magazine's persons of the year 2002. According to Linda Chatman Thomsen, deputy director for enforcement at the Securities and Exchange Commission, "Whistle-blowers give us an insider's perspective and have advanced our investigation immeasurably."

Meet Senators Sarbanes and Oxley. The Sarbanes-Oxley Act of 2002 adopted tough new provisions to deter and punish corporate and accounting fraud and corruption. Here, Senator Paul S. Sarbanes and John LaFalce congratulate each other as Senator Michael J. Oxley (middle) looks on. The legislation passed with near unanimous support.

© Scott J. Ferrell/Newscom

Whistle-blowing could have averted disaster and prevented needless deaths in the *Challenger* space shuttle disaster, for example. How could employees have known about life-threatening problems and let them pass? Whistle-blowing, however, can have serious repercussions for employees: Those who "blow whistles" sometimes lose their jobs. However, the Sarbanes-Oxley Act of 2002 protects whistle-blowers who report corporate misconduct. Any executive who retaliates against a whistle-blower can be held criminally liable and imprisoned for up to ten years.

Retaliations do occur, however. For example, in 2005, the U.S. Court of Appeals for the 8th Circuit unanimously upheld the right of Jane Turner, a 25-year veteran FBI agent, to obtain monetary damages and a jury trial against the FBI. The court held that Ms. Turner presented sufficient facts to justify a trial by jury based on the FBI's retaliatory transfer of Ms. Turner from her investigatory position in Minot, North Dakota, to a demeaning desk job in Minneapolis. Kris Kolesnik, executive director of the National Whistle Blower Center, said, "Jane Turner is an American hero. She refused to be silent when her co-agents committed misconduct in a child rape case. She refused to be silent when her co-agents stole property from Ground Zero. She paid the price and lost her job. The 8th Circuit Court did the right thing and insured that justice will take place in her case." In 2008, the U.S. government was ordered to pay $1 million in legal fees to Turner's lawyers. In 2010, the Obama administration was attempting to pass a law that would further protect the government whistle-blowers, however, the bill was killed in the final hours of the last Congress.[8]

When firms set up anonymous hotlines to handle ethically questionable situations, employees actually may be more likely to engage in whistle-blowing. When firms instead create an environment that educates employees and nurtures ethical behavior, fewer ethical problems arise. Ultimately, the need for whistle-blowing is greatly reduced.

It is difficult for an organization to develop ethics codes, policies, and procedures to deal with all relationships and every situation. When no company policies or procedures exist or apply, a quick test to determine if a behavior is ethical is to see if others—co-workers, customers, and suppliers—approve of it. Ethical decisions will always withstand scrutiny. Openness and communication about choices will often build trust and strengthen business relationships. Table 2-1 provides some general guidelines for making ethical decisions.

whistle-blowing informing the press or government officials about unethical practices within one's organization

TABLE 2-1: Guidelines for Making Ethical Decisions

1. Listen and learn.	Recognize the problem or decision-making opportunity that confronts your company, team, or unit. Don't argue, criticize, or defend yourself—keep listening and reviewing until you are sure that you understand others.
2. Identify the ethical issues.	Examine how co-workers and consumers are affected by the situation or decision at hand. Examine how you feel about the situation, and attempt to understand the viewpoint of those involved in the decision or in the consequences of the decision.
3. Create and analyze options.	Try to put aside strong feelings such as anger or a desire for power and prestige and come up with as many alternatives as possible before developing an analysis. Ask everyone involved for ideas about which options offer the best long-term results for you and the company. Then decide which option will increase your self-respect even if, in the long run, things don't work out the way you hope.
4. Identify the best option from your point of view.	Consider it and test it against some established criteria, such as respect, understanding, caring, fairness, honesty, and openness.
5. Explain your decision and resolve any differences that arise.	This may require neutral arbitration from a trusted manager or taking "time out" to reconsider, consult, or exchange written proposals before a decision is reached.

Source: Tom Rusk with D. Patrick Miller, "Doing the Right Thing," *Sky* (Delta Airlines), August 1993, 18–22.

SOCIAL RESPONSIBILITY

Social responsibility is the recognition that business activities have an impact on society and the consideration of that impact in business decision making. In the first few days after Hurricane Katrina hit New Orleans, Walmart delivered $20 million in cash (including $4 million to employees displaced by the storm), 100 truckloads of free merchandise, and food for 100,000 meals. The company also promised a job elsewhere for every one of its workers affected by the catastrophe. Obviously, social responsibility costs money. It is perhaps not so obvious—except in isolated cases—that social responsibility is also good business. Customers eventually find out which firms act responsibly and which do not. Just as easily as they can purchase a product made by a company that is socially responsible, they can choose against buying from the firm that is not.

Personal App When businesses take actions that affect our society, they're touching your life, too. You can make a difference by speaking up about the issues that matter to you. And you can vote with your wallet by buying from companies that act in socially responsible ways.

Consider the following examples of organizations that are attempting to be socially responsible:

- Social responsibility can take many forms—including flying lessons. Through Young Eagles, underwritten by S. C. Johnson, Phillips Petroleum, Lockheed Martin, Jaguar, and other corporations, 22,000 volunteer pilots have taken a half million youngsters on free flights designed to teach flying basics and inspire excitement about flying careers. Young Eagles is just one of the growing number of education projects undertaken by businesses building solid records as good corporate citizens.
- The General Mills Foundation, created in 1954, is one of the nation's largest company-sponsored foundations. Since the General Mills Foundation was created, it has awarded more than $420 million to its communities.

In the Twin Cities, the General Mills Foundation provides grants for youth nutrition and fitness, education, arts and culture, social services, and the United Way. Beyond financial resources, the General Mills Foundation also supports organizations with volunteers and mentors who share their expertise and talents. For example, General Mills plays a leadership role in supporting education, arts, and cultural organizations by matching employee and retiree contributions dollar for dollar. In 2010, the foundation contributed over $22 million in grants

social responsibility the recognition that business activities have an impact on society and the consideration of that impact in business decision making

in its communities; its total contributions in 2010 were $100 million.[9]

- As part of Dell's commitment to the community, the Michael and Susan Dell Foundation contributes significantly to the quality of life in communities where Dell employees live and work. The Dell Foundation supports innovative and effective programs that provide fundamental prerequisites to equip youth to learn and excel in a world driven by the digital economy. The Dell Foundation supports a wide range of programs that benefit children from newborn to 17 years of age in Dell's principal U.S. locations and welcomes proposals from non-profit organizations that address health and human services, education, and technology access for youth.

  Globally, the Michael and Susan Dell Foundation has contributed more than $658 million to improve student performance and increase access to education so that all children have the opportunity to achieve their dreams.[10]

Social responsibility is good business. ICAP, the world's largest interdealer broker in Jersey City, New Jersey, hosts its 16th annual global Charity Day during which the company revenues are donated to over 100 charities around the world.

© Jacob Silberg/Reuters/Landov

- Improving public schools around the world continues to be IBM's top social priority. Its efforts are focused on preparing the next generation of leaders and workers. Through Reinventing Education and other strategic efforts, IBM is solving education's toughest problems with solutions that draw on advanced information technologies and the best minds IBM can apply. Its programs are paving the way for reforms in school systems around the world.

  IBM launched the World Community Grid in November 2004. It combines excess processing power from thousands of computers into a virtual supercomputer. This grid enables researchers to gather and analyze unprecedented quantities of data aimed at advancing research on genomics, diseases, and natural disasters. The first project, the Human Proteome Folding Project, assists in identifying cures for diseases such as malaria and tuberculosis and has registered 85,000 devices around the world to date.

  In 2011, as IBM celebrated its centennial, the company announced that Africa is the destination for is 100th team and 1,000th employee involved in the company's Corporate Service Corps. Often called a "corporate version" of the Peace Corps, this program has made a direct economic impact in many of the 20 countries it has helped. Participants, who are selected from among IBM's highest performing employees, provide technology-related assistance to both local governments and community organizations. Issues they tackle include local economic development, entrepreneurship, transportation, education, citizen services, health care, and disaster recovery. Stanley S. Litow, IBM's vice president of Corporate Citizenship and Corporate Affairs, and president of IBM's Foundation stated, "Our Corporate Service Corps program epitomizes the progressive ethics of IBM's employees, both today and 100 years ago."[11]

- General Electric Company (GE) has a long history of supporting the communities where its employees work and live through GE's unique combination of resources, equipment, and employees' and retirees' hearts and souls. Today GE's responsibility extends to communities around the world.

  GE applies its long-standing spirit of innovation and unique set of capabilities to take on tough challenges in its communities. For example, in 2011, GE awarded a five-year grant of $20 million to Milwaukee Public Schools to improve academic achievement and better prepare students for college and career opportunities, with a focus on math and science programs. This grant is a part of the GE Foundation Developing Futures™ in Education program, an initiative to ensure that U.S. students are prepared to compete in an increasingly competitive global economy.[12]

going
for
SUCCESS

© Neil Sullivan/iStockphoto.com

American Express "Crowdsources" Philanthropy

American Express, well known for its charge cards, is also known for getting the public involved in its philanthropy. During its 1983 campaign to raise money for restoring the Statue of Liberty, the company donated a penny each time an American Express card was used to make a purchase. Cardholders responded so enthusiastically that the company wound up donating more than $1 million to the cause.

More recently, it has expanded its Partners in Preservation program, working with the National Trust for Historic Preservation and the World Monuments Fund to save and restore dozens of local landmarks. Each year since 2006, the company has pledged $1 million to refurbish historic sites in a particular metropolitan area through an unusual combination of philanthropy and "crowdsourcing." After choosing the city, American Express sets up a special Web site and asks the public to vote for the local landmarks they think should receive the money. This gets stakeholders actively involved in the company's social responsibility efforts—and in their communities, as well.

When American Express focused on the Boston area, it posted a list of 25 historic sites online, along with their plans for preservation. During the month-long voting period, the public was invited to view the plans, visit the sites in person, click to vote, and encourage others to vote. All 25 sites received some funding, but the big winner was the Paragon Carousel, which used American Express's $100,000 contribution to restore its 1928 merry-go-round building.

Sources: Taryn Plumb, "Calling All Hands to Back Mayflower for Online Prize," *Boston Globe*, December 12, 2010, www.boston.com; Kerry A. Dolan, "American Express Re-Upping Its 'Crowdsourced' Philanthropy," *Forbes*, November 15, 2010, http://blogs.forbes.com; Partners in Preservation Web site, www.partnersinpreservation.com.

- With the help of dedicated Schwab volunteers, the Charles Schwab Foundation provides programs and funding to help individuals fill the information gap. For example, Schwab MoneyWise helps adults teach—and children learn—the basics of financial literacy. Interactive tools are available at http://schwabmoneywise.com, and local workshops cover topics such as getting kids started on a budget. In addition to these efforts, widely distributed publications and news columns by foundation President Carrie Schwab Pomerantz promote financial literacy on a wide range of topics—from saving for a child's education to bridging the health insurance gap for retirees. Since its founding in 1993, Charles Schwab Foundation has made contributions averaging $4 million a year to more than 2,300 nonprofit organizations.[13]

- In recognition of 2011 International Women's Day, ExxonMobil granted $6 million to support economic opportunities for women around the world. In announcing the grant, Suzanne McCarron, president of ExxonMobil Foundation said, "Research tells us that the success of women entrepreneurs is key to building communities. When women thrive economically, entire societies are transformed by becoming healthier, more stable and more prosperous." In 2010, ExxonMobil, its employees, and retirees provided $238 million in contributions worldwide.[14]

- AT&T has built a tradition of supporting education, health and human services, the environment, public policy, and the arts in the communities it serves since Alexander Graham Bell founded the company over a century ago. Since 1984, AT&T has invested more than $600 million in support of education. Currently, more than half the company's contribution dollars, employee volunteer time, and community-service activities are directed toward education. Since 1911, AT&T has been a sponsor to the Telephone Pioneers of America, the world's largest industry-based volunteer organization consisting of nearly 750,000 employees and retirees from the telecommunications industry. Each year, the Pioneers volunteer millions of hours and raise millions of dollars for health and human services and the environment. In schools and neighborhoods, the Pioneers strengthen connections and build communities.

To respond to the high school drop-out crisis, AT&T launched Aspire, a $100 million philanthropic program that focuses on the crisis. It is the biggest and most significant investment in education in the company's history. The job shadowing program had reached more than 23,000 students in more than 200 cities. By summer of 2013, the program will provide 100,000 students with the opportunity to learn more about career options and what it takes to be successful in today's workforce.[15]

- At Merck & Co., Inc., the Patient Assistance Program makes the company's medicines available to low-income Americans and their families at no cost. When patients do not have health insurance or a prescription drug plan and are unable to afford the Merck medicines their doctors prescribe, they can work with their physicians to contact the Merck Patient Assistance Program. For more than 50 years, Merck has provided its medicines completely free of charge to people in need through this program. Patients can get information through www.merck .com; by calling a toll-free number, 1-800-727-5400; or from their physician's office. For eligible patients, the medicines are shipped directly to their home or the prescribing physician's office. Each applicant may receive up to one year of medicines, and patients may reapply to the program if their need continues.

Established in 1957, the Merck Company Foundation has contributed more than $560 million to develop and initiate programs that help improve the health and well-being of people around the world. According to Richard T. Clark, chairman, president, and CEO, "Merck established the Foundation more than 50 years ago because we knew that along with corporate success comes social responsibility."

Education programs often link social responsibility with corporate self-interest. For example, Bayer and Merck, two major pharmaceuticals firms, promote science education as a way to enlarge the pool of future employees. Students who visit the Bayer Science Forum in Elkhart, Indiana, work alongside scientists conducting a variety of experiments. Workshops created by the Merck Institute for Science Education show teachers how to put scientific principles into action through hands-on experiments.

These are just a few illustrations from the long list of companies, big and small, that attempt to behave in socially responsible ways. In general, people are more likely to want to work for and buy from such organizations.

Concept Check ✳

☐ How can the government encourage the ethical behavior of organizations?

☐ What is trade associations' role in encouraging ethics?

☐ What is whistle-blowing? Who protects the whistle blowers?

☐ What is social responsibility? How can business be socially responsible?

THE EVOLUTION OF SOCIAL RESPONSIBILITY IN BUSINESS

Business is far from perfect in many respects, but its record of social responsibility today is much better than that in past decades. In fact, present demands for social responsibility have their roots in outraged reactions to the abusive business practices of the early 1900s.

Historical Evolution of Business Social Responsibility

During the first quarter of the 20th century, businesses were free to operate pretty much as they chose. Government protection of workers and consumers was minimal. As a result, people either accepted what business had to offer or they did without. Working conditions often were deplorable by today's standards. The average workweek in most industries exceeded 60 hours, no minimum-wage law existed, and employee benefits were almost nonexistent. Work areas were crowded and unsafe, and industrial accidents were the rule rather than the exception. To improve working conditions, employees organized and joined labor unions. During the early 1900s, however, businesses—with the help of government—were able to use court orders, brute force, and even the few existing antitrust laws to defeat union attempts to improve working conditions.

During this period, consumers generally were subject to the doctrine of **caveat emptor**, a Latin phrase meaning "let the buyer beware." In other words, "what you

LEARNING OBJECTIVE

5 Describe how our current views on the social responsibility of business have evolved.

caveat emptor a Latin phrase meaning "let the buyer beware"

Breaking away from fossil fuels. Today's consumers are more open to transportation alternatives, such as the electric or hybrid cars, because they are concerned about the negative impact of gasoline-run vehicles.

© Boykov/Shutterstock

✱ Concept Check

☐ Outline the historical evolution of business social responsibility.

☐ What is the doctrine of caveat emptor?

☐ What are the six important business-related federal laws passed between 1887 and 1914?

see is what you get," and if it is not what you expected, too bad. Although victims of unscrupulous business practices could take legal action, going to court was very expensive, and consumers rarely won their cases. Moreover, no consumer groups or government agencies existed to publicize their consumers' grievances or to hold sellers accountable for their actions.

Personal App You, the customer, are the strongest possible consumer protection. No laws, agencies, policies, or advocates can replace your common sense in applying caveat emptor, especially in today's complex business world.

Before the 1930s, most people believed that competition and the action of the marketplace would, in time, correct abuses. Government, therefore, became involved in day-to-day business activities only in cases of obvious abuse of the free-market system. Six of the more important business-related federal laws passed between 1887 and 1914 are described in Table 2-2. As you can see, these laws were aimed more at encouraging competition than at correcting abuses, although two of them did deal with the purity of food and drug products.

The collapse of the stock market on October 29, 1929, triggered the Great Depression and years of dire economic problems for the United States. Factory production fell by almost half, and up to 25 percent of the nation's workforce was unemployed. Before long, public pressure mounted for the government to "do something" about the economy and about worsening social conditions.

Soon after Franklin D. Roosevelt became president in 1933, he instituted programs to restore the economy and improve social conditions. The government passed laws to correct what many viewed as the monopolistic abuses of big business, and provided various social services for individuals. These massive federal programs became the foundation for increased government involvement in the dealings between business and society.

As government involvement has increased, so has everyone's awareness of the social responsibility of business. Today's business owners are concerned about the return on their investment, but at the same time most of them demand ethical behavior from employees. In addition, employees demand better working conditions, and consumers want safe, reliable products. Various advocacy groups echo these concerns and also call for careful consideration of Earth's delicate ecological balance. Therefore,

TABLE 2-2: Early Government Regulations that Affected American Business

Six of the important business-related federal laws passed between 1887 and 1914 were aimed more at encouraging competition than at correcting abuses.

Government Regulation	Major Provisions
Interstate Commerce Act (1887)	First federal act to regulate business practices; provided regulation of railroads and shipping rates
Sherman Antitrust Act (1890)	Prevented monopolies or mergers where competition was endangered
Pure Food and Drug Act (1906)	Established limited supervision of interstate sales of food and drugs
Meat Inspection Act (1906)	Provided for limited supervision of interstate sales of meat and meat products
Federal Trade Commission Act (1914)	Created the Federal Trade Commission to investigate illegal trade practices
Clayton Antitrust Act (1914)	Eliminated many forms of price discrimination that gave large businesses a competitive advantage over smaller firms

© Cengage Learning 2013

managers must operate in a complex business environment—one in which they are just as responsible for their managerial actions as for their actions as individual citizens. Interestingly, today's high-tech and Internet-based firms fare relatively well when it comes to environmental issues, worker conditions, the representation of minorities and women in upper management, animal testing, and charitable donations.

TWO VIEWS OF SOCIAL RESPONSIBILITY

LEARNING OBJECTIVE
6 Explain the two views on the social responsibility of business and understand the arguments for and against increased social responsibility.

Government regulation and public awareness are *external* forces that have increased the social responsibility of business. However, business decisions are made within the firm—there, social responsibility begins with the attitude of management. Two contrasting philosophies, or models, define the range of management attitudes toward social responsibility.

The Economic Model

According to the traditional concept of business, a firm exists to produce quality goods and services, earn a reasonable profit, and provide jobs. In line with this concept, the **economic model of social responsibility** holds that society will benefit most when business is left alone to produce and market profitable products that society needs. The economic model has its origins in the 18th century, when businesses were owned primarily by entrepreneurs or owner-managers. Competition was vigorous among small firms, and short-run profits and survival were the primary concerns.

To the manager who adopts this traditional attitude, social responsibility is someone else's job. After all, stockholders invest in a corporation to earn a return on their investment, not because the firm is socially responsible, and the firm is legally obligated to act in the economic interest of its stockholders. Moreover, profitable firms pay federal, state, and local taxes that are used to meet the needs of society. Thus, managers who concentrate on profit believe that they fulfill their social responsibility indirectly through the taxes paid by their firms. As a result, social responsibility becomes the problem of the government, various environmental groups, charitable foundations, and similar organizations.

The Socioeconomic Model

In contrast, some managers believe that they have a responsibility not only to stockholders but also to customers, employees, suppliers, and the general public. This broader view is referred to as the **socioeconomic model of social responsibility**, which places emphasis not only on profits but also on the impact of business decisions on society.

Recently, increasing numbers of managers and firms have adopted the socioeconomic model, and they have done so for at least three reasons. First, business is dominated by the corporate form of ownership, and the corporation is a creation of society. If a corporation does not perform as a good citizen, society can and will demand changes. Second, many firms have begun to take pride in their social responsibility records, among them Starbucks Coffee, Hewlett-Packard, Colgate-Palmolive, and Coca-Cola. Each of these companies is a winner of a Corporate Conscience Award in the areas of environmental concern, responsiveness to employees, equal opportunity, and community involvement. Of course, many other corporations are much more socially responsible today than they were ten years ago. Third, many businesspeople believe that it is in their best interest to take the initiative in this area. The alternative may be legal action brought against the firm by some special-interest group; in such a situation, the firm may lose control of its activities.

The Pros and Cons of Social Responsibility

Business owners, managers, customers, and government officials have debated the pros and cons of the economic and socioeconomic models for years. Each side seems to have four major arguments to reinforce its viewpoint.

economic model of social responsibility the view that society will benefit most when business is left alone to produce and market profitable products that society needs

socioeconomic model of social responsibility the concept that business should emphasize not only profits but also the impact of its decisions on society

SUSTAIN THE PLANET

Sustainability

What are major companies and non-profit groups doing to preserve the environment? Hundreds of organizations, including AT&T, Burt's Bees, General Mills, Hitachi America, Microsoft, PepsiCo, Union Bank, Vivendi, and Yahoo!, post the latest news about their sustainability initiatives and accomplishments on Corporate Social Responsibility Newswire. Take a look: www.csrwire.com/.

ARGUMENTS FOR INCREASED SOCIAL RESPONSIBILITY Proponents of the socioeconomic model maintain that a business must do more than simply seek profits. To support their position, they offer the following arguments:

1. Because business is a part of our society, it cannot ignore social issues.
2. Business has the technical, financial, and managerial resources needed to tackle today's complex social issues.
3. By helping resolve social issues, business can create a more stable environment for long-term profitability.
4. Socially responsible decision making by firms can prevent increased government intervention, which would force businesses to do what they fail to do voluntarily.

These arguments are based on the assumption that a business has a responsibility to all its stakeholders, not just to its stockholders but also to its customers, employees, suppliers, and the general public.

ARGUMENTS AGAINST INCREASED SOCIAL RESPONSIBILITY Opponents of the socioeconomic model argue that business should do what it does best: earn a profit by manufacturing and marketing products that people want. Those who support this position argue as follows:

1. Business managers are responsible primarily to stockholders, so management must be concerned with providing a return on owners' investments.
2. Corporate time, money, and talent should be used to maximize profits, not to solve society's problems.
3. Social problems affect society in general, so individual businesses should not be expected to solve these problems.
4. Social issues are the responsibility of government officials who are elected for that purpose and who are accountable to the voters for their decisions.

These arguments obviously are based on the assumption that the primary objective of business is to earn profits and that government and social institutions should deal with social problems.

Table 2-3 compares the economic and socioeconomic viewpoints in terms of business emphasis. Today, few firms are either purely economic or purely socioeconomic in outlook; most have chosen some middle ground between the two extremes.

✱ Concept Check

☐ Explain the two views on the social responsibility of business.

☐ What are the arguments for increased social responsibility?

☐ What are the arguments against increased social responsibility?

TABLE 2-3: A Comparison of the Economic and Socioeconomic Models of Social Responsibility as Implemented in Business

Economic Model Primary Emphasis		Socioeconomic Model Primary Emphasis
1. Production		1. Quality of life
2. Exploitation of natural resources		2. Conservation of natural resources
3. Internal, market-based decisions	Middle ground	3. Market-based decisions, with some community controls
4. Economic return (profit)		4. Balance of economic return and social return
5. Firm's or manager's interest		5. Firm's and community's interests
6. Minor role for government		6. Active government

Source: Adapted from Keith Davis, William C. Frederick, and Robert L. Blomstron, *Business and Society: Concepts and Policy Issues* (New York: McGraw-Hill, 1980), 9. Used by permission of McGraw-Hill Book Company.

However, our society generally seems to want—and even to expect—some degree of social responsibility from business. Thus, within this middle ground, businesses are leaning toward the socioeconomic view. In the next several sections, we look at some results of this movement in four specific areas: consumerism, employment practices, concern for the environment, and implementation of social responsibility programs.

CONSUMERISM

LEARNING OBJECTIVE
7 Discuss the factors that led to the consumer movement and list some of its results.

Consumerism consists of all activities undertaken to protect the rights of consumers. The fundamental issues pursued by the consumer movement fall into three categories: environmental protection, product performance and safety, and information disclosure. Although consumerism has been with us to some extent since the early 19th century, the consumer movement became stronger in the 1960s. It was then that President John F. Kennedy declared that the consumer was entitled to a new "Bill of Rights."

The Six Basic Rights of Consumers

President Kennedy's Consumer Bill of Rights asserted that consumers have a right to safety, to be informed, to choose, and to be heard. Two additional rights added since 1975 are the right to consumer education and the right to courteous service. These six rights are the basis of much of the consumer-oriented legislation passed during the last 50 years. These rights also provide an effective outline of the objectives and accomplishments of the consumer movement.

Personal App Keep these consumer rights in mind when you shop around for goods or services, buy something, or have a problem with a purchase. You're entitled to be informed, to have choices, to be heard, to buy safe products, to have responsive service, and to know your rights.

THE RIGHT TO SAFETY The consumers' right to safety means that the products they purchase must be safe for their intended use, must include thorough and explicit directions for proper use, and must be tested by the manufacturer to ensure product quality and reliability. There are several reasons why American business firms must be concerned about product safety.

Corrective Actions Can Be Expensive. Federal agencies, such as the Food and Drug Administration and the Consumer Product Safety Commission, have the power to force businesses that make or sell defective products to take corrective actions. Such actions include offering refunds, recalling defective products, issuing public warnings, and reimbursing consumers—all of which can be expensive.

Increasing Number of Lawsuits. Business firms also should be aware that consumers and the government have been winning an increasing number of product-liability lawsuits against sellers of defective products. Moreover, the amount of the awards in these suits has been increasing steadily. Fearing the outcome of numerous lawsuits filed around the nation, tobacco giants Philip Morris and R. J. Reynolds, which for decades had denied that cigarettes cause illness, began negotiating in 1997 with state attorneys general, plaintiffs' lawyers, and antismoking activists. The tobacco giants proposed sweeping curbs on their sales and advertising practices and the payment of hundreds of billions of dollars in compensation.

Consumer Demand. Yet another major reason for improving product safety is consumers' demand for safe products. People simply will stop buying a product they believe is unsafe or unreliable.

The right to be informed. The Consumer Bill of Rights asserts consumers' basic rights. The right to be informed and the right to choose means that consumers must have complete information about a product and a choice of products.

© Monkey Business Images/Shutterstock

consumerism all activities undertaken to protect the rights of consumers

THE RIGHT TO BE INFORMED The right to be informed means that consumers must have access to complete information about a product before they buy it. Detailed information about ingredients and nutrition must be provided on food containers, information about fabrics and laundering methods must be attached to clothing, and lenders must disclose the true cost of borrowing the money they make available to customers who purchase merchandise on credit.

In addition, manufacturers must inform consumers about the potential dangers of using their products. Manufacturers that fail to provide such information can be held responsible for personal injuries suffered because of their products. For example, Maytag provides customers with a lengthy booklet that describes how they should use an automatic clothes washer. Sometimes such warnings seem excessive, but they are necessary if user injuries (and resulting lawsuits) are to be avoided.

THE RIGHT TO CHOOSE The right to choose means that consumers must have a choice of products, offered by different manufacturers and sellers, to satisfy a particular need. The government has done its part by encouraging competition through antitrust legislation. The greater the competition, the greater is the choice available to consumers.

Competition and the resulting freedom of choice provide additional benefits for customers by reducing prices. For example, when personal computers were introduced, they cost more than $5,000. Thanks to intense competition and technological advancements, personal computers today can be purchased for less than $500.

THE RIGHT TO BE HEARD This fourth right means that someone will listen and take appropriate action when customers complain. Actually, management began to listen to consumers after World War II, when competition between businesses that manufactured and sold consumer goods increased. One way that firms got a competitive edge was to listen to consumers and provide the products they said they wanted and needed. Today, businesses are listening even more attentively, and many larger firms have consumer relations departments that can be contacted easily via toll-free telephone numbers. Other groups listen, too. Most large cities and some states have consumer affairs offices to act on citizens' complaints.

ADDITIONAL CONSUMER RIGHTS In 1975, President Gerald Ford added to the Consumer Bill of Rights the right to consumer education, which entitles people to be fully informed about their rights as consumers. In 1994, President Bill Clinton added a sixth right, the right to service, which entitles consumers to convenience, courtesy, and responsiveness from manufacturers and sellers of consumer products.

Major Consumerism Forces

The major forces in consumerism are individual consumer advocates and organizations, consumer education programs, and consumer laws. Consumer advocates, such as Ralph Nader, take it on themselves to protect the rights of consumers. They band together into consumer organizations, either independently or under government sponsorship. Some organizations, such as the National Consumers' League and the Consumer Federation of America, operate nationally, whereas others are active at state and local levels. They inform and organize other consumers, raise issues, help businesses to develop consumer-oriented programs, and pressure lawmakers to enact consumer protection laws. Some consumer advocates and organizations encourage consumers to boycott products and businesses to which they have objections. Today, the consumer movement has adopted corporate-style marketing and addresses a broad range of issues. Current campaigns include efforts (1) to curtail the use of animals for testing purposes, (2) to reduce liquor and cigarette billboard advertising in low-income, inner-city neighborhoods, and (3) to encourage recycling.

Educating consumers to make wiser purchasing decisions is perhaps one of the most far-reaching aspects of consumerism. Increasingly, consumer education is becoming a part of high school and college curricula and adult-education programs. These programs cover many topics—for instance, what major factors should be considered when buying specific products, such as insurance, real estate, automobiles, appliances and furniture, clothes, and food; the provisions of certain consumer-protection laws; and the sources of information that can help individuals become knowledgeable consumers.

Major advances in consumerism have come through federal legislation. Some laws enacted in the last 50 years to protect your rights as a consumer are listed and described in Table 2-4.

TABLE 2-4: Major Federal Legislation Protecting Consumers Since 1960

Legislation	Major Provisions
Federal Hazardous Substances Labeling Act (1960)	Required warning labels on household chemicals if they were highly toxic
Kefauver-Harris Drug Amendments (1962)	Established testing practices for drugs and required manufacturers to label drugs with generic names in addition to trade names
Cigarette Labeling Act (1965)	Required manufacturers to place standard warning labels on all cigarette packages and advertising
Fair Packaging and Labeling Act (1966)	Called for all products sold across state lines to be labeled with net weight, ingredients, and manufacturer's name and address
Motor Vehicle Safety Act (1966)	Established standards for safer cars
Truth in Lending Act (1968)	Required lenders and credit merchants to disclose the full cost of finance charges in both dollars and annual percentage rates
Credit Card Liability Act (1970)	Limited credit-card holder's liability to $50 per card and stopped credit-card companies from issuing unsolicited cards
Fair Credit Reporting Act (1971)	Required credit bureaus to provide credit reports to consumers regarding their own credit files; also provided for correction of incorrect information
Consumer Product Safety Commission Act (1972)	Established an abbreviated procedure for registering certain generic drugs
Fair Credit Billing Act (1974)	Amended the Truth in Lending Act to enable consumers to challenge billing errors
Equal Credit Opportunity Act (1974)	Provided equal credit opportunities for males and females and for married and single individuals
Magnuson-Moss Warranty-Federal Trade Commission Act (1975)	Provided for minimum disclosure standards for written consumer-product warranties for products that cost more than $15
Amendments to the Equal Credit Opportunity Act (1976, 1994)	Prevented discrimination based on race, creed, color, religion, age, and income when granting credit
Fair Debt Collection Practices Act (1977)	Outlawed abusive collection practices by third parties
Nutrition Labeling and Education Act (1990)	Required the Food and Drug Administration to review current food labeling and packaging focusing on nutrition label content, label format, ingredient labeling, food descriptors and standards, and health messages
Telephone Consumer Protection Act (1991)	Prohibited the use of automated dialing and prerecorded-voice calling equipment to make calls or deliver messages
Consumer Credit Reporting Reform Act (1997)	Placed more responsibility for accurate credit data on credit issuers; required creditors to verify that disputed data are accurate and to notify a consumer before reinstating the data
Children's Online Privacy Protection Act (2000)	Placed parents in control over what information is collected online from their children younger than 13 years; required commercial Web site operators to maintain the confidentiality, security, and integrity of personal information collected from children
Do Not Call Implementation Act (2003)	Directed the FCC and the FTC to coordinate so that their rules are consistent regarding telemarketing call practices including the Do Not Call Registry and other lists, as well as call abandonment
Credit Card Accountability, Responsibility, and Disclosure Act (2009)	Provided the most sweeping changes in credit card protections since the Truth in Lending Act of 1968
Wall Street Reform and Consumer Protection Act of 2010	Promoted the financial stability of the United States by improving accountability and responsibility in the financial system; established a new Consumer Financial Protection Agency to regulate home mortgages, car loans, and credit cards; became Public Law on July 21, 2010

Here is the 2010 list of proposed legislation to protect consumers and investors:[16]

- Bank and Savings Association Holding Company and Depository Institution Regulatory Improvements Act of 2010
- Consumer Financial Protection Act of 2010
- Enhancing Financial Institution Safety and Soundness Act of 2010
- Expand and Preserve Home Ownership Through Counseling Act
- Federal Insurance Office Act of 2010
- Financial Stability Act of 2010
- Improving Access to Mainstream Financial Institutions Act of 2010
- Investor Protection and Securities Reform Act of 2010
- Mortgage Reform and Anti-Predatory Lending Act of 2010
- Nonadmitted and Reinsurance Reform Act of 2010
- Payment, Clearing, and Settlement Supervision Act of 2010
- Private Fund Investment Advisers Registration Act of 2010
- Wall Street Transparency and Accountability Act of 2010

Most businesspeople now realize that they ignore consumer issues only at their own peril. Managers know that improper handling of consumer complaints can result in lost sales, bad publicity, and lawsuits.

✳ Concept Check

☐ Describe the six basic rights of consumers.

☐ What are the major forces in consumerism today?

☐ What are some of the federal laws enacted in the last 50 years to protect your rights as a consumer?

LEARNING OBJECTIVE

8 Analyze how present employment practices are being used to counteract past abuses.

EMPLOYMENT PRACTICES

Managers who subscribe to the socioeconomic view of a business's social responsibility, together with significant government legislation enacted to protect the buying public, have broadened the rights of consumers. The last five decades have seen similar progress in affirming the rights of employees to equal treatment in the workplace.

Everyone should have the opportunity to land a job for which he or she is qualified and to be rewarded on the basis of ability and performance. This is an important issue for society, and it also makes good business sense. Yet, over the years, this opportunity has been denied to members of various minority groups. A **minority** is a racial, religious, political, national, or other group regarded as different from the larger group of which it is a part and that is often singled out for unfavorable treatment.

The federal government responded to the outcry of minority groups during the 1960s and 1970s by passing a number of laws forbidding discrimination in the workplace. (These laws are discussed in Chapter 9 in the context of human resources management.) Now, 46 years after passage of the first of these (the Civil Rights Act of 1964), abuses still exist. An example is the disparity in income levels for whites, blacks, Hispanics, and Asians, as illustrated in Figure 2-3. Lower incomes and higher unemployment rates also characterize Native Americans, handicapped persons, and women. Responsible managers have instituted a number of programs to counteract the results of discrimination.

Affirmative Action Programs

An **affirmative action program** is a plan designed to increase the number of minority employees at all levels within an organization. Employers with federal contracts of more than $50,000 per year must have written affirmative action plans. The objective of such programs is to ensure that minorities are represented within the organization in approximately the same proportion as in the surrounding community. If 25 percent of the electricians in a geographic area in which a company is located are African-Americans, then approximately 25 percent of the electricians it employs also should be African-Americans. Affirmative action plans encompass all areas of human resources management: recruiting, hiring, training, promotion, and pay.

Unfortunately, affirmative action programs have been plagued by two problems. The first involves quotas. In the beginning, many firms pledged to recruit

minority a racial, religious, political, national, or other group regarded as different from the larger group of which it is a part and that is often singled out for unfavorable treatment

affirmative action program a plan designed to increase the number of minority employees at all levels within an organization

FIGURE 2-3: Comparative Income Levels

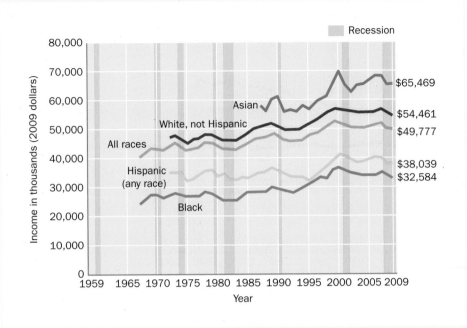

Source: U.S. Census Bureau, Current Population Survey, 1968 to 2010 Annual Social and Economic Supplements, www.census.gov/newsroom/releases/archives/income_wealth/cb10-144.html, (accessed August 14, 2011).

and hire a certain number of minority members by a specific date. To achieve this goal, they were forced to consider only minority applicants for job openings; if they hired nonminority workers, they would be defeating their own purpose. However, the courts have ruled that such quotas are unconstitutional even though their purpose is commendable. They are, in fact, a form of discrimination called *reverse discrimination.*

The second problem is that although most such programs have been reasonably successful, not all businesspeople are in favor of affirmative action programs. Managers not committed to these programs can "play the game" and still discriminate against workers. To help solve this problem, Congress created (and later strengthened) the **Equal Employment Opportunity Commission (EEOC)**, a government agency with the power to investigate complaints of employment discrimination and sue firms that practice it.

The threat of legal action has persuaded some corporations to amend their hiring and promotional policies, but the discrepancy between men's and women's salaries still exists, as illustrated in Figure 2-4. For more than 52 years, women have consistently earned only about 77 cents for each dollar earned by men.

Training Programs for the Hard-Core Unemployed

For some firms, social responsibility extends far beyond placing a help-wanted advertisement in the local newspaper. These firms have assumed the task of helping the **hard-core unemployed**, workers with little education or vocational training and a long history of

Equal Employment Opportunity Commission (EEOC) a government agency with the power to investigate complaints of employment discrimination and the power to sue firms that practice it

hard-core unemployed workers with little education or vocational training and a long history of unemployment

Training unemployed veterans. Meet Floretta Brown, an unemployed secretary living in Silver Springs, MD. Here, she prepares for a Microsoft training class Governor Martin O'Malley's administration helped create for unemployed veterans.

FIGURE 2-4: Relative Earnings of Male and Female Workers

Source: U.S. Census Bureau, Current Population Survey, 1968 to 2009 Annual Social and Economic Supplements, www.census.gov/prod/2010pubs/p60-238.pdf, (accessed August 14, 2011).

unemployment. For example, a few years ago, General Mills helped establish Si-yeza, a frozen soul-food processing plant in North Minneapolis. Through the years, Siyeza has provided stable, high-quality full-time jobs for a permanent core of 80 unemployed or underemployed minority inner-city residents. In addition, groups of up to 100 temporary employees are called in when needed. In the past, such workers often were turned down routinely by personnel managers, even for the most menial jobs.

Obviously, such workers require training; just as obviously, this training can be expensive and time-consuming. To share the costs, business and community leaders have joined together in a number of cooperative programs. One particularly success-ful partnership is the **National Alliance of Business (NAB)**, a joint business–government program to train the hard-core unemployed. The alliance's 5,000 members include companies of all sizes and industries, their CEOs and senior executives, as well as educators and community leaders. NAB, founded in 1968 by President Lyndon Johnson and Henry Ford II, is a major national business organization focusing on education and workforce issues.

✳ Concept Check

☐ What is an affirmative action program? What is its purpose?

☐ Why did Congress create (and later strengthen) the Equal Employment Opportunity Commission?

☐ What is the National Alliance of Business?

LEARNING OBJECTIVE

9 Describe the major types of pollution, their causes, and their cures.

National Alliance of Business (NAB) a joint business–government program to train the hard-core unemployed

pollution the contamination of water, air, or land through the actions of people in an industrialized society

CONCERN FOR THE ENVIRONMENT

The social consciousness of responsible business managers, the encouragement of a concerned government, and an increasing concern on the part of the public have led to a major effort to reduce environmental pollution, conserve natural resources, and reverse some of the worst effects of past negligence in this area. **Pollution** is the contamination of water, air, or land through the actions of people in an in-dustrialized society. For several decades, environmentalists have been warning us about the dangers of industrial pollution. Unfortunately, business and government leaders either ignored the problem or were not concerned about it until pollution became a threat to life and health in America. Today, Americans expect business and government leaders to take swift action to clean up our environment—and to keep it clean.

TABLE 2-5: Summary of Major Environmental Laws

Legislation	Major Provisions
National Environmental Policy Act (1970)	Established the Environmental Protection Agency (EPA) to enforce federal laws that involve the environment
Clean Air Amendment (1970)	Provided stringent automotive, aircraft, and factory emission standards
Water Quality Improvement Act (1970)	Strengthened existing water pollution regulations and provided for large monetary fines against violators
Resource Recovery Act (1970)	Enlarged the solid-waste disposal program and provided for enforcement by the EPA
Water Pollution Control Act Amendment (1972)	Established standards for cleaning navigable streams and lakes and eliminating all harmful waste disposal by 1985
Noise Control Act (1972)	Established standards for major sources of noise and required the EPA to advise the Federal Aviation Administration on standards for airplanes
Clean Air Act Amendment (1977)	Established new deadlines for cleaning up polluted areas; also required review of existing air-quality standards
Resource Conservation and Recovery Act (1984)	Amended the original 1976 act and required federal regulation of potentially dangerous solid-waste disposal
Clean Air Act Amendment (1987)	Established a national air-quality standard for ozone
Oil Pollution Act (1990)	Expanded the nation's oil-spill prevention and response activities; also established the Oil Spill Liability Trust Fund
Clean Air Act Amendments (1990)	Required that motor vehicles be equipped with onboard systems to control about 90 percent of refueling vapors
Food Quality Protection Act (1996)	Amended the Federal Insecticide, Fungicide and Rodenticide Act and the Federal Food Drug and Cosmetic Act; the requirements included a new safety standard—reasonable certainty of no harm—that must be applied to all pesticides used on foods
American Recovery and Reinvestment Act (2009)	Provided $7.22 billion to the EPA to protect and promote "green" jobs and a healthier environment

© Cengage Learning 2013

Effects of Environmental Legislation

As in other areas of concern to our society, legislation and regulations play a crucial role in pollution control. The laws outlined in Table 2-5 reflect the scope of current environmental legislation: laws to promote clean air, clean water, and even quiet work and living environments. Of major importance was the creation of the Environmental Protection Agency (EPA), the federal agency charged with enforcing laws designed to protect the environment.

When they are aware of a pollution problem, many firms respond to it rather than wait to be cited by the EPA. Other owners and managers, however, take the position that environmental standards are too strict. (Loosely translated, this means that compliance with present standards is too expensive.) Consequently, it often has been necessary for the EPA to take legal action to force firms to install antipollution equipment and to clean up waste storage areas.

Experience has shown that the combination of environmental legislation, voluntary compliance, and EPA action can succeed in cleaning up the environment and keeping it clean. However, much still remains to be done.

WATER POLLUTION The Clean Water Act has been credited with greatly improving the condition of the waters in the United States. This success comes largely from the control of pollutant discharges from industrial and wastewater treatment plants. Although the quality of our nation's rivers, lakes, and streams has improved significantly in recent years, many of these surface waters remain severely polluted. Currently, one of the most serious water-quality problems results from the high level of toxic pollutants found in these waters.

SPOT LIGHT

Recession and Responsibility

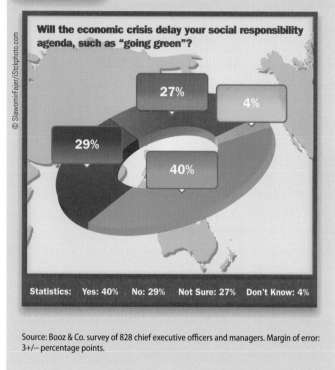

Will the economic crisis delay your social responsibility agenda, such as "going green"?

27%

4%

29%

40%

Statistics: Yes: 40%   No: 29%   Not Sure: 27%   Don't Know: 4%

Source: Booz & Co. survey of 828 chief executive officers and managers. Margin of error: 3+/− percentage points.

© Slawomir Fajer/iStockphoto.com

Corporate concern for the environment. Motorola Co-CEO Sanjay Jha helps clear brush at the Old School Forest Preserve in Libertyville, Illinois, as part of the company's fourth Annual Global Day of Services. Employees from 41 countries volunteered in their communities, with their focus on the environment.

PRNewsFoto/Motorola, Inc.

Among the serious threats to people posed by water pollutants are respiratory irritation, cancer, kidney and liver damage, anemia, and heart failure. Toxic pollutants also damage fish and other forms of wildlife. In fish, they cause tumors or reproductive problems; shellfish and wildlife living in or drinking from toxin-laden waters also have suffered genetic defects. Recently, the Pollution Control Board of Kerala in India ordered Coca-Cola to close its major bottling plant. For years, villagers in the nearby areas had accused Coke of depleting local groundwater and producing other local pollution. The village council president said, "We are happy that the government is finally giving justice to the people who are affected by the plant."

One of the worst environmental disasters in 2010 was the explosion of the *Deepwater Horizon*, in which 11 people died. The British Petroleum (BP) catastrophe led to an oil spill in the Gulf of Mexico that contaminated a vast area of the United States marine environment. It caused a serious impact on wildlife, the local fishing industry, and regional tourism. British Petroleum was held liable for property damaged by the oil spill and the cleanup efforts; loss of income or earning capacity; loss of income to boat owners, hotel owners, and restaurant owners; removal and cleanup costs of property; and claims of bodily injury caused by the spill.

The task of water cleanup has proved to be extremely complicated and costly because of pollution runoff and toxic contamination. Yet, improved water quality is not only necessary, it is also achievable. Consider Cleveland's Cuyahoga River. A few years ago, the river was so contaminated by industrial wastes that it burst into flames one hot summer day! Now, after a sustained community cleanup effort, the river is pure enough for fish to thrive in.

Another serious issue is acid rain, which is contributing significantly to the deterioration of coastal waters, lakes, and marine life in the eastern United States. Acid rain forms when sulfur emitted by smokestacks in industrialized areas combines with moisture in the atmosphere to form acids that are spread by winds. The acids eventually fall to Earth in rain, which finds its way into streams, rivers, and lakes. The acid-rain problem has spread rapidly in recent years, and experts fear that the situation will worsen if the nation begins to burn more coal to generate electricity. To solve the problem, investigators first must determine where the sulfur is being emitted. The costs of this vital investigation and cleanup are going to be high. The human costs of having ignored the problem so long may be higher still.

AIR POLLUTION Aviation emissions are a potentially significant and growing percentage of greenhouse gases that contribute to global warming. Aircraft emissions are significant for several reasons. First, jet aircraft are the main source of human emissions deposited directly into the upper atmosphere, where they may have a greater warming effect than if they were released at Earth's surface. Second, carbon dioxide—the primary aircraft emission—is the main focus of international concern. For example, it survives in the atmosphere for nearly 100 years and contributes to global warming, according to the Intergovernmental Panel on Climate Change. The carbon dioxide emissions from worldwide aviation roughly equal those of some industrialized countries. Third, carbon dioxide emissions combined with other gases and particles emitted by jet aircraft could have two to four times as great an effect on the atmosphere as carbon dioxide alone. Fourth, the Intergovernmental Panel recently concluded that the rise in aviation emissions owing to the growing demand for air travel would not be fully offset by reductions in emissions achieved solely through technological improvements.

Usually, two or three factors combine to form air pollution in any given location. The first factor is large amounts of carbon monoxide and hydrocarbons emitted by motor vehicles concentrated in a relatively small area. The second is the smoke and other pollutants emitted by manufacturing facilities. These two factors can be eliminated in part through pollution control devices on cars, trucks, and smokestacks.

A third factor that contributes to air pollution—one that cannot be changed—is the combination of weather and geography. The Los Angeles Basin, for example, combines just the right weather and geographic conditions for creating dense smog. Los Angeles has strict regulations regarding air pollution. Even so, Los Angeles still struggles with air pollution problems because of uncontrollable conditions.

How effective is air pollution control? The EPA estimates that the Clean Air Act and its amendments will eventually result in the removal of 56 billion pounds of pollution from the air each year, thus measurably reducing lung disease, cancer, and other serious health problems caused by air pollution. Other authorities note that we have already seen improvement in air quality. A number of cities have cleaner air today than they did 30 years ago. Even in southern California, bad air-quality days have dropped to less than 40 days a year, about 60 percent lower than that observed just a decade ago. Numerous chemical companies have recognized that they must take responsibility for operating their plants in an environmentally safe manner; some now devote considerable capital to purchasing antipollution devices. For example, 3M's pioneering Pollution Prevention Pays (3P) program, designed to find ways to avoid the generation of pollutants, marked its 30th anniversary in 2005. Since 1975, more than 5,600 employee-driven 3P projects have prevented the generation of more than 2.2 billion pounds of pollutants and produced first-year savings of nearly $1 billion.

LAND POLLUTION Air and water quality may be improving, but land pollution is still a serious problem in many areas. The fundamental issues are (1) how to restore damaged or contaminated land at a reasonable cost and (2) how to protect unpolluted land from future damage.

The land pollution problem has been worsening over the past few years because modern technology has continued to produce increasing amounts of chemical and radioactive waste. U.S. manufacturers produce an estimated 40 to 60 million tons of contaminated oil, solvents, acids, and sludge each year. Service businesses, utility companies, hospitals, and other industries also dump vast amounts of wastes into the environment.

Individuals in the United States contribute to the waste-disposal problem, too. A shortage of landfills, owing to stricter regulations, makes garbage disposal a serious problem in some areas. Incinerators help to solve the landfill-shortage problem, but they bring with them their own problems. They reduce the amount of garbage but also leave tons of ash to be buried—ash that often has a higher concentration of toxicity than the original garbage. Other causes of land pollution include strip mining of coal, nonselective cutting of forests, and development of agricultural land for housing and industry.

To help pay the enormous costs of cleaning up land polluted with chemicals and toxic wastes, Congress created a $1.6 billion Superfund in 1980. Originally, money was to flow into the Superfund from a tax paid by 800 oil and chemical companies that produce toxic waste. The EPA was to use the money in the Superfund to finance the cleanup of hazardous waste sites across the nation. To replenish the Superfund, the EPA had two options: It could sue companies guilty of dumping chemicals at specific waste sites, or it could negotiate with guilty companies and thus completely avoid the legal system. During the 1980s, officials at the EPA came under fire because they preferred negotiated settlements. Critics referred to these settlements as "sweetheart deals" with industry. They felt that the EPA should be much more aggressive in reducing land pollution. Of course, most corporate executives believe that cleanup efficiency and quality might be improved if companies were more involved in the process. Many firms, including Delphi Automotive Systems Corporation and 3M, have modified or halted the production and sale of products that have a negative impact on the environment. For example, after tests showed that Scotch-Guard does not decompose in the environment, 3M announced a voluntary end to production of the 40-year-old product, which had generated $300 million in sales.

NOISE POLLUTION Excessive noise caused by traffic, aircraft, and machinery can do physical harm to human beings. Research has shown that people who are exposed to loud noises for long periods of time can suffer permanent hearing loss. The Noise Control Act of 1972 established noise emission standards for aircraft and airports, railroads, and interstate motor carriers. The act also provided funding for noise research at state and local levels.

Noise levels can be reduced by two methods. The source of noise pollution can be isolated as much as possible. (Thus, many metropolitan airports are located outside the cities.) Engineers can also modify machinery and equipment to reduce noise levels. If it is impossible to reduce industrial noise to acceptable levels, workers should be required to wear earplugs to guard them against permanent hearing damage.

Who Should Pay for a Clean Environment?

Governments and businesses are spending billions of dollars annually to reduce pollution—more than $45 billion to control air pollution, $33 billion to control water pollution, and $12 billion to treat hazardous wastes. To make matters worse, much of the money required to purify the environment is supposed to come from already depressed industries, such as the chemical industry. A few firms have discovered that it is cheaper to pay a fine than to install expensive equipment for pollution control.

Who, then, will pay for the environmental cleanup? Many business leaders offer one answer—tax money should be used to clean up the environment and to keep it clean. They reason that business is not the only source of pollution, so business should not be forced to absorb the entire cost of the cleanup. Environmentalists disagree. They believe that the cost of proper treatment and disposal of industrial wastes is an expense of doing business. In either case, consumers probably will pay a large part of the cost—either as taxes or in the form of higher prices for goods and services.

Personal App Consumers—you, your family, your friends—will wind up paying a lot of the costs for keeping the planet clean. Is social responsibility a matter of dollars and cents or dollars and sense?

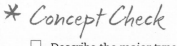

✱ *Concept Check*

☐ Describe the major types of pollution? What are their causes, and their cures?

☐ Summarize major provisions of federal environmental laws enacted since 1970?

☐ Who should pay for a clean environment?

LEARNING OBJECTIVE

10 Identify the steps a business must take to implement a program of social responsibility.

IMPLEMENTING A PROGRAM OF SOCIAL RESPONSIBILITY

A firm's decision to be socially responsible is a step in the right direction—but only the first step. The firm then must develop and implement a program to reach this goal. The program will be affected by the firm's size, financial resources, past record in the area of social responsibility, and competition. Above all, however, the program must have the firm's total commitment or it will fail.

Developing a Program of Social Responsibility

An effective program for social responsibility takes time, money, and organization. In most cases, developing and implementing such a program will require four steps: securing the commitment of top executives, planning, appointing a director, and preparing a social audit.

COMMITMENT OF TOP EXECUTIVES Without the support of top executives, any program will soon falter and become ineffective. For example, the Boeing Company's Ethics and Business Conduct Committee is responsible for the ethics program. The committee is appointed by the Boeing board of directors, and its members include the company chairman and CEO, the president and chief operating officer, the presidents of the operating groups, and senior vice presidents. As evidence of their commitment to social responsibility, top managers should develop a policy statement that outlines key areas of concern. This statement sets a tone of positive support and later will serve as a guide for other employees as they become involved in the program.

PLANNING Next, a committee of managers should be appointed to plan the program. Whatever form their plan takes, it should deal with each of the issues described in the top managers' policy statement. If necessary, outside consultants can be hired to help develop the plan.

APPOINTMENT OF A DIRECTOR After the social responsibility plan is established, a top-level executive should be appointed to implement the organization's plan. This individual should be charged with recommending specific policies and helping individual departments to understand and live up to the social responsibilities the firm has assumed. Depending on the size of the firm, the director may require a staff to handle the program on a day-to-day basis. For example, at the Boeing Company, the director of ethics and business conduct administers the ethics and business conduct program.

THE SOCIAL AUDIT At specified intervals, the program director should prepare a social audit for the firm. A **social audit** is a comprehensive report of what an organization has done and is doing with regard to social issues that affect it. This document provides the information the firm needs to evaluate and revise its social responsibility program. Typical subject areas include human resources, community involvement, the quality and safety of products, business practices, and efforts to reduce pollution and improve the environment. The information included in a social audit should be as accurate and as quantitative as possible, and the audit should reveal both positive and negative aspects of the program.

Today, many companies listen to concerned individuals within and outside the company. For example, the Boeing Ethics Line listens to and acts on concerns expressed by employees and others about possible violations of company policies, laws, or regulations, such as improper or unethical business practices, as well as health, safety, and environmental issues. Employees are encouraged to communicate their concerns, as well as ask questions about ethical issues. The Ethics Line is available to all Boeing employees, including Boeing subsidiaries. It is also available to concerned individuals outside the company.

Funding the Program

We have noted that social responsibility costs money. Thus, just like any other corporate undertaking, a program to improve social responsibility must be funded. Funding can come from three sources:

1. Management can pass the cost on to consumers in the form of higher prices.
2. The corporation may be forced to absorb the cost of the program if, for example, the competitive situation does not permit a price increase. In this case, the cost is treated as a business expense, and profit is reduced.
3. The federal government may pay for all or part of the cost through tax reductions or other incentives.

social audit a comprehensive report of what an organization has done and is doing with regard to social issues that affect it

Concept Check ✱

☐ What steps must a business take to implement a program of social responsibility?

☐ What is the social audit? Who should prepare a social audit for the firm?

☐ What are the three sources of funding for a social responsibility program?

Get Flashcards, Quizzes, Games, Crosswords, and more @ **www.cengagebrain.com**

SUMMARY

1 Understand what is meant by *business ethics*.

Ethics is the study of right and wrong and of the morality of choices. Business ethics is the application of moral standards to business situations.

2 Identify the types of ethical concerns that arise in the business world.

Ethical issues arise often in business situations out of relationships with investors, customers, employees, creditors, or competitors. Businesspeople should make every effort to be fair, to consider the welfare of customers and others within the firm, to avoid conflicts of interest, and to communicate honestly.

3 Discuss the factors that affect the level of ethical behavior in organizations.

Individual, social, and opportunity factors all affect the level of ethical behavior in an organization. Individual factors include knowledge level, moral values and attitudes, and personal goals. Social factors include cultural norms and the actions and values of co-workers and significant others. Opportunity factors refer to the amount of leeway that exists in an organization for employees to behave unethically if they choose to do so.

4 Explain how ethical decision making can be encouraged.

Governments, trade associations, and individual firms can establish guidelines for defining ethical behavior. Governments can pass stricter regulations. Trade associations provide ethical guidelines for their members. Companies provide codes of ethics—written guides to acceptable and ethical behavior as defined by an organization—and create an atmosphere in which ethical behavior is encouraged. An ethical employee working in an unethical environment may resort to whistle-blowing to bring a questionable practice to light.

5 Describe how our current views on the social responsibility of business have evolved.

In a socially responsible business, management realizes that its activities have an impact on society and considers that impact in the decision-making process. Before the 1930s, workers, consumers, and government had very little influence on business activities; as a result, business leaders gave little thought to social responsibility. All this changed with the Great Depression. Government regulations, employee demands, and consumer awareness combined to create a demand that businesses act in socially responsible ways.

6 Explain the two views on the social responsibility of business and understand the arguments for and against increased social responsibility.

The basic premise of the economic model of social responsibility is that society benefits most when business is left alone to produce profitable goods and services. According to the socioeconomic model, business has as much responsibility to society as it has to its owners. Most managers adopt a viewpoint somewhere between these two extremes.

7 Discuss the factors that led to the consumer movement and list some of its results.

Consumerism consists of all activities undertaken to protect the rights of consumers. The consumer movement generally has demanded—and received—attention from business in the areas of product safety, product information, product choices through competition, and the resolution of complaints about products and business practices. Although concerns over consumer rights have been around to some extent since the early 19th century, the movement became more powerful in the 1960s when President John F. Kennedy initiated the Consumer Bill of Rights. The six basic rights of consumers include the right to safety, the right to be informed, the right to choose, the right to be heard, and the rights to consumer education and courteous service.

8 Analyze how present employment practices are being used to counteract past abuses.

Legislation and public demand have prompted some businesses to correct past abuses in employment practices—mainly with regard to minority groups. Affirmative action and training of the hard-core unemployed are two types of programs that have been used successfully.

9 Describe the major types of pollution, their causes, and their cures.

Industry has contributed to noise pollution and pollution of our land and water through the dumping of wastes, and to air pollution through vehicle and smokestack emissions. This contamination can be cleaned up and controlled, but the big question is: Who will pay? Present cleanup efforts are funded partly by government tax revenues, partly by business, and in the long run by consumers.

10 Identify the steps a business must take to implement a program of social responsibility.

A program to implement social responsibility in a business begins with total commitment by top management. The program should be planned carefully, and a capable director should be appointed to implement it. Social audits should be prepared periodically as a means of evaluating and revising the program. Programs may be funded through price increases, reduction of profit, or federal incentives.

KEY TERMS

You should now be able to define and give an example relevant to each of the following terms:

ethics (36)
business ethics (36)
Sarbanes-Oxley Act of 2002 (40)
code of ethics (41)
whistle-blowing (43)
social responsibility (44)

caveat emptor (47)
economic model of social responsibility (49)
socioeconomic model of social responsibility (49)
consumerism (51)
minority (54)

affirmative action program (54)
Equal Employment Opportunity Commission (EEOC) (55)
hard-core unemployed (55)

National Alliance of Business (NAB) (56)
pollution (56)
social audit (61)

DISCUSSION QUESTIONS

1. When a company acts in an ethically questionable manner, what types of problems are caused for the organization and its customers?
2. How can an employee take an ethical stand regarding a business decision when his or her superior already has taken a different position?
3. Overall, would it be more profitable for a business to follow the economic model or the socioeconomic model of social responsibility?
4. Why should business take on the task of training the hard-core unemployed?
5. To what extent should the blame for vehicular air pollution be shared by manufacturers, consumers, and government?
6. Why is there so much government regulation involving social responsibility issues? Should there be less?

TEST YOURSELF

Matching Questions

1. _____ An application of moral standards to business situations.
2. _____ Provides legal protection for employees who report corporate misconduct.
3. _____ A guide to acceptable and ethical behavior as defined by the organization.
4. _____ All activities undertaken to protect the rights of consumers.
5. _____ Informing the press or government officials about unethical practices within one's organization.
6. _____ A Latin phrase meaning "let the buyer beware."
7. _____ A racial, religious, political, national, or other group regarded as different from the larger group of which it is a part.
8. _____ A plan designed to increase the number of minority employees at all levels within an organization.
9. _____ A joint business-government program to train the hard-core unemployed.
10. _____ The contamination of water, air, or land.

a. whistle-blowing
b. pollution
c. social audit
d. minority
e. code of ethics
f. National Alliance of Business (NAB)
g. Sarbanes-Oxley Act of 2002
h. economic model of social responsibility
i. affirmative action program
j. business ethics
k. consumerism
l. caveat emptor

True False Questions

11. **T F** The field of business ethics applies moral standards to business situations.

12. **T F** Business ethics rarely involves the application of moral standards to the business activity of a normal company.

13. **T F** The economic model of social responsibility emphasizes the effect of business decisions on society.

14. **T F** Consumerism consists of all activities undertaken to protect the rights of consumers.

15. **T F** Manufacturers are not required by law to inform consumers about the potential dangers of using their products.

16. **T F** Affirmative-action plans encompass all areas of human resources management, including recruiting, hiring, training, promotion, and pay.

17. **T F** A successful program for training hard-core unemployed people is the National Alliance of Business.

18. **T F** The EPA was created by the government to develop new improved ways to clean and improve the environment.

19. **T F** Consumers will probably pay in large part for cleaning up our environment through increased taxes or increased product cost.

20. **T F** A key step in developing and implementing a social responsibility program is the environmental audit.

Multiple-Choice Questions

21. _____ Business ethics
    a. is laws and regulations that govern business.
    b. is the application of moral standards to business situations.
    c. do not vary from one person to another.
    d. is most important for advertising agencies.
    e. is well-defined rules for appropriate business behavior.

22. _____ Customers expect a firm's products to
    a. boost sales.
    b. be profitable.
    c. earn a reasonable return on investment
    d. be available everywhere.
    e. be safe, reliable, and reasonably priced.

23. _____ Some AIG executives were aware of the financial problems the company was facing and yet failed to reveal this information to the public. These actions taken by AIG executives were
    a. moral.
    b. normal.
    c. in the best interests of shareholders.
    d. unethical.
    e. in the best interests of the employees.

24. _____ Bribes are
    a. unethical.
    b. ethical only under certain circumstances.
    c. uncommon in many foreign countries.
    d. economic returns.
    e. ethical.

25. _____ What are three sets of factors that influence the standards of behavior in an organization?
    a. Organizational norms, circumstances, morals
    b. Peer pressure, attitudes, social factors
    c. Historical factors, management attitudes, opportunity
    d. Opportunity, individual factors, social factors
    e. Financial factors, opportunity, morals

26. _____ Informing the press or government officials about unethical practices within one's organization is called
    a. unethical behavior.
    b. whistling.
    c. whistle-blowing.
    d. trumpeting.
    e. a company violation.

27. _____ Social responsibility
    a. has little or no associated costs.
    b. can be extremely expensive and provides very little benefit to a company.
    c. has become less important as businesses become more competitive.
    d. is generally a crafty scheme to put competitors out of business.
    e. is costly but provides tremendous benefits to society and the business.

28. _____ *Caveat emptor*
    a. is a French term that implies *laissez faire*.
    b. implies disagreements over peer evaluations.
    c. is a Latin phrase meaning "let the buyer beware."
    d. is a Latin phrase meaning "let the seller beware."
    e. is a Latin phrase meaning "the cave is empty."

29. _____ Where does social responsibility of business have to begin?
    a. Government
    b. Management
    c. Consumers
    d. Consumer protection groups
    e. Society

30. _____ Primary emphasis in the economic model of social responsibility is on
    a. quality of life.
    b. conservation of resources.
    c. market-based decisions.
    d. production.
    e. firm's and community's interests.

Answers to the Test Yourself questions appear at the end of the book on page TY-1.

VIDEO CASE
Scholfield Honda—Going Green with Honda

Signs of green marketing can be found everywhere today: reusable shopping bags are the rule rather than the exception, organic and natural products fill grocers' shelves, and socially responsible companies are increasing their efforts to reduce pollution, conserve water and energy, and recycle waste paper, plastic, and other reusable materials.

Of course, some companies have always been ahead of the curve. Since the early 1970s, Honda has been producing the low-emissions, fuel-efficient Civic model, and the company has never strayed from its roots. Today's Honda line consists of four classes of vehicles: Good, Better, Best, and Ultimate. Its regular gas cars are Good, with about 30 mpg; hybrids are Better at about 45 mpg; and its Best solution is a natural gas-powered Civic GX, which gets about 220 miles to a tank. Honda also has Ultimate solutions in the works, such as the new Honda FCX Clarity—a hydrogen fuel cell car that uses hydrogen and oxygen to create electricity. Although the Civic GX and Clarity models are available to consumers, neither vehicle is practical for the average driver as fueling stations are scarce.

Alternative energy vehicles are making their way to the Midwest. Lee Lindquist, an alternative fuels specialist at Scholfield Honda in Wichita, Kansas, was researching alternative fuel vehicles for a local Sierra Club meeting when he learned that municipalities in New York and California used the natural gas Civic GX to address air-quality issues. Although Lee recognized that his own Wichita market was not teeming with green consumers, he knew that people needed ways to combat rising fuel prices—so he proposed the Civic GX for use at his dealership.

Lee's boss was skeptical of the idea. Although management was open to clever ways to promote the dealership, owner Roger Scholfield did not want to risk muddying the waters with a new and somewhat impractical vehicle. Nevertheless, he agreed to offer the car to his fleet and corporate customers, and in time fate offered another opportunity for Scholfield Honda to go green.

In May 2007, a devastating tornado hit the nearby town of Greensburg, Kansas, leveling the area. Once again Lee Lindquist approached his boss. This time, he proposed donating both a Honda Civic GX and a natural-gas fueling station to Greensburg as a way of helping the town rebuild. Upon careful reflection, Roger realized that Lee's idea would benefit his dealership through good publicity and higher awareness of alternative fuel vehicles. Scholfield made the Civic model and fuel station available to Greensburg residents free of charge, and the dealership has been on the green bandwagon ever since.

Although there are more cost-effective ways of advertising, Roger Scholfield notes that customers are becoming more interested in alternative fuel vehicles since he donated the Civic GX. In addition, his dealership has generated plenty of goodwill in the press and among local residents—Scholfield Honda has developed a good reputation for its commitment to the environment and the people of Greensburg, even opening a "Honda Green Zone" conference room on the premises. The room can hold several hundred people. It includes a digital projector, sound system, and kitchenette and is available free to local firms and organizations for meetings and conferences. Its chairs, tables, tiles, and flooring are all made from recycled materials.[17]

Questions

1. How would you rate Scholfield Honda's sense of social responsibility? Does the dealership meet all the criteria for a socially responsible company?
2. What is Scholfield Honda's primary ethical responsibility in situations where a proposed green initiative is cost-prohibitive or even detrimental to the company's bottom line?
3. Should the government regulate companies' claims that their products are green? Should official classifications for environmental friendliness be defined?

BUILDING SKILLS FOR CAREER SUCCESS

1. Exploring The Internet

Socially responsible business behavior can be as simple as donating unneeded older computers to schools, mentoring interested learners in good business practices, or supplying public speakers to talk about career opportunities. Students, as part of the public at large, perceive a great deal of information about a company, its employees, and its owners by the positive social actions taken, and perhaps even more by actions not taken. Microsoft donates millions of dollars of computers and software to educational institutions every year. Some people consider this level of corporate giving to be insufficient given the scale of the wealth of the corporation. Others believe that firms have no obligation to give back any more than they wish and that recipients should be grateful. Visit the text Web site for updates to this exercise.

Assignment

1. Select any firm involved in high technology and the Internet such as Microsoft or IBM. Examine its Web site and report its corporate position on social responsibility and

giving as it has stated it. What activities is it involved in? What programs does it support, and how does it support them?

2. Search the Internet for commentary on business social responsibility, form your own opinions, and then evaluate the social effort demonstrated by the firm you have selected. What more could the firm have done?

2. Building Team Skills

A firm's code of ethics outlines the kinds of behaviors expected within the organization and serves as a guideline for encouraging ethical behavior in the workplace. It reflects the rights of the firm's workers, shareholders, and consumers.

Assignment

1. Working in a team of four, find a code of ethics for a business firm. Start the search by asking firms in your community for a copy of their codes, by visiting the library, or by searching and downloading information from the Internet.

2. Analyze the code of ethics you have chosen, and answer the following questions:
   a. What does the company's code of ethics say about the rights of its workers, shareholders, consumers, and suppliers? How does the code reflect the company's attitude toward competitors?
   b. How does this code of ethics resemble the information discussed in this chapter? How does it differ?
   c. As an employee of this company, how would you personally interpret the code of ethics? How might the code influence your behavior within the workplace? Give several examples.

3. Researching Different Careers

Business ethics has been at the heart of many discussions over the years and continues to trouble employees and shareholders. Stories about dishonesty and wrongful behavior in the workplace appear on a regular basis in newspapers and on the national news.

Assignment

Prepare a written report on the following:

1. Why can it be so difficult for people to do what is right?

2. What is your personal code of ethics? Prepare a code outlining what you believe is morally right. The document should include guidelines for your personal behavior.

3. How will your code of ethics affect your decisions about:
   a. The types of questions you should ask in a job interview?
   b. Selecting a company in which to work?

CHAPTER 3 EXPLORING GLOBAL BUSINESS

© Paul Precott/Shutterstock

Why should you care?

Free trade—are you for or against it? Most economists support free-trade policies, but public support can be lukewarm, and certain groups are adamantly opposed, alleging that "trade harms large segments of U.S. workers," "degrades the environment," and "exploits the poor."

Learning Objectives

What you will be able to do once you complete this chapter:

1 Explain the economic basis for international business.

2 Discuss the restrictions nations place on international trade, the objectives of these restrictions, and their results.

3 Outline the extent of international business and the world economic outlook for trade.

4 Discuss international trade agreements and international economic organizations working to foster trade.

5 Define the methods by which a firm can organize for and enter into international markets.

6 Describe the various sources of export assistance.

7 Identify the institutions that help firms and nations finance international business.

PepsiCo Gobbles Up Growth in Global Markets

PepsiCo—the company responsible for Doritos, Gatorade, Lipton, Mountain Dew, Tropicana, and 14 other billion-dollar food and beverage brands—has moved international business to the top of its menu for long-term growth. It's been active in global markets for decades, selling soft drinks in Canada for more than 75 years and in Russia for more than half a century. Today, nearly $21 billion of PepsiCo's $43 billion in annual revenue comes from sales outside the United States, and the company aims to increase its international presence in the coming decade.

China is one of PepsiCo's top business priorities. Health-conscious, increasingly prosperous Chinese consumers are looking for alternatives to high-fat, high-sugar foods and drinks. In response, PepsiCo is investing $2.5 billion to develop a variety of nutritious products featuring traditional ingredients. For example, one of its new Quaker Herbal Oatmeal flavors incorporates a tree fungus commonly used in local remedies. By catering to Chinese preferences, PepsiCo is boosting its sales volume in this fast-growing market.

Another key market is Russia, where consumers have even more buying power than consumers in China. In 2008, the company paid $1.4 billion to buy a major Russian juice producer. Two years later, it paid $3.8 billion for a majority stake in a top Russian dairy and juice company. These acquisitions helped PepsiCo take a commanding competitive lead over Coca-Cola in Russia, where the two rivals have long battled for market share. In addition, the acquisitions gave PepsiCo a pantryful of healthy beverages to supplement its carbonated drink business.

To better manage its international activities, PepsiCo has organized the various units into four major divisions: PepsiCo Americas Beverage and PepsiCo Americas Food (which include businesses in North and South America); PepsiCo Europe (including Russia and 44 other nations); and PepsiCo Asia, Middle East, and Africa. Looking ahead, PepsiCo's worldwide expansion will continue to be driven by its proven strategy of building global brands adapted to local tastes, interests, and customs.[1]

Did you know?

Nearly half of PepsiCo's $43 billion in annual revenue comes from sales outside the United States.

PepsiCo is just one of a growing number of companies, large and small, that are doing business with firms in other countries. Some companies, such as General Electric, sell to firms in other countries; others, such as Pier 1 Imports, buy goods around the world to import into the United States. Whether they buy or sell products across national borders, these companies are all contributing to the volume of international trade that is fueling the global economy.

Theoretically, international trade is every bit as logical and worthwhile as interstate trade between, say, California and Washington. Yet, nations tend to restrict the import of certain goods for a variety of reasons. For example, in the early 2000s, the United States restricted the import of Mexican fresh tomatoes because they were undercutting price levels of domestic fresh tomatoes.

Despite such restrictions, international trade has increased almost steadily since World War II. Many of the industrialized nations have signed trade agreements intended to eliminate problems in international business and to help less-developed nations participate in world trade. Individual firms around the world have seized the opportunity to compete in foreign markets by exporting products and increasing foreign production, as well as by other means.

Signing the Trade Act of 2002, President George W. Bush remarked, "Trade is an important source of good jobs for our workers and a source of higher growth for our economy. Free trade is also a proven strategy for building global prosperity and adding to the momentum of political freedom. Trade is an engine of economic growth. In our lifetime, trade has helped lift millions of people and whole nations out of poverty and put them on the path of prosperity".[2] In his national best seller, *The World Is Flat,* Thomas L. Friedman states, "The flattening of the world has presented us with new opportunities, new challenges, new partners but, also, alas new dangers, particularly as Americans it is imperative that we be the best global citizens that we can be—because in a flat world, if you don't visit a bad neighborhood, it might visit you."

We describe international trade in this chapter in terms of modern specialization, whereby each country trades the surplus goods and services it produces most efficiently for products in short supply. We also explain the restrictions nations place on products and services from other countries and present some of the possible advantages and disadvantages of these restrictions. We then describe the extent of international trade and identify the organizations working to foster it. We describe several methods of entering international markets and the various sources of export assistance available from the federal government. Finally, we identify some of the institutions that provide the complex financing necessary for modern international trade.

THE BASIS FOR INTERNATIONAL BUSINESS

LEARNING OBJECTIVE

1 Explain the economic basis for international business.

International business encompasses all business activities that involve exchanges across national boundaries. Thus, a firm is engaged in international business when it buys some portion of its input from, or sells some portion of its output to, an organization located in a foreign country. (A small retail store may sell goods produced in some other country. However, because it purchases these goods from American distributors, it is not engaged in international trade.)

international business all business activities that involve exchanges across national boundaries

absolute advantage the ability to produce a specific product more efficiently than any other nation

Absolute and Comparative Advantage

Some countries are better equipped than others to produce particular goods or services. The reason may be a country's natural resources, its labor supply, or even customs or a historical accident. Such a country would be best off if it could specialize in the production of such products so that it can produce them most efficiently. The country could use what it needed of these products and then trade the surplus for products it could not produce efficiently on its own.

Saudi Arabia thus has specialized in the production of crude oil and petroleum products; South Africa, in diamonds; and Australia, in wool. Each of these countries is said to have an absolute advantage with regard to a particular product. An **absolute advantage** is the ability to produce a specific product more efficiently than any other nation.

One country may have an absolute advantage with regard to several products, whereas another country may have no absolute advantage at all. Yet it is still worthwhile for these two countries to specialize and trade with each other. To see why this is so, imagine that you are the president of a successful manufacturing firm and that you can accurately type 90 words per minute. Your assistant can type 80 words per minute but would

Exploiting absolute advantage. Mir Mine, also called Mirny Mine is an open pit diamond mine in Mirny, Eastern Siberia, Russia. In the 1960s the mine was producing 10,000,000 carats (2,000 kg) of diamonds annually. The mine's present owner, Alrosa, accounts for about 25 percent of the world's rough diamond supply and 97 percent of Russia's rough diamond production.

© Tatiana Grozetskaya/Shutterstock

run the business poorly. Thus, you have an absolute advantage over your assistant in both typing and managing. However, you cannot afford to type your own letters because your time is better spent in managing the business. That is, you have a **comparative advantage** in managing. A comparative advantage is the ability to produce a specific product more efficiently than any other product.

Your assistant, on the other hand, has a comparative advantage in typing because he or she can do that better than managing the business. Thus, you spend your time managing, and you leave the typing to your assistant. Overall, the business is run as efficiently as possible because you are each working in accordance with your own comparative advantage.

> (Personal App) On the job, keep your comparative advantage in mind. What do you do more efficiently and more effectively than anyone else? This is an especially important consideration for entrepreneurs who have to juggle so many business roles.

The same is true for nations. Goods and services are produced more efficiently when each country specializes in the products for which it has a comparative advantage. Moreover, by definition, every country has a comparative advantage in some product. The United States has many comparative advantages—in research and development, high-technology industries, and identifying new markets, for instance.

Exporting and Importing

Suppose that the United States specializes in producing corn. It then will produce a surplus of corn, but perhaps it will have a shortage of wine. France, on the other hand, specializes in producing wine but experiences a shortage of corn. To satisfy both needs—for corn and for wine—the two countries should trade with each other. The United States should export corn and import wine. France should export wine and import corn.

Exporting is selling and shipping raw materials or products to other nations. The Boeing Company, for example, exports its airplanes to a number of countries for use by their airlines. Figure 3-1 shows the top ten merchandise-exporting states in this country.

Importing is purchasing raw materials or products in other nations and bringing them into one's own country. Thus, buyers for Macy's department stores may purchase rugs in India or raincoats in England and have them shipped back to the United States for resale.

Importing and exporting are the principal activities in international trade. They give rise to an important concept called the *balance of trade*. A nation's **balance of trade** is the total value of its exports minus the total value of its imports over some period of time. If a country imports more than it exports, its balance of trade is negative and is said to be *unfavorable*. (A negative balance of trade is unfavorable because the country must export money to pay for its excess imports.)

In 2010, the United States imported $2,330 billion worth of goods and services and exported $1,832 billion worth. It thus had a trade deficit of $498 billion. A **trade deficit** is a negative balance of trade (see Figure 3-2). However, the United States has consistently enjoyed a large and rapidly growing surplus in services. For example, in 2010, the United States imported $394 billion worth of services and exported $543 billion worth, thus creating a favorable balance of $149 billion.[3]

Question: *Are trade deficits bad?*

Answer: In testimony before the Senate Finance Committee, Daniel T. Griswold, associate director of the Center for Trade Policy at the Cato Institute, remarked, "The trade deficit is not a sign of economic distress, but of

comparative advantage the ability to produce a specific product more efficiently than any other product

exporting selling and shipping raw materials or products to other nations

importing purchasing raw materials or products in other nations and bringing them into one's own country

balance of trade the total value of a nation's exports minus the total value of its imports over some period of time

trade deficit a negative balance of trade

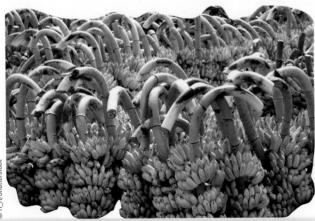
© R_R/Shutterstock

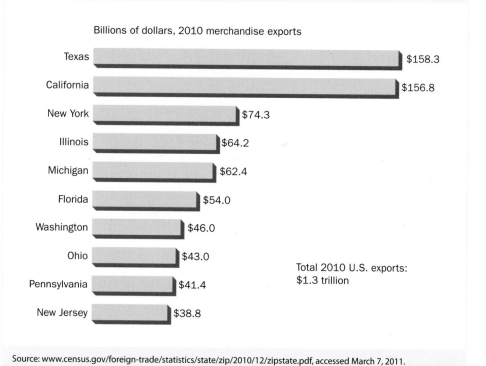

FIGURE 3-1: **The Top Ten Merchandise-Exporting States**

Texas and California accounted for almost one-fourth of all 2010 U.S. merchandise exports.

Billions of dollars, 2010 merchandise exports

Texas	$158.3
California	$156.8
New York	$74.3
Illinois	$64.2
Michigan	$62.4
Florida	$54.0
Washington	$46.0
Ohio	$43.0
Pennsylvania	$41.4
New Jersey	$38.8

Total 2010 U.S. exports: $1.3 trillion

Source: www.census.gov/foreign-trade/statistics/state/zip/2010/12/zipstate.pdf, accessed March 7, 2011.

rising domestic demand and investment. Imposing new trade barriers will only make Americans worse off while leaving the trade deficit virtually unchanged."

On the other hand, when a country exports more than it imports, it is said to have a *favorable* balance of trade. This has consistently been the case for Japan over the last two decades or so.

A nation's **balance of payments** is the total flow of money into a country minus the total flow of money out of that country over some period of time. Balance of payments, therefore, is a much broader concept than balance of trade. It includes imports and exports, of course. However, it also includes investments, money spent by foreign tourists, payments by foreign governments, aid to foreign governments, and all other receipts and payments.

A continual deficit in a nation's balance of payments (a negative balance) can cause other nations to lose confidence in that nation's economy. Alternatively, a continual surplus may indicate that the country encourages exports but limits imports by imposing trade restrictions.

RESTRICTIONS TO INTERNATIONAL BUSINESS

Specialization and international trade can result in the efficient production of want-satisfying goods and services on a worldwide basis. As we have noted, international business generally is increasing. Yet the nations of the world continue to erect barriers to free trade. They do so for reasons ranging from internal political and economic pressures to simple mistrust of other nations. We examine first the types of restrictions that are applied and then the arguments for and against trade restrictions.

Concept Check ✱

☐ Why do firms engage in international trade?

☐ What is the difference between an absolute advantage and a comparative advantage?

☐ What is the difference between balance of trade and balance of payments?

LEARNING OBJECTIVE

2 Discuss the restrictions nations place on international trade, the objectives of these restrictions, and their results.

balance of payments the total flow of money into a country minus the total flow of money out of that country over some period of time

FIGURE 3-2: U.S. International Trade in Goods and Services

If a country imports more goods than it exports, the balance of trade is negative, as it was in the United States from 1987 to 2010.

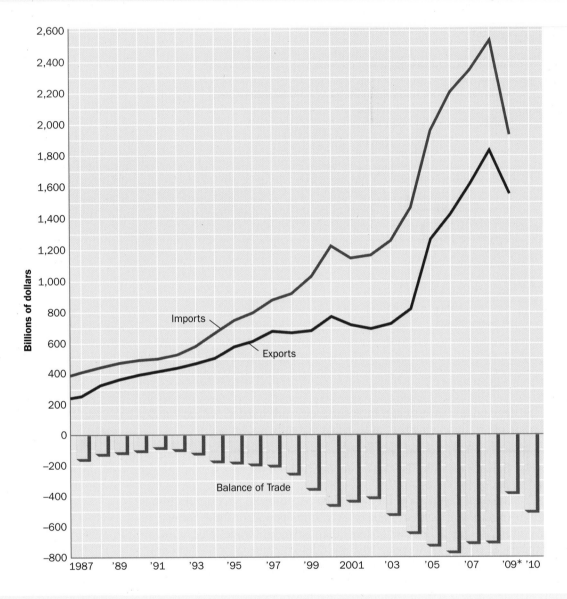

Source: U.S. Department of Commerce, International Trade Administration, U.S. Bureau of Economic Analysis, http://census.gov/foreign-trade/Press-Release/current_press_release, accessed March 7, 2011.

Types of Trade Restrictions

Nations generally are eager to export their products. They want to provide markets for their industries and to develop a favorable balance of trade. Hence, most trade restrictions are applied to imports from other nations.

TARIFFS Perhaps the most commonly applied trade restriction is the customs (or import) duty. An **import duty** (also called a **tariff**) is a tax levied on a particular foreign product entering a country. For example, the United States imposes a 2.2 percent import duty on fresh Chilean tomatoes, an 8.7 percent duty if tomatoes are dried and packaged, and nearly 12 percent if tomatoes are made into ketchup or salsa. The two types of tariffs are revenue tariffs and protective tariffs; both have

import duty (tariff) a tax levied on a particular foreign product entering a country

the effect of raising the price of the product in the importing nations, but for different reasons. *Revenue tariffs* are imposed solely to generate income for the government. For example, the United States imposes a duty on Scotch whiskey solely for revenue purposes. *Protective tariffs,* on the other hand, are imposed to protect a domestic industry from competition by keeping the price of competing imports level with or higher than the price of similar domestic products. Because fewer units of the product will be sold at the increased price, fewer units will be imported. The French and Japanese agricultural sectors would both shrink drastically if their nations abolished the protective tariffs that keep the price of imported farm products high. Today, U.S. tariffs are the lowest in history, with average tariff rates on all imports under 3 percent.

Some countries rationalize their protectionist policies as a way of offsetting an international trade practice called *dumping*. **Dumping** is the exportation of large quantities of a product at a price lower than that of the same product in the home market.

The United States-Brazil cotton dispute. After a series of fruitless discussions between the United States and Brazil, the World Trade Organization ruled that the United States and European Union have been dumping cotton in developing countries, hurting poor farmers in the developing country.

© Noam Armonn/Shutterstock

Thus, dumping drives down the price of the domestic item. Recently, for example, the Pencil Makers Association, which represents eight U.S. pencil manufacturers, charged that low-priced pencils from Thailand and the People's Republic of China were being sold in the United States at less than fair value prices. Unable to compete with these inexpensive imports, several domestic manufacturers had to shut down. To protect themselves, domestic manufacturers can obtain an antidumping duty through the government to offset the advantage of the foreign product. In 2010, for example, the U.S. Department of Commerce imposed antidumping duties of up to 99 percent on a variety of steel products imported from China, following allegations by U.S. Steel Corp. and other producers that the products were being dumped at unfair prices.

NONTARIFF BARRIERS A **nontariff barrier** is a nontax measure imposed by a government to favor domestic over foreign suppliers. Nontariff barriers create obstacles to the marketing of foreign goods in a country and increase costs for exporters. The following are a few examples of government-imposed nontariff barriers:

- An **import quota** is a limit on the amount of a particular good that may be imported into a country during a given period of time. The limit may be set in terms of either quantity (so many pounds of beef) or value (so many dollars' worth of shoes). Quotas also may be set on individual products imported from specific countries. Once an import quota has been reached, imports are halted until the specified time has elapsed.
- An **embargo** is a complete halt to trading with a particular nation or of a particular product. The embargo is used most often as a political weapon. At present, the United States has import embargoes against Iran and North Korea—both as a result of extremely poor political relations.
- A **foreign-exchange control** is a restriction on the amount of a particular foreign currency that can be purchased or sold. By limiting the amount of foreign currency importers can obtain, a government limits the amount of goods importers can purchase with that currency. This has the effect of limiting imports from the country whose foreign exchange is being controlled.
- A nation can increase or decrease the value of its money relative to the currency of other nations. **Currency devaluation** is the reduction of the value of a nation's currency relative to the currencies of other countries.

dumping exportation of large quantities of a product at a price lower than that of the same product in the home market

nontariff barrier a nontax measure imposed by a government to favor domestic over foreign suppliers

import quota a limit on the amount of a particular good that may be imported into a country during a given period of time

embargo a complete halt to trading with a particular nation or in a particular product

foreign-exchange control a restriction on the amount of a particular foreign currency that can be purchased or sold

currency devaluation the reduction of the value of a nation's currency relative to the currencies of other countries

Devaluation increases the cost of foreign goods, whereas it decreases the cost of domestic goods to foreign firms. For example, suppose that the British pound is worth $2. In this case, an American-made $2,000 computer can be purchased for £1,000. However, if the United Kingdom devalues the pound so that it is worth only $1, that same computer will cost £2,000. The increased cost, in pounds, will reduce the import of American computers—and all foreign goods—into England.

On the other hand, before devaluation, a £500 set of English bone china will cost an American $1,000. After the devaluation, the set of china will cost only $500. The decreased cost will make the china—and all English goods—much more attractive to U.S. purchasers. Bureaucratic red tape is more subtle than the other forms of nontariff barriers. Yet it can be the most frustrating trade barrier of all. A few examples are the unnecessarily restrictive application of standards and complex requirements related to product testing, labeling, and certification.

Another type of nontariff barrier is related to cultural attitudes. Cultural barriers can impede acceptance of products in foreign countries. For example, illustrations of feet are regarded as despicable in Thailand. When customers are unfamiliar with particular products from another country, their general perceptions of the country itself affect their attitude toward the product and help to determine whether they will buy it. Because Mexican cars have not been viewed by the world as being quality products, Volkswagen, for example, may not want to advertise that some of its models sold in the United States are made in Mexico. Many retailers on the Internet have yet to come to grips with the task of designing an online shopping site that is attractive and functional for all global customers.

Personal App What's your reaction when you see "Made in America" on a pickup truck? Would your reaction be the same if the truck had been made elsewhere? Clearly, cultural attitudes can influence how people feel about goods in the global marketplace.

Reasons for Trade Restrictions

Various reasons are given for trade restrictions either on the import of specific products or on trade with particular countries. We have noted that political considerations usually are involved in trade embargoes. Other frequently cited reasons for restricting trade include the following:

- To *equalize a nation's balance of payments*. This may be considered necessary to restore confidence in the country's monetary system and in its ability to repay its debts.
- To *protect new or weak industries*. A new, or infant, industry may not be strong enough to withstand foreign competition. Temporary trade restrictions may be used to give it a chance to grow and become self-sufficient. The problem is that once an industry is protected from foreign competition, it may refuse to grow, and "temporary" trade restrictions will become permanent. For example, a recent report by the Government Accountability Office (GAO), the congressional investigative agency, has accused the federal government of routinely imposing quotas on foreign textiles without "demonstrating the threat of serious damage" to U.S. industry. The GAO said that the Committee for the Implementation of Textile Agreements sometimes applies quotas even though it cannot prove the textile industry's claims that American companies have been hurt or jobs have been eliminated.
- To *protect national security*. Restrictions in this category generally apply to technological products that must be kept out of the hands of potential enemies. For example, strategic and defense-related goods cannot be exported to unfriendly nations.
- To *protect the health of citizens*. Products may be embargoed because they are dangerous or unhealthy (e.g., farm products contaminated with insecticides).
- To *retaliate for another nation's trade restrictions*. A country whose exports are taxed by another country may respond by imposing tariffs on imports from that country.

- *To protect domestic jobs.* By restricting imports, a nation can protect jobs in domestic industries. However, protecting these jobs can be expensive. For example, protecting 9,000 jobs in the U.S. carbon-steel industry costs $6.8 billion, or $750,000 per job. In addition, Gary Hufbauer and Ben Goodrich, economists at the Institute for International Economics, estimate that the tariffs could temporarily save 3,500 jobs in the steel industry, but at an annual cost to steel users of $2 billion, or $584,000 per job saved. Yet recently the United States imposed tariffs of up to 616 percent on steel pipes imported from China, South Korea, and Mexico. Similarly, it is estimated that we spent more than $100,000 for every job saved in the apparel manufacturing industry—jobs that seldom paid more than $35,000 a year.

Restrictions or not, international business is booming. Globalization is the reality of our time. As trade barriers decrease, ever-increasing numbers of U.S. companies are entering the global marketplace, creating more choices for consumers.

© Amy Nichole Harris/Shutterstock

Reasons Against Trade Restrictions

Trade restrictions have immediate and long-term economic consequences—both within the restricting nation and in world trade patterns. These include the following:

- *Higher prices for consumers.* Higher prices may result from the imposition of tariffs or the elimination of foreign competition, as described earlier. For example, imposing quota restrictions and import protections adds $25 billion annually to U.S. consumers' apparel costs by directly increasing costs for imported apparel.
- *Restriction of consumers' choices.* Again, this is a direct result of the elimination of some foreign products from the marketplace and of the artificially high prices that importers must charge for products that are still imported.
- *Misallocation of international resources.* The protection of weak industries results in the inefficient use of limited resources. The economies of both the restricting nation and other nations eventually suffer because of this waste.
- *Loss of jobs.* The restriction of imports by one nation must lead to cutbacks—and the loss of jobs—in the export-oriented industries of other nations. Furthermore, trade protection has a significant effect on the composition of employment. U.S. trade restrictions—whether on textiles, apparel, steel, or automobiles—benefit only a few industries while harming many others. The gains in employment accrue to the protected industries and their primary suppliers, and the losses are spread across all other industries. A few states gain employment, but many other states lose employment.

Concept Check ✱

☐ List and briefly describe the principal restrictions that may be applied to a nation's imports.

☐ What reasons are generally given for imposing trade restrictions?

☐ What are the general effects of import restrictions on trade?

THE EXTENT OF INTERNATIONAL BUSINESS

LEARNING OBJECTIVE

3 Outline the extent of international business and the world economic outlook for trade.

Restrictions or not, international business is growing. Although the worldwide recessions of 1991 and 2001–2002 slowed the rate of growth, and the 2008–2009 global economic crisis caused the sharpest decline in more than 70 years, globalization is a reality of our time. In the United States, international trade now accounts for over one-fourth of GDP. As trade barriers decrease, new competitors enter the global marketplace, creating more choices for consumers and new opportunities for job seekers. International business will grow along with the expansion of commercial use of the Internet.

The World Economic Outlook for Trade

Although the global economy continued to grow robustly until 2007 economic performance was not equal: growth in the advanced economies slowed and then stopped in 2009, whereas emerging and developing economies continued to grow. Looking ahead, the International Monetary Fund (IMF), an international bank with 186 member nations, expected growth to continue in 2011 and 2012 in both advanced and emerging developing economies.[4]

Although the U.S. economy had been growing steadily since 2000 and recorded the longest peacetime expansion in the nation's history, the worldwide recession which began in December 2007 had slowed the rate of growth. The IMF estimated that the U.S. economy grew by less than half of 1 percent in 2008 and, because of subprime mortgage lending and other global financial problems, declined 2.6 percent in 2009. The U.S. growth was expected to be 3.0 percent in 2011 and 2.7 percent in 2012. International experts expected global economic growth of 4.4 percent in 2011 and 4.5 percent in 2012, despite the high oil prices.

CANADA AND WESTERN EUROPE Our leading export partner, Canada, is projected to show a growth rate of 2.7 percent in 2011. The euro area, which declined by 4.1 percent in 2009, grew by 1.7 percent in 2010, and is expected to grow 1.5 percent in 2011. The United Kingdom and smaller European countries, such as Austria, the Netherlands, Norway, and Switzerland, are expected to experience a modest recovery.

MEXICO AND LATIN AMERICA Our second-largest export customer, Mexico, suffered its sharpest recession ever in 1995, and experienced another major setback in 2009. However, its growth rate in 2010 and 2011 was expected to be 5.0 percent and 3.9 percent, respectively. Brazil escaped the recent global economic crisis with only minor setbacks: its growth in 2008 was more than 5.0 percent, and in 2009 it declined only 0.4 percent. Growth of about 7.5 percent and 4.1 percent was expected in 2010 and 2011, respectively. In general, the Latin American and the Caribbean economies are recovering at a robust pace.

JAPAN Japan's economy is regaining momentum. Stronger consumer demand and business investment make Japan less reliant on exports for growth. The IMF estimates the growth for Japan at 1.6 percent in 2011 and 1.8 percent in 2012. (The devastating March 11, 2011, earthquake, tsunami, and nuclear radiation leaks may lower these projections.)

OTHER ASIAN COUNTRIES The economic growth in Asia remained strong in 2008–2010 despite the global recession. Growth was led by China, where its economy expanded by 10.5 percent in 2010, and was expected to grow at 9.6 percent in 2011. Growth in India was 9.7 percent in 2010, but was predicted to grow at 8.4 percent in 2011. Growth in Indonesia, Malaysia, the Philippines, Thailand, and Vietnam was 6.6 percent in 2010 and was predicted to grow at 5.4 percent in 2011. In short, the key emerging economies in Asia are leading the global recovery.

China's emergence as a global economic power has been among the most dramatic economic developments of recent decades. Just imagine that in 2010, we imported almost $365 billion worth of goods from China, making it our number one supplier. And, China is our third leading country for U.S. exports ($91.9 billion in 2010). In 2009, China surpassed Germany as the leading exporter of merchandise. China's share of world merchandise imports increased by 7.9 percent in 2009, thus making China the second largest world importer.[5]

EMERGING EUROPE The global economic crisis that plagued this region finally came to an end in 2010 and most countries in the region are expected to see positive growth of 3.7 percent and 3.1 percent, in 2010 and 2011, respectively. The economies in Poland and Turkey continue to gain strength; however, Bulgaria, Latvia, Hungary, and Romania are expected to recover more slowly.

COMMONWEALTH OF INDEPENDENT STATES The growth in this region was expected to be 4.7 percent in 2011 and 4.6 percent in 2012. Strong growth is expected to continue in Azerbaijan and Armenia, whereas growth is projected to remain stable in Moldova, Tajikistan, and Uzbekistan.

After World War II, trade between the United States and the communist nations of Central and Eastern Europe was minimal. The United States maintained high tariff barriers on imports from most of these countries and also restricted their exports. However, since the disintegration of the Soviet Union and the collapse of communism, trade between the United States and Central and Eastern Europe has expanded substantially.

The countries that made the transition from communist to market economies quickly have recorded positive growth for several years—those that did not continue to struggle. Among the nations that have enjoyed several years of positive economic growth are the member countries of the Central European Free Trade Association: Hungary, the Czech Republic, Poland, Slovenia, and Slovakia.

U.S. exports to Central and Eastern Europe and Russia will increase, as will U.S. investment in these countries, as demand for capital goods and technology opens new markets for U.S. products. There already has been a substantial expansion in trade between the United States and the Czech Republic, Slovakia, Hungary, and Poland. Table 3-1 shows the growth rates from 2009 to 2012 for most regions of the world.

EXPORTS AND THE U.S. ECONOMY In 2008, U.S. exports supported more than 10.3 million full- and part-time jobs during a historic time, when exports as a percentage of GDP reached the highest levels since 1916. This new record, 12.8 percent of GDP, shows that U.S. businesses have great opportunities in the global marketplace. Even though the global economic crisis caused the number of jobs supported by exports to decline sharply to 8.5 million in 2009, globalization represents a huge opportunity for all countries—rich or poor. Today, exports support ten million jobs

TABLE 3-1: Global Growth Is Picking Up

Growth has been led by developing countries and emerging markets.

	Annual Percent Change			
	2009	2010	Projected 2011	Projected 2012
World	−0.6	5.0	4.4	4.5
United States	−2.6	2.8	3.0	2.7
Euro area	−4.1	1.8	1.5	1.7
United Kingdom	−4.9	1.7	2.0	2.3
Japan	−6.3	4.3	1.6	1.8
Canada	−2.5	2.9	2.3	2.7
Other advanced economies	−1.2	5.6	3.8	3.7
Newly industrialized Asian economies	−0.9	8.2	4.7	4.3
Developing countries and emerging markets	2.6	7.1	6.5	6.5
Developing Asia	7.0	9.3	8.4	8.4
Commonwealth of Independent States	−6.5	4.2	4.7	4.6
Middle East and North Africa	1.8	3.9	4.6	4.7
Latin America and the Caribbean	−1.8	5.9	4.3	4.1

Source: *International Monetary Fund: World Economic Outlook* by International Monetary Fund. Copyright 2010 by International Monetary Fund. Reproduced with permission of International Monetary Fund via Copyright Clearance Center. www.imf.org/external/pubs/ft/weo/2011/update/01/#tbl1, (accessed March 12, 2011).

Today's Global Career Path

career SUCCESS

As international business continues to expand, you'll have many more opportunities to work abroad. Taking a job or an internship in another country can give you valuable hands-on experience in global business activities, enhance your resume so it stands out, help you polish your communication skills, and offer you new professional challenges to meet and master.

Succeeding in a global career path requires resilience and adaptability, the ability to listen carefully, a positive attitude, a large dash of patience and persistence, and the willingness to try new things. Even if you don't know a foreign language, your employer may offer training before or during your international assignment. The accounting firm Deloitte Touche Tohmatsu, for example, provides intensive language instruction for employees who work abroad. "We really encourage international exposure and experience," says the firm's global managing director of talent. "It creates a more well-rounded professional."

Many U.S. companies have an ever-growing presence in other countries, which opens the door to employees who want to pursue a global career path. Caterpillar and UPS, for instance, both have a sizable workforce abroad. Non-profit agencies and

businesses that emphasize social responsibility over profitability also court employees who seek international experience. If you have entrepreneurial spirit, you may want to start your own business or set up a socially-responsible organization in another country. There's a world of career choices out there—so think global as you think about your work future.

Sources: Phyllis Korkki, "When a Career Path Leads Abroad," *New York Times*, December 5, 2010, p. Bu-9; Pallavi Gogoi, "Where Are the Jobs? Overseas, of Course," *Salon.com*, December 28, 2010, www.salon.com; Stacie Nevadomski Berdan, "I've Got an International Job—Now What?" *Huffington Post*, December 8, 2010, www. huffingtonpost.com.

in America, including almost seven million manufacturing jobs. Exports as a percentage of our GDP were 12.5 percent in 2010, up from 11.2 percent in 2009, but we are still far behind countries like Germany where exports account for 40 percent or Canada where 30 percent of its GDP is from exports. Less than one percent of America's 30 million companies export, and of those that do, 58 percent export only to one country. The National Export Initiative, the Obama administration's plan to create jobs, will double exports over the next five years and support millions of new jobs in the United States. Our exports to developing and newly industrialized countries are on the rise. Table 3-2 shows the value of U.S. merchandise exports

General Agreement on Tariffs and Trade (GATT) an international organization of 153 nations dedicated to reducing or eliminating tariffs and other barriers to world trade

✳ *Concept Check*

☐ According to the IMF, what are the world economic growth projections for 2011 and 2012?

☐ What is the importance of exports to the U.S. economy?

☐ Which nations are the principal trading partners of the United States? What are the major U.S. imports and exports?

TABLE 3-2: **Value of U.S. Merchandise Exports and Imports, 2010**

Rank/Trading Partner	Exports ($ billions)	Rank/Trading Partner	Imports ($ billions)
1/Canada	248.8	1/China	364.9
2/Mexico	163.3	2/Canada	276.5
3/China	91.9	3/Mexico	229.7
4/Japan	60.5	4/Japan	120.3
5/United Kingdom	48.5	5/Germany	82.7
6/Germany	48.2	6/United Kingdom	49.8
7/South Korea	38.8	7/South Korea	48.9
8/Brazil	35.4	8/France	38.6
9/Netherlands	35.0	9/Taiwan	35.9
10/Singapore	29.1	10/Ireland	33.9

Source: U.S. Department of Commerce, International Trade Administration, www.census.gov/foreign-trade/statistics/highlights/top/top1012yr.html (accessed March 9, 2011).

to, and imports from, each of the nation's ten major trading partners. Note that Canada and Mexico are our best partners for our exports; China and Canada, for imports.

Figure 3-3 shows the U.S. goods export and import shares in 2010. Major U.S. exports and imports are manufactured goods, agricultural products, and mineral fuels.

INTERNATIONAL TRADE AGREEMENTS

The General Agreement on Tariffs and Trade and the World Trade Organization

At the end of World War II, the United States and 22 other nations organized the body that came to be known as GATT. The **General Agreement on Tariffs and Trade (GATT)** was an international organization of 153 nations dedicated to reducing or eliminating tariffs and other barriers to world trade. These 153 nations accounted for more than 97 percent of the world's merchandise trade (see Figure 3-4). GATT, headquartered in Geneva, Switzerland, provided a forum for tariff negotiations and a means for settling international trade disputes and problems. *Most-favored-nation status* (MFN) was the famous principle of GATT. It meant that each GATT member nation was to be treated equally by all contracting nations. Therefore, MFN ensured that any tariff

Leading Exporters in World Merchandise Trade, 2009

Source: World Trade Organization, *World Trade Developments in 2009*, Table 1.8, at www .wto.org, accessed March 13, 2011.

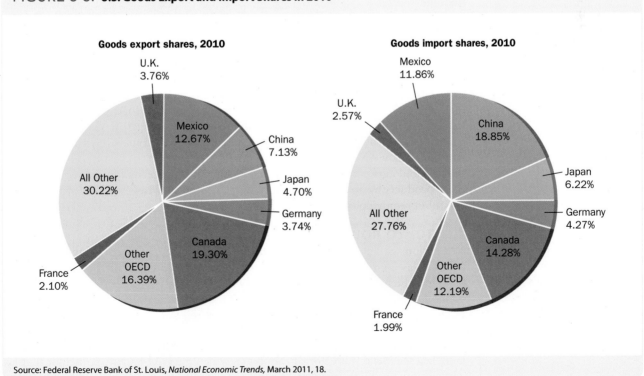

Source credit text on right side of leading exporters image: © Slawomir Fajer/iStockphoto 3163103

LEARNING OBJECTIVE
4 Discuss international trade agreements and international economic organizations working to foster trade.

FIGURE 3-3: U.S. Goods Export and Import Shares in 2010

Source: Federal Reserve Bank of St. Louis, *National Economic Trends,* March 2011, 18.

FIGURE 3-4: WTO Members Share in World Merchandise Trade, 2009

The 153 member nations account for more than 97 percent of the world's merchandise trade.

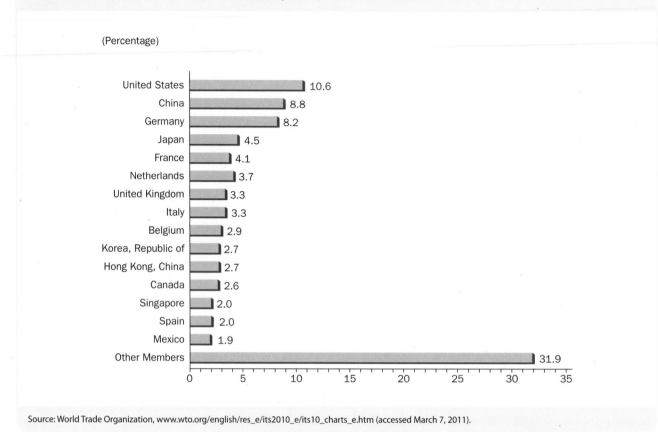

(Percentage)

United States	10.6
China	8.8
Germany	8.2
Japan	4.5
France	4.1
Netherlands	3.7
United Kingdom	3.3
Italy	3.3
Belgium	2.9
Korea, Republic of	2.7
Hong Kong, China	2.7
Canada	2.6
Singapore	2.0
Spain	2.0
Mexico	1.9
Other Members	31.9

Source: World Trade Organization, www.wto.org/english/res_e/its2010_e/its10_charts_e.htm (accessed March 7, 2011).

reductions or other trade concessions were extended automatically to all GATT members. From 1947 to 1994, the body sponsored eight rounds of negotiations to reduce trade restrictions. Three of the most fruitful were the Kennedy Round, the Tokyo Round, and the Uruguay Round.

THE KENNEDY ROUND (1964–1967) In 1962, the U.S. Congress passed the Trade Expansion Act. This law gave President John F. Kennedy the authority to negotiate reciprocal trade agreements that could reduce U.S. tariffs by as much as 50 percent. Armed with this authority, which was granted for a period of five years, President Kennedy called for a round of negotiations through GATT.

These negotiations, which began in 1964, have since become known as the Kennedy Round. They were aimed at reducing tariffs and other barriers to trade in both industrial and agricultural products. The participants succeeded in reducing tariffs on these products by an average of more than 35 percent. However, they were less successful in removing other types of trade barriers.

THE TOKYO ROUND (1973–1979) In 1973, representatives of approximately 100 nations gathered in Tokyo for another round of GATT negotiations. The *Tokyo Round* was completed in 1979. The participants negotiated tariff cuts of 30 to 35 percent, which were to be implemented over an eight-year period. In addition, they were able to remove or ease such nontariff barriers as import quotas, unrealistic quality standards for imports, and unnecessary red tape in customs procedures.

THE URUGUAY ROUND (1986–1993) In 1986, the *Uruguay Round* was launched to extend trade liberalization and widen the GATT treaty to include textiles, agricultural products, business services, and intellectual-property rights. This most ambitious and comprehensive global commercial agreement in history concluded overall negotiations on December 15, 1993, with delegations on hand from 109 nations. The agreement included provisions to lower tariffs by greater than one-third, to reform trade in agricultural goods, to write new rules of trade for intellectual property and services, and to strengthen the dispute-settlement process. These reforms were expected to expand the world economy by an estimated $200 billion annually.

The Uruguay Round also created the **World Trade Organization (WTO)** on January 1, 1995. The WTO was established by GATT to oversee the provisions of the Uruguay Round and resolve any resulting trade disputes. Membership in the WTO obliges 153 member nations to observe GATT rules. The WTO has judicial powers to mediate among members disputing the new rules. It incorporates trade in goods, services, and ideas and exerts more binding authority than GATT.

THE DOHA ROUND (2001) On November 14, 2001, in Doha, Qatar, the WTO members agreed to further reduce trade barriers through multilateral trade negotiations over the next three years. This new round of negotiations focuses on industrial tariffs and nontariff barriers, agriculture, services, and easing trade rules. U.S. exporters of industrial and agricultural goods and services should have improved access to overseas markets. The Doha Round has set the stage for WTO members to take an important step toward significant new multilateral trade liberalization. It is a difficult task, but the rewards—lower tariffs, more choices for consumers, and further integration of developing countries into the world trading system—are sure to be worth the effort. Some experts suggest that U.S. exporters of industrial and agricultural goods and services should have improved access to overseas markets, whereas others disagree. Negotiations between the developed and developing countries continued in 2011.

World Trade and Global Economic Crisis

After the sharpest decline in more than 70 years, world trade was set to rebound in 2010 by growing at 9.5 percent, according to the WTO economists. According to WTO Director-General Pascal Lamy, "WTO rules and principles have assisted governments in keeping markets open and they now provide a platform for which trade can grow as the global economy improves. We see the light at the end of the tunnel and trade promises to be an important part of the recovery. But we must avoid derailing any economic revival through protectionism."[6]

Exports from developed economies are expected to rise whereas exports from the rest of the world, including developing economies and the Commonwealth of Independent States, should increase by 11 percent as the world emerges from recession. This strong expansion will help recover some, but not all, of the loss in 2009, when the global economic crisis caused a 12.2 percent decline in the volume of global trade—the largest such decline since World War II.

International Economic Organizations Working to Foster Trade

The primary objective of the WTO is to remove barriers to trade on a worldwide basis. On a smaller scale, an **economic community** is an organization of nations formed to promote the free movement of resources and products among its members and to create common economic policies. A number of economic communities now exist.

- The European Union (EU), also known as the *European Economic Community* and the *Common Market*, was formed in 1957 by six countries—France, the Federal Republic of Germany, Italy, Belgium, the Netherlands, and Luxembourg. Its objective was freely conducted commerce among these nations and others that might later join. As shown in Figure 3-5, many more nations have joined the EU since then.

World Trade Organization (WTO) powerful successor to GATT that incorporates trade in goods, services, and ideas

economic community an organization of nations formed to promote the free movement of resources and products among its members and to create common economic policies

FIGURE 3-5: The Evolving European Union

The Evolving European Union: The European Union is now an economic force, with a collective economy larger than that of the United States or Japan.

Source: http://europa.eu/abc/european_countries/index_en.htm (accessed March 14, 2011).

- On January 1, 2007, the 25 nations of the EU became the EU27 as Bulgaria and Romania became new members. The EU, with a population of nearly half a billion, is now an economic force with a collective economy larger than much of the United States or Japan.

  In celebrating the EU's 50th anniversary in 2007, the president of the European Commission, Jose Manuel Durao Barraso, declared, "Let us first recognize 50 years of achievement. Peace, liberty, and prosperity, beyond the dreams of even the most optimistic founding fathers of Europe. In 1957, 15 of our 27 members were either under dictatorship or were not allowed to exist as independent countries. Now we are all prospering democracies. The EU of today is around 50 times more prosperous and with three times the population of the EU of 1957."

  Since January 2002, 15 member nations of the EU have been participating in the new common currency, the euro. The euro is the single currency of the European Monetary Union nations. However, three EU members, Denmark, the United Kingdom, and Sweden, still keep their own currencies.

- A second community in Europe, the *European Economic Area* (EEA), became effective in January 1994. This pact consists of Iceland, Norway, Liechtenstein, and the 27 member nations of the EU. The EEA, encompassing an area inhabited by more than 500 million people, allows for the free movement of goods throughout all 30 countries.

- The *North American Free Trade Agreement* (NAFTA) joined the United States with its first- and second-largest export trading partners, Canada and Mexico. Implementation of NAFTA on January 1, 1994, created a market of more than 458 million people. This market consists of Canada (population 34 million), the United States (311 million), and Mexico (113 million). According to the Office of the U.S. Trade Representative, trade among NAFTA countries has more than tripled from $297 billion to over $941 billion since 1994. Each day the three countries conduct over $2.6 billion in trilateral trade. Canada and Mexico were the two top buyers of U.S. exports in 2010 and accounted for 32.2 percent of overall U.S. exports in 2010. Canada and Mexico remain the second and third largest suppliers of U.S. imports in 2010.[7]

  NAFTA is built on the Canadian Free Trade Agreement, signed by the United States and Canada in 1989, and on the substantial trade and investment reforms undertaken by Mexico since the mid-1980s. Initiated by the Mexican government, formal negotiations on NAFTA began in June 1991 among the three governments. The support of NAFTA by President Bill Clinton, past U.S. Presidents Ronald Reagan and Jimmy Carter, and Nobel Prize–winning economists provided the impetus for U.S. congressional ratification of NAFTA in November 1993. NAFTA has gradually eliminated all tariffs on goods produced and traded among Canada, Mexico, and the United States to provide for a totally free-trade area by 2009. Chile is expected to become the fourth member of NAFTA, but political forces may delay its entry into the agreement for several years.

  However, NAFTA is not without its critics. Critics maintain that NAFTA:

  - has not achieved its goals
  - has resulted in job losses
  - hurt workers by eroding labor standards and lowering wages
  - undermines national sovereignty and independence
  - does nothing to help the environment, and
  - hurts the agricultural sector

  The proponents of NAFTA call the agreement a remarkable economic success story for all three partners. They maintain that NAFTA:

  - has contributed to significant increases in trade and investment
  - has benefited companies in all three countries
  - has resulted in increased sales, new partnerships, and new opportunities
  - has created high-paying export-related jobs, and
  - better prices and selection in consumer goods
- The *Central American Free Trade Agreement* (CAFTA) was created in 2003 by the United States and four Central American countries—El Salvador, Guatemala, Honduras, and Nicaragua. The CAFTA became CAFTA-DR when the Dominican Republic joined the group in 2007. On January 1, 2009, Costa Rica joined CAFTA-DR as the sixth member. CAFTA-DR creates the third-largest U.S. export market in Latin America, behind only Mexico and Brazil. U.S. agricultural export growth to this region in the last five years exceeded the growth rate of top agricultural export markets such as Canada, Mexico, and China. Reduced tariffs and a growing middle class is expanding demand in this region.[8]
- The *Association of Southeast Asian Nations*, with headquarters in Jakarta, Indonesia, was established in 1967 to promote political, economic, and social cooperation among its seven member countries: Indonesia, Malaysia, the Philippines, Singapore, Thailand, Brunei, and Vietnam. With the three new members, Cambodia, Laos, and Myanmar, this region is already our fifth-largest trading partner. The ten-member region, with a population of 592 million, has $1.5 trillion in GDP and accounts for more than $203 billion worth of trade with the United States. This region supports nearly 800,000 jobs in the United States. All ten ASEAN economies are expected to grow in 2011, and the future of U.S.-ASEAN trade looks positive.[9]

Celebrating OPEC's 50th anniversary. Secretary General of OPEC Abdalla Salem El-Badri and Iranian Oil Minister Masoud Mir Kazemi attend a ceremony to celebrate the 50th anniversary of the founding of OPEC, in Tehran, Iran, on April 19th, 2011.

© EPA/Landov

- The *Pacific Rim,* referring to countries and economies bordering the Pacific Ocean, is an informal, flexible term generally regarded as a reference to East Asia, Canada, and the United States. At a minimum, the Pacific Rim includes Canada, Japan, China, Taiwan, and the United States. In 2010, our exports to the Pacific Rim were $326.5 billion; our imports $653.8 billion.
- The *Commonwealth of Independent States* was established in December 1991 by the newly independent states as an association of 11 republics of the former Soviet Union.
- The *Caribbean Basin Initiative* (CBI) is an inter-American program led by the United States to give economic assistance and trade preferences to the Caribbean and Central American countries. CBI provides duty-free access to the U.S. market for most products from the region and promotes private-sector development in member nations.
- The *Common Market of the Southern Cone* (MERCOSUR) was established in 1991 under the Treaty of Asuncion to unite Argentina, Brazil, Paraguay, and Uruguay as a free-trade alliance; Colombia, Ecuador, Peru, Bolivia, and Chile joined later as associates. The alliance represents more than 267 million consumers—67 percent of South America's population, making it the third-largest trading block behind NAFTA and the EU. Like NAFTA, MERCOSUR promotes "the free circulation of goods, services and production factors among the countries" and established a common external tariff and commercial policy.
- The *Organization of Petroleum Exporting Countries* was founded in 1960 in response to reductions in the prices that oil companies were willing to pay for crude oil. The organization was conceived as a collective bargaining unit to provide oil-producing nations with some control over oil prices.
- The *Organization for Economic Cooperation and Development* (OECD) is a group of 30 industrialized market-economy countries of North America, Europe, the Far East, and the South Pacific. OECD, headquartered in Paris, was established in 1961 to promote economic development and international trade.

✳ Concept Check

☐ Define and describe the major objectives of the World Trade Organization (WTO) and the international economic communities.

☐ What is the North American Free Trade Agreement (NAFTA)? What is its importance for the United States, Canada, and Mexico?

LEARNING OBJECTIVE

5 Define the methods by which a firm can organize for and enter into international markets.

METHODS OF ENTERING INTERNATIONAL BUSINESS

A firm that has decided to enter international markets can do so in several ways. We will discuss several different methods. These different approaches require varying degrees of involvement in international business. Typically, a firm begins its international operations at the simplest level. Then, depending on its goals, it may progress to higher levels of involvement.

Licensing

licensing a contractual agreement in which one firm permits another to produce and market its product and use its brand name in return for a royalty or other compensation

Licensing is a contractual agreement in which one firm permits another to produce and market its product and use its brand name in return for a royalty or other compensation. For example, Yoplait yogurt is a French yogurt licensed for production in the United States. The Yoplait brand maintains an appealing French image, and in return, the U.S. producer pays the French firm a percentage of its income from sales of the product.

LEGO Builds on Licensing for Global Growth

Over the past 15 years, Luke Skywalker, Batman, and Spider-Man have all helped fuel the global growth of Denmark's LEGO Group. Founded in 1932 to market wooden toys, LEGO patented its now iconic interlocking plastic bricks in 1958. The brick system became an instant sensation.

Decades later, with high-tech toys such as robots and video games crowding store shelves, LEGO executives began looking for a way to connect the timeless appeal of their bricks to pop-culture trends worldwide. The answer: licensing. The first license they arranged was with Lucasfilm, covering popular characters such as Luke Skywalker and R2-D2, as well as spaceships and weapons in LEGO form, based on the blockbuster Star Wars films. These licensed products became so popular in so many countries that LEGO pursued additional licenses.

Today the company offers all kinds of licensed products featuring fictional favorites, such as Harry Potter, Indiana Jones, Batman, Spider-Man, and SpongeBob SquarePants. LEGO's license with Walt Disney allows it to market

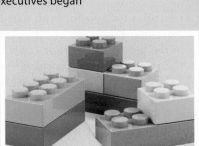

plastic blocks and figures based on Toy Story, Cars, and Prince of Persia. Even as many competitors struggled during the recent economic turmoil, LEGO has prospered because more than half of its global sales come from products linked to such brand licenses.

Sources: Lauren McKay, "Where Does Innovation Come From?" *CRM Magazine*, January 2010, 24ff; "Toymaker Grows by Listening to Customers," *Advertising Age*, November 9, 2009, 15; "LEGO: Always Listening," *Advertising Age*, October 19, 2009, 4; "Disney, LEGO Strike Licensing Deal," *Triangle Business Journal*, February 16, 2009, http://triangle .bizjournals.com; LEGO Web site and company profile, www.lego.com.

© tavi/Shutterstock.com

Personal App If you spot Buzz Lightyear or Tinkerbell on pillowcases or pajamas, you're seeing licensing in action. Did you know that Walt Disney licenses its characters for use on many different products around the world?

Licensing is especially advantageous for small manufacturers wanting to launch a well-known domestic brand internationally. For example, all Spalding sporting products are licensed worldwide. The licensor, the Questor Corporation, owns the Spalding name but produces no goods itself. Licensing thus provides a simple method for expanding into a foreign market with virtually no investment. On the other hand, if the licensee does not maintain the licensor's product standards, the product's image may be damaged. Another possible disadvantage is that a licensing arrangement may not provide the original producer with any foreign marketing experience.

Exporting

A firm also may manufacture its products in its home country and export them for sale in foreign markets. As with licensing, exporting can be a relatively low-risk method of entering foreign markets. Unlike licensing, however, it is not a simple method; it opens up several levels of involvement to the exporting firm.

At the most basic level, the exporting firm may sell its products outright to an *export–import merchant*, which is essentially a merchant wholesaler. The merchant assumes all the risks of product ownership, distribution, and sale. It may even purchase the goods in the producer's home country and assume responsibility for exporting the goods. An important and practical issue for domestic firms dealing with foreign customers is securing payment. This is a two-sided issue that

© Caitlin Mirra/Shutterstock

reflects the mutual concern rightly felt by both parties to the trade deal: The exporter would like to be paid before shipping the merchandise, whereas the importer obviously would prefer to know that it has received the shipment before releasing any funds. Neither side wants to take the risk of fulfilling its part of the deal only to discover later that the other side has not. The result would lead to legal costs and complex, lengthy dealings that would waste everyone's resources. This mutual level of mistrust, in fact, makes good business sense and has been around since the beginning of trade centuries ago. The solution then was the same as it still is today—for both parties to use a mutually trusted go-between who can ensure that the payment is held until the merchandise is in fact delivered according to the terms of the trade contract. The go-between representatives employed by the importer and exporter are still, as they were in the past, the local domestic banks involved in international business.

Here is a simplified version of how it works. After signing contracts detailing the merchandise sold and terms for its delivery, an importer will ask its local bank to issue a **letter of credit** for the amount of money needed to pay for the merchandise. The letter of credit is issued "in favor of the exporter," meaning that the funds are tied specifically to the trade contract involved. The importer's bank forwards the letter of credit to the exporter's bank, which also normally deals in international transactions. The exporter's bank then notifies the exporter that a letter of credit has been received in its name, and the exporter can go ahead with the shipment. The carrier transporting the merchandise provides the exporter with evidence of the shipment in a document called a **bill of lading**. The exporter signs over title to the merchandise (now in transit) to its bank by delivering signed copies of the bill of lading and the letter of credit.

In exchange, the exporter issues a **draft** from the bank, which orders the importer's bank to pay for the merchandise. The draft, bill of lading, and letter of credit are sent from the exporter's bank to the importer's bank. Acceptance by the importer's bank leads to return of the draft and its sale by the exporter to its bank, meaning that the exporter receives cash and the bank assumes the risk of collecting the funds from the foreign bank. The importer is obliged to pay its bank on delivery of the merchandise, and the deal is complete.

In most cases, the letter of credit is part of a lending arrangement between the importer and its bank. Of course, both banks earn fees for issuing letters of credit and drafts and for handling the import–export services for their clients. Furthermore, the process incorporates the fact that both importer and exporter will have different local currencies and might even negotiate their trade in a third currency. The banks look after all the necessary exchanges. For example, the vast majority of international business is negotiated in U.S. dollars, even though the trade may be between countries other than the United States. Thus, although the importer may end up paying for the merchandise in its local currency and the exporter may receive payment in another local currency, the banks involved will exchange all necessary foreign funds in order to allow the deal to take place.

Alternatively, the exporting firm may ship its products to an *export–import agent*, which arranges the sale of the products to foreign intermediaries for a commission or fee. The agent is an independent firm—like other agents—that sells and may perform other marketing functions for the exporter. The exporter, however, retains title to the products during shipment and until they are sold.

An exporting firm also may establish its own *sales offices*, or *branches*, in foreign countries. These installations are international extensions of the firm's distribution system. They represent a deeper involvement in international business than the other exporting techniques we have discussed—and thus they carry a greater risk. The exporting firm maintains control over sales, and it gains both experience in and

letter of credit issued by a bank on request of an importer stating that the bank will pay an amount of money to a stated beneficiary

bill of lading document issued by a transport carrier to an exporter to prove that merchandise has been shipped

draft issued by the exporter's bank, ordering the importer's bank to pay for the merchandise, thus guaranteeing payment once accepted by the importer's bank

knowledge of foreign markets. Eventually, the firm also may develop its own sales force to operate in conjunction with foreign sales offices.

Joint Ventures

A *joint venture* is a partnership formed to achieve a specific goal or to operate for a specific period of time. A joint venture with an established firm in a foreign country provides immediate market knowledge and access, reduced risk, and control over product attributes. However, joint-venture agreements established across national borders can become extremely complex. As a result, joint-venture agreements generally require a very high level of commitment from all the parties involved.

A joint venture may be used to produce and market an existing product in a foreign nation or to develop an entirely new product. Recently, for example, Archer Daniels Midland Company (ADM), one of the world's leading food processors, entered into a joint venture with Gruma SA, Mexico's largest corn flour and tortilla company. Besides a 22 percent stake in Gruma, ADM also received stakes in other joint ventures operated by Gruma. One of them will combine both companies' U.S. corn flour operations, which account for about 25 percent of the U.S. market. ADM also has a 40 percent stake in a Mexican wheat flour mill. ADM's joint venture increased its participation in the growing Mexican economy, where ADM already produces corn syrup, fructose, starch, and wheat flour.

Totally Owned Facilities

At a still deeper level of involvement in international business, a firm may develop *totally owned facilities*, that is, its own production and marketing facilities in one or more foreign nations. This *direct investment* provides complete control over operations, but it carries a greater risk than the joint venture. The firm is really establishing a subsidiary in a foreign country. Most firms do so only after they have acquired some knowledge of the host country's markets.

Direct investment may take either of two forms. In the first, the firm builds or purchases manufacturing and other facilities in the foreign country. It uses these facilities to produce its own established products and to market them in that country and perhaps in neighboring countries. Firms such as General Motors, Union Carbide, and Colgate-Palmolive are multinational companies with worldwide manufacturing facilities. Colgate-Palmolive factories are becoming *Eurofactories*, supplying neighboring countries as well as their own local markets.

A second form of direct investment in international business is the purchase of an existing firm in a foreign country under an arrangement that allows it to operate independently of the parent company. When Sony Corporation (a Japanese firm) decided to enter the motion picture business in the United States, it chose to purchase Columbia Pictures Entertainment, Inc., rather than start a new motion picture studio from scratch.

strategic alliance a partnership formed to create competitive advantage on a worldwide basis

Strategic alliance for mutual benefits. Chairman and Managing Director of Air India, V. Thulasidas, and Chairman of Lufthansa AG, Wolfgang Mayrhuber, sign a strategic alliance agreement in Mumbai, India. The alliance improves their market leadership position on India-Europe-U.S.A. routes.

© Reuters/Landov

Strategic Alliances

A **strategic alliance**, the newest form of international business structure, is a partnership formed to create competitive advantage on a worldwide basis. Strategic alliances are very similar to joint ventures. The number of strategic alliances is growing at an estimated rate of about 20 percent per year. In fact, in the automobile and computer industries, strategic alliances are becoming the predominant means of competing. International competition is so fierce and the costs of competing on a global basis are so high that few firms have all the resources needed to do it alone. Thus, individual firms that lack the internal resources essential for international success may seek to collaborate with other companies.

An example of such an alliance is the New United Motor Manufacturing, Inc. (NUMMI), formed by Toyota and General Motors to make automobiles of both firms. This enterprise united the quality engineering of Japanese cars with the marketing expertise and market access of General Motors.[10]

Trading Companies

A **trading company** provides a link between buyers and sellers in different countries. A trading company, as its name implies, is not involved in manufacturing or owning assets related to manufacturing. It buys products in one country at the lowest price consistent with quality and sells to buyers in another country. An important function of trading companies is taking title to products and performing all the activities necessary to move the products from the domestic country to a foreign country. For example, large grain-trading companies operating out of home offices both in the United States and overseas control a major portion of the world's trade in basic food commodities. These trading companies sell homogeneous agricultural commodities that can be stored and moved rapidly in response to market conditions.

Countertrade

In the early 1990s, many developing nations had major restrictions on converting domestic currency into foreign currency. Therefore, exporters had to resort to barter agreements with importers. **Countertrade** is essentially an international barter transaction in which goods and services are exchanged for different goods and services. Examples include Saudi Arabia's purchase of ten 747 jets from Boeing with payment in crude oil and Philip Morris' sale of cigarettes to Russia in return for chemicals used to make fertilizers.

Multinational Firms

A **multinational enterprise** is a firm that operates on a worldwide scale without ties to any specific nation or region. The multinational firm represents the highest level of involvement in international business. It is equally "at home" in most countries of the world. In fact, as far as the operations of the multinational enterprise are concerned, national boundaries exist only on maps. It is, however, organized under the laws of its home country.

(**Personal App**) Multinational enterprises bring the best of the world to you. Because they operate in so many countries, they can make smart buys and sell here, there, and everywhere. Keep your eyes open for products from multinational firms.

Table 3-3 shows the ten largest foreign and U.S. public multinational companies; the ranking is based on a composite score reflecting each company's best three out of four rankings for sales, profits, assets, and market value. Table 3-4 describes steps in entering international markets.

According to the chairman of the board of Dow Chemical Company, a multinational firm of U.S. origin, "The emergence of a world economy and of the multinational corporation has been accomplished hand in hand." He sees multinational enterprises moving toward what he calls the "anational company," a firm that has no nationality but belongs to all countries. In recognition of this movement, there already have been international conferences devoted to the question of how such enterprises would be controlled.

trading company provides a link between buyers and sellers in different countries

countertrade an international barter transaction

multinational enterprise a firm that operates on a worldwide scale without ties to any specific nation or region

*

☐ Two methods of engaging in international business may be categorized as either direct or indirect. How would you classify each of the methods described in this chapter? Why?

☐ What is a letter of credit? A bill of lading? A draft?

☐ In what ways is a multinational enterprise different from a large corporation that does business in several countries?

☐ What are the steps in entering international markets?

TABLE 3-3: The Ten Largest Foreign and U.S. Multinational Corporations

2010 Rank	Company	Business	Country	Revenue ($ millions)
1	Walmart Stores	General Merchandiser	United States	408,214
2	Royal Dutch/Shell Group	Energy	Netherlands/United Kingdom	285,129
3	ExxonMobil	Energy	United States	284,650
4	BP	Energy	United Kingdom	246,138
5	Toyota Motor	Automobiles	Japan	204,106
6	Japan Post Holdings	Financial Services	Japan	202,196
7	Sinopec	Energy	China	187,518
8	State Grid	Power Grids	China	184,496
9	AXA	Insurance	France	175,257
10	China National Petroleum	Energy	China	165,496

Source: http://money.cnn.com/magazines/fortune/global500/2010/snapshots/10939.html (accessed March 14, 2011).

TABLE 3-4: Steps in Entering International Markets

Step	Activity	Marketing Tasks
1	Identify exportable products.	Identify key selling features. Identify needs that they satisfy. Identify the selling constraints that are imposed.
2	Identify key foreign markets for the products.	Determine who the customers are. Pinpoint what and when they will buy. Do market research. Establish priority, or "target," countries.
3	Analyze how to sell in each priority market (methods will be affected by product characteristics and unique features of country/market).	Locate available government and private-sector resources. Determine service and backup sales requirements.
4	Set export prices and payment terms, methods, and techniques.	Establish methods of export pricing. Establish sales terms, quotations, invoices, and conditions of sale. Determine methods of international payments, secured and unsecured.
5	Estimate resource requirements and returns.	Estimate financial requirements. Estimate human resources requirements (full- or part-time export department or operation?). Estimate plant production capacity. Determine necessary product adaptations.
6	Establish overseas distribution network.	Determine distribution agreement and other key marketing decisions (price, repair policies, returns, territory, performance, and termination). Know your customer (use U.S. Department of Commerce international marketing services).
7	Determine shipping, traffic, and documentation procedures and requirements.	Determine methods of shipment (air or ocean freight, truck, rail). Finalize containerization. Obtain validated export license. Follow export-administration documentation procedures.
8	Promote, sell, and be paid.	Use international media, communications, advertising, trade shows, and exhibitions. Determine the need for overseas travel (when, where, and how often?). Initiate customer follow-up procedures.
9	Continuously analyze current marketing, economic, and political situations.	Recognize changing factors influencing marketing strategies. Constantly re-evaluate.

Source: U.S. Department of Commerce, International Trade Administration, Washington, DC.

SOURCES OF EXPORT ASSISTANCE

LEARNING OBJECTIVE

6 Describe the various sources of export assistance.

In September 1993, President Bill Clinton announced the *National Export Strategy* (NES) to revitalize U.S. exports. Under the NES, the *Trade Promotion Coordinating Committee* (TPCC) assists U.S. firms in developing export-promotion programs. The export services and programs of the 19 TPCC agencies can help American firms to compete in foreign markets and create new jobs in the United States. Table 3-5 provides an overview of selected export assistance programs.

These and other sources of export information enhance the business opportunities of U.S. firms seeking to enter expanding foreign markets. Another vital energy factor is financing.

TABLE 3-5: U.S. Government Export Assistance Programs

1	U.S. Export Assistance Centers, www.sba.gov/oit/export/useac.html	Provides assistance in export marketing and trade finance
2	International Trade Administration, www.ita.doc.gov/	Offers assistance and information to exporters through its domestic and overseas commercial officers
3	U.S. and Foreign Commercial Services, www.export.gov/	Helps U.S. firms compete more effectively in the global marketplace and provides information on foreign markets
4	Advocacy Center, www.ita.doc.gov/advocacy	Facilitates advocacy to assist U.S. firms competing for major projects and procurements worldwide
5	Trade Information Center, www.ita.doc.gov/td/tic/	Provides U.S. companies information on federal programs and activities that support U.S. exports
6	STAT-USA/Internet, www.stat-usa.gov/	Offers a comprehensive collection of business, economic, and trade information on the Web
7	Small Business Administration, www.sba.gov/oit/	Publishes many helpful guides to assist small- and medium-sized companies
8	National Trade Data Bank, www.stat-usa.gov/tradtest.nsf	Provides international economic and export-promotion information supplied by more than 20 U.S. agencies

© Cengage Learning 2013

* Concept Check

☐ How does the Trade Promotion Coordinating Committee (TPCC) assist the U.S. firms?

☐ List some key sources of export assistance. How can these sources be useful to small business firms?

LEARNING OBJECTIVE

7 Identify the institutions that help firms and nations finance international business.

FINANCING INTERNATIONAL BUSINESS

International trade compounds the concerns of financial managers. Currency exchange rates, tariffs and foreign exchange controls, and the tax structures of host nations all affect international operations and the flow of cash. In addition, financial managers must be concerned both with the financing of their international operations and with the means available to their customers to finance purchases.

Fortunately, along with business in general, a number of large banks have become international in scope. Many have established branches in major cities around the world. Thus, like firms in other industries, they are able to provide their services where and when they are needed. In addition, financial assistance is available from U.S. government and international sources.

Several of today's international financial organizations were founded many years ago to facilitate free trade and the exchange of currencies among nations. Some, such as the Inter-American Development Bank, are supported internationally and focus on developing countries. Others, such as the Export-Import Bank, are operated by one country but provide international financing.

The Export-Import Bank of the United States

The **Export-Import Bank of the United States**, created in 1934, is an independent agency of the U.S. government whose function is to assist in financing the exports of American firms. *Ex-Im Bank*, as it is commonly called, extends and guarantees credit to overseas buyers of American goods and services and guarantees short-term financing for exports. It also cooperates with commercial banks in helping American exporters to offer credit to their overseas customers.

According to Fred P. Hochberg, chairman and president of Ex-Im Bank, "Working with private lenders we are helping U.S. exporters put Americans to work producing the high quality goods and services that foreign buyers prefer. As part of President Obama's National Export Initiative, Ex-Im Bank's export financing is contributing to the goal of doubling of U.S. exports within the next five years."

Multilateral Development Banks

A **multilateral development bank (MDB)** is an internationally supported bank that provides loans to developing countries to help them grow. The most familiar is the World Bank, which operates worldwide. Established in 1944 and headquartered in Washington, DC, the bank provides low-interest loans, interest-free credits, and grants to developing countries. In 2010, the World Bank and its affiliates, the International Bank for Reconstruction and Development (IBRD) and the International Development Association (IDA), provided $72.9 billion to developing countries. The loans and grants helped these countries to:

- supply safe drinking water
- build schools and train teachers
- increase agricultural productivity
- expand citizens' access to markets, jobs, and housing
- improve health care and access to water and sanitation
- manage forests and other natural resources
- build and maintain roads, railways, and ports
- reduce air pollution and protect the environment[11]

Four other MDBs operate primarily in Central and South America, Asia, Africa, and Eastern and Central Europe. All five are supported by the industrialized nations, including the United States.

The *Inter-American Development Bank* (IDB), the oldest and largest regional bank, was created in 1959 by 19 Latin American countries and the United States. The bank, which is headquartered in Washington, DC, makes loans and provides technical advice and assistance to countries. Today, the IDB is owned by 48 member states.

With 67 member nations, the *Asian Development Bank* (ADB), created in 1966 and headquartered in the Philippines, promotes economic and social progress in Asian and Pacific regions. The U.S. government is the second-largest contributor to the ADB's capital, after Japan.

The *African Development Bank* (AFDB), also known as *Banque Africaines de Development,* was established in 1964 with headquarters in Abidjan, Ivory Coast.

Selling Eco-Friendly Goods, Services, and Technologies

SUSTAIN THE PLANET

Since 1994, the Export-Import Bank's Environmental Export Financing Program has been promoting sustainability by helping U.S. businesses obtain the funding they need to sell their eco-friendly goods, services, and technologies to overseas buyers around the world. Take a look: www .exim.gov/products/policies/environment/index .cfm.

Export-Import Bank of the United States an independent agency of the U.S. government whose function is to assist in financing the exports of American firms

multilateral development bank (MDB) an internationally supported bank that provides loans to developing countries to help them grow

Its members include 53 African and 24 non-African countries from the Americas, Europe, and Asia. The AFDB's goal is to foster the economic and social development of its African members. The bank pursues this goal through loans, research, technical assistance, and the development of trade programs.

Established in 1991 to encourage reconstruction and development in the Eastern and Central European countries, the London-based *European Bank for Reconstruction and Development* is owned by 61 countries and 2 intergovernmental institutions (the European Union and the European Investment Bank). Its loans are geared toward developing market-oriented economies and promoting private enterprise.

The International Monetary Fund

The **International Monetary Fund (IMF)** is an international bank with 187 member nations that makes short-term loans to developing countries experiencing balance-of-payment deficits. This financing is contributed by member nations, and it must be repaid with interest. Loans are provided primarily to fund international trade. Created in 1945 and headquartered in Washington, DC, the bank's main goals are to:

- promote international monetary cooperation,
- facilitate the expansion and balanced growth of international trade,
- promote exchange rate stability,
- assist in establishing a multilateral system of payments, and
- make resources available to members experiencing balance-of-payment difficulties.

✱ Concept Check

☐ What is the Export-Import Bank of the United States? How does it assist U.S. exporters?

☐ What is a multilateral development bank (MDB)? Who supports these banks?

☐ What is the International Monetary Fund? What types of loans does the IMF provide?

Get Flashcards, Quizzes, Games, Crosswords and more @ www.cengagebrain.com

SUMMARY

1 Explain the economic basis for international business.

International business encompasses all business activities that involve exchanges across national boundaries. International trade is based on specialization, whereby each country produces the goods and services that it can produce more efficiently than any other goods and services. A nation is said to have a comparative advantage relative to these goods. International trade develops when each nation trades its surplus products for those in short supply.

A nation's balance of trade is the difference between the value of its exports and the value of its imports. Its balance of payments is the difference between the flow of money into and out of the nation. Generally, a negative balance of trade is considered unfavorable.

2 Discuss the restrictions nations place on international trade, the objectives of these restrictions, and their results.

Despite the benefits of world trade, nations tend to use tariffs and nontariff barriers (import quotas, embargoes, and other restrictions) to limit trade. These restrictions typically are justified as being needed to protect a nation's economy, industries, citizens, or security. They can result in the loss of jobs, higher prices, fewer choices in the marketplace, and the misallocation of resources.

3 Outline the extent of international business and the world economic outlook for trade.

World trade is generally increasing. Trade between the United States and other nations is increasing in dollar value but decreasing in terms of our share of the world market. Exports as a percentage of U.S. GDP have increased steadily since 1985, except in the 2001 and 2008 recessions.

4 Discuss international trade agreements and international economic organizations working to foster trade.

The General Agreement on Tariffs and Trade (GATT) was formed to dismantle trade barriers and provide an environment in which international business can grow. Today, the World Trade Organization (WTO) and various economic communities carry on this mission. These world economic communities include the European Union, the NAFTA, the CAFTA, the Association of Southeast Asian Nations, the Pacific Rim, the Commonwealth of Independent States, the Caribbean Basin Initiative, the Common Market of the Southern Cone, the Organization of Petroleum Exporting Countries, and the Organization for Economic Cooperation and Development.

5 Define the methods by which a firm can organize for and enter into international markets.

A firm can enter international markets in several ways. It may license a foreign firm to produce and market its products. It may export its products and sell them through foreign intermediaries or its own sales organization abroad, or it may sell its exports outright to an export–import merchant. It may enter into a joint venture with a foreign firm. It may establish its own foreign subsidiaries, or it may develop into a multinational enterprise.

Generally, each of these methods represents an increasingly deeper level of involvement in international business, with licensing being the simplest and the development of a multinational corporation the most involved.

6 Describe the various sources of export assistance.

Many government and international agencies provide export assistance to U.S. and foreign firms. The export services and programs of the 19 agencies of the U.S. Trade Promotion Coordinating Committee (TPCC) can help U.S. firms to compete in foreign markets and create new jobs in the United States. Sources of export assistance include U.S. Export Assistance Centers, the International Trade Administration, U.S. and Foreign Commercial Services, Export Legal Assistance Network, Advocacy Center, National Trade Data Bank, and other government and international agencies.

7 Identify the institutions that help firms and nations finance international business.

The financing of international trade is more complex than that of domestic trade. Institutions such as the Ex-Im Bank and the International Monetary Fund have been established to provide financing and ultimately to increase world trade for American and international firms.

KEY TERMS

You should now be able to define and give an example relevant to each of the following terms:

international business (69)
absolute advantage (69)
comparative advantage (70)
exporting (70)
importing (70)
balance of trade (70)
trade deficit (70)
balance of payments (71)
import duty (tariff) (72)
dumping (73)

nontariff barrier (73)
import quota (73)
embargo (73)
foreign-exchange control (73)
currency devaluation (73)
General Agreement on Tariffs and Trade (GATT) (79)

World Trade Organization (WTO) (81)
economic community (81)
licensing (84)
letter of credit (86)
bill of lading (86)
draft (86)
strategic alliance (87)
trading company (88)
countertrade (88)

multinational enterprise (88)
Export-Import Bank of the United States (91)
multilateral development bank (MDB) (91)
International Monetary Fund (IMF) (92)

DISCUSSION QUESTIONS

1. The United States restricts imports but, at the same time, supports the WTO and international banks whose objective is to enhance world trade. As a member of Congress, how would you justify this contradiction to your constituents?
2. What effects might the devaluation of a nation's currency have on its business firms, its consumers, and the debts it owes to other nations?

3. Should imports to the United States be curtailed by, say, 20 percent to eliminate our trade deficit? What might happen if this were done?
4. When should a firm consider expanding from strictly domestic trade to international trade? When should it consider becoming further involved in international trade? What factors might affect the firm's decisions in each case?
5. How can a firm obtain the expertise needed to produce and market its products in, for example, the EU?

TEST YOURSELF

Matching Questions

1. _____ The total value of a nation's exports minus the total value of its imports over some period of time.

2. _____ The ability to produce a specific product more efficiently than any other nation.

3. _____ Selling and shipping raw materials or products to other nations.

4. _____ The ability to produce a specific product more efficiently than any other product.

5. _____ All business activities that involve exchanges across national boundaries.

6. _____ The total flow of money into a country minus the total flow of money out of that country over the same period of time.

7. _____ A tax levied on a particular foreign product entering a country.

8. _____ A complete halt to trading with a particular nation or in a particular product.

9. _____ An international barter transaction.

10. _____ An internationally supported bank that provides loans to developing countries to help them grow.

    a. countertrade
    b. foreign exchange control
    c. multilateral development bank (MDB)
    d. absolute advantage
    e. import duty
    f. embargo
    g. importing
    h. international business
    i. balance of trade
    j. comparative advantage
    k. Export-Import Bank of the United States
    l. balance of payments

True False Questions

11. **T F** The United States has enjoyed a trade surplus during the last two decades.

12. **T F** Tariff is a tax levied on a particular foreign product entering a country.

13. **T F** Quotas may be set on worldwide imports or on imports from a specific country.

14. **T F** The participants in the Kennedy Round have succeeded in reducing tariffs by less than 20 percent.

15. **T F** Licensing and exporting can be considered relatively low-risk methods of entering foreign markets.

16. **T F** A letter of credit is issued in favor of the importer.

17. **T F** A letter of credit is issued by the transport carrier to the exporter to prove that merchandise has been shipped.

18. **T F** Strategic alliances are partnerships formed to create competitive advantage on a worldwide basis.

19. **T F** A firm that has no ties to a specific nation or region and operates on a worldwide scale is called a national enterprise.

20. **T F** The International Monetary Fund (IMF) makes short-term loans to developing countries experiencing balance-of-payment deficits.

Multiple-Choice Questions

21. _____ By definition, every country has a(n) _____ advantage in some product.
    a. relative
    b. absolute
    c. comparative
    d. superior
    e. inferior

22. _____ Purchasing products or materials in other nations and bringing them into one's own country is
    a. trading.
    b. balancing.
    c. exporting.
    d. importing.
    e. dumping.

23. _____ General Motors and Ford products produced in the United States are found around the world. The United States is _____ these automobiles.
    a. tariffing
    b. importing
    c. exporting
    d. releasing
    e. dumping

24. _____ is the exportation of large quantities of a product at a price lower than that of the same product in the home market.
    a. Embargo
    b. Duty
    c. Dumping
    d. Export quota
    e. Dropping

25. _____ A complete halt to trading with a particular nation or in a particular product is called a(n)
   a. embargo.
   b. stoppage.
   c. stay.
   d. closure.
   e. barricade.

26. _____ Because it has not been around long enough to establish itself, the Russian automobile industry could be classified as a(n)
   a. hopeless industry.
   b. soft industry.
   c. infant industry.
   d. protected industry.
   e. toddler industry.

27. _____ The World Trade Organization was created by the
   a. Kennedy Round.
   b. United Nations.
   c. League of Nations.
   d. Tokyo Round.
   e. Uruguay Round.

28. _____ CAFTA, NAFTA, OECD, and OPEC are all examples of
   a. political organizations.
   b. peace treaties.
   c. international economic communities.
   d. World Trade Organization members.
   e. democratic organizations.

29. _____ Foreign licensing is similar to
   a. starting from scratch.
   b. franchising.
   c. wholesaling.
   d. establishing a subsidiary in another country.
   e. establishing a sales office in a foreign country.

30. _____ The World Bank is an example of a(n) _____, owned by 185 nations, including the United States.
   a. Eximbank
   b. IMF
   c. MDB
   d. EFTA
   e. LAFTA

Answers to the Test Yourself questions appear at the end of the book on page TY-1.

VIDEO CASE
Evo: Creatively Exceeding Customer Expectations Here and Abroad

Evo is proof that a company does not have to be large or operate worldwide in order to run a successful global business. Based in Seattle, Evo is an online and brick-and-mortar retailer of skiing, wakeboarding, skateboarding, and snowboarding equipment and clothing that recently reached $10 million in annual sales. It employs about 70 people and has been growing more than 70 percent a year since moving beyond founder Bryce Phillips' apartment eight years ago.

Evo now maintains a 40,000-square-foot distribution center and a busy Seattle store, along with a highly successful retail Web site, EvoGear.com. It is through the Web site that Evo started the global side of its operations, serving customers as far away as Bahrain, Turkey, Bali, Europe, and Australia and New Zealand. Because taxes, duties, exchange rates, and shipping requirements are so complex, for now customers in countries other than the United States and Canada must call the company's customer-service line to personally place their orders and arrange shipping and payment individually. Although for the present these customers account for a very small percentage of Evo's annual orders (5 percent including Canada), the company's managers hope that the growth of e-commerce will eventually ease order-handling and payment procedures enough to let this side of the business grow.

Another factor that might continue to limit Evo's international growth in the meantime is the business practices of Evo's suppliers. Most of these equipment manufacturers want to protect their own brands, so they restrict the amount of their products that any one retailer can sell to avoid saturating markets and to keep competition fair. Thus, Evo sometimes has to turn down requests for particular products, though the company hopes that this problem too will some day be overcome. For now the firm is able to keep its customer-service lines open for less than 24 hours a day and still remain accessible to most of its international callers.

The firm does not have plans to open any overseas operations because its shipping partners are already located everywhere that Evo needs assistance abroad. Most of the company's overseas suppliers have offices or representatives in the United States, so Evo team members usually travel only within the country for trade shows and the like. One exception is founder Bryce Phillips himself.

Evo has recently begun offering extreme skiing, snowboarding, and surfing expeditions to its customers through a new operation called EvoTrip. By outsourcing the logistics of these trips to a separate international travel company called JustFares.com, Evo is able to focus on choosing destinations like Japan, Indonesia, Switzerland, and South

America, many of which Phillips has visited and enjoyed, and arranging for professional athletes to accompany each group. Each of these trips, Phillips feels, is an opportunity for Evo's "ambassadors" to seamlessly spread the word about the company to potential new customers in every country they visit.

Despite management's conviction that its domestic business probably brings a better return on investment for now than its global operations, Evo can still proudly call itself a multinational firm.[12]

Questions

1. Do you think Evo's decision not to set up any physical operations overseas is a good one? Why or why not?
2. What political and economic challenges could EvoTrip encounter in other countries?
3. Would you recommend that Evo expand the international side of its business? If so, how, and if not, why not?

BUILDING SKILLS FOR CAREER SUCCESS

1. Exploring the Internet

A popular question debated among firms actively involved on the Internet is whether there exists a truly global Internet-based customer, irrespective of any individual culture, linguistic, or nationality issues. Does this Internet-based universal customer see the Internet and products sold there in pretty much the same way? If so, then one model might fit all customers. For example, although Yahoo.com translates its Web pages so that they are understood around the world, the pages look pretty much the same regardless of which international site you use. Is this good strategy, or should the sites reflect local customers differently? Visit the text Web site for updates to this exercise.

Assignment

1. Examine a Web site such as Yahoo! (www.yahoo.com) and its various international versions that operate in other languages around the world. Compare their similarities and differences as best you can, even if you do not understand the individual languages.
2. After making your comparison, do you now agree that there are indeed universal Internet products and customers? Explain your decision.

2. Building Team Skills

The North American Free Trade Agreement among the United States, Mexico, and Canada went into effect on January 1, 1994. It has made a difference in trade among the countries and has affected the lives of many people.

Assignment

1. Working in teams and using the resources of your library, investigate NAFTA. Answer the following questions:
    a. What are NAFTA's objectives?
    b. What are its benefits?
    c. What impact has NAFTA had on trade, jobs, and travel?
    d. Some Americans were opposed to the implementation of NAFTA. What were their objections? Have any of these objections been justified?
    e. Has NAFTA influenced your life? How?
2. Summarize your answers in a written report. Your team also should be prepared to give a class presentation.

3. Researching Different Careers

Today, firms around the world need employees with special skills. In some countries, such employees are not always available, and firms then must search abroad for qualified applicants. One way they can do this is through global workforce databases. As business and trade operations continue to grow globally, you may one day find yourself working in a foreign country, perhaps for an American company doing business there or for a foreign company. In what foreign country would you like to work? What problems might you face?

Assignment

1. Choose a country in which you might like to work.
2. Research the country. The National Trade Data Bank is a good place to start. Find answers to the following questions:
    a. What language is spoken in this country? Are you proficient in it? What would you need to do if you are not proficient?
    b. What are the economic, social, and legal systems like in this nation?
    c. What is its history?
    d. What are its culture and social traditions like? How might they affect your work or your living arrangements?
3. Describe what you have found out about this country in a written report. Include an assessment of whether you would want to work there and the problems you might face if you did.

Running a Business: Part 1

Let's Go Get a Graeter's!

Only a tiny fraction of family-owned businesses are still viable four generations after their founding, but happily for lovers of premium-quality ice cream, Graeter's is one of them.

Graeter's, now a $20 million firm, was founded in Cincinnati in 1870 by a young couple named Charlie and Regina Graeter, who made ice cream and chocolate candies in the back room of their shop, sold them in the front room, and lived upstairs. Refrigeration was unknown at the time, and ice cream was a novelty. Regina carried on the business for more than 30 years after her husband's death, at a time when women didn't run companies, opening not only a factory but also 20 additional stores. Her sons followed her into the firm, and three of her great-grandsons now share the responsibility for continuing to bring the company's original dense and creamy ice cream recipe to an ever-growing customer base.

The company currently operates a few dozen stores in Cincinnati and several neighboring cities, and its products are also available in hundreds of supermarkets thanks to distribution through big supermarket chains like Kroger's. Graeter's is currently building an additional factory to support its continued expansion, and it even operates a retail Web site where customers can order ice cream shipped anywhere in the continental United States, via UPS, guaranteed frozen on arrival.

Simple Secrets of Success

Several factors make Graeter's unique and account for its long success. Perhaps the most important is product quality. Throughout its history, Graeter's has focused on using a unique manufacturing process that produces its signature ice cream flavors in small batches of about two gallons every 20 minutes. "Our competition is making thousands and thousands of gallons a day," says Chip Graeter, the company's vice president of retail stores. "We are making hundreds of gallons a day at the most. All of our ice cream is packed by hand, so it's a very laborious process." Graeter's "French pot" manufacturing method ensures that very little air gets into the product, producing the same creamy texture all ice cream used to have but few other brands can still achieve. The product is so dense that each pint of Graeter's weighs nearly a pound.

Another success factor is the use of simple, fresh ingredients. Fresh eggs, high-grade chocolate, pure cane sugar, and the choicest raspberries, strawberries, and other fruits in season are among the basic ingredients, and the company gets its milk and cream only from local farmers who guarantee their cows are not fed artificial growth hormones. (These hormones are believed to have environmental effects and health effects on humans.) "We use a really great grade of chocolate," says Bob Graeter, vice president of manufacturing. "We don't cut corners on that. . . . Specially selected great black raspberries, strawberries, blueberries, cherries, go into our ice cream because we feel that we want to provide flavor not from artificial or unnatural ingredients but from really quality ripe rich fruits."

Welcoming Change

Finally, while many things about Graeter's—like its recipes—have stayed simple, its recent expansion and future growth plans have resulted from something quite new to the firm: outside advice. The current generation of owners hired management consultants to help them achieve the kind of productivity increases that allowed for greatly increased capacity so that when Kroger's, for instance, suggested expanding Graeter's to a chain of supermarkets Kroger owns in Denver, the company could quickly ramp up production to fill the increased orders.

In recent years, change has come quickly to this small firm, which prospered for three prior generations by staying essentially the same. But, says Bob Graeter, success does require balancing consistency—what he calls "preserving the core"—with innovation. "If you just preserve the core," he says, "ultimately you stagnate. And if you are constantly stimulating progress and looking for new ideas, well, then you risk losing what was important. . . . Part of your secret to long-term success is knowing what your core is and holding to that. Once you know what you're really all about and what is most important to you, you can change everything else." One of those "important" things is giving back to the community and its families via local charities and other initiatives. Graeter's recently celebrated a new store opening by making a cash donation to the local public library, for instance, and has given a research foundation for pediatric brain cancer the proceeds from sales of a limited-time flavor created by the winner of a special drawing created for the purpose.

© Liudmila Chernova/iStockphoto

© DNY59 / iStockphoto 16941138

Defining the Competitive Landscape

The company recognizes that while it produces a premium product in the ice cream category, its competition includes offerings other than ice cream. "We would be compared to Ben & Jerry's and Haagen Dazs," says Bob Graeter. "From a sales standpoint and from a shelf-space allocation, that is how [supermarkets] rank us, but . . . in my opinion that is really not our competition. Our competition is the upscale treats. It's like New York Cheesecake. That is our competition in my opinion. What is it that you are going to have when you want that indulgence, when you are willing to spend a thousand calories on dessert? It's going to be something that is fabulous. Graeter's in Cincinnati is synonymous with ice cream. People will say, 'Let's go get a Graeter's.' They don't say, 'Let's go get an ice cream.'"[13]

Questions

1. Think about the elements of Graeter's business that have stayed the same over its long history and those that have changed. Do you think the company's owners have chosen the right factors to change over time? Why or why not?

2. Which view of social responsibility does Graeter's management appear to take—the economic view or the socioeconomic view? What evidence in the case supports your answer?

3. Do you agree with Bob Graeter about what the company's real competition is? Why or why not?

Building a Business Plan: Part 1

A *business plan* is a carefully constructed guide for a person starting a business. The purpose of a well-prepared business plan is to show how practical and attainable the entrepreneur's goals are. It also serves as a concise document that potential investors can examine to see if they would like to invest or assist in financing a new venture. A business plan should include the following 12 components:

- Introduction
- Executive summary
- Benefits to the community
- Company and industry
- Management team
- Manufacturing and operations plan
- Labor force
- Marketing plan
- Financial plan
- Exit strategy
- Critical risks and assumptions
- Appendix

A brief description of each of these sections is provided in Chapter 5 (see also Table 5-4 on page 145).

This is the first of seven exercises that appear at the ends of each of the seven major parts in this textbook. The goal of these exercises is to help you work through the preceding components to create your own business plan. For example, in the exercise for this part, you will make decisions and complete the research that will help you to develop the introduction for your business plan and the benefits to the community that your business will provide. In the exercises for Parts 2 through 7, you will add more components to your plan and eventually build a plan that actually could be used to start a business. The flowchart shown in Figure 3-6 gives an overview of the steps you will be taking to prepare your business plan.

The First Step: Choosing Your Business

One of the first steps for starting your own business is to decide what type of business you want to start. Take some time to think about this decision. Before proceeding, answer the following questions:

- Why did you choose this type of business?
- Why do you think this business will be successful?
- Would you enjoy owning and operating this type of business?

Warning: Do not rush this step. This step often requires much thought, but it is well worth the time and effort. As an added bonus, you are more likely to develop a quality business plan if you really want to open this type of business.

Now that you have decided on a specific type of business, it is time to begin the planning process. The goal for this part is to complete the introduction and benefits-to-the-community components of your business plan.

Before you begin, it is important to note that the business plan is not a document that is written and then set aside. It is a living document that an entrepreneur should refer to continuously in order to ensure that plans are being carried through appropriately. As the entrepreneur begins to execute the plan, he or she should monitor the business environment continuously and make changes to the plan to address any challenges or opportunities that were not foreseen originally.

Throughout this course, you will, of course, be building your knowledge about business. Therefore, it will be appropriate for you to continually revisit parts of the plan that you have already written in order to refine them based on your more comprehensive knowledge. You will find that writing your plan is not a simple matter of starting at the beginning and moving chronologically through to the end. Instead, you probably will find yourself jumping around the various components, making refinements as you go. In fact, the second component—the executive summary—should be written last, but because of its comprehensive nature and its importance to potential investors, it appears after the introduction in the final business plan. By the end of this course, you should be able to put the finishing touches on your plan, making sure that all the parts create a comprehensive and sound whole so that you can present it for evaluation.

The Introduction Component

1.1. Start with the cover page. Provide the business name, street address, telephone number, Web address (if any), name(s) of owner(s) of the business, and the date the plan is issued.

1.2. Next, provide background information on the company and include the general nature of the business: retailing, manufacturing, or service; what your product or service is; what is unique about it; and why you believe that your business will be successful.

1.3. Then include a summary statement of the business's financial needs, if any. You probably will need to revise your financial needs summary after you complete a detailed financial plan later in Part 6.

1.4. Finally, include a statement of confidentiality to keep important information away from potential competitors.

FIGURE 3-6: **Business Plan**

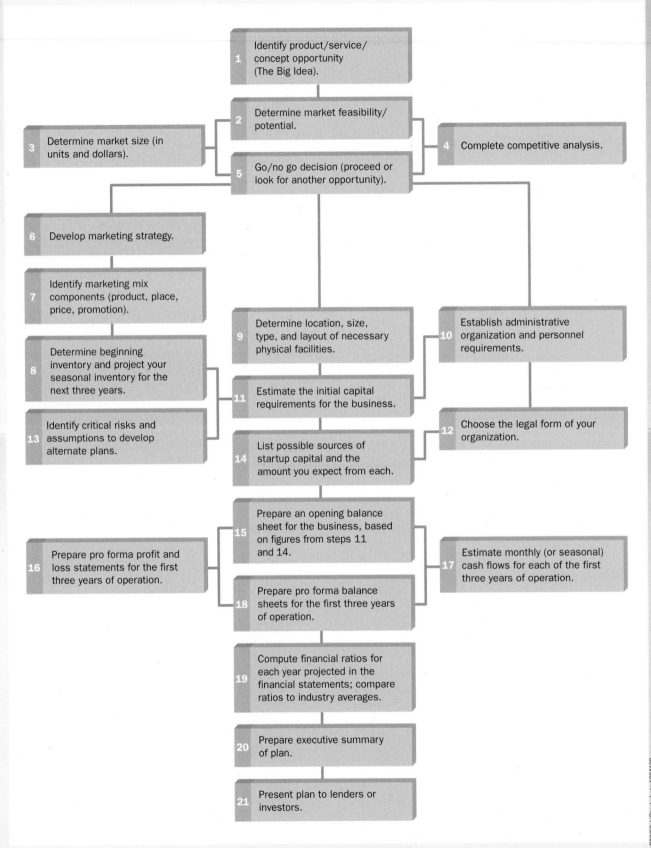

1 Identify product/service/concept opportunity (The Big Idea).

2 Determine market feasibility/potential.

3 Determine market size (in units and dollars).

4 Complete competitive analysis.

5 Go/no go decision (proceed or look for another opportunity).

6 Develop marketing strategy.

7 Identify marketing mix components (product, place, price, promotion).

8 Determine beginning inventory and project your seasonal inventory for the next three years.

9 Determine location, size, type, and layout of necessary physical facilities.

10 Establish administrative organization and personnel requirements.

11 Estimate the initial capital requirements for the business.

12 Choose the legal form of your organization.

13 Identify critical risks and assumptions to develop alternate plans.

14 List possible sources of startup capital and the amount you expect from each.

15 Prepare an opening balance sheet for the business, based on figures from steps 11 and 14.

16 Prepare pro forma profit and loss statements for the first three years of operation.

17 Estimate monthly (or seasonal) cash flows for each of the first three years of operation.

18 Prepare pro forma balance sheets for the first three years of operation.

19 Compute financial ratios for each year projected in the financial statements; compare ratios to industry averages.

20 Prepare executive summary of plan.

21 Present plan to lenders or investors.

Source: Hatten, Timothy, *Small Business Management,* Fifth Edition. Copyright © 2012 Cengage Learning.

© DNY59 / iStockphoto 1694138

© aleksandar velasevic / iStockphoto 14545705

The Benefits-to-the-Community Component

In this section, describe the potential benefits to the community that your business could provide. Chapter 2 in your textbook, "Being Ethical and Socially Responsible," can help you in answering some of these questions. At the very least, address the following issues:

1.5. Describe the number of skilled and nonskilled jobs the business will create, and indicate how purchases of supplies and other materials can help local businesses.

1.6. Next, describe how providing needed goods or services will improve the community and its standard of living.

1.7. Finally, state how your business can develop new technical, management, or leadership skills; offer attractive wages; and provide other types of individual growth.

Review of Business Plan Activities

Read over the information that you have gathered. Because the Building a Business Plan exercises at the end of Parts 2 through 7 are built on the work you do in Part 1, make sure that any weaknesses or problem areas are resolved before continuing. Finally, write a brief statement that summarizes all the information for this part of the business plan.

The information contained in "Building a Business Plan" will also assist you in completing the online *Interactive Business Plan*.

PART TWO
BUSINESS OWNERSHIP AND ENTREPRENEURSHIP

SUCCESS

© Tetra Images / Alamy / BJGX1B

In Part 2 of *Business*, we look at a very practical aspect of business: How businesses are owned. Issues related to ownership are particularly interesting in today's world, where large global businesses coexist with small businesses. In addition, because the majority of businesses are small, we look at specific issues related to small business.

Chapter 4 Choosing a Form of Business Ownership
Chapter 5 Small Business, Entrepreneurship, and Franchises

CHAPTER 4 CHOOSING A FORM OF BUSINESS OWNERSHIP

© mangostock/Shutterstock

Why should you care?

There's a good chance that during your lifetime you will work for a business or start a business. With this fact in mind, the material in this chapter can help you to understand how and why businesses are organized.

Learning Objectives

What you will be able to do once you complete this chapter:

1 Describe the advantages and disadvantages of sole proprietorships.

2 Explain the different types of partners and the importance of partnership agreements.

3 Describe the advantages and disadvantages of partnerships.

4 Summarize how a corporation is formed.

5 Describe the advantages and disadvantages of a corporation.

6 Examine special types of corporations, including S-corporations, limited-liability companies, and not-for-profit corporations.

7 Discuss the purpose of a joint venture and syndicate.

8 Explain how growth from within and growth through mergers can enable a business to expand.

Raising Cane's Serves Up Small Business Success

Todd Graves got the idea for a chicken-finger restaurant while in college. Although his professor didn't think much of the business concept, Graves kept the idea in mind as he found work and saved his money. A year later, he returned home to Baton Rouge, Louisiana, and refined his business plan with the help of counselors at the local non-profit SCORE counseling office. Going over the details with SCORE volunteers gave Graves invaluable insights, boosted his confidence, and helped him make the leap from plan to startup to success.

"The counselors were able to give me a reality check on the business world that I didn't have experience with," Graves remembers. "Running a business is very hard. SCORE challenged me to be ready and know what to expect."

Graves organized his restaurant as a limited liability company (LLC), a form of business ownership that caps the owner's financial liability in case the firm fails. With his own capital plus money from investors and a Small Business Administration-backed loan, the entrepreneur refurbished a building opposite the entrance to Louisiana State University. In 1996, when he opened that first Raising Cane's restaurant, so many customers crowded in that Graves didn't close the doors until 3:30 A.M.

That was only the beginning. In addition to opening more Raising Cane's restaurants, Graves decided to offer licenses to franchisees. Today, there are more than 100 Raising Cane's chicken-finger restaurants in 15 states, stretching outward from the Louisiana headquarters as far north as Minnesota and as far east as Massachusetts.

Raising Cane's actively supports the communities in which it operates. The parent company and its franchisees donate more than $1 million annually to community-based causes and colleges. Many managers and employees volunteer with local groups, as well. In recognition of the company's commitment to community involvement, it recently received the SCORE Award for Outstanding Socially-Progressive Business.

What advice does Todd Graves have for would-be entrepreneurs? "Know what you want and have the willingness and determination to see it through. There will always be obstacles and people who will tell you that it can't work. But for every road block, there is a clear path."[1]

Did you Know?

Todd Graves named his fast-growing chicken-finger restaurant chain after Raising Cane, his people-loving yellow Labrador retriever.

According to Todd Graves, "I got the worst grade on my business plan for a college class. The professor said a chicken finger restaurant would never work. The banks said the same."[2] Despite some pretty discouraging advice, Graves went on to build a successful restaurant chain. For would-be entrepreneurs and business owners, his advice in the last paragraph of the Inside Business opening case for this chapter is worth remembering: "Know what you want and have the willingness and determination to see it through."[3] In effect, Todd Graves is telling you that you can do the same thing he did. You can be successful if you decide to start a business.

Deciding to start a business is only the first step. It takes hard work, and there are many decisions that you must make to build a successful business. For example, a new (or an old) business must meet the needs of its customers. You also must have financing and a business plan that helps you convert your dream to a reality. And you must choose the right type of business ownership.

We begin this chapter by describing the three common forms of business ownership: sole proprietorships, partnerships, and corporations. We discuss how these types of businesses are formed and note the advantages and disadvantages of each.

Next, we consider several types of business ownership usually chosen for special purposes, including S-corporations, limited-liability companies, not-for-profit corporations, joint ventures, and syndicates. We conclude the chapter with a discussion of how businesses can grow through internal expansion or through mergers with other companies.

SOLE PROPRIETORSHIPS

A **sole proprietorship** is a business that is owned (and usually operated) by one person. Although a few sole proprietorships are large and have many employees, most are small. Sole proprietorship is the simplest form of business ownership and the easiest to start. In most instances, the owner (the *sole* proprietor) simply decides that he or she is in business and begins operations. Some of today's largest corporations, including Walmart, JCPenney, H.J. Heinz Company, and Procter & Gamble Company, started out as tiny—and in many cases, struggling—sole proprietorships.

As you can see in Figure 4-1, there are approximately 23 million nonfarm sole proprietorships in the United States. They account for 72 percent of the country's business firms. Although the most popular form of ownership when compared with partnerships and corporations, they rank last in total sales revenues. As shown in Figure 4-2, sole proprietorships account for just over $1 trillion, or about 4 percent of total annual sales.

Sole proprietorships are most common in retailing, service, and agriculture. Thus, the clothing boutique, television-repair shop down the street, and small, independent farmers are likely to be sole proprietorships.

Advantages of Sole Proprietorships

Most of the advantages of sole proprietorships arise from the two main characteristics of this form of ownership: simplicity and individual control.

LEARNING OBJECTIVE

1 Describe the advantages and disadvantages of sole proprietorships.

FIGURE 4-1: **Relative Percentages of Nonfarm Sole Proprietorships, Partnerships, and Corporations in the United States**

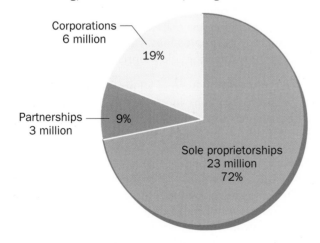

Sole proprietorships, the most common form of business ownership, are most common in retailing, the service industries, and agriculture.

Corporations
6 million
19%

Partnerships — 9%
3 million

Sole proprietorships
23 million
72%

Source: U.S. Bureau of the Census, *Statistical Abstract of the United States* (Washington, DC: Bureau of the Census, 2011), table 743 (www.census.gov).

sole proprietorship a business that is owned (and usually operated) by one person

FIGURE 4-2: Total Sales Receipts of American Businesses

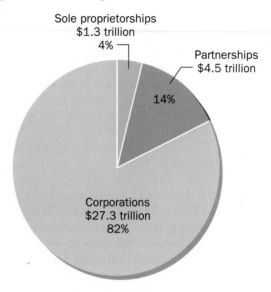

Although corporations account for only about 19 percent of U.S. businesses, they bring in 83 percent of sales receipts.

Sole proprietorships
$1.3 trillion
4%

Partnerships
$4.5 trillion
14%

Corporations
$27.3 trillion
82%

Source: U.S. Bureau of the Census, *Statistical Abstract of the United States* (Washington, DC: Bureau of the Census, 2011), table 743 (www.census.gov).

EASE OF START-UP AND CLOSURE Sole proprietorship is the simplest and cheapest way to start a business. Often, start-up requires no contracts, agreements, or other legal documents. Thus, a sole proprietorship can be, and most often is, established without the services of an attorney. The legal requirements often are limited to registering the name of the business and obtaining any necessary licenses or permits.

If the enterprise does not succeed, the firm can be closed as easily as it was opened. Creditors must be paid, of course, but generally, the owner does not have to go through any legal procedure before hanging up an "Out of Business" sign.

PRIDE OF OWNERSHIP A successful sole proprietor is often very proud of her or his accomplishments—and rightfully so. In almost every case, the owner deserves a great deal of credit for assuming the risks and solving the day-to-day problems associated with operating sole proprietorships. Unfortunately, the reverse is also true. When the business fails, it is often the sole proprietor who is to blame.

RETENTION OF ALL PROFITS Because all profits become the personal earnings of the owner, the owner has a strong incentive to succeed. This direct financial reward attracts many entrepreneurs to the sole proprietorship form of business and, if the business succeeds, is a source of great satisfaction.

NO SPECIAL TAXES Profits earned by a sole proprietorship are taxed as the personal income of the owner. As a result, sole proprietors must report certain financial information on their personal income tax returns and make estimated quarterly tax payments to the federal government. Thus, a sole proprietorship does not pay the special state and federal income taxes that corporations pay.

FLEXIBILITY OF BEING YOUR OWN BOSS A sole proprietor is completely free to make decisions about the firm's operations. Without asking or waiting for anyone's approval, a sole proprietor can switch from retailing to wholesaling, move a shop's location, open a new store, or close an old one. Suppose that the sole proprietor of an appliance store finds that many customers now prefer to shop on Sunday afternoons. He or she can make an immediate change in business hours to take advantage of this information (provided that state laws allow such stores to open on Sunday). The manager of a store in a large corporate chain such as Best Buy Company may have to seek the approval of numerous managers and company officials before making such a change.

Personal App Do you dream of being your own boss? If you become a sole proprietor, you'll have all the flexibility that comes with making your own decisions. But remember: Although you'll have the final say, you'll also be responsible if something goes wrong.

Disadvantages of Sole Proprietorships

The disadvantages of a sole proprietorship stem from the fact that these businesses are owned and often managed by one person. Some capable sole proprietors experience no problems. Individuals who start out with few management skills and little money are most at risk for failure.

A builder with a dream. As a homebuilder, Shelley Reynolds, owner and president of Reynolds Signature Homes, has faced new challenges since the downturn in home sales that began four years ago. In most areas of the United States, there are fewer homeowners that can qualify for home mortgages, which makes it hard for business owners like Reynolds to construct upscale homes and sell them for a profit.

© Michael Ainsworth/Dallas Morning News/MCT/Newscom

UNLIMITED LIABILITY Unlimited liability is a legal concept that holds a business owner personally responsible for all the debts of the business. There is legally no difference between the debts of the business and the debts of the proprietor. If the business fails, or if the business is involved in a lawsuit and loses, the owner's personal property—including savings and other assets—can be seized (and sold if necessary) to pay creditors.

Unlimited liability is perhaps the major factor that tends to discourage would-be entrepreneurs with substantial personal wealth from using the sole proprietor form of business organization.

LACK OF CONTINUITY Legally, the sole proprietor *is* the business. If the owner retires, dies, or is declared legally incompetent, the business essentially ceases to exist. In many cases, however—especially when the business is a profitable enterprise—the owner's heirs take it over and either sell it or continue to operate it. The business also can suffer if the sole proprietor becomes ill and cannot work for an extended period of time. If the owner, for example, has a heart attack, there is often no one who can step in and manage the business. An illness can be devastating if the sole proprietor's personal skills are what determine if the business is a success or a failure.

LACK OF MONEY Banks, suppliers, and other lenders usually are unwilling to lend large sums of money to sole proprietorships. Only one person—the sole proprietor—can be held responsible for repaying such loans, and the assets of most sole proprietors usually are limited. Moreover, these assets may have been used already as the basis for personal borrowing (a home mortgage or car loan) or for short-term credit from suppliers. Lenders also worry about the lack of continuity of sole proprietorships: Who will repay a loan if the sole proprietor dies? Finally, many lenders are concerned about the large number of sole proprietorships that fail—a topic discussed in Chapter 5.

The limited ability to borrow money can prevent a sole proprietorship from growing. It is the main reason that many business owners, when in need of relatively large amounts of capital, change from a sole proprietorship to a partnership or corporate form of ownership.

unlimited liability a legal concept that holds a business owner personally responsible for all the debts of the business

entrepreneurial SUCCESS

© Jon Schulte/iStockphoto 6184858

Student Business Incubators

Whether you're starting a new venture or expanding an existing company, you may be able to get expert help, office space, and even some funding without leaving your campus, if your school has a student business incubator. A growing number of colleges and universities are setting up incubators to help student entrepreneurs choose an appropriate form of business ownership and proceed to develop, test, implement, and refine their business ideas in a supportive environment.

The incubator at the University of Northern Iowa, for instance, invites student entrepreneurs to apply for a semester of on-campus assistance, including legal and accounting services, management training, and access to seed funds. Carlos Arguello was the first student entrepreneur to "graduate" from this incubator, working with his mother to successfully launch the Spanish-language newspaper *La Prensa* in northern Iowa.

At the University of Wisconsin-Madison, student entrepreneurs compete for six spaces in the on-campus incubator by submitting a written application and making a presentation to the Student Business Incubator Board. At the University of Michigan, the TechArb incubator houses up to 12 student-owned high-tech businesses at a time. One recent tenant was Mobil33t, which designed the iPhone app DoGood to encourage people to do a good deed every day. Can an incubator set you on the path toward entrepreneurial success?

Sources: Melissa Domsic, "East Lansing's The Hatch Gets Its First Student Tenant," *Lansing State Journal*, December 29, 2010, www.lansingstatejournal.com; Nathan Bomey, "University of Michigan Strikes Deal to Establish Permanent Student Business Incubator," *AnnArbor.com*, November 5, 2009, www.annarbor.com/business-review/university-of-michigan-strikes-deal-to-establish-permanent-student-business-incubator/; University of Wisconsin-Madison Student Business Incubator, www.asm.wisc.edu/sbi.html; University of Northern Iowa Student Business Incubator, www.bcs.uni.edu/jpec/sbi.htm.

LIMITED MANAGEMENT SKILLS The sole proprietor is often the sole manager—in addition to being the only salesperson, buyer, accountant, and, on occasion, janitor. Even the most experienced business owner is unlikely to have expertise in all these areas. Unless he or she obtains the necessary expertise by hiring employees, assistants, or consultants, the business can suffer in the areas in which the owner is less knowledgeable. For the many sole proprietors who cannot hire the help they need, there just are not enough hours in the day to do everything that needs to be done.

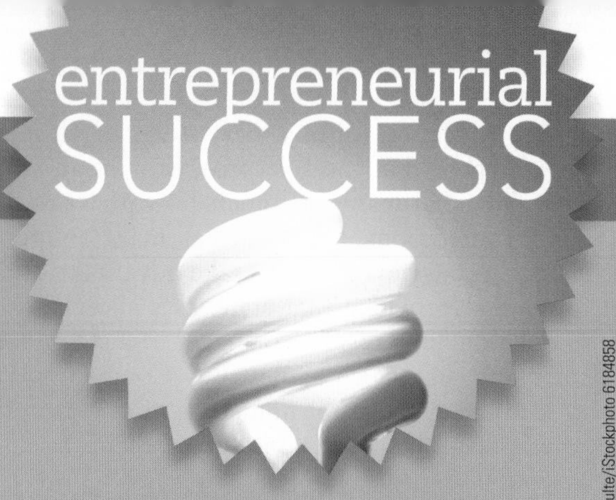

DIFFICULTY IN HIRING EMPLOYEES The sole proprietor may find it hard to attract and keep competent help. Potential employees may feel that there is no room for advancement in a firm whose owner assumes all managerial responsibilities. And when those who *are* hired are ready to take on added responsibility, they may find that the only way to do so is to quit the sole proprietorship and go to work for a larger firm or start up their own businesses. The lure of higher salaries and increased benefits (especially health insurance) also may cause existing employees to change jobs.

*** Concept Check**

- ☐ What is a sole proprietorship?
- ☐ What are the advantages of a sole proprietorship?
- ☐ What are the disadvantages of a sole proprietorship?

Beyond the Sole Proprietorship

Like many others, you may decide that the major disadvantage of a sole proprietorship is the limited amount that one person can do in a workday. One way to reduce the effect of this disadvantage (and retain many of the advantages) is to have more than one owner.

LEARNING OBJECTIVE

2 Explain the different types of partners and the importance of partnership agreements.

partnership a voluntary association of two or more persons to act as co-owners of a business for profit

PARTNERSHIPS

A person who would not think of starting and running a business alone may enthusiastically seize the opportunity to enter into a business partnership. The U.S. Uniform Partnership Act defines a **partnership** as a voluntary association of two or more persons to act as co-owners of a business for profit. For example, in 1990, two young African-American entrepreneurs named Janet Smith and Gary Smith started Ivy Planning Group—a company that provides strategic planning and performance measurement for clients. Today, more than 20 years later, the

company has evolved into a multimillion-dollar company that has hired a diverse staff of employees and provides cultural diversity training for *Fortune* 1,000 firms, large not-for-profit organizations, and government agencies. In recognition of its efforts, Ivy Planning Group has been honored by Diversity-Business.com as one of the top 50 minority-owned companies and by *Black Enterprise* and *Working Mother* magazines. And both Janet Smith and Gary Smith—Ivy Planning Group's founders—have been named "1 of 50 Most Influential Minorities in Business" by Minority Business and Professionals Network.[4]

As shown in Figures 4-1 and 4-2, there are approximately 3 million partnerships in the United States, and this type of ownership accounts for about $4.5 trillion in sales receipts each year. Note, however, that this form of ownership is much less common than the sole proprietorship or the corporation. In fact, as Figure 4-1 shows, partnerships represent only about 9 percent of all American businesses. Although there is no legal maximum on the number of partners a partnership may have, most have only two. Regardless of the number of people involved, a partnership often represents a pooling of special managerial skills and talents; at other times, it is the result of a sole proprietor's taking on a partner for the purpose of obtaining more capital.

Personal App In many cases, two heads really are better than one. If you've ever teamed up with a classmate on a school project, you know the benefits of sharing the work and learning from your partner's ideas. You also know that partners don't always see eye to eye.

Types of Partners

All partners are not necessarily equal. Some may be active in running the business, whereas others may have a limited role.

GENERAL PARTNERS A **general partner** is a person who assumes full or shared responsibility for operating a business. General partners are active in day-to-day business operations, and each partner can enter into contracts on behalf of the other partners. He or she also assumes unlimited liability for all partnership debts, including debts incurred by any other general partner without his or her knowledge or consent. A *general partnership* is a business co-owned by two or more general partners who are liable for everything the business does. To avoid future liability, a general partner who withdraws from the partnership must give notice to creditors, customers, and suppliers.

LIMITED PARTNERS A **limited partner** is a person who invests money in a business but who has no management responsibility or liability for losses beyond his or her investment in the partnership. A *limited partnership* is a business co-owned by one or more general partners who manage the business and limited partners who invest money in it. Limited partnerships may be formed to finance real estate, oil and gas, motion picture, and other business ventures. Typically, the general partner or partners collect management fees and receive a percentage of profits. Limited partners receive a portion of profits and tax benefits.

Because of potential liability problems, special rules apply to limited partnerships. These rules are intended to protect customers and creditors who deal with limited partnerships. For example, prospective partners in a limited partnership must file a formal declaration, usually with the secretary of state, that describes the

general partner a person who assumes full or shared responsibility for operating a business

limited partner a person who invests money in a business but has no management responsibility or liability for losses beyond the amount he or she invested in the partnership

essential details of the partnership and the liability status of each partner involved in the business. At least one general partner must be responsible for the debts of the limited partnership. Also, some states prohibit the use of the limited partner's name in the partnership's name.

The Partnership Agreement

Articles of partnership refers to an agreement listing and explaining the terms of the partnership. Although both oral and written partnership agreements are legal and can be enforced in the courts, a written agreement has an obvious advantage. It is not subject to lapses of memory.

Figure 4-3 shows a typical partnership agreement. The partnership agreement should state

FIGURE 4-3: Articles of Partnership

The articles of partnership is a written or oral agreement that lists and explains the terms of a partnership.

PARTNERSHIP AGREEMENT

Names of partners — This agreement, made June 20, 2011, between Penelope Wolfburg of 783A South Street, Hazelton, Idaho, and Ingrid Swenson of RR 5, Box 96, Hazelton, Idaho.

Nature, name, and address of business — 1. The above named persons have this day formed a partnership that shall operate under the name of W-S Jewelers, located at 85 Broad Street, Hazelton, Idaho 83335, and shall engage in jewelry sales and repairs.

Duration of partnership — 2. The duration of this agreement will be for a term of fifteen (15) years, beginning June 20, 2011, or for a shorter period if agreed upon in writing by both partners.

Contribution of capital — 3. The initial investment by each partner will be as follows: Penelope Wolfburg, assets and liabilities of Wolfburg's Jewelry Store, valued at a capital investment of $40,000; Ingrid Swenson, cash of $20,000. These investments are partnership property.

Duties of each partner — 4. Each partner will give her time, skill, and attention to the operation of this partnership and will engage in no other business enterprise unless permission is granted in writing by the other partner.

Salaries, withdrawals, and distribution of profits — 5. The salary for each partner will be as follows: Penelope Wolfburg, $40,000 per year; Ingrid Swenson, $30,000 per year. Neither partner may withdraw cash or other assets from the business without express permission in writing from the other partner. All profits and losses of the business will be shared as follows: Penelope Wolfburg, 60 percent; Ingrid Swenson, 40 percent.

Termination — 6. Upon the dissolution of the partnership due to termination of this agreement, or to written permission by each of the partners, or to the death or incapacitation of one or both partners, a new contract may be entered into by the partners or the sole continuing partner has the option to purchase the other partner's interest in the business at a price that shall not exceed the balance in the terminating partner's capital account. The payment shall be made in cash in equal quarterly installments from the date of termination.

7. At the conclusion of this contract, unless it is agreed by both partners to continue the operation of the business under a new contract, the assets of the partnership, after the liabilities are paid, will be divided in proportion to the balance in each partner's capital account on that date.

Signatures — *Penelope Wolfburg*   *Ingrid Swenson*

Penelope Wolfburg   Ingrid Swenson

Date — *June 20, 2011*   *June 20, 2011*

Date   Date

Source: Adapted from Goldman and Sigismond, *Business Law*, 8th ed. (Mason, OH: South-Western Cengage Learning, 2011). Copyright © 2011 by Cengage Learning Company. Reprinted with permission.

- Who will make the final decisions
- What each partner's duties will be
- The investment each partner will make
- How much profit or loss each partner receives or is responsible for
- What happens if a partner wants to dissolve the partnership or dies

Although the people involved in a partnership can draft their own agreement, most experts recommend consulting an attorney.

When entering into a partnership agreement, partners would be wise to let a neutral third party—a consultant, an accountant, a lawyer, or a mutual friend—assist with any disputes that might arise.

Concept Check ✱

☐ How does a sole proprietorship differ from a partnership?

☐ Explain the difference between a general partner and a limited partner?

☐ Describe the issues that should be included in a partnership agreement?

Advantages of Partnerships

Partnerships have many advantages. The most important are described below.

EASE OF START-UP Partnerships are relatively easy to form. As with a sole proprietorship, the legal requirements often are limited to registering the name of the business and obtaining any necessary licenses or permits. It may not even be necessary to prepare written articles of partnership, although doing so is generally a good idea.

AVAILABILITY OF CAPITAL AND CREDIT Because partners can pool their funds, a partnership usually has more capital available than a sole proprietorship does. This additional capital, coupled with the general partners' unlimited liability, can form the basis for a better credit rating. Banks and suppliers may be more willing to extend credit or approve larger loans to such a partnership than to a sole proprietor. This does not mean that partnerships can borrow all the money they need. Many partnerships have found it hard to get long-term financing simply because lenders worry about the possibility of management disagreements and lack of continuity.

PERSONAL INTEREST General partners are very concerned with the operation of the firm—perhaps even more so than sole proprietors. After all, they are responsible for the actions of all other general partners, as well as for their own. The pride of ownership from solving the day-to-day problems of operating a business—with the help of another person(s)—is a strong motivating force and often makes all the people involved in the partnership work harder to become more successful.

COMBINED BUSINESS SKILLS AND KNOWLEDGE Partners often have complementary skills. The weakness of one partner—in manufacturing, for example—may be offset by another partner's strength in that area. Moreover, the ability to discuss important decisions with another concerned individual often relieves some pressure and leads to more effective decision making.

RETENTION OF PROFITS As in a sole proprietorship, all profits belong to the owners of the partnership. The partners share directly in the financial rewards and therefore are highly motivated to do their best to make the firm succeed. As noted, the partnership agreement should state how much profit or loss each partner receives or is responsible for.

NO SPECIAL TAXES Although a partnership pays no income tax, the Internal Revenue Service requires partnerships to file an annual information return that states the names and addresses of all partners involved in the

LEARNING OBJECTIVE

3 Describe the advantages and disadvantages of partnerships.

Two entrepreneurs with one goal. The goal for Matt Flannery (right) and Premal Shah (left) when they co-founded Kiva.org was to create an organization that would connect people, through lending, for the sake of alleviating poverty. Have the two partners been successful? You bet—at the beginning of 2011, Kiva.org had facilitated over $230 million in loans. For more information about Kiva.org or to become a lender and get involved, go to www.kiva.org.

© Gary Reyes/San Jose Mercury News/MCT/Newscom

business. The return also must provide information about income and expenses and distributions made to each partner. Then each partner is required to report his or her share of profit (or loss) from the partnership business on his or her individual tax return and is taxed on his or her share of the profit—in the same way a sole proprietor is taxed.

Disadvantages of Partnerships

Although partnerships have many advantages when compared with sole proprietorships and corporations, they also have some disadvantages, which anyone thinking of forming a partnership should consider.

UNLIMITED LIABILITY As we have noted, each *general* partner has unlimited liability for all debts of the business. Each partner is legally and personally responsible for the debts, taxes, and actions of any other partner conducting partnership business, even if that partner did not incur those debts or do anything wrong. General partners thus run the risk of having to use their personal assets to pay creditors. *Limited* partners, however, risk only their original investment.

Today, many states allow partners to form a *limited-liability partnership* (LLP), in which a partner may have limited-liability protection from legal action resulting from the malpractice or negligence of the other partners. Most states that allow LLPs restrict this type of ownership to certain types of professionals such as accountants, architects, attorneys, and similar professionals. (Note the difference between a limited partnership and a limited-liability partnership. A limited partnership must have at least one general partner that has unlimited liability. On the other hand, all partners in a limited-liability partnership may have limited liability *for the malpractice or negligence of the other partners*.)

MANAGEMENT DISAGREEMENTS What happens to a partnership if one of the partners brings a spouse or a relative into the business? What happens if a partner wants to withdraw more money from the business? Notice that each of the preceding situations—and for that matter, most of the other problems that can develop in a partnership—involves one partner doing something that disturbs the other partner(s). This human factor is especially important because business partners—with egos, ambitions, and money on the line—are especially susceptible to friction. When partners begin to disagree about decisions, policies, or ethics, distrust may build and get worse as time passes—often to the point where it is impossible to operate the business successfully.

LACK OF CONTINUITY Partnerships are terminated if any one of the general partners dies, withdraws, or is declared legally incompetent. However, the remaining partners can purchase that partner's ownership share. For example, the partnership agreement may permit surviving partners to continue the business after buying a deceased partner's interest from his or her estate. However, if the partnership loses an owner whose specific management or technical skills cannot be replaced, it is not likely to survive.

FROZEN INVESTMENT It is easy to invest money in a partnership, but it is sometimes quite difficult to get it out. This is the case, for example, when remaining partners are unwilling to buy the share of the business that belongs to a partner who retires or wants to relocate to another city. To avoid such difficulties, the partnership agreement should include some procedure for buying out a partner.

In some cases, a partner must find someone outside the firm to buy his or her share. How easy or difficult it is to find an outsider depends on how successful the business is and how willing existing partners are to accept a new partner.

Beyond the Partnership

The main advantages of a partnership over a sole proprietorship are the added capital and management expertise of the partners. However, some of the basic disadvantages of the sole proprietorship also plague the general partnership. One disadvantage in particular—unlimited liability—can cause problems for a partner with substantial personal wealth. A third form of business ownership, the corporation, overcomes this disadvantage.

* ***Concept Check***

☐ What are the advantages of a partnership?

☐ What are the disadvantages of a partnership?

CORPORATIONS

Back in 1837, William Procter and James Gamble—two sole proprietors—formed a partnership called Procter & Gamble (P&G) and set out to compete with 14 other soap and candle makers in Cincinnati, Ohio. Then, in 1890, Procter & Gamble incorporated to raise additional capital for expansion that eventually allowed the company to become a global giant. Today, 4 billion times a day, Procter & Gamble brands touch the lives of people in 180 countries around the globe.[5] Like many large corporations, P&G's market capitalization is greater than the gross domestic product of many countries. Although this corporation is a corporate giant, the firm's executives and employees believe it also has a responsibility to be an ethical corporate citizen. For example, P&G's purpose statement (or mission) is

> We will provide branded products and services of superior quality and value that improve the lives of the world's consumers, now and for generations to come. As a result, consumers will reward us with leadership sales, profit and value creation, allowing our people, our shareholders and the communities in which we live and work to prosper.[6]

In today's competitive environment, it's common to hear of large companies that are profitable. It is less common to hear of profitable companies that are held in high regard because they are good corporate citizens.

While not all sole proprietorships and partnerships become corporations, there are reasons why business owners choose the corporate form of ownership. Let's begin with a definition of a corporation. Perhaps the best definition of a corporation was given by Chief Justice John Marshall in a famous Supreme Court decision in 1819. A corporation, he said, "is an artificial person, invisible, intangible, and existing only in contemplation of the law." In other words, a **corporation** (sometimes referred to as a *regular* or *C-corporation*) is an artificial person created by law, with most of the legal rights of a real person. These include:

- The right to start and operate a business
- The right to buy or sell property
- The right to borrow money
- The right to sue or be sued
- The right to enter into binding contracts

Would you believe a major corporation was started in this building? The building in this photo was once used by Bill Hewlett and Dave Packard as a research lab, development workshop, and manufacturing facility. Their efforts paid off, and today Hewlett-Packard Corporation is one of the world's leading technology companies. By the way, this building is now a historic landmark and is considered to be the birthplace of Silicon Valley.

© David Paul Morris/Getty Images

Unlike a real person, however, a corporation exists only on paper. There are approximately 6 million corporations in the United States. They comprise about 19 percent of all businesses, but they account for 82 percent of sales revenues (see Figures 4-1 and 4-2).

Corporate Ownership

The shares of ownership of a corporation are called **stock**. The people who own a corporation's stock—and thus own part of the corporation—are called **stockholders**. Once a corporation has been formed, it may sell its stock to individuals or other companies that want to invest in the corporation. It also may issue stock as a reward to key employees in return for certain services or as a return to investors in place of cash payments.

A **closed corporation** is a corporation whose stock is owned by relatively few people and is not sold to the general public. As an example, DeWitt and Lila Wallace owned virtually all the stock of Reader's Digest Association, making it one of the

corporation an artificial person created by law with most of the legal rights of a real person, including the rights to start and operate a business, to buy or sell property, to borrow money, to sue or be sued, and to enter into binding contracts

stock the shares of ownership of a corporation

stockholder a person who owns a corporation's stock

closed corporation a corporation whose stock is owned by relatively few people and is not sold to the general public

TABLE 4-1: **Ten Aspects of Business that May Require Legal Help**

1. Choosing either the sole proprietorship, partnership, corporate, or some special form of ownership	6. Filing for licenses or permits at the local, state, and federal levels
2. Constructing a partnership agreement	7. Purchasing an existing business or real estate
3. Incorporating a business	8. Creating valid contracts
4. Registering a corporation's stock	9. Hiring employees and independent contractors
5. Obtaining a trademark, patent, or copyright	10. Extending credit and collecting debts

© Cengage Learning 2013

largest corporations of this kind. A person who wishes to sell the stock of a closed corporation generally arranges to sell it privately to another stockholder or a close acquaintance.

Although founded in 1922 as a closed corporation, the Reader's Digest Association became an open corporation when it sold stock to investors for the first time in 1990. (*Note:* In 2007, Reader's Digest Association was purchased by a group of investors who returned the company to private ownership.[7])

An **open corporation** is one whose stock can be bought and sold by any individual. Examples of open corporations include General Electric, Microsoft, and Johnson & Johnson.

Forming a Corporation

Although you may think that incorporating a business guarantees success, it does not. There is no special magic about placing the word *Incorporated* or the abbreviation *Inc.* after the name of a business. Unfortunately, like sole proprietorships or partnerships, corporations can go broke. The decision to incorporate a business therefore should be made only after carefully considering whether the corporate form of ownership suits your needs better than the sole proprietorship or partnership forms.

If you decide that the corporate form is the best form of organization for you, most experts recommend that you begin the incorporation process by consulting a lawyer to be sure that all legal requirements are met. While it may be possible to incorporate a business without legal help, it is well to keep in mind the old saying, "A man who acts as his own attorney has a fool for a client." Table 4-1 lists some aspects of starting and running a business that may require legal help.

WHERE TO INCORPORATE A business is allowed to incorporate in any state that it chooses. Most small- and medium-sized businesses are incorporated in the state where they do the most business. The founders of larger corporations or of those that will do business nationwide often compare the benefits that various states provide to corporations. The decision on where to incorporate usually is based on two factors: (1) the cost of incorporating in one state compared with the cost in another state and (2) the advantages and disadvantages of each state's corporate laws and tax structure. Some states are more hospitable than others, and some offer fewer restrictions, lower taxes, and other benefits to attract new firms. Delaware and Nevada are often chosen by corporations that do business in more than one state because of their corporation-friendly laws.[8]

An incorporated business is called a **domestic corporation** in the state in which it is incorporated. In all other states where it does business, it is called a **foreign corporation**. Sears Holdings Corporation, the parent company of Sears and Kmart, is incorporated in Delaware, where it is a domestic corporation. In the remaining 49 states, Sears is a foreign corporation. Sears must register in all states where it does business and also pay taxes and annual fees to each state. A corporation chartered by a foreign government and conducting business in the United States is an **alien corporation**. Volkswagen AG, Sony Corporation, and the Royal Dutch/Shell Group are examples of alien corporations.

open corporation a corporation whose stock can be bought and sold by any individual

domestic corporation a corporation in the state in which it is incorporated

foreign corporation a corporation in any state in which it does business except the one in which it is incorporated

alien corporation a corporation chartered by a foreign government and conducting business in the United States

Part 2: Business Ownership and Entrepreneurship

THE CORPORATE CHARTER Once a home state has been chosen, the incorporator(s) submits *articles of incorporation* to the secretary of state. When the articles of incorporation are approved, they become a contract between a corporation and the state in which the state recognizes the formation of the artificial person that is the corporation. Usually, the articles of incorporation include the following information:

- The firm's name and address
- The incorporators' names and addresses
- The purpose of the corporation
- The maximum amount of stock and types of stock to be issued
- The rights and privileges of stockholders
- The length of time the corporation is to exist

To help you to decide if the corporate form of organization is the right choice, you may want to use a search engine like Yahoo! (www.yahoo.com). Once at the site, enter "types of business ownership" in the search box. In addition, before making a decision to organize your business as a corporation, you may want to consider two additional areas: stockholders' rights and the importance of the organizational meeting.

Question: How much can a sheet of paper be worth?
Answer: A sheet of paper can be worth thousands (or even millions) of dollars if it is a stock certificate like those in this picture. Often corporations issue common stock to obtain financing. When investors purchase stock, they have the right to receive dividends, to profit from an increase in the stock's value, and to vote on corporate matters.

© Tupungato/Shutterstock

STOCKHOLDERS' RIGHTS There are two basic types of stock. Owners of **common stock** may vote on corporate matters. Generally, an owner of common stock has one vote for each share owned. However, any claims of common stockholders on profits and assets of the corporation are subordinate to the claims of others. The owners of **preferred stock** usually have no voting rights, but their claims on dividends are paid before those of common-stock owners. Although large corporations may issue both common and preferred stock, generally small corporations issue only common stock.

Personal App Even if you own a single share of common stock, you're legally a part-owner of the corporation. You're entitled to vote on important matters such as electing the board of directors. Your vote is counted—and it counts!

Perhaps the most important right of owners of both common and preferred stock is to share in the profit earned by the corporation through the payment of dividends. A **dividend** is a distribution of earnings to the stockholders of a corporation. Other rights include receiving information about the corporation, voting on changes to the corporate charter, and attending the corporation's annual stockholders' meeting, where they may exercise their right to vote.

Because common stockholders usually live all over the nation, very few actually may attend a corporation's annual meeting. Instead, they vote by proxy. A **proxy** is a legal form listing issues to be decided at a stockholders' meeting and enabling stockholders to transfer their voting rights to some other individual or individuals. The stockholder can register a vote and transfer voting rights simply by signing and returning the form. Today, most corporations also allow stockholders to exercise their right to vote by proxy by accessing the Internet or using a toll-free phone number.

ORGANIZATIONAL MEETING As the last step in forming a corporation, the incorporators and original stockholders meet to adopt corporate by-laws and elect their first board of directors. (Later, directors will be elected or reelected at the corporation's annual meetings.) The board members are directly responsible to the stockholders for the way they operate the firm.

common stock stock owned by individuals or firms who may vote on corporate matters but whose claims on profits and assets are subordinate to the claims of others

preferred stock stock owned by individuals or firms who usually do not have voting rights but whose claims on dividends are paid before those of common-stock owners

dividend a distribution of earnings to the stockholders of a corporation

proxy a legal form listing issues to be decided at a stockholders' meeting and enabling stockholders to transfer their voting rights to some other individual or individuals

* *Concept Check*

☐ Explain the difference between an open corporation and a closed corporation.

☐ How is a domestic corporation different from a foreign corporation and an alien corporation?

☐ Outline the incorporation process, and describe the basic corporate structure.

☐ What rights do stockholders have?

LEARNING OBJECTIVE

5 Describe the advantages and disadvantages of a corporation.

board of directors the top governing body of a corporation, the members of which are elected by the stockholders

corporate officers the chairman of the board, president, executive vice presidents, corporate secretary, treasurer, and any other top executive appointed by the board of directors

limited liability a feature of corporate ownership that limits each owner's financial liability to the amount of money that he or she has paid for the corporation's stock

Corporate Structure

The organizational structure of most corporations is more complicated than that of a sole proprietorship or partnership. This is especially true as the corporation begins to grow and expand. In a corporation, both the board of directors and the corporate officers are involved in management.

BOARD OF DIRECTORS As an artificial person, a corporation can act only through its directors, who represent the corporation's stockholders. The **board of directors** is the top governing body of a corporation and is elected by the stockholders. In theory, then, the stockholders are able to control the activities of the entire corporation through its directors because they are the group that elects the board of directors (see Figure 4-4).

Board members can be chosen from within the corporation or from outside it. *Note:* For a small corporation, only one director is required in many states although you can choose to have more. Directors who are elected from within the corporation are usually its top managers—the president and executive vice presidents, for example. Those elected from outside the corporation generally are experienced managers or entrepreneurs with proven leadership ability and/or specific talents the organization seems to need. In smaller corporations, majority stockholders usually serve as board members.

The major responsibilities of the board of directors are to set company goals and develop general plans (or strategies) for meeting those goals. The board also is responsible for the firm's overall operation and appointing corporate officers.

CORPORATE OFFICERS **Corporate officers** are appointed by the board of directors. Although a small corporation may not have all of the following officers, the chairman of the board, president, executive vice presidents, corporate secretary, and treasurer are all corporate officers. They help the board to make plans, carry out strategies established by the board, hire employees, and manage day-to-day business activities. Periodically (usually each month), they report to the board of directors. And at the annual meeting, the directors report to the stockholders.

Advantages of Corporations

Back in October 2000, Manny Ruiz decided that it was time to start his own company. With the help of a team of media specialists, he founded Miami-based Hispanic PR Wire. In a business where hype is the name of the game, Hispanic PR Wire is the real thing and has established itself as the nation's premier news distribution service reaching U.S. Hispanic media and opinion leaders. Today, the business continues to build on its early success.[9] Mr. Ruiz chose to incorporate this business because it provided a number of advantages that other forms of business ownership did not offer. Typical advantages include limited liability, ease of raising capital, ease of transfer of ownership, perpetual life, and specialized management.

LIMITED LIABILITY One of the most attractive features of corporate ownership is **limited liability**. With few exceptions, each owner's financial liability is limited to the amount of money he or she has paid for the corporation's stock. This feature

FIGURE 4-4: **Hierarchy of Corporate Structure**

Stockholders exercise a great deal of influence through their right to elect the board of directors.

© Cengage Learning 2013

arises from the fact that the corporation is itself a legal person, separate from its owners. If a corporation fails or is involved in a lawsuit and loses, creditors have a claim only on the corporation's assets, not on the owners' (stockholders') personal assets. Because it overcomes the problem of unlimited liability connected with sole proprietorships and general partnerships, limited liability is one of the chief reasons why entrepreneurs often choose the corporate form of organization.

EASE OF RAISING CAPITAL The corporation is by far the most effective form of business ownership for raising capital. Like sole proprietorships and partnerships, corporations can borrow from lending institutions. However, they also can raise additional sums of money by selling stock. Individuals are more willing to invest in corporations than in other forms of business because of limited liability, and they can sell their stock easily—hopefully for a profit.

EASE OF TRANSFER OF OWNERSHIP Accessing a brokerage firm Web site or a telephone call to a stockbroker is all that is required to put most stock up for sale. Willing buyers are available for most stocks at the market price. Ownership is transferred when the sale is made, and practically no restrictions apply to the sale and purchase of stock issued by an open corporation. Remember: An open corporation is one whose stock can be bought and sold by any individual.

Business Profits

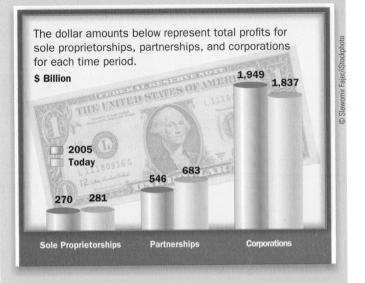

The dollar amounts below represent total profits for sole proprietorships, partnerships, and corporations for each time period.

$ Billion

☐ 2005
☐ Today

Sole Proprietorships: 270, 281
Partnerships: 546, 683
Corporations: 1,949, 1,837

Source: U.S. Bureau of the Census, *Statistical Abstract of the United States* (Washington, DC: Bureau of the Census, 2011), table 743 (www.census.gov).

PERPETUAL LIFE Since it is essentially a legal "person," a corporation exists independently of its owners and survives them. The withdrawal, death, or incompetence of a key executive or owner does not cause the corporation to be terminated. Sears, Roebuck and Co. incorporated in 1893 and is one of the nation's largest retailing corporations, even though its original co-founders, Richard Sears and Alvah Roebuck, have been dead for decades.

SPECIALIZED MANAGEMENT Typically, corporations are able to recruit more skilled, knowledgeable, and talented managers than proprietorships and partnerships. This is so because they pay bigger salaries, offer excellent employee benefits, and are large enough to offer considerable opportunity for advancement. Within the corporate structure, administration, human resources, finance, marketing, and operations are placed in the charge of experts in these fields.

Disadvantages of Corporations

Like its advantages, many of a corporation's disadvantages stem from its legal definition as an artificial person or legal entity. The most serious disadvantages are described in the following text. (See Table 4-2 for a comparison of some of the advantages and disadvantages of a sole proprietorship, general partnership, and corporation.)

TABLE 4-2: **Some Advantages and Disadvantages of a Sole Proprietorship, Partnership, and Corporation**

	Sole Proprietorship	General Partnership	Regular C-Corporation
Protecting against liability for debts	Difficult	Difficult	Easy
Raising money	Difficult	Difficult	Easy
Ownership transfer	Difficult	Difficult	Easy
Preserving continuity	Difficult	Difficult	Easy
Government regulations	Few	Few	Many
Formation	Easy	Easy	Difficult
Income taxation	Once	Once	Twice

© Cengage Learning 2013

DIFFICULTY AND EXPENSE OF FORMATION Forming a corporation can be a relatively complex and costly process. The use of an attorney is usually necessary to complete the legal forms that are submitted to the secretary of state. Application fees, attorney's fees, registration costs associated with selling stock, and other organizational costs can amount to thousands of dollars for even a medium-sized corporation. The costs of incorporating, in terms of both time and money, discourage many owners of smaller businesses from forming corporations.

GOVERNMENT REGULATION AND INCREASED PAPERWORK A corporation must meet various government standards before it can sell its stock to the public. Then it must file many reports on its business operations and finances with local, state, and federal governments. In addition, the corporation must make periodic reports to its stockholders about various aspects of the business. To prepare all the necessary reports, even small corporations often need the help of an attorney, certified public accountant, and other professionals on a regular basis. In addition, a corporation's activities are restricted by law to those spelled out in its charter.

CONFLICT WITHIN THE CORPORATION Because a large corporation may employ thousands of employees, some conflict is inevitable. For example, the pressure to increase sales revenue, reduce expenses, and increase profits often leads to increased stress and tension for both managers and employees. This is especially true when a corporation operates in a competitive industry, attempts to develop and market new products, or must downsize the workforce to reduce employee salary expense during an economic crisis.

DOUBLE TAXATION Corporations must pay a tax on their profits. In addition, stockholders must pay a personal income tax on profits received as dividends. Corporate profits thus are taxed twice—once as corporate income and a second time as the personal income of stockholders. *Note:* Both the S-corporation and the limited-liability company discussed in the next section eliminate the disadvantage of double taxation because they are taxed like a partnership. These special types of ownership still provide limited liability for the personal assets of the owners.

LACK OF SECRECY Because open corporations are required to submit detailed reports to government agencies and to stockholders, they cannot keep their operations confidential. Competitors can study these corporate reports and then use the information to compete more effectively. In effect, every public corporation has to share some of its secrets with its competitors.

✳ *Concept Check*

☐ What are the advantages of a corporation?

☐ What are the disadvantages of a corporation?

SPECIAL TYPES OF BUSINESS OWNERSHIP

In addition to the sole proprietorship, partnership, and the regular corporate form of organization, some entrepreneurs choose other forms of organization that meet their special needs. Additional organizational options include S-corporations, limited-liability companies, and not-for-profit corporations.

LEARNING OBJECTIVE

6 Examine special types of corporations, including S-corporations, limited-liability companies, and not-for-profit corporations.

S-Corporations

If a corporation meets certain requirements, its directors may apply to the Internal Revenue Service for status as an S-corporation. An **S-corporation** is a corporation that is taxed as though it were a partnership. In other words, the corporation's income is taxed only as the personal income of its stockholders. Corporate profits or losses "pass through" the business and are reported on the owners' personal income tax returns.

To qualify for the special status of an S-corporation, a firm must meet the following criteria:[10]

1. No more than 100 stockholders are allowed.
2. Stockholders must be individuals, estates, or certain trusts.
3. There can be only one class of outstanding stock.
4. The firm must be a domestic corporation eligible to file for S-corporation status.
5. There can be no partnerships, corporations, or nonresident-alien stockholders.
6. All stockholders must agree to the decision to form an S-corporation.

Becoming an S-corporation can be an effective way to avoid double taxation while retaining the corporation's legal benefit of limited liability.

Limited-Liability Companies

A new form of ownership called a *limited-liability company* has been approved in all 50 states—although each state's laws may differ. A **limited-liability company (LLC)** is a form of business ownership that combines the benefits of a corporation and a partnership while avoiding some of the restrictions and disadvantages of those forms of ownership. In an LLC, business owners are called members. Chief advantages of an LLC are as follows:

1. Like a sole proprietorship or partnership, an LLC enjoys pass-through taxation. This means that owners report their share of profits or losses in the company on their individual tax returns and avoid the double taxation imposed on most corporations. LLCs with at least two members are taxed like a partnership. LLCs with just one member are taxed like a sole proprietorship. In some cases, members can even elect to be taxed as a corporation or an S-corporation if there are benefits to offset the corporate double taxation.
2. Like a corporation, it provides limited-liability protection for acts and debts of the LLC. An LLC thus extends the concept of personal-asset protection to small business owners.
3. The LLC type of organization provides more management flexibility when compared with corporations. A corporation, for example, is required to hold annual meetings and record meeting minutes; an LLC is not.
4. Like a corporation, LLCs can live beyond the death of their owners. This feature avoids the problems of terminating a business when a partner or sole proprietor dies.

S-corporation a corporation that is taxed as though it were a partnership

limited-liability company (LLC) a form of business ownership that combines the benefits of a corporation and a partnership while avoiding some of the restrictions and disadvantages of those forms of ownership

Chrysler Group: a limited liability company. Sergio Marchionne, the current CEO of Chrysler Group LLC, helped steer the auto maker out of bankruptcy and back to profitability. When Chrysler emerged from bankruptcy, it chose the LLC form of business ownership because this type of business ownership provided limited liability for investors and avoided some of the restrictions and disadvantages of other forms of business ownership.

© Rebecca Cook/Reuters/Landov

Although many experts believe that the LLC is nothing more than a variation of the S-corporation, there is a difference. An LLC is not restricted to 100 stockholders—a common drawback of the S-corporation. LLCs are also less restricted and have more flexibility than S-corporations in terms of who can become an owner. Although the owners of an LLC may file the required articles of organization in any state, most choose to file in their home state—the state where they do most of their business. While forming an LLC is typically a very simple process, the *decision* whether to choose an LLC or another form of ownership is not. Most experts recommend that you consult an attorney before actually taking the steps required to form an LLC. For more information about the benefits of forming an LLC, go to www.llc.com.

Because of the increased popularity of the LLC form of organization, experts are predicting that LLCs may become one of the most popular forms of business ownership available. For help in understanding the differences between a regular corporation, S-corporation, and limited-liability company, see Table 4-3.

Not-for-Profit Corporations

A **not-for-profit corporation** (sometimes referred to as *non-profit*) is a corporation organized to provide a social, educational, religious, or other service rather than to earn a profit. Various charities, museums, private schools, colleges, and charitable organizations are organized in this way, primarily to ensure limited liability.

Personal App Have you ever gone trick-or-treating for UNICEF, bought Girl Scout cookies, or donated during a Red Cross blood drive? By supporting the not-for-profit corporations of your choice, you're helping them to help others.

While the process used to organize a not-for-profit corporation is similar to the process used to create a regular corporation, each state does have different laws. In fact, many of the requirements are different than the requirements for establishing a regular corporation. Once approved by state authorities, not-for-profit corporations must meet specific Internal Revenue Service guidelines in order to obtain tax-exempt status.

Today, there is a renewed interest in not-for-profits because these organizations are formed to improve communities and change lives. For example, Habitat for Humanity is a not-for-profit corporation and was formed to provide homes for qualified lower income people who cannot afford housing. Even though this corporation may receive more money than it spends, any surplus funds are "reinvested" in building activities to provide low-cost housing to qualified individuals. Other examples of not-for-profit corporations include the SeaWorld and Busch Gardens Conservation

not-for-profit corporation a corporation organized to provide a social, educational, religious, or other service rather than to earn a profit

* Concept Check

☐ Explain the difference between an S-corporation and a limited liability company.

☐ How does a regular (C) corporation differ from a not-for-profit corporation?

TABLE 4-3: **Some Advantages and Disadvantages of a Regular Corporation, S-Corporation, and Limited-Liability Company**

	Regular C-Corporation	S-Corporation	Limited-Liability Company
Double taxation	Yes	No	No
Limited liability and personal asset protection	Yes	Yes	Yes
Management and ownership flexibility	No	No	Yes
Restrictions on the number of owners/ stockholders	No	Yes	No
Internal Revenue Service tax regulations	Many	Many	Fewer

© Cengage Learning 2013

going
for
SUCCESS

© Neil Sullivan/iStockphoto 2412286

In search of higher revenue and profits, a growing number of U.S. companies are forming joint ventures with local partners in countries with fast-growing economies. Not only does this give the U.S. firms new opportunities to expand internationally, it allows them to benefit from their local partners' market knowledge and business strengths. With careful planning and execution, the result can be a big win for the partners and their customers.

General Electric, which owns many businesses that fortify the world's infrastructure, recently formed two joint ventures in Russia. With the Russian energy firm Inter RAO and the government-owned Rostekhnologii, GE will produce, market, and service gas turbines. This joint venture will take advantage of the country's drive to modernize and upgrade its energy grid during the coming decade. A second joint venture, with

© AFP/Getty Images

Russian Prime Minister Putin meets with GE Executives.

Rostekhnologii, will manufacture diagnostic devices such as CT scanners to meet the growing need for medical services.

General Motors has been active in international joint ventures for some time. Eyeing strong demand for cars in China, it recently increased its stake in a joint venture with SAIC and the Wuling Group to produce small cars and vans locally. In addition, GM has other joint ventures to make and market vehicles elsewhere in Asia.

Service businesses are embracing international joint ventures, as well. UPS, for instance, formed a joint venture in Vietnam with local partner P&T Express. The new company offers express delivery services to customers throughout the country. With the economy doing well and buying power on the rise, UPS expects Vietnam to deliver revenue growth in the coming years.

Sources: Ira Iosebashvili and Paul Glader, "GE Forms Joint Ventures with Two Russian Firms," *Wall Street Journal*, December 28, 2010, www.wsj.com; "UPS announces Joint Venture in Vietnam," *Associated Press*, May 14, 2010, http://vietnambusiness.asia/ups-announces-joint-venture-in-vietnam/; Norihiko Shirouzu, "GM to Strengthen China Stake," *Wall Street Journal*, November 12, 2010, www.wsj.com.

Fund, the Girl Scouts, the Bill and Melinda Gates Foundation, and many local not-for-profits designed to meet specific needs within a community.

JOINT VENTURES AND SYNDICATES

LEARNING OBJECTIVE

7 Discuss the purpose of a joint venture and syndicate.

Today, two additional types of business organizations—joint ventures and syndicates—are used for special purposes. Each of these forms of organization is unique when compared with more traditional forms of business ownership.

Joint Ventures

A **joint venture** is an agreement between two or more groups to form a business entity in order to achieve a specific goal or to operate for a specific period of time. Both the scope of the joint venture and the liabilities of the people or businesses involved usually are limited to one project. Once the goal is reached, the period of time elapses, or the project is completed, the joint venture is dissolved.

Corporations, as well as individuals, may enter into joint ventures. Major oil producers often have formed a number of joint ventures to share the extremely high cost of exploring for offshore petroleum deposits. And many U.S. companies are forming joint ventures with foreign firms in order to enter new markets around the globe. For example, Walmart has joined forces with India's Bharti Enterprises to establish wholesale cash-and-carry stores that sell directly to local retailers in different

joint venture an agreement between two or more groups to form a business entity in order to achieve a specific goal or to operate for a specific period of time

cities and towns in India. Plans are for each store to offer an assortment of approximately 6,000 items including food and nonfood items at competitive wholesale prices, allowing retailers and small business owners to lower their cost of operation. The first cash-and-carry store was named Best Price Modern Wholesale and opened in Amritsar, India, in May 2009. Over the next two years, the joint venture plans to open 10 to 12 cash-and-carry stores that will employ approximately 5,000 to 6,000 people.[11]

Syndicates

A **syndicate** is a temporary association of individuals or firms organized to perform a specific task that requires a large amount of capital. The syndicate is formed because no one person or firm is willing to put up the entire amount required for the undertaking. Like a joint venture, a syndicate is dissolved as soon as its purpose has been accomplished.

Syndicates are used most commonly to underwrite large insurance policies, loans, and investments. To share the risk of default, banks have formed syndicates to provide loans to developing countries. Stock brokerage firms usually join together in the same way to market a new issue of stock. For example, ten Wall Street firms including Morgan Stanley, J.P. Morgan Chase, Bank of America, and Goldman Sachs formed a syndicate to sell shares of stock in the "new" General Motors. With the help of the syndicate, GM was able to raise over $20 billion—one of the largest IPOs in U.S. history.[12] (An *initial public offering (IPO)* is the term used to describe the first time a corporation sells stock to the general public.)

CORPORATE GROWTH

Growth seems to be a basic characteristic of business. One reason for seeking growth has to do with profit: A larger firm generally has greater sales revenue and thus greater profit. Another reason is that in a growing economy, a business that does not grow is actually shrinking relative to the economy. A third reason is that business growth is a means by which some executives boost their power, prestige, and reputation.

Growth poses new problems and requires additional resources that first must be available and then must be used effectively. The main ingredient in growth is capital—and as we have noted, capital is most readily available to corporations.

Growth from Within

Most corporations grow by expanding their present operations. Some introduce and sell new but related products. Others expand the sale of present products to new geographic markets or to new groups of consumers in geographic markets already served. Although Walmart was started by Sam Walton in 1962 with one discount store, today Walmart has over 8,900 stores in the United States and 14 other countries and has long-range plans for expanding into additional international markets.[13]

Growth from within, especially when carefully planned and controlled, can have relatively little adverse effect on a firm. For the most part, the firm continues to do what it has been doing, but on a larger scale. For instance, Larry Ellison, co-founder and CEO of Oracle Corporation of Redwood Shores, California, built the firm's annual revenues up from a mere $282 million in 1988 to approximately $27 billion today.[14] Much of this growth has taken place over the last ten years as Oracle capitalized on its global leadership in information management software.

Growth Through Mergers and Acquisitions

Another way a firm can grow is by purchasing another company. The purchase of one corporation by another is called a **merger**. An *acquisition* is essentially the same thing as a merger, but the term usually is used in reference to a large corporation's purchases of other corporations. Although most mergers and acquisitions are friendly, hostile takeovers also occur. A **hostile takeover** is a situation in which the

LEARNING OBJECTIVE

8 Explain how growth from within and growth through mergers can enable a business to expand.

syndicate a temporary association of individuals or firms organized to perform a specific task that requires a large amount of capital

merger the purchase of one corporation by another

hostile takeover a situation in which the management and board of directors of a firm targeted for acquisition disapprove of the merger

management and board of directors of a firm targeted for acquisition disapprove of the merger.

Personal App What do mergers have to do with you? If you're a manager or an employee of one of the corporations, your job may change. If you're a customer, the products you buy may change. If you're a stockholder, your ownership stake will change.

When a merger or acquisition becomes hostile, a corporate raider—another company or a wealthy investor—may make a tender offer or start a proxy fight to gain control of the target company. A **tender offer** is an offer to purchase the stock of a firm targeted for acquisition at a price just high enough to tempt stockholders to sell their shares. Corporate raiders also may initiate a proxy fight. A **proxy fight** is a technique used to gather enough stockholder votes to control a targeted company.

If the corporate raider is successful and takes over the targeted company, existing management usually is replaced. Faced with this probability, existing management may take specific actions, sometimes referred to as "poison pills," "shark repellents," or "porcupine provisions," to maintain control of the firm and avoid the hostile takeover. Whether mergers are friendly or hostile, they are generally classified as *horizontal, vertical,* or *conglomerate* (see Figure 4-5).

A $39 billion acquisition. AT&T's purchase of rival T-Mobile would create the largest wireless carrier in the United States. While the mega-merger would be good for shareholders of both companies, consumer advocates worry about reduced competition and fewer choices for consumers. Because of these concerns, the "$39 billion deal" had not been approved by government regulators at the time of publication.

© Peter Foley/EPA/Landov

FIGURE 4-5: **Three Types of Growth by Merger**

Today, mergers are classified as horizontal, vertical, or conglomerate.

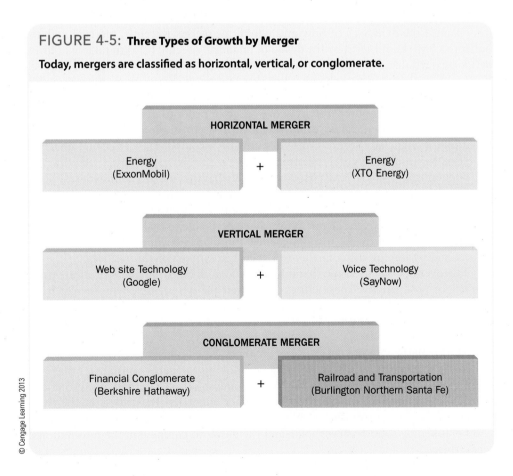

tender offer an offer to purchase the stock of a firm targeted for acquisition at a price just high enough to tempt stockholders to sell their shares

proxy fight a technique used to gather enough stockholder votes to control a targeted company

© Cengage Learning 2013

HORIZONTAL MERGERS A *horizontal merger* is a merger between firms that make and sell similar products or services in similar markets. The merger between ExxonMobil and XTO Energy is an example of a horizontal merger because both firms are in the energy industry. This type of merger tends to reduce the number of firms in an industry—and thus may reduce competition. Most horizontal mergers are reviewed carefully by federal agencies before they are approved in order to protect competition in the marketplace.

VERTICAL MERGERS A *vertical merger* is a merger between firms that operate at different but related levels in the production and marketing of a product. Generally, one of the merging firms is either a supplier or a customer of the other. A vertical merger occurred when Google acquired SayNow. At the time of the 2011 merger, SayNow, a company based in Palo Alto, California, was a leading provider of applications for voice messaging, conversations, and group calls that could be integrated into Facebook, Twitter, and iPhone apps. By acquiring SayNow's existing technology, Google will be able to develop social networking applications and extend Google's current consumer and business services. Rather than develop its own applications or purchase applications from SayNow, Google simply purchased the company.[15]

CONGLOMERATE MERGERS A *conglomerate merger* takes place between firms in completely different industries. One of the largest conglomerate mergers in recent history occurred when Berkshire Hathaway acquired Burlington Northern Santa Fe Railway. While both companies were recognized as successful companies that have a history of increasing sales revenues and profits, they operate in different industries. The Berkshire Hathaway–Burlington Northern Santa Fe merger was friendly because it was beneficial for both firms.

Merger and Acquisition Trends During an Economic Crisis

While there have always been mergers and acquisitions, the recent economic crisis has changed the dynamics of how and why firms merge. Recently, mergers and acquisitions have been fueled by the desire of financially secure firms to take over firms in financial trouble. For a firm experiencing financial difficulties, a merger or acquisition is often a better option than bankruptcy. During the recent economic crisis, this trend was especially evident in the financial services and banking industry. For example, Wachovia was purchased by Wells Fargo in order to avoid a Wachovia bank failure or a government takeover of Wachovia's assets and loan portfolio. In other situations, a financially secure firm will purchase a company experiencing financial problems because it is a good investment.

Economists, financial analysts, corporate managers, and stockholders still hotly debate whether mergers and acquisitions are good for the economy—or for individual companies—in the long run. Takeover advocates argue that for companies that have been taken over, the purchasers have been able to make the company more profitable and productive by installing a new top-management team, by reducing expenses, and by forcing the company to concentrate on one main business.

Takeover opponents argue that takeovers do nothing to enhance corporate profitability or productivity. These critics argue that the only people who benefit from takeovers are investment bankers, brokerage firms, and takeover "artists," who receive financial rewards by manipulating corporations rather than by producing tangible products or services.

Most experts now predict that mergers and acquisitions after the economic crisis will be the result of cash-rich companies looking to acquire businesses that will enhance their position in the marketplace. Analysts also anticipate more mergers that involve companies or investors from other countries. Regardless of the companies involved or where the companies are from, future mergers and acquisitions will be driven by solid business logic and the desire to compete in the international marketplace.

✱ Concept Check

☐ What happens when a firm makes a decision to grow from within?

☐ What is a hostile takeover? How is it related to a tender offer and a proxy fight?

☐ Explain the three types of mergers.

☐ Describe current merger trends and how they affect the businesses involved and their stockholders.

Whether they are sole proprietorships, partnerships, corporations, or some other form of business ownership, most U.S. businesses are small. In the next chapter, we focus on these small businesses. We examine, among other things, the meaning of the word *small* as it applies to business and the place of small business in the American economy.

Get Flashcards, Quizzes, Games, Crosswords, and more @ www.cengagebrain.com

SUMMARY

1 Describe the advantages and disadvantages of sole proprietorships.

In a sole proprietorship, all business profits become the property of the owner, but the owner is also personally responsible for all business debts. A successful sole proprietorship can be a great source of pride for the owner. When comparing different types of business ownership, the sole proprietorship is the simplest form of business to enter, control, and leave. It also pays no special taxes. Perhaps for these reasons, 72 percent of all American business firms are sole proprietorships. Sole proprietorships nevertheless have disadvantages, such as unlimited liability and limits on one person's ability to borrow or to be an expert in all fields. As a result, this form of ownership accounts for only 4 percent of total revenues when compared with partnerships and corporations.

2 Explain the different types of partners and the importance of partnership agreements.

Like sole proprietors, general partners are responsible for running the business and for all business debts. Limited partners receive a share of the profit in return for investing in the business. However, they are not responsible for business debts beyond the amount they have invested. Regardless of the type of partnership, it is always a good idea to have a written agreement (or articles of partnership) setting forth the terms of a partnership.

3 Describe the advantages and disadvantages of partnerships.

Although partnership eliminates some of the disadvantages of sole proprietorship, it is the least popular of the major forms of business ownership. The major advantages of a partnership include ease of start-up, availability of capital and credit, personal interest, combined skills and knowledge, retention of profits, and possible tax advantages. The effects of management disagreements are one of the major disadvantages of a partnership. Other disadvantages include unlimited liability (in a general partnership), lack of continuity, and frozen investment. By forming a limited partnership, the disadvantage of unlimited liability

may be eliminated for the limited partner(s). This same disadvantage may be eliminated for partners that form a limited-liability partnership (LLP). Of course, special requirements must be met if partners form either the limited partnership or the limited-liability partnership.

4 Summarize how a corporation is formed.

A corporation is an artificial person created by law, with most of the legal rights of a real person, including the right to start and operate a business, to own property, to borrow money, to be sued or sue, and to enter into contracts. With the corporate form of ownership, stock can be sold to individuals to raise capital. The people who own a corporation's stock—and thus own part of the corporation—are called stockholders. Generally, corporations are classified as closed corporations (few stockholders) or open corporations (many stockholders).

The process of forming a corporation is called incorporation. Most experts believe that the services of a lawyer are necessary when making decisions about where to incorporate and about obtaining a corporate charter, issuing stock, holding an organizational meeting, and all other legal details involved in incorporation. In theory, stockholders are able to control the activities of the corporation because they elect the board of directors who appoint the corporate officers.

5 Describe the advantages and disadvantages of a corporation.

Perhaps the major advantage of the corporate form is limited liability—stockholders are not liable for the corporation's debts beyond the amount they paid for its stock. Other important advantages include ease of raising capital, ease of transfer of ownership, perpetual life, and specialized management. A major disadvantage of a large corporation is double taxation: All profits are taxed once as corporate income and again as personal income because stockholders must pay a personal income tax on the profits they receive as dividends. Other disadvantages include difficulty and expense of formation, government regulation and increased paperwork, conflict within the corporation, and lack of secrecy.

6 Examine special types of corporations, including S-corporations, limited-liability companies, and not-for-profit corporations.

S-corporations are corporations that are taxed as though they were partnerships but that enjoy the benefit of limited liability. To qualify as an S-corporation, a number of criteria must be met. A limited-liability company (LLC) is a form of business ownership that provides limited liability and has fewer restrictions. LLCs with at least two members are taxed like a partnership and thus avoid the double taxation imposed on most corporations. LLCs with just one member are taxed like a sole proprietorship. When compared with a regular corporation or an S-corporation, an LLC is more flexible. Not-for-profit corporations are formed to provide social services and to improve communities and change lives rather than to earn profits.

7 Discuss the purpose of a joint venture and syndicate.

Two additional forms of business ownership—the joint venture and syndicate—are used by their owners to meet special needs. A joint venture is formed when two or more groups form a business entity in order to achieve a specific goal or to operate for a specific period of time. Once the goal is reached, the period of time elapses, or the project is completed, the joint venture is dissolved. A syndicate is a temporary association of individuals or firms organized to perform a specific task that requires large amounts of capital. Like a joint venture, a syndicate is dissolved as soon as its purpose has been accomplished.

8 Explain how growth from within and growth through mergers can enable a business to expand.

A corporation may grow by expanding its present operations or through a merger or an acquisition. Although most mergers are friendly, hostile takeovers also occur. A hostile takeover is a situation in which the management and board of directors of a firm targeted for acquisition disapprove of the merger. Mergers generally are classified as horizontal, vertical, or conglomerate.

During the recent economic crisis, mergers and acquisitions have been fueled by the desire of financially secure firms to take over firms in financial trouble. In other situations, a financially secure firm will purchase a company experiencing financial problems because it is a good investment.

While economists, financial analysts, corporate managers, and stockholders debate the merits of mergers, some trends should be noted. First, experts predict that future mergers will be the result of cash-rich companies looking to acquire businesses that will enhance their position in the marketplace. Second, more mergers are likely to involve foreign companies or investors. Third, mergers will be driven by business logic and the desire to compete in the international marketplace.

KEY TERMS

You should now be able to define and give an example relevant to each of the following terms:

sole proprietorship (105)
unlimited liability (107)
partnership (108)
general partner (109)
limited partner (109)
corporation (113)
stock (113)
stockholder (113)

closed corporation (113)
open corporation (114)
domestic corporation (114)
foreign corporation (114)
alien corporation (114)
common stock (115)
preferred stock (115)

dividend (115)
proxy (115)
board of directors (116)
corporate officers (116)
limited liability (116)
S-corporation (119)
limited-liability company (LLC) (119)

not-for-profit corporation (120)
joint venture (121)
syndicate (122)
merger (122)
hostile takeover (122)
tender offer (123)
proxy fight (123)

DISCUSSION QUESTIONS

1. If you were to start a business, which ownership form would you choose? What factors might affect your choice?
2. Why might an investor choose to become a partner in a limited partnership business instead of purchasing the stock of an open corporation?
3. Discuss the following statement: "Corporations are not really run by their owners."
4. What kinds of services do not-for-profit corporations provide? Would a career in a not-for-profit corporation appeal to you?
5. Is growth a good thing for all firms? How does management know when a firm is ready to grow?

TEST YOURSELF

Matching Questions

1. _____ It is an association of two or more business owners.

2. _____ A distribution of earnings to the stockholders of a corporation.

3. _____ This type of ownership is the simplest type of business to start.

4. _____ A person who invests only money in a partnership.

5. _____ The concept of being personally responsible for all debts of a business.

6. _____ A business entity or artificial being with most of the legal rights of a person.

7. _____ A legal document that describes the purpose of the corporation.

8. _____ An offer to purchase the stock of a firm targeted for acquisition.

9. _____ A temporary association of individuals or firms organized to perform a specific task.

10. _____ A company chartered in a foreign country doing business in the United States.

a. alien corporation
b. articles of incorporation
c. syndicate
d. tender offer
e. vertical venture
f. limited partner
g. voluntary association
h. corporation
i. dividend
j. partnership
k. sole proprietorship
l. unlimited liability

True False Questions

11. **T** **F** Unlimited liability is an advantage of a sole proprietorship.

12. **T** **F** Preferred stockholders manage the day-to-day business activities of a corporation.

13. **T** **F** A conglomerate merger takes place between firms in completely different industries.

14. **T** **F** A limited partner is responsible for any debts of the partnership, regardless of whether he or she was directly involved in the transaction that created the debt.

15. **T** **F** The articles of partnership is a written contract describing the terms of a partnership.

16. **T** **F** Compared to a corporation, a partnership is more difficult and expensive to establish.

17. **T** **F** The S-corporation form of organization allows a corporation to avoid double taxation.

18. **T** **F** Corporate officers are elected by the firm's stockholders.

19. **T** **F** The board of directors is directly responsible to the stockholders.

20. **T** **F** The amount paid for stock is the most a shareholder can lose in the corporate form of ownership.

Multiple-Choice Questions

21. _____ During college, Elyssa Wood earned extra money by using her culinary skills to cater special parties. After graduation, she decided to turn her part-time job into a full-time business that she plans to expand in the future. In the meantime, she wants to maintain complete control of the business. She will most likely organize the business as a
a. limited partnership.
b. corporation.
c. general partnership.
d. sole proprietorship.
e. not-for-profit corporation.

22. _____ Which of the following is not an advantage of a corporate form of ownership?
a. It is easier to raise capital.
b. Ownership can be transferred easily and quickly.
c. The death of an owner does not terminate the corporation.
d. Profits are taxed twice.
e. The liability of the owners is limited.

23. _____ A corporation incorporated in Texas doing business in New York is known in
a. New York as a domestic corporation.
b. Texas as a foreign corporation.
c. Texas as a domestic corporation.
d. New York as an alien corporation.
e. The firm cannot do business in New York.

24. _____ PepsiCo acquired Pizza Hut. What type of merger was this?
   a. Limited
   b. Syndicated
   c. Joint venture
   d. Horizontal
   e. Vertical

25. _____ J. R. Imax, a financial investor, wants to control the Simex Company. So far he has been unsuccessful in purchasing enough stock to give him control. To reach his goal, which technique should he use to gather enough stockholder votes to control the company?
   a. Poison pill
   b. Liability takeover
   c. Merger
   d. Acquisition
   e. Proxy fight

26. _____ A corporation whose stock is owned by relative few people is called a(n)
   a. limited corporation.
   b. open corporation.
   c. closed corporation.
   d. domestic corporation.
   e. friendly corporation.

27. _____ When two business firms need large sums of money to finance a major project, they are likely to establish a
   a. closed corporation.
   b. syndicate.
   c. new sole proprietorship business.
   d. legal tender corporation.
   e. conglomerate venture.

28. _____ The ability to combine skills and knowledge is an advantage of a
   a. partnership.
   b. sole proprietorship.
   c. limited venture.
   d. an enterprise venture.
   e. a horizontal business.

29. _____ One of the advantages of an LLC is that owners have _____ liability.
   a. unlimited
   b. restricted
   c. special
   d. limited
   e. taxable

30. _____ Unlimited liability means
   a. there is no limit on the amount an owner can borrow.
   b. creditors will absorb any loss from nonpayment of debt.
   c. the business can borrow money for any type of purchase.
   d. the owner is responsible for all business debts.
   e. stockholders can borrow money from the business.

Answers to the Test Yourself questions appear at the end of the book on page TY-1.

VIDEO CASE

Annie's Homegrown: A Corporation with Entrepreneurial Spirit

When Annie Withey's first husband suggested she create a snack food to go into the resalable bag he'd invented, the 21-year-old newlywed developed an all-natural, cheddar cheese-flavored popcorn. The bag never made it to market, but Annie's popcorn, called Smartfood, became one of the fastest-selling snack foods in U.S. history. In fact, in 1989 PepsiCo Inc's Frito-Lay division bought the brand for about $15 million.

Annie, an organic farmer and mother of two children, cashed out stock worth $1 million and created the all-natural white-cheddar macaroni and cheese product she had been thinking about for some time. She and her husband initially marketed it by knocking on supermarket doors and canvassing ski lodges, outdoor folk concerts, store parking lots, and wherever people gathered. Thus Annie's Homegrown, a pioneering entrepreneurial company in the natural and organic food industry, was born.

This venture was also a success for Annie, and even though her firm has gone on to become part of a larger conglomerate, Annie remains the entrepreneurial heart of the brand. "I learned a lot and took a lot with me," says Annie of her early experience running the operation. Now she delegates day-to-day management, as well as public appearances, to others, and concentrates on what she does best—creating new recipes and providing inspiration to her co-workers. Being a public figure? "That's just not me," she says. "I'm not very good at making presentations and selling," she feels.

Annie's Homegrown offers 80 natural and organic pasta and canned products, as well as snack crackers and a microwaveable version of its now-famous macaroni and cheese, designed for college dorm room convenience. Its products are found in Costco and Target, as well as in 18,000 grocery and 6,000 natural food stores nationwide. Yet Annie's still has only about 3 percent of the macaroni and cheese market compared with the leader, Kraft, which has 80 percent.

"We could never compete directly," says CEO John Foraker. "We appeal to a consumer who is less price conscious and willing to pay more to feel good about what they eat." Because Annie's mac and cheese also costs 30 percent more than Kraft's, the company's marketing focuses on product attributes. The nation's leading brand of organic and natural pasta meals and snacks, Annie's Homegrown represents what *Customer Relationship Magazine* calls "an unmistakable shift toward organic products, green marketing, and sustainability efforts." Annie's story, well known to many of the company's customers, also helps build loyalty to the company's brands.

But for Annie Withey, becoming successful meant taking some risks. Annie had to personally guarantee all loans to her company early on. "Your entire career and reputation are on the line," says previous company president Paul Nardone. But Annie has always trusted her instincts, and events have usually proven her right. She is "our moral compass," says Nardone, and a continuing inspiration. By 1998 a capital infusion from two small food companies, Consorzio and Fantastic Foods, was helping fuel growth, but choosing the right investment company would become critical to the company's long-term expansion goals.

CEO Foraker says Solera Capital LLC, a $250 million private-equity firm run by women, was looking to enter the fast-growing organic food market and took a majority stake in the company with an initial $20 million investment in 2002. "It's a perfect fit," says Molly Ashby, Solera's chief executive officer. "It's a great brand, very authentic, with tremendous crossover into both mainstream and natural markets." The remaining interest in the company is held by Withey, current management, and a small group of founding investors. Solera recently bought Consorzio and Fantastic Foods and combined them with Annie's Homegrown to form Homegrown Naturals Inc., based in Napa, California.

As founder, Annie Withey has assumed the role of "inspirational president." She still writes the text on every product box, and Bernie the Bunny, inspired by her brother's illustration, still appears on every package. As she continues to fill the role of creative leader of the company she started, Annie has been described as its "quality gatekeeper" and a humble person whose creative instincts are "right on." When customers write or e-mail to suggest new products, each idea is still considered, and the "real" Annie never gets tired of hearing how much people enjoy her products.[16]

Questions

1. What personal traits does Annie Withey exhibit that entrepreneurs need to succeed? How have her personal characteristics helped shape the success of her business?
2. How did the company evolve from a small business into a multimillion dollar leader in the natural organic food industry? What long-term growth strategies is the company pursuing as it moves into the future?
3. Explore Annie's Web site at www.annies.com. What unique features did you find? How does this Web site support Annie's mission?

BUILDING SKILLS FOR CAREER SUCCESS

1. Exploring the Internet

Arguments about mergers and acquisitions often come down to an evaluation of who benefits and by how much. Sometimes the benefits include access to new products, talented management, new customers, or new sources of capital. Often, the debate is complicated by the involvement of firms based in different countries.

The Internet is a fertile environment for information and discussion about mergers. The firms involved will provide their view about who will benefit and why it is either a good thing or not. Journalists will report facts and offer commentary as to how they see the future result of any merger, and of course, chat rooms located on the Web sites of many journals promote discussion about the issues.

Assignment

1. Using an Internet search engine such as Google or Yahoo!, locate two or three sites providing information about a recent merger (use a keyword such as *merger* or *acquisition*).

2. After examining these sites and reading journal articles, report information about the merger, such as the dollar value, the reasons behind the merger, and so forth.
3. Based on your assessment of the information you have read, do you think the merger is a good idea or not for the firms involved, the employees, the investors, the industry, and society as a whole? Explain your reasoning.

2. Building Team Skills

Suppose that you have decided to quit your job as an insurance adjuster and open a bakery. Your business is now growing, and you have decided to add a full line of catering services. This means more work and responsibility. You will need someone to help you, but you are undecided about what to do. Should you hire an employee or find a partner? If you add a partner, what type of decisions should be made to create a partnership agreement?

Assignment

1. In a group, discuss the following questions:
   a. What are the advantages and disadvantages of adding a partner versus hiring an employee?
   b. Assume that you have decided to form a partnership. What articles should be included in a partnership agreement?
   c. How would you go about finding a partner?
2. As a group, prepare an articles-of-partnership agreement. Be prepared to discuss the pros and cons of your group's agreement with other groups from your class, as well as to examine their agreements.
3. Summarize your group's answers to these questions, and present them to your class.

3. Researching Different Careers

Many people spend their entire lives working in jobs that they do not enjoy. Why is this so? Often, it is because they have taken the first job they were offered without giving it much thought. How can you avoid having this happen to you? First, you should determine your "personal profile" by identifying and analyzing your own strengths, weaknesses, things you enjoy, and things you dislike. Second, you should identify the types of jobs that fit your profile. Third, you should identify and research the companies that offer those jobs.

Assignment

1. Take two sheets of paper and draw a line down the middle of each sheet, forming two columns on each page. Label column 1 "Things I Enjoy or Like to Do," column 2 "Things I Do Not Like Doing," column 3 "My Strengths," and column 4 "My Weaknesses."
2. Record data in each column over a period of at least one week. You may find it helpful to have a relative or friend give you input.
3. Summarize the data, and write a profile of yourself.
4. Take your profile to a career counselor at your college or to the public library and ask for help in identifying jobs that fit your profile. Your college may offer testing to assess your skills and personality. The Internet is another resource.
5. Research the companies that offer the types of jobs that fit your profile.
6. Write a report on your findings.

CHAPTER 5 SMALL BUSINESS, ENTREPRENEURSHIP, AND FRANCHISES

© Susan Van Etten

Why should you care?

America's small businesses drive the U.S. economy. Small businesses represent 99.7 percent of all employer firms, and there is a good probability that you will work for a small business or perhaps even start your own business. This chapter can help you to become a good employee or a successful entrepreneur.

Learning Objectives

What you will be able to do once you complete this chapter:

1 Define what a small business is and recognize the fields in which small businesses are concentrated.

2 Identify the people who start small businesses and the reasons why some succeed and many fail.

3 Assess the contributions of small businesses to our economy.

4 Judge the advantages and disadvantages of operating a small business.

5 Explain how the Small Business Administration helps small businesses.

6 Appraise the concept and types of franchising.

7 Analyze the growth of franchising and franchising's advantages and disadvantages.

Small Businesses Get Boost from Big Business

Who goes to Home Depot for business advice? Small business owner Gwen Thomas does—and she's not the only one. For nearly a decade, Home Depot managers in Georgia have served as mentors to a number of startups and small companies. Gwen Thomas, who owns a consulting firm, received free advice from Home Depot executives as she formulated and implemented plans to expand her Atlanta-based business. "I had a wish list of what I wanted to learn, and they helped me with it," she says. In addition to spending time with Home Depot's legal and financial experts, Thomas was able to call on her mentors for guidance when facing difficult business decisions.

Home Depot isn't the only corporate giant giving small businesses a boost. AT&T, Bank of America, Citigroup, IBM, Pfizer, and UPS have banded together to form the Supplier Connection (www.supplier-connection.net/), which smoothes the way for small businesses to become suppliers to these big businesses. Navigating all the twists and turns of individual corporations' procedures and requirements can be cumbersome and time-consuming when a small business is trying to break in as a supplier. Now, thanks to the Supplier Connection, entrepreneurs can easily submit one online application to become an authorized supplier to any of the participants.

One way American Express helps small businesses is by offering free online tools, information, and resources to make their operations more efficient. It also launched the nationwide "Small Business Saturday" movement, which encourages shoppers to buy at local independent businesses on the Saturday after Thanksgiving.

Why would giant corporations offer a helping hand to small businesses? First, small businesses make good customers, suppliers, and partners. AT&T and other Supplier Connection participants are actually helping themselves when they help small businesses qualify as authorized suppliers. "Hopefully over the long term, hundreds of large companies will come in with billions and billions of dollars worth of spending and make it easier for small business to jumpstart themselves," says the head of IBM's Corporate Citizenship and Corporate Affairs group. A second key reason is that big businesses can enhance their reputations as good corporate citizens by assisting small businesses in their communities.[1]

Did you know?

American Express, AT&T, Bank of America, Citigroup, Home Depot, IBM, Pfizer, and UPS are only some of the corporate giants that help local entrepreneurs build their small businesses.

Just as Gwen Thomas' consulting business in Atlanta, most businesses start small, and those that survive usually stay small. They provide a solid foundation for our economy—as employers, as suppliers and purchasers of goods and services, and as taxpayers.

In this chapter, we do not take small businesses for granted. Instead, we look closely at this important business sector—beginning with a definition of small business, a description of industries that often attract small businesses, and a profile of some of the people who start small businesses. Next, we consider the importance of small businesses in our economy. We also present the advantages and disadvantages of smallness in business. We then describe services provided by the Small Business Administration, a government agency formed to assist owners and managers of small businesses. We conclude the chapter with a discussion of the pros and cons of franchising, an approach to small-business ownership that has become very popular in the last 40 years.

SMALL BUSINESS: A PROFILE

LEARNING OBJECTIVE

1 Define what a small business is and recognize the fields in which small businesses are concentrated.

The Small Business Administration (SBA) defines a **small business** as "one which is independently owned and operated for profit and is not dominant in its field." How small must a firm be not to dominate its field? That depends on the particular industry it is in. The SBA has developed the following specific "smallness" guidelines for the various industries, as shown in Table 5-1.[2] The SBA periodically revises and simplifies its small-business size regulations. For example, in 2011, the SBA proposed to increase small business size standards for 35 industries.

Annual sales in millions of dollars may not seem very small. However, for many firms, profit is only a small percentage of total sales. Thus, a firm may earn only $40,000 or $50,000 on yearly sales of $1 million—and that *is* small in comparison with the profits earned by most medium-sized and large firms. Moreover, most small firms have annual sales well below the maximum limits in the SBA guidelines.

Small businesses are very important to the U.S. economy. For example, small businesses:

- Represent 99.7 percent of all employer firms.
- Employ about half of all private sector employees.
- Pay 43 percent of total U.S. private payroll.
- Have generated 65 percent of net new jobs over the past 17 years.
- Create more than half of the nonfarm private GDP.
- Hire 43 percent of high-tech workers (scientists, engineers, computer programmers, and others).
- Are 52 percent home-based and 2 percent franchises.
- Made up 97.5 percent of all identified exporters and produced 31 percent of export value in FY 2008.
- Produced 16.5 times more patents per employee than large patenting firms.[3]

The Small-Business Sector

In the United States, it typically takes four days and $210 to establish a business as a legal entity. The steps include registering the name of the business, applying for tax IDs, and setting up unemployment and workers' compensation insurance. In Japan,

TABLE 5-1: Industry Group-Size Standards

Small-business size standards are usually stated in number of employees or average annual sales. In the United States, 99.7 percent of all businesses are considered small.

Industry Group	Size Standard
Manufacturing, mining industries	500 employees
Wholesale trade	100 employees
Agriculture	$750,000
Retail trade	$7 million
General and heavy construction (except dredging)	$33.5 million
Dredging	$20 million
Special trade contractors	$14 million
Travel agencies	$3.5 million (commissions and other income)
Business and personal services except	$7 million
• Architectural, engineering, surveying, and mapping services	$4.5 million
• Dry cleaning and carpet cleaning services	$4.5 million

Source: www.sba.gov/content/summary-size-standards-industry (accessed March 15, 2011).

small business one that is independently owned and operated for profit and is not dominant in its field

however, a typical entrepreneur spends more than $3,500 and 31 days to follow 11 different procedures.

A surprising number of Americans take advantage of their freedom to start a business. There are, in fact, about 27.5 million businesses in this country. Only 18,469 of these employ more than 500 workers—enough to be considered large.

Interest in owning or starting a small business has never been greater than it is today. During the last decade, the number of small businesses in the United States has increased 49 percent. For the last few years, new-business formation in the United States has broken successive records, except during the 2001–2002 and 2008 recessions. Recently, nearly 552,600 new businesses were incorporated. Furthermore, part-time entrepreneurs have increased fivefold in recent years; they now account for one-third of all small businesses.[4]

According to a recent study, approximately 70 percent of small business firms fail within the first seven years; 34 percent survive at least ten years.[5] The primary reason for these failures is mismanagement resulting from a lack of business know-how. The makeup of the small-business sector thus is constantly changing. Despite the high failure rate, many small businesses succeed modestly. Some, like Apple Computer, Inc., are extremely successful—to the point where they can no longer be considered small. Taken together, small businesses are also responsible for providing a high percentage of the jobs in the United States. According to some estimates, the figure is about 50 percent.

Industries that Attract Small Businesses

Some industries, such as auto manufacturing, require huge investments in machinery and equipment. Businesses in such industries are big from the day they are started—if an entrepreneur or group of entrepreneurs can gather the capital required to start one.

By contrast, a number of other industries require only a low initial investment and some special skills or knowledge. It is these industries that tend to attract new businesses. Growing industries, such as outpatient-care facilities, are attractive because of their profit potential. However, knowledgeable entrepreneurs choose areas with which they are familiar, and these are most often the more established industries.

Small enterprise spans the gamut from corner newspaper vending to the development of optical fibers. The owners of small businesses sell gasoline, flowers, and coffee to go. They publish magazines, haul freight, teach languages, and program computers. They make wines, movies, and high-fashion clothes. They build new homes and restore old ones. They fix appliances, recycle metals, and sell used cars. They drive cabs and fly planes. They make us well when we are ill, and they sell us the products of corporate giants. In fact, 74 percent of real estate, rental, and leasing industries; 61 percent of the businesses in the leisure and hospitality services; and 86 percent of the construction industries are dominated by small businesses.[6] The various kinds of businesses generally fall into three broad categories of industry: distribution, service, and production.

Personal App Sometime in your career, you're likely to have a job in a small business. You might work in a store, in a service business, or in production. If you're thinking of starting your own business, be sure to watch how these entrepreneurs manage their companies.

DISTRIBUTION INDUSTRIES This category includes retailing, wholesaling, transportation, and communications—industries concerned with the movement of goods from producers to consumers. Distribution industries account for approximately 33 percent of all small businesses. Of these, almost three-quarters are involved in retailing, that is, the sale of goods directly to consumers. Clothing and jewelry stores, pet shops, bookstores, and grocery stores, for example, are all retailing firms. Slightly less than one-quarter of the small distribution firms are wholesalers. Wholesalers purchase products in quantity from manufacturers and then resell them to retailers.

SERVICE INDUSTRIES This category accounts for more than 48 percent of all small businesses. Of these, about three-quarters provide such nonfinancial services as medical and dental care; watch, shoe, and TV repairs; haircutting and styling; restaurant meals; and dry cleaning. About 8 percent of the small service firms offer financial services, such as accounting, insurance, real estate, and investment counseling. An increasing number of self-employed Americans are running service businesses from home.

PRODUCTION INDUSTRIES This last category includes the construction, mining, and manufacturing industries. Only about 19 percent of all small businesses are in this group, mainly because these industries require relatively large initial investments. Small firms that do venture into production generally make parts and subassemblies for larger manufacturing firms or supply special skills to larger construction firms.

Concept Check ✳

☐ What information would you need to determine whether a particular business is small according to SBA guidelines?

☐ Which two areas of business generally attract the most small business? Why are these areas attractive to small business?

☐ Distinguish among service industries, distribution industries, and production industries.

THE PEOPLE IN SMALL BUSINESSES: THE ENTREPRENEURS

LEARNING OBJECTIVE

2 Identify the people who start small businesses and the reasons why some succeed and many fail.

The entrepreneurial spirit is alive and well in the United States. A recent study revealed that the U.S. population is quite entrepreneurial when compared with those of other countries. More than 70 percent of Americans would prefer being an entrepreneur to working for someone else. This compares with 46 percent of adults in Western Europe and 58 percent of adults in Canada. Another study on entrepreneurial activity for 2002 found that of 36 countries studied, the United States was in the top third in entrepreneurial activity and was the leader when compared with Japan, Canada, and Western Europe.[7]

Small businesses typically are managed by the people who started and own them. Most of these people have held jobs with other firms and still could be so employed if they wanted. Yet owners of small businesses would rather take the risk of starting and operating their own firms, even if the money they make is less than the salaries they otherwise might earn.

Researchers have suggested a variety of personal factors as reasons why people go into business for themselves. These are discussed below.

Characteristics of Entrepreneurs

Entrepreneurial spirit is the desire to create a new business. For example, Nikki Olyai always knew that she wanted to create and develop her own business. Her father, a successful businessman in Iran, was her role model. She came to the United States at the age of 17 and lived with a host family in Salem, Oregon, attending high school there. Undergraduate and graduate degrees in computer science led her to start Innovision Technologies while she held two other jobs to keep the business going and took care of her four-year-old son. Recently, Nikki Olyai's business was honored by the Women's Business Enterprise National Council's "Salute to Women's Business Enterprises" as one of 11 top successful firms. For three consecutive years, her firm was selected as a "Future 50 of Greater Detroit Company."

Meet Sir Richard Branson, founder and chairperson of the Virgin Group. Born in 1950, Richard set up *Student* magazine at age 16. Then, at age 20, he founded Virgin as a small mailorder record retailer. Today, Virgin is a leading venture capital organization and is one of the world's most recognized and respected brands. Sir Branson established Branson School of Entrepreneurship to identify and support the most promising young entrepreneurs to launch successful businesses of their own.

© Alex Gallardo/Landov

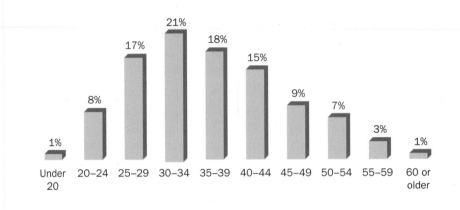

FIGURE 5-1: How Old Is the Average Entrepreneur?

People in all age groups become entrepreneurs, but more than 70 percent are between 24 and 44 years of age.

Source: Data developed and provided by the National Federation of Independent Business Foundation and sponsored by the American Express Travel Related Services Company, Inc.

Personal App Do you have what it takes to succeed as an entrepreneur? You'll need more than a good idea and the desire to be your own boss. Even if you don't start your own business, entrepreneurial spirit will serve you well in any work situation.

Other Personal Factors

Other personal factors in small-business success include

- Independence
- A desire to determine one's own destiny
- A willingness to find and accept a challenge
- Family background (In particular, researchers think that people whose families have been in business, successfully or not, are most apt to start and run their own businesses.)
- Age (Those who start their own businesses also tend to cluster around certain ages—more than 70 percent are between 24 and 44 years of age; see Figure 5-1.)

Motivation

There must be some motivation to start a business. A person may decide that he or she simply has "had enough" of working and earning a profit for someone else. Another may lose his or her job for some reason and decide to start the business he or she has always wanted rather than to seek another job. Still another person may have an idea for a new product or a new way to sell an existing product. Or the opportunity to go into business may arise suddenly, perhaps as a result of a hobby. For example, Cheryl Strand started baking and decorating cakes from her home while working full time as a word processor at Clemson University. Her cakes became so popular that she soon found herself working through her lunch breaks and late into the night to meet customer demand.

Women as Small-Business Owners

- Women are 51 percent of the U.S. population, and according to the SBA, they owned at least 50 percent of all small businesses in 2008.
- Women already own 66 percent of the home-based businesses in this country, and the number of men in home-based businesses is growing rapidly.

Looking for an Internship? Think Small

career SUCCESS

If you think only giant corporations hire interns, think again. Small businesses across the country have begun recruiting interns for both paid and unpaid positions, creating opportunities for students and recent graduates to gain valuable work experience and first-hand knowledge of their chosen industry or career.

Raven Kauffman was an intern 15 years ago. Once she started her own luxury handbag business in Los Angeles, she decided to hire a college student for an unpaid summer intern position. "I really want to teach someone something, to mentor someone, because it really worked for me," she explained.

If you pursue an internship with a small business, be sure to ask about the training you can expect to receive on the job. Also, whether your internship is paid or unpaid, find out whether your work will qualify for course credit. Finally, don't forget that completing a successful internship in your field is a great way to enhance your resume and your professional credentials.

Competition for internships can be intense, but your school may be able to help you identify good opportunities for intern positions with small businesses in your area. For example, Texas A&M University-Corpus Christi places interns with local businesses through its Small Business Internship Program. The University of Central Florida has an Enterprising Interns Program that puts fast-growing small businesses in contact with entrepreneurial undergraduate and graduate students seeking internship experiences. So if you're interested in an internship, think small—there may be a small business that needs just your combination of skills and education.

Sources: Ralph Coker, "A&M Intern Program Is Win-Win for Student Workers, Businesses," *Corpus Christi Caller Times (TX),* January 3, 2011, www.caller.com/news; Cyndia Zwahlen, "Unpaid Summer Internships Gaining Popularity at Small Firms," *Los Angeles Times,* June 28, 2010, http://articles.latimes.com; Joanna L. Krotz, "The Do's and Don'ts of Unpaid Internships," *Fox News Small Business Center,* November 5, 2010, www.foxsmallbusinesscenter.com; www.cei.ucf.edu/education/internships.

- According to the SBA, 7.8 million women-owned businesses in the United States provide almost 7.6 million jobs and generate $1.2 trillion in sales.
- Women-owned businesses in the United States have proven that they are more successful; more than 40 percent have been in business for 12 years or more.
- According to Dun and Bradstreet, women-owned businesses are financially sound and credit-worthy, and their risk of failure is lower than average.
- Compared to other working women, self-employed women are older, better educated, and have more managerial experience.
- Just over one-half of small businesses are home based, and 91 percent have no employees. About 60 percent of home-based businesses are in service industries, 16 percent in construction, 14 percent in retail trade, and the rest in manufacturing, finance, transportation, communications, wholesaling, and other industries.[8]

Teenagers as Small-Business Owners

High-tech teen entrepreneurship is definitely exploding. "There's not a period in history where we've seen such a plethora of young entrepreneurs," comments Nancy F. Koehn, associate professor of business administration at Harvard Business School. Still, teen entrepreneurs face unique pressures in juggling their schoolwork, their social life, and their high-tech workload. Some ultimately quit school, whereas others quit or cut back on their business activities. Consider Brian Hendricks at Winston

Leanna Archer—A child entrepreneur. Thirteen-year-old Leanna Archer, child entrepreneur, owner, and CEO of Leanna's Hair Inc., developed and runs her own natural hair care products company, which she founded at age nine in New York. She invented a line of five green hair care products whose profits she plans to use for tuition at Harvard University.

© Newscom

Churchill High School in Potomac, Maryland. He is the founder of StartUpPc and VB Solutions, Inc. StartUpPc, founded in 2001, sells custom-built computers and computer services for home users, home offices, small businesses, and students. Brian's services include design, installation of systems, training, networking, and on-site technical support. In October 2002, Brian founded VB Solutions, Inc., which develops and customizes Web sites and message boards. The firm sets up advertising contracts and counsels Web site owners on site improvements. The company has designed corporate ID kits, logos, and Web sites for clients from all over the world. Brian learned at a very young age that working for yourself is one of the best jobs available. According to Brian, a young entrepreneur must possess "the five P's of entrepreneurship"—planning, persistence, patience, people, and profit. Brian knows what it takes to be a successful entrepreneur. His accolades include Junior Achievement's "National Youth Entrepreneur of the Year" and SBA's 2005 "Young Entrepreneur of the Year" awards.[9]

In some people, the motivation to start a business develops slowly as they gain the knowledge and ability required for success as a business owner. Knowledge and ability—especially, management ability—are probably the most important factors involved. A new firm is very much built around the entrepreneur. The owner must be able to manage the firm's finances, its personnel (if there are any employees), and its day-to-day operations. He or she must handle sales, advertising, purchasing, pricing, and a variety of other business functions. The knowledge and ability to do so are acquired most often through experience working for other firms in the same area of business.

Why Some Entrepreneurs and Small Businesses Fail

Small businesses are prone to failure. Capital, management, and planning are the key ingredients in the survival of a small business, as well as the most common reasons for failure. Businesses can experience a number of money-related problems. It may take several years before a business begins to show a profit. Entrepreneurs need to have not only the capital to open a business but also the money to operate it in its possibly lengthy start-up phase. One cash flow obstacle often leads to others. Moreover, a series of cash flow predicaments usually ends in a business failure. This scenario is played out all too often by small and not-so-small start-up Internet firms that fail to meet their financial backers' expectations and so are denied a second wave of investment dollars to continue their drive to establish a profitable online firm. According to Maureen Borzacchiello, co-owner of Creative Display Solutions, a trade show products company, "Big businesses such as Bear Stearns, Fannie Mae and Freddie Mac, and AIG can get bailouts, but small-business owners are on their own when times are tough and credit is tight."

Many entrepreneurs lack the management skills required to run a business. Money, time, personnel, and inventory all need to be managed effectively if a small business is to succeed. Starting a small business requires much more than optimism and a good idea.

Success and expansion sometimes lead to problems. Frequently, entrepreneurs with successful small businesses make the mistake of overexpansion. Fast growth often results in dramatic changes in a business. Thus, the entrepreneur must plan carefully and adjust competently to new and potentially disruptive situations.

Every day, and in every part of the country, people open new businesses. For example, 552,600 new businesses recently opened their doors. At the same time,

TABLE 5-2: U.S. Business Start-ups, Closures, and Bankruptcies

	New	Closures	Bankruptcies
2009	552,600[e]	660,990[e]	60,837
2008	626,400[e]	663,900[e]	43,546
2007	668,395	592,410	28,322
2006	670,058	599,333	19,695
2005	644,122	565,745	39,201
e = Advocacy estimate.			

Source: Small Business Administration, Office of Advocacy, *Frequently Asked Questions*, www.sba.gov/sites/default/files/files/sbfaq.pdf (accessed March 15, 2011).

Concept Check *

☐ What kinds of factors encourage certain people to start new businesses?

☐ What are the major causes of small-business failure? Do these causes also apply to larger businesses?

however, 660,900 businesses closed their business and 60,837 businesses declared bankruptcy (see Table 5-2).[10] Although many fail, others represent well-conceived ideas developed by entrepreneurs who have the expertise, resources, and determination to make their businesses succeed. As these well-prepared entrepreneurs pursue their individual goals, our society benefits in many ways from their work and creativity. Billion-dollar companies such as Apple Computer, McDonald's Corporation, and Procter & Gamble are all examples of small businesses that expanded into industry giants.

THE IMPORTANCE OF SMALL BUSINESSES IN OUR ECONOMY

LEARNING OBJECTIVE

3 Assess the contributions of small businesses to our economy.

This country's economic history abounds with stories of ambitious men and women who turned their ideas into business dynasties. The Ford Motor Company started as a one-man operation with an innovative method for industrial production. L.L. Bean, Inc., can trace its beginnings to a basement shop in Freeport, Maine. Both Xerox and Polaroid began as small firms with a better way to do a job. More recently, Mark Zuckerberg created Facebook in his Harvard University dorm room. Indeed, every year since 1963, the President of the United States has proclaimed National Small Business Week to recognize the contributions of small businesses to the economic well-being of America.

Providing Technical Innovation

Invention and innovation are part of the foundations of our economy. The increases in productivity that have characterized the past 200 years of our history are all rooted in one principal source: new ways to do a job with less effort for less money. Studies show that the incidence of innovation among small-business workers is significantly higher than among workers in large businesses. Small firms produce two-and-a-half times as many innovations as large firms relative to the number of persons employed. In fact, small firms employ 43 percent of all high-tech workers such as scientists, engineers, and computer specialists. No wonder small firms produce over 16 times more patents per employee than large patenting firms.

Consider Waymon Armstrong, the owner of a small business that uses computer simulations to help government and other clients prepare for and respond to natural disasters, medical emergencies, and combat. In presenting the 2010 National Small Business Person of the Year award, Karen Mills, Administrator of the U.S. Small Business Administration, said, "Waymon Armstrong is a perfect example of the innovation, inspiration, and determination that exemplify America's most successful entrepreneurs. He believed in his brainchild to the point where he deferred his own salary for three years to keep it afloat. When layoffs loomed for his staff after 9/11, their loyalty and belief in the company was so great that they were willing to work without pay for four months."

"Waymon's commitment to his employees and to his business—Engineering & Computer Simulations, Inc.—demonstrates the qualities that make small businesses such a powerful force for job creation in the American economy and in their local communities," said Mills. "It's the same qualities that will lead us to economic recovery. We are especially proud that his company benefited from two grants under SBA's Small Business Innovation and Research Program."[11]

According to the U.S. Office of Management and Budget, more than half the major technological advances of the 20th century originated with individual inventors and small companies. Even just a sampling of those innovations is remarkable:

Providing technical innovation. Meet *Time* magazine's Person of the Year, entrepreneur Mark Zuckerberg, who founded Facebook while still a student at Harvard. In 2008, Zuckerberg became the world's youngest billionaire at age 25.

© WireImage/Getty Images

- Air conditioning
- Airplane
- Automatic transmission
- FM radio
- Heart valve
- Helicopter
- Instant camera
- Insulin
- Jet engine
- Penicillin
- Personal computer
- Power steering

Perhaps even more remarkable—and important—is that many of these inventions sparked major new U.S. industries or contributed to an established industry by adding some valuable service.

Providing Employment

Small firms traditionally have added more than their proportional share of new jobs to the economy. Seven out of the ten industries that added the most new jobs were small-business-dominated industries. Small businesses creating the most new jobs recently included business services, leisure and hospitality services, and special trade contractors. Small firms hire a larger proportion of employees who are younger workers, older workers, women, or workers who prefer to work part time. Furthermore, small businesses provide 67 percent of workers with their first jobs and initial on-the-job training in basic skills. According to the SBA, small businesses represent 99.7 percent of all employers, employ more than 50 percent of the private workforce, and provide about two-thirds of the net new jobs added to our economy.[12] Small businesses thus contribute significantly to solving unemployment problems.

The business cycle, as discussed in Chapter 1, is an important factor in the net creation or loss of jobs. During the 2008–2009 recession, businesses with fewer than 20 employees began losing jobs as early as mid-2007. From 2008 to mid-2009, these smallest businesses accounted for 24 percent of the net job losses, while those with 20–499 employees accounted for 36 percent; the remaining 40 percent of job losses were in larger firms with more than 500 employees.[13]

Getting personal. For those who like dealing with people, small business is the place to be. Here, a business-owner-manager provides personal service to a happy customer.

© Monkey Business Images/Shutterstock

Providing Competition

Small businesses challenge larger, established firms in many ways, causing them to become more efficient and more responsive to consumer needs. A small business cannot, of course, compete with a large firm in all respects. However, a number of small firms, each competing in its own particular area and its own particular way, together have the desired competitive effect. Thus, several small janitorial companies together add up to reasonable competition for the no-longer-small ServiceMaster.

Filling Needs of Society and Other Businesses

Small firms also provide a variety of goods and services to each other and to much larger firms. Sears, Roebuck & Co. purchases merchandise from approximately 12,000 suppliers—and most of them are small businesses. General Motors relies on more than 32,000 companies for parts and supplies and depends on more than 11,000 independent dealers to sell its automobiles and trucks. Large firms generally buy parts and assemblies from smaller firms for one very good reason: It is less expensive than manufacturing the parts in their own factories. This lower cost eventually is reflected in the price that consumers pay for their products.

It is clear that small businesses are a vital part of our economy and that, as consumers and as members of the labor force, we all benefit enormously from their existence. Now let us look at the situation from the viewpoint of the owners of small businesses.

Concept Check ✱

☐ Briefly describe four contributions of small business to the American economy.

☐ Give examples of how small businesses fill needs of society and other businesses.

THE PROS AND CONS OF SMALLNESS

LEARNING OBJECTIVE
4 Judge the advantages and disadvantages of operating a small business.

Do most owners of small businesses dream that their firms will grow into giant corporations—managed by professionals—while they serve only on the board of directors? Or would they rather stay small, in a firm where they have the opportunity (and the responsibility) to do everything that needs to be done? The answers depend on the personal characteristics and motivations of the individual owners. For many, the advantages of remaining small far outweigh the disadvantages.

Advantages of Small Business

Small-business owners with limited resources often must struggle to enter competitive new markets. They also have to deal with increasing international competition. However, they enjoy several unique advantages.

PERSONAL RELATIONSHIPS WITH CUSTOMERS AND EMPLOYEES For those who like dealing with people, small business is the place to be. The owners of retail shops get to know many of their customers by name and deal with them on a personal basis. Through such relationships, small-business owners often become involved in the social, cultural, and political life of the community.

Relationships between owner-managers and employees also tend to be closer in smaller businesses. In many cases, the owner is a friend and counselor as well as the boss.

These personal relationships provide an important business advantage. The personal service small businesses offer to customers is a major competitive weapon—one that larger firms try to match but often cannot. In addition, close relationships with employees often help the small-business owner to keep effective workers who might earn more with a larger firm.

ABILITY TO ADAPT TO CHANGE Being his or her own boss, the owner-manager of a small business does not need anyone's permission to adapt to change. An owner may add or discontinue merchandise or services, change store hours, and experiment with various price strategies in response to changes in market conditions. And through personal relationships with customers, the owners of small businesses quickly become aware of changes in people's needs and interests, as well as in the activities of competing firms.

Tips from the Environmental Protection Agency

© kryczka/iStockphoto 13403524

The Environmental Protection Agency's Small Business Gateway offers a multitude of resources and ideas for small businesses going green. The site offers links to state and local environmental experts plus the latest information about complying with environmental laws and regulations. Take a look: www.epa.gov/smallbusiness/.

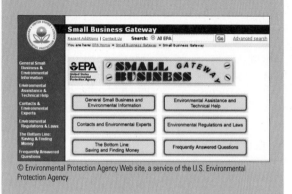

© Environmental Protection Agency Web site, a service of the U.S. Environmental Protection Agency

SIMPLIFIED RECORD KEEPING Many small firms need only a simple set of records. Record keeping might consist of a checkbook, a cash-receipts journal in which to record all sales, and a cash-disbursements journal in which to record all amounts paid out. Obviously, enough records must be kept to allow for producing and filing accurate tax returns.

INDEPENDENCE Small-business owners do not have to punch in and out, bid for vacation times, take orders from superiors, or worry about being fired or laid off. They are the masters of their own destinies—at least with regard to employment. For many people, this is the prime advantage of owning a small business.

OTHER ADVANTAGES According to the SBA, the most profitable companies in the United States are small firms that have been in business for more than ten years and employ fewer than 20 people. Small-business owners also enjoy all the advantages of sole proprietorships, which were discussed in Chapter 4. These include being able to keep all profits, the ease and low cost of going into business and (if necessary) going out of business, and being able to keep business information secret.

Disadvantages of Small Business

Personal contacts with customers, closer relationships with employees, being one's own boss, less cumbersome record-keeping chores, and independence are the bright side of small business. In contrast, the dark side reflects problems unique to these firms.

RISK OF FAILURE As we have noted, small businesses (especially new ones) run a heavy risk of going out of business—about two out of three close their doors within the first six years. Older, well-established small firms can be hit hard by a business recession mainly because they do not have the financial resources to weather an extended difficult period.

LIMITED POTENTIAL Small businesses that survive do so with varying degrees of success. Many are simply the means of making a living for the owner and his or her family. The owner may have some technical skill—as a hair stylist or electrician, for example—and may have started a business to put this skill to work. Such a business is unlikely to grow into big business. In addition, employees' potential for advancement is limited.

LIMITED ABILITY TO RAISE CAPITAL Small businesses typically have a limited ability to obtain capital. Figure 5-2 shows that most small-business financing comes out of the owner's pocket. Personal loans from lending institutions provide only about one-fourth of the capital required by small businesses. About 50 percent of all new firms begin with less than $30,000 in total capital, according to Census Bureau and Federal Reserve surveys. In fact, almost 36 percent of new firms begin with less than $20,000, usually provided by the owner or family members and friends.[14]

Although every person who considers starting a small business should be aware of the hazards and pitfalls we have noted, a well-conceived business plan may help to avoid the risk of failure. The U.S. government is also dedicated to helping small businesses make it. It expresses this aim most actively through the SBA.

Developing a Business Plan

Lack of planning can be as deadly as lack of money to a new small business. Planning is important to any business, large or small, and never should be overlooked or taken lightly. A **business plan** is a carefully constructed guide for the person starting a business. Consider it as a tool with three basic purposes: communication, management, and planning. As a communication tool, a business plan serves as a concise

business plan a carefully constructed guide for the person starting a business

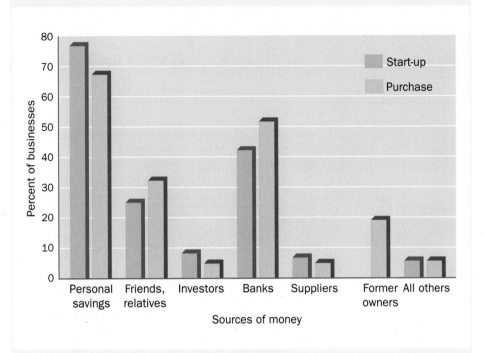

FIGURE 5-2: Sources of Capital for Entrepreneurs

Small businesses get financing from various sources; the most important is personal savings.

Source: Data developed and provided by the National Federation of Independent Business Foundation and sponsored by the American Express Travel Related Services Company, Inc.

document that potential investors can examine to see if they would like to invest or assist in financing a new venture. It shows whether a business has the potential to make a profit. As a management tool, the business plan helps to track, monitor, and evaluate the progress. The business plan is a living document; it is modified as the entrepreneur gains knowledge and experience. It also serves to establish time lines and milestones and allows comparison of growth projections against actual accomplishments. Finally, as a planning tool, the business plan guides a businessperson through the various phases of business. For example, the plan helps to identify obstacles to avoid and to establish alternatives. According to Robert Krummer, Jr., chairman of First Business Bank in Los Angeles, "The business plan is a necessity. If the person who wants to start a small business can't put a business plan together, he or she is in trouble."

Personal App Although writing a business plan won't guarantee your success, it will help you think through many of the issues that can trip up entrepreneurs. And if you work for a big company, you may find yourself writing a kind of business plan for a product or project.

Components of a Business Plan

Table 5-3 shows the 12 sections that a business plan should include. Each section is further explained at the end of each of the seven major parts in the text. The goal of each end-of-the-part exercise is to help a businessperson create his or her own business plan. When constructing a business plan, the businessperson should strive to keep it easy to read, uncluttered, and complete. Like other busy executives, officials of financial institutions do not have the time to wade through pages of extraneous data. The business plan should answer the four questions banking officials and

entrepreneurial SUCCESS

Prep Your Elevator Pitch

Imagine that you've just stepped into an elevator with a potential investor. You have a mere 60 seconds to pitch your business idea before the ride is over and the doors open. Are you ready?

Successful entrepreneurs are always perfecting their "elevator pitch," a quick, to-the-point summary of the business proposition. In just a minute or two, you should be able to clearly and succinctly explain what your business is about and the opportunity or problem you're addressing. Practice until you can project confidence and high energy without appearing rushed or overly aggressive. Just as important, a good elevator pitch should end with a "call to action," such as asking for a meeting to discuss more details.

"Entrepreneur Idol" Jordan Leahy knows how to make every second count. A student at the University of Wisconsin–Whitewater, Leahy recently won the Northwestern University "elevator pitch" competition with a one-minute summary of his newest business venture. In addition to a cash prize, Leahy won an internship at a venture-capital firm. The day after his win, he received a call from one of the judges, a potential investor who requested more details about the business idea. That's the point of having your elevator pitch ready: "You never know when or where you'll meet your next investor," Leahy explains.

Sources: Scott Austin, "How to Pitch a Venture Capitalist on a Napkin," *Wall Street Journal Blog,* January 11, 2010, http://blogs.wsj.com/venturecapital/2010/01/11/how-to-pitch-a-venture-capitalist-on-a-napkin/?mod5rss_WSJBlog; "UW-Whitewater Student Entrepreneur Wins 'Entrepreneur Idol' Elevator Pitch Competition," *WisBusiness.com (Wisconsin),* November 24, 2009, www.wisbusiness.com/index.iml?Article5177894; Scott Andron, "Entrepreneurs Seek Success in a Minute," *Miami Herald,* November 20, 2009, www.miamiherald.com/business/small-business/story/1342790.html; Daisy Wademan Dowling, "How to Perfect an Elevator Pitch about Yourself," *Harvard Business Review Blog,* May 4, 2009, http://blogs.harvardbusiness.org/dowling/2009/05/how-to-perfect-an-elevator-pit.html.

TABLE 5-3: Components of a Business Plan

1. *Introduction.* Basic information such as the name, address, and phone number of the business; the date the plan was issued; and a statement of confidentiality to keep important information away from potential competitors.

2. *Executive Summary.* A one- to two-page overview of the entire business plan, including a justification why the business will succeed.

3. *Benefits to the Community.* Information on how the business will have an impact on economic development, community development, and human development.

4. *Company and Industry.* The background of the company, choice of the legal business form, information on the products or services to be offered, and examination of the potential customers, current competitors, and the business's future.

5. *Management Team.* Discussion of skills, talents, and job descriptions of management team, managerial compensation, management training needs, and professional assistance requirements.

6. *Manufacturing and Operations Plan.* Discussion of facilities needed, space requirements, capital equipment, labor force, inventory control, and purchasing requirement.

7. *Labor Force.* Discussion of the quality of skilled workers available and the training, compensation, and motivation of workers.

8. *Marketing Plan.* Discussion of markets, market trends, competition, market share, pricing, promotion, distribution, and service policy.

9. *Financial Plan.* Summary of the investment needed, sales and cash flow forecasts, breakeven analysis, and sources of funding.

10. *Exit Strategy.* Discussion of a succession plan or going public. Who will take over the business?

11. *Critical Risks and Assumptions.* Evaluation of the weaknesses of the business and how the company plans to deal with these and other business problems.

12. *Appendix.* Supplementary information crucial to the plan, such as résumés of owners and principal managers, advertising samples, organization chart, and any related information.

Source: Adapted from Timothy S. Hatten, *Small Business Management: Entrepreneurship and Beyond,* 4th ed. Copyright © 2009 by Houghton Mifflin Company, 93–118. Reprinted with permission.

TABLE 5-4: Business Plan Checklist

1. Does the executive summary grab the reader's attention and highlight the major points of the business plan?
2. Does the business-concept section clearly describe the purpose of the business, the customers, the value proposition, and the distribution channel and convey a compelling story?
3. Do the industry and market analyses support acceptance and demand for the business concept in the marketplace and define a first customer in depth?
4. Does the management team plan persuade the reader that the team could implement the business concept successfully? Does it assure the reader that an effective infrastructure is in place to facilitate the goals and operations of the company?
5. Does the product/service plan clearly provide details on the status of the product, the time line for completion, and the intellectual property that will be acquired?
6. Does the operations plan prove that the product or service could be produced and distributed efficiently and effectively?
7. Does the marketing plan successfully demonstrate how the company will create customer awareness in the target market and deliver the benefit to the customer?
8. Does the financial plan convince the reader that the business model is sustainable—that it will provide a superior return on investment for the investor and sufficient cash flow to repay loans to potential lenders?
9. Does the growth plan convince the reader that the company has long-term growth potential and spin-off products and services?
10. Does the contingency and exit-strategy plan convince the reader that the risk associated with this venture can be mediated? Is there an exit strategy in place for investors?

Source: Kathleen R. Allen, *Launching New Ventures: An Entrepreneurial Approach,* 4th ed. Copyright © 2006 by Houghton Mifflin Company, 197. Reprinted with permission.

investors are most interested in: (1) What exactly is the nature and mission of the new venture? (2) Why is this new enterprise a good idea? (3) What are the business-person's goals? (4) How much will the new venture cost?

The great amount of time and consideration that should go into creating a business plan probably will end up saving time later. For example, Sharon Burch, who was running a computer software business while earning a degree in business administration, had to write a business plan as part of one of her courses. Burch has said, "I wish I'd taken the class before I started my business. I see a lot of things I could have done differently. But it has helped me since because I've been using the business plan as a guide for my business." Table 5-4 provides a business plan checklist. Accuracy and realistic expectations are crucial to an effective business plan. It is unethical to deceive loan officers, and it is unwise to deceive yourself.

THE SMALL BUSINESS ADMINISTRATION

The **Small Business Administration (SBA)**, created by Congress in 1953, is a governmental agency that assists, counsels, and protects the interests of small businesses in the United States. It helps people get into business and stay in business. The agency provides assistance to owners and managers of prospective, new, and established small businesses. Through more than 1,000 offices and resource centers throughout the nation, the SBA provides both financial assistance and management counseling. Recently, the SBA provided training, technical assistance, and education to more than 3 million small businesses. It helps small firms to bid for and obtain government contracts, and it helps them to prepare to enter foreign markets.

SBA Management Assistance

Statistics show that most failures in small business are related to poor management. For this reason, the SBA places special emphasis on improving the management ability of the owners and managers of small businesses. The SBA's Management Assistance Program is extensive and diversified. It includes free individual counseling, courses, conferences, workshops, and a wide range of publications. Recently, the

Concept Check ✱

☐ What are the major advantages and disadvantages of smallness in business?

☐ What are the major components of a business plan? Why should an individual develop a business plan?

LEARNING OBJECTIVE

5 Explain how the Small Business Administration helps small businesses.

Small Business Administration (SBA) a governmental agency that assists, counsels, and protects the interests of small businesses in the United States

SBA provided management and technical assistance to nearly 1 million small businesses through its 1,100 Small Business Development Centers and 13,000 volunteers from the Service Corps of Retired Executives.[15]

MANAGEMENT COURSES AND WORKSHOPS The management courses offered by the SBA cover all the functions, duties, and roles of managers. Instructors may be teachers from local colleges and universities or other professionals, such as management consultants, bankers, lawyers, and accountants. Fees for these courses are quite low. The most popular such course is a general survey of eight to ten different areas of business management. In follow-up studies, businesspeople may concentrate in-depth on one or more of these areas depending on their particular strengths and weaknesses. The SBA occasionally offers one-day conferences. These conferences are aimed at keeping owner-managers up-to-date on new management developments, tax laws, and the like. The Small Business Training Network (SBTN) is an online training network consisting of 83 SBA-run courses, workshops, and resources. Some of the most requested courses include Entrepreneurship, Starting and Managing Your Own Business, Developing a Business Plan, Managing the Digital Enterprise, Identify Your Target Market, and Analyze Profitability. Find out more at www.sba.gov/training. Recently, more than 240,000 small-business owners benefited from SBA's free online business courses.

SCORE The **Service Corps of Retired Executives (SCORE)**, created in 1964, is a group of more than 13,000 retired and active businesspeople including more than 2,000 women who volunteer their services to small businesses through the SBA. The collective experience of SCORE volunteers spans the full range of American enterprise. These volunteers have worked for such notable companies as Eastman Kodak, General Electric, IBM, and Procter & Gamble. Experts in areas of accounting, finance, marketing, engineering, and retailing provide counseling and mentoring to entrepreneurs.

A small-business owner who has a particular problem can request free counseling from SCORE. An assigned counselor visits the owner in his or her establishment and, through careful observation, analyzes the business situation and the problem. If the problem is complex, the counselor may call on other volunteer experts to assist. Finally, the counselor offers a plan for solving the problem and helping the owner through the critical period.

Consider the plight of Elizabeth Halvorsen, a mystery writer from Minneapolis. Her husband had built up the family advertising and graphic arts firm for 17 years when he was called in 1991 to serve in the Persian Gulf War. The only one left behind who could run the business was Mrs. Halvorsen, who admittedly had no business experience. Enter SCORE. With a SCORE management expert at her side, she kept the business on track. Recently, SCORE volunteers served more than 523,800 small-business people like Mrs. Halvorsen through its 364 offices. The 13,000 counselors provided 203,000 face-to-face counseling sessions, 119,000 online counseling sessions, and more than 49,500 online workshops to more than 201,000 workshop participants. Since its inception, SCORE has assisted more than 9 million small-business people with online and face-to-face small business counseling.[16]

Help for Minority-Owned Small Businesses

Americans who are members of minority groups have had difficulty entering the nation's economic mainstream. Raising money is a nagging problem for minority business owners, who also may lack adequate training. Members of minority groups are, of course, eligible for all SBA programs, but the SBA makes a special effort to assist those minority groups who want to start small businesses or expand existing ones. For example, the Minority Business Development Agency awards grants to develop and increase business opportunities for members of racial and ethnic minorities.

Helping women become entrepreneurs is also a special goal of the SBA. Emily Harrington, one of nine children, was born in Manila, the Philippines. She

Service Corps of Retired Executives (SCORE) a group of businesspeople who volunteer their services to small businesses through the SBA

arrived in the United States in 1972 as a foreign-exchange student. Convinced that there was a market for hard-working, dedicated minorities and women, she launched Qualified Resources, Inc. *Inc.* magazine selected her firm as one of "America's Fastest Growing Private Companies" just six years later. Harrington credits the SBA with giving her the technical support that made her first loan possible. Finding a SCORE counselor who worked directly with her, she refined her business plan until she got a bank loan. Before contacting the SBA, Harrington was turned down for business loans "by all the banks I approached," even though she worked as a manager of loan credit and collection for a bank. Later, Emily Harrington was SBA's winner of the local, regional, and national Small Business Entrepreneurial Success Award for Rhode Island, the New England region, and the nation! For several years in a row, Qualified Resources, Inc., was named one of the fastest growing private companies in Rhode Island. Now with more than 100 Women's Business Centers, entrepreneurs like Harrington can receive training and technical assistance, access to credit and capital, federal contracts, and international markets. The SBA's Online Women's Business Center (www.sba.gov/content/womens-business-centers) is a state-of-the-art Internet site to help women expand their businesses. This free, interactive Web site offers women information about business principles and practices, management techniques, networking, industry news, market research and technology training, online counseling, and hundreds of links to other sites, as well as information about the many SBA services and resources available to them.

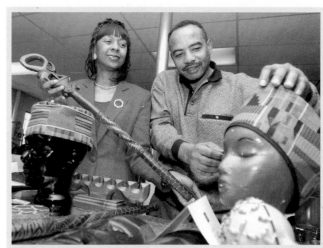

Banking on the Banks. Meet Marilyn and Dwayne Banks, owners of Marilyn's Gift Gallery and Sound World Music in their East Waco, TX, gift shop. Since opening their business in 1989, they have helped start many community projects including an association to help minority business owners in the area.

SMALL-BUSINESS INSTITUTES Small-business institutes (SBIs), created in 1972, are groups of senior and graduate students in business administration who provide management counseling to small businesses. SBIs have been set up on more than 520 college campuses as another way to help business owners. The students work in small groups guided by faculty advisers and SBA management-assistance experts. Like SCORE volunteers, they analyze and help solve the problems of small-business owners at their business establishments.

SMALL-BUSINESS DEVELOPMENT CENTERS Small-business development centers (SBDCs), created in July 1980, are university-based groups that provide individual counseling and practical training to owners of small businesses. SBDCs draw from the resources of local, state, and federal governments, private businesses, and universities. These groups can provide managerial and technical help, data from research studies, and other types of specialized assistance of value to small businesses. In 2011, there were more than 1,000 SBDC locations, primarily at colleges and universities, assisting people such as Kathleen DuBois. After scribbling a list of her abilities and the names of potential clients on a napkin in a local restaurant, Kathleen DuBois decided to start her own marketing firm. Beth Thornton launched her engineering firm after a discussion with a colleague in the ladies room of the Marriott. When Richard Shell was laid off after 20 years of service with Nisource (Columbia Gas), he searched the Internet tirelessly before finding the right franchise option. Introduced by mutual friends, Jim Bostic and Denver McMillion quickly connected, built a high level of trust, and combined their diverse professional backgrounds to form a manufacturing company. Although these entrepreneurs took different routes in starting their new businesses in West Virginia, all of them turned to the West Virginia Small Business Development Center for the technical assistance to make their dreams become a reality.

small-business institutes (SBIs) groups of senior and graduate students in business administration who provide management counseling to small businesses

small-business development centers (SBDCs) university-based groups that provide individual counseling and practical training to owners of small businesses

Are you a student entrepreneur? Find out whether your local small-business development center has a special program for students who start their own firms. Many do—and they're an excellent source of information, advice, and assistance.

SBA PUBLICATIONS The SBA issues management, marketing, and technical publications dealing with hundreds of topics of interest to present and prospective managers of small firms. Most of these publications are available from the SBA Web site at www.sba.gov. Others can be obtained for a small fee from the U.S. Government Printing Office.

SBA Financial Assistance

Small businesses seem to be constantly in need of money. An owner may have enough capital to start and operate the business. But then he or she may require more money to finance increased operations during peak selling seasons, to pay for required pollution control equipment, to finance an expansion, or to mop up after a natural disaster such as a flood or a terrorist attack. For example, the Supplemental Terrorist Activity Relief program has made $3.7 billion in loans to 8,202 small businesses harmed or disrupted by the September 11 terrorist attacks. In October 2005, the SBA guaranteed loans of up to $150,000 to small businesses affected by Hurricanes Katrina and Rita. Since the 2005 hurricanes, SBA has made more than $4.9 billion in disaster loans to 102,903 homeowners and renters in the Gulf region. Businesses in the area received 16,828 business disaster loans with disbursements worth $1.5 billion.[17] In 2010, the SBA offered economic injury loans to fishing and fishing-dependent small businesses as a result of the Deepwater BP spill that shut down commercial and recreational fishing waters. According to the SBA Administrator Karen Mills, "SBA remains committed to taking every step to help small businesses deal with the financial challenges they are facing as a result of the Deepwater BP oil spill."[18] The SBA offers special financial-assistance programs that cover all these situations. However, its primary financial function is to guarantee loans to eligible businesses.

venture capital money that is invested in small (and sometimes struggling) firms that have the potential to become very successful

small-business investment companies (SBICs) privately owned firms that provide venture capital to small enterprises that meet their investment standards

REGULAR BUSINESS LOANS Most of the SBA's business loans are actually made by private lenders such as banks, but repayment is partially guaranteed by the agency. That is, the SBA may guarantee that it will repay the lender up to 90 percent of the loan if the borrowing firm cannot repay it. Guaranteed loans approved on or after October 1, 2002, may be as large as $1.5 million (this loan limit may be increased in the future). The average size of an SBA-guaranteed business loan is about $300,000, and its average duration is about eight years.

SMALL-BUSINESS INVESTMENT COMPANIES Venture capital is money that is invested in small (and sometimes struggling) firms that have the potential to become very successful. In many cases, only a lack of capital keeps these firms from rapid and solid growth. The high net-worth people (angel investors) who invest in such firms expect that their investments will grow with the firms and become quite profitable.

The popularity of these investments has increased over the past 40 years, but most small firms still have difficulty obtaining venture capital. To help such businesses, the SBA licenses, regulates, and provides financial assistance to **small-business investment companies (SBICs)**. The 2011 complete listing of all licensees by state is available at www.sba.gov/content/all-sbc-licensees-state.

Making music at the Modesto Academy of Music & Design. After giving private piano lessons for more than 25 years, Pam Tallman of Modesto, California, used an SBA loan to help finance the purchase of a building to open the academy. The school offers music, art, design, and computer classes for students aged two years and older.

© Newscom

Part 2: Business Ownership and Entrepreneurship

An SBIC is a privately owned firm that provides venture capital to small enterprises that meet its investment standards. Such firms as America Online, Apple Computer, Federal Express, Compaq Computer, Intel Corporation, Outback Steakhouse, and Staples, Inc., all were financed through SBICs during their initial growth period. SBICs are intended to be profit-making organizations. The aid that SBA offers allows them to invest in small businesses that otherwise would not attract venture capital. Since Congress created the program in 1958, SBICs have financed more than 102,000 small businesses for a total of about $50.6 billion. Recently, SBIC benefited 1,477 businesses, and 24 percent of these firms were less than two years old.[19]

State of Small Business During the Recession

Celebrating the 47th annual observance of National Small Business Week in May 2010, President Obama stated,

> Our nation is still emerging from one of the worst recessions in our history, and small businesses were among the hardest hit. From mom-and-pop stores to high tech start-ups, countless small businesses have been forced to lay off employees or shut their doors entirely. In these difficult times, we must do all we can to help these firms recover from the recession and put Americans back to work. Our government cannot guarantee a company's success, but it can help create market conditions that allow small businesses to thrive.
>
> My Administration is committed to helping small businesses drive our economy toward recovery and long-term growth. The American Recovery and Reinvestment Act has supported billions of dollars in loans and Federal contracts for small businesses across the country. The Affordable Care Act makes it easier for small business owners to provide health insurance to their employees, and gives entrepreneurs the security they need to innovate and take risks. We have enacted new tax cuts and tax credits for small firms. Still, we must do more to empower these companies. Small businesses are the engine of our prosperity and a proud reflection of our character. A healthy small business sector will give us vibrant communities, cutting-edge technology, and an American economy that can compete and win in the 21st century.[20]

As if the recession was not enough, in the states near the Gulf of Mexico, many small businesses suffered financial losses following the April 20, 2010, Deepwater BP oil spill that shut down commercial and recreational fishing along the coasts. According to the SBA Administrator, Karen Mills, "With the region still recovering from previous devastation and the national recession of the last couple of years, it's critical that we take every step we can to provide small businesses with resources to make it through this latest crisis so that they can continue to drive local economic growth and provide good-paying jobs." The SBA is offering working capital loans up to $2 million at an interest rate of 4 percent with terms up to 30 years.[21]

We have discussed the importance of the small-business segment of our economy. We have weighed the advantages and drawbacks of operating a small business as compared with a large one. But is there a way to achieve the best of both worlds? Can one preserve one's independence as a business owner and still enjoy some of the benefits of "bigness"? Let's take a close look at franchising.

FRANCHISING

A **franchise** is a license to operate an individually owned business as if it were part of a chain of outlets or stores. Often, the business itself is also called a *franchise*. Among the most familiar franchises are McDonald's, H&R Block, AAMCO Transmissions, GNC (General Nutrition Centers), and Dairy Queen. Many other franchises carry familiar names; this method of doing business has become very popular in the last 30 years or so. It is an attractive means of starting and operating a small business.

Concept Check ✱

☐ Identify six ways in which the SBA provides management assistance to small businesses.

☐ Identify two ways in which the SBA provides financial assistance to small businesses.

☐ Why does the SBA concentrate on providing management and financial assistance to small business?

☐ What is venture capital? How does the SBA help small businesses to obtain it?

LEARNING OBJECTIVE

6 Appraise the concept and types of franchising.

franchise a license to operate an individually owned business as though it were part of a chain of outlets or stores

TABLE 5-5: Basic Rights and Obligations Delineated in a Franchise Agreement

Franchisee rights include:

1. use of trademarks, trade names, and patents of the franchisor.
2. use of the brand image and the design and decor of the premises developed by the franchisor.
3. use of the franchisor's secret methods.
4. use of the franchisor's copyrighted materials.
5. use of recipes, formulae, specifications, processes, and methods of manufacture developed by the franchisor.
6. conducting the franchised business upon or from the agreed premises strictly in accordance with the franchisor's methods and subject to the franchisor's directions
7. guidelines established by the franchisor regarding exclusive territorial rights.
8. rights to obtain supplies from nominated suppliers at special prices.

Franchisee obligations include:

1. to carry on the business franchised and no other business upon the approved and nominated premises.
2. to observe certain minimum operating hours.
3. to pay a franchise fee.
4. to follow the accounting system laid down by the franchisor.
5. not to advertise without prior approval of the advertisements by the franchisor.
6. to use and display such point-of-sale advertising materials as the franchisor stipulates.
7. to maintain the premises in good, clean, and sanitary condition and to redecorate when required to do so by the franchisor.
8. to maintain the widest possible insurance coverage.
9. to permit the franchisor's staff to enter the premises to inspect and see if the franchisor's standards are being maintained.
10. to purchase goods or products from the franchisor or his designated suppliers.
11. to train the staff in the franchisor's methods to ensure that they are neatly and appropriately clothed.
12. not to assign the franchise contract without the franchisor's consent.

Source: Excerpted from the SBA's "Is Franchising for Me?" http://ftp.sbaonline.sba.gov/idc/groups/public/documents/sba_homepage/serv_sbp_isfforme.pdf (accessed March 17, 2011).

What Is Franchising?

Franchising is the actual granting of a franchise. A **franchisor** is an individual or organization granting a franchise. A **franchisee** is a person or organization purchasing a franchise. The franchisor supplies a known and advertised business name, management skills, the required training and materials, and a method of doing business. The franchisee supplies labor and capital, operates the franchised business, and agrees to abide by the provisions of the franchise agreement. Table 5-5 lists the basic franchisee rights and obligations that would be covered in a typical franchise agreement.

Types of Franchising

Franchising arrangements fall into three general categories. In the first approach, a manufacturer authorizes a number of retail stores to sell a certain brand-name item. This type of franchising arrangement, one of the oldest, is prevalent in sales of passenger cars and trucks, farm equipment, shoes, paint, earth-moving equipment, and petroleum. About 90 percent of all gasoline is sold through franchised, independent retail service stations, and franchised dealers handle virtually all sales of new cars and trucks. In the second type of franchising arrangement, a producer licenses distributors to sell a given product to retailers. This arrangement is common in the soft drink industry. Most national manufacturers of soft drink syrups— The Coca-Cola Company, Dr. Pepper/Seven-Up Companies, PepsiCo, Royal Crown

franchising the actual granting of a franchise

franchisor an individual or organization granting a franchise

franchisee a person or organization purchasing a franchise

Companies, Inc.—franchise independent bottlers who then serve retailers. In a third form of franchising, a franchisor supplies brand names, techniques, or other services instead of a complete product. Although the franchisor may provide certain production and distribution services, its primary role is the careful development and control of marketing strategies. This approach to franchising, which is the most typical today, is used by Holiday Inns, Howard Johnson Company, AAMCO Transmissions, McDonald's, Dairy Queen, Avis, Hertz Corporation, KFC (Kentucky Fried Chicken), and SUBWAY, to name but a few.

Concept Check *

☐ Explain the relationships among a franchise, the franchisor, and the franchisee.

☐ Describe the three general categories of franchising arrangements.

THE GROWTH OF FRANCHISING

Franchising, which began in the United States around the time of the Civil War, was used originally by large firms, such as the Singer Sewing Company, to distribute their products. Franchising has been increasing steadily in popularity since the early 1900s, primarily for filling stations and car dealerships; however, this retailing strategy has experienced enormous growth since the mid-1970s. The franchise proliferation generally has paralleled the expansion of the fast-food industry. As Table 5-6 shows, three of *Entrepreneur* magazine's top-rated franchises for 2010 were in this category.

LEARNING OBJECTIVE

7 Analyze the growth of franchising and franchising's advantages and disadvantages.

Of course, franchising is not limited to fast foods. Hair salons, tanning parlors, and dentists and lawyers are expected to participate in franchising arrangements in growing numbers. Franchised health clubs, pest exterminators, and campgrounds are already widespread, as are franchised tax preparers and travel agencies. The real estate industry also has experienced a rapid increase in franchising.

Also, franchising is attracting more women and minority business owners in the United States than ever before. One reason is that special outreach programs designed to encourage franchisee diversity have developed. Consider Angela Trammel, a young mother of two. She had been laid off from her job at the Marriott after 9/11. Since she was a member of a Curves Fitness Center and liked the concept of empowering women to become physically fit, she began researching the cost of purchasing a Curves

TABLE 5-6: Entrepreneur's Top Ten Franchises in 2011

Rank	Franchise	Total Investment	Franchise Fee	Royalty Fee	Net-Worth Requirement	Cash Requirement	Comments
1	Hampton Hotels	$3,716,000–$13,148,800	$50,000	5%			22-years renewable
2	Ampm	$1,786,929–$7,596,688	$30,000–$70,000	5%		$700,000–$1,000,000	20-years renewable
3	McDonald's	$1,057,200–$1,885,000	$45,000	12.5%+		$500,000	20-years renewable
4	7-Eleven Inc.	$30,800–$604,500	$10,000–$440,400	Varies	$127,000		15-years renewable
5	Supercuts	$119,350–$196,550	$22,500	6%	$300,000	$100,000	Conditional renewable
6	Days Inn	$192,291–$6,479,764	$36,000–$37,500	5.5%			15- to 20-years renewable
7	Vanguard Cleaning Systems	$8,200–$38,100	$7,650–$37,000	5%		$2,800–$9,000	10-years renewable
8	Servpro	$127,300–$174,700	$41,000	3–10%	$100,000	$60,000	5-years renewable
9	Subway	$84,300–$258,300	$15,000	8%	$30,000–$90,000	$80,000–$310,000	20-years renewable
10	Denny's Inc.	$1,125,609–$2,396,419	$40,000	4%	$1,000,000	$350,000	20-years renewable

Source: www.entrepreneur.com/franchise500/index.html (accessed March 15, 2011).

© Stephen Shaver/Landov

franchise and ways to finance the business. "I was online looking for financing, and I linked to Enterprise Development Group in Washington, DC. I knew that they had diverse clients." The cost for the franchise was $19,500, but it took $60,000 to open the doors to her fitness center. "Applying for a loan to start the business was much harder than buying a house," said Trammel. Just three years later, Angela and her husband, Ernest, own three Curves Fitness Centers with 12 employees. Recently, since giving birth to her third child, she has found the financial freedom and flexibility needed to care for her busy family. In fact, within a three-year period, the Trammels grew their annual household income from $80,000 to $250,000.[22]

Franchisors such as Wendy's, McDonald's, Burger King, and Church's Chicken all have special corporate programs to attract minority and women franchisees. Just as important, successful women and minority franchisees are willing to get involved by offering advice and guidance to new franchisees.

Herman Petty, the first African-American McDonald's franchisee, remembers that the company provided a great deal of help while he worked to establish his first units. In turn, Petty traveled to help other black franchisees, and he invited new franchisees to gain hands-on experience in his Chicago restaurants before starting their own establishments. Petty also organized a support group, the National Black McDonald's Operators Association, to help black franchisees in other areas. Today, this support group has 33 local chapters and more than 330 members across the country. "We are really concentrating on helping our operators to be successful both operationally and financially," says Craig Welburn, the McDonald's franchisee who leads the group.

Dual-branded franchises, in which two franchisors offer their products together, are a new small-business trend. For example, in 1993, pleased with the success of its first cobranded restaurant with Texaco in Beebe, Arkansas, McDonald's now has more than 400 cobranded restaurants in the United States. Also, an agreement between franchisors Doctor's Associates, Inc., and TCBY Enterprises, Inc., now allows franchisees to sell SUBWAY sandwiches and TCBY yogurt in the same establishment.

Are Franchises Successful?

Franchising is designed to provide a tested formula for success, along with ongoing advice and training. The success rate for businesses owned and operated by franchisees is significantly higher than the success rate for other independently owned small businesses. In a recent nationwide Gallup poll of 944 franchise owners, 94 percent of franchisees indicated that they were very or somewhat successful, only 5 percent believed that they were very unsuccessful or somewhat unsuccessful, and 1 percent did not know. Despite these impressive statistics, franchising is not a guarantee of success for either franchisees or franchisors. Too rapid expansion, inadequate capital or management skills, and a host of other problems can cause failure for both franchisee and franchisor. Thus, for example, the Dizzy Dean's Beef and Burger franchise is no longer in business. Timothy Bates, a Wayne State University economist, warns, "Despite the hype that franchising is the safest way to go when starting a new business, the research just doesn't bear that out." Just consider Boston Chicken, which once had more than 1,200 restaurants before declaring bankruptcy in 1998.

Advantages of Franchising

Franchising plays a vital role in our economy and soon may become the dominant form of retailing. Why? Because franchising offers advantages to both the franchisor and the franchisee.

TO THE FRANCHISOR The franchisor gains fast and well-controlled distribution of its products without incurring the high cost of constructing and operating its own outlets. The franchisor thus has more capital available to expand production and to use for advertising. At the same time, it can ensure, through the franchise agreement, that outlets are maintained and operated according to its own standards.

The franchisor also benefits from the fact that the franchisee—a sole proprietor in most cases—is likely to be very highly motivated to succeed. The success of the franchise means more sales, which translate into higher royalties for the franchisor.

© Susan Van Etten

TO THE FRANCHISEE The franchisee gets the opportunity to start a business with limited capital and to make use of the business experience of others. Moreover, an outlet with a nationally advertised name, such as Radio Shack, McDonald's, or Century 21 Real Estate, has guaranteed customers as soon as it opens.

Personal App Local business owners who become franchisees of well-known brands are hoping for an edge that will help them succeed. But having a well-known brand is only the start. Franchisees must give you good service if they want to keep you as a customer.

If business problems arise, the franchisor gives the franchisee guidance and advice. This counseling is primarily responsible for the very high degree of success enjoyed by franchises. In most cases, the franchisee does not pay for such help.

The franchisee also receives materials to use in local advertising and can take part in national promotional campaigns sponsored by the franchisor. McDonald's and its franchisees, for example, constitute one of the nation's top 20 purchasers of advertising. Finally, the franchisee may be able to minimize the cost of advertising, supplies, and various business necessities by purchasing them in cooperation with other franchisees.

Disadvantages of Franchising

The main disadvantage of franchising affects the franchisee, and it arises because the franchisor retains a great deal of control. The franchisor's contract can dictate every aspect of the business: decor, design of employee uniforms, types of signs, and all the details of business operations. All Burger King French fries taste the same because all Burger King franchisees have to make them the same way.

Contract disputes are the cause of many lawsuits. For example, Rekha Gabhawala, a Dunkin' Donuts franchisee in Milwaukee, alleged that the franchisor was forcing her out of business so that the company could profit by reselling the downtown franchise to someone else; the company, on the other hand, alleged that Gabhawala breached the contract by not running the business according to company standards. In another case, Dunkin' Donuts sued Chris Romanias, its franchisee in Pennsylvania, alleging that Romanias intentionally underreported gross sales to the company. Romanias, on the other hand, alleged that Dunkin' Donuts, Inc., breached the contract because it failed to provide assistance in operating the franchise. Other franchisees claim that contracts are unfairly tilted toward the franchisors. Yet others have charged that they lost their franchise and investment because their franchisor would not approve the sale of the business when they found a buyer.

To arbitrate disputes between franchisors and franchisees, the National Franchise Mediation Program was established in 1993 by 30 member firms, including Burger King Corporation, McDonald's Corporation, and Wendy's International, Inc. Negotiators have since resolved numerous cases through mediation. Recently, Carl's Jr. brought in one of its largest franchisees to help set its system straight, making most franchisees happy for the first time in years. The program also helped PepsiCo settle a long-term contract dispute and renegotiate its franchise agreements.

Because disagreements between franchisors and franchisees have increased in recent years, many franchisees have been demanding government regulation of

SPOTLIGHT

SUBWAY's Foreign Franchising Around the World

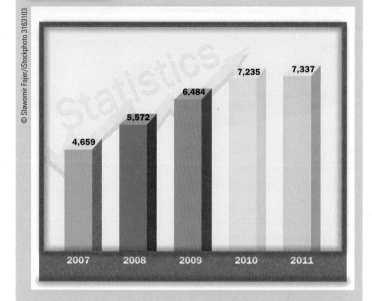

© Slawomir Fajer/iStockphoto 3163103

4,659 — 2007
5,572 — 2008
6,484 — 2009
7,235 — 2010
7,337 — 2011

Source: www.entrepreneur.com/franchises/subway/282839-0.html (accessed March 18, 2011).

franchising. In 1997, to avoid government regulation, some of the largest franchisors proposed a new self-policing plan to the Federal Trade Commission.

Franchise holders pay for their security, usually with a one-time franchise fee and continuing royalty and advertising fees, collected as a percentage of sales. As Table 5-6 shows, a SUBWAY franchisee pays an initial franchise fee of $15,000 and an annual fee of 8 percent of gross sales. In Table 5-6, you can see how much money a franchisee needs to start a new franchise for selected organizations. In some fields, franchise agreements are not uniform. One franchisee may pay more than another for the same services.

Even success can cause problems. Sometimes a franchise is so successful that the franchisor opens its own outlet nearby, in direct competition—although franchisees may fight back. For example, a court recently ruled that Burger King could not enter into direct competition with the franchisee because the contract was not specific on the issue. A spokesperson for one franchisor contends that the company "gives no geographical protection" to its franchise holders and thus is free to move in on them. Franchise operators work hard. They often put in 10- and 12-hour days, six days a week. The International Franchise Association advises prospective franchise purchasers to investigate before investing and to approach buying a franchise cautiously. Franchises vary widely in approach as well as in products. Some, such as Dunkin' Donuts and Baskin-Robbins, demand long hours. Others, such as Great Clips hair salons and Albert's Family Restaurants, are more appropriate for those who do not want to spend many hours at their stores.

Global Perspectives in Small Business

For small American businesses, the world is becoming smaller. National and international economies are growing more and more interdependent as political leadership and national economic directions change and trade barriers diminish or disappear. Globalization and instant worldwide communications are rapidly shrinking distances at the same time that they are expanding business opportunities. According to a recent study, the Internet is increasingly important to small-business strategic thinking, with more than 50 percent of those surveyed indicating that the Internet represented their most favored strategy for growth. This was more than double the next-favored choice, strategic alliances reflecting the opportunity to reach both global and domestic customers. The Internet and online payment systems enable even very small businesses to serve international customers. In fact, technology now gives small businesses the leverage and power to reach markets that were once limited solely to large corporations. No wonder the number of businesses exporting their goods and services has tripled since 1990, with two-thirds of that boom coming from companies with fewer than 20 employees.[23]

Personal App Thanks to the Internet, you don't need a passport to buy and sell in the global marketplace. Whether you're running your own business or working for someone else, now you can find suppliers and customers online, on any continent.

The SBA offers help to the nation's small-business owners who want to enter the world markets. The SBA's efforts include counseling small firms on how and where to market overseas, matching U.S. small-business executives with potential overseas customers, and helping exporters to secure financing. The agency brings small U.S. firms into direct contact with potential overseas buyers and partners. The SBA International Trade Loan program provides guarantees of up to $1.75 million in loans to small-business owners. These loans help small firms in expanding or developing new export markets. The U.S. Commercial Service, a Commerce Department division, aids small and medium-sized businesses in selling overseas. The division's global network includes more than 100 offices in the United States and 151 others in 80 countries around the world.[24]

Consider Daniel J. Nanigian, President of Nanmac Corporation in Framingham, Massachusetts. This company manufactures temperature sensors used in a wide range of industrial applications. With an export strategy aimed at growing revenues in diverse foreign markets including China, the Nanmac Corporation experienced explosive growth in 2009. The company nearly doubled its sales from $2.7 million in 2008 to $5.1 million in 2009. The company's international sales, at $300,000 in 2004, reached $700,000 in 2009 and were expected to reach $1.7 million in 2010. Its administrative, sales, and manufacturing employees have increased by 80 percent.

The company has a strong presence in China and is expanding in other markets, as well, including Latin America, Singapore, and Russia. Under Nanigian's guidance, the company has developed creative solutions and partnerships to help maximize its presence internationally. As part of its China strategy, Nanmac partners with distributors, recruits European and in-country sales representatives, uses a localized Chinese Web site, and relies for advice on the export assistance programs of the Massachusetts Small Business Development Center Network's Massachusetts Export Center. The strategy, along with travel to China to conduct technical training seminars and attend trade shows and technical conferences, has helped to grow Nanmac's Chinese client list from 1 in 2003 to more than 30 accounts today. Mr. Nanigian received SBA's 2010 Small Business Exporter of the Year Award.[25]

International trade will become more important to small-business owners as they face unique challenges in the new century. Small businesses, which are expected to remain the dominant form of organization in this country, must be prepared to adapt to significant demographic and economic changes in the world marketplace.

This chapter ends our discussion of American business today. From here on, we shall be looking closely at various aspects of business operations. We begin, in the next chapter, with a discussion of management—what management is, what managers do, and how they work to coordinate the basic economic resources within a business organization.

Concept Check ✻

☐ What does the franchisor receive in a franchising agreement? What does the franchisee receive? What does each provide?

☐ Cite one major benefit of franchising for the franchisor. Cite one major benefit of franchising for the franchisee.

☐ How does the SBA help small business-owners who want to enter the world markets?

Get Flashcards, Quizzes, Games, Crosswords, and more @ www.cengagebrain.com

SUMMARY

1 Define what a small business is and recognize the fields in which small businesses are concentrated.

A small business is one that is independently owned and operated for profit and is not dominant in its field. There are about 23 million businesses in this country, and more than 90 percent of them are small businesses. Small businesses employ more than half the nation's workforce, even though about 70 percent of new businesses can be expected to fail within five years. More than half of all small businesses are in retailing and services.

2 Identify the people who start small businesses and the reasons why some succeed and many fail.

Such personal characteristics as independence, desire to create a new enterprise, and willingness to accept a challenge may encourage individuals to start small businesses. Various external circumstances, such as special expertise or even the loss of a job, also can supply the motivation to strike out on one's own. Poor planning and lack of capital and management experience are the major causes of small-business failures.

3 Assess the contributions of small businesses to our economy.

Small businesses have been responsible for a wide variety of inventions and innovations, some of which have given rise to new industries. Historically, small businesses have created the bulk of the nation's new jobs. Further, they have mounted effective competition to larger firms. They provide things that society needs, act as suppliers to larger firms, and serve as customers of other businesses, both large and small.

4 Judge the advantages and disadvantages of operating a small business.

The advantages of smallness in business include the opportunity to establish personal relationships with customers and employees, the ability to adapt to changes quickly, independence, and simplified record keeping. The major disadvantages are the high risk of failure, the limited potential for growth, and the limited ability to raise capital.

5 Explain how the Small Business Administration helps small businesses.

The Small Business Administration (SBA) was created in 1953 to assist and counsel the nation's millions of small-business owners. The SBA offers management courses and workshops; managerial help, including one-to-one counseling through SCORE; various publications; and financial assistance through guaranteed loans and SBICs. It places special emphasis on aid to minority-owned businesses, including those owned by women.

6 Appraise the concept and types of franchising.

A franchise is a license to operate an individually owned business as though it were part of a chain. The franchisor provides a known business name, management skills, a method of doing business, and the training and required materials. The franchisee contributes labor and capital, operates the franchised business, and agrees to abide by the provisions of the franchise agreement. There are three major categories of franchise agreements.

7 Analyze the growth of franchising and franchising's advantages and disadvantages.

Franchising has grown tremendously since the mid-1970s. The franchisor's major advantage in franchising is fast and well-controlled distribution of products with minimal capital outlay. In return, the franchisee has the opportunity to open a business with limited capital, to make use of the business experience of others, and to sell to an existing clientele. For this, the franchisee usually must pay both an initial franchise fee and a continuing royalty based on sales. He or she also must follow the dictates of the franchise with regard to operation of the business.

Worldwide business opportunities are expanding for small businesses. The SBA assists small-business owners in penetrating foreign markets. The next century will present unique challenges and opportunities for small-business owners.

KEY TERMS

You should now be able to define and give an example relevant to each of the following terms:

small business (133)	Service Corps of Retired	small-business development	franchise (149)
business plan (142)	Executives (SCORE) (146)	centers (SBDCs) (147)	franchising (150)
Small Business	small-business institutes	venture capital (148)	franchisor (150)
Administration	(SBIs) (147)	small-business investment	franchisee (150)
(SBA) (145)		companies (SBICs) (148)	

DISCUSSION QUESTIONS

1. Most people who start small businesses are aware of the high failure rate and the reasons for it. Why, then, do some take no steps to protect their firms from failure? What steps should they take?
2. Are the so-called advantages of small business really advantages? Wouldn't every small-business owner like his or her business to grow into a large firm?
3. Do average citizens benefit from the activities of the SBA, or is the SBA just another way to spend our tax money?
4. Would you rather own your own business independently or become a franchisee? Why?

TEST YOURSELF

Matching Questions

1. _____ A carefully constructed guide for the person starting a business.

2. _____ A group of retired business people who volunteer their services to small businesses through the SBA.

3. _____ A government agency that assists, counsels, and protects the interests of small businesses in the United States.

4. _____ Money that is invested in small (and sometimes struggling) firms that have the potential to become very successful.

5. _____ Group of senior and graduate students in business administration who provide management counseling to small businesses.

6. _____ A business that is independently owned and operated for profit and is not dominant in its field.

7. _____ A person or organization purchasing a franchise.

8. _____ A license to operate an individually owned business as though it were a part of a chain of outlets or stores.

9. _____ The actual granting of a franchise.

10. _____ An individual or organization granting a franchise.

    a. venture capital
    b. franchise
    c. joint venture
    d. Small Business Institutes (SBIs)
    e. SCORE
    f. small business
    g. franchise
    h. strategic alliance
    i. business plan
    j. franchising
    k. SBA
    l. franchisor

True False Questions

11. **T F** The SBA has defined a small business as one independently owned, operated for profit, and not dominant in its field.

12. **T F** The various types of businesses attracting small business are generally grouped into service industries, distribution industries, and financial industries.

13. **T F** Small businesses are generally managed by professional managers.

14. **T F** Small firms have traditionally added more than their proportional share of new jobs to the economy.

15. **T F** Economically, the U.S government is not concerned with whether or not small businesses make it.

16. **T F** SCORE is a group of active business executives offering their services to small businesses for a fee.

17. **T F** A small-business investment company (SBIC) is a government agency that provides venture capital to small enterprises.

18. **T F** The purchaser of a franchise is called the franchisor.

19. **T F** An agreement between two franchisors in which the two franchisors offer their products together is called double franchising.

20. **T F** International trade will become more important to small-business owners in the new century.

Multiple-Choice Questions

21. _____ What is the primary reason that so many new businesses fail?
    a. Owner does not work hard enough
    b. Mismanagement resulting from lack of business know-how
    c. Low employee quality for new businesses
    d. Lack of brand-name recognition
    e. Inability to compete with well-established brand names

22. _____ Businesses such as flower shops, restaurants, bed and breakfasts, and automobile repair are good candidates for entrepreneurs because they
    a. do not require any skills.
    b. are the most likely to succeed.
    c. can obtain financing easily.
    d. require no special equipment.
    e. have a relatively low initial investment.

23. _____ An individual's desire to create a new business is referred to as
    a. the entrepreneurial spirit.
    b. the desire for ownership.
    c. self-determination.
    d. self-evaluation.
    e. the *laissez-faire* spirit.

24. _____ What is a common mistake that small-business owners make when their businesses begin growing?
   a. They sell more goods and services.
   b. They put too much money in advertising.
   c. They move beyond their local area.
   d. They overexpand without proper planning.
   e. They invest too much of their own money.

25. _____ The fact that insulin and power steering both originated with individual inventors and small companies is testimony to the power of small businesses as providers of
   a. employment.
   b. competition.
   c. technical innovation.
   d. capital.
   e. quality products.

26. _____ In her small retail shop, Jocelyn knows most of her best customers by name and knows their preferences in clothing and shoes. This demonstrates which advantage of a small business?
   a. Ability to adapt to change
   b. Independence from customer's desires
   c. Simplified record keeping
   d. Personal relationships with customers
   e. Small customer base

27. _____ Shonta started a graphic design firm a year ago. The business has done well, but it needs a lot more equipment, computers, and employees to continue expanding. Shonta thinks she can get all the money she will need from her bank. What advice might you give to her?
   a. She is right—the bank is likely to lend her as much as she needs because banks primarily focus on supporting small businesses.
   b. She is crazy—banks do not lend money to small businesses but only to well-known, well-established organizations.
   c. She should sell her business immediately before it fails because most small businesses fail during the first five years.

   d. She should not accept any new clients so that she can end the need to add additional equipment and employees.
   e. She should consider alternative sources of financing because banks provide only about one-fourth of the total capital to small businesses.

28. _____ Volunteers for SCORE are
   a. mostly university business professors.
   b. active executives from large corporations.
   c. generally either lawyers or accountants.
   d. graduate business students working on projects.
   e. retired businesspeople from different industries.

29. _____ An individual or organization granting a license to operate an individually owned business as though it were part of a chain of outlets or stores is a(n)
   a. franchise.
   b. franchisor.
   c. franchisee.
   d. venture capitalist.
   e. entrepreneur.

30. _____ Manju Iyer asks for your advice in opening a new business. She plans to provide tax-related services to individuals and small-business owners in her community. Of course, she wants an attractive means of starting and operating her business with a reasonable hope of succeeding in it. What will be your advice?
   a. Start your own independent business.
   b. Form a partnership with a CPA.
   c. Consider purchasing a franchise.
   d. Forget about opening the business because it is too risky.
   e. First secure a loan from the Small Business Administration.

Answers to the Test Yourself questions appear at the end of the book on page TY-1.

VIDEO CASE
Murray's Cheese: More Cheese Please

Murray's Cheese began in New York's Greenwich Village in 1940, as a wholesale butter and egg shop owned by a Jewish veteran of the Spanish Civil War named Murray Greenberg. When the current president Rob Kaufelt purchased the shop in 1991, it was little more than a local hole-in-the-wall. Kaufelt and his staff made the decision to focus on high-quality gourmet cheeses from around the world. Today, people come from all over to sample Murray's cheeses and to take classes or attend its Cheese U bootcamp to learn about cheese. Although Murray's has extended its product line

to include gourmet meats, crackers, olives, and dried fruit, cheese remains its core product. In fact, Murray's Cheese has been voted by *Forbes* as "the best cheese shop" and it is expanding to three other stores. Its success prompted Kroger to seek it out as a partner in its chain of supermarkets, a step that included intensively training Kroger employees in the fine points of selling Murray's products and the creation of a 300-page cheese service guide for them.

"We are little and they are very big," says Murray's managing director, Liz Thorpe, in speaking of Kroger. "So it's a very interesting model for us. We've begun operating cheese shops in Kroger delis that are similar to our New York shops. This allows us to bring our knowledge and expertise on sourcing, production selection, education, and customer service to a different format.... We're actually going to be opening 50 of these shops in the next 36 months."

Murray's is still small, with about 70 employees, and has an advertising budget of zero dollars. Instead of advertising, Murray's relies on providing great customer service and creating positive word of mouth to promote its products and to secure its reputation. Personal selling is key. The company recruits salespeople who are passionate about both cheese and people and trains them carefully. The key is to inform customers about the store's many unique products and persuade them to taste and then purchase. The staff enjoys listening to customers, gaining an understanding of their interests, and trying to find the right product to satisfy their needs. Their efforts often succeed in getting customers to purchase more and to make repeat buys.

All customers get to taste free samples of cheese before they buy it. "We like knowing the folks who walk in our door and having everyone taste the cheese," said the managing director. "It's part of the shopping experience. That said, we are getting more sophisticated about how we communicate with people. E-mail marketing continues to be really critical,

and we're starting to take advantage of social networking outlets like Twitter. For people who are into cheese and into Murray's, it's a great way for them to be directly tapped into knowing what's going on right this second."

What continues to appeal to sophisticated shoppers about Murray's is that cheese is an affordable luxury. A wine and cheese party for a dozen people, for instance, can fit almost any budget, and Murray's salespeople are happy to provide suggestions and samples to assist in the selection. Murray's manager also credits popular media like the Food Network with helping to popularize food in general, and cheese in particular. After all, he says, cheeses "don't have to be improved upon or fortified. They are naturally good for you."[26]

Questions

1. How does Murray's overcome one of the most common limitations facing small companies, its nonexistent advertising budget?
2. What are some of the advantages of being a small business that Murray's can (or does) take advantage of? What disadvantages might it face as a small firm?
3. Do you think the partnership with Kroger will have a negative or a positive effect on the unique experience customers expect from Murray's? Why?

BUILDING SKILLS FOR CAREER SUCCESS

1. Exploring the Internet

To provide information and point small-business operators in the right direction, many Internet sites offer helpful products and services. The SBA within the U.S. Department of Commerce provides a wide array of free information and resources. You can find your way to the SBA through www.sbaonline.sba.gov or www.sba.gov.

Assignment

1. Describe the various services provided by the SBA site.
2. What sources of funding are there?
3. What service would you like to see improved? How?

2. Building Team Skills

A business plan is a written statement that documents the nature of a business and how that business intends to achieve its goals. Although entrepreneurs should prepare a business plan *before* starting a business, the plan also serves as an effective guide later on.

Assignment

1. Working in a team of four students, identify a company in your community that would benefit from using a business plan, or create a scenario in which a hypothetical entrepreneur wants to start a business.

2. Using the resources of the library or the Internet and/or interviews with business owners, write a business plan incorporating the information in Table 5-4.
3. Present your business plan to the class.

3. Researching Different Careers

Do you know which personal characteristics make some entrepreneurs succeed and others fail?

Assignment

1. Use the resources of the library or the Internet to establish what a successful entrepreneur's profile is and to determine whether your personal characteristics fit that profile.
2. Interview several small-business owners. Ask them to describe the characteristics they think are necessary for being a successful entrepreneur.
3. Using your findings, write a report that includes the following:
   a. A profile of a successful small-business owner
   b. A comparison of your personal characteristics with the profile of the successful entrepreneur
   c. A discussion of your potential as a successful small-business owner

Running a Business: Part 2

Graeter's: A Fourth-Generation Family Business

Graeter's, headquartered in Cincinnati, is a small, privately owned fourth-generation family business that has been making premium ice cream for about 140 years. Though the company has grown and expanded, particularly in the last ten years (it is now worth $20 million), its small-batch manufacturing remains similar to an original handmade process, and each machine still churns out only about two gallons every 20 minutes. Compared to the competition, which mass produces its ice cream, Graeter's takes time with every batch and packs it by hand. Two brothers and a cousin, all great-grandsons of the founders, share responsibility for the firm's day-to-day operations and its future direction.

"Even though I have the title of CEO, in a family business titles don't mean a whole lot," says CEO Richard Graeter II. "The functions that I am doing now as CEO, I was doing as executive vice president for years . . . . It really was and remains a partnership with my two cousins . . . . Our fathers brought us into the business at an early age . . . . One summer I was on the maintenance crew, another summer I worked at the store, another summer I worked up in the bakery, and my cousins all did the same thing. We were just around this business all of our lives. I think most important is we saw our fathers and their dedication and the fact that, you know, they came home later, they came home tired, they got up early and went to work before we ever got up to go to school in the morning, and you see that dedication and appreciate that—that is what keeps your business going."

Growing the Business

From one small store in 1870, Graeter's has expanded to a few dozen small stores in Ohio, Kentucky, Indiana, Texas, and Colorado; an online retail operation that ships ice cream overnight to 48 states; and multi-state distribution to about 1,700 supermarkets through big supermarket chains like Kroger's. The kitchen in the back of the original store has grown to three factories; the newest is an $11 million Cincinnati plant being built to support the expanded distribution the company is planning. Because the new factory will create 50 new jobs, the city helped pay for the land and lent money for the construction.

What Graeter's no longer has, however, is a franchise operation. It had licensed a handful of franchise operators over the past 20 years, which were quite successful, and at one time the owners thought of franchising as a good expansion strategy. One franchise operation had even opened its own factory. Recently, however, the company repurchased all the stores of its last remaining franchisee. "When you think about Graeter's," says the CEO, "the core of Graeter's is the quality of the product. You can't franchise your core. So by franchising our manufacturing, that created substantial risk for the organization, because the customer doesn't know that it is a franchise . . . . They know it is Graeter's. . . . You really have to rely on the intention and goodwill of the individual franchisees to make the product the way you would make it, and that is not an easy thing to guarantee."[27]

Questions

1. Graeter's current management team—Richard, Robert, and Chip Graeter—took the business over from their parents, who did not have a formal succession plan in place to indicate who would do what. Do you think the current team should have such a plan specifying who is to step into the business, when, and with what responsibilities? Why or why not?

2. Graeter's has recently hired management consultants to help improve its hiring and training processes and especially to assist in the continued expansion of its distribution chain. "I think my cousins and I all have come to realize we can't do it alone," says the CEO. Why do you think the management team made this decision? Does bringing these outsiders into the firm make Graeter's less of a family company than it has been?

3. Do you think Graeter's made the right decision to close its franchise operation? Why or why not?

© Liudmila Chernova / iStockphoto 12864114

© DNY59 / iStockphoto 1694138

Building a Business Plan: Part 2

After reading Part 2, "Business Ownership and Entrepreneurship," you should be ready to tackle the company and industry component of your business plan. In this section, you will provide information about the background of the company, choice of the legal business form, information on the product or services to be offered, and descriptions of potential customers, current competitors, and the business's future. Chapter 4 in your textbook, "Choosing a Form of Business Ownership," and Chapter 5, "Small Business, Entrepreneurship, and Franchises," can help you to answer some of the questions in this part of the business plan.

The Company and Industry Component

The company and industry analysis should include the answers to at least the following questions:

2.1. What is the legal form of your business? Is your business a sole proprietorship, a partnership, or a corporation?

2.2. What licenses or permits will you need, if any?

2.3. Is your business a new independent business, a take-over, an expansion, or a franchise?

2.4. If you are dealing with an existing business, how did your company get to the point where it is today?

2.5. What does your business do, and how does it satisfy customers' needs?

2.6. How did you choose and develop the products or services to be sold, and how are they different from those currently on the market?

2.7. What industry do you operate in, and what are the industry-wide trends?

2.8. Who are the major competitors in your industry?

2.9. Have any businesses recently entered or exited? Why did they leave?

2.10. Why will your business be profitable, and what are your growth opportunities?

2.11. Does any part of your business involve e-business?

Review of Business Plan Activities

Make sure to check the information you have collected, make any changes, and correct any weaknesses before beginning Part 3. *Reminder:* Review the answers to questions in the preceding part to make sure that all your answers are consistent throughout the business plan. Finally, write a summary statement that incorporates all the information for this part of the business plan.

The information contained in "Building a Business Plan" will also assist you in completing the online *Interactive Business Plan.*

PART THREE
MANAGEMENT AND ORGANIZATION

SUCCESS

© Duncan Babbage/iStockphoto.com

This part of the book deals with the organization—the "thing" that is a business. We begin with a discussion of the management functions involved in developing and operating a business. Next, we analyze the organization's elements and structure. Then we consider a firm's operations that are related to the production of goods and services.

Chapter 6   Understanding the Management Process
Chapter 7   Creating a Flexible Organization
Chapter 8   Producing Quality Goods and Services

CHAPTER 6 UNDERSTANDING THE MANAGEMENT PROCESS

© Tony Freeman/PhotoEdit

Why should you care?

Most of the people who read this chapter will not spend much time at the bottom of organizations. They will advance upward and become managers. Thus an overview of the field of management is essential.

Learning Objectives

What you will be able to do once you complete this chapter:

1 Define what management is.

2 Describe the four basic management functions: planning, organizing, leading and motivating, and controlling.

3 Distinguish among the various kinds of managers in terms of both level and area of management.

4 Identify the key management skills of successful managers.

5 Explain the different types of leadership.

6 Discuss the steps in the managerial decision-making process.

7 Describe how organizations benefit from total quality management.

How H.J. Heinz Manages for a Healthy Company, People, and Planet

The company that made bottled ketchup famous, H.J. Heinz, rings up more than $10 billion in annual revenues, employs 30,000 people worldwide, and is active in more than 200 countries. In addition to making products under its own brands, including Heinz, Ore-Ida, Classico, and Lea & Perrins, Heinz also sells foods under licensed brands such as Boston Market, TGI Friday's, and Weight Watchers. Here's how the company sees its mission: "As the trusted leader in nutrition and wellness, Heinz—the original Pure Food Company—is dedicated to the sustainable health of people, the planet, and our company."

CEO William Johnson notes that his job as head of the company is not to run the day-to-day business but to "lead the people and manage the process." He's very involved in selecting senior executives because "it's that level—the business-unit managers, the country managers—who really make this company work." Johnson likes to sample new products in the pipeline—he tastes more than 300 new foods every year—but he delegates the final decisions on product introductions to his marketing experts.

Johnson and his top executives know that keeping this multinational food giant nimble, competitive, and profitable over the long run requires careful coordination and constant innovation. In addition to having managers supervise their own functions or departments, Johnson insists they collaborate across functions to develop cost-cutting, time-saving efficiencies that will benefit the overall organization. The company has several senior-level groups working on priorities such as improving productivity, boosting profit margins, and reducing the environmental impact of the business.

Looking ahead, Heinz has a strategic plan for expanding its reach and spicing up revenues through new product innovation and accelerated growth in emerging countries such as China, India, and Indonesia. By 2016, as much as 25 percent of Heinz's revenue could come from sales in emerging nations, which is why management pays close attention to cultural, technological, political, and financial trends that affect it locally and globally. At the same time, the firm is also maintaining its growth momentum within the United States, where Heinz has a long history of success and scores high on customer satisfaction surveys.[1]

Did you know?

H.J. Heinz first bottled ketchup in 1876 and now rings up more than $10 billion in annual revenue from operations in more than 200 nations.

The leadership employed at H.J. Heinz illustrates that management can be one of the most exciting and rewarding professions available today. Depending on its size, a firm may employ a number of specialized managers who are responsible for particular areas of management, such as marketing, finance, and operations. That same organization also includes managers at several levels within the firm. In this chapter, we define *management* and describe the four basic management functions of planning, organizing, leading and motivating, and controlling. Then we focus on the types of managers with respect to levels of responsibility and areas of expertise. Next, we focus on the skills of effective managers and the different roles managers must play. We examine several styles of leadership and explore the process by which managers make decisions. We also describe how total quality management can improve customer satisfaction.

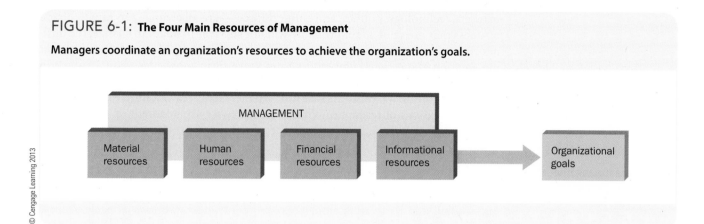

© Cengage Learning 2013

WHAT IS MANAGEMENT?

Management is the process of coordinating people and other resources to achieve the goals of an organization. As we saw in Chapter 1, most organizations make use of four kinds of resources: material, human, financial, and informational (see Figure 6-1).

LEARNING OBJECTIVE
1 Define what management is.

Personal App Maybe you've never thought of yourself as a manager. But if you've ever headed a committee or organized a new school club, you've actually been involved in management. Understanding more about the way management works can make you more successful in the daily business of *your* life.

Material resources are the tangible, physical resources an organization uses. For example, General Motors uses steel, glass, and fiberglass to produce cars and trucks on complex machine-driven assembly lines. A college or university uses books, classroom buildings, desks, and computers to educate students. And the Mayo Clinic uses beds, operating room equipment, and diagnostic machines to provide health care.

Perhaps the most important resources of any organization are its *human resources*—people. In fact, some firms live by the philosophy that their employees are their most important assets. One such firm is Southwest Airlines. Southwest treats its employees with the same respect and attention it gives its passengers. Southwest selectively seeks employees with upbeat attitudes and promotes from within 80 percent of the time. In decision making, everyone who will be affected is encouraged to get involved in the process. In an industry in which deregulation, extreme price competition, and fluctuating fuel costs have eliminated several major competitors, Southwest keeps growing and making a profit because of its employees. Many experts would agree with Southwest's emphasis on employees. Some managers believe that the way employees are developed and managed may have more impact on an organization than other vital components such as marketing, sound financial decisions about large expenditures, production, or use of technology.

© Kurhan/Shutterstock

Financial resources are the funds an organization uses to meet its obligations to investors and creditors. A 7-Eleven convenience store obtains money from customers at the checkout counters and uses a portion of that money to pay its suppliers. Citicorp, a large New York bank, borrows and lends money. Your college obtains money in the form of tuition, income from its endowments, and state and federal grants. It uses the money to pay utility bills, insurance premiums, and professors' salaries.

Finally, many organizations increasingly find that they cannot afford to ignore *information*. External environmental conditions—including the economy, consumer

management the process of coordinating people and other resources to achieve the goals of an organization

markets, technology, politics, and cultural forces—are all changing so rapidly that a business that does not adapt probably will not survive. To adapt to change, the business must know what is changing and how it is changing. Most companies gather information about their competitors to increase their knowledge about changes in their industry and to learn from other companies' failures and successes.

It is important to realize that the four types of resources described earlier are only general categories of resources. Within each category are hundreds or thousands of more specific resources. It is this complex mix of specific resources—and not simply "some of each" of the four general categories—that managers must coordinate to produce goods and services.

Another interesting way to look at management is in terms of the different functions managers perform. These functions have been identified as planning, organizing, leading and motivating employees, and controlling. We look at each of these management functions in the next section.

* Concept Check

☐ What is management?

☐ What are the four kinds of resources?

LEARNING OBJECTIVE

2 Describe the four basic management functions: planning, organizing, leading and motivating, and controlling.

BASIC MANAGEMENT FUNCTIONS

Pharmaceutical company Eli Lilly recently made a decision to focus on the emerging market of China. The company reorganized its structure so that one of its six units would handle emerging markets, doubled its employee count from 1,100 to 2,200, and began construction on a second manufacturing plant in Suzhou, China. The company also implemented a partnering strategy in China to handle research and development. Eli Lilly's key strategies include maximizing their core assets, accelerating new product launches, capitalizing on longer product life-cycles in areas like China, and establishing local alliances to access fast-growing market segments.[2]

Management functions such as those just described do not occur according to some rigid, preset timetable. Managers do not plan in January, organize in February, lead and motivate in March, and control in April. At any given time, managers may engage in a number of functions simultaneously. However, each function tends to lead naturally to others. Figure 6-2 provides a visual framework for a more detailed discussion of the four basic management functions. How well managers perform these key functions determines whether a business is successful.

Personal App Do you make New Year's resolutions? Then you know a little about planning, a basic management function. But planning alone won't get you where you want to go. In managing your personal and your professional lives, you need to know about all four of the management functions.

FIGURE 6-2: **The Management Process**

Note that management is not a step-by-step procedure but a process with a feedback loop that represents a flow.

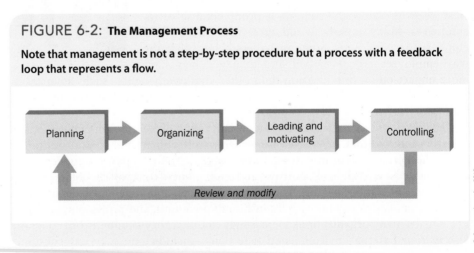

© Cengage Learning 2013

Planning

Planning, in its simplest form, is establishing organizational goals and deciding how to accomplish them. It is often referred to as the "first" management function because all other management functions depend on planning. Organizations such as Starbucks, Houston Community Colleges, and Facebook begin the planning process by developing a mission statement.

An organization's **mission** is a statement of the basic purpose that makes that organization different from others. Starbucks' mission statement, for example, is "to inspire and nurture the human spirit—one person, one cup, and one neighborhood at a time." Houston Community College's mission is to provide an education for local citizens. Facebook's mission statement is "to give people the power to share and make the world more open and connected."[3] Once an organization's mission has been described in a mission statement, the next step is to engage in strategic planning.

STRATEGIC PLANNING PROCESS The **strategic planning process** involves establishing an organization's major goals and objectives and allocating resources to achieve them. Top management is responsible for strategic planning, although customers, products, competitors, and company resources are some of the factors that are analyzed in the strategic planning process.

In today's rapidly changing business environment, constant internal or external changes may necessitate changes in a company's goals, mission, or strategy. The time line for strategic plans is generally one to two years and can be as long as ten years. Strategic plans should be flexible and include action items, such as outlining how plans will be implemented.

ESTABLISHING GOALS AND OBJECTIVES A **goal** is an end result that an organization is expected to achieve over a one- to ten-year period. An **objective** is a specific statement detailing what the organization intends to accomplish over a shorter period of time.

A mission statement communicates an organization's basic purpose. The mission of Darden Restaurants, for example, which is the parent company of Red Lobster, Olive Garden, and other casual eateries, is "to nourish and delight everyone we serve." Companies often present their mission statements to their employees to serve as a reminder of what is expected of them.

© Jeff Greenberg/PhotoEdit

Goals and objectives can deal with a variety of factors, such as sales, company growth, costs, customer satisfaction, and employee morale. Whereas a small manufacturer may focus primarily on sales objectives for the next six months, a large firm may be more interested in goals that impact several years in the future. Starbucks, for example, has established several goals under its "Shared Planet" program to be completed in the next few years, specifically in the areas of ethical sourcing, environmental stewardship, and community involvement. By 2015, Starbucks hopes to purchase 100 percent of its coffee from ethical sources or farmers who grow their coffee responsibly without permanently harming the environment. The company also hopes to combat climate change by encouraging farmers to prevent deforestation through the use of incentive programs. Starbucks hopes to develop a recyclable cup by 2012. Also, the company hopes to use their stores to lead volunteer programs in each store's community.[4] Finally, goals are set at every level of an organization. Every member of an organization—the president of the company, the head of a department, and an operating employee at the lowest level—has a set of goals that he or she hopes to achieve.

The goals developed for these different levels must be consistent. However, it is likely that some conflict will arise. A production department, for example, may have a goal of minimizing costs. One way to do this is to produce only one type of product and offer "no frills." Marketing may have a goal of maximizing sales. One way to implement this goal is to offer customers a wide range of products and options. As part of goal setting, the manager who is responsible for *both* departments

planning establishing organizational goals and deciding how to accomplish them

mission a statement of the basic purpose that makes an organization different from others

strategic planning process the establishment of an organization's major goals and objectives and the allocation of resources to achieve them

goal an end result that an organization is expected to achieve over a one- to ten-year period

objective a specific statement detailing what an organization intends to accomplish over a shorter period of time

must achieve some sort of balance between conflicting goals. This balancing process is called *optimization*.

The optimization of conflicting goals requires insight and ability. Faced with the marketing-versus-production conflict just described, most managers probably would not adopt either viewpoint completely. Instead, they might decide on a reasonably diverse product line offering only the most widely sought-after options. Such a compromise would seem to be best for the whole organization.

SWOT ANALYSIS **SWOT analysis** is the identification and evaluation of a firm's strengths, weaknesses, opportunities, and threats. Strengths and weaknesses are internal factors that affect a company's capabilities. Strengths refer to a firm's favorable characteristics and core competencies. **Core competencies** are approaches and processes that a company performs well that may give it an advantage over its competitors. These core competencies may help the firm attract financial and human resources and be more capable of producing products that better satisfy customers. Weaknesses refer to any internal limitations a company faces in developing or implementing plans. At times, managers have difficulty identifying and understanding the negative effects of weaknesses in their organizations.

External opportunities and threats exist independently of the firm. Opportunities refer to favorable conditions in the environment that could produce rewards for the organization. That is, opportunities are situations that exist but must be exploited for the firm to benefit from them. Threats, on the other hand, are conditions or barriers that may prevent the firm from reaching its objectives. Opportunities and threats can stem from many sources within the business environment. For example, competitor's actions, new laws, economic changes, or new technology can be threats. Threats for some firms may be opportunities for others. Examples of strengths, weaknesses, opportunities, and threats are shown in Figure 6-3.

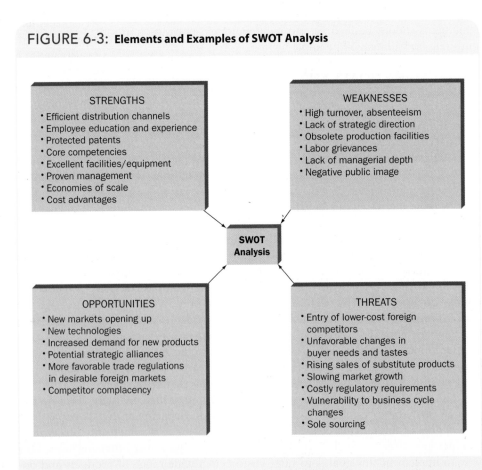

FIGURE 6-3: **Elements and Examples of SWOT Analysis**

STRENGTHS
- Efficient distribution channels
- Employee education and experience
- Protected patents
- Core competencies
- Excellent facilities/equipment
- Proven management
- Economies of scale
- Cost advantages

WEAKNESSES
- High turnover, absenteeism
- Lack of strategic direction
- Obsolete production facilities
- Labor grievances
- Lack of managerial depth
- Negative public image

SWOT Analysis

OPPORTUNITIES
- New markets opening up
- New technologies
- Increased demand for new products
- Potential strategic alliances
- More favorable trade regulations in desirable foreign markets
- Competitor complacency

THREATS
- Entry of lower-cost foreign competitors
- Unfavorable changes in buyer needs and tastes
- Rising sales of substitute products
- Slowing market growth
- Costly regulatory requirements
- Vulnerability to business cycle changes
- Sole sourcing

© Cengage Learning 2013

SWOT analysis the identification and evaluation of a firm's strengths, weaknesses, opportunities, and threats

core competencies approaches and processes that a company performs well that may give it an advantage over its competitors

TYPES OF PLANS Once goals and objectives have been set for the organization, managers must develop plans for achieving them. A **plan** is an outline of the actions by which an organization intends to accomplish its goals and objectives. Just as it has different goals and objectives, the organization also develops several types of plans, as shown in Figure 6-4.

Resulting from the strategic planning process, an organization's **strategic plan** is its broadest plan, developed as a guide for major policy setting and decision-making. Strategic plans are set by the board of directors and top management and are generally designed to achieve the organization's long-term goals. Thus, a firm's strategic plan defines what business the company is in or wants to be in and the kind of company it is or wants to be. When top management at the world's biggest retailer, Walmart, wanted to manage their stores more efficiently, they decided to focus on three priorities—growth, leverage, and returns—in order to provide more value for customers and shareholders. First, management consolidated the company's logistics, real estate, and store operations. Then, stores in the United States were divided into three new business units: Walmart West, Walmart South, and Walmart North. Finally, a new division called Global.com was created to regulate global e-commerce and business. This long-term strategy has been adopted to facilitate the company's future growth as it expands.[5]

The Internet has challenged traditional strategic thinking. For example, reluctant to move from a face-to-face sales approach to a less personal Web site approach, Allstate has created an Internet presence to support its established sales force.

In addition to strategic plans, most organizations also employ several narrower kinds of plans. A **tactical plan** is a smaller scale plan developed to implement a strategy.

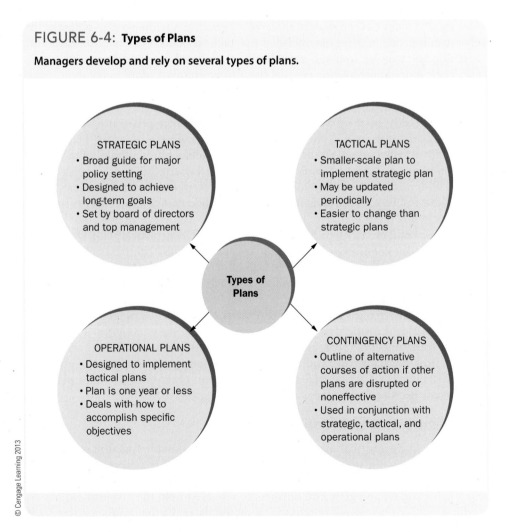

FIGURE 6-4: **Types of Plans**

Managers develop and rely on several types of plans.

STRATEGIC PLANS
- Broad guide for major policy setting
- Designed to achieve long-term goals
- Set by board of directors and top management

TACTICAL PLANS
- Smaller-scale plan to implement strategic plan
- May be updated periodically
- Easier to change than strategic plans

Types of Plans

OPERATIONAL PLANS
- Designed to implement tactical plans
- Plan is one year or less
- Deals with how to accomplish specific objectives

CONTINGENCY PLANS
- Outline of alternative courses of action if other plans are disrupted or noneffective
- Used in conjunction with strategic, tactical, and operational plans

© Cengage Learning 2013

plan an outline of the actions by which an organization intends to accomplish its goals and objectives

strategic plan an organization's broadest plan, developed as a guide for major policy setting and decision making

tactical plan a smaller scale plan developed to implement a strategy

Going for SUCCESS

Be Prepared with a Contingency Plan

Managers have to be prepared for all kinds of twists and turns as they move their organizations toward the future in today's highly dynamic business environment. Strategic, tactical, and operational plans are vital for keeping the company on track toward its long-term and short-term goals. However, the future doesn't always unfold the way managers expected. That's why successful companies formulate a variety of contingency plans to deal with possible problems due to economic volatility, extreme weather conditions, prolonged power outages, a pandemic, fire or flood, or other major challenges.

The Danish toymaker Lego, for example, has used contingency plans to effectively adapt to a range of economic circumstances. First, its top managers take a close look at several possible economic scenarios and estimate how each might disrupt Lego's performance. Next, they create contingency plans to minimize the disruption under each scenario. Then every month, the managers meet to review key economic indicators, examine Lego's performance in the context of these trends, and determine whether and when to put one of their contingency plans into operation. Thanks to good contingency planning, Lego has been able to preserve profits even during periods of economic turmoil.

Many businesses have contingency plans to check on employees and continue operations despite severe weather conditions. When a major blizzard blanketed Chicago not long ago, Ariel Investments activated its plan, starting with e-mails and phone calls to be sure employees were safe. Because employees used company laptops to work from home, the normal flow of business was only slightly interrupted.

Sources: Barry B. Burr, "Snowstorm Puts Pension Plans in Remote Mode," *Pensions & Investments*, February 2, 2011, www.pionline.com/article/20110202/DAILYREG/110209976; Joann S. Lublin and Dana Mattioli, "Strategic Plans Lose Favor," *Wall Street Journal*, January 25, 2010, www.wsj.com; "Managing in the Fog," *The Economist*, February 28, 2009, pp. 67–68; Phyllis Furman, "In Case of Emergency: Business Contingency Plan Needed," *New York Daily News*, July 27, 2009, www.nydailynews.com.

Most tactical plans cover a one- to three-year period. If a strategic plan will take five years to complete, the firm may develop five tactical plans, one covering each year. Tactical plans may be updated periodically as dictated by conditions and experience. Their more limited scope permits them to be changed more easily than strategies. Volkswagen, for example, recently began constructing a new assembly plant in Guangzhou, China. The 300,000-unit plant is expected to begin operations in 2013, and is expected to increase Volkswagen's sales and market penetration in southern China, which is currently dominated by Toyota, Honda, and Nissan. This tactical plan is part of Volkswagen's recent strategic plan to achieve annual sales of more than 2 million units in southern China by 2018. China is currently Volkswagen's largest market, with nearly 1.5 million units of annual sales, more than the company's market in Germany or the United States. The automobile manufacturer hopes that this newest assembly plant will help Volkswagen achieve its long-term goal.[6]

An **operational plan** is a type of plan designed to implement tactical plans. Operational plans are usually established for one year or less and deal with how to accomplish the organization's specific objectives. Procter & Gamble has adopted the *Go-to-Market plan* in order to speed up the availability of products to retailers and thus to consumers. The strategic and tactical plans have been kept in mind in order to achieve this plan. It includes making significant changes in the way that Procter & Gamble distributes its products.[7]

Regardless of how hard managers try, sometimes business activities do not go as planned. Today, most corporations also develop contingency plans along with strategies, tactical plans, and operational plans. A **contingency plan** is a plan that outlines alternative courses of action that may be taken if an organization's other plans are disrupted or become ineffective.

Organizing the Enterprise

After goal setting and planning, the manager's second major function is organization. **Organizing** is the grouping of resources and activities to accomplish some end result in an efficient and effective manner. Consider the case of an inventor who creates a new product and goes into business to sell it. At first, the inventor will do everything on his or her own—purchase raw materials, make the product, advertise it,

operational plan a type of plan designed to implement tactical plans

contingency plan a plan that outlines alternative courses of action that may be taken if an organization's other plans are disrupted or become ineffective

organizing the grouping of resources and activities to accomplish some end result in an efficient and effective manner

sell it, and keep business records. Eventually, as business grows, the inventor will need help. To begin with, he or she might hire a professional sales representative and a part-time bookkeeper. Later, it also might be necessary to hire sales staff, people to assist with production, and an accountant. As the inventor hires new personnel, he or she must decide what each person will do, to whom each person will report, and how each person can best take part in the organization's activities. We discuss these and other facets of the organizing function in much more detail in Chapter 7.

Leading and Motivating

The leading and motivating function is concerned with the human resources within an organization. Specifically, **leading** is the process of influencing people to work toward a common goal. **Motivating** is the process of providing reasons for people to work in the best interests of an organization. Together, leading and motivating are often referred to as **directing**.

We have already noted the importance of an organization's human resources. Because of this importance, leading and motivating are critical activities. Obviously, different people do things for different reasons—that is, they have different *motivations*. Some are interested primarily in earning as much money as they can. Others may be spurred on by opportunities to get promoted. Part of a manager's job, then, is to determine what factors motivate workers and to try to provide those incentives to encourage effective performance. Jeffrey R. Immelt, GE's chairperson and CEO, has worked to transform GE into a leader in essential themes tied to world development, such as emerging markets, environmental solutions, demographics, and digital connections. He believes in giving freedom to his teams and wants them to come up with their own solutions. However, he does not hesitate to intervene if the situation demands. He believes that a leader's primary role is to teach, and he makes people feel that he is willing to share what he has learned. Immelt also laid the vision for GE's ambitious "ecomagination initiative" and has been named one of the "World's Best CEOs" three times by *Barron's*.[8] A lot of research has been done on both motivation and leadership. As you will see in Chapter 10, research on motivation has yielded very useful information. However, research on leadership has been less successful. Despite decades of study, no one has discovered a general set of personal traits or characteristics that makes a good leader. Later in this chapter, we discuss leadership in more detail.

At Google's Kirkland, Washington, facility, employees eat for free in the company's cafeteria. This employee benefit contributes to the company's famously collaborative atmosphere by making it easy for coworkers to socialize together during the day, building personal bonds that strengthen teamwork. What would contribute to a satisfying work environment for you?

Controlling Ongoing Activities

Controlling is the process of evaluating and regulating ongoing activities to ensure that goals are achieved. To see how controlling works, consider a rocket launched by NASA to place a satellite in orbit. Do NASA personnel simply fire the rocket and then check back in a few days to find out whether the satellite is in place? Of course not. The rocket is monitored constantly, and its course is regulated and adjusted as needed to get the satellite to its destination.

The control function includes three steps (see Figure 6-5). The first is *setting standards* with which performance can be compared. The second is *measuring actual performance* and comparing it with the standard. The third is *taking corrective action* as necessary. Notice that the control function is circular in nature. The steps in the control function must be repeated periodically until the goal is achieved. For example, suppose that Southwest Airlines establishes a goal of increasing profits

leading the process of influencing people to work toward a common goal

motivating the process of providing reasons for people to work in the best interests of an organization

directing the combined processes of leading and motivating

controlling the process of evaluating and regulating ongoing activities to ensure that goals are achieved

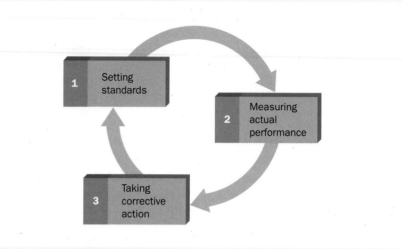

FIGURE 6-5: **The Control Function**

The control function includes three steps: setting standards, measuring actual performance, and taking corrective action.

1 Setting standards

2 Measuring actual performance

3 Taking corrective action

© Cengage Learning 2013

by 12 percent. To ensure that this goal is reached, Southwest's management might monitor its profit on a monthly basis. After three months, if profit has increased by 3 percent, management might be able to assume that plans are going according to schedule. In this case, it is likely that no action will be taken. However, if profit has increased by only 1 percent after three months, some corrective action is needed to get the firm on track. The particular action that is required depends on the reason for the small increase in profit.

KINDS OF MANAGERS

LEARNING OBJECTIVE
3 Distinguish among the various kinds of managers in terms of both level and area of management.

Managers can be classified in two ways: according to their level within an organization and according to their area of management. In this section, we use both perspectives to explore the various types of managers.

(**Personal App**) As a customer and as an employee, you'll meet all kinds of managers. What do they do and why are some at a higher level than others?

Levels of Management

For the moment, think of an organization as a three-story structure (as illustrated in Figure 6-6). Each story corresponds to one of the three general levels of management: top managers, middle managers, and first-line managers.

TOP MANAGERS A **top manager** is an upper-level executive who guides and controls an organization's overall fortunes. Top managers constitute a small group. In terms of planning, they are generally responsible for developing the organization's mission. They also determine the firm's strategy. It takes years of hard work, long hours, and perseverance, as well as talent and no small share of good luck, to reach the ranks of top management in large companies. Common job titles associated with top managers are president, vice president, chief executive officer (CEO), and chief operating officer (COO).

MIDDLE MANAGERS Middle managers probably make up the largest group of managers in most organizations. A **middle manager** is a manager who implements the strategy and major policies developed by top management. Middle

top manager an upper-level executive who guides and controls the overall fortunes of an organization

middle manager a manager who implements the strategy and major policies developed by top management

172

managers develop tactical plans and operational plans, and they coordinate and supervise the activities of first-line managers. Titles at the middle-management level include division manager, department head, plant manager, and operations manager.

FIRST-LINE MANAGERS A **first-line manager** is a manager who coordinates and supervises the activities of operating employees. First-line managers spend most of their time working with and motivating their employees, answering questions, and solving day-to-day problems. Most first-line managers are former operating employees who, owing to their hard work and potential, were promoted into management. Many of today's middle and top managers began their careers on this first management level. Common titles for first-line managers include office manager, supervisor, and foreman.

Areas of Management Specialization

Organizational structure can also be divided into areas of management specialization (see Figure 6-7). The most common areas are finance, operations, marketing, human resources, and administration. Depending on its mission, goals, and objectives, an organization may include other areas as well—research and development (R&D), for example.

FINANCIAL MANAGERS A **financial manager** is primarily responsible for an organization's financial resources. Accounting and investment are specialized areas within financial management. Because financing affects the operation of the entire firm, many of the CEOs and presidents of this country's largest companies are people who got their "basic training" as financial managers.

OPERATIONS MANAGERS An **operations manager** manages the systems that convert resources into goods and services. Traditionally, operations management has been equated with manufacturing—the production of goods. However, in recent years, many of the techniques and procedures of operations management have been applied to the production of services and to a variety of nonbusiness activities. As with financial management, operations management has produced a large percentage of today's company CEOs and presidents.

MARKETING MANAGERS A **marketing manager** is responsible for facilitating the exchange of products between an organization and its customers or clients. Specific areas within marketing are marketing research, product management, advertising, promotion, sales, and distribution. A sizable number of today's company presidents have risen from the ranks of marketing management.

HUMAN RESOURCES MANAGERS A **human resources manager** is charged with managing an organization's human resources programs. He or she engages in human resources planning; designs systems for hiring, training, and evaluating the

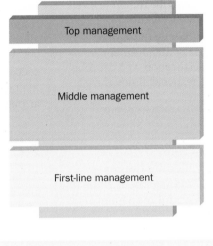

FIGURE 6-6: Management Levels Found in Most Companies

The coordinated effort of all three levels of managers is required to implement the goals of any company.

©Cengage Learning 2013

first-line manager a manager who coordinates and supervises the activities of operating employees

financial manager a manager who is primarily responsible for an organization's financial resources

operations manager a manager who manages the systems that convert resources into goods and services

marketing manager a manager who is responsible for facilitating the exchange of products between an organization and its customers or clients

human resources manager a person charged with managing an organization's human resources programs

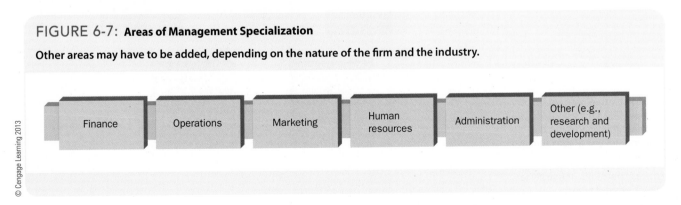

FIGURE 6-7: Areas of Management Specialization

Other areas may have to be added, depending on the nature of the firm and the industry.

© Cengage Learning 2013

performance of employees; and ensures that the organization follows government regulations concerning employment practices. Some human resources managers make effective use of technology. For example, more than 1 million job openings are posted on Monster.com, which attracts about 15 million visitors monthly.[9]

ADMINISTRATIVE MANAGERS An **administrative manager** (also called a *general manager*) is not associated with any specific functional area but provides overall administrative guidance and leadership. A hospital administrator is an example of an administrative manager. He or she does not specialize in operations, finance, marketing, or human resources management but instead coordinates the activities of specialized managers in all these areas. In many respects, most top managers are really administrative managers.

Whatever their level in the organization and whatever area they specialize in, successful managers generally exhibit certain key skills and are able to play certain managerial roles. However, as we shall see, some skills are likely to be more critical at one level of management than at another.

KEY SKILLS OF SUCCESSFUL MANAGERS

As shown in Figure 6-8, managers need a variety of skills, including conceptual, analytic, interpersonal, technical, and communication skills.

Personal App Whether you're co-captain of your softball team or taking a step upward on your career ladder, you won't succeed unless you can think beyond today, reason things out, get along with people, do a good job, and make yourself understood.

Conceptual Skills

Conceptual skills involve the ability to think in abstract terms. Conceptual skills allow a manager to see the "big picture" and understand how the various parts of an organization or idea can fit together. These skills are useful in a wide range of situations, including the optimization of goals described earlier.

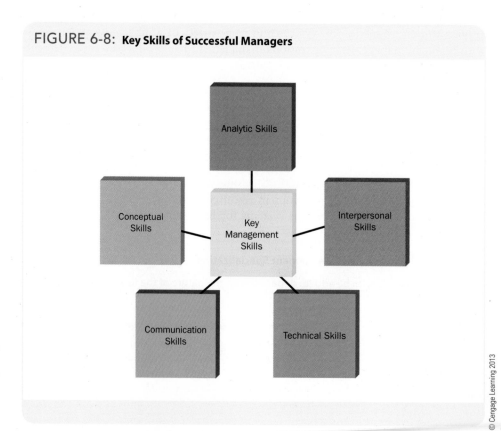

FIGURE 6-8: **Key Skills of Successful Managers**

Analytic Skills

Conceptual Skills

Key Management Skills

Interpersonal Skills

Communication Skills

Technical Skills

© Cengage Learning 2013

Concept Check

☐ Describe the three levels of management.

☐ Identify the various areas of management specialization, and describe the responsibilities of each.

LEARNING OBJECTIVE
4 Identify the key management skills of successful managers.

administrative manager a manager who is not associated with any specific functional area but who provides overall administrative guidance and leadership

conceptual skills the ability to think in abstract terms

First-time Manager? Avoid These Rookie Mistakes!

Congratulations! You've moved into your first management position. Launch yourself on the road to management success by avoiding these rookie mistakes:

- *Plunging ahead without a plan.* Find out what your department or team is expected to accomplish, set specific goals and objectives, investigate the situation, and create a plan before you take action.

- *Neglecting your professional development.* Invest in your management future by taking courses, attending training sessions, and reading industry publications to keep your knowledge and skills up to date. And be sure your employees have access to development opportunities, as well.

- *Communicating too little, too late.* "So often, new managers are scared to relay bad news to their higher-ups, and that usually results in the worst outcome possible," says an executive with the global consulting firm Accenture. Speaking up early and being honest with your management—and your employees—is the best way to get the guidance and resources you need to fix the situation. And when things are going well, don't be shy about putting the spotlight on

the employees who are responsible. When they look good, you look good.

- *Doing too much on your own.* Although it's tempting to take on the most difficult or tricky tasks yourself, learn to delegate activities that can be handled more efficiently or effectively by your capable employees.

- *Not building internal relationships.* You can't be successful without the cooperation of other departments, so reach out and cultivate connections with managers and employees in many other parts of the organization.

Sources: Sarah H. Needleman, "Management Flubs Made by Rookie Bosses," *Wall Street Journal,* January 3, 2011, www.wsj.com; Jeff Schmitt, "Twenty Tips for First-Time Managers," *Bloomberg BusinessWeek,* October 8, 2010, www.businessweek.com; Meghan Casserly, "Congratulations! You're a Manager . . . Now What?" *Forbes.com,* April 5, 2010, www.forbes.com.

Analytic Skills

Employers expect managers to use **analytic skills** to identify problems correctly, generate reasonable alternatives, and select the "best" alternatives to solve problems. Top-level managers especially need these skills because they need to discern the important issues from the less important ones, as well as recognize the underlying reasons for different situations. Managers who use these skills not only address a situation but also correct the initial event or problem that caused it to occur. Thus, these skills are vital to run a business efficiently and logically.

Interpersonal Skills

Interpersonal skills involve the ability to deal effectively with other people, both inside and outside an organization. Examples of interpersonal skills are the ability to relate to people, understand their needs and motives, and show genuine compassion. One reason why Steve Jobs, founder of Apple, has been so successful is his ability to motivate his employees and to inspire their loyalty to his vision for the firm. Although it is obvious that a CEO such as Steve Jobs must be able to work with employees throughout the organization, what is not so obvious is that middle and first-line managers must also possess interpersonal skills. For example, a first-line manager on an assembly line at Procter & Gamble must rely on employees to manufacture Tide detergent. The better the manager's interpersonal skills, the more likely the manager will be able to lead and motivate those employees. When all

analytic skills the ability to identify problems correctly, generate reasonable alternatives, and select the "best" alternatives to solve problems

interpersonal skills the ability to deal effectively with other people

To be successful, an effective manager must be able to simultaneously employ and integrate several skills. Technical skills that aid specialized work, conceptual skills that foster abstract thinking, and interpersonal skills for interacting with others are all important to develop. Which of these skills are you already good at, and which will you work on as you build your career?

© Elena Elisseva/Shutterstock

other things are equal, the manager who is able to exhibit these skills will be more successful than the arrogant and brash manager who does not care about others.

Technical Skills

Technical skills involve specific skills needed to accomplish a specialized activity. For example, the skills engineers and machinists need to do their jobs are technical skills. First-line managers (and, to a lesser extent, middle managers) need the technical skills relevant to the activities they manage. Although these managers may not perform the technical tasks themselves, they must be able to train subordinates, answer questions, and otherwise provide guidance and direction. A first-line manager in the accounting department of the Hyatt Corporation, for example, must be able to perform computerized accounting transactions and help employees complete the same accounting task. In general, top managers do not rely on technical skills as heavily as managers at other levels. Still, understanding the technical side of a business is an aid to effective management at every level.

Communication Skills

Communication skills, both oral and written, involve the ability to speak, listen, and write effectively. Managers need both oral and written communication skills. Because a large part of a manager's day is spent conversing with others, the ability to speak *and* listen is critical. Oral communication skills are used when a manager makes sales presentations, conducts interviews, and holds press conferences. Written communication skills are important because a manager's ability to prepare letters, e-mails, memos, sales reports, and other written documents may spell the difference between success and failure. In order to further communicate within an organization, most managers should know how to use a computer to prepare written and statistical reports and to communicate with other managers and employees.

LEADERSHIP

Leadership has been defined broadly as the ability to influence others. A leader can use his or her power to affect the behavior of others. Leadership is different from management in that a leader strives for voluntary cooperation, whereas a manager may have to depend on coercion to change employee behavior.

technical skills specific skills needed to accomplish a specialized activity

communication skills the ability to speak, listen, and write effectively

leadership the ability to influence others

✳ *Concept Check*

☐ What are the key skills that successful managers should have?

☐ For each skill, provide two reasons why a successful manager should have that skill.

Formal and Informal Leadership

Some experts make distinctions between formal leadership and informal leadership. Formal leaders have legitimate power of position. They have *authority* within an organization to influence others to work for the organization's objectives. Informal leaders usually have no such authority and may or may not exert their influence in support of the organization. Both formal and informal leaders make use of several kinds of power, including the ability to grant rewards or impose punishments, the possession of expert knowledge, and personal attraction or charisma. Informal leaders who identify with the organization's goals are a valuable asset to any organization. However, a business can be brought to its knees by informal leaders who turn work groups against management.

Styles of Leadership

For many years, leadership was viewed as a combination of personality traits, such as self-confidence, concern for people, intelligence, and dependability. Achieving a consensus on which traits were most important was difficult, however, so attention turned to styles of leadership behavior. In recent years, several styles of leadership have emerged, including *autocratic, participative,* and *entrepreneurial.*

Autocratic leadership is very task oriented. Decisions are made confidently, with little concern about employee opinions. Employees are told exactly what is expected from them and given specific guidelines, rules, and regulations on how to achieve their tasks. At one time, managers at UPS used autocratic leadership. Managers at Hyundai USA also successfully employ the authoritarian leadership style.[10]

Participative leadership is common in today's business organizations. Participative leaders consult workers before making decisions. This helps workers understand which goals are important and fosters a sense of ownership and commitment to reach those goals. Participative leaders can be classified into three groups: consultative, consensus, and democratic. *Consultative leaders* discuss issues with workers but retain the final authority for decision making. *Consensus leaders* seek input from almost all workers and make final decisions based on their support. *Democratic leaders* give final authority to the group. They collect opinions and base their decisions on the vote of the group. Google co-founders Larry Page and Sergey Brin are known for their democratic decision-making styles.[11] Communication is active upward and downward in participative organizations. Coaching, collaborating, and negotiating are important skills for participative leaders.

Entrepreneurial leadership is personality dependent. Although each entrepreneur is different, this leadership style is generally task-oriented, driven, charismatic, and enthusiastic.[12] The entrepreneurial personality tends to take initiative, venture into new areas, be visionary, and focus on the next deal. Their enthusiasm energizes and inspires their people. Entrepreneurial leaders take responsibility for the success or failure of their firm, and often don't understand why their employees don't always share their passion for their work.[13]

Executives Rank Men and Women Differently on Workplace Characteristics

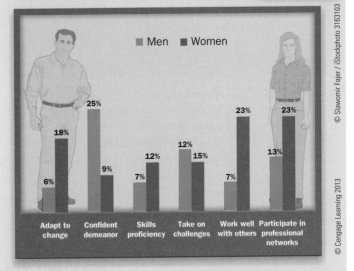

© Slawomir Fajer / iStockphoto 3163103

© Cengage Learning 2013

Source: Accenture 2010 International Women's Day Survey of 524 senior executives from 20 countries around the world. These results are from the U.S. only. Margin of error ±4 percentage points. www.accenture.com/SiteCollectionDocuments/PDF/Accenture_Womens_Research_Women_Leaders_and_Resilience3.pdf

autocratic leadership task-oriented leadership style in which workers are told what to do and how to accomplish it; workers have no say in the decision-making process

participative leadership leadership style in which all members of a team are involved in identifying essential goals and developing strategies to reach those goals

entrepreneurial leadership personality-based leadership style in which the manager seeks to inspire workers with a vision of what can be accomplished to benefit all stakeholders

Leadership style. Apple co-founder, Steve Jobs, was always known for his leadership style that helped to create an environment that nurtured and enhanced the creation of technology-based products. The people at Apple will miss his leadership skills, but the world will miss his creative genius.

© Ryan Anson/AFP/Getty Images

Which Leadership Style Is the Best?

Today, most management experts agree that no "best" managerial leadership style exists. Each of the styles described—autocratic, participative, and entrepreneurial—has advantages and disadvantages. Participative leadership can motivate employees to work effectively because they are implementing their own decisions. However, the decision-making process in participative leadership takes time that subordinates could be devoting to the work itself. Table 6-1 presents tips for effective leadership. Most of these tips are consistent with the participative leadership style.

Although hundreds of research studies have been conducted to prove which leadership style is best, there are no definite conclusions. The "best" leadership seems to occur when the leader's style matches the situation. Each of the leadership styles can be effective in the right situation. The *most* effective style depends on interaction among employees, characteristics of the work situation, and the manager's personality.

* *Concept Check*

☐ Describe the major leadership styles.

☐ Which one is best?

LEARNING OBJECTIVE

6 Discuss the steps in the managerial decision-making process.

MANAGERIAL DECISION MAKING

Decision making is the act of choosing one alternative from a set of alternatives.[14] In ordinary situations, decisions are made casually and informally. We encounter a problem, mull it over, settle on a solution, and go on. Managers, however, require a more systematic method for solving complex problems. As shown in Figure 6-9, managerial decision making involves four steps: (1) identifying the problem or opportunity, (2) generating alternatives, (3) selecting an alternative, and (4) implementing and evaluating the solution.

decision making the act of choosing one alternative from a set of alternatives

TABLE 6-1: Tips for Successful Leadership

1. Walk the talk. Make your actions consistent with your words.
2. Be truthful, fair, and respectful, and honor confidences.
3. Demonstrate a vision and values worth following.
4. Co-workers make mistakes. So do you. Admit to them and learn from them.
5. Be open to what others have to offer. Ask questions and take time to listen to co-workers.
6. Know your weaknesses, so you can build a team to make up for them.
7. All work and no fun can reduce productivity.
8. Help workers do their best by encouraging them to grow and learn.
9. Never publicly blame anyone but yourself.
10. Stay positive and expect it of your people. Negativity leads downhill fast.
11. Involve people in decisions—especially those regarding change.
12. Be open to new ways of doing things. Embrace change—it's inevitable.
13. Recognize and celebrate individual and team successes, both big and not so big.
14. Embrace and benefit from diversity.
15. Empower your workers. They will have greater self-respect, responsibility, and accountability.
16. Take your work, but not yourself, seriously.

© Cengage Learning 2013

178

Part 3 : Management and Organization

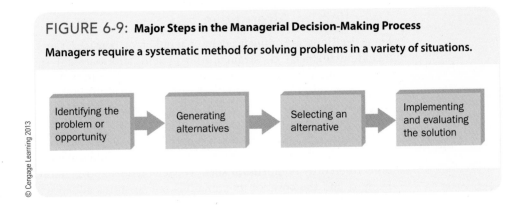

FIGURE 6-9: **Major Steps in the Managerial Decision-Making Process**

Managers require a systematic method for solving problems in a variety of situations.

© Cengage Learning 2013

Personal App You make dozens of decisions every single day. Although some are very big (such as which school to attend or what company to work for), most are quite small (which snack to eat, which shoes to wear). Knowing how to make a decision will help you do a better job of managing the business of *your* life.

Identifying the Problem or Opportunity

A **problem** is the discrepancy between an actual condition and a desired condition—the difference between what is occurring and what one wishes would occur. For example, a marketing manager at Campbell Soup Company has a problem if sales revenues for Campbell's Hungry Man frozen dinners are declining (the actual condition). To solve this problem, the marketing manager must take steps to increase sales revenues (desired condition). Most people consider a problem to be "negative;" however, a problem also can be "positive." A positive problem should be viewed as an "opportunity."

Although accurate identification of a problem is essential before it can be solved or turned into an opportunity, this stage of decision making creates many difficulties for managers. Sometimes managers' preconceptions of the problem prevent them from seeing the actual situation. They produce an answer before the proper question has been asked. In other cases, managers overlook truly significant issues by focusing on unimportant matters. Also, managers may mistakenly analyze problems in terms of symptoms rather than underlying causes.

Effective managers learn to look ahead so that they are prepared when decisions must be made. They clarify situations and examine the causes of problems, asking whether the presence or absence of certain variables alters a situation. Finally, they consider how individual behaviors and values affect the way problems or opportunities are defined.

Generating Alternatives

After a problem has been defined, the next task is to generate alternatives. The more important the decision, the more attention that must be devoted to this stage. Managers should be open to fresh, innovative ideas as well as obvious answers.

Certain techniques can aid in the generation of creative alternatives. Brainstorming, commonly used in group discussions, encourages participants to produce many new ideas. During brainstorming, other group members are not permitted to criticize or ridicule. Another approach, developed by the U.S. Navy, is called "Blast! Then Refine." Group members tackle a recurring problem by erasing all previous solutions and procedures. The group then re-evaluates its original objectives, modifies them if necessary, and devises new solutions. Other techniques—including trial and error—are also useful in this stage of decision making.

problem the discrepancy between an actual condition and a desired condition

SOCIAL MEDIA @

Through Social Media, Do Workers Create Problems for Their Employers?

© Eray Haciosmanoglu/iStockphoto 4968487

How should managers handle employee use of social media? Despite the growing popularity of Facebook, LinkedIn, Twitter, and other sites, some companies are concerned that employees will disclose proprietary information or become involved in controversial conversations that could harm the company's image. They also worry that employees will be distracted during the workday.

Employers in a few industries—such as financial services—are required to monitor business-related messages posted by employees to ensure compliance with government regulations. In most cases, however, companies are free to set their own policies. For example, IBM's policy requires employees to use respectful language, obey copyright laws, and indicate that their views are personal.

© Juan Camilo Bernal/Shutterstock

Sources: Melinda J. Caterine, "Your Business: Make Your Social Media Policy Clear," *Portland Press Herald (Maine)*, January 25, 2011, www.pressherald.com; Tamara Schweitzer, "Do You Need a Social Media Policy?" *Inc.*, January 25, 2010, www.inc.com; David Scheer, "Brokers' Facebook, Twitter Posts Must Be Tracked by Employers," *BusinessWeek*, January 25, 2010, www.businessweek.com.

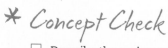

Concept Check

☐ Describe the major steps in the managerial decision-making process.

☐ Why does a manager need to evaluate the solution and look for problems after a solution has been implemented?

Selecting an Alternative

Final decisions are influenced by a number of considerations, including financial constraints, human and informational resources, time limits, legal obstacles, and political factors. Managers must select the alternative that will be most effective and practical. Starbucks, for example, was experiencing high profits a few years ago as it continued to expand to more than 17,000 stores. However, the recession eventually caught up with the company, as more of its customers turned to less expensive options offered by competition such as McDonald's and Dunkin' Donuts, and the costs of its numerous failing stores added up. In an effort to turn Starbucks around, Howard Schultz, the man who bought the first six stores in 1987, returned to the CEO position and rehired many of the original top management staff to help lead the company's renovation. Starbucks then began an extensive process of closing low-producing stores and laying off workers, as management tried to return the company's focus back to urban areas. New stores were no longer cookie cutouts of each other, but instead were each specifically targeted to their community, with the product offering and store appearance varying by location. Many new locations didn't even carry the Starbucks name, such as the 15th Avenue Coffee and Tea in Seattle. One year later, Starbucks' net income had nearly quadrupled as it began to see the effects of its changes.[15]

At times, two or more alternatives or some combination of alternatives will be equally appropriate. Managers may choose solutions to problems on several levels. The coined word *satisfice* describes solutions that are only adequate and not ideal. When lacking time or information, managers often make decisions that "satisfice." Whenever possible, managers should try to investigate alternatives carefully and select the ideal solution.

Implementing and Evaluating the Solution

Implementation of a decision requires time, planning, preparation of personnel, and evaluation of results. Managers usually deal with unforeseen consequences even when they have carefully considered the alternatives.

The final step in managerial decision making entails evaluating a decision's effectiveness. If the alternative that was chosen removes the difference between the actual condition and the desired condition, the decision is considered effective. If the problem still exists, managers may select one of the following choices:

- Decide to give the chosen alternative more time to work.
- Adopt a different alternative.
- Start the problem identification process all over again.

Failure to evaluate decisions adequately may have negative consequences. For example, Toyota suffered negative consequences after its focus on rapid growth led to a series of recalls that damaged the company's reputation for quality. In 2002, Toyota executives announced plans to become the largest automaker by attaining 15 percent of the global market share for automobiles. Although the company reached their goal less than eight years later, their choice to cut costs by switching to less-expensive suppliers for parts led to recent issues with faulty accelerator pedals. These issues temporarily stopped production in several countries and caused Toyota to recall over eight million vehicles worldwide, making it the largest automobile recall in history.[16]

MANAGING TOTAL QUALITY

Personal App **As a customer, you don't want a defective computer or erratic cell phone service. That's why quality matters. As a customer, you can make a difference by speaking up about problems. And as an employee, you can make a difference by helping to improve whatever you're working on.**

The management of quality is a high priority in some organizations today. Major reasons for a greater focus on quality include foreign competition, more demanding customers, and poor financial performance resulting from reduced market shares and higher costs. Over the last few years, several U.S. firms have lost the dominant competitive positions they had held for decades.

Total quality management. Starbucks CEO Howard Schultz, who espouses the importance and methods of total quality management, addresses the company's shareholders.

© AP Images/Elaine Thompson

Total quality management is a much broader concept than just controlling the quality of the product itself (which is discussed in Chapter 8). **Total quality management (TQM)** is the coordination of efforts directed at improving customer satisfaction, increasing employee participation, strengthening supplier partnerships, and facilitating an organizational atmosphere of continuous quality improvement. For TQM programs to be effective, management must address each of the following components:

- *Customer satisfaction.* Ways to improve include producing higher-quality products, providing better customer service, and showing customers that the company cares.
- *Employee participation.* This can be increased by allowing employees to contribute to decisions, develop self-managed work teams, and assume responsibility for improving the quality of their work.
- *Strengthening supplier partnerships.* Developing good working relationships with suppliers can ensure that the right supplies and materials will be delivered on time at lower costs.
- *Continuous quality improvement.* This should not be viewed as achievable through one single program that has a target objective. A program based on continuous improvement has proven to be the most effective long-term approach.

LEARNING OBJECTIVE

7 Describe how organizations benefit from total quality management.

One tool that is used for TQM is called benchmarking. **Benchmarking** is the process of evaluating the products, processes, or management practices of another organization for the purpose of improving quality. The focal organization may be superior in safety, customer service, productivity, innovativeness, or in some other way.

For example, competitor's products might be disassembled and evaluated, or wage and benefit plans might be surveyed to measure compensation packages against the labor market. The four basic steps of benchmarking are identifying objectives, forming a benchmarking team, collecting data, analyzing data, and acting on the results. Best practices may be discovered in any industry or organization.

Although many factors influence the effectiveness of a TQM program, two issues are crucial. First, top management must make a strong commitment to a TQM program by treating quality improvement as a top priority and giving it frequent

total quality management (TQM) the coordination of efforts directed at improving customer satisfaction, increasing employee participation, strengthening supplier partnerships, and facilitating an organizational atmosphere of continuous quality improvement

benchmarking a process used to evaluate the products, processes, or management practices of another organization that is superior in some way in order to improve quality

❋ *Concept Check*

☐ Why does top management need to be strongly committed to TQM programs?

☐ Describe the major components of a TQM program.

attention. Firms that establish a TQM program but then focus on other priorities will find that their quality-improvement initiatives will fail. Second, management must coordinate the specific elements of a TQM program so that they work in harmony with each other.

Although not all U.S. companies have TQM programs, these programs provide many benefits. Overall financial benefits include lower operating costs, higher return on sales and on investments, and an improved ability to use premium pricing rather than competitive pricing. Motorola has successfully implemented a TQM program, which helps the company reduce defects and keep up with its competitors technologically.[17]

Get Flashcards, Quizzes, Games, Crosswords, and more @ **www.cengagebrain.com**

SUMMARY

1 Define what management is.

Management is the process of coordinating people and other resources to achieve an organization's goals. Managers are concerned with four types of resources—material, human, financial, and informational.

2 Describe the four basic management functions: planning, organizing, leading and motivating, and controlling.

Managers perform four basic functions. Management functions do not occur according to some rigid, preset timetable, though. At any time, managers may engage in a number of functions simultaneously. However, each function tends to lead naturally to others. First, managers engage in planning—determining where the firm should be going and how best to get there. One method of planning that can be used is SWOT analysis, which identifies and evaluates a firm's strengths, weaknesses, opportunities, and threats. Three types of plans, from the broadest to the most specific, are strategic plans, tactical plans, and operational plans. Managers also organize resources and activities to accomplish results in an efficient and effective manner, and they lead and motivate others to work in the best interests of the organization. In addition, managers control ongoing activities to keep the organization on course. There are three steps in the control function: setting standards, measuring actual performance, and taking corrective action.

3 Distinguish among the various kinds of managers in terms of both level and area of management.

Managers—or management positions—may be classified from two different perspectives. From the perspective of level within the organization, there are top managers, who control the fortunes of the organization; middle managers, who implement strategies and major policies; and first-line managers, who supervise the activities of operating employees. From the viewpoint of area of management, managers most often deal with the areas of finance, operations, marketing, human resources, and administration.

4 Identify the key management skills of successful managers.

Managers need a variety of skills in order to run a successful and efficient business. Conceptual skills are used to think in abstract terms or see the "big picture." Analytic skills are used to identify problems correctly, generate reasonable alternatives, and select the "best" alternatives to solve problems. Interpersonal skills are used to deal effectively with other people, both inside and outside an organization. Technical skills are needed to accomplish a specialized activity, whether they are used to actually do the task or used to train and assist employees. Communication skills are used to speak, listen, and write effectively.

5 Explain the different types of leadership.

Managers' effectiveness often depends on their styles of leadership—that is, their ability to influence others, either formally or informally. Autocratic leaders are very task oriented; they tell their employees exactly what is expected from them and give them specific instructions on how to do their assigned tasks. Participative leaders consult their employees before making decisions and can be classified into three groups: consultative, consensus, and democratic. Entrepreneurial leaders are different depending on their personalities, but they are generally enthusiastic and passionate about their work and tend to take initiative.

6 Discuss the steps in the managerial decision-making process.

Decision making, an integral part of a manager's work, is the process of developing a set of possible alternative solutions to a problem and choosing one alternative from among the set. Managerial decision making involves four steps: Managers must accurately identify problems, generate several possible solutions, choose the solution that will be most effective under the circumstances, and implement and evaluate the chosen course of action.

7 Describe how organizations benefit from total quality management.

Total quality management (TQM) is the coordination of efforts directed at improving customer satisfaction, increasing employee participation, strengthening supplier partnerships, and facilitating an organizational atmosphere of continuous quality improvement. Another tool used for TQM is benchmarking, which is used to evaluate the products, processes, or management practices of another organization that is superior in some way in order to improve quality. The five basic steps in benchmarking are identifying objectives, forming a benchmarking team, collecting data, analyzing data, and acting on the results. To have an effective TQM program, top management must make a strong, sustained commitment to the effort and must be able to coordinate all the program's elements so that they work in harmony. Overall financial benefits of TQM include lower operating costs, higher return on sales and on investment, and an improved ability to use premium pricing rather than competitive pricing.

KEY TERMS

You should now be able to define and give an example relevant to each of the following terms:

management (165)
planning (167)
mission (167)
strategic planning process (167)
goal (167)
objective (167)
SWOT analysis (168)
core competencies (168)
plan (169)
strategic plan (169)
tactical plan (169)

operational plan (170)
contingency plan (170)
organizing (170)
leading (171)
motivating (171)
directing (171)
controlling (171)
top manager (172)
middle manager (172)
first-line manager (173)
financial manager (173)
operations manager (173)

marketing manager (173)
human resources manager (173)
administrative manager (174)
conceptual skills (174)
analytic skills (175)
interpersonal skills (175)
technical skills (176)
communication skills (176)
leadership (176)

autocratic leadership (177)
participative leadership (177)
entrepreneurial leadership (177)
decision making (178)
problem (179)
total quality management (TQM) (181)
benchmarking (181)

DISCUSSION QUESTIONS

1. Define the word *manager* without using the word *management* in your definition.
2. Does a healthy firm (one that is doing well) have to worry about effective management? Explain.
3. What might be the mission of a neighborhood restaurant? Of the Salvation Army? What might be reasonable objectives for these organizations?
4. What are the major elements of SWOT analysis?
5. How do a strategic plan, a tactical plan, and an operational plan differ? What do they all have in common?
6. Why are leadership and motivation necessary in a business in which people are paid for their work?
7. Compare and contrast the major styles of leadership.

8. According to this chapter, the leadership style that is *most* effective depends on interaction among the employees, characteristics of the work situation, and the manager's personality. Do you agree or disagree? Explain your answer.
9. What are the major benefits of a total quality management program?
10. Do you think that people are really as important to an organization as this chapter seems to indicate?
11. Discuss what happens during each of the four steps of the managerial decision-making process.
12. As you learned in this chapter, managers often work long hours at a hectic pace. Would this type of career appeal to you? Explain.

TEST YOURSELF

Matching Questions

1. _____ The process of accomplishing objectives through people.

2. _____ The process of establishing an organization's goals and objectives.

3. _____ Its purpose is to implement a strategy.

4. _____ Its purpose is to outline alternative courses of action.

5. _____ Process of influencing people to work.

6. _____ It is a combination of leading and motivating.

7. _____ A vast amount of time is spent motivating employees.

8. _____ Specific skills needed to work a computer.

9. _____ The ability to influence others.

10. _____ Improving customer satisfaction and increasing employee participation are two objectives of this process.

   a. conceptual skills
   b. contingency plan
   c. directing
   d. first-line manager
   e. leadership
   f. leading
   g. management
   h. operations manager
   i. strategic planning
   j. tactical plan
   k. technical skills
   l. total quality management (TQM)

True False Questions

11. **T** **F** Management functions occur according to a rigid, preset timetable.

12. **T** **F** As managers carry out their functions, the first step is to control, the second to organize, and the third to plan.

13. **T** **F** An organization's mission is the means by which it fulfills its purpose.

14. **T** **F** SWOT analysis is the identification and evaluation of a firm's internal strengths, weaknesses, opportunities, and tactics.

15. **T** **F** Operational plans aimed at increasing sales would include specific advertising activities.

16. **T** **F** Measuring actual performance is the first step in the control process.

17. **T** **F** Top managers rely on technical skills more than managers at other levels.

18. **T** **F** A democratic leader makes all the decisions and tells subordinates what to do.

19. **T** **F** Brainstorming is a common technique used to generate alternatives in solving problems.

20. **T** **F** Implementation of a decision requires time, planning, preparation of personnel, and evaluation of results.

Multiple-Choice Questions

21. _____ The process of developing a set of goals and committing an organization to them is called
   a. organizing.
   b. planning.
   c. motivating.
   d. controlling.
   e. directing.

22. _____ Grouping resources and activities to accomplish some goal is called
   a. motivating.
   b. directing.
   c. leading.
   d. planning.
   e. organizing.

23. _____ Acme Houseware established a goal to increase its sales by 20 percent in the next year. To ensure that the firm reaches its goal, the sales reports are monitored on a weekly basis. When sales show a slight decline, the sales manager takes actions to correct the problem. Which management function is the manager using?
   a. Leading
   b. Controlling
   c. Directing
   d. Organizing
   e. Planning

24. _____ Who is responsible for developing a firm's mission?
   a. Top managers
   b. First-level managers
   c. Operations managers
   d. Middle managers
   e. Supervisors

25. _____ The chief executive officer of Southwest Airlines provides the company with leadership and overall guidance and is responsible for developing its mission and establishing its goals. Which area of management is being used?
   a. Human resources
   b. Operations
   c. Financial
   d. Administrative
   e. Marketing

26. _____ This manager is responsible for facilitating the exchange of products between an organization and its customers or clients.
   a. Human resources manager
   b. Marketing manager
   c. Operations manager
   d. Financial manager
   e. Administrative manager

27. _____ These types of skills allow a manager to see the "big picture" and understand how the various parts of an organization or idea can fit together.
   a. Interpersonal skills
   b. Conceptual skills
   c. Technical skills
   d. Communication skills
   e. Analytical skills

28. _____ Because a large part of the manager's day is spent conversing with others, it is important for the managers to have
   a. conceptual skills.
   b. analytical skills.
   c. technical skills.
   d. communication skills.
   e. interpersonal skills.

29. _____ What leadership style is task-oriented, driven, charismatic, and enthusiastic?
   a. Autocratic leadership
   b. Participative leadership
   c. Entrepreneurial leadership
   d. Democratic leadership

30. _____ Which of the following statements is correct about TQM?
   a. Top management must make a strong commitment to a TQM program by treating quality improvement as a top priority.
   b. Employees should be aware of TQM movement, not necessarily involved in it.
   c. Managers need to ask for input occasionally in order to practice TQM.
   d. The top administration should appear to be interested in TQM.
   e. In order for TQM to function effectively, you need a lot of resources.

Answers to the Test Yourself questions appear at the end of the book on page TY-1.

VIDEO CASE
L.L. Bean Relies on Its Core Values and Effective Leadership

L.L. Bean's first product was a waterproof boot, designed by Maine outdoorsman Leon Leonwood Bean, who promised complete customer satisfaction. One hundred pairs were sold—and 90 pairs were returned because of a defect. Bean refunded the customers' money and went to work perfecting the product, now one of the most popular in the firm's long and successful history.

L.L. Bean began in 1912 as a tiny mail-order company and has grown to include 14 retail stores in ten states, an online store, and a popular catalog showcasing many of the company's 20,000 items, including high-quality clothing, accessories, outdoor gear, luggage, linens, and furniture. It is still privately owned and family run and has had just three presidents in its history—L.L. Bean himself, his grandson Leon Gorman, and now Chris McCormick, the first nonfamily member to lead the firm. New England is the core of L.L. Bean's market, and its selling cycle accelerates sharply every year around the winter holidays. Headquartered in Freeport, Maine, near its original store, the company reports annual sales of over $1.5 billion.

Managers at L.L. Bean today have many opportunities for using their planning, organizing, leading, and controlling skills. During the preholiday selling season, for instance, temporary workers hired to handle the increased workload bring the normal staff of about 4,600 to almost double its size, so managers have to reorganize the teams of 25 to 30 front-line employees who work in the call centers. Regular employees not currently in leadership positions are asked to head the teams of temps, ensuring they have an experienced person to help them develop their skills and perform to expectations. This organizing strategy works so well that many temps return year after year.

Planning skills come to the fore when top management decides when and where to open new retail stores, whether to expand the number of outlet stores offering discontinued items and overstocks, and how much to invest in ensuring that L.L. Bean buildings meet the highest standards of environmental stewardship. One recent strategic planning project resulted in the creation of a new clothing and accessories collection called L.L. Bean Signature, featuring updated versions of classic items from the company's 100-year heritage.

With respect to the control function, managers assess employee performance with a continuous evaluation process. Corporate-level goals are broken down to the level of the individual store and employee. If something isn't on track, the supervisor is expected to let the employee know and help figure out a solution. However, control at L.L. Bean is not entirely a top-down process. Employees are encouraged to develop their own personal goals, such as learning a new skill or gaining a better appreciation of the way L.L. Bean makes business decisions. Managers help them find ways to meet these personal objectives as well, through a temporary reassignment within the firm or participation in a special company project.

L.L. Bean has a strong collaborative work culture in which it is equally important to work through your supervisor, your co-workers, and your subordinates. That means everyone is a leader to some extent. Formal management candidates are asked to demonstrate both analytical and interpersonal skills and to model the company's six core values: outdoor heritage, integrity, service, respect, perseverance, and safe and healthy living. In the early days of the company, L.L. Bean lived above the store and would come downstairs in the middle of the night to help a customer who rang the bell. "A customer is the most important person ever in this office—in person or by mail," he was fond of saying. So, true to his beliefs, leadership style continues to revolve around serving the customer's needs. As one L.L. Bean manager said, the company is all about salespeople and customer service representatives so that they can better serve customers.[18]

Questions

1. What style of leadership do you think most L.L. Bean managers probably employ?
2. To produce hot water in L.L. Bean's flagship store, the company recently installed a solar hot water system that will offset almost 11,000 pounds of carbon dioxide emissions every year. Suggest some of the questions the company's managers might have asked at each level of planning (strategic, tactical, operational, and contingency) for this project.
3. Which managerial role or roles do you think the leaders of L.L. Bean's temp teams fill?

BUILDING SKILLS FOR CAREER SUCCESS

1. Exploring the Internet

Most large companies call on a management consulting firm for a variety of services, including employee training, help in the selection of an expensive purchase such as a computer system, recruitment of employees, and direction in reorganization and strategic planning.

Large consulting firms generally operate globally and provide information to companies considering entry into foreign countries or business alliances with foreign firms. They use their Web sites, along with magazine-style articles, to celebrate achievements and present their credentials to clients. Business students can acquire an enormous amount of up-to-date information in the field of management by perusing these sites.

Assignment

1. Explore each of the following Web sites:

    Accenture: www.accenture.com
    BearingPoint (formerly KPMG Consulting):
    www.bearingpoint.com
    Cap Gemini Ernst & Young: www.capgemini.com
    Visit the text Web site for updates to this exercise.

2. Judging from the articles and notices posted, what are the current areas of activities of one of these firms?

3. Explore one of these areas in more detail by comparing postings from each firm's site. For instance, if "global business opportunities" appears to be a popular area of management consulting, how has each firm distinguished itself in this area? Who would you call first for advice?

4. Given that consulting firms are always trying to fill positions for their clients and to meet their own recruitment needs, it is little wonder that employment postings are a popular area on their sites. Examine these in detail. Based on your examination of the site and the registration format, what sort of recruit are they interested in?

2. Building Team Skills

Over the past few years, an increasing number of employees, stockholders, and customers have been demanding to know what their companies are about. As a result, more companies have been taking the time to analyze their operations and to prepare mission statements that focus on the purpose of the company. The mission statement is becoming a critical planning tool for successful companies. To make effective decisions, employees must understand the purpose of their company.

Assignment

1. Divide into teams and write a mission statement for one of the following types of businesses:

    Food service, restaurant
    Banking
    Airline
    Auto repair
    Cabinet manufacturing

2. Discuss your mission statement with other teams. How did the other teams interpret the purpose of your company? What is the mission statement saying about the company?

3. Write a one-page report on what you learned about developing mission statements.

186

3. Researching Different Careers

A successful career requires planning. Without a plan, or roadmap, you will find it very difficult, if not impossible, to reach your desired career destination. The first step in planning is to establish your career goal. You then must set objectives and develop plans for accomplishing those objectives. This kind of planning takes time, but it will pay off later.

Assignment

Complete the following statements:

1. My career goal is to

_____

_____

_____

_____

This statement should encapsulate what you want to accomplish over the long run. It may include the type of job you want and the type of business or industry you want to work in. Examples include the following:

- My career goal is to work as a top manager in the food industry.
- My career goal is to supervise aircraft mechanics.
- My career goal is to win the top achievement award in the advertising industry.

2. My career objectives are to

_____

_____

_____

_____

Objectives are benchmarks along the route to a career destination. They are more specific than a career goal. A statement about a career objective should specify what you want to accomplish, when you will complete it, and any other details that will serve as criteria against which you can measure your progress. Examples include the following:

- My objective is to enroll in a management course at Main College in the spring semester 2012.
- My objective is to earn an A in the management course at Main College in the spring semester 2012.
- My objective is to be promoted to supervisor by January 1, 2013.
- My objective is to prepare a status report by September 30 covering the last quarter's activities by asking Charlie in Quality Control to teach me the procedures.

3. Exchange your goal and objectives statements with another class member. Can your partner interpret your objectives correctly? Are the objectives concise and complete? Do they include criteria against which you can measure your progress? If not, discuss the problem and rewrite the objective.

CHAPTER 7 CREATING A FLEXIBLE ORGANIZATION

© Mozgova /Shutterstock

Why should you care?

To operate a business at an acceptable level of profitability, those in charge must create an organization that not only operates efficiently but also is able to attract resources, such as employees, and to develop long-term relationships with customers.

Learning Objectives

What you will be able to do once you complete this chapter:

1 Understand what an organization is and identify its characteristics.

2 Explain why job specialization is important.

3 Identify the various bases for departmentalization.

4 Explain how decentralization follows from delegation.

5 Understand how the span of management describes an organization.

6 Describe the four basic forms of organizational structure.

7 Describe the effects of corporate culture.

8 Understand how committees and task forces are used.

9 Explain the functions of the informal organization and the grapevine in a business.

Get Flashcards, Quizzes, Games, Crosswords, and more @ www.cengagebrain.com

Why Nokia Needed a New Structure

Although Nokia was founded in Finland during the nineteenth century, its management has a very global, very twenty-first century outlook on the business world. The company was started as a paper manufacturer in 1865. A century later, after merging with a rubber company and a cable company, Nokia entered the electronics industry. By 1992, it had restructured to concentrate exclusively on telecommunications. This strategic decision drove revenues and profits to new heights year after year as Nokia expanded and strengthened its position as a worldwide mobile-phone leader.

However, Nokia's lineup of cell phones soon ran into intense competition from cutting-edge smart-phones introduced by fast-moving rivals such as Apple and Samsung. The company moved into smart-phones even as its profit margins were being squeezed by higher costs and it was feeling pressure to cut prices. Now, with multiple management layers and an international workforce of 130,000 employees, decision making was getting bogged down just when Nokia needed to be nimble and innovative. Despite its well-known brand, its huge customer base, and its impressive production efficiency, the firm wouldn't be able to grow as quickly and compete as effectively without rapid, radical change.

Early in 2011, the CEO announced that "Nokia is at a critical juncture, where significant change is necessary and inevitable in our journey forward to make the most of emerging opportunities." He reorganized the company into two major product divisions, smart devices and mobile phones, and began selling off business units that weren't a good fit with the new organization. He also forged a strategic alliance by adopting Microsoft's Bing search technology and its Windows Phone software for new multi-function smart-phones. Moreover, Nokia is partnering with Microsoft to market digital applications for next-generation communications devices. This cuts Nokia's costs for development while opening the door to lucrative new revenue possibilities for both partners. Finally, Nokia is allowing local executives to make decisions that previously had to be referred to top management. This will help make the company more responsive to trends, competition, and opportunities that emerge in any market, at any time.[1]

Did you know?

Nokia, founded in 1865, was named for the river that flows near the firm's second production plant in Finland.

To survive and to grow, companies such as Nokia must constantly look for ways to improve their methods of doing business. Managers at Nokia, like those at many other organizations, deliberately reorganized the company to achieve its goals and to create satisfying products that foster long-term customer relationships.

When firms are organized, or reorganized, the focus is sometimes on achieving low operating costs. Other firms, such as Nike, emphasize providing high-quality products to ensure customer satisfaction. A firm's organization influences its performance. Thus, the issue of organization is important.

We begin this chapter by examining the business organization—what it is and how it functions in today's business environment. Next, we focus one by one on five characteristics that shape an organization's structure. We discuss job specialization within a company, the grouping of jobs into manageable units or departments, the delegation of power from management to workers, the span of management, and establishment of a chain of command. Then we step back for an overall view of organizational structure, describe the effects of corporate culture, and focus in on how committees and task forces are used. Finally, we look at the network of social interactions—the informal organization—that operates within the formal business structure.

FIGURE 7-1: A Typical Corporate Organization Chart

A company's organization chart represents the positions and relationships within the organization and shows the managerial chains of command.

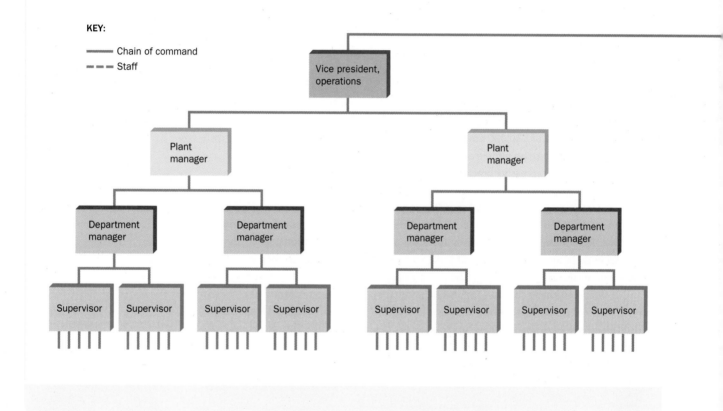

KEY:

— Chain of command

- - - Staff

WHAT IS AN ORGANIZATION?

LEARNING OBJECTIVE

1 Understand what an organization is and identify its characteristics.

We used the term *organization* throughout Chapter 6 without really defining it mainly because its everyday meaning is close to its business meaning. Here, however, let us agree that an **organization** is a group of two or more people working together to achieve a common set of goals. A neighborhood dry cleaner owned and operated by a husband-and-wife team is an organization. IBM and Home Depot, which employ thousands of workers worldwide, are also organizations in the same sense. Although each corporation's organizational structure is more complex than the dry-cleaning establishment, all must be organized to achieve their goals.

An inventor who goes into business to produce and market a new invention hires people, decides what each will do, determines who will report to whom, and so on. These activities are the essence of organizing, or creating, the organization. One way to create this "picture" is to create an organization chart.

organization a group of two or more people working together to achieve a common set of goals

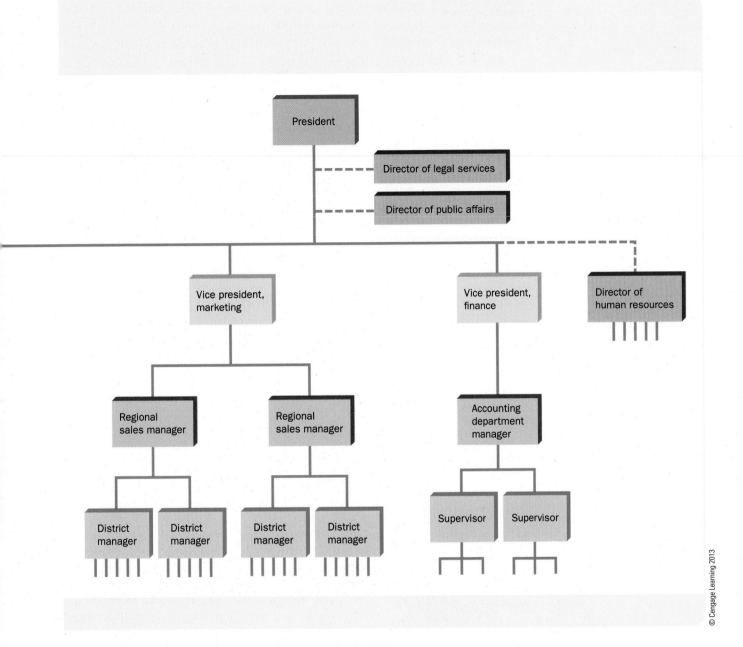

Developing Organization Charts

An **organization chart** is a diagram that represents the positions and relationships within an organization. An example of an organization chart is shown in Figure 7-1. Each rectangle represents a particular position or person in the organization. At the top is the president, at the next level are the vice presidents. The solid vertical lines connecting the vice presidents to the president indicate that the vice presidents are in the chain of command. The **chain of command** is the line of authority that extends from the highest to the lowest levels of the organization. Moreover, each vice president reports directly to the president. Similarly, the plant managers, regional sales managers, and accounting department manager report to the vice presidents. The chain of command can be short or long. For example, at Royer's Roundtop Café, an independent restaurant in Roundtop, Texas, the chain of command is very short. Bud Royer, the owner, is responsible only to himself and can alter his hours or change his menu quickly. On the other hand, the chain of command at McDonald's is long. Before making certain types of changes, a McDonald's franchisee seeks permission from regional management, which, in turn, seeks approval from corporate headquarters.

organization chart a diagram that represents the positions and relationships within an organization

chain of command the line of authority that extends from the highest to the lowest levels of an organization

In the chart, the connections to the directors of legal services, public affairs, and human resources are shown as broken lines; these people are not part of the direct chain of command. Instead, they hold *advisory*, or *staff*, positions. This difference will be examined later in this chapter when we discuss line-and-staff positions.

Most smaller organizations find organization charts useful. They clarify positions and report relationships for everyone in the organization, and they help managers to track growth and change in the organizational structure. However, many large organizations, such as ExxonMobil, Kellogg's, and Procter & Gamble, do not maintain complete, detailed charts for two reasons. First, it is difficult to chart even a few dozen positions accurately, much less the thousands that characterize larger firms. Second, larger organizations are almost always changing parts of their structure. An organization chart would be outdated before it was completed. However, organization must exist even without a chart in order for a business to be successful. Technology is helping large companies implement up-to-date organization charts.

Major Considerations for Organizing a Business

When a firm is started, management must decide how to organize the firm. These decisions focus on job design, departmentalization, delegation, span of management, and chain of command. In the next several sections, we discuss major issues associated with these dimensions.

JOB DESIGN

In Chapter 1, we defined *specialization* as the separation of a manufacturing process into distinct tasks and the assignment of different tasks to different people. Here we are extending that concept to *all* the activities performed within an organization.

Job Specialization

Job specialization is the separation of all organizational activities into distinct tasks and the assignment of different tasks to different people. Adam Smith, the 18th-century economist whose theories gave rise to capitalism, was the first to emphasize the power of specialization in his book, *The Wealth of Nations*. According to Smith, the various tasks in a particular pin factory were arranged so that one worker drew the wire for the pins, another straightened the wire, a third cut it, a fourth ground the point, and a fifth attached the head. Smith claimed that 10 men were able to produce 48,000 pins per day. Before specialization, they could produce only 200 pins per day because each worker had to perform all five tasks!

The Rationale for Specialization

For a number of reasons, some job specialization is necessary in every organization because the "job" of most organizations is too large for one person to handle. In a firm such as Chrysler, thousands of people are needed to manufacture automobiles. Others are needed to sell the cars, control the firm's finances, and so on.

Second, when a worker has to learn one specific, highly specialized task, that individual should be able to learn it very efficiently. Third, a worker repeating the same job does not lose time changing from operations,

LEARNING OBJECTIVE

2 Explain why job specialization is important.

job specialization the separation of all organizational activities into distinct tasks and the assignment of different tasks to different people

This employee has a highly specialized job and performs it many times a day. Specialization is highly efficient for the firm, but it can have drawbacks, such as employee boredom and dissatisfaction. What does job rotation provide that can help offset these negative consequences?

© AFP/Getty Images

as the pin workers did when producing complete pins. Fourth, the more specialized the job, the easier it is to design specialized equipment. And finally, the more specialized the job, the easier is the job training.

Alternatives to Job Specialization

Unfortunately, specialization can have negative consequences as well. The most significant drawback is the boredom and dissatisfaction employees may feel when repeating the same job. Bored employees may be absent from work frequently, may not put much effort into their work, and may even sabotage the company's efforts to produce quality products.

To combat these problems, managers often turn to job rotation. **Job rotation** is the systematic shifting of employees from one job to another. For example, a worker may be assigned a different job every week for a four-week period and then return to the first job in the fifth week. Job rotation provides a variety of tasks so that workers are less likely to become bored and dissatisfied. Pharmaceutical company Eli Lilly, for example, uses a form of job rotation for its managers in which it gives them short-term assignments outside their field of expertise to further develop their skills.[2]

Two other approaches—job enlargement and job enrichment—also can provide solutions to the problems caused by job specialization. These topics, along with other methods used to motivate employees, are discussed in Chapter 10.

These co-workers are members of the same department. Some organizations use more than one base for creating departments. If your school or university has more than one campus, for example, it is organized by location, but also by function such as business, social science, math, and perhaps by customer such as undergraduate, graduate, and continuing education students.

© AFP/Getty Images

DEPARTMENTALIZATION

After jobs are designed, they must be grouped together into "working units," or departments. This process is called *departmentalization*. More specifically, **departmentalization** is the process of grouping jobs into manageable units. Several departmentalization bases are used commonly. In fact, most firms use more than one. Today, the most common bases for organizing a business into effective departments are by function, by product, by location, and by customer.

By Function

Departmentalization by function groups jobs that relate to the same organizational activity. Under this scheme, all marketing personnel are grouped together in the marketing department, all production personnel in the production department, and so on.

Most smaller and newer organizations departmentalize by function. Supervision is simplified because everyone is involved in the same activities, and coordination is easy. The disadvantages of this method of grouping jobs are that it can lead to slow decision making and that it tends to emphasize the department over the whole organization.

By Product

Departmentalization by product groups activities related to a particular good or service. This approach is used often by older and larger firms that produce and sell a variety of products. Each department handles its own marketing, production, financial management, and human resources activities.

Departmentalization by product makes decision making easier and provides for the integration of all activities associated with each product. However, it causes some

Concept Check *

☐ What are the positive and negative effects of specialization?

☐ What are three ways to reduce the negative effects of specialization?

LEARNING OBJECTIVE

3 Identify the various bases for departmentalization.

job rotation the systematic shifting of employees from one job to another

departmentalization the process of grouping jobs into manageable units

departmentalization by function grouping jobs that relate to the same organizational activity

departmentalization by product grouping activities related to a particular product or service

duplication of specialized activities—such as finance—from department to department. Moreover, the emphasis is placed on the product rather than on the whole organization.

By Location

Departmentalization by location groups activities according to the defined geographic area in which they are performed. Departmental areas may range from whole countries (for international firms) to regions within countries (for national firms) to areas of several city blocks (for police departments organized into precincts). Departmentalization by location allows the organization to respond readily to the unique demands or requirements of different locations. Nevertheless, a large administrative staff and an elaborate control system may be needed to coordinate operations in many locations.

By Customer

Departmentalization by customer groups activities according to the needs of various customer populations. A local Chevrolet dealership, for example, may have one sales staff to deal with individual consumers and a different sales staff to work with corporate fleet buyers. The obvious advantage of this approach is that it allows the firm to deal efficiently with unique customers or customer groups. The biggest drawback is that a larger-than-usual administrative staff is needed.

Combinations of Bases

Many organizations use more than one of these departmentalization bases.

Take a moment to examine Figure 7-2. Notice that departmentalization by customer is used to organize New-Wave Fashions, Inc., into three major divisions:

departmentalization by location grouping activities according to the defined geographic area in which they are performed

departmentalization by customer grouping activities according to the needs of various customer populations

FIGURE 7-2: **Multibase Departmentalization for New-Wave Fashions, Inc.**

Most firms use more than one basis for departmentalization to improve efficiency and to avoid overlapping positions.

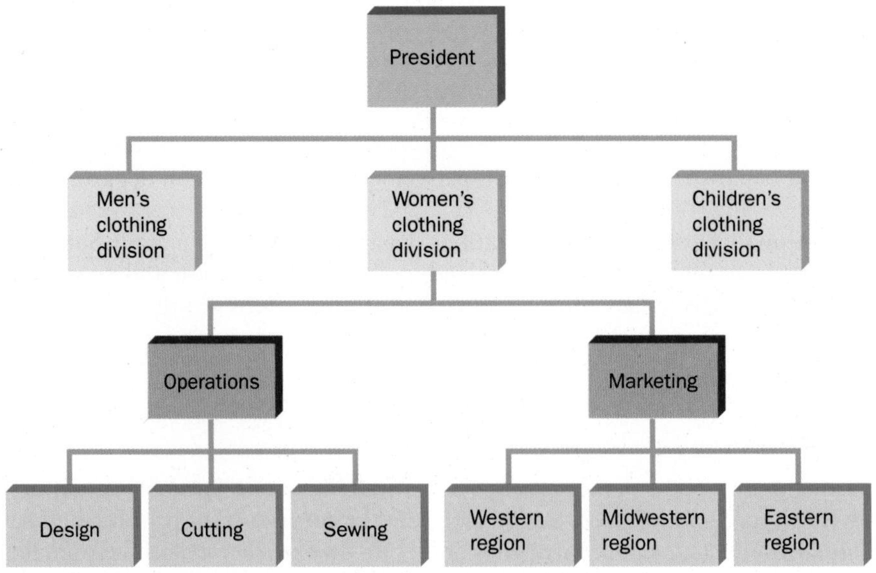

© Cengage Learning 2013

* Concept Check

☐ What are the four most common bases for departmentalization?

☐ Give an example of each.

Part 3: Management and Organization

men's, women's, and children's clothing. Then functional departmentalization is used to distinguish the firm's production and marketing activities. Finally, location is used to organize the firm's marketing efforts.

LEARNING OBJECTIVE
4 Explain how decentralization follows from delegation.

DELEGATION, DECENTRALIZATION, AND CENTRALIZATION

The third major step in the organizing process is to distribute power in the organization. **Delegation** assigns part of a manager's work and power to other workers. The degree of centralization or decentralization of authority is determined by the overall pattern of delegation within the organization.

Delegation of Authority

Because no manager can do everything, delegation is vital to completion of a manager's work. Delegation is also important in developing the skills and abilities of subordinates. It allows those who are being groomed for higher-level positions to play increasingly important roles in decision making.

STEPS IN DELEGATION The delegation process generally involves three steps (see Figure 7-3). First, the manager must *assign responsibility*. **Responsibility** is the duty to do a job or perform a task. In most job settings, a manager simply gives the worker a job to do. Typical job assignments might range from having a worker prepare a report on the status of a new quality control program to placing the person in charge of a task force. Second, the manager must *grant authority*. **Authority** is the power, within the organization, to accomplish an assigned job or task. This might include the power to obtain specific information, order supplies, authorize relevant expenditures, or make certain decisions. Finally, the manager must *create accountability*. **Accountability** is the obligation of a worker to accomplish an assigned job or task.

delegation assigning part of a manager's work and power to other workers

responsibility the duty to do a job or perform a task

authority the power, within an organization, to accomplish an assigned job or task

accountability the obligation of a worker to accomplish an assigned job or task

Personal App Delegation can be tricky in nonbusiness situations. How do you get things done when you're put in charge of a volunteer or school project? What happens if you're accountable but you don't have the authority to make things happen?

Note that accountability is created, but it cannot be delegated. Suppose that you are an operations manager for Target and are responsible for performing a specific task. You, in turn, delegate this task to someone else. You nonetheless remain accountable to your immediate supervisor for getting the task done properly. If the other person fails to complete the assignment, you—not the person to whom you delegated the task—will be held accountable.

BARRIERS TO DELEGATION For several reasons, managers may be unwilling to delegate work. Many managers are reluctant to delegate because they want to be sure that the work gets done. Another reason for reluctance stems from the opposite situation. The manager fears that the worker will do the work well and attract the

FIGURE 7-3: Steps in the Delegation Process

To be successful, a manager must learn how to delegate. No one can do everything alone.

THE DELEGATION PROCESS

Manager

1 Assign responsibility

2 Grant authority

3 Assign accountability

Worker

career SUCCESS

Your Green Career Path?

If you want to pursue a green career path, you have more choices and opportunities than ever before, extending up to the very top of the management ranks. The post of chief sustainability officer (CSO) is the newest C-level position in the organizational hierarchy—a green management job that reports directly to the president or chief executive officer.

AT&T, Avon Products, Google, Dow Chemical, DuPont, and many other businesses have appointed a CSO to plan and coordinate companywide environmental initiatives, ensure proper compliance with government regulations, and manage internal and external communications about sustainability goals and issues. Just as important, the CSO is responsible for inserting sustainability into corporate strategy and making it part of the business case for new goods and services. Some colleges, universities, and municipalities are hiring sustainability officers to handle such diverse issues as switching to clean power sources, improving recycling programs, reducing waste, and minimizing the environmental impact of buildings, supplies, and operations.

Rather than isolate responsibility for sustainability in a single top-management role, companies are increasingly adding sustainability to job descriptions throughout the organization.

As Levi Strauss's vice president for social and environmental sustainability explains: "We're successful when sustainability gets embedded in all the roles in the company." Even if your job description doesn't explicitly include corporate environmental actions, you can show your interest and commitment by participating in recycling, saving energy, and taking other earth-friendly steps during the work day.

Sources: Tilde Herrera, "Wanted: Chief Sustainability Officer," *GreenBiz.com,* February 3, 2011, www.greenbiz.com; Henry Fountain, "Sustainability Comes of Age," *New York Times Education Life Supplement,* January 3, 2010, p. 20; Tiffany Hsu, "Eco-officers Are Moving into Executive Suites," *Los Angeles Times,* December 30, 2009, www.latimes.com/business/la-fi-green-officers30-2009dec30,0,3283781.story; Geoff Colvin, "Linda Fisher, C-Suite Strategies," *Fortune,* November 23, 2009, p. 45ff.

---

approving notice of higher-level managers. Finally, some managers do not delegate because they are so disorganized that they simply are not able to plan and assign work effectively.

Decentralization of Authority

The pattern of delegation throughout an organization determines the extent to which that organization is decentralized or centralized. In a **decentralized organization**, management consciously attempts to spread authority widely across various organization levels. A **centralized organization**, on the other hand, systematically works to concentrate authority at the upper levels. For example, many publishers of college-level textbooks are centralized organizations, with authority concentrated at the top. Large organizations may have characteristics of both decentralized and centralized organizations.

A number of factors can influence the extent to which a firm is decentralized. One is the external environment in which the firm operates. The more complex and unpredictable this environment, the more likely it is that top management will let lower-level managers make important decisions. After all, lower-level managers are closer to the problems. Another factor is the nature of the decision itself. The riskier or more important the decision, the greater is the tendency to centralize decision making. A third factor is the abilities of lower-level managers. If these managers do not have strong decision-making skills, top managers will be reluctant to decentralize. And, in contrast, strong lower-level decision-making skills encourage decentralization. Finally, a firm that traditionally has practiced centralization or decentralization is likely to maintain that posture in the future.

In principle, neither decentralization nor centralization is right or wrong. What works for one organization may or may not work for another. Kmart Corporation and McDonald's are very successful—and both practice centralization. But decentralization has worked very well for General Electric and Sears. Every organization must assess its own situation and then choose the level of centralization or decentralization that will work best.

decentralized organization an organization in which management consciously attempts to spread authority widely in the lower levels of the organization

centralized organization an organization that systematically works to concentrate authority at the upper levels of the organization

✱ Concept Check

☐ Identify and describe the three steps in the delegation process.

☐ Differentiate decentralized organization and centralized organization.

Part 3: Management and Organization

THE SPAN OF MANAGEMENT

LEARNING OBJECTIVE

5 Understand how the span of management describes an organization.

The fourth major step in organizing a business is establishing the **span of management (or span of control)**, which is the number of workers who report directly to one manager. For hundreds of years, theorists have searched for an ideal span of management. When it became apparent that there is no perfect number of subordinates for a manager to supervise, they turned their attention to the general issue of whether the span should be wide or narrow. This issue is complicated because the span of management may change by department within the same organization.

Wide and Narrow Spans of Management

A *wide* span of management exists when a manager has a larger number of subordinates. A *narrow* span exists when the manager has only a few subordinates. Several factors determine the span that is better for a particular manager (see Figure 7-4). Generally, the span of control may be wide when (1) the manager and the subordinates are very competent, (2) the organization has a well-established set of standard operating procedures, and (3) few new problems are expected to arise. The span should be narrow when (1) workers are physically located far from one another, (2) the manager has much work to do in addition to supervising workers, (3) a great deal of interaction is required between supervisor and workers, and (4) new problems arise frequently.

Organizational Height

The span of management has an obvious impact on relations between managers and workers. It has a more subtle but equally important impact on the height of the organization. **Organizational height** is the number of layers, or levels, of management in a firm. The span of management plays a direct role in determining the height of the organization (see Figure 7-4). If spans of management are wider, fewer levels are needed, and the organization is *flat*. If spans of management generally are narrow, more levels are needed, and the resulting organization is *tall*.

span of management (or span of control) the number of workers who report directly to one manager

organizational height the number of layers, or levels, of management in a firm

Personal App You can expect to hold a good deal of responsibility in a flat organization. You'll probably have frequent contact with higher-level managers, along with many opportunities to apply your skills and make a noticeable difference.

In a taller organization, administrative costs are higher because more managers are needed. Communication among levels may become distorted because information has to pass up and down through more people. When companies are cutting costs, one option is to decrease organizational height in order to reduce related administrative expenses. For example, when cosmetics

FIGURE 7-4: **The Span of Management**

Several criteria determine whether a firm uses a wide span of management, in which a number of workers report to one manager, or a narrow span, in which a manager supervises only a few workers.

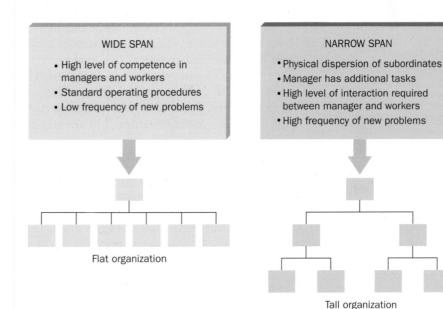

WIDE SPAN
- High level of competence in managers and workers
- Standard operating procedures
- Low frequency of new problems

Flat organization

NARROW SPAN
- Physical dispersion of subordinates
- Manager has additional tasks
- High level of interaction required between manager and workers
- High frequency of new problems

Tall organization

© Cengage Learning 2013

provider Avon experienced declining sales, the company began a series of long and extensive restructuring programs. The programs focused on increasing efficiency and organizational effectiveness. While the original restructuring plan saved the company approximately $200 million per year, the newer plan has saved the company an estimated $350 million per year.[3] Although flat organizations avoid these problems, their managers may perform more administrative duties simply because there are fewer managers. Wide spans of management also may require managers to spend considerably more time supervising and working with subordinates.

FORMS OF ORGANIZATIONAL STRUCTURE

LEARNING OBJECTIVE

6 Describe the four basic forms of organizational structure.

Up to this point, we have focused our attention on the major characteristics of organizational structure. In many ways, this is like discussing the parts of a jigsaw puzzle one by one. It is now time to put the puzzle together. In particular, we discuss four basic forms of organizational structure: line, line-and-staff, matrix, and network.

The Line Structure

The simplest and oldest form of organizational structure is the **line structure**, in which the chain of command goes directly from person to person throughout the organization. Thus, a straight line could be drawn down through the levels of management, from the chief executive down to the lowest level in the organization. In a small retail store, for example, an hourly employee might report to an assistant manager, who reports to a store manager, who reports to the owner.

Managers within a line structure, called **line managers**, make decisions and give orders to subordinates to achieve the organization's goals. A line structure's simplicity and clear chain of command allow line managers to make decisions quickly with direct accountability because the decision-maker only has one supervisor to report to.

Line-and-staff organization structure. Ronald McDonald occupies a staff position and does not have direct authority over other employees at McDonald's. The other individuals shown here occupy line positions and do have direct authority over some of the other McDonald's employees.

The downside of a line structure, however, is that line managers are responsible for many activities, and therefore must have a wide range of knowledge about all of them. While this may not be a problem for small organizations with a lower volume of activities, in a larger organization, activities become more numerous and complex, thus making it more difficult for line managers to fully understand what they are in charge of. Therefore, line managers in a larger organization would have a hard time making an educated decision without expert advice from outside sources. As a result, line structures are not very effective in medium- or large-size organizations, but are very popular in small organizations.

The Line-and-Staff Structure

A **line-and-staff structure** not only utilizes the chain of command from a line structure but also provides line managers with specialists, called staff managers. Therefore, this structure works much better for medium- and large-size organizations than line management alone. **Staff managers** provide support, advice, and expertise to line managers, thus eliminating the previous drawback of line structures. Staff managers are not part of the chain of command like line managers are, but they do have authority over their assistants (see Figure 7-5).

Both line and staff managers are needed for effective management, but the two positions differ in important ways. The basic difference is in terms of authority. Line managers have *line authority*, which means that they can make decisions and issue directives relating to the organization's goals. Staff managers seldom have this kind of authority. Instead, they usually have either advisory authority or functional authority. *Advisory*

line structure an organizational structure in which the chain of command goes directly from person to person throughout the organization

line manager a position in which a person makes decisions and gives orders to subordinates to achieve the organization's goals

line-and-staff structure an organizational structure that utilizes the chain of command from a line structure in combination with the assistance of staff managers

staff manager a position created to provide support, advice, and expertise within an organization

authority is the expectation that line managers will consult the appropriate staff manager when making decisions. Functional authority is stronger. *Functional authority* is the authority of staff managers to make decisions and issue directives about their areas of expertise. For example, a legal adviser for Nike can decide whether to retain a particular clause in a contract but not product pricing.

For a variety of reasons, conflict between line managers and staff managers is fairly common in business. Staff managers often have more formal education and sometimes are younger (and perhaps more ambitious) than line managers. Line managers may perceive staff managers as a threat to their own authority and thus may resent them. For their part, staff managers may become annoyed or angry if their expert recommendations—for example, in public relations or human resources management—are not adopted by line management.

Personal App If you're looking to move up, try to get some advice from co-workers in both line and staff positions. Not only will this broaden your understanding of the organization, it will also help you bridge the gaps between line and staff and connect with both groups.

Fortunately, there are several ways to minimize the likelihood of such conflict. One way is to integrate line and staff managers into one team. Another is to ensure that the areas of responsibility of line and staff managers are clearly defined. Finally, line and staff managers both can be held accountable for the results of their activities.

Green Citizenship at General Electric

General Electric views sustainability as essential to being a good corporate citizen. The company has woven environmental stewardship into the fabric of its organizational structure and made sustainability an integral part of its corporate culture. Take a look: www.ge.com/citizenship/index.jsp

© kryczka / iStockphoto 13403524

Courtesy, General Electric/credit

FIGURE 7-5: Line and Staff Managers

A line manager has direct responsibility for achieving the company's goals and is in the direct chain of command. A staff manager supports and advises the line managers.

LINE

President

STAFF

Director of legal services

Director of public affairs

Vice president, marketing

Vice president, finance

Regional sales manager

Regional sales manager

Accounting department manager

© Cengage Learning 2013

The Matrix Structure

When the matrix structure is used, individuals report to more than one superior at the same time. The **matrix structure** combines vertical and horizontal lines of authority, which is why it is called a matrix structure. The matrix structure occurs when product departmentalization is superimposed on a functionally departmentalized organization. In a matrix organization, authority flows both down and across. Martha Stewart Living Omnimedia, for example, utilizes the matrix structure to combine the management of its functional departments (publishing, Internet, broadcasting, and merchandising) with its product departments (food, crafts, entertaining, gardening, etc.).[4] Another example of a matrix organization could be an automobile manufacturer, whose company may be divided into functional departments, such as production, sales, marketing, distribution, and accounting, which co-manage with product departments (the vehicle models).

To understand the structure of a matrix organization, consider the usual functional arrangement, with people working in departments such as engineering, finance, and marketing. Now suppose that we assign people from these departments to a special group that is working on a new project as a team—a cross-functional team. A **cross-functional team** consists of individuals with varying specialties, expertise, and skills that are brought together to achieve a common task. Frequently, cross-functional teams are charged with the responsibility of developing new products. For example, Ford Motor Company assembled a special project team to design and manufacture its global cars. The manager in charge of a team is usually called a *project manager*. Any individual who is working with the team reports to *both* the project manager and the individual's superior in the functional department (see Figure 7-6).

FIGURE 7-6: A Matrix Structure

A matrix is usually the result of combining product departmentalization with function departmentalization. It is a complex structure in which employees have more than one supervisor.

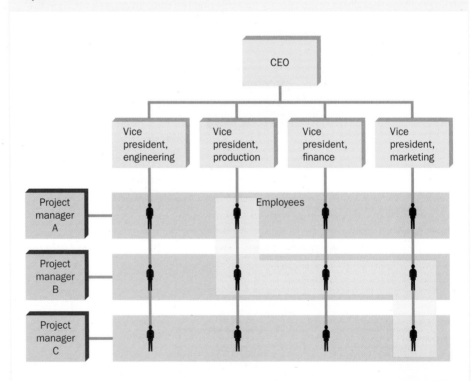

Source: Ricky W. Griffin, *Management*, 10th ed. Copyright © 2011 by South-Western/Cengage Learning, Mason, OH. Adapted with permission.

matrix structure an organizational structure that combines vertical and horizontal lines of authority, usually by superimposing product departmentalization on a functionally departmentalized organization

cross-functional team a team of individuals with varying specialties, expertise, and skills that are brought together to achieve a common task

Cross-functional team projects may be temporary, in which case the team is disbanded once the mission is accomplished, or they may be permanent. These teams often are empowered to make major decisions. When a cross-functional team is employed, prospective team members may receive special training because effective teamwork can require different skills. For cross-functional teams to be successful, team members must be given specific information on the job each performs. The team also must develop a sense of cohesiveness and maintain good communications among its members.

Matrix structures offer advantages over other organizational forms. Added flexibility is probably the most obvious advantage. The matrix structure also can increase productivity, raise morale, and nurture creativity and innovation. In addition, employees experience personal development through doing a variety of jobs.

The matrix structure also has disadvantages. Having employees report to more than one supervisor can cause confusion about who is in charge. Like committees, teams may take longer to resolve problems and issues than individuals working alone. Other difficulties include personality clashes, poor communication, undefined individual roles, unclear responsibilities, and finding ways to reward individual and team performance simultaneously. Because more managers and support staff may be needed, a matrix structure may be more expensive to maintain.

Top-Ranked Barriers to Women in the Workplace

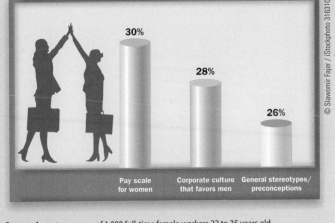

Source: Accenture survey of 1,000 full-time female workers 22 to 35 years old.

The Network Structure

In a **network structure** (sometimes called a *virtual organization*), administration is the primary function performed, and other functions such as engineering, production, marketing, and finance are contracted out to other organizations. Frequently, a network organization does not manufacture the products it sells. This type of organization has a few permanent employees consisting of top management and hourly clerical workers. Leased facilities and equipment, as well as temporary workers, are increased or decreased as the organization's needs change. Thus, there is rather limited formal structure associated with a network organization.

An obvious strength of a network structure is flexibility that allows the organization to adjust quickly to changes. Some of the challenges faced by managers in network-structured organizations include controlling the quality of work performed by other organizations, low morale and high turnover among hourly workers, and the vulnerability associated with relying on outside contractors.

Concept Check ✱

☐ Describe the four forms of organizational structure.

☐ Give an example of each form.

CORPORATE CULTURE

Most managers function within a corporate culture. A **corporate culture** is generally defined as the inner rites, rituals, heroes, and values of a firm. An organization's culture has a powerful influence on how employees think and act. It also can determine public perception of the organization.

Personal App When you are searching for a new job, look for clues that reveal the inner workings of the firm's corporate culture. You'll want to be in step with the culture, understand what the organization values, and if those values fit your own.

Corporate culture generally is thought to have a very strong influence on a firm's performance over time. Hence, it is useful to be able to assess a firm's corporate culture.

LEARNING OBJECTIVE
7 Describe the effects of corporate culture.

network structure an organizational structure in which administration is the primary function, and most other functions are contracted out to other firms

corporate culture the inner rites, rituals, heroes, and values of a firm

FIGURE 7-7: Types of Corporate Culture

Which corporate culture would you choose?

<table>
<tr>
<td>Networked Culture
• Extrovert energized by relationships
• Tolerant of ambiguities and have low needs for structure
• Can spot politics and act to stop "negative" politics
• Consider yourself easygoing, affable, and loyal to others</td>
<td>Communal Culture
• You consider yourself passionate
• Strong need to identify with something bigger than yourself
• You enjoy being in teams
• Prepared to make sacrifices for the greater good</td>
</tr>
<tr>
<td>Fragmented Culture
• Are a reflective and self-contained introvert
• Have a high autonomy drive and strong desire to work independently
• Have a strong sense of self</td>
<td>Mercenary Culture
• Goal-oriented and have an obsessive desire to complete tasks
• Thrive on competitive energy
• Keep "relationships" out of work—develop them</td>
</tr>
</table>

Vertical axis: Sociability (Low to High)

Source: "Types of Corporate Culture," in Rob Goffee and Gareth Jones, *The Character of a Corporation* (New York: HarperCollins, 1998). Copyright © 1998 by Rob Goffee and Gareth Jones. Permission granted by Rob Goffee and Gareth Jones by arrangement with The Helen Rees Literary Agency.

Common indicators include the physical setting (building, office layouts), what the company says about its corporate culture (in advertising and news releases), how the company greets guests (does it have formal or informal reception areas?), and how employees spend their time (working alone in an office or working with others).

Goffee and Jones have identified four distinct types of corporate cultures (see Figure 7-7). One is called the *networked culture,* characterized by a base of trust and friendship among employees, a strong commitment to the organization, and an informal environment. The *mercenary culture* embodies the feelings of passion, energy, sense of purpose, and excitement for one's work. The term *mercenary* does not imply that employees are motivated to work only for the money, but this is part of it. In this culture, employees are very intense, focused, and determined to win. In the *fragmented culture,* employees do not become friends, and they work "at" the organization, not "for" it. Employees have a high degree of autonomy, flexibility, and equality. The *communal culture* combines the positive traits of the networked culture and the mercenary culture—those of friendship, commitment, high focus on performance, and high energy. People's lives revolve around the product in this culture, and success by anyone in the organization is celebrated by all.[5]

Some experts believe that cultural change is needed when a company's environment changes, when the industry becomes more competitive, the company's performance is mediocre, and when the company is growing or is about to become a truly large organization. For example, top executives at Dell Computer allocated considerable time and resources to develop a strong, positive corporate culture aimed at increasing employee loyalty and the success of the company. Organizations in the future will look quite different. Experts predict that tomorrow's businesses will comprise small, task-oriented work groups, each with control over its own activities. These small groups will be

Food and fun are a part of the corporate culture at Google. This company believes satisfied employees produce the best and most innovative ideas. How would you describe Google's corporate culture in Goffee and Jones' terms—as networked, mercenary, fragmented, or communal? Why?

entrepreneurial SUCCESS

Building Innovation and Involvement into the Corporate Culture

Even the smallest business can create a corporate culture that encourages employees to be innovative and to get actively involved with the business and its customers. How? First, management must tolerate failure. If employees fear being penalized for taking a risk that doesn't pay off, they'll shy away from innovation. On the other hand, if employees know that the firm welcomes new thinking, they'll be more likely to contribute their ideas. For example, Bazaarvoice, a fast-growing tech business in Austin, expects employees to think boldly about challenges and possibilities. One of the values on which its corporate culture is based is: "Thinking beyond status quo and without precedence."

Another way entrepreneurs can build this type of corporate culture is by sharing their vision of what they hope the business will some day become. When founders talk about the brainstorms behind new businesses and the innovations that have helped transform the vision into reality, their employees feel a sense of excitement about being part of that vision.

Finally, it's important to reward innovation and involvement at every level. Any employee might have a great idea for a new product or a new way to serve customers. To reinforce this element of the corporate culture, entrepreneurs have to make a point of listening carefully and responding thoughtfully to suggestions from employees (and other stakeholders). For example, the owners of Aubree's Pizzeria and Tavern, a Michigan-based restaurant chain, say they "manage from the bottom up," taking all employees' ideas into consideration when making business decisions such as adding new menu items.

Sources: Tom Perkins, "Aubree's Restaurant Owners Examine Franchise Plans with Hope of Expanding beyond Michigan," *AnnArbor.com*, February 10, 2011, www.annarbor.com; Sam Decker, "Don't Wait to Build a Corporate Culture of Charitable Giving," *Austin Entrepreneur Network*, January 14, 2011, http://austinentrepreneurnetwork.org; Lisa Jackson, "Corporate Culture: Your Growth Depends on It," *Colorado Business*, October 11, 2010, www.cobizmag.com; www.bazaarvoice.com.

---

coordinated through an elaborate computer network and held together by a strong corporate culture. Businesses operating in fast-changing industries will require leadership that supports trust and risk taking. Creating a culture of trust in an organization can lead to increases in growth, profit, productivity, and job satisfaction. A culture of trust can retain the best people, inspire customer loyalty, develop new markets, and increase creativity.

Another area where corporate culture plays a vital role is the integration of two or more companies. Business leaders often cite the role of corporate cultures in the integration process as one of the primary factors affecting the success of a merger or acquisition. Experts note that corporate culture is a way of conducting business both within the company and externally. If two merging companies do not address differences in corporate culture, they are setting themselves up for missed expectations and possibly failure.

Concept Check ✱

☐ What is corporate culture?

☐ Explain the four types of corporate cultures.

COMMITTEES AND TASK FORCES

Today, business firms use several types of committees that affect organizational structure. An **ad hoc committee** is created for a specific short-term purpose, such as reviewing the firm's employee benefits plan. Once its work is finished, the ad hoc committee disbands. A **standing committee** is a relatively permanent committee charged with performing a recurring task. A firm might establish a budget review committee, for example, to review departmental budget requests on an ongoing basis. Finally, a **task force** is a committee established to investigate a major problem or pending decision. A firm contemplating a merger with another company might form a task force to assess the pros and cons of the merger.

Committees offer some advantages over individual action. Their several members are able to bring information and knowledge to the task at hand. Furthermore, committees tend to make more accurate decisions and to transmit their results through the organization more effectively. However, committee deliberations take

LEARNING OBJECTIVE

8 Understand how committees and task forces are used.

ad hoc committee a committee created for a specific short-term purpose

standing committee a relatively permanent committee charged with performing some recurring task

task force a committee established to investigate a major problem or pending decision

✳ *Concept Check*

☐ What is the difference between a committee and a task force?

☐ What are the advantages and disadvantages of using committees?

LEARNING OBJECTIVE

9 **Explain the functions of the informal organization and the grapevine in a business.**

Informal groups. Informal groups can be a source of information and camaraderie for participants. These groups can create both challenges and benefits for an organization.

informal organization the pattern of behavior and interaction that stems from personal rather than official relationships

informal group a group created by the members themselves to accomplish goals that may or may not be relevant to an organization

grapevine the informal communications network within an organization

✳ *Concept Check*

☐ In what ways can informal groups affect a business?

☐ How is the grapevine used in a business organization?

longer than individual actions. In addition, unnecessary compromise may take place within the committee, or the opposite may occur, as one person dominates (and thus negates) the committee process.

THE INFORMAL ORGANIZATION AND THE GRAPEVINE

So far, we have discussed the organization as a formal structure consisting of inter-related positions. This is the organization that is shown on an organization chart. There is another kind of organization, however, that does not show up on any chart. We define this **informal organization** as the pattern of behavior and interaction that stems from personal rather than official relationships. Firmly embedded within every informal organization are informal groups and the notorious grapevine.

An **informal group** is created by the group members themselves to accomplish goals that may or may not be relevant to the organization. Workers may create an informal group to go bowling, form a union, get a particular manager fired or transferred, or meet for lunch. The group may last for several years or a few hours.

Informal groups can be powerful forces in organizations. They can restrict output, or they can help managers through tight spots. They can cause disagreement and conflict, or they can help to boost morale and job satisfaction. They can show new people how to contribute to the organization, or they can help people to get away with substandard performance. Clearly, managers should be aware of these informal groups. Those who make the mistake of fighting the informal organization have a major obstacle to overcome.

The **grapevine** is the informal communications network within an organization. It is completely separate from—and sometimes much faster than—the organization's formal channels of communication. Formal communications usually follow a path that parallels the organizational chain of command. Information can be transmitted through the grapevine in any direction—up, down, diagonally, or horizontally across the organizational structure. Subordinates may pass information to their bosses, an executive may relay something to a maintenance worker, or there may be an exchange of information between people who work in totally unrelated departments. Grapevine information may be concerned with topics ranging from the latest management decisions to gossip.

Personal App When you are searching for a new job, look for clues that reveal the inner workings of the firm's corporate culture. You'll want to be in step with the culture, understand what the organization values, and if those values fit your own.

How should managers treat the grapevine? Certainly, it would be a mistake to try to eliminate it. People working together, day in and day out, are going to communicate. A more rational approach is to recognize its existence. For example, managers should respond promptly and aggressively to inaccurate grapevine information to minimize the damage that such misinformation might do. Moreover, the grapevine can come in handy when managers are on the receiving end of important communications from the informal organization.

In the next chapter, we apply these and other management concepts to an extremely important business function: the production of goods and services.

Get Flashcards, Quizzes, Games, Crosswords, and more @ www.cengagebrain.com

© i love images/Photolibrary

SUMMARY

1 Understand what an organization is and identify its characteristics.

An organization is a group of two or more people working together to achieve a common set of goals. The relationships among positions within an organization can be illustrated by means of an organization chart. Five specific characteristics—job design, departmentalization, delegation, span of management, and chain of command—help to determine what an organization chart and the organization itself look like.

2 Explain why job specialization is important.

Job specialization is the separation of all the activities within an organization into smaller components and the assignment of those different components to different people. Several factors combine to make specialization a useful technique for designing jobs, but high levels of specialization may cause employee dissatisfaction and boredom. One technique for overcoming these problems is job rotation.

3 Identify the various bases for departmentalization.

Departmentalization is the grouping of jobs into manageable units. Typical bases for departmentalization are by function, product, location, or customer. Because each of these bases provides particular advantages, most firms—especially larger ones—use a combination of different bases in different organizational situations.

4 Explain how decentralization follows from delegation.

Delegation is the assigning of part of a manager's work to other workers. It involves the following three steps: (1) assigning responsibility, (2) granting authority, and (3) creating accountability. A decentralized firm is one that delegates as much power as possible to people in the lower management levels. In a centralized firm, on the other hand, power is systematically retained at the upper levels.

5 Understand how the span of management describes an organization.

The span of management is the number of workers who report directly to a manager. Spans generally are characterized as wide (many workers per manager) or narrow (few workers per manager). Wide spans generally result in flat organizations (few layers of management); narrow spans generally result in tall organizations (many layers of management).

6 Describe the four basic forms of organizational structure.

There are four basic forms of organizational structure. The line structure is the oldest and most simple structure, in which the chain of command goes in a straight line from person to person down through the levels of management. The line-and-staff structure is similar to the line structure, but adds specialists called staff managers to assist the line managers in decision making. The line structure works most efficiently for smaller organizations, whereas the line-and-staff structure is used by medium- and large-size organizations. The matrix structure may be visualized as product departmentalization superimposed on functional departmentalization. With the matrix structure, an employee on a cross-functional team reports to both the project manager and the individual's supervisor in a functional department. In an organization with a network structure, the primary function performed internally is administration, and other functions are contracted out to other firms.

7 Describe the effects of corporate culture.

Corporate culture has both internal and external effects on an organization. An organization's culture can influence the way employees think and act, and it can also determine the public's perception of the organization. Corporate culture can affect a firm's performance over time, either negatively or positively. Creating a culture of trust, for example, can lead to increased growth, profits, productivity, and job satisfaction, while retaining the best employees, inspiring customer loyalty, developing new markets, and increasing creativity. In addition, when two or more companies undergo the integration process, their different or similar corporate cultures can affect the success of a merger or acquisition.

8 Understand how committees and task forces are used.

Committees and task forces are used to develop organizational structure within an organization. An ad hoc committee is created for a specific short-term purpose, whereas a standing committee is relatively permanent. A task force is created to investigate a major problem or pending decision.

9 Explain the functions of the informal organization and the grapevine in a business.

Informal groups are created by group members to accomplish goals that may or may not be relevant to the organization, and they can be very powerful forces. The grapevine—the informal communications network within an organization—can be used to transmit information (important or gossip) through an organization much faster than through the formal communication network. Information transmitted through the grapevine can go in any direction across the organizational structure, skipping up or down levels of management and even across departments.

KEY TERMS

You should now be able to define and give an example relevant to each of the following terms:

organization (190)
organization chart (191)
chain of command (191)
job specialization (192)
job rotation (193)
departmentalization (193)
departmentalization by
function (193)
departmentalization by
product (193)

departmentalization by
location (194)
departmentalization by
customer (194)
delegation (195)
responsibility (195)
authority (195)
accountability (195)
decentralized organization
(196)

centralized organization
(196)
span of management (or
span of control) (197)
organizational height (197)
line structure (198)
line manager (198)
line-and-staff structure
(198)
staff manager (198)

matrix structure (200)
cross-functional team (200)
network structure (201)
corporate culture (201)
ad hoc committee (203)
standing committee (203)
task force (203)
informal organization (204)
informal group (204)
grapevine (204)

DISCUSSION QUESTIONS

1. In what way do organization charts create a picture of an organization?
2. What determines the degree of specialization within an organization?
3. Describe how job rotation can be used to combat the problems caused by job specialization.
4. Why do most firms employ a combination of departmentalization bases?
5. What three steps are involved in delegation? Explain each.
6. How does a firm's top management influence its degree of centralization?

7. How is organizational height related to the span of management?
8. Contrast line-and-staff and matrix forms of organizational structure.
9. How does the corporate culture of a local Best Buy store compare to that of a local McDonald's?
10. Which kinds of firms probably would operate most effectively as centralized firms? As decentralized firms?
11. How do decisions concerning span of management and the use of committees affect organizational structure?

TEST YOURSELF

Matching Questions

1. _____ Line of authority from the highest to lowest levels.
2. _____ Two or more people working toward a common goal.
3. _____ Grouping jobs into manageable units.
4. _____ Assigns part of the manager's work to others.
5. _____ The power to accomplish an assigned task.
6. _____ The duty to do a job or perform a task.
7. _____ Combines vertical and horizontal lines of authority.
8. _____ Charged with the responsibility of developing new products.
9. _____ An informal communications network.

10. _____ Committee that investigates major problems or pending decisions.

a. ad hoc committee
b. authority
c. chain of command
d. cross-functional team
e. delegation
f. departmentalization
g. grapevine
h. matrix structure
i. network structure
j. organization
k. responsibility
l. task force

True False Questions

11. **T F** A benefit of specialization is improved efficiency and increased productivity.

12. **T F** Job rotation involves assigning an employee more tasks and greater control.

13. **T F** The power to make decisions is granted through authority.

14. **T F** Accountability is created, not delegated.

15. **T F** The span of management should be wide when a great deal of interaction is required between the supervisor and worker.

16. **T F** Line positions support staff positions in decision making.

17. **T F** Many firms find that by using matrix organization, the motivation level is lowered, and personal growth of employees is limited.

18. **T F** In the mercenary culture, employees work "at" the organization, not "for" it.

19. **T F** Creating a culture of trust can lead to decreased productivity and job satisfaction.

20. **T F** Ad hoc committees can be used effectively to review a firm's employee benefits plan.

Multiple-Choice Questions

21. _____ The process of dividing work to be done by an entire organization into separate parts and assigning the parts to positions within the organization is called
    a. departmentalization.
    b. delegation.
    c. job design.
    d. specialization.
    e. organizing.

22. _____ Who was the first to recognize the power of specialization?
    a. Karl Marx
    b. Max Weber
    c. John Kenneth Galbraith
    d. Adam Smith
    e. Thomas Friedman

23. _____ ABC Distributors is reorganizing to better control costs. The company decided to group hospitals, schools, and churches together into one department. Which departmentalization base is the company using?
    a. Location
    b. Function
    c. Employees
    d. Product
    e. Customer

24. _____ Older and larger firms that produce and sell a variety of products organize by
    a. location.
    b. product.
    c. customer.
    d. function.
    e. executive decisions.

25. _____ A supervisor assigned to Wendy, the most proficient employee in the accounting department, a project on cost control that was due in three weeks. For Wendy to be accountable for the project, what must Wendy be given?
    a. Responsibility
    b. Power
    c. Authority
    d. Training
    e. Control

26. _____ Many managers are reluctant to delegate. Which one of the following is *not* one of the reasons they are reluctant to do so?
    a. They want to be sure that the work gets done.
    b. They fear that workers will do the work well and attract the approving notice of higher-level managers.
    c. They are so disorganized that they simply are not able to plan and assign work.
    d. Most managers are workaholics.
    e. Most subordinates are reluctant to accept delegated tasks.

27. _____ A narrow span of management works best when
    a. subordinates are located close together.
    b. the manager has few responsibilities outside of supervision.
    c. little interaction is required between the manager and the worker.
    d. new problems arise frequently.
    e. few problems arise on a daily basis.

28. _____ A relatively permanent committee charged with performing some recurring task is called
    a. an ad hoc committee.
    b. a standing committee.
    c. a task force.
    d. a managerial committee.
    e. a permanent committee.

29. _____ A committee is organized to review applications for scholarships. The group will award two scholarships to recent high school graduates. What type of committee would work best?
    a. Ad hoc committee
    b. Task force
    c. Liaison committee
    d. Standing committee
    e. Self-managed team

30. _____ In order to best handle the grapevine, managers should
    a. try to eliminate it.
    b. respond slowly to inaccurate information.
    c. respond aggressively to accurate information.
    d. recognize its existence.
    e. reprimand employees who pass on important information.

Answers to the Test Yourself questions appear at the end of the book on page TY-1.

VIDEO CASE
At Numi Organic Tea, Teams and Organizational Culture Are Critical

You might expect a company specializing in marketing organic teas to have a distinctive corporate culture. In the case of Numi Organic Tea, a progressive seller of premium organic and Fair Trade teas based in Oakland, California, you'd be right.

With a relatively small staff of about 50 people and a recent growth rate of 180 percent a year, Numi needs to remain nimble and responsive. Its founders, the brother-and-sister team of Ahmed and Reem Rahim, were inspired to create a tea company after Ahmed had spent some years operating tea houses in Europe while Reem studied art in the United States. Combining both their interests led to a unique firm dedicated to quality, sustainability, and community. Numi occupies offices that include a tea garden where employees often gather to relax, and it has won awards for many achievements including its unique teas, its innovative packaging, and its commitment to the environment. Numi's 25 different tea and flowering tea products and gift packs are sold in Whole Foods and Safeway markets, as well as in individual natural food and grocery stores throughout the United States, and in 20 other countries overseas.

The prevailing attitude in the company, which maintains a blog and a presence on Facebook and MySpace, is a can-do, team-oriented spirit. Because it's a small firm where everyone works hard, Numi can't afford rapid employee turnover and the time that would be lost in recruiting, interviewing, and training. Employees are thus carefully chosen for their willingness to do whatever it takes to get the job done and to remain upbeat and positive despite the occasional stress of working for a small company with customers around the world. Workers must also be able to devote long hours when necessary and share the company's goals.

Employees in Numi's distribution center, for instance, recently found themselves under pressure because it was taking nearly two weeks to fill international orders. With a new manager and a new focus on everyone's understanding how each job fit into the big picture, however, a sense of teamwork began to grow. Soon each employee had been trained to perform all the critical tasks in order fulfillment, so instead of working in isolation they were able to pitch in during crunch times. Their new flexibility reduced lead times for overseas orders to about five days and cut the time for domestic orders in half. Sometimes the team can ship them the same day.

At Numi, managers who communicate well and who are out working alongside their staff are the norm. They must also communicate well with customers and demonstrate a high level of emotional maturity. Some meet with their teams on a regular basis, to review project status against deadlines and due dates and to make changes in workload and procedures where necessary. The company offers flex-time to help employees retain a balance between their work and personal life, and when things get overwhelming at the office, there's always the tea garden and a freshly brewed cup of organic tea.[6]

Questions

1. Numi's customer service manager, Cindy Graffort, says the company is like a "living, breathing organism." What does she mean? How does the company's culture reflect this belief?
2. Numi's distribution manager, Dannielle Oviedo, says her philosophy of management means she gets involved in what her team is doing: "I do what I ask folks to do." Do you think she is a good delegator? Why or why not?
3. What can you infer about Numi's basis for departmentalization and its chain of command?

BUILDING SKILLS FOR CAREER SUCCESS

1. Exploring the Internet

After studying the various organizational structures described in this chapter and the reasons for employing them, you may be interested in learning about the organizational structures in place at large firms. As noted in the chapter, departmentalization typically is based on function, product, location, and customer. Many large firms use a combination of these organizational structures successfully. You can gain a good sense of which organizational theme prevails in an industry by looking at several corporate sites.

Assignment

1. Explore the Web site of any large firm that you believe is representative of its industry, and find its organization chart or a description of its organization. Create a brief organization chart from the information you have found.
2. Describe the bases on which this firm is departmentalized.

2. Building Team Skills

An organization chart is a diagram showing how employees and tasks are grouped and how the lines of communication and authority flow within an organization. These charts can look very different depending on a number of factors, including the nature and size of the business, the way it is departmentalized, its patterns of delegating authority, and its span of management.

Assignment

1. Working in a team, use the following information to draw an organization chart: The KDS Design Center works closely with two home-construction companies, Amex and Highmass. KDS's role is to help customers select materials for their new homes and to ensure that their selections are communicated accurately to the builders. The company is also a retailer of wallpaper, blinds, and drapery. The retail department, the Amex accounts, and the Highmass accounts make up KDS's three departments. The company has the following positions: President, executive vice president, managers, 2 appointment coordinators, 2 Amex coordinators, 2 Highmass coordinators, 2 consultants/designers for the Amex and Highmass accounts, 15 retail positions, and 4 payroll and billing personnel.

2. After your team has drawn the organization chart, discuss the following:
   a. What type of organizational structure does your chart depict? Is it a bureaucratic, matrix, cluster, or network structure? Why?
   b. How does KDS use departmentalization?
   c. To what extent is authority in the company centralized or decentralized?
   d. What is the span of management within KDS?
   e. Which positions are line positions and which are staff? Why?

3. Prepare a three-page report summarizing what the chart revealed about relationships and tasks at the KDS Design Center and what your team learned about the value of organization charts. Include your chart in your report.

3. Researching Different Careers

In the past, company loyalty and the ability to assume increasing job responsibility usually ensured advancement within an organization. While the reasons for seeking advancement (the desire for a better-paying position, more prestige, and job satisfaction) have not changed, the qualifications for career advancement have. In today's business environment, climbing the corporate ladder requires packaging and marketing yourself. To be promoted within your company or to be considered for employment with another company, it is wise to improve your skills continually. By taking workshops and seminars or enrolling in community college courses, you can keep up with the changing technology in your industry. Networking with people in your business or community can help you to find a new job. Most jobs are filled through personal contacts, who you know can be important.

A list of your accomplishments on the job can reveal your strengths and weaknesses. Setting goals for improvement helps to increase your self-confidence.

Be sure to recognize the signs of job dissatisfaction. It may be time to move to another position or company.

Assignment

Are you prepared to climb the corporate ladder? Do a self-assessment by analyzing the following areas and summarize the results in a two-page report.

1. Skills
   - What are your most valuable skills?
   - What skills do you lack?
   - Describe your plan for acquiring new skills and improving your skills.

2. Networking
   - How effective are you at using a mentor?
   - Are you a member of a professional organization?
   - In which community, civic, or church groups are you participating?
   - Whom have you added to your contact list in the last six weeks?

3. Accomplishments
   - What achievements have you reached in your job?
   - What would you like to accomplish? What will it take for you to reach your goal?

4. Promotion or new job
   - What is your likelihood for getting a promotion?
   - Are you ready for a change? What are you doing or willing to do to find another job?

CHAPTER 8 PRODUCING QUALITY GOODS AND SERVICES

© Mikheyev Viktor/Shutterstock

Why should you care?

Think for a moment about the products and services you bought in the past week. If it weren't for the production activities described in this chapter, those products and services would not be available.

Learning Objectives

What you will be able to do once you complete this chapter:

1 Explain the nature of production.

2 Outline how the conversion process transforms raw materials, labor, and other resources into finished products or services.

3 Understand the importance of service businesses to consumers, other business firms, and the nation's economy.

4 Describe how research and development lead to new products and services.

5 Discuss the components involved in planning the production process.

6 Explain how purchasing, inventory control, scheduling, and quality control affect production.

7 Summarize how productivity and technology are related.

Get Flashcards, Quizzes, Games, Crosswords, and more @ www.cengagebrain.com

Unilever's Bold Plans for New Products, Greener Production

Can Unilever double sales by 2020 while simultaneously slashing its environmental impact by 50 percent? These are only two of the ambitious goals the Anglo-Dutch consumer products giant aims to achieve in the coming years. With worldwide annual sales exceeding $55 billion, the company also has long-term plans to introduce more nutritional versions of its food products and buy all of its agricultural raw materials from sustainable sources.

Some of the biggest stars in Unilever's pantry of famous brands are Axe, Bertolli, Ben & Jerry's, Dove, Hellman's, Knorr, Lipton, and Sunlight. Founded more than 120 years ago, Unilever now operates in 180 countries. More than half its revenue comes from sales in developing countries within Asia, Africa, Europe, and Latin America. In every market, the company competes with local firms as well as one or more global giants such as Procter & Gamble, Kraft, or Nestlé.

To reach its aggressive goals, Unilever spends more than $1.3 billion annually on research and development. It is particularly interested in improving the nutritional value of its food products and has invested heavily to stuff its product pipeline full of new foods featuring lower fat and salt content, fewer calories, and less sugar. Unilever is also speeding up new product introductions and building new production facilities in fast-growing markets. For example, in Indonesia, where the company sees great potential for sales growth, it can build a factory and begin manufacturing new food, personal care, or household products in a matter of months.

Although meeting its aggressive sustainability goals will be a challenge, Unilever has made a good start by drastically reducing the amount of water and energy used in manufacturing as well as cutting harmful emissions. Through regular audits, Unilever is ensuring that its factories are progressing toward their environmental targets while maintaining high quality. Finally, Unilever is making the most of its connections with environmentally-conscious retailers such as Walmart and Tesco to share practical ideas about best green practices and implement effective methods of protecting the environment throughout the production and distribution process.[1]

Did you know?

Every year, Unilever spends more than $1.3 billion on research and development to put new products into its global pipeline.

There's a good chance when you saw the name Unilever in the opening case for this chapter you didn't recognize a company that operates in 180 countries around the globe. And yet, this company generates annual sales exceeding $55 billion by producing consumer products that you may use on a regular basis including Axe, Bertolli, Ben & Jerry's, Dove, Hellman's, Knorr, Lipton, and Sunlight. Although the company was founded more than 120 years ago, Unilever continues to innovate and introduce new products to compete with not only local firms but also global giants Procter & Gamble, Kraft, and Nestlé. In fact, Unilever is an excellent example of what this chapter's content—the production of quality goods and services—is all about.

We begin this chapter with an overview of operations management—the activities required to produce goods and services that meet the needs of customers. In this section, we also discuss the role of manufacturing in the U.S. economy, competition in the global marketplace, and careers in operations management. Next, we describe the conversion process that makes production possible and also note the growing role of services in our economy. Then we examine more closely three important aspects of operations management: developing ideas for new products and services, planning for production, and effectively controlling operations after production has begun. We close the chapter with a look at the productivity trends and the ways that productivity can be improved through the use of technology.

WHAT IS PRODUCTION?

Have you ever wondered where a new pair of Levi jeans comes from? Or a new Mitsubishi high-definition television, Izod pullover sweater, or Uniroyal tire for your car? Even factory service on a Hewlett-Packard computer or a Maytag clothes dryer would be impossible if it weren't for the activities described in this chapter. In fact, these products and services and millions of others like them would not exist if it weren't for production activities.

Where did these blue toy rabbits come from?
Answer: China. In today's competitive global marketplace, many products like these stuffed animals are manufactured in China and then shipped to nations around the globe. Today, people in all nations want to sell the products and services they produce to customers in their own nation and to customers in the global marketplace. In fact, experts say the world has become a smaller place because of increased global trade.

Let's begin this chapter by reviewing what an operating manager does. In Chapter 6, we described an *operations manager* as a person who manages the systems that convert resources into goods and services. This area of management is usually referred to as **operations management**, which consists of all the activities required to produce goods and services.

To produce a product or service successfully, a business must perform a number of specific activities. For example, suppose that Chevrolet has an idea for a new version of the sporty Camaro convertible that will cost approximately $35,000. Marketing research must determine not only if customers are willing to pay the price for this product but also what special features they want. Then Chevrolet's operations managers must turn the idea into reality.

Chevrolet's managers cannot just push the "start button" and immediately begin producing the new automobile. Production must be planned. As you will see, planning takes place both *before* anything is produced and *during* the production process.

Managers also must concern themselves with the control of operations to ensure that the organization's goals are achieved. For a product such as Chevrolet's Camaro, control of operations involves a number of important issues, including product quality, performance standards, the amount of inventory of both raw materials and finished products, and production costs.

We discuss each of the major activities of operations management later in this chapter. First, however, let's take a closer look at American manufacturers and how they compete in the global marketplace.

How American Manufacturers Compete in the Global Marketplace

After World War II, the United States became the most productive country in the world. For almost 30 years, until the late 1970s, its leadership was never threatened. By then, however, manufacturers in Japan, Germany, Great Britain, Taiwan, Korea, Sweden, and other industrialized nations were offering U.S. firms increasing competition. Now the Chinese are manufacturing everything from sophisticated electronic equipment and automobiles to less expensive everyday items—often at a lower cost than the same goods can be manufactured in other countries.

When assessing manufacturing in the United States, there is both good and bad news. First, the bad news: The number of Americans employed in the manufacturing

operations management all activities required to produce goods and services

sector has decreased. Currently, approximately 12 million U.S. workers are employed in manufacturing jobs—down from just over 19 million back in 1979.[2] Many of the manufacturing jobs that were lost were outsourced to low-wage workers in nations where there are few labor and environmental regulations. Finally, the number of unemployed factory workers increased during the recent economic crisis because of decreased consumer demand for manufactured goods. As a result of the previously noted factors, manufacturing accounts for only about 11 percent of the private workforce.[3] Since 1979, 7 million jobs have been lost, and many of those jobs aren't coming back.

Now, the good news. The United States remains the largest manufacturing country in the world—producing approximately 20 percent of total global manufacturing output.[4] As a result, the manufacturing sector is still a very important part of the U.S. economy. Although the number of manufacturing jobs has declined, productivity has increased. At least two very important factors account for increases in productivity: First, innovation—finding a better way to produce products—is the key factor that has enabled American manufacturers to compete in the global marketplace. Often, innovation is the result of manufacturers investing money to purchase new, state-of-the-art equipment that helps employees improve productivity. Second, today's workers in the manufacturing sector are highly skilled in order to operate sophisticated equipment. Simply put, Americans are making more goods, but with fewer employees.

Personal App If you decide to order a customized product, you'll get it more quickly if it's made in America. In fact, many businesses, large and small, are thriving by tailoring products to the needs of customers like you and your friends.

Even more good news. Many American manufacturers that outsourced work to factories in foreign nations are once again beginning to manufacture goods in the United States. For example, General Electric (GE) built a new plant in Louisville, Kentucky, to manufacture hybrid electric water heaters. Before the Kentucky plant was built, the water heaters were manufactured in China.[5] Increasing labor costs in foreign nations, faster product development when goods are produced in the United States, the ability to quickly customize existing products to meet customer needs, and federal and state subsidies all help account for this trend in U.S. manufacturing.

Although the global marketplace has never been more competitive, the most successful U.S. firms have focused on the following:

1. Motivating employees to cooperate with management and improve productivity.
2. Reducing costs by selecting suppliers that offer higher quality raw materials and components at reasonable prices.
3. Using computer-aided and flexible manufacturing systems that allow a higher degree of customization.
4. Improving control procedures to help ensure lower manufacturing costs and improved quality in products and services.
5. Using green manufacturing to conserve natural resources and sustain the planet.

Although competing in the global economy is a major challenge, it is a worthwhile pursuit. For most firms, competing in the global marketplace is not only profitable but also an essential activity that requires the cooperation of everyone within the organization.

Careers in Operations Management

Although it is hard to provide information about specific career opportunities in operations management, some generalizations do apply to this management area. First, you must appreciate the manufacturing process and the steps required to produce a product or service. A basic understanding of mass production and the difference between an analytical process and a synthetic process is essential. **Mass production** is a manufacturing process that lowers the cost required to produce

mass production a manufacturing process that lowers the cost required to produce a large number of identical or similar products over a long period of time

Concept Check ✱

☐ List the major activities in operations management.

☐ What steps have U.S. firms taken to regain a competitive edge in the global marketplace?

☐ What is the difference between an analytical and a synthetic manufacturing process? Give an example of each type of process.

a large number of identical or similar products over a long period of time. An **analytical process** breaks raw materials into different component parts. For example, a barrel of crude oil refined by Marathon Oil Corporation—a Texas-based oil and chemical refiner—can be broken down into gasoline, oil, and lubricants and many other petroleum by-products. A **synthetic process** is just the opposite of the analytical one; it combines raw materials or components to create a finished product. Connecticut-based Black & Decker uses a synthetic process when it combines plastic, steel, rechargeable batteries, and other components to produce a cordless drill.

Once you understand that operations managers are responsible for producing tangible products or services that customers want, you must determine how you fit into the production process. Today's successful operations managers must:

1. Be able to motivate and lead people.
2. Understand how technology can make a manufacturer more productive and efficient.
3. Appreciate the control processes that help lower production costs and improve product quality.
4. Understand the relationship between the customer, the marketing of a product, and the production of a product.

If operations management seems like an area you might be interested in, why not do more career exploration? You could take an operations management course if your college or university offers one, or you could obtain a part-time job during the school year or a summer job in a manufacturing company.

analytical process a process in operations management in which raw materials are broken into different component parts

synthetic process a process in operations management in which raw materials or components are combined to create a finished product

utility the ability of a good or service to satisfy a human need

form utility utility created by people converting raw materials, finances, and information into finished products

LEARNING OBJECTIVE

2 Outline how the conversion process transforms raw materials, labor, and other resources into finished products or services.

THE CONVERSION PROCESS

The purpose of manufacturing is to provide utility to customers. **Utility** is the ability of a good or service to satisfy a human need. Although there are four types of utilities—form, place, time, and possession—operations management focuses primarily on form utility. **Form utility** is created by people converting raw materials, finances, and information into finished products. The other types of utility—place, time, and possession—are discussed in Chapter 11.

But how does the conversion take place? How does Kellogg's convert grain, sugar, salt, and other ingredients; money from previous sales and stockholders' investments; production workers and managers; and economic and marketing forecasts into Frosted Flakes cereal products? How does New York Life Insurance convert office buildings, insurance premiums, actuaries, and mortality tables into life insurance policies? They do so through the use of a conversion process like the one illustrated in Figure 8-1. As indicated by our New York Life Insurance example, the conversion process is not limited to manufacturing products. The conversion process also can be used to produce services.

Empty cans, but not for long. For food manufacturers, it's not enough just to make a product. They must also combine metal and technology to create a can in order to package and preserve their product. Ultimately, the food "stored" in the cans can be delivered to wholesalers, retailers, and other distributors so customers can purchase the product for personal consumption.

Manufacturing Using a Conversion Process

The conversion of resources into products and services can be described in several ways. We limit our discussion here to three: the focus or major resource used in the conversion process, its magnitude of change, and the number of production processes employed.

FIGURE 8-1: The Conversion Process

The conversion process converts ideas and resources into useful goods and services. The ability to create ideas and to produce products and services is a crucial step in the economic development of any nation.

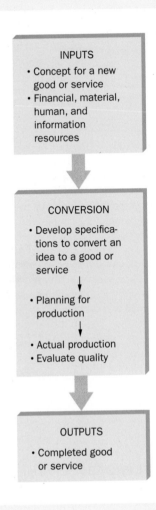

INPUTS
- Concept for a new good or service
- Financial, material, human, and information resources

CONVERSION
- Develop specifications to convert an idea to a good or service
- Planning for production
- Actual production
- Evaluate quality

OUTPUTS
- Completed good or service

FOCUS By the *focus* of a conversion process, we mean the resource or resources that make up the major or most important *input*. The resources are financial, material, information, and people—the same resources discussed in Chapters 1 and 6. For a bank such as Citibank, financial resources are the major resource. A chemical and energy company such as Chevron concentrates on material resources. Your college or university is concerned primarily with information. And temporary employment services, such as Manpower, Inc., focus on the use of human resources.

MAGNITUDE OF CHANGE The *magnitude* of a conversion process is the degree to which the resources are physically changed. At one extreme lie such processes as the one by which the Glad Products Company produces Glad Cling Wrap. Various chemicals in liquid or powder form are combined to produce long, thin sheets of plastic Glad Cling Wrap. Here, the original resources are totally unrecognizable in the finished product. At the other extreme, Southwest Airlines produces *no* physical change in its original resources. The airline simply provides a service and transports people from one place to another.

ETHICAL
challenges & successful
SOLUTIONS

The Ethics of Ecotourism Services

From boat trips to the remote Galapagos Islands to hikes through the rugged Canadian back-country, ecotourism to regions of natural beauty is a fast-growing segment of the service economy. Specialized service businesses—large and small—have sprung up to cater to the needs of adventurous travelers who want to visit pristine places all over the planet.

Yet the ecotourism boom has intensified the controversy over bringing travelers to ecologically sensitive destinations. Some people worry that increased tourism will overwhelm fragile ecosystems, increase pollution, and lead to over-commercialization. Proponents say ecotourism attracts much-needed economic development, with more job opportunities and more money to preserve the unique character of scenic areas. This is why Florida, for example, is seeking to create jobs by attracting

ecotourists while protecting the natural environment through more support for state parks and other eco-destinations.

Many local governments strive for balance by limiting the number of tourists at sensitive sites and setting environmental-protection standards for travel firms. Some ecotourism services showcase their ethical side by going beyond the basics. Lindblad Expeditions, for example, donates to conservation groups in the Galapagos and other areas where it operates. Karisia, a safari firm in Kenya, gets visitors out of gas-guzzling all-terrain vehicles with tours on mountain bikes and on foot. "The idea is to get people to appreciate nature through traveling here and supporting the local communities, so they in turn become inspired to protect the animals and everything around them," says one of the owners.

Sources: "Ecotourism in Florida: Take Birding, Biking to the Bank," *The Ledger* (Lakeland, FL), January 2, 2011, p. A14; Lucy Siegle, "Is It Possible to Be an Eco-Friendly Tourist?" *The Observer (UK)*, November 22, 2009, www.guardian.co.uk; Simon Horsford, "Hump Day," *Time International*, August 24, 2009, p. 49; Lindblad Expeditions, www.expeditions.com.

✳ Concept Check

☐ Explain how utility is related to form utility?

☐ In terms of focus, magnitude of change, and number, characterize the production processes used by a local pizza parlor, a dry-cleaning establishment, and an auto repair shop.

NUMBER OF PRODUCTION PROCESSES A single firm may employ one production process or many. In general, larger firms that make a variety of products use multiple production processes. For example, GE manufactures some of its own products, buys other merchandise from suppliers, and operates multiple divisions including a finance division, a lighting division, an energy division, a health care division, and other divisions responsible for the products and services that customers associate with the GE name. Smaller firms, by contrast, may use one production process. For example, Texas-based Advanced Cast Stone, Inc., manufactures one basic product: building materials made from concrete.

THE INCREASING IMPORTANCE OF SERVICES

LEARNING OBJECTIVE

3 Understand the importance of service businesses to consumers, other business firms, and the nation's economy.

service economy an economy in which more effort is devoted to the production of services than to the production of goods

The application of the basic principles of operations management to the production of services has coincided with a dramatic growth in the number and diversity of service businesses. In 1900, only 28 percent of American workers were employed in service firms. By 1950, this figure had grown to 40 percent, and by 2011, it had risen to 86 percent.[6] In fact, the American economy is now characterized as a **service economy** (see Figure 8-2). A service economy is one in which more effort is devoted to the production of services than to the production of goods.

Planning Quality Services

Today, the managers of restaurants, laundries, real estate agencies, banks, movie theaters, airlines, travel bureaus, and other service firms have realized that they can benefit from the experience of manufacturers. And while service firms are different from manufacturing firms, both types of businesses must plan in order to provide products *and* services that their customers want.

For a service firm, planning often begins with determining who the customer is and what needs the customer has. After customer needs are identified, the next step for successful service firms is to develop a plan that will enable the firm to deliver the services that their customers want or need. For example, a swimming pool repair business must develop a business plan that includes a process for hiring and training qualified employees, obtaining necessary parts and supplies, marketing the firm's services, and creating management and accounting systems to control the firm's activities. Once the firm provides a service to a customer, successful firms evaluate their operating systems and measure customer satisfaction. And if necessary, redesign their operating systems *and* their services to improve the customer's experience.

Evaluating the Quality of a Firm's Services

The production of services is very different from the production of manufactured goods in the following four ways:

1. Services are consumed immediately and, unlike manufactured goods, cannot be stored. For example, a hair stylist cannot store completed haircuts.
2. Services are provided when and where the customer desires the service. In many cases, customers will not travel as far to obtain a service.
3. Services are usually labor-intensive because the human resource is often the most important resource used in the production of services.
4. Services are intangible, and it is therefore more difficult to evaluate customer satisfaction.[7]

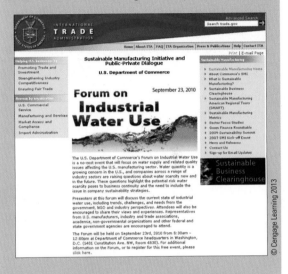
FIGURE 8-2: Service Industries

The growth of service firms has increased so dramatically that we now live in what is referred to as a service economy.

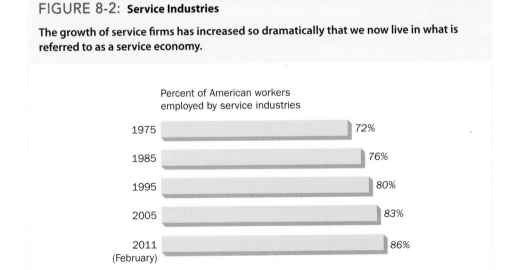

Percent of American workers employed by service industries

Year	Percent
1975	72%
1985	76%
1995	80%
2005	83%
2011 (February)	86%

Source: U.S. Bureau of Labor Statistics Web site, www.bls.gov (accessed March 16, 2011).

✳ *Concept Check*

- ☐ How is the production of services similar to the production of manufactured goods?
- ☐ How is production of services different from the production of manufactured goods?
- ☐ How can service firms measure customer satisfaction?

Although it is often more difficult to measure customer satisfaction, today's successful service firms work hard at providing the services customers want. Compared with manufacturers, service firms often listen more carefully to customers and respond more quickly to the market's changing needs. For example, Maggiano's Little Italy restaurant is a chain of eating establishments owned by Brinker International. This restaurant prides itself on customer service and wants customers to have an enjoyable dining experience. In order to continuously improve customer service, the restaurant encourages diners to complete online surveys that prompt diners to evaluate the food, atmosphere, service, and other variables. The information from the surveys is then used to fine-tune the way Maggiano's meets its customers' needs.

Now that we understand something about the production process that is used to transform resources into goods and services, we can consider three major activities involved in operations management: product development, planning for production, and operations control.

LEARNING OBJECTIVE
4 Describe how research and development lead to new products and services.

WHERE DO NEW PRODUCTS AND SERVICES COME FROM?

No firm can produce a product or service until it has an idea. In other words, someone first must come up with a new way to satisfy a need—a new product or an improvement in an existing product. Both Apple's iPad and Amazon's Kindle began as an idea. Although no one can predict with 100 percent accuracy what types of products will be available in the next five years, it is safe to say that companies will continue to introduce new products that will change our everyday lives.

Personal App Your idea for a new good or service may be your ticket to a small business of your own, if you have entrepreneurial spirit. But don't forget that big corporations also value people with new product ideas.

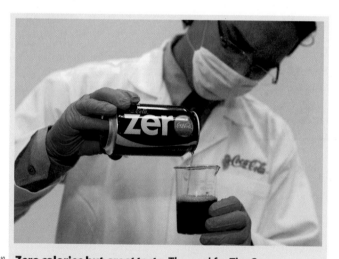

Zero calories but *great* taste. The goal for The Coca-Cola Company was to develop a soft drink that had real Coke taste, but zero calories. As a result of hard work by the company's product research and development team, Coca-Cola Zero is one of the most successful new products in the company's history. Today, the company sells more than 600 million cases of Coca-Cola Zero each year in more than 130 countries.

© Susana Gonzalez/Bloomberg via Getty Images

research and development (R&D) a set of activities intended to identify new ideas that have the potential to result in new goods and services

Research and Development

How did we get the iPad and the Kindle? We got them as a result of people working with new ideas that developed into useful products. In the same way, scientists and researchers working in businesses, colleges, and universities have produced many of the newer products we already take for granted.

These activities generally are referred to as *research and development*. For our purposes, **research and development (R&D)** involves a set of activities intended to identify new ideas that have the potential to result in new goods and services.

Today, business firms use three general types of R&D activities. *Basic research* consists of activities aimed at uncovering new knowledge. The goal of basic research is scientific advancement, without regard for its potential use in the development of goods and services. *Applied research*, in contrast, consists of activities geared toward discovering new knowledge with some potential use. *Development and implementation* involves research activities undertaken specifically to put new or existing knowledge to use in producing goods and services. The 3M Company has always been known for its development and implementation research activities. Currently, the company employs 7,350 researchers worldwide and has invested more than $7 billion over the last five years to develop new products designed to make people's lives easier and safer.[8]

Product Extension and Refinement

When a brand-new product is first marketed, its sales are zero and slowly increase from that point. If the product is successful, annual sales increase more and more rapidly until they reach some peak. Then, as time passes, annual sales begin to decline, and they continue to decline until it is no longer profitable to manufacture the product. (This rise-and-decline pattern, called the *product life-cycle*, is discussed in more detail in Chapter 12.)

© David Thyberg/Shutterstock

If a firm sells only one product, when that product reaches the end of its life-cycle, the firm will die, too. To stay in business, the firm must, at the very least, find ways to refine or extend the want-satisfying capability of its product. Consider television sets. Since they were introduced in the late 1930s, television sets have been constantly *refined* so that they now provide clearer, sharper pictures with less dial adjusting. During the same time, television sets also were extended. There are television-only sets and others that include DVD players. And the latest development—high-definition television—has already become the standard.

For most firms, extension and refinement are expected results of their research, development, and implementation activities. Often, product extensions and refinements result from the application of new knowledge to existing products. Each refinement or extension results in an essentially "new" product whose sales make up for the declining sales of a product that was introduced earlier. When consumers discovered that the original five varieties of Campbell's Soup were of the highest quality, as well as inexpensive, the soups were an instant success. Although one of the most successful companies at the beginning of the 1900s, Campbell's had to continue to innovate, refine, and extend its product line. For example, many consumers in the United States live in what is called an on-the-go society. To meet this need, Campbell's Soup has developed ready-to-serve products that can be popped into a microwave at work or school.

Concept Check ✱

☐ Describe how research and development lead to new products.

☐ What is the difference between basic research, applied research, and development and implementation?

☐ Explain why product extension and refinement are important.

HOW DO MANAGERS PLAN PRODUCTION?

Only a few of the many ideas for new products, refinements, and extensions ever reach the production stage. For those ideas that do, however, the next step is planning for production. Once a new product idea has been identified, planning for production involves three different phases: design planning, site selection and facilities planning, and operational planning (see Figure 8-3).

Design Planning

When the R&D staff at Hewlett-Packard recommended to top management that the firm produce and market an affordable netbook computer, the company could not simply swing into production the next day. Instead, a great deal of time and energy had to be invested in determining what the new computer would look like, where and how it would be produced, and what options would be included. These decisions are a part of design planning. **Design planning** is the development of a plan for converting an idea into an actual product or service. The major decisions involved in design planning deal with product line, required capacity, and use of technology.

PRODUCT LINE A **product line** is a group of similar products that differ only in relatively minor characteristics. During the design-planning stage, a computer manufacturer such as Hewlett-Packard must determine how many different models to produce and what major options to offer. Likewise, a restaurant chain such as Pizza Hut must decide how many menu items to offer.

LEARNING OBJECTIVE

5 Discuss the components involved in planning the production process.

design planning the development of a plan for converting an idea into an actual product or service

product line a group of similar products that differ only in relatively minor characteristics

FIGURE 8-3: Planning for Production

Once research and development identifies an idea that meets customer needs, manufacturers then use three additional phases to convert the idea to an actual product or service.

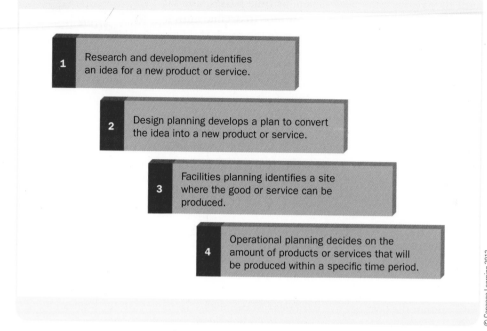

1. Research and development identifies an idea for a new product or service.

2. Design planning develops a plan to convert the idea into a new product or service.

3. Facilities planning identifies a site where the good or service can be produced.

4. Operational planning decides on the amount of products or services that will be produced within a specific time period.

© Cengage Learning 2013

An important issue in deciding on the product line is to balance customer preferences and production requirements. For this reason, marketing managers play an important role in making product-line decisions. Typically, marketing personnel want a "long" product line that offers customers many options. Because a long product line with more options gives customers greater choice, it is easier to sell products that meet the needs of individual customers. On the other hand, production personnel generally want a "short" product line with fewer options because products are easier to produce. In many cases, the actual choice between a long and short product line involves balancing customer preferences with the cost and problems associated with a more complex production process.

Once the product line has been determined, each distinct product within the product line must be designed. **Product design** is the process of creating a set of specifications from which a product can be produced. When designing a new product, specifications are extremely important. For example, product engineers for Whirlpool Corporation must make sure that a new frost-free refrigerator keeps food frozen in the freezer compartment. At the same time, they must make sure that lettuce and tomatoes do not freeze in the crisper section of the refrigerator. The need for a complete product design is fairly obvious; products that work cannot be manufactured without it. But services should be designed carefully as well—and *for the same reason.*

REQUIRED PRODUCTION CAPACITY **Capacity** is the amount of products or services that an organization can produce in a given period of time. (For example, the capacity of a Panasonic assembly plant might be 1.3 million high-definition televisions per year.) Operations managers—again working with the firm's marketing managers—must determine the required capacity. This, in turn, determines the size of the production facility. If the facility is built with too much capacity, valuable resources (plant, equipment, and money) will lie idle. If the facility offers insufficient capacity, additional capacity may have to be added later when it is much more expensive than in the initial building stage.

product design the process of creating a set of specifications from which a product can be produced

capacity the amount of products or services that an organization can produce in a given time

Personal App Have you ever waited in line to buy a movie ticket or see a bank teller? Waiting time is one of the issues that designers of these services take into account when thinking about capacity.

Capacity means about the same thing to service businesses. For example, the capacity of a restaurant such as the Hard Rock Cafe in Nashville, Tennessee, is the number of customers it can serve at one time. As with the manufacturing facility described earlier, if the restaurant is built with too much capacity—too many tables and chairs—valuable resources will be wasted. If the restaurant is too small, customers may have to wait for service; if the wait is too long, they may leave and choose another restaurant.

USE OF TECHNOLOGY During the design-planning stage, management must determine the degree to which *automation* and *technology* will be used to produce a product or service. Here, there is a trade-off between high initial costs and low operating costs (for automation) and low initial costs and high operating costs (for human labor). Ultimately, management must choose between a labor-intensive technology and a capital-intensive technology. A **labor-intensive technology** is a process in which people must do most of the work. Housecleaning services and the New York Yankees baseball team, for example, are labor-intensive. A **capital-intensive technology** is a process in which machines and equipment do most of the work. A Sony automated assembly plant is capital-intensive.

Site Selection and Facilities Planning

Generally, a business will choose to produce a new product in an existing factory as long as (1) the existing factory has enough capacity to handle customer demand for both the new product and established products and (2) the cost of refurbishing an existing factory is less than the cost of building a new one.

After exploring the capacity of existing factories, management may decide to build a new production facility. In determining where to locate new production facilities, management must consider a number of variables, including the following:

- Locations of major customers and suppliers.
- Availability and cost of skilled and unskilled labor.
- Quality of life for employees and management in the proposed location.
- The cost of land and construction to build a new facility.
- Local and state taxes, environmental regulations, and zoning laws.
- The amount of financial support and subsidies, if any, offered by local and state governments.
- Special requirements, such as great amounts of energy or water used in the production process.

Personal App Is your state or city courting a manufacturer who's planning to build a new production facility? New facilities are bringing new jobs and tax dollars to communities all around the country.

Before making a final decision about where a proposed plant will be located and how it will be organized, two other factors—human resources and plant layout—should be examined.

HUMAN RESOURCES Several issues involved in facilities planning and site selection fall within the province of the human resources manager. Thus, at this stage, human resources and operations managers work closely together. For example, suppose that a firm such as Reebok wants to lower labor costs by constructing a sophisticated production plant in China. The human resources manager will have to recruit managers and employees with the appropriate skills who are willing to relocate to a foreign country, develop training programs for local Chinese workers, or both.

labor-intensive technology a process in which people must do most of the work

capital-intensive technology a process in which machines and equipment do most of the work

FIGURE 8-4: Facilities Planning

The process layout is used when small batches of different products are created or when working on different parts of a product. The product layout (assembly line) is used when all products undergo the same operations in the same sequence. The fixed-position layout is used in producing a product too large to move.

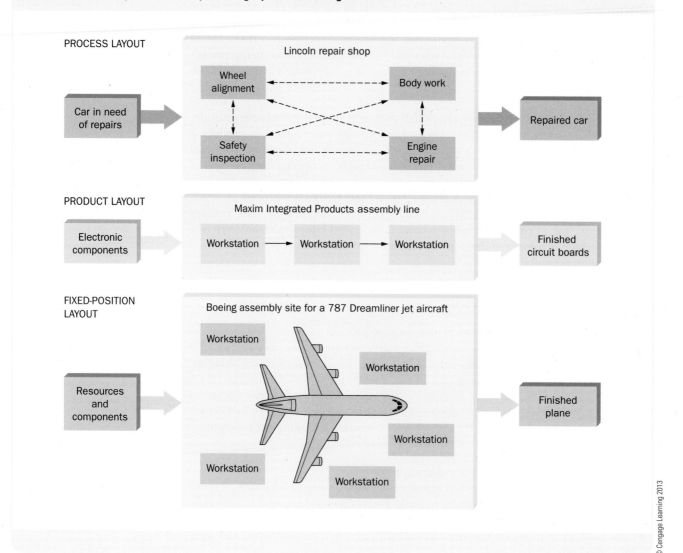

PROCESS LAYOUT

Lincoln repair shop

Car in need of repairs → Wheel alignment, Body work, Safety inspection, Engine repair → Repaired car

PRODUCT LAYOUT

Maxim Integrated Products assembly line

Electronic components → Workstation → Workstation → Workstation → Finished circuit boards

FIXED-POSITION LAYOUT

Boeing assembly site for a 787 Dreamliner jet aircraft

Resources and components → Workstation, Workstation, Workstation, Workstation, Workstation, Workstation → Finished plane

© Cengage Learning 2013

PLANT LAYOUT **Plant layout** is the arrangement of machinery, equipment, and personnel within a production facility. Three general types of plant layout are used (see Figure 8-4).

The *process layout* is used when different operations are required for creating small batches of different products or working on different parts of a product. The plant is arranged so that each operation is performed in its own particular area. An auto repair facility at a local automobile dealership provides an example of a process layout. The various operations may be engine repair, bodywork, wheel alignment, and safety inspection. If you take your Lincoln Navigator for a wheel alignment, your car "visits" only the area where alignments are performed.

A *product layout* (sometimes referred to as an *assembly line*) is used when all products undergo the same operations in the same sequence. Workstations are arranged to match the sequence of operations, and work flows from station to station. An assembly line is the best example of a product layout. For example, California-based Maxim Integrated Products, Inc., uses a product layout to manufacture components for consumer and business electronic products.

plant layout the arrangement of machinery, equipment, and personnel within a production facility

Part 3: Management and Organization

A *fixed-position layout* is used when a very large product is produced. Aircraft manufacturers and shipbuilders apply this method because of the difficulty of moving a large product such as an airliner or a ship. The product remains stationary, and people and machines are moved as needed to assemble the product. Boeing, for example, uses the fixed-position layout to build 787 Dreamliner jet aircraft at its Everett, Washington, manufacturing facility.

Operational Planning

The objective of operational planning is to decide on the amount of products or services each facility will produce during a specific period of time. Four steps are required.

STEP 1: SELECTING A PLANNING HORIZON A **planning horizon** is simply the time period during which an operational plan will be in effect. A common planning horizon for production plans is one year. Then, before each year is up, management must plan for the next. A planning horizon of one year generally is long enough to average out seasonal increases and decreases in sales. At the same time, it is short enough for planners to adjust production to accommodate long-range sales trends.

Ice cream that tastes as good as home made. The goal for Roundy's Supermarkets is to make their ice cream taste just like Mom's—but production is on a much larger scale. To accomplish the task, the Wisconsin-based company uses a stainless steel assembly line that snakes through the company's food manufacturing and processing plant in Kenosha, Wisconsin.

© AP Photo/Mark Hertzberg

STEP 2: ESTIMATING MARKET DEMAND The *market demand* for a product is the quantity that customers will purchase at the going price. This quantity must be estimated for the time period covered by the planning horizon. Sales projections developed by marketing managers are the basis for market-demand estimates.

STEP 3: COMPARING MARKET DEMAND WITH CAPACITY The third step in operational planning is to compare the estimated market demand with the facility's capacity to satisfy that demand. (Remember that capacity is the amount of products or services that an organization can produce in a given time period.) One of three outcomes may result: Demand may exceed capacity, capacity may exceed demand, or capacity and demand may be equal. If they are equal, the facility should be operated at full capacity. However, if market demand and capacity are not equal, adjustments may be necessary.

STEP 4: ADJUSTING PRODUCTS OR SERVICES TO MEET DEMAND The biggest reason for changes to a firm's production schedule is changes in the amount of products or services that a company sells to its customers. For example, Indiana-based Berry Plastics manufactures all kinds of plastic products. One particularly successful product line for Berry Plastics is drink cups that can be screen-printed to promote a company or the company's products or services.[9] If Berry Plastics obtains a large contract to provide promotional cups to a large fast-food chain such as Whataburger or McDonald's, the company may need to work three shifts a day, seven days a week, until the contract is fulfilled. Unfortunately, the reverse is also true. If the company's sales force does not generate new sales, there may be only enough work for the employees on one shift.

When market demand exceeds capacity, several options are available to a firm. Production of products or services may be increased by operating the facility overtime with existing personnel or by starting a second or third work shift. For manufacturers, another response is to subcontract or outsource a portion of the work to other manufacturers. If the excess demand is likely to be permanent, the firm may expand the current facility or build another facility.

What happens when capacity exceeds market demand? Again, there are several options. To reduce output temporarily, workers may be laid off and part of the

planning horizon the period during which an operational plan will be in effect

Concept Check *

☐ What are the major elements of design planning?

☐ Define capacity. Why is it important for a manufacturing business or a service business?

☐ What factors should be considered when selecting a site for a new manufacturing facility?

☐ What is the objective of operational planning? What four steps are used to accomplish this objective?

facility shut down, or the facility may be operated on a shorter-than-normal work-week for as long as the excess capacity persists. To adjust to a permanently decreased demand, management may shift the excess capacity of a manufacturing facility to the production of other goods or services. The most radical adjustment is to eliminate the excess capacity by selling unused manufacturing facilities.

OPERATIONS CONTROL

LEARNING OBJECTIVE

6 Explain how purchasing, inventory control, scheduling, and quality control affect production.

We have discussed the development of an idea for a product or service and the planning that translates that idea into the reality. Now we are ready to push the "start button" to begin the production process. In this section, we examine four important areas of operations control: purchasing, inventory control, scheduling, and quality control (see Figure 8-5).

Purchasing

Purchasing consists of all the activities involved in obtaining required materials, supplies, components (or subassemblies), and parts from other firms. Levi Strauss, for example, must purchase denim cloth, thread, and zippers before it can produce a single pair of jeans. For all firms, the purchasing function is far from routine, and its importance should not be underestimated. For some products, purchased materials make up more than 50 percent of their wholesale costs.

The objective of purchasing is to ensure that required materials are available when they are needed, in the proper amounts, and at minimum cost. Generally, the company with purchasing needs and suppliers must develop a working relationship built on trust. In addition to a working relationship built on trust, many companies believe that purchasing is one area where they can promote diversity. For example, AT&T developed a Supplier Diversity Program that includes minorities, women, and disabled veteran business enterprises in 1968. Today, more than 40 years later, goals for the AT&T program include purchasing a total of 21.5 percent of all products and services from these three groups. As a result of its Supplier Diversity Program, the company is now recognized as one of the nation's leading companies in supplier diversity.[10]

Purchasing personnel should constantly be on the lookout for new or backup suppliers, even when their needs are being met by their present suppliers, because problems such as strikes and equipment breakdowns can cut off the flow of purchased materials from a primary supplier at any time.

The choice of suppliers should result from careful analysis of a number of factors. The following are especially critical:

- *Price.* Comparing prices offered by different suppliers is always an essential part of selecting a supplier. Even tiny differences in price add up to enormous sums when large quantities are purchased.

FIGURE 8-5: Four Aspects of Operations Control

Implementing the operations control system in any business requires the effective use of purchasing, inventory control, scheduling, and quality control.

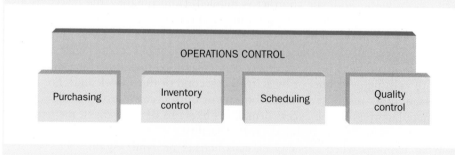

© Cengage Learning 2013

purchasing all the activities involved in obtaining required materials, supplies, components, and parts from other firms

- *Quality.* Purchasing specialists always try to buy materials at a level of quality in keeping with the type of product being manufactured. The minimum acceptable quality is usually specified by product designers.
- *Reliability.* An agreement to purchase high-quality materials at a low price is the purchaser's dream. However, the dream becomes a nightmare if the supplier does not deliver.
- *Credit terms.* Purchasing specialists should determine if the supplier demands immediate payment or will extend credit. Also, does the supplier offer a cash discount or reduction in price for prompt payment?
- *Shipping costs.* Low prices and favorable credit terms offered by a supplier can be wiped out when the buyer must pay the shipping costs. Above all, the question of who pays the shipping costs should be answered before any supplier is chosen.

Personal App When you buy for yourself, you're probably accustomed to comparing price, quality, reliability, payment terms, and shipping costs. Industrial purchasing follows these basics, but with much larger quantities and more complicated procedures.

Inventory Control

Can you imagine what would happen if a Coca-Cola manufacturing plant ran out of the company's familiar red-and-white aluminum cans? It would be impossible to complete the manufacturing process and ship the cases of Coke to retailers. Management would be forced to shut the assembly line down until the next shipment of cans arrived from a supplier. The simple fact is that shutdowns are expensive because costs such as rent, wages, insurance, and other expenses still must be paid.

Operations managers are concerned with three types of inventories. A *raw-materials inventory* consists of materials that will become part of the product during the production process. The *work-in-process inventory* consists of partially completed products. The *finished-goods inventory* consists of completed goods. Each type of inventory also has a *holding cost*, or storage cost, and a *stock-out cost*, the cost of running out of inventory. **Inventory control** is the process of managing inventories in such a way as to minimize inventory costs, including both holding costs and potential stock-out costs.

Today, computer systems are being used to keep track of inventories and alert managers to impending stock-outs. One of the most sophisticated methods of inventory control used today is materials requirements planning. **Materials requirements planning (MRP)** is a computerized system that integrates production planning and inventory control. One of the great advantages of an MRP system is its ability to juggle delivery schedules and lead times effectively. For a complex product such as an automobile, it is virtually impossible for individual managers to oversee the hundreds of parts that go into the finished product. However, a manager using an MRP system can arrange both order and delivery schedules so that materials, parts, and supplies arrive when they are needed.

Because large firms can incur huge inventory costs, much attention has been devoted to inventory control. The just-in-time system being used by some businesses is one result of all this attention. A **just-in-time inventory system** is designed to ensure

Sometimes being overstocked is a good thing! For Patrick Byrne, Executive Chairman and CEO of Overstock.com, the concept of having too much inventory may be a good thing. This online retailer obtains merchandise from its suppliers and manufacturers when they have too much inventory. Then Overstock.com generates sales revenues *and* profits by offering merchandise to its online customers at discount prices. To see if the company does offer lower prices on something you may want or need, go to www.overstock.com

© AP Photo/Geroge Frey

inventory control the process of managing inventories in such a way as to minimize inventory costs, including both holding costs and potential stock-out costs

materials requirements planning (MRP) a computerized system that integrates production planning and inventory control

just-in-time inventory system a system designed to ensure that materials or supplies arrive at a facility just when they are needed so that storage and holding costs are minimized

that materials or supplies arrive at a facility just when they are needed so that storage and holding costs are minimized. The customer must specify what will be needed, when, and in what amounts. The supplier must be sure that the right supplies arrive at the agreed-upon time and location. For example, managers using a just-in-time inventory system at a Ford assembly plant determine the number of automobiles that will be assembled in a specified time period. Then Ford purchasing personnel order just the parts needed to produce those automobiles. In turn, suppliers deliver the parts in time or when they are needed on the assembly line.

Without proper inventory control, it is impossible for operations managers to schedule the work required to produce goods that can be sold to customers.

Scheduling

Scheduling is the process of ensuring that materials and other resources are at the right place at the right time. The materials and resources may be moved from a warehouse to the workstations, they may move from station to station along an assembly line, or they may arrive at workstations "just in time" to be made part of the work-in-process there.

As our definition implies, both place and time are important to scheduling. The *routing* of materials is the sequence of workstations that the materials will follow. Assume that Drexel-Heritage—one of America's largest and oldest furniture manufacturers—is scheduling production of an oval coffee table made from cherry wood. Operations managers route the needed materials (wood, screws, packaging materials, etc.) through a series of individual workstations along an assembly line. At each workstation, a specific task is performed, and then the partially finished coffee table moves to the next workstation. When routing materials, operations managers are especially concerned with the sequence of each step of the production process. For the coffee table, the top and legs must be cut to specifications before the wood is finished. (If the wood were finished before being cut, the finish would be ruined, and the coffee table would have to be stained again.)

When scheduling production, managers also are concerned with timing. The *timing* function specifies when the materials will arrive at each station and how long they will remain there. For the cherry coffee table, it may take workers 30 minutes to cut the table top and legs and another 30 minutes to drill the holes and assemble the table. Before packaging the coffee table for shipment, it must be finished with cherry stain and allowed to dry. This last step may take as long as three days depending on weather conditions and humidity. Only after the product is completely dry can the coffee table be packaged and shipped to wholesalers and retailers.

Regardless of whether the finished product requires a simple or complex production process, operations managers are responsible for monitoring schedules—called *follow-up*—to ensure that the work flows according to a timetable.

Quality Control

As mentioned earlier in this chapter, American business firms that compete in the very competitive global marketplace have taken another look at the importance of improving quality. Today, there is even a national quality award. The **Malcolm Baldrige National Quality Award** is given by the U.S. president to organizations that apply and are judged to be outstanding in specific managerial tasks that lead to improved quality for both products and services. Past winners include Ritz-Carlton Hotels, Boeing, Motorola, Nestlé Purina Petcare, Cargill Corn Milling North America, Richland Community College (part of the Dallas Community College District), and many others. For many organizations, using the Baldrige criteria results in

- better employee relations,
- higher productivity,
- greater customer satisfaction,
- increased market share, and
- improved profitability.[11]

scheduling the process of ensuring that materials and other resources are at the right place at the right time

Malcolm Baldrige National Quality Award an award given by the U.S. president to organizations that apply and are judged to be outstanding in specific managerial tasks that lead to improved quality for both products and services

Although winning the "Baldrige" can mean prestige and lots of free media coverage, the winners all have one factor in common: They use quality control to improve their firm's products or services.

Quality control is the process of ensuring that goods and services are produced in accordance with design specifications. The major objective of quality control is to see that the organization lives up to the standards it has set for itself on quality. Some firms, such as Mercedes-Benz, have built their reputations on quality. Customers pay more for their products in return for assurances of high quality. Other firms adopt a strategy of emphasizing lower prices along with reasonable (but not particularly high) quality.

Personal App You don't want to buy a shoddy product, and any company you work for doesn't want to gain a reputation for poor quality. That's why strict quality control is so important.

INSPECTION Increased effort is also being devoted to **inspection**, which is the examination of the quality of work-in-process. Inspections are performed at various times during production. Purchased materials may be inspected when they arrive at the production facility. Subassemblies and manufactured parts may be inspected before they become part of a finished product. In addition, finished goods may be inspected before they are shipped to customers. Items that are within design specifications continue on their way. Those that are not within design specifications are removed from production.

IMPROVING QUALITY THROUGH EMPLOYEE PARTICIPATION Over the years, more and more managers have realized that quality is an essential "ingredient" of the good or service being provided. This view of quality provides several benefits. The number of defects decreases, which causes profits to increase. Furthermore, making products right the first time reduces many of the rejects and much of the rework. In addition, making employees responsible for quality often eliminates the need for inspection. An employee is encouraged to accept full responsibility for the quality of his or her work.

The use of a **quality circle**, a team of employees who meet on company time to solve problems of product quality, is another way manufacturers are achieving better quality at the operations level. Quality circles have been used successfully in companies such as IBM, Northrop Grumman Corporation, Lockheed Martin, and GE.

Total quality management (TQM) can also be used to improve the quality of a firm's products or services. As noted in Chapter 6, a TQM program coordinates the efforts directed at improving customer satisfaction, increasing employee participation, strengthening supplier partnerships, and facilitating an organizational atmosphere of continuous quality improvement. Firms such as American Express, AT&T, Motorola, and Hewlett-Packard all have used TQM to improve product quality and, ultimately, customer satisfaction.

Another technique that businesses may use to improve not only quality but also overall performance is Six Sigma. **Six Sigma** is a disciplined approach that relies on statistical data and improved methods to eliminate defects for a firm's products and services. Although many experts agree that Six Sigma is similar to TQM and other methods used to improve quality, Six Sigma often has more top-level support, much more teamwork, and a new corporate attitude or culture. The companies that developed, refined, and have the most experience with Six Sigma are Motorola, GE, and Honeywell. Although each of these companies is a corporate giant, the underlying principles of Six Sigma can be used by all firms regardless of size.[12]

WORLD QUALITY STANDARDS: ISO 9000 AND ISO 14000 Different companies have different perceptions of quality. Without a common standard of quality, however, customers may be at the mercy of manufacturers, service providers, and vendors. To deal with the problem of standardization, the International Organization for Standardization, a nongovernmental organization with headquarters in Geneva, Switzerland, was created. The **International Organization for Standardization (ISO)** is

quality control the process of ensuring that goods and services are produced in accordance with design specifications

inspection the examination of the quality of work-in-process

quality circle a team of employees who meet on company time to solve problems of product quality

Six Sigma a disciplined approach that relies on statistical data and improved methods to eliminate defects for a firm's products and services

International Organization for Standardization (ISO) a network of national standards institutes and similar organizations from 162 different countries that is charged with developing standards for quality products and services that are traded throughout the globe

Measuring Reliability by the Nines

Decade after decade, AT&T's landline telephone system has achieved an astounding record of reliability. The system was designed so that a dial tone would be available 99.999 percent of the time. At this "Five 9s" level of quality, customers might miss a dial tone for about 5 minutes per year. In contrast, a quality level of Four 9s would mean no dial tone for about 52 minutes per year, and a level of Three 9s would mean no dial tone for more than 8 hours per year.

In today's Internet-fueled business environment, high reliability is critical. Google knows that millions of firms and individuals really depend on its search site, its e-mail, and many of its other services. In fact, Google's Gmail e-mail service was available 99.984 percent of the time during one recent year. In the quest for Four 9s reliability, Google has two perfectly synchronized Gmail systems running in tandem at all times, with extra backup copies ready to be loaded if problems occur. However, a Google executive observes that the company is unlikely to aspire to Five 9s quality because "we don't believe Five 9s is attainable in a commercial service, if measured correctly."

Amazon, a pioneer of online retailing and online technology, aims for exceptionally high reliability for the data storage services it offers other businesses. "We talk of 'durability' of data—it's designed for Eleven 9s durability," says an Amazon executive. Because businesses that store data on its servers expect around-the-clock access at all times, Amazon does everything it can to deliver reliability measured in as many 9s as possible.

Sources: Randall Stross, "99.999% Reliable? Don't Hold Your Breath," *New York Times*, January 9, 2011, www.nytimes.com; Tony Kontzer, "Cloud Forecast 2015," *CIO Insight*, January 7, 2011, www.cioinsight.com/c/a/Infrastructure/Cloud-Forecast-2015-431830.

a network of national standards institutes and similar organizations from 162 different countries that is charged with developing standards for quality products and services that are traded throughout the globe. According to the organization,

> ISO's work makes a positive difference to the world we live in. ISO standards add value to all types of business operations. They contribute to making the development, manufacturing and supply of products and services more efficient, safer and cleaner. They make trade between countries easier and fairer. ISO standards also serve to safeguard consumers and users of products and services in general, as well as making their lives simpler.[13]

Standardization is achieved through consensus agreements between national delegations representing all the economic stakeholders—suppliers, customers, and often governments. The member organization for the United States is the American National Standards Institute located in Washington, D.C.

In 1987, the panel published ISO 9000 (*iso* is Greek for "equal"), which sets the guidelines for quality procedures that businesses must use to receive certification. Certification by independent auditors and laboratory testing services serves as evidence that a company meets the standards for quality control procedures in design, production processes, and product testing.

Although certification is not a legal requirement to do business globally, the organization's 162 member countries have approved the ISO standards. In fact, ISO standards are so prevalent around the globe that many customers refuse to do business with noncertified companies. As an added bonus, companies completing the certification process often discover new, cost-efficient ways to improve their existing quality-control programs.

As a continuation of this standardization process, the International Organization for Standardization has developed ISO 14000. ISO 14000 is a family of international standards for incorporating environmental concerns into operations and product standards. Other standards include ISO 26000 (social responsibility) and ISO 31000 (risk management). All ISO standards are updated periodically to reflect changing conditions in the changing global business world.[14]

TABLE 8-1: Production Planning: A Summary

Both planning for production and operations control are necessary if a firm is to produce a successful product or service.

The Process Begins with Planning for Production
1. *Research and Development* identifies ideas for a product or service.
2. *Design Planning* develops a plan for producing a product or service.
3. *Site Selection and Facilities Planning* identifies a production site, a plant layout, and if human resources are available.
4. *Operational Planning* decides on the amount of products or services that will be produced.

Then Four Operations Control Steps Are Used to Produce a Product or Service
1. *Purchasing* obtains required materials, supplies, and parts from other firms.
2. *Inventory Control* ensures that materials, supplies, and parts are available when needed.
3. *Scheduling* ensures that materials and other resources are at the right place and at the right time in the production process.
4. *Quality Control* determines if the firm has lived up to the standards it has set for itself on the quality of its products or services.

The End Result: A Successful Product or Service

© Cengage Learning 2013

Production Planning: A Summary

In this chapter, the activities that firms use to produce products and services have been described. And yet, it is often hard to determine how the individual activities fit together in a logical sequence. Now, toward the end of the chapter, it may help to look at a table to see how all of the "pieces of the puzzle" fit together. At the top of Table 8-1, planning for production begins with research and development, design planning, facilities planning, and operational planning—all topics described in this chapter. In the middle section of Table 8-1, activities that were described in the Operations Control section (purchasing, inventory control, scheduling, and quality control) are summarized. The goal of all the planning activities in the top section and operations control activities in the middle section is to create and produce a successful product or service. Of course, the steps for planning production and operations control should always be evaluated to determine if the firm's activities can be improved in order to increase the firm's productivity.

IMPROVING PRODUCTIVITY WITH TECHNOLOGY

No coverage of production and operations management would be complete without a discussion on productivity. Productivity concerns all managers, but it is especially important to operations managers, the people who must oversee the creation of a firm's products or services. We define **productivity** as the average level of output per worker per hour. Hence, if each worker at plant A produces 75 units per day and each worker at plant B produces only 70 units per day, the workers at plant A are more productive. If one bank teller serves 25 customers per hour and another serves 28 per hour, the second teller is more productive.

Productivity Trends

Overall productivity growth for the U.S. business sector averaged 4.2 percent for the period 1979-2009.[15] More specifically, productivity in 2009 increased 7.7 percent.[16] (*Note:* At the time of publication, 2009 was the last year that complete statistics were available.) The 7.7 percent increase in the United States in 2009 was the largest productivity increase for the 19 countries tracked by the U.S. Bureau of Labor Statistics.

Concept Check ✱

☐ Why is selecting a supplier important? What factors should be considered when selecting a supplier?

☐ What costs must be balanced and minimized through inventory control?

☐ Explain in what sense scheduling is a control function of operations managers.

☐ How can a business firm improve the quality of its products or services?

LEARNING OBJECTIVE

7 Summarize how productivity and technology are related.

productivity the average level of output per worker per hour

SPOT LIGHT

Productivity Growth Rates

Statistics represent average annual productivity growth rates for manufacturing output per hour in the leading five countries for the last year that complete results are available.

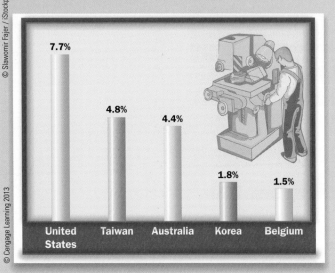

Source: "International Comparisons of Manufacturing Productivity and Unit Labor Cost Trends, 2009," The Bureau of Labor Statistics at www.bls.gov (accessed March 26, 2011).

By comparison, productivity in 2009 decreased in 12 of the 19 countries. In addition to the United States, only Australia, Belgium, Canada, Korea, Norway, and Taiwan had productivity increases.[17]

While the 7.7 percent productivity gain is above average when compared to other countries around the globe, there is always room for improvement. And, there are a number of factors that can limit productivity growth for any country. For example, the recent economic crisis caused many businesses to reduce the rate of investment in new equipment and technology. As workers had to use increasingly outdated equipment, their ability to increase productivity declined. Now that the U.S. economy shows signs of improvement, business firms are once again beginning to invest in new equipment and machinery. As a result, economic experts predict that the productivity increase in 2009 will continue to increase in the future.

Another important factor that has hurt the U.S. productivity growth rate is the tremendous growth of the service sector in the United States. Although this sector grew in the number of employees and economic importance, its productivity levels did not grow as fast. Today, many economic experts agree that improving service-sector productivity can lead to higher overall productivity growth for the nation.

Finally, increased government regulation is frequently cited as a factor affecting productivity. Federal agencies such as the Occupational Safety and Health Administration, the Environmental Protection Agency, and the Food and Drug Administration are increasingly regulating business practices. Often, the time employees spend complying with government reporting requirements can reduce productivity growth rates. Even though executives, managers, and business owners often cite increased regulation from all levels of government as a reason for low productivity, the general public believes there is need for effective government regulations that improve working conditions, product safety, and the environment. For example, the recent British Petroleum oil spill in the Gulf of Mexico and its effect on nearby beaches and wetlands may have been prevented or at least reduced if there had been more government regulation of off-shore drilling. Although there are two sides to the regulatory argument, it may be beneficial to take a new look at existing and proposed regulations to ensure all the regulations are needed and compliance is no more time-consuming and expensive than absolutely necessary.

Improving Productivity Growth Rates

Several techniques and strategies have been suggested to improve current productivity growth rates. For example:

- Government policies that may be hindering productivity growth could be eliminated or at least modified.
- Changing the incentives for work and altering the reward system so that people are paid for what they contribute rather than for the time they put in may motivate employees to produce at higher levels.
- Increased cooperation between labor and management could be fostered to improve productivity.
- Investing more money in facilities, equipment, technology and automation, and employee training could improve productivity.

In addition to the above techniques and strategies, many business firms have adopted lean manufacturing techniques to improve productivity. **Lean manufacturing** (sometimes referred to as lean production or just lean) is a manufacturing approach that enhances efficiency, identifies and eliminates waste, and increases profits. The most important factor in a lean manufacturing process is value. Any step or process that adds value to the end product or service is kept. Anything that does not add value is considered waste and is eliminated. Engineers at the Toyota Corporation are often given credit for creating the lean manufacturing concept. Despite the company's recent quality crisis, the use of lean manufacturing concepts along with empowering workers and improved methods of inventory control have enabled the company to grow from a small company to one of the world's largest automakers.

Automated assembly lines and robots increase productivity! Today, Chrysler—like most domestic and foreign automobile manufacturers—uses very sophisticated (and expensive) robotics to increase productivity and lower costs. In this photo, robotic arms are welding the front cab on the chassis of a Dodge Ram pickup truck at the Warren truck plant in Warren, Michigan.

The Impact of Computers and Robotics on Productivity

Automation is the total or near-total use of machines to do work. The rapid increase in automated procedures has been made possible by the microprocessor, a silicon chip that led to the production of desktop computers for businesses, homes, and schools. In factories, microprocessors are used in robotics and in computer manufacturing systems.

ROBOTICS **Robotics** is the use of programmable machines to perform a variety of tasks by manipulating materials and tools. Robots work quickly, accurately, and steadily. For example, Illumina, Inc., a San Diego company, uses robotics to perform medical laboratory tests. The information then is sold to some of the world's largest pharmaceutical companies, where it is used to alter existing prescription drugs, develop new drug therapies, and customize diagnoses and treatments for all kinds of serious diseases. As an added bonus, Illumina's robots can work 24 hours a day at much lower costs than if human lab workers performed the same tests.[18]

Robots are especially effective in tedious, repetitive assembly-line jobs, as well as in handling hazardous materials. They are also useful as artificial "eyes" that can check the quality of products as they are being processed on the assembly lines. To date, the automotive industry has made the most extensive use of robotics, but robots also have been used to mine coal, inspect the inner surfaces of pipes, assemble computer components, provide certain kinds of patient care in hospitals, and clean and guard buildings at night.

COMPUTER MANUFACTURING SYSTEMS People are quick to point out how computers have changed their everyday lives, but most people do not realize the impact computers have had on manufacturing. In simple terms, the factory of the future has already arrived. For most manufacturers, the changeover began with the use of computer-aided design and computer-aided manufacturing. **Computer-aided design (CAD)** is the use of computers to aid in the development of products. Ford speeds up car design, Canon designs new photocopiers, and American Greetings creates new birthday cards by using CAD. **Computer-aided manufacturing (CAM)** is the use of computers to plan and control manufacturing processes. A well-designed CAM system allows manufacturers to become much more productive. Not only are a greater number of products produced, but speed and quality also increase. Toyota, Hasbro, Oneida, and Apple Computer all have used CAM to increase productivity.

If you are thinking that the next logical step is to combine the CAD and CAM computer systems, you are right. Today, the most successful manufacturers use CAD

lean manufacturing (sometimes referred to as lean production or just lean) a manufacturing approach that enhances efficiency, identifies and eliminates waste, and increases profits

automation the total or near-total use of machines to do work

robotics the use of programmable machines to perform a variety of tasks by manipulating materials and tools

computer-aided design (CAD) the use of computers to aid in the development of products

computer-aided manufacturing (CAM) the use of computers to plan and control manufacturing processes

and CAM together to form a computer-integrated manufacturing system. Specifically, **computer-integrated manufacturing (CIM)** is a computer system that not only helps to design products but also controls the machinery needed to produce the finished product. For example, Liz Claiborne, Inc., uses CIM to design clothing, to establish patterns for new fashions, and then to cut the cloth needed to produce the finished product. Other advantages of using CIM include improved flexibility, more efficient scheduling, and higher product quality—all factors that make a production facility more competitive in today's global economy.

FLEXIBLE MANUFACTURING SYSTEMS Manufacturers have known for a number of years that the old-style, mass-production, and traditional assembly lines used to manufacture products present a number of problems. For example, although traditional assembly lines turn out extremely large numbers of identical products economically, the system requires expensive, time-consuming retooling of equipment whenever a new product is to be manufactured. This type of manufacturing is often referred to as a continuous process. **Continuous process** is a manufacturing process in which a firm produces the same product(s) over a long period of time. Now it is possible to use flexible manufacturing systems to solve such problems. A **flexible manufacturing system (FMS)** combines electronic machines and computer-integrated manufacturing in a single production system. Instead of having to spend vast amounts of time and effort to retool the traditional mechanical equipment on an assembly line for each new product, an FMS is rearranged simply by reprogramming electronic machines. Because FMSs require less time and expense to reprogram than traditional systems, manufacturers can produce smaller batches of a variety of products without raising the production cost. Flexible manufacturing is sometimes referred to as an intermittent process. An **intermittent process** is a manufacturing process in which a firm's manufacturing machines and equipment are changed to produce different products. When compared with the continuous process (longer production runs), an intermittent process has a shorter production run.

For most manufacturers, the driving force behind FMSs is the customer. In fact, the term *customer-driven production* is often used by operations managers to describe a manufacturing system that is driven by customer needs and what customers want to buy. For example, advanced software and a flexible manufacturing system have enabled Dell Computer to change to a more customer-driven manufacturing process. The process starts when a customer phones a sales representative on a toll-free line or accesses Dell's Web site. Then the representative or the customer enters the specifications for the new product directly into a computer. The order then is sent to a nearby plant. Once the order is received, a team of employees, with the help of a FMS can build the product just the way the customer wants it. Products include desktop computers, notebook computers, and other Dell equipment.[19] Although the costs of designing and installing an FMS such as this are high, the electronic equipment is used more frequently and efficiently than the machinery on a traditional assembly line.

TECHNOLOGICAL DISPLACEMENT In the future, most experts agree that, because U.S. manufacturers will continue to innovate, workers who have manufacturing jobs will be highly skilled and can work with the automated and computer-assisted manufacturing systems. Those that don't possess high-tech skills will not be needed and may become unemployed. Many workers will be faced with the choice of retraining for new jobs or seeking jobs in other sectors of the economy. Government, business, and education will have to cooperate to prepare workers for new roles in an automated workplace.

The next chapter discusses many of the issues caused by technological displacement. In addition, a number of major components of human resources management are described, and we see how managers use various reward systems to boost motivation, productivity, and morale.

computer-integrated manufacturing (CIM) a computer system that not only helps to design products but also controls the machinery needed to produce the finished product

continuous process a manufacturing process in which a firm produces the same product(s) over a long period of time

flexible manufacturing system (FMS) a single production system that combines electronic machines and computer-integrated manufacturing

intermittent process a manufacturing process in which a firm's manufacturing machines and equipment are changed to produce different products

✳ *Concept Check*

☐ How might productivity be measured in a restaurant? In a department store? In a public school system?

☐ How can robotics, computer manufacturing systems, and flexible manufacturing systems help a manufacturer to produce products?

SUMMARY

1 Explain the nature of production.

Operations management consists of all the activities that managers engage in to create goods and services. Operations are as relevant to service organizations as to manufacturing firms. Today, U.S. companies are forced to compete in an ever-smaller world to meet the needs of more-demanding customers. As a result, U.S. manufacturers have used innovation to improve productivity. Because of innovation, fewer workers are needed, but those workers who are needed must possess the skills to use automation and technology. In an attempt to regain a competitive edge, manufacturers have taken another look at the importance of improving quality and meeting the needs of their customers. They also have used new techniques to motivate employees, reduced costs, used computer-aided and flexible manufacturing systems, improved control procedures, and used green manufacturing. Competing in the global economy is not only profitable but also an essential activity that requires the cooperation of everyone within an organization.

2 Outline how the conversion process transforms raw materials, labor, and other resources into finished products or services.

A business transforms resources into goods and services in order to provide utility to customers. Utility is the ability of a good or service to satisfy a human need. Form utility is created by people converting raw materials, finances, and information into finished products. Conversion processes vary in terms of the major resources used to produce goods and services (focus), the degree to which resources are changed (magnitude of change), and the number of production processes that a business uses.

3 Understand the importance of service businesses to consumers, other business firms, and the nation's economy.

The application of the basic principles of operations management to the production of services has coincided with the growth and importance of service businesses in the United States. Today 86 percent of American workers are employed in the service industry. In fact, the American economy is now characterized as a service economy. For a service firm, planning often begins with determining who the customer is and what needs the customer has. After customer needs are identified, the next step is to develop a plan that will enable the firm to deliver the services that their customers want or need.

Although it is often more difficult to measure customer satisfaction, today's successful service firms work hard at providing the services customers want. For example, compared with manufacturers, service firms often listen more carefully to customers and respond more quickly to the market's changing needs.

4 Describe how research and development lead to new products and services.

Operations management often begins with product research and development (R&D). The results of R&D may be entirely new products or extensions and refinements of existing products. R&D activities are classified as basic research (aimed at uncovering new knowledge), applied research (discovering new knowledge with some potential use), and development and implementation (using new or existing knowledge to produce goods and services). If a firm sells only one product or service, when that product or service reaches the end of its life-cycle, the firm will die, too. To stay in business, the firm must, at the very least, find ways to refine or extend the want-satisfying capability of its product.

5 Discuss the components involved in planning the production process.

Planning for production involves three major phases: design planning, facilities planning, and operational planning. First, design planning is undertaken to address questions related to the product line, required production capacity, and the use of technology. Then production facilities, human resources, and plant layout must be considered. Operational planning focuses on the use of production facilities and resources. The steps for operational planning include (1) selecting a planning horizon, (2) estimating market demand, (3) comparing market demand with capacity, and (4) adjusting production of products or services to meet demand.

6 Explain how purchasing, inventory control, scheduling, and quality control affect production.

The major areas of operations control are purchasing, inventory control, scheduling, and quality control. Purchasing involves selecting suppliers. The choice of suppliers should result from careful analysis of a number of factors, including price, quality, reliability, credit terms, and shipping costs. Inventory control is the management of stocks of raw materials, work-in-process, and finished goods to minimize the total inventory cost. Scheduling ensures that materials and other resources are at the right place at the right time. Quality control guarantees that products meet the design specifications for those products. The major objective of quality control is to see that the organization lives up to the standards it has set for itself on quality. A number of different activities can be used to improve quality.

7 Summarize how productivity and technology are related.

Productivity is the average level of output per worker per hour. From 1979 to 2009, U.S. productivity growth averaged a 4.2 percent increase. More specifically, productivity in 2009 increased 7.7 percent. While the 7.7 percent productivity gain is above average when compared to other countries around the globe, there is always room for improvement. Several factors have been cited as possible causes for lower productivity growth, and managers have begun to explore solutions for overcoming them. Possible solutions include less government regulation, increased cooperation between management and labor, changing the incentives for employees, and additional investment by business to fund new or renovated facilities, equipment, employee training, and the use of automation and technology.

Automation, the total or near-total use of machines to do work, has for some years been changing the way work is done in factories. A growing number of industries are using programmable machines called robots. Computer-aided design, computer-aided manufacturing, and computer-integrated manufacturing use computers to help design and manufacture products. FMS combines electronic machines and computer-integrated manufacturing to produce smaller batches of products more efficiently than on the traditional assembly line. Instead of having to spend vast amounts of time and effort to retool the traditional mechanical equipment on an assembly line for each new product, an FMS is rearranged simply by reprogramming electronic machines.

KEY TERMS

You should now be able to define and give an example relevant to each of the following terms:

operations management (212)
mass production (213)
analytical process (214)
synthetic process (214)
utility (214)
form utility (214)
service economy (216)
research and development (R&D) (218)
design planning (219)
product line (219)
product design (220)

capacity (220)
labor-intensive technology (221)
capital-intensive technology (221)
plant layout (222)
planning horizon (223)
purchasing (224)
inventory control (225)
materials requirements planning (MRP) (225)
just-in-time inventory system (225)

scheduling (226)
Malcolm Baldrige National Quality Award (226)
quality control (227)
inspection (227)
quality circle (227)
Six Sigma (227)
International Organization for Standardization (ISO) (227)
productivity (229)
lean manufacturing (231)
automation (231)

robotics (231)
computer-aided design (CAD) (231)
computer-aided manufacturing (CAM) (231)
computer-integrated manufacturing (CIM) (232)
continuous process (232)
flexible manufacturing system (FMS) (232)
intermittent process (232)

DISCUSSION QUESTIONS

1. Why would Rubbermaid—a successful U.S. company—need to expand and sell its products to customers in foreign countries?
2. Do certain kinds of firms need to stress particular areas of operations management? Explain.
3. Is it really necessary for service firms to engage in research and development? In planning for production and operations control?
4. How are the four areas of operations control interrelated?
5. In what ways can employees help to improve the quality of a firm's products?
6. Is operations management relevant to nonbusiness organizations such as colleges and hospitals? Why or why not?

TEST YOURSELF

Matching Questions

1. _____ It is a plan for converting a product idea into an actual product or service.

2. _____ Raw materials are broken into different components.

3. _____ Its focus is minimizing holding costs and potential stock-out costs.

4. _____ It is created by people converting materials, finances, and information into finished goods.

5. _____ A manufacturing process in which a firm's manufacturing machines and equipment are changed to produce different products.

6. _____ Work is accomplished mostly by equipment.

7. _____ Input from workers is used to improve the workplace.

8. _____ The average level of output per worker per hour.

9. _____ Computers are the main tool used in the development of products.

10. _____ The time period during which an operational plan will be in effect.

a. analytical process
b. capital-intensive technology
c. product line
d. computer-aided design
e. design planning
f. form utility
g. inventory control
h. plant layout
i. planning horizon
j. productivity
k. quality circle
l. intermittent process

True False Questions

11. **T F** Capacity is the degree to which input resources are physically changed by the conversion process.

12. **T F** The rise-and-decline pattern of sales for an existing product is called the product life-cycle.

13. **T F** Operations management is the process of creating a set of specifications from which the product can be produced.

14. **T F** A purchasing agent need not worry about a tiny difference in price when a large quantity is being bought.

15. **T F** A synthetic process combines raw materials or components to create a finished product.

16. **T F** When work stations are arranged to match the sequence of operations, a process layout is being used.

17. **T F** Work-in-process inventories are raw materials and supplies waiting to be processed.

18. **T F** The purpose of research and development is to identify new ideas that have the potential to result in new goods and services.

19. **T F** For a food-processing plant such as Kraft Foods, capacity refers to the number of employees working on an assembly line.

20. **T F** Labor-intensive technology is accompanied by low initial costs and high operating costs.

Multiple-Choice Questions

21. _____ One worker in Department A produces 45 units of work per day on a computer, whereas a coworker produces only 40 units of work per day on a computer. Since the first worker produces more units, that worker has a
    a. lower capacity to use technology.
    b. higher productivity rate.
    c. desire to help the coworker.
    d. computer-integrated system.
    e. computer-aided system

22. _____ Services differ from the production of manufactured goods in all ways except that services
    a. are consumed immediately and cannot be stored.
    b. aren't as important as manufactured products to the U.S. economy.
    c. are provided when and where the customer desires the service.
    d. are usually labor-intensive.
    e. are intangible, and it's more difficult to evaluate customer service.

23. _____ The goal of basic research is to
   a. uncover new knowledge without regard for its potential use.
   b. discover new knowledge with regard for potential use in development.
   c. discover knowledge for potential use.
   d. put new or existing knowledge to use.
   e. combine ideas.

24. _____ Two important components of scheduling are
   a. lead time and planning.
   b. designing and arranging.
   c. monitoring and controlling.
   d. place and time.
   e. logistics and flow.

25. _____ A common planning horizon for production activities is
   a. one day.
   b. a week.
   c. a month.
   d. six months.
   e. one year.

26. A_____ manufacturing system combines electronic machines and computer-integrated manufacturing in a single-production system.
   a. continuous
   b. analytic
   c. synthetic
   d. flexible
   e. automation

27. _____ The process of acquiring materials, supplies, components, and parts from other firms is known as
   a. acquisition.
   b. planning.
   c. purchasing.
   d. inventory requisition.
   e. materials requirements planning.

28. Procter & Gamble uses _____ production to produce household products.
   a. efficient order
   b. demand
   c. supply order
   d. mass
   e. effective

29. _____ If a good or service satisfies a human need, it has
   a. form.
   b. value.
   c. focus.
   d. magnitude.
   e. utility.

30. The American economy is now characterized as a(n) _____ economy.
   a. civilized
   b. stagnant
   c. service
   d. bureaucratic
   e. industrialized

Answers to the Test Yourself questions appear at the end of the book on page TY-1.

VIDEO CASE
Burton Snowboards' High-Quality Standards

"The people at Burton are a powerful, inspiring, and fun group, and I will miss that," said the recently departing CEO of Vermont's fabled Burton Snowboards. In fact, the company's nearly 900 employees are some of the many reasons the firm has grown to be the world's leading snowboard and accessories company. Many are snowboard enthusiasts, not least among them Jake Burton Carpenter, founder and currently interim CEO. Despite his management responsibilities, Jake still rides a snowboard about 100 days of the year, sometimes to test new products, but sometimes just for fun. "There are a lot of vibrant folks," at the company "and it rubs off on you," he says.

The company began as an entrepreneurial venture housed in a barn in 1977. Jake, who says he was a failure in shop class while in school, handmade his own boards for a sport that had few followers and was yet to be recognized. Snowboarding has since come a long way, having made its Olympic debut during the 1998 Winter Games at Nagano, Japan. Burton Snowboards has grown, too. With world headquarters in Burlington, the company operates a factory in Austria and stores in Chicago, Los Angeles, New

York, Wrentham (MA), Orlando, and of course Burlington, as well as in Tokyo and Innsbruck (Austria). It also works with thousands of retail dealers in more than 30 countries around the world and offers products for sale online as well.

A major factor in the company's success is the high-quality standards to which it has adhered from its very beginning. These have made Burton Snowboards a premium supplier whose name is synonymous with quality. Its snowboards are made to exacting specifications from wood, fiberglass, and steel, not cheaper foam materials, and with unrelenting attention to every step, including the finishing details. "We don't cut corners," says a company spokesperson, though that sometimes means its products will cost a bit more than competitors'. The prevailing philosophy at the firm is that "you get what you pay for," and by listening to its core customers, who fall between 12 and 35 years of age, Burton remains confident that its high standards meet the expectations of those for whom snowboarding is not just a sport but also a lifestyle. "We've always based our decisions around snowboarders and what's best for them," says Jake.

Quality is further assured by the company's policy of redesigning every product every year in order to retain its position as "an innovator, not an imitator" and to keep up with changing customers' needs and desires as well as with competitors' efforts to grow their own market share. One such threat comes from ski companies that have decided to move into the snowboarding industry. Burton's managers credit much of the company's success to its ability to respond well to change. According to Jake, "As a company we've always thrived on opportunity."

One new opportunity the firm faces is the need to control its production costs without sacrificing quality. Burton recently announced that it is closing its Burlington factory and will manufacture exclusively at the Austrian plant it has operated for the past 25 years. "It costs us significantly more to produce a board in Vermont than we are capable of selling it for," a company statement said, "and sadly, this is not sustainable in the current economy." Nearly 400 employees will remain at the Burlington facility, however, which has "excelled at prototyping and developing product" in the past and will

still carry that responsibility. "Here in Vermont," said the then-CEO, "we will continue to focus on advanced product development, which will allow us to bring the latest snowboard technology to riders faster than ever before."[20]

Questions

1. About 40 people will lose their jobs when Burton closes its Burlington factory, and the company is working with the state of Vermont to provide them with help in finding new employment. How do you think the factory closing might affect the productivity of the remaining headquarters staff? What impact could it have on product quality?

2. Do you think there will be an impact on quality when the design and development staff are separated from the factory floor by so many miles? Why or why not?

3. Can you reconcile the company's focus on product quality with its decision to concentrate manufacturing in a place where it's less expensive to operate? If so, how, and if not, why not?

BUILDING SKILLS FOR CAREER SUCCESS

1. Exploring the Internet

Improvements in the quality of products and services is an ever-popular theme in business management. Besides the potential increase to profitability to be gained by such improvements, a company's demonstration of its continuous search for ways to improve operations can be a powerful statement to customers, suppliers, and investors. Two of the larger schools of thought in this field are Six Sigma and Total Quality Management.

Assignment

1. Use Internet search engines to find more information about each of these topics.
2. From the information on the Internet, can you tell whether there is any real difference between these two approaches?
3. Describe one success story of a firm that realized improvement by adopting either approach.

2. Building Team Skills

Suppose that you are planning to build a house in the country. It will be a brick, one-story structure of approximately 2,000 square feet, centrally heated and cooled. It will have three bedrooms, two bathrooms, a family room, a dining room, a kitchen with a breakfast nook, a study, a utility room, an entry foyer, a two-car garage, a covered patio, and a fireplace. Appliances will operate on electricity and propane fuel. You have received approval and can be connected to the cooperative water system at any time. Public sewerage services are not available; therefore, you must rely on

a septic system. You want to know how long it will take to build the house.

Assignment

1. Identify the major activities involved in the project and sequence them in the proper order.
2. Estimate the time required for each activity.
3. Present your list of activities to the class and ask for comments and suggestions.

3. Researching Different Careers

Because service businesses are now such a dominant part of our economy, job seekers sometimes overlook the employment opportunities available in production. Two positions often found in these plants are quality-control inspector and purchasing agent.

Assignment

1. Using the *Occupational Outlook Handbook* at your local library or on the Internet (http://stats.bls.gov/oco/home.htm), find the following information for the jobs of quality-control inspector and purchasing agent:

   Nature of work, including main activities and responsibilities
   Job outlook
   Earnings
   Training, qualifications, and advancement.

2. Look for other production jobs that may interest you and compile the same sort of information about them.

3. Summarize in a two-page report the key things you learned about jobs in production.

Running a Business: Part 3

Graeter's Leadership and Management Efforts Enhance Performance

Graeter's, the premier ice-cream maker based in Cincinnati, is a special organization. A small company ($20 million in annual sales) currently unfolding ambitious plans for national expansion, it is also a fourth-generation family firm with an entrepreneurial spirit. "What is unique to Graeter's, I believe, is that they are just the best out there," says one food industry analyst.

A Family Affair

Graeter's top-management team consists of CEO Richard Graeter II and his two cousins, (brothers) Bob and Chip Graeter. All are great grandsons of the original founders. As vice president of manufacturing, Bob is responsible for sourcing the fresh fruits, cream, eggs, sugar, and top-quality chocolates that go into Graeter's products, whereas Chip oversees the 45 company-owned retail stores in Cincinnati and neighboring cities. All three Graeters grew up by working their way through various jobs within the company, sometimes making packing boxes and stamping the names of flavors on ice-cream containers. "I think I always knew that I'd be here," says Richard. "Looking back, I can't imagine not being here. It is just such a part of who I am." He observes, "It can be challenging to work with your family. My father and I didn't always see things the same way. But on the other hand, there is a lot of strength in the family relationship. . . we certainly had struggles, and family businesses do struggle, especially with transition . . . but we found people to help us, including lawyers, accountants, and a family-business psychologist."

Richard describes the current management structure as "an equal partnership" of himself and his two cousins. He says of their collaborative decision-making process, "Every major decision, we make on a consensus basis. That doesn't mean we don't have a different point of view from time to time, but. . . we learn to see each other's view and discuss, debate, and get down to a decision that all of us support. The other thing that we have learned to do, something that is a little different than our parents' generation [did], is bring in outside people into the. . . executive level of the management team. . . . We now work with a couple of consultants to help us plan our strategy to look for a new vision, to develop training programs. . . all those systems that big companies have."

Says another of the company's managers about problem solving and decision making at Graeter's, "If I can get the right resources in the room, there is no problem that cannot be solved. . . . Sometimes that means the operators on the floor. . . because they are in touch with what is really going on. So I ask a lot of questions. I understand what the barriers are, and I find resources to come to a solution."

Embracing Opportunities for Growth

After three generations of local mom-and-pop style operations, the company is poised for what it hopes will be rapid nationwide expansion of its supermarket distribution operation, which currently puts Graeter's ice cream in the freezers of about 1,700 Kroger's supermarkets in the Midwest, Texas, and Colorado. A new factory to help increase production was already being built when an unexpected opportunity arose: to buy out the last franchise company operating Graeter's retail stores and take over the franchisor's factory as well. The management team jumped at the chance. "A few months ago our strategy was just operate one plant," says Richard. "Now our strategy is, adapt to the opportunity that came along. . . we are operating three plants. The goal is to keep all of your assets deployed productively, so if we have these three plants, what is the most we can do out of those plants to be generating product and profit? One example would be supplying restaurants in other cities, which we really weren't considering originally because our new plant was really geared for pints, but if we have this excess capacity, the smart thing to do is figure out what we can do with that."

As the company looks forward to the possibility of opening Graeter's stores as far away as Dallas, Los Angeles, and New York, the management team is carefully considering the risk. "Our family has always been contented to make a little less profit in order to ensure our long-term survival," says Richard. "It is a trait that we intend to drum into the fifth generation the same way that our fathers drummed it into us."[21]

Questions

1. What do you think is Graeter's current basis of departmentalization? Do you think this basis might change as Graeter's begins to expand across the country?
2. How would you describe the decision-making process at Graeter's?
3. How many types of planning can you observe in the case? How well do you think Graeter's team handles the planning function of management?

Building a Business Plan: Part 3

Now you should be ready to provide evidence that you have a management team with the necessary skills and experience to execute your business plan successfully. Only a competent management team can transform your vision into a successful business. You also should be able to describe your manufacturing and operations plans. The three chapters in Part 3 of your textbook, "Understanding the Management Process," "Creating a Flexible Organization," and "Producing Quality Goods and Services," should help you in answering some of the questions in this part of the business plan.

The Management Team Component

The management team component should include the answers to at least the following questions:

3.1. How is your team balanced in technical, conceptual, interpersonal, and other special skills needed in your business?

3.2. What will be your style of leadership?

3.3. How will your company be structured? Include a statement of the philosophy of management and company culture.

3.4. What are the key management positions, compensation, and key policies?

3.5. Include a job description for each management position and specify who will fill that position. *Note:* Prepare an organization chart and provide the résumé of each key manager for the appendix.

3.6. What other professionals, such as a lawyer, an insurance agent, a banker, and a certified public accountant, will you need for assistance?

The Manufacturing and Operations Plan Component

If you are in a manufacturing business, now is a good time to describe your manufacturing and operations plans, space requirements, equipment, labor force, inventory control, and purchasing requirements. Even if you are in a service-oriented business, many of these questions still may apply.

The manufacturing and operations plan component should include the answers to at least the following questions:

3.7. What are the advantages and disadvantages of your planned location in terms of
- Wage rates
- Unionization
- Labor pool
- Proximity to customers and suppliers
- Types of transportation available
- Tax rates
- Utility costs
- Zoning requirements

3.8. What facilities does your business require? Prepare a floor plan for the appendix. Will you rent, lease, or purchase the facilities?

3.9. Will you make or purchase component parts to be assembled into the finished product? Make sure to justify your "make-or-buy decision."

3.10. Who are your potential subcontractors and suppliers?

3.11. How will you control quality, inventory, and production? How will you measure your progress?

3.12. Is there a sufficient quantity of adequately skilled people in the local labor force to meet your needs?

Review of Business Plan Activities

Be sure to go over the information you have gathered. Check for any weaknesses and resolve them before beginning Part 4. Also, review all the answers to the questions in Parts 1, 2, and 3 to be certain that they are consistent throughout the entire business plan. Finally, write a brief statement that summarizes all the information for this part of the business plan.

The information contained in "Building a Business Plan" will also assist you in completing the online *Interactive Business Plan.*

PART FOUR
HUMAN RESOURCES

This part of *Foundations of Business* is concerned with the most important and least predictable of all resources—people. We begin by examining the human resources efforts that organizations use to hire, develop, and retain their best employees. Then we discuss employee motivation and satisfaction.

Chapter 9   Attracting and Retaining the Best Employees
Chapter 10 Motivating and Satisfying Employees and Teams

CHAPTER 9 ATTRACTING AND RETAINING THE BEST EMPLOYEES

© Konstantin Chagin/Shutterstock.com

Why should you care?

Being able to understand how to attract and keep the right people is crucial. Also, you can better understand about your own interactions with your co-workers.

Learning Objectives

What you will be able to do once you complete this chapter:

1 Describe the major components of human resources management.

2 Identify the steps in human resources planning.

3 Describe cultural diversity and understand some of the challenges and opportunities associated with it.

4 Explain the objectives and uses of job analysis.

5 Describe the processes of recruiting, employee selection, and orientation.

6 Discuss the primary elements of employee compensation and benefits.

7 Explain the purposes and techniques of employee training and development.

8 Discuss performance appraisal techniques and performance feedback.

9 Outline the major legislation affecting human resources management.

Get Flashcards, Quizzes, Games, Crosswords, and more @ www.cengagebrain.com

Good Employees Keep Southwest Airlines on Growth Course

Southwest Airlines pioneered the low-cost carrier concept that has kept it on a flight path to growth for more than four decades. Today, Southwest employs 43,000 people, flies to 72 cities in 37 states, and rings up $10 billion in annual revenue. Its mission is to deliver high-quality customer service "with a sense of warmth, friendliness, individual pride, and company spirit." No wonder Southwest's stock-market symbol is LUV.

Given the airline industry's financial ups and downs over the years, Southwest's stability and its legendary corporate culture are two key reasons why it attracts tens of thousands of resumes every year. Management looks carefully at growth plans, economic conditions, and other elements when determining how many new hires will be needed in the coming year. As the recent recession got underway, Southwest stopped hiring new pilots and flight attendants. Two years later, with the recession receding, Southwest got back on the fast track path to growth by buying low-cost carrier AirTran and hiring new employees for its renewed focus on expansion.

Although merging two airlines into one can be a human resources challenge, Southwest was up to the task. Just weeks after the purchase was announced, Southwest's pilots invited Airtran's pilots to a party in Airtran's headquarters city. The purpose was "to welcome them to the family," according to a Southwest pilot. The Southwest "family" is famous for good-natured fun on the ground and in the air. For example, many employees (including the CEO) dress up for Halloween.

When making hiring decisions, the carrier is more concerned about attitude than about technical skills. "The first thing we look for is the 'warrior spirit,'" says a senior executive in Southwest's People Department. "We would rather take an eager, hungry, customer-oriented mind and mold it to what works well at Southwest, than try to change the habits of someone who's come up through an organization that views life differently." Once hired, employees receive intensive training in Southwest's procedures and in its special brand of corporate culture. "If we're treating employees right, they're going to be keeping the customers happy," explains Southwest's head of culture and communications.[1]

Did you know?

Southwest Airlines, whose stock trades under the symbol LUV, receives more than 90,000 resumes annually but hires fewer than 1 percent of applicants.

Southwest Airlines devotes considerable time and resources to hire the right people and to take actions to make them satisfied with their jobs. We begin our study of human resources management (HRM) with an overview of how businesses acquire, maintain, and develop their human resources. After listing the steps by which firms match their human resources needs with the supply available, we explore several dimensions of cultural diversity. Then we examine the concept of job analysis. Next, we focus on a firm's recruiting, selection, and orientation procedures as the means of acquiring employees. We also describe forms of employee compensation that motivate employees to remain with a firm and to work effectively. Then we discuss methods of employee training, management development, and performance appraisal. Finally, we consider legislation that affects HRM practices.

HUMAN RESOURCES MANAGEMENT: AN OVERVIEW

LEARNING OBJECTIVE

1 Describe the major components of human resources management.

The human resource is not only unique and valuable but also an organization's most important resource. It seems logical that an organization would expend a great deal of effort to acquire and make full use of such a resource. This effort is known as *human resources management*. It also has been called *staffing* and *personnel management*.

Human resources management (HRM) consists of all the activities involved in acquiring, maintaining, and developing an organization's human resources. As the definition implies, HRM begins with acquisition—getting people to work for the organization. The acquisition process can be quite competitive for certain types of qualified employees. Next, steps must be taken to keep these valuable resources. (After all, they are the only business resources that can leave an organization.) Finally, the human resources should be developed to their full capacity.

HRM Activities

Each of the three phases of HRM—acquiring, maintaining, and developing human resources—consists of a number of related activities. Acquisition, for example, includes planning, as well as the various activities that lead to hiring new personnel. Altogether this phase of HRM includes five separate activities:

- *Human resources planning*—determining the firm's future human resources needs
- *Job analysis*—determining the exact nature of the positions
- *Recruiting*—attracting people to apply for positions
- *Selection*—choosing and hiring the most qualified applicants
- *Orientation*—acquainting new employees with the firm

Maintaining human resources consists primarily of encouraging employees to remain with the firm and to work effectively by using a variety of HRM programs, including the following:

- *Employee relations*—increasing employee job satisfaction through satisfaction surveys, employee communication programs, exit interviews, and fair treatment
- *Compensation*—rewarding employee effort through monetary payments
- *Benefits*—providing rewards to ensure employee well-being

The development phase of HRM is concerned with improving employees' skills and expanding their capabilities. The two important activities within this phase are:

- *Training and development*—teaching employees new skills, new jobs, and more effective ways of doing their present jobs
- *Performance appraisal*—assessing employees' current and potential performance levels

These activities are discussed in more detail shortly, when we have completed this overview of HRM.

Responsibility for HRM

In general, HRM is a shared responsibility of line managers and staff HRM specialists. In very small organizations, the owner handles all or most HRM activities. As a firm grows in size, a human resources manager is hired to take over staff responsibilities. In firms as large as Disney, HRM activities tend to be very highly specialized. There are separate groups to deal with compensation, benefits, training and development, and other staff activities.

Specific HRM activities are assigned to those who are in the best position to perform them. Human resources planning and job analysis usually are done by staff

human resources management (HRM) all the activities involved in acquiring, maintaining, and developing an organization's human resources

✻ *Concept Check*

☐ What are the three phases of human resource management?

☐ Identify the activities associated with each phase.

☐ How does the responsibility of HRM change with the size of a firm?

LEARNING OBJECTIVE

2 Identify the steps in human resources planning.

specialists, with input from line managers. Similarly, recruiting and selection are handled by staff experts, although line managers are involved in hiring decisions. Orientation programs are devised by staff specialists and carried out by both staff specialists and line managers. Compensation systems (including benefits) most often are developed and administered by the HRM staff. However, line managers recommend pay increases and promotions. Training and development activities are the joint responsibility of staff and line managers. Performance appraisal is the job of the line manager, although HRM personnel design the firm's appraisal system in many organizations.

HUMAN RESOURCES PLANNING

Human resources planning is the development of strategies to meet a firm's future human resources needs. The starting point is the organization's overall strategic plan. From this, human resources planners can forecast future demand for human resources. Next, the planners must determine whether the needed human resources will be available. Finally, they have to take steps to match supply with demand.

Forecasting Human Resources Demand

Planners should base forecasts of the demand for human resources on as much relevant information as available. The firm's overall strategic plan will provide information about future business ventures, new products, and projected expansions or contractions of specific product lines. Information on past staffing levels, evolving technologies, industry staffing practices, and projected economic trends also can be helpful.

HRM staff use this information to determine both the number of employees required and their qualifications. Planners use a wide range of methods to forecast specific personnel needs. For example, with one simple method, personnel requirements are projected to increase or decrease in the same proportion as sales revenue. Thus, if a 30 percent increase in sales volume is projected over the next two years, then up to a 30 percent increase in personnel requirements may be expected for the same period. (This method can be applied to specific positions as well as to the workforce in general. It is not, however, a very precise forecasting method.) At the other extreme are elaborate, computer-based personnel planning models used by some large firms such as ExxonMobil Corporation.

Forecasting Human Resources Supply

The forecast of the supply of human resources must take into account both the present workforce and any changes that may occur within it. For example, suppose that planners project that in five years a firm that currently employs 100 engineers will need to employ a total of 200 engineers. Planners simply cannot assume that they will have to hire 100 engineers; during that period, some of the firm's present engineers are likely to be promoted, leave the firm, or move to other jobs within the firm. Thus, planners may project the supply of engineers in five years at 87, which means that the firm will have to hire a total of 113 new engineers. When forecasting supply, planners should analyze the organization's existing employees to determine who can be retrained to perform the required tasks.

Two useful techniques for forecasting human resources supply are the replacement chart and the skills inventory. A **replacement chart** is a list of key personnel and their possible replacements within a firm. The chart is maintained to ensure that top-management positions can be filled fairly quickly in the event of an unexpected death, resignation, or retirement. Some firms also provide additional training for employees who might eventually replace top managers.

human resources planning the development of strategies to meet a firm's future human resources needs

replacement chart a list of key personnel and their possible replacements within a firm

© iofoto/Shutterstock

A **skills inventory** is a computerized data bank containing information on the skills and experience of all present employees. It is used to search for candidates to fill available positions. For a special project, a manager may be seeking a current employee with specific information technology skills, at least six years of experience, and fluency in French. The skills inventory can quickly identify employees who possess such qualifications. Skill-assessment tests can be administered inside an organization, or they can be provided by outside vendors. For example, SkillView Technologies, Inc., and Bookman Testing Services, Inc., are third-party information technology skill-assessment providers.

Personal App The more skills you develop, the more valuable you are to any employer. Do your own personal skills inventory before you write a resume or interview for a job. Then you'll be prepared to explain the special skills you can bring to an employer.

Matching Supply with Demand

Once they have forecasted the supply and demand for personnel, planners can devise a course of action for matching the two. When demand is predicted to be greater than supply, they must make plans to recruit new employees. The timing of these actions depends on the types of positions to be filled. Suppose that we expect to open another plant in five years that will need, along with other employees, a plant manager and 25 maintenance workers. We probably can wait quite a while before we begin to recruit maintenance personnel. However, because the job of a plant manager is so critical, we may start searching for the right person for that position immediately.

When supply is predicted to be greater than demand, the firm must take steps to reduce the size of its workforce. When the oversupply is expected to be temporary, some employees may be *laid off*—dismissed from the workforce until they are needed again.

Perhaps the most humane method for making personnel cutbacks is through attrition. *Attrition* is the normal reduction in the workforce that occurs when employees leave a firm. Over the last five years, Ford, for example, has cut its number of hourly workers by more than 50 percent. Tens of thousands of employees left the company through a combination of involuntary layoffs, buyouts, and normal attrition, which allowed the company to cut salary costs and avoid declaring bankruptcy during the recent recession.[2]

Early retirement is another option. Under early retirement, people who are within a few years of retirement are permitted to retire early with full benefits. Depending on the age makeup of the workforce, this may or may not reduce the staff enough.

As a last resort, unneeded employees are sometimes simply *fired*. However, because of its negative impact, this method generally is used only when absolutely necessary.

CULTURAL DIVERSITY IN HUMAN RESOURCES

Today's workforce is made up of many types of people. Firms can no longer assume that every employee has similar beliefs or expectations. Whereas North American white males may believe in challenging authority, Asians tend to respect and defer to it. In Hispanic cultures, people often bring music, food, and family members to work, a custom that U.S. businesses traditionally have not allowed. A job applicant who will not make eye contact during an interview may be rejected for being unapproachable, when, according to his or her culture, he or she was just being polite.

Because a larger number of women, minorities, and immigrants have entered the U.S. workforce, the workplace is more diverse. It is estimated that women make up

Concept Check ✳

☐ How do firms forecast the demand for human resources?

☐ What are the techniques used to forecast human resources supply?

☐ To match human resources supply and demand, how is attrition used?

LEARNING OBJECTIVE
3 Describe cultural diversity and understand some of the challenges and opportunities associated with it.

skills inventory a computerized data bank containing information on the skills and experience of all present employees

TABLE 9-1: Advantages of Cultural Diversity

Cost	As organizations become more diverse, the cost of doing a poor job of integrating workers will increase. Companies that handle this well thus can create cost advantages over those that do a poor job. In addition, companies also experience cost savings by hiring people with knowledge of various cultures as opposed to having to train Americans, for example, about how Germans do business.
Resource acquisition	Companies develop reputations as being favorable or unfavorable prospective employers for women and ethnic minorities. Those with the best reputations for managing diversity will win the competition for the best personnel.
Marketing edge	For multinational organizations, the insight and cultural sensitivity that members with roots in other countries bring to marketing efforts should improve these efforts in important ways. The same rationale applies to marketing subpopulations domestically.
Flexibility	Culturally diverse employees often are open to a wider array of positions within a company and are more likely to move up the corporate ladder more rapidly, given excellent performance.
Creativity	Diversity of perspectives and less emphasis on conformity to norms of the past should improve the level of creativity.
Problem solving	Differences within decision-making and problem-solving groups potentially produce better decisions through a wider range of perspectives and more thorough critical analysis of issues.
Bilingual skills	Cultural diversity in the workplace brings with it bilingual and bicultural skills, which are very advantageous to the ever-growing global marketplace. Employees with knowledge about how other cultures work not only can speak to them in their language but also can prevent their company from making embarrassing moves owing to a lack of cultural sophistication. Thus, companies may seek job applicants with a background in cultures in which the company does business.

Sources: Taylor H. Cox and Stacy Blake, "Managing Cultural Diversity: Implications for Organizational Competitiveness," *Academy of Management Executive* 5(3): 46, 1991; Ricky Griffin and Gregory Moorhead, *Organizational Behavior* (Mason, OH: South-Western/Cengage Learning, 2010), 40; and Richard L. Daft, *Management* (Mason, OH: South-Western/Cengage Learning, 2010), 348–349.

about 47 percent of the U.S. workforce; African Americans and Hispanics each make up about 11 and 14 percent of U.S. workers, respectively.[3]

Cultural (or workplace) diversity refers to the differences among people in a work-force owing to race, ethnicity, and gender. Increasing cultural diversity is forcing managers to learn to supervise and motivate people with a broader range of value systems. The high proportion of women in the workforce, combined with a new emphasis on participative parenting by men, has brought many family-related issues to the workplace. Today's more educated employees also want greater independence and flexibility. In return for their efforts, they want both compensation and a better quality of life.

Although cultural diversity presents a challenge, managers should view it as an opportunity rather than a limitation. When managed properly, cultural diversity can provide advantages for an organization. Table 9-1 shows several benefits that creative management of cultural diversity can offer. A firm that manages diversity properly can develop cost advantages over other firms. Moreover, organizations that manage diversity creatively are in a much better position to attract the best personnel. A culturally diverse organization may gain a marketing edge because it understands different cultural groups. Proper guidance and management of diversity in an organization also can improve the level of creativity. Culturally diverse people frequently are more flexible in the types of positions they will accept.

Because cultural diversity creates challenges along with advantages, it is important for an organization's employees to understand it. To accomplish this goal, numerous U.S. firms have trained their managers to respect and manage diversity. Diversity training programs may include recruiting minorities, training minorities to be managers, training managers to view diversity positively, teaching English

※ *Concept Check*

☐ What is cultural diversity in an organization?

☐ What are some of the benefits and challenges of cultural diversity in an organization?

cultural (workplace) diversity differences among people in a workforce owing to race, ethnicity, and gender

as a second language, and facilitating support groups for immigrants. Many companies are realizing the necessity of having diversity training span beyond just racial issues. For example, companies such as PricewaterhouseCoopers and PepsiCo require annual diversity training and use company-sanctioned global employee-resource groups.[4] Companies such as these are continuously expanding their business worldwide and therefore need to meld a cohesive workforce from a labor pool whose demographics are constantly becoming more diverse.

A diversity program will be successful only if it is systematic, is ongoing, and has a strong, sustained commitment from top leadership. Cultural diversity is here to stay. Its impact on organizations is widespread and will continue to grow within corporations. Management must learn to overcome the obstacles and capitalize on the advantages associated with culturally diverse human resources.

Cultural diversity can be valuable to an organization. Organizations that are dedicated to diversity gain significant benefits from their efforts.

© Dan Lamont/Alamy

JOB ANALYSIS

There is no sense in hiring people unless we know what we are hiring them for. In other words, we need to know the nature of a job before we can find the right person to do it.

Job analysis is a systematic procedure for studying jobs to determine their various elements and requirements. Consider the position of a clerk, for example. In a large corporation, there may be 50 kinds of clerk positions. They all may be called "clerks," but each position may differ from the others in the activities performed, the level of proficiency required for each activity, and the particular set of qualifications that the position demands. These distinctions are the focus of job analysis. Some companies, such as HR.BLR.COM, help employers with preparing the material for job analysis and keeping them updated about state and federal HR employment laws. They provide employers with easy-to-use online service for the resources needed for HR success.[5]

The job analysis for a particular position typically consists of two parts—a job description and a job specification. A **job description** is a list of the elements that make up a particular job. It includes the duties to be performed, the working conditions, the responsibilities, and the tools and equipment that must be used on the job (see Figure 9-1).

A **job specification** is a list of the qualifications required to perform a particular job, such as certain skills, abilities, education, and experience. When attempting to hire a financial analyst, the Bank of America might use the following job specification: "Requires eight to ten years of financial experience, a broad-based financial background, strong customer focus, the ability to work confidently with the client's management team, strong analytical skills. Must have strong Excel and Word skills. Personal characteristics should include strong desire to succeed, impact performer (individually and as a member of a team), positive attitude, high energy level and ability to influence others."

Personal App Remember your personal skills inventory? When you apply for an open position, tailor your resume and cover letter to highlight how well your skills match those listed in the job specification. Don't stop there—also show how you can help the employer achieve its goals through your skills and past experiences.

The job analysis is not only the basis for recruiting and selecting new employees; it is also used in other areas of HRM, including evaluation and the determination of equitable compensation levels.

job analysis a systematic procedure for studying jobs to determine their various elements and requirements

job description a list of the elements that make up a particular job

job specification a list of the qualifications required to perform a particular job

Concept Check *

☐ What is job analysis?

☐ What is job specification? How can it be used to hire the right person for the job?

FIGURE 9-1: **Job Description and Job Specification**

This job description explains the job of sales coordinator and lists the responsibilities of the position. The job specification is contained in the last paragraph.

SOUTH-WESTERN
JOB DESCRIPTION

TITLE:	Georgia Sales Coordinator	**DATE:**	3/25/11
DEPARTMENT:	College, Sales	**GRADE:**	12
REPORTS TO:	Regional Manager	**EXEMPT/NONEXEMPT:**	Exempt

BRIEF SUMMARY:

Supervise one other Georgia-based sales representative to gain supervisory experience. Captain the four members of the outside sales rep team that are assigned to territories consisting of colleges and universities in Georgia. Oversee, coordinate, advise, and make decisions regarding Georgia sales activities. Based upon broad contact with customers across the state and communication with administrators of schools, the person will make recommendations regarding issues specific to the needs of higher education in the state of Georgia such as distance learning, conversion to the semester system, potential statewide adoptions, and faculty training.

PRINCIPAL ACCOUNTABILITIES:

1. Supervises/manages/trains one other Atlanta-based sales rep.
2. Advises two other sales reps regarding the Georgia schools in their territories.
3. Increases overall sales in Georgia as well as his or her individual sales territory.
4. Assists regional manager in planning and coordinating regional meetings and Atlanta conferences.
5. Initiates a dialogue with campus administrators, particularly in the areas of the semester conversion, distance learning, and faculty development.

DIMENSIONS:

This position will have one direct report in addition to the leadership role played within the region. Revenue most directly impacted will be within the individually assigned territory, the supervised territory, and the overall sales for the state of Georgia.

KNOWLEDGE AND SKILLS:

Must have displayed a history of consistently outstanding sales in personal territory. Must demonstrate clear teamwork and leadership skills and be willing to extend beyond the individual territory goals. Should have a clear understanding of the company's systems and product offerings in order to train and lead other sales representatives. Must have the communication skills and presence to communicate articulately with higher education administrators and to serve as a bridge between the company and higher education in the state.

© Cengage Learning 2013

LEARNING OBJECTIVE

5 Describe the processes of recruiting, employee selection, and orientation.

RECRUITING, SELECTION, AND ORIENTATION

In an organization with jobs waiting to be filled, HRM personnel need to (1) find candidates for the jobs and (2) match the right candidate with each job. Three activities are involved: recruiting, selection, and new employee orientation.

Recruiting

Recruiting is the process of attracting qualified job applicants. Because it is a vital link in a costly process (the cost of hiring an employee can be several thousand dollars), recruiting needs to be a systematic process. One goal of recruiters is to attract the "right number" of applicants. The right number is enough to allow a good match between applicants and open positions but not so many that matching them requires too much time and effort. For example, if there are five open positions and five applicants, the firm essentially has no choice. It must hire those five applicants (qualified or not), or the positions will remain open. At the other extreme, if several hundred job seekers apply for the five positions, HRM personnel will have to spend weeks processing their applications.

Recruiters may seek applicants outside the firm, within the firm, or both. The source used depends on the nature of the position, the situation within the firm, and sometimes the firm's established or traditional recruitment policies.

recruiting the process of attracting qualified job applicants

EXTERNAL RECRUITING **External recruiting** is the attempt to attract job applicants from outside an organization. External recruiting may include recruiting via newspaper advertising, employment agencies, and online employment organizations; recruiting on college campuses; soliciting recommendations from present employees; and conducting "open houses." The biggest of the online job-search sites is Monster.com, which has almost all the *Fortune* 500 companies, as well as small- and medium-sized businesses, as clients. In addition, many people simply apply at a firm's employment office.

Clearly, it is best to match the recruiting means with the kind of applicant being sought. For example, private employment agencies most often handle professional people, whereas public employment agencies (operated by state or local governments) are more concerned with operations personnel. We might approach a private agency when looking for a vice president but contact a public agency to hire a machinist. Procter & Gamble hires graduates directly out of college. It picks the best and brightest—those not "tainted" by another company's culture. It promotes its own "inside" people. This policy makes sure that the company retains the best and brightest and trains new recruits. Procter & Gamble pays competitively and offers positions in many countries. Employee turnover is very low.[6]

The primary advantage of external recruiting is that it brings in people with new perspectives and varied business backgrounds. A disadvantage of external recruiting is that it is often expensive, especially if private employment agencies must be used. External recruiting also may provoke resentment among present employees.

INTERNAL RECRUITING **Internal recruiting** means considering present employees as applicants for available positions. Generally, current employees are considered for *promotion* to higher-level positions. However, employees may be considered for *transfer* from one position to another at the same level. Among leading companies, 85 percent of CEOs are promoted from within. In the companies that hire CEOs from outside, 40 percent of the CEOs are gone after 18 months.[7]

Personal App Even if you're working part-time for a company, watch for job postings and network with colleagues. If a position opens up, you may be able move into full-time work or shift to a different job that interests you.

Promoting from within provides strong motivation for current employees and helps the firm to retain quality personnel. General Electric, ExxonMobil, and Eastman Kodak are companies dedicated to promoting from within. The practice of *job posting*, or informing current employees of upcoming openings, may be a company policy or required by union contract. The primary disadvantage of internal recruiting is that promoting a current employee leaves another position to be filled. Not only does the firm still incur recruiting and selection costs, but it also must train two employees instead of one.

In many situations it may be impossible to recruit internally. For example, a new position may be such that no current employee is qualified, or the firm may be growing so rapidly that there is no time to reassign positions that promotion or transfer requires.

Selection

Selection is the process of gathering information about applicants for a position and then using that information to choose the most appropriate applicant. Note the use of the word *appropriate*. In selection, the idea is not to hire the person with the *most* qualifications but rather the applicant who is *most appropriate*. The selection of an applicant is made by line managers responsible for the position. However,

Salesforce.com's Social Recruiting Strategy

Recruiting is a highly social activity at fast-growing Salesforce.com, a high-tech company specializing in Web-based software for sales management and other corporate functions. To attract job applicants, Salesforce.com posts openings on a multitude of public social media sites. Using internal blogs, the company invites its workforce to suggest good candidates for open positions. Of the 1,000 new employees hired during the past two years, 40 percent came through employee referrals. The company knows that its success can continue only if its employees succeed. That's why the top human resources executive holds the title of "Senior Vice President of Employee Success."

Sources: Milton Moskowitz, Robert Levering, and Christopher Tkaczyk, "100 Best Companies to Work For: No. 52, Salesforce.com" *Fortune*, February 7, 2011, p. 94; Milton Moskowitz, Robert Levering, and Christopher Tkaczyk, "100 Best Companies to Work For: No. 43, Salesforce.com," *Fortune*, February 8, 2010, p. 82; Steve Hamm, "The King of the Cloud," *BusinessWeek*, November 30, 2009, p. 77; www.salesforce.com.

external recruiting the attempt to attract job applicants from outside an organization

internal recruiting considering present employees as applicants for available positions

selection the process of gathering information about applicants for a position and then using that information to choose the most appropriate applicant

What Can a Career Coach Do for You?

career
SUCCESS

Whether you're hunting for your first job, getting ready to change jobs, or testing the waters in a new industry, consider consulting a career coach. Like a sports coach, a career coach can offer good advice and provide guidance from the sidelines as you take the field and move ahead with key career decisions.

Working with a career coach can open the door to new career possibilities, help you focus your networking efforts, provide feedback to polish your interviewing skills, and help you get ready for on-the-job challenges. Career coaches can also offer insights into what recruiters look for when they read resumes and recommend ways to demonstrate the value of your skills and education to a potential employer. To get the most

from coaching, have your resume handy, prepare questions in advance, and take notes as your coach makes suggestions.

Although you should expect to pay an experienced, professional career coach, don't rule out the idea of asking a trusted mentor to coach you through an important career decision, as a favor. Depending on your goals, you may decide on a single coaching session or meet more than once to continue the discussion. No career coach will hand you a listing of job openings, but you should come away with a definite direction for your job search, fresh perspectives on your choices, more concrete career goals, and more confidence in your abilities.

Sources: Carolyn Kepcher, "Partnering Up With Career Coach, Mentor or Advisor Can Give You Inside Track to Career Success," *New York Daily News*, February 4, 2011, www .nydailynews.com; Nick Corcodilos, "When Someone You Respect Offers to Be Your Career Coach, What's the Best Response?" *Seattle Times NW Jobs*, February 28, 2010, http:// blog.marketplace.nwsource.com/careercenter; Karina Diaz Cano, "Is a Career Coach Really Worth the Investment?" *Wall Street Journal*, May 28, 2009, http://blogs.wsj.com.

HRM personnel usually help by developing a pool of applicants and by expediting the assessment of these applicants. Common means of obtaining information about applicants' qualifications are employment applications, interviews, references, and assessment centers.

EMPLOYMENT APPLICATIONS An employment application is useful in collecting factual information on a candidate's education, work experience, and personal history (see Figure 9-2). The data obtained from applications usually are used for two purposes: to identify applicants who are worthy of further scrutiny and to familiarize interviewers with their backgrounds.

Many job candidates submit résumés, and some firms require them. A *résumé* is a one or two-page summary of the candidate's background and qualifications. It may include a description of the type of job the applicant is seeking. A résumé may be sent to a firm to request consideration for available jobs, or it may be submitted along with an employment application.

To improve the usefulness of information, HRM specialists ask current employees about factors in their backgrounds most related to their current jobs. Then these factors are included on the applications and may be weighted more heavily when evaluating new applicants' qualifications.

EMPLOYMENT TESTS Tests administered to job candidates usually focus on aptitudes, skills, abilities, or knowledge relevant to the job. Such tests (basic computer skills tests, for example) indicate how well the applicant will do the job. Occasionally, companies use general intelligence or personality tests, but these are seldom helpful in predicting specific job performance. However, *Fortune* 500 companies, as well as an increasing number of medium and small-sized companies, are using predictive behavior personality tests as administration costs decrease.

FIGURE 9-2: **Typical Employment Application**

Employers use applications to collect factual information on a candidate's education, work experience, and personal history.

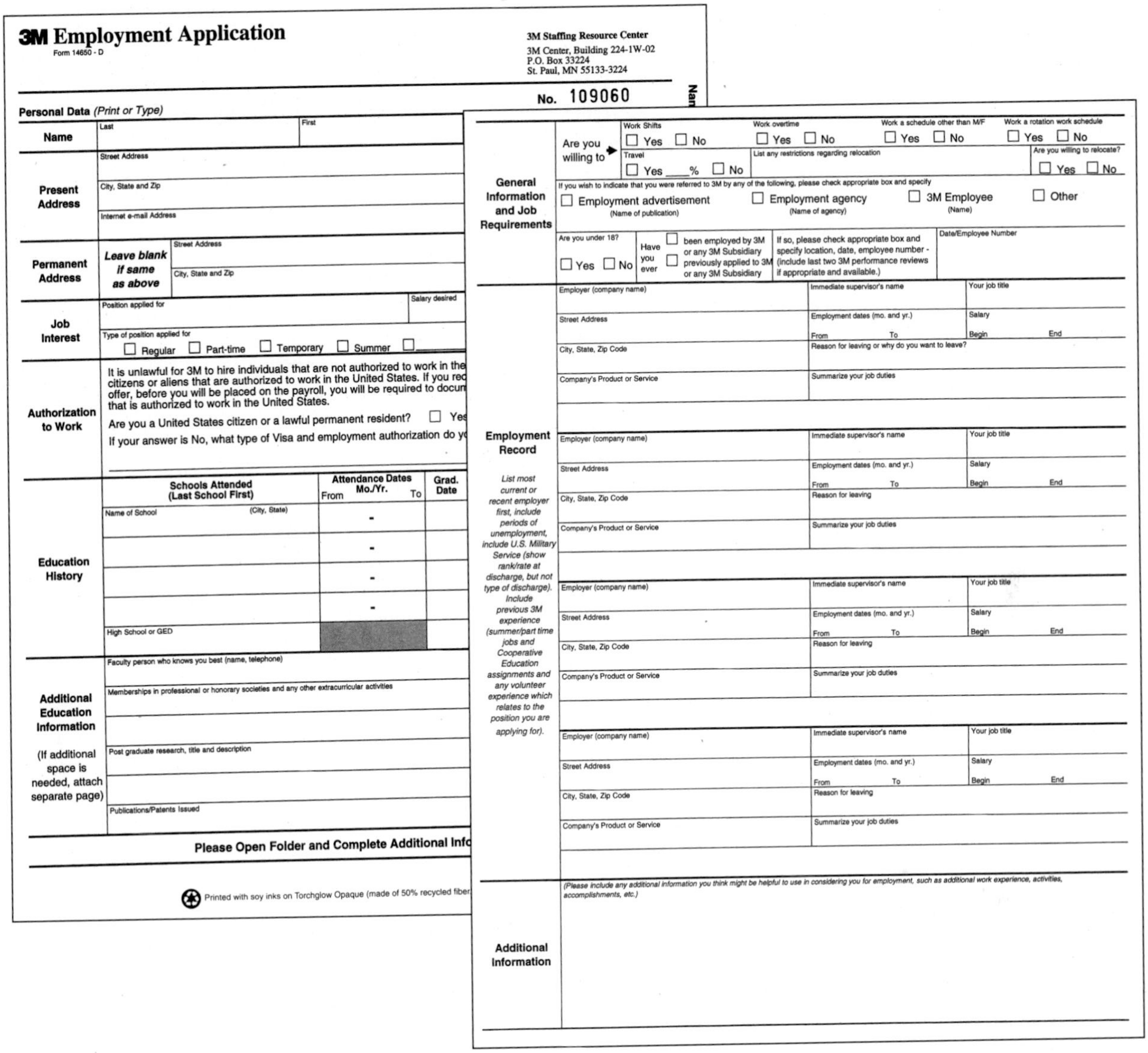

3M Employment Application
Form 14650 - D

3M Staffing Resource Center
3M Center, Building 224-1W-02
P.O. Box 33224
St. Paul, MN 55133-3224

No. 109060

Personal Data *(Print or Type)*

Name — Last / First

Present Address — Street Address / City, State and Zip / Internet e-mail Address

Permanent Address — *Leave blank if same as above* — Street Address / City, State and Zip

Job Interest — Position applied for / Salary desired / Type of position applied for: ☐ Regular ☐ Part-time ☐ Temporary ☐ Summer ☐

Authorization to Work — It is unlawful for 3M to hire individuals that are not authorized to work in the … citizens or aliens that are authorized to work in the United States. If you rec… offer, before you will be placed on the payroll, you will be required to docum… that is authorized to work in the United States.
Are you a United States citizen or a lawful permanent resident? ☐ Yes
If your answer is No, what type of Visa and employment authorization do y…

Education History — Schools Attended (Last School First) / Attendance Dates Mo./Yr. From To / Grad. Date — Name of School (City, State) … High School or GED

Additional Education Information (If additional space is needed, attach separate page) — Faculty person who knows you best (name, telephone) / Memberships in professional or honorary societies and any other extracurricular activities / Post graduate research, title and description / Publications/Patents Issued

Please Open Folder and Complete Additional Inf…

Printed with soy inks on Torchglow Opaque (made of 50% recycled fiber…

General Information and Job Requirements — Are you willing to: Work Shifts ☐ Yes ☐ No; Work overtime ☐ Yes ☐ No; Work a schedule other than M/F ☐ Yes ☐ No; Work a rotation work schedule ☐ Yes ☐ No; Travel ☐ Yes ___% ☐ No; List any restrictions regarding relocation; Are you willing to relocate? ☐ Yes ☐ No
If you wish to indicate that you were referred to 3M by any of the following, please check appropriate box and specify: ☐ Employment advertisement (Name of publication) ☐ Employment agency (Name of agency) ☐ 3M Employee (Name) ☐ Other
Are you under 18? ☐ Yes ☐ No — Have you ever ☐ been employed by 3M or any 3M Subsidiary ☐ previously applied to 3M or any 3M Subsidiary — If so, please check appropriate box and specify location, date, employee number - (include last two 3M performance reviews if appropriate and available.) — Date/Employee Number

Employment Record — *List most current or recent employer first, include periods of unemployment, include U.S. Military Service (show rank/rate at discharge, but not type of discharge). Include previous 3M experience (summer/part time jobs and Cooperative Education assignments and any volunteer experience which relates to the position you are applying for).*
Employer (company name) / Immediate supervisor's name / Your job title / Street Address / Employment dates (mo. and yr.) From To / Salary Begin End / City, State, Zip Code / Reason for leaving or why do you want to leave? / Company's Product or Service / Summarize your job duties

Additional Information — *(Please include any additional information you think might be helpful to use in considering you for employment, such as additional work experience, activities, accomplishments, etc.)*

Source: Courtesy of 3M.

At one time, a number of companies were criticized for using tests that were biased against certain minority groups—in particular, African Americans. The test results were, to a great extent, unrelated to job performance. Today, a firm must be able to prove that a test is not discriminatory by demonstrating that it accurately measures one's ability to perform. Applicants who believe that they have been discriminated against through an invalid test may file a complaint with the Equal Employment Opportunity Commission (EEOC).

INTERVIEWS The interview is perhaps the most widely used selection technique. Job candidates are interviewed by at least one member of the HRM staff and by the person for whom they will be working. Candidates for higher-level jobs may meet with a department head or vice president over several interviews.

Tough Questions, Honest Answers

In today's economy, competition for jobs is so fierce that applicants may be tempted to stretch the truth simply to get an interview. According to one study, nearly half of the resumes investigated by employers inaccurately described the applicants' job history, educational background, or professional credentials. "It's easy to falsify or embellish beyond a point that would be an ethical representation of your accomplishments," says John Challenger, CEO of the outplacement firm Challenger, Gray & Christmas.

Even when applicants don't exaggerate or lie, "what we often see is people omitting the truth" on applications, says an executive at RoyOMartin Plywood in Chopin, Louisiana. For example, applicants might not list all of their previous jobs or might give the impression that they were laid off when they were actually fired.

However, honesty is the best policy, because employers must be able to trust the people they hire. Catching an applicant in a lie violates that trust and leads management to wonder whether that person would also lie to customers or co-workers. In fact, a lot of companies have zero-tolerance policies and will dismiss any employee found to have lied on a resume or application.

These days, most companies thoroughly check out applicants before they make a job offer. To gauge attitudes toward honesty, interviewers sometimes ask applicants how they handled ethically questionable situations in previous jobs, such as seeing someone steal from the company. The best advice for applicants is: Even the toughest question deserves an honest answer.

Sources: Anna Prior, "In Job Hunting, Honesty Is Still the Best Policy," *Wall Street Journal*, April 25, 2010, www.wsj.com; David Dinsmore, "Self-confidence, Honesty Are Key to Successful Job Search," *Town Talk (Louisiana)*, February 12, 2011, www.thetowntalk.com; "How to Hire an Honest Staff," *Lahontan Valley News (Nevada)*, March 3, 2011, www.lahontanvalleynews.com.

Interviews provide an opportunity for applicants and the firm to learn more about each other. Interviewers can pose problems to test the candidate's abilities, probe employment history, and learn something about the candidate's attitudes and motivation. The candidate has a chance to find out more about the job and potential co-workers.

Unfortunately, interviewing may be the stage at which discrimination begins. For example, suppose that a female applicant mentions that she is the mother of small children. Her interviewer may assume that she would not be available for job-related travel. In addition, interviewers may be unduly influenced by such factors as appearance, or they may ask different questions of different applicants so that it becomes impossible to compare candidates' qualifications. Table 9-2 contains interview questions that are difficult to answer.

Some of these problems can be solved through better interviewer training and use of structured interviews. In a *structured interview*, the interviewer asks only a prepared set of job-related questions. The firm also may consider using several different interviewers for each applicant, but this is likely to be costly.

REFERENCES A job candidate generally is asked to furnish the names of references—people who can verify background information and provide personal evaluations. Naturally, applicants tend to list only references who are likely to say good things. Thus, personal evaluations obtained from references may not be of much value. However, references are often contacted to verify such information as previous job responsibilities and the reason an applicant left a former job.

Interviews are a normal part of the recruiting process. Interviews can occur in a variety of locations and through several formats. They also provide an opportunity for the job seeker and the company to find out about each other. Can you think of any other selection methods that benefit *both* parties in the recruiting process?

TABLE 9-2: Interview Questions that May Be Difficult to Answer

1. Tell me about yourself.
2. What do you know about our organization?
3. What can you do for us? Why should we hire you?
4. What qualifications do you have that make you feel that you will be successful in your field?
5. What have you learned from the jobs that you have held?
6. Where do you see your career in 5 or 10 years?
7. What are your special skills, and how did you acquire them?
8. Have you had any special accomplishments in your lifetime that you are particularly proud of?
9. Why did you leave your most recent job?
10. How do you spend your spare time? What are your hobbies?
11. What are your strengths and weaknesses?
12. Discuss five major accomplishments.
13. What kind of box would you like? Why?
14. If you could spend a day with someone you have known or known of, who would it be?
15. What personality characteristics rub you the wrong way?
16. How do you show your anger? What type of things make you angry?
17. With what type of person do you spend the majority of your time?
18. What activities have you ever quit?
19. Define cooperation.

Source: Adapted from GREENE, *The Ultimate Job Hunter's Guidebook*, 5E. © 2008 South-Western, a part of Cengage Learning, Inc. Reproduced by permission. www.cengage.com/permissions

ASSESSMENT CENTERS An assessment center is used primarily to select current employees for promotion to higher-level positions. Typically, a group of employees is sent to the center for a few days. While there, they participate in activities designed to simulate the management environment and to predict managerial effectiveness. Trained observers make recommendations regarding promotion possibilities. Although this technique is gaining popularity, the expense involved limits its use.

Orientation

Once all information about job candidates has been collected and analyzed, the company extends a job offer. If it is accepted, the candidate becomes an employee.

Soon after a candidate joins a firm, he or she goes through the firm's orientation program. **Orientation** is the process of acquainting new employees with an organization. Orientation topics range from the location of the company cafeteria to career paths within the firm. The orientation itself may consist of a half-hour informal presentation by a human resources manager, or it may be an elaborate program involving dozens of people and lasting several days or weeks.

Personal App As a freshman, you probably had an orientation before you started classes. Job orientation serves the same purpose: to show you around, give you an overview of the organization, and introduce you to the main policies and procedures.

orientation the process of acquainting new employees with an organization

Concept Check ✱

☐ What are the differences between internal and external recruiting?

☐ Under what conditions are each one of these used?

☐ Identify and briefly describe the types of practices and tools that are used in the selection process.

COMPENSATION AND BENEFITS

An effective employee reward system must (1) enable employees to satisfy basic needs, (2) provide rewards comparable with those offered by other firms, (3) be distributed fairly within the organization, and (4) recognize that different people have different needs.

LEARNING OBJECTIVE
6 Discuss the primary elements of employee compensation and benefits.

When Should Compensation and Benefits Be Discussed with Job Applicants?

Senior Executives Tell Us...

- Phone interview: 14%
- First interview: 19%
- Second interview: 33%
- Third interview or after: 9%
- Once job offer is made: 22%
- Other/ Don't know: 3%

Source: Accountemps Survey 2009. Information compiled from telephone interiews with 150 senior executives from the nation's 1,000 largest companies. http://accountemps.rhi. mediaroom.com/index.php?s=189&item=165.

A firm's compensation system can be structured to meet the first three of these requirements. The fourth is more difficult because it must account for many variables. Most firms offer a number of benefits that, taken together, generally help to provide for employees' varying needs.

Compensation Decisions

Compensation is the payment employees receive in return for their labor. Its importance to employees is obvious. Because compensation may account for up to 80 percent of a firm's operating costs, it is equally important to the management. Therefore, the firm's **compensation system**, the policies and strategies that determine employee compensation, must be designed carefully to provide for employees' needs while keeping labor costs within reasonable limits. For most firms, designing an effective compensation system requires three separate management decisions—wage level, wage structure, and individual wages.

WAGE LEVEL Management first must position the firm's general pay level relative to pay levels of comparable firms. Most firms choose a pay level near the industry average. However, a firm that is not in good financial shape may pay less than average, and large, prosperous organizations may pay more than average.

To determine the average pay for a job, the firm may use wage surveys. A **wage survey** is a collection of data on prevailing wage rates within an industry or a geographic area. Such surveys are compiled by industry associations, local governments, personnel associations, and (occasionally) individual firms.

WAGE STRUCTURE Next, management must decide on relative pay levels for all the positions within the firm. Will managers be paid more than secretaries? Will secretaries be paid more than custodians? The result of this set of decisions is often called the firm's *wage structure*.

The wage structure almost always is developed on the basis of a job evaluation. **Job evaluation** is the process of determining the relative worth of the various jobs within a firm. Most observers probably would agree that a secretary should make more money than a custodian, but how much more? Job evaluation should provide the answer to this question.

A number of techniques may be used to evaluate jobs. The simplest is to rank all the jobs within the firm according to value. A more frequently used method is based on the job analysis. Points are allocated to each job for each of its elements and requirements. For example, "college degree required" might be worth 50 points, whereas the need for a high school education might count for only 25 points. The more points a job is allocated, the more important it is presumed to be (and the higher its level in the firm's wage structure).

INDIVIDUAL WAGES Finally, the company must determine the specific payments individual employees will receive. Consider the case of two secretaries working side by side. Job evaluation has been used to determine the relative level of secretarial pay within the firm's wage structure. However, suppose that one secretary has 15 years of experience and can type 80 words per minute accurately and the other has two years of experience and can type only 55 words per minute; in most firms, these two people would not receive the same pay. Instead, a wage range would be

compensation the payment employees receive in return for their labor

compensation system the policies and strategies that determine employee compensation

wage survey a collection of data on prevailing wage rates within an industry or a geographic area

job evaluation the process of determining the relative worth of the various jobs within a firm

established for the secretarial position. In this case, the range might be $8.50 to $12.50 per hour. The more experienced and proficient secretary then would be paid an amount near the top of the range (say, $12.25 per hour); the less experienced secretary would receive an amount that is lower but still within the range (say, $8.75 per hour).

Two wage decisions come into play here. First, the employee's initial rate must be established. It is based on experience, other qualifications, and expected performance. Later, the employee may be given pay increases based on seniority and performance.

Comparable Worth

One reason women in the workforce are paid less may be that a proportion of women occupy female-dominated jobs—nurses, secretaries, and medical records analysts, for example—that require education, skills, and training equal to higher-paid positions but are undervalued. **Comparable worth** is a concept that seeks equal compensation for jobs that require about the same level of education, training, and skill. Several states have enacted laws requiring equal pay for comparable work in government positions. Critics of comparable worth argue that the market has determined the worth of jobs and laws should not tamper with the market's pricing mechanism. The Equal Pay Act, discussed later in this chapter, does not address the issue of comparable worth. Critics also argue that inflating salaries artificially for female-dominated occupations encourages women to keep these jobs rather than seek out higher-paying jobs.

© Alexander Kalina/Shutterstock

Types of Compensation

Compensation can be paid in a variety of forms. Most forms of compensation fall into the following categories: hourly wage, weekly or monthly salary, commissions, incentive payments, lump-sum salary increases, and profit sharing.

HOURLY WAGE An **hourly wage** is a specific amount of money paid for each hour of work. People who earn wages are paid their hourly wage for the first 40 hours worked in any week. They are then paid one-and-one-half times their hourly wage for time worked in excess of 40 hours (i.e., they are paid "time-and-a-half" for overtime). Workers in retailing and fast-food chains, on assembly lines, and in clerical positions usually are paid an hourly wage.

WEEKLY OR MONTHLY SALARY A **salary** is a specific amount of money paid for an employee's work during a set calendar period, regardless of the actual number of hours worked. Salaried employees receive no overtime pay, but they do not lose pay when they are absent from work. Most professional and managerial positions are salaried.

COMMISSIONS A **commission** is a payment that is a percentage of sales revenue. Sales representatives and sales managers often are paid entirely through commissions or through a combination of commissions and salary.

INCENTIVE PAYMENTS An **incentive payment** is a payment in addition to wages, salary, or commissions. Incentive payments are really extra rewards for outstanding job performance. They may be distributed to all employees or only to certain employees. Some firms distribute incentive payments to all employees annually. The size of the payment depends on the firm's earnings and, at times, on the particular employee's length of service with the firm. Firms sometimes offer incentives to employees who exceed specific sales or production goals, a practice called *gain sharing*.

To avoid yearly across-the-board salary increases, some organizations reward outstanding workers individually through *merit pay*. This pay-for-performance approach allows management to control labor costs while encouraging employees to work more efficiently. An employee's merit pay depends on his or her achievements relative to those of others.

comparable worth a concept that seeks equal compensation for jobs requiring about the same level of education, training, and skills

hourly wage a specific amount of money paid for each hour of work

salary a specific amount of money paid for an employee's work during a set calendar period, regardless of the actual number of hours worked

commission a payment that is a percentage of sales revenue

incentive payment a payment in addition to wages, salary, or commissions

Employee benefits can be used to compete for the best employees. Companies provide different types of employee benefits. For example, some provide child-care services.

LUMP-SUM SALARY INCREASES In traditional reward systems, an employee who receives an annual pay increase is given part of the increase in each pay period. For example, suppose that an employee on a monthly salary gets a 10 percent annual pay hike. He or she actually receives 10 percent of the former monthly salary added to each month's paycheck for a year. Companies that offer a **lump-sum salary increase** give the employee the option of taking the entire pay raise in one lump sum. The employee then draws his or her "regular" pay for the rest of the year. The lump-sum payment typically is treated as an interest-free loan that must be repaid if the employee leaves the firm during the year.

PROFIT-SHARING **Profit-sharing** is the distribution of a percentage of a firm's profit among its employees. The idea is to motivate employees to work effectively by giving them a stake in the company's financial success. Some firms—including Sears, Roebuck—have linked their profit-sharing plans to employee retirement programs; that is, employees receive their profit-sharing distributions, with interest, when they retire.

Employee Benefits

An **employee benefit** is a reward in addition to regular compensation that is provided indirectly to employees. Employee benefits consist mainly of services (such as insurance) that are paid for partially or totally by employers and employee expenses (such as college tuition) that are reimbursed by employers. Currently, the average cost of these benefits is 29.4 percent of an employee's total compensation, which includes wages plus benefits.[8] Thus, a person who received total compensation (including benefits) of $50,000 a year earned $35,300 in wages and received an additional $14,700 in benefits.

(**Personal App**) When you're applying for a new job, wait to ask about benefits until you've been offered the position. During your first interview, stay focused on the company and how you can be an asset in this position, not on the benefits or compensation.

TYPES OF BENEFITS Employee benefits take a variety of forms. *Pay for time not worked* covers such absences as vacation time, holidays, and sick leave. *Insurance packages* may include health, life, and dental insurance for employees and their families. Some firms pay the entire cost of the insurance package, and others share the cost with the employee. The costs of *pension and retirement programs* also may be borne entirely by the firm or shared with the employee.

Some benefits are required by law. For example, employers must maintain *workers' compensation insurance,* which pays medical bills for injuries that occur on the job and provides income for employees who are disabled by job-related injuries. Employers must also pay for *unemployment insurance* and contribute to each employee's federal *Social Security* account.

Other benefits provided by employers include tuition-reimbursement plans, credit unions, child-care services, company cafeterias, exercise rooms, and broad stock-option plans available to all employees. Some companies offer special benefits to U.S. military reservists who are called up for active duty.

Some companies offer unusual benefits to attract and retain employees. Paychex, a payroll-processing company, gives awards of up to $300 to its employees for participating in healthy activities, such as receiving flu shots, going to the dentist, attending exercise classes, running a race, and riding their bike to work. Kimpton

lump-sum salary increase an entire pay raise taken in one lump sum

profit-sharing the distribution of a percentage of a firm's profit among its employees

employee benefit a reward in addition to regular compensation that is provided indirectly to employees

Hotels and Restaurants lets hotel employees bring their pets to work (provided they play well with others) and leave them with onsite pet care specialists. The company has also partnered with Pet Assure to offer veterinary health insurance. Employees at SC Johnson have access to an on-site concierge service that will run errands for them, such as mailing packages, getting groceries, and changing their car's oil. A wine bar is installed in all 17 of the DPR Construction offices, where employees can pop a bottle of red to toast major accomplishments or a project's completion. The only exception is the construction company's Texas branch, which features an in-house saloon instead. SAS, which is highly ranked in *Fortune* magazine's "Top 100 Companies to Work For," offers unlimited sick days, a medical center that provides free services, a free 66,000-square-foot fitness center and natatorium, a lending library, on-site saunas, discounted massages, classes on Wii bowling, and even a summer camp for children of employees. Google is known for its unusual perks and fun activities, which include foosball, pool, volleyball, video games, ping pong, and gymnasiums that offer yoga and dance classes.[9]

FLEXIBLE BENEFIT PLANS Through a **flexible benefit plan**, an employee receives a predetermined amount of benefit dollars and may allocate those dollars to various categories of benefits in the mix that best fits his or her needs. Some flexible benefit plans offer a broad array of benefit options, including health care, dental care, life insurance, accidental death and dismemberment coverage for both the worker and dependents, long-term disability coverage, vacation benefits, retirement savings, and dependent-care benefits. Other firms offer limited options, primarily in health and life insurance and retirement plans.

Although the cost of administering flexible plans is high, a number of organizations, including Quaker Oats and Coca-Cola, have implemented this option for several reasons. Because employees' needs are so diverse, flexible plans help firms to offer benefit packages that more specifically meet their employees' needs. Flexible plans can, in the long run, help a company to contain costs because a specified amount is allocated to cover the benefits of each employee. Furthermore, organizations that offer flexible plans with many choices may be perceived as being employee-friendly. Thus, they are in a better position to attract and retain qualified employees.

TRAINING AND DEVELOPMENT

Training and development are extremely important at the Container Store. Because great customer service is so important, every first-year full-time salesperson receives about 185 hours of formal training as opposed to the industry standard, which is approximately seven hours. Training and development continue throughout a person's career. Each store has a full-time trainer called the *super sales trainer*. This trainer provides product training, sales training, and employee-development training. A number of top managers believe that the financial and human resources invested in training and development are well worth it.

Both training and development are aimed at improving employees' skills and abilities. However, the two are usually differentiated as either employee training or management development. **Employee training** is the process of teaching operations and technical employees how to do their present jobs more effectively and efficiently. **Management development** is the process of preparing managers and other professionals to assume increased responsibility in both present and future positions. Thus, training and development differ in who is being taught and the purpose of the teaching. However, both are necessary for personal and organizational growth. Companies that hope to stay competitive typically make huge commitments to employee training and development. Internet-based e-learning is growing. Driven by cost, travel, and time savings, online learning alone (and in conjunction with face-to-face situations) is a strong alternative strategy. Development of a training program usually has three components: analysis of needs, determination of training and development methods, and creation of an evaluation system to assess the program's effectiveness.

Concept Check ✻

☐ Identify the major compensation decisions that HRM managers make.

☐ What are the different forms of compensation?

☐ What are the major types of employee benefits?

☐ How do flexible benefit plans work?

LEARNING OBJECTIVE

7 Explain the purposes and techniques of employee training and development.

flexible benefit plan compensation plan whereby an employee receives a predetermined amount of benefit dollars to spend on a package of benefits he or she has selected to meet individual needs

employee training the process of teaching operations and technical employees how to do their present jobs more effectively and efficiently

management development the process of preparing managers and other professionals to assume increased responsibility in both present and future positions

Employees are trained through numerous methods including simulations, classroom teaching, role playing, and on-the-job coaching. Training may take just a few hours, a few weeks, or many months. What job training methods have you experienced, and how effective were they?

© AP Photo/Chattanooga Times Free Press, Dan Henry

Analysis of Training Needs

When thinking about developing a training program, managers first must determine if training is needed and, if so, what types of training needs exist. At times, what at first appears to be a need for training is actually, on assessment, a need for motivation. Training needs can vary considerably. For example, some employees may need training to improve their technical skills, or they may need training about organizational procedures. Training also may focus on business ethics, product information, or customer service. Because training is expensive, it is critical that the correct training needs be identified.

Training and Development Methods

A number of methods are available for employee training and management development. Some of these methods may be more suitable for one or the other, but most can be applied to both training and management development.

- *On-the-job methods.* The trainee learns by doing the work under the supervision of an experienced employee.
- *Simulations.* The work situation is simulated in a separate area so that learning takes place away from the day-to-day pressures of work.
- *Classroom teaching and lectures.* You probably already know these methods quite well.
- *Conferences and seminars.* Experts and learners meet to discuss problems and exchange ideas.
- *Role-playing.* Participants act out the roles of others in the organization for better understanding of those roles (primarily a management development tool).

Evaluation of Training and Development

Training and development are very expensive. The training itself costs quite a bit, and employees are usually not working—or are working at a reduced load and pace—during training sessions. To ensure that training and development are cost-effective, the managers responsible should evaluate the company's efforts periodically.

The starting point for this evaluation is a set of verifiable objectives that are developed before the training is undertaken. Suppose that a training program is expected to improve the skills of machinists. The objective of the program might be stated as follows: "At the end of the training period, each machinist should be able to process 30 parts per hour with no more than one defective part per 90 parts completed." This objective clearly specifies what is expected and how training results may be measured or verified. Evaluation then consists of measuring machinists' output and the ratio of defective parts produced after the training.

The results of training evaluations should be made known to all those involved in the program—including trainees and upper management. For trainees, the results of evaluations can enhance motivation and learning. For upper management, the results may be the basis for making decisions about the training program itself.

performance appraisal the evaluation of employees' current and potential levels of performance to allow managers to make objective human resources decisions

* *Concept Check*

☐ What is the difference between employee training and management development?

☐ What are the primary training and development methods used by firms?

PERFORMANCE APPRAISAL

Performance appraisal is the evaluation of employees' current and potential levels of performance to allow managers to make objective human resources decisions. The process has three main objectives. First, managers use performance appraisals to let

FIGURE 9-3: **Performance Appraisal**

3M **Contribution and Development Summary**
FORM 37450 - B

Employee Name	Employee Number	Job Title
Department		Location
Coach/Supervisor(s) Name(s)		Review Period
		From :

Major Job Responsibilities

Goals/Expectations	Contributions/

Contribution (To be completed by coach/supervisor)

☐ Good Level of Contribution for this year   ☐ Exceptional

☐ Unsatisfactory Level of Contribution for this year

Development Summary

Areas of Strength	Development Priorities

Career Interests

Next job	Longer Range

Current Mobility

☐ 0 - Currently Unable to Relocate
☐ 1 - Position In Home Country Only (Use if Home Country is Outside U.S.)
☐ 2 - Position Within O.U.S. Region (e: Nordic, SEA...)

☐ 3 - Position Within O.U.S. Area (ex: Europe, Asia)
☐ 4 - Position In U.S.
☐ 5 - Position Anywhere In The World

Development

☐ W - Well placed. Development plans achievable in current role for at least the next year
☐ C - Ready now for a move to a different job for career broadening experience
☐ I - Ready now for a move to a different job involving increased responsibility

☐ X - Not well placed. Action required to resolve placement issues.
Comments on Development

Employee Comments

Coach/Supervisor Comments | **Other Supervisor (if applicable) and/or Reviewer**

Signatures

Coach/Supervisor	Date	Other Coach/Supervisor or Reviewer	Date
Employee			Date

page 4

Source: Courtesy of 3M.

workers know how well they are doing and how they can do better in the future. Second, a performance appraisal provides an effective basis for distributing rewards, such as pay raises and promotions. Third, performance appraisal helps the organization monitor its employee selection, training, and development activities. If large numbers of employees continually perform below expectations, the firm may need to revise its selection process or strengthen its training and development activities. Most performance appraisal processes include a written document. An example appears in Figure 9-3.

Common Evaluation Techniques

The various techniques and methods for appraising employee performance are either objective or judgmental in nature.

OBJECTIVE METHODS Objective appraisal methods use some measurable quantity as the basis for assessing performance. Units of output, dollar volume of sales, number of defective products, and number of insurance claims processed are all objective, measurable quantities. Thus, an employee who processes an average of 26 insurance claims per week is given a higher evaluation than one whose average is 19 claims per week.

Such objective measures may require some adjustment for the work environment. Suppose that the first of our insurance claims' processors works in New York City and the second works in rural Iowa. Both must visit each client because they are processing homeowners' insurance claims. The difference in their average weekly output may be entirely because of the long distances the Iowan must travel to visit clients. In this case, the two workers may very well be equally competent and motivated. Thus, a manager must take into account circumstances that may be hidden by a purely statistical measurement.

JUDGMENTAL METHODS Judgmental appraisal methods are used much more frequently than objective methods. They require that the manager judge or estimate the employee's performance level. However, judgmental methods are not capricious. These methods are based on employee ranking or rating scales. When ranking is used, the manager ranks subordinates from best to worst. This approach has a number of drawbacks, including the lack of any absolute standard. Use of rating scales is the most popular judgmental appraisal technique. A *rating scale* consists of a number of statements; each employee is rated on the degree to which the statement applies. For example, one statement might be, "This employee always does high-quality work." The supervisor would give the employee a rating, from 5 down to 1, corresponding to gradations ranging from "strongly agree" to "strongly disagree." The ratings on all the statements are added to obtain the employee's total evaluation.

AVOIDING APPRAISAL ERRORS Managers must be cautious if they are to avoid making mistakes when appraising employees. It is common to overuse one portion of an evaluation instrument, thus overemphasizing some issues and underemphasizing others. A manager must guard against allowing an employee's poor performance on one activity to influence his or her judgment of that subordinate's work on other activities. Similarly, putting too much weight on recent performance distorts an employee's evaluation. For example, if the employee is being rated on performance over the last year, a manager should not permit last month's disappointing performance to overshadow the quality of the work done in the first 11 months of the year. Finally, a manager must guard against discrimination on the basis of race, age, gender, religion, national origin, or sexual orientation.

Performance Feedback

No matter which appraisal technique is used, the results should be discussed with the employee soon after the evaluation is completed. The manager should explain the basis for present rewards and should let the employee know what he or she can do to be recognized as a better performer in the future. The information provided to an employee in such discussions is called *performance feedback*, and the process is known as a *performance feedback interview*.

Personal App Nobody's perfect. Think of performance feedback as a way to learn about any additional training, practice, and experience that could help you become even more valuable as an employee.

There are three major approaches to performance feedback interviews: tell-and-sell, tell-and-listen, and problem solving. In a *tell-and-sell* feedback interview, the superior tells the employee how good or bad the employee's performance has been and then attempts to persuade the employee to accept the evaluation. Because the employee has no input into the evaluation, the tell-and-sell interview can lead to defensiveness, resentment, and frustration on the part of the subordinate. The employee may not accept the results of the interview and may not be committed to achieving the goals that are set.

With the *tell-and-listen* approach, the supervisor tells the employee what has been right and wrong with the employee's performance and then gives the employee a chance to respond. The subordinate may simply be given an opportunity to react to the supervisor's statements or may be permitted to offer a full self-appraisal, challenging the supervisor's assessment.

In the *problem-solving* approach, employees evaluate their own performance and set their own goals for future performance. The supervisor is more a colleague than a judge and offers comments and advice in a noncritical manner. An active and open dialogue ensues in which goals for improvement are mutually established. The problem-solving interview is most likely to result in the employee's commitment to the established goals.

To avoid some of the problems associated with the tell-and-sell interview, supervisors sometimes use a mixed approach. The mixed interview uses the tell-and-sell approach to communicate administrative decisions and the problem-solving approach to discuss employee-development issues and future performance goals.[10]

An appraisal approach that has become popular is called a *360-degree evaluation*. A 360-degree evaluation collects anonymous reviews about an employee from his or her peers, subordinates, and supervisors and then compiles these reviews into a feedback report that is given to the employee. Companies that invest significant resources in employee-development efforts are especially likely to use 360-degree evaluations. An employee should not be given a feedback report without first having a one-on-one meeting with his or her supervisor. The most appropriate way to introduce a 360-degree evaluation system in a company is to begin with upper-level management. Then managers should be trained on how to interpret feedback reports so that they can coach their employees on how to use the feedback to achieve higher-level job-related skills and behaviors.[11]

Finally, we should note that many managers find it difficult to discuss the negative aspects of an appraisal. Unfortunately, they may ignore performance feedback altogether or provide it in a very weak and ineffectual manner. In truth, though, most employees have strengths that can be emphasized to soften the discussion of their weaknesses. An employee may not even be aware of the weaknesses and their consequences. If such weaknesses are not pointed out through performance feedback, they cannot possibly be eliminated. Only through tactful, honest communication can the results of an appraisal be fully used.

Concept Check ✳

☐ What are the main objectives of performance appraisal?

☐ What methods are used?

☐ Describe the three approaches to performance feedback interviews.

LEARNING OBJECTIVE
9 Outline the major legislation affecting human resources management.

THE LEGAL ENVIRONMENT OF HRM

Legislation regarding HRM practices has been passed mainly to protect the rights of employees, to promote job safety, and to eliminate discrimination in the workplace. The major federal laws affecting HRM are described in Table 9-3.

National Labor Relations Act and Labor–Management Relations Act

These laws are concerned with dealings between business firms and labor unions. This general area is, in concept, a part of HRM. However, because of its importance, it is often treated as a separate set of activities.

Numerous laws and regulations help to protect workers. The Occupational Safety and Health Act (OSHA), for instance, specifies required safety equipment on the job and protects employees from exposure to hazardous substances. How are OSHA regulations enforced, and what happens when a company is not in compliance with them?

© AP Photo/Daniel Miller

TABLE 9-3: Federal Legislation Affecting Human Resources Management

Law	Purpose
National Labor Relations Act (1935)	Established a collective-bargaining process in labor–management relations as well as the National Labor Relations Board (NLRB).
Fair Labor Standards Act (1938)	Established a minimum wage and an overtime pay rate for employees working more than 40 hours per week.
Labor–Management Relations Act (1947)	Provides a balance between union power and management power; also known as the Taft–Hartley Act.
Equal Pay Act (1963)	Specifies that men and women who do equal jobs must be paid the same wage.
Title VII of the Civil Rights Act (1964)	Prohibits discrimination in employment practices based on sex, race, color, religion, or national origin.
Age Discrimination in Employment Act (1967–1986)	Prohibits personnel practices that discriminate against people aged 40 years and older; the 1986 amendment eliminated a mandatory retirement age.
Occupational Safety and Health Act (1970)	Regulates the degree to which employees can be exposed to hazardous substances and specifies the safety equipment that the employer must provide.
Employment Retirement Income Security Act (1974)	Regulates company retirement programs and provides a federal insurance program for retirement plans that go bankrupt.
Worker Adjustment and Retraining Notification (WARN) Act (1988)	Requires employers to give employees 60 days notice regarding plant closure or layoff of 50 or more employees.
Americans with Disabilities Act (1990)	Prohibits discrimination against qualified individuals with disabilities in all employment practices, including job-application procedures, hiring, firing, advancement, compensation, training, and other terms, conditions, and privileges of employment.
Civil Rights Act (1991)	Facilitates employees' suing employers for sexual discrimination and collecting punitive damages.
Family and Medical Leave Act (1993)	Requires an organization with 50 or more employees to provide up to 12 weeks of leave without pay on the birth (or adoption) of an employee's child or if an employee or his or her spouse, child, or parent is seriously ill.
Affordable Care Act (2010)	Requires an organization with 50 or more employees to make health insurance available to employees or pay an assessment and gives employees the right to buy health insurance from another provider if an organization's health insurance is too expensive.

© Cengage Learning 2013

Fair Labor Standards Act

This act, passed in 1938 and amended many times since, applies primarily to wages. It established minimum wages and overtime pay rates. Many managers and other professionals, however, are exempt from this law. Managers, for example, seldom get paid overtime when they work more than 40 hours a week.

Equal Pay Act

Passed in 1963, this law overlaps somewhat with Title VII of the Civil Rights Act (see next section). The Equal Pay Act specifies that men and women who are doing equal jobs must be paid the same wage. Equal jobs are jobs that demand equal effort, skill, and responsibility and are performed under the same conditions. Differences in pay are legal if they can be attributed to differences in seniority, qualifications, or performance. However, women cannot be paid less (or more) for the same work solely because they are women.

Civil Rights Acts

Title VII of the Civil Rights Act of 1964 applies directly to selection and promotion. It forbids organizations with 15 or more employees to discriminate in those areas on the basis of sex, race, color, religion, or national origin. The purpose of Title VII is to ensure that employers make personnel decisions on the basis of employee qualifications only. As a result of this act, discrimination in employment (especially against African Americans) has been reduced in this country.

The EEOC is charged with enforcing Title VII. A person who believes that he or she has been discriminated against can file a complaint with the EEOC. The commission then investigates the complaint and, if it finds that the person has, in fact, been the victim of discrimination, the commission can take legal action on his or her behalf.

The Civil Rights Act of 1991 facilitates an employee's suing and collecting punitive damages for sexual discrimination. Discriminatory promotion and termination decisions as well as on-the-job issues, such as sexual harassment, are covered by this act.

Age Discrimination in Employment Act

The general purpose of this act, which was passed in 1967 and amended in 1986, is the same as that of Title VII—to eliminate discrimination. However, as the name implies, the Age Discrimination in Employment Act is concerned only with discrimination based on age. It applies to companies with 20 or more employees. In particular, it outlaws personnel practices that discriminate against people aged 40 years or older. (No federal law forbids discrimination against people younger than 40 years, but several states have adopted age discrimination laws that apply to a variety of age groups.) Also outlawed are company policies that specify a mandatory retirement age. Employers must base employment decisions on ability and not on a number.

Occupational Safety and Health Act

Passed in 1970, this act is mainly concerned with issues of employee health and safety. For example, the act regulates the degree to which employees can be exposed to hazardous substances. It also specifies the safety equipment that the employer must provide.

The Occupational Safety and Health Administration (OSHA) was created to enforce this act. Inspectors from OSHA investigate employee complaints regarding unsafe working conditions. They also make spot checks on companies operating in particularly hazardous industries, such as chemical and mining industries, to ensure compliance with the law. A firm found to be in violation of federal standards can be heavily fined or shut down. Nonetheless, many people feel that issuing OSHA violations is not enough to protect workers from harm.

Employee Retirement Income Security Act

This act was passed in 1974 to protect the retirement benefits of employees. It does not require that firms provide a retirement plan. However, it does specify that if a retirement plan is provided, it must be managed in such a way that the interests of employees are protected. It also provides federal insurance for retirement plans that go bankrupt.

Affirmative Action

Affirmative action is not one act but a series of executive orders issued by the President of the United States. These orders established the requirement for affirmative action in personnel practices. This stipulation applies to all employers with 50 or more employees holding federal contracts in excess of $50,000. It prescribes that such employers (1) actively encourage job applications from members of minority groups and (2) hire qualified employees from minority groups who are not fully represented in their organizations. Many firms that do not hold government contracts voluntarily take part in this affirmative action program.

Americans with Disabilities Act

The Americans with Disabilities Act (ADA) prohibits discrimination against qualified individuals with disabilities in all employment practices—including job-application procedures, hiring, firing, advancement, compensation, training, and other terms and conditions of employment. All private employers and government agencies with 15 or more employees are covered by the ADA. Defining who is a qualified individual with a disability is, of course, difficult. Depending on how *qualified individual with a disability* is interpreted, up to 43 million Americans can be included under this law. This law also mandates that all businesses that serve the public must make their facilities accessible to people with disabilities.

ADA not only protects individuals with obvious physical disabilities but also safeguards those with less visible conditions, such as heart disease, diabetes, epilepsy, cancer, AIDS, and mental illnesses. Because of this law, many organizations no longer require job applicants to pass physical examinations as a condition of employment.

Employers are required to provide disabled employees with reasonable accommodation. *Reasonable accommodation* is any modification or adjustment to a job or work environment that will enable a qualified employee with a disability to perform a central job function. Examples of reasonable accommodation include making existing facilities readily accessible to and usable by an individual confined to a wheelchair. Reasonable accommodation also might mean restructuring a job, modifying work schedules, acquiring or modifying equipment, providing qualified readers or interpreters, or changing training programs.

* Concept Check

☐ How is the National Labor Relations Act different from the Fair Labor Standards Act?

☐ How does the Civil Rights Act influence the selection and promotion of employees?

☐ What is the Occupational Safety and Health Act?

☐ What is the purpose of the Americans with Disabilities Act?

Get Flashcards, Quizzes, Games, Crosswords, and more @ www.cengagebrain.com

SUMMARY

1 Describe the major components of human resources management.

Human resources management (HRM) is the set of activities involved in acquiring, maintaining, and developing an organization's human resources. Responsibility for HRM is shared by specialized staff and line managers. HRM activities include human resources planning, job analysis, recruitment, selection, orientation, compensation, benefits, training and development, and performance appraisal.

2 Identify the steps in human resources planning.

Human resources planning consists of forecasting the human resources that a firm will need and those that it will have available and then planning a course of action to match supply with demand. Layoffs, attrition,

early retirement, and (as a last resort) firing are ways to reduce the size of the workforce. Supply is increased though hiring.

3 Describe cultural diversity and understand some of the challenges and opportunities associated with it.

Cultural diversity refers to the differences among people in a workforce owing to race, ethnicity, and gender. With an increasing number of women, minorities, and immigrants entering the U.S. workforce, management is faced with both challenges and competitive advantages. Some organizations are implementing diversity-related training programs and working to make the most of cultural diversity. With proper guidance and management, a culturally diverse organization can prove beneficial to all involved.

4 Explain the objectives and uses of job analysis.

Job analysis provides a job description and a job specification for each position within a firm. A job description is a list of the elements that make up a particular job. A job specification is a list of qualifications required to perform a particular job. Job analysis is used in evaluation and in the determination of compensation levels and serves as the basis for recruiting and selecting new employees.

5 Describe the processes of recruiting, employee selection, and orientation.

Recruiting is the process of attracting qualified job applicants. Candidates for open positions may be recruited from within or outside a firm. In the selection process, information about candidates is obtained from applications, resumes, tests, interviews, references, or assessment centers. This information then is used to select the most appropriate candidate for the job. Newly hired employees will then go through a formal or an informal orientation program to acquaint themselves with the firm.

6 Discuss the primary elements of employee compensation and benefits.

Compensation is the payment employees receive in return for their labor. In developing a system for paying employees, management must decide on the firm's general wage level (relative to other firms), the wage structure within the firm, and individual wages. Wage surveys and job analyses are useful in making these decisions. Employees may be paid hourly wages, salaries, or commissions. They also may receive incentive payments, lump-sum salary increases, and profit-sharing payments. Employee benefits, which are nonmonetary rewards to employees, add about 28 percent to the cost of compensation.

7 Explain the purposes and techniques of employee training and development.

Employee-training and management-development programs enhance the ability of employees to contribute to a firm. When developing a training program, the company should analyze training needs and then select training methods. Because training is expensive, an organization should periodically evaluate the effectiveness of its training programs.

8 Discuss performance appraisal techniques and performance feedback.

Performance appraisal, or evaluation, is used to provide employees with performance feedback, to serve as a basis for distributing rewards, and to monitor selection and training activities. Both objective and judgmental appraisal techniques are used. Their results are communicated to employees through three performance feedback approaches: tell-and-sell, tell-and-listen, and problem solving.

9 Outline the major legislation affecting human resources management.

A number of laws have been passed that affect HRM practices and that protect the rights and safety of employees. Some of these are the National Labor Relations Act of 1935, the Labor–Management Relations Act of 1947, the Fair Labor Standards Act of 1938, the Equal Pay Act of 1963, Title VII of the Civil Rights Act of 1964, the Age Discrimination in Employment Acts of 1967 and 1986, the Occupational Safety and Health Act of 1970, the Employment Retirement Income Security Act of 1974, the Worker Adjustment and Retraining Notification Act of 1988, the Americans with Disabilities Act of 1990, the Civil Rights Act of 1991, and the Family and Medical Leave Act of 1993.

KEY TERMS

You should now be able to define and give an example relevant to each of the following terms:

human resources management (HRM) (243)
human resources planning (244)
replacement chart (244)
skills inventory (245)
cultural (workplace) diversity (246)

job analysis (247)
job description (247)
job specification (247)
recruiting (248)
external recruiting (249)
internal recruiting (249)
selection (249)
orientation (253)
compensation (254)

compensation system (254)
wage survey (254)
job evaluation (254)
comparable worth (255)
hourly wage (255)
salary (255)
commission (255)
incentive payment (255)

lump-sum salary increase (256)
profit-sharing (256)
employee benefit (256)
flexible benefit plan (257)
employee training (257)
management development (257)
performance appraisal (258)

DISCUSSION QUESTIONS

1. In general, on what basis is responsibility for HRM divided between line and staff managers?
2. How is a forecast of human resources demand related to a firm's organizational planning?
3. How do human resources managers go about matching a firm's supply of workers with its demand for workers?
4. What are the major challenges and benefits associated with a culturally diverse workforce?
5. What are the advantages and disadvantages of external recruiting? Of internal recruiting?
6. How is a job analysis used in the process of job evaluation?
7. Suppose that you have just opened a new Ford sales showroom and repair shop. Which of your employees would be paid wages, which would receive salaries, and which would receive commissions?
8. Why is it so important to provide feedback after a performance appraisal?
9. How accurately can managers plan for future human resources needs?
10. Are employee benefits really necessary? Why?
11. As a manager, what actions would you take if an operations employee with six years of experience on the job refused ongoing training and ignored performance feedback?
12. Why are there so many laws relating to HRM practices?
13. Which are the most important laws, in your opinion?

TEST YOURSELF

Matching Questions

1. _____ Jobs are studied to determine specific tasks.
2. _____ People are acquired, maintained, and developed for the firm.
3. _____ Personal qualifications required in a job are described.
4. _____ Potential applicants are made aware of available positions.
5. _____ The reward employees receive for their labor.
6. _____ The process for teaching employees to do their jobs more efficiently.
7. _____ An employee's work performance is evaluated.
8. _____ Gain sharing is an example.
9. _____ It seeks equal compensation for similar jobs.
10. _____ Employees may choose from a variety of benefit options.

a. comparable worth
b. compensation
c. employee training
d. flexible benefit plan
e. human resources management
f. incentive payment
g. wage survey
h. job analysis
i. job specification
j. performance appraisal
k. recruiting
l. profit sharing

True False Questions

11. **T F** Staffing, personnel management, and human resources management are synonymous terms.
12. **T F** Attrition is the process of acquiring information on applicants.
13. **T F** Recruiting is an activity of human resources acquisition.
14. **T F** The selection process matches the right candidate with each job.
15. **T F** The most widely used selection technique is the employment test.
16. **T F** In a structured interview, the interviewer uses a prepared set of questions.
17. **T F** Employee benefits such as vacation and sick leave are required by law.
18. **T F** Transfers involve moving employees into higher level positions.
19. **T F** The purpose of Title VII is to ensure that employers make personnel decisions on the basis of employee qualifications.
20. **T F** The Employee Retirement Income Security Act requires firms to provide a retirement plan for their employees.

Multiple-Choice Questions

21. _____ Human resources planning requires the following steps *except*
    a. using the firm's strategic plan.
    b. forecasting the firm's future demand.
    c. determining availability of human resources.
    d. acquiring funds for implementation.
    e. matching supply with demand.

22. _____ Which of the following is *least likely* to be the responsibility of a line manager?
    a. Developing a compensation system
    b. Implementing an orientation program
    c. Job analysis
    d. Recommending a promotion
    e. Hiring employees

23. _____ Melinda walked into First National Bank to pick up an application for an administrative assistant position. When she asked about the duties and working conditions, the busy receptionist handed her a job
    a. description.
    b. inventory.
    c. analysis.
    d. orientation.
    e. specification.

24. _____ Companies develop reputations as being favorable or unfavorable prospective employers for women and ethnic minorities. Based on this understanding or company reputation, what advantage do companies that have a good record for managing diversity have over others?
    a. Resource acquisition
    b. Flexibility
    c. Bilingual skills
    d. Cost saving
    e. Creativity

25. _____ Which of the following is the term used to describe a process of "recruiting minorities, training minorities to be managers, training managers to view diversity positively, and teaching English as a second language"?
    a. Problem solving
    b. Flexibility
    c. Resource acquisition
    d. Diversity training programs
    e. Acquiring bilingual skills

26. _____ A one-page summary of an applicant's qualifications is known as a(n)
    a. application form.
    b. data sheet.
    c. summary sheet.
    d. resume.
    e. qualification sheet.

27. _____ Which of the following is the best way to describe "employee-development training"?
    a. Attracting the best people to apply for positions
    b. Using satisfaction surveys and employee communication programs
    c. Recruiting experienced employees from other firms
    d. Providing rewards to ensure employee well-being
    e. Improving employees' skills and expanding their capabilities

28. _____ Which of the following is a good example of the "judgmental method" of evaluation?
    a. Each employee is rated on the degree to which the statement applies.
    b. The number of insurance claims processed is evaluated.
    c. The units of output per employee are calculated.
    d. An employee's dollar volume of sales per week is assessed.
    e. The number of defective products an employee produces, on average, is counted.

29. _____ Required retirement before age 70 was outlawed in the
    a. Age Discrimination in Employment Act.
    b. Equal Pay Act.
    c. Fair Labor Standards Act.
    d. Employee Retirement Income Security Act.
    e. Civil Rights Act.

30. _____ Larry was hurt while playing football in his senior year in high school. Since then, he has been confined to a wheelchair. After receiving his college diploma, he applied for a supervision job in a local warehouse. Under ADA, the employer must provide *reasonable accommodation* for disabled employees. Which activity will not legally cover Larry?
    a. Providing adequate home medical care
    b. Making existing facilities accessible
    c. Modifying work schedules
    d. Providing qualified readers
    e. Changing examinations

Answers to the Test Yourself questions appear at the end of the book on page TY-1.

Whirlpool's Award-Winning Diversity Program Is Facilitated Through Employee Network

In today's global marketplace, managers interact with people of different cultures, languages, beliefs, and values. Whirlpool Corporation has shown that a diverse workforce can be a powerful advantage.

Since its establishment in 1911, Whirlpool, headquartered in Michigan, has grown into a global corporation with manufacturing locations on every major continent and annual revenues in excess of $19 billion. Approximately 60 percent of Whirlpool's 70,000+ employees work outside North America. The development of this broad workforce is aided by the company's award-winning diversity program, which gathers workers into support groups based on personal affiliations. To enter the program, workers join a particular employee network of their choosing, such as the Hispanic network, the young professionals network, the Asian or African American networks, the women's network, the Native American network, or the Pride network, which includes gay, lesbian, bisexual, and transgender (GLBT) employees.

These networks give employees access to a world of new career resources and training opportunities. For instance, according to the company's Web site, "Our primary objective is to become the employer of choice for GLBT and affirming employees." Despite the program's obvious focus on employee well-being, leaders at Whirlpool say the networks also offer a competitive advantage in global marketing. "Having diverse people making decisions and giving input to the factors that we consider on a daily basis is extremely important to the business," according to the company's vice president of consumer and appliance care, Kathy Nelson. "It's important because we need to make sure that the people who are making business decisions are reflective of who our consumers are."

This belief is fully in keeping with the company's Diversity Mission Statement, expressed by Chairman and CEO Jeff Fettig: "We best serve the unique needs of our customers through diverse, inclusive, and engaged employees who truly reflect our global customer base."[12]

Questions

1. What are the three main objectives of Whirlpool's diversity networks?
2. What challenges do managers face in establishing a diverse workplace, and how might they respond to these challenges?
3. Do you think formation of Whirlpool's employee networks is the best way to promote a positive culture of diversity? Explain.

BUILDING SKILLS FOR CAREER SUCCESS

1. Exploring the Internet

Although you may believe that your formal learning will end when you graduate and enter the working world, it will not. Companies both large and small spend billions of dollars annually in training employees and updating their knowledge and skills. Besides supporting employees who attend accredited continuing-education programs, companies also may provide more specialized in-house course work on new technologies, products, and markets for strategic planning. The Internet is an excellent search tool to find out about course work offered by private training organizations, as well as by traditional academic institutions. Learning online is a fast-growing alternative, especially for busy employees requiring updates to skills in the information technology field, where software knowledge must be refreshed continuously. Visit the text Web site for updates to this exercise.

Assignment

1. Visit the Web sites of several academic institutions and examine their course work offerings. Also examine the offerings of some of the following private consulting firms:

   Learning Tree International: www.learningtree.com
   Accenture: www.accenture.com
   KPMG: www.kpmg.com
   Ernst & Young: www.ey.com/global

2. What professional continuing-education training and services are provided by any one of the academic institutions whose site you have visited?
3. What sort of training is offered by one of the preceding consulting firms?
4. From the company's point of view, what is the total real cost of a day's worth of employee training? What is the money value of one day of study for a full-time college

student? Can you explain why firms are willing to pay higher starting salaries for employees with higher levels of education?

5. The American Society for Training & Development (www .astd.org/) and the Society for Human Resource Management (www.shrm.org/) are two good sources of information about online training programs. Describe what you found out at these and other sites providing online learning solutions.

2. Building Team Skills

The New Therapy Company is soliciting a contract to provide five nursing homes with physical, occupational, speech, and respiratory therapy. The therapists will float among the five nursing homes. The therapists have not yet been hired, but the nursing homes expect them to be fully trained and ready to go to work in three months. The previous therapy company lost its contract because of high staff turnover owing to "burnout" (a common problem in this type of work), high costs, and low-quality care. The nursing homes want a plan specifying how the New Therapy Company will meet staffing needs, keep costs low, and provide high-quality care.

Assignment

1. Working in a group, discuss how the New Therapy Company can meet the three-month deadline and still ensure that the care its therapists provide is of high quality. Also discuss the following:

   a. How many of each type of therapist will the company need?

   b. How will it prevent therapists from "burning out"?

   c. How can it retain experienced staff and still limit costs?

   d. Are promotions available for any of the staff? What is the career ladder?

   e. How will the company manage therapists at five different locations? How will it keep in touch with them (computer, voice mail, or monthly meetings)? Would it make more sense to have therapists work permanently at each location rather than rotate among them?

   f. How will the company justify the travel costs? What other expenses might it expect?

2. Prepare a plan for the New Therapy Company to present to the nursing homes.

3. Researching Different Careers

A resume provides a summary of your skills, abilities, and achievements. It also may include a description of the type of job you want. A well-prepared resume indicates that you know what your career objectives are, shows that you have given serious thought to your career, and tells a potential employer what you are qualified to do. The way a resume is prepared can make a difference in whether you are considered for a job.

Assignment

1. Prepare a resume for a job that you want using the information in Appendix A (see text Web site).

   a. First, determine what your skills are and decide which skills are needed to do this particular job.

   b. Decide which type of format—chronological or functional—would be most effective in presenting your skills and experience.

   c. Keep the resume to one page, if possible (definitely no more than two pages). (Note that portfolio items may be attached for certain types of jobs, such as artwork.)

2. Have several people review the resume for accuracy.

3. Ask your instructor to comment on your resume.

CHAPTER 10 MOTIVATING AND SATISFYING EMPLOYEES AND TEAMS

Why should you care?

As you move up into management positions or operate your own business, you will need to understand what motivates others in an organization.

© StockLite/Shutterstock

Learning Objectives

What you will be able to do once you complete this chapter:

1 Explain what motivation is.

2 Understand some major historical perspectives on motivation.

3 Describe three contemporary views of motivation: equity theory, expectancy theory, and goal-setting theory.

4 Explain several techniques for increasing employee motivation.

5 Understand the types, development, and uses of teams.

Get Flashcards, Quizzes, Games, Crosswords, and more @ www.cengagebrain.com

How Google, Now Teenaged, Drives Employee Motivation

Can a well-established Silicon Valley company with $29 billion in annual revenue get its 24,500 employees worldwide to act like they work for a start-up? That's the thinking behind Google's recent moves to enhance employee motivation. Incorporated in 1998, and still on the fast track to growth, Google wants to instill a sense of urgency and encourage high performance inside what has become a teenaged company.

This is a critical time for Google. Despite more than a decade of success in Web-based search services and other offerings, the company faces fierce competition from Facebook, Microsoft, Yahoo!, Apple, and other high-tech rivals. Google has deep pockets—more than $35 billion in the bank—and has gone on a global recruitment spree to attract thousands of talented engineers, software experts, advertising salespeople, and others who can help Google expand its offerings and serve new customers.

Hiring is only the start, however; Google must also retain its experienced Googlers (employees), keep them satisfied, and renew their sense of excitement about the company's goals and opportunities. To reward loyalty and performance during a highly profitable year, Google gave the entire workforce a 10 percent raise and a $1,000 bonus at the end of 2010. That same year, two-thirds of Googlers took advantage of the firm's "peer spot bonus" program to award colleagues $175 in cash for special effort.

Googlers are expected to work hard but they also can take advantage of many on-site extras that make everyday life a little easier. These include free lunch and dinner, free any-time snacks, free laundry services, free workout and sports facilities, and other benefits. Google has built teamwork into its corporate culture and as a result, few Googlers occupy individual offices. Instead, employees get a sense of satisfaction from collaborating on cutting-edge projects.

The head of human resources explains that although Google may be a global giant, "it's still a company that wants to change the world." By empowering its employees, Google gives them a powerful motivation to use their skills and capabilities to make a difference—to the company and to the world.[1]

Did you know?

Although Google's annual revenues top $29 billion, it wants to motivate its 24,500 employees to think and act like they work for a scrappy start-up company.

To achieve its goals, any organization—whether it is Google, FedEx, or a local convenience store—must be sure that its employees have more than the right raw materials, adequate facilities, and equipment that works. The organization also must ensure that its employees are *motivated*. To some extent, a high level of employee motivation derives from effective management practices.

In this chapter, after first explaining what motivation is, we present several views of motivation that have influenced management practices over the years: Taylor's ideas of scientific management, Mayo's Hawthorne Studies, Maslow's hierarchy of needs, Herzberg's motivation–hygiene theory, McGregor's Theory X and Theory Y, Ouchi's Theory Z, and reinforcement theory. Then, turning our attention to contemporary ideas, we examine equity theory, expectancy theory, and goal-setting theory. Finally, we discuss specific techniques managers can use to foster employee motivation and satisfaction.

WHAT IS MOTIVATION?

A *motive* is something that causes a person to act. A successful athlete is said to be "highly motivated." A student who avoids work is said to be "unmotivated." We define **motivation** as the individual internal process that energizes, directs, and sustains behavior. It is the personal "force" that causes you or me to act in a particular way. For example, although job rotation may increase your job satisfaction and your enthusiasm for your work so that you devote more energy to it, job rotation may not have the same impact on me.

Morale is an employee's attitude or feelings about the job, about superiors, and about the firm itself. To achieve organizational goals effectively, employees need more than the right raw materials, adequate facilities, and efficient equipment. High morale results mainly from the satisfaction of needs on the job or as a result of the job. One need that might be satisfied on the job is the need *to be recognized* as an important contributor to the organization. A need satisfied as a result of the job is the need for *financial security*. High morale, in turn, leads to dedication and loyalty, as well as to the desire to do the job well. Low morale, however, can lead to shoddy work, absenteeism, and high turnover rates as employees leave to seek more satisfying jobs with other firms. A study conducted by the Society for Human Resource Management showed that 75 percent of all employees are actively or passively seeking new employment opportunities. To offset this turnover trend, companies are creating work environments focused on increasing employee satisfaction. One obvious indicator of satisfaction at a specific organization is whether employees like working there and whether other people want to work there. In the most recent *Fortune* magazine's "Top 100 Companies to Work For" list, the top ten best companies to work for were SAS, Boston Consulting Group, Wegmans Food Markets, Google, Net App, Zappos.com, Camden Property Trust, Nugget Market, Recreational Equipment (REI), and DreamWorks Animation SKG.[2]

Personal App What do you want to gain from your work? Besides money, are you working because you find satisfaction in gaining new skills or in helping customers? What else affects your morale?

Motivation, morale, and the satisfaction of employees' needs are thus intertwined. Along with productivity, they have been the subject of much study since the end of the 19th century. We continue our discussion of motivation by outlining some landmarks of the early research.

HISTORICAL PERSPECTIVES ON MOTIVATION

Researchers often begin a study with a fairly narrow goal in mind. After they develop an understanding of their subject, however, they realize that both their goal and their research should be broadened. This is exactly what happened when early research into productivity blossomed into the more modern study of employee motivation.

Scientific Management

Toward the end of the 19th century, Frederick W. Taylor became interested in improving the efficiency of individual workers. This interest, which stemmed from his own experiences in manufacturing plants, eventually led to **scientific management**, the application of scientific principles to management of work and workers.

One of Taylor's first jobs was with the Midvale Steel Company in Philadelphia, where he developed a strong distaste for waste and inefficiency. He also observed a practice he called "soldiering." Workers "soldiered," or worked slowly, because they feared that if they worked faster, they would run out of work and lose their jobs. Taylor realized that managers were not aware of this practice because they had no idea what the workers' productivity levels *should* be.

motivation the individual internal process that energizes, directs, and sustains behavior; the personal "force" that causes you or me to behave in a particular way

morale an employee's feelings about his or her job and superiors and about the firm itself

scientific management the application of scientific principles to management of work and workers

Taylor later left Midvale and spent several years at Bethlehem Steel. While there, he made his most significant contribution to the field of motivation. He suggested that each job should be broken down into separate tasks. Then management should determine (1) the best way to perform each task and (2) the job output to expect when employees performed the tasks properly. Next, management should carefully choose the best person for each job and train that person in how to do the job properly. Finally, management should cooperate with workers to ensure that jobs were performed as planned.

Taylor also developed the idea that most people work only to earn money. He therefore reasoned that pay should be tied directly to output. The more a person produced, the more he or she should be paid. This gave rise to the **piece-rate system**, under which employees are paid a certain amount for each unit of output they produce. Under Taylor's piece-rate system, each employee was assigned an output quota. Those exceeding the quota were paid a higher per-unit rate for all units they produced (see Figure 10-1). Today, the piece-rate system is still used by some manufacturers and by farmers who grow crops that are harvested by farm laborers.

When Taylor's system was put into practice at Bethlehem Steel, the results were dramatic. Average earnings per day for steel handlers rose from $1.15 to $1.88. (Do not let the low wages that prevailed at the time obscure the fact that this was an increase of better than 60 percent!) The average amount of steel handled per day increased from 16 to 57 tons.

Taylor's revolutionary ideas had a profound impact on management practice. However, his view of motivation was soon recognized as overly simplistic and narrow. It is true that most people expect to be paid for their work, but it is also true that people work for a variety of reasons other than pay. Therefore, simply increasing a person's pay may not increase that person's motivation or productivity.

Employee satisfaction. Is anyone happy? A century ago employee satisfaction was not a major concern in many businesses. Today, employee satisfaction is a major consideration in a number of business organizations. Why do you think attitudes about employee motivation and satisfaction have changed?

© Getty

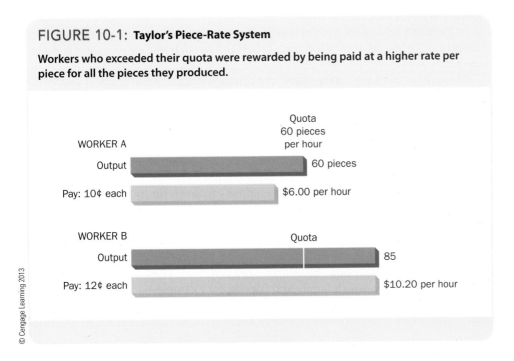

FIGURE 10-1: **Taylor's Piece-Rate System**

Workers who exceeded their quota were rewarded by being paid at a higher rate per piece for all the pieces they produced.

WORKER A

Quota 60 pieces per hour

Output — 60 pieces

Pay: 10¢ each — $6.00 per hour

WORKER B

Quota

Output — 85

Pay: 12¢ each — $10.20 per hour

© Cengage Learning 2013

piece-rate system a compensation system under which employees are paid a certain amount for each unit of output they produce

The Hawthorne Studies

Between 1927 and 1932, Elton Mayo conducted two experiments at the Hawthorne plant of the Western Electric Company in Chicago. The original objective of these studies, now referred to as the *Hawthorne Studies*, was to determine the effects of the work environment on employee productivity.

In the first set of experiments, lighting in the workplace was varied for one group of workers but not for a second group. Then the productivities of both groups were measured to determine the effect of light. To the amazement of the researchers, productivity increased for both groups. For the group whose lighting was varied, productivity remained high until the light was reduced to the level of moonlight!

The second set of experiments focused on the effectiveness of the piece-rate system in increasing the output of groups of workers. Researchers expected that output would increase because faster workers would put pressure on slower workers to produce more. Again, the results were not as expected. Output remained constant no matter what "standard" rates management set.

The researchers came to the conclusion that *human factors* were responsible for the results of the two experiments. In the lighting experiments, researchers had given both groups of workers a *sense of involvement* in their jobs merely by asking them to participate in the research. These workers—perhaps for the first time—felt as though they were an important part of the organization. In the piece-rate experiments, each group of workers informally set the acceptable rate of output for the group. To gain or retain the *social acceptance* of the group, each worker had to produce at that rate. Slower or faster workers were pressured to maintain the group's pace.

The Hawthorne Studies showed that such human factors are at least as important to motivation as pay rates. From these and other studies, the *human relations movement* in management was born. Its premise was simple: Employees who are happy and satisfied with their work are motivated to perform better. Hence, management is best served by providing a work environment that maximizes employee satisfaction.

Maslow's Hierarchy of Needs

Abraham Maslow, an American psychologist whose best-known works were published in the 1960s and 1970s, developed a theory of motivation based on a hierarchy of needs. A **need** is a personal requirement. Maslow assumed that humans are "wanting" beings who seek to fulfill a variety of needs. He observed that these needs can be arranged according to their importance in a sequence now known as **Maslow's hierarchy of needs** (see Figure 10-2).

At the most basic level are **physiological needs**, the things we require to survive. They include food and water, clothing, shelter, and sleep. In the employment context, these needs usually are satisfied through adequate wages.

At the next level are **safety needs**, the things we require for physical and emotional security. Safety needs may be satisfied through job security, health insurance, pension plans, and safe working conditions. Many companies are facing increasing insurance premiums for employee health care. Both GE and Hershey recently endured strikes centered on the issue of increased health care costs. Reduced health care coverage is a threat to employees' need for safety. Some companies are trying to find unique solutions to the health care question. For example, SAS, a software company recently ranked as the number one company to work for by *Fortune*, covers 90 percent of its employees' health care premiums and maintains its own medical center that provides several services at no cost to employees.[3]

Next are the **social needs**, the human requirements for love and affection and a sense of belonging. To an extent, these needs can be satisfied through relationships in the work environment and the informal organization. However, social networks beyond the workplace—with family and friends, for example—are needed, too. Restaurant chain Texas Roadhouse uses fun corporate retreats to help employees meet their social needs. The company regularly holds retreats that are fun and exciting.

need a personal requirement

Maslow's hierarchy of needs a sequence of human needs in the order of their importance

physiological needs the things we require for survival

safety needs the things we require for physical and emotional security

social needs the human requirements for love and affection and a sense of belonging

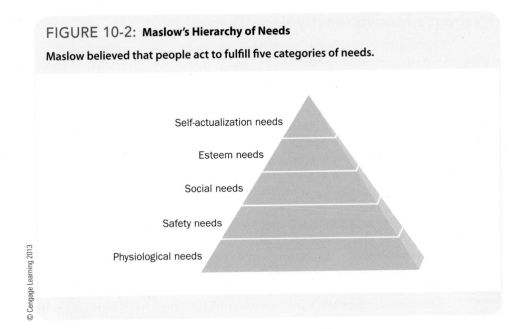

FIGURE 10-2: Maslow's Hierarchy of Needs

Maslow believed that people act to fulfill five categories of needs.

Self-actualization needs

Esteem needs

Social needs

Safety needs

Physiological needs

© Cengage Learning 2013

During the company's most recent retreat, several of their top-performing employees went to New York, where they watched a meat-cutting contest at Rockefeller Plaza and spent a day at Ellis Island. Although the recession caused many companies to cancel retreats in order to save money, Texas Roadhouse CEO G. J. Hart believes the company retreats are beneficial because motivating and caring for employees results in much happier restaurant guests. This mentality seems to be working, as evidenced by the chain opening 20 new restaurants during the recession and employee turnover rates dropping by 80 percent in the past ten years.[4]

At the level of **esteem needs**, we require respect and recognition from others and a sense of our own accomplishment and worth (self-esteem). These needs may be satisfied through personal accomplishment, promotion to more responsible jobs, various honors and awards, and other forms of recognition.

At the top of the hierarchy are the **self-actualization needs**, the need to grow, develop, and become all that we are capable of being. These are the most difficult needs to satisfy, and the means of satisfying them tend to vary with the individual. For some people, learning a new skill, starting a new career after retirement, or becoming "the best there is" at some endeavor may be the way to realize self-actualization.

Personal App Every time you take a step toward your personal or professional goals, you move a little closer to being the best that you can be. Celebrate your achievements, but remember that self-actualization is a journey, not a destination.

Maslow suggested that people work to satisfy their physiological needs first, then their safety needs, and so on up the "needs ladder." In general, they are motivated by the needs at the lowest level that remain unsatisfied. However, needs at one level do not have to be satisfied completely before needs at the next higher level come into play. If the majority of a person's physiological and safety needs are satisfied, that person will be motivated primarily by social needs. However, any physiological and safety needs that remain unsatisfied also will be important.

Maslow's hierarchy of needs provides a useful way of viewing employee motivation, as well as a guide for management. By and large, American business has been able to satisfy workers' basic needs, but the higher-order needs present more of a challenge. These needs are not satisfied in a simple manner, and the means of satisfaction vary from one employee to another.

esteem needs our need for respect, recognition, and a sense of our own accomplishment and worth

self-actualization needs the need to grow and develop and to become all that we are capable of being

Herzberg's Motivation–Hygiene Theory

In the late 1950s, Frederick Herzberg interviewed approximately 200 accountants and engineers in Pittsburgh. During the interviews, he asked them to think of a time when they had felt especially good about their jobs and their work. Then he asked them to describe the factor or factors that had caused them to feel that way. Next, he did the same regarding a time when they had felt especially bad about their work. He was surprised to find that feeling good and feeling bad resulted from entirely different sets of factors; that is, low pay may have made a particular person feel bad, but it was some factor other than high pay that made that person feel good.

SATISFACTION AND DISSATISFACTION Before Herzberg's interviews, the general assumption was that employee satisfaction and dissatisfaction lay at opposite ends of the same scale. People felt satisfied, dissatisfied, or somewhere in between. However, Herzberg's interviews convinced him that satisfaction and dissatisfaction may be different dimensions altogether. One dimension might range from satisfaction to no satisfaction, and the other might range from dissatisfaction to no dissatisfaction. In other words, the opposite of satisfaction is not dissatisfaction. The idea that satisfaction and dissatisfaction are separate and distinct dimensions is referred to as the **motivation–hygiene theory** (see Figure 10-3).

The job factors that Herzberg found most frequently associated with satisfaction were achievement, recognition, responsibility, advancement, growth, and the work itself. These factors generally are referred to as **motivation factors** because their presence increases motivation. However, their absence does not necessarily result in feelings of dissatisfaction. When motivation factors are present, they act as *satisfiers*.

Job factors cited as causing dissatisfaction were supervision, working conditions, interpersonal relationships, pay, job security, company policies, and administration. These factors, called **hygiene factors**, reduce dissatisfaction when they are present to an acceptable degree. However, they do not necessarily result in high levels of motivation. When hygiene factors are absent, they act as *dissatisfiers*.

motivation–hygiene theory the idea that satisfaction and dissatisfaction are separate and distinct dimensions

motivation factors job factors that increase motivation, although their absence does not necessarily result in dissatisfaction

hygiene factors job factors that reduce dissatisfaction when present to an acceptable degree but that do not necessarily result in high levels of motivation

FIGURE 10-3: Herzberg's Motivation–Hygiene Theory

Herzberg's theory takes into account that there are different dimensions to job satisfaction and dissatisfaction and that these factors do not overlap.

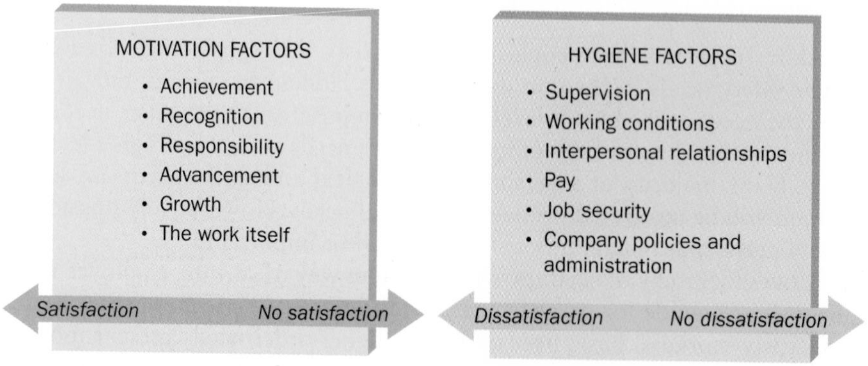

MOTIVATION FACTORS	HYGIENE FACTORS
• Achievement	• Supervision
• Recognition	• Working conditions
• Responsibility	• Interpersonal relationships
• Advancement	• Pay
• Growth	• Job security
• The work itself	• Company policies and administration
Satisfaction ← → No satisfaction	Dissatisfaction ← → No dissatisfaction

© Cengage Learning 2013

USING HERZBERG'S MOTIVATION–HYGIENE THEORY Herzberg provides explicit guidelines for using the motivation–hygiene theory of employee motivation. He suggests that the hygiene factors must be present to ensure that a worker can function comfortably. He warns, however, that a state of *no dissatisfaction* never exists. In any situation, people always will be dissatisfied with something.

According to Herzberg, managers should make hygiene as positive as possible, but then should expect only short-term, rather than long-term, improvement in motivation. Managers must focus instead on providing those motivation factors that presumably will enhance motivation and long-term effort.

We should note that employee pay has more effect than Herzberg's theory indicates. He suggests that pay provides only short-term change and not true motivation. Yet, in many organizations, pay constitutes a form of recognition and reward for achievement—and recognition and achievement are both motivation factors. The effect of pay may depend on how it is distributed. If a pay increase does not depend on performance (as in across-the-board or cost-of-living raises), it may not motivate people. However, if pay is increased as a form of recognition (as in bonuses or incentives), it may play a powerful role in motivating employees to higher performance.

Motivation–hygiene theory. Companies sometimes use travel awards as incentives for better employee performance. According to the motivation–hygiene theory, when an incentive for higher performance is not provided, is that a dissatisfier?

© Arvind Balaraman/Shutterstock

Theory X and Theory Y

The concepts of Theory X and Theory Y were advanced by Douglas McGregor in his book *The Human Side of Enterprise*. They are, in essence, sets of assumptions that underlie management's attitudes and beliefs regarding workers' behavior.[5]

Theory X is a concept of employee motivation generally consistent with Taylor's scientific management. Theory X assumes that employees dislike work and will function effectively only in a highly controlled work environment.

Theory X is based on the following assumptions:

1. People dislike work and try to avoid it.
2. Because people dislike work, managers must coerce, control, and frequently threaten employees to achieve organizational goals.
3. People generally must be led because they have little ambition and will not seek responsibility; they are concerned mainly about security.

The logical outcome of such assumptions will be a highly controlled work environment—one in which managers make all the decisions and employees take all the orders.

On the other hand, **Theory Y** is a concept of employee motivation generally consistent with the ideas of the human relations movement. Theory Y assumes that employees accept responsibility and work toward organizational goals, and by doing so they also achieve personal rewards. Theory Y is based on the following assumptions:

1. People do not naturally dislike work; in fact, work is an important part of their lives.
2. People will work toward goals to which they are committed.
3. People become committed to goals when it is clear that accomplishing the goals will bring personal rewards.
4. People often seek out and willingly accept responsibility.
5. Employees have the potential to help accomplish organizational goals.
6. Organizations generally do not make full use of their human resources.

Theory X a concept of employee motivation generally consistent with Taylor's scientific management; assumes that employees dislike work and will function only in a highly controlled work environment

Theory Y a concept of employee motivation generally consistent with the ideas of the human relations movement; assumes that employees accept responsibility and work toward organizational goals, and by doing so they also achieve personal rewards

TABLE 10-1: Theory X and Theory Y Contrasted

Area	Theory X	Theory Y
Attitude toward work	Dislike	Involvement
Control systems	External	Internal
Supervision	Direct	Indirect
Level of commitment	Low	High
Employee potential	Ignored	Identified
Use of human resources	Limited	Not limited

Obviously, this view is quite different from—and much more positive than—that of Theory X. McGregor argued that most managers behave in accordance with Theory X, but he maintained that Theory Y is more appropriate and effective as a guide for managerial action (see Table 10-1).

The human relations movement and Theories X and Y increased managers' awareness of the importance of social factors in the workplace. However, human motivation is a complex and dynamic process to which there is no simple key. Neither money nor social factors alone can provide the answer. Rather, a number of factors must be considered in any attempt to increase motivation.

Theory Z

William Ouchi, a management professor at UCLA, studied business practices in American and Japanese firms. He concluded that different types of management systems dominate in these two countries.[6] In Japan, Ouchi found what he calls *type J* firms. They are characterized by lifetime employment for employees, collective (or group) decision making, collective responsibility for the outcomes of decisions, slow evaluation and promotion, implied control mechanisms, nonspecialized career paths, and a holistic concern for employees as people.

American industry is dominated by what Ouchi calls *type A* firms, which follow a different pattern. They emphasize short-term employment, individual decision making, individual responsibility for the outcomes of decisions, rapid evaluation and promotion, explicit control mechanisms, specialized career paths, and a segmented concern for employees only as employees.

A few very successful American firms represent a blend of the type J and type A patterns. These firms, called *type Z* organizations, emphasize long-term employment, collective decision making, individual responsibility for the outcomes of decisions, slow evaluation and promotion, informal control along with some formalized measures, moderately specialized career paths, and a holistic concern for employees.

Ouchi's **Theory Z** is the belief that some middle ground between his type A and type J practices is best for American business (see Figure 10-4). A major part of Theory Z is the emphasis on participative decision making. The focus is on "we" rather than on "us versus them." Theory Z employees and managers view the organization as a family. This participative spirit fosters cooperation and the dissemination of information and organizational values.

Theory Z the belief that some middle ground between type A and type J practices is best for American business

reinforcement theory a theory of motivation based on the premise that rewarded behavior is likely to be repeated, whereas punished behavior is less likely to recur

Reinforcement Theory

Reinforcement theory is based on the premise that behavior that is rewarded is likely to be repeated, whereas behavior that is punished is less likely to recur. A *reinforcement* is an action that follows directly from a particular behavior. It may be a pay raise after a particularly large sale to a new customer or a reprimand for coming to work late.

FIGURE 10-4: The Features of Theory Z

The best aspects of Japanese and American management theories combine to form the nucleus of Theory Z.

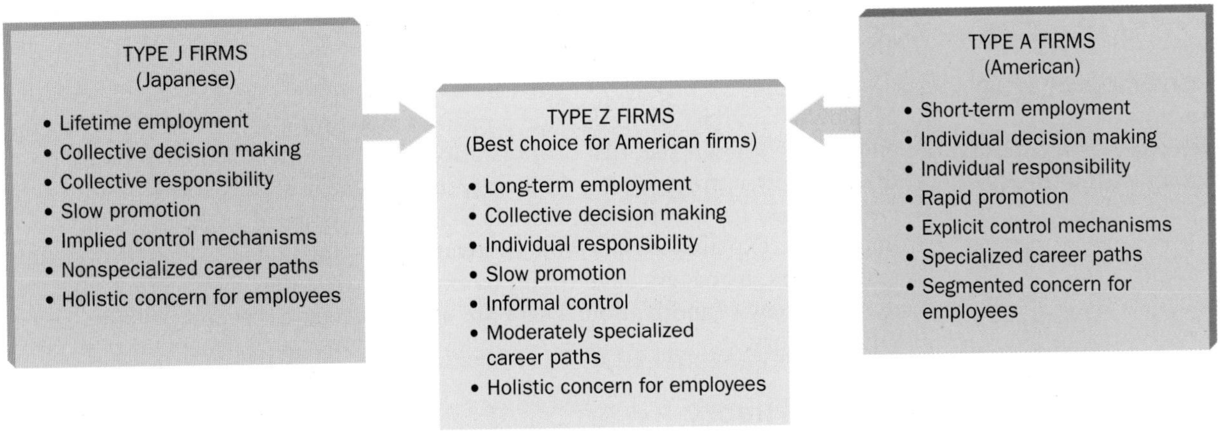

TYPE J FIRMS
(Japanese)

- Lifetime employment
- Collective decision making
- Collective responsibility
- Slow promotion
- Implied control mechanisms
- Nonspecialized career paths
- Holistic concern for employees

TYPE Z FIRMS
(Best choice for American firms)

- Long-term employment
- Collective decision making
- Individual responsibility
- Slow promotion
- Informal control
- Moderately specialized career paths
- Holistic concern for employees

TYPE A FIRMS
(American)

- Short-term employment
- Individual decision making
- Individual responsibility
- Rapid promotion
- Explicit control mechanisms
- Specialized career paths
- Segmented concern for employees

© Cengage Learning 2013

Reinforcements can take a variety of forms and can be used in a number of ways. A *positive reinforcement* is one that strengthens desired behavior by providing a reward. For example, many employees respond well to praise; recognition from their supervisors for a job done well increases (strengthens) their willingness to perform well in the future. A *negative reinforcement* strengthens desired behavior by eliminating an undesirable task or situation. Suppose that a machine shop must be cleaned thoroughly every month—a dirty, miserable task. During one particular month when the workers do a less-than-satisfactory job at their normal work assignments, the boss requires the workers to clean the factory rather than bringing in the usual private maintenance service. The employees will be motivated to work harder the next month to avoid the unpleasant cleanup duty again.

Personal App You'll see reinforcement theory at work in many situations. When a sports team receives recognition for winning a championship game, that's positive reinforcement. When a student receives a low mark for a paper and must redo it, that's negative reinforcement.

Punishment is an undesired consequence of undesirable behavior. Common forms of punishment used in organizations include reprimands, reduced pay, disciplinary layoffs, and termination (firing). Punishment often does more harm than good. It tends to create an unpleasant environment, fosters hostility and resentment, and suppresses undesirable behavior only until the supervisor's back is turned.

Managers who rely on *extinction* hope to eliminate undesirable behavior by not responding to it. The idea is that the behavior eventually will become "extinct." Suppose, for example, that an employee writes memo after memo to his or her manager about insignificant events. If the manager does not respond to any of these memos, the employee probably will stop writing them, and the behavior will be squelched.

The effectiveness of reinforcement depends on which type is used and how it is timed. One approach may work best under certain conditions, although some situations lend themselves to the use of more than one approach. Generally, positive reinforcement is considered the most effective, and it is recommended when the manager has a choice.

Continual reinforcement can become tedious for both managers and employees, especially when the same behavior is being reinforced over and over again in the

Concept Check ✱

☐ What are the major elements of Taylor's "scientific management"?

☐ What were Elton Mayo's conclusions from the Hawthorne Studies?

☐ What are the different levels in Maslow's hierarchy of needs?

☐ What are the major elements of Herzberg's motivation–hygiene theory?

☐ What are the underlying assumptions of Theory X and Theory Y?

same way. At the start, it may be necessary to reinforce a desired behavior every time it occurs. However, once a desired behavior has become more or less established, occasional reinforcement seems to be most effective.

CONTEMPORARY VIEWS ON MOTIVATION

LEARNING OBJECTIVE
3 Describe three contemporary views of motivation: equity theory, expectancy theory, and goal-setting theory.

Maslow's hierarchy of needs and Herzberg's motivation–hygiene theory are popular and widely known theories of motivation. Each is also a significant step up from the relatively narrow views of scientific management and Theories X and Y. However, they do have one weakness: Each attempts to specify *what* motivates people, but neither explains *why* or *how* motivation develops or is sustained over time. In recent years, managers have begun to explore three other models that take a more dynamic view of motivation. These are equity theory, expectancy theory, and goal-setting theory.

Equity Theory

The **equity theory** of motivation is based on the premise that people are motivated to obtain and preserve equitable treatment for themselves. As used here, *equity* is the distribution of rewards in direct proportion to each employee's contribution to the organization. Everyone need not receive the same rewards, but the rewards should be in accordance with individual contributions.

According to this theory, we tend to implement the idea of equity in the following way: First, we develop our own input-to-outcome ratio. *Inputs* are the time, effort, skills, education, experience, and so on, that we contribute to the organization. *Outcomes* are the rewards we get from the organization, such as pay, benefits, recognition, and promotions. Next, we compare this ratio with what we perceive as the input-to-outcome ratio for some other person. It might be a co-worker, a friend who works for another firm, or even an average of all the people in our organization. This person is called the *comparison other*. Note that our perception of this person's input-to-outcome ratio may be absolutely correct or completely wrong. However, we believe that it is correct.

If the two ratios are roughly the same, we feel that the organization is treating us equitably. In this case, we are motivated to leave things as they are. However, if our ratio is the higher of the two, we feel underrewarded and are motivated to make changes. We may (1) decrease our own inputs by not working so hard, (2) try to increase our total outcome by asking for a raise in pay, (3) try to get the comparison other to increase some inputs or receive decreased outcomes, (4) leave the work situation, or (5) do a new comparison with a different comparison other.

Equity theory is most relevant to pay as an outcome. Because pay is a very real measure of a person's worth to an organization, comparisons involving pay are a natural part of organizational life. Managers can try to avoid problems arising from inequity by making sure that rewards are distributed on the basis of performance and that everyone clearly understands the basis for his or her own pay.

Expectancy Theory

Expectancy theory, developed by Victor Vroom, is a very complex model of motivation based on a deceptively simple assumption. According to expectancy theory, motivation depends on how much we want something and on how likely we think we are to get it (see Figure 10-5). Consider, for example, the case of three sales representatives who are candidates for promotion to one sales manager's job.

equity theory a theory of motivation based on the premise that people are motivated to obtain and preserve equitable treatment for themselves

expectancy theory a model of motivation based on the assumption that motivation depends on how much we want something and on how likely we think we are to get it

© James Steidl/Shutterstock

FIGURE 10-5: Expectancy Theory

Vroom's theory is based on the idea that motivation depends on how much people want something and on how likely they think they are to get it.

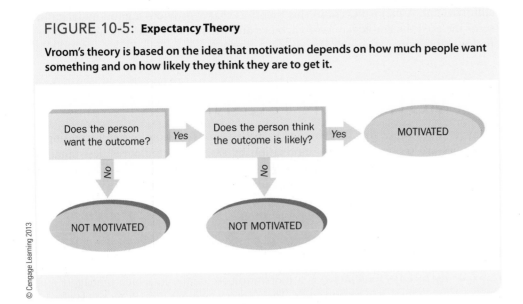

© Cengage Learning 2013

Bill has had a very good sales year and always gets good performance evaluations. However, he is not sure that he wants the job because it involves a great deal of travel, long working hours, and much stress and pressure. Paul wants the job badly but does not think he has much chance of getting it. He has had a terrible sales year and gets only mediocre performance evaluations from his present boss. Susan wants the job as much as Paul, and she thinks that she has a pretty good shot at it. Her sales have improved significantly this past year, and her evaluations are the best in the company.

Expectancy theory would predict that Bill and Paul are not very motivated to seek the promotion. Bill does not really want it, and Paul does not think that he has much of a chance of getting it. Susan, however, is very motivated to seek the promotion because she wants it and thinks that she can get it.

Expectancy theory is complex because each action we take is likely to lead to several different outcomes; some we may want, and others we may not want. For example, a person who works hard and puts in many extra hours may get a pay raise, be promoted, and gain valuable new job skills. However, that person also may be forced to spend less time with his or her family and be forced to cut back on his or her social life.

For one person, the promotion may be paramount, the pay raise and new skills fairly important, and the loss of family and social life of negligible importance. For someone else, the family and social life may be most important, the pay raise of moderate importance, the new skills unimportant, and the promotion undesirable because of the additional hours it would require. The first person would be motivated to work hard and put in the extra hours, whereas the second person would not be motivated at all to do so. In other words, it is the entire bundle of outcomes—and the individual's evaluation of the importance of each outcome—that determines motivation.

Expectancy theory is difficult to apply, but it does provide several useful guidelines for managers. It suggests that managers must recognize that (1) employees work for a variety of reasons; (2) these reasons, or expected outcomes, may change over time; and (3) it is necessary to clearly show employees how they can attain the outcomes they desire.

Goal-Setting Theory

Goal-setting theory suggests that employees are motivated to achieve goals that they and their managers establish together. The goal should be very specific, moderately difficult, and one the employee will be committed to achieve.[7] Rewards should be tied directly to goal achievement. Using goal-setting theory, a manager can design rewards that fit employee needs, clarify expectations, maintain equity, and provide

goal-setting theory a theory of motivation suggesting that employees are motivated to achieve goals that they and their managers establish together

Concept Check

☐ What is equity theory?

☐ How do managers use it in order to decide the pay structure of employees?

☐ What is expectancy theory and how is it different from goal-setting theory?

LEARNING OBJECTIVE

4 Explain several techniques for increasing employee motivation.

management by objectives (MBO) a motivation technique in which managers and employees collaborate in setting goals

Motivation through Profit-Sharing. At Free Wave Technologies in Boulder, Colorado, employees are rewarded through a profit-sharing plan based on individual performance.

reinforcement. A major benefit of this theory is that it provides a good understanding of the goal the employee has to achieve and the rewards that will accrue to the employee if the goal is accomplished.

KEY MOTIVATION TECHNIQUES

Today, it takes more than a generous salary to motivate employees. Increasingly, companies are trying to provide motivation by satisfying employees' less-tangible needs. At times, businesses use simple, low- or no-cost approaches such as those listed in Table 10-2 to motivate workers. Organizations also use more complex approaches. In this section, we discuss several specific techniques that help managers to boost employee motivation and job satisfaction.

Management by Objectives

Management by objectives (MBO) is a motivation technique in which managers and employees collaborate in setting goals. The primary purpose of MBO is to clarify the roles employees are expected to play in reaching the organization's goals.

By allowing individuals to participate in goal setting and performance evaluation, MBO increases their motivation. Most MBO programs consist of a series of five steps. The first step in setting up an MBO program is to secure the acceptance of top management. It is essential that top managers endorse and participate in the program if others in the firm are to accept it. The commitment of top management also provides a natural starting point for educating employees about the purposes and mechanics of MBO.

Next, preliminary goals must be established. Top management also plays a major role in this activity because the preliminary goals reflect the firm's mission and strategy. The intent of an MBO program is to have these goals filter down through the organization.

The third step, which actually consists of several smaller steps, is the heart of MBO:

1. The manager explains to each employee that he or she has accepted certain goals for the group (the manager as well as the employees) and asks the individual to think about how he or she can help to achieve these goals.
2. The manager later meets with each employee individually. Together they establish goals for the employee. Whenever possible, the goals should be measurable and should specify the time frame for completion (usually one year).
3. The manager and the employee decide what resources the employee will need to accomplish his or her goals.

As the fourth step, the manager and each employee meet periodically to review the employee's progress. They may agree to modify certain goals during these meetings if circumstances have changed. For example, a sales representative may have accepted a goal of increasing sales by 20 percent. However, an aggressive competitor may have entered the marketplace, making this goal unattainable. In light of this circumstance, the goal may be revised downward to 10 or 15 percent.

The fifth step in the MBO process is evaluation. At the end of the designated time period, the manager and each employee meet again to determine which of the individual's goals were met and which were not met, and why. The employee's reward (in

© AP Photo/David Zalubowski

TABLE 10-2: No-Cost/Low-Cost Motivation Techniques

1. Acknowledge and celebrate birthdays and other important events.

2. Allow an employee to choose his/her next assignment.

3. Call an employee to your office to thank him or her (do not discuss any other issue).

4. In the department newsletter, publish a "kudos" column and ask for nominations throughout the department.

5. Nominate the employee for a formal award program.

6. Plan a surprise achievement celebration for an employee or group of employees.

7. Pop in at the first meeting of a special project team and express your appreciation for their involvement.

8. Send a letter to all team members at the conclusion of a project, thanking them for their participation.

9. When you hear a positive remark about someone, repeat it to that person as soon as possible in person or electronically.

10. Widely publicize suggestions used and their positive impact on your department.

11. Support flexible work schedules.

12. Ask the employee to be a mentor to a new hire.

13. Put up a bulletin board in your department and post letters of thanks from customers.

14. Take the opportunity to learn what your people are working on and recognize their efforts.

15. Interview your people and capture their wisdom. Compile the quotes and stories in a booklet and hand it out to employees.

16. Send a letter of praise to the employee's spouse/family.

17. Honor employee subgroups in your department with their own day or week (e.g., Administrative Staff Week, Custodian Week) and present them with flowers, candy, breakfast, and so on.

18. Recognize highly skilled employees with increased responsibility that will develop new skills that may be helpful for advancement.

19. Pass around an office trophy to the employee of the week or other traveling awards.

20. Volunteer to do an employee's least favorite task.

21. Wash the employee's car.

22. Give the person tickets to a ball game, golf lessons, movie tickets, a book by his or her favorite author, "Lunch on me" coupons, and so on.

23. Reserve the best parking spot for employees who have done something truly worthwhile.

24. Send a handwritten note or praise about a specific action, not "thanks for all you do."

25. Create a yearbook for your team with pictures and stories of accomplishments during the year.

26. Copy senior management on your thank-you note to the employee, to advise them of an employee's efforts/accomplishments.

27. Introduce employees to key suppliers, customers, or someone in senior management.

28. Reward ideas even if they fail.

29. Set aside a public space inside your firm as a "wall of fame" and place photos of employees who have accomplished something truly special along with the details of what they did to earn that space.

30. Say, "Thank you."

Sources: Texas A&M University Human Resources Department, http://employees.tamu.edu/docs/employment/classComp/614recognitionIdeas.pdf; HRWorld, www.hrworld.com/features/25-employee-rewards/; Michigan Office of Great Workplace Development, www.michigan.gov/documents/firstgentleman/50_242400_7.pdf.

the form of a pay raise, praise, or promotion) is based primarily on the degree of goal attainment.

As with every other management method, MBO has advantages and disadvantages. MBO can motivate employees by involving them actively in the life of the firm. The collaboration on goal setting and performance appraisal improves communication and makes employees feel that they are an important part of the organization. Periodic review of progress also enhances control within an organization. A major problem with MBO is that it does not work unless the process begins at the top of an organization. In some cases, MBO results in excessive paperwork. Also, a manager

Job enrichment. Volvo was one of the first automobile companies to deviate from the traditional assembly line system and adopt a more employee-centric approach for manufacturing automobiles.

© Casper Hedberg/Bloomberg via Getty Images

may not like sitting down and working out goals with subordinates and may instead just assign them goals. Finally, MBO programs prove difficult to implement unless goals are quantifiable.

Job Enrichment

Job enrichment is a method of motivating employees by providing them with variety in their tasks while giving them some responsibility for, and control over, their jobs. At the same time, employees gain new skills and acquire a broader perspective about how their individual work contributes to the goals of the organization. Earlier in this chapter, we noted that Herzberg's motivation–hygiene theory is one rationale for the use of job enrichment; that is, the added responsibility and control that job enrichment confers on employees increases their satisfaction and motivation. For example, engineers at Google get to spend 20 percent of their time at work on projects of their choosing.[8] This type of enrichment can motivate employees and create a variety of benefits for the company. At times, **job enlargement**, expanding a worker's assignments to include additional but similar tasks, can lead to job enrichment. Job enlargement might mean that a worker on an assembly line who used to connect three wires to components moving down the line now connects five wires. Unfortunately, the added tasks often are just as routine as those the worker performed before the change. In such cases, enlargement may not be effective.

Whereas job enlargement does not really change the routine and monotonous nature of jobs, job enrichment does. Job enrichment requires that added tasks give an employee more responsibility for what he or she does. It provides workers with both more tasks to do and more control over how they perform them. In particular, job enrichment removes many controls from jobs, gives workers more authority, and assigns work in complete, natural units. Moreover, employees frequently are given fresh and challenging job assignments. By blending more planning and decision making into jobs, job enrichment gives work more depth and complexity.

Job redesign is a type of job enrichment in which work is restructured in ways that cultivate the worker–job match. Job redesign can be achieved by combining tasks, forming work groups, or establishing closer customer relationships. Employees often are more motivated when jobs are combined because the increased variety of tasks presents more challenge and therefore more reward. Work groups motivate employees by showing them how their jobs fit within the organization as a whole and how they contribute to its success. Establishing client relationships allows employees to interact directly with customers. This type of redesign not only adds a personal dimension to employment but also provides workers with immediate and relevant feedback about how they are doing their jobs.

Job enrichment works best when employees seek more challenging work. Of course, not all workers respond positively to job-enrichment programs. Employees must desire personal growth and have the skills and knowledge to perform enriched jobs. Lack of self-confidence, fear of failure, and distrust of management's intentions are likely to lead to ineffective performance on enriched jobs. In addition, some workers do not view their jobs as routine and boring, and others even prefer routine jobs because they find them satisfying. Companies that use job enrichment as an alternative to specialization also face extra expenses, such as the cost of retraining. Another motivation for job redesign is to reduce employees' stress at work. A job redesign that carefully matches worker to job can prevent stress-related injuries, which constitute about 60 to 80 percent of all work-related injuries.

job enrichment a motivation technique that provides employees with more variety and responsibility in their jobs

job enlargement expanding a worker's assignments to include additional but similar tasks

job redesign a type of job enrichment in which work is restructured to cultivate the worker–job match

entrepreneurial SUCCESS

Motivation Gives Bonobos a Competitive Edge

Although Andy Dunn and Brian Spaly named their Web-based business Bonobos, they don't monkey around when it comes to employee motivation. Bonobos, co-founded by roommates at Stanford Business School, is a fast-growing young company that manufactures and sells men's clothing. The entrepreneurs' continued success depends on the ability of their employees to make the most of every opportunity, solve problems quickly, and turn first-time buyers into loyal repeat customers through outstanding service.

The co-founders have motivation on their minds from the moment they sit down to design a new job or enrich an existing job. Their goal, says Dunn, is to create "an environment where people can come alive every day" and be empowered to deliver

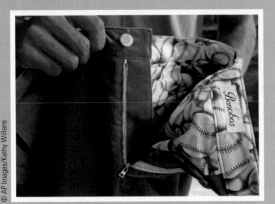

© AP Images/Kathy Willens

the best possible service. The first step is to seek out highly qualified candidates who possess skills and expertise that complement the company's strengths. Dunn begins job interviews with one simple statement: "I am not good at what you do, and I need your help."

Because the high-energy culture encourages delegation at all organizational levels, Bonobos prepares new hires with training and on-the-job coaching so they can make informed decisions on their own. Employees are motivated by being respected by their managers and peers, challenged to do their best, and delegated responsibility for meeting their objectives. Only with such empowerment can Bonobos keep growing beyond $15 million in annual sales, with the kind of exceptional service that sets it apart from its competition.

Sources: Owen Thomas, "Silicon Valley's Shopping Spree: One Kings Lane, Abe's Market and More," *Venture Beat*, February 11, 2011, http://venturebeat.com; "To Recruit the Best, Admit Weaknesses," *BusinessWeek*, December 29, 2009, www.businessweek.com; Bambi Francisco Roizen, "Can Friends Be Business Partners?" *VatorNews*, November 10, 2009, http://vator.tv/news/show/2009-11-10-can-friends-be-business-partners; Matt Kinsey, "Bonobos: An America's Hottest Brands Case Study," *Advertising Age*, November 16, 2009, www.adage.com.

Behavior Modification

Behavior modification is a systematic program of reinforcement to encourage desirable behavior. Behavior modification involves both rewards to encourage desirable actions and punishments to discourage undesirable actions. However, studies have shown that rewards, such as compliments and expressions of appreciation, are much more effective behavior modifiers than punishments, such as reprimands and scorn.

When applied to management, behavior modification strives to encourage desirable organizational behavior. Use of this technique begins with identification of a *target behavior*—the behavior that is to be changed. (It might be low production levels or a high rate of absenteeism, for example.) Existing levels of this behavior are then measured. Next, managers provide positive reinforcement in the form of a reward when employees exhibit the *desired behavior* (such as increased production or less absenteeism). The reward might be praise or a more tangible form of recognition, such as a gift, meal, or trip. Apple Company created the Corporate Gifting and Rewards Program in order to give companies the ability to reward their staff with iPods, iPod accessories, and iTunes gift cards.[9] Finally, the levels of the target behavior are measured again to determine whether the desired changes have been achieved. If they have been achieved, the reinforcement is maintained. However, if the target behavior has not changed significantly in the desired direction, the reward system must be changed to one that is likely to be more effective. The key is to devise effective rewards that will not only modify employees' behavior in desired ways but also motivate them. To this end, experts suggest that management should reward quality, loyalty, and productivity.

behavior modification a systematic program of reinforcement to encourage desirable behavior

Flextime

To most people, a work schedule means the standard nine-to-five, 40-hour work week. In reality, though, many people have work schedules that are quite different from this. SC Johnson's Flexible Work Schedule Program allows employees to create their own work schedule around their personal lives.[10] Police officers, firefighters, restaurant personnel, airline employees, and medical personnel usually have work schedules that are far from standard. Some manufacturers also rotate personnel from shift to shift. Many professional people—such as managers, artists, and lawyers—need more than 40 hours each week to get their work done.

The needs and lifestyles of today's workforce are changing. Dual-income families make up a much larger share of the workforce than ever before, and women are one of its fastest-growing sectors. In addition, more employees are responsible for the care of elderly relatives. Recognizing that these changes increase the demand for family time, many employers are offering flexible work schedules that not only help employees to manage their time better but also increase employee motivation and job satisfaction.

Flextime is a system in which employees set their own work hours within certain limits determined by employers. Typically, the firm establishes two bands of time: the *core time,* when all employees must be at work, and the flexible *time,* when employees may choose whether to be at work. The only condition is that every employee must work a total of eight hours each day. For example, the hours between 9 and 11 a.m. and 1 and 3 p.m. might be core times, and the hours between 6 and 9 a.m., 11 a.m. and 1 p.m., and 3 and 6 p.m. might be flexible times. This would give employees the option of coming in early and getting off early, coming in later and leaving later, or taking an extra long lunch break. But flextime also ensures that everyone is present at certain times, when conferences with supervisors and department meetings can be scheduled. Another type of flextime allows employees to work a 40-hour work week in four days instead of five. Workers who put in ten hours a day instead of eight get an extra day off each week. More than three-quarters of companies currently offer flextime.[11]

At times, smaller firms use flextime to attract and retain employees, especially when they cannot match the salaries and benefit package provided by larger companies. Other companies view flextime as an entitlement, given out on a case-by-case basis. For example, Sodexo, a provider of food and facilities management solutions, allows employees with a history of good work performance to propose a flexible schedule to their managers, who then monitor the new schedule through a trial period and semiannual performance reviews. Flextime has been used not only by corporations but also by local governments. For example, the "Flex in the City" event in Houston, Texas, began a few years ago in an effort to lighten the city's congested commutes. The two-week program involving over 200 companies has been held every year since then and is estimated to reduce workers' stress by 58 percent while nearly doubling their productivity.[12]

The sense of independence and autonomy employees gain from having a say in what hours they work can be a motivating factor. In addition, employees who have enough time to deal with non-work issues often work more productively and with greater satisfaction when they are on the job. Two common problems associated with using flextime are (1) supervisors sometimes find their jobs complicated by having employees who come and go at different times and (2) employees without flextime sometimes resent co-workers who have it.

Part-Time Work and Job Sharing

Part-time work is permanent employment in which individuals work less than a standard work week. The specific number of hours worked varies, but part-time jobs are structured so that all responsibilities can be completed in the number of hours an employee works. Part-time work is of special interest to parents who want more time with their children and people who simply desire more leisure time. One

flextime a system in which employees set their own work hours within employer-determined limits

part-time work permanent employment in which individuals work less than a standard work week

disadvantage of part-time work is that it often does not provide the benefits that come with a full-time position. This is not, however, the case at Starbucks, where approximately 80 percent of its employees work part-time. Starbucks does not treat its part-time employees any differently from its full-time employees; all receive the same access to numerous benefits, which even includes a free pound of coffee every week.[13]

Job sharing (sometimes referred to as *work sharing*) is an arrangement whereby two people share one full-time position. One job sharer may work from 8 a.m. to noon, and the other may work from 1 to 5 p.m., or they may alternate workdays. Dr. Jennifer Stahl and Dr. Suzy McNulty, two pediatricians in California, recently established their own practice where they can share their work. Dr. Stahl and Dr. McNulty each work two-and-a-half days a week doing clinical duties, and while one of them is working, the other remains on-call in case of an emergency. Any additional paperwork is done when they are not busy with their children, usually in the evenings from home or during a child's practice. They divide the management-related work based on their individual skills: Dr. Stahl handles accounting and marketing, whereas Dr. McNulty

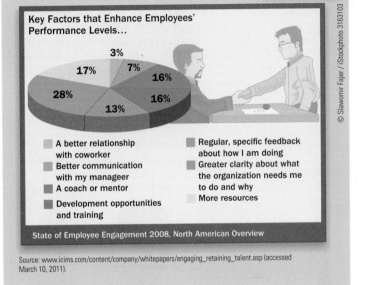

Key Factors that Enhance Employees' Performance Levels...

3% | 7% | 17% | 28% | 13% | 16% | 16%

- A better relationship with coworker
- Better communication with my manageer
- A coach or mentor
- Development opportunities and training
- Regular, specific feedback about how I am doing
- Greater clarity about what the organization needs me to do and why
- More resources

State of Employee Engagement 2008, North American Overview

Source: www.icims.com/content/company/whitepapers/engaging_retaining_talent.asp (accessed March 10, 2011).

takes care of human resources and information technology. Not only do they share their job, but their employees share jobs with each other. This way, everyone has more time to spend with their families.[14] Job sharing combines the security of a full-time position with the flexibility of a part-time job. For firms, job sharing provides a unique opportunity to attract highly skilled employees who might not be available on a full-time basis. In addition, companies can save on expenses by reducing the cost of benefits and avoiding the disruptions of employee turnover. For employees, opting for the flexibility of job sharing may mean giving up some of the benefits received for full-time work. In addition, job sharing is difficult if tasks are not easily divisible or if two people do not work or communicate well with one another.

Telecommuting

A growing number of companies allow **telecommuting**, working at home all the time or for a portion of the work week. Personal computers, modems, fax machines, voice mail, cellular phones, and overnight couriers all facilitate the work-at-home trend. Working at home means that individuals can set their own hours and have more time with their families.

Companies that allow telecommuting experience several benefits, including increased productivity, lower real estate and travel costs, reduced employee absenteeism and turnover, increased work/life balance, improved morale, and access to additional labor pools. Telecommuting also helps improve the community by decreasing air pollutants, reducing traffic congestion, and lowering consumption of fossil fuels, which can give a company a green factor. Also, by having fewer employees commuting to work, the Reason Public Policy Institute estimates that approximately 350 lives are saved per year. Of all the companies that give employees the option to telecommute or work from home, Deloitte is ranked number one with 86 percent of its employees classified as "regular" telecommuters.[15]

Among the disadvantages of telecommuting are feelings of isolation, putting in longer hours, and being distracted by family or household responsibilities. Although most bosses say that they trust their staff to work from home, many think that home

job sharing an arrangement whereby two people share one full-time position

telecommuting working at home all the time or for a portion of the work week

Get Ready to Telecommute

career **SUCCESS**

At some point in your career, you'll be a telecommuter, so get ready. More than 30 million U.S. workers telecommute occasionally or regularly. Telecommuters are often more productive than on-site workers because they don't have to spend time traveling to the office or moving from one building to another for a meeting (or for lunch). In fact, the ability to telecommute at least once a week is one of the top preferences of job-seekers—and a powerful source of motivation, as employers such as AT&T have discovered. More than 95 percent of AT&T's telecommuters surveyed say that the ability to work from home is important to their job satisfaction.

Telecommuters are already adept at using digital devices to work from anywhere, which means they have the tools and experience to team up with co-workers located hundreds or even thousands of miles away. Another benefit: When commuters

are delayed by severe weather or traffic tie-ups, telecommuters can start work right on time, as long as they have Internet access.

Employees who telecommute are just as pleased with their higher productivity as their employers are. Still, managers may not know quite how to supervise employees who are among the first to telecommute. This is where telecommuters can take the initiative. For example, when an Atlanta government employee began telecommuting, she and her manager agreed on her agenda for each working day. At the end of the day, she reported on what she'd accomplished and what was left to do, showing her manager that telecommuting was both efficient and effective.

Sources: Ariel Hart, "Telecommuting Now Metro Area's Main Alternative to Driving Solo," *Atlanta Journal-Constitution*, February 24, 2011, www.ajc.com/business; Daniel Walsh, "How Telecommuting Lets Workers Mobilize for Sustainability," *Greener World Media*, February 17, 2011, www.reuters.com.

workers are work-shy and less productive than office-based staff. A survey conducted in the United Kingdom found that up to 38 percent of managers surveyed believe that home workers are less productive, and 22 percent think that working from home is an excuse for time off. In addition, some supervisors have difficulty monitoring productivity.[16]

Cisco, for example, is an industry leader at providing a virtual work environment. Approximately 85 percent of the company's 37,000-member U.S. workforce connects to the company remotely on a regular basis. Cisco's employees use many of the company's own products, including WebEx and TelePresence, which allow employees to attend meetings, do training, and hold video conferences online. Cisco's telecommuting program has boosted employee satisfaction, reduced turnover, and earned the company numerous sustainability awards. Telecommuting has saved the company over $277 million and lowers employees' fuel costs by an estimated $10 million annually.[17]

Employee Empowerment

Many companies are increasing employee motivation and satisfaction through the use of empowerment. **Empowerment** means making employees more involved in their jobs and in the operations of the organization by increasing their participation in decision making. With empowerment, control no longer flows exclusively from the top level of the organization downward. Empowered employees have a voice in what they do and how and when they do it. In some organizations, employees' input is restricted to individual choices, such as when to take breaks. In other companies,

empowerment making employees more involved in their jobs by increasing their participation in decision making

their responsibilities may encompass more far-reaching issues. For example, at W. L. Gore & Associates, a product-development company, workers are "associates" and never referred to as "employees." Gore's unique lattice management structure creates a nonhierarchical system free from traditional bosses or managers. At Gore, there is no assigned authority, and people become leaders by gaining the respect of their peers. Everyone owns a part of the company through the corporate stock plan. Associates at Gore are never told what to do or given assignments. Instead, they are encouraged to work on their own projects, developing innovative new products and technologies. It is this unique corporate culture at Gore that inspires their associates to explore, discover, and invent.[18]

Personal App With empowerment, you're the boss of you. Of course you may not be empowered to act on your own in every situation, and your company may have guidelines to follow, but you get more of a say in what you do on the job and how you do it.

For empowerment to work effectively, management must be involved. Managers should set expectations, communicate standards, institute periodic evaluations, and guarantee follow-up. If effectively implemented, empowerment can lead to increased job satisfaction, improved job performance, higher self-esteem, and increased organizational commitment. Obstacles to empowerment include resistance on the part of management, distrust of management on the part of workers, insufficient training, and poor communication between management and employees.

Employee Ownership

Some organizations are discovering that a highly effective technique for motivating employees is **employee ownership**—that is, employees own the company they work for by virtue of being stockholders. Employee-owned businesses directly reward employees for success. When the company enjoys increased sales or lower costs, employees benefit directly. The National Center for Employee Ownership, an organization that studies employee-owned American businesses, reports that employee stock ownership plans (ESOPs) provide considerable employee incentive and increase employee involvement and commitment. In the United States today, about 13.7 million employees participate in 11,400 ESOPs and stock bonus plans.[19] As a means to motivate top executives and, frequently, middle-ranking managers who are working long days for what are generally considered poor salaries, some firms provide stock options as part of the employee compensation package. The option is simply the right to buy shares of the firm within a prescribed time at a set price. If the firm does well and its stock price rises past the set price (presumably because of all the work being done by the employee), the employee can exercise the option and immediately sell the stock and cash in on the company's success.

The difficulties of such companies as United Airlines have damaged the idea of employee ownership. United Airlines' ESOP failed to solve problems between employees and management. In addition, Lowe's, the home-improvement retailer, recently stopped its long-running and mostly successful ESOP and transferred the remaining money into 401(k) plans.

TEAMS AND TEAMWORK

The concepts of teams and teamwork may be most commonly associated with sports, but they are also integral parts of business organizations. This organizational structure is popular because it encourages employees to participate more fully in business decisions. The growing number of companies organizing their workforces into teams reflects an effort to increase employee productivity and creativity because team members are working on specific goals and are given greater autonomy. This leads to greater job satisfaction as employees feel more involved in the management process.[20]

Concept Check ✱

☐ What are the five steps of most MBO programs?

☐ How can companies use job enrichment as a method for motivating employees?

☐ What is behavior modification and how is it used in organizations?

☐ What benefits does a company receive when using flextime, job sharing, and telecommuting?

☐ How do employee ownership and employee empowerment help in increasing employee motivation and satisfaction?

LEARNING OBJECTIVE

5 Understand the types, development, and uses of teams.

---

employee ownership a situation in which employees own the company they work for by virtue of being stockholders

---

Good Green Fun

At the online auction site eBay, a Green Team promotes sustainability worldwide using the slogan "Inspiring the world to buy, sell, and think green every day." Through blog entries and Twitter posts, the Green Team offers tips for greener living and highlights eco-friendly activities. Take a look: www.ebaygreenteam.com.

What Is a Team?

In a business organization, a **team** is two or more workers operating as a coordinated unit to accomplish a specific task or goal.[21] A team may be assigned any number of tasks or goals, from development of a new product to selling that product. A team can also be created to identify or solve a problem that an organization is experiencing. Toyota, for example, assembled a team of seven experts in the fields of business, transportation, automobile safety, and technology to help the company after an unprecedented number of vehicles needed to be recalled because of the possibility of sudden acceleration. The team analyzed the company from top to bottom, evaluating Toyota's quality-control methods to figure out how unsafe acceleration problems in certain vehicles went unnoticed during development and testing.[22] Although teamwork may seem like a simple concept learned on soccer or football fields, teams function as a microcosm of the larger organization. Therefore, it is important to understand the types, development, and general nature of teams.

Types of Teams

There are several types of teams within businesses that function in specific ways to achieve different purposes, including problem-solving teams, self-managed teams, cross-functional teams, and virtual teams.

PROBLEM-SOLVING TEAMS The most common type of team in business organizations is the **problem-solving team**. It is generally used temporarily in order to bring knowledgeable employees together to tackle a specific problem. Once the problem is solved, the team typically is disbanded.

In some extraordinary cases, an expert team may be needed to generate groundbreaking ideas. A **virtuoso team** consists of exceptionally highly skilled and talented individuals brought together to produce significant change. As with other kinds of problem-solving teams, virtuoso teams are usually assembled on a temporary basis. Instead of being task-oriented, they focus on producing ideas and provoking change that could have an effect on the company and its industry. Because of the high skill level of their members, virtuoso teams can be difficult to manage. Unlike traditional teams, virtuoso teams place an emphasis on individuality over teamwork, which can cause further conflict. However, their conflicts usually are viewed as competitive and therefore productive in generating the most substantial ideas.[23]

SELF-MANAGED WORK TEAMS **Self-managed teams** are groups of employees with the authority and skills to manage themselves. Experts suggest that workers on self-managed teams are more motivated and satisfied because they have more task variety and job control. On many work teams, members rotate through all the jobs for which the team is responsible. Some organizations cross-train the entire team so that everyone can perform everyone else's job. In a traditional business structure, management is responsible for hiring and firing employees, establishing budgets, purchasing supplies, conducting performance reviews, and taking corrective action. When self-managed teams are in place, they take over some or all of these management functions. Xerox, Procter & Gamble, Ferrari, and numerous other companies have used self-managed teams successfully. The major advantages and disadvantages of self-managed teams are mentioned in Figure 10-6.

team two or more workers operating as a coordinated unit to accomplish a specific task or goal

problem-solving team a team of knowledgeable employees brought together to tackle a specific problem

virtuoso team a team of exceptionally highly skilled and talented individuals brought together to produce significant change

self-managed teams groups of employees with the authority and skills to manage themselves

FIGURE 10-6: Advantages and Disadvantages of Self-Managed Teams

While self-managed teams provide advantages, managers must recognize their disadvantages.

ADVANTAGES	DISADVANTAGES
• Boosts employee morale • Increases productivity • Aids innovation • Reduces employee boredom	• Additional training costs • Teams may be disorganized • Conflicts may arise • Leadership role may be unclear

© Cengage Learning 2013

CROSS-FUNCTIONAL TEAMS Traditionally, businesses have organized employees into departments based on a common function or specialty. However, increasingly, business organizations are faced with projects that require a diversity of skills not available within a single department. A **cross-functional team** consists of individuals with varying specialties, expertise, and skills that are brought together to achieve a common task. For example, a purchasing agent might create a cross-functional team with representatives from various departments to gain insight into useful purchases for the company. This structure avoids departmental separation and allows greater efficiency when there is a single goal. Although cross-functional teams are not necessarily self-managed, most self-managed teams are cross-functional. They can also be cross-divisional, such as at Dow Chemical Company, which created a cross-divisional team at their West Alexandria plant to improve energy efficiency. The team was able to look throughout the plant's divisions to find ways to save energy, including turning off unnecessary equipment and optimizing various processes, which resulted in 14 percent annual energy savings.[24] Cross-functional teams can also include a variety of people from outside the company, such as the cross-functional team of ergonomists, users, and university scientists that developed a new natural ergonomic keyboard for Microsoft.[25] Because of their speed, flexibility, and increased employee satisfaction, it is likely that the use of cross-functional teams will increase.

© Andreas Rodriquez/iStockphoto.com

VIRTUAL TEAMS With the advent of sophisticated communications technology, it is no longer necessary for teams to be geographically close. A **virtual team** consists of members who are geographically dispersed but communicate electronically. In fact, team members may never meet in person but rely solely on e-mail, teleconferences, faxes, voice mail, and other technological interactions. In the modern global environment, virtual teams connect employees on a common task across continents, oceans, time zones, and organizations. For example, Mozilla, the software provider responsible for Firefox, regularly requests the help of volunteers to test and improve their products virtually. Some of these volunteers become employees of the organization based on their performance in the project they did.[26] In some cases, the physical distances between participants and the lack of face-to-face interaction can be difficult when deadlines approach or communication is not clear.

cross-functional team a team of individuals with varying specialties, expertise, and skills that are brought together to achieve a common task

virtual team a team consisting of members who are geographically dispersed but communicate electronically

Developing and Using Effective Teams

When a team is first developed, it takes time for the members to establish roles, relationships, delegation of duties, and other attributes of an effective team. As a team matures, it passes through five stages of development, as shown in Figure 10-7.

FORMING In the first stage, *forming,* team members are introduced to one another and begin to develop a social dynamic. The members of the team are still unsure about how to relate to one another, what behaviors are considered acceptable, and what the ground rules are for the team. Through group member interaction over time, team members become more comfortable and a group dynamic begins to emerge.

STORMING During the *storming* stage, the interaction may be volatile and the team may lack unity. Because the team is still relatively new, this is the stage at which goals and objectives begin to develop. Team members will brainstorm to develop ideas and plans and establish a broad-ranging agenda. It is important at this stage for team members to grow more comfortable around the others so that they can contribute openly. At this time, the leadership role likely will be formally undefined. A team member may emerge as the informal leader. The success or failure of the ideas in storming determines how long the team will take to reach the next stage.

NORMING After storming and the first large burst of activity, the team begins to stabilize during the *norming* stage. During this process, each person's role within the group starts to become apparent, and members begin to recognize the roles of others. A sense of unity will become stronger. If it has not occurred already, an identified leader will emerge. The group still may be somewhat volatile at this point and may regress back to the second stage if any conflict, especially over the leadership role, occurs.

PERFORMING The fourth stage, *performing,* is when the team achieves its full potential. It is usually slow to develop and occurs when the team begins to focus strongly on the assigned task and away from team-development issues. The members of the team work in harmony under the established roles to accomplish the necessary goals.

ADJOURNING In the final stage, *adjourning,* the team is disbanded because the project has been completed. Team members may be reassigned to other teams or tasks. This stage does not always occur if the team is placed together for a task with no specific date of completion. For example, a marketing team for Best Buy may continue to develop promotional efforts for a store even after a specific promotional task has been accomplished.

FIGURE 10-7: Stages of Team Development

When attempting to develop teams, managers must understand that multiple stages are generally required.

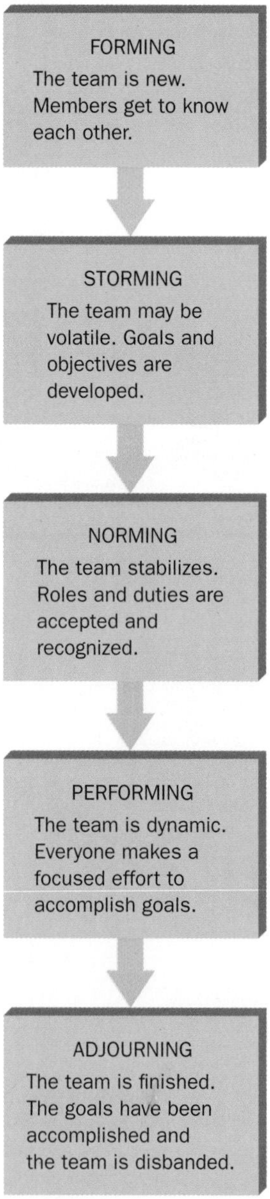

FORMING
The team is new. Members get to know each other.

↓

STORMING
The team may be volatile. Goals and objectives are developed.

↓

NORMING
The team stabilizes. Roles and duties are accepted and recognized.

↓

PERFORMING
The team is dynamic. Everyone makes a focused effort to accomplish goals.

↓

ADJOURNING
The team is finished. The goals have been accomplished and the team is disbanded.

©Cengage Learning 2013

This stage is especially common in problem-solving teams that are dismantled after the assigned problem has been resolved.

Roles Within a Team

Within any team, each member has a role to play in helping the team attain its objectives. Each of these roles adds important dimensions to team member interactions. The group member who pushes forward toward goals and places the objective first plays the *task-specialist role* by concentrating fully on the assigned task. In a cross-functional team, this might be the person with the most expertise relating to the current task. The *socioemotional role* is played by the individual who supports and encourages the emotional needs of the other members. This person places the team members' personal needs over the task of the team. Although this may sound unimportant, the socioemotional member's dedication to team cohesiveness will lead to greater unity and higher productivity. The leader of the team, and possibly others as well, will play a *dual role*. This dual role is a combination of both the socioemotional and task-specialist roles because this individual focuses on both the task and the team. The team leader might not always play a dual role, but the team is likely to be most successful when he or she does. Sometimes an individual assumes the *nonparticipant role*. This role behavior is characterized by a person who does not contribute to accomplishing the task and does not provide favorable input with respect to team members' socioemotional needs.

Personal App Think about how you generally act in teams. Do you stay focused on the task or do you try to get other people more involved? How do you balance the need to get things done with the personal needs of all the team members?

Team Cohesiveness

Developing a unit from a diverse group of personalities, specialties, backgrounds, and work styles can be challenging and complicated. In a cohesive team, the members get along and are able to accomplish their tasks effectively. There are factors that affect cohesiveness within a team. Teams generally are ideal when they contain 5 to 12 people. Teams with fewer than 5 people often fail to accomplish tasks and generate a variety of ideas. Teams with more than 12 are too large because members do not develop relationships, may feel intimidated to speak, or may disconnect. It also may be beneficial to have team members introduce themselves and describe their past work experiences. This activity will foster familiarity and shared experiences. One of the most reliable ways to build cohesiveness within a team is through competition with other teams. When two teams are competing for a single prize or recognition, they are forced to put aside conflict and accomplish their goal. By adding an incentive to finishing the task, the team automatically becomes more goal oriented. Also, a favorable appraisal from an outsider may strengthen team cohesiveness. Because the team is being praised as a group, team members recognize their contribution as a unit. Teams are also more successful when goals have been agreed upon. A team that is clear about its objective will focus more on accomplishing it. Frequent interaction also builds cohesiveness as relationships strengthen and familiarity increases.

Team Conflict and How to Resolve It

Conflict occurs when a disagreement arises between two or more team members. Conflict traditionally has been viewed as negative; however, if handled properly, conflict can work to improve a team. For example, if two team members disagree about a certain decision, both may analyze the situation more closely to determine the best choice. As long as conflict is handled in a respectful and professional manner, it can improve the quality of work produced. However, if conflict turns hostile and affects the work environment, then steps must be taken to arrive at a suitable compromise. Compromises can be difficult in a business organization because neither party ends up getting everything he or she wants. The best solution is a middle-ground

☐ What are the major types of teams?

☐ Highlight some differences between cross-functional teams and virtual teams.

☐ Identify and describe the stages of team development.

☐ How can team conflict be reduced?

☐ What are some of the benefits and limitations of a team?

alternative in which each party is satisfied to some degree. It is best to avoid attempting to minimize or ignore conflicts within a group because this may cause the conflict to grow as members concentrate on the problem instead of the task. However the conflict is resolved, it is important to remember that conflict must be acknowledged if it is to either be resolved or serve a constructive purpose.

Benefits and Limitations of Teams

Teamwork within a company has been credited as a key to reducing turnover and costs and increasing production, quality, and customer service. There is also evidence that working in teams leads to higher levels of job satisfaction among employees and a harmonious work environment. Thus, an increasingly large number of companies are considering teams as a viable organizational structure. However, the process of reorganizing into teams can be stressful and time consuming with no guarantee that the team will develop effectively. If a team lacks cohesiveness and is unable to resolve conflict, the company may experience lower productivity.

Get Flashcards, Quizzes, Games, Crosswords, and more @ www.cengagebrain.com

SUMMARY

1 Explain what motivation is.

Motivation is the individual internal process that energizes, directs, and sustains behavior. Motivation is affected by employee morale—that is, the employee's feelings about the job, superiors, and the firm itself. Motivation, morale, and job satisfaction are closely related.

2 Understand some major historical perspectives on motivation.

One of the first approaches to employee motivation was Frederick Taylor's scientific management, the application of scientific principles to the management of work and workers. Taylor believed that employees work only for money and that they must be closely supervised and managed. This thinking led to the piece-rate system, under which employees are paid a certain amount for each unit they produce. The Hawthorne Studies attempted to determine the effects of the work environment on productivity. Results of these studies indicated that human factors affect productivity more than do physical aspects of the workplace.

Maslow's hierarchy of needs suggests that people are motivated by five sets of needs. In ascending order of importance, these motivators are physiological, safety, social, esteem, and self-actualization needs. People are motivated by the lowest set of needs that remains unfulfilled. As needs at one level are satisfied, people try to satisfy needs at the next level.

Frederick Herzberg found that job satisfaction and dissatisfaction are influenced by two distinct sets of factors. Motivation factors, including recognition and responsibility, affect an employee's degree of satisfaction, but their absence does not necessarily cause dissatisfaction. Hygiene factors, including pay and working conditions, affect an employee's degree of dissatisfaction but do not affect satisfaction.

Theory X is a concept of motivation that assumes that employees dislike work and will function effectively only in a highly controlled work environment. Thus, to achieve an organization's goals, managers must coerce, control, and threaten employees. This theory generally is consistent with Taylor's ideas of scientific management. Theory Y is more in keeping with the results of the Hawthorne Studies and the human relations movement. It suggests that employees can be motivated to behave as responsible members of the organization. Theory Z emphasizes long-term employment, collective decision making, individual responsibility for the outcomes of decisions, informal control, and a holistic concern for employees. Reinforcement theory is based on the idea that people will repeat behavior that is rewarded and will avoid behavior that is punished.

3 Describe three contemporary views of motivation: equity theory, expectancy theory, and goal-setting theory.

Equity theory maintains that people are motivated to obtain and preserve equitable treatment for themselves. Expectancy theory suggests that our motivation depends on how much we want something and how likely we think we are to get it. Goal-setting theory suggests that employees are motivated to achieve a goal that they and their managers establish together.

4 Explain several techniques for increasing employee motivation.

Management by objectives (MBO) is a motivation technique in which managers and employees collaborate in setting goals. MBO motivates employees by getting them more involved in their jobs and in the organization as a whole. Job enrichment seeks to motivate employees by varying their tasks and giving them more responsibility for and control over their jobs. Job enlargement, expanding a worker's assignments to include additional tasks, is one aspect of job enrichment. Job redesign is a type of job enrichment in which work is restructured to improve the worker–job match.

Behavior modification uses reinforcement to encourage desirable behavior. Rewards for productivity, quality, and loyalty change employees' behavior in desired ways and also increase motivation.

Allowing employees to work more flexible hours is another way to build motivation and job satisfaction. Flextime is a system of work scheduling that allows workers to set their own hours as long as they fall within the limits established by employers. Part-time work is permanent employment in which individuals work less than a standard work week. Job sharing is an arrangement whereby two people share one full-time position. Telecommuting allows employees to work at home all or part of the work week. All these types of work arrangements give employees more time outside the workplace to deal with family responsibilities or to enjoy free time.

Employee empowerment, self-managed work teams, and employee ownership are also techniques that boost employee motivation. Empowerment increases employees' involvement in their jobs by increasing their decision-making authority. Self-managed work teams are groups of employees with the authority and skills to manage themselves. When employees participate in ownership programs, such as employee stock ownership plans (ESOPs), they have more incentive to make the company succeed and therefore work more effectively.

5 Understand the types, development, and uses of teams.

A large number of companies use teams to increase their employees' productivity. In a business organization, a team is a group of workers functioning together as a unit to complete a common goal or purpose.

There are several types of teams within businesses that function in specific ways to achieve different purposes. A problem-solving team is a team of knowledgeable employees brought together to tackle a specific problem. A virtuoso team is a team of highly skilled and talented individuals brought together to produce significant change. A virtual team is a team consisting of members who are geographically dispersed but communicate electronically. A cross-functional team is a team of individuals with varying specialties, expertise, and skills.

The five stages of team development are forming, storming, norming, performing, and adjourning. As a team develops, it should become more productive and unified. The four roles within teams are task specialist, socioemotional, dual, and nonparticipative. Each of these roles plays a specific part in the team's interaction. For a team to be successful, members must learn how to resolve and manage conflict so that the team can work cohesively to accomplish goals.

KEY TERMS

You should now be able to define and give an example relevant to each of the following terms:

motivation (272)	self-actualization	expectancy theory (280)	telecommuting (287)
morale (272)	needs (275)	goal-setting theory (281)	empowerment (288)
scientific management	motivation–hygiene	management by	employee ownership (289)
(272)	theory (276)	objectives (MBO) (282)	team (290)
piece-rate system (273)	motivation factors (276)	job enrichment (284)	problem-solving
need (274)	hygiene factors (276)	job enlargement (284)	team (290)
maslow's hierarchy of	Theory X (277)	job redesign (284)	virtuoso team (290)
needs (274)	Theory Y (277)	behavior modification	self-managed
physiological needs (274)	Theory Z (278)	(285)	teams (290)
safety needs (274)	reinforcement	flextime (286)	cross-functional
social needs (274)	theory (278)	part-time work (286)	team (291)
esteem needs (275)	equity theory (280)	job sharing (287)	virtual team (291)

1. How did the results of the Hawthorne Studies influence researchers' thinking about employee motivation?
2. What are the five sets of needs in Maslow's hierarchy? How are a person's needs related to motivation?
3. What are the two dimensions in Herzberg's theory? What kinds of elements affect each dimension?
4. According to equity theory, how does an employee determine whether he or she is being treated equitably?
5. According to expectancy theory, what two variables determine motivation?
6. Describe the steps involved in the MBO process.
7. What are the objectives of MBO? What do you think might be its disadvantages?
8. How does employee participation increase motivation?
9. Identify and describe the major types of teams.
10. What are the major benefits and limitations associated with the use of self-managed teams?
11. Explain the major stages of team development.
12. What combination of motivational techniques do you think would result in the best overall motivation and reward system?
13. In what ways are team cohesiveness and team conflict related?

TEST YOURSELF

Matching Questions

1. _____ A force that causes people to behave in a particular way
2. _____ Based on an assumption that people dislike work.
3. _____ Employees believe they will receive the rewards.
4. _____ When not provided, they become dissatisfiers.
5. _____ Needs that can be met by health care benefits.
6. _____ Promotions and rewards can fulfill these needs.
7. _____ Behavior that is rewarded is likely to be repeated.
8. _____ Employees become more involved in the decision-making process.
9. _____ Employees are given more variety and responsibility in their jobs.
10. _____ Groups that have more task variety and greater job control.

a. virtuoso teams
b. empowerment
c. esteem needs
d. expectancy theory
e. hygiene factors
f. job enrichment
g. motivation
h. reinforcement theory
i. self-managed teams
j. safety needs
k. Theory X
l. morale

True False Questions

11. **T F** Giving employee recognition builds employee morale.
12. **T F** Frederick W. Taylor made his most significant contribution to management practice by his involvement with the Hawthorne Studies.
13. **T F** The Hawthorne Studies concluded that human factors were responsible for the results.
14. **T F** Maslow's higher-level needs are the easiest to satisfy.
15. **T F** Self-actualization needs are the most basic needs that Maslow discovered.
16. **T F** Herzberg's theory suggests that pay is a strong motivator.
17. **T F** Theory X is a set of assumptions that are consistent with the human relations movement.
18. **T F** According to the expectancy theory, motivation depends on how much we want something and how likely we think we are to get it.
19. **T F** MBO is an inflexible system that requires all goals to be met; if not, the employee is fired.
20. **T F** A systematic program of reinforcement that encourages desirable behavior is called behavior modification.

Multiple-Choice Questions

21. _____ If Delta Airlines ticket agents discovered that they were being paid a lot less per ticket sold than United Airlines ticket agents, we might expect the Delta ticket agents to
    a. increase their sales so that they will make as much as their United peers.
    b. think their outcome-to-input ratios are lower than those of the United ticket agents.
    c. have as a group very different personal needs than United ticket agents.
    d. be very satisfied because they work for a great airline.
    e. feel that rewards are being distributed fairly and equitably.

22. _____ Randi Wood wants to become the best manager in the firm. She takes every available opportunity to learn new skills and improve her knowledge about management. Which need is Randi attempting to satisfy?
    a. Social
    b. Esteem
    c. Self-actualization
    d. Physiological
    e. Safety

23. _____ The idea that satisfaction and dissatisfaction are separate and distinct dimensions comes from which of the following theories?
    a. Frederick Herzberg's motivation–hygiene theory
    b. Maslow's hierarchy of needs
    c. Frederick Taylor's scientific management
    d. Reinforcement theory
    e. Hawthorne Studies

24. _____ Herzberg cited _____ as a cause of dissatisfaction.
    a. working conditions
    b. promotions
    c. pay for special projects
    d. rewards
    e. challenging work

25. _____ According to Theory Y, which type of behavior would a supervisor expect from an employee?
    a. Delegate most of the work to others.
    b. Avoid working too hard.
    c. Spend time discussing job security.
    d. Ask to leave early several times a month.
    e. Seek opportunities to learn new skills.

26. _____ Developing an input-to-output ratio is the basis of the _____ theory.
    a. equity
    b. expectancy
    c. reward
    d. reinforcement
    e. quality circle

27. _____ Expectancy theory is difficult to apply, but it does provide several useful guidelines for managers. One such outcome that managers must realize is that
    a. everyone expects the same things.
    b. employees expect to be financially rewarded for hard work.
    c. employees work for a variety of reasons.
    d. most employees tend to be unreasonable in their expectations.
    e. managers need to use the authoritarian style to get tasks accomplished.

28. _____ Which of the following is a motivation technique that provides employees with more variety and responsibility in their jobs?
    a. Job rotation
    b. Job enrichment
    c. Job redesign
    d. Job enlargement
    e. Job analysis

29. _____ What stage of a team is usually slow to develop and occurs when the team begins to focus strongly on the assigned task and away from team-development issues?
    a. Norming
    b. Storming
    c. Performing
    d. Adjourning
    e. Unifying

30. _____ The group member who pushes forward toward goals and places the objective first is playing the
    a. task-specialist role.
    b. socioemotional role.
    c. nonparticipant role.
    d. dual role.
    e. aggressor role.

Answers to the Test Yourself questions appear at the end of the book on page TY-1.

VIDEO CASE
At L.L. Bean, Everyone Is Family

From a tiny mail-order company begun 100 years ago, L.L. Bean has grown into a well-known retail firm with net sales of over $1.5 billion a year. It encompasses 14 stores in 10 states, continues its ever-popular catalog, has a thriving online store, and sells some 20,000 high-quality items, including clothing for the whole family, accessories, outdoor and camping gear, and even luggage, linens, and furniture. Employees at L.L. Bean share a sense of purpose that closely reflects the values of the company's founders and managers, making them feel like they are part of a large family.

Although its online store has grown enormously in popularity, the company continues to field a huge number of mail and telephone orders year-round, which puts employees in constant direct contact with customers. The company has a world-class training program, so employees' skills are not an issue. In addition, employees' motivation brought the company to the top of *BusinessWeek*'s list of companies with outstanding customer service. Why are they so motivated? "Our frontline employees are the face of L.L. Bean and the voice of L.L. Bean to our customers," says the company's vice president of e-commerce, "so they need to feel that they're supported in making the right decisions on behalf of the customer and the company." Describing the way many other firms require their telephone call center employees to bring in a supervisor to resolve customers' problems, the vice president explains why L.L. Bean does things differently. "We expect that the person you talk to on the phone will make it right. Other places you have to say, 'Let me talk to your supervisor,' and we really can't stand that. We look on elevated calls as a bad thing."

Empowering employees to resolve customer problems on their own not only speeds the handling of calls and leaves L.L. Bean's customers more satisfied, it also increases employees' decision-making authority and the pride and satisfaction they feel in their work. The company offers annual bonuses and profit sharing for all year-round employees. However, as one company executive explained, the sense of ownership Bean employees feel in the company isn't founded on money. "It's definitely not based on that kind of incentive. . . . We select employees based on their ability

to feel that kind of ownership, based on their investment in delivering the right customer experience. . . . They have this sort of underlying sense of values that drives them to deliver and . . . act as if they are an owner of the company. I talk about that a lot with my frontline employees."

Communication at the firm goes both ways. L.L. Bean employees also know they are empowered to speak up when they think a product or a business process can be improved. As one manager says, "They would be very clear to the chain of command that 'this doesn't work, and you need to change it so that it better suits the customer.'"

Other ways in which L.L. Bean rewards its employees are the company-owned fitness centers, walking trails, and sporting camps for fishing, kayaking, and skiing that encourage everyone at the firm to stay healthy and active. Ergonomic workstations bring the company's commitment to its employees' well-being right to their desks. During his tenure as president, in fact, Leon Gorman defined the company's stakeholders as including not just customers, stockholders, vendors, communities, and the natural environment, but employees as well. Benefits, wages, discounts, and pensions are competitive, even generous. Some employees have worked for the company for as long as 30 years, and nearly 800 applicants turned out for 130 jobs created by the opening of a new L.L. Bean store in upstate New York. It all comes back to what Gorman calls the power of L.L.'s personality: "His personal charisma, based on down-home honesty, a true love for the outdoors, and a genuine enthusiasm for people inspired all who worked for him." In that respect, the founder's legacy is very much alive today.[27]

Questions

1. What role do you think empowerment plays at L.L. Bean?
2. Because the company's retail Web site has proven to be so successful, L.L. Bean recently announced the closing of one of its four call centers, but the 220 employees there will have the option to work at another site or telecommute. What net effect do you think closing of the call center will have on employee morale and motivation?
3. What else could L.L. Bean do to motivate its employees?

BUILDING SKILLS FOR CAREER SUCCESS

1. Exploring the Internet

There are few employee incentives as motivating as owning "a piece of the action." Either through profit sharing or equity, many firms realize that the opportunity to share in the wealth generated by their effort is a primary force to drive

employees toward better performance and a sense of ownership. The Foundation for Enterprise Development (www .fed.org/) is a non-profit organization dedicated to helping entrepreneurs and executives use employee ownership and equity compensation as a fair and effective means of motivating the workforce and improving corporate performance.

You can learn more about this approach at the foundation's Web site. Visit the text Web site for updates to this exercise.

Assignment
1. Describe the content and services provided by the Foundation for Enterprise Development through its Web site.
2. Do you agree with this orientation toward motivation of employees/owners, or does it seem contrived to you? Discuss.
3. How else might employees be motivated to improve their performance?

2. Building Team Skills

By increasing employees' participation in decision making, empowerment makes workers feel more involved in their jobs and the operations of the organization. Although empowerment may seem like a commonsense idea, it is a concept not found universally at the workplace. If you had empowerment in your job, how would you describe it?

Assignment
1. Brainstorm to explore the concept of empowerment.
   a. Write each letter of the word *empowerment* in a vertical column on a sheet of paper or on the classroom chalkboard.
   b. Think of several words that begin with each letter.
   c. Write the words next to the appropriate letter.
2. Formulate a statement by choosing one word from each letter that best describes what empowerment means to you.
3. Analyze the statement.
   a. How relevant is the statement for you in terms of empowerment? Or empowerment in your workplace?

b. What changes must occur in your workplace for you to have empowerment?
   c. How would you describe yourself as an empowered employee?
   d. What opportunities would empowerment give to you in your workplace?
4. Prepare a report of your findings.

3. Researching Different Careers

Because a manager's job varies from department to department within firms, as well as among firms, it is virtually impossible to write a generic description of a manager's job. If you are contemplating becoming a manager, you may find it very helpful to spend time on the job with several managers learning firsthand what they do.

Assignment
1. Make an appointment with managers in three firms, preferably firms of different sizes. When you make the appointments, request a tour of the facilities.
2. Ask the managers the following questions:
   a. What do you do in your job?
   b. What do you like most and least about your job? Why?
   c. What skills do you need in your job?
   d. How much education does your job require?
   e. What advice do you have for someone thinking about pursuing a career in management?
3. Summarize your findings in a two-page report. Include answers to these questions:
   a. Is management a realistic field of study for you? Why?
   b. What might be a better career choice? Why?

Running a Business: Part 4

Graeter's: Where Tenure Is "a Proud Number"

Although you might think working for an ice-cream company would be motivating under almost any circumstances, Graeter's doesn't take its employees' commitment for granted. Including full-time and part-time seasonal workers, Graeter's employs about 800 hourly workers in nearly 30 retail stores in Cincinnati and surrounding areas. Over the last few years, it has benefitted from tightening up some of its long-standing human resource management (HRM) procedures, including those for hiring and evaluating employees.

Improving Training and Performance Measurement

According to an HR consultant who works with top management at this fourth-generation family-owned firm, in past years the company ran more or less on unquestioned directives from the top down. There was a Laissez-Faire attitude, and goals and measurement systems weren't strongly emphasized. "If [employees] came in and they made ice cream, if they made enough for the week, for the day, that was enough," says the consultant. Now "that has really radically changed. If you walk around now we have measurement systems up. People understand what their expectation is, and we have defined the behaviors that are acceptable and not acceptable within the company. We communicate that. We teach and educate people. We've done a lot of work in retail about exceptional customer service and what that looks like and how you do that…. Employees are going to engage you…and you are going to have a good time."

Turnover is low. "We don't hire based on race," says David Blink, the company's controller. "We don't hire based on gender. We hire based on potential…. We are looking for people who are conscientious about their work, who do a good job, who show up every day. We are a fun place to work…. We have turnover based on seasonal work only because we hire a lot of college kids [and] high school kids that are here for the summer and then they come back for the holidays." Each store is staffed with a manager and an assistant manager as well as team leaders. Some employees spend their entire working careers with Graeter's and eventually retire from the firm.

Raising The Bar for Production

Graeter's looks for people with baking industry skills for its factories, which recently grew from one to three as the company has undertaken a major and possibly nationwide expansion of its supermarket distribution system. Higher production goals have given newly empowered factory employees achievements to boast about on the slogan T-shirts they wear. Employee suggestions for improvement pour in, and morale is going up. Employees also wear badges with their names and the number of years they have worked for the firm, "and that is a proud number," says Blink. Some factory employees have been with Graeter's for 25 years, a milestone that merits a party. Birthdays and anniversaries are also celebrated with flair.

Benefits That Pay

The benefits package is competitive. Graeter's offers its employees profit sharing, and it has made a profit every year. It also has a 401k retirement plan that matches employees' contributions and a rolling allowance for paid time off that is separate from paid vacations and based on the employee's tenure with the firm. The health care plan covers 65 percent of employees' medical expenses; dental insurance, life insurance, and short- and long-term disability insurance are offered. Employees who don't use the company's insurance plan (because they are covered by a spouse's plan, for instance) are rewarded with a stipend. Store employees wear uniforms for which the company pays as well.

Adding Executives Because "You Can't Do It Alone"

Hiring at the executive level is largely the province of CEO Richard Graeter II, who, like his cousins Robert (vice president of manufacturing) and Chip (vice president of retail stores), is a great grandson of the 140-year-old company's founders. The company has adopted ambitious expansion plans and has taken advantage of the unexpected opportunity to purchase several Graeter's stores and a factory from the last of its franchisees, increasing its production capacity overnight. Therefore, the management team has also grown, altering the structure of the growing firm.

"In the last few months," says Richard, "I have hired a vice president of sales and marketing…we now work with a food broker…we hired a vice president of finance, basically a CFO [chief financial officer] because we are big enough to support that. Actually when we bought the franchisee we kept his entire team, so we added another vice president of sales for the Columbus area. We elevated our director of sales to a vice president level here in Cincinnati, and I think we are going to find someone to be our marketing director,

(continued on bottom of next page)

© Liudmila Chernova / iStockphoto 12864114

© DNY59 / iStockphoto 1694138

Building a Business Plan: Part 4

In this section of your business plan, you will expand on the type and quantity of employees that will be required to operate the business. Your human resources requirements are determined by the type of business and by the size and scale of your operation. From the preceding section, you should have a good idea of how many people you will need. Part 4 of your textbook, "Human Resources," especially Chapters 9 and 10, should help you in answering some of the questions in this part of the business plan.

The Human Resources Component

To ensure successful performance by employees, you must inform workers of their specific job requirements. Employees must know what is expected of the job, and they are entitled to expect regular feedback on their work. It is vital to have a formal job description and job specification for every position in your business. Also, you should establish procedures for evaluating performance.

The labor force component should include the answers to at least the following questions:

4.1 How many employees will you require, and what qualifications should they have—including skills, experience, and knowledge? How many jobs will be full-time? Part-time?

4.2 Will you have written job descriptions for each position?

4.3 Have you prepared a job-application form? Do you know what can legally be included in it?

4.4 What criteria will you use in selecting employees?

4.5 Have you made plans for the orientation process?

4.6 Who will do the training?

4.7 What can you afford to pay in wages and salaries? Is this in line with the going rate in your region and industry?

4.8 Who will evaluate your employees?

4.9 Will you delegate any authority to employees?

4.10 Have you developed a set of disciplinary rules?

4.11 Do you plan to interview employees when they resign?

Review of Business Plan Activities

Remember that your employees are the company's most valuable and important resource. Therefore, make sure that you expend a great deal of effort to acquire and make full use of this resource. Check and resolve any issues in this component of your business plan before beginning Part 5. Again, make sure that your answers to the questions in each part are consistent with the entire business plan. Finally, write a brief statement that summarizes all the information for this part of the business plan.

The information contained in "Building a Business Plan" will also assist you in completing the online *Interactive Business Plan*.

Running a Business: Part 4, con't

which is a position we've never had on our staff before.... Identifying the gaps in your executive team and your talent pool, and going out and finding people to fill those gaps, is probably one of my most critical functions in addition to looking out to define the strategic direction of the company. I've got some wonderful people on the team now, and they are really helping us make the jump from a small business to a medium-sized business.... People at that level, you've got to pay them well. It's worth it, though.... They can command the kind of salary they do because they bring the talent you need to navigate the waters."

"You can't do it alone," Richard concludes. "That is the other thing that I think my cousins and I all have come to realize; we can't do it alone. Our fathers and aunt and the folks that came before them... they did it all, from figuring out where to build the next store to hanging up the laundry at the end of the day." But now, as the company's growth begins to surge, "you need to rely on talent that is beyond just you."[28]

Questions

1. If you were a Graeter's human resource executive, would you expect to do more internal recruiting or external recruiting for the company's retail stores? Why?

2. Graeter's controller believes the company "must be doing something right" because employee turnover is low. What are some of the factors that might be contributing to Graeter's low turnover?

3. Graeter's is currently a non-union company. How might the experience of working there change if a union were to be introduced?

PART FIVE
MARKETING

The business activities that make up a firm's marketing efforts are those most directly concerned with satisfying customers' needs. In this part, we explore these activities in some detail. Initially, we discuss markets, marketing mixes, marketing environment forces, marketing plans, and buying behavior. Then, we discuss the four elements that together make up a marketing mix: product, price, distribution, and promotion.

Chapter 11   Building Customer Relationships Through Effective Marketing
Chapter 12   Creating and Pricing Products that Satisfy Customers
Chapter 13   Distributing and Promoting Products

CHAPTER 11 BUILDING CUSTOMER RELATIONSHIPS THROUGH EFFECTIVE MARKETING

© Kayte M. Deioma/PhotoEdit

Why should you care?

Marketers are concerned about building long-term customer relationships. To develop competitive product offerings, business people must identify acceptable target customer groups and understand their behaviors.

Learning Objectives

What you will be able to do once you complete this chapter:

1 Understand the meaning of *marketing* and the importance of management of customer relationships.

2 Explain how marketing adds value by creating several forms of utility.

3 Trace the development of the marketing concept and understand how it is implemented.

4 Understand what markets are and how they are classified.

5 Identify the four elements of the marketing mix and be aware of their importance in developing a marketing strategy.

6 Explain how the marketing environment affects strategic market planning.

7 Understand the major components of a marketing plan.

8 Describe how market measurement and sales forecasting are used.

9 Distinguish between a marketing information system and marketing research.

10 Identify the major steps in the consumer buying decision process and the sets of factors that may influence this process.

Domino's Pizza Cooks Up Marketing Turnaround

What pizza company would admit—publicly—that some customers think its pizza crust tastes like cardboard and its sauce tastes like ketchup? Only one: Domino's Pizza. With more than 9,000 stores in 60 nations, Domino's delivers 1.3 million pizzas every day. Yet after research revealed how many pizza lovers were unhappy with its pies, Domino's marketers decided they needed a bold new strategy for winning customers back and encouraging noncustomers to give their pizza a try.

In an unusually candid marketing campaign called the "Pizza Turnaround," Dominos acknowledged the complaints and responded by ripping up its 49-year-old recipe. Its television commercials showed real customers griping and real Domino's chefs cooking up a fresh new recipe. To top it off, Domino's offered a money-back guarantee on every pie. The campaign worked remarkably well: Within weeks, Domino's sales and profits were on the rise as consumers rushed to try the new taste.

The company also got customers involved by inviting them to send in their photos of Domino's pizza, exactly as the pie looked when delivered. The idea was to show that a Domino's pizza is as mouth-watering in real life as it looks in any ad. Customers whose photos were chosen to be featured in Domino's ads received $500.

Knowing that its customers like online interaction, Domino's now invites orders on its Web site, maintains an active Facebook page (with 2 million "likes"), and tweets about special offers and new products via Twitter. It also provides a convenient app for smart phone users who want to order while on the go.

Domino's marketers continue to study their customers closely and respond. For example, the company recently introduced breakfast pizzas without sauce, a product line that's especially popular on college campuses. Domino's also examines order trends to anticipate and prepare for peaks and valleys of demand. On Super Bowl Sunday, the year's biggest pizza delivery day, members of the kitchen staff watch the game so they will know exactly when to expect an avalanche of orders (at the start of half-time, for instance).[1]

Did you know?

On Super Bowl Sunday, the single biggest pizza delivery day of the year, customers eat up 9 million slices of Domino's pizza.

Numerous organizations, like Domino's Pizza, use marketing efforts to provide customer satisfaction and value. Understanding customers' needs, such as "what's cool," is crucial to provide customer satisfaction. Although marketing encompasses a diverse set of decisions and activities performed by individuals as well as both business and nonbusiness organizations, marketing always begins and ends with the customer. The American Marketing Association defines **marketing** as "The activity, set of institutions, and processes for creating, communicating, delivering, and exchanging offerings that have value for customers, clients, partners, and society at large."[2] The marketing process involves eight major functions and numerous related activities (see Table 11-1). All these functions are essential if the marketing process is to be effective.

In this chapter, we examine marketing activities that add value to products. We trace the evolution of the marketing concept and describe how organizations practice it. Next, our focus shifts to market classifications and marketing strategy. We analyze the four elements of a marketing mix and also discuss uncontrollable factors in the marketing environment. Then we examine the major components of a marketing

marketing the activity, set of institutions, and processes for creating, communicating, delivering, and exchanging offerings that have value for customers, clients, partners, and society at large

TABLE 11-1: Eight Major Marketing Functions

Exchange functions: All companies—manufacturers, wholesalers, and retailers—buy and sell to market their merchandise.

1. Buying includes obtaining raw materials to make products, knowing how much merchandise to keep on hand, and selecting suppliers.

2. Selling creates possession utility by transferring the title of a product from seller to customer.

Physical distribution functions: These functions involve the flow of goods from producers to customers. Transportation and storage provide time utility and place utility and require careful management of inventory.

3. Transporting involves selecting a mode of transport that provides an acceptable delivery schedule at an acceptable price.

4. Storing goods is often necessary to sell them at the best selling time.

Facilitating functions: These functions help the other functions to take place.

5. Financing helps at all stages of marketing. To buy raw materials, manufacturers often borrow from banks or receive credit from suppliers. Wholesalers may be financed by manufacturers, and retailers may receive financing from the wholesaler or manufacturer. Finally, retailers often provide financing to customers.

6. Standardization sets uniform specifications for products or services. Grading classifies products by size and quality, usually through a sorting process. Together, standardization and grading facilitate production, transportation, storage, and selling.

7. Risk taking—even though competent management and insurance can minimize risks—is a constant reality of marketing because of such losses as bad-debt expense, obsolescence of products, theft by employees, and product-liability lawsuits.

8. Gathering market information is necessary for making all marketing decisions.

© Cengage Learning 2013

plan. We consider tools for strategic market planning, including market measurement, sales forecasts, marketing information systems, and marketing research. Last, we look at the forces that influence consumer and organizational buying behavior.

MANAGING CUSTOMER RELATIONSHIPS

LEARNING OBJECTIVE

1 Understand the meaning of *marketing* and the importance of management of customer relationships.

Marketing relationships with customers are the lifeblood of all businesses. Maintaining positive relationships with customers is an important goal for marketers. The term **relationship marketing** refers to "marketing decisions and activities focused on achieving long-term, satisfying relationships with customers." Relationship marketing continually deepens the buyer's trust in the company, which, as the customer's loyalty grows, increases a company's understanding of the customer's needs and desires. Successful marketers respond to customers' needs and strive to continually increase value to buyers over time. Eventually, this interaction becomes a solid relationship that allows for cooperation and mutual trust. Sears, for example, offers Shop Your Way Rewards, a card-based program that provides incentives for frequent shoppers at any Sears or Kmart store, as well as their online sites. Members of this program receive rewards totaling 1 percent of their purchases, which can be used in a store, spent online, or saved for later use. Members are allowed to return any items they purchase without presenting a receipt, can take part in exclusive promotional events, and are also entered to win prizes. Such initiatives give stores the opportunity to build stronger relationships with customers.[3]

To build long-term customer relationships, marketers are increasingly turning to marketing research and information technology. **Customer relationship management (CRM)** focuses on using information about customers to create marketing strategies that develop and sustain desirable customer relationships. By increasing customer value over time, organizations try to retain and increase long-term profitability through customer loyalty.

Managing customer relationships requires identifying patterns of buying behavior and using this information to focus on the most promising and profitable customers. Companies must be sensitive to customers' requirements and desires and

relationship marketing establishing long-term, mutually satisfying buyer–seller relationships

customer relationship management (CRM) using information about customers to create marketing strategies that develop and sustain desirable customer relationships

Concept Check ✱

☐ How can technology help to build long-term customer relationships?

☐ What are the benefits of retaining customers?

Building long-term customer relationships. L.L. Bean has been building long-term customer relationships for 100 years. As indicated in this ad, L.L Bean provides free shipping, a long-term warranty, and three ways to shop.

LEARNING OBJECTIVE

2 Explain how marketing adds value by creating several forms of utility.

customer lifetime value a measure of a customer's worth (sales minus costs) to a business over one's lifetime

utility the ability of a good or service to satisfy a human need

form utility utility created by converting production inputs into finished products

place utility utility created by making a product available at a location where customers wish to purchase it

time utility utility created by making a product available when customers wish to purchase it

possession utility utility created by transferring title (or ownership) of a product to a buyer

establish communication to build customers' trust and loyalty. In some instances, it may be more profitable for a company to focus on satisfying a valuable existing customer than to attempt to attract a new one who may never develop the same level of loyalty. This involves determining how much the customer will spend over his or her lifetime. The **customer lifetime value** is a measure of a customer's worth (sales minus costs) to a business during one's lifetime.[4] However, there are also intangible benefits of retaining lifetime-value customers, such as their ability to provide feedback to a company and refer new customers of similar value. The amount of money a company is willing to spend to retain such customers is also a factor. In general, when marketers focus on customers chosen for their lifetime value, they earn higher profits in future periods than when they focus on customers selected for other reasons.[5] Because the loss of a potential lifetime customer can result in lower profits, managing customer relationships has become a major focus of marketers.

UTILITY: THE VALUE ADDED BY MARKETING

As defined in Chapter 8, **utility** is the ability of a good or service to satisfy a human need. A lunch at a Pizza Hut, an overnight stay at a Holiday Inn, and a Mercedes S500L all satisfy human needs. Thus, each possesses utility. There are four kinds of utility.

Form utility is created by converting production inputs into finished products. Marketing efforts may influence form utility indirectly because the data gathered as part of marketing research are frequently used to determine the size, shape, and features of a product.

Personal App One glance down the food aisle of any store will show you the importance of form utility. When you're hungry, form utility is the way marketers satisfy your need for a sweet or salty snack, a single-serving size or a giant family size, a no-fat, low-fat, or reduced-fat food.

The three kinds of utility that are created directly by marketing are place, time, and possession utility. **Place utility** is created by making a product available at a location where customers wish to purchase it. A pair of shoes is given place utility when it is shipped from a factory to a department store.

Time utility is created by making a product available when customers wish to purchase it. For example, Halloween costumes may be manufactured in April but not displayed until late September, when consumers start buying them. By storing the costumes until they are wanted, the manufacturer or retailer provides time utility.

Possession utility is created by transferring title (or ownership) of a product to a buyer. For a product as simple as a pair of shoes, ownership usually is transferred by means of a sales slip or receipt. For such products as automobiles and homes, the transfer of title is a more complex process. Along with the title to its products, the seller transfers the right to use that product to satisfy a need (see Figure 11-1).

Place, time, and possession utility have real value in terms of both money and convenience. This value is created and added to goods and services through a wide variety of marketing activities—from research indicating what customers want to product warranties ensuring that customers get what they pay for. Overall, these marketing activities account for about half of every dollar spent by consumers. When they are part of an integrated marketing program that delivers maximum utility to the customer, many would agree that they are worth the cost.

Place, time, and possession utility are only the most fundamental applications of marketing activities. In recent years, marketing activities have been influenced by a broad business philosophy known as the *marketing concept*.

THE MARKETING CONCEPT

The **marketing concept** is a business philosophy that a firm should provide goods and services that satisfy customers' needs through a coordinated set of activities that allow the firm to achieve its objectives. Thus, initially, the firm must communicate with potential customers to assess their product needs. Then, the firm must develop a good or service to satisfy those needs. Finally, the firm must continue to seek ways to provide customer satisfaction. This process is an application of the marketing concept or marketing orientation. Ben & Jerry's, for example, constantly assesses customer demand for ice cream and sorbet. On its Web site, it maintains a "flavor graveyard" listing combinations that were tried and ultimately failed. It also notes its top ten flavors each month. Thus, the marketing concept emphasizes that marketing begins and ends with customers.

© Getty Images

Evolution of the Marketing Concept

From the start of the Industrial Revolution until the early 20th century, business effort was directed mainly toward the production of goods. Consumer demand for manufactured products was so great that manufacturers could almost bank on selling everything they produced. Business had a strong *production orientation*, in which emphasis was placed on increased output and production efficiency. Marketing was limited to taking orders and distributing finished goods.

LEARNING OBJECTIVE

3 Trace the development of the marketing concept and understand how it is implemented.

FIGURE 11-1: **Types of Utility**

Form utility is created by the production process, but marketing creates place, time, and possession utility.

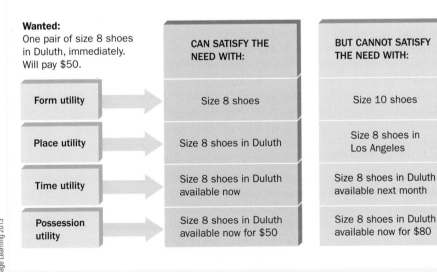

	CAN SATISFY THE NEED WITH:	BUT CANNOT SATISFY THE NEED WITH:
Wanted: One pair of size 8 shoes in Duluth, immediately. Will pay $50.		
Form utility	Size 8 shoes	Size 10 shoes
Place utility	Size 8 shoes in Duluth	Size 8 shoes in Los Angeles
Time utility	Size 8 shoes in Duluth available now	Size 8 shoes in Duluth available next month
Possession utility	Size 8 shoes in Duluth available now for $50	Size 8 shoes in Duluth available now for $80

© Cengage Learning 2013

marketing concept a business philosophy that a firm should provide goods and services that satisfy customers' needs through a coordinated set of activities that allow the firm to achieve its objectives

The marketing concept. Being focused on the customer and providing customer satisfaction is at the heart of the marketing concept.

© Stew Leonard's

In the 1920s, production caught up with and began to exceed demand. Now producers had to direct their efforts toward selling goods rather than just producing goods that consumers readily bought. This new *sales orientation* was characterized by increased advertising, enlarged sales forces, and, occasionally, high-pressure selling techniques. Manufacturers produced the goods they expected consumers to want, and marketing consisted primarily of promoting products through personal selling and advertising, taking orders, and delivering goods.

During the 1950s, however, businesspeople started to realize that even enormous advertising expenditures and the most thoroughly proven sales techniques were not enough. Something else was needed if products were to sell as well as expected. It was then that business managers recognized that they were not primarily producers or sellers but rather were in the business of satisfying customers' needs. Marketers realized that the best approach was to adopt a customer orientation—in other words, the organization had to first determine what customers need and then develop goods and services to fill those particular needs (see Table 11-2).

All functional areas—research and development, production, finance, human resources, and, of course, marketing—are viewed as playing a role in providing customer satisfaction.

TABLE 11-2: Evolution of Customer Orientation

Business managers recognized that they were not primarily producers or sellers but were rather in the business of satisfying customers' wants.

Production Orientation	Sales Orientation	Customer Orientation
Take orders	Increase advertising	Determine customer needs
Distribute goods	Enlarge sales force	Develop products to fill these needs
	Intensify sales techniques	Achieve the organization's goals

© Cengage Learning 2013

Marketing Yourself via Webcam

career SUCCESS

All kinds of companies are saving money and time by interviewing job candidates via webcam. Zappos, the online retailer, screens job applicants by calling them on Skype. While its recruiters listen to candidates talk, they also learn a lot by observing body language and facial expressions.

Here are some tips for marketing yourself via webcam:

● Check that your equipment is in working order.

● Wear appropriate business attire to make a good impression.

● Sit facing a good light source so your face can be seen.

● Tidy up the area visible on camera and remove any inappropriate or distracting decorations.

● Close the windows and doors to keep out noise.

Do a run-through with a friend to be sure that you look professional on screen and that your answers can be heard. Remember, your interview may be replayed several times before managers make any hiring decisions. Are you ready for your webcam close-up?

Sources: Dakshana Bascaramurty, "The Video Job Interview: When Your Face Precedes the Face-to-face," *The Globe and Mail (Toronto, Canada)*, September 13, 2010, www.theglobeandmail.com; Patrick J. Kiger, "Webcam Job Interviews: How to Survive and Thrive," *Fast Company*, January 12, 2010, www.fastcompany.com; Barbara Kiviat, "Résumé? Check. Nice Suit? Check. Webcam?" *Time*, November 9, 2009, pp. 49–50.

Implementing the Marketing Concept

The marketing concept has been adopted by many of the most successful business firms. Some firms, such as Ford Motor Company and Apple Computer, have gone through minor or major reorganizations in the process. Because the marketing concept is essentially a business philosophy, anyone can say, "I believe in it." To make it work, however, management must fully adopt and then implement it.

To implement the marketing concept, a firm first must obtain information about its present and potential customers. The firm must determine not only what customers' needs are but also how well these needs are being satisfied by products currently in the market—both its own products and those of competitors. It must ascertain how its products might be improved and what opinions customers have about the firm and its marketing efforts.

The firm then must use this information to pinpoint the specific needs and potential customers toward which it will direct its marketing activities and resources. (Obviously, no firm can expect to satisfy all needs. Also, not every individual or firm can be considered a potential customer for every product manufactured or sold by a firm.) Next, the firm must mobilize its marketing resources to (1) provide a product that will satisfy its customers, (2) price the product at a level that is acceptable to buyers and that will yield an acceptable profit, (3) promote the product so that potential customers will be aware of its existence and its ability to satisfy their needs, and (4) ensure that the product is distributed so that it is available to customers where and when needed.

Finally, the firm must again obtain marketing information—this time regarding the effectiveness of its efforts. Can the product be improved? Is it being promoted properly? Is it being distributed efficiently? Is the price too high or too low? The firm must be ready to modify any or all of its marketing activities based on information about its customers and competitors. Sears' Kenmore brand, for example, has become an iconic American brand of appliances, known for its high quality, dependability, and innovation. However, as the brand neared its 85-year mark, managers at Sears noticed that the aging brand was not in very high demand among the younger population. The company decided to rebrand Kenmore, modernizing it with a focus on sophisticated, contemporary styling and increased energy efficiency. Sears decided to market its new brand's vision mostly to women in their 20s to 50s, specifically "savvy moms" and young first-time home buyers. The company launched a new advertising campaign, with television advertisements, as well as online advertisements on Facebook, YouTube, and Twitter. All advertisements featured real customers or actual engineers at Kenmore, and used the tagline "Kenmore, That's Genius." Sears also launched the Kenmore.com site, where customers could view and purchase Kenmore products and use the "help me choose" tool to help them find the best model for their needs. Sears hopes that this rebranding will help Kenmore appeal to the younger generations as the market adjusts.[6]

MARKETS AND THEIR CLASSIFICATION

LEARNING OBJECTIVE

4 Understand what markets are and how they are classified.

A **market** is a group of individuals or organizations, or both, that need products in a given category and that have the ability, willingness, and authority to purchase such products. The people or organizations must want the product. They must be able to purchase the product by exchanging money, goods, or services for it. They must be willing to use their buying power. Finally, they must be socially and legally authorized to purchase the product.

Markets are broadly classified as consumer or business-to-business markets. These classifications are based on the characteristics of the individuals and organizations within each market. Because marketing efforts vary depending on the intended market, marketers should understand the general characteristics of these two groups.

Personal App Think about the purchases you've made this year. From books and beverages to movies and music, you're part of the consumer market for many types of products. You want these products, and you also have the ability, authority, and money to buy them.

Consumer markets consist of purchasers and/or household members who intend to consume or benefit from the purchased products and who do not buy products to make profits. *Business-to-business markets*, also called *industrial markets*, are grouped broadly into producer, reseller, governmental, and institutional categories. These markets purchase specific kinds of products for use in making other products for resale or for day-to-day operations. *Producer markets* consist of individuals and business organizations that buy certain products to use in the manufacture of other products. *Reseller markets* consist of intermediaries such as wholesalers and retailers, who buy finished products and sell them for a profit. *Governmental markets* consist of federal, state, county, and local governments. They buy goods and services to maintain internal operations and to provide citizens with such products as highways, education, water, energy, and national defense. Governmental purchases total billions of dollars each year. *Institutional markets* include churches, not-for-profit private schools and hospitals, civic clubs, fraternities and sororities, charitable organizations, and foundations. Their goals are different from such typical business goals as profit, market share, or return on investment.

DEVELOPING MARKETING STRATEGIES

A **marketing strategy** is a plan that will enable an organization to make the best use of its resources and advantages to meet its objectives. A marketing strategy consists of (1) the selection and analysis of a target market and (2) the creation and maintenance of an appropriate **marketing mix**, a combination of product, price, distribution, and promotion developed to satisfy a particular target market.

market a group of individuals or organizations, or both, that need products in a given category and that have the ability, willingness, and authority to purchase such products

marketing strategy a plan that will enable an organization to make the best use of its resources and advantages to meet its objectives

marketing mix a combination of product, price, distribution, and promotion developed to satisfy a particular target market

Target Market Selection and Evaluation

A **target market** is a group of individuals or organizations, or both, for which a firm develops and maintains a marketing mix suitable for the specific needs and preferences of that group. In selecting a target market, marketing managers examine potential markets for their possible effects on the firm's sales, costs, and profits. The managers attempt to determine whether the organization has the resources to produce a marketing mix that meets the needs of a particular target market and whether satisfying these needs is consistent with the firm's overall objectives. They also analyze the strengths and number of competitors already marketing to people in this target market. Marketing managers may define a target market as a sizable number of people or a relatively small group. The Nissan Cube, for example, definitely has features to attract the teens and early 20-somethings, including an upgraded Rockford Fosgate subwoofer, an interface system

Segmentation based on gender and age. Dooney & Bourke handbags are not aimed at everyone. Instead, they are targeted at a specific market segment—teenage girls and young women under 35 years old.

for the iPod, smaller cup holders for energy drinks, and the option to add more than 40 accessories. Nissan also ensured that its promotion, price, and distribution were appropriate for this target market. The price point for the Cube starts at just under $14,000. Ideas for promoting this vehicle came straight from U.S. college students who competed to have their marketing strategy adopted by Nissan and are part of this vehicle's target market.[7] On the other hand, Rolls-Royce targets its automobiles toward a small, very exclusive market: wealthy people who want the ultimate in prestige in an automobile. Other companies target multiple markets with different products, prices, distribution systems, and promotion for each one. Nike uses this strategy, marketing different types of shoes to meet specific needs of cross-trainers, rock climbers, basketball players, aerobics enthusiasts, and other athletic-shoe buyers. When selecting a target market, marketing managers generally take either the undifferentiated approach or the market segmentation approach.

UNDIFFERENTIATED APPROACH A company that designs a single marketing mix and directs it at the entire market for a particular product is using an **undifferentiated approach** (see Figure 11-2). This approach assumes that individual customers in the target market for a specific kind of product have similar needs and that the organization therefore can satisfy most customers with a single marketing mix. This single marketing mix consists of one type of product with little or no variation, one price, one promotional program aimed at everyone, and one distribution system to reach all customers in the total market. Products that can be marketed successfully with the undifferentiated approach include staple food items, such as sugar and salt, and certain kinds of farm produce. An undifferentiated approach is useful in only a limited number of situations because for most product categories buyers have different needs. When customers' needs vary, a company should use the market segmentation approach.

MARKET SEGMENTATION APPROACH A firm that is marketing 40-foot yachts would not direct its marketing effort toward every person in the total boat market. Some might want a sailboat or a canoe. Others might want a speedboat or an outboard-powered fishing boat. Still others might be looking for something resembling a small ocean liner. Marketing efforts directed toward such boat buyers would be wasted.

target market a group of individuals or organizations, or both, for which a firm develops and maintains a marketing mix suitable for the specific needs and preferences of that group

undifferentiated approach directing a single marketing mix at the entire market for a particular product

FIGURE 11-2: General Approaches for Selecting Target Markets

The undifferentiated approach assumes that individual customers have similar needs and that most customers can be satisfied with a single marketing mix. When customers' needs vary, the market segmentation approach—either concentrated or differentiated—should be used.

UNDIFFERENTIATED APPROACH

Organization → Single marketing mix (Product, Price, Distribution, Promotion) → Target market

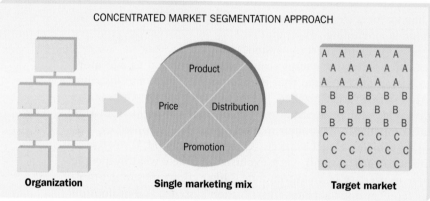

CONCENTRATED MARKET SEGMENTATION APPROACH

Organization → Single marketing mix (Product, Price, Distribution, Promotion) → Target market

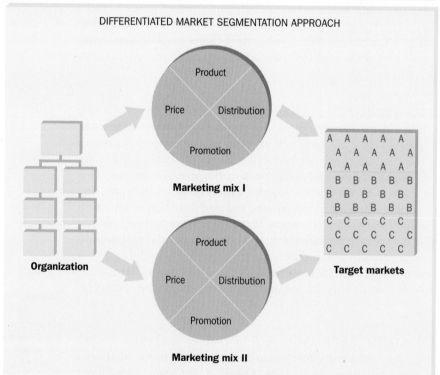

DIFFERENTIATED MARKET SEGMENTATION APPROACH

Organization → Marketing mix I (Product, Price, Distribution, Promotion) / Marketing mix II (Product, Price, Distribution, Promotion) → Target markets

NOTE: The letters in each target market represent potential customers. Customers that have the same letters have similar characteristics and similar product needs.

Source: William M. Pride and O. C. Ferrell, *Marketing: Concepts and Strategies,* 16th ed. (Mason, OH: South-Western/Cengage Learning, 2012). Adapted with permission.

Instead, the firm would direct its attention toward a particular portion, or *segment*, of the total market for boats. A **market segment** is a group of individuals or organizations within a market that shares one or more common characteristics. The process of dividing a market into segments is called **market segmentation**. As shown in Figure 11-2, there are two types of market segmentation approaches: concentrated and differentiated. When an organization uses *concentrated* market segmentation, a single marketing mix is directed at a single market segment. If *differentiated* market segmentation is used, multiple marketing mixes are focused on multiple market segments.

Personal App Do you and your friends wear the same types of clothing, listen to the same music, and shop in the same stores? Even small differences in behavior can signal needs to be addressed through market segmentation.

In our boat example, one common characteristic, or *basis*, for segmentation might be "end use of a boat." The firm would be interested primarily in the market segment whose uses for a boat could lead to the purchase of a 40-foot yacht. Another basis for segmentation might be income, still another might be geographic location. Each of these variables can affect the type of boat an individual might purchase. When choosing a basis for segmentation, it is important to select a characteristic that relates to differences in people's needs for a product. The yacht producer, for example, would not use religion to segment the boat market because people's needs for boats do not vary based on religion.

Marketers use a wide variety of segmentation bases. Bases most commonly applied to consumer markets are shown in Table 11-3. Each may be used as a single basis for market segmentation or in combination with other bases. OfficeMax, for example, is typically considered to be in a not-so-dazzling industry with a very broad

Undifferentiated approach. The producer of Morton Salt uses an undifferentiated approach because people's needs for salt are homogeneous.

Image courtesy of Susan Van Etten

TABLE 11-3: Common Bases of Market Segmentation

Demographic	Psychographic	Geographic	Behavioristic
Age	Personality attributes	Region	Volume usage
Gender	Motives	Urban, suburban, rural	End use
Race	Lifestyles	Market density	Benefit expectations
Ethnicity		Climate	Brand loyalty
Income		Terrain	Price sensitivity
Education		City size	
Occupation		County size	
Family size		State size	
Family life cycle			
Religion			
Social class			

Source: William M. Pride and O. C. Ferrell, *Marketing: Concepts and Strategies,* 16th ed. (Mason, OH: South-Western/Cengage Learning, 2012). Adapted with permission.

market segment a group of individuals or organizations within a market that share one or more common characteristics

market segmentation the process of dividing a market into segments and directing a marketing mix at a particular segment or segments rather than at the total market

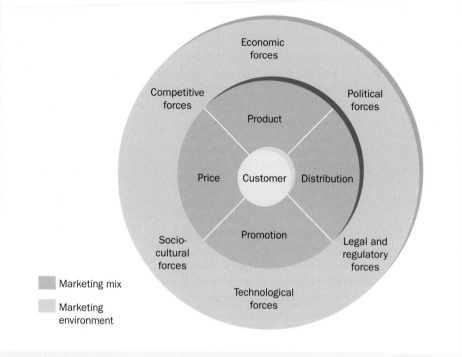

FIGURE 11-3: The Marketing Mix and the Marketing Environment

The marketing mix consists of elements that the firm controls—product, price, distribution, and promotion. The firm generally has no control over forces in the marketing environment.

Source: William M. Pride and O. C. Ferrell, *Marketing: Concepts and Strategies,* 16th ed. (Mason, OH: South-Western/ Cengage Learning, 2012). Adapted with permission.

definition for its target market (people and businesses that need office supplies). Therefore, the company recently decided to completely reposition itself. No longer a dull office supply store, it is now a fun, more intimate, retail outlet that appeals to women. The company repositioned itself through its campaign called "Life Is Beautiful, Work Can Be Too," which featured stylish new private-label product lines, a spiced up catalog, and appearances at venues like Mercedes-Benz Fashion Week in New York. OfficeMax has made a huge effort to separate itself from other office supply stores by further defining its target market and centering all of its marketing around "her."[8]

LEARNING OBJECTIVE
5 Identify the four elements of the marketing mix and be aware of their importance in developing a marketing strategy.

Creating a Marketing Mix

A business firm controls four important elements of marketing that it combines in a way that reaches the firm's target market. These are the *product* itself, the *price* of the product, the means chosen for its *distribution,* and the *promotion* of the product. When combined, these four elements form a marketing mix (see Figure 11-3). Nissan, for example, recently released the LEAF and developed a marketing mix that included an affordable, zero-emission electric vehicle with seating for five; a price starting at just over $25,000; distribution through straightforward online reservations and orders; and promotion through an extensive and interactive global tour, which included 63 stops in the United States.[9]

A firm can vary its marketing mix by changing any one or more of these ingredients. Thus, a firm may use one marketing mix to reach one target market and a second, somewhat different, marketing mix to reach another target market. For example, most automakers produce several different types and models of vehicles and aim them at different market segments based on the potential customers' age, income, and other factors.

The *product* ingredient of the marketing mix includes decisions about the product's design, brand name, packaging, warranties, and the like. When McDonald's decides on brand names, package designs, sizes of orders, flavors of sauces, and recipes, these choices are all part of the product ingredient.

The *pricing* ingredient is concerned with both base prices and discounts of various kinds. Pricing decisions are intended to achieve particular goals, such as to maximize profit or even to make room for new models. The rebates offered by automobile manufacturers are a pricing strategy developed to boost low auto sales. Product and pricing are discussed in detail in Chapter 12.

The *distribution* ingredient involves not only transportation and storage but also the selection of intermediaries. How many levels of intermediaries should be used in the distribution of a particular product? Should the product be distributed as widely as possible or should distribution be restricted to a few specialized outlets in each area? Video rental retailers have had to make numerous decisions regarding distribution. Currently, vending machines like Redbox make up 19 percent of the video rental market, mail rental services like Netflix have 36 percent, and brick-and-mortar stores like Blockbuster own 45 percent. Fifteen years ago, almost all videos were distributed through brick-and-mortar stores. Distribution decisions and activities are discussed in more detail in Chapter 13.[10]

The *promotion* ingredient focuses on providing information to target markets. The major forms of promotion are advertising, personal selling, sales promotion, and public relations. These four forms are discussed in Chapter 13.

These ingredients of the marketing mix are controllable elements. A firm can vary each of them to suit its organizational goals, marketing goals, and target markets. As we extend our discussion of marketing strategy, we will see that the marketing environment includes a number of *uncontrollable* elements.

Recognizing marketing environmental forces. In this ad, Denny's marketing strategy recognizes that customers are experiencing difficulties during adverse economic conditions, and that Denny's wants to provide products with good customer value.

Marketing Strategy and the Marketing Environment

LEARNING OBJECTIVE
6 Explain how the marketing environment affects strategic market planning.

The marketing mix consists of elements that a firm controls and uses to reach its target market. In addition, the firm has control over such organizational resources as finances and information. These resources may be used to accomplish marketing goals, too. However, the firm's marketing activities are also affected by a number of external—and generally uncontrollable—forces. As Figure 11-3 illustrates, the following forces make up the external *marketing environment*:

- *Economic forces*—the effects of economic conditions on customers' ability and willingness to buy
- *Sociocultural forces*—influences in a society and its culture that result in changes in attitudes, beliefs, norms, customs, and lifestyles
- *Political forces*—influences that arise through the actions of elected and appointed officials
- *Competitive forces*—the actions of competitors, who are in the process of implementing their own marketing plans
- *Legal and regulatory forces*—laws that protect consumers and competition and government regulations that affect marketing
- *Technological forces*—technological changes that can create new marketing opportunities or cause products to become obsolete almost overnight

Online Videos Add Vitality to Marketing Mix

Online videos can add vitality to any marketing mix, helping companies engage, educate, and persuade customers. Whether a video shows a product demonstration or a customer testimonial, it can capture attention, build buzz, and highlight key features and benefits. Ford, for example, posts videos on YouTube, Facebook, and its Web site to spotlight its vehicles' innovative features. Blendtec demonstrates the power of its blenders through its popular "Will it blend?" videos. Viewers can't take their eyes off the screen as the CEO puts an iPod and other unlikely objects into a blender, turns it on, and the item is pulverized in just a few seconds.

Sources: Andrew Hampp, "Super Bowl Buzz Wears Off the Viral Video Chart," *Advertising Age*, March 3, 2011, www.adage.com; Erik Bratt, "Social Media: Adding Video to Your Digital Marketing Plan," *San Diego Union-Tribune*, February 6, 2011, www.signonsandiego.com; David Kiley, "Ford Kicks Off Social-Media Push for Explorer," *Advertising Age*, February 9, 2011, www.adage.com. www.youtube.com/user/Honda#p/c/1F2F88164C76470D/11/5gmzECyp7nA

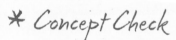
✱ Concept Check

☐ What are the major components of a marketing strategy?

☐ Describe the major approaches used in target market selection.

☐ Identify the four elements of the marketing mix.

☐ Describe the environmental forces that affect a firm's marketing activities.

LEARNING OBJECTIVE

7 Understand the major components of a marketing plan.

---

marketing plan a written document that specifies an organization's resources, objectives, strategy, and implementation and control efforts to be used in marketing a specific product or product group

---

These forces influence decisions about marketing-mix ingredients. Changes in the environment can have a major impact on existing marketing strategies. In addition, changes in environmental forces may lead to abrupt shifts in customers' needs. Consider the effect technological forces have had on printed newspapers: years ago, very few people would have predicted that consumers would one day have no need for their daily newspaper. However, that day has come; with 24-hour up-to-the-second news online, fewer people are buying newspapers. Consumers want today's news now and are able to access it, most of the time for free, from computers, smartphones, and other devices with Internet access.[11]

Personal App Don't underestimate the power of competitive forces. When companies compete, you—the consumer—wind up with more choices. In many cases, you'll also pay less because of competition.

DEVELOPING A MARKETING PLAN

A **marketing plan** is a written document that specifies an organization's resources, objectives, marketing strategy, and implementation and control efforts to be used in marketing a specific product or product group. The marketing plan describes the firm's current position or situation, establishes marketing objectives for the product, and specifies how the organization will attempt to achieve these objectives. Marketing plans vary with respect to the time period involved. Short-range plans are for one year or less, medium-range plans cover from over one year to five years, and long-range plans cover periods of more than five years.

Although time-consuming, developing a clear, well-written marketing plan is important. The plan will be used for communication among the firm's employees. It covers the assignment of responsibilities, tasks, and schedules for implementation. It specifies how resources are to be allocated to achieve marketing objectives. It helps marketing managers monitor and evaluate the performance of the marketing strategy. Because the forces of the marketing environment are subject to change, marketing plans have to be updated frequently. Disney, for example, recently made changes

TABLE 11-4: Components of the Marketing Plan

Plan Component	Component Summary	Highlights
Executive summary	One- to two-page synopsis of the entire marketing plan	
Environmental analysis	Information about the company's current situation with respect to the marketing environment	1. Assessment of marketing environment factors 2. Assessment of target market(s) 3. Assessment of current marketing objectives and performance
SWOT analysis	Assessment of the organization's strengths, weaknesses, opportunities, and threats	1. Strengths 2. Weaknesses 3. Opportunities 4. Threats
Marketing objectives	Specification of the firm's marketing objectives	Qualitative measures of what is to be accomplished
Marketing strategies	Outline of how the firm will achieve its objectives	1. Target market(s) 2. Marketing mix
Marketing implementation	Outline of how the firm will implement its marketing strategies	1. Marketing organization 2. Activities and responsibilities 3. Implementation timetable
Evaluation and control	Explanation of how the firm will measure and evaluate the results of the implemented plan	1. Performance standards 2. Financial controls 3. Monitoring procedures (audits)

Source: William M. Pride and O. C. Ferrell, *Marketing: Concepts and Strategies,* 16th ed. (Mason, OH: South-Western/Cengage Learning, 2012). Reprinted with permission.

to its marketing plans by combining all activities and licensing associated with the Power Rangers, Winnie the Pooh, and Disney Princess into one marketing plan with a $500 million budget. The primary goal is to send consistent messages about branding to customers. As the new marketing plan is implemented, Disney will have to respond quickly to customers' reactions and make adjustments to the plan. The major components of a marketing plan are shown in Table 11-4.

MARKET MEASUREMENT AND SALES FORECASTING

Measuring the sales potential of specific types of market segments helps an organization to make some important decisions, such as the feasibility of entering new segments. The organization can also decide how best to allocate its marketing resources and activities among market segments in which it is already active. All such estimates should identify the relevant time frame. As with marketing plans, these estimates may be short-range plans, covering periods of less than one year; medium-range plans, covering one to five years; or long-range plans, covering more than five years. The estimates should also define the geographic boundaries of the forecast. For example, sales potential can be estimated for a city, county, state, or group of nations. Finally, analysts should indicate whether their estimates are for a specific product item, a product line, or an entire product category.

A **sales forecast** is an estimate of the amount of a product that an organization expects to sell during a certain period of time based on a specified level of marketing

Concept Check ✱

☐ What are the major components of a marketing plan?

☐ Why is developing a well-written marketing plan important?

LEARNING OBJECTIVE
8 Describe how market measurement and sales forecasting are used.

sales forecast an estimate of the amount of a product that an organization expects to sell during a certain period of time based on a specified level of marketing effort

SPOT LIGHT

Most Promising Growth Opportunities in the Technology Industry

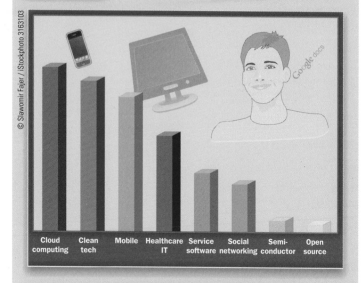

Cloud computing | Clean tech | Mobile | Healthcare IT | Service software | Social networking | Semi-conductor | Open source

Source: Fall 2010 DLA Piper Technology Leaders Forecast Survey was distributed via e-mail to a group of thousands of senior executives and advisors in the technology industry. www.dlapiper.com/files/upload/DLA_Piper_Tech_Survey_Report_2010.pdf (accessed March 23, 2011).

effort. Managers in different divisions of an organization rely on sales forecasts when they purchase raw materials, schedule production, secure financial resources, consider plant or equipment purchases, hire personnel, and plan inventory levels. Because the accuracy of a sales forecast is so important, organizations often use several forecasting methods, including executive judgments, surveys of buyers or sales personnel, time-series analyses, correlation analyses, and market tests. The specific methods used depend on the costs involved, type of product, characteristics of the market, time span of the forecast, purposes for which the forecast is used, stability of historical sales data, availability of the required information, and expertise and experience of forecasters.

MARKETING INFORMATION

The availability and use of accurate and timely information are critical to make effective marketing decisions. A wealth of marketing information is obtainable. There are two general ways to obtain it: through a marketing information system and through marketing research.

Marketing Information Systems

A **marketing information system** is a system for managing marketing information that is gathered continually from internal and external sources. Most of these systems are computer based because of the amount of data the system must accept, store, sort, and retrieve. *Continual* collection of data is essential if the system is to incorporate the most up-to-date information.

In concept, the operation of a marketing information system is not complex. Data from a variety of sources are fed into the system. Data from *internal* sources include sales figures, product and marketing costs, inventory levels, and activities of the sales force. Data from *external* sources relate to the organization's suppliers, intermediaries, and customers; competitors' marketing activities; and economic conditions. All these data are stored and processed within the marketing information system. Its output is a flow of information in the form that is most useful for making marketing decisions. This information might include daily sales reports by territory and product, forecasts of sales or buying trends, and reports on changes in market share for the major brands in a specific industry. Both the information outputs and their form depend on the requirements of the personnel in the organization. Anheuser-Busch, for example, uses a system called BudNet that compiles information about past sales at individual stores, inventory, competitors' displays and prices, and a host of other information collected by distributors' sales representatives on handheld computers. BudNet allows managers to respond quickly to changes in social trends or competitors' strategies with an appropriate promotional message, package, display, or discount.[12]

Marketing Research

Marketing research is the process of systematically gathering, recording, and analyzing data concerning a particular marketing problem. Thus, marketing research is used in specific situations to obtain information not otherwise available to decision makers. It is an intermittent, rather than a continual, source of marketing information.

* **Concept Check**

☐ Why is sales forecasting important?

☐ What methods do businesses use to forecast sales?

LEARNING OBJECTIVE

9 Distinguish between a marketing information system and marketing research.

marketing information system a system for managing marketing information that is gathered continually from internal and external sources

marketing research the process of systematically gathering, recording, and analyzing data concerning a particular marketing problem

Personal App If you're ever asked to participate in a survey, remember that by responding, you're helping a marketer understand your needs and do a better job of giving you what you want. Your answers and comments can make a real difference.

JCPenney, for example, conducted extensive research to learn more about a core segment of shoppers who were not being adequately reached by department stores: middle-income mothers between 35 and 54 years old. The research involved asking 900 women about their casual clothes preferences. Later, the firm conducted in-depth interviews with 30 women about their clothing needs, feelings about fashion, and shopping experiences. The research helped the company recognize that this "missing middle" segment of shoppers was frustrated with the choices and quality of the clothing available in their price range and stressed out by the experience of shopping for clothes for themselves. Armed with this information, JCPenney launched two new lines of moderately priced, quality casual women's clothing, including one by designer Nicole Miller.[13] A study by SPSS Inc. found that the most common reasons for conducting marketing research surveys included determining satisfaction (43 percent); product development (29 percent); branding (23 percent); segmentation (18 percent); awareness, trend tracking, and concept testing (18 percent); and business markets (11 percent).[14]

Table 11-5 outlines a six-step procedure for conducting marketing research. This procedure is particularly well-suited to test new products, determine various characteristics of consumer markets, and evaluate promotional activities. Food-processing companies, such as Kraft Foods and Kellogg's, use a variety of marketing research methods to avoid costly mistakes in introducing the wrong products, not to mention introducing products in the wrong way or at the wrong time. They have been particularly interested in using marketing research to learn more about the African-American and Hispanic markets. Understanding of the food preferences, loyalties, and purchase motivators of these groups enables companies to serve them better.

TABLE 11-5: The Six Steps of Marketing Research

1. Define the problem.	In this step, the problem is stated clearly and accurately to determine what issues are involved in the research, what questions to ask, and what types of solutions are needed. This is a crucial step that should not be rushed.
2. Make a preliminary investigation.	The objective of preliminary investigation is to develop both a sharper definition of the problem and a set of tentative answers. The tentative answers are developed by examining internal information and published data and by talking with persons who have some experience with the problem. These answers will be tested by further research.
3. Plan the research.	At this stage, researchers know what facts are needed to resolve the identified problem and what facts are available. They make plans on how to gather needed but missing data.
4. Gather factual information.	Once the basic research plan has been completed, the needed information can be collected by mail, telephone, or personal interviews; by observation; or from commercial or government data sources. The choice depends on the plan and the available sources of information.
5. Interpret the information.	Facts by themselves do not always provide a sound solution to a marketing problem. They must be interpreted and analyzed to determine the choices available to management.
6. Reach a conclusion.	Sometimes the conclusion or recommendation becomes obvious when the facts are interpreted. However, in other cases, reaching a conclusion may not be so easy because of gaps in the information or intangible factors that are difficult to evaluate. If and when the evidence is less than complete, it is important to say so.

Limits to Online Privacy?

Can online targeting go too far? When consumers do an online search or download a digital coupon, marketers can follow their electronic movements. For example, Jackson Hewitt recently offered digital coupons for its tax preparation services. Each coupon's bar code was unique, allowing the company's ad agency to track an individual consumer's search history leading up to the download.

The purpose of tracking online behavior is to do a better job of targeting communications and tailoring offers to customers' needs and interests. However, consumers are not always aware of exactly what information is being gathered, how it will be used, who will see it, and how long it will be retained. This raises questions about the limits of online privacy.

"Imagine that you were walking through a shopping mall, and there was someone that was walking behind you . . . taking notes on everywhere you went," says the head of the Federal Trade Commission. Moreover, the data would be available "to every shop or anyone who was interested, for a small fee." Privacy advocates also worry about identity theft and about the possibility of "online redlining," marketers restricting access to products based on what consumers do or say on the Internet. As experts debate the limits of online privacy, regulators are

formulating new privacy protections, makers of Web browsers are adding new anti-tracking features, and industry groups are developing new ways for consumers to opt out of tracking systems if they choose.

Sources: Julia Angwin, Scott Thurm, and Michael Hickins, "Lawmaker Introduces New Privacy Bill," *Wall Street Journal,* February 11, 2011, www.wsj.com; Wendy Davis, "Report: Marketers Limit Behavioral Targeting Due To Privacy Worries," *Media Post,* May 2, 2010, www.mediapost.com; Bob Garfield, "FTC Privacy Review Could Mean Trouble for Online Marketing," *Advertising Age,* April 19, 2010, www.adage.com; Stephanie Clifford, "Web Coupons Know Lots about You, and They Tell," *New York Times,* April 16, 2010, www.nytimes.com; Laurie Burkitt, "Ad Industry To Regulators: We Can Take Care Of Ourselves," *Forbes,* April 14, 2010, www.forbes.com; Steve Lohr, "How Privacy Vanishes Online," *New York Times,* March 16, 2010, www.nytimes.com.

Using Technology to Gather and Analyze Marketing Information

Technology is making information for marketing decisions increasingly accessible. The ability of firms to track the purchase behaviors of customers electronically and to better determine what they want is changing the nature of marketing. The integration of telecommunications with computing technology provides marketers with access to accurate information not only about customers and competitors but also about industry forecasts and business trends. Among the communication tools that are radically changing the way marketers obtain and use information are databases, online information services, and the Internet.

A *database* is a collection of information arranged for easy access and retrieval. Using databases, marketers tap into internal sales reports, newspaper articles, company news releases, government economic reports, bibliographies, and more. Many marketers use commercial databases, such as LEXIS-NEXIS, to obtain useful information for marketing decisions. Many of these commercial databases are available in printed form (for a fee), online (for a fee), or on purchasable CD-ROMs. Other marketers develop their own databases in-house. Some firms sell their databases to other organizations. *Reader's Digest*, for example, markets a database that provides information on 100 million households. Dunn & Bradstreet markets a database that includes information on the addresses, phone numbers, and contacts of businesses located in specific areas.

Information provided by a single firm on household demographics, purchases, television viewing behavior, and responses to promotions such as coupons and free samples is called *single-source data*. For example, Behavior Scan, offered by Information Resources, Inc., screens about 60,000 households in 26 U.S. markets. This single-source information service monitors household televisions and records the programs and commercials viewed. When buyers from these households shop in stores equipped with scanning registers, they present Hotline cards (similar to credit cards) to cashiers. This enables each customer's identification to be coded electronically so that the firm can track each product purchased and store the information in a database.

Online information services offer subscribers access to e-mail, Web sites, files for downloading (such as with Acrobat Reader), news, databases, and research materials. By subscribing to mailing lists, marketers can receive electronic newsletters and participate in online discussions with other network users. This ability to communicate online with customers, suppliers, and employees improves the capability of a firm's marketing information system and helps the company track its customers' changing desires and buying habits.

The *Internet* has evolved as a powerful communication medium, linking customers and companies around the world via computer networks with e-mail, forums, Web pages, and more. Growth in Internet use has given rise to an entire industry that makes marketing information easily accessible to both companies and customers. Among the many Web pages useful for marketing research are the home pages of Nielsen marketing research and *Advertising Age*. While most Web pages are open to all Internet users, some companies, such as U.S. West and Turner Broadcasting System, also maintain internal Web pages, called *intranets,* that allow employees to access internal data and facilitate communication among departments.

Table 11-6 contains a variety of sources of secondary information, which is existing information that has been gathered by other organizations. Many of these

TABLE 11-6: Sources of Secondary Information

Government sources	
Economic census	www.census.gov/econ/census07/
Export.gov—country and industry market research	www.export.gov/mrktresearch/index.asp
National Technical Information Services	www.ntis.gov/
STAT-USA	www.stat-usa.gov/
Strategis—Canadian trade	http://strategis.ic.gc.ca/engdoc/main.html
Trade associations and shows	
American Society of Association Executives	www.asaecenter.org/
Directory of Associations	www.marketingsource.com/associations/
Trade Show News Network	www.tsnn.com/
Magazines, newspapers, video, and audio news programming	
Blinkx	www.blinkx.com/
FindArticles.com	http://findarticles.com/p/articles/tn_bus/?tag=trunk
Google Video Search	http://video.google.com/
Media Jumpstation	www.directcontactpr.com/jumpstation/
Google News Directory	www.google.com/Top/News/
Yahoo! Video Search	http://video.search.yahoo.com/
Corporate information	
Annual Report Service	www.annualreportservice.com/
Bitpipe	www.bitpipe.com/
Business Wire—press releases	www.businesswire.com/
Hoover's Online	www.hoovers.com/
Open Directory Project	www.dmoz.org/
PR Newswire—press releases	www.prnewswire.com/

Source: Adapted from "Data Collection: Low-Cost Secondary Research," *KnowThis.com,* www.knowthis.com/principles-of-marketing-tutorials/data-collection-low-cost-secondary-research/ (accessed January 18, 2011).

Recognizing a problem. Some advertisements, such as this one for Olay Definity, are aimed at a particular stage of the consumer buying-decision process. This ad is meant to stimulate the problem-recognition stage of the buying-decision process.

✱ Concept Check

☐ Data from a marketing information system is collected from which internal and external sources?

☐ What are the major reasons for conducting marketing research?

☐ Identify and describe the six steps of the marketing research process.

☐ How does technology facilitate collecting and analyzing marketing information?

LEARNING OBJECTIVE

10 Identify the major steps in the consumer buying decision process and the sets of factors that may influence this process.

buying behavior the decisions and actions of people involved in buying and using products

consumer buying behavior the purchasing of products for personal or household use, not for business purposes

business buying behavior the purchasing of products by producers, resellers, governmental units, and institutions

sources are available through Web sites. As can be seen in Table 11-6, secondary information can be obtained from a variety of sources including government sources, trade associations, general publications and news sources, and corporate information.

A tool that has recently gained popularity as a means of marketing research is social media. There are many companies that have begun using various social media outlets to solicit feedback from customers on the company's existing or upcoming products. Not all information that a company receives will be solicited, however. A part of being involved in social media is exposing your company to unwanted or negative information from the general public. Nevertheless, these comments need to be regarded as useful and viable information from a marketing research standpoint. Customer complaints are opportunities for improvement; if handled correctly, they can be an invaluable source of data.

TYPES OF BUYING BEHAVIOR

Buying behavior may be defined as the decisions and actions of people involved in buying and using products.[15] **Consumer buying behavior** refers to the purchasing of products for personal or household use, not for business purposes. **Business buying behavior** is the purchasing of products by producers, resellers, governmental units, and institutions. Because a firm's success depends greatly on buyers' reactions to a particular marketing strategy, it is important to understand buying behavior. Marketing managers are better able to predict customer responses to marketing strategies and to develop a satisfying marketing mix if they are aware of the factors that affect buying behavior.

Consumer Buying Behavior

Consumers' buying behaviors differ when they buy different types of products. For frequently purchased low-cost items, a consumer uses routine response behavior involving very little search or decision-making effort. The buyer uses limited decision making for purchases made occasionally or when more information is needed about an unknown product in a well-known product category. When buying an unfamiliar, expensive item or one that is seldom purchased, the consumer engages in extensive decision making.

FIGURE 11-4: Consumer Buying Decision Process and Possible Influences on the Process

A buyer goes through some or all of these steps when making a purchase.

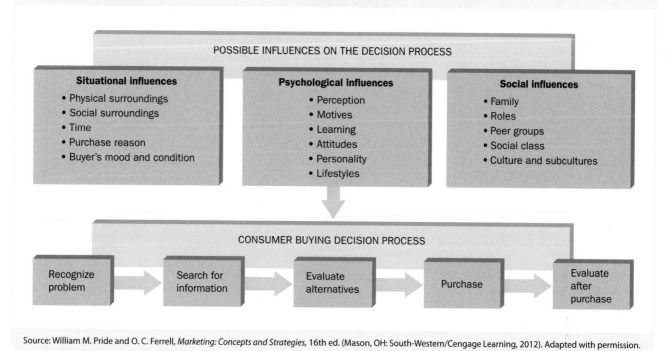

Source: William M. Pride and O. C. Ferrell, *Marketing: Concepts and Strategies,* 16th ed. (Mason, OH: South-Western/Cengage Learning, 2012). Adapted with permission.

Personal App Whether you're about to buy a pair of shoelaces or a digital camera, the process starts when you realize you've got some kind of problem. If it's a minor problem—such as a broken shoelace—it won't take you long to make your purchase. You'll usually spend more time and effort on a bigger problem, such as buying a new digital camera.

A person deciding on a purchase goes through some or all of the steps shown in Figure 11-4. First, the consumer acknowledges that a problem exists. A problem is usually the lack of a product or service that is desired or needed. Then, the buyer looks for information, which may include brand names, product characteristics, warranties, and other features. Next, the buyer weighs the various alternatives he or she has discovered and then finally makes a choice and acquires the item. In the after-purchase stage, the consumer evaluates the suitability of the product. This judgment will affect future purchases. As Figure 11-4 shows, the buying process is influenced by situational factors (physical surroundings, social surroundings, time, purchase reason, and buyer's mood and condition), psychological factors (perception, motives, learning, attitudes, personality, and lifestyle), and social factors (family, roles, reference groups, online social networks, social class, culture, and subculture).

Consumer buying behavior is also affected by the ability to buy or one's buying power, which is largely determined by income. As every taxpayer knows, not all income is available for spending. For this reason, marketers consider income in three different ways. **Personal income** is the income an individual receives from all sources *less* the Social Security taxes the individual must pay. **Disposable income** is personal income *less* all additional personal taxes. These taxes include income, estate, gift, and property taxes levied by local, state, and federal governments. About 3 percent of all disposable income is saved. **Discretionary income** is disposable income *less* savings and expenditures on food, clothing, and housing. Discretionary income is of particular interest to marketers because consumers have the most choice in spending

personal income the income an individual receives from all sources *less* the Social Security taxes the individual must pay

disposable income personal income *less* all additional personal taxes

discretionary income disposable income *less* savings and expenditures on food, clothing, and housing

Concept Check ✳

☐ Why is it important to understand buying behavior?

☐ How does a customer's decision-making time vary with the type of product?

☐ What are the five stages of the consumer buying decision process?

☐ What are the possible influences on this process?

☐ What is the difference between disposable income and discretionary income?

it. Consumers use their discretionary income to purchase items ranging from automobiles and vacations to movies and pet food.

Business Buying Behavior

Business buyers consider a product's quality, its price, and the service provided by suppliers. Business buyers are usually better informed than consumers about products and generally buy in larger quantities. In a business, a committee or a group of people, rather than just one person, often decides on purchases. Committee members must consider the organization's objectives, purchasing policies, resources, and personnel. Business buying occurs through description, inspection, sampling, or negotiation. A number of organizations buy a variety of products online.

Get Flashcards, Quizzes, Games, Crosswords, and more @ www.cengagebrain.com

SUMMARY

1 Understand the meaning of *marketing* and the importance of management of customer relationships.

Marketing is an organizational function and a set of processes for creating, communicating, and delivering value to customers and for managing customer relationships in ways that benefit the organization and its stakeholders. Maintaining positive relationships with customers is crucial. Relationship marketing is establishing long-term, mutually satisfying buyer–seller relationships. Customer relationship management uses information about customers to create marketing strategies that develop and sustain desirable customer relationships. Managing customer relationships requires identifying patterns of buying behavior and focusing on the most profitable customers. Customer lifetime value is a combination of purchase frequency, average value of purchases, and brand-switching patterns over the entire span of a customer's relationship with the company.

2 Explain how marketing adds value by creating several forms of utility.

Marketing adds value in the form of utility or the power of a product or service to satisfy a need. It creates place utility by making products available where customers want them, time utility by making products available when customers want them, and possession utility by transferring the ownership of products to buyers.

3 Trace the development of the marketing concept and understand how it is implemented.

From the Industrial Revolution until the early 20th century, businesspeople focused on the production of goods; from the 1920s to the 1950s, the emphasis moved to the selling of goods. During the 1950s, however, businesspeople recognized that their enterprises involved not only producing and selling products but also satisfying customers' needs. They began to implement the marketing concept, a business philosophy that involves the entire organization in the dual processes of meeting the customers' needs and achieving the organization's goals.

Implementation of the marketing concept begins and ends with customers—first to determine what customers' needs are and then to evaluate how well the firm is meeting these needs.

4 Understand what markets are and how they are classified.

A market consists of people with needs, the ability to buy, and the desire and authority to purchase. Markets are classified as consumer and industrial (producer, reseller, governmental, and institutional) markets.

5 Identify the four elements of the marketing mix and be aware of their importance in developing a marketing strategy.

A marketing strategy is a plan for the best use of an organization's resources to meet its objectives. Developing a marketing strategy involves selecting and analyzing a target market and creating and maintaining a marketing mix that will satisfy the target market. A target market is chosen through either the undifferentiated approach or the market segmentation approach. A market segment is a group of individuals or organizations within a market that have similar characteristics and needs. Businesses that use an undifferentiated approach design a single marketing mix and direct it at the entire market for a particular product. The market segmentation approach directs a marketing mix at a segment of a market.

The four elements of a firm's marketing mix are product, price, distribution, and promotion. The product ingredient includes decisions about the product's design, brand name, packaging, and warranties. The pricing ingredient is concerned with both base prices and various types of discounts. Distribution involves not only transportation and storage but also the selection of intermediaries. Promotion focuses on providing information to target markets. The elements of the marketing mix can be varied to suit broad organizational goals, marketing objectives, and target markets.

6 Explain how the marketing environment affects strategic market planning.

To achieve a firm's marketing objectives, marketing-mix strategies must begin with an assessment of the marketing environment, which, in turn, will influence decisions about marketing-mix ingredients. Marketing activities are affected by a number of external forces that make up the marketing environment. These forces include economic forces, sociocultural forces, political forces, competitive forces, legal and regulatory forces, and technological forces. Economic forces affect customers' ability and willingness to buy. Sociocultural forces are societal and cultural factors, such as attitudes, beliefs, and lifestyles, that affect customers' buying choices. Political forces and legal and regulatory forces influence marketing planning through laws that protect consumers and regulate competition. Competitive forces are the actions of competitors who are implementing their own marketing plans. Technological forces can create new marketing opportunities or quickly cause a product to become obsolete.

7 Understand the major components of a marketing plan.

A marketing plan is a written document that specifies an organization's resources, objectives, strategy, and implementation and control efforts to be used in marketing a specific product or product group. The marketing plan describes a firm's current position, establishes marketing objectives, and specifies the methods the organization will use to achieve these objectives. Marketing plans can be short-range plans, covering one year or less; medium-range plans, covering two to five years; or long-range plans, covering periods of more than five years.

8 Describe how market measurement and sales forecasting are used.

Market measurement and sales forecasting are used to estimate sales potential and predict product sales in specific market segments.

9 Distinguish between a marketing information system and marketing research.

Strategies are monitored and evaluated through marketing research and the marketing information system that stores and processes internal and external data in a form that aids marketing decision making. A marketing information system is a system for managing marketing information that is gathered continually from internal and external sources. Marketing research is the process of systematically gathering, recording, and analyzing data concerning a particular marketing problem. It is an intermittent rather than a continual source of marketing information. Technology is making information for marketing decisions more accessible. Electronic communication tools can be very useful for accumulating accurate information with minimal customer interaction. Information technologies that are changing the way marketers obtain and use information are databases, online information services, and the Internet. Some companies are using social media to obtain feedback from customers.

10 Identify the major steps in the consumer buying decision process and the sets of factors that may influence this process.

Buying behavior consists of the decisions and actions of people involved in buying and using products. Consumer buying behavior refers to the purchase of products for personal or household use. Organizational buying behavior is the purchase of products by producers, resellers, governments, and institutions. Understanding buying behavior helps marketers to predict how buyers will respond to marketing strategies. The consumer buying decision process consists of five steps, that is, recognizing the problem, searching for information, evaluating alternatives, purchasing, and evaluating after purchase. Factors affecting the consumer buying decision process fall into three categories: situational influences, psychological influences, and social influences.

KEY TERMS

You should now be able to define and give an example relevant to each of the following terms:

marketing (304)
relationship marketing (305)
customer relationship management (CRM) (305)
customer lifetime value (306)
utility (306)

form utility (306)
place utility (306)
time utility (306)
possession utility (306)
marketing concept (307)
market (310)
marketing strategy (310)
marketing mix (310)
target market (311)

undifferentiated approach (311)
market segment (313)
market segmentation (313)
marketing plan (316)
sales forecast (317)
marketing information system (318)
marketing research (318)

buying behavior (322)
consumer buying behavior (322)
business buying behavior (322)
personal income (323)
disposable income (323)
discretionary income (323)

DISCUSSION QUESTIONS

1. What is relationship marketing?
2. How is a marketing-oriented firm different from a production-oriented firm or a sales-oriented firm?
3. What are the major requirements for a group of individuals and organizations to be a market? How does a consumer market differ from a business-to-business market?
4. What are the major components of a marketing strategy?
5. What is the purpose of market segmentation? What is the relationship between market segmentation and the selection of target markets?
6. Describe the forces in the marketing environment that affect an organization's marketing decisions.
7. What is a marketing plan, and what are its major components?

8. What new information technologies are changing the ways that marketers keep track of business trends and customers?
9. Why do marketers need to understand buying behavior?
10. Are there any problems for a company that focuses mainly on the most profitable customers?
11. How might adoption of the marketing concept benefit a firm? How might it benefit the firm's customers?
12. Is marketing information as important to small firms as it is to larger firms? Explain.
13. How does the marketing environment affect a firm's marketing strategy?

TEST YOURSELF

Matching Questions

1. _____ The process of planning and executing the conception, pricing, promotion, and distribution of ideas, goods, and services.
2. _____ A business philosophy that involves the satisfying of customers' needs while achieving a firm's goals.
3. _____ Value is added through converting raw materials into finished goods.
4. _____ It is the individuals in a market who share common characteristics.
5. _____ Income that is left after savings, food, clothing, and housing are paid.
6. _____ It is a combination of marketing elements designed to reach a target market.
7. _____ It is a plan of actions intended to accomplish a marketing goal.
8. _____ The decision-making process that is used when purchasing personal-use items.

9. _____ Marketing activities that focus on a particular group such as teenagers.
10. _____ The marketing objectives for a product are established.

a. consumer buying behavior
b. discretionary income
c. form utility
d. possession utility
e. market segment
f. marketing
g. marketing concept
h. customer lifetime value
i. marketing mix
j. marketing plan
k. marketing strategy
l. target market

True False Questions

11. **T** **F** Marketing is a process that fulfills consumers' needs.

12. **T** **F** Financing and risk taking are physical distribution functions of marketing.

13. **T** **F** The first step in implementing the marketing concept is to provide a product that satisfies customers.

14. **T** **F** Markets are classified as consumer markets or business-to-business markets.

15. **T** **F** The marketing mix is composed of product, price, distribution, and promotion.

16. **T** **F** When Toyota focuses its advertising for the Corolla on the population between the ages of 20 and 34, it is targeting a market.

17. **T** **F** The four common bases of market segmentation are demographic, strategic, geographic, and discretionary.

18. **T** **F** Pricing is an uncontrollable element of the marketing environment.

19. **T** **F** *Advertising Age* and *Hoover's* are important resources for marketing research.

20. **T** **F** Understanding factors that affect buying behavior helps marketing managers to predict consumer responses to marketing strategies and helps to develop a market mix.

Multiple-Choice Questions

21. _____ Which facilitating function of marketing is riddled with thefts, obsolescence, and lawsuits?
    a. Risk taking
    b. Standardizing
    c. Financing
    d. Information gathering
    e. Selling

22. _____ When fresh vegetables are shipped to Oklahoma from Mexico, which utility is added?
    a. Form
    b. Place
    c. Price
    d. Possession
    e. Time

23. _____ Sales orientation was predominate during the
    a. late 1800s.
    b. 1920s.
    c. 1940s.
    d. late 1950s.
    e. 1970s.

24. _____ To implement the marketing concept, the firm must mobilize its marketing resources to
    a. price the product at a level that is acceptable to buyers.
    b. provide a product that will not satisfy the firm's objectives.
    c. minimize promotion.
    d. reduce the number of distribution sites.
    e. obtain incorrect marketing information.

25. _____ Women in the market can be classified as
    a. market segmentation.
    b. a marketing mix.
    c. a market segment.
    d. an independent market.
    e. a producer market.

26. _____ What element in the market mix provides information to consumers?
    a. Product
    b. Price
    c. Promotion
    d. Distribution
    e. Quality

27. _____ Which ingredient in the marketing mix focuses on transportation, storage, and intermediaries?
    a. Product
    b. Price
    c. Distribution
    d. Promotion
    e. Buying

28. _____ Which environmental force influences change in consumers' attitudes, customs, and lifestyles?
    a. Legal, political, and regulatory
    b. Competitive
    c. Technological
    d. Economic
    e. Sociocultural

29. _____ What situational influence can affect the consumer buying process?
    a. They have uses for the products.
    b. They like the convenience that products provide.
    c. They take pride in ownership of products.
    d. They believe that products will enhance their wealth.
    e. All of the above.

30. _____ What type of income is Ramona's $2,450 monthly take-home amount *after* taxes?
    a. Ordinary
    b. Personal
    c. Disposable
    d. Gross
    e. Discretionary

Answers to the Test Yourself questions appear at the end of the book on page TY-1.

VIDEO CASE

E*Trade Focuses on Building Long-Term Customer Relationships, Even from the Crib

Even if you are not an active investor, you probably already know e*Trade, the online investing service, from its wildly successful series of funny television commercials. The ads feature an irreverent talking baby wielding a laptop and boasting about his investing expertise to all his admiring baby friends. The commercials were inspired by e*Trade's desire to come up with a marketing message that would not only be memorable and funny but would also create an overall sense of unity in its marketing efforts. (Before the baby appeared, each new advertisement was a start-from-scratch proposition.)

The theme of ease of use that the baby conveys has proven effective through several e*Trade advertising campaigns and Super Bowl spots. The ads' light-hearted appeal has also helped the company strengthen its brand name, particularly among hard-to-reach and highly desirable 20-somethings. Even the outtake reels have proven popular, and an online "Baby Mail" campaign in which viewers can insert their own words or their own pictures and share them with friends has successfully extended the marketing message from television to the Internet and from passive to interactive. "We are one of the largest online advertisers," says the company's senior vice president of marketing. "And we're an online company, so it stands to reason that we'd find different types of interactive ways to be able to reach consumers through the Internet as well."

E*Trade is a publicly traded financial and banking services company that encourages customers to take control of their own financial futures with an array of quick and easy-to-use online tools, products, and services. These are available online and also through a network of customer service representatives reachable both via telephone and in person at one of e*Trade's 28 retail branches across the United States. Mobile applications for the iPhone and the BlackBerry include access to a stripped-down e*Trade Web site and target

both experienced and novice investors. Securities can be traded instantaneously (when the stock exchanges are open; otherwise, the next trading day) or when a particular security meets the customer's desired buy or sell price.

E*Trade can accommodate customers' long- and short-term financial goals and prides itself on its ability to offer customers exactly what they need, often by replicating, as nearly as possible, the experience of talking to a financial advisor. Even if a user is just looking for information about investing, the company's online Investor Resource Center provides free educational articles, brief three-minute videos, webinars, and seminars about many different types of investment topics, from basic to sophisticated, as well as access to independent research about investment options. "Education has become a really major component for us and for our customers," says one of the company's vice presidents. A new feedback link on the company's Web site allows users to tell e*Trade what they like or don't like about a page on the Resource Center so improvements can be made. "It's really a core lesson in listening to your customers, what they want, and not always thinking that you know what they want," says a company executive.

Meanwhile, e*Trade's baby is unlikely to grow up very soon. "When people see that baby," says a company executive, "they stop their DVRs and they watch. I think the real challenge for us is being able to blend the combination of humor, magic, and the overall value proposition and message in a way that none of it gets buried."[16]

Questions

1. How does e*Trade manage its customer relationships?
2. How many different kinds of utility does e*Trade provide for its customers?
3. Why are young adults a desirable target market for a company like e*Trade?

BUILDING SKILLS FOR CAREER SUCCESS

1. Exploring the Internet

Consumer products companies with a variety of famous brand names known around the world are making their presence known on the Internet through Web sites and online banner advertising. The giants in consumer products include U.S.-based Procter & Gamble (www.pg.com/), Swiss-based Nestlé (www.nestle.com/), and U.K.-based Unilever (www.unilever.com/).

According to a spokesperson for the Unilever Interactive Brand Center in New York, the firm is committed to making the Internet part of its marketing strategy. The center carries out research and development and serves as a model for others now in operation in the Netherlands and Singapore. Information is shared with interactive marketers assigned to specific business units. Eventually, centers will be established globally, reflecting the fact that most of Unilever's $52 billion in sales takes place in about 100 countries around the world.

Unilever's view that online consumer product sales are the way of the future was indicated by online alliances established with Microsoft Network, America Online, and NetGrocer.com. Creating an online dialogue with consumers on a global scale is no simple task. Cultural differences are often subtle and difficult to explain but nonetheless are perceived by the viewers interacting with a site. Unilever's Web site, which is its connection to customers all over the world, has a global feel to it. The question is whether it is satisfactory to each target audience. Visit the text Web site for updates to this exercise.

Assignment
1. Examine the Unilever, Procter & Gamble, and Nestlé sites and describe the features that you think would be most interesting to consumers.
2. Describe the features you do not like and explain why.
3. Do you think that the sites can contribute to better consumer buyer behavior? Explain your thinking.

2. Building Team Skills

Review the text definitions of *market* and *target market*. Markets can be classified as consumer or industrial. Buyer behavior consists of the decisions and actions of those involved in buying and using products or services. By examining aspects of a company's products, you usually can determine the company's target market and the characteristics important to members of that target market.

Assignment
1. Working in teams of three to five, identify a company and its major products.
2. List and discuss characteristics that customers may find important. These factors may include price, quality, brand name, variety of services, salespeople, customer service, special offers, promotional campaign, packaging, convenience of use, convenience of purchase, location, guarantees, store/office decor, and payment terms.
3. Write a description of the company's primary customer (target market).

3. Researching Different Careers

Before interviewing for a job, you should learn all you can about the company. With this information, you will be prepared to ask meaningful questions about the firm during the interview, and the interviewer no doubt will be impressed with your knowledge of the business and your interest in it. To find out about a company, you can conduct some market research.

Assignment
1. Choose at least two local companies for which you might like to work.
2. Contact your local Chamber of Commerce. (The Chamber of Commerce collects information about local businesses, and most of its services are free.) Ask for information about the companies.
3. Call the Better Business Bureau in your community and ask if there are any complaints against the companies.
4. Prepare a report summarizing your findings.

CHAPTER 12 CREATING AND PRICING PRODUCTS THAT SATISFY CUSTOMERS

Why should you care?

To be successful, a business person must understand how to develop and manage a mix of appropriately priced products and to change the mix of products as customers' needs change.

© Konstantin Chagin/Shutterstock

Learning Objectives

What you will be able to do once you complete this chapter:

1 Explain what a product is and how products are classified.

2 Discuss the product life-cycle and how it leads to new-product development.

3 Define *product line* and *product mix* and distinguish between the two.

4 Identify the methods available for changing a product mix.

5 Explain the uses and importance of branding, packaging, and labeling.

6 Describe the economic basis of pricing and the means by which sellers can control prices and buyers' perceptions of prices.

7 Identify the major pricing objectives used by businesses.

8 Examine the three major pricing methods that firms employ.

9 Explain the different strategies available to companies for setting prices.

10 Describe three major types of pricing associated with business products.

Get Flashcards, Quizzes, Games, Crosswords, and more @ **www.cengagebrain.com**

E-Book Readers Battle On

How low can e-book reader prices go? Several electronic devices for buying, downloading, and reading digital books were available before Amazon.com decided to market its own. Once the Web-based retail giant jumped into e-book readers, however, its clout changed both the product and the pricing—forever.

Amazon released its first Kindle e-book reader in November, 2007. That first Kindle was priced at $399, yet all inventory sold out within weeks and orders continued to flood in long after the Christmas buying season was over. Even as the company struggled to produce enough Kindles to meet demand, it was already designing a second E-generation Kindle, with more memory (to hold more digital books) and a slimmer case. The Kindle 2 launched in 2009 with an initial price of $359, lowered in stages as Amazon's e-book reader took on a new competitor: the Nook.

The company behind the Nook is Barnes & Noble, a national bookstore chain that also has a major presence on the Internet. When Barnes & Noble began marketing the Nook at a lower price than the Kindle, Amazon quickly matched the Nook's $259 price. In turn, both the Nook and the Kindle soon felt a bit of competitive heat from the Apple iPad, a tablet computer that can double as an e-book reader. The iPad is priced higher than the Nook or the Kindle, but it has more functions, not to mention the Apple brand cachet.

By Christmas 2010, Amazon was selling its third-generation Kindle, improved with more memory, better battery life, and a more readable screen. The price was a wallet-pleasing $139 for the basic Kindle model. Sales skyrocketed and when the year was over, Amazon had sold an estimated 8 million Kindles and captured nearly half of the fast-growing U.S. e-book reader market. Meanwhile, the iPad 2 was in stores, and Barnes & Noble had a new color Nook.

These days, digital book sales are booming and competition among e-book readers is as fierce as ever. Buyers will be the big winners as marketers battle on, adding features and lowering prices on their e-book readers to capture or defend market share.[1]

Did you know?

Amazon's Kindle e-book readers account for nearly half of all e-book readers sold in the United States.

A **product**, like a Kindle or Nook, is everything one receives in an exchange, including all tangible and intangible attributes and expected benefits. An Apple iPod purchase, for example, includes not only the iPod itself but also earphones, instructions, and a warranty. A new car includes a warranty, an owner's manual, and perhaps free emergency road service for a year. Some of the intangibles that may go with an automobile include the status associated with ownership and the memories generated from past rides. Developing and managing products effectively are crucial to an organization's ability to maintain successful marketing mixes.

A product may be a good, a service, or an idea. A *good* is a real, physical thing that we can touch, such as a Classic Sport football. A *service* is the result of applying human or mechanical effort to a person or thing. Basically, a *service* is a change we pay others to make for us. A real estate agent's services result in a change in the ownership of real property. A barber's services result in a change in your appearance. An *idea* may take the form of philosophies, lessons, concepts, or advice. Often ideas are included with a good or service. Thus, we might buy a book (a good) that provides ideas on how to lose weight. Alternatively, we might join Weight Watchers for ideas on how to lose weight and for help (services) in doing so.

product everything one receives in an exchange, including all tangible and intangible attributes and expected benefits; it may be a good, a service, or an idea

We look first in this chapter at products. We examine product classifications and describe the four stages, or life-cycles, through which every product moves. Next, we illustrate how firms manage products effectively by modifying or deleting existing products and by developing new products. We also discuss branding, packaging, and labeling of products. Then our focus shifts to pricing. We explain competitive factors that influence sellers' pricing decisions and also explore buyers' perceptions of prices. After considering organizational objectives that can be accomplished through pricing, we outline several methods for setting prices. Finally, we describe pricing strategies by which sellers can reach target markets successfully.

CLASSIFICATION OF PRODUCTS

LEARNING OBJECTIVE

1 Explain what a product is and how products are classified.

Different classes of products are directed at particular target markets. A product's classification largely determines what kinds of distribution, promotion, and pricing are appropriate in marketing the product.

Products can be grouped into two general categories: consumer and business (also called *business-to-business* or *industrial products*). A product purchased to satisfy personal and family needs is a **consumer product**. A product bought for resale, for making other products, or for use in a firm's operations is a **business product**. The buyer's use of the product determines the classification of an item. Note that a single item can be both a consumer and a business product. A broom is a consumer product if you use it in your home. However, the same broom is a business product if you use it in the maintenance of your business. After a product is classified as a consumer or business product, it can be categorized further as a particular type of consumer or business product.

© AP Photo/Paul Cancya

Specialty products. Most cars are classified as shopping products. However, a few automobiles, such as the Bentley, are extremely expensive, have distinctive styling and amenities, and are distributed exclusively through just a few dealers. These distinctive vehicles are specialty products.

Consumer Product Classifications

The traditional and most widely accepted system of classifying consumer products consists of three categories: convenience, shopping, and specialty products. These groupings are based primarily on characteristics of buyers' purchasing behavior.

A **convenience product** is a relatively inexpensive, frequently purchased item for which buyers want to exert only minimal effort. Examples include bread, gasoline, newspapers, soft drinks, and chewing gum. The buyer spends little time in planning the purchase of a convenience item or in comparing available brands or sellers.

A **shopping product** is an item for which buyers are willing to expend considerable effort on planning and making the purchase. Buyers allocate ample time for comparing stores and brands with respect to prices, product features, qualities, services, and perhaps warranties. Appliances, upholstered furniture, men's suits, bicycles, and cellular phones are examples of shopping products. These products are expected to last for a fairly long time and thus are purchased less frequently than convenience items.

A **specialty product** possesses one or more unique characteristics for which a group of buyers is willing to expend considerable purchasing effort. Buyers actually plan the purchase of a specialty product; they know exactly what they want and will not accept a substitute. In searching for specialty products, purchasers do not compare alternatives. Examples include unique sports cars, a specific type of antique dining table, a rare imported beer, or perhaps special handcrafted stereo speakers.

consumer product a product purchased to satisfy personal and family needs

business product a product bought for resale, for making other products, or for use in a firm's operations

convenience product a relatively inexpensive, frequently purchased item for which buyers want to exert only minimal effort

shopping product an item for which buyers are willing to expend considerable effort on planning and making the purchase

specialty product an item that possesses one or more unique characteristics for which a significant group of buyers is willing to expend considerable purchasing effort

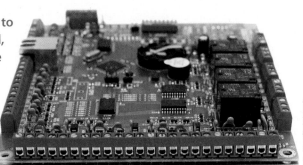
© Kurilina/Shutterstock

Personal App Nothing else will do when you're looking to buy a specialty product. It might be handmade, it might be old, but most of all, it's unique—possibly one of a kind. Because the item is so special, shopping around for it is well worth the effort.

One problem with this approach to classification is that buyers may behave differently when purchasing a specific type of product. Thus, a single product can fit into more than one category. To minimize this problem, marketers think in terms of how buyers are most likely to behave when purchasing a specific item.

Business Product Classifications

Based on their characteristics and intended uses, business products can be classified into the following categories: raw materials, major equipment, accessory equipment, component parts, process materials, supplies, and services.

A **raw material** is a basic material that actually becomes part of a physical product. It usually comes from mines, forests, oceans, or recycled solid wastes. Raw materials are usually bought and sold according to grades and specifications.

Major equipment includes large tools and machines used for production purposes. Examples of major equipment are lathes, cranes, and stamping machines. Some major equipment is custom-made for a particular organization, but other items are standardized products that perform one or several tasks for many types of organizations.

Accessory equipment is standardized equipment used in a firm's production or office activities. Examples include hand tools, fax machines, fractional horsepower motors, and calculators. Compared with major equipment, accessory items are usually much less expensive and are purchased routinely with less negotiation.

A **component part** becomes part of a physical product and is either a finished item ready for assembly or a product that needs little processing before assembly. Although it becomes part of a larger product, a component part can often be identified easily. Clocks, tires, computer chips, and switches are examples of component parts.

A **process material** is used directly in the production of another product. Unlike a component part, however, a process material is not readily identifiable in the finished product. Like component parts, process materials are purchased according to industry standards or to the specifications of the individual purchaser. Examples include industrial glue and food preservatives.

A **supply** facilitates production and operations but does not become part of a finished product. Paper, pencils, oils, and cleaning agents are examples.

A **business service** is an intangible product that an organization uses in its operations. Examples include financial, legal, online, janitorial, and marketing research services. Purchasers must decide whether to provide their own services internally or to hire them from outside the organization.

THE PRODUCT LIFE-CYCLE

In a way, products are like people. They are born, they live, and they die. Every product progresses through a **product life-cycle**, a series of stages in which a product's sales revenue and profit increase, reach a peak, and then decline. A firm must be able to launch, modify, and delete products from its offering of products in response to changes in product life-cycles. Otherwise, the firm's profits will disappear, and the firm will fail. Depending on the product, life-cycle stages will vary in length. In this section, we discuss the stages of the life-cycle and how marketers can use this information.

raw material a basic material that actually becomes part of a physical product; usually comes from mines, forests, oceans, or recycled solid wastes

major equipment large tools and machines used for production purposes

accessory equipment standardized equipment used in a firm's production or office activities

component part an item that becomes part of a physical product and is either a finished item ready for assembly or a product that needs little processing before assembly

process material a material that is used directly in the production of another product but is not readily identifiable in the finished product

supply an item that facilitates production and operations but does not become part of a finished product

business service an intangible product that an organization uses in its operations

product life-cycle a series of stages in which a product's sales revenue and profit increase, reach a peak, and then decline

Concept Check ✱

☐ Identify the general categories of products.

☐ Describe the classifications of consumer products.

☐ Based on their characteristics, business products can be classified into what categories?

LEARNING OBJECTIVE

2 Discuss the product life-cycle and how it leads to new-product development.

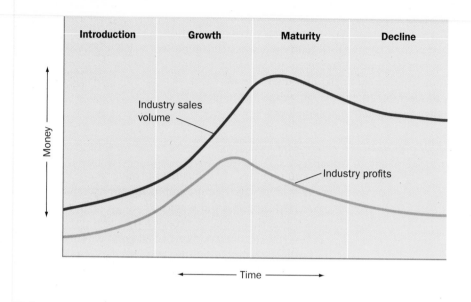

FIGURE 12-1: Product Life-Cycle

The graph shows sales volume and profits during the life-cycle of a product.

Source: William M. Pride and O. C. Ferrell, *Marketing: Concepts and Strategies,* 16th ed. (Mason, OH: South-Western/ Cengage Learning, 2012). Adapted with permission.

Stages of the Product Life-Cycle

Generally, the product life-cycle is assumed to be composed of four stages—introduction, growth, maturity, and decline—as shown in Figure 12-1. Some products progress through these stages rapidly, in a few weeks or months. Others may take years to go through each stage. The Rubik's Cube had a relatively short life-cycle. In contrast, Parker Brothers' Monopoly game, which was introduced over 70 years ago, is still going strong.

INTRODUCTION In the *introduction stage,* customer awareness and acceptance of the product are low. Sales rise gradually as a result of promotion and distribution activities; initially, however, high development and marketing costs result in low profit or even in a loss. There are relatively few competitors. The price is sometimes high, and purchasers are primarily people who want to be "the first" to own the new product. The marketing challenge at this stage is to make potential customers aware of the product's existence and its features, benefits, and uses. Apple, for example, recently introduced the iPad, a highly portable tablet computer. The iPad was described as revolutionary by many—combining the touch screen and features of an iPod Touch with the hard drive space of a Mac computer. In addition, the product can function as an e-reader, able to display electronic books. Apple created a new iBooks application for their iPad, where customers can purchase and download books from a large electronic library. With the release of the iPad, Apple further improved their market penetration in the personal computer market while also entering the e-reader market. The product's starting price of $499, although high compared to its e-reader market competitors, reflected the iPad's impressive additional features. The product's introduction was a success, with Apple selling its one-millionth iPad just 28 days after the product was introduced to the market.[2]

A new product is seldom an immediate success. Marketers must watch early buying patterns carefully and be prepared to modify the new product promptly if necessary. The product should be priced to attract the particular market segment that has the greatest desire and ability to buy the product. Plans for distribution and promotion should suit the targeted market segment. As with the product itself, the initial price, distribution channels, and promotional efforts may need to be adjusted quickly to maintain sales growth during the introduction stage.

GROWTH In the *growth stage,* sales increase rapidly as the product becomes well-known. Other firms have probably begun to market competing products. The competition and lower unit costs (owing to mass production) result in a lower price, which reduces the profit per unit. Note that industry profits reach a peak and begin to decline during this stage. To meet the needs of the growing market, the originating firm offers modified versions of its product and expands its distribution. For example, the 3M Company, the maker of Post-it Notes, has developed a variety of sizes, colors, and designs.

Management's goal in the growth stage is to stabilize and strengthen the product's position by encouraging brand loyalty. To beat the competition, the company may further improve the product or expand the product line to appeal to additional market segments. Apple, for example, has introduced several variations of its wildly popular iPod MP3 player. The iPod Shuffle is the smallest and most affordable version, whereas the iPod Nano offers song, photo, and video support in a thin, lightweight version that has a built-in video camera. The iPod Classic provides up to 160 GB of hard drive space, the most of any of the versions. The iPod Touch has a large, vibrant touch screen and an additional Wi-Fi connection that can use GPS technology and download applications. Apple has expanded its iTunes Music Store to include downloadable versions of popular TV shows that can be purchased per episode or as an entire season, exclusive music video downloads, and movies that can be purchased or rented online. Apple greatly expanded its product mix with the release of the iPhone, a combination iPod Touch and cell phone. Continuous product innovation and service expansion have helped to expand Apple's market penetration in the competitive MP3 player market.[3]

Management also may compete by lowering prices if increased production efficiency has resulted in savings for the company. As the product becomes more widely accepted, marketers may be able to broaden the network of distributors. Marketers can also emphasize customer service and prompt credit for defective products. During this period, promotional efforts attempt to build brand loyalty among customers.

MATURITY Sales are still increasing at the beginning of the *maturity stage,* but the rate of increase has slowed. Later in this stage, the sales curve peaks and begins to decline. Industry profits decline throughout this stage. Product lines are simplified, markets are segmented more carefully, and price competition increases. The increased competition forces weaker competitors to leave the industry. Refinements and extensions of the original product continue to appear on the market.

During a product's maturity stage, its market share may be strengthened by redesigned packaging or style changes. In addition, consumers may be encouraged to use the product more often or in new ways. Pricing strategies are flexible during this stage. Markdowns and price incentives are not uncommon, although price increases may work to offset production and distribution costs. Marketers may offer incentives and assistance of various kinds to dealers to encourage them to support mature products, especially in the face of competition from private-label brands. New promotional efforts and aggressive personal selling may be necessary during this period of intense competition.

DECLINE During the *decline stage,* sales volume decreases sharply. Profits continue to fall. The number of competing firms declines, and the only survivors in the marketplace are firms that specialize in marketing the product. Production and marketing costs become the most important determinant of profit.

When a product adds to the success of the overall product line, the company may retain it; otherwise, management must determine when to eliminate the product. A product usually declines because of technological advances or environmental factors or because consumers have switched to competing brands. Therefore, few

© Jeremy Hoare/Superstock

Product life-cycle. The pay telephone is in the decline stage of the product life-cycle.

changes are made in the product itself during this stage. Instead, management may raise the price to cover costs, reprice to maintain market share, or lower the price to reduce inventory. Similarly, management will narrow distribution of the declining product to the most profitable existing markets. During this period, the company probably will not spend heavily on promotion, although it may use some advertising and sales incentives to slow the product's decline. The company may choose to eliminate less-profitable versions of the product from the product line or may decide to drop the product entirely. General Motors (GM), for example, recently had to discontinue its Hummer brand. The company originally tried to sell the brand to a Chinese manufacturer, but the deal fell through, and GM had to begin phasing out Hummer vehicles. Although the brand had several loyal customers, GM claimed declining sales, the recession, and increased customer value of sustainability as reasons for the discontinuation. The CEO of GM himself acknowledged that the brand had developed a negative stigma as being a gas-guzzling icon of wealth and didn't think the brand could be salvaged.[4]

Personal App Think back to toys that were wildly popular when you were younger, such as Beanie Babies and Tickle Me Elmo. How many do you still see in stores? This shows how quickly some products can pass through the stages of the product life-cycle.

Using the Product Life-Cycle

Marketers should be aware of the life-cycle stage of each product for which they are responsible. Moreover, they should try to estimate how long the product is expected to remain in that stage. Both must be taken into account in making decisions about the marketing strategy for a product. If a product is expected to remain in the maturity stage for a long time, a replacement product might be introduced later in the maturity stage. If the maturity stage is expected to be short, however, a new product should be introduced much earlier. In some cases, a firm may be willing to take the chance of speeding up the decline of existing products. In other situations, a company will attempt to extend a product's life-cycle. For example, General Mills has extended the life of Bisquick baking mix (launched in the mid-1930s) by improving the product's formulation significantly and creating and promoting a variety of uses.

✱ *Concept Check*

☐ Explain the four stages of the product life-cycle.

☐ How does knowledge of product life-cycle relate to introduction of new products?

LEARNING OBJECTIVE

3 Define *product line* and *product mix* and distinguish between the two

product line a group of similar products that differ only in relatively minor characteristics

product mix all the products a firm offers for sale

PRODUCT LINE AND PRODUCT MIX

A **product line** is a group of similar products that differ only in relatively minor characteristics. Generally, the products within a product line are related to each other in the way they are produced, marketed, or used. Procter & Gamble, for example, manufactures and markets several shampoos, including Prell, Head & Shoulders, and Ivory.

Many organizations tend to introduce new products within existing product lines. This permits them to apply the experience and knowledge they have acquired to the production and marketing of new products. Other firms develop entirely new product lines.

An organization's **product mix** consists of all the products the firm offers for sale. For example, Procter & Gamble, which acquired Gillette, has over 85 brands that fall into one of three product line categories: beauty and grooming, health and well-being, and household care.[5] Two "dimensions" are often applied to a firm's product mix. The *width* of the mix is the number of product lines it contains. The *depth* of the mix is the average number of individual products within each line. These are general measures; we speak of a *broad* or a *narrow* mix rather than a mix of exactly three or five product lines. Some organizations provide broad product mixes to be competitive.

MANAGING THE PRODUCT MIX

LEARNING OBJECTIVE
4 Identify the methods available for changing a product mix.

To provide products that satisfy people in a firm's target market or markets and that also achieve the organization's objectives, a marketer must develop, adjust, and maintain an effective product mix. Seldom can the same product mix be effective for long. Because customers' product preferences and attitudes change, their desire for a product may diminish or grow. In some cases, a firm needs to alter its product mix to adapt to competition. A marketer may have to eliminate a product from the mix because one or more competitors dominate that product's specific market segment. Similarly, an organization may have to introduce a new product or modify an existing one to compete more effectively. A marketer may also expand the firm's product mix to take advantage of excess marketing and production capacity. For example, both Coca-Cola and Pepsi have expanded their lines by adding to their existing brands and acquiring new brands as well. In response to the increasing popularity of energy drinks, Coca-Cola acquired the Full Throttle brand, whereas Pepsi acquired AMP. In an effort to seem more health conscious, both companies came out with new sugar-free or zero-calorie soda products, along with more juice brands. Coca-Cola contains brands such as Minute Maid, Simply Orange, and FUZE, whereas Pepsi contains Tropicana, Ocean Spray, Dole, and SoBe. For tea and coffee brands, Coca-Cola has Nestea and Caribou Iced Coffee, whereas Pepsi has partnerships with Lipton and Starbucks. Both companies are also involved in the fast-growing sports drink category, with Coca-Cola's POWERADE and Pepsi's Gatorade and Propel among the top competitors. Coca-Cola even has a brand in the alcohol category: BACARDI Mixers.[6] For whatever reason a product mix is altered, the product mix must be managed to bring about improvements in the mix. There are three major ways to improve a product mix: change an existing product, delete a product, or develop a new product.

Product lines. Burberry produces several product lines including shoes, handbags, sunglasses, watches, and apparel.

Image Courtesy of The Advertising Archives

Managing Existing Products

A product mix can be changed by deriving additional products from existing ones. This can be accomplished through product modifications and by line extensions.

PRODUCT MODIFICATIONS Product modification refers to changing one or more of a product's characteristics. For this approach to be effective, several conditions must be met. First, the product must be modifiable. Second, existing customers must be able to perceive that a modification has been made, assuming that the modified item is still directed at the same target market. Third, the modification should make the product more consistent with customers' desires so that it provides greater

product modification the process of changing one or more of a product's characteristics

satisfaction. For example, Energizer increased its product's durability by using better materials—a larger cathode and anode interface—that make batteries last longer.

Personal App Few products remain the same forever, and that's to your advantage. When car companies add the latest safety features to their vehicles, for example, they're making product modifications that benefit you.

Existing products can be altered in three primary ways: in quality, function, and aesthetics. *Quality modifications* are changes that relate to a product's dependability and durability and are usually achieved by alterations in the materials or production process. *Functional modifications* affect a product's versatility, effectiveness, convenience, or safety; they usually require redesign of the product. Typical product categories that have undergone extensive functional modifications include home appliances, office and farm equipment, and consumer electronics. *Aesthetic modifications* are directed at changing the sensory appeal of a product by altering its taste, texture, sound, smell, or visual characteristics. Because a buyer's purchasing decision is affected by how a product looks, smells, tastes, feels, or sounds, an aesthetic modification may have a definite impact on purchases. Through aesthetic modifications, a firm can differentiate its product from competing brands and perhaps gain a sizable market share if customers find the modified product more appealing.

LINE EXTENSIONS A **line extension** is the development of a product closely related to one or more products in the existing product line but designed specifically to meet somewhat different customer needs. For example, Nabisco extended its cookie line to include Reduced Fat Oreos and Double Stuf Oreos.

Product line extension. Nabisco, the maker of Oreos, developed a product line extension when it launched Oreo Fudge Cremes. It did not delete its other Oreo products from its Oreo product line.

© Susan Van Etten

Many of the so-called new products introduced each year are in fact line extensions. Line extensions are more common than new products because they are a less-expensive, lower-risk alternative for increasing sales. A line extension may focus on a different market segment or be an attempt to increase sales within the same market segment by more precisely satisfying the needs of people in that segment. Line extensions are also used to take market share from competitors.

Deleting Products

To maintain an effective product mix, an organization often has to eliminate some products. This is called **product deletion**. A weak product costs a firm time, money, and resources that could be used to modify other products or develop new ones. In addition, when a weak product generates an unfavorable image among customers, the negative image may rub off on other products sold by the firm.

Most organizations find it difficult to delete a product. Some firms drop weak products only after they have become severe financial burdens. A better approach is to conduct some form of systematic review of the product's impact on the overall effectiveness of a firm's product mix. Such a review should analyze a product's contribution to a company's sales for a given period. It should include estimates of future sales, costs, and profits associated with the product and a consideration of whether changes in the marketing strategy could improve the product's performance.

A product-deletion program can definitely improve a firm's performance. Condé Nast, for example, recently discontinued its *Gourmet* magazine. The magazine, which had been around since 1940, was experiencing declining ad sales and suffering from the move to digital media. However, Condé Nast plans to continue the brand in book publishing and television programming as well as online.[7]

line extension development of a new product that is closely related to one or more products in the existing product line but designed specifically to meet somewhat different customer needs

product deletion the elimination of one or more products from a product line

Developing New Products

Developing and introducing new products frequently is time-consuming, expensive, and risky. Thousands of new products are introduced annually. Depending on how we define it, the failure rate for new products ranges between 60 and 75 percent. Although developing new products is risky, failing to introduce new products can be just as hazardous. Successful new products bring a number of benefits to an organization, including survival, profits, a sustainable competitive advantage, and a favorable public image. Consider the numerous ways that the producers of the products in Table 12-1 have benefited.

New products are generally grouped into three categories on the basis of their degree of similarity to existing products. *Imitations* are products designed to be similar to—and to compete with—existing products of other firms. Examples are the various brands of whitening toothpastes that were developed to compete with Rembrandt. *Adaptations* are variations of existing products that are intended for an established market. Product refinements and extensions are the adaptations considered most often, although imitative products may also include some refinement and extension. *Innovations* are entirely new products. They may give rise to a new industry or revolutionize an existing one. The introduction of digital music, for example, has brought major changes to the recording industry. Innovative products take considerable time, effort, and money to develop. They are therefore less common than adaptations and imitations. As shown in Figure 12-2, the process of developing a new product consists of seven phases.

Fan blades 'chop' the airflow, causing buffeting. The new Dyson fan works differently. An annular jet accelerates the surrounding air and amplifies it fifteen times. There are no blades to chop the air so the airflow is smooth – it cools without the unpleasant buffeting.

Blades cause buffeting.

No blades means no buffeting.

dyson air multiplier

No blades. No buffeting.

Learn more at www.dyson.co.uk
Or experience in-store

New-product development. Dyson developed a new product when it created its Air Multiplier, a bladeless fan.

IDEA GENERATION Idea generation involves looking for product ideas that will help a firm to achieve its objectives. Although some organizations get their ideas almost by chance, firms trying to maximize product-mix effectiveness usually develop systematic approaches for generating new-product ideas. Ideas may come

TABLE 12-1: **Top Ten New Products of the Decade**

Rank	Product Name	Year Introduced
1	iPod	2001
2	Wii	2006
3	Axe	2002
4	$5 Footlong	2008
5	Activia	2006
6	Mini Cooper	2002
7	Crest Whitestrips	2000
8	Guitar Hero	2005
9	Toyota Prius	2000
10	7 For All Mankind	2000

Source: *Advertising Age,* December 14, 2009, http://adage.com/article?article_id=141032 (accessed March 23, 2011).

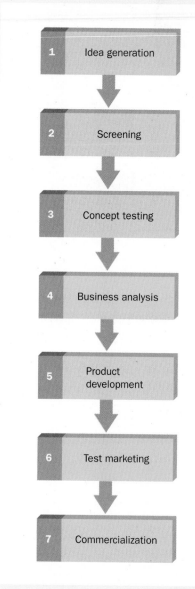

FIGURE 12-2: Phases of New-Product Development

Generally, marketers follow these seven steps to develop a new product.

1. Idea generation
2. Screening
3. Concept testing
4. Business analysis
5. Product development
6. Test marketing
7. Commercialization

Source: William M. Pride and O. C. Ferrell, *Marketing: Concepts and Strategies*, 16th ed. (Mason, OH: South-Western/Cengage Learning, 2012). Adapted with permission.

from managers, researchers, engineers, competitors, advertising agencies, management consultants, private research organizations, customers, salespersons, or top executives. For example, Fahrenheit 212 serves as an "idea factory" that provides ready-to-go product ideas, including market potential analysis, to its clients, which include Procter & Gamble, Coca-Cola, Hershey, Samsung, Starbucks, Capital One Financial, General Mills, Nestlé, Clorox, and Adidas.[8]

SCREENING During screening, ideas that do not match organizational resources and objectives are rejected. In this phase, a firm's managers consider whether the organization has personnel with the expertise to develop and market the proposed product. Management may reject a good idea because the company lacks the necessary skills and abilities. The largest number of product ideas are rejected during the screening phase.

CONCEPT TESTING Concept testing is a phase in which a product idea is presented to a small sample of potential buyers through a written or oral description (and perhaps a few drawings) to determine their attitudes and initial buying intentions regarding the product. For a single product idea, an organization can test one or several concepts of the same product. Concept testing is a low-cost means for an organization to determine consumers' initial reactions to a product idea before investing considerable resources in product research and development (R&D). Product development personnel can use the results of concept testing to improve product attributes and product benefits that are most important to potential customers. The types of questions asked vary considerably depending on the type of product idea being tested. The following are typical questions:

- Which benefits of the proposed product are especially attractive to you?
- Which features are of little or no interest to you?
- What are the primary advantages of the proposed product over the one you currently use?
- If this product were available at an appropriate price, how often would you buy it?
- How could this proposed product be improved?

BUSINESS ANALYSIS Business analysis provides tentative ideas about a potential product's financial performance, including its probable profitability. During this stage, the firm considers how the new product, if it were introduced, would affect the firm's sales, costs, and profits. Marketing personnel usually work up preliminary sales and cost projections at this point, with the help of R&D and production managers.

PRODUCT DEVELOPMENT In the product development phase, the company must find out first if it is technically feasible to produce the product and then if the product can be made at costs low enough to justify a reasonable price. If a product idea makes it to this point, it is transformed into a working model, or *prototype*. For example, Aptera, a California-based vehicle manufacturer, recently developed a prototype electric vehicle called the 2e. The 2e is an innovative three-wheeled, two-seat vehicle that uses an electric motor with phosphate-based lithium-ion batteries. The 2e is expected to operate at about 200 MPG and travel about 100 miles on a single charge.[9] Often, this step is time-consuming and expensive for the organization. If a product successfully moves through this step, then it is ready for test marketing.

TEST MARKETING Test marketing is the limited introduction of a product in several towns or cities chosen to be representative of the intended target market. Its aim is to determine buyers' probable reactions. The product is left in the test markets

going for SUCCESS

Where Do Big Companies Get New Product Ideas?

Big companies routinely launch hundreds or even thousands of new products every year. But where do their new product ideas come from? At 3M, a global research-and-development team of 7,300 specialists pursues new technologies while simultaneously looking for new ways to apply existing materials and technologies to solve customers' problems. Recently the company used a production process it perfected in the 1960s to create material for golf gloves that helps the user grip clubs more tightly with less effort. Looking backward for innovation possibilities has helped 3M build revenue beyond $26 billion, with more than 1,000 new products introduced each year.

Although big companies like 3M have large and well-funded new-product-development groups, they also reach outside to consider ideas from entrepreneurs and customers. Procter & Gamble's decade-old Connect & Develop program invites small businesses and inventors to submit ideas for potential new-product partnerships. Thanks to the company's international presence and marketing expertise, promising ideas can become profitable realities for both partners. In fact, within a few years, new products introduced through this program will account for $3 billion in annual revenue.

Increasingly, corporate giants such as Dell and Starbucks are asking consumers to get involved by submitting new-product ideas online. Dell has already launched more than 400 new products based on ideas submitted through its special IdeaStorm Web site and Twitter account. Starbucks has launched more than 100 new products based on ideas submitted through its MyStarbucksIdea Web site and Twitter account. Where will the next big new-product idea come from?

Sources: Dave Evans, "Brands That Listen," *ClickZ*, February 9, 2011, www.clickz.com; Lee G. Demuth III, "New Method Approach Toward Efficiency," *Journal of American Academy of Business*, Volume 17, September 2011; Jonathan Birchall, "Open Innovation Powers Growth," *Financial Times*, December 27, 2010, www.ft.com; Marc Gunther, "3M's Innovation Revival," *Fortune*, September 27, 2010, pp. 73–76.

long enough to give buyers a chance to repurchase the product if they are so inclined. Marketers can experiment with advertising, pricing, and packaging in different test areas and can measure the extent of brand awareness, brand switching, and repeat purchases that result from alterations in the marketing mix.

COMMERCIALIZATION During commercialization, plans for full-scale manufacturing and marketing must be refined and completed, and budgets for the project must be prepared. In the early part of the commercialization phase, marketing management analyzes the results of test marketing to find out what changes in the marketing mix are needed before the product is introduced. The results of test marketing may tell the marketers, for example, to change one or more of the product's physical attributes, to modify the distribution plans to include more retail outlets, to alter promotional efforts, or to change the product's price. Products are usually not introduced nationwide overnight. Most new products are marketed in stages, beginning in selected geographic areas and expanding into adjacent areas over a period of time.

Why Do Products Fail?

Despite this rigorous process for developing product ideas, most new products end up as failures. In fact, many well-known companies have produced market failures (see Table 12-2).

Why does a new product fail? Mainly because the product and its marketing program are not planned and tested as completely as they should be. For example, to save on development costs, a firm may market-test its product but not its entire marketing mix. Alternatively, a firm may market a new product before all the "bugs" have been worked out. Or, when problems show up in the testing stage, a firm may try to recover its product development costs by pushing ahead with full-scale marketing anyway. Finally, some firms try to market new products with inadequate financing.

☐ What are the ways to improve a product mix? Describe two approaches to use existing products to strengthen a product mix.

☐ Why is it important to delete certain products? The largest number of product ideas are rejected during which stage?

☐ What is the aim of test marketing?

☐ Describe seven phases of new-product development.

TABLE 12-2: Examples of Product Failures

Company	Product
Gillette	For Oily Hair shampoo
3M	Floptical storage disk
IncrEdibles Breakaway Foods	Push n' Eat
General Mills	Betty Crocker MicroRave Singles
Adams (Pfizer)	Body Smarts nutritional bars
Ford	Edsel
Anheuser-Busch	Bud Dry and Michelob Dry beer
Coca-Cola	New Coke
Heinz	Ketchup Salsa
Noxema	Noxema Skin Fitness

Sources: Robert McMath and Thom Forbes, "What Were They Thinking," Reed Business Information, 1998. Robert M. McMath, "Copycat Cupcakes Don't Cut It," *American Demographics,* January 1997, 60; Eric Berggren and Thomas Nacher, "Why Good Ideas Go Bust," *Management Review,* February 2000, 32–36.

LEARNING OBJECTIVE

5 Explain the uses and importance of branding, packaging, and labeling

BRANDING, PACKAGING, AND LABELING

Three important features of a product (particularly a consumer product) are its brand, package, and label. These features may be used to associate a product with a successful product line or to distinguish it from existing products. They may be designed to attract customers at the point of sale or to provide information to potential purchasers. Because the brand, package, and label are very real parts of the product, they deserve careful attention during product planning.

What Is a Brand?

A **brand** is a name, term, symbol, design, or any combination of these that identifies a seller's products and distinguishes it from other sellers' products. A **brand name** is the part of a brand that can be spoken. It may include letters, words, numbers, or pronounceable symbols, such as the ampersand in *Procter & Gamble.* A **brand mark**, on the other hand, is the part of a brand that is a symbol or distinctive design, such as the Nike "swoosh." A **trademark** is a brand name or brand mark that is registered with the U.S. Patent and Trademark Office and thus is legally protected from use by anyone except its owner. A **trade name** is the complete and legal name of an organization, such as Pizza Hut or Cengage Learning (the publisher of this text).

Types of Brands

Brands are often classified according to who owns them: manufacturers or stores. A **manufacturer** (or **producer**) **brand**, as the name implies, is a brand that is owned by a manufacturer. Many foods (Frosted Flakes), major appliances (Whirlpool), gasolines (Exxon), automobiles (Honda), and clothing (Levi's) are sold as manufacturers' brands. Some consumers prefer manufacturer brands because they are usually nationally known, offer consistent quality, and are widely available.

Personal App Do you know exactly what your favorite brand of candy looks like? Now that it's so familiar, you can grab it and go without looking at all the other brands on the shelf. That's how brands save you time.

A **store** (or **private**) **brand** is a brand that is owned by an individual wholesaler or retailer. Among the better-known store brands are Kenmore and Craftsman, both owned by Sears, Roebuck. Owners of store brands claim that they can offer

brand a name, term, symbol, design, or any combination of these that identifies a seller's products as distinct from those of other sellers

brand name the part of a brand that can be spoken

brand mark the part of a brand that is a symbol or distinctive design

trademark a brand name or brand mark that is registered with the U.S. Patent and Trademark Office and thus is legally protected from use by anyone except its owner

trade name the complete and legal name of an organization

manufacturer (or producer) brand a brand that is owned by a manufacturer

store (or private) brand a brand that is owned by an individual wholesaler or retailer

lower prices, earn greater profits, and improve customer loyalty with their own brands. Some companies that manufacture private brands also produce their own manufacturer brands. They often find such operations profitable because they can use excess capacity and at the same time avoid most marketing costs. Many private-branded grocery products are produced by companies that specialize in making private-label products. About 25 percent of products sold in supermarkets are private-branded items.[10]

Consumer confidence is the most important element in the success of a branded product, whether the brand is owned by a producer or by a retailer. Because branding identifies each product completely, customers can easily repurchase products that provide satisfaction, performance, and quality. Moreover, they can just as easily avoid or ignore products that do not. In supermarkets, the products most likely to keep their shelf space are the brands with large market shares and strong customer loyalty.

Manufacturer brand. Duracell is a manufacturer's brand and is distributed through numerous retailers.

A **generic product** (sometimes called a **generic brand**) is a product with no brand at all. Its plain package carries only the name of the product—applesauce, peanut butter, potato chips, or whatever. Generic products, available in supermarkets since 1977, sometimes are made by the major producers that manufacture name brands. Even though generic brands may have accounted for as much as 10 percent of all grocery sales several years ago, they currently represent less than one-half of 1 percent.

Benefits of Branding

Both buyers and sellers benefit from branding. Because brands are easily recognizable, they reduce the amount of time buyers must spend shopping; buyers can quickly identify the brands they prefer. Choosing particular brands, such as Tommy Hilfiger, Polo, Nautica, and Nike, can be a way of expressing oneself. When buyers are unable to evaluate a product's characteristics, brands can help them to judge the quality of the product. For example, most buyers are not able to judge the quality of stereo components but may be guided by a well-respected brand name. Brands can symbolize a certain quality level to a customer, allowing that perception of quality to represent the actual quality of the item. Brands thus help to reduce a buyer's perceived risk of purchase. Finally, customers may receive a psychological reward that comes from owning a brand that symbolizes status. The Lexus brand is an example.

Because buyers are already familiar with a firm's existing brands, branding helps a firm to introduce a new product that carries the same brand name. Branding aids sellers in their promotional efforts because promotion of each branded product indirectly promotes other products of the same brand. H.J. Heinz, for example, markets many products with the Heinz brand name, such as ketchup, vinegar, vegetarian beans, gravies, barbecue sauce, and steak sauce. Promotion of one Heinz product indirectly promotes the others.

One chief benefit of branding is the creation of **brand loyalty**, the extent to which a customer is favorable toward buying a specific brand. The stronger the brand loyalty, the greater is the likelihood that buyers will consistently choose the brand. For example, Toyota is expected to survive as a company, despite the massive recalls affecting several million vehicles, because of its historically high perceived brand quality. Even though this is a huge mark against the brand, the company is relying on its loyalists and previously perceived brand quality to survive.[11] There are three levels of brand loyalty: recognition, preference, and insistence. *Brand recognition* is the level of loyalty at which customers are aware that the brand exists and will purchase it if their preferred brands are unavailable or if they are unfamiliar with available brands. This is the weakest form of brand loyalty. *Brand preference* is the level of brand loyalty at which a customer prefers one brand over competing brands. However, if the preferred

generic product (or brand) a product with no brand at all

brand loyalty extent to which a customer is favorable toward buying a specific brand

SOCIAL MEDIA @

Local Businesses Use Social Media to Build Brand Loyalty

More than 70 percent of small businesses now use Facebook to reach their customers. Twitter, YouTube, and other social media tools are also popular among local firms around the country. Why? Because they're an affordable way to interact with customers, build brand recognition, and reinforce loyalty.

AJ Bombers, a Milwaukee burger restaurant, became a local favorite within a year of its opening, thanks to its crowd-pleasing menu and its social-media activity. The business has earned thousands of Twitter followers, Facebook "likes," and YouTube video views. Most important, AJ Bombers uses social media for two-way conversation, engaging customers and showing the brand's playful personality.

Sources: Donna DeClemente, "Facebook Pages: 4 Strategic Marketing Tips to Engage Fans," *Social Media Today*, February 16, 2011, http://socialmediatoday.com; Dave Folkens, "How Social Media Really Works for Small Business," *Top Rank*, January 20, 2011, www.toprankblog.com; Augie Ray, "Word of Mouth and Social Media: A Tale of Two Burger Joints," *Forrester.com*, March 28, 2010, http://blogs.forrester.com/augie_ray.

brand is unavailable, the customer is willing to substitute another brand. *Brand insistence* is the strongest level of brand loyalty. Brand-insistent customers strongly prefer a specific brand and will not buy substitutes. Brand insistence is the least common type of brand loyalty. Partly owing to marketers' increased dependence on discounted prices, coupons, and other short-term promotions, and partly because of the enormous array of new products with similar characteristics, brand loyalty in general seems to be declining.

Brand equity is the marketing and financial value associated with a brand's strength in a market. Although difficult to measure, brand equity represents the value of a brand to an organization. The top ten most highly valued brands in the world are shown in Table 12-3. The four major factors that contribute to brand equity are brand awareness, brand associations, perceived brand quality, and brand loyalty. Brand awareness leads to brand familiarity, and buyers are more likely to select a familiar brand than an unfamiliar one. The associations linked to a brand can connect a personality type or lifestyle with a particular brand. For example, customers associate Michelin tires with protecting family members; a De Beers diamond with a loving, long-lasting relationship ("A Diamond Is Forever"); and Dr Pepper with a unique taste. When consumers are unable to judge for themselves the quality of a product, they may rely on their perception of the quality of the product's brand. Finally, brand loyalty is a valued element of brand equity because it reduces both a brand's vulnerability to competitors and the need to spend tremendous resources to attract new customers; it also provides brand visibility and encourages retailers to carry the brand. Companies have much work to do in establishing new brands to compete with well-known brands. For example, Coca-Cola decided that it would be a better business decision to buy the established brand Glaceau than to create a new brand of its own. The company acquired Glaceau, which included the Vitaminwater and Smartwater brands, to strengthen Coca-Cola's water and energy drink product line.[12]

Marketing on the Internet is sometimes best done in collaboration with a better-known Web brand. For instance, Tire Rack, Razor Gator, Audible.com, and Shutterfly all rely on partnerships with Internet retail giant Amazon to increase their sales. Amazon provides special sections on its Web site to promote its partners and their products. As with its own products, Amazon gives users the ability to post online reviews of its partners' products or to add them to an Amazon "wish list" that can be saved or e-mailed to friends. Amazon even labels its partners as "Amazon Trusted" when customers browse their sites, giving even these well-known real-world companies credibility in the online marketplace.[13]

Choosing and Protecting a Brand

A number of issues should be considered when selecting a brand name. The name should be easy for customers to say, spell, and recall. Short, one-syllable names such as *Tide* often satisfy this requirement. Letters and numbers are used to create such brands as Volvo's S60 sedan or RIM's BlackBerry 8100. Words, numbers, and letters are combined to yield brand names such as Motorola's RAZR V3 phone or BMW's Z4 Roadster. The brand name should suggest, in a positive way, the product's uses, special characteristics, and major benefits and should be distinctive enough to set it apart from competing brands. Choosing the right brand name has become a challenge because many obvious product names already have been used.

It is important that a firm select a brand that can be protected through registration, reserving it for exclusive use by that firm. Some brands, because of their

brand equity marketing and financial value associated with a brand's strength in a market

designs, are infringed on more easily than others. Although registration protects trademarks domestically for ten years and can be renewed indefinitely, a firm should develop a system for ensuring that its trademarks will be renewed as needed. To protect its exclusive right to the brand, the company must ensure that the selected brand will not be considered an infringement on any existing brand already registered with the U.S. Patent and Trademark Office. This task may be complicated by the fact that infringement is determined by the courts, which base their decisions on whether a brand causes consumers to be confused, mistaken, or deceived about the source of the product. McDonald's is one company that aggressively protects its trademarks against infringement; it has brought charges against a number of companies with *Mc* names because it fears that the use of the prefix will give consumers the impression that these companies are associated with or owned by McDonald's.

A firm must guard against having its brand name become a generic term that refers to a general product category. Generic terms cannot be legally protected as exclusive brand names. For example, names such as *yo-yo, aspirin, escalator,* and *thermos*—all exclusively brand names at one time—eventually were declared generic terms that refer to product categories. As such, they can no longer be protected. To ensure that a brand name does not become a generic term, the firm should spell the name with a capital letter and use it as an adjective to modify the name of the general product class, as in Jell-O Brand Gelatin. An organization can deal directly with this problem by advertising that its brand is a trademark and should not be used generically. Firms also can use the registered trademark symbol® to indicate that the brand is trademarked.

Branding Strategies

The basic branding decision for any firm is whether to brand its products. A producer may market its products under its own brands, private brands, or both. A retail store may carry only producer brands, its own brands, or both. Once either type of firm decides to brand, it chooses one of two branding strategies: individual branding or family branding.

Individual branding is the strategy in which a firm uses a different brand for each of its products. For example, Procter & Gamble uses individual branding for its line of bar soaps, which includes Ivory, Camay, Zest, Safeguard, Coast, and Olay. Individual branding offers two major advantages. A problem with one product will not affect the good name of the firm's other products, and the different brands can be directed toward different market segments. For example, Marriott's Fairfield Inns are directed toward budget-minded travelers, whereas Marriott Hotels are aimed toward upscale customers.

Family branding is the strategy in which a firm uses the same brand for all or most of its products. Sony, Dell, IBM, and Xerox use family branding for their entire product mixes. A major advantage of family branding is that the promotion of any one item that carries the family brand tends to help all other products with the same brand name. In addition, a new product has a head start when its brand name is already known and accepted by customers.

Brand Extensions

A **brand extension** occurs when an organization uses one of its existing brands to brand a new product in a different product category. For example, Procter & Gamble employed a brand extension when it named a new product Ivory Body Wash. A brand extension should not be confused with a line extension. A *line extension* refers to using an existing brand on a new product in the same product category, such as a new flavor or new sizes. For example, when the makers of Tylenol introduced Extra Strength Tylenol PM, the new product was a line extension because it was in the same product category. One thing marketers must be careful of, however, is extending a brand too many times or extending too far outside the original product

TABLE 12-3: Top Ten Most Valuable Brands in the World

Brand	Brand Value (in billion $)
Coca-Cola	70.5
IBM	64.7
Microsoft	60.9
Google	43.6
GE	42.8
McDonald's	33.6
Intel	32.0
Nokia	29.5
Disney	28.7
Hewlett-Packard	26.9

Source: "Best Global Brands," *Interbrand,* www.interbrand.com/en/best-global-brands/Best-Global-Brands-2010.aspx (accessed March 23, 2011).

individual branding the strategy in which a firm uses a different brand for each of its products

family branding the strategy in which a firm uses the same brand for all or most of its products

brand extension using an existing brand to brand a new product in a different product category

Package design. The original design of the ketchup bottle is inconvenient for customers because it is difficult to get the ketchup out of the bottle. Heinz designed a ketchup bottle to make it more convenient for customers to use it. This package has a bottom cap with a wide mouth.

© Susan Van Etten

category, which may weaken the brand. For example, Kellogg's extended its brand name to a line of hip-hop street clothing that was later named one of the worst brand extensions that year.[14]

Packaging

Packaging consists of all the activities involved in developing and providing a container with graphics for a product. The package is a vital part of the product. It can make the product more versatile, safer, or easier to use. Through its shape, appearance, and printed message, a package can influence purchasing decisions.

PACKAGING FUNCTIONS Effective packaging means more than simply putting products in containers and covering them with wrappers. The basic function of packaging materials is to protect the product and maintain its functional form. Fluids such as milk, orange juice, and hair spray need packages that preserve and protect them; the packaging should prevent damage that could affect the product's usefulness and increase costs. Because product tampering has become a problem for marketers of many types of goods, several packaging techniques have been developed to counter this danger. Some packages are also designed to foil shoplifting.

Another function of packaging is to offer consumer convenience. For example, small, aseptic packages—individual-serving boxes or plastic bags that contain liquids and do not require refrigeration—appeal strongly to children and to young adults with active lifestyles. The size or shape of a package may relate to the product's storage, convenience of use, or replacement rate. Small, single-serving cans of vegetables, for instance, may prevent waste and make storage easier. A third function of packaging is to promote a product by communicating its features, uses, benefits, and image. Sometimes a firm develops a reusable package to make its product more desirable. For example, the Cool Whip package doubles as a food-storage container.

PACKAGE DESIGN CONSIDERATIONS Many factors must be weighed when developing packages. Obviously, one major consideration is cost. Although a number of packaging materials, processes, and designs are available, some are rather expensive. Although U.S. buyers have shown a willingness to pay more for improved packaging, there are limits.

Marketers also must decide whether to package the product in single or multiple units. Multiple-unit packaging can increase demand by increasing the amount of the product available at the point of consumption (in the home, for example). However, multiple-unit packaging does not work for infrequently used products because buyers do not like to tie up their dollars in an excess supply or to store those products for a long time. However, multiple-unit packaging can make storage and handling easier (as in the case of six-packs used for soft drinks); it can also facilitate special price offers, such as two-for-one sales. In addition, multiple-unit packaging may increase consumer acceptance of a product by encouraging the buyer to try it several times. On the other hand, customers may hesitate to try the product at all if they do not have the option to buy just one.

Marketers should consider how much consistency is desirable among an organization's package designs. To promote an overall company image, a firm may decide that all packages must be similar or include one major element of the design. This approach, called *family packaging,* is sometimes used only for lines of products, as with Campbell's soups, Weight Watchers entrées, and Planters nuts. The best policy is sometimes no consistency, especially if a firm's products are unrelated or aimed at vastly different target markets.

packaging all the activities involved in developing and providing a container with graphics for a product

Packages also play an important promotional role. Through verbal and nonverbal symbols, the package can inform potential buyers about the product's content, uses, features, advantages, and hazards. Firms can create desirable images and associations by choosing particular colors, designs, shapes, and textures. Many cosmetics manufacturers, for example, design their packages to create impressions of richness, luxury, and exclusiveness. The package performs another promotional function when it is designed to be safer or more convenient to use, especially if such features help to stimulate demand.

Packaging also must meet the needs of intermediaries. Wholesalers and retailers consider whether a package facilitates transportation, handling, and storage. Resellers may refuse to carry certain products if their packages are cumbersome.

Finally, firms must consider the issue of environmental responsibility when developing packages. Companies must balance consumers' desires for convenience against the need to preserve the environment. About one-half of all garbage consists of discarded plastic packaging, such as plastic soft drink bottles and carryout bags. Plastic packaging material is not biodegradable, and paper necessitates destruction of valuable forest lands. Consequently, many companies are exploring packaging alternatives and recycling more materials. Last year, Naked Juice became the first beverage with national distribution to produce its packaging completely from recycled plastic.[15]

Labeling

Labeling is the presentation of information on a product or its package. The *label* is the part that contains the information. This information may include the brand name and mark, the registered trademark symbol ®, the package size and contents, product claims, directions for use and safety precautions, a list of ingredients, the name and address of the manufacturer, and the Universal Product Code (UPC) symbol, which is used for automated checkout and inventory control.

A number of federal regulations specify information that *must* be included in the labeling for certain products. For example,

- Garments must be labeled with the name of the manufacturer, country of manufacture, fabric content, and cleaning instructions.
- Food labels must contain the most common term for ingredients.
- Any food product for which a nutritional claim is made must have nutrition labeling that follows a standard format.
- Food product labels must state the number of servings per container, the serving size, the number of calories per serving, the number of calories derived from fat, and the amounts of specific nutrients.
- Non-edible items such as shampoos and detergents must carry safety precautions as well as instructions for their use.

Such regulations are aimed at protecting customers from both misleading product claims and the improper (and thus unsafe) use of products. A product that has come under fire in 2010 is the printer cartridge. Consumers are pushing for more disclosure on labels about the amount of ink in each cartridge. Currently, it is difficult for consumers to compare offerings and prices without knowing the amount of ink contained in each cartridge. Companies have responded by saying ink does not fall under the Fair Packaging and Labeling Act. This dispute is currently under review.[16]

Labels also may carry the details of written or express warranties. An **express warranty** is a written explanation of the producer's responsibilities in the event that a product is found to be defective or otherwise unsatisfactory. As a result of consumer discontent (along with some federal legislation), firms have begun to simplify the wording of warranties and to extend their duration. The L.L.Bean warranty states, "Our products are guaranteed to give 100 percent satisfaction in every way. Return anything purchased from us at any time if it proves otherwise. We will replace it, refund your purchase price or credit your credit card, as you wish."

labeling the presentation of information on a product or its package

express warranty a written explanation of the producer's responsibilities in the event that a product is found to be defective or otherwise unsatisfactory

Concept Check ✶

☐ Describe the major types of brands.

☐ How do brands help customers in product selection? How do brands help companies introduce new products? Explain the three levels of brand loyalty.

☐ Define brand equity and describe the four major factors that contribute toward brand equity. What issues must be considered while choosing a brand name?

☐ What are the major functions of packaging?

PRICING PRODUCTS

A product is a set of attributes and benefits that has been carefully designed to satisfy its market while earning a profit for its seller. No matter how well a product is designed, however, it cannot help an organization to achieve its goals if it is priced incorrectly. Few people will purchase a product with too high a price, and a product with too low a price will earn little or no profit. Somewhere between too high and too low there is a "proper," effective price for each product. Let's take a closer look at how businesses go about determining a product's right price.

The Meaning and Use of Price

The **price** of a product is the amount of money a seller is willing to accept in exchange for the product at a given time and under given circumstances. At times, the price results from negotiations between buyer and seller. In many business situations, however, the price is fixed by the seller. Suppose that a seller sets a price of $10 for a particular product. In essence, the seller is saying, "Anyone who wants this product can have it here and now in exchange for $10."

Each interested buyer then makes a personal judgment regarding the product's utility, often in terms of some dollar value. A particular person who feels that he or she will get at least $10 worth of want satisfaction (or value) from the product is likely to buy it. If that person can get more want satisfaction by spending $10 in some other way, however, he or she will not buy the product.

Price competition. Price competition is common among general merchandise retailers such as supermarkets and discount stores.

Price thus serves the function of *allocator*. First, it allocates goods and services among those who are willing and able to buy them. (As we noted in Chapter 1, the answer to the economic question "For whom to produce?" depends primarily on prices.) Second, price allocates financial resources (sales revenue) among producers according to how well they satisfy customers' needs. Third, price helps customers to allocate their own financial resources among various want-satisfying products.

Supply and Demand Affects Prices

In Chapter 1, we defined the **supply** of a product as the quantity of the product that producers are willing to sell at each of various prices. We can draw a graph of the supply relationship for a particular product, say, jeans (see the left graph in Figure 12-3). Note that the quantity supplied by producers *increases* as the price increases along this *supply curve*.

As defined in Chapter 1, the **demand** for a product is the quantity that buyers are willing to purchase at each of various prices. We can also draw a graph of the demand relationship (see the center graph in Figure 12-3). Note that the quantity demanded by purchasers *increases* as the price decreases along the *demand curve*. The buyers and sellers of a product interact in the marketplace. We can show this interaction by superimposing the supply curve onto the demand curve for our product, as shown in the right graph in Figure 12-3. The two curves intersect at point *E*, which represents a quantity of 15 million pairs of jeans and a price of $30 per pair. Point *E* is on the *supply curve;* thus, producers are willing to supply 15 million pairs at $30 each. Point *E* is also on the demand curve; thus, buyers are willing to purchase 15 million pairs at $30 each. Point *E* represents *equilibrium*. If 15 million pairs are produced and priced at $30, they all will be sold. In addition, everyone who is willing to pay $30 will be able to buy a pair of jeans.

price the amount of money a seller is willing to accept in exchange for a product at a given time and under given circumstances

supply the quantity of a product that producers are willing to sell at each of various prices

demand the quantity of a product that buyers are willing to purchase at each of various prices

348

Part 5: Marketing

FIGURE 12-3: Supply and Demand Curves

Supply curve (*left*): The upward slope means that producers will supply more jeans at higher prices. Demand curve (*center*): The downward slope (to the right) means that buyers will purchase fewer jeans at higher prices. Supply and demand curves together (*right*): Point *E* indicates equilibrium in quantity and price for both sellers and buyers.

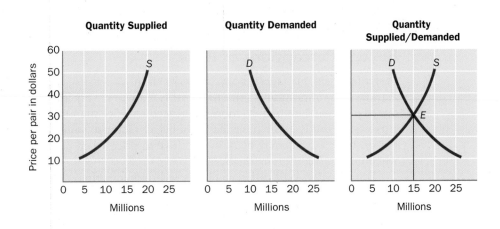

Personal App When a band you like releases a new album, do you rush to buy it? Or do you wait for a sale? Your willingness to buy is what drives demand for the album (or any product) at each price level.

Price and Non-Price Competition

Before a product's price can be set, an organization must determine the basis on which it will compete—whether on price alone or some combination of factors. The choice influences pricing decisions as well as other marketing-mix variables.

Price competition occurs when a seller emphasizes a product's low price and sets a price that equals or beats competitors' prices. To use this approach most effectively, a seller must have the flexibility to change prices often and must do so rapidly and aggressively whenever competitors change their prices. Price competition allows a marketer to set prices based on demand for the product or in response to changes in the firm's finances. Competitors can do likewise, however, which is a major drawback of price competition. They, too, can quickly match or outdo an organization's price cuts. In addition, if circumstances force a seller to raise prices, competing firms may be able to maintain their lower prices. For example, when increasing numbers of coffee sellers entered the market, competition increased. Starbucks needed to counter the widespread perception that it was the home of the $4 cup of coffee, especially during the economic downturn. In order to compete with McDonald's inexpensive coffee, Starbucks cut its coffee prices and started selling discounted breakfast foods for $3.95, including coffee.[17]

The Internet makes price comparison relatively easy for users. This ease of price comparison helps to drive competition. Examples of Web sites where customers can compare prices include http://mysimon.com, http://pricescan.com, http://bizrate.com, http://pricegrabber.com, http://pricecomparison.com, http://shopping.yahoo.com, http://nextag.com, and http://froogle.google.com.

Non-price competition is competition based on factors other than price. It is used most effectively when a seller can make its product stand out from the competition by distinctive product quality, customer service, promotion, packaging, or other features. Buyers must be able to perceive these distinguishing characteristics and consider them desirable. Once customers have chosen a brand for non-price reasons, they may not be attracted as easily to competing firms and brands. In this way, a

price competition an emphasis on setting a price equal to or lower than competitors' prices to gain sales or market share

non-price competition competition based on factors other than price

seller can build customer loyalty to its brand. A method of non-price competition, **product differentiation**, is the process of developing and promoting differences between one's product and all similar products. Apple, for example, is known for producing products that demand a premium price because of the capabilities and service that comes with its products. One writer went as far as to say that Linux will not be able to compete with the Apple iPad because it lacks the "magic" that Apple products have. It is difficult to define and therefore imitate Apple's magic; it is a combination of several qualities including the appearance of its products, ease of use, and product integration.[18]

Buyers' Perceptions of Price

In setting prices, managers should consider the price sensitivity of people in the target market. How important is price to them? Is it always "very important?" Members of one market segment may be more influenced by price than members of another. For a particular product, the price may be a bigger factor to some buyers than to others. For example, buyers may be more sensitive to price when purchasing gasoline than when purchasing running shoes.

Buyers will accept different ranges of prices for different products; that is, they will tolerate a narrow range for certain items and a wider range for others. Consider the wide range of prices that consumers pay for soft drinks—from 15 cents per ounce at the movies down to 1.5 cents per ounce on sale at the grocery store. Management should be aware of these limits of acceptability and the products to which they apply. The firm also should take note of buyers' perceptions of a given product in relation to competing products. A premium price may be appropriate if a product is considered superior to others in its category or if the product has inspired strong brand loyalty. On the other hand, if buyers have even a hint of a negative view of a product, a lower price may be necessary.

Sometimes buyers relate price to quality. They may consider a higher price to be an indicator of higher quality. Managers involved in pricing decisions should determine whether this outlook is widespread in the target market. If it is, a higher price may improve the image of a product and, in turn, make the product more desirable.

PRICING OBJECTIVES

Before setting prices for a firm's products, management must decide what it expects to accomplish through pricing. That is, management must set pricing objectives that are in line with both organizational and marketing objectives. Of course, one objective of pricing is to make a profit, but this may not be a firm's primary objective. One or more of the following factors may be just as important.

Survival

A firm may have to price its products to survive—either as an organization or as a player in a particular market. This usually means that the firm will cut its price to attract customers, even if it then must operate at a loss. Obviously, such a goal hardly can be pursued on a long-term basis, for consistent losses would cause the business to fail. Even Abercrombie and Fitch (A&F) had to resort to price reductions on its luxury priced clothing to stay in business during the recent economic downturn. Last year, A&F's first quarter result was a loss of almost $27 million, compared to the previous year's income of over $62 million. This drastic difference forced the retailer to adjust prices to better complement customer's smaller budgets.[19]

Profit Maximization

Many firms may state that their goal is to maximize profit, but this goal is impossible to define (and thus impossible to achieve). What, exactly, is the *maximum* profit? How does a firm know when it has been reached? Firms that wish to set profit goals should express them as either specific dollar amounts, or percentage increases, over previous profits.

* Concept Check

☐ What factors must be considered when pricing products?

☐ How does a change in price affect the demand and supply of a product?

☐ Differentiate price competition and non-price competition.

☐ Why is it important to consider the buyer's sensitivity to price when pricing products?

LEARNING OBJECTIVE

7 Identify the major pricing objectives used by businesses.

product differentiation the process of developing and promoting differences between one's product and all similar products

Target Return on Investment

The *return on investment* (ROI) is the amount earned as a result of that investment. Some firms set an annual percentage ROI as their pricing goal. ConAgra, the company that produces Healthy Choice meals and a multitude of other products, has a target after-tax ROI of 20 percent.

Market-Share Goals

A firm's *market share* is its proportion of total industry sales. Some firms attempt, through pricing, to maintain or increase their market shares. Both U.S. cola giants try to gain market share through aggressive pricing and other marketing efforts.

Status-Quo Pricing

In pricing their products, some firms are guided by a desire to avoid "making waves," or to maintain the status quo. This is especially true in industries that depend on price stability. If such a firm can maintain its profit or market share simply by meeting the competition—charging about the same price as competitors for similar products—then it will do so.

Concept Check ✱

☐ Explain the various types of pricing objectives.

☐ Which ones usually will result in a firm having lower prices?

PRICING METHODS

Once a firm has developed its pricing objectives, it must select a pricing method to reach that goal. Two factors are important to every firm engaged in setting prices. The first is recognition that the market, and not the firm's costs, ultimately determines the price at which a product will sell. The second is awareness that costs and expected sales can be used only to establish some sort of *price floor,* the minimum price at which the firm can sell its product without incurring a loss. In this section, we look at three kinds of pricing methods: cost-based, demand-based, and competition-based pricing.

LEARNING OBJECTIVE

8 Examine the three major pricing methods that firms employ.

Cost-Based Pricing

Using the simplest method of pricing, *cost-based pricing,* the seller first determines the total cost of producing (or purchasing) one unit of the product. The seller then adds an amount to cover additional costs (such as insurance or interest) and profit. The amount that is added is called the **markup**. The total of the cost plus the markup is the product's selling price.

A firm's management can calculate markup as a percentage of its total costs. Suppose, for example, that the total cost of manufacturing and marketing 1,000 DVD players is $100,000, or $100 per unit. If the manufacturer wants a markup that is 20 percent above its costs, the selling price will be $100 plus 20 percent of $100, or $120 per unit.

Markup pricing is easy to apply, and it is used by many businesses (mostly retailers and wholesalers). However, it has two major flaws. The first is the difficulty of determining an effective markup percentage. If this percentage is too high, the product may be overpriced for its market; then too few units may be sold to return the total cost of producing and marketing the product. In contrast, if the markup percentage is too low, the seller is "giving away" profit it could have earned simply by assigning a higher price. In other words, the markup percentage needs to be set to account for the workings of the market, and that is very difficult to do.

The second problem with markup pricing is that it separates pricing from other business functions. The product is priced after production quantities are determined, after costs are incurred, and almost without regard for the market or the marketing mix. To be most effective, the various business functions should be integrated. Each should have an impact on all marketing decisions.

markup the amount a seller adds to the cost of a product to determine its basic selling price

Cost-based pricing can also be facilitated through the use of breakeven analysis. For any product, the **breakeven quantity** is the number of units that must be sold for the total revenue (from all units sold) to equal the total cost (of all units sold). **Total revenue** is the total amount received from the sales of a product. We can estimate projected total revenue as the selling price multiplied by the number of units sold.

The costs involved in operating a business can be broadly classified as either fixed or variable costs. A **fixed cost** is a cost incurred no matter how many units of a product are produced or sold. Rent, for example, is a fixed cost; it remains the same whether 1 or 1,000 units are produced. A **variable cost** is a cost that depends on the number of units produced. The cost of fabricating parts for a stereo receiver is a variable cost. The more units produced, the more parts that will be needed, and thus the higher cost of fabricating parts. The **total cost** of producing a certain number of units is the sum of the fixed costs and the variable costs attributed to those units.

If we assume a particular selling price, we can find the breakeven quantity either graphically or by using a formula. Figure 12-4 graphs the total revenue earned and the total cost incurred by the sale of various quantities of a hypothetical product. With fixed costs of $40,000, variable costs of $60 per unit, and a selling price of $120, the breakeven quantity is 667 units. To find the breakeven quantity, first deduct the variable cost from the selling price to determine how much money the sale of one unit contributes to offsetting fixed costs. Then divide that contribution into the total fixed costs to arrive at the breakeven quantity. (The breakeven quantity in Figure 12-4 is the quantity represented by the intersection of the total revenue and total cost axes.) If the firm sells more than 667 units at $120 each, it will earn a profit. If it sells fewer units, it will suffer a loss.

breakeven quantity the number of units that must be sold for the total revenue (from all units sold) to equal the total cost (of all units sold)

total revenue the total amount received from sales of a product

fixed cost a cost incurred no matter how many units of a product are produced or sold

variable cost a cost that depends on the number of units produced

total cost the sum of the fixed costs and the variable costs attributed to a product

FIGURE 12-4: Breakeven Analysis

Breakeven analysis answers the question: What is the lowest level of production and sales at which a company can break even on a particular product?

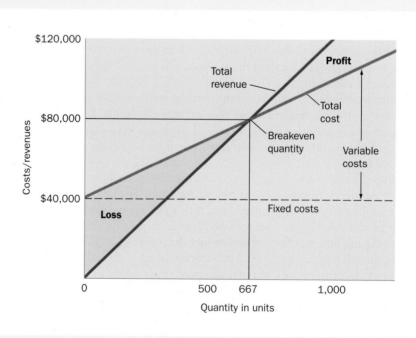

Demand-Based Pricing

Rather than basing the price of a product on its cost, companies sometimes use a pricing method based on the level of demand for the product: *demand-based pricing.* This method results in a high price when product demand is strong and a low price when demand is weak. Some long-distance telephone companies use demand-based pricing. Buyers of new cars that are in high demand, such as the Chevrolet Camaro, Dodge Charger, Ford Mustang GT, and Toyota Prius, pay sticker prices plus a premium. To use this method, a marketer estimates the amount of a product that customers will demand at different prices and then chooses the price that generates the highest total revenue. Obviously, the effectiveness of this method depends on the firm's ability to estimate demand accurately.

A firm may favor a demand-based pricing method called *price differentiation* if it wants to use more than one price in the marketing of a specific product. Price differentiation can be based on such considerations as time of the purchase, type of customer, or type of distribution channel. For example, Florida hotel accommodations are more expensive in winter than in summer, a home owner pays more for air conditioner filters than does an apartment complex owner purchasing the same size filters in greater quantity, and Christmas tree ornaments usually are cheaper on December 26 than on December 16. For price differentiation to work correctly, the company first must be able to segment a market on the basis of different strengths of demand. The company must then be able to keep the segments separate enough so that those who buy at lower prices cannot sell to buyers in segments that are charged a higher price. This isolation can be accomplished, for example, by selling to geographically separated segments.

Compared with cost-based pricing, demand-based pricing places a firm in a better position to attain higher profit levels, assuming that buyers value the product at levels sufficiently above the product's cost. To use demand-based pricing, however, management must be able to estimate demand at different price levels, which may be difficult to do accurately.

Demand-based pricing. Many airlines employ demand-based pricing. The price of an airline ticket will usually be higher when demand for that specific flight is higher.

© iStockphoto.com/Igor Marx

Competition-Based Pricing

In using *competition-based pricing,* an organization considers costs and revenue secondary to competitors' prices. The importance of this method increases if competing products are quite similar and the organization is serving markets in which price is the crucial variable of the marketing strategy. A firm that uses competition-based pricing may choose to be below competitors' prices, slightly above competitors' prices, or at the same level. The price that your bookstore paid to the publishing company of this text was determined using competition-based pricing. Competition-based pricing can help to attain a pricing objective to increase sales or market share. Competition-based pricing may also be combined with other cost approaches to arrive at profitable levels.

PRICING STRATEGIES

A *pricing strategy* is a course of action designed to achieve pricing objectives. Generally, pricing strategies help marketers to solve the practical problems of setting prices. The extent to which a business uses any of the following strategies depends on its pricing and marketing objectives, the markets for its products, the degree of product differentiation, the product's life-cycle stage, and other factors. Figure 12-5 contains a list of the major types of pricing strategies. We discuss these strategies in the remainder of this section.

Concept Check ✱

☐ List and explain the three kinds of pricing methods.

☐ Give an advantage and a disadvantage for each method.

LEARNING OBJECTIVE

9 Explain the different strategies available to companies for setting prices.

FIGURE 12-5: Types of Pricing Strategies

Companies have a variety of pricing strategies available to them.

PRICING STRATEGIES				
New-Product Pricing	**Differential Pricing**	**Psychological Pricing**	**Product-Line Pricing**	**Promotional Pricing**
• Price skimming • Penetration pricing	• Negotiated pricing • Secondary-market pricing • Periodic discounting • Random discounting	• Odd-number pricing • Multiple-unit pricing • Reference pricing • Bundle pricing • Everyday low prices • Customary pricing	• Captive pricing • Premium pricing • Price lining	• Price leaders • Special-event pricing • Comparison discounting

© Cengage Learning 2013

New-Product Pricing

The two primary types of new-product pricing strategies are price skimming and penetration pricing. An organization can use either one, or even both, over a period of time.

PRICE SKIMMING Some consumers are willing to pay a high price for an innovative product either because of its novelty or because of the prestige or status that ownership confers. **Price skimming** is the strategy of charging the highest possible price for a product during the introduction stage of its life-cycle. The seller essentially "skims the cream" off the market, which helps to recover the high costs of R&D more quickly. In addition, a skimming policy may hold down demand for the product, which is helpful if the firm's production capacity is limited during the introduction stage. The greatest disadvantage is that a skimming price may make the product appear lucrative to potential competitors, who then may attempt to enter that market.

PENETRATION PRICING At the opposite extreme, **penetration pricing** is the strategy of setting a low price for a new product. The main purpose of setting a low price is to build market share for the product quickly. The seller hopes that the building of a large market share quickly will discourage competitors from entering the market. If the low price stimulates sales, the firm also may be able to order longer production runs, which result in lower production costs per unit. A disadvantage of penetration pricing is that it places a firm in a less-flexible position. It is more difficult to raise prices significantly than it is to lower them.

Differential Pricing

An important issue in pricing decisions is whether to use a single price or different prices for the same product. A single price is easily understood by both employees and customers. Since many salespeople and customers do not like having to negotiate a price, having a single price reduces the chance of a marketer developing an adversarial relationship with a customer.

Differential pricing means charging different prices to different buyers for the same quality and quantity of product. For differential pricing to be effective, the market must consist of multiple segments with different price sensitivities. When this

price skimming the strategy of charging the highest possible price for a product during the introduction stage of its life-cycle

penetration pricing the strategy of setting a low price for a new product

New Day, New Deal

Small businesses are getting big attention on dozens of "deal-a-day" Web sites such as Groupon and Group Swoop. The idea is to promote one eye-catching local discount every day, with one important catch: The deal is valid only if a minimum number of consumers click to buy. The deal sites keep a commission on each sale, which entrepreneurs must factor into their pricing plans.

These daily-deal sites can be a good way for small businesses to introduce their goods or services to a large number of new customers. Mission Minis, a San Francisco bakery specializing in tiny cupcakes, recently offered a half-price deal on Groupon. Although the owner set the minimum number of customers at 100, more than 3,000 consumers had clicked to buy by the end of the day. The unexpectedly strong response caught the bakery

by surprise. Scrambling to keep up with demand, bakers had to buy additional ingredients twice a day for the first few weeks. Despite the higher costs and the strain on the workforce, the owner says the deal was worthwhile because many customers came back to buy cupcakes at full price.

Satisfying deal-a-day buyers today can lead to profits tomorrow. More than 80 percent of the customers who responded to a deal for MindBody Fitness in Washington, D.C., purchased additional services at regular prices. Endeavor Personal Concierge in Chicago found that 25 percent of its deal-a-day buyers turned into repeat customers, a good deal for all.

Sources: Tim Donnelly, "How Groupon Can Boost Your Company's Exposure," *Inc.*, January 24, 2011, www.inc.com; Angela Kilduff, "Collective Buys by Groupon and Others = Customers + More," *Mission Local* (San Francisco), May 11, 2010, http://missionlocal .org; Kunur Patel, "Groupon Takes Coupons into the Social-Media Age," *Advertising Age*, December 21, 2009, www.adage.com.

method is employed, caution should be used to avoid confusing or antagonizing customers. Differential pricing can occur in several ways, including negotiated pricing, secondary-market pricing, periodic discounting, and random discounting.

NEGOTIATED PRICING **Negotiated pricing** occurs when the final price is established through bargaining between the seller and the customer. Negotiated pricing occurs in a number of industries and at all levels of distribution. Even when there is a predetermined stated price or a price list, manufacturers, wholesalers, and retailers still may negotiate to establish the final sales price. Consumers commonly negotiate prices for houses, cars, and used equipment.

SECONDARY-MARKET PRICING **Secondary-market pricing** means setting one price for the primary target market and a different price for another market. Often the price charged in the secondary market is lower. However, when the costs of serving a secondary market are higher than normal, secondary-market customers may have to pay a higher price. Examples of secondary markets include a geographically isolated domestic market, a market in a foreign country, and a segment willing to purchase a product during off-peak times (such as "early bird" diners at restaurants and off-peak users of cellular phones).

PERIODIC DISCOUNTING **Periodic discounting** is the temporary reduction of prices on a patterned or systematic basis. For example, many retailers have annual holiday sales, and some women's apparel stores have two seasonal sales each year— a winter sale in the last two weeks of January and a summer sale in the first two weeks of July. From the marketer's point of view, a major problem with periodic discounting is that customers can predict when the reductions will occur and may delay their purchases until they can take advantage of the lower prices.

negotiated pricing establishing a final price through bargaining

secondary-market pricing setting one price for the primary target market and a different price for another market

periodic discounting temporary reduction of prices on a patterned or systematic basis

Bundle pricing. Bundle pricing is commonly used in the telecommunications industry. In this ad, Verizon promotes bundle pricing of its phone and internet services.

RANDOM DISCOUNTING To alleviate the problem of customers' knowing when discounting will occur, some organizations employ **random discounting**. That is, they reduce their prices temporarily on a nonsystematic basis. When price reductions of a product occur randomly, current users of that brand are unlikely to predict when the reductions will occur; therefore, they will not delay their purchases in anticipation of buying the product at a lower price. Marketers also use random discounting to attract new customers.

Psychological Pricing

Psychological pricing strategies encourage purchases based on emotional responses rather than on economically rational responses. These strategies are used primarily for consumer products rather than business products.

ODD-NUMBER PRICING Many retailers believe that consumers respond more positively to odd-number prices such as $4.99 than to whole-dollar prices such as $5. **Odd-number pricing** is the strategy of setting prices using odd numbers that are slightly below whole-dollar amounts. Nine and five are the most popular ending figures for odd-number prices.

Sellers who use this strategy believe that odd-number prices increase sales. The strategy is not limited to low-priced items. Auto manufacturers may set the price of a car at $11,999 rather than $12,000. Odd-number pricing has been the subject of various psychological studies, but the results have been inconclusive.

MULTIPLE-UNIT PRICING Many retailers (and especially supermarkets) practice **multiple-unit pricing**, setting a single price for two or more units, such as two cans for 99 cents rather than 50 cents per can. Especially for frequently purchased products, this strategy can increase sales. Customers who see the single price and who expect eventually to use more than one unit of the product regularly purchase multiple units to save money.

Personal App Quick—what does "BOGO" stand for? It's short for "buy one, get one free," a type of multiple-unit pricing used by clothing stores, shoe stores, and other marketers. Sometimes you'll see a "buy one, get the second for half price" variation, as well.

REFERENCE PRICING **Reference pricing** means pricing a product at a moderate level and positioning it next to a more expensive model or brand in the hope that the customer will use the higher price as a reference price (i.e., a comparison price). Because of the comparison, the customer is expected to view the moderate price favorably. When you go to Sears to buy a DVD recorder, a moderately priced DVD recorder may appear especially attractive because it offers most of the important attributes of the more expensive alternatives on display and at a lower price.

BUNDLE PRICING **Bundle pricing** is the packaging together of two or more products, usually of a complementary nature, to be sold for a single price. To be attractive to customers, the single price usually is considerably less than the sum of the prices of the individual products. Being able to buy the bundled combination of products in a single transaction may be of value to the customer as well. Bundle pricing is used commonly for banking and travel services, computers, and

random discounting
temporary reduction of prices on an unsystematic basis

odd-number pricing the strategy of setting prices using odd numbers that are slightly below whole-dollar amounts

multiple-unit pricing the strategy of setting a single price for two or more units

reference pricing pricing a product at a moderate level and positioning it next to a more expensive model or brand

bundle pricing packaging together two or more complementary products and selling them for a single price

automobiles with option packages. Bundle pricing can help to increase customer satisfaction. By bundling slow-moving products with ones with a higher turnover, an organization can stimulate sales and increase its revenues. Selling products as a package rather than individually also may result in cost savings. As regulations in the telecommunications industry continue to evolve, many experts agree that telecom services will be provided together using bundled pricing in the near future. The new term *all-distance* has emerged; however, the bundling of services goes beyond just combined pricing for local and long-distance services. Verizon, for example, is offering the Verizon Triple Play plan that gives customers unlimited local, long-distance, wireless, high speed Internet, and DirectTV for a bundled price of about $85 per month.[20]

EVERYDAY LOW PRICES (EDLPs) To reduce or eliminate the use of frequent short-term price reductions, some organizations use an approach referred to as **everyday low prices (EDLPs)**. When EDLPs are used, a marketer sets a low price for its products on a consistent basis rather than setting higher prices and frequently discounting them. EDLPs, though not deeply discounted, are set far enough below competitors' prices to make customers feel confident that they are receiving a fair price. EDLPs are employed by retailers such as Walmart and by manufacturers such as Procter & Gamble. A company that uses EDLPs benefits from reduced promotional costs, reduced losses from frequent markdowns, and more stability in its sales. A major problem with this approach is that customers have mixed responses to it. In some instances, customers simply do not believe that EDLPs are what they say they are but are instead a marketing gimmick.

CUSTOMARY PRICING In **customary pricing**, certain goods are priced primarily on the basis of tradition. Examples of customary, or traditional, prices would be those set for candy bars and chewing gum.

Product-Line Pricing

Rather than considering products on an item-by-item basis when determining pricing strategies, some marketers employ product-line pricing. *Product-line pricing* means establishing and adjusting the prices of multiple products within a product line. Product-line pricing can provide marketers with flexibility in price setting. For example, marketers can set prices so that one product is quite profitable, whereas another increases market share by virtue of having a lower price than competing products.

When marketers employ product-line pricing, they have several strategies from which to choose. These include captive pricing, premium pricing, and price lining.

CAPTIVE PRICING When **captive pricing** is used, the basic product in a product line is priced low, but the price on the items required to operate or enhance it are set at a higher level. Some razors are relatively inexpensive, but the razor blade replacement cartridges are priced to be highly profitable for the manufacturer. It is estimated that if a person replaces the cartridges as suggested by the manufacturer, the annual cost to the consumer will exceed $50.

PREMIUM PRICING **Premium pricing** occurs when the highest-quality product or the most-versatile version of similar products in a product line is given the highest price. Other products in the line are priced to appeal to price-sensitive shoppers or to those who seek product-specific features. Marketers that use premium pricing often realize a significant portion of their profits from premium-priced products. Examples of product categories in which premium pricing is common are small kitchen appliances, beer, ice cream, and television cable service.

PRICE LINING **Price lining** is the strategy of selling goods only at certain predetermined prices that reflect definite price breaks. For example, a shop may sell men's ties only at $22 and $37. This strategy is used widely in clothing and

everyday low prices (EDLPs) setting a low price for products on a consistent basis

customary pricing pricing on the basis of tradition

captive pricing pricing the basic product in a product line low, but pricing related items at a higher level

premium pricing pricing the highest-quality or most-versatile products higher than other models in the product line

price lining the strategy of selling goods only at certain predetermined prices that reflect definite price breaks

SPOT LIGHT

Which Online Content Are People Willing to Pay for?

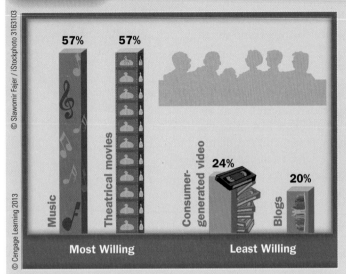

Source: Data from Nielsen survey of 27,548 consumers in 54 countries, http://blog.nielsen.com/nielsenwire/consumer/whats-your-online-content-worth-global-consumers-say-it-depends/, (accessed March 23, 2011).

accessory stores. It eliminates minor price differences from the buying decision—both for customers and for managers who buy merchandise to sell in these stores.

Promotional Pricing

Price, as an ingredient in the marketing mix, often is coordinated with promotion. The two variables sometimes are so interrelated that the pricing policy is promotion oriented. Examples of promotional pricing include price leaders, special-event pricing, and comparison discounting.

PRICE LEADERS Sometimes a firm prices a few products below the usual markup, near cost, or below cost, which results in prices known as **price leaders**. This type of pricing is used most often in supermarkets and restaurants to attract customers by giving them especially low prices on a few items. Management hopes that sales of regularly priced products will more than offset the reduced revenues from the price leaders.

SPECIAL-EVENT PRICING To increase sales volume, many organizations coordinate price with advertising or sales promotions for seasonal or special situations. **Special-event pricing** involves advertised sales or price cutting linked to a holiday, season, or event. If the pricing objective is survival, then special sales events may be designed to generate the necessary operating capital.

COMPARISON DISCOUNTING **Comparison discounting** sets the price of a product at a specific level and simultaneously compares it with a higher price. The higher price may be the product's previous price, the price of a competing brand, the product's price at another retail outlet, or a manufacturer's suggested retail price. Customers may find comparative discounting informative, and it can have a significant impact on them. However, because this pricing strategy on occasion has led to deceptive pricing practices, the Federal Trade Commission has established guidelines for comparison discounting. If the higher price against which the comparison is made is the price formerly charged for the product, sellers must have made the previous price available to customers for a reasonable period of time. If sellers present the higher price as the one charged by other retailers in the same trade area, they must be able to demonstrate that this claim is true. When they present the higher price as the manufacturer's suggested retail price, then the higher price must be similar to the price at which a reasonable proportion of the product was sold. Some manufacturers' suggested retail prices are so high that very few products actually are sold at those prices. In such cases, it would be deceptive to use comparison discounting.

PRICING BUSINESS PRODUCTS

Many of the pricing issues discussed thus far in this chapter deal with pricing in general. However, setting prices for business products can be different from setting prices for consumer products owing to several factors such as size of purchases, transportation considerations, and geographic issues. We examine three types of pricing associated with business products: geographic pricing, transfer pricing, and discounting.

✳ Concept Check

☐ Identify the five categories of pricing strategies.

☐ Describe two specific pricing strategies in each category.

price leaders products priced below the usual markup, near cost, or below cost

special-event pricing advertised sales or price cutting linked to a holiday, season, or event

comparison discounting setting a price at a specific level and comparing it with a higher price

LEARNING OBJECTIVE

10 Describe three major types of pricing associated with business products.

TABLE 12-4: Discounts Used for Business Markets

Type	Reasons for Use	Examples
Trade (functional)	To attract and keep effective resellers by compensating them for performing certain functions, such as transportation, warehousing, selling, and providing credit.	A college bookstore pays about one-third less for a new textbook than the retail price a student pays.
Quantity	To encourage customers to buy large quantities when making purchases and, in the case of cumulative discounts, to encourage customer loyalty.	Numerous companies serving business markets allow a 2 percent discount if an account is paid within ten days.
Seasonal	To allow a marketer to use resources more efficiently by stimulating sales during off-peak periods.	Florida hotels provide companies holding national and regional sales meetings with deeply discounted accommodations during the summer months.
Allowance	In the case of a trade-in allowance, to assist the buyer in making the purchase and potentially earn a profit on the resale of used equipment; in the case of a promotional allowance, to ensure that dealers participate in advertising and sales support programs.	A farm equipment dealer takes a farmer's used tractor as a trade-in on a new one. Nabisco pays a promotional allowance to a supermarket for setting up and maintaining a large end-of-aisle display for a two-week period.

Source: William M. Pride and O. C. Ferrell, *Foundations of Marketing* (Mason, OH: South-Western/Cengage Learning, 2011), 279.

Geographic Pricing

Geographic pricing strategies deal with delivery costs. The pricing strategy that requires the buyer to pay the delivery costs is called *FOB origin pricing*. It stands for "free on board at the point of origin," which means that the price does not include freight charges, and thus the buyer must pay the transportation costs from the seller's warehouse to the buyer's place of business. *FOB destination* indicates that the price does include freight charges, and thus the seller pays these charges.

Transfer Pricing

When one unit in an organization sells a product to another unit, **transfer pricing** occurs. The price is determined by calculating the cost of the product. A transfer price can vary depending on the types of costs included in the calculations. The choice of the costs to include when calculating the transfer price depends on the company's management strategy and the nature of the units' interaction. An organization also must ensure that transfer pricing is fair to all units involved in the purchases.

Discounting

A **discount** is a deduction from the price of an item. Producers and sellers offer a wide variety of discounts to their customers, including trade, quantity, cash, and seasonal discounts as well as allowances. *Trade discounts* are discounts from the list prices that are offered to marketing intermediaries, or middlemen. *Quantity discounts* are discounts given to customers who buy in large quantities. The seller's per-unit selling cost is lower for larger purchases. *Cash discounts* are discounts offered for prompt payment. A seller may offer a discount of "2/10, net 30," meaning that the buyer may take a 2 percent discount if the bill is paid within ten days and that the bill must be paid in full within 30 days. A *seasonal discount* is a price reduction to buyers who purchase out of season. This discount lets the seller maintain steadier production during the year. An *allowance* is a reduction in price to achieve a desired goal. Trade-in allowances, for example, are price reductions granted for turning in used equipment, like aircraft, when purchasing new equipment. Table 12-4 describes some of the reasons for using these discounting techniques as well as some examples.

transfer pricing prices charged in sales between an organization's units

discount a deduction from the price of an item

Concept Check ✱

☐ Describe the three types of pricing associated with business products.

☐ Differentiate between FOB origin and FOB destination pricing.

☐ Explain the five types of discounts for business products.

Get Flashcards, Quizzes, Games, Crosswords, and more @ www.cengagebrain.com

SUMMARY

1 Explain what a product is and how products are classified.

A product is everything one receives in an exchange, including all attributes and expected benefits. The product may be a manufactured item, a service, an idea, or some combination of these.

Products are classified according to their ultimate use. Classification affects a product's distribution, promotion, and pricing. Consumer products, which include convenience, shopping, and specialty products, are purchased to satisfy personal and family needs. Business products are purchased for resale, for making other products, or for use in a firm's operations. Business products can be classified as raw materials, major equipment, accessory equipment, component parts, process materials, supplies, and services.

2 Discuss the product life-cycle and how it leads to new-product development.

Every product moves through a series of four stages—introduction, growth, maturity, and decline—which together form the product life-cycle. As the product progresses through these stages, its sales and profitability increase, peak, and then decline. Marketers keep track of the life-cycle stage of products in order to estimate when a new product should be introduced to replace a declining one.

3 Define *product line* and *product mix* and distinguish between the two.

A product line is a group of similar products marketed by a firm. The products in a product line are related to each other in the way they are produced, marketed, and used. The firm's product mix includes all the products it offers for sale. The width of a mix is the number of product lines it contains. The depth of the mix is the average number of individual products within each line.

4 Identify the methods available for changing a product mix.

Customer satisfaction and organizational objectives require marketers to develop, adjust, and maintain an effective product mix. Marketers may improve a product mix by changing existing products, deleting products, and developing new products.

New products are developed through a series of seven steps. The first step, idea generation, involves the accumulation of a pool of possible product ideas. Screening, the second step, removes from consideration those product ideas that do not mesh with organizational goals or resources. Concept testing, the third step, is a phase in which a small sample of potential buyers is exposed to a proposed product through a written or oral description in order to determine their initial reaction and buying intentions. The fourth step, business analysis, generates information about the potential sales, costs, and profits. During the development step, the product idea is transformed into mock-ups and actual prototypes to determine if the product is technically feasible to build and can be produced at reasonable costs. Test marketing is an actual launch of the product in several selected cities. Finally, during commercialization, plans for full-scale production and marketing are refined and implemented. Most product failures result from inadequate product planning and development.

5 Explain the uses and importance of branding, packaging, and labeling.

A brand is a name, term, symbol, design, or any combination of these that identifies a seller's products as distinct from those of other sellers. Brands can be classified as manufacturer brands, store brands, or generic brands. A firm can choose between two branding strategies—individual branding or family branding. Branding strategies are used to associate (or *not* associate) particular products with existing products, producers, or intermediaries. Packaging protects goods, offers consumer convenience, and enhances marketing efforts by communicating product features, uses, benefits, and image. Labeling provides customers with product information, some of which is required by law.

6 Describe the economic basis of pricing and the means by which sellers can control prices and buyers' perceptions of prices.

Under the ideal conditions of pure competition, an individual seller has no control over the price of its products. Prices are determined by the workings of supply and demand. In our real economy, however, sellers do exert some control, primarily through product differentiation. Product differentiation is the process of developing and promoting differences between one's product and all similar products. Firms also attempt to gain some control over pricing through advertising. A few large sellers have considerable control over prices because each controls a large proportion of the total supply of the product. Firms must consider the relative importance of price to buyers in the target market before setting prices. Buyers' perceptions of prices are affected by the importance of the product to them, the range of prices they consider acceptable, their perceptions of competing products, and their association of quality with price.

7 Identify the major pricing objectives used by businesses.

Objectives of pricing include survival, profit maximization, target return on investment, achieving market goals, and maintaining the status quo. Firms sometimes have to price products to survive, which usually requires cutting prices to attract customers. ROI is the amount earned as a result of the investment in developing and marketing the product. The firm sets an annual percentage ROI as the pricing goal. Some firms use pricing to maintain or increase their market share. And in industries in which price stability is important, firms oftenprice their products by charging about the same as competitors.

8 Examine the three major pricing methods that firms employ.

The three major pricing methods are cost-based pricing, demand-based pricing, and competition-based pricing. When cost-based pricing is employed, a proportion of the cost is added to the total cost to determine the selling price. When demand-based pricing is used, the price will be higher when demand is higher, and the price will be lower when demand is lower. A firm that uses competition-based pricing may choose to price below competitors' prices, at the same level as competitors' prices, or slightly above competitors' prices.

9 Explain the different strategies available to companies for setting prices.

Pricing strategies fall into five categories: new-product pricing, differential pricing, psychological pricing, product-line pricing, and promotional pricing. Price skimming and penetration pricing are two strategies used for pricing new products. Differential pricing can be accomplished through negotiated pricing, secondary-market pricing, periodic discounting, and random discounting. The types of psychological pricing strategies are odd-number pricing, multiple-unit pricing, reference pricing, bundle pricing, everyday low prices, and customary pricing. Product-line pricing can be achieved through captive pricing, premium pricing, and price lining. The major types of promotional pricing are price-leader pricing, special-event pricing, and comparison discounting.

10 Describe three major types of pricing associated with business products.

Setting prices for business products can be different from setting prices for consumer products as a result of several factors, such as size of purchases, transportation considerations, and geographic issues. The three types of pricing associated with the pricing of business products are geographic pricing, transfer pricing, and discounting.

KEY TERMS

You should now be able to define and give an example relevant to each of the following terms:

product (331)
consumer product (332)
business product (332)
convenience product (332)
shopping product (332)
specialty product (332)
raw material (333)
major equipment (333)
accessory equipment (333)
component part (333)
process material (333)
supply (333)
business service (333)
product life-cycle (333)
product line (336)
product mix (336)
product modification (337)
line extension (338)
product deletion (338)

brand (342)
brand name (342)
brand mark (342)
trademark (342)
trade name (342)
manufacturer (or producer) brand (342)
store (or private) brand (342)
generic product (or brand) (343)
brand loyalty (343)
brand equity (344)
individual branding (345)
family branding (345)
brand extension (345)
packaging (346)
labeling (347)
express warranty (347)

price (348)
supply (348)
demand (348)
price competition (349)
non-price competition (349)
product differentiation (350)
markup (351)
breakeven quantity (352)
total revenue (352)
fixed cost (352)
variable cost (352)
total cost (352)
price skimming (354)
penetration pricing (354)
negotiated pricing (355)
secondary-market pricing (355)
periodic discounting (355)

random discounting (356)
odd-number pricing (356)
multiple-unit pricing (356)
reference pricing (356)
bundle pricing (356)
everyday low prices (EDLPs) (357)
customary pricing (357)
captive pricing (357)
premium pricing (357)
price lining (357)
price leaders (358)
special-event pricing (358)
comparison discounting (358)
transfer pricing (359)
discount (359)

DISCUSSION QUESTIONS

1. What does the purchaser of a product obtain besides the good, service, or idea itself?
2. What major factor determines whether a product is a consumer or a business product?
3. What are the four stages of the product life-cycle? How can a firm determine which stage a particular product is in?
4. Under what conditions does product modification work best?
5. Why do products have to be deleted from a product mix?
6. Why must firms introduce new products?
7. What is the difference between manufacturer brands and store brands? Between family branding and individual branding?
8. What is the difference between a line extension and a brand extension?
9. For what purposes is labeling used?
10. Compare and contrast the characteristics of price and non-price competition.
11. How might buyers' perceptions of price influence pricing decisions?
12. What are the five major categories of pricing strategies? Give at least two examples of specific strategies that fall into each category.
13. Identify and describe the main types of discounts that are used in the pricing of business products.
14. Some firms do not delete products until they become financially threatening. What problems may result from relying on this practice?
15. Under what conditions would a firm be most likely to use non-price competition?
16. Under what conditions would a business most likely decide to employ one of the differential pricing strategies?
17. For what types of products are psychological pricing strategies most likely to be used?

TEST YOURSELF

Matching Questions

1. _____ Quantities of products that producers are willing to sell.
2. _____ Quantities of products that buyers are willing to purchase.
3. _____ Presentation of information on a package.
4. _____ The amount earned for investing.
5. _____ Changes that make a product more dependable.
6. _____ Different prices are set for each market.
7. _____ It represents the value of an organization's brand.
8. _____ Customers consistently choose specific brands.
9. _____ It is the legal name of an organization.
10. _____ Bargaining occurs between seller and buyer.

a. labeling
b. supply
c. demand
d. product differentiation
e. return on investment (ROI)
f. secondary-market pricing
g. quality product modification
h. trade name
i. brand loyalty
j. brand equity
k. consumer product
l. negotiated pricing

True False Questions

11. **T F** Tobacco products, alcoholic beverages, and Del Monte brand fruits are considered a product line.
12. **T F** Once established, a product mix remains effective.
13. **T F** Screening is the first step in the evolution of a new product.
14. **T F** Commercialization is the final stage in the development of a new product.
15. **T F** "Peanut Butter" written on a plain white wrapper is an example of a generic product.
16. **T F** Packaging has little influence on buying decisions.
17. **T F** Labels may carry details of written or express warranties.
18. **T F** Product differentiation makes products more competitive with similar products.
19. **T F** Total revenue is the selling price times the number of units sold.
20. **T F** The breakeven quantity includes the desired profit level.

Multiple-Choice Questions

21. _____ Western Day was a special day at the office. Janice wanted to dress in the latest western fashion, but she had limited funds. She visited several shops before finding the right outfit. For Janice, what type of product is the clothing?
a. Specialty product
b. Major equipment
c. Industrial product
d. Shopping product
e. Convenience product

22. _____ Sales rise gradually as a result of promotion and distribution activities, but initially, high development and marketing costs result in low profit or even in a loss. This best describes which stage of the product life-cycle?
a. Maturity
b. Introduction
c. Decline
d. Growth
e. Steady

23. _____ Product modification makes changes to existing products in three primary ways. They are
a. screening, testing, and changing.
b. growth, maturity, and decline.
c. quality, function, and aesthetics.
d. quantity, description, and appearance.
e. product, price, and service.

24. _____ The largest number of new product ideas is rejected during this phase.
a. Concept testing
b. Screening
c. Test marketing
d. Idea generation
e. Business analysis

25. _____ The manager of a local restaurant wants to add new desserts to the menu. Customers were asked to complete a survey about what they like. The restaurant is in which stage of the new-product development process?
a. Test marketing
b. Product development
c. Idea generation
d. Screening
e. Business analysis

26. _____ A customer who consistently buys Sony televisions whenever he or she needs to replace his or her TV set demonstrates
a. the importance of trademarks.
b. the importance of trade names.
c. the importance of brand awareness.
d. brand loyalty.
e. brand equity.

27. _____ Dell, IBM, and Xerox use a strategy that helps promote all their products. This strategy is called
a. family branding.
b. generic brands.
c. store brands.
d. individual branding.
e. none of the above.

28. _____ Plastic water bottles, while convenient for customers, are a clear example that manufacturers are not considering _____ when designing packaging.
a. the needs of intermediaries
b. the needs of retailers
c. environmental consciousness
d. family needs
e. cost-effectiveness

29. _____ When there is a shortage of citrus fruit, the economic forces of supply and demand would suggest that
a. price will stay constant.
b. price will decrease.
c. price will increase.
d. price, all things remaining equal, will increase.
e. it will take a long time before the shortage is felt in the market.

30. _____ Like many other food establishments, Denny's offers a senior citizen's discount. This is an example of
a. periodic discounting.
b. random discounting.
c. differential pricing.
d. negotiated pricing.
e. senior market pricing.

Answers to the Test Yourself questions appear at the end of the book on page TY-1.

VIDEO CASE
From Artistic Roots, Blu Dot Styles Marketing Strategy

When a trio of college friends with backgrounds in art and architecture started moving into their first apartments in the late 1990s, they were frustrated to find that when it came to furniture, they couldn't afford what they liked and didn't like what they could afford. Happily for many future furniture shoppers, however, this frustration led the three to found Blu Dot, a Minneapolis-based furniture design and manufacturing company that has flourished and grown.

Blu Dot specializes in the creation of furniture that is attractive, high quality, and affordable. Its modern, streamlined pieces use off-the-shelf materials and simple manufacturing processes that keep the company's costs and prices down. The company also contracts with suppliers that make industrial rather than consumer products, because they use more efficient and cost-effective processes and technology. These strategies, plus designs that pack flat and are easy to ship, allow the firm to combine what Maurice Blanks, one of the founders, describes as the affordability of the low end of the market and the craftsmanship of the high end. Anyone can design a $600 or $700 coffee table, Blu Dot believes. It's the $99 one the company is aiming for that's more of a challenge.

The company sells seven product lines—tables, storage, accessories, desks, beds, seating, and shelving. Its pricing strategy for each of these is straightforward. Managers add their fixed and variable costs, plus the markup they believe they'll need to keep the business functioning. They then usually look at what competitors are doing with similar products and try to identify three or four different pieces of pricing information to help them settle on a profitable price. The company also uses some creative pricing strategies to make its margins. For instance, one coffee table in a set might have a higher markup, whereas another has a slightly lower one for more price-conscious customers. Overall, then, the target margins are often met.

Blu Dot thinks of its total product offering as consisting of three interdependent elements: the core product, its supplemental features, and its symbolic or experiential value. Although some customers are attracted by the design aspects of the products, others are more concerned with value. That's one reason the company recently introduced a separate brand, called 1oo ("too"), and priced it slightly below the original Blu Dot line. These items have been marketed through Urban Outfitters, and Blu Dot has adjusted the prices over time after seeing how sales progressed. Co-founder John Christakos likens Blu Dot's pricing practice to cooking, in that both are processes that allow for fine-tuning as events develop.

In an interesting recent promotion that flirted with the price of zero, Blu Dot celebrated the opening of its new store in New York's hip SoHo district by leaving 25 brand-new units of its iconic "Real Good Chair," normally priced at $129, on various street corners in the city. Most of the chairs were equipped with GPS devices that allowed the company's marketing agency to trace the chairs to those who "rescued" them and brought them home. The company's Web site proclaims that all the chairs found good homes, and those "scavengers" who agreed to chat with the firm about its products received a second free chair in thanks.[21]

Questions

1. What challenges does Blu Dot face in selling consumer products (as opposed to business products)?
2. Do you think the product life-cycle is an important marketing concept in developing and managing Blu Dot products? Why or why not?
3. Describe the product mix and the role different product lines play in Blu Dot's marketing strategy.

BUILDING SKILLS FOR CAREER SUCCESS

1. Exploring the Internet

The Internet has quickly taken comparison shopping to a new level. Several Web sites such as http://bizrate.com, http://pricescan.com, and http://mysimon.com have emerged boasting that they can find the consumer the best deal on any product. From computers to watches, these sites offer unbiased price and product information to compare virtually any product. Users may read reviews about products as well as provide their own input from personal experience. Some of these sites also offer special promotions and incentives in exchange for user information. Visit the text Web site for updates to this exercise.

Assignment

1. Search all three of the Web sites listed above for the same product.
2. Did you notice any significant differences between the sites and the information they provide?
3. What percentage of searches do you think lead to purchases as opposed to browsing? Explain your answer.

4. Which site are you most likely to use on a regular basis? Why?
5. In what ways do these Web sites contribute to price competition?

2. Building Team Skills

In This book, *The Post-Industrial Society,* Peter Drucker wrote:

Society, community, and family are all conserving institutions. They try to maintain stability and to prevent, or at least slow down, change. But the organization of the post-capitalist society of organizations is a destabilizer. Because its function is to put knowledge to work—on tools, processes, and products; on work; on knowledge itself—it must be organized for constant change. It must be organized for innovation.

New product development is important in this process of systematically abandoning the past and building a future. Current customers can be sources of ideas for new products and services and ways of improving existing ones.

Assignment

1. Working in teams of five to seven, brainstorm ideas for new products or services for your college.
2. Construct questions to ask currently enrolled students (your customers). Sample questions might include:
   a. Why did you choose this college?
   b. How can this college be improved?
   c. What products or services do you wish were available?
3. Conduct the survey and review the results.
4. Prepare a list of improvements and/or new products or services for your college.

3. Researching Different Careers

Standard & Poor's Industry Surveys, designed for investors, provides insight into various industries and the companies that compete within those industries. The "Basic Analysis" section gives overviews of industry trends and issues. The other sections define some basic industry terms, report the latest revenues and earnings of more than 1,000 companies, and occasionally list major reference books and trade associations.

Assignment

1. Identify an industry in which you might like to work.
2. Find the industry in *Standard & Poor's.* (*Note: Standard & Poor's* uses broad categories of industry. For example, an apparel or home-furnishings store would be included under "Retail" or "Textiles.")
3. Identify the following:
   a. Trends and issues in the industry
   b. Opportunities and/or problems that might arise in the industry in the next five years
   c. Major competitors within the industry (These companies are your potential employers.)
4. Prepare a report of your findings.

CHAPTER 13 DISTRIBUTING AND PROMOTING PRODUCTS

© Chen Fei/Xinhua/Xinhua Press/Corbis

Why should you care?

Not only is it important to create and maintain a mix of products that satisfies customers but also to make these products available at the *right place* and *time* and to communicate with customers effectively.

Learning Objectives

1 Identify the various distribution channels and explain the concept of market coverage.

2 Understand how supply chain management facilitates partnering among channel members.

3 Discuss the need for wholesalers, describe the services they provide, and identify the major types of wholesalers.

4 Distinguish among the major types of retailers and shopping centers.

5 Explain the five most important physical distribution activities.

6 Explain how integrated marketing communications works to have the maximum impact on the customer.

7 Understand the basic elements of the promotion mix.

8 Explain the three types of advertising and describe the major steps of developing an advertising campaign.

9 Recognize the kinds of salespersons, the steps in the personal selling process, and the major sales management tasks.

10 Describe sales promotion objectives and methods.

11 Understand the types and uses of public relations.

Get Flashcards, Quizzes, Games, Crosswords, and more @ www.cengagebrain.com

Macy's Blends the Best of National and Local Marketing

Crowds have gathered every Thanksgiving Day since 1924 to enjoy the huge Macy's parade that winds its way through New York City, ending with the arrival of Santa Claus to kick off the Christmas season. These days, millions of viewers also watch the parade on television or online. This special event is indelibly connected with the Macy's brand and its star logo, which now shines over 810 department stores from coast to coast. Macy's also owns the Bloomingdale's department store chain, which consists of 40 stores featuring upscale fashions for men, women, and children.

Macy's, first founded in 1858, is on the upswing, ringing up $25 billion in annual sales (including online revenue) and gaining sales momentum year by year. Its situation contrasts with the struggles of some other department stores, which have had difficulty coping with a challenging economy and with increased competition from specialty stores and discount stores. How does Macy's do it?

One key marketing strategy is My Macy's, a drive to tailor the merchandise in each store to local customers' tastes. This was needed because over the previous decades, Macy's had acquired a number of department store companies and changed their names to Macy's to take advantage of that brand's equity. Although some local customers were initially unhappy with the switch, My Macy's has largely won them over. Now the assortment of national and regional brands more closely fits the needs and preferences of each store's shoppers. "The ultimate goal is to have you walk in the store and say, 'They *get* me! This is MY Macy's!'" explains a district vice president. Thanks to My Macy's, even the smallest stores are enjoying sizable sales and profit increases.

Another key marketing strategy is a promotion mix that appeals to local audiences while building on the national recognition and heritage of the Macy's brand. For consistency, every Macy's promotion features the same red-star logo, whether swim suits are being promoted in a Southern store or ski jackets are being promoted in a Northern store. And the same logo tops Macy's online store, Facebook page, Twitter account, and YouTube channel. [1]

Did you know?

Macy's, established in 1858, rings up more than $24 billion in annual sales through two major retailing divisions, Macy's and Bloomingdale's.

Some companies, like Macy's, use a particular approach to distribution and marketing channels that gives them a sustainable competitive advantage. More than two million firms in the United States help to move products from producers to consumers. Store chains such as Dollar General Stores, Starbucks, Sears, and Walmart operate retail outlets where consumers make purchases. Some retailers, such as Avon Products and Amway, send their salespeople to the homes of customers. Other retailers, such as Lands' End and L. L. Bean, sell online, through catalogs, or both. Still others, such as Amazon, sell online to customers.

In this chapter, we initially examine various distribution channels that products follow as they move from producer to ultimate user. Then we discuss wholesalers and retailers and examine the major types of shopping centers. Next, we explore the physical distribution function and the major modes of transportation that are used to move goods. Then we discuss integrated marketing communication and the major elements that can be a part of a promotion mix: advertising, personal selling, sales promotion, and public relations.

DISTRIBUTION CHANNELS AND MARKET COVERAGE

A **distribution channel, or marketing channel**, is a sequence of marketing organizations that directs a product from the producer to the ultimate user. Every marketing channel begins with the producer and ends with either the consumer or the business user.

A marketing organization that links a producer and user within a marketing channel is called a **middleman, or marketing intermediary**. For the most part, middlemen are concerned with the transfer of *ownership* of products. A **merchant middleman** (or, more simply, a *merchant*) is a middleman that actually takes title to products by buying them. A **functional middleman** on the other hand, helps in the transfer of ownership of products but does not take title to the products.

Commonly Used Distribution Channels

Different channels of distribution generally are used to move consumer and business products. The four most commonly used channels for consumer products and the two most commonly used business product channels are illustrated in Figure 13-1.

PRODUCER TO CONSUMER This channel, often called the *direct channel*, includes no marketing intermediaries. Practically all services and a few consumer goods are distributed through a direct channel. Examples of marketers that sell goods directly to consumers include Dell Computer, Mary Kay Cosmetics, and Avon Products.

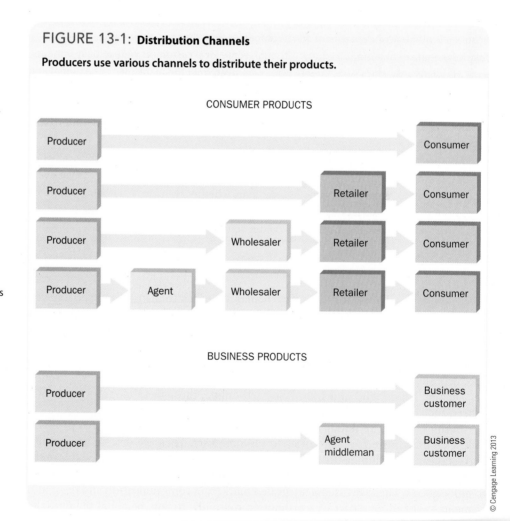

FIGURE 13-1: Distribution Channels

Producers use various channels to distribute their products.

CONSUMER PRODUCTS

BUSINESS PRODUCTS

© Cengage Learning 2013

distribution channel (or marketing channel) a sequence of marketing organizations that directs a product from the producer to the ultimate user

middleman (or marketing intermediary) a marketing organization that links a producer and user within a marketing channel

merchant middleman a middleman that actually takes title to products by buying them

functional middleman a middleman that helps in the transfer of ownership of products but does not take title to the products

Furniture Store? That Used to Be Our Roller-Skating Rink!

entrepreneurial SUCCESS

It takes entrepreneurial spirit to see a cavernous roller-skating rink as a future furniture store. However, an out-of-the-ordinary location was part of the appeal for Mary Liz Curtin and Stephen Scannell, the husband-and-wife owners of Leon & Lulu, an upscale furniture shop in Clawsen, Michigan. Curtin and Scannell liked the size and character of the Ambassador Roller Rink, a local landmark more than 60 years old. Although they had to renovate it for its new purpose, they left the rink's original scoreboard and floor intact.

Since the store's grand opening in 2006, Curtin and Scannell have incorporated the rink's heritage into their marketing efforts. They put hundreds of the old skates on display and, during busy sales, their employees skate around serving cookies to customers. The location has become a major draw, helping build the store's annual sales beyond $2 million in just a few years. "We get letters from people who thank us for keeping the history alive," Curtin says.

Beacham's Clock Company is also unusual, located in an updated, old-fashioned home with a wrap-around porch just a few steps from Main Street in Sisters, Oregon. The house complements master clockmaker Ed Beacham's inventory of hand-crafted clocks and adds to the word of mouth about his store. The town attracts thousands of visitors during tourist season, and customers from as far away as New Zealand find their way to Beacham's unique store, ready to pay up to $30,000 for his one-of-a-kind clocks.

Sources: Saverio Mancina, "A Store That's Fun to Visit," *Fox Business*, January 2, 2011, www.foxbusiness.com; Sarah E. Needleman, "Entrepreneurs Make Use of Odd Spaces," *Wall Street Journal*, May 4, 2010, www.wsj.com; Kristian Foden-Vencil, "The Old Clock Shop Thrives in Sisters," *Oregon Public Broadcasting*, May 11, 2010, http://news.opb.org/article/7278-clock-shop/; http://leonandlulu.com.

Producers sell directly to consumers for several reasons. They can better control the quality and price of their products. They do not have to pay (through discounts) for the services of intermediaries. Also, they can maintain closer ties with customers.

PRODUCER TO RETAILER TO CONSUMER A **retailer** is a middleman that buys from producers or other middlemen and sells to consumers. Producers sell directly to retailers when retailers (such as Walmart) can buy in large quantities. This channel is used most often for products that are bulky, such as furniture and automobiles, for which additional handling would increase selling costs. It is also the usual channel for perishable products, such as fruits and vegetables, and for high-fashion products that must reach the consumer in the shortest possible time.

PRODUCER TO WHOLESALER TO RETAILER TO CONSUMER This channel is known as the *traditional channel* because many consumer goods (especially convenience goods) pass through wholesalers to retailers. A **wholesaler** is a middleman that sells products to other firms. These firms may be retailers, industrial users, or other wholesalers. A producer uses wholesalers when its products are carried by so many retailers that the producer cannot deal with all of them. For example, the maker of Wrigley's gum uses this type of channel.

PRODUCER TO AGENT TO WHOLESALER TO RETAILER TO CONSUMER Producers may use agents to reach wholesalers. Agents are functional middlemen that do not take title to products and that are compensated by commissions paid by producers. Often these products are inexpensive, frequently purchased items. For example, to reach a large number of potential customers, a small manufacturer of gas-powered lawn edgers might choose to use agents to market its product to wholesalers, which, in turn, sell the lawn edgers to a large number of retailers. This channel is also used for highly seasonal products (such as Christmas tree ornaments) and by producers that do not have their own sales forces.

retailer a middleman that buys from producers or other middlemen and sells to consumers

wholesaler a middleman that sells products to other firms

Intensive distribution. M&M's candies are distributed through intensive distribution. This product can be purchased in superstores, supermarkets, discount stores, convenience stores, and through vending machines.

© Susan Van Etten

intensive distribution the use of all available outlets for a product

selective distribution the use of only a portion of the available outlets for a product in each geographic area

exclusive distribution the use of only a single retail outlet for a product in a large geographic area

✱ *Concept Check*

☐ How do the different types of middlemen link a producer to a user within a marketing channel?

☐ Describe the six distribution channels. Give an example of each.

☐ Explain the three intensities of market coverage. Which types of products are generally associated with each of the different intensity levels (convenience, shopping, or specialty)?

PRODUCER TO BUSINESS USER In this direct channel, the manufacturer's own sales force sells directly to business users. Heavy machinery, airplanes, and major equipment usually are distributed in this way. The very short channel allows the producer to provide customers with expert and timely services, such as delivery, machinery installation, and repairs.

PRODUCER TO AGENT MIDDLEMAN TO BUSINESS USER Manufacturers use this channel to distribute such items as operating supplies, accessory equipment, small tools, and standardized parts. The agent is an independent intermediary between the producer and the user. Generally, agents represent sellers.

USING MULTIPLE CHANNELS Often a manufacturer uses different distribution channels to reach different market segments. For example, candy bars are sold through channels containing wholesalers and retailers as well as channels in which the producer sells them directly through large retailers. Multiple channels are also used to increase sales or to capture a larger share of the market with the goal of selling as much merchandise as possible.

Level of Market Coverage

How does a producer decide which distribution channels (and which particular intermediaries) to use? As with every other marketing decision, this one should be based on all relevant factors. These include the firm's production capabilities and marketing resources, the target market and buying patterns of potential customers, and the product itself. After evaluating these factors, the producer can choose a particular *intensity of market coverage*. Then the producer selects channels and intermediaries to implement that coverage.

Intensive distribution is the use of all available outlets for a product. The producer that wants to give its product the widest possible exposure in the marketplace chooses intensive distribution. The manufacturer saturates the market by selling to any intermediary of good financial standing that is willing to stock and sell the product. For the consumer, intensive distribution means being able to shop at a convenient store and spend minimum time buying the product. Many convenience goods, including candy, gum, and soft drinks, are distributed intensively. Companies such as Procter & Gamble that produce consumer packaged items rely on intensive distribution for many of their products because consumers want ready availability.

Personal App Wherever you are—at school, at work, at a ball game, or at a movie—you're likely to see bottled water and snacks for sale. So many people buy these items in so many situations that marketers use intensive distribution to make them available just about everywhere.

Selective distribution is the use of only a portion of the available outlets for a product in each geographic area. Manufacturers of goods such as furniture, major home appliances, and clothing typically prefer selective distribution. For example, Apple distributes its iPhone through Verizon, Best Buy, AT&T, and Apple retail stores in the United States.

Exclusive distribution is the use of only a single retail outlet for a product in a large geographic area. Exclusive distribution usually is limited to very prestigious products. It is appropriate, for instance, for specialty goods such as upscale pianos, fine china, and expensive jewelry. The producer usually places many requirements (such as inventory levels, sales training, service quality, and warranty procedures) on exclusive dealers. For example, Patek Philippe watches, which may sell for $10,000 or more, are available in only a few select locations.

PARTNERING THROUGH SUPPLY-CHAIN MANAGEMENT

LEARNING OBJECTIVE

2 Understand how supply-chain management facilitates partnering among channel members.

Supply-chain management is a long-term partnership among channel members working together to create a distribution system that reduces inefficiencies, costs, and redundancies while creating a competitive advantage and satisfying customers. Supply-chain management requires cooperation throughout the entire marketing channel, including manufacturing, research, sales, advertising, and shipping. Supply chains focus not only on producers, wholesalers, retailers, and customers but also on component-parts suppliers, shipping companies, communication companies, and other organizations that participate in product distribution. Suppliers are having a greater impact on determining what items retail stores carry. This phenomenon, called *category management,* is becoming common for mass merchandisers, supermarkets, and convenience stores. Through category management, the retailer asks a supplier in a particular category how to stock the shelves. Many retailers and suppliers claim this process delivers maximum efficiency.

Traditionally, buyers and sellers have been adversarial when negotiating purchases. Supply-chain management, however, encourages cooperation in reducing the costs of inventory, transportation, administration, and handling; in speeding order-cycle times; and in increasing profits for all channel members. When buyers, sellers, marketing intermediaries, and facilitating agencies work together, customers' needs regarding delivery, scheduling, packaging, and other requirements are better met. Home Depot, North America's largest home-improvement retailer, is working to help its suppliers improve productivity and thereby supply Home Depot with better-quality products at lower costs. The company has even suggested a cooperative partnership with its competitors so that regional trucking companies making deliveries to all these organizations can provide faster, more efficient delivery.

Technology has enhanced the implementation of supply-chain management significantly. Through computerized integrated information sharing, channel members reduce costs and improve customer service. At Walmart, for example, supply-chain management has almost eliminated the occurrence of out-of-stock items. Using barcode and electronic data interchange (EDI) technology, stores, warehouses, and suppliers communicate quickly and easily to keep Walmart's shelves stocked with items customers want. Furthermore, there are currently about 400 electronic trading communities made up of businesses selling to other businesses, including auctions, exchanges, e-procurement hubs, and multisupplier online catalogs. As many major industries transform their processes over the next five to ten years, the end result will be increased productivity by reducing inventory, shortening cycle time, and removing wasted human effort.

Concept Check ✱

☐ How does supply-chain management encourage cooperation between buyers and sellers?

☐ How has technology enhanced the implementation of supply-chain management?

MARKETING INTERMEDIARIES: WHOLESALERS

LEARNING OBJECTIVE

3 Discuss the need for wholesalers, describe the services they provide, and identify the major types of wholesalers.

supply-chain management long-term partnership among channel members working together to create a distribution system that reduces inefficiencies, costs, and redundancies while creating a competitive advantage and satisfying customers

Wholesalers may be the most misunderstood of marketing intermediaries. Producers sometimes try to eliminate them from distribution channels by dealing directly with retailers or consumers. Yet wholesalers provide a variety of essential marketing services. Although wholesalers can be eliminated, their functions cannot be eliminated; these functions *must* be performed by other channel members or by the consumer or ultimate user. Eliminating a wholesaler may or may not cut distribution costs.

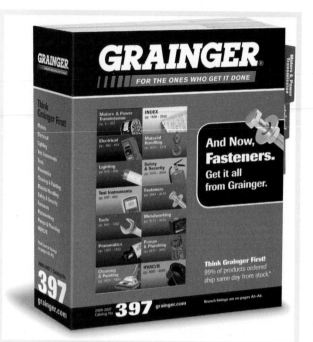

Limited-line wholesaler. A limited-line wholesaler carries a few product lines but many product items within each line.

Wholesalers Provide Services to Retailers and Manufacturers

Wholesalers help retailers

- Buying in large quantities and then selling to retailers in smaller quantities and by delivering goods to retailers.
- Stocking in one place the variety of goods that retailers otherwise would have to buy from many producers.
- Providing assistance in other vital areas, including promotion, market information, and financial aid.

Wholesalers help manufacturers by

- Performing functions similar to those provided to retailers.
- Providing a sales force, reducing inventory costs, assuming credit risks, and furnishing market information.

Types of Wholesalers

Wholesalers generally fall into two categories: merchant wholesalers; agents and brokers. Of these, merchant wholesalers constitute the largest portion. They account for about four-fifths of all wholesale establishments and employees.

MERCHANT WHOLESALERS A **merchant wholesaler** is a middleman that purchases goods in large quantities and then sells them to other wholesalers or retailers and to institutional, farm, government, professional, or industrial users.

Characteristics of a Merchant Wholesaler

- Merchant wholesalers usually operate one or more warehouses at which they receive, take title to, and store goods. These wholesalers are sometimes called *distributors* or *jobbers*.
- Most merchant wholesalers are businesses composed of salespeople, order takers, receiving and shipping clerks, inventory managers, and office personnel.
- The successful merchant wholesaler must analyze available products and market needs. It must be able to adapt the type, variety, and quality of its products to changing market conditions.
- Merchant wholesalers may be classified as full-service or limited-service wholesalers depending on the number of services they provide. A **full-service wholesaler** performs the entire range of wholesaler functions described earlier in this section. These functions include delivering goods, supplying warehousing, arranging for credit, supporting promotional activities, and providing general customer assistance.

A full-service wholesaler can be of three different types:

- A **general-merchandise wholesaler** deals in a wide variety of products, such as drugs, hardware, nonperishable foods, cosmetics, detergents, and tobacco.
- A **limited-line wholesaler** stocks only a few product lines but carries numerous product items within each line.
- A **specialty-line wholesaler** carries a select group of products within a single line. Food delicacies such as shellfish represent the kind of product handled by this type of wholesaler.

AGENTS AND BROKERS Agents and brokers are functional middlemen. Functional middlemen do not take title to products. They perform a small number of marketing activities and are paid a commission that is a percentage of the sales price.

merchant wholesaler a middleman that purchases goods in large quantities and then sells them to other wholesalers or retailers and to institutional, farm, government, professional, or industrial users

full-service wholesaler a middleman that performs the entire range of wholesaler functions

general-merchandise wholesaler a middleman that deals in a wide variety of products

limited-line wholesaler a middleman that stocks only a few product lines but carries numerous product items within each line

specialty-line wholesaler a middleman that carries a select group of products within a single line

An **agent** is a middleman that expedites exchanges, represents a buyer or a seller, and often is hired permanently on a commission basis. When agents represent producers, they are known as *sales agents* or *manufacturer's agents*. As long as the products represented do not compete, a sales agent may represent one or several manufacturers on a commission basis. The agent solicits orders for the manufacturers within a specific territory. As a rule, the manufacturers ship the merchandise and bill the customers directly. The manufacturers also set the prices and other conditions of the sales.

What do the manufacturers gain by using a sales agent? The sales agent provides immediate entry into a territory, regular calls on customers, selling experience, and a known, predetermined selling expense (a commission that is a percentage of sales revenue).

A **broker** is a middleman that specializes in a particular commodity, represents either a buyer or a seller, and is likely to be hired on a temporary basis. However, food brokers, which sell grocery products to resellers, generally have long-term relationships with their clients. Brokers may perform only the selling function or both buying and selling using established contacts or special knowledge of their fields.

Concept Check ✳

☐ What services do wholesalers provide to producers and to retailers?

☐ Identify and describe the various types of wholesalers.

MARKETING INTERMEDIARIES: RETAILERS

LEARNING OBJECTIVE

4 Distinguish among the major types of retailers and shopping centers.

Retailers are the final link between producers and consumers. Retailers may buy from either wholesalers or producers. They sell not only goods but also such services as auto repairs, haircuts, and dry cleaning. Some retailers sell both. Sears, Roebuck sells consumer goods, financial services, and repair services for home appliances bought at Sears.

Of approximately 3 million retailers in the United States, about 90 percent have annual sales of less than $1 million. On the other hand, some large retail organizations realize well over $1 million in sales revenue per day. Table 13-1 lists the ten largest retail organizations and their approximate sales revenues and yearly profits.

Types of Retail Stores

One way to classify retailers is by the number of stores owned and operated by the firm.

1. An **independent retailer** is a firm that operates only one retail outlet. Approximately three-fourths of retailers are independent. One-store operators, like all small businesses, generally provide personal service and a convenient location.

TABLE 13-1: **The Ten Largest Retail Firms in the United States**

Rank	Company	Sales (000)	Operating Income (000)	Store Count
1	Walmart	$304,939,000	$21,034,000	4,304
2	Kroger	$76,733,000	$1,091,000	3,619
3	Target	$63,435,000	$4,376,000	1,740
4	Walgreen's	$63,335,000	$3,247,000	7,397
5	The Home Depot	$59,176,000	$4,803,000	1,966
6	Costco	$56,548,000	$1,273,000	406
7	CVS Caremark	$55,355,000	$4,159,000	7,025
8	Lowe's	$47,220,000	$2,825,000	1,694
9	Sears Holdings	$44,043,000	$713,000	3,519
10	Best Buy	$37,314,000	$2,071,000	1,192

Source: "Top 100 Retailers," Stores, July 2009, www.stores.org/2009/Top-100-Retailers. Reprinted with permission from Wrights Reprints.

agent a middleman that expedites exchanges, represents a buyer or a seller, and often is hired permanently on a commission basis

broker a middleman that specializes in a particular commodity, represents either a buyer or a seller, and is likely to be hired on a temporary basis

independent retailer a firm that operates only one retail outlet

2. A **chain retailer** is a company that operates more than one retail outlet. By adding outlets, chain retailers attempt to reach new geographic markets. As sales increase, chains usually buy merchandise in larger quantities and thus take advantage of quantity discounts. They also wield more power in their dealings with suppliers. About one-fourth of retail organizations operate chains.

Personal App Stop by any shopping center and you'll see dozens of stores operated by chain retailers. If you've ever been in other outlets operated by these chains, you'll know what type of merchandise the local branches carry even before you step inside.

Another way to classify retail stores is by store size and the kind and number of products carried. Let's take a closer look at store types based on these dimensions.

DEPARTMENT STORES These large retail establishments consist of several sections, or departments, that sell a wide assortment of products. According to the U.S. Bureau of the Census, a **department store** is a retail store that (1) employs 25 or more persons and (2) sells at least home furnishings, appliances, family apparel, and household linens and dry goods, each in a different part of the store. Marshall Field's in Chicago (and several other cities), Harrods in London, and Au Printemps in Paris are examples of large department stores. Sears, Roebuck and JCPenney are also department stores. Traditionally, department stores have been service oriented. Along with the goods they sell, these retailers provide credit, delivery, personal assistance, liberal return policies, and pleasant shopping atmospheres.

Department store. Macy's is an example of a department store.

chain retailer a company that operates more than one retail outlet

department store a retail store that (1) employs 25 or more persons and (2) sells at least home furnishings, appliances, family apparel, and household linens and dry goods, each in a different part of the store

discount store a self-service general-merchandise outlet that sells products at lower-than-usual prices

warehouse showroom a retail facility in a large, low-cost building with a large on-premises inventory and minimal service

convenience store a small food store that sells a limited variety of products but remains open well beyond normal business hours

supermarket a large self-service store that sells primarily food and household products

DISCOUNT STORES A **discount store** is a self-service general-merchandise outlet that sells products at lower-than-usual prices. These stores can offer lower prices by operating on smaller markups and by offering minimal customer services. To keep prices low, discount stores operate on the basic principle of high turnover of such items as appliances, toys, clothing, automotive products, and sports equipment. Popular discount stores include Kmart, Walmart, Dollar General, and Target.

WAREHOUSE SHOWROOMS A **warehouse showroom** is a retail facility with five basic characteristics: (1) a large, low-cost building, (2) warehouse materials-handling technology, (3) vertical merchandise displays, (4) a large, on-premises inventory, and (5) minimal service. Some of the best-known showrooms are operated by big furniture retailers. These operations employ few personnel and offer few services. Most customers carry away purchases in the manufacturer's carton, although some warehouse showrooms will deliver for a fee.

CONVENIENCE STORES A **convenience store** is a small food store that sells a limited variety of products but remains open well beyond normal business hours. Almost 70 percent of convenience store customers live within a mile of the store. White Hen Pantry, 7-Eleven, Circle K, and Open Pantry stores, for example, are found in some areas, as are independent convenience stores. Their limited product mixes and higher prices keep convenience stores from becoming a major threat to other grocery retailers. There are over 117,000 convenience stores in the United States.[2]

SUPERMARKETS A **supermarket** is a large self-service store that sells primarily food and household products. It stocks canned, fresh, frozen, and processed foods; paper products; and cleaning supplies. Supermarkets also may sell such items as housewares, toiletries, toys and games, drugs, stationery, books and magazines, plants and flowers, and a few clothing items. Supermarkets are large-scale operations that emphasize low prices and one-stop shopping for household needs.

SUPERSTORES A **superstore** is a large retail store that carries not only food and nonfood products ordinarily found in supermarkets but also additional product lines—housewares, hardware, small appliances, clothing, personal-care products, garden products, and automotive merchandise. Superstores also provide a number of services to entice customers. Typically, these include automotive repair, snack bars and restaurants, film developing, and banking.

Category killer. Home Depot, a building materials retailer, is an example of a category killer.

© Susan Van Etten

WAREHOUSE CLUBS The **warehouse club** is a large-scale members-only establishment that combines features of cash-and-carry wholesaling with discount retailing. For a nominal annual fee (about $25), small retailers may purchase products at wholesale prices for business use or for resale. Warehouse clubs also sell to ultimate consumers. Individual purchasers usually can choose to pay yearly dues for membership cards that allow them to avoid the 5 percent additional charge.

Because their product lines are shallow and sales volumes are high, warehouse clubs can offer a broad range of merchandise, including perishable and nonperishable foods, beverages, books, appliances, housewares, automotive parts, hardware, furniture, and sundries.

TRADITIONAL SPECIALTY STORES A **traditional specialty store** carries a narrow product mix with deep product lines. Traditional specialty stores are sometimes called *limited-line retailers*. If they carry depth in one particular product category, they may be called *single-line retailers*. Specialty stores usually sell such products as clothing, jewelry, sporting goods, fabrics, computers, flowers, baked goods, books, and pet supplies. Specialty stores usually offer deeper product mixes than department stores. They attract customers by emphasizing service, atmosphere, and location. Consumers who are dissatisfied with the impersonal atmosphere of large retailers often find the attention offered by small specialty stores appealing. Specialty stores include the Gap, Radio Shack, Bath and Body Works, and Foot Locker.

OFF-PRICE RETAILERS An **off-price retailer** is a store that buys manufacturers' seconds, overruns, returns, and off-season merchandise at below-wholesale prices and sells them to consumers at deep discounts. Off-price retailers sell limited lines of national-brand and designer merchandise, usually clothing, shoes, or house wares. Off-price retailers include T.J. Maxx, Burlington Coat Factory, and Marshalls. Off-price stores charge up to 50 percent less than department stores do for comparable merchandise but offer few customer services. They often include community dressing rooms and central checkout counters, and some off-price retailers have a no-returns, no-exchanges policy.

CATEGORY KILLERS A **category killer** is a very large specialty store that concentrates on a single product line and competes by offering low prices and an enormous number of products. These stores are called *category killers* because they take business away from smaller, high-cost retail stores. Category killers include Home Depot (building materials), Office Depot (office supplies and equipment), and Best Buy (electronics), all of which are leaders in their niche. These specialty chains that grew so aggressively in the 1990s and early 2000s—that bankrupted thousands of independent businesses—are now themselves rapidly losing ground to a handful of giant mass merchandisers, namely, Walmart, Amazon, Target, and Costco.[3]

superstore a large retail store that carries not only food and nonfood products ordinarily found in supermarkets but also additional product lines

warehouse club a large-scale members-only establishment that combines features of cash-and-carry wholesaling with discount retailing

traditional specialty store a store that carries a narrow product mix with deep product lines

off-price retailer a store that buys manufacturers' seconds, overruns, returns, and off-season merchandise for resale to consumers at deep discounts

category killer a very large specialty store that concentrates on a single product line and competes on the basis of low prices and product availability

Nonstore Selling Gets Facebook Friendly

Facebook isn't just for staying in touch with friends and family: Now users can browse and buy without clicking away from the site. Roots, the Canadian clothing retailer, has created special "pop up" stores on Facebook to preview merchandise, season by season. To begin shopping, users simply click "like" on the Roots Facebook page (www.facebook.com/roots) and they're admitted to the shopping pages. The French Connection and other retailers are also selling to consumers via social media. With a fast-growing user base of more than 600 million people worldwide, Facebook has the potential to be an extremely important aspect of nonstore selling in the years ahead.

Sources: Jake Hird, "What Does the Future Hold for F-Commerce?" *E-Consultancy*, March 4, 2011, http://econsultancy.com/us; Dana Flavelle, "Facebook 'Pop Up' Stores Latest Social Media Trend," *Toronto Star*, February 8, 2011, www.thestar.com; Sarah Shearman, "French Connection to Launch Facebook Store," *Marketing*, February 9, 2011, www.marketingmagazine.co.uk.

nonstore retailing a type of retailing whereby consumers purchase products without visiting a store

direct selling the marketing of products to customers through face-to-face sales presentations at home or in the workplace

direct marketing the use of the telephone, Internet, and nonpersonal media to introduce products to customers, who then can purchase them via mail, telephone, or the Internet

catalog marketing a type of marketing in which an organization provides a catalog from which customers make selections and place orders by mail, telephone, or the Internet

Types of Nonstore Selling

Nonstore retailing is selling that does not take place in conventional store facilities; consumers purchase products without visiting a store. This form of retailing accounts for an increasing percentage of total retail sales. Nonstore retailers use direct selling, direct marketing, and vending machines.

DIRECT SELLING **Direct selling** is the marketing of products to customers through face-to-face sales presentations at home or in the workplace. Traditionally called *door-to-door selling*, direct selling in the United States began with peddlers more than a century ago and has grown to about $30 billion in U.S. sales annually.[4] Instead of the door-to-door approach, many companies today—such as Mary Kay, Kirby, Amway, and Avon—use other approaches. They identify customers by mail, telephone, the Internet, or at shopping malls and then set up appointments. Direct selling sometimes involves the "party plan," which can occur in the customer's home or workplace. Direct selling through the party plan requires effective salespeople who can identify potential hosts and provide encouragement and incentives for them to organize a gathering of friends and associates. Companies that commonly use the party plan are Tupperware, Stanley Home Products, Pampered Chef, and Sarah Coventry.

DIRECT MARKETING **Direct marketing** is the use of the telephone, Internet, and nonpersonal media to communicate product and organizational information to customers, who then can purchase products via mail, telephone, or the Internet. Direct marketing is one type of nonstore retailing. Direct marketing can occur through catalog marketing, direct-response marketing, telemarketing, television home shopping, and online retailing.

In **catalog marketing**, an organization provides a catalog from which customers make selections and place orders by mail, telephone, or the Internet. Catalog marketing began in 1872 when Montgomery Ward issued its first catalog to rural families. Today, there are more than 7,000 catalog marketing companies in the United States, as well as a number of retail stores, such as JCPenney, that engage in catalog marketing. While some organizations offer a broad array of products spread over multiple product lines, JCPenney recently revamped its catalog strategy, doing away with the "Big Book," a 1,000-page catalog, and replacing it with smaller specialty catalogs.[5] Catalog companies such as Lands' End, Pottery Barn, and J. Crew offer considerable depth in one major line of products. Still other catalog companies specialize in only a few products within a single line. The advantages of catalog marketing include efficiency and convenience for customers. The retailer benefits by being able to locate in remote, low-cost areas, save on expensive store fixtures, and reduce both personal selling and store operating expenses. Disadvantages, on the other hand, are that catalog marketing is inflexible, provides limited service, and is most effective for only a selected set of products.

Direct-response marketing occurs when a retailer advertises a product and makes it available through mail, telephone, or online orders. Examples of direct-response marketing would include a television commercial offering a recording artist's musical collection or a newspaper or magazine advertisement for a series of children's books. Direct-response marketing is also conducted by sending letters, samples, brochures, or booklets to prospects on a mailing list and asking that they order the advertised products by mail, by telephone, or online.

Telemarketing is the performance of marketing-related activities by telephone. Some organizations use a prescreened list of prospective clients. Telemarketing has many advantages such as generating sales leads, improving customer service, speeding up payments on past-due accounts, raising funds for nonprofit organizations, and gathering market data.

Currently, the laws and regulations regarding telemarketing, while in a state of flux, are becoming more restrictive. On October 1, 2003, the U.S. Congress implemented a national do-not-call registry for consumers who do not want to receive telemarketing calls. So far, the do-not-call registry has listed about 200 million phone numbers. Regulations associated with the national do-not-call registry are enforced by the Federal Trade Commission (FTC). Companies are subject to fines of up to $16,000 for each call made to consumers listed on the national do-not-call registry. Since the registry went into effect, the FTC and FCC have collected over $22 million in penalties and $13 million in restitution from violators. Companies can access data for up to five area codes for free, but each additional area code costs $55 with a maximum annual fee of $15,058.[6] Certain exceptions apply to no-call lists. A company still can use telemarketing to communicate with existing customers. In addition, charitable, political, and telephone survey organizations are not restricted by the national registry.

Television home shopping presents products to television viewers, encouraging them to order through toll-free numbers and pay with credit cards. Home Shopping Network (HSN) originated and popularized this format. The most popular products sold through television home shopping are jewelry (40 percent of total sales), clothing, housewares, and electronics. Home shopping channels have grown so rapidly in recent years that more than 60 percent of U.S. households have access to home shopping programs.

HSN and QVC are two of the largest home shopping networks. Approximately 60 percent of home shopping sales revenues come from repeat purchasers.

Online retailing makes products available to buyers through computer connections. Most bricks-and-mortar retailers have websites to sell products, provide information about their company, or distribute coupons. Netflix has changed the video rental industry by offering its completely online movie rental service. Customers pay a monthly fee for unlimited rentals and browse the Netflix site to compose a list of videos they want to rent. Selections are mailed to their home, and customers are free to keep the rental as long as they want without the late fees typically charged by traditional stores.[7] Although online retailing represents a major retailing venue, security remains an issue. In a recent survey conducted by the Business Software Alliance, some Internet users still expressed concerns about shopping online. The major problems are identity theft and credit-card theft.

Personal App Thanks to online retailing, you can buy or rent just about anything with a few clicks of your mouse. The global marketplace is open 24/7 with online retailing. And you can also shop on the go if your cell phone has wireless capabilities.

Automatic vending is the use of machines to dispense products. It accounts for less than 2 percent of all retail sales. Video game machines provide an entertainment service, and many banks offer automatic teller machines (ATMs), which dispense cash and perform other services.

Automatic vending is one of the most impersonal forms of retailing. Small, standardized, routinely purchased products (e.g., chewing gum, candy, newspapers,

Direct marketing. Crate & Barrel engages in direct marketing through catalog and online retailing. It also operates over 160 retail stores.

direct-response marketing a type of marketing in which a retailer advertises a product and makes it available through mail, telephone, or online orders

telemarketing the performance of marketing-related activities by telephone

television home shopping a form of selling in which products are presented to television viewers, who can buy them by calling a toll-free number and paying with a credit card

online retailing retailing that makes products available to buyers through computer connections

automatic vending the use of machines to dispense products

cigarettes, soft drinks, and coffee) can be sold in machines because consumers usually buy them at the nearest available location. Machines in areas of heavy traffic provide efficient and continuous service to consumers. Such high-volume areas may have more diverse product availability—for example, hot and cold sandwiches, DVD rentals, or even iPods (yes, $200 iPods are available in machines with coin slots). San Francisco–based Zoom Systems has expanded its vending machine offerings from snacks to digital cameras, iPods and iPod accessories, Sephora-brand beauty products, Rosetta Stone language learning software, and Proactiv skin care products.[8]

Types of Shopping Centers

The *planned shopping center* is a self-contained retail facility constructed by independent owners and consisting of various stores. Shopping centers are designed and promoted to serve diverse groups of customers with widely differing needs. The management of a shopping center strives for a coordinated mix of stores, a comfortable atmosphere, adequate parking, pleasant landscaping, and special events to attract customers. The convenience of shopping for most family and household needs in a single location is an important part of shopping-center appeal.

A planned shopping center is one of four types: lifestyle, neighborhood, community, or regional. Although shopping centers vary, each offers a complementary mix of stores for the purpose of generating consumer traffic.

Lifestyle shopping centers. The Village of Rochester Hills shopping center is one example of a lifestyle shopping center.

LIFESTYLE SHOPPING CENTERS A **lifestyle shopping center** is a shopping center that has an open-air configuration and is occupied by upscale national chain specialty stores.

The lifestyle center is more convenient than a traditional enclosed mall but offers the same quality of upscale retail and department stores, movie theaters, and dining. A strong emphasis is placed on the architecture of the center and creating a pleasant and "hip" shopping environment. Most lifestyle centers are found in affluent neighborhoods.[9]

NEIGHBORHOOD SHOPPING CENTERS A **neighborhood shopping center** typically consists of several small convenience and specialty stores. Businesses in neighborhood shopping centers might include small grocery stores, drugstores, gas stations, and fast-food restaurants. These retailers serve consumers who live less than ten minutes away, usually within a two to three-mile radius of the stores. Because most purchases in the neighborhood shopping center are based on convenience or personal contact, these retailers generally make only limited efforts to coordinate promotional activities among stores in the shopping center.

COMMUNITY SHOPPING CENTERS A **community shopping center** includes one or two department stores and some specialty stores, along with convenience stores. It attracts consumers from a wider geographic area who will drive longer distances to find products and specialty items unavailable in neighborhood shopping centers. Community shopping centers, which are carefully planned and coordinated, generate traffic with special events such as art exhibits, automobile shows, and sidewalk sales. The management of a community shopping center maintains a balance of tenants so that the center can offer wide product mixes and deep product lines.

lifestyle shopping center an open-air-environment shopping center with upscale chain specialty stores

neighborhood shopping center a planned shopping center consisting of several small convenience and specialty stores

community shopping center a planned shopping center that includes one or two department stores and some specialty stores, along with convenience stores

REGIONAL SHOPPING CENTERS A **regional shopping center** usually has large department stores, numerous specialty stores, restaurants, movie theaters, and sometimes even hotels. It carries most of the merchandise offered by a downtown shopping district. Downtown merchants, in fact, often have renovated their stores and enlarged their parking facilities to meet the competition of successful regional shopping centers. Urban expressways and improved public transportation also have helped many downtown shopping areas to remain vigorous.

Regional shopping centers carefully coordinate management and marketing activities to reach the 150,000 or more customers in their target market. These large centers usually advertise, hold special events, and provide transportation to certain groups of customers. They also maintain a suitable mix of stores. National chain stores can gain leases in regional shopping centers more easily than small independent stores because they are better able to meet the centers' financial requirements.

Concept Check ✱

☐ Describe the major types of retail stores. Give an example of each.

☐ How does nonstore retailing occur?

☐ What are the four most common types of shopping centers, and what type of store does each typically contain?

PHYSICAL DISTRIBUTION

Physical distribution is all those activities concerned with the efficient movement of products from the producer to the ultimate user. Physical distribution therefore is the movement of the products themselves—both goods and services—through their channels of distribution. It is a combination of several interrelated business functions. The most important of these are inventory management, order processing, warehousing, materials handling, and transportation. These functions and their costs are highly interrelated. For example, using expensive air freight may reduce warehousing and inventory costs. Because of such interrelationships, marketers view physical distribution as an integrated effort that supports other important marketing activities, such as getting the right product to the right place at the right time and at minimal total cost.

LEARNING OBJECTIVE
5 Explain the five most important physical distribution activities.

Inventory Management

In Chapter 8 we discussed inventory management from the standpoint of operations. We defined **inventory management** as the process of managing inventories in such a way as to minimize inventory costs, including both holding costs and potential stock-out costs. Both the definition and the objective of inventory control apply here as well.

Holding costs are the costs of storing products until they are purchased or shipped to customers. *Stock-out costs* are the costs of sales lost when items are not in inventory. Of course, holding costs can be reduced by minimizing inventories, but then stock-out costs could be financially threatening to the organization. And stock-out costs can be minimized by carrying very large inventories, but then holding costs would be enormous.

Inventory management therefore is a sort of balancing act between stock-out costs and holding costs. The latter include the cost of money invested in inventory, the cost of storage space, insurance costs, and inventory taxes. Often even a relatively small reduction in inventory investment can provide a relatively large increase in working capital. And sometimes this reduction can best be accomplished through a willingness to incur a reasonable level of stock-out costs. Companies frequently rely on technology and software to help manage inventory on a regular basis.

Order Processing

Order processing consists of activities involved in receiving and filling customers' purchase orders. It may include not only the means by which customers order products but also procedures for billing and for granting credit.

Fast, efficient order processing is an important marketing service—one that can provide a dramatic competitive edge. The people who purchase goods for intermediaries are especially concerned with their suppliers' promptness and reliability in

regional shopping center a planned shopping center containing large department stores, numerous specialty stores, restaurants, movie theaters, and sometimes even hotels

physical distribution all those activities concerned with the efficient movement of products from the producer to the ultimate user

inventory management the process of managing inventories in such a way as to minimize inventory costs, including both holding costs and potential stock-out costs

order processing activities involved in receiving and filling customers' purchase orders

order processing. To them, promptness and reliability mean minimal inventory costs as well as the ability to order goods when they are needed rather than weeks in advance. The Internet is providing new opportunities for improving services associated with order processing.

Warehousing

Warehousing is the set of activities involved in receiving and storing goods and preparing them for reshipment. Goods are stored to create time utility; that is, they are held until they are needed for use or sale. Warehousing includes the following activities:

- *Receiving goods.* The warehouse accepts delivered goods and assumes responsibility for them.
- *Identifying goods.* Records are made of the quantity of each item received. Items may be marked, coded, or tagged for identification.
- *Sorting goods.* Delivered goods may have to be sorted before being stored.
- *Dispatching goods to storage.* Items must be moved to specific storage areas, where they can be found later.
- *Holding goods.* The goods are kept in storage under proper protection until needed.
- *Recalling, picking, and assembling goods.* Items that are to leave the warehouse must be selected from storage and assembled efficiently.
- *Dispatching shipments.* Each shipment is packaged suitably and directed to the proper transport vehicle. Shipping and accounting documents are prepared.

A firm may use its own private warehouses or rent space in public warehouses. A *private warehouse*, owned and operated by a particular firm, can be designed to serve the firm's specific needs. However, the organization must take on the task of financing the facility, determining the best location for it, and ensuring that it is used fully. Generally, only companies that deal in large quantities of goods can justify private warehouses. With a total of almost 96 million square feet in warehouse space, United Parcel Service (UPS) owns the largest amount of private warehouse space in the world. Walmart is second with 80 million, and Sears is third with 40 million.[10]

Public warehouses offer their services to all individuals and firms. Most are huge, one-story structures on the outskirts of cities, where rail and truck transportation is easily available. They provide storage facilities, areas for sorting and assembling shipments, and office and display spaces for wholesalers and retailers. Public warehouses also will hold—and issue receipts for—goods used as collateral for borrowed funds.

Materials Handling

Materials handling is the actual physical handling of goods—in warehouses as well as during transportation. Proper materials-handling procedures and techniques can increase the usable capacity of a warehouse or that of any means of transportation. Proper handling can reduce breakage and spoilage as well.

Modern materials handling attempts to reduce the number of times a product is handled. One method is called *unit loading.* Several smaller cartons, barrels, or boxes are combined into a single standard-size load that can be handled efficiently by forklift, conveyer, or truck.

Transportation

As a part of physical distribution, **transportation** is simply the shipment of products to customers. The greater the distance between seller and purchaser, the more important is the choice of the means of transportation and the particular carrier.

warehousing the set of activities involved in receiving and storing goods and preparing them for reshipment

materials handling the actual physical handling of goods, in warehouses as well as during transportation

transportation the shipment of products to customers

TABLE 13-2: Characteristics of Transportation Modes

Selection Criteria	Railroads	Trucks	Pipelines	Waterways	Airplanes
Cost	Moderate	High	Low	Very low	Very high
Speed	Average	Fast	Slow	Very slow	Very fast
Dependability	Average	High	High	Average	High
Load flexibility	High	Average	Very low	Very high	Low
Accessibility	High	Very high	Very limited	Limited	Average
Frequency	Low	High	Very high	Very low	Average
Percent of use	39.5%	28.6%	19.6%	12.0%	0.3%
Products carried	Coal, grain, lumber, heavy equipment, paper and pulp products, chemicals	Clothing, computers, books, groceries and produce, livestock	Oil, processed coal, natural gas, wood chips	Chemicals, bauxite, grain, motor vehicles, agricultural implements	Flowers, food (highly perishable), technical instruments, emergency parts and equipment, overnight mail

Sources: U.S. Bureau of Transportation Statistics, National Transportation Statistics 2005, www.bts.gov/publications/national_transportation_statistics/html/table_01_46b .html (accessed March 23, 2011).

A firm that offers transportation services is called a **carrier**. A *common carrier* is a transportation firm whose services are available to all shippers. Railroads, airlines, and most long-distance trucking firms are common carriers. A *contract carrier* is available for hire by one or several shippers. Contract carriers do not serve the general public. Moreover, the number of firms they can handle at any one time is limited by law. A *private carrier* is owned and operated by the shipper.

In addition, a shipper can hire agents called *freight forwarders* to handle its transportation. Freight forwarders pick up shipments from the shipper, ensure that the goods are loaded on selected carriers, and assume responsibility for safe delivery of the shipments to their destinations. Freight forwarders often can group a number of small shipments into one large load (which is carried at a lower rate). This, of course, saves money for shippers.

The six major criteria used for selecting transportation modes are compared in Table 13-2. These six criteria are cost, speed, dependability, load flexibility, accessibility, and frequency.

Obviously, the *cost* of a transportation mode is important to marketers. At times, marketers choose higher-cost modes of transportation because of the benefits they provide. *Speed* is measured by the total time that a carrier possesses the products, including time required for pickup and delivery, handling, and movement between point of origin and destination. Usually there is a direct relationship between cost and speed; that is, faster modes of transportation are more expensive. A transportation mode's *dependability* is determined by the consistency of service provided by that mode. *Load flexibility* is the degree to which a transportation mode can provide appropriate equipment and conditions for moving specific kinds of products and can be adapted for moving other kinds of products. For example, certain types of products may need controlled temperatures or humidity levels. *Accessibility* refers to a transportation mode's ability to move goods over a specific route or network. *Frequency* refers to how often a marketer can ship products by a specific transportation mode. Whereas pipelines provide continuous shipments, railroads and waterways follow specific schedules for moving products from one location to another. In Table 13-2, each transportation mode is rated on a relative basis for these six selection criteria and the percentage of use (ton-miles) for each mode.

carrier a firm that offers transportation services

Transportation. Numerous products are transported by waterways using containers. This provides shippers with efficiencies because containers can be transported by ships, railroads, and trucks.

RAILROADS In terms of total freight carried, railroads are America's most important mode of transportation. They are also the least expensive for many products. Almost all railroads are common carriers, although a few coal-mining companies operate their own lines. Many commodities carried by railroads could not be transported easily by any other means.

TRUCKS The trucking industry consists of common, contract, and private carriers. Trucks can move goods to suburban and rural areas not served by railroads. They can handle freight quickly and economically, and they carry a wide range of shipments. Many shippers favor this mode of transportation because it offers door-to-door service, less stringent packaging requirements than ships and airplanes, and flexible delivery schedules. Railroad and truck carriers have teamed up to provide a form of transportation called *piggyback*. Truck trailers are carried from city to city on specially equipped railroad flatcars. Within each city, the trailers are then pulled in the usual way by truck tractors.

AIRPLANES Air transport is the fastest but most expensive means of transportation. All certified airlines are common carriers. Supplemental or charter lines are contract carriers. Because of the high cost, lack of airport facilities in many areas, and reliance on weather conditions, airlines carry less than 1 percent of all intercity freight. Only high-value, perishable items or goods that are needed immediately usually are shipped by air.

WATERWAYS Cargo ships and barges offer the least expensive but slowest form of transportation. They are used mainly for bulky, nonperishable goods such as iron ore, bulk wheat, motor vehicles, and agricultural implements. Of course, shipment by water is limited to cities located on navigable waterways.

PIPELINES Pipelines are a highly specialized mode of transportation. They are used primarily to carry petroleum and natural gas. Pipelines have become more important as the nation's need for petroleum products has increased. Such products as semiliquid coal and wood chips also can be shipped through pipelines continuously, reliably, and with minimal handling.

* Concept Check

☐ How is inventory management a balancing act between stock-out costs and holding costs?

☐ Explain the seven major warehousing activities.

☐ What is the goal of materials handling?

☐ Describe the major characteristics of the primary transportation modes.

LEARNING OBJECTIVE

6 Explain how integrated marketing communications works to have the maximum impact on the customer.

WHAT IS INTEGRATED MARKETING COMMUNICATIONS?

Integrated marketing communications is the coordination of promotion efforts to ensure maximal informational and persuasive impact on customers. A major goal of integrated marketing communications is to send a consistent message to customers.

Integrated marketing communications provides an organization with a way to coordinate and manage its promotional efforts to ensure that customers do receive consistent messages. This approach fosters not only long-term customer relationships but also the efficient use of promotional resources. The concept of integrated marketing communications has been increasingly accepted for several reasons. Mass-media advertising, a very popular promotional method in the past, is used less today because of its high costs and less predictable audience sizes. Marketers now can take advantage of more precisely targeted promotional tools, such as cable TV, direct mail, DVDs, the Internet, special-interest magazines, and podcasts. Database marketing is also allowing marketers to be more precise in targeting individual customers. Until recently, suppliers of marketing communications were specialists.

integrated marketing communications coordination of promotion efforts to ensure maximal informational and persuasive impact on customers

Advertising agencies provided advertising campaigns, sales promotion companies provided sales promotion activities and materials, and public-relations organizations engaged in public-relations efforts. Today, a number of promotion-related companies provide one-stop shopping to the client seeking advertising, sales promotion, and public relations, thus reducing coordination problems for the sponsoring company.

Because the overall costs of marketing communications are significant, management demands systematic evaluations of communications efforts to ensure that promotional resources are being used efficiently. Although the fundamental role of promotion is not changing, the specific communication vehicles employed and the precision with which they are used are changing.

Concept Check ✴

☐ What is the major goal of integrated marketing communications?

☐ Why is integrated marketing communications being increasingly accepted?

THE PROMOTION MIX: AN OVERVIEW

LEARNING OBJECTIVE

7 Understand the basic elements of the promotion mix.

Promotion is communication about an organization and its products that is intended to inform, persuade, or remind target-market members. The promotion with which we are most familiar—advertising—is intended to inform, persuade, or remind us to buy particular products. But there is more to promotion than advertising, and it is used for other purposes as well. Charities use promotion to inform us of their need for donations, to persuade us to give, and to remind us to do so in case we have forgotten. Even the Internal Revenue Service uses promotion (in the form of publicity) to remind us of its April 15 deadline for filing tax returns.

A **promotion mix** (sometimes called a *marketing-communications mix*) is the particular combination of promotion methods a firm uses to reach a target market. The makeup of a mix depends on many factors, including the firm's promotional resources and objectives, the nature of the target market, the product characteristics, and the feasibility of various promotional methods. The four major elements that can be a part of an organization's mix are advertising, personal selling, sales promotion, and public relations (see Figure 13-2).

Advertising is a paid nonpersonal message communicated to a select audience through a mass medium. Advertising is flexible enough that it can reach a very large

---

FIGURE 13-2: **Possible Elements of a Promotion Mix**

Depending on the type of product and target market involved, one or more of these ingredients are used in a promotion mix.

Source: Wiliam M. Pride and O. C. Ferrell, *Marketing: Concepts and Strategies* (Mason, OH: South-Western/Cengage Learning), 2012.

promotion communication about an organization and its products that is intended to inform, persuade, or remind target-market members

promotion mix the particular combination of promotion methods a firm uses to reach a target market

advertising a paid nonpersonal message communicated to a select audience through a mass medium

target group or a small, carefully chosen one. **Personal selling** is personal communication aimed at informing customers and persuading them to buy a firm's products. It is more expensive to reach a consumer through personal selling than through advertising, but this method provides immediate feedback and often is more persuasive than advertising. **Sales promotion** is the use of activities or materials as direct inducements to customers or salespersons. It adds extra value to the product or increases the customer's incentive to buy the product. **Public relations** is a broad set of communication activities used to create and maintain favorable relationships between an organization and various public groups, both internal and external. Public-relations activities are numerous and varied and can be a very effective form of promotion.

While it is possible that one ingredient may be used, it is likely that two, three, or four of these ingredients will be used in a promotion mix depending on the type of product and target market involved.

★ Concept Check

☐ What are the major elements of a promotion mix?

☐ How can each element help a firm reach a target market?

ADVERTISING

LEARNING OBJECTIVE

8 Explain the three types of advertising and describe the major steps of developing an advertising campaign.

In 2010, U.S. organizations spent $168.5 billion on advertising and are expected to spend $188.5 billion in 2014.[11] In this section, we discuss the types of advertising and how to develop an advertising campaign.

Types of Advertising by Purpose

Depending on its purpose and message, advertising may be classified into one of three groups: primary demand, selective demand, or institutional.

PRIMARY-DEMAND ADVERTISING **Primary-demand advertising** is advertising aimed at increasing the demand for all brands of a product within a specific industry. Trade and industry associations, such as the California Milk Processor Board ("got milk?"), are the major users of primary-demand advertising. Their advertisements promote broad product categories, such as beef, milk, pork, potatoes, and prunes, without mentioning specific brands.

SELECTIVE-DEMAND ADVERTISING **Selective-demand (or brand) advertising** is advertising that is used to sell a particular brand of product. It is by far the most common type of advertising, and it accounts for the lion's share of advertising expenditures. Producers use brand-oriented advertising to convince us to buy everything from Bubble Yum to Buicks.

Selective-demand advertising that aims at persuading consumers to make purchases within a short time is called *immediate-response advertising*. Most local advertising is of this type.

Often local advertisers promote products with immediate appeal. Selective advertising aimed at keeping a firm's name or product before the public is called *reminder advertising*.

Comparative advertising compares the sponsored brand with one or more identified competing brands. Of course, the comparison shows the sponsored brand to be as good as or better than the other identified competing brands.

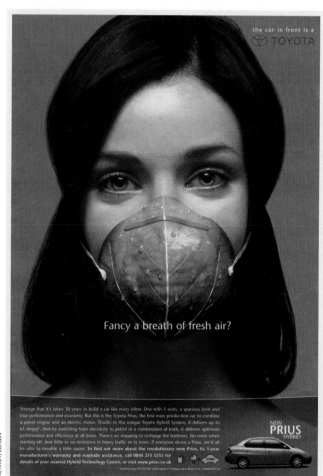

Selective demand advertisement. This Prius ad promotes a specific automobile brand, which means that Toyota is attempting to stimulate selective demand.

INSTITUTIONAL ADVERTISING Institutional advertising is advertising designed to enhance a firm's image or reputation. Many public utilities and larger firms use part of their advertising dollars to build goodwill rather than to stimulate sales directly. A positive public image helps an organization to attract customers, employees, and investors.

Major Steps in Developing an Advertising Campaign

An advertising campaign is developed in several stages. These stages may vary in number and the order in which they are implemented depending on the company's resources, products, and audiences. The development of a campaign in any organization, however, will include the following steps in some form:

1. IDENTIFY AND ANALYZE THE TARGET AUDIENCE The target audience is the group of people toward which a firm's advertisements are directed. To pinpoint the organization's target audience and develop an effective campaign, marketers must analyze such information as the geographic distribution of potential customers; their age, sex, race, income, and education; and their attitudes toward both the advertiser's product and competing products. How marketers use this information will be influenced by the features of the product to be advertised and the nature of the competition. Precise identification of the target audience is crucial to the proper development of subsequent stages and, ultimately, to the success of the campaign itself.

2. DEFINE THE ADVERTISING OBJECTIVES The goals of an advertising campaign should be stated precisely and in measurable terms. The objectives should include the current position of the firm, indicate how far and in what direction from that original reference point the company wishes to move, and specify a definite period of time for the achievement of the goals. Advertising objectives that focus on sales will stress increasing sales by a certain percentage or dollar amount or expanding the firm's market share. Communication objectives will emphasize increasing product or brand awareness, improving consumer attitudes, or conveying product information.

3. CREATE THE ADVERTISING PLATFORM An advertising platform includes the important selling points or features that an advertiser wishes to incorporate into the advertising campaign. These features should be important to customers in their selection and use of a product, and if possible, they should be features that competing products lack. Although research into what consumers view as important issues is expensive, it is the most productive way to determine which issues to include in an advertising platform.

4. DETERMINE THE ADVERTISING APPROPRIATION The advertising appropriation is the total amount of money designated for advertising in a given period. This stage is critical to the success of the campaign because advertising efforts based on an inadequate budget will understimulate customer demand, and a budget too

Internet Advertising on the Rise

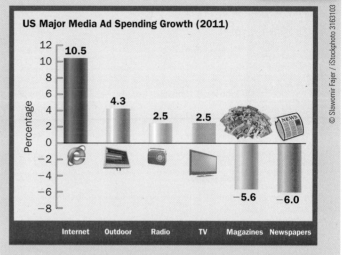

US Major Media Ad Spending Growth (2011)

Source: eMarketer, http://totalaccess.emarketer.com/Chart.aspx?R=107058&dsNav=Rpp:50, Ro:3,N:779&xsrc=TopicsPanel (accessed March 24, 2011).

personal selling personal communication aimed at informing customers and persuading them to buy a firm's products

sales promotion the use of activities or materials as direct inducements to customers or salespersons

public relations communication activities used to create and maintain favorable relationships between an organization and various public groups, both internal and external

primary-demand advertising advertising whose purpose is to increase the demand for *all* brands of a product within a specific industry

selective-demand (or brand) advertising advertising that is used to sell a particular brand of product

institutional advertising advertising designed to enhance a firm's image or reputation

TABLE 13-3: **Advertising Expenditures and Sales Volume for the Top Ten National Advertisers**

Rank	Company	Advertising Expenditures (in millions)	Sales (in millions)	Advertising Expenditures as Percentage of Sales
1	Procter & Gamble	$4,188.9	$31,080	13.5
2	Verizon Communications	3,020.0	107,808	2.8
3	AT&T	2,797.0	123,018	2.3
4	General Motors Co.	2,214.9	49,159	4.5
5	Pfizer	2,097.0	21,749	9.6
6	Johnson & Johnson	2,060.9	30,889	6.7
7	Walt Disney Co.	2,003.8	27,508	7.3
8	Time Warner	1,848.1	18,085	10.2
9	L'Oréal	1,833.6	5,945	30.8
10	Kraft Foods	1,748.4	21,165	8.3

Source: *Advertising Age,* June 21, 2010. Used by permission of Crain Communications.

large will waste a company's resources. Advertising appropriations may be based on last year's (or next year's forecasted) sales, on what competitors spend on advertising, or on executive judgment. The top ten U.S. companies that spend the most on advertising are shown in Table 13-3.

5. DEVELOP THE MEDIA PLAN A media plan specifies exactly which media will be used in the campaign and when advertisements will appear. Although cost-effectiveness is not easy to measure, the primary concern of the media planner is to reach the largest number of persons in the target audience for each dollar spent. In addition to cost, media planners must consider the location and demographics of people in the advertising target, the content of the message, and the characteristics of the audiences reached by various media. The media planner begins with general media decisions, selects subclasses within each medium, and finally chooses particular media vehicles for the campaign. The advantages and disadvantages of the major media classes are shown in Table 13-4.

Personal App Think about the media plan an advertiser might use to reach you. When do you watch television? Do you ever pass any billboards? Which printed or online newspapers or magazines do you read? These are all questions a media planner would consider when choosing media for a target audience.

6. CREATE THE ADVERTISING MESSAGE The content and form of a message are influenced by the product's features, the characteristics of people in the target audience, the objectives of the campaign, and the choice of media. An advertiser must consider these factors to choose words and illustrations that will be meaningful and appealing to persons in the advertising target. The copy, or words, of an advertisement will vary depending on the media choice but should attempt to move the audience through attention, interest, desire, and action. Artwork and visuals should complement copy by attracting the audience's attention and communicating an idea quickly. Creating a cohesive advertising message is especially difficult for a company such as eBay that offers such a broad mix of products. eBay developed a "whatever it is" campaign that features a variety of consumers of every age using a variety of products (a car, a television, a dress, and a laptop) all shaped like the letters "it". The tagline, "Whatever it is, you can get it on eBay," emphasizes the massive range of products available from the site and showcases the service that the company provides effectively.

TABLE 13-4: Advantages and Disadvantages of Major Media Classes

	Advantages	Disadvantages
Television	Reaches large audiences; high frequency available; dual impact of audio and video; highly visible; high prestige; geographic and demographic selectivity; difficult to ignore	Very expensive; highly perishable message; size of audience not guaranteed; amount of prime time limited; lack of selectivity in target market
Direct mail	Little wasted circulation; highly selective; circulation controlled by advertiser; few distractions; personal; stimulates actions; use of novelty; relatively easy to measure performance; hidden from competitors	Very expensive; lacks editorial content to attract readers; often thrown away unread as junk mail; criticized as invasion of privacy; consumers must choose to read the ad
Newspapers	Reaches large audience; purchased to be read; geographic flexibility; short lead time; frequent publication; favorable for cooperative advertising; merchandising services	Not selective for socioeconomic groups or target market; short life; limited reproduction capabilities; large advertising volume limits exposure to any one advertisement
Radio	Reaches 95 percent of consumers; highly mobile and flexible; very low relative costs; ad can be changed quickly; high level of geographic and demographic selectivity; encourages use of imagination	Lacks visual imagery; short life of message; listeners' attention limited because of other activities; market fragmentation; difficult buying procedures; limited media and audience research
Yellow Pages	Wide availability; action and product category oriented; low relative costs; ad frequency and longevity; nonintrusive	Market fragmentation; extremely localized; slow updating; lack of creativity; long lead times; requires large space to be noticed
Magazines	Demographic selectivity; good reproduction; long life; prestige; geographic selectivity when regional issues are available; read in leisurely manner	High costs; 30- to 90-day average lead time; high level of competition; limited reach; communicates less frequently
Internet	Immediate response; potential to reach a precisely targeted audience; ability to track customers and build databases; highly interactive medium	Costs of precise targeting are high; inappropriate ad placement; effects difficult to measure; concerns about security and privacy
Outdoor	Allows for frequent repetition; low cost; message can be placed close to point of sale; geographic selectivity; operable 24 hours a day; high creativity and effectiveness	Message must be short and simple; no demographic selectivity; seldom attracts readers' full attention; criticized as traffic hazard and blight on countryside; much wasted coverage; limited capabilities
Social Media	Target, interact, and connect more personally with customers; receive real-time feedback from customers; able to direct messages to specific individuals; more effectively reach target market/followers	Restricted number of contacts reached per message because it's so personal/targeted; unsure of the best way to use this medium; unsure how to measure return on investment (ROI); large time commitment to constantly monitor activity

Sources: William F. Arens, Michael Weigold, and Christian Arens, *Contemporary Advertising* (Burr Ridge, IL: Irwin/McGraw-Hill, 2008); George E. Belch and Michael Belch, *Advertising and Promotion* (Burr Ridge, IL: Irwin/McGraw-Hill, 2009).

7. EXECUTE THE CAMPAIGN Execution of an advertising campaign requires extensive planning, scheduling, and coordinating because many tasks must be completed on time. The efforts of many people and firms are involved. Production companies, research organizations, media firms, printers, photoengravers, and commercial artists are just a few of the people and firms that may contribute to a campaign. Advertising managers constantly must assess the quality of the work and take corrective action when necessary. In some instances, advertisers make changes during the campaign to meet objectives more effectively.

8. EVALUATE ADVERTISING EFFECTIVENESS A campaign's success should be measured in terms of its original objectives before, during, and/or after the campaign. An advertiser should at least be able to estimate whether sales or market share went up because of the campaign or whether any change occurred in customer attitudes or brand awareness. Data from past and current sales and responses to coupon offers

Marketing and Media Jobs Beyond *Mad Men*

career **SUCCESS**

Although the television success of *Mad Men* has put the spotlight on advertising agencies, marketing and media jobs are available everywhere from Madison Avenue to Madison, Wisconsin, and beyond. In addition to traditional agencies, your career possibilities include working for companies that specialize in Internet marketing, media buying, specialty advertising, public relations, direct marketing, and personal sales. When *Advertising Age* compiled its first-ever list of "Best Places to Work in Marketing and Media," 30 firms of all sizes were cited for their career-building opportunities, creative workplaces, and employee-friendly policies.

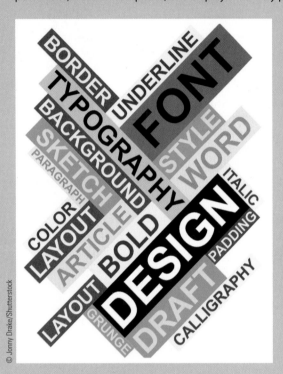

One firm on the list is BGT Partners, a digital advertising agency based in Miami, Florida. Its motto is "Trade your job for a career"—and, in fact, few employees ever want to leave. Why? Because the agency encourages professional development and offers both bonuses and salary increases to reward creativity and innovation. BGT also livens up its workplace with free-lunch Fridays, complete with music or other entertainment for all staffers to enjoy.

Another firm on the list is Hiebing, a marketing and advertising agency in Madison, Wisconsin. The agency, which develops and implements branding, advertising, public relations, and social media campaigns, maintains a collaborative atmosphere that attracts talented employees from all over. Hiebing also offers its services for free to several nonprofit groups, including the local United Way agency. In addition, it actively promotes eco-friendly practices such as bicycling to work and recycling materials.

Wherever you want to live and work, these two examples give you a taste of the diverse marketing and media career possibilities beyond *Mad Men*.

Sources: "2011 Best Places to Work: Medium Company Winner, BGT Partners," *South Florida Business Journal*, February 25, 2011, www.bizjournals.com/southflorida; Jennifer Rooney, "Best Places to Work in Marketing and Media 2010," *Advertising Age*, September 20, 2010, www.adage.com; Beth Snyder Bulick, "Encouraging Individuality Keeps BGT Staff Locked In," *Advertising Age*, September 20, 2010, www.adage.com; Caitlin Fitzsimmons, "In the Church of Hiebing, Faithful Keep Coming Back," *Advertising Age*, September 20, 2010, www.adage.com.

and customer surveys administered by research organizations are some of the ways in which advertising effectiveness can be evaluated.

Advertising Agencies

Advertisers can plan and produce their own advertising with help from media personnel, or they can hire advertising agencies. An **advertising agency** is an independent firm that plans, produces, and places advertising for its clients. Many large ad agencies offer help with sales promotion and public relations as well. The media usually pay a commission of 15 percent to advertising agencies. Thus the cost to the agency's client can be quite moderate. The client may be asked to pay for selected services that the agency performs. Other methods for compensating agencies are also used.

Firms that do a lot of advertising may use both an in-house advertising department and an independent agency. This approach gives the firm the advantage of being able to call on the agency's expertise in particular areas of advertising. An agency also can bring a fresh viewpoint to a firm's products and advertising plans.

advertising agency an independent firm that plans, produces, and places advertising for its clients

Social and Legal Considerations in Advertising

Critics of U.S. advertising have two main complaints—that it is wasteful and that it can be deceptive. Although advertising (like any other activity) can be performed inefficiently, it is far from wasteful. Let's look at the evidence:

- Advertising is the most effective and least expensive means of communicating product information to a large number of individuals and organizations.
- Advertising encourages competition and is, in fact, a means of competition. It thus leads to the development of new and improved products, wider product choices, and lower prices.
- Advertising revenues support our mass-communications media—newspapers, magazines, radio, and television. This means that advertising pays for much of our news coverage and entertainment programming.
- Advertising provides job opportunities in fields ranging from sales to film production.

A number of government and private agencies scrutinize advertising for false or misleading claims or offers. At the national level, the Federal Trade Commission (FTC), the Food and Drug Administration (FDA), and the Federal Communications Commission (FCC) oversee advertising practices. The FDA conducted a survey of doctors about the impact of direct-to-consumer advertising for prescription drugs and found that 92 percent could recall a patient initiating conversation about a drug he or she had seen advertised. Direct-to-consumer prescription ads, a controversial type of advertising, make patients more aware of potential treatments according to 72 percent of the physicians surveyed, and they also caused 47 percent of these doctors to feel pressured into prescribing a particular drug.[12] Advertising also may be monitored by state and local agencies, better business bureaus, and industry associations.

Concept Check ✱

☐ Describe the major types of advertising by purpose.

☐ Explain the eight major steps in developing an advertising campaign.

PERSONAL SELLING

Personal selling is the most adaptable of all promotional methods because the person who is presenting the message can modify it to suit the individual buyer. However, personal selling is also the most expensive method of promotion. Most successful salespeople are able to communicate with others on a one-to-one basis and are strongly motivated. They strive to have a thorough knowledge of the products they offer for sale. And they are willing and able to deal with the details involved in handling and processing orders. Sales managers tend to emphasize these qualities when recruiting and hiring. Many selling situations demand the face-to-face contact and adaptability of personal selling. This is especially true of industrial sales, in which a single purchase may amount to millions of dollars. Obviously, sales of that size must be based on carefully planned sales presentations, personal contact with customers, and thorough negotiations.

LEARNING OBJECTIVE

9 Recognize the kinds of salespersons, the steps in the personal-selling process, and the major sales management tasks.

Kinds of Salespersons

Because most businesses employ different salespersons to perform different functions, marketing managers must select the kinds of sales personnel that will be most effective in selling the firm's products. Salespersons may be identified as order getters, order takers, and support personnel. A single individual can, and often does, perform all three functions.

ORDER GETTERS An **order getter** is responsible for what is sometimes called **creative selling**—selling a firm's products to new customers and increasing sales to current customers. An order getter must perceive buyers' needs, supply customers with information about the firm's product, and persuade them to buy the product. Some order getters focus on current customers, whereas others focus on new customers.

order getter a salesperson who is responsible for selling a firm's products to new customers and increasing sales to present customers

creative selling selling products to new customers and increasing sales to present customers

ORDER TAKERS An **order taker** handles repeat sales in ways that maintain positive relationships with customers. An order taker sees that customers have products when and where they are needed and in the proper amounts. *Inside order takers* receive incoming mail and telephone orders in some businesses; salespersons in retail stores are also inside order takers. *Outside* (or *field*) *order takers* travel to customers. Often the buyer and the field salesperson develop a mutually beneficial relationship of placing, receiving, and delivering orders. Both inside and outside order takers are active salespersons and often produce most of their companies' sales.

SUPPORT PERSONNEL **Sales support personnel** aid in selling but are more involved in locating prospects (likely first-time customers), educating customers, building goodwill for the firm, and providing follow-up service. The most common categories of support personnel are missionary, trade, and technical salespersons.

A **missionary salesperson**, who usually works for a manufacturer, visits retailers to persuade them to buy the manufacturer's products. If the retailers agree, they buy the products from wholesalers, who are the manufacturer's actual customers.

A **trade salesperson**, who generally works for a food producer or processor, assists customers in promoting products, especially in retail stores. A trade salesperson may obtain additional shelf space for the products, restock shelves, set up displays, and distribute samples. Because trade salespersons usually are order takers as well, they are not strictly support personnel.

A **technical salesperson** assists a company's current customers in technical matters. He or she may explain how to use a product, how it is made, how to install it, or how a system is designed. A technical salesperson should be formally educated in science or engineering.

Marketers usually need sales personnel from several of these categories. Factors that affect hiring and other personnel decisions include the number of customers and their characteristics; the product's attributes, complexity, and price; the distribution channels used by the company; and the company's approach to advertising.

The Personal-Selling Process

No two selling situations are exactly alike, and no two salespeople perform their jobs in exactly the same way. Most salespeople, however, follow the six-step procedure illustrated in Figure 13-3.

PROSPECTING The first step in personal selling is to research potential buyers and choose the most likely customers, or prospects. Sources of prospects include business associates and customers, public records, telephone and trade-association directories, and company files. The salesperson concentrates on those prospects who have the financial resources, willingness, and authority to buy the product.

APPROACHING THE PROSPECT First impressions are often lasting impressions. Thus the salesperson's first contact with the prospect is crucial to successful selling. The best approach is one based on knowledge of the product, of the prospect's needs, and of how the product can meet those needs. Salespeople who understand each customer's particular situation are likely to make a good first impression—and to make a sale.

MAKING THE PRESENTATION The next step is actual delivery of the sales presentation. In many cases this includes demonstrating the product. The salesperson points out the product's features, its benefits, and how it is superior to competitors'

order taker a salesperson who handles repeat sales in ways that maintain positive relationships with customers

sales support personnel employees who aid in selling but are more involved in locating prospects, educating customers, building goodwill for the firm, and providing follow-up service

missionary salesperson a salesperson—generally employed by a manufacturer—who visits retailers to persuade them to buy the manufacturer's products

trade salesperson a salesperson—generally employed by a food producer or processor—who assists customers in promoting products, especially in retail stores

technical salesperson a salesperson who assists a company's current customers in technical matters

merchandise. If the product has been used successfully by other firms, the salesperson may mention this as part of the presentation.

During a demonstration, the salesperson may suggest that the prospect try out the product personally. The demonstration and product trial should underscore specific points made during the presentation.

ANSWERING OBJECTIONS The prospect is likely to raise objections or ask questions at any time. This gives the salesperson a chance to eliminate objections that might prevent a sale, to point out additional features, or to mention special services the company offers.

CLOSING THE SALE To close the sale, the salesperson asks the prospect to buy the product. This is considered the critical point in the selling process. Many experienced salespeople make use of a *trial closing,* in which they ask questions based on the assumption that the customer is going to buy the product. The questions "When would you want delivery?" and "Do you want the standard model or the one with the special options package?" are typical of trial closings. They allow the reluctant prospect to make a purchase without having to say, "I'll take it."

FOLLOWING UP The salesperson must follow up after the sale to ensure that the product is delivered on time, in the right quantity, and in proper operating condition. During follow-up, the salesperson also makes it clear that he or she is available in case problems develop. Follow-up leaves a good impression and eases the way toward future sales. Hence it is essential to the selling process. The salesperson's job does not end with a sale. It continues as long as the seller and the customer maintain a working relationship.

Major Sales Management Tasks

A firm's success often hinges on the competent management of its sales force. Although some companies operate efficiently without a sales force, most firms rely on a strong sales force—and the sales revenue it brings in—for their success.

Responsibilities of Sales Managers

- Sales managers must set sales objectives in concrete, quantifiable terms and specify a certain period of time and a certain geographic area.
- Sales managers must adjust the size of the sales force to meet changes in the firm's marketing plan and the marketing environment.
- Sales managers must attract and hire effective salespersons. Guitar Center, the largest musical instrument chain in the United States, has only one requirement for members of its sales force—that they be able to play a musical instrument. The company believes that a rocking sales force will care more deeply about the product and sell it more effectively to customers.[13]
- Sales managers must develop a training program and decide where, when, how, and for whom to conduct the training.
- Sales managers must formulate a fair and adequate compensation plan to keep qualified employees.
- Sales managers must motivate salespersons to boost their productivity.
- Sales managers must define sales territories and determine scheduling and routing of the sales force.
- Finally, sales managers must evaluate the operation as a whole through sales reports, communications with customers, and invoices.

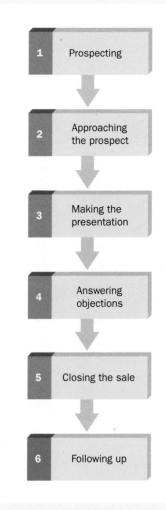

FIGURE 13-3: **The Six Steps of the Personal-Selling Process**

Personal selling is not only the most adaptable of all promotional methods but also the most expensive.

1. Prospecting
2. Approaching the prospect
3. Making the presentation
4. Answering objections
5. Closing the sale
6. Following up

Source: William M. Pride and O. C. Ferrell, *Marketing: Concepts and Strategies* (Mason, OH: South-Western/Cengage Learning) 2010. Adapted with permission.

© Cengage Learning 2013

Concept Check ✱

☐ What are the advantages and disadvantages of using personal selling?

☐ Identify the three types of salespersons.

☐ Describe the six steps of the personal-selling process.

SALES PROMOTION

LEARNING OBJECTIVE

10 Describe sales promotion objectives and methods.

Sales promotion consists of activities or materials that are direct inducements to customers or salespersons. Are you a member of an airline frequent-flyer program? Did you recently receive a free sample in the mail or at a supermarket? Have you recently received a rebate from a manufacturer? Do you use coupons? All these are examples of sales promotion efforts. Sales promotion techniques often are used to enhance and supplement other promotional methods. They can have a significant impact on sales.

The dramatic increase in spending for sales promotion shows that marketers have recognized the potential of this promotional method. Many firms now include numerous sales promotion efforts as part of their overall promotion mix.

Coupons. Numerous marketers offer coupons to promote product trial and to increase the quantities purchased.

© Susan Van Etten

Sales Promotion Objectives

Sales promotion activities may be used singly or in combination, both offensively and defensively, to achieve one goal or a set of goals. Marketers use sales promotion activities and materials for a number of purposes, including

1. To attract new customers
2. To encourage trial of a new product
3. To invigorate the sales of a mature brand
4. To boost sales to current customers
5. To reinforce advertising
6. To increase traffic in retail stores
7. To steady irregular sales patterns
8. To build up reseller inventories
9. To neutralize competitive promotional efforts
10. To improve shelf space and displays[14]

Any sales promotion objectives should be consistent with the organization's general goals and with its marketing and promotional objectives.

Sales Promotion Methods

Most sales promotion methods can be classified as promotional techniques for either consumer sales or trade sales.

A **consumer sales promotion method** attracts consumers to particular retail stores and motivates them to purchase certain new or established products.

A **trade sales promotion method** encourages wholesalers and retailers to stock and actively promote a manufacturer's product. Incentives such as money, merchandise, marketing assistance, and gifts are commonly awarded to resellers who buy products or respond positively in other ways. Of the combined dollars spent on sales promotion and advertising last year, about one-half was spent on trade promotions, one-fourth on consumer promotions, and one-fourth on advertising.

Selection of Sales Promotion Methods

Several factors affect the choice of sales promotion methods to be used. Of greatest importance are

1. The objectives of the promotional effort
2. Product characteristics—size, weight, cost, durability, uses, features, and hazards
3. Target-market profiles—age, gender, income, location, density, usage rate, and buying patterns
4. Distribution channels and availability of appropriate resellers
5. The competitive and regulatory forces in the environment

consumer sales promotion method a sales promotion method designed to attract consumers to particular retail stores and to motivate them to purchase certain new or established products

trade sales promotion method a sales promotion method designed to encourage wholesalers and retailers to stock and actively promote a manufacturer's product

REBATES A **rebate** is a return of part of the purchase price of a product. Usually the refund is offered by the producer to consumers who send in a coupon along with a specific proof of purchase. Rebating is a relatively low-cost promotional method.

One problem with rebates is that many people perceive the redemption process as too complicated. Only about half of individuals who purchase rebated products actually apply for the rebates.

COUPONS A **coupon** reduces the retail price of a particular item by a stated amount at the time of purchase. Coupons may be worth anywhere from a few cents to a few dollars. They are made available to customers through newspapers, magazines, direct mail, online, and shelf dispensers in stores. Some coupons are precisely targeted at customers. All Online Coupons is an Internet site that provides visitors with links to all online coupons currently being offered. Customers can find coupons by category or store name. Other companies, such as Old Navy and The Gap, offer coupons on their websites that can be used online or in stores. Coupon use has been declining steadily since the early 1990s, but in 2009, consumers redeemed 3.3 billion coupons, a 27% increase over the previous year. This was the first time in 17 years that consumers used more coupons than they did the year before.[15]

Samples. A large number of consumer convenience products are promoted through free samples. Often, food items are sampled in retail stores. Nonfood products are more likely to be sampled by sending them to people's homes.

© Jeff Greenberg/PhotoEdit

SAMPLES A **sample** is a free product given to customers to encourage trial and purchase. Marketers use free samples to stimulate trial of a product, increase sales volume in the early stages of a product's life cycle, and obtain desirable distribution. Samples may be offered via online coupons, direct mail, or in stores. Many customers prefer to receive their samples by mail. It is the most expensive sales promotion technique, and while it is used often to promote new products, it can be used to promote established brands, too, such as cosmetics companies that use samples to attract customers. In designing a free sample, organizations must consider such factors as seasonal demand for the product, market characteristics, and prior advertising.

Personal App Samples go far beyond the supermarket or drug store. If you've ever downloaded a trial version of new software or a new digital game, you've taken advantage of a free sample. This is a great way to try before you buy.

PREMIUMS A **premium** is a gift that a producer offers a customer in return for buying its product. They are used to attract competitors' customers, introduce different sizes of established products, add variety to other promotional efforts, and stimulate consumer loyalty. Creativity is essential when using premiums; to stand out and achieve a significant number of redemptions, the premium must match both the target audience and the brand's image. Premiums also must be easily recognizable and desirable. Premiums are placed on or inside packages and also can be distributed through retailers or through the mail.

FREQUENT-USER INCENTIVES A **frequent-user incentive** is a program developed to reward customers who engage in repeat (frequent) purchases. Such programs are used commonly by service businesses such as airlines, hotels, and auto rental agencies. Frequent-user incentives foster customer loyalty to a specific company or group of cooperating companies because the customer is given an additional reason to continue patronizing the business. For example, most major airlines offer frequent-flier programs that reward customers who have flown a specified number of miles with free tickets for additional travel. Research shows

rebate a return of part of the purchase price of a product

coupon reduces the retail price of a particular item by a stated amount at the time of purchase

sample a free product given to customers to encourage trial and purchase

premium a gift that a producer offers a customer in return for buying its product

frequent-user incentive a program developed to reward customers who engage in repeat (frequent) purchases

Event sponsorship. Event sponsorship is a public relations tool. It can be tied in with advertising, personal selling, and sales promotion.

that 93 percent of people with household incomes above $100,000 participate in frequent-user programs, whereas only 58 percent of people with incomes below $50,000 participate.[16]

POINT-OF-PURCHASE DISPLAYS A **point-of-purchase display** is promotional material placed within a retail store. The display is usually located near the product being promoted. It actually may hold merchandise (as do L'eggs hosiery displays) or inform customers about what the product offers and encourage them to buy it. Most point-of-purchase displays are prepared and set up by manufacturers and wholesalers.

TRADE SHOWS A **trade show** is an industry-wide exhibit at which many sellers display their products. Some trade shows are organized exclusively for dealers—to permit manufacturers and wholesalers to show their latest lines to retailers. Others are promotions designed to stimulate consumer awareness and interest. Among the latter are boat shows, home shows, and flower shows put on each year in large cities.

BUYING ALLOWANCES A **buying allowance** is a temporary price reduction to resellers for purchasing specified quantities of a product. A laundry detergent manufacturer might give retailers $1 for each case of detergent purchased. A buying allowance may serve as an incentive to resellers to handle new products and may stimulate purchase of items in large quantities. While the buying allowance is simple, straightforward, and easily administered, competitors can respond quickly by offering a better buying allowance.

COOPERATIVE ADVERTISING **Cooperative advertising** is an arrangement whereby a manufacturer agrees to pay a certain amount of a retailer's media cost for advertising the manufacturer's products. To be reimbursed, a retailer must show proof that the advertisements actually did appear. A large percentage of all cooperative advertising dollars are spent on newspaper advertisements. Not all retailers take advantage of available cooperative advertising offers because they cannot afford to advertise or do not choose to do so.

PUBLIC RELATIONS

As noted earlier, public relations is a broad set of communication activities used to create and maintain favorable relationships between an organization and various public groups, both internal and external. These groups can include customers, employees, stockholders, suppliers, educators, the media, government officials, and society in general.

Types of Public-Relations Tools

Organizations use a variety of public-relations tools to convey messages and to create images. Public-relations professionals prepare written materials such as brochures, newsletters, company magazines, annual reports, and news releases. They also create corporate-identity materials such as logos, business cards, signs, and stationery. Speeches are another public-relations tool. Speeches can affect an organization's image and therefore must convey the desired message clearly.

Another public-relations tool is event sponsorship, in which a company pays for all or part of a special event such as a concert, sports competition, festival, or

---

✳ Concept Check

☐ Why do marketers use sales promotion?

☐ What are the two classifications of sales promotion methods?

☐ What factors affect the choice of sales promotion used?

LEARNING OBJECTIVE

11 Understand the types and uses of public relations.

point-of-purchase display promotional material placed within a retail store

trade show an industry-wide exhibit at which many sellers display their products

buying allowance a temporary price reduction to resellers for purchasing specified quantities of a product

cooperative advertising an arrangement whereby a manufacturer agrees to pay a certain amount of a retailer's media cost for advertising the manufacturer's products

© Doug James/Shutterstock.com

play. Sponsoring special events is an effective way for organizations to increase brand recognition and receive media coverage with comparatively little investment. Pharmaceutical company Bristol-Myers Squibb sponsored the Tour of Hope, a nine-day bike trek from San Diego, California, to Washington, D.C., to raise money for cancer research. Bristol-Myers spokesman, seven-time Tour de France winner and cancer survivor Lance Armstrong, led 24 other bikers on the tour.[17]

Some public-relations tools traditionally have been associated specifically with publicity, which is a part of public relations. **Publicity** is communication in news-story form about an organization, its products, or both. Publicity is transmitted through a mass medium, such as newspapers or radio, at no charge. Organizations use publicity to provide information about products; to announce new product launches, expansions, or research; and to strengthen the company's image. Public-relations personnel sometimes organize events, such as grand openings with prizes and celebrities, to create news stories about a company.

The most widely used type of publicity is the **news release**. It is generally one typed page of about 300 words provided by an organization to the media as a form of publicity. The release includes the firm's name, address, phone number, and contact person. There are also several other kinds of publicity-based public-relations tools. A **feature article**, which may run as long as 3,000 words, is usually written for inclusion in a particular publication. For example, a software firm might send an article about its new product to a computer magazine. A **captioned photograph**, a picture accompanied by a brief explanation, is an effective way to illustrate a new or improved product. A **press conference** allows invited media personnel to hear important news announcements and to receive supplementary textual materials and photographs. Finally, letters to the editor, special newspaper or magazine editorials, films, and tapes may be prepared and distributed to appropriate media for possible use.

publicity communication in news-story form about an organization, its products, or both

news release a typed page of about 300 words provide by an organization to the media as a form of publicity

feature article a piece (of up to 3,000 words) prepared by an organization for inclusion in a particular publication

captioned photograph a picture accompanied by a brief explanation

press conference a meeting at which invited media personnel hear important news announcements and receive supplementary textual materials and photographs

Uses of Public Relations

Public relations can be used to promote people, places, activities, ideas, and even countries. Public relations focuses on enhancing the reputation of the total organization by making people aware of a company's products, brands, or activities and by creating specific company images such as that of innovativeness or dependability. Ice-cream maker Ben and Jerry's uses news stories and other public-relations efforts to reinforce its reputation as a socially responsible company. By getting the media to report on a firm's accomplishments, public relations helps a company to maintain positive public visibility. Effective management of public-relations efforts also can reduce the unfavorable effects of negative events.

Concept Check *

☐ What are the common tools of public relations?

☐ What is publicity, and why do organizations use it?

☐ What are the four common types of publicity?

Get Flashcards, Quizzes, Games, Crosswords, and more @ **www.cengagebrain.com**

SUMMARY

1 **Identify the various distribution channels and explain the concept of market coverage.**

A marketing channel is a sequence of marketing organizations that directs a product from producer to ultimate user. The marketing channel for a particular product is concerned with the transfer of ownership of that product. Merchant middlemen (merchants) actually take title to products, whereas functional middlemen simply aid in the transfer of title.

The channels used for consumer products include the direct channel from producer to consumer; the channel from producer to retailer to consumer; the channel from producer to wholesaler to retailer to consumer; and the channel from producer to agent to wholesaler to retailer to consumer. There are two major channels of industrial products: (1) producer to user and (2) producer to agent middleman to user.

Channels and intermediaries are chosen to implement a given level of market coverage. Intensive distribution is the use of all available outlets for a product, providing the widest market coverage. Selective distribution uses only a portion of the available outlets in an area. Exclusive distribution uses only a single retail outlet for a product in a large geographic area.

2 Understand how supply chain management facilitates partnering among channel members.

Supply-chain management is a long-term partnership among channel members working together to create a distribution system that reduces inefficiencies, costs, and redundancies while creating a competitive advantage and satisfying customers. Cooperation is required among all channel members, including manufacturing, research, sales, advertising, and shipping. When all channel partners work together, delivery, scheduling, packaging, and other customer requirements are better met. Technology, such as bar coding and electronic data interchange (EDI), makes supply-chain management easier to implement.

3 Discuss the need for wholesalers, describe the services they provide, and identify the major types of wholesalers.

Wholesalers are intermediaries that purchase from producers or other intermediaries and sell to industrial users, retailers, or other wholesalers. Wholesalers perform many functions in a distribution channel. If they are eliminated, other channel members—such as the producer or retailers—must perform these functions. Wholesalers provide retailers with help in promoting products, collecting information and financing. They provide manufacturers with sales help, reduce their inventory costs, furnish market information, and extend credit to retailers.

Merchant wholesalers buy and then sell products. Commission merchants and brokers are essentially agents and do not take title to the goods they distribute. Sales branches and offices are owned by the manufacturers and resemble merchant wholesalers and agents, respectively.

4 Distinguish among the major types of retailers and shopping centers.

Retailers are intermediaries that buy from producers or wholesalers and sell to consumers. In-store retailers include department stores, discount stores, catalog and warehouse showrooms, convenience stores, supermarkets, superstores, warehouse clubs, traditional specialty stores, off-price retailers, and category killers. Non store retailers do not sell in conventional store facilities. Instead they use direct selling, direct marketing, and automatic vending. Types of direct marketing include catalog marketing, direct response marketing, telemarketing, television home shopping, and online retailing.

There are four major types of shopping centers: lifestyle, neighborhood, community, and regional. A center fits one of these categories based on its mix of stores and the size of the geographic area it serves.

5 Explain the five most important physical distribution activities.

Physical distribution consists of activities designed to move products from producers to ultimate users. Its five major functions are inventory management, order processing, warehousing, materials handling, and transportation. These interrelated functions are integrated into the marketing effort.

6 Explain how integrated marketing communications works to have the maximum impact on the customer.

Integrated marketing communications is the coordination of promotion efforts to achieve maximum informational and persuasive impact on customers.

7 Understand the basic elements of the promotion mix.

Promotion is communication about an organization and its products that is intended to inform, persuade, or remind target market members. The major ingredients of a promotion mix are advertising, personal selling, sales promotion, and public relations. The role of promotion is to facilitate exchanges directly or indirectly and to help an organization maintain favorable relationship with groups in the marketing environment.

8 Explain the three types of advertising and describe the major steps of developing an advertising campaign.

Advertising is a paid nonpersonal message communicated to a specific audience through a mass medium. Primary-demand advertising promotes the products of an entire industry rather than just a single brand. Selective demand advertising promotes a particular brand of product. Institutional advertising is image-building advertising for a firm.

An advertising campaign is developed in several stages. A firm's first task is to identify and analyze its advertising target. The goals of the campaign also must be clearly defined. Then the firm must develop the advertising platform, or statement of important selling points, and determine the size of advertising budget. The next steps are to develop a media plan, to create the advertising message, and to execute the campaign. Finally, promotion managers must evaluate the effectiveness of the advertising efforts before, during, and/or after the campaign.

9 Recognize the kinds of salespersons, the steps in the personal selling process, and the major sales management tasks.

Personal selling is personal communication aimed at informing customers and persuading them to buy a firm's products. It is the most adaptable promotional method because the salesperson can modify the message to fit each buyer. Three major kinds of salespeople are order getters, order takers, and support personnel. The six steps in the personal-selling process are prospecting, approaching the prospect, making the presentation, answering objections, closing the sale, and following up. Sales managers are involved directly in setting sales force objectives; recruiting; selecting, and training salespersons; compensating and motivating sales personnel; creating sales territories; and evaluating sales performance.

10 Describe sales promotion objectives and methods.

Sales promotion is the use of activities and materials as direct inducements to customers and salespersons. The primary objective of sales promotion methods is to enhance and supplement other promotional methods. Methods of sales promotion include rebates, coupons, samples, premiums, frequent-user incentives, point-of-purchase displays, trade shows, buying allowances, and cooperative advertising.

11 Understand the types and uses of public relations.

Public relations is a broad set of communication activities used to create and maintain favorable relationships between an organization and various public groups, both internal and external. Organizations use a variety of public relations tools to convey messages and create images. Brochures, newsletters, company magazines and annual reports are written public-relations tools. Speeches, event sponsorship, and publicity are other public-relations tools. Publicity is communication in news-story form about an organization, its products, or both. Types of publicity include news releases, feature articles, captioned photographs, and press conferences. Public relations can also be used to promote people, places, activities, ideas, and even countries. It can be used to enhance the reputation of an organization and also to reduce the unfavorable effects of negative events.

KEY TERMS

You should now be able to define and give an example relevant to each of the following terms:

distribution channel, or marketing channel (368)
middleman (or marketing intermediary) (368)
merchant middleman (368)
functional middleman (368)
retailer (369)
wholesaler (369)
intensive distribution (370)
selective distribution (370)
exclusive distribution (370)
supply-chain management (371)
merchant wholesaler (372)
full-service wholesaler (372)
general-merchandise wholesaler (372)
limited-line wholesaler (372)
specialty-line wholesaler (372)
agent (373)
broker (373)
independent retailer (373)
chain retailer (374)
department store (374)
discount store (374)
warehouse showroom (374)

convenience store (374)
supermarket (374)
superstore (375)
warehouse club (375)
traditional specialty store (375)
off-price retailer (375)
category killer (375)
nonstore retailing (376)
direct selling (376)
direct marketing (376)
catalog marketing (376)
direct-response marketing (376)
telemarketing (377)
television home shopping (377)
online retailing (377)
automatic vending (377)
lifestyle shopping center (378)
neighborhood shopping center (378)
community shopping center (378)
regional shopping center (379)
physical distribution (379)

inventory management (379)
order processing (379)
warehousing (380)
materials handling (380)
transportation (380)
carrier (381)
integrated marketing communications (382)
promotion (383)
promotion mix (383)
advertising (383)
personal selling (384)
sales promotion (384)
public relations (384)
primary-demand advertising (384)
selective-demand (or brand) advertising (384)
institutional advertising (385)
advertising agency (388)
order getter (389)
creative selling (389)
order taker (390)
sales support personnel (390)

missionary salesperson (390)
trade salesperson (390)
technical salesperson (390)
consumer sales promotion method (392)
trade sales promotion method (392)
rebate (393)
coupon (393)
sample (393)
premium (393)
frequent-user incentive (393)
point-of-purchase display (394)
trade show (394)
buying allowance (394)
cooperative advertising (394)
publicity (395)
news release (395)
feature article (395)
captioned photograph (395)
press conference (395)

DISCUSSION QUESTIONS

1. What are the most common marketing channels for consumer products? For industrial products?
2. What are the three levels of market coverage? What types of products is each used for?
3. List the services performed by wholesalers. For whom is each service performed?
4. Identify three kinds of full-service wholesalers. What factors are used to classify wholesalers into one of these categories?
5. What can nonstore retailers offer their customers that in-store retailers cannot?
6. What is physical distribution? Which major functions does it include?
7. Many producers sell to consumers both directly and through middlemen. How can such a producer justify competing with its own middlemen?
8. In what situations might a producer use agents or commission merchants rather than its own sales offices or branches.
9. If a middleman is eliminated from a marketing channel, under what conditions will costs decrease? Under what conditions will costs increase? Will the middleman's functions be eliminated? Explain.
10. What is integrated marketing communications, and why is it becoming increasingly accepted?
11. Identify and describe the major ingredients of a promotion mix.
12. Identify and give examples of the three major types of salespersons.
13. What are the major tasks involved in managing a sales force?
14. What are the major differences between consumer and trade sales promotion methods? Give examples of each.
15. What is the difference between publicity and public relations? What is the purpose of each?
16. Why do firms use event sponsorship?

TEST YOURSELF

Matching Questions

1. _____ This type of market coverage provides the widest possible exposure in the marketplace.
2. _____ A middleman often hired on a commission basis.
3. _____ This middleman carries a few lines with many products within each line.
4. _____ The process involves receiving and filling customers' purchase orders.
5. _____ Manufacturers' seconds or off-season merchandise are examples of products sold.
6. _____ The process includes any nonpersonal, paid form of communication.
7. _____ The purpose is to increase demand for all brands of a product.
8. _____ A large specialty store that concentrates on a single product line and has low prices.
9. _____ A salesperson who handles repeat sales to maintain positive relationships with customers.
10. _____ News stories about products, employees, or a company that appear in the newspaper are examples.

a. agent
b. intensive distribution
c. limited-line wholesaler
d. category killer
e. off-price retailer
f. order processing
g. advertising
h. distribution channel
i. catalog marketing
j. primary-demand advertising
k. publicity
l. order taker

True False Questions

11. **T F** A direct channel of distribution includes both wholesalers and retailers.
12. **T F** A retailer buys and sells merchandise.
13. **T F** Exclusive distribution makes use of all available outlets for a product.
14. **T F** Inventory holding costs are the costs of storing products until they are purchased or shipped to customers.
15. **T F** Piggyback service is unique to air freight.
16. **T F** Institutional advertising promotes specific brands of products.
17. **T F** Advertising can be broadly classified into three groups: selective-demand, institutional, and primary-demand.
18. **T F** A major disadvantage of magazines is their lack of timeliness.
19. **T F** Radio advertising offers a high degree of selectivity.
20. **T F** News releases are the least used type of publicity.

Multiple-Choice Questions

21. _____ A women's apparel manufacturer most likely will use
    a. intensive distribution.
    b. selective distribution.
    c. exclusive distribution.
    d. high-style distribution.
    e. popular style distribution.

22. _____ Category management is
    a. a producer deciding which category to concentrate on for the next season.
    b. a retailer asking the supplier in a particular category how to stock the shelves.
    c. when suppliers tell the manufacturer which category to produce more of.
    d. when Home Depot decides which category sells the best and decides to concentrate on that category of goods.
    e. the combined efforts of producers and wholesalers to manage the wholesaler's inventory.

23. _____ Haley is shopping for a new outfit to wear to an awards banquet where she will be honored. She has found a beautiful outfit at The Gap and a new pair of shoes at the Foot Locker. What type of stores are these?
    a. Warehouse club
    b. Convenience
    c. Specialty
    d. Department
    e. Off-price

24. _____ Which one of the following is an example of a category killer?
    a. Kmart
    b. 7-Eleven
    c. Home Depot
    d. Burlington Coat Factory
    e. Macy's

25. _____ Which activity combines inventory management, order processing, warehousing, material handling, and transportation?
    a. Marketing
    b. Merchandising
    c. Warehousing
    d. Physical distribution
    e. Transporting

26. _____ Choose the correct order of the following three of the eight steps in developing an advertising campaign.
    a. Create the advertising platform; identify and analyze the target audience; define the advertising objectives.
    b. Identify and analyze the target audience; create the advertising platform; define the advertising objectives.
    c. Identify and analyze the target audience; define the advertising objectives; create the advertising platform.
    d. Define the advertising objectives; identify and analyze the target audience; create the advertising platform.
    e. Define the advertising objectives; create the advertising platform; identify and analyze the target audience.

27. _____ Salespeople may be identified as
    a. experts, order makers, and support personnel.
    b. order preparers, order trackers, and order receivers.
    c. order getters, order takers, and support personnel.
    d. order getters, order makers, and order receivers.
    e. order getters, order dictators, and support personnel.

28. _____ The first step in the personal selling process is
    a. product display.
    b. prospecting.
    c. approaching the prospect.
    d. organizing the sales pitch.
    e. making the presentation.

29. _____ Closing the sale is considered the critical point in the selling process. Many salespeople use a trial closing. Based on an assumption that the customer is going to buy, which of the following statements is an appropriate trial closing?
    a. "Will you be placing an order, Mrs. Johnston?"
    b. "Would you like the standard or the deluxe model?"
    c. "Here's my card. Give me a call if you would like to place an order."
    d. "Shall I give you a week to consider the offer?"
    e. "I'll put you down for the deluxe model. Is that your natural hair color?"

30. _____ Deloitte, a public accounting firm, helps to underwrite the musical production "Mama Mia" currently playing at the Theater Center. Why would the accounting firm do this? What is Deloitte creating?
    a. Point-of-purchase activity
    b. Sales promotion
    c. Public-relations activity
    d. Community-service activity
    e. Cooperative advertising

Answers to the Test Yourself questions appear at the end of the book on page TY-1.

L.L.Bean Employs a Variety of Promotion Methods to Communicate with Customers

Perhaps best known for its beloved mail-order catalog, L.L.Bean was recently placed near the top of Photobrand's list of New England's most powerful brands, beating Ethan Allen and Yankee Candle. L.L.Bean has grown from its founding as a one-product firm in 1912 to a national brand with 14 stores in 10 different states and a thriving online store. Net sales are over $1.5 billion a year.

Marketing communications are more sophisticated now than they were when L.L.Bean created his first product, a waterproof boot, and publicized it with a homemade brochure. In its early days, the firm thrived on word-of-mouth communication about its reliability and the expert advice of its founder, himself an avid outdoorsman. Determined to build his company and his mailing list, L.L.Bean poured all the company's profits into advertising and talked about the company with one and all. Said one neighbor at the time, "If you drop in just to shake his hand, you get home to find his catalog in your mailbox."

Now the company makes use of marketing database systems to manage and update its mailing lists. The L.L.Bean catalog swelled in size in the 1980s and 1990s, but it has slimmed down as the company's Web site has taken over some of the task of promoting the company's products. Still a major communication tool for the firm, the catalog is also a multiple-industry award-winner. The company uses computer-modeling tools to help it identify what customers want and sends them only the catalogs they desire. Still, says the vice president of stores, "What we find is most customers want some sort of touch point," and the catalog remains very popular.

Online orders recently surpassed mail and phone orders for the first time in the company's history. The relationship between the catalog and the Web site is complicated. As L.L.Bean's vice president for e-commerce explains, customers have begun to shift much of their buying to the Internet, but they still rely on the catalog to browse, plan, and get ideas. Customers take their L.L.Bean catalogs "to soccer games, they read them in the car," she says. "What's changed is what they do next"—often they go online to find more details about an item or to place an order.

L.L.Bean still places print advertising, sometimes small ads that simply offer a free catalog or remind customers that they already have the catalog at home. Since the catalog is expensive to produce, the company tries to support it with other marketing media so it doesn't get lost among all the other messages demanding customers' attention.

A big and growing area for the company's promotion efforts is the Internet, where it uses banner ads on popular sites like Hulu.com that let customers click through to the L.L.Bean online store. It also maintains a Facebook page, a Twitter account, and a YouTube channel. The company invests heavily in television advertising as well, particularly around the holidays. Local TV ads are concentrated in the areas around the company's retail stores.

L.L.Bean doesn't take the wide familiarity of its brand for granted. It also promotes its name through partnerships with environmentally conscious companies and organizations and through charitable giving, mainly to organizations committed to maintaining and protecting Earth's natural resources. The company recognizes, however, that a good product is at the heart of its success. "We really want to sell a good product, and we really guarantee that product," says the company's vice president of e-commerce. "We want to keep . . . the customer happy and keep that customer coming back to L.L.Bean over and over."[18]

Questions

1. What are the ingredients of L.L.Bean's promotion mix?
2. L.L.Bean is reaching into "alternative" promotions, including outfitting Weather Channel meteorologists around the United States and emblazoning its name on the tarp used by the Red Sox baseball team to protect the field during rain delays. What other kinds of promotional activities do you think would suit the company's outdoors image?
3. Do you think L.L.Bean's Web site will ever entirely take the place of its mail-order catalog? Why or why not?

BUILDING SKILLS FOR CAREER SUCCESS

1. Exploring the Internet

One reason the Internet has generated so much excitement and interest among both buyers and distributors of products is that it is a highly effective method of direct marketing. Already a multibillion dollar industry, e-commerce is growing as more businesses recognize the power of the Internet to reach customers 24 hours a day anywhere in the world. In addition to using the Internet to provide product information to potential customers, businesses can use it to process orders and accept payment from customers. Quick delivery from warehouses or stores by couriers such as UPS and FedEx adds to the convenience of Internet shopping.

Businesses whose products traditionally have sold well through catalogs are clear leaders in the electronic marketplace. Books, CDs, clothing, and other frequently purchased, relatively low-cost items sell well through both the Internet and catalogs. As a result, many successful catalog companies are including the Internet as a means of communicating about products. Many of their customers are finding that they prefer the more dynamic online versions of the catalogs.

Assignment

1. Explore the websites listed below, or just enter "shopping" on one of the web search engines—then stand back! Also visit the text website for updates to this exercise.
   www.llbean.com
   www.jcpenney.com
   www.sears.com
   www.landsend.com
   www.barnesandnoble.com
   www.amazon.com
2. Which website does the best job of marketing merchandise? Explain your answer.
3. Find a product that you would be willing to buy over the Internet, and explain why you would buy it. Name the website and describe the product.
4. Find a product that you would be unwilling to buy over the Internet, and again, explain your reasoning. Name the website and describe the product.

2. Building Team Skills

Surveys are a commonly used tool in marketing research. The information they provide can reduce business risk and facilitate decision making. Retail outlets often survey their customers' wants and needs by distributing comment cards or questionnaires. The customer survey (below) is an example of a survey that a local photography shop might distribute to its customers.

Assignment

1. Working in teams of three to five, choose a local retailer.
2. Classify the retailer according to the major types of retailers.
3. Design a survey to help the retailer improve customer service. (You may find it beneficial to work with the retailer and actually administer the survey to the retailer's customers. Prepare a report of the survey results for the retailer.)
4. Present your findings to the class.

3. Researching Different Careers

Most public libraries maintain relatively up-to-date collections of occupational or career materials. Begin your library search by looking at the computer listings under "vocations" or "careers" and then under specific fields. Check the library's periodicals section, where you will find trade and professional magazines and journals about specific occupations and industries. (*Business Periodicals Index,* published by H. W. Wilson, is an index to articles in major business publications. Arranged alphabetically, it is easy to use.) Familiarize yourself with the concerns and activities of potential employers by skimming their annual reports and other information they distribute to the public. You can also find occupational information on videocassettes, in kits, and through computerized information systems.

Assignment

1. Choose a specific occupation.
2. Conduct a library search of the occupation.
3. Prepare an annotated bibliography for the occupation.

Customer Survey

To help us serve you better, please take a few minutes while your photographs are being developed to answer the following questions. Your opinions are important to us.

1. Do you live/work in the area? (Circle one or both if they apply.)
2. Why did you choose us? (Circle all that apply.)
   Close to home
   Close to work Convenience
   Good service
   Quality
   Full-service photography shop
   Other
3. How did you learn about us? (Circle one.)

   Newspaper
   Flyer/coupon
   Passing by
   Recommended by someone
   Other

4. How frequently do you have film developed? (Please estimate.)
   _____ Times per month
   _____ Times per year
5. Which aspects of our photography shop do you think need improvement?
6. Our operating hours are from 8:00 A.M. to 7:00 P.M. weekdays and Saturdays from 9:30 A.M. to 6:00 P.M. We are closed on Sundays and legal holidays. If changes in our operating hours would serve you better, please specify how you would like them changed.
7. Age (Circle one.)
   Under 25
   26–39
   40–59
   Over 60

   Comments:

Graeter's Is "Synonymous with Ice Cream"

When a 140-year-old company finally redesigns its logo, that's big news. Graeter's, the beloved Cincinnati-based maker of premium, hand-packed ice cream, is still managed by direct descendants of its founders. Its new logo is just one part of a major rebranding effort to support the company's first big planned expansion. "If we don't continue to improve and innovate, somebody will come and do it better than us," says Chip Graeter, the company's vice president of retail stores. "And we don't want that to happen."

Quality Builds the Brand

Graeter's considers as its competitors not only Häagen-Dazs and Ben & Jerry's, national premium ice-cream brands that have much bigger marketing budgets, but also all kinds of premium-quality desserts and edible treats. Taking that wide-angle view means its competition is both broad and fierce. One thing the company is firm about, however, is maintaining the quality of its dense, creamy product (it's so dense that one pint of Graeter's ice cream weighs about a pound). Graeter's quality standards call for adhering to its simple, original family recipe—which now includes more all-natural ingredients, like beet juice instead of food dye and dairy products from hormone-free cows—and an original, artisanal production process that yields only about two gallons per machine every 20 minutes. "We were always all-natural," says CEO Richard Graeter II, "but now we're being militant about it."

That hard-earned premium quality is what built the Graeter's brand from its earliest days when refrigeration was unknown and ice cream was a true novelty. Today, "Graeter's in Cincinnati is synonymous with ice cream," says a company executive. "People will say, 'Let's go get a Graeter's.' They don't say, 'Let's go get an ice cream.'" Quality is also what the current management team hopes will propel Graeter's beyond its current market, which consists of a few dozen company-owned retail stores in Ohio, Missouri, Kentucky, and nearby states, and the freezer cases of about 1,700 supermarkets and grocery stores, particularly the Kroger chain. Graeter's is also on the menu in some fine restaurants and country clubs. The company operates an online store and will ship ice cream overnight via UPS to any of the 48 continental states (California is its biggest shipping market). Graeter's also sells a limited line of candies, cakes, and other bakery goods, and its ice-cream line includes smoothies and sorbets.

Expanding to New Markets

Graeter's ambitious expansion plans are backed by a recent increase in production capacity from one factory to three (one of the new factories was built, and the other purchased). The plans call for distributing Graeter's delectable, seasonal flavors to even more supermarkets and grocery stores, and for gradually opening new retail stores, perhaps as far away as Los Angeles and New York. The Kroger chain is Graeter's biggest distribution partner. Of the tens of thousands of brands Kroger carries, says the chain, pricey Graeter's commands the strongest brand loyalty. It was through Kroger, in fact, that Graeter's managers hit upon the idea of conducting a trial expansion to Denver, a new market for the brand.

Kroger owns the King Soopers chain of grocery stores in Denver, and research showed that more Denver ice-cream buyers choose premium brands than cheaper choices, suggesting that Graeter's might do well there. So Graeter's chose 12 flavors to send to 30 King Soopers stores in Denver as a test market, with the goal of selling two or three gallons a week. The test was an unqualified success. Within a few weeks, the company was selling an average of five gallons a week per store.

"I'd like to be coast to coast," admits Graeter's CEO. In fact, the management team would like to explore selling Graeter's in Canada, perhaps within the next five years. "The challenge, of course, is to preserve the integrity of the product as we grow. But we have done that for more than 100 years, and I'd argue that it's better now than ever."

Promoting the Brand

Graeter's had already gotten a big free boost from a positive mention on the *Oprah Winfrey Show* in 2002, when the influential talk-show host called it the best ice cream she had ever tasted. "We were shipping about 40 orders a day," says CEO Richard Graeter II. "After her show, the next day we probably shipped 400." National attention continues with occasional exposure on the Food Network, the Fine Living Channel, the Travel Channel, and even the History Channel. "How does that happen?" asks one of the firm's executives. "It happens because we have a product and a process and a growth that is exciting."

© Liudmila Chernova / iStockphoto 12864114

© DNY59 / iStockphoto 1694138

Still, says George Denman, the company's vice president of sales and marketing, Graeter's faces the same challenge in new markets as any "small, regional niche player" and one with a limited marketing budget: "establishing a relationship with the consumer, building brand awareness [through] trial and repeat. . . . So obviously when we roll into a marketplace one of the first things we do is we demo the product. We get it out in front of the consumer and get them to taste it, because the product sells itself." The company has also been reducing its price to distributors, who pass the savings along to stores that can then advertise that Graeter's pints are on sale. "If a consumer has maybe been buying Ben & Jerry's and never considered ours, because maybe that dollar price point difference was too high, this gives her the opportunity to try us. And once she tries us, we know we've brand-switched that consumer right then," says Denman.

Marketing Communications

Through its Cincinnati-based ad agency, Graeter's does some local advertising, including attractive point-of-sale displays in supermarkets and grocery stores and some radio ads, occasional print ads, and billboards. The company launches small-scale promotions for the introduction of a new flavor or to celebrate National Ice Cream Month or other occasions. However, brand loyalty for this family business has grown mostly through word of mouth that endures across generations. "We are the beneficiary of that loyalty that our customers have built up over so many years, multiple generations," says one of the company's executives. "Our customers have told us they were introduced to the product through their grandmother, or a special time . . . . They don't come to our stores because they have to; they come because they want to."

"We use the traditional [marketing] methods," says Denman. "We are also doing nontraditional methods. We are looking at electronic couponing, where consumers will be able to go to our Web site as a new consumer . . . and secure a dollar-off coupon to try Graeter's, just for coming to our Web site or joining up on Facebook. We've done loyalty programs with Kroger where they have actually direct-mailed loyal consumers and offered . . . discounts as well . . . . So far it's worked well for us. We've had to go back and look at the return on investment on each of these programs and cut some things out and improve on some other things, but in the end we have been very pleased with the results."

"Quality . . . We Never Changed"

"We ship our product, and that was something that for the first hundred years you never thought about. I mean, who would think about shipping ice cream from Cincinnati to California? But it is our number-one market for shipping, so all those things you can change," says Richard Graeter, the CEO. "The most important thing, the quality of the product and how we make it, that we never changed."[19]

Questions

1. How might Graeter's capitalize on its valuable capacity for word-of-mouth promotion in expanding to new markets where, despite some national publicity like the *Oprah Winfrey Show*, its name is still not widely known?

2. Graeter's ice-cream line includes smoothies and sorbets. Do you think it should consider other brand extensions such as yogurt, low-fat ice cream, coffee drinks, or other related products? Why or why not?

3. What are the elements of Graeter's marketing mix? Which are most likely to be affected by external forces in the marketing environment?

Building a Business Plan: Part 5

This part is one of the most important components of your business plan. In this part, you will present the facts that you have gathered on the size and nature of your market(s). State market size in dollars and units. How many units and what is the dollar value of the products you expect to sell in a given time period? Indicate your primary and secondary sources of data and the methods you used to estimate total market size and your market share. Part 5 of your textbook covers all marketing-related topics. These chapters should help you to answer the questions in this part of the business plan.

The Marketing Plan Component

The marketing plan component is and should be unique to your business. Many assumptions or projections used in the analysis may turn out differently; therefore, this component should be flexible enough to be adjusted as needed. The marketing plan should include answers to at least the following questions:

5.1 What are your target markets, and what common identifiable need(s) can you satisfy?

5.2 What are the competitive, legal, political, economic, technological, and sociocultural factors affecting your marketing efforts?

5.3 What are the current needs of each target market? Describe the target market in terms of demographic, geographic, psychographic, and product-usage characteristics. What changes in the target market are anticipated?

5.4 What advantages and disadvantages do you have in meeting the target market's needs?

5.5 How will your product distribution, promotion, and price satisfy customer needs?

5.6 How effectively will your products meet these needs?

5.7 What are the relevant aspects of consumer behavior and product use?

5.8 What are your company's projected sales volume, market share, and profitability?

5.9 What are your marketing objectives? Include the following in your marketing objectives:
- Product introduction, improvement, or innovation
- Sales or market share
- Profitability
- Pricing
- Distribution
- Advertising (Prepare advertising samples for the appendix.)

Make sure that your marketing objectives are clearly written, measurable, and consistent with your overall marketing strategy.

5.10 How will the results of your marketing plan be measured and evaluated?

Review of Business Plan Activities

Remember that even though it will be time-consuming, developing a clear, well-written marketing plan is important. Therefore, make sure that you have checked the plan for any weaknesses or problems before proceeding to Part 6. Also, make certain that all your answers to the questions in this and other parts are consistent throughout the business plan. Finally, write a brief statement that summarizes all the information for this part of the business plan.

The information contained in this section will also assist you in completing the online *Interactive Business Plan*.

PART SIX

MANAGING INFORMATION, ACCOUNTING, AND FINANCE

In this part of the book, we focus on information and finances, two of the four essential resources on which all businesses rely. First, we discuss the information necessary for effective decision making, where it can be found, how it is organized, and how it can be used throughout an organization by those who need it. We also investigate the world of e-business in Chapter 14. In Chapter 15, we then examine the role of accounting and how financial information is used to better control managerial decision making. Then we examine the concept of financial management in Chapter 16.

Chapter 14   Understanding Information and e-Business
Chapter 15   Using Accounting Information
Chapter 16   Mastering Financial Management

©Lauren Dadayustv/iShutterstock.com (12728883)

CHAPTER 14 UNDERSTANDING INFORMATION AND E-BUSINESS

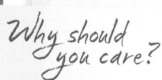

Why should you care?

Question: How important is information for a successful business?

Answer: It would be extremely difficult to manage even a small business without information.

© Rido/Shutterstock

Learning Objectives

What you will be able to do once you complete this chapter:

1 Examine how information can reduce risk when making a decision.

2 Discuss management's information requirements.

3 Outline the five functions of an information system.

4 Describe how computers and technology help improve productivity, decision making, communications, sales, and recruiting and training.

5 Analyze how computers and technology change the way information is acquired, organized, and used.

6 Explain the meaning of e-business.

7 Describe the fundamental models of e-business.

8 Explore the factors that will affect the future of e-business.

Get Flashcards, Quizzes, Games, Crosswords, and more @ www.cengagebrain.com

How Mars Built My M&M's into a Sweet E-Business

Those Ms on M&M's don't simply appear—parent company Mars has been printing them on every bite-size chocolate-coated candy since 1950. A $30 billion corporation based in McLean, Virginia, Mars makes foods for people and pets under such well-known brands as M&M's, Dove, Uncle Ben's, Pedigree, and Whiskas.

Back in 2000, a Mars executive began thinking about how to print something other than Ms on M&M's. The company already had candy-printing technology—what it didn't have was the ability to take orders from individuals or businesses for customized M&M's. The next step was building an e-business around this capability.

Mars gave the team a tiny budget to begin testing custom-printed M&M's internally to the company's 65,000 employees. This was an opportunity to obtain information about how much candy should be in each package, how much to charge, and other details. On the first day, the team sold 800 pounds of custom-printed M&M's at $12 per pound, $4 more per pound than the usual price of M-only M&M's. Information obtained from employees indicated that demand would be even higher if the custom-printed candies were offered in a wider variety of colors, with fancier packaging, and with a smaller minimum order size.

Months later, Mars added a link to its public Web site to invite custom orders, and the new e-business was officially launched. Even without marketing hoopla, the custom-printed M&M's were a hit. Mars named the e-business Mars Direct and has since expanded it to Europe and beyond.

Today, consumers can order M&M's online from www.mymms.com in more than a dozen colors, printed with special messages plus images (such as Disney characters, NFL team emblems, or personal photos), in a variety of bags or boxes. Businesses can have their logos or corporate names or slogans printed on M&M's for distribution to clients or employees. Mars is also showing its commitment to social responsibility by switching to certified eco-friendly cocoa for all its chocolates by 2020, making Mars Direct an even sweeter e-business for customers interested in sustainability.[1]

Did you know?

Mars has eleven billion-dollar brands: M&M's, Snickers, Dove, Mars, Extra, Orbit, Twix, Uncle Ben's, Pedigree, Royal Canin, and Whiskas.

How did Mars—the company profiled in the Inside Business opening case for this chapter—decide to begin manufacturing customized M&M's? The decision-making process began by gathering information. Although they had the ability to print M&M's with customized names, photos, dates, NFL team emblems, and even Disney characters, they had to determine if customers would buy customized candy. To obtain much needed information about consumer demand, price, packaging, and other factors, Mars began by testing custom-printed M&M's internally to the company's 65,000 employees. The information the company obtained from its initial research and development activities was used to "fine-tune" its business plan for its custom-printed M&M's. For example, initial research indicated that consumers wanted a wider variety of colors, fancier packaging, and a smaller minimum order size. Only after Mars gathered information did they add a link to its Web site where customers could order customized M&Ms. Today, Mars Direct is an important division of the company and customized M&M's are sold in the United States, Europe, and beyond. For more information about Mars Direct and customized M&M's, go to www.mymms.com.

To improve the decision-making process, the information used by both individuals and business firms must be relevant or useful to meet a specific need. Using relevant information results in better decisions.

Relevant information → Better intelligence and knowledge → Better decisions

For businesses, better intelligence and knowledge that lead to better decisions are especially important because they can provide a *competitive edge* over competitors and improve a firm's *profits*. We begin this chapter by describing why employees need information.

The first three major sections in this chapter answer the following questions:

- How can information reduce risk when making a decision?
- What is a management information system?
- How do employees use a management information system?

Next, we discuss how computers, the Internet, and software—all topics covered in this chapter—are used to obtain the information needed to make decisions and improve productivity on a daily basis. In the last part of this chapter, we take a close look at how firms conduct business on the Internet and what growth opportunities and challenges affect both new and existing e-business firms.

LEARNING OBJECTIVE

1 Examine how information can reduce risk when making a decision.

HOW CAN INFORMATION REDUCE RISK WHEN MAKING A DECISION?

As we noted in Chapter 1, information is one of the four major resources (along with material, human, and financial resources) managers must have to operate a business. Although a successful business uses all four resources efficiently, it is information that helps managers reduce risk when making a decision.

Information and Risk

Theoretically, with accurate and complete information, there is no risk whatsoever. On the other hand, a decision made without any information is a gamble. These two extreme situations are rare in business. For the most part, business decision makers see themselves located someplace between either extreme. As illustrated in Figure 14-1, when the amount of available information is high, there is less risk; when the amount of available information is low, there is more risk.

Personal App You can reduce the risk in any decision you make—a decision about school, a decision about work, or a decision about buying something expensive—by doing your homework. The more you know about the situation and your alternatives, the better your decision will be.

FIGURE 14-1: **The Relationship Between Information and Risk**

When the amount of available information is high, managers tend to make better decisions. On the other hand, when the amount of information is low, there is a high risk of making a poor decision.

© Cengage Learning 2013

Suppose that a marketing manager for Procter & Gamble responsible for the promotion of a well-known shampoo such as Pantene Pro-V has called a meeting of her department team to consider the selection of a new magazine advertisement. The company's advertising agency has submitted two new advertisements in sealed envelopes. Neither the manager nor any of her team has seen them before. Only one selection will be made for the new advertising campaign. Which advertisement should be chosen?

Without any further information, the team might as well make the decision by flipping a coin. If, however, team members were allowed to open the envelopes and examine the advertisements, they would have more information. If, in addition to allowing them to examine the advertisements, the marketing manager circulated a report containing the reactions of a group of target consumers to each of the two advertisements, the team would have even more information with which to work. Thus, information, when understood properly, produces knowledge and empowers managers and employees to make better decisions.

Information Rules

Marketing research continues to show that discounts influence almost all car buyers. Simply put, if dealers lower their prices, they will sell more cars. This relationship between buyer behavior and price can be thought of as an information rule that usually will guide the marketing manager correctly. An information rule emerges when research confirms the same results each time that it studies the same or a similar set of circumstances.

Because of the volume of information they receive each day and their need to make decisions on a daily basis, businesspeople try to accumulate information rules to shorten the time they spend analyzing choices. Information rules are the "great simplifiers" for all decision makers. Business research is continuously looking for new rules that can be put to good use and looking to discredit old ones that are no longer valid. This ongoing process is necessary because business conditions rarely stay the same for very long.

The Difference Between Data and Information

Many people use the terms *data* and *information* interchangeably, but the two differ in important ways. **Data** are numerical or verbal descriptions that usually result from some sort of measurement. (The word *data* is plural; the singular form is datum.) Your current wage level, the amount of last year's after-tax profit for Motorola, and the current retail prices of Honda automobiles are all data. Most people think of data as being numerical only, but they can be nonnumerical as well. A description of an individual as a "tall, athletic person with short, dark hair" certainly would qualify as data.

Information is data presented in a form that is useful for a specific purpose. Suppose that a human resources manager wants to compare the wages paid to male and female employees over a period of five years. The manager might begin with a stack of computer printouts listing every person employed by the firm, along with each employee's current and past wages. The manager would be hard pressed to make any sense of all the names and numbers. Such printouts consist of data rather than information.

Now suppose that the manager uses a computer and software to graph the average wages paid to men and to women in each of the five years. The result is information because the manager can use it for the purpose at hand—to compare

© weknow/Shutterstock

data numerical or verbal descriptions that usually result from some sort of measurement

information data presented in a form that is useful for a specific purpose

wages paid to men with those paid to women over the five-year period. For a manager, information presented in a practical, useful form such as a graph simplifies the decision-making process.

Personal App If you're thinking about buying a car, a listing of vehicles for sale would be *data*. Put that data into a table that ranks each vehicle by price and fuel efficiency, and you've got *information* you can use to narrow down the field and make your decision.

Knowledge Management

The average company maintains a great deal of data that can be transformed into information. Typical data include records pertaining to personnel, inventory, sales, and accounting. Often each type of data is stored in individual departments within an organization. However, the data can be used more effectively when they are organized into a database. A **database** is a single collection of data and information stored in one place that can be used by people throughout an organization to make decisions. Although databases are important, the way the data and information are used is even more important—and more valuable to the firm. As a result, management information experts now use the term **knowledge management (KM)** to describe a firm's procedures for generating, using, and sharing the data and information. The basic principle of knowledge management is that real knowledge is more than just a collection of data and information. When compared to data and information stored in a database, knowledge management takes the next step and attempts to determine meaningful and useful relationships between available data and information. As a result, KM helps the firm's employees and managers make more effective and intelligent decisions. Typically, data, information, databases, and KM all become important parts of a firm's management information system.

WHAT IS A MANAGEMENT INFORMATION SYSTEM?

A **management information system (MIS)** is a system that provides managers and employees with the information they need to perform their jobs as effectively as possible. The purpose of an MIS (sometimes referred to as an information technology system or simply IT system) is to distribute timely and useful information from both internal and external sources to the managers and employees who need it (see Figure 14-2). Today, most medium-sized to large business firms have an information technology (IT) officer. An **information technology (IT) officer** is a manager at the executive level who is responsible for ensuring that a firm has the equipment necessary to provide the information the firm's employees and managers need to make effective decisions.

Today's typical MIS is built around a computerized system of record-keeping and communications software so that it can provide information based on a wide variety of data. After all, the goal is to provide needed information to all employees and managers.

A Firm's Information Requirements

Employees and managers have to plan for the future, implement their plans in the present, and evaluate results against what has been accomplished in the past. Of course, the specific types of information they need depend on their work area and on their level within the firm.

Today, many firms are organized into five areas of management: *finance, operations, marketing, human resources,* and *administration.* Managers in each of these areas need specific information in order to make decisions.

* *Concept Check*

☐ In your own words, describe how information reduces risk when you make a personal or work-related decision.

☐ What are information rules? How do they simplify the process of making decisions?

☐ What is the difference between data and information? Give one example of accounting data and one example of accounting information.

LEARNING OBJECTIVE
2 Discuss management's information requirements.

database a single collection of data and information stored in one place that can be used by people throughout an organization to make decisions

knowledge management (KM) a firm's procedures for generating, using, and sharing the data and information

management information system (MIS) a system that provides managers and employees with the information they need to perform their jobs as effectively as possible

information technology (IT) officer a manager at the executive level who is responsible for ensuring that a firm has the equipment necessary to provide the information the firm's employees and managers need to make effective decisions

FIGURE 14-2: Management Information System (MIS)

After an MIS is installed, employers and managers can get information directly from the MIS without having to go through other people in the organization.

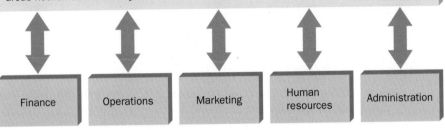

MANAGEMENT INFORMATION SYSTEM

Integrated database capable of receiving, organizing, summarizing, and calculating data and information from functional areas, and providing information to managers from functional areas networked into the system.

| Finance | Operations | Marketing | Human resources | Administration |

Source: Ricky W. Griffin, *Management*, 10/e (Mason, OH: Cengage Learning, 2011). Reprinted by permission.

- *Financial managers* obviously are most concerned with their firm's finances. They study its debts and receivables, cash flow, future financial needs, financial statements, and other accounting information. Of equal importance to financial managers is information about the present state of the economy, interest rates, and predictions of business conditions in the future.

- *Operations managers* are concerned with present and future sales levels, current inventory levels of work in process and finished goods, and the availability and cost of the resources required to produce products and services. They also must keep abreast of any innovative production technology that might be useful to the firm.

- *Marketing managers* need to have detailed information about their firm's products and the products offered by competitors. Such information includes pricing strategies, new promotional campaigns, and products that competitors are test marketing. Information concerning the firm's customers, current and projected market share, and new and pending product legislation is also important to marketing managers.

- *Human resources managers* must be aware of anything that pertains to the firm's employees. Key examples include current wage levels and benefits packages both within the firm and in firms that compete for valuable employees, current legislation and court decisions that affect employment practices, union activities, and the firm's plans for growth, expansion, or mergers.

- *Administrative managers* are responsible for the overall management of the organization. Thus, they are concerned with the coordination of information—just as they are concerned with the coordination of material, human, and financial resources.

Numbers and charts. What does it all mean? Good question. The fact is that few managers and employees would be able to perform their jobs without accurate and up-to-date information. Because it is so important, most organizations invest large amounts of money to ensure that the firm's employees have access to the information they need to make decisions on a daily basis.

© Francesco Ridolfi/iStockphoto.com

Administrators must ensure that all employees have access to the information they need to do their jobs. Administrative managers must also ensure that the information is used in a consistent manner throughout the firm. Suppose, for example, that General Electric (GE) is designing a new plant that will open in five years. GE's management will want answers to many questions: Is the capacity of the plant consistent with marketing plans based on sales projections? Will human resources managers be able to staff the plant on the basis of employment forecasts? And do sales projections indicate enough income to cover the expected cost of the plant? Next, administrative managers must make sure that all managers and employees are able to use the IT that is available. Certainly, this requires that all employees receive the skills training required to use the firm's MIS. Finally, administrative managers must commit to the costs of updating the firm's MIS and providing additional training when necessary.

Size and Complexity of the System

An MIS must be tailored to the needs of the organization it serves. In some firms, a tendency to save on initial costs may result in a system that is too small or overly simple. Such a system generally ends up serving only one or two management levels or a single department. Managers in other departments "give up" on the system as soon as they find that it cannot process their data.

Almost as bad is an MIS that is too large or too complex for the organization. Unused capacity and complexity do nothing but increase the cost of owning and operating the system. In addition, a system that is difficult to use probably will not be used at all.

✳ *Concept Check*

☐ How do the information requirements of managers differ by management area?

☐ What happens if a business has a management information system that is too large?

☐ What happens if a business has a management information system that is too small?

LEARNING OBJECTIVE

3 Outline the five functions of an information system.

HOW DO EMPLOYEES USE A MANAGEMENT INFORMATION SYSTEM?

To provide information, a management information system (MIS) must perform five specific functions. It must (1) collect data, (2) store the data, (3) update the data, (4) process the data into information, and (5) present the information to users (see Figure 14-3).

Step 1: Collecting Data

A firm's employees, with the help of an MIS system, must gather the data and information needed to establish the firm's *database*. The database should include all past and current data that may be useful in managing the firm. Clearly, the data entered into the system must be *relevant* to the needs of the firm's managers. And perhaps most important, the data must be *accurate*. Irrelevant data are simply useless; inaccurate data can be disastrous. There are two data sources: *internal* and *external*.

INTERNAL SOURCES OF DATA Typically, most of the data gathered for an MIS come from internal sources. The most common internal sources of information are managers and employees, company records and reports, and minutes of meetings.

Past and present accounting data can also provide information about the firm's transactions with customers, creditors, and suppliers. Sales reports are a source of data on sales, pricing strategies, and the effectiveness of promotional campaigns. Human resources records are useful as a source of data on wage and benefits levels, hiring patterns, employee turnover, and other personnel variables.

Present and past production forecasts also should be included in the firm's data bank, along with data indicating how well these forecasts predicted actual events. Specific plans and management decisions—regarding capital expansion and new product development, for example—should be incorporated into the MIS system.

EXTERNAL SOURCES OF DATA External sources of data include customers, suppliers, financial institutions and banks, trade and business publications, industry conferences, online computer services, government sources, and firms that specialize in gathering data for organizations. For example, a marketing research company may acquire forecasts pertaining to product demand, consumer tastes, and other marketing variables. Suppliers are also an excellent source of information about the future availability and costs of raw materials and component parts. Bankers often can provide valuable economic insights and projections. The information furnished by trade and business publications and industry conferences is usually concerned as much with future projections as with present conditions. Legal issues and court decisions that may affect a firm are discussed occasionally in local newspapers and, more often, in specialized publications such as *The Wall Street Journal*, *Fortune*, and *Business Week*. Government publications such as the *Monthly Labor Review* and the *Federal Reserve Bulletin* are also quite useful as sources of external data, as are a number of online computer services.

Whether the source of the data is internal or external, always remember the following three cautions:

1. The cost of obtaining data from some external sources, such as marketing research firms, can be quite high.
2. Outdated or incomplete data usually yield inaccurate information.
3. Although computers generally do not make mistakes, the people who use them can make or cause errors. When data (or information) and your judgment disagree, always check the data.

Personal App When gathering external data for important professional or personal decisions, ask yourself: Are you using reliable, timely, and objective sources? Can the data be double-checked? Are more up-to-date details available? What additional data do you need to make a more informed decision?

Step 2: Storing Data

An MIS must be capable of storing data until they are needed. Typically, the method chosen to store data depends on the size and needs of the organization. Small businesses may enter data and then store them directly on the hard drive inside an employee's computer. Generally, medium-sized to large businesses store data in a larger computer system and provide access to employees through a computer network. Today, networks take on many configurations and are designed by specialists who work with a firm's IT personnel to decide on what's best for the company.

Step 3: Updating Data

Today, an MIS must be able to update stored data regularly to ensure that the information presented to managers and employees is accurate, complete, and up-to-date. The frequency with which the data are updated depends on how fast they change and how often they are used. When it is vital to have current data, updating may occur as soon as the new data are available. For example, Giant Food, a grocery store chain operating in the eastern part of the United States, has cash registers that automatically transmit data on each item sold to a central computer. The computer adjusts the store's inventory records accordingly. In some systems, the computer may even be programmed to reorder items whose inventories fall below some specified level. Data and information may also be entered into a firm's data bank at certain intervals—every 24 hours, weekly, or monthly.

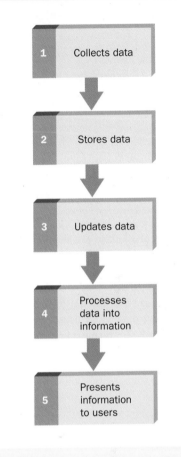

FIGURE 14-3: **Five Management Information System Functions**

Every MIS must be tailored to the organization it serves and must perform five functions.

1 Collects data

2 Stores data

3 Updates data

4 Processes data into information

5 Presents information to users

© Cengage Learning 2013

HOW AMERICA STACKS UP

COUNTRY	PERCENT OF BUDGET SPENT ON FOOD
United States	10%
Finland	16%
France	18%
New Zealand	20%
Germany	21%
Australia	21%
United Kingdom	22%
Italy	23%
Spain	25%
Japan	26%
Israel	26%
South Africa	28%
Mexico	33%
India	51%

Source: USDA Economic Research Service

Why visual displays are important! Visual displays, like the bar chart in this photo, are often more interesting than if the same information was described in a written report. Here, food costs (as a percent of budget) for people in different countries are illustrated using a bar chart. Because it's easier to compare data when visual displays are used, the eye can quickly pick out the most important information.

PRNewFoto/Corn Growers Association

* *Concept Check*

☐ List the five functions of an MIS.

☐ What are the components of a typical business report?

☐ What types of information could be illustrated in a visual display? In a tabular display?

data processing the transformation of data into a form that is useful for a specific purpose

statistic a measure that summarizes a particular characteristic of an entire group of numbers

Step 4: Processing Data

Some data are used in the form in which they are stored, whereas other data require processing to extract, highlight, or summarize the information they contain. **Data processing** is the transformation of data into a form that is useful for a specific purpose.

For verbal data, this processing consists mainly of extracting the pertinent material from storage and combining it into a report. Most business data, however, are in the form of numbers—large groups of numbers, such as daily sales totals or production costs for a specific product. Fortunately, computers can be programmed to process such large volumes of numbers quickly. While such groups of numbers may be difficult to handle and to comprehend, their contents can be summarized through the use of statistics. A **statistic** is a measure that summarizes a particular characteristic of an entire group of numbers.

Step 5: Presenting Information

An MIS must be capable of presenting information in a usable form. That is, the method of presentation—reports, tables, graphs, or charts, for example—must be appropriate for the information itself and for the uses to which it will be put.

BUSINESS REPORTS Verbal information may be presented in list or paragraph form. Employees often are asked to prepare formal business reports. A typical business report includes (1) an introduction, (2) the body of the report, (3) the conclusions, and (4) the recommendations.

The *introduction*, which sets the stage for the remainder of the report, describes the problem to be studied in the report, identifies the research techniques that were used, and previews the material that will be presented in the report. The *body* of the report should objectively describe the facts that were discovered in the process of completing the report. The body also should provide a foundation for the conclusions and the recommendations. The *conclusions* are statements of fact that describe the findings contained in the report. They should be specific, practical, and based on the evidence contained in the report. The *recommendations* section presents suggestions on how the problem might be solved. Like the conclusions, the recommendations should be specific, practical, and based on the evidence.

VISUAL DISPLAYS AND TABLES A visual display can also be used to present information and may be a diagram that represents several items of information in a manner that makes comparison easier. Figure 14-4 illustrates examples of visual displays generated by a computer. Typical visual displays include:

- Graphs
- Bar charts
- Pie charts

A tabular display is used to present verbal or numerical information in columns and rows. It is most useful in presenting information about two or more related variables. A table, for example, can be used to illustrate the number of salespeople in each region of the country, sales for different types of products, and total sales for all products (see Table 14-1). Information that is to be manipulated—for example, to calculate loan payments—is usually displayed in tabular form.

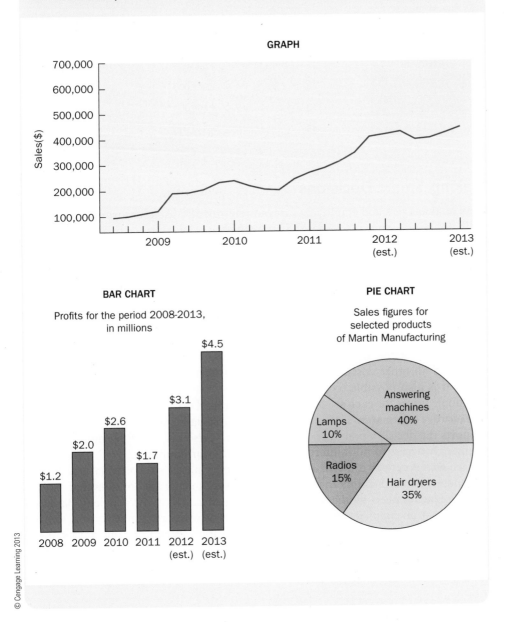

FIGURE 14-4: **Typical Visual Displays Used in Business Presentations**

Visual displays help businesspeople to present information in a form that can be understood easily.

GRAPH

BAR CHART

Profits for the period 2008-2013, in millions

PIE CHART

Sales figures for selected products of Martin Manufacturing

Answering machines 40%

Lamps 10%

Radios 15%

Hair dryers 35%

© Cengage Learning 2013

Tabular displays generally have less impact than visual displays. However, displaying the information that could be contained in a multicolumn table such as Table 14-1 would require several bar or pie charts.

IMPROVING PRODUCTIVITY WITH THE HELP OF COMPUTERS AND TECHNOLOGY

In this section, we examine several practical applications of computer technology. In each case, a specific application is always evaluated in terms of its costs and compared with the benefits a firm receives, generally referred to as a *cost/benefit analysis.* Typical applications for a business include decision making, communications, sales, recruiting and training employees, business software, and virtual offices.

LEARNING OBJECTIVE

4 Describe how computers and technology help improve productivity, decision making, communications, sales, and recruiting and training.

TABLE 14-1: **Typical Three-Column Table Used in Business Presentations**

Tables are most useful for displaying information about two or more variables.

All-Star Technology Projected Sales			
Section of the Country	Number of Salespeople	Consumer Products ($)	Industrial Products ($)
Eastern territory	15	1,500,000	3,500,000
Midwestern territory	20	2,000,000	5,000,000
Western territory	10	1,000,000	4,000,000
TOTAL	45	4,500,000	12,500,000

© Cengage Learning 2013

Making Smart Decisions

How do managers and employees sort out relevant and useful information from the spam, junk mail, and useless data? Three different applications can actually help to improve and speed the decision-making process for people at different levels within an organization. First, a **decision-support system (DSS)** is a type of computer program which provides relevant data and information to help a firm's employees make decisions. It also can be used to determine the effect of changing different variables and answer "what if" type questions. For example, a manager at Michigan-based Pulte Homes may use a DSS to determine prices for new homes built in an upscale, luxury subdivision. By entering the number of homes that will be built along with different costs associated with land, labor, materials, building permits, promotional costs, and all other costs, a DSS can help to determine a base price for each new home. It is also possible to increase or decrease the building costs and determine new home prices for each set of assumptions with a DSS. Although similar to a DSS, an **executive information system (EIS)** is a computer-based system that facilitates and supports the decision-making needs of top managers and senior executives by providing easy access to both internal and external information.

An **expert system** is a type of computer program that uses artificial intelligence to imitate a human's ability to think. An expert system uses a set of rules that analyze information supplied by the user about a particular activity or problem. Based on the information supplied, the expert system then provides recommendations or suggests specific actions in order to help make decisions. Expert systems, for example, have been used to schedule manufacturing tasks, diagnose illnesses, determine credit limits for credit-card customers, evaluate loan applications, and develop electronic games.

Helping Employees Communicate

One of the first business applications of computer technology was e-mail. Once software was chosen and employees trained, communications could be carried out globally within and outside a firm at any time, 24 hours a day, seven days a week. Today, e-mail is also being used as a direct link between businesses and customers. For example, many brokerage and financial firms like Charles Schwab and Fidelity Investments use e-mail to stay in contact with customers and promote different investment products.

Today, employers expect that their employees will be able to use e-mail to communicate with other employees and customers. Although it takes practice, the seven tips provided in Table 14-2 will help you improve your ability to effectively use e-mails.

Groupware is one of the latest types of software that facilitates the management of large projects among geographically dispersed employees, as well as such group activities as problem solving and brainstorming. Suppose that the home office of a software development firm in a major city has been hired to prepare customized

decision-support system (DSS) a type of computer program that provides relevant data and information to help a firm's employees make decisions

executive information system (EIS) a computer-based system that facilitates and supports the decision-making needs of top managers and senior executives by providing easy access to both internal and external information

expert system a type of computer program that uses artificial intelligence to imitate a human's ability to think

groupware one of the latest types of software that facilitates the management of large projects among geographically dispersed employees as well as such group activities as problem solving and brainstorming

TABLE 14-2: Seven Tips for Effective E-mail Communication

It takes practice to develop effective e-mail communication skills that you will need in the workplace.

1.	*Most Important:* Think about what you are really saying in an e-mail. Don't put something in an e-mail that you wouldn't say face-to-face to another person. In addition, remember that it is very easy for the reader to forward your e-mail to everyone in the company—even when it was meant for just the original reader.
2.	Write perfect subject lines. After your name, the subject line is often the next information the reader sees. Make sure your subject line captures the reader's attention.
3.	Talk about one subject in an e-mail. Including more than one idea, concept, or issue in an e-mail can make your e-mail confusing.
4.	Keep e-mails short. Long e-mails with long sentences intimidate readers. Often, readers skip important information and miss the most important point because they get tired of reading.
5.	Be careful when using all caps. Using ALL CAPS is like shouting and should only be used when you really want to emphasize an important point.
6.	Do not use the reply all option unless everyone needs to see your response. Send your response to only the people who really need to see it.
7.	Don't hit the send button until you are ready to send the e-mail. Often, people accidentally hit the send button before they are finished writing an e-mail. A better approach is to leave the address line blank until you have finished and reread your e-mail. Once completed, enter the address of the recipient(s) and hit send.

© Cengage Learning 2013

software for a client in another city. The project team leader uses groupware to establish guidelines for the project, check availability of employees around the world, give individuals specific work assignments, and set up a schedule for work completion, testing, and final installation on the client's computer. The team leader is able to monitor work progress and may intervene if asked or if problems develop. When needed, people from various locations, possessing an array of knowledge and skills, can be called to the "workspace" created on the computer system for their contribution. When the work is finally completed, it can be forwarded to the client's computer and installed.

Besides being useful in project management, groupware provides an opportunity to establish a collaborative learning system to help solve a specific problem. A **collaborative learning system** is a work environment that allows problem-solving participation by all team members. By posting a question or problem on the groupware site, the team leader invites members, who may be located anywhere in the world, to submit messages that can help to move the group toward a solution.

Assisting the Firm's Sales Force

Internet-based software application programs, sometimes referred to as customer relationship management programs, focus on the special information needs of sales personnel. For example, sales force automation programs support sales representatives with organized databases of information such as names of clients, status of pending orders, and sales leads and opportunities, as well as any related advice or recommendations from other company personnel. Consider what happens when a sales representative for the pharmaceutical division of Johnson & Johnson is planning to visit doctors, health care providers, and hospitals in the Chicago area. A sales force automation software program can provide information about what the results were of the last contacts, who else in the firm has interacted with the client, and previous purchases the client has made. As sales representatives complete their visits, information about what was learned should be entered into the sales force automation system as soon as possible so that everyone can use the latest information.

collaborative learning system a work environment that allows problem solving participation by all team members

Apps Become Big Business

Apps—small software programs that users download to run on cell phones and iPods—are becoming big business. Some apps, such as the game *Trism*, are just for fun; some, such as *Recorder*, which records voices with the touch of a button, have both business and personal uses.

Since Apple first started its App Store, users have downloaded more than 10 billion apps for its iPhones, iPods, and iPads. Apps are so popular that on the very first day Apple opened its Mac App Store, users downloaded 1 million apps created exclusively for Macintosh computers. With Microsoft, Google, and many other companies setting up sites featuring apps for digital devices, experts see app sales soaring to $30 billion within a few years. No wonder thousands of entrepreneurs are busy developing and marketing apps for consumer and business use.

Steve Demeter, who created *Trism* for the iPhone, is a successful app entrepreneur. When he began, he was employed as a software developer for a major bank but spent nights and weekends writing and polishing the code for *Trism*. After his game was ready for release, Demeter submitted it for App Store approval and sent copies to influential

reviewers. The game was an instant sensation, generating thousands of dollars in sales in its first two months. Now Demeter is a full-time app developer, with a number of promising ideas in the works. He tells budding app entrepreneurs to ask themselves: "Does my app convey something unique and interesting in ten to fifteen seconds?"

Sources: Gregg Keizer, "Apple to Give Away $10K as App Store Nears 10B Downloads," *ComputerWorld*, January 14, 2011, www.computerworld.com; Bill Shea, "New iPad May Fuel 'Gold Rush' for App Makers," *Crain's Detroit Business*, February 1, 2010, p. 1; Douglas MacMillan, Peter Burrows, and Spencer E. Ante, "Inside the App Economy," *BusinessWeek*, October 22, 2009, www.businessweek.com; Gary Marshall, "App Store Millionaires Share Their Secrets," *Tech Radar*, February 5, 2009, www.techradar.com/news/; Kira Bindrim, "Big App-le, indeed: Rush is on," *Crain's New York Business*, October 19, 2009, p. 2.

Recruiting and Training Employees

A common icon on most corporate Web sites is a link to "Careers" or "Employment Opportunities." Firms looking for people with specialized skills can post their employee needs on their Web sites and reach potential candidates from around the globe. This is an extremely important method of recruiting employees for positions where labor shortages are common and individuals with the *right* skills are in high demand.

Furthermore, software programs can help large firms such as GE, ExxonMobil, and General Mills to establish a database of potential employees. This is an especially important function for a firm that receives thousands of unsolicited employment applications from people all over the world. The cost of organizing and processing this information is high, but software can reduce this expense when compared with a paper-based system.

Large and midsize companies also spend a great deal of money on educational and training programs for employees. By distributing information about the firm, products and services, new procedures, and general information to employees through the Internet for reading and study at convenient times and places, firms can reduce training costs dramatically. Furthermore, revision and distribution of changes to this type of information are much easier if the information is provided on the company's Web site.

Telecommuting, Virtual Offices, and Technology

Today more and more employees are using telecommuting, virtual offices, and technology to perform typical work activities. In Chapter 10, *telecommuting* was defined as employees working at home all the time or for a portion of the work week. Although we do not want to cover the same topic again, it is important to understand how technology enables workers to work any place—at home, in an airport,

✳ Concept Check

☐ Describe the three types of computer applications that help employees, managers, and executives make smart decisions.

☐ How can computers and software help a firm's employees communicate, increase sales, and recruit and train employees?

☐ What are the advantages and disadvantages of telecommuting and virtual offices?

in a hotel room, or even in an automobile. Simply put: The ability to use technology—computers, e-mail, software, the Internet, and phones—makes telecommuting and virtual offices a reality. Although there are different definitions of a virtual office, for our purposes a **virtual office** allows employees to work at any place where they have access to computers, software, and other technology that enables them to perform their normal work activities.

For both employees and employers, the chief benefits of telecommuting and virtual offices include:

- Higher job satisfaction and increased productivity.
- Greater independence and flexible work hours.
- Reduced commuting costs and time required to commute to an office.
- Lower employee turnover.
- New employment opportunities for employees with physical disabilities, new mothers, and people living in remote areas.

Typical challenges for telecommuters include feelings of isolation and exploitation, working too many hours, lack of support from managers, inability to access needed files and information, and fear of performance evaluations. Still, employers have found that if the right person is selected, the benefits of telecommuting and virtual offices outweigh the disadvantages. The key is often finding the right person.

Business Applications Software

Early software typically performed a single function. Today, however, *integrated* software combines many functions in a single package. Integrated packages allow for the easy *linking* of text, numerical data, graphs, photographs, and even audiovisual clips. A business report prepared using the Microsoft Office package, for instance, can include all these components.

Integration offers at least two other benefits. Once data have been entered into an application in an integrated package, the data can be used in another integrated package without having to reenter the data again. In addition, once a user learns one application, it is much easier to learn another application in an integrated package. From a career standpoint, you should realize that employers will assume that you possess, or will possess after training, a high degree of working comfort with several of the software applications described in Table 14-3.

Why do you need a laptop and a cell phone?
Answer: While there are many reasons why people purchase laptops and cell phones, new technology enables people to obtain information, improve communications, and increase productivity. For many employees, the use of technology has enabled them to work at home or any place where they have access to computers, software, and other technology.

© michaeljung/Shutterstock

TABLE 14-3: Current Business Application Software Used to Improve Productivity

Word processing	Users can prepare and edit written documents and store them in the computer or on a memory device.
Desktop publishing	Users can combine text and graphics in professional reports, newsletters, and pamphlets.
Accounting	Users can record routine financial transactions and prepare financial reports at the end of the accounting period.
Database management	Users can electronically store large amounts of data and transform the data into information.
Graphics	Users can display and print pictures, drawings, charts, and diagrams.
Spreadsheets	Users can organize numerical data into a grid of rows and columns.

© Cengage Learning 2013

virtual office allows employees to work at any place where they have access to computers, software, and other technology that enables them to perform their normal work activities

SUSTAIN THE PLANET

The Green Grid

IT is going green. Cisco, IBM, Verizon, Walt Disney, and the other corporate members of the Green Grid are embracing sustainability by learning how to improve the efficiency of their information networks and data centers. Take a look: www.thegreengrid.org.

USING COMPUTERS AND THE INTERNET TO OBTAIN INFORMATION

We live in a rapidly changing **information society**—that is, a society in which large groups of employees generate or depend on information to perform their jobs. Today, businesses are using the Internet to find and distribute information to global users. The Internet is also used for communicating between the firm's employees and its customers. Finally, businesses use the Internet to gather information about competitors' products, prices, and other business strategies. Clearly, computers, software, and the Internet are here to stay.

Computers, Software, the Internet, and Networks

Before beginning our discussion of how both individuals and business firms are using the Internet, let's begin with a basic review of the components—computer hardware, system software, and application software—needed to access the Internet.

- *Computer hardware* is the physical components of a computer. Examples include the hard disk drive, keyboard, mouse, and monitor.
- *System software* is computer software designed to operate the computer hardware. Examples include Microsoft Windows and Mac OS X operating systems.
- *Application software (also known as application or simply "app")* is computer software designed to help the user perform specific tasks. Examples include Quicken accounting software and Microsoft Office software.

Using a computer and software, it is now possible to access the Internet. The **Internet** is a worldwide network of computers linked through telecommunications. Enabling users around the world to communicate with each other electronically, the Internet provides access to a huge array of information sources. The Internet's most commonly used network for finding information is the World Wide Web. The **World Wide Web** (or more simply, **the Web**) is the Internet's multimedia environment of audio, visual, and text data.

In addition to business sites, the World Wide Web has a wide array of government and institutional sites that provide information to a firm's employees and the general public. There are also online sites available for most of the popular business periodicals.

An **intranet** is a smaller version of the Internet for use within a firm. Using a series of customized Web pages, employees can quickly find information about their firm as well as connect to external sources. For instance, an employee might use the intranet to access the firm's policy documents on customer warranties or even take a company-designed course on new products and how to introduce them to customers. Generally, intranet sites are protected, and users must supply both a user name and a password to gain access to a company's intranet site. *Note:* Although the term *intranet* was popular in the 1990s, it was often confused with the Internet. Although still used today, many computer experts use the term *LAN* (which stands for local-area network) to describe intranet applications used within a company. More information about different types of computer networks, including LANs, is provided below.

Both the Internet and intranets are examples of a computer network. A **computer network** is a group of two or more computers linked together that allows users

LEARNING OBJECTIVE

5 Analyze how computers and technology change the way information is acquired, organized, and used.

information society a society in which large groups of employees generate or depend on information to perform their jobs

Internet a worldwide network of computers linked through telecommunications

World Wide Web (the Web) the Internet's multimedia environment of audio, visual, and text data

intranet a smaller version of the Internet for use within a firm's computer network

computer network a group of two or more computers linked together that allows users to share data and information

to share data and information. Today, two basic types of networks affect the way employees and the general public obtain data and information. A **wide-area network (WAN)** is a network that connects computers over a large geographic area, such as a city, a state, or even the world. The world's largest public WAN is the Internet.[2] In addition to the Internet, other WANs include private corporate networks (sometimes referred to as virtual private networks, or VPNs) and research networks. A **local-area network (LAN)** is a network that connects computers that are in close proximity to each other, such as an office building or a college campus. LANs allow users to share files, printers, games, or other applications.[3] Typically, LANs also allow users to connect to the Internet.

Accessing the Internet

The search for available information often begins with a specific Web site address or a search engine. Every Web site on the Internet is identified by its Uniform Resource Locator (URL), which acts as its address. To connect to a site, you enter its URL in your Web browser. A Web browser such as Windows Internet Explorer or Mozilla Firefox is software that helps users to navigate around the Internet and connect to different Web sites. The URLs of most corporate sites are similar to the organizations' real names. For instance, you can reach IBM by entering www.ibm.com. The first part of the entry, *http*, sets the software protocols for proper transfer of information between your computer and the one at the site to which you are connecting. *Http* stands for *HyperText Transfer Protocol*. Both http and www are frequently omitted from a URL because your computer adds them automatically when you enter the rest of the address. *HyperText* refers to words or phrases highlighted or underlined on a Web page; when you select these, they link you to other Web sites.

To find a particular Web site, you can take advantage of several free search programs available on the Web, such as Google, Yahoo!, and AltaVista. To locate a search engine, enter its URL in your browser. Some URLs for popular search engines are www.altavista.com, www.google.com, and www.yahoo.com.

The home page for many search engines provides a short list of primary topic divisions, such as careers, news, shopping, yellow pages, and weather, as well as a search window where you can enter the particular topic you are looking for.

Creating Web Sites

Today, employees and the general public connect to the Internet, enter a Web address, or use a search engine to access information. That information is presented on a Web site created and maintained by business firms; agencies of federal, state, or local governments; or educational or similar organizations. Because a Web site should provide accurate information, great care is required when creating a Web site.

Personal App Do you use your smart-phone to look at Web sites? How many of the sites use layouts and graphics that look particularly good on the small screen? Some companies now design "mobile" sites especially for smart-phone users, so watch for these as you surf the Web.

What the Web site says about a company is important and should be developed carefully to portray the "right" image. Therefore, it is understandable that a firm

Top Two U.S. Web Sites

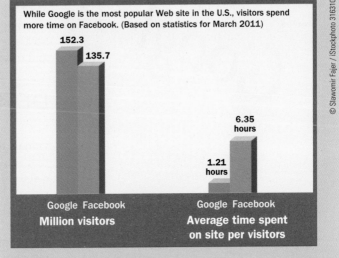

While Google is the most popular Web site in the U.S., visitors spend more time on Facebook. (Based on statistics for March 2011)

152.3   135.7

6.35 hours

1.21 hours

Google Facebook
Million visitors

Google Facebook
Average time spent on site per visitors

© Slawomir Fajer / iStockphoto 3163103

Source: "Top U.S. Web Brands," The Nielsen.com Web site at www.nielsen.com (accessed April 13, 2011).

Concept Check ✱

☐ Explain the difference between the Internet and an intranet. What types of information does each of these networks provide?

☐ What is the difference between a wide area network (WAN) and a local area network (LAN)?

☐ What factors should be considered when a firm is developing a Web page?

wide-area network (WAN) a network that connects computers over a large geographic area, such as a city, a state, or even the world

local-area network (LAN) a network that connects computers that are in close proximity to each other, such as an office building or a college campus

Google—the number 1 search engine. When Google created its now famous Web site, developers chose a rather simple opening screen with just the Google name, a search box, and very little else. Users enter terms or words to describe the type of information they want. Then with the click of their mouse, they can find information about products and services, the latest news stories, investment research, and even information about new movies and the current weather.

© Bloomberg via Getty Images

6 Explain the meaning of e-business.

e-business (electronic business) the organized effort of individuals to produce and sell, for a profit, the products and services that satisfy society's needs *through the facilities available on the Internet*

outsourcing the process of finding outside vendors and suppliers that provide professional help, parts, or materials at a lower cost

without the internal human resources to design and launch its Web site will turn to the talents of creative experts available through Web consulting firms. Regardless of whether the Web site is developed by the firm's employees or outside consultants, the suggestions listed in Table 14-4 should be considered when creating materials for a firm's Web site.

Once a Web site is established, most companies prefer to manage their sites on their own computers. An alternative approach is to pay a hosting service that often will provide guaranteed user accessibility, e-business shopping software, site-updating services, and other specialized services.

DEFINING E-BUSINESS

In Chapter 1, we defined *business* as the organized effort of individuals to produce and sell, for a profit, the products and services that satisfy society's needs. In a simple sense, then, **e-business**, or **electronic business,** can be defined as the organized effort of individuals to produce and sell, for a profit, the products and services that satisfy society's needs *through the facilities available on the Internet*. Sometimes people use the term *e-commerce* instead of *e-business*. In a strict sense, e-business is used when one is speaking about all business activities and practices conducted on the Internet by an individual firm or industry. On the other hand, e-commerce is a part of e-business and usually refers only to buying and selling activities conducted online. In this chapter, we generally use the term *e-business* because of its broader definition and scope. As you will see in the remainder of this chapter, e-business is transforming key business activities.

Organizing e-Business Resources

As noted in Chapter 1, to be organized, a business must combine *human, material, informational,* and *financial resources*. This is true of e-business, too (see Figure 14-5), but in this case, the resources may be more specialized than in a typical business. For example, people who can design, create, and maintain Web sites are only a fraction of the specialized human resources required by e-businesses. Material resources must include specialized computers, sophisticated equipment and software, and high-speed Internet connections. Computer programs that track the number of customers who view a firm's Web site are generally among the specialized informational resources required. Financial resources, the money required to start and maintain the firm and allow it to grow, usually reflect greater participation by individual entrepreneurs, venture capitalists, and investors willing to invest in a high-tech firm instead of conventional financial sources such as banks.

In an effort to reduce the cost of specialized resources that are used in e-business, many firms have turned to outsourcing. **Outsourcing** is the process of finding outside vendors and suppliers that provide professional help, parts, or materials at a lower cost. For example, a firm that needs specialized software to complete a project may turn to an outside firm located in another part of the United States, India, or an Eastern European country.

Satisfying Needs Online

Think for a moment about this question: "Why do people use the Internet?" For most people, the Internet can be used to purchase products or services and as a source of information and interaction with other people. Today, more people use the Internet to satisfy these needs than ever before. Let's start with two basic assumptions.

TABLE 14-4: Tips for Web Site Development

Whether you build your site from scratch, use a Web design software program, or hire outside professionals, make sure that your Web site conveys not only the "right" image but also useful information about your company or organization.

1.	Develop a theme.	A Web site is like a book and needs a theme to tie ideas together and tell an interesting story.
2.	Determine how much information to include on your site.	Get a handle on the type and amount of information that will be contained on your site. Although it is tempting to include everything, you must be selective.
3.	Plan the layout of your site.	Think about how you want your site to look. Web sites that combine color, art, and links to narrative material are the most useful.
4.	Add graphics.	Obtain graphics that illustrate the types of data and information contained on your site. Choose colors and photographs carefully to make sure that they add rather than detract from the site.
5.	Outline the material for each page.	Generally, the opening, or home, page contains basic information with links to additional pages that provide more detailed information.
6.	Develop plans to update the site.	It is important to develop a plan to update your site on a regular basis. Too often, sites are "forgotten" and contain dated or inaccurate material.
7.	Make sure that your site is easy to use.	Stand back and take a look at your site. Is your site confusing, or does it provide a road map to get from point A to point B? If you have trouble getting information, others will too.

FIGURE 14-5: Combining e-Business Resources

While all businesses use four resources (human, material, informational, and financial), these resources typically are more specialized when used in an e-business.

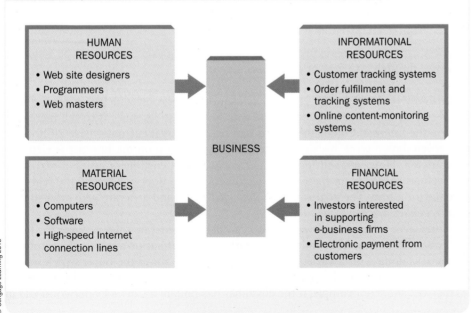

One way to reduce customer service costs. Many American companies are outsourcing customer service to high-tech companies in India. The main reason: lower labor costs for educated and affordable customer service representatives. In this photo, future customer service employees attend a class at Infosys Technologies' training center at its sprawling corporate campus in Mysore, India.

© AP Images/Gurinder Osan

- The Internet has created some new customer needs that did not exist before creation of the Internet.
- e-Businesses can satisfy those needs, as well as more traditional ones.

Personal App These days, you can find e-businesses that buy or sell almost anything. Many will help you recognize a new need by offering free trials of apps, games, or other digital products. This is a great way to find out whether the digital product is useful, convenient, and worth buying.

Restoration Hardware (www.restorationhardware.com), for instance, gives customers anywhere in the world access to the same virtual store of hardware and decorative items. And at eBay's global auction site, customers can, for a small fee, buy and sell almost anything. In each of these examples, customers can use the Internet to purchase a product or service.

In addition to purchasing products, the Internet can be used by both individuals and business firms to obtain information. For example:

- Internet users can access newspapers, magazines, and radio and television programming at a time and place convenient to them.
- The Internet provides the opportunity for two-way interaction between an Internet firm and the viewer. A Web site like www.cnn.com and other news-content sites encourage dialogue among users in chat rooms and exchanges with the writers of articles posted to the site.
- Customers can respond to information on the Internet by requesting more information about a product or posing specific questions, which may lead to purchasing a product or service.
- Finally, the Internet allows customers to choose the content they are offered. Knowing the interests of a customer allows an Internet firm to direct appropriate, smart advertising to a specific customer. For the advertiser, knowing that its advertisements are being directed to the most likely customers represents a better way to spend advertising dollars.

Creating e-Business Profit

Business firms can increase profits either by increasing sales revenue or by reducing expenses through a variety of e-business activities.

INCREASING SALES REVENUE Each source of sales revenue flowing into a firm is referred to as a **revenue stream**. One way to increase revenues is to sell merchandise on the Internet. Online merchants can reach a global customer base 24 hours a day, seven days a week because the opportunity to shop on the Internet is virtually unrestricted. However, shifting revenues earned from customers inside a real store to revenues earned from these same customers online does not create any real new revenue for a firm. The goal is to find *new customers* and generate *new sales* so that *total revenues are increased*.

Intelligent information systems also can help to generate sales revenue for Internet firms such as Amazon.com. Such systems store information about each customer's purchases, along with a variety of other information about the buyer's preferences. Using this information, the system can assist the customer the next time he or she visits the Web site. For example, if the customer has bought a Carrie Underwood CD in

revenue stream a source of revenue flowing into a firm

Want to shop 24 hours a day, seven days a week? Then go to the Kohl's Web site. For many retailers, a new way to increase sales revenues (and profits) is to sell merchandise on the Internet. Online customers can shop 24 hours a day, seven days a week. Ultimately, the goal for a retailer like Kohl's is to use their Web site to find *new* customers and generate new sales so that *total revenues are increased.*

the past, the system might suggest CDs by similar artists who have appeared on the popular televised talent-search program *American Idol.*

Although some customers in certain situations may not make a purchase online, the existence of the firm's Web site and the services and information it provides may lead to increased sales in the firm's physical stores. For example, www.honda.com can provide basic comparative information for shoppers so that they are better prepared for their visit to an automobile showroom.

In addition to selling products or services online, e-business revenue streams are created by advertising placed on Web pages and by subscription fees charged for access to online services and content. For example, Hoover's Online (www.hoovers.com), a comprehensive source for company and industry information, makes some of its online content free for anyone who visits the site, but more detailed data are available only by paid subscription. In addition, it receives revenue from companies that are called sponsors, who advertise their products and services on Hoover's Web site.

Many Internet firms that distribute news, magazine and newspaper articles, and similar content generate revenue from commissions earned from sellers of products linked to the site. Online shopping malls, for example, now provide groups of related vendors of electronic equipment and computer hardware and software with a new method of selling their products and services. In many cases, the vendors share online sales revenues with the site owners.

REDUCING EXPENSES Reducing expenses is the second major way in which e-business can help to increase profitability. Providing online access to information that customers want can reduce the cost of dealing with customers. Sprint Nextel (www.sprint.com), for instance, is just one company that maintains an extensive Web site where potential customers can learn more about cell phone products and services and current customers can access personal account information, send e-mail questions to customer service, and purchase additional products or services.

Concept Check *

☐ What are the four factors contained in the definition of e-business?

☐ How do e-businesses generate revenue streams, reduce expenses, and earn a profit?

With such extensive online services, Sprint Nextel does not have to maintain as many physical store locations as it would without these online services. We examine more examples of how e-business contributes to profitability throughout this chapter, especially as we focus on some of the business models for activity on the Internet.

LEARNING OBJECTIVE
7 Describe the fundamental models of e-business.

FUNDAMENTAL MODELS OF E-BUSINESS

One way to get a better sense of how businesses are adapting to the opportunities available on the Internet is to identify e-business models. A **business model** represents a group of common characteristics and methods of doing business to generate sales revenues and reduce expenses. Each of the models discussed in this section represents a primary e-business model. Regardless of the type of business model, planning often depends on if the e-business is a new firm or an existing firm adding an online presence—see Figure 14-6. It also helps to remember the definition of e-business that was included at the beginning of the last section. Finally, keep in mind that to generate sales revenues and earn profits, a business—especially an e-business—must meet the needs of its customers.

FIGURE 14-6 **Planning for a New Internet Business or Building an Online Presence for an Existing Business**

The approach taken to creating an e-business plan will depend on whether you are establishing a new Internet business or adding an online component to an existing business.

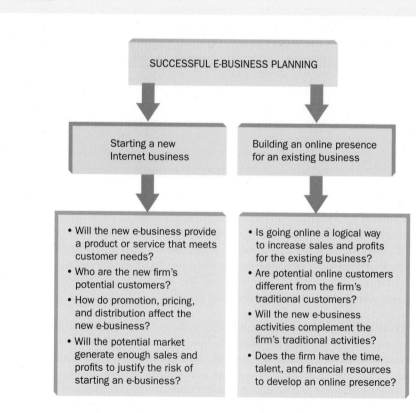

SUCCESSFUL E-BUSINESS PLANNING

Starting a new Internet business

Building an online presence for an existing business

- Will the new e-business provide a product or service that meets customer needs?
- Who are the new firm's potential customers?
- How do promotion, pricing, and distribution affect the new e-business?
- Will the potential market generate enough sales and profits to justify the risk of starting an e-business?

- Is going online a logical way to increase sales and profits for the existing business?
- Are potential online customers different from the firm's traditional customers?
- Will the new e-business activities complement the firm's traditional activities?
- Does the firm have the time, talent, and financial resources to develop an online presence?

© Cengage Learning 2013

business model represents a group of common characteristics and methods of doing business to generate sales revenues and reduce expenses

Business-to-Business (B2B) Model

Many e-businesses can be distinguished from others simply by their customer focus. For instance, some firms use the Internet mainly to conduct business with other businesses. These firms are generally referred to as having a **business-to-business** (or **B2B**) **model**.

When examining B2B firms, two clear types emerge. In the first type, the focus is simply on facilitating sales transactions between businesses. For example, Dell manufactures computers to specifications that customers enter on the Dell Web site. A large portion of Dell's online orders are from corporate clients who are well-informed about the products they need and are looking for fairly priced, high-quality computer products that will be delivered quickly. Basically, by building only what is ordered, Dell reduces storage and carrying costs and rarely is stuck with unsold inventory. By dealing directly with Dell, customers eliminate costs associated with wholesalers, suppliers, and retailers, thereby helping to reduce the price they pay for equipment.

A second, more complex type of B2B model involves a company and its suppliers. Today, suppliers use the Internet to bid on products and services they wish to sell to a customer and learn about the customer's rules and procedures that must be followed. For example, Ford has developed a B2B model to link thousands of suppliers that sell the automobile maker parts worth billions of dollars each year. Although the B2B site is expensive to start and maintain, there are significant savings for Ford. Given the potential savings, it is no wonder that many other manufacturers and their suppliers are beginning to use the same kind of B2B systems that are used by Ford. In fact, suppliers know that to be a "preferred" supplier for a large firm that may purchase large quantities of parts, supplies, or raw materials, they must be tied into the purchaser's B2B system.

Business-to-Consumer (B2C) Model

In contrast to the B2B model, firms such as Barnesandnoble.com and Landsend.com clearly are focused on individual consumers. These companies are referred to as having a **business-to-consumer** (or **B2C**) **model**. In a B2C situation, understanding how consumers behave online is critical to a firm's success. Typically, a business firm that uses a B2C model must answer the following questions:

- Will consumers use Web sites merely to simplify and speed up comparison shopping?
- Will consumers purchase services and products online or end up buying at a traditional retail store?
- What sorts of products and services are best suited for online consumer shopping?

In addition to providing round-the-clock global access to all kinds of products and services, B2C firms often attempt to build long-term relationships with their customers. Often, firms will make a special effort to make sure that the customer is satisfied and that problems, if any, are solved quickly. Specialized software also can help build good customer relationships. Tracking the decisions and buying preferences as customers navigate a Web site, for instance, helps management to make well-informed decisions about how best to serve such customers. In essence, this is Orbitz's (www.orbitz.com) online selling approach. By tracking and analyzing customer data, Orbitz can provide individualized service to its customers. Although a "little special attention" may increase the cost of doing business for a B2C firm, the customer's repeated purchases will repay the investment many times over.

Today, B2B and B2C models are the most popular business models for e-business. And yet, there are other business models that perform specialized e-business activities to generate revenues. Most of the business models described in Table 14-5 are modified versions of the B2B and B2C models.

Apple iTunes—everything consumers need to be entertained. One company that uses the business-to-consumer (B2C) model is Apple. By making music, videos, and other electronic media available in its iTunes Store, the company generates sales revenues and profits while meeting the needs of its customers.

Image courtesy of Susan Van Etten

Concept Check ✱

☐ What are the two fundamental e-business models?

☐ Assume that you are the owner of a small company that produces outdoor living furniture. Describe how you could use the B2C business model to sell your products to consumers.

business-to-business (or B2B) model a model used by firms that conduct business with other businesses

business-to-consumer (or B2C) model a model used by firms that focus on conducting business with individual consumers

TABLE 14-5: Other Business Models that Perform Specialized e-Business Activities

Although modified versions of B2B or B2C, these business models perform specialized e-business activities to generate revenues.

Advertising e-business model	Advertisements that are displayed on a firm's Web site in return for a fee. Examples include pop-up and banner advertisements on search engines and other popular Internet sites.
Brokerage e-business model	Online marketplaces where buyers and sellers are brought together to facilitate exchange of goods and services. Examples include eBay (www.ebay.com), which provides a site for buying and selling virtually anything.
Peer-to-peer (P2P) model	Peer-to-peer software allows individuals to share information over the Internet. Examples include BitTorrent (www.bittorrent.com) which allows users to share large amounts of data.
Subscription and pay-per-view e-business models	Content that is available only to users who pay a fee to gain access to a Web site. Examples include investment information provided by Standard & Poor's (www.standardandpoors.com) and business research provided by Forrester Research, Inc. (www.forrester.com).

© Cengage Learning 2013

LEARNING OBJECTIVE

8 Explore the factors that will affect the future of e-business.

THE FUTURE OF COMPUTER TECHNOLOGY, THE INTERNET, AND E-BUSINESS

Since the beginning of commercial activity on the Internet, developments in computer technology and e-business have been rapid and formidable with spectacular successes such as Google, eBay, and Yahoo! However, a larger-than-usual number of technology companies and e-business firms struggled or even failed during the recent economic crisis. Today, most firms involved in computer technology and e-business use a more intelligent approach to development. The long-term view held by the vast majority of analysts is that the Internet and e-business will continue to expand along with related computer technologies. For example, according to Forrester Research, Inc., the popularity and growth of consumer broadband access to the Internet have pushed marketers to allocate more money to interactive marketing that utilizes computer technology to understand the customer's purchasing decisions. As a result, Forrester predicts that advertisers will spend approximately $55 billion on interactive marketing in 2014.[4] Marketers will shift away from traditional media and spend more advertising dollars on search engines, social media sites, other Internet sites, and e-mail marketing.

Internet Growth Potential

To date, only a small percentage of the global population uses the Internet. In 2010, estimates suggest that about 2 billion of the nearly 7 billion people in the world use the Web.[5] Clearly, there is much more growth opportunity. Americans comprise 12 percent of all users.[6] Of the 310 million people making up the American population, 240 million use the Internet. With approximately 77 percent of the American population already being Internet users, potential growth in the United States is limited.[7] On the other hand, the number of Internet users in the world's developing countries is expected to increase dramatically. There will also be additional growth as more people begin to use smart-phones and mobile devices. Because of worldwide growth and an increase in wireless computing devices, Computer Industry Almanac projects that worldwide users will exceed 2.6 billion by 2015.[8]

Firms that adapt existing business models to an online environment will continue to dominate development. For example, books, CDs, clothing, hotel accommodations, car rentals, and travel reservations are products and services well-suited to online buying and selling. These products or services will continue to be sold in the traditional way, as well as in a more cost-effective and efficient fashion over the Internet.

Although the number of global Internet users is expected to increase by 2015, that's only part of the story. Perhaps the more important question is why people are using the Internet. Internet users may want to obtain information about a firm's products or services. As mentioned earlier in this chapter, all experts agree that the number of businesses using the e-business B2B or B2C models to sell products or services or to provide customers with information is increasing. All experts agree that this trend will continue.

Social Media

In addition to purchasing products or services online or obtaining information about products or services, many people use the Internet to become part of a social network. In addition to advertising through social media—a topic discussed in the marketing chapters—the Internet is often used to promote social network sites. A **social network site** is a Web site (often called a social site) that functions like an online community of Internet

A new use for Facebook. Today many retailers like The Container Store are using Facebook and other social network sites to reach out and "touch" consumers. It's just one more way to provide information to consumers that want to purchase the firm's products or services.

users where you can share your personal profile, messages, and photographs with family and friends. All social sites also provide users with a method to meet other people and gather and share information about special interests, hobbies, religion, and politics. For businesses, social networks represent a marketing opportunity that is different than more traditional marketing activities. And using social media for advertising and marketing activities is often less expensive than traditional marketing activities. As a result, more and more firms like Dell Computer, Starbucks, and Macy's use social sites to post information about products and services and obtain information from customers. The most common social networking sites include Facebook, Twitter, MySpace, and blogs. Some social sites, like LinkedIn, can also be useful when you are looking for employment or developing a network of professionals to help you advance your career. *CAUTION:* Prospective employers often use information on social sites to learn about future employees. Reading profiles and viewing photographs has become standard procedure for human resources departments in many companies. Therefore, think before you post inappropriate language or photographs on your social site.

Personal App Although marketing may not be the first thing that comes to mind when you use social media, lots of companies want you to "like" them and spread the word about their products. Keep your eyes open for companies on social networking sites, and you just might grab a special deal.

Ethical and Legal Concerns

The social and legal concerns for the Internet and e-business extend beyond those shared by all businesses. Essentially, the Internet is a new "frontier" without borders and without much control by governments or other organizations.

ETHICS AND SOCIAL RESPONSIBILITY Socially responsible and ethical behavior by individuals and businesses on the Internet are major concerns. For example, **spamming**, the sending of massive amounts of unsolicited e-mails, is an ethical issue. Sorting through what many recipients view as *junk e-mail* is, if nothing else, a waste of resources that costs the individual time and their employer money.

Another ethically questionable practice in cyberspace is the unauthorized access and use of information discovered through computerized tracking of users once they

social network site a Web site (often called a social site) that functions like an online community of Internet users where you can share your profile, messages, and photographs with family and friends

spamming the sending of massive amounts of unsolicited e-mails

are connected to the Internet. Essentially, a user may visit a Web page and unknowingly receive a small piece of software code called a **cookie**. This cookie can track where the user goes on the Internet and measure how long the user stays at any particular Web site. Although this type of software may produce valuable customer information, it also can be viewed as an invasion of privacy, especially since users may not even be aware that their movements are being monitored.

Besides the unauthorized use of cookies to track online behavior, there are several other threats to users' privacy and confidentiality. Monitoring an employee's **log-file records**, which record the Web sites visited, may be intended to help employers police unauthorized Internet use on company time. However, the same records can also give a firm the opportunity to observe what otherwise might be considered private and confidential information. Today, legal experts suggest that, at the very least, employers need to disclose the level of surveillance to their employees and consider the corporate motivation for monitoring employees' behavior.

Some firms also practice data mining. **Data mining** refers to the practice of searching through data records looking for useful information. For instance, assume an individual frequents multiple Web sites that provide information about a life-threatening disease. If this information is sent to an insurance company, the company might refuse to insure this individual, thinking that there is a higher risk associated with someone who wants more information about this disease.

INTERNET CRIME Because the Internet is often regarded as an unregulated frontier, both individuals and business users must be particularly aware of online risks and dangers. For example, a general term that describes software designed to infiltrate a computer system without the user's consent is **malware**. Malware is often based on the creator's criminal or malicious intent and can include computer viruses, spyware, deceptive adware, and other software capable of criminal activities. A more specific term used to describe disruptive software is computer virus. A **computer virus**, which can originate anywhere in the world, is a software code designed to disrupt normal computer activities. The potentially devastating effects of both malware and computer viruses have given rise to a software security industry.

In addition to the risk of computer viruses, identity theft is one of the most common computer crimes that affects both individuals and business users. A 2011 study conducted by Javelin Strategy and Research determined that more than 8 million Americans had personal information (Social Security number, bank or credit card account number, name and address, driver's license number, etc.) used by criminals for illegal activity.[9] Most consumers are also concerned about fraud. Because the Internet allows easy creation of Web sites, access from anywhere in the world, and anonymity for the creator, it is almost impossible to know with certainty that the Web site, organization, or individuals that you believe you are interacting with are what they seem. As always, caveat emptor ("let the buyer beware") is a good suggestion to follow whether on the Internet or not.

Future Challenges for Computer Technology and e-Business

Today, there is more information available than ever before. Although individuals and business users may think we are at the point of information overload, the amount of information will only increase in the future. In order to obtain more information in the future, both individuals and business users must consider the cost of obtaining information and computer technology. In an effort to reduce expenses, some companies are using cloud computing. **Cloud computing** is a type of computer usage in which services stored on the Internet are provided to users on a temporary basis. Today, many new and existing technology companies, including Amazon, Rackspace, Microsoft, and Google, are offering cloud computing services. When cloud computing is used, a third party makes processing power, software applications, databases, and storage available for use on-demand from anywhere, via the Internet. Instead of running

cookie a small piece of software sent by a Web site that tracks an individual's Internet use

log-file records files that store a record of the Web sites visited

data mining the practice of searching through data records looking for useful information

malware a general term that describes software designed to infiltrate a computer system without the user's consent

computer virus a software code designed to disrupt normal computer operations

cloud computing a type of computer usage in which services stored on the Internet are provided to users on a temporary basis

ETHICAL
challenges & successful
SOLUTIONS

How Green Is Cloud Computing?

Are businesses and consumers helping to protect the planet by shifting to cloud computing? Certainly, a lot of trees and energy would be saved if business firms and people stored documents, photos, and other items in the cloud instead of printing them. And the centralized data facilities that house cloud-computing services are designed for maximum efficiency, with industrial-strength equipment and the latest power-saving technology. According to a report from the IT consulting firm Accenture, commissioned by Microsoft, businesses of all sizes could dramatically reduce their energy consumption by moving to the cloud.

Yet cloud computing is far from squeaky green. An enormous amount of electricity is needed to keep even the most efficient cloud-computing facility running smoothly on a 24/7 basis. With demand rising and many new cloud-computing facilities being built worldwide, the industry's energy consumption is skyrocketing. Even worse, depending on where data centers are located, that electricity may be generated by coal rather than by more eco-friendly sources such as water or wind. Cloud-computing companies rarely disclose specifics about energy sources and consumption, however, which means users have few hard facts on which to base their decisions.

Although choosing between traditional technology and cloud computing poses an ethical dilemma for green-tech fans today, the situation may be quite different in a few years. Cloud-computing giants such as Google and Amazon are already stepping up their investments in green energy. They're also in discussions with environmental activists and government policy-makers to find new ways of making the cloud greener, year by year.

Sources: Corbin Hiar, "How Green Is Facebook, Microsoft Push into Cloud Computing?" *PBS MediaShift*, January 12, 2011, www.pbs.org/mediashift; Heather Clancy, "More Apparent Evidence of Cloud Computing's Inherent Green-ness," *ZDNet*, December 6, 2010, www.zdnet.com; Heather Clancy, "Microsoft-backed Research Suggests Big Energy Reductions from Cloud," *ZDNet*, November 4, 2010, www.zdnet.com.

---

software and storing data on their employer's computer network or their individual computers, employees log onto the third party's system and use (and pay for) only the applications and data storage they actually need. In addition to just cost, there are a number of external and internal factors that a business must consider.

Although the environmental forces at work are complex, it is useful to think of them as either *internal* or *external* forces that affect computer technology and e-business. Internal environmental forces are those that are closely associated with the actions and decisions taking place within a firm. As shown in Figure 14-7, typical internal forces include a firm's planning activities, organization structure, human resources, management decisions, information database, and available financing. A shortage of skilled employees needed for a specialized project, for instance, can undermine a firm's ability to sell its services to clients. Unlike the external environmental forces affecting the firm, internal forces such as this one are more likely to be under the direct control of management. In this case, management can either hire the needed staff or choose to pass over a prospective project.

In contrast, external environmental forces are factors affecting e-business planning that originate from outside the organization. These forces are unlikely to be controllable by an e-business firm. Instead, managers and employees of an e-business firm generally will react to these forces, attempting to shield the organization from any undue negative effects and finding ways to take advantage of opportunities in the ever-changing e-business environment. The primary external environmental forces affecting e-business planning include globalization, demographic, societal, economic, competitive, technological, and political and legal forces.

In this chapter, we have explored a business firm's need for information and how a computer, the Internet, and technology can help people to obtain the information they need. We also examined how e-business is changing the way that firms do business. In Chapter 15, we examine the accounting process, which is a major source of information for business.

Concept Check ✱

☐ Experts predict that the Internet will continue to expand along with related technologies. What effect will this expansion have on businesses in the future?

☐ What is the difference between internal and external forces that affect an e-business? How do they change the way an e-business operates?

FIGURE 14-7: **Internal and External Forces that Affect an e-Business**

Today, managers and employees of an e-business must respond to internal forces within the organization and external forces outside the organization.

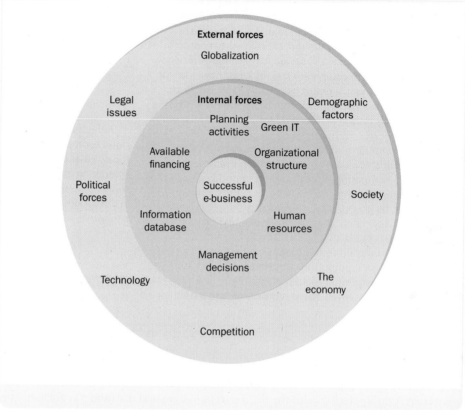

Get Flashcards, Quizzes, Games, Crosswords, and more @ **www.cengagebrain.com**

SUMMARY

1 Examine how information can reduce risk when making a decision.

The more information a manager has, the less risk there is that a decision will be incorrect. Information produces knowledge and empowers managers and employees to make better decisions. Without accurate and timely information, individual performance will be undermined. Consequently, so will the performance of the entire organization. Because of the volume of information they receive each day and their need to make decisions on a daily basis, businesspeople use information rules to shorten the time spent analyzing choices. Information rules emerge when business research confirms the same results each time it studies the same or a similar set of circumstances. Although many people use the terms *data* and *information* interchangeably, there is a difference. Data are numerical or verbal descriptions that usually result from some sort of measurement. Information is data presented in a form that is useful for a specific purpose. A database is a single collection of data and information stored in one place that can be used by people throughout an organization to make decisions. Management information experts now use the term *knowledge management* (KM) to incorporate a firm's procedures for generating, using, and sharing the data and information contained in the firm's databases.

2 Discuss management's information requirements.

A management information system (MIS) is a means of providing managers with the information they need to perform their jobs as effectively as possible. The purpose of an MIS (sometimes referred to as an information technology system or simply IT system) is to distribute timely and useful information from both internal and external sources to the decision makers who need it. The specific types of information managers need depend on their area of management and level within the firm. The size and complexity of an MIS must be tailored to the information needs of the organization it serves.

3 Outline the five functions of an information system.

The five functions performed by an MIS system are collecting data, storing data, updating data, processing data into information, and presenting information. Data may be collected from such internal sources as company records, reports, and minutes of meetings, as well as from the firm's managers and employees. External sources include customers, suppliers, financial institutions and banks, trade and business publications, industry conferences, online computer services, and information-gathering organizations. An MIS must be able to store data until they are needed and to update them regularly to ensure that the information presented to managers is accurate, complete, and timely. Data processing is the MIS function that transforms stored data into a form useful for a specific purpose. Finally, the processed data (which now can be called information) must be presented for use. Verbal information generally is presented in the form of a report. Numerical information most often is displayed in graphs, charts, or tables.

4 Describe how computers and technology help improve productivity, decision making, communications, sales, and recruiting and training.

Today, many employees use computers and the Internet to improve productivity and performance and communicate with other employees while at the office or away from the office. Three different applications—decision-support systems, executive information systems, and expert systems—can help managers and employees to speed and improve the decision-making process. Another application in the workplace is e-mail, which provides for communication within and outside the firm at any time, 24 hours a day, seven days a week. An extension of e-mail is groupware, which is software that facilitates the management of large projects among geographically dispersed employees as well as such group activities as problem solving and brainstorming. The Internet and a customer relationship management program can provide a database of information that can be used to assist a sales representative. The Internet also can be used to improve employee training and recruitment while lowering costs. Now, with the help of technology, more and more employees are telecommuting and using virtual offices. A number of software applications—word processing, desktop publishing, accounting, database management, graphics, and spreadsheets—can all help employees improve productivity.

5 Analyze how computers and technology change the way information is acquired, organized, and used.

We live in an information society—one in which large groups of employees generate or depend on information to perform their jobs. To find needed information, many businesses and individuals use the Internet. The Internet is a worldwide network of computers linked through telecommunications. Firms also can use an intranet (local-area network) to distribute information within the firm. Both the Internet and intranets are examples of a computer network. A computer network is a group of two or more computers linked together to allow users to share data and information. Today, employees and the general public connect to the Internet, enter a Web address, or use a Web search engine to access information. That information is presented on a Web site created and maintained by business firms; agencies of federal, state, and local governments; or educational or similar organizations. Because a Web site should provide accurate information, great care is required when creating a Web site.

6 Explain the meaning of e-business.

e-Business, or electronic business, can be defined as the organized effort of individuals to produce and sell, for a profit, the goods and services that satisfy society's needs *through the facilities available on the Internet*. The human, material, information, and financial resources that any business requires are highly specialized for e-business. In an effort to reduce the cost of e-business resources, many firms have turned to outsourcing.

Using e-business activities, it is possible to satisfy new customer needs created by the Internet as well as traditional ones in unique ways. Meeting customer needs is especially important when an e-business is trying to earn profits by increasing sales and reducing expenses. Each source of revenue flowing into the firm is referred to as a revenue stream.

7 Describe the fundamental models of e-business.

e-Business models focus attention on the identity of a firm's customers. Firms that use the Internet mainly to conduct business with other businesses generally are referred to as having a business-to-business, or B2B, model.

When examining B2B firms, two clear types emerge. In the first type of B2B, the focus is simply on facilitating sales transactions between businesses. A second, more complex type of the B2B model involves a company and its suppliers. In contrast to the focus of the B2B model, firms such as Amazon or eBay clearly are focused on individual buyers and so are referred to as having a business-to-consumer, or B2C, model. In a B2C situation, understanding how consumers behave online is critical to the firm's success. While B2B and B2C models are the most popular e-business models, there are other models that perform specialized e-business activities to generate revenues (see Table 14-5).

8 Explore the factors that will affect the future of e-business.

Because of the advent of commercial activity on the Internet, developments in e-business have been rapid and formidable. However, a larger-than-usual number of technology companies and e-business firms struggled or even failed during the recent economic crisis. Today, most firms involved in e-business use a more intelligent approach to development. The long-term view held by the vast majority of analysts is that the Internet will continue to expand along with related technologies. While approximately 77 percent of Americans now have access to the Internet, it is expected that worldwide users will exceed 2.6 billion by 2015. When you consider the future of computer technology, the Internet, and e-business, social networks, ethics and social responsibility, and Internet crime are all factors that must be considered in the future. Although the environmental forces at work are complex, it is useful to think of them as either internal or external forces that affect an e-business. Internal environmental forces are those that are closely associated with the actions and decisions taking place within a firm. In contrast, external environmental forces are those factors affecting an e-business originating outside an organization.

KEY TERMS

You should now be able to define and give an example relevant to each of the following terms:

data (409)
information (409)
database (410)
knowledge management (KM) (410)
management information system (MIS) (410)
information technology (IT) officer (410)
data processing (414)
statistic (414)
decision-support system (DSS) (416)

executive information system (EIS) (416)
expert system (416)
groupware (416)
collaborative learning system (417)
virtual office (419)
information society (420)
Internet (420)
World Wide Web (the Web) (420)
intranet (420)
computer network (420)

wide-area network (WAN) (421)
local-area network (LAN) (421)
e-business (electronic business) (422)
outsourcing (422)
revenue stream (424)
business model (426)
business-to-business (or B2B) model (427)
business-to-consumer (or B2C) model (427)

social network site (429)
spamming (429)
cookie (430)
log-file records (430)
data mining (430)
malware (430)
computer virus (430)
cloud computing (430)

DISCUSSION QUESTIONS

1. Do managers really need all the kinds of information discussed in this chapter? If not, which kinds can they do without?

2. How can confidential data and information (such as the wages of individual employees) be kept confidential and yet still be available to managers who need them?

3. Why are computers so well suited to management information systems (MISs)? What are some things computers cannot do in dealing with data and information?

4. How could the Internet help you to find information about employment opportunities at Coca-Cola, Johnson & Johnson, or Microsoft? Describe the process you would use to access this information.

5. Can advertising provide enough revenue for an e-business to succeed in the long run?

6. Is outsourcing good for an e-business firm? The firm's employees? Explain your answer.

7. What distinguishes a B2B from a B2C e-business model?

TEST YOURSELF

Matching Questions

1. _____ Data that have been processed.

2. _____ It incorporates a firm's procedures for generating, using, and sharing the data and information contained in the firm's database.

3. _____ It is a work environment that allows groups to solve problems.

4. _____ It transforms data into useful information.

5. _____ This tool organizes numerical data into grids of rows and columns.

6. _____ All business activities that are conducted on the Internet.

7. _____ Its focus is to facilitate sales transactions between businesses.

8. _____ Amazon.com makes a special effort to build long-term relationships with its customers.

9. _____ Allows employees to work any place where they have access to a computer and technology.

10. _____ Two or more computers that are linked together.

    a. data processing
    b. business-to-business model
    c. knowledge management
    d. spreadsheet program
    e. convergence of technologies
    f. e-business
    g. social networking
    h. information
    i. virtual office
    j. business-to-consumer model
    k. collaborative learning system
    l. computer network

True False Questions

11. **T F** The more information a manager has, the less risk there is that a decision will be incorrect.

12. **T F** Information rules help businesspeople make everyday decisions.

13. **T F** Most data gathered for an MIS come from external sources.

14. **T F** An expert system uses artificial intelligence to imitate a human's ability to think.

15. **T F** A society in which large groups of employees generate or depend on information to perform their jobs is referred to as a data society.

16. **T F** A LAN is a network that connects computers over a large geographic area.

17. **T F** Companies such as Sprint reduce their expenses by offering product information online.

18. **T F** Sources of revenue flowing into the firm are referred to as channels.

19. **T F** Firms that tend to focus on conducting e-business with other businesses are referred to as having a B2B focus.

20. **T F** When Ford Motor Company uses the Internet to purchase materials from its suppliers, it is using a B2C business model.

Multiple-Choice Questions

21. _____ You are a purchasing manager in a large firm and are responsible for deciding on and ordering the appropriate software program that allows the user to prepare and edit letters and store them on a computer memory stick. What type of program will you order?
    a. Spreadsheet
    b. Word processing
    c. Graphics
    d. Communications
    e. Database

22. _____ Management information systems
    a. collect data, hire personnel, and compensate workers.
    b. store data, present data to users, and make final decisions.
    c. collect, store, update, process, and present data.
    d. supervise personnel, reprimand workers, and conduct follow-ups.
    e. collect relevant information.

23. _____ As an MIS manager, you are charged with establishing a management information system that is capable of presenting information in a useable form. Which item below do you feel Is not appropriate for presenting information in business report format?
    a. The introduction describes the problem and techniques used to gather data.
    b. The body of the report describes the facts.
    c. The conclusions describe the findings.
    d. The recommendations present suggestions for solving the problem.
    e. The database of research methods used by the author of the report.

24. _____ As an information manager, you must ensure that
   a. information is protected from employees.
   b. information is used in a consistent manner.
   c. the smart group receives the data first.
   d. the promotional campaigns are aired on time.
   e. new product planning is on schedule.

25. _____ A single collection of data stored in one place and used by employees throughout an organization is called a(n)
   a. data collection.
   b. information center.
   c. database.
   d. data center.
   e. management data center.

26. _____ A manager at the executive level responsible for ensuring that a firm has the equipment necessary to provide the information the firm's employees and managers need to make effective decisions is often called a(n)
   a. information expert.
   b. technology expert.
   c. MIS officer.
   d. information technology officer.
   e. database manager.

27. _____ A customer tracking system is an example of e-business _____ resources.
   a. human
   b. informational
   c. material
   d. financial
   e. supplemental

28. _____ Which of the types of resources needed for an e-business is Storybook.com most likely to receive from a venture capitalist?
   a. Financial
   b. Human
   c. Software
   d. Material
   e. Informational

29. _____ When Microsoft allows workers in a foreign country to provide technical assistance to its customers, it is engaging in
   a. external recruiting.
   b. employment sourcing.
   c. insourcing.
   d. outsourcing
   e. revenue stream buildup.

30. _____ An Internet distributor of office supplies has a system of bidding and awarding contracts online for its purchases and acquisitions from suppliers. This is most likely a _____ model.
   a. B2B
   b. C2C
   c. B2C
   d. C2B
   e. Cross functional

Answers to the Test Yourself questions appear at the end of the book on page TY-1.

VIDEO CASE

E*Trade Provides Information to Its e-Business Customers

E*Trade, the highly successful online financial and banking services company, offers many quick and easy-to-use online investment and financial planning tools that provide research information for its millions of customers. The company has only 28 brick-and-mortar retail branches around the United States for in-person service, but E*Trade online customers hold nearly five million bank and brokerage accounts with the company. E*Trade is so adept at e-business that it sees the Internet as "just another medium," though it's a particularly useful one and the one most of its customers choose.

E*Trade's free research and educational materials cater to the novice investor, the very experienced investor, and the investor in between by means of webinars, short videos, written articles, and other resources that users can access online at their own convenience. Customers can also make long-term investment plans, conduct quick trades for short-term gains, or track the performance of stocks and other

securities they are thinking of buying or selling in the future. Increasingly, their customers are using mobile phone applications, called Mobile-Pro, to contact E*Trade, get investing information and company and market statistics, and conduct their investment trades and financial transactions. The company has made investing as quick and convenient as accessing its Web site from a computer, but now more portable.

Another E*Trade's tool, the automated Online Advisor, asks a short series of questions to provide information that help investors gauge their own risk tolerance for each investment, while also identifying its goal and its time horizon. One key question, for instance, is how soon the investor expects to start drawing money out of his or her investment program, and for how many years thereafter. Another is the investor's age, and yet another is the investor's likely response to a sudden drop in the value of his or her investment. Whether the investor wants to start college savings for a child, put money away for retirement, or manage an inheritance or other windfall, assessing risk tolerance and goals is the first step for which E*Trade provides guidance.

Additional investment tools and services available from E*Trade's Web site around the clock provide even more information and include trading charts, streaming news and stock quotes, live "watch" lists, and screening tools, as well as a new customer-feedback link. Global markets on which E*Trade's customers can buy and sell securities are in Canada, France, Germany, Hong Kong, Japan, and the UK. Speed and reliability are the key characteristics E*Trade builds into its securities transactions. Securities trade instantaneously online when the stock exchanges are open, on the next trading day if not, or when a particular security meets the customer's stated buy or sell price. And if a customer has a problem or a question, E*Trade maintains customer service teams and an online customer service center 24 hours a day and 7days a week.

SmartMoney magazine recently gave E*Trade its highest rating for excellence based on its trading tools, banking services, and customer service. Barron's also gave the firm high marks for trade experience and technology, usability, customer service, and cost. The company is also a model citizen of today's information society: "At E*Trade you'll never stop learning," says the company's website, "and that's a good thing."

Discussion Questions

1. Each year E*Trade helps millions of individuals obtain investment research information and invest in publicly traded companies. It also operates a Corporate Services business that helps firms, from startups to Fortune 500 companies, manage their stock plans. What type of business model(s) is E*Trade using?
2. What are some of the ways in which E*Trade works to strengthen its competitive position as an e-business?
3. What are some of the advantages offered by E*Trade's mobile apps? How do these capitalize on the capabilities of the Internet?

Sources: Company website, www.etrade.com, accessed September 8, 2011; Whitney Kisling, "E*Trade Gains Most Since December on Return to Profit," Bloomberg BusinessWeek, www.businessweek.com, July 23, 2010; Matt Ackerman, "E*Trade to Target Long-Term Investors," American Banker, www.americanbanker.com, January 29, 2010; and interviews with company employees and the video "E*Trade Uses e-Business to Meet Customer Needs."

BUILDING SKILLS FOR CAREER SUCCESS

1. Exploring the Internet

Millions of people around the world belong to social networks. And yet, you may want to consider the following facts before joining or sharing personal information on a social site.

- Prospective or current employers often use the information you post on social sites to learn more about you.
- People who you do not know (or want to know) often can view your personal information.
- Although social sites have revised or improved their privacy policies, there are still too many reports of serious privacy abuses that affect too many users.

Today, the two most popular social sites are Facebook and Twitter. Both sites have privacy statements and attempt to protect users.

Assignment

1. Go to the Facebook Web site (www.facebook.com) and the Twitter Web site (www.twitter.com), and examine each site's privacy policy. (Hint: Scroll down to the bottom of the home page and look for the link marked "privacy.")
2. Read each site's privacy policy. Note any concerns that you feel could restrict the type of information you might want to share or lead to a violation of your personal privacy.

3. In a two-page report, answer at least the following questions.
   a. What specific actions has each site taken to protect your privacy?
   b. Are there weaknesses in the policies that could lead to abuses of your personal privacy?
   c. Based on your research, which site do you think has the most effective privacy policy? Why?
   d. How has this exercise changed the type of information you would share on the Facebook or Twitter Web site? Explain your answer.

2. Building Team Skills

To provide marketing managers with information about consumer reactions to a particular product or service, business researchers often conduct focus groups. The participants in these groups are representative of the target market for the product or service under study. The leader poses questions and lets members of the group express their feelings and ideas about the product or service. The ideas are recorded, transcribed, and analyzed.

Assignment

1. Working in a small team, select a product or service to research—for example, your college's food service or bookstore or a new item you would like to see stocked in your local grocery store.

2. Create a list of questions that can be used to generate discussion about the product or service with focus-group members.

3. Form a focus group of five to seven people representative of the market for the product or service your team has selected.

4. During the group sessions, record the input. Later, transcribe it into printed form, analyze it, and process it into information. On the basis of this information, make recommendations for improving the product or service.

5. In a report, describe your team's experiences in forming the focus groups and the value of focus groups in collecting data. Use the report as the basis for a three- to five-minute class presentation.

3. Researching Different Careers

Firms today expect employees to be proficient in using computers and software. Typical business applications include e-mail, word processing, spreadsheets, and graphics. By improving your skills in these areas, you can increase your chances not only of being employed but also of being promoted once you are employed.

Assignment

1. Assess your computer skills by placing a check in the appropriate column in the following table:

Software	Skill Level			
	None	Low	Average	High
e-Mail				
Word processing				
Desktop publishing				
Accounting				
Database management				
Graphics				
Spreadsheet				
Groupware				
Internet research				

2. Describe your self-assessment in a written report. Specify the skills in which you need to become more proficient, and outline a plan for doing this.

CHAPTER 15 USING ACCOUNTING INFORMATION

135.844
7,496

537.745
21.200

83.336
5.325

62.411
2.249

8.798
1.390

312

© Juan Guertes/Shutterstock

Why should you care?

Although lenders, suppliers, stockholders, and government agencies all rely on the information generated by a firm's accounting system, the primary users of accounting information are managers and employees.

Learning Objectives

What you will be able to do once you complete this chapter:

1 Explain why accurate accounting information and audited financial statements are important.

2 Identify the people who use accounting information and possible careers in the accounting industry.

3 Discuss the accounting process.

4 Read and interpret a balance sheet.

5 Read and interpret an income statement.

6 Describe business activities that affect a firm's cash flow.

7 Summarize how managers evaluate the financial health of a business.

KPMG Helps Keep Businesses Running Smoothly

Companies of all sizes—from the multinational giant General Electric to locally-owned family restaurants—keep their businesses running smoothly by seeking accounting, tax, or consulting services from KPMG. One of the world's largest accounting firms, Switzerland-based KPMG has $21 billion in annual revenues and nearly 140,000 employees working with businesses in 144 countries. The firm is truly international, formed from the merger of Peat Marwick International and Klynveld Main Goerdeler in 1987, and is growing especially quickly in Brazil, Russia, India, and China.

KPMG's mission is "to turn knowledge into value for the benefit of our clients, our people, and the capital markets." Its specialists are trained to carefully examine and interpret accounting information and other key data to identify important trends and issues for management attention. Although it may be best known for its expertise in all things financial, KPMG has the know-how to advise management about a wide range of matters, from detecting fraud and developing new products to going green and global infrastructure.

Every year, KPMG recruits several thousand new college graduates to fill job openings in accounting, corporate finance, international tax, and related areas. Bruce Pfau, vice chair of human resources, explains that KPMG reaches out to students and experienced candidates through on-campus interviews, electronic job boards, and social media sites such as LinkedIn. "We're looking firstly for highly competent, very bright people to come work for us and secondly for people that share our same values," he says.

KPMG's values include a commitment to continuous learning and professional development, a dedication to good corporate citizenship worldwide, and high standards of professional integrity throughout the workforce. To allow employees to balance their personal and professional lives, the company offers flexible working arrangements such as telecommuting, job sharing, and other alternatives to the traditional 9-to-5 in-office workday. Travel-minded employees can apply to participate in KPMG's "global opportunities" program and earn an assignment abroad for several months or even several years. KPMG's global expansion—to meet the growing needs of its client base—will create even more career opportunities in the coming years.[1]

Did you know?

KPMG is one of the world's largest accounting firms, with $21 billion in annual revenues and nearly 140,000 employees in 144 countries.

Wanted: An individual with at least two years of college accounting courses. Must be honest, dependable, and willing to complete all routine accounting activities for a manufacturing business. Salary dependent on experience. Want a job? Positions such as the one described in this newspaper advertisement are increasingly becoming available to those with the required training. In fact, firms like KPMG—the accounting firm profiled in the Inside Business opening case for this chapter—employ thousands of new employees each year. KPMG is proud of its people culture where employees from all kinds of backgrounds find a culture in which they have the freedom and flexibility to grow while helping their clients solve their toughest accounting problems.

The fact is that without accounting information, managers can't make decisions, investors can't evaluate potential investments, and lenders and suppliers can't extend credit to a business firm. Although accurate accounting information has always been important, it is even more important now in the wake of the recent accounting scandals and the crisis in the banking and financial industries.

We begin this chapter by looking at why accounting information is important, the recent problems in the accounting industry, and attempts to improve financial reporting. Then we look at how managers, employees, individuals, and groups outside a firm use accounting information. We also identify different types of accountants and career opportunities in the accounting industry. Next, we focus on the accounting process and the basics of an accounting system. We also examine the three most important financial statements: the balance sheet, the income statement, and the statement of cash flows. Finally, we show how ratios are used to measure specific aspects of a firm's financial health.

WHY ACCOUNTING INFORMATION IS IMPORTANT

Accounting is the process of systematically collecting, analyzing, and reporting financial information. Just for a moment, think about the following three questions:

1. How much profit did a business earn last year?
2. How much tax does a business owe the Internal Revenue Service?
3. How much cash does a business have to pay lenders and suppliers?

In each case, the firm's accountants and its accounting system provide the answers to these questions and many others. Although accounting information can be used to answer questions about what has happened in the past, it can also be used to help make decisions about the future. For these reasons, accounting is one of the most important areas within a business organization.

Because the information provided by a firm's accountants and its accounting system is so important, managers and other groups interested in a business firm's financial records must be able to "trust the numbers." Unfortunately, a large number of accounting scandals have caused people to doubt not only the numbers but also the accounting industry.

Personal App Whether you're investing money in a company or applying for a job there, you must be able to "trust the numbers." The same holds true for any business you start: Your investors, employees, and lenders will count on the fact that your accounting information is both complete and accurate.

Recent Accounting Scandals

Which of the following firms has been convicted or accused of accounting fraud?

a. Enron
b. Lehman Brothers
c. Fannie Mae
d. AIG
e. All of the above

Unfortunately, the answer to the question is e—all of the above. Each company is a major U.S. business that has been plagued by accounting problems. These problems led to bankruptcy for Enron and Lehman Brothers and a massive federal bailout for mortgage giant Fannie Mae and insurance giant AIG. The accounting problems at these companies—and similar problems at even more companies—have forced many investors, lenders and suppliers, and government regulators to question the motives behind fraudulent and unethical accounting practices.

Today, much of the pressure on corporate executives to "cook" the books is driven by the desire to look good to Wall Street analysts and investors. Every three months companies report their revenues, expenses, profits, and projections for the future. If a company meets or exceeds "the street's" expectations, everything is usually fine. However, if a company reports financial numbers that are lower than expected, the company's stock value can drop dramatically. An earnings report that is lower

LEARNING OBJECTIVE

1 Explain why accurate accounting information and audited financial statements are important.

accounting the process of systematically collecting, analyzing, and reporting financial information

Question: Was Lehman Brothers too big to fail? Answer: No. The once proud Wall Street financial firm filed for bankruptcy in September 2008. While there are many reasons why the firm failed, many experts believe that top executives regularly used fraudulent accounting tactics to enhance Lehman Brother's balance sheet and improve the firm's bottom line profit amount reported on the firm's income statement. The experts also point out that without accurate accounting records, it's hard to run a successful business.

by even a few pennies per share than what is expected can cause a company's stock value to drop immediately by as much as 20 to 30 percent or more. Greed—especially when executive salaries and bonuses are tied to a company's stock value—is another factor that can lead some corporate executives to use questionable accounting methods to inflate a firm's sales revenues and profit amount.

Unfortunately, the ones hurt when companies (and their accountants) report inaccurate or misleading accounting information often are not the high-paid corporate executives. In many cases, it's the employees who lose their jobs, as well as the money they invested in the company's retirement program. In addition, investors, lenders, and suppliers who relied on fraudulent accounting information in order to make a decision to invest in or lend money to the company also usually experience a loss.

In an indirect way, the recent accounting scandals underscore how important accurate accounting information is for a corporation. To see how the auditing process can improve accounting information, read the next section.

Why Audited Financial Statements Are Important

An **audit** is an examination of a company's financial statements and the accounting practices that produced them. The purpose of an audit is to make sure that a firm's financial statements have been prepared in accordance with **generally accepted accounting principles (GAAPs)**. GAAPs have been developed to provide an accepted set of guidelines and practices for U.S. companies reporting financial information and the accounting profession.[2] At the time of publication, the Financial Accounting Standards Board (FASB), which establishes and improves accounting standards for U.S. companies, is working toward establishing a new set of standards that combines GAAPs with the International Financial Reporting Standards (IFRS) to create one set of accounting standards that can be used by both U.S. and multinational firms. Created by the International Accounting Standards Board, IFRS are now used in more than 100 different countries around the world. For multinational firms, the benefits of global accounting standards are huge because preparing financial statements and accounting records that meet global standards saves both time and money. According to many accounting experts, it's not a question of whether IFRS guidelines will be adopted in the United States but when.[3]

If an accountant determines that a firm's financial statements present financial information fairly and conform to GAAPs, then he or she will issue the following statement:

In our opinion, the financial statements . . . present fairly, in all material respects . . . in conformity with generally accepted accounting principles.

Although an audit and the resulting report do not *guarantee* that a company has not "cooked" the books, it does imply that, on the whole, the company has followed GAAPs. Bankers, creditors, investors, and government agencies are willing to rely on an auditor's opinion because of the historically ethical reputation and independence of auditors and accounting firms. Finally, it should be noted that without the audit function and GAAPs, there would be very little oversight or supervision. The validity of a firm's financial statements and its accounting records would drop quickly, and firms would find it difficult to obtain debt financing, acquire goods and services

audit an examination of a company's financial statements and the accounting practices that produced them

generally accepted accounting principles (GAAPs) an accepted set of guidelines and practices for companies reporting financial information and for the accounting profession

from suppliers, find investor financing, or prepare documents requested by government agencies.

Reform: The Sarbanes-Oxley Act of 2002

According to John Bogle, founder of Vanguard Mutual Funds, "Investing is an act of faith. Without that faith—that reported numbers reflect reality, that companies are being run honestly, that Wall Street is playing it straight, and that investors aren't being hoodwinked—our capital markets simply can't function."[4] In reality, what Mr. Bogle says is true. To help ensure that corporate financial information is accurate and in response to the many accounting scandals that surfaced in the last few years, Congress enacted the Sarbanes-Oxley Act. Key components include the following:[5]

- The Securities and Exchange Commission (SEC) is required to establish a full-time five-member federal oversight board that will police the accounting industry.
- Chief executive and financial officers are required to certify periodic financial reports and are liable for intentional violations of securities reporting requirements.
- Accounting firms are prohibited from providing many types of non-audit and consulting services to the companies they audit.
- Auditors must maintain financial documents and audit work papers for five years.
- Auditors, accountants, and employees can be imprisoned for up to 20 years and subject to fines for destroying financial documents and willful violations of the securities laws.
- A public corporation must change its lead auditing firm every five years.
- There is added protection for whistle-blowers who report violations of the Sarbanes-Oxley Act.

Although most people welcome the Sarbanes-Oxley Act, complex rules make compliance more expensive and time-consuming for corporate management and

Concept Check ✱

☐ What purpose do audits and generally accepted accounting principles (GAAPs) serve in today's business world?

☐ How do the major provisions of the Sarbanes-Oxley Act affect a public company's audit procedures?

more difficult for accounting firms. Yet, most people agree that the cost of compliance is justified. As you read the next section, you will see the importance of maintaining accurate accounting information.

LEARNING OBJECTIVE

2 Identify the people who use accounting information and possible careers in the accounting industry.

WHO USES ACCOUNTING INFORMATION

Managers and employees, lenders, suppliers, stockholders, and government agencies all rely on the information contained in three financial statements, each no more than one page in length. These three reports—the balance sheet, the income statement, and the statement of cash flows—are concise summaries of a firm's activities during a specific time period. This information has a variety of uses both within the firm and outside it. However, first and foremost, accounting information is management information.

The People Who Use Accounting Information

The primary users of accounting information are *managers*. The firm's accounting system provides information that can be compiled for the entire firm—for each product; for each sales territory, store, or salesperson; for each division or department; and generally in any way that will help those who manage the organization. At a company such as Kraft Foods, for example, financial information is gathered for all its hundreds of food products: Maxwell House Coffee, A1 Steak Sauce, Chips Ahoy Cookies, Jell-O Desserts, Kool Aid, and so on. The president of the company is interested in total sales for all these products. The vice president for marketing for Maxwell House Coffee is interested in national sales. The northeastern sales manager might want to look at sales figures for Kool Aid in New England. For a large, complex organization like Kraft, the accounting system must enable managers to get the information they need.

Much of this accounting information is *proprietary*; it is not divulged to anyone outside the firm. This type of information is used by a firm's managers and employees to plan and set goals, organize, lead and motivate, and control—all the management functions that were described in Chapter 6.

Personal App Just as you don't tell the world how much money is in your wallet or how much you owe on a student loan, not all accounting information you work with on the job is for public discussion. Your manager and coworkers may talk about some details, but outsiders don't need to know everything you know.

In addition to proprietary information used inside the firm, certain financial information must be supplied to lenders, suppliers, stockholders, potential investors, government agencies, and other stakeholders. For more information about the type of information these individuals and organizations need, take a look at Table 15-1.

An important function of accountants is to ensure that such information is accurate and thorough enough to satisfy these outside groups.

Why do stockholders attend annual meetings? There are many reasons why stockholders—the actual owners of a corporation—attend an annual meeting. For starters, most stockholders want to learn more about the company. Others want to vote in person for the board of directors and approve or reject major corporate actions. Still other stockholders want a chance to ask questions about the corporation's future plans.

Different Types of Accounting

Although many people think that all accountants do the same tasks, there are special areas of expertise within the accounting industry. In fact, accounting is usually broken down into two broad categories: managerial and financial.

TABLE 15-1: Users of Accounting Information

The primary users of accounting information are a company's managers and employees, although individuals and organizations outside the company also require information on its finances.

Management and Employees	Lenders and Suppliers	Stockholders and Potential Investors	Government Agencies
• Plan and set goals • Organize • Lead and motivate • Control	• Evaluate credit applicants before committing to short- or long-term financing • Evaluate the risk of non-payment before selling goods or services to a firm	• Evaluate the financial health of the firm before purchasing stocks or bonds • Evaluate the risk associated with investing in a company's stocks, bonds, or securities	• Confirm tax liabilities • Confirm payroll deductions • Approve new issues of stocks and bonds

Managerial accounting provides managers and employees within the organization with the information needed to make decisions about a firm's financing, investing, marketing, and operating activities. By using managerial accounting information, both managers and employees can evaluate how well they have done in the past and what they can expect in the future. **Financial accounting**, on the other hand, generates financial statements and reports for interested people outside of an organization. Typically, stockholders, financial analysts, bankers, lenders, suppliers, government agencies, and other interested groups use the information provided by financial accounting to determine how well a business firm has achieved its goals and if the company is financially healthy. In addition to managerial and financial accounting, additional special areas of accounting include the following:

- *Cost accounting*—determining the cost of producing specific products or services
- *Tax accounting*—planning tax strategy and preparing tax returns for firms or individuals
- *Government accounting*—providing basic accounting services to ensure that tax revenues are collected and used to meet the goals of state, local, and federal agencies
- *Not-for-profit accounting*—helping not-for-profit organizations to account for all donations and expenditures

Careers in Accounting

Many people have the idea that accountants spend their day working with endless columns of numbers in a small office locked away from other people. Accountants do spend a lot of time at their desks, but their job entails far more than just adding or subtracting numbers. Accountants are expected to share their ideas and the information they possess with people who need the information.

According to the *Occupational Outlook Handbook*, published by the Department of Labor, job opportunities for accountants, as well as auditors in the accounting area, are expected to experience much faster-than-average employment growth between now and the year 2018. According to a recent salary survey conducted by the National Association of Colleges and Employers, starting salaries for accountants with a bachelor's degree average $48,993 a year.[6] Job applicants with a two-year degree or with some college accounting courses make less, but still higher than the starting salaries for other entry-level positions.

managerial accounting provides managers and employees with the information needed to make decisions about a firm's financing, investing, marketing, and operating activities

financial accounting generates financial statements and reports for interested people outside an organization

SPOT LIGHT

Accounting Careers Are Attracting More Students!

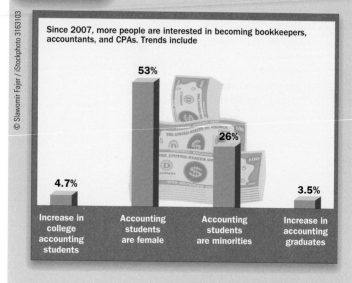

Since 2007, more people are interested in becoming bookkeepers, accountants, and CPAs. Trends include

- **4.7%** Increase in college accounting students
- **53%** Accounting students are female
- **26%** Accounting students are minorities
- **3.5%** Increase in accounting graduates

Source: The American Institute of Certified Public Accountants Web site at www.aicpa.org (accessed April 5, 2011).

© Slawomir Fajer / iStockphoto 3163103

Accounting can be an exciting and rewarding career—one that offers higher-than-average starting salaries. To be successful in the accounting industry, employees must

- Be responsible, honest, and ethical.
- Have a strong background in financial management.
- Know how to use a computer and software to process data into accounting information.
- Be able to communicate with people who need accounting information.

Today, accountants generally are classified as either private accountants or public accountants. A *private accountant* is employed by a specific organization. A medium-sized or a large firm may employ one or more private accountants to design its accounting information system and provide managers with accounting information, advice, and assistance.

Individuals, self-employed business owners, and smaller firms that do not require their own full-time accountants can hire the services of public accountants. A *public accountant* works on a fee basis for clients and may be self-employed or be the employee of an accounting firm. Accounting firms range in size from one-person operations to huge international firms with hundreds of accounting partners and thousands of employees. Today, the largest accounting firms, sometimes referred to as the "Big Four," are PricewaterhouseCoopers, Ernst & Young, KPMG, and Deloitte Touche Tohmatsu.

Typically, public accounting firms include on their staffs at least one **certified public accountant (CPA)**, an individual who has met state requirements for accounting education and experience and has passed a rigorous accounting examination. The AICPA uniform CPA examination covers four areas: (1) regulation, taxation, business law, ethics, and professional and legal responsibilities; (2) auditing; (3) business environment and concepts; and (4) financial accounting and reporting.[7] More information about general requirements, the CPA examination, and the accounting profession can be obtained by contacting the AICPA at www.aicpa.org. Details regarding specific state requirements for practice as a CPA can be obtained by contacting the state's board of accountancy.

Certification as a CPA brings both status and responsibility. Publicly traded corporations must hire an independent certified public accountant to audit their financial statements. In addition to auditing a corporation's financial statements, typical services performed by CPAs include planning and preparing tax returns, determining the true cost of producing and marketing a firm's goods or services, and compiling the financial information needed to make major management decisions. Fees for the services provided by CPAs generally range from $50 to $300 an hour.

In addition to CPAs, there are also certified management accountants (CMAs). A **certified management accountant (CMA)** is an accountant who has met the requirements for education and experience, passed a rigorous exam, and is certified by the Institute of Management Accountants. The CMA exam is designed to develop and measure not only accounting skills but also decision-making, financial planning, analysis, and critical-thinking skills. For more information about the CMA exam, visit the Institute of Management Accountants Web site at www.imanet.org. Although both CPAs and CMAs can work for the public, a CMA is more likely to work within a large organization. In addition, both types of accountants are excellent career choices.

certified public accountant (CPA) an individual who has met state requirements for accounting education and experience and has passed a rigorous accounting examination prepared by the AICPA

certified management accountant (CMA) an accountant who has met the requirements for education and experience, passed a rigorous exam, and is certified by the Institute of Management Accountants

✱ Concept Check

☐ List four groups that use accounting information, and briefly explain why each group has an interest in the information.

☐ What is the difference between a private accountant and a public accountant?

☐ What are certified public accountants and certified management accountants?

U.S. businesses and not-for-profit organizations will soon need the services of many more accountants and auditors. The *Occupational Outlook Handbook* forecasts a 22 percent increase in the number of accountants and auditors needed in the nation's workforce by 2018—a much faster-than-average occupational growth rate.

Already, the "Big Four" (Deloitte Touche Tohmatsu, Ernst & Young, KPMG, and PricewaterhouseCoopers) accounting firms are actively recruiting to fill open positions and prepare for the coming boom in demand for their services. All four appear on *Fortune*'s annual list of 100 Best Companies to Work For. And all four appear on *BusinessWeek*'s annual list of Best Places to Launch a Career.

Here's a taste of what the Big Four are doing to attract, develop, and retain career-minded accountants and auditors. Deloitte (www.deloitte.com) offers options such as telecommuting and reduced work hours for employees who want to advance their careers while juggling family obligations. It has also created Deloitte University, a state-of-the-art $300 million learning center for companywide technical and leadership training. Ernst & Young (www.ey.com) has a wide variety of international assignments to develop, challenge, and motivate its personnel.

KPMG (www.kpmg.com) encourages employees to pursue their outside interests by granting sabbatical leaves for up to three months at 20 percent pay. Pricewaterhouse Coopers (www.pwc.com) provides on-the-job coaching and networking opportunities to help employees sharpen their skills, learn from experts throughout the organization, and identify new job opportunities internally. Is a Big Four career in your future?

Sources: Steven Greenhouse, "Flex Time Flourishes in Accounting Industry," *New York Times*, January 11, 2011, www.nytimes.com; Alison Maitland, "A Different Way of Working," *Financial Times*, March 22, 2010, www.ft.com; Milton Moskowitz, Robert Levering, and Christopher Tkaczyk, "100 Best Companies to Work for in America," *Fortune*, February 8, 2010, pp. 75–88; Lindsey Gerdes, "Best Places to Launch a Career," *BusinessWeek*, September 14, 2009, pp. 32ff; "Accountants and Auditors," *Occupational Outlook Handbook*, December 17, 2009, www.bls.gov/oco/ocos001.htm.

THE ACCOUNTING PROCESS

LEARNING OBJECTIVE

3 Discuss the accounting process.

In Chapter 14, *information* was defined as data presented in a form that is useful for a specific purpose. In this section, we examine accounting as the system for transforming raw financial *data* into useful financial *information*. Then, in the next sections, we describe the three most important financial statements—the balance sheet, income statement, and statement of cash flows—provided by the accounting process.

Steps in the Accounting Cycle

The purpose of an accounting system is to (1) analyze daily transactions, (2) record the transactions, and (3) summarize the accounting information that is included in a firm's financial statements. The first two steps—analyzing and recording—are performed on a regular basis throughout the accounting period. The third step—preparation of the financial statements—is performed at the end of the accounting period.

STEP 1: ANALYZING SOURCE DOCUMENTS Basic accounting data are contained in *source documents*, the receipts, invoices, sales slips, and other documents that show the dollar amounts of day-to-day business transactions. The accounting cycle begins with the analysis of each of these documents. The purpose of the analysis is to determine which accounts are affected by the documents and how they are affected.

STEP 2: RECORDING AND POSTING TRANSACTIONS Every financial transaction then is recorded in a journal—a process called *journalizing*. Transactions must be recorded in the firm's general journal or in specialized journals. The *general* *journal* is a book of original entry in which typical transactions are recorded in order of their occurrence. An accounting system also may include *specialized journals* for specific types of transactions that occur frequently. Thus, a retail store might have journals for cash receipts, cash disbursements, purchases, and sales in addition to its general journal.

After the information is recorded in the general journal and specialized journals, it is transferred to the general ledger. The *general ledger* is a book of accounts containing a separate sheet or section for each account. Today, most businesses use a computer and software to record accounting entries in the general journal or specialized journals and then to post journal entries to the general ledger.

STEP 3: PREPARING FINANCIAL STATEMENTS The firm's financial statements are prepared from the information contained in the firm's general ledger accounts. This information is presented in a standardized format to make the statements as accessible as possible to the various people who may be interested in the firm's financial affairs—managers, employees, lenders, suppliers, stockholders, potential investors, and government agencies. In fact, the form of the financial statements is pretty much the same for all businesses, from a neighborhood video store or small dry cleaner to giant conglomerates such as Home Depot, Boeing, and Bank of America. A firm's financial statements are prepared at least once a year and included in the firm's annual report. An **annual report** is a report distributed to stockholders and other interested parties that describes a firm's operating activities and its financial condition. Most firms also have financial statements prepared semiannually, quarterly, or monthly.

(**Personal App**) Before you accept a company's job offer or buy its stock, check the Web site to view or download the latest annual report and learn more about its financials and its business situation. Are profits increasing or decreasing? How is it handling its debt? What are its plans for expansion?

With this brief information about the steps of the accounting cycle in mind, let's now examine the fundamental accounting equation.

The Accounting Equation

The accounting equation is a simple statement that forms the basis for the accounting process. This important equation shows the relationship between a firm's assets, liabilities, and owners' equity.

- **Assets** are the resources a business owns—cash, inventory, equipment, and real estate.
- **Liabilities** are the firm's debts—borrowed money that it owes to others that must be repaid.
- **Owners' equity** is the difference between total assets and total liabilities—what would be left for the owners if the firm's assets were sold and the money used to pay off its liabilities.

The relationship between assets, liabilities, and owners' equity is shown by the following **accounting equation**:

$$\text{Assets} = \text{liabilities} + \text{owners' equity}$$

The dollar total of all a firm's assets cannot equal more than the total funds obtained by borrowing money (liabilities) and the investment of the owner(s). Whether a business is a small corner grocery store or a giant corporation such as General Mills, its assets must equal the sum of its liabilities and owners' equity.

To use this equation, a firm's accountants must record raw data—that is, the firm's day-to-day financial transactions—using the double-entry system of bookkeeping. The **double-entry bookkeeping system** is a system in which each financial transaction is recorded as two separate accounting entries to maintain the balance shown in the accounting equation. All of this financial information can now be summarized in the firm's financial statements.

---

annual report a report distributed to stockholders and other interested parties that describes a firm's operating activities and its financial condition

assets the resources that a business owns

liabilities a firm's debts and obligations

owners' equity the difference between a firm's assets and its liabilities

accounting equation the basis for the accounting process: *assets = liabilities + owners' equity*

double-entry bookkeeping system a system in which each financial transaction is recorded as two separate accounting entries to maintain the balance shown in the accounting equation

✳ *Concept Check*

☐ Briefly describe the three specific steps of the accounting cycle in order.

☐ State the accounting equation, and list two specific examples of each term in the equation.

☐ How is double-entry bookkeeping related to the accounting equation?

Part 6: Managing Information, Accounting, and Finance

THE BALANCE SHEET

LEARNING OBJECTIVE

4 Read and interpret a balance sheet.

Question: *Where could you find the total amount of assets, liabilities, and owners' equity for Hershey Foods Corporation?*

Answer: The firm's balance sheet.

A **balance sheet** (sometimes referred to as a **statement of financial position**) is a summary of the dollar amounts of a firm's assets, liabilities, and owners' equity accounts at the end of a specific accounting period. The balance sheet must demonstrate that assets are equal to liabilities plus owners' equity. Most people think of a balance sheet as a statement that reports the financial condition of a business firm such as the Home Depot or Hershey Foods Corporation, but balance sheets apply to individuals, too. For example, Marty Campbell graduated from college three years ago and obtained a position as a sales representative for an office supply firm. After going to work, he established a checking and savings account and purchased an automobile, stereo, television, and a few pieces of furniture. Marty paid cash for some purchases, but he had to borrow money to pay for the larger ones. Figure 15-1 shows Marty's current personal balance sheet.

Marty Campbell's assets total $26,500, and his liabilities amount to $10,000. Although the difference between total assets and total liabilities is referred to as *owners' equity or stockholders' equity* for a business, it is normally called *net worth* for an individual. As reported on Marty's personal balance sheet, net worth is $16,500. The total assets ($26,500) and the total liabilities plus net worth ($26,500) are equal. Thus, the accounting equation (Assets = liabilities + owners' equity) is still in balance.

Figure 15-2 shows the balance sheet for Northeast Art Supply, a small corporation that sells picture frames, paints, canvases, and other artists' supplies to retailers in New England. Note that assets are reported on the left side of the statement, and liabilities and stockholders' equity are reported on the right side. Let's work through the different accounts in Figure 15-2.

balance sheet (or statement of financial position) a summary of the dollar amounts of a firm's assets, liabilities, and owners' equity accounts at the end of a specific accounting period

---

FIGURE 15-1: Personal Balance Sheet

Often individuals determine their net worth, or owners' equity, by subtracting the value of their liabilities from the value of their assets. After all amounts are included, the total for assets equals the total for liabilities + net worth (owners' equity).

		Marty Campbell		
		Personal Balance Sheet		
		December 31, 20XX		
ASSETS		**LIABILITIES**		
Cash	$ 2,500	Automobile loan	$ 9,500	
Savings account	5,000	Credit card balance	500	
Automobile	15,000	TOTAL LIABILITIES		$10,000
Stereo	1,000			
Television	500	NET WORTH (Owners' Equity)		16,500
Furniture	2,500	TOTAL LIABILITIES AND NET WORTH		$26,500
TOTAL ASSETS	$26,500			

FIGURE 15-2: Business Balance Sheet

A balance sheet (sometimes referred to as a statement of financial position) summarizes a firm's accounts at the end of an accounting period, showing the various dollar amounts that enter into the accounting equation. Note that assets ($340,000) equal liabilities plus owners' equity ($340,000) and the accounting equation is still in balance.

NORTHEAST ART SUPPLY, INC.

Balance Sheet
December 31, 20XX

ASSETS

Current assets

Cash		$ 59,000
Marketable securities		10,000
Accounts receivable	$ 40,000	
Less allowance for doubtful accounts	2,000	38,000
Notes receivable		32,000
Merchandise inventory		41,000
Prepaid expenses		2,000
Total current assets		$182,000

Fixed assets

Delivery equipment	$110,000		
Less accumulated depreciation	20,000	$ 90,000	
Furniture and store equipment	$62,000		
Less accumulated depreciation	15,000	47,000	
Total fixed assets			137,000

Intangible assets

Patents	$ 21,000	
Total intangible assets		21,000
TOTAL ASSETS		$340,000

LIABILITIES AND STOCKHOLDERS' EQUITY

Current liabilities

Accounts payable	$ 35,000	
Notes payable	25,675	
Salaries payable	4,000	
Taxes payable	5,325	
Total current liabilities		$ 70,000

Long-term liabilities

Mortgage payable on store equipment	$ 40,000	
Total long-term liabilities		$ 40,000
TOTAL LIABILITIES		$110,000

Stockholders' equity

Common stock (25,000×$6)	$ 150,000	
Retained earnings	80,000	
TOTAL OWNERS' EQUITY		230,000
TOTAL LIABILITIES AND OWNERS' EQUITY		$340,000

© Cengage Learning 2013

Assets

On a balance sheet, assets are listed in order from the *most liquid* to the *least liquid*. The **liquidity** of an asset is the ease with which it can be converted into cash.

CURRENT ASSETS Current assets are assets that can be converted quickly into cash or that will be used in one year or less. Because cash is the most liquid asset, it is listed first. Next are *marketable securities*—stocks, bonds, and other investments—that can be converted into cash in a matter of days.

Next are the firm's receivables. Its *accounts receivable,* which result from allowing customers to make credit purchases, generally are paid within 30 to 60 days. However, the firm expects that some of these debts will not be collected. Thus, it has reduced its accounts receivables by a 5 percent *allowance for doubtful accounts.* The firm's *notes receivable* are receivables for which customers have signed promissory notes. They generally are repaid over a longer period of time than the firm's accounts receivable.

Northeast's *merchandise inventory* represents the value of goods on hand for sale to customers. Since Northeast Art Supply is a wholesale operation, the inventory listed in Figure 15-2 represents finished goods ready for sale to retailers. For a manufacturing firm, merchandise inventory also may represent raw materials that will become part of a finished product or work that has been partially completed but requires further processing.

Northeast's last current asset is *prepaid expenses,* which are assets that have been paid for in advance but have not yet been used. An example is insurance premiums.

liquidity the ease with which an asset can be converted into cash

current assets assets that can be converted quickly into cash or that will be used in one year or less

They are usually paid at the beginning of the policy year. The unused portion (say, for the last four months of the time period covered by the policy) is a prepaid expense. For Northeast Art, all current assets total $182,000.

FIXED ASSETS **Fixed assets** are assets that will be held or used for a period longer than one year. They generally include land, buildings, and equipment used in the continuing operation of the business. Although Northeast owns no land or buildings, it does own delivery equipment that originally cost $110,000. It also owns furniture and store equipment that originally cost $62,000.

Note that the values of both fixed assets are decreased by their *accumulated depreciation.* **Depreciation** is the process of apportioning the cost of a fixed asset over the period during which it will be used, that is, its useful life. The depreciation amount allotted to each year is an expense for that year, and the value of the asset must be reduced by the amount of depreciation expense. In the case of Northeast's delivery equipment, $20,000 of its value has been depreciated (or used up) since it was purchased. Its value at this time is thus $110,000 less $20,000, or $90,000. In a similar fashion, the original value of furniture and store equipment ($62,000) has been reduced by depreciation totaling $15,000. Furniture and store equipment now has a reported value of $47,000. For Northeast Art, all fixed assets total $137,000.

INTANGIBLE ASSETS **Intangible assets** are assets that do not exist physically but that have a value based on the rights or privileges they confer on a firm. They include patents, copyrights, trademarks, and goodwill. Note: Goodwill normally is not listed on a balance sheet unless the firm has been purchased from previous owners. By their nature, intangible assets are long-term assets—they are of value to the firm for a number of years.

Northeast Art Supply lists a *patent* for a special oil paint that the company purchased from the inventor. The firm's accountants estimate that the patent has a current market value of $21,000. Since the firm has only one intangible asset, the firm's intangible assets total $21,000. Now it is possible to total all three types of assets for Northeast Art. As calculated in Figure 15-2, total assets are $340,000.

Liabilities and Owners' Equity

The liabilities and the owners' equity accounts complete the balance sheet. The firm's liabilities are separated into two categories—current and long-term liabilities.

CURRENT LIABILITIES A firm's **current liabilities** are debts that will be repaid in one year or less. Northeast Art Supply purchased merchandise from its suppliers on credit. Thus, its balance sheet includes an entry for accounts payable. *Accounts payable* are short-term obligations that arise as a result of a firm making credit purchases.

Notes payable are obligations that have been secured with promissory notes. They are usually short-term obligations, but they may extend beyond one year. Only those that must be paid within the year are listed under current liabilities.

Northeast also lists *salaries payable* and *taxes payable* as current liabilities. These are both expenses that have been incurred during the current accounting period but will be paid in the next accounting period. For Northeast Art, current liabilities total $70,000.

LONG-TERM LIABILITIES **Long-term liabilities** are debts that need not be repaid for at least one year. Northeast lists only one long-term liability—a $40,000 *mortgage payable* for store equipment. As you can see in Figure 15-2, Northeast's current and long-term liabilities total $110,000.

fixed assets assets that will be held or used for a period longer than one year

depreciation the process of apportioning the cost of a fixed asset over the period during which it will be used

intangible assets assets that do not exist physically but that have a value based on the rights or privileges they confer on a firm

current liabilities debts that will be repaid in one year or less

long-term liabilities debts that need not be repaid for at least one year

© Elnur/Shutterstock

☐ How are current assets distinguished from fixed assets?

☐ Why are fixed assets depreciated on a firm's balance sheet?

☐ How do you determine the dollar amount of owner's equity for a sole proprietorship, or a partnership, or a corporation?

LEARNING OBJECTIVE

5 Read and interpret an income statement.

OWNERS' OR STOCKHOLDERS' EQUITY For a sole proprietorship or partnership, the owners' equity is shown as the difference between assets and liabilities. In a partnership, each partner's share of the ownership is reported separately in each owner's name. For a corporation, the owners' equity usually is referred to as *stockholders' equity*. The dollar amount reported on the balance sheet is the total value of stock plus retained earnings that have accumulated to date. **Retained earnings** are the portion of a business's profits not distributed to stockholders.

The original investment by the owners of Northeast Art Supply was $150,000 and was obtained by selling 25,000 shares at $6 per share. In addition, $80,000 of Northeast's earnings has been reinvested in the business since it was founded. Thus, owners' equity totals $230,000.

As the two grand totals in Figure 15-2 show, Northeast's assets and the sum of its liabilities and owners' equity are equal—at $340,000. The accounting equation (Assets = liabilities + owners' equity) is still in balance.

THE INCOME STATEMENT

Question: *Where can you find the profit or loss amount for Gap Inc.?*

Answer: The firm's income statement.

An **income statement** is a summary of a firm's revenues and expenses during a specified accounting period—one month, three months, six months, or a year. The income statement is sometimes called the *earnings statement* or *the statement of income and expenses*. Let's begin our discussion by constructing a personal income statement for Marty Campbell. Having worked as a sales representative for an office supply firm for the past three years, Marty now earns $33,600 a year, or $2,800 a month. After deductions, his take-home pay is $1,900 a month. As illustrated in Figure 15-3, Marty's typical monthly expenses include payments for an automobile loan, credit card purchases, apartment rent, utilities, food, clothing, and recreation and entertainment.

Although the difference between income and expenses is referred to as *profit* or *loss* for a business, it is normally referred to as a *cash surplus* or *cash deficit* for an individual. Fortunately for Marty, he has a surplus of $250 at the end of each month. He can use this surplus for savings, investing, or paying off debts. The information on a personal income statement like the one illustrated in Figure 15-3 can also be used to construct a personal budget in order to plan for the future. A **personal budget** is a specific plan for spending your income.

Figure 15-4 shows the income statement for Northeast Art Supply. For a business, revenues *less* cost of goods sold *less* operating expenses equals net income.

$$\text{Revenues} - \text{cost of goods sold} - \text{operating expenses} = \text{net income}$$

Revenues

Revenues are the dollar amounts earned by a firm from selling goods, providing services, or performing business activities. Like most businesses, Northeast Art obtains its revenues solely from the sale of its products or services. The revenues section of its income statement begins with gross sales. **Gross sales** are the total dollar amount of all goods and services sold during the accounting period. Deductions made from this amount are

- *Sales returns*—merchandise returned to the firm by its customers
- *Sales allowances*—price reductions offered to customers who accept slightly damaged or soiled merchandise
- *Sales discounts*—price reductions offered to customers who pay their bills promptly

retained earnings the portion of a business's profits not distributed to stockholders

income statement a summary of a firm's revenues and expenses during a specified accounting period

personal budget a specific plan for spending your income

revenues the dollar amounts earned by a firm from selling goods, providing services, or performing business activities

gross sales the total dollar amount of all goods and services sold during the accounting period

FIGURE 15-3: Personal Income Statement

By subtracting expenses from income, anyone can construct a personal income statement and determine if he or she has a surplus or deficit at the end of each month.

```
                    Marty Campbell
                Personal Income Statement
             For the month ended December 31, 20XX


    INCOME (Take-home pay)                              $1,900

    LESS MONTHLY EXPENSES
        Automobile loan                 $  250
        Credit card payment                100
        Apartment rent                     500
        Utilities                          200
        Food                               250
        Clothing                           100
        Recreation & entertainment         250
                                        _____

    TOTAL MONTHLY EXPENSES                               1,650
                                                        _____

    CASH SURPLUS (or profit)                           $   250
                                                        _____
```

© Cengage Learning 2013

net sales the actual dollar amounts received by a firm for the goods and services it has sold after adjustment for returns, allowances, and discounts

cost of goods sold the dollar amount equal to beginning inventory *plus* net purchases *less* ending inventory

The remainder is the firm's net sales. **Net sales** are the actual dollar amounts received by the firm for the goods and services it has sold after adjustment for returns, allowances, and discounts. For Northeast Art, net sales are $451,000.

Cost of Goods Sold

The standard method of determining the **cost of goods sold** by a retailing or a wholesaling firm can be summarized as follows:

Cost of goods sold = beginning inventory + net purchases
– ending inventory

According to Figure 15-4, Northeast began its accounting period on January 1 with a merchandise inventory that cost $40,000. During the next 12 months, the firm purchased merchandise valued at $346,000. After deducting *purchase discounts*, however, it paid only $335,000 for this merchandise. Thus, during the year, Northeast had total *goods available for sale* valued at $40,000 plus $335,000, for a total of $375,000.

Twelve months later, at the end of the accounting period on December 31, Northeast had sold all but $41,000 worth of the available goods. The cost of goods sold by Northeast

Inventory by the numbers. For most retailers, determining the level of available inventory in a store is a very important accounting function. In this photo, Chenille English-Boswell, an executive team leader at a Chicago-area Target Store, checks not only inventory levels but also prices to make sure merchandise is correctly priced.

© AP Photo/Charles Rex Arbogast

FIGURE 15-4: Business Income Statement

An income statement summarizes a firm's revenues and expenses during a specified accounting period. For Northeast Art, net income after taxes is $30,175.

NORTHEAST ART SUPPLY, INC.

Income Statement
For the Year Ended
December 31, 20XX

Revenues			
Gross sales		$465,000	
Less sales returns and allowances	$ 9,500		
Less sales discounts	4,500	14,000	
Net sales			$451,000
Cost of goods sold			
Beginning inventory, January 1, 20XX		$ 40,000	
Purchases	$346,000		
Less purchase discounts	11,000		
Net purchases		335,000	
Cost of goods available for sale		$375,000	
Less ending inventory December 31, 20XX		41,000	
Cost of goods sold			334,000
Gross profit			$117,000
Operating expenses			
Selling expenses			
Sales salaries	$ 22,000		
Advertising	4,000		
Sales promotion	2,500		
Depreciation—store equipment	3,000		
Depreciation—delivery equipment	4,000		
Miscellaneous selling expenses	1,500		
Total selling expenses		$ 37,000	
General expenses			
Office salaries	$ 28,500		
Rent	8,500		
Depreciation—furniture	1,500		
Utilities expense	2,500		
Insurance expense	1,000		
Miscellaneous expense	500		
Total general expense		42,500	
Total operating expenses			79,500
Net income from operations			$ 37,500
Less interest expense			2,000
NET INCOME BEFORE TAXES			$ 35,500
Less federal income taxes			5,325
NET INCOME AFTER TAXES			$ 30,175

was therefore $375,000 less ending inventory of $41,000, or $334,000. It is now possible to calculate gross profit. A firm's **gross profit** is its net sales *less* the cost of goods sold. For Northeast, gross profit was $117,000.

Operating Expenses

A firm's **operating expenses** are all business costs other than the cost of goods sold. Total operating expenses generally are divided into two categories: selling expenses or general expenses.

Selling expenses are costs related to the firm's marketing activities. For Northeast Art, selling expenses total $37,000. *General expenses* are costs incurred in

gross profit a firm's net sales *less* the cost of goods sold

operating expenses all business costs other than the cost of goods sold

managing a business. For Northeast Art, general expenses total $42,500. Now it is possible to total both selling and general expenses. As Figure 15-4 shows, total operating expenses for the accounting period are $79,500.

Net Income

When revenues exceed expenses, the difference is called **net income**. When expenses exceed revenues, the difference is called **net loss**. As Figure 15-4 shows, Northeast Art's *net income from operations* is computed as gross profit ($117,000) less total operating expenses ($79,500). For Northeast Art, net income from operations is $37,500. From this amount, *interest expense* of $2,000 is deducted to obtain a *net income before taxes* of $35,500. The interest expense is deducted in this section of the income statement because it is not an operating expense. Rather, it is an expense that results from financing the business.

Personal App Is a net loss always a red flag? Amazon.com, one of the most successful e-businesses ever, reported net losses in its early years as it geared up for rapid growth by investing heavily in technology, facilities, and equipment. So when you see a net loss on the income statement, dig deeper to find out why.

Would you like to drive one of these to college or work? Although not your typical commuter vehicle, these trucks represent a necessary investment for an electric utility company. Without these "bucket trucks", a utility company would be unable to repair existing electric transmission lines or build new ones. In fact, dollar values for all equipment purchases are reported on a firm's statement of cash flows.

© Tom McNemar/Shutterstock

Northeast's *federal income taxes* are $5,325. Although these taxes may or may not be payable immediately, they are definitely an expense that must be deducted from income. This leaves Northeast Art with a *net income after taxes* of $30,175. This amount may be used to pay a dividend to stockholders, it may be retained or reinvested in the firm, it may be used to reduce the firm's debts, or all three.

THE STATEMENT OF CASH FLOWS

Cash is vital to any business. In 1987, the SEC and the FASB required all publicly traded companies to include a statement of cash flows, along with their balance sheet and income statement, in their annual report. The **statement of cash flows** illustrates how the company's operating, investing, and financing activities affect cash during an accounting period. Whereas a firm's balance sheet reports dollar values for assets, liabilities, and owners' equity and an income statement reports the firm's dollar amount of profit or loss, the statement of cash flow focuses on how much cash is on hand to pay the firm's bills. Executives and managers can also use the information on a firm's statement of cash flows to determine how much cash is available to pay dividends to stockholders. Finally, the information on the statement of cash flows can be used to evaluate decisions related to a firm's future investments and financing needs. Outside stakeholders including investors, lenders, and suppliers are also interested in a firm's statement of cash flows. Investors want to know if a firm can pay dividends in the future. Before extending credit to a firm, lenders and suppliers often use the information on the statement of cash flows to evaluate the firm's ability to repay its debts.

A statement of cash flows for Northeast Art Supply is illustrated in Figure 15-5. It provides information concerning the company's cash receipts and cash payments and is organized around three different activities: operating, investing, and financing.

- *Cash flows from operating activities.* This is the first section of a statement of cash flows. It addresses the firm's primary revenue source—providing goods and services. Typical adjustments include adding the amount of depreciation

FIGURE 15-5: Statement of Cash Flows

A statement of cash flows summarizes how a firm's operating, investing, and financing activities affect its cash during a specified period—one month, three months, six months, or a year. For Northeast Art, the amount of cash at the end of the year reported on the statement of cash flows is $59,000—the same amount reported for the cash account on the firm's balance sheet.

NORTHEAST ART SUPPLY, INC.

Statement of Cash Flows
For the Year Ended
December 31, 20XX

Cash flows from operating activities		
Net Income		$30,175
Adjustments to reconcile net income to net cash flows		
Depreciation	$ 8,500	
Decrease in accounts receivable	1,000	
Increase in inventory	(5,000)	
Increase in accounts payable	6,000	
Increase in income taxes payable	3,000	13,500
Net cash provided by operating activities		$43,675
Cash flows from investing activities		
Purchase of equipment	$ (2,000)	
Purchase of investments	(10,000)	
Sale of investments	20,000	
Net cash provided by investing activities		8,000
Cash flows from financing activities		
Payments on debt	$(23,000)	
Payment of dividends	(5,000)	
Net cash provided by financing activities		(28,000)
NET INCREASE IN CASH		$23,675
Cash at beginning of year		35,325
CASH AT END OF YEAR		$59,000

to a firm's net income. Other adjustments for increase or decrease in amounts for accounts receivable, inventory, accounts payable, and income taxes payable are also required to reflect a true picture of cash flows from operating activities.

- *Cash flows from investing activities.* The second section of the statement is concerned with cash flow from investments. This includes the purchase and sale of land, equipment, and other assets and investments.
- *Cash flows from financing activities.* The third and final section deals with the cash flow from all financing activities. It reports changes in debt obligation and owners' equity accounts. This includes loans and repayments, the sale and repurchase of the company's own stock, and cash dividends.

The totals of all three activities are added to the beginning cash balance to determine the ending cash balance. For Northeast Art Supply, the ending cash balance is $59,000. Note that this is the same amount reported for the cash account on the firm's balance sheet. Together, the statement of cash flows, balance sheet, and income statement illustrate the results of past business decisions and reflect the firm's ability to pay debts and dividends and to finance new growth.

✳ Concept Check

☐ What is the purpose of the statement of cash flows?

☐ In a statement of cash flows, what is included in the operating activities section? In the investing activities section? In the financing activities section?

EVALUATING FINANCIAL STATEMENTS

LEARNING OBJECTIVE

7 Summarize how managers evaluate the financial health of a business.

All three financial statements—the balance sheet, the income statement, and the statement of cash flows—can provide answers to a variety of questions about a firm's ability to do business and stay in business, its profitability, and its value as an investment.

Using Accounting Information to Evaluate a Potential Investment

Many investors rely on accounting information to gauge the financial health of a business. Today, all three financial statements are included in a corporation's annual report. You can request a current annual report by contacting the corporation by mail or telephone. You can also obtain an annual report and additional accounting information by accessing the firm's Web site. Once at the corporate Web site, click on the button for "Investor Relations" or "Financial Information." Accounting information about a corporation is also available from many professional investment advisory services.

To help evaluate potential investments, investors often use a firm's three financial statements—the information on the balance sheet, income statement, and statement of cash flows. Although the numbers may be frightening, it helps to take a commonsense approach to evaluating accounting information. For example, consider the following questions:

1. Is an increase in sales revenues a healthy sign for a corporation? (Answer: yes)
2. Should a firm's net profit increase or decrease over time? (Answer: increase)
3. Should a corporation's retained earnings increase or decrease over time? (Answer: increase)

Although the answers to these questions are obvious, you will be surprised by how much you can learn from accounting information if you just spend some time with the numbers. In addition to a commonsense approach to evaluating a firm's accounting information, it helps to remember the following suggestions:

- All three financial statements should be audited by an outside source. The amounts reported on audited financial statements have been examined by an accountant(s) in order to determine if the firm used GAAPs.
- The balance sheet is a snapshot of the corporation's financial position at a single point in time. The dollar amounts for each asset, liability, and owners' equity account reported on a balance sheet will change over time. Therefore, be sure to use the most recent balance sheet available.
- The income statement reports sales revenues, expenses, and profit or loss for a specific period of time. Smart investors look for companies that are not only profitable, but also using new strategies to reduce operating expenses.
- The statement of cash flows indicates how much cash the business has and how it manages the cash that flows into and out of the business. This statement can help you determine if the firm can pay its debts and maintain its ability to borrow money in the future.
- Look at how the numbers relate to each other. For example, investors generally like to see that current assets are greater than current liabilities. This means the firm can pay its short-term liabilities quickly and maintain its ability to borrow additional money when needed.
- Learn how to calculate and interpret financial ratios. Some of the most important financial ratios are discussed in the last part of this chapter.

Personal App Your personal finances change day to day, and the same goes for any business's finances. Remember that financial statements are a "snapshot" of the company's money situation as of a certain day. Its finances may have changed a little (or a lot) since the statements were made public, so double-check when possible.

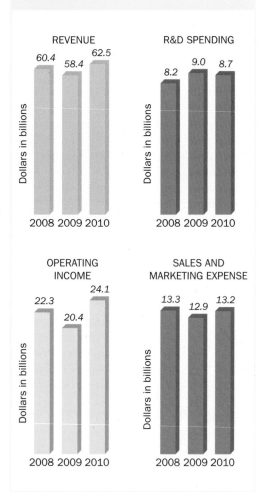

FIGURE 15-6: Comparisons of Present and Past Financial Statements for Microsoft Corporation

Most corporations include in their annual reports comparisions of the important elements of their financial statements for recent years.

REVENUE
60.4 58.4 62.5
Dollars in billions
2008 2009 2010

R&D SPENDING
8.2 9.0 8.7
Dollars in billions
2008 2009 2010

OPERATING INCOME
22.3 20.4 24.1
Dollars in billions
2008 2009 2010

SALES AND MARKETING EXPENSE
13.3 12.9 13.2
Dollars in billions
2008 2009 2010

Source: Adapted from the Microsoft Corporation 2010 Annual Report, www.microsoft.com (accessed April 4, 2011).

financial ratio a number that shows the relationship between two elements of a firm's financial statements

Sometimes additional information can be obtained by digging deeper into a firm's annual report. Be sure and read the letters from the chairman of the board and chief executive officer that describe the corporation's operations, prospects for the future, new products or services, financial strengths, and any potential problems. In addition, examine the footnotes closely, and look for red flags that may be in the fine print. Often, the footnotes contain (and sometimes hide) important information about the company and its finances. As one expert put it, "the footnotes are where they bury the bodies."

Finally, most corporations include in their annual reports comparisons of the important elements of their financial statements for recent years. Figure 15-6 shows such comparisons—of revenue, research and development (R&D), operating income, and sales and marketing expenses—for Microsoft Corporation, a world leader in the computer software industry. By examining these data, an operating manager can tell whether R&D expenditures have been increasing or decreasing over the past three years. The vice president of marketing can determine if the total amount of sales and marketing expenses is changing. Stockholders and potential investors, on the other hand, may be more concerned with increases or decreases in Microsoft's revenues and operating income over the same time period.

Comparing Data with Other Firms' Data

Many firms also compare their financial results with those of competing firms and with industry averages. Comparisons are possible as long as accountants follow GAAPs.

Except for minor differences in format and terms, the balance sheet, income statement, and statement of cash flows of Procter & Gamble, for example, will be similar to those of other large corporations, such as Church & Dwight, Clorox, Colgate-Palmolive, and Unilever, in the consumer goods industry. Comparisons among firms give managers a general idea of a firm's relative effectiveness and its standing within the industry. Competitors' financial statements can be obtained from their annual reports—if they are public corporations. Industry averages are published by reporting services such as D&B (formerly Dun & Bradstreet) and Standard & Poor's, as well as by some industry trade associations.

Still another type of analysis of a firm's financial health involves computation of financial ratios. A **financial ratio** is a number that shows the relationship between two elements of a firm's financial statements. Often business students are afraid of the math required to calculate ratios. In reality, the math usually requires that you add, subtract, multiply, and divide numbers. And with the help of a calculator, ratio analysis is easier than you might think.

Among the most useful ratios are profitability ratios, short-term financial ratios, activity ratios, and the debt-to-owners'-equity ratio. Like the individual elements in financial statements, these ratios can be compared with the firm's past ratios, with those of competitors, and with industry averages. The information required to form these ratios is found in a firm's balance sheet, income statement, and statement of cash flows (in our examples for Northeast Art Supply, Figures 15-2, 15-4, and 15-5).

Profitability Ratios

A firm's net income after taxes indicates whether the firm is profitable. It does not, however, indicate how effectively the firm's resources are being used. For this latter purpose, three ratios can be computed.

RETURN ON SALES **Return on sales (or profit margin)** is a financial ratio calculated by dividing net income after taxes by net sales. For Northeast Art Supply,

$$\text{Return on sales} = \frac{\text{net income after taxes}}{\text{net sales}} = \frac{\$30,175}{\$451,000}$$
$$= 0.067, \text{ or } 6.7 \text{ percent}$$

The return on sales indicates how effectively the firm is transforming sales into profits. A higher return on sales is better than a low one. Today, the average return on sales for all business firms is between 4 and 5 percent. With a return on sales of 6.7 percent, Northeast Art Supply is above average. A low return on sales can be increased by reducing expenses, increasing sales, or both.

RETURN ON OWNERS' (STOCKHOLDERS') EQUITY **Return on owners' equity** is a financial ratio calculated by dividing net income after taxes by owners' equity. For Northeast Art Supply,

$$\text{Return on owners' equity} = \frac{\text{net income after taxes}}{\text{owners' equity}} = \frac{\$30,175}{\$230,000}$$
$$= 0.13, \text{ or } 13 \text{ percent}$$

Return on owners' equity indicates how much income is generated by each dollar of equity. Northeast is providing income of 13 cents per dollar invested in the business. The average for all businesses is between 12 and 15 cents. A higher return on owners' equity is better than a low one, and the only practical ways to increase return on owners' equity is to reduce expenses, increase sales, or both.

EARNINGS PER SHARE From the point of view of stockholders, **earnings per share** is one of the best indicators of a corporation's success. It is calculated by dividing net income after taxes by the number of shares of common stock outstanding. For Northeast Art Supply,

$$\text{Earnings per share} = \frac{\text{net income after taxes}}{\text{common stock shares outstanding}} = \frac{\$30,175}{\$25,000}$$
$$= \$1.21 \text{ per share}$$

There is no meaningful average for this ratio mainly because the number of outstanding shares of a firm's stock is subject to change as a result of stock splits and stock dividends. In addition, some corporations choose to issue more stock than others. As a general rule, however, an increase in earnings per share is a healthy sign for any corporation.

Short-Term Financial Ratios

Two short-term financial ratios permit managers (and lenders) to evaluate a firm's ability to pay its current liabilities. Before we discuss these ratios, we should examine one other easily determined measure: working capital.

WORKING CAPITAL **Working capital** is the difference between current assets and current liabilities. For Northeast Art,

Current assets	$182,000
Less current liabilities	70,000
Equals working capital	$112,000

Why does a CPA tweet? All of the Big Four accounting firms are active on Twitter, as well as posting messages, contests, and photos on Facebook, listing job openings on LinkedIn, and posting videos and commercials on YouTube. The idea is to connect with potential job candidates, interact with clients and potential clients, engage employees, showcase the firms' expertise, and polish their reputations.

For example, PricewaterhouseCoopers, Ernst & Young, KPMG, and Deloitte Touche Tohmatsu recruit new graduates and experienced professionals by posting job openings on Facebook. They also use Twitter and LinkedIn to publicize studies they've conducted, comment on business conditions, and announce company news. And local affiliates often have special Facebook pages just for "alumni"— former staff members—to network.

Sources: Luis Gallardo, "Fueling the Social Media Engine," *Social Media Marketing Magazine*, January 17, 2011, www.smmmagazine.com; Karl Flinders, "How Deloitte Is Using Facebook, Twitter, and LinkedIn to Recruit," *ComputerWeekly*, July 2, 2010, www.computerweekly.com.

return on sales (or profit margin) a financial ratio calculated by dividing net income after taxes by net sales

return on owners' (stockholders') equity a financial ratio calculated by dividing net income after taxes by owners' equity

earnings per share a financial ratio calculated by dividing net income after taxes by the number of shares of common stock outstanding

working capital the difference between current assets and current liabilities

The next step: Going beyond a firm's financial statements. Often accountants must calculate financial ratios to determine the financial "health" of a firm. Among the most useful (and informative) are ratios that measure a firm's profitability, its ability to pay its debts, and how well it manages its inventory and receivables.

© Denis Opolja/Shutterstock

Working capital indicates how much would remain if a firm paid off all current liabilities with cash and other current assets. The "proper" amount of working capital depends on the type of firm, its past experience, and its particular industry. A firm with too little working capital may have to borrow money to finance its operations.

CURRENT RATIO A firm's **current ratio** is computed by dividing current assets by current liabilities. For Northeast Art Supply,

$$\text{Current ratio} = \frac{\text{current assets}}{\text{current liabilities}} = \frac{\$182,000}{\$70,000} = 2.6$$

This means that Northeast Art Supply has $2.60 of current assets for every $1 of current liabilities. The average current ratio for all industries is 2.0, but it varies greatly from industry to industry. A high current ratio indicates that a firm can pay its current liabilities. A low current ratio can be improved by repaying current liabilities, by reducing dividend payments to stockholders to increase the firm's cash balance, or by obtaining additional cash from investors.

ACID-TEST RATIO This ratio, sometimes called the *quick ratio*, is a measure of the firm's ability to pay current liabilities *quickly*—with its cash, marketable securities, and receivables. The **acid-test ratio** is calculated by adding cash, marketable securities, and receivables and dividing the total by current liabilities. The value of inventory and other current assets is "removed" from current assets because these assets are not converted into cash as easily as cash, marketable securities, and receivables. For Northeast Art Supply,

$$\text{Acid-test ratio} = \frac{\text{cash} + \text{marketable securities} + \text{receivables}}{\text{current liabilities}} = \frac{\$139,000}{\$70,000}$$
$$= 1.99$$

For all businesses, the desired acid-test ratio is 1.0. Northeast Art Supply is above average with a ratio of 1.99, and the firm should be well-able to pay its current liabilities. To increase a low acid-test ratio, a firm would have to repay current liabilities, reduce dividend payments to stockholders to increase the firm's cash balance, or obtain additional cash from investors.

(Personal App) Try the acid test on *your* finances to see how you stand. First, add up the amount in your savings and checking accounts plus any cash on hand and income you've earned but not yet received. Divide that total by the amount you owe on credit cards or other debts due within a year. Is the ratio 1 (or higher)?

Activity Ratios

Two activity ratios permit managers to measure how many times each year a company collects its accounts receivables or sells its inventory.

ACCOUNTS RECEIVABLE TURNOVER A firm's **accounts receivable turnover** is the number of times the firm collects its accounts receivable in one year. This ratio can be calculated by dividing net sales by accounts receivable. For Northeast Art,

current ratio a financial ratio computed by dividing current assets by current liabilities

acid-test ratio a financial ratio calculated by adding cash, marketable securities, and receivables and dividing the total by current liabilities

accounts receivable turnover a financial ratio calculated by dividing net sales by accounts receivable

$$\text{Accounts receivable turnover} = \frac{\text{net sales}}{\text{accounts receivable}} = \frac{\$451,000}{\$38,000}$$

$$= 11.9 \text{ times per year}$$

Northeast Art Supply collects its accounts receivables 11.9 times each year, or about every 30 days. If a firm's credit terms require customers to pay in 25 days, a collection period of 30 days is considered acceptable. There is no meaningful average for this measure mainly because credit terms differ among companies. A high accounts receivable turnover is better than a low one. As a general rule, a low accounts receivable turnover ratio can be improved by pressing for payment of past-due accounts and by tightening requirements for prospective credit customers.

INVENTORY TURNOVER A firm's **inventory turnover** is the number of times the firm sells its merchandise inventory in one year. It is approximated by dividing the cost of goods sold in one year by the average value of the inventory.

The average value of the inventory can be found by adding the beginning inventory value and the ending inventory value (given on the income statement) and dividing the sum by 2. For Northeast Art Supply, average inventory is $40,500. Thus

$$\text{Inventory turnover} = \frac{\text{cost of goods sold}}{\text{average inventory}} = \frac{\$334,000}{\$40,500}$$

$$= 8.2 \text{ times per year}$$

Northeast Art Supply sells its merchandise inventory 8.2 times each year, or about once every 45 days. The average inventory turnover for all firms is about 9 times per year, but turnover rates vary widely from industry to industry. For example, supermarkets may have inventory turnover rates of 20 or higher, whereas inventory turnover rates for furniture stores are generally well below the national average. The quickest way to improve inventory turnover is to order merchandise in smaller quantities at more frequent intervals.

Debt-to-Owners'-Equity Ratio

Our final category of financial ratios indicates the degree to which a firm's operations are financed through borrowing. Although other ratios can be calculated, the debt-to-owners'-equity ratio is used often to determine whether a firm has too much debt. The **debt-to-owners'-equity ratio** is calculated by dividing total liabilities by owners' equity. For Northeast Art Supply,

$$\text{Debt-to-owners'-equity ratio} = \frac{\text{total liabilities}}{\text{owners' equity}} = \frac{\$110.000}{\$230.000}$$

$$= 0.48, \text{ or } 48 \text{ percent}$$

A debt-to-owners'-equity ratio of 48 percent means that creditors have provided about 48 cents of financing for every dollar provided by the owners. The higher this ratio, the riskier the situation is for lenders. A high debt-to-owners'-equity ratio may make borrowing additional money from lenders difficult. It can be reduced by paying off debts or by increasing the owners' investment in the firm.

Northeast's Financial Ratios: A Summary

Table 15-2 compares the financial ratios of Northeast Art Supply with the average financial ratios for all businesses. It also lists the formulas we used to calculate Northeast's ratios. Northeast seems to be in good financial shape. Its return on sales, current ratio, and acid-test ratio are all above average. Its other ratios are about average, although its inventory turnover and debt-to-equity ratio could be improved.

inventory turnover a financial ratio calculated by dividing the cost of goods sold in one year by the average value of the inventory

debt-to-owners'-equity ratio a financial ratio calculated by dividing total liabilities by owners' equity

Concept Check *

☐ What type of information is contained in an annual report? How does the information help to identify financial trends?

☐ Explain the calculation procedure for and significance of each of the following:
    a. One of the profitability ratios.
    b. A short-term financial ratio.
    c. An activity ratio.
    d. Debt-to-owners'-equity ratio.

TABLE 15-2: Financial Ratios of Northeast Art Supply Compared with Average Ratios for All Businesses

Ratio	Formula	Northeast Ratio	Average Business Ratio	Direction for Improvement
Profitability Ratios				
Return on sales	$\dfrac{\text{net income after taxes}}{\text{net sales}}$	6.7%	4%–5%	Higher
Return on owners' equity	$\dfrac{\text{net income after taxes}}{\text{owners' equity}}$	13%	12%–15%	Higher
Earnings per share	$\dfrac{\text{net income after taxes}}{\text{common stock shares outstanding}}$	$1.21 per share	—	Higher
Short-Term Financial Ratios				
Working capital	current assets – current liabilities	$112,000	—	Higher
Current ratio	$\dfrac{\text{current assets}}{\text{current liabilities}}$	2.6	2.0	Higher
Acid-test ratio	$\dfrac{\text{cash + marketable securities + receivables}}{\text{current liabilities}}$	1.99	1.0	Higher
Activity Ratios				
Accounts receivable turnover	$\dfrac{\text{net sales}}{\text{accounts receivable}}$	11.9	—	Higher
Inventory turnover	$\dfrac{\text{cost of goods sold}}{\text{average inventory}}$	8.2	9	Higher
Debt-to-owners'-equity ratio	$\dfrac{\text{total liabilities}}{\text{owners' equity}}$	48%	—	Lower

This chapter ends our discussion of accounting information. In Chapter 16, we see why firms need financing, how they obtain it, and how they ensure that funds are used efficiently in keeping with their organizational goals.

Get Flashcards, Quizzes, Games, Crosswords, and more @ www.cengagebrain.com

SUMMARY

1 Explain why accurate accounting information and audited financial statements are important.

Accounting is the process of systematically collecting, analyzing, and reporting financial information. It can be used to answer questions about what has happened in the past; it also can be used to help make decisions about the future. Unfortunately, a large number of accounting scandals have caused people to doubt the financial information reported by a corporation. The purpose of an audit is to make sure that a firm's financial statements have been prepared in accordance with GAAPs. To help ensure that corporate financial information is accurate and in response to the accounting

scandals that have surfaced, the Sarbanes-Oxley Act was signed into law. This law contains a number of provisions designed to restore public confidence in the accounting industry.

2 Identify the people who use accounting information and possible careers in the accounting industry.

To be successful in the accounting industry, employees must be responsible, honest, and ethical; have a strong background in financial management; know how to use a computer and software to process data into accounting information; and be able to communicate with people who need accounting information. Primarily, management uses accounting information, but it is also demanded by lenders, suppliers, stockholders, potential investors, and government agencies. Although many people think that all accountants do the same tasks, there are special areas of expertise within the accounting industry. Typical areas of expertise include managerial, financial, cost, tax, government, and not-for-profit accounting. A private accountant is employed by a specific organization to operate its accounting system. A public accountant performs these functions for various individuals or firms on a fee basis. Most accounting firms include on their staffs at least one CPA. In addition to CPAs, there are also CMAs.

3 Discuss the accounting process.

The purpose of an accounting system is to (1) analyze daily transactions, (2) record the transactions, and (3) summarize accounting information that is included in a firm's financial statements. Step 1 requires analysis of source documents including receipts, invoices, sales slips, and other documents that show the dollar amounts of day-to-day business transactions. Step 2 is to record financial transactions in a general journal or specialized journals. Once all transactions are recorded in the firm's ledger accounts, step 3 is to summarize financial information in the firm's financial statements. The accounting process is based on the accounting equation: Assets = liabilities + owners' equity. Double-entry bookkeeping ensures that the balance shown by the accounting equation is maintained.

A firm's financial statements are included in its annual report. An annual report is a report distributed to stockholders and other interested parties that describes a firm's operating activities and its financial condition. Once statements are prepared, the books are closed. A new accounting cycle then is begun for the next accounting period.

4 Read and interpret a balance sheet.

A balance sheet (sometimes referred to as a statement of financial position) is a summary of a firm's assets, liabilities, and owners' equity accounts at the end of an accounting period. This statement must demonstrate that the accounting equation is in balance and that assets = liabilities + owners' equity. On the balance sheet, assets are categorized as current, fixed, or intangible. Similarly, liabilities can be divided into current liabilities and long-term ones. For a sole proprietorship or partnership, owners' equity is shown as the difference between assets and liabilities. For corporations, the owners' equity section reports the values of stock and retained earnings.

5 Read and interpret an income statement.

An income statement is a summary of a firm's financial operations during the specified accounting period. On the income statement, the company's gross profit is computed by subtracting the cost of goods sold from net sales. To determine the cost of goods sold for a retailing or a wholesaling firm, beginning inventory is added to net purchases, and then ending inventory is subtracted. Operating expenses and interest expense then are deducted to compute net income before taxes. Finally, income taxes are deducted to obtain the firm's net income after taxes.

6 Describe business activities that affect a firm's cash flow.

Since 1987, the Securities and Exchange Commission (SEC) and the FASB have required all publicly traded companies to include a statement of cash flows in their annual reports. This statement illustrates how the company's operating, investing, and financing activities affect cash during an accounting period. Together, the cash flow statement, balance sheet, and income statement illustrate the results of past decisions and the business's ability to pay debts and dividends as well as to finance new growth.

7 Summarize how managers evaluate the financial health of a business.

The firm's financial statements and its accounting information become more meaningful when compared with corresponding information for previous years, for competitors, and for the industry in which the firm operates. Such comparisons permit managers, employees, lenders, investors, and other interested people to pick out trends in growth, borrowing, income, and other business variables and to determine whether the firm is on the way to accomplishing its long-term goals. A number of financial ratios can be computed from the information in a firm's financial statements. These ratios provide a picture of the firm's profitability, its short-term financial position, its activity in the area of accounts receivable and inventory, and its debt financing. Like the information on the firm's financial statements, these ratios can and should be compared with those of past accounting periods, those of competitors, and those representing the average of the industry as a whole.

KEY TERMS

You should now be able to define and give an example relevant to each of the following terms:

accounting (441)
audit (442)
generally accepted accounting principles (GAAPs) (442)
managerial accounting (445)
financial accounting (445)
certified public accountant (CPA) (446)
certified management accountant (CMA) (446)
annual report (448)
assets (448)
liabilities (448)

owners' equity (448)
accounting equation (448)
double-entry bookkeeping system (448)
balance sheet (or statement of financial position) (449)
liquidity (450)
current assets (450)
fixed assets (451)
depreciation (451)
intangible assets (451)
current liabilities (451)
long-term liabilities (451)
retained earnings (452)

income statement (452)
personal budget (452)
revenues (452)
gross sales (452)
net sales (453)
cost of goods sold (453)
gross profit (454)
operating expenses (454)
net income (455)
net loss (455)
statement of cash flows (455)
financial ratio (458)
return on sales (or profit margin) (459)

return on owners' (stockholders') equity (459)
earnings per share (459)
working capital (459)
current ratio (460)
acid-test ratio (460)
accounts receivable turnover (460)
inventory turnover (461)
debt-to-owners'-equity ratio (461)

DISCUSSION QUESTIONS

1. Why do you think there have been so many accounting scandals in recent years?
2. Bankers usually insist that prospective borrowers submit audited financial statements along with a loan application. Why should financial statements be audited by a CPA?
3. What can be said about a firm whose owners' equity is a negative amount? How could such a situation come about?
4. Do the balance sheet, income statement, and statement of cash flows contain all the information you might want

as a potential lender or stockholder? What other information would you like to examine?
5. Why is it so important to compare a firm's current financial statements with those of previous years, those of competitors, and the average of all firms in the industry in which the firm operates?
6. Which do you think are the two or three most important financial ratios? Why?

TEST YOURSELF

Matching Questions

1. _____ It is the process of collecting, analyzing, and reporting data.
2. _____ All the firm's debts are included.
3. _____ It is the difference between a firm's assets and its liabilities.
4. _____ A person who is employed by PricewaterhouseCoopers.
5. _____ Inventories are an example.
6. _____ The ease with which assets can be converted into cash.
7. _____ This statement reveals the financial position of the firm.
8. _____ It illustrates how operating, investing, and financing activities affect cash.

9. _____ A promissory note secures this obligation.
10. _____ The result of dividing current assets by current liabilities.

a. accounting
b. assets
c. balance sheet
d. cost of goods sold
e. current ratio
f. double-entry bookkeeping
g. liabilities
h. liquidity
i. notes payable
j. owners' equity
k. public accountant
l. statement of cash flows

Part 6: Managing Information, Accounting, and Finance

True False Questions

11. **T F** A private accountant is an accountant whose services may be hired on a fee basis by individuals or business firms.

12. **T F** The accounting equation is assets + liabilities = owners' equity.

13. **T F** A cash receipts journal is a specialized journal.

14. **T F** Return on owners' equity indicates a measure of the amount earned per share.

15. **T F** An acid-test ratio is a measure of the firm's ability to pay current liabilities.

16. **T F** There is added protection for whistle-blowers who report violations of the Sarbanes-Oxley Act.

17. **T F** The debt-to-owners'-equity ratio is used to indicate the degree to which a firm's operations are financed through borrowing.

18. **T F** Recording transactions in the general ledger is the first step in the accounting cycle.

19. **T F** Marketable securities can be converted into cash in a matter of days.

20. **T F** Stockholders' equity represents the total value of a corporation's stock plus retained earnings that have accumulated to date.

Multiple-Choice Questions

21. _____ Which statement is not true about a balance sheet?
   a. It provides proof that assets = liabilities + owners' equity.
   b. It lists the current, fixed, and intangible assets.
   c. It summarizes the firm's revenues and expenses during one accounting period.
   d. It gives the liabilities of the firm.
   e. It shows the owners' equity in the business.

22. _____ The board of directors decided to pay 50 percent of the firm's $460,000 earnings in dividends to the stockholders. The firm has retained earnings of $680,000 on the books. After the dividends are paid, which of the following statements is true about the firm's retained earnings account?
   a. The new value of the firm's retained earnings is $910,000.
   b. The new value of the firm's retained earnings is $450,000.
   c. The firm failed to reach its profit goal.
   d. Each shareholder will receive more than he or she received last year.
   e. The firm's retained earnings are too high.

23. _____ A firm had gross profits from sales in the amount of $180,000, operating expenses of $90,000, and federal income taxes of $20,000. What was the firm's net income after taxes?
   a. $10,000
   b. $20,000
   c. $70,000
   d. $90,000
   e. $200,000

24. _____ The Sarbanes-Oxley Act
   a. requires the SEC to police the accounting industry.
   b. requires CEOs to certify periodic financial statements.
   c. subjects auditors, accountants, and employees to imprisonment for destroying financial documents.
   d. prohibits many types of consulting services by accounting firms.
   e. All of the above are true.

25. _____ A high debt-to-owners'-equity ratio
   a. reduces the risk for lenders.
   b. will increase as debts are paid off.
   c. will increase the owner's investment.
   d. makes borrowing money from lenders difficult.
   e. makes investors want to invest more money in the firm.

26. _____ An income statement is sometimes called the
   a. statement of financial position.
   b. owners' equity statement.
   c. earnings statement.
   d. statement of cash inflow.
   e. statement of revenues.

27. _____ When a company reports financial numbers that are lower than expected, generally
   a. the company's stock value will increase.
   b. the company's stock value will decrease.
   c. the company will restate its earnings amount.
   d. the stockholders' will immediately ask for an audit.
   e. the corporate officers will resign and new officers will be appointed.

28. _____ An audit is
   a. performed by the firm's private bookkeepers.
   b. not necessary if the firm used accepted bookkeeping procedures.
   c. required by many lenders who are trying to validate a firm's accounting statements.
   d. a waste of the firm's resources.
   e. a guarantee that a firm hasn't "cooked" the books.

29. _____ People who purchased stock in Morgan Oil Exploration are most interested in its _____ reports.
   a. financial accounting
   b. schedule of accounting
   c. cost accounting
   d. managerial accounting
   e. tax accounting

30. _____ The process of transferring information from source documents to a general journal or specialized journals is referred to as
   a. posting.
   b. journalizing.
   c. constructing a balance sheet.
   d. debiting.
   e. crediting.

Answers to the Test Yourself questions appear at the end of the book on page TY-1.

VIDEO CASE

Accounting Information Helps Level the Playing Field for The Little Guys

As the "leading supplier of exclusive, high-end audio and video electronics for homes, businesses, educational institutions, and other organizations in greater Chicagoland," The Little Guys has built an enviable reputation since its founding in 1994. The Little Guys sells and installs top-brand home audio and theater equipment and does it well. The company prides itself on its highly knowledgeable salespeople and outstanding customer service, and these have helped it survive strong competition from "big guys" like the Best Buy electronics chain, which has a store not far away, and economic downturns that have cut consumers' buying power. "We have the best employees," says the company's Web site, and "how we treat our customers makes us great."

David Wexler, the store's co-owner, describes how one of the firm's award-winning salespeople deals with his customers, for instance: "If a guy comes in to buy a $50 DVD player, Ed treats him the same as the guy who's spending $500,000 with us. I think that's what keeps people coming back over and over and over. He fights for them. Frankly, sometimes he fights too much for them. But he's their advocate, and they know it."

In response to recession-slowed sales, the company was recently forced to lay some people off and has reorganized departments from advertising to payroll (the latter is a major and complex expense for The Little Guys because its salespeople earn base pay plus a percentage of their sales). In another cost-cutting move, the company also recently moved to a new location not far from its original store, and it's keeping close track of its cash flows in and out. Salespeople are careful about customers' change orders, too, which often cost the company money.

"We're in survival mode as opposed to growth mode," says David Wexler of the downturn. "You can try to put cherries or chocolate sauce on it, but the fact is, it's…brutal out there right now….But if there's a thin silver lining to the whole thing, it's that you are cleaning things up and eliminating waste and finding ways to do business better."

With the help of QuickBooks accounting software and a professional accountant who visits regularly, David Wexler and co-owner Evie Wexler have deepened their knowledge of accounting and finance as the business has grown. In the beginning, for instance, they checked sales figures every day, but David quickly realized that this practice created instant information overload. Now he looks at the numbers about every week or ten days, comparing each set with past results, and the accountant comes in at least once each quarter to help with more complex issues like depreciation of assets and equipment for tax purposes. Taxes are a big concern. As Evie Wexler points out, sometimes the firm has to make a special push to sell off inventory in order to generate extra cash flow when taxes are due, or when it wants to purchase new merchandise that customers are asking for and that will therefore sell faster. Keeping warehoused inventory low saves money, too.

One reason cash flow can be slow is that customers often negotiate prices at The Little Guys, so that an expensive system might not only be sold at a discount, but the customer may also be given extra time to pay. That certainly helps make customers happy, but if it means the company is paying its own suppliers on time while customers lag in their payments, cash can get tight. As David explains, that's partly why The Little Guys limits the number of brands it sells and works with only a few suppliers. Establishing good relationships with these suppliers, largely by ordering regularly and paying on time, allows the company to ask them for special discounts or improved payment terms—even when other retailers aren't getting them—and find yet another way to earn a little more profit on the same volume of sales.[8]

Questions

1. Do you think a fairly small company like The Little Guys still needs a professional accountant after its owners have had so much experience running a successful business? Why or why not?
2. Do you think The Little Guys is doing a good job of managing its cash flow? If so, why, and if not, how can the company improve this function?
3. What are some of the factors that contribute to The Little Guys' operating expenses?

BUILDING SKILLS FOR CAREER SUCCESS

1. Exploring the Internet

In this chapter, we discussed a number of very important financial ratios that can help managers, employees, lenders, suppliers, and investors examine the financial health of a company. Although the formulas and mathematical calculations can be intimidating, in reality most of the ratios require that you simply divide one number by another number. And as pointed out in this chapter, the information needed to perform ratio analysis is reported on a firm's financial statements.

Assignment

1. Use the information contained on the Yahoo! Finance Web site to obtain financial information about Target—the parent company of Target and Super Target discount stores. In order to complete this exercise, follow these steps:
   a. Visit the Yahoo! Finance Web site at www.finance.yahoo.com.
   b. Enter the stock symbol (TGT) for the Target Corporation in the search box at the top on the left side of the screen. Then click "Get Quotes."
2. Look on the left side of the screen and scroll down to the bottom and click on the buttons for "Balance Sheet," "Income Statement," or "Cash Flow." Using this information reported on the Target's financial statements, calculate amounts for the following.
   a. Return on sales
   b. Return on owners' (stockholders') equity
   c. Working capital
   d. Current ratio
3. In a two-page report, summarize your calculations. Be sure to indicate the date you obtained the information and how your calculations could help managers and employees, investors, lenders, and suppliers determine the financial health of the Target Corporation.

2. Building Team Skills

This has been a bad year for Miami-based Park Avenue Furniture. The firm increased sales revenues to $1,400,000, but total expenses ballooned to $1,750,000. Although management realized that some of the firm's expenses were out of control, including cost of goods sold ($700,000), salaries ($450,000), and advertising costs ($140,000), it could not contain expenses. As a result, the furniture retailer lost $350,000. To make matters worse, the retailer applied for a $350,000 loan at Fidelity National Bank and was turned down. The bank officer, Mike Nettles, said that the firm already had too much debt. At that time, liabilities totaled $420,000; owners' equity was $600,000.

Assignment

1. In groups of three or four, analyze the financial condition of Park Avenue Furniture.
2. Discuss why you think the bank officer turned down Park Avenue's loan request.
3. Prepare a detailed plan of action to improve the financial health of Park Avenue Furniture over the next 12 months.

3. Researching Different Careers

As pointed out in this chapter, job opportunities for accountants and auditors in the accounting area are expected to experience much faster-than-average employment growth between now and the year 2018. Employment opportunities range from entry-level positions for clerical workers and technicians to professional positions that require a college degree in accounting, management consulting, or computer technology. Typical job titles in the accounting field include bookkeeper, corporate accountant, public accountant, auditor, managerial accountant, and controller.

Assignment

1. Answer the following questions based on information obtained from interviews with people employed in accounting, from research in the library or by using the Internet, or from information gained from your college's career center.
   a. What types of activities would a person employed in one of the accounting positions listed above perform on a daily basis?
   b. Would you choose this career? Why or why not?
2. Summarize your findings in a report.

CHAPTER 16 MASTERING FINANCIAL MANAGEMENT

Why should you care?

The old saying goes, "Money makes the world go around." For business firms, this is true. It's hard to operate a business without money. In this chapter, we discuss how financial management is used to obtain money and ensure that it is used effectively.

Learning Objectives

What you will be able to do once you complete this chapter:

1 Explain the need for financial management in business.

2 Summarize the process of planning for financial management.

3 Identify the services provided by banks and financial institutions for their business customers.

4 Describe the advantages and disadvantages of different methods of short-term debt financing.

5 Evaluate the advantages and disadvantages of equity financing.

6 Evaluate the advantages and disadvantages of long-term debt financing.

Get Flashcards, Quizzes, Games, Crosswords, and more @ www.cengagebrain.com

General Motors Goes Public—Again

General Motors (GM), the market-leader among the "Big Three" U.S. automakers for most of its corporate life, is known for such iconic car brands as Cadillac, Buick, and Chevrolet. In 2010, the automaker made headlines for a different reason: It raised more than $20 billion from a public stock offering, seeking to pay down debt and fuel growth in the aftermath of the previous year's huge bankruptcy proceeding.

GM's financial woes had been building for some time. From 2004 to 2009, the car company operated at a loss, as fuel prices soared and consumers reeling from the global recession put the brakes on buying. Late in 2008, GM's financial position was so poor that it applied for, and received, billions of dollars in low-cost U.S. government loans.

Finally, GM filed for bankruptcy protection in mid-2009 after top management concluded that the company had to significantly downsize before it could turn its financial fortunes around. In the words of GM's chief financial officer, the bankruptcy filing gave the firm a "once-in-a-lifetime opportunity to get our balance sheet healthy" by reorganizing its business affairs and cutting costs through factory closings and layoffs. Now, after decades of market leadership followed by a painful period of financial hardship, GM would have no shares being traded on the stock exchanges.

By 2010, GM was refashioning its product lines and getting ready for such major introductions as the electric Chevy Volt car. Just as important, the company was again reporting profits. In November, GM's position was so strong that it could make a successful public stock offering. It began selling shares on the New York Stock Exchange once again at an offering price of $33 for each share of common stock. Much of the $20 billion raised in the stock offering went to pay off some of the government loans. In fact, one of management's top financial objectives in the wake of the automaker's newfound profit momentum was to steer in the direction of a debt-free future.

Only a few months after the stock offering, GM declared a dividend for holders of its preferred stock. Looking ahead, GM is gearing up for higher sales and profits as new models drive into showrooms across America and recession-weary consumers begin to open their wallets and buy.[1]

Did you know?

GM's public stock offering in 2010 raised more than $20 billion and put the automaker on the road toward a debt-free future.

Although most managers and employees have been affected by the economic crisis, the last few years have been especially difficult for financial managers. After all, they are the ones that must be able to raise the money needed to pay bills and expenses to keep a company's doors open. In fact, executives at General Motors—the company profiled in the Inside Business case for this chapter—were forced to obtain low-cost loans from the government and eventually filed for bankruptcy protection in 2009. And yet because of effective financial management after the bankruptcy, the American automaker's financial picture was so strong that it could make a successful public stock offering and raise $20 billion in 2010. Did their financial plan work? The answer: A definite yes! Today, General Motors is selling more cars, developing environmentally friendly engines, creating concept cars for the future, and has returned to profitability. Although there are many factors that account for General Motor's success, most experts agree that the firm's financial planning enabled it to weather the economic storm and build for the future.

In reality, the crisis was a wake-up call for all corporate executives, managers, and business owners because one factor became obvious. The ability to borrow money (debt capital) or obtain money from the owners of a business (equity capital) is necessary for the efficient operation of a business firm *and* our economic system. In this chapter we focus on how firms find the financing required to meet two needs of all business organizations: the need for money to start a business and keep it going, and the need to manage that money effectively. We also look at how firms develop financial plans and evaluate financial performance. Then we examine typical banking services and compare various methods of obtaining short-term financing. We also examine sources of long-term financing.

LEARNING OBJECTIVE

1 Explain the need for financial management in business.

WHAT IS FINANCIAL MANAGEMENT?

Financial management consists of all the activities concerned with obtaining money and using it effectively. Within a business organization, the financial manager not only must determine the best way (or ways) to raise money, but he or she also must ensure that projected uses are in keeping with the organization's goals.

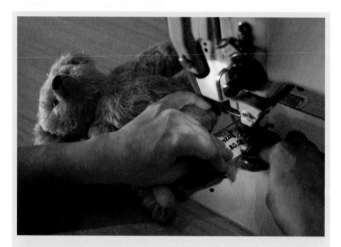

Someone's favorite toy! Before this toy teddy bear becomes someone's favorite toy, it has to be manufactured. And today manufacturing even small stuffed animals requires a great deal of money. To meet this need, most manufacturers rely on short-term financing to reduce cash-flow problems and pay for materials, labor, and other necessary business expenses.

The Need for Financing

Money is needed both to start a business and to keep it going. The original investment of the owners, along with money they may have borrowed, should be enough to open the doors. After that, ideally sales revenues should be used to pay the firm's expenses and provide a profit as well.

This is exactly what happens in a successful firm—over the long run. However, income and expenses may vary from month to month or from year to year. Temporary financing may be needed when expenses are high or sales are low. Then, too, situations such as the opportunity to purchase a new facility or expand an existing plant may require more money than is currently available within a firm.

SHORT-TERM FINANCING Short-term financing is money that will be used for one year or less. As illustrated in Table 16-1, there are many short-term financing needs, but two deserve special attention. First, certain business practices may affect a firm's cash flow and create a need for short-term financing. **Cash flow** is

financial management all the activities concerned with obtaining money and using it effectively

short-term financing money that will be used for one year or less

cash flow the movement of money into and out of an organization

TABLE 16-1: Comparison of Short- and Long-Term Financing

Whether a business seeks short- or long-term financing depends on what the money will be used for.

Type of Cash Needs	
Short-Term Financing Needs	Long-Term Financing Needs
Cash-flow problems	Business start-up costs
Current inventory needs	Mergers and acquisitions
Speculative production	New product development
Monthly expenses	Long-term marketing activities
Short-term promotional needs	Replacement of equipment
Unexpected emergencies	Expansion of facilities

© Cengage Learning 2013

© Alexandra Beier/Reuters/Landov

FIGURE 16-1: Cash Flow for a Manufacturing Business

Manufacturers such as Stanley Black & Decker often use short-term financing to pay expenses during the production process. Once goods are shipped to retailers and wholesalers and payment is received, sales revenues are used to repay short-term financing.

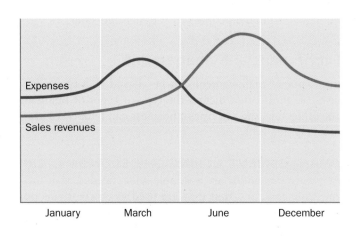

the movement of money into and out of an organization. The ideal is to have sufficient money coming into the firm in any period to cover the firm's expenses during that period. This ideal, however, is not always achieved. For example, California-based Callaway Golf offers credit to retailers and wholesalers that carry the firm's golf clubs, balls, clothing, and golf accessories. Credit purchases made by Callaway's retailers generally are not paid until 30 to 60 days (or more) after the transaction. Callaway therefore may need short-term financing to pay its bills until its customers have paid theirs.

A second major need for short-term financing is speculative production. **Speculative production** refers to the time lag between the actual production of goods and when the goods are sold. Consider what happens when a firm such as Stanley Black & Decker begins to manufacture electric tools and small appliances for sale during the Christmas season. Manufacturing begins in February, March, and April, and the firm negotiates short-term financing to buy materials and supplies, to pay wages and rent, and to cover inventory costs until its products eventually are sold to wholesalers and retailers later in the year. Take a look at Figure 16-1. Although Stanley Black & Decker manufactures and sells finished products all during the year, expenses peak during the first part of the year. During this same period, sales revenues are low. Once the firm's finished products are shipped to retailers and wholesalers and payment is received (usually within 30 to 60 days), sales revenues are used to repay short-term financing.

Retailers that range in size from Walmart to the neighborhood drugstore also need short-term financing to build up their inventories before peak selling periods. For example, Dallas-based Bruce Miller Nurseries must increase the number of shrubs, trees, and flowering plants that it makes available for sale during the spring and summer growing seasons. To obtain this merchandise inventory from growers or wholesalers, it uses short-term financing and repays the loans when the merchandise is sold.

LONG-TERM FINANCING **Long-term financing** is money that will be used for longer than one year. Long-term financing obviously is needed to start a new business. As Table 16-1 shows, it is also needed for business mergers and acquisitions, new product development, long-term marketing activities, replacement of equipment that has become obsolete, and expansion of facilities.

speculative production the time lag between the actual production of goods and when the goods are sold

long-term financing money that will be used for longer than one year

Personal App Take a moment to write down your short-term and long-term financing needs. Paying for college is a long-term need, for example, as is buying a home. What kinds of short-term financing needs do you have? What can you do to meet your short- and long-term needs in the coming months and years?

The amounts of long-term financing needed by large firms can seem almost unreal. The 3M Company—a large multinational corporation known for research and development—has invested more than $7 billion over the last five years to develop new products designed to make people's lives easier and safer.[2]

The Need for Financial Management

To some extent, financial management can be viewed as a two-sided problem. On one side, the uses of funds often dictate the type or types of financing needed by a business. On the other side, the activities a business can undertake are determined by the types of financing available.

FINANCIAL MANAGEMENT DURING THE ECONOMIC CRISIS Financial managers must ensure that funds are available when needed, that they are obtained at the lowest possible cost, and that they are used as efficiently as possible. During the recent economic crisis, many companies found it was increasingly difficult to use many of the traditional sources of short- and long-term financing described later in this chapter. In some cases, banks stopped making loans even to companies that had always been able to borrow money. Even companies that had always been able to sell commercial paper had difficulty finding buyers. For example, both GE and AT&T—two premier names in corporate America—could not get the short-term financing they were looking for. Furthermore, the number of corporations selling stock for the first time to the general public decreased because investors were afraid to invest in new companies. The worst case scenario: There was an increase in the number of businesses that filed for bankruptcy during the economic crisis as illustrated in Figure 16-2.

Although the number of business bankruptcies increased, fortunately there were many more business firms that were able to weather the economic storm and keep operating because of their ability to manage their finances. Proper financial management during both good and bad times must ensure the following:

- Financing priorities are established in line with organizational goals and objectives.
- Spending is planned and controlled.
- Sufficient financing is available when it is needed, both now and in the future.
- A firm's credit customers pay their bills on time, and the number of past due or delinquent accounts is reduced.
- Bills are paid promptly to protect the firm's credit rating and its ability to borrow money.
- The funds required for paying the firm's taxes are available when needed to meet tax deadlines.
- Excess cash is invested in certificates of deposit (CDs), government securities, or conservative, marketable securities.

FINANCIAL REFORM AFTER THE ECONOMIC CRISIS At the time of publication of this text, it has been more than a year since the financial crisis peaked during 2009. As the economy began to improve, it became apparent that something needed to be done to stabilize the financial system and prevent future economic meltdowns. In the wake of the crisis that affected both business firms and individuals, a cry for more regulations and reforms became a high priority.

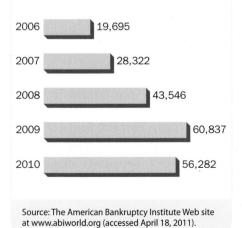

FIGURE 16-2: Business Bankruptcies in the United States

The number of businesses that filed for bankruptcy increased during the economic crisis. (*Note*: At the time of publication, 2010 was the most recent year for which complete statistics were available.)

Year	Bankruptcies
2006	19,695
2007	28,322
2008	43,546
2009	60,837
2010	56,282

Source: The American Bankruptcy Institute Web site at www.abiworld.org (accessed April 18, 2011).

On July 21, 2010, President Obama signed the Dodd-Frank Wall Street Reform and Consumer Protection Act into law. Still some experts say the law went too far while others argue the new law did not go far enough. Although the U.S. House of Representatives and Senate debate additional regulations, the goals are to hold Wall Street firms accountable for their actions, end taxpayer bailouts, tighten regulations for major financial firms, and increase government oversight. There has also been debate about limiting the amount of executive pay and bonuses, limiting the size of the largest financial firms, and curbing speculative investment techniques that were used by banks before the crisis. The new regulations will protect American families from unfair, abusive financial and banking practices. For business firms, the impact of new regulations could increase the time and cost of obtaining both short- and long-term financing.

Case closed—25 years in prison. The common phrase "Don't do the crime if you can't do the time," explains why Bernard Ebbers is so unhappy in this photo. Mr. Ebbers, former CEO of WorldCom, was sentenced to 25 years in prison for his part in the financial fraud and accounting scandal that led to World-Com's bankruptcy.

THE RISK-RETURN RATIO According to financial experts, business firms will find it more difficult to raise capital in the future for two reasons. First, financial reform and increased regulations will lengthen the process required to obtain financing. Second, both lenders and investors are more cautious about who receives financing. As a result of these two factors, financial managers must develop a strong financial plan that describes how the money will be used and how it will be repaid. When developing a financial plan for a business, a financial manager must also consider the risk-return ratio when making decisions that affect the firm's finances.

The **risk-return ratio** is based on the principle that a high-risk decision should generate higher financial returns for a business. On the other hand, more conservative decisions (with less risk) often generate lesser returns. Although financial managers want higher returns, they often must strive for a balance between risk and return. For example, American Electric Power may consider investing millions of dollars to fund research into new solar technology that could enable the company to use the sun to generate electrical power. Yet, financial managers (along with other managers throughout the organization) must determine the potential return before committing to such a costly research project.

Careers in Finance

When you hear the word *finance,* you may think of highly paid executives who determine what a corporation can afford to do and what it cannot. At the executive level, most large business firms have a **chief financial officer (CFO)** for financial management. A CFO is a high-level corporate executive who manages a firm's finances and reports directly to the company's chief executive officer or president. Some firms prefer to use the titles vice president of financial management, treasurer, or controller instead of the CFO title for executive-level positions in the finance area.

 **Personal App** You're the CFO of your life: You're already putting your math skills to work when you balance your checkbook, and you're using your communication skills when you apply for a job and negotiate pay. It's a lifelong position that can pay off in so many ways!

Although some executives in finance do make $300,000 a year or more, many entry-level and lower-level positions that pay quite a bit less are available. Banks, insurance companies, and investment firms obviously have a need for workers who can manage and analyze financial data. So do businesses involved in manufacturing, services, and marketing. Colleges and universities, not-for-profit organizations, and government entities at all levels also need finance workers.

People in finance must have certain traits and skills. One of the most important priorities for someone interested in a finance career is honesty. Be warned: Investors,

risk-return ratio a ratio based on the principle that a high-risk decision should generate higher financial returns for a business and more conservative decisions often generate lower returns

chief financial officer (CFO) a high-level corporate executive who manages a firm's finances and reports directly to the company's chief executive officer or president

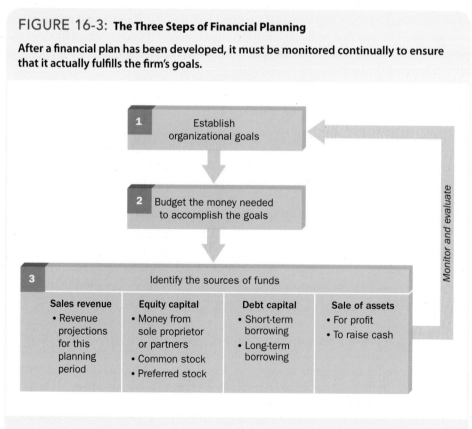

Concept Check

☐ How does short-term financing differ from long-term financing? Give two business uses for each type of financing.

☐ What is speculative production? How is it related to a firm's cash-flow problems?

☐ In your own words, define the risk-return ratio.

☐ To be successful, what traits and skills does an employee in the finance area need?

LEARNING OBJECTIVE

2 Summarize the process of planning for financial management.

lenders, and other corporate executives expect financial managers to be above reproach. Moreover, both federal and state government entities have enacted legislation to ensure that corporate financial statements reflect the "real" status of a firm's financial position. In addition to honesty, managers and employees in the finance area must:

1. Have a strong background in accounting or mathematics.
2. Know how to use a computer to analyze data.
3. Be an expert at both written and oral communication.

Typical job titles in finance include bank officer, consumer credit officer, financial analyst, financial planner, loan officer, insurance analyst, and investment account executive. Depending on qualifications, work experience, and education, starting salaries generally begin at $25,000 to $35,000 a year, but it is not uncommon for college graduates to earn higher salaries. In addition to salary, many employees have attractive benefits and other perks that make a career in financial management attractive.

PLANNING—THE BASIS OF SOUND FINANCIAL MANAGEMENT

In Chapter 6, we defined a *plan* as an outline of the actions by which an organization intends to accomplish its goals. A **financial plan**, then, is a plan for obtaining and using the money needed to implement an organization's goals.

Developing the Financial Plan

Financial planning (like all planning) begins with establishing a set of valid goals. Financial managers must then determine how much money is needed to accomplish each goal. Finally, financial managers must identify available sources of financing and decide which to use. The three steps involved in financial planning are illustrated in Figure 16-3.

FIGURE 16-3: **The Three Steps of Financial Planning**

After a financial plan has been developed, it must be monitored continually to ensure that it actually fulfills the firm's goals.

1 Establish organizational goals

2 Budget the money needed to accomplish the goals

3 Identify the sources of funds

Sales revenue	Equity capital	Debt capital	Sale of assets
• Revenue projections for this planning period	• Money from sole proprietor or partners • Common stock • Preferred stock	• Short-term borrowing • Long-term borrowing	• For profit • To raise cash

Monitor and evaluate

© Cengage Learning 2013

---

financial plan a plan for obtaining and using the money needed to implement an organization's goals

ESTABLISHING ORGANIZATIONAL GOALS As pointed out in Chapter 6, a *goal* is an end result that an organization expects to achieve over a one- to ten-year period. If goals are not specific and measurable, they cannot be translated into dollar costs, and financial planning cannot proceed. Goals also must be realistic. Otherwise, they may be impossible to finance or achieve. For large corporations, goals can be expensive. For example, ever wonder how much Geico's advertising program costs? Well, the clever advertisements featuring the green gecko are not cheap. In fact, Berkshire Hathaway, the parent company of Geico Insurance, spends over $600 million each year to attract new customers and to increase Geico's market share in the very competitive insurance industry.[3]

Personal App What are your personal and professional goals? Just like a business, you should be looking ahead to what you want to achieve in the next few years and writing down specific goals for yourself. If one goal is to buy a home, for example, this will help you think about how much you'll need and when you'll need it.

To be a successful retailer, it takes a financial plan. Many would-be business owners assume that if they have enough money, they will be successful. The truth is that effective financial planning involves more than just spending money. In fact, sound financial planning is built on the firm's goals and objectives, different types of budgets, and available sources of funds.

© Tomaz_Levstek/iStockphoto.com

BUDGETING FOR FINANCIAL NEEDS Once planners know what the firm's goals are for a specific period—say, the next calendar year—they can budget the costs the firm will incur and the sales revenues it will receive. Specifically, a **budget** is a financial statement that projects income, expenditures, or both over a specified future period.

Usually, the budgeting process begins with the construction of departmental budgets for sales and various types of expenses. Financial managers can easily combine each department's budget for sales and expenses into a company-wide cash budget. A **cash budget** estimates cash receipts and cash expenditures over a specified period. Notice in the cash budget for Stars and Stripes Clothing, shown in Figure 16-4, that cash sales and collections are listed at the top for each calendar quarter. Payments for purchases and routine expenses are listed in the middle section. Using this information, it is possible to calculate the anticipated cash gain or loss at the end of each quarter for this small retail clothing store.

Most firms today use one of two approaches to budgeting. In the *traditional* approach, each new budget is based on the dollar amounts contained in the budget for the preceding year. These amounts are modified to reflect any revised goals, and managers are required to justify only new expenditures. The problem with this approach is that it leaves room for padding budget items to protect the (sometimes selfish) interests of the manager or his or her department. This problem is essentially eliminated through zero-base budgeting. **Zero-base budgeting** is a budgeting approach in which every expense in every budget must be justified.

To develop a plan for long-term financing needs, managers often construct a capital budget. A **capital budget** estimates a firm's expenditures for major assets, including new product development, expansion of facilities, replacement of obsolete equipment, and mergers and acquisitions. For example, satellite television company Dish Network Corporation constructed a capital budget to determine the best way to finance the $320 million acquisition of Blockbuster Video in 2011. Although the Dish takeover was part of a bankruptcy settlement, Dish plans to keep some Blockbuster stores open and also many of the bankrupt firm's DVD rental kiosks. For Dish, the Blockbuster takeover represents a new way to market Dish satellite services.[4]

IDENTIFYING SOURCES OF FUNDS The four primary sources of funds, listed in Figure 16-3, are sales revenue, equity capital, debt capital, and proceeds from the sale of assets. Future sales revenue generally provides the greatest part of a firm's financing. Figure 16-4 shows that for Stars and Stripes Clothing, sales for the year are expected to

budget a financial statement that projects income, expenditures, or both over a specified future period

cash budget a financial statement that estimates cash receipts and cash expenditures over a specified period

zero-base budgeting a budgeting approach in which every expense in every budget must be justified

capital budget a financial statement that estimates a firm's expenditures for major assets and its long-term financing needs

FIGURE 16-4: Cash Budget for Stars and Stripes Clothing

A company-wide cash budget projects sales, collections, purchases, and expenses over a specified period to anticipate cash surpluses and deficits.

STARS AND STRIPES CLOTHING
Cash Budget   From January 1, 2011 to December 31, 2011

	First Quarter ($)	Second Quarter ($)	Third Quarter ($)	Fourth Quarter ($)	Total ($)
Cash sales and collections	150,000	160,000	150,000	185,000	645,000
Less payments					
Purchases	110,000	80,000	90,000	60,000	340,000
Wages/salaries	25,000	20,000	25,000	30,000	100,000
Rent	10,000	10,000	12,000	12,000	44,000
Other expenses	4,000	4,000	5,000	6,000	19,000
Taxes	8,000	8,000	10,000	10,000	36,000
Total payments	157,000	122,000	142,000	118,000	539,000
Cash gain or (loss)	(7,000)	38,000	8,000	67,000	106,000

cover all expenses and to provide a cash gain of $106,000. However, Stars and Stripes has a problem in the first quarter, when sales are expected to fall short of expenses by $7,000. In fact, one of the primary reasons for financial planning is to provide management with adequate lead time to solve this type of cash-flow problem.

A second type of funding is **equity capital**. For a sole proprietorship or partnership, equity capital is provided by the owner or owners of the business. For a corporation, equity capital is money obtained from the sale of shares of ownership in the business. Equity capital is used almost exclusively for long-term financing. Thus, it would not be considered for short-term financing needs, such as Stars and Stripes Clothing's first-quarter $7,000 shortfall.

A third type of funding is **debt capital**, which is borrowed money. Debt capital may be borrowed for either short- or long-term use—and a short-term loan seems made to order for Stars and Stripes Clothing's shortfall problem. The firm probably would borrow the needed $7,000 (or perhaps a bit more) at some point during the first quarter and repay it from second-quarter sales revenue.

Proceeds from the sale of assets are the fourth type of funding. Selling assets is a drastic step. However, it may be a reasonable last resort when sales revenues are declining, the firm is operating at a loss, or additional equity capital or debt capital cannot be found. Assets also may be sold when they are no longer needed or do not "fit" with the company's core business. Faced with sagging sales and an uncertain financial future, Ford Motor Company sold luxury brands Jaguar, Land Rover, and Aston Martin as part of a corporate plan to generate the financial fuel it needed during the recent economic crisis.

equity capital money received from the owners or from the sale of shares of ownership in a business

debt capital borrowed money obtained through loans of various types

Monitoring and Evaluating Financial Performance

It is important to ensure that financial plans are being implemented properly and to catch potential problems before they become major ones. Despite efforts to raise additional financing, reduce expenses, and increase sales, retail and online bookseller Borders filed for bankruptcy protection in early 2011. Eventually, the firm was forced to liquidate its inventory and close all its stores because a buyer could not be found for the bankrupt firm.

> **★ Concept Check**
>
> ☐ What is the function of a cash budget? A capital budget?
>
> ☐ What is the difference between equity capital and debt capital?
>
> ☐ Describe the four sources of funds for a business.
>
> ☐ How does a financial manager monitor and evaluate a firm's financing?

To prevent problems such as those just described, financial managers should establish a means of monitoring financial performance. Interim budgets (weekly, monthly, or quarterly) may be prepared for comparison purposes. These comparisons point up areas that require additional or revised planning—or at least areas calling for a more careful investigation. Budget comparisons can also be used to improve the firm's future budgets.

FINANCIAL SERVICES PROVIDED BY BANKS AND OTHER FINANCIAL INSTITUTIONS

For a business owner, it helps to know your banker. Banking services can be divided into three broad categories: traditional services, electronic banking services, and international services.

Traditional Banking Services for Business Clients

Traditional services provided by banks and other financial institutions include savings and checking accounts, loans, processing credit- and debit-card transactions, and providing professional advice.

SAVINGS AND CHECKING ACCOUNTS Savings accounts provide a safe place to store money and a very conservative means of investing. The usual *passbook savings account* earns between 0.15 and 0.40 percent in banks and savings and loan associations (S&Ls) and slightly more in credit unions. A business with excess cash can also purchase a certificate of deposit. A **certificate of deposit (CD)** is a document stating that the bank will pay the depositor a guaranteed interest rate on money left on deposit for a specified period of time. The rate always depends on how much is invested and for how long. At the time of publication, CDs earned between 0.50 and 2 percent. Generally, the rule is: the longer the period of time until maturity, the higher is the rate. Depositors are penalized for early withdrawal of funds invested in CDs.

Business firms (and individuals) also deposit money in checking accounts so that they can write checks to pay for purchases. A **check** is a written order for a bank or other financial institution to pay a stated dollar amount to the business or person indicated on the face of the check. For businesses, monthly charges are based on the average daily balance in the checking account and/or the number of checks written.

BUSINESS LOANS Banks, savings and loan associations, credit unions, and other financial institution provide short- and long-term loans to businesses. *Short-term business loans* must be repaid within one year or less. Typical uses for the money obtained through short-term loans include solving cash-flow problems, purchasing inventory, and meeting unexpected emergencies. To help ensure that short-term money will be available when needed, many firms establish a line of credit. A **line of credit** is a loan that is approved before the money is actually needed. Because all the necessary paperwork is already completed and the loan is preapproved, the business can obtain the money later without delay, as soon as it is required. Even with a line of credit, a firm may not be able to borrow money if the bank does not have sufficient funds available. For this reason, some firms prefer a **revolving credit agreement**, which is a guaranteed

Borders bookstores—no more! After 40 years, Borders is closing. The firm filed for bankruptcy in early 2011 and was forced to close a large number of stores in order to reorganize. Then in the summer of 2011, the bookseller was forced to liquidate its inventory and remaining stores despite revised financial plans, new financial goals, and its reorganizational efforts. Simply put: A buyer could not be found for the bankrupt firm.

LEARNING OBJECTIVE

3 Identify the services provided by banks and financial institutions for their business customers.

certificate of deposit (CD) a document stating that the bank will pay the depositor a guaranteed interest rate on money left on deposit for a specified period of time

check a written order for a bank or other financial institution to pay a stated dollar amount to the business or person indicated on the face of the check

line of credit a loan that is approved before the money is actually needed

revolving credit agreement a guaranteed line of credit

line of credit. Under this type of agreement, the bank guarantees that the money will be available when the borrower needs it. In return for the guarantee, the bank charges a commitment fee ranging from 0.25 to 1.0 percent of the *unused* portion of the revolving credit agreement. The usual interest is charged for the portion that *is* borrowed.

Long-term business loans are repaid over a period of years. The average length of a long-term business loan is generally three to seven years but sometimes as long as fifteen to twenty years. Long-term loans are used most often to finance the expansion of buildings and retail facilities, mergers and acquisitions, replacement of equipment, or product development. Most lenders require some type of collateral for long-term loans. **Collateral** is real estate or property (e.g., stocks, bonds, equipment, or any other asset of value) pledged as security for a loan.

Repayment terms and interest rates for both short- and long-term loans are arranged between the lender and the borrower. For businesses, repayment terms may include monthly, quarterly, semiannual, or annual payments.

Why Has the Use of Credit Transactions Increased?

By 2011, 188 million Americans will use credit cards to pay for everything from tickets on American Airlines to Zebco fishing gear.[5] Why have credit cards become so popular? For a merchant, the answer is obvious. By depositing charge slips in a bank or other financial institution, the merchant can convert credit-card sales into cash. In return for processing the merchant's credit-card transactions, the financial institution charges a fee that generally ranges between 1.5 and 4 percent. Typically, small, independent businesses pay more than larger stores or chain stores. Let's assume that you use a Visa credit card to purchase a microwave oven for $300 from Gold Star Appliances, a small retailer in Richardson, Texas. At the end of the day, the retailer deposits your charge slip, along with other charge slips, checks, and currency collected during the day, at its bank. If the bank charges Gold Star Appliances 4 percent to process each credit-card transaction, the bank deducts a processing fee of $12 ($300 × 0.04 = $12) for your credit-card transaction and immediately deposits the remainder ($288) in Gold Star Appliances' account. The number of credit-card transactions, the total dollar amount of credit sales, and how well the merchant can negotiate the fees the financial institution charges determine actual fees.

Do not confuse debit cards with credit cards. Although they may look alike, there are important differences. A **debit card** electronically subtracts the amount of a customer's purchase from her or his bank account at the moment the purchase is made. (By contrast, when you use your credit card, the credit-card company extends short-term financing, and you do not make payment until you receive your next statement.) Debit cards are used most commonly to obtain cash at automatic teller machines (ATMs) and to purchase products and services from retailers.

Electronic Banking Services

An **electronic funds transfer (EFT) system** is a means of performing financial transactions through a computer terminal or telephone hookup. The following three EFT applications are changing how banks help firms do business:

1. *Automated clearinghouses (ACHs).* Designed to reduce the number of paper checks, automated clearinghouses process checks, recurring bill payments, Social Security benefits, and employee salaries. For example, large companies use ACHs to transfer wages and salaries directly into their employees' bank accounts, thus eliminating the need to make out individual paychecks.

collateral real estate or property pledged as security for a loan

debit card a card that electronically subtracts the amount of a customer's purchase from her or his bank account at the moment the purchase is made

electronic funds transfer (EFT) system a means of performing financial transactions through a computer terminal or telephone hookup

2. *Point-of-sale (POS) terminals.* A POS terminal is a computerized cash register located in a retail store and connected to a bank's computer. At the cash register, you pull your bank credit or debit card through a magnetic card reader. A central processing center notifies a computer at your bank that you want to make a purchase. The bank's computer immediately adds the amount to your account for a credit-card transaction. In a similar process, the bank's computer deducts the amount of the purchase from your bank account if you use a debit card. Finally, the amount of your purchase is added to the store's account. The store then is notified that the transaction is complete, and the cash register prints out your receipt.

Convenient banking. For both customers and employees, banking is different than it used to be. Bank customers, like the people in this photo, expect banks to provide ATM machines where customers can withdraw money and complete many banking activities. For employees, the name of the game is customer service whether the customer is standing at a bank teller's window or banking online.

© Richard B. Levine/Newscom

3. *Electronic check conversion (ECC).* Electronic check conversion is a process used to convert information from a paper check into an electronic payment for merchandise, services, or bills. When you give your completed check to a store cashier, the check is processed through an electronic system that captures your banking information and the dollar amount of the check. Once the check is processed, you are asked to sign a receipt, and you get a voided (canceled) check back for your records. Finally, the funds to pay for your transaction are transferred into the business firm's account. ECC also can be used for checks you mail to pay for a purchase or to pay on an account.

Bankers and business owners generally are pleased with EFT systems. EFTs are fast, and they eliminate the costly processing of checks. However, many customers are reluctant to use online banking or EFT systems. Some simply do not like "the technology," whereas others fear that the computer will garble their accounts. Early on, in 1978, Congress responded to such fears by passing the Electronic Funds Transfer Act, which protects the customer in case the bank makes an error or the customer's credit or debit card information is stolen.

International Banking Services

For international businesses, banking services are extremely important. Depending on the needs of an international firm, a bank can help by providing a letter of credit or a banker's acceptance.

A **letter of credit** is a legal document issued by a bank or other financial institution guaranteeing to pay a seller a stated amount for a specified period of time—usually 30 to 60 days. (With a letter of credit, certain conditions, such as delivery of the merchandise, may be specified before payment is made.)

A **banker's acceptance** is a written order for a bank to pay a third party a stated amount of money on a specific date. (With a banker's acceptance, no conditions are specified. It is simply an order to pay guaranteed by a bank without any strings attached.)

Both a letter of credit and a banker's acceptance are popular methods of paying for import and export transactions. Imagine that you are a business owner in the United States who wants to purchase some leather products from a small business in Florence, Italy. You offer to pay for the merchandise with your company's check drawn on an American bank, but the Italian business owner is worried about payment. To solve the problem, your bank can issue either a letter of credit or a banker's acceptance to guarantee that payment will be made. In addition to a letter of credit and a banker's acceptance, banks also can use EFT technology to speed international banking transactions.

One other international banking service should be noted. Banks and other financial institutions provide for currency exchange. If you place an order for

letter of credit a legal document issued by a bank or other financial institution guaranteeing to pay a seller a stated amount for a specified period of time

banker's acceptance a written order for a bank to pay a third party a stated amount of money on a specific date

Concept Check ✱

☐ Describe the traditional banking services provided by financial institutions.

☐ What are the major advantages of electronic banking services?

☐ How can a bank or other financial institution help American businesses to compete in the global marketplace?

Japanese merchandise valued at $50,000, how do you pay for the order? Do you use U.S. dollars or Japanese yen? To solve this problem, you can use the bank's currency-exchange service. To make payment, you can use either currency, and if necessary, the bank will exchange one currency for the other to complete your transaction.

LEARNING OBJECTIVE

4 Describe the advantages and disadvantages of different methods of short-term debt financing.

SOURCES OF SHORT-TERM DEBT FINANCING

Typically, short-term debt financing is money that will be repaid in one year or less. During the economic crisis, many business firms found that it was much more difficult to borrow money for short periods of time to purchase inventory, buy supplies, pay salaries, and meet everyday expenses. Today the amount of available short-term financing has increased. Nevertheless, a business must be able to repay borrowed funds before lenders and investors will provide this type of financing.

The decision to borrow money does not necessarily mean that a firm is in financial trouble. On the contrary, astute financial management often means regular, responsible borrowing of many different kinds to meet different needs. In this section, we examine the sources of *short-term debt financing* available to businesses. In the next two sections, we look at long-term financing options: equity capital and debt capital.

Sources of Unsecured Short-Term Financing

Short-term debt financing is usually easier to obtain than long-term debt financing for three reasons:

1. For the lender, the shorter repayment period means less risk of non-payment.
2. The dollar amounts of short-term loans are usually smaller than those of long-term loans.
3. A close working relationship normally exists between the short-term borrower and the lender.

Most lenders do not require collateral for short-term financing. If they do, it is usually because they are concerned about the size of a particular loan, the borrowing firm's poor credit rating, or the general prospects of repayment.

Unsecured financing is financing that is not backed by collateral. A company seeking unsecured short-term financing has several options.

TRADE CREDIT Manufacturers and wholesalers often provide financial aid to retailers by allowing them 30 to 60 days (or more) in which to pay for merchandise. This delayed payment, known as **trade credit**, is a type of short-term financing extended by a seller who does not require immediate payment after delivery of merchandise. It is the most popular form of short-term financing, because most manufacturers and wholesalers do not charge interest for trade credit. In fact, from 70 to 90 percent of all transactions between businesses involve some trade credit.

Let us assume that Discount Tire Store receives a shipment of tires from a manufacturer. Along with the merchandise, the manufacturer sends an invoice that states the terms of payment. Discount Tire now has two options for payment. First, the retailer may pay the invoice promptly and take advantage of any cash discount the manufacturer offers. Cash-discount terms are specified on the invoice. For instance, "2/10, net 30" means that the customer—Discount Tire—may take a "2" percent discount if it pays the invoice within ten days of the invoice date. Let us assume that the dollar amount of the invoice is $200,000. In this case, the cash discount is $4,000 ($200,000 × 0.02 = $4,000).

unsecured financing financing that is not backed by collateral

trade credit a type of short-term financing extended by a seller who does not require immediate payment after delivery of merchandise

A second option is to wait until the end of the credit period before making payment. If payment is made between 11 and 30 days after the date of the invoice, Discount Tire must pay the entire amount. As long as payment is made before the end of the credit period, the customer maintains the ability to purchase additional merchandise using the trade-credit arrangement.

PROMISSORY NOTES ISSUED TO SUPPLIERS A **promissory note** is a written pledge by a borrower to pay a certain sum of money to a creditor at a specified future date. Suppliers uneasy about extending trade credit may be less reluctant to offer credit to customers who sign promissory notes. Unlike trade credit, however, promissory notes usually require the borrower to pay interest. Although repayment periods may extend to one year, most short-term promissory notes are repaid in 60 to 180 days.

A promissory note offers two important advantages to the firm extending the credit.

1. A promissory note is legally binding and an enforceable contract.
2. A promissory note is a negotiable instrument.

Because a promissory note is negotiable, the supplier (or company extending credit) may be able to discount, or sell, the note to its own bank. If the note is discounted, the dollar amount the supplier receives is slightly less than the maturity value because the bank charges a fee for the service. The supplier recoups most of its money immediately, and the bank collects the maturity value when the note matures.

UNSECURED BANK LOANS Banks and other financial institutions offer unsecured short-term loans to businesses at interest rates that vary with each borrower's credit rating. The **prime interest rate**, sometimes called the *reference rate*, is the lowest rate charged by a bank for a short-term loan. Figure 16-5 traces the fluctuations in the average prime rate charged by U.S. banks from 1990 to March 2011. This lowest rate generally is reserved for large corporations with excellent credit ratings. Organizations with good to high credit ratings may pay the prime rate plus "2" percent. Firms with questionable credit ratings may have to pay the prime rate plus "4" percent. (The fact that a banker charges a higher interest rate for a higher-risk loan is a practical application of the risk-return ratio discussed earlier in this chapter.) Of course, if the banker believes that loan repayment may be a problem, the borrower's loan application may well be rejected.

Personal App You should follow changes in the prime interest rate because sometimes the interest charged on consumer credit (such as a credit card, auto loan, or home mortgage loan) is based on the prime rate as of a certain date. Of course, as a consumer, you'll pay more than the prime rate on money you borrow, even if you have a great credit score.

When a business obtains an unsecured short-term bank loan, interest rates and repayment terms may be negotiated between the borrower and a bank. A bank may also require that a *compensating balance* be kept on deposit at the bank. Compensating balances, if required, are typically 10 to 20 percent of the borrowed funds. Finally, the bank may require that every commercial borrower *clean up* (pay off completely) its short-term promissory note or line of credit at least once each year and not use it again for a period of 30 to 60 days.

COMMERCIAL PAPER **Commercial paper** is a short-term promissory note issued by a large corporation. Commercial paper is secured only by the reputation of the issuing firm; no collateral is involved. It is usually issued in large denominations, ranging from $5,000 to $100,000. Corporations issuing commercial paper pay interest rates slightly below the interest rates charged by banks for short-term loans.

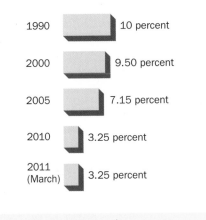

FIGURE 16-5: Average Prime Interest Rate Paid by U.S. Businesses, 1990 to March 2011

The prime rate is the interest rate charged by U.S. banks when businesses with the "best" credit ratings borrow money. All other businesses pay higher interest rates than the prime rate.

1990	10 percent
2000	9.50 percent
2005	7.15 percent
2010	3.25 percent
2011 (March)	3.25 percent

Source: Federal Reserve Bank Web site, www.federalreserve.gov (accessed April 20, 2011).

promissory note a written pledge by a borrower to pay a certain sum of money to a creditor at a specified future date

prime interest rate the lowest rate charged by a bank for a short-term loan

commercial paper a short-term promissory note issued by a large corporation

Thus, issuing commercial paper is cheaper than getting short-term financing from a bank. The interest rate a corporation pays when it issues commercial paper is tied to its credit rating and its ability to repay the commercial paper. It is most often used to purchase inventory, pay salaries and other necessary expenses, and solve cash-flow problems.

Large firms with excellent credit reputations like Microsoft, Procter & Gamble, and Caterpillar can raise large sums of money quickly by issuing commercial paper. However, during the recent economic crisis, even companies that had always been able to sell commercial paper had difficulty finding buyers. To help provide additional short-term financing, the Federal Reserve Bank stepped in and began to purchase the commercial paper from firms in need of financing to pay for day-to-day business operations.[6]

Sources of Secured Short-Term Financing

If a business cannot obtain enough capital through unsecured financing, it must put up collateral to obtain additional short-term financing. Almost any asset can serve as collateral. However, *inventories* and *accounts receivable* are the assets most commonly pledged for short-term financing. Even when it is willing to pledge collateral to back up a loan, a firm that is financially weak may have difficulty obtaining short-term financing.

LOANS SECURED BY INVENTORY Normally, manufacturers, wholesalers, and retailers have large amounts of money invested in finished goods. In addition, manufacturers carry raw materials and work-in-process inventories. All three types of inventory may be pledged as collateral for short-term loans. However, lenders prefer the much more salable finished merchandise to raw materials or work-in-process inventories.

A lender may insist that inventory used as collateral be stored in a public warehouse. In such a case, the receipt issued by the warehouse is retained by the lender. Without this receipt, the public warehouse will not release the merchandise. The lender releases the warehouse receipt—and the merchandise—to the borrower when the borrowed money is repaid. In addition to paying the interest on the loan, the borrower must pay for storage in the public warehouse. As a result, this type of loan is more expensive than an unsecured short-term loan.

LOANS SECURED BY RECEIVABLES As defined in Chapter 15, *accounts receivable* are amounts owed to a firm by its customers. A firm can pledge its accounts receivable as collateral to obtain short-term financing. A lender may advance 70 to 80 percent of the dollar amount of the receivables. First, however, it conducts a thorough investigation to determine the *quality* of the receivables. (The quality of the receivables is the credit standing of the firm's customers, coupled with the customers' ability to repay their credit obligations when they are due.) If a favorable determination is made, the loan is approved. When the borrowing firm collects from a customer whose account has been pledged as collateral, generally it must turn the money over to the lender as partial repayment of the loan. An alternative approach is to notify the borrower's credit customers to make their payments directly to the lender.

Factoring Accounts Receivable

Accounts receivable may be used in one other way to help raise short-term financing: They can be sold to a factoring company (or factor). A **factor** is a firm that specializes in buying other firms' accounts receivable. The factor buys the accounts receivable for less than their face value; however, it collects the full dollar amount when each account is due. The factor's profit thus is the difference between the face value of the accounts receivable and the amount the factor has paid for them. Generally, the

factor a firm that specializes in buying other firms' accounts receivable

TABLE 16-2: **Comparison of Short-Term Financing Methods**

Type of Financing	Cost	Repayment Period	Businesses that May Use It	Comments
Trade credit	Low, if any	30–60 days	All businesses with good credit	Usually no finance charge
Promissory note issued to suppliers	Moderate	One year or less	All businesses	Usually unsecured but requires legal document
Unsecured bank loan	Moderate	One year or less	All businesses	Promissory note, a line of credit, or revolving credit agreement generally required
Commercial paper	Moderate	One year or less	Large corporations with high credit ratings	Available only to large firms
Secured loan	High	One year or less	Firms with questionable credit ratings	Inventory or accounts receivable often used as collateral
Factoring	High	None	Firms that have large numbers of credit customers	Accounts receivable sold to a factor

amount of profit the factor receives is based on the risk the factor assumes. Risk, in this case, is the probability that the accounts receivable will not be repaid when they mature.

Even though the firm selling its accounts receivable gets less than face value, it does receive needed cash immediately. Moreover, it has shifted both the task of collecting and the risk of non-payment to the factor, which now owns the accounts receivable. Generally, customers whose accounts receivable have been factored are given instructions to make their payments directly to the factor.

Cost Comparisons

Table 16-2 compares the various types of short-term financing. As you can see, trade credit is the least expensive. Factoring of accounts receivable is typically the highest-cost method shown.

For many purposes, short-term financing suits a firm's needs perfectly. At other times, however, long-term financing may be more appropriate. In this case, a business may try to raise equity capital or long-term debt capital.

SOURCES OF EQUITY FINANCING

Sources of long-term financing vary with the size and type of business. As mentioned earlier, a sole proprietorship or partnership acquires equity capital when the owner or owners invest money in the business. For corporations, equity-financing options include the sale of stock and the use of profits not distributed to owners. All three types of businesses can also obtain venture capital and use long-term debt capital (borrowed money) to meet their financial needs. Different types of debt capital are discussed in the next section.

Selling Stock

Some equity capital is used to start every business—sole proprietorship, partnership, or corporation. In the case of corporations, stockholders who buy shares in the company provide equity capital.

INITIAL PUBLIC OFFERING AND THE PRIMARY MARKET An **initial public offering (IPO)** occurs when a corporation sells common stock to the general public for the first time. To raise money, 21Vianet Group—a cloud computing and

Concept Check ✱

☐ How important is trade credit as a source of short-term financing?

☐ Why would a supplier require a customer to sign a promissory note?

☐ What is the prime rate? Who gets the prime rate?

☐ Explain how factoring works. Of what benefit is factoring to a firm that sells its receivables?

LEARNING OBJECTIVE
5 Evaluate the advantages and disadvantages of equity financing.

initial public offering (IPO) occurs when a corporation sells common stock to the general public for the first time

SPOT LIGHT

The roller coaster ride for IPOs

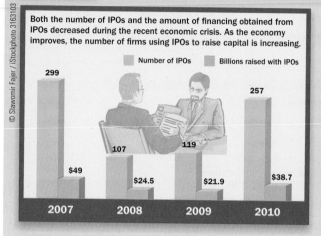

Both the number of IPOs and the amount of financing obtained from IPOs decreased during the recent economic crisis. As the economy improves, the number of firms using IPOs to raise capital is increasing.

■ Number of IPOs   ■ Billions raised with IPOs

299

257

107

119

$49

$24.5

$21.9

$38.7

2007   2008   2009   2010

Source: The Renaissance Capital IPO Home Web site at www.renaissancecapital.com (accessed April 22, 2011).

technology company based in China—used a 2011 IPO to raise almost $200 million that it could use to fund expansion and other business activities.[7] Established companies that plan to raise capital by selling subsidiaries and operating divisions to the public can also use IPOs. In early 2011, Sunoco—a large oil and gas company located in Pennsylvania—filed a registration statement with the Securities and Exchange Commission (SEC) to raise up to $100 million by selling shares in its metallurgical division. The new corporation—SunCoke Energy—will be a separate company and will produce metallurgical coke—a necessary component for manufacturing steel. Monies from the IPO will be used to increase the parent company's cash balance and provide funding for growth opportunities and expansion. The SunCoke Energy IPO was scheduled to be completed by the end of 2011.[8] In addition to using an IPO to increase the cash balance for the parent company, corporations often sell shares in a subsidiary when shares can be sold at a profit or when the subsidiary no longer fits with its current business plan.

When a corporation uses an IPO to raise capital, the stock is sold in the primary market. The **primary market** is a market in which an investor purchases financial securities (via an investment bank) directly from the issuer of the securities. An **investment banking firm** is an organization that assists corporations in raising funds, usually by helping to sell new issues of stocks, bonds, or other financial securities.

Although a corporation can have only one IPO, it can sell additional stock after the IPO, assuming that there is a market for the company's stock. Even though the cost of selling stock (often referred to as *flotation costs*) is high, the *ongoing* costs associated with this type of equity financing are low for two reasons. First, the corporation does not have to repay money obtained from the sale of stock because the corporation is under no legal obligation to do so. If you purchase corporate stock and later decide to sell your stock, you may sell it to another investor—not the corporation.

A second advantage of selling stock is that a corporation is under no legal obligation to pay dividends to stockholders. As noted in Chapter 4, a *dividend* is a distribution of earnings to the stockholders of a corporation. For any reason (e.g., if a company has a bad year), the board of directors can vote to omit dividend payments. Earnings then are retained for use in funding business operations. Of course, corporate management may hear from unhappy stockholders if expected dividends are omitted too frequently.

primary market a market in which an investor purchases financial securities (via an investment bank) directly from the issuer of those securities

investment banking firm an organization that assists corporations in raising funds, usually by helping to sell new issues of stocks, bonds, or other financial securities

secondary market a market for existing financial securities that are traded between investors

THE SECONDARY MARKET Although a share of corporate stock is only sold one time in the primary market, the stock can be sold again and again in the secondary market. The **secondary market** is a market for existing financial securities that are traded between investors. Although a corporation does not receive money each time its stock is bought or sold in the secondary market, the ability to obtain cash by selling stock investments is one reason why investors purchase corporate stock. Without the secondary market, investors would not purchase stock in the primary market because there would be no way to sell shares to other investors. Usually, secondary-market transactions are completed through a securities exchange or the over-the-counter (OTC) market.

© Slawomir Fajer / iStockphoto 3163103

A **securities exchange** is a marketplace where member brokers meet to buy and sell securities. Generally, securities issued by larger corporations are traded at the New York Stock Exchange (NYSE) (now owned by the NYSE Euronext holding company), or at regional exchanges located in different parts of the country. The securities of very large corporations may be traded at more than one of these exchanges. Securities of firms also may be listed on foreign securities exchanges—in Tokyo or London, for example.

Stocks issued by several thousand companies are traded in the OTC market. The **over-the-counter (OTC) market** is a network of dealers who buy and sell the stocks of corporations that are not listed on a securities exchange. The term *over-the-counter* was coined more than 100 years ago when securities actually were sold "over the counter" in stores and banks. Most OTC securities today are traded through an *electronic* exchange called the NASDAQ (pronounced "nazzdack"). The NASDAQ quotation system provides price information on more than 3,600 different stocks. Begun in 1971, the NASDAQ is now one of the largest securities markets in the world.

There are two types of stock: common and preferred. Each type has advantages and drawbacks as a means of long-term financing.

One way to raise capital. The Walt Disney Company, like many corporations, chose to sell stock to raise the money it needed to expand and become one of the largest entertainment companies in the world. On the other hand, investors purchase stock because they can profit from their investment if the price for a share of the corporation's stock increases and a corporation pays dividends.

© Amy Etra/PhotoEdit

COMMON STOCK A share of **common stock** represents the most basic form of corporate ownership. In return for the financing provided by selling common stock, management must make certain concessions to stockholders that may restrict or change corporate policies. Every corporation must hold an annual meeting, at which the holders of common stock may vote for the board of directors and approve or disapprove major corporate actions. Among such actions are:

1. Amendments to the corporate charter or corporate by-laws
2. Sale of certain assets
3. Mergers and acquisitions
4. New issues of preferred stock or bonds
5. Changes in the amount of common stock issued

Few investors will buy common stock unless they believe that their investment will increase in value. Information on the reasons why investors purchase stocks and how to evaluate stock investments is provided in Appendix A.

PREFERRED STOCK As noted in Chapter 4, the owners of **preferred stock** must receive their dividends before holders of common stock receive theirs. Also, preferred stockholders know the dollar amount of the dividend because it is stated on the stock certificate.

When compared to common stockholders, preferred stockholders also have first claim (after creditors) on assets if the corporation is dissolved or declares bankruptcy. Even so, as with common stock, the board of directors must approve dividends on preferred stock, and this type of financing does not represent a debt that must be legally repaid. In return for preferential treatment, preferred stockholders generally give up the right to vote at a corporation's annual meeting.

Although a corporation usually issues only one type of common stock, it may issue many types of preferred stock with varying dividends or dividend rates. For example, New York–based Consolidated Edison has one common-stock issue but three preferred-stock issues.

securities exchange a marketplace where member brokers meet to buy and sell securities

over-the-counter (OTC) market a network of dealers who buy and sell the stocks of corporations that are not listed on a securities exchange

common stock stock whose owners may vote on corporate matters but whose claims on profits and assets are subordinate to the claims of others

preferred stock stock whose owners usually do not have voting rights but whose claims on dividends and assets are paid before those of common-stock owners

going for SUCCESS

Who's Getting Venture Capital?

Venture capital firms make no secret of where they're looking to invest, and these days, they're investing heavily in "I" industries—information technology and infrastructure. According to a recent report, software companies are attracting considerable venture capital, as are companies that provide a wide range of consumer information services (such as Zynga, the fast-growing company behind such popular Facebook games as Farmville).

Venture capital money is also flowing to companies that handle power-grid improvements and companies creating new equipment to generate or transmit renewable energy. These include manufacturers of solar-energy panels and electronics firms that create sophisticated sensors and switches for wind and solar energy projects. Particularly hot are companies at the intersection of cutting-edge technology and eco-friendly energy. This, says one venture capital expert, is a sign of the "corporatization of clean tech." In addition, venture capital firms are working with companies developing infrastructure innovations such as "smart" parking meters that alert drivers when spots open up.

Given the aging of the U.S. population, it's not surprising that health-care companies are receiving large infusions of venture capital. Among the types of companies receiving venture-capital funding are firms with new technology for delivering better medical care, firms with systems for efficiently digitizing, organizing, and managing patient records, and firms with products that help improve the quality of life for consumers who have chronic conditions.

Looking ahead, venture capitalists will continue to monitor the business environment for clues to the next big opportunities for successful investment.

Sources: Colleen DeBaise, "What's Hot in Venture Capital in 2011," *Wall Street Journal*, February 9, 2011, www.wsj.com; Martin LaMonica, "IBM: 'Internet of Things' To Improve Infrastructure," *CNet News*, February 9, 2011, http://news.cnet.com; Tiffany Hsu, "Venture Capital Funding and Deals Rise in 2010, "*Los Angeles Times*, January 24, 2011, http://articles.latimes.com.

Retained Earnings

Most large corporations distribute only a portion of their after-tax earnings to stockholders. The portion of a corporation's profits *not* distributed to stockholders is called **retained earnings**. Because they are undistributed profits, retained earnings are considered a form of equity financing.

The amount of retained earnings in any year is determined by corporate management and approved by the board of directors. Most small and growing corporations pay no cash dividend—or a very small dividend—to their stockholders. All or most earnings are reinvested in the business for research and development, expansion, or the funding of major projects. Reinvestment tends to increase the value of the firm's stock while it provides essentially cost-free financing for the business. More mature corporations may distribute 40 to 60 percent of their after-tax profits as dividends. Utility companies and other corporations with very stable earnings often pay out as much as 80 to 90 percent of what they earn. For a large corporation, retained earnings can amount to a hefty bit of financing. For

retained earnings the portion of a corporation's profits not distributed to stockholders

example, on December 31, 2010, the total amount of retained earnings for General Electric was over $131 billion.[9]

Venture Capital and Private Placements

To establish a new business or expand an existing one, an entrepreneur may try to obtain venture capital. In Chapter 5, we defined *venture capital* as money invested in small (and sometimes struggling) firms that have the potential to become very successful. Most venture capital firms do not invest in the typical small business—a neighborhood convenience store or a local dry cleaner—but in firms that have the potential to become extremely profitable. Although venture capital firms are willing to take chances, they have also been more selective about where they invest their money after the recent economic crisis.

Generally, a venture capital firm consists of a pool of investors, a partnership established by a wealthy family, or a joint venture formed by corporations with money to invest. In return for financing, these investors generally receive an equity or ownership position in the business and share in its profits. Venture capital firms vary in size and scope of interest. Some offer financing for start-up businesses, whereas others finance only established businesses.

Another method of raising capital is through a private placement. A **private placement** occurs when stock and other corporate securities are sold directly to insurance companies, pension funds, or large institutional investors. When compared with selling stocks and other corporate securities to the public, there are often fewer government regulations and the cost is generally less when the securities are sold through a private placement. Typically, terms between the buyer and seller are negotiated when a private placement is used to raise capital.

SOURCES OF LONG-TERM DEBT FINANCING

As pointed out earlier in this chapter, businesses borrow money on a short-term basis for many valid reasons other than desperation. There are equally valid reasons for long-term borrowing. In addition to using borrowed money to meet the long-term needs listed in Table 16-1, successful businesses often use the financial leverage it creates to improve their financial performance. **Financial leverage** is the use of borrowed funds to increase the return on owners' equity. The principle of financial leverage works as long as a firm's earnings are larger than the interest charged for the borrowed money.

To understand how financial leverage can increase a firm's return on owners' equity, study the information for Texas-based Cypress Springs Plastics presented in Table 16-3. Pete Johnston, the owner of the firm, is trying to decide how best to finance a $100,000 purchase of new high-tech manufacturing equipment. He could borrow the money and pay 7 percent annual interest. As a second option, Johnston could invest an additional $100,000 in the firm. Assuming that the firm earns $95,000 a year and that annual interest for this loan totals $7,000 ($100,000 × 0.07 = $7,000), the return on owners' equity for Cypress Springs Plastics would be higher if the firm borrowed the additional financing. Return on owners' equity—a topic covered in Chapter 15— is determined by dividing a firm's net income by the

Concept Check ✱

☐ What are the advantages of financing through the sale of stock?

☐ From a corporation's point of view, how does preferred stock differ from common stock?

☐ Where do a corporation's retained earnings come from? What are the advantages of this type of financing?

☐ What is venture capital?

LEARNING OBJECTIVE

6 Evaluate the advantages and disadvantages of long-term debt financing.

private placement occurs when stock and other corporate securities are sold directly to insurance companies, pension funds, or large institutional investors

financial leverage the use of borrowed funds to increase the return on owners' equity

A big loan for a big auto manufacturer. Ford Motor Company President and CEO Alan Mulally (left) and U.S. Energy Secretary Steven Chu announce that the U.S. Department of Energy will loan the company $5.9 billion dollars. The government financing will be used to retool and upgrade automobile manufacturing plants so Ford can produce more fuel-efficient vehicles.

© Bill Pugliano/Getty Images

dollar amount of owners' equity. Based on the calculations illustrated in Table 16-3, Cypress Springs Plastics' return on owners' equity equals 17.6 percent if Johnston borrows the additional $100,000. The firm's return on owners' equity would decrease to 15.8 percent if Johnston invests an additional $100,000 in the business.

The most obvious danger when using financial leverage is that the firm's earnings may be less than expected. If this situation occurs, the fixed interest charge actually works to reduce or eliminate the return on owners' equity. Of course, borrowed money eventually must be repaid.

For a small business, long-term debt financing is generally limited to loans. Large corporations have the additional option of issuing corporate bonds.

TABLE 16-3: **Analysis of the Effect of Additional Capital from Debt or Equity for Cypress Springs Plastics, Inc.**

Additional Debt		Additional Equity	
Owners' equity	$ 500,000	Owners' equity	$ 500,000
Additional equity	+ 0	Additional equity	+ 100,000
Total equity	$ 500,000	Total equity	$ 600,000
Loan (@ 7%)	+ 100,000	No loan	+ 0
Total capital	$ 600,000	Total capital	$ 600,000
Year-End Earnings			
Gross profit	$ 95,000	Gross profit	$ 95,000
Less loan interest	− 7,000	No interest	− 0
Operating profit	$ 88,000	Operating profit	$ 95,000
Return on owners' equity	17.6%	Return on owners' equity	15.8%
($88,000 ÷ $500,000 = 17.6%)		($95,000 ÷ $600,000 = 15.8%)	

© Cengage Learning 2013

Long-Term Loans

Many businesses satisfy their long-term financing needs, such as those listed in Table 16-1, with loans from commercial banks, insurance companies, pension funds, and other financial institutions. Manufacturers and suppliers of heavy machinery may also provide long-term debt financing by granting credit to their customers.

TERM-LOAN AGREEMENTS A **term-loan agreement** is a promissory note that requires a borrower to repay a loan in monthly, quarterly, semiannual, or annual installments. Although repayment may be as long as 15 to 20 years, long-term business loans normally are repaid in 3 to 7 years.

Assume that Pete Johnston, the owner of Cypress Springs Plastics, decides to borrow $100,000 and take advantage of the principle of financial leverage illustrated in Table 16-3. Although the firm's return on owners' equity does increase, interest must be paid each year and, eventually, the loan must be repaid. To pay off a $100,000 loan over a three-year period with annual payments, Cypress Springs Plastics must pay $33,333 on the loan balance plus $7,000 annual interest, or a total of $40,333 the first year. Although the amount of interest decreases each year because of the previous year's payment on the loan balance, annual payments of this amount are still a large commitment for a small firm such as Cypress Springs Plastics.

The interest rate and repayment terms for term loans often are based on factors such as the reasons for borrowing, the borrowing firm's credit rating, and the value of collateral. Although long-term loans occasionally may be unsecured, the lender usually requires some type of collateral. Acceptable collateral includes real estate, stocks, bonds, equipment, or any asset of value. Lenders may also require that borrowers maintain a minimum amount of working capital.

THE BASICS OF GETTING A LOAN According to many financial experts, preparation is the key when applying for a long-term business loan. In reality, preparation begins before you ever apply for the loan. To begin the process, you should get to know potential lenders before requesting debt financing. Although there may be many potential lenders that can provide the money you need, the logical place to borrow money is where your business does its banking. This fact underscores the importance of maintaining adequate balances in the firm's bank accounts. Before applying for a loan, you may also want to check your firm's credit rating with a national credit bureau such as D&B (formerly known as Dun & Bradstreet).

Typically, business owners will be asked to fill out a loan application. In addition to the loan application, the lender will also want to see your current business plan. Be sure to explain what your business is, how much funding you require to accomplish your goals, and how the loan will be repaid. Next, have your certified public accountant (CPA) prepare financial statements. Most lenders insist that you submit current financial statements that have been prepared by an independent CPA. Then compile a list of references that includes your suppliers, other lenders, or the professionals with whom you are associated. You may also be asked to discuss the loan request with a loan officer. Hopefully, your loan request will be approved. If not, try to determine why your loan request was rejected. Think back over the loan process and determine what you could do to improve your chances of getting a loan the next time you apply.

(**Personal App**) As CFO of your life, you should put your financial house in order before you apply for any loan. Be sure to check your credit report in advance to see how it looks, and think about how you'll repay the loan. Apply only when you know your finances are ready for the spotlight.

Corporate Bonds

In addition to loans, large corporations may choose to issue bonds in denominations of $1,000 to $50,000. Although the usual face value for corporate bonds is $1,000, the total face value of all the bonds in an issue usually amounts to millions of dollars. In fact, one of the reasons why corporations sell bonds is that they can borrow a lot of money from a lot of different bondholders and raise larger amounts

term-loan agreement a promissory note that requires a borrower to repay a loan in monthly, quarterly, semiannual, or annual installments

of money than could be borrowed from one lender. A **corporate bond** is a corporation's written pledge that it will repay a specified amount of money with interest. The **maturity date** is the date on which the corporation is to repay the borrowed money. Today, most corporate bonds are registered bonds. A **registered bond** is a bond registered in the owner's name by the issuing company. Many corporations do not issue actual bonds. Instead, the bonds are recorded electronically, and the specific details regarding the bond issue, along with the current owner's name and address, are maintained by computer. Computer entries are safer because they cannot be stolen, misplaced, or destroyed, and make it easier to transfer ownership when bonds are sold.

Until a bond's maturity, a corporation pays interest to the bond owner at the stated rate. For example, owners of the American & Foreign Power Company bonds that mature in 2030 receive 5 percent per year for each bond. For each $1,000 bond issued, the corporation must pay bondholders $50 ($1,000 × 0.05 = $50) interest each year. Generally, interest on corporate bonds is paid semiannually—every six months in equal installments. On the maturity date, the registered owner receives cash equaling the face value.

TYPES OF BONDS Corporate bonds are generally classified as debentures, mortgage bonds, or convertible bonds. Most corporate bonds are debenture bonds. A **debenture bond** is a bond backed only by the reputation of the issuing corporation. To make its bonds more appealing to investors, a corporation may issue mortgage bonds. A **mortgage bond** is a corporate bond secured by various assets of the issuing firm. Typical corporate assets that are used as collateral for a mortgage bond include real estate, machinery, and equipment that is not pledged as collateral for other debt obligations. The corporation can also issue convertible bonds. A **convertible bond** can be exchanged, at the owner's option, for a specified number of shares of the corporation's common stock. An Advanced Micro Devices (AMD) bond that matures in 2015 is convertible: Each bond can be converted to 35.6125 shares of AMD common stock.[10] A corporation can gain in three ways by issuing convertible bonds. First, convertibles usually carry a lower interest rate than nonconvertible bonds. Second, the conversion feature attracts investors who are interested in the speculative gain that conversion to common stock may provide. Third, if the bondholder converts to common stock, the corporation no longer has to redeem the bond at maturity.

REPAYMENT PROVISIONS FOR CORPORATE BONDS Maturity dates for bonds generally range from 10 to 30 years after the date of issue. Some bonds are callable before the maturity date; that is, a corporation can buy back, or redeem, them. For these bonds, the corporation may pay the bond owner a call premium. The amount of the call premium is specified, along with other provisions, in the bond indenture. The **bond indenture** is a legal document that details all the conditions relating to a bond issue.

Before deciding if bonds are the best way to obtain corporate financing, managers must determine if the company can afford to pay the interest on the corporate bonds. It should be obvious that the larger the bond issue, the higher the dollar amount of interest. For example, assume that American Express issues bonds with a face value of $100 million. If the interest rate is 4.875 percent, the interest on this bond issue is $4,875,000 ($100 million × 0.04875 = $4,875,000) each year until the bonds are repaid. In addition, the American Express corporate bonds must all be redeemed for their face value ($100 million) at maturity. If the corporation defaults on (does not pay) either interest payments or repayment of the bonds at maturity, owners of bonds can force the firm into bankruptcy. And, if the firm goes bankrupt, bond owners' claims on the assets of the corporation take precedence over the claims of both common and preferred stockholders.

A corporation may use one of three methods to ensure that it has sufficient funds available to redeem a bond issue. First, it can issue the bonds as **serial bonds**, which

---

corporate bond a corporation's written pledge that it will repay a specified amount of money with interest

maturity date the date on which a corporation is to repay borrowed money

registered bond a bond registered in the owner's name by the issuing company

debenture bond a bond backed only by the reputation of the issuing corporation

mortgage bond a corporate bond secured by various assets of the issuing firm

convertible bond a bond that can be exchanged, at the owner's option, for a specified number of shares of the corporation's common stock

bond indenture a legal document that details all the conditions relating to a bond issue

serial bonds bonds of a single issue that mature on different dates

TABLE 16-4: Comparison of Long-Term Financing Methods

Type of Financing	Repayment	Repayment Period	Cost/Dividends or Interest	Businesses that May Use It
Equity				
Common stock	No	None	High initial cost; low ongoing costs because dividends and repayment not required	All corporations that sell stock to investors
Preferred stock	No	None	Dividends not required but must be paid before common stockholders receive any dividends	Large corporations that have an established investor base of common stockholders
Debt				
Long-term loan	Yes	Usually 3–7 years	Interest rates between 3.25 and 12 percent depending on economic conditions and the financial stability of the company requesting the loan	All firms that can meet the lender's repayment and collateral requirements
Corporate bond	Yes	Usually 10–30 years	Interest rates between 3 and 9 percent depending on economic conditions and the financial stability of the company issuing the bonds	Large corporations that are financially healthy

© Cengage Learning 2013

are bonds of a single issue that mature on different dates. For example, a company may use a 25-year $50 million bond issue to finance its expansion. None of the bonds mature during the first 15 years. Thereafter, 10 percent of the bonds mature each year until all the bonds are retired at the end of the 25th year. Second, the corporation can establish a sinking fund. A **sinking fund** is a sum of money to which deposits are made each year for the purpose of redeeming a bond issue. When Union Pacific Corporation sold a $275 million bond issue, the company agreed to contribute to a sinking fund until the bond's maturity in the year 2025.[11] Third, a corporation can pay off an old bond issue by selling new bonds. Although this may appear to perpetuate the corporation's long-term debt, a number of utility companies and railroads use this repayment method.

A corporation that issues bonds must also appoint a **trustee**, an individual or an independent firm that acts as the bond owner's representative. A trustee's duties are handled most often by a commercial bank or other large financial institution. The corporation must report to the trustee periodically regarding its ability to make interest payments and eventually redeem the bonds. In turn, the trustee transmits this information to the bond owners, along with its own evaluation of the corporation's ability to pay.

Cost Comparisons

Table 16-4 compares some of the methods that can be used to obtain long-term equity *and* debt financing. Although the initial flotation cost of issuing stock is high, selling common stock is generally a popular option for most financial managers. Once the stock is sold and upfront costs are paid, the *ongoing* costs of using stock to finance a business are low. The type of long-term financing that generally has the highest *ongoing* costs is a long-term loan (debt).

To a great extent, firms are financed through the investments of individuals—money that people have deposited in banks or have used to purchase stocks, mutual funds, and bonds. In Appendix A we look at how securities markets help people invest their money in business.

sinking fund a sum of money to which deposits are made each year for the purpose of redeeming a bond issue

trustee an individual or an independent firm that acts as a bond owner's representative

Concept Check ✱

☐ Describe how financial leverage can increase return on owners' equity.

☐ For a corporation, what are the advantages of corporate bonds over long-term loans?

☐ Describe the three methods used to ensure that funds are available to redeem corporate bonds at maturity.

Get Flashcards, Quizzes, Games, Crosswords, and more @ **www.cengagebrain.com**

SUMMARY

1 Explain the need for financial management in business.

Financial management consists of all activities concerned with obtaining money and using it effectively. Short-term financing is money that will be used for one year or less. There are many short-term needs, but cash flow and speculative production are two for which financing is often required. Long-term financing is money that will be used for more than one year. Such financing may be required for a business start-up, for a merger or an acquisition, for new product development, for long-term marketing activities, for replacement of equipment, or for expansion of facilities. Financial management can be viewed as a two-sided problem. On one side, the uses of funds often dictate the type or types of financing needed by a business. On the other side, the activities a business can undertake are determined by the types of financing available. Financial managers must also consider the risk-return ratio when making decisions. The risk-return ratio is based on the principle that a high-risk decision should generate higher financial returns for a business. On the other hand, more conservative decisions generate lesser returns. Financial managers must ensure that funds are available when needed, that they are obtained at the lowest possible cost, and that they are available for the repayment of debts. During the recent economic crisis, the number of business bankruptcies increased. Fortunately, there were many more business firms that were able to weather the economic storm and keep operating because of their ability to manage their finances.

2 Summarize the process of planning for financial management.

A financial plan begins with an organization's goals. Next, these goals are "translated" into departmental budgets that detail expected income and expenses. From these budgets, which may be combined into an overall cash budget, the financial manager determines what funding will be needed and where it may be obtained. Whereas departmental and cash budgets emphasize short-term financing needs, a capital budget can be used to estimate a firm's expenditures for major assets and its long-term financing needs. The four principal sources of financing are sales revenues, equity capital, debt capital, and proceeds from the sale of assets. Once the needed funds have been obtained, the financial manager is responsible for monitoring and evaluating the firm's financial activities.

3 Identify the services provided by banks and financial institutions for their business customers.

Banks and other financial institutions offer today's business customers a tempting array of services. Among the most important and attractive banking services are savings accounts, checking accounts, short- and long-term loans, and credit-card and debit-card processing. Increased use of electronic funds transfer systems (automated clearinghouses, point-of-sale terminals, and electronic check conversion) also will change the way that business firms bank and conduct typical business transactions. For firms in the global marketplace, a bank can provide letters of credit and banker's acceptances that will reduce the risk of nonpayment for sellers. Banks and financial institutions also can provide currency exchange to reduce payment problems for import or export transactions.

4 Describe the advantages and disadvantages of different methods of short-term debt financing.

Most short-term financing is unsecured; that is, no collateral is required. Sources of unsecured short-term financing include trade credit, promissory notes issued to suppliers, unsecured bank loans, and commercial paper. Sources of secured short-term financing include loans secured by inventory and accounts receivable. A firm may also sell its receivables to factors. Trade credit is the least-expensive source of short-term financing. Factoring is generally the most expensive approach.

5 Evaluate the advantages and disadvantages of equity financing.

A corporation can raise equity capital by selling either common or preferred stock. The first time a corporation sells stock to the general public is referred to as an initial public offering (IPO). With an IPO, the stock is sold in the primary market. Once sold in the primary market, investors buy and sell stock in the secondary market. Usually, secondary market transactions are completed through a securities exchange or the over-the-counter market. Common stock is voting stock; holders of common stock elect the corporation's directors and must approve changes to the corporate charter. Holders of preferred stock must be paid dividends before holders of common stock are paid any dividends. Another source of equity funding is retained earnings, which is the portion of a business's profits not distributed to stockholders. Venture capital—money invested in small (and sometimes struggling) firms that have the potential to become very successful—is yet another source of equity funding. Finally, a private placement can be used to sell stocks and other corporate securities.

6 Evaluate the advantages and disadvantages of long-term debt financing.

Regardless of whether the business is small or large, it can take advantage of financial leverage. Financial leverage is the use of borrowed funds to increase the return on owners' equity. The rate of interest for long-term loans usually depends on the financial status of the borrower, the reason for borrowing, and the kind of collateral pledged to back up the loan. Long-term business loans are normally repaid in 3 to 7 years but can be as long as 15 to 20 years. Money realized from the sale of corporate bonds must be repaid when the bonds mature. In addition, the corporation must pay interest on that money from the time the bonds are sold until maturity. Maturity dates for bonds generally range from 10 to 30 years after the date of issue. Three types of bonds—debentures, mortgage bonds, and convertible bonds—are sold to raise debt capital. When comparing the cost of equity and debt long-term financing, the ongoing costs of using stock (equity) to finance a business are low. The most expensive is a long-term loan (debt).

KEY TERMS

You should now be able to define and give an example relevant to each of the following terms:

financial management (470)	debt capital (476)	promissory note (481)	retained earnings (486)
short-term financing (470)	certificate of deposit (CD) (477)	prime interest rate (481)	private placement (487)
cash flow (470)		commercial paper (481)	financial leverage (487)
speculative production (471)	check (477)	factor (482)	term-loan agreement (489)
	line of credit (477)	initial public offering (IPO) (483)	corporate bond (490)
long-term financing (471)	revolving credit agreement (477)	primary market (484)	maturity date (490)
risk-return ratio (473)	collateral (478)	investment banking firm (484)	registered bond (490)
chief financial officer (CFO) (473)	debit card (478)	secondary market (484)	debenture bond (490)
financial plan (474)	electronic funds transfer (EFT) system (478)	securities exchange (485)	mortgage bond (490)
budget (475)	letter of credit (479)	over-the-counter (OTC) market (485)	convertible bond (490)
cash budget (475)	banker's acceptance (479)		bond indenture (490)
zero-base budgeting (475)	unsecured financing (480)	common stock (485)	serial bonds (490)
capital budget (475)	trade credit (480)	preferred stock (485)	sinking fund (491)
equity capital (476)			trustee (491)

DISCUSSION QUESTIONS

1. During the recent economic crisis, many financial managers and corporate officers have been criticized for (a) poor decisions, (b) lack of ethical behavior, (c) large salaries, (d) lucrative severance packages worth millions of dollars, and (e) extravagant lifestyles. Is this criticism justified? Justify your opinion.
2. What does a financial manager do? How can he or she monitor a firm's financial success?
3. If you were the financial manager of Stars and Stripes Clothing, what would you do with the excess cash that the firm expects in the second and fourth quarters? (See Figure 16-4.)
4. Develop a *personal* cash budget for the next six months. Explain what you would do if there are budget shortfalls or excess cash amounts at the end of any month during the six-month period.
5. Why would a lender offer unsecured loans when it could demand collateral?
6. How can a small-business owner or corporate manager use financial leverage to improve the firm's profits and return on owners' equity?
7. In what circumstances might a large corporation sell stock rather than bonds to obtain long-term financing? In what circumstances would it sell bonds rather than stock?

TEST YOURSELF

Matching Questions

1. _____ It is the movement of money into and out of a business organization.

2. _____ Determining a firm's financial needs is one of its important functions.

3. _____ A loan that is approved before the money is actually needed.

4. _____ Funding that comes from the sale of stock.

5. _____ Payments are usually made in 30 to 60 days from the invoice date.

6. _____ Must receive dividends before common stockholders.

7. _____ It is pledged as security for a loan.

8. _____ A method of financing that is legally binding and enforceable and often issued to suppliers.

9. _____ The deposits are used for redeeming a bond issue.

10. _____ This investment is backed by the reputation of the issuing corporation.

a. cash flow
b. collateral
c. debenture bond
d. equity capital
e. financial management
f. letter of credit
g. line of credit
h. preferred stock
i. private placement
j. promissory note
k. sinking fund
l. trade credit

True False Questions

11. **T F** Long-term financing is generally used to open new businesses.

12. **T F** A budget is a historical record of the previous year's financial activities.

13. **T F** When you use a debit card to make a purchase, a financial institution is extending credit to you and expects to be paid in the future.

14. **T F** With a banker's acceptance, certain conditions, such as delivery of the merchandise, may be specified before payment is made.

15. **T F** Most lenders do not require collateral for short-term financing.

16. **T F** A revolving credit agreement is a guaranteed line of credit.

17. **T F** Factoring of accounts receivable typically is the highest cost method of short-term financing.

18. **T F** Normally, the usual repayment period for a long-term loan is 3 to 7 years.

19. **T F** The face value for most corporate bonds is $5,000.

20. **T F** A capital budget estimates a firm's expenditures for labor costs.

Multiple-Choice Questions

21. _____ A written order for a bank or other financial institution to pay a stated dollar amount to a specified business or person is called a
a. check
b. deposit slip
c. notes receivable
d. receipt
e. debit memorandum

22. _____ Judy Martinez, owner of Judy's Fashions, received a $12,000 tax refund. She deposited the money in Chase Bank. The terms of the agreement are that she must leave the money on deposit for three years and the bank will pay her 3 percent interest. Her account is a
a. line of credit.
b. certificate of deposit.
c. checking account.
d. commercial paper agreement.
e. savings account.

23. _____ An invoice in the amount of $200 carries cash terms of "2/10, net 30." If the buyer takes advantage of the discount terms, how much will the buyer pay?
a. $100
b. $120
c. $140
d. $160
e. $196

24. _____ When a firm sells its accounts receivable to raise short-term cash, it is engaging in a strategy called
a. factoring.
b. financial planning.
c. equity financing
d. debt financing.
e. drafting.

25. _____ Retained earnings, as a form of equity financing, are
   a. gross earnings.
   b. profits before taxes.
   c. profits after taxes.
   d. undistributed profits.
   e. total owners' equity.

26. _____ Since prices are extremely low, the Pipeline Supply Company wants to purchase a special line of pipes from a company going out of business. Pipeline, however, will need to borrow money to make this deal. Which assets will Pipeline most commonly pledge as collateral for this short-term loan?
   a. delivery equipment
   b. notes payable
   c. manufacturing equipment
   d. owners' equity
   e. inventory

27. _____ The most basic form of corporate ownership that has voting rights is
   a. preferred stock.
   b. common stock.
   c. retained stock.
   d. deferred value stock.
   e. treasury stock.

28. _____ A short-term promissory note issued by large corporations is known as
   a. debenture agreement.
   b. equity agreement.
   c. commercial paper.
   d. draft agreement.
   e. loan commitment.

29. _____ Each of the following causes a cash-flow problem except
   a. embezzlement of company funds.
   b. an unexpected slow selling season.
   c. a large number of credit sales.
   d. slow-paying customers.
   e. customers who pay early.

30. _____ The primary sources of funds available to a business include all of the following *except*
   a. debt capital.
   b. equity capital.
   c. sales revenue.
   d. government grants.
   e. sale of assets.

Answers to the Test Yourself questions appear at the end of the book on page TY-1.

VIDEO CASE
Financial Planning Equals Profits for Nederlander Concerts

Nederlander Concerts is in the business of booking, promoting, and producing live music shows in the western United States. The company presents artists from James Taylor to Flogging Molly, Bruce Springsteen, Bonnie Raitt, and the Allman Brothers Band. But, says its CEO, "We're not trying to be necessarily a national player or an international player. We seek out opportunities that fit within and leverage our existing portfolio of small- to mid-size venues . . . . It's one of the few remaining family-run entertainment enterprises worldwide . . . . What this means for us on a day-to-day basis is that we can focus on running the business. We're not as guided by Wall Street, we don't have the same constraints, we don't have the same reporting responsibilities, and it allows us to focus on . . . our business strategy for development."

Of course, being a privately owned company and not needing to respond to shareholders (Wall Street) doesn't mean that Nederlander has *no* reporting responsibilities. As the CEO explains, "We assess at the beginning of the year not only concert revenue and expenses but also special event revenue. What kind of expenses are attended to generating that revenue? What's our fixed overhead for the year? Who's on the payroll, whether full-time, or part-time, or seasonal, and how much does it cost us to run the business on a day-to-day basis in order to secure those revenues and pay those

expenses? That's wrapped up into an annual budget at the beginning of every year, which is kind of a guideline for me to know how we achieve growth. It also allows me to communicate to our owners what our growth orientation is for that given year."

In addition to daily, weekly, and quarterly event reports, Nederlander's financial team generates daily and weekly reports of ticket sales. Monthly reports on company-wide performance feed into quarterly and annual reports. Each annual report is compared to that year's budget. The finance department tallies hundreds of transactions in order to arrive at some of these annual numbers, which are reported to the company's owners to ensure that the company is running as profitably as it can be.

Nederlander's managers say growth in the concert industry must be measured in the long term because the business is cyclical and the cost of real estate is so high that short-term profit is hard to generate. Still, the company is in a strong financial position (it is part of a profitable global theater-owning company called the Nederlander Organization), so it can afford to fund its own growth and expansion, or it can borrow on favorable terms. "We're very fortunate to have an ownership that is very well capitalized with over 80 years in the business," says the "CEO."

It can be thrilling to meet some of the artists the company books. "But at the end of the day it's a business," the CEO points out. "If we're not successful in growing our revenue and managing our expense, ultimately we won't be profitable, and our ownership will not be happy with those results."[12]

Questions

1. Here's what Nederlander's chief operating officer has to say about its business model: "A show has a short lifetime. You go and sell two months out, and the tickets have no value on any day but the day of the show. So it's a very interesting model in that sense." How do you think the short life of the company's products affects its financial planning?

2. The company uses its own arenas and theaters about 90 percent of the time. What are some of the possible disadvantages of owning its own venues?

3. Why would Nederlander choose to sometimes borrow funds for expansion if it has capital of its own?

BUILDING SKILLS FOR CAREER SUCCESS

1. Exploring the Internet

For many Americans, technology has changed the way they conduct their banking transactions. For example, an increasing number of individuals and businesses are using computers and the Internet to improve financial management activities, apply for loans, and pay their bills. Banking with the help of a computer is continually being made easier, giving both individuals and business customers access to their accounts 24 hours a day and seven days a week. As a result, bank customers have more control over their money.

Assignment

1. Examine the Web sites of several major banks with which you are familiar. Describe their online banking services. Are they worthwhile and could they help a small business owner manage a firm's finances.

2. How has technology changed the way you handle your money, such as depositing your paychecks, paying your monthly bills, obtaining cash, paying for purchases, and applying for loans? What impact have the same activities had on the banks and business firms that you interact with on a regular basis?

3. In the next five to ten years, what will the banking industry be like? How will these changes affect a small business owner and the way he or she banks in the future? The Internet and the library can help you to learn what is in the forefront of banking technology.

4. Prepare a report explaining your answers to these questions.

2. Building Team Skills

Suppose that for the past three years you have been repairing lawn mowers in your garage. Your business has grown steadily, and you recently hired two part-time workers. Your garage is no longer adequate for your business; it is also in violation of the city code, and you have already been fined for noncompliance. You have decided that it is time to find another location for your shop and that it also would be a good time to expand your business. You are concerned, however, about how you will get the money to move your shop and get it established in a new location.

Assignment

1. With all class members participating, use brainstorming to identify the following:
   a. The funds you will need to accomplish your business goals
   b. The sources of short-term financing available to you
   c. Problems that might prevent you from getting a short-term loan
   d. How you will repay the money if you get a loan
2. Have a classmate write the ideas on the board.
3. Discuss how you can overcome any problems that might hamper your current chances of getting a loan and how your business can improve its chances of securing short-term loans in the future.
4. Summarize what you learned from participating in this exercise.

3. Researching Different Careers

Financial managers are responsible for determining the best way to raise funds, for ensuring that the funds are used to accomplish their firm's goals and objectives, and for developing and implementing their firm's financial plan. Their decisions have a direct impact on the firm's level of success. When managers do not pay enough attention to finances, a firm is likely to fail.

Assignment

1. Investigate the job of financial manager by searching the library or Internet, by interviewing a financial manager, or both.
2. Find answers to the following questions:
   a. What skills do financial managers need?
   b. How much education is required?
   c. What is the starting salary? Top salary?
   d. What will the job of financial manager be like in the future?
   e. What opportunities are available?
   f. What types of firms are most likely to hire financial managers? What is the employment potential?
3. Prepare a report on your findings.

Running a Business: Part 6

Graeter's Adds MIS and Financing to the Recipe

A rapidly growing company often must accommodate new goals and capabilities. That's true for Graeter's, the Cincinnati-based family-owned maker of premium ice cream, now worth about $20 million in annual sales.

MIS Will Transform Decision Making

For three generations, Graeter's grew slowly and changed little. Today its ice cream is still hand-packed, but in almost every other respect, the company is changing rapidly under the leadership of a new generation. It has expanded capacity from one factory to three; its staff has grown; it operates a Web site and ships online orders nationwide; it nurtures customer relationships via Facebook and Twitter; it expanded its retail operation to several nearby states; and it has become a wholesaler, distributing its products to supermarkets as far away as Denver, Dallas, and Houston.

Says Paul Porcino, a management consultant to Graeter's, "We have done a lot of work up front to define what performances we are going to develop, what are the sales measures, how do we understand the data and information that is out there in terms of helping us run the organization from a strategic perspective, where are we getting margins from? We need to understand that first, so we had to pull together a lot of information."

This information will become input for new management information systems, giving Graeter's powerful decision-making tools. Says Porcino, "We are going to be . . . bringing in probably a variety of different information systems, both point-of-sale in retail, so we fully have an understanding of what we are selling, as well as some other financial systems, and probably some human resources information systems. . . . There will be a fairly radical transformation . . . .We'll be in a very different place."

Upgrading the Accounting Systems

Graeter's controller David Blink is responsible for preparing "all financial statements, all reports, payroll, [and] any ad hoc reports that any of the managers would need. I handle a lot of the reporting for the retail side as well as the manufacturing side," says Blink. Although an outside payroll company cuts the paychecks, Blink's department conducts its own information-gathering. "We are really tracking payroll right now. We are really working sales and payroll trying to get a real handle on that so I can produce reports for all the managers . . . biweekly, so it keeps them current and up to date." An outside accounting company also prepares the company's financial statements, with information collected by Blink and his staff.

From One Factory to Two

For many years one factory met all Graeter's production needs, but a few years ago, for its first major expansion, the company built a second plant, an $11 million, 28,000-square-foot facility in Cincinnati. The city contributed $3.3 million in financial incentives, some as loans, to help pay for the land and the new building; Graeter's sought outside financing for the rest. Besides adding 50 new jobs to the local economy, Graeter's also committed to "stay and grow" in Cincinnati for at least 20 years.

"We are incredibly grateful [for the City's assistance]," says, CEO Richard Graeter II, because not only will their support help us expand nationally, but it is also helping us create jobs locally."

From Two Factories to Three

A few months before opening the new plant, Graeter's faced an unexpected opportunity. Its remaining franchisee, who operated several stores and a factory, offered to sell his operation back to the company. Graeter's could operate not one, not two, but three production facilities. The timing was almost perfect for growth. But how would the company pay for this unanticipated acquisition?

Says Richard Graeter, "We had to come up with several millions of dollars in additional financing over and above what we had borrowed to build our new plant. So that means working with the bankers and lawyers and accountants to model how the business would look after the acquisition to determine if it makes financial sense, and then going out and raising the investment that you need to make the acquisition."

It was clear the firm would buy back the franchise and its factory. All its stores are now company-owned, and management is happy to keep it that way. "There is something about the personal touch on a product that you just can't replace," says a management consultant who works with the firm. Richard Graeter agrees. "We've never really been in it just to make the most money or to be everywhere. We've really been all about the quality of the product and our connection to the product, which tends to be pretty hands-on."[13]

© Liudmila Chernova / iStockphoto 12864114

© DNY59 / iStockphoto 1694138

Questions

1. Graeter's uses information to track cash, sales revenue, and expenses on a daily basis. How does this type of accounting system encourage effective decision-making and discourage store-level theft?

2. Which of the financial ratios might Graeter's, as a small privately owned business, want to track especially closely? Why?

3. Graeter's needed to raise several millions of dollars to buy out its franchisee after borrowing to build its new plant. One of the strategies it did *not* use to raise the needed funds was going public, that is, issuing an initial public offering or IPO to sell ownership shares in the firm. What are the advantages and disadvantages of issuing stock to obtain the money needed to expand a business?

Building a Business Plan: Part 6

Now that you have a marketing plan, the next big and important step is to prepare an information and financial plan. One of the biggest mistakes an entrepreneur makes when faced with a need for financing is not being prepared. The information contained in Chapters 14 (Understanding Information and e-Business), Chapter 15 (Using Accounting Information), and Chapter 16 (Mastering Financial Management) will help you prepare this section of the business plan and determine the amount of financing you need to start your business. With the help of information in the last three chapters of the text, the task may be easier than you think.

In this last section, you should also provide some information about your exit strategy, and discuss any potential trends, problems, or risks that you may encounter. Now is also the time to go back and prepare the executive summary, which should be placed at the beginning of the business plan.

The Information and Accounting Plan Component

Information and accounting systems are important if your business is to succeed. Your information plan should answer at least the following questions.

6.1 How will you gather information about competitors, their products, and the prices that they charge for their products and services?

6.2 Explain how you will develop a management information system to collect, store, update, and process data, and present information.

6.3 Will your business have an e-business component? If so, explain how you will sell your products or services online.

6.4 Who will create and maintain the accounting system that you will use to record routine business transactions for your business?

6.5 Will you hire an accountant to prepare financial statements for your firm?

The Financial Plan Component

Your financial plan should answer at least the following questions about the investment needed, sales and cash-flow forecasts, breakeven analysis, and sources of funding.

6.6 What is the actual amount of money you need to open your business (start-up budget) and the amount needed to keep it open (operating budget)? Prepare a realistic budget.

6.7 How much money do you have, and how much money will you need to start your business and stay in business?

6.8 Prepare a projected income statement by month for the first year of operation and by quarter for the second and third years.

6.9 Prepare projected balance sheets for each of the first three years of operation.

6.10 Prepare a breakeven analysis. How many units of your product or service will have to be sold to cover your costs?

6.11 Reinforce your final projections by comparing them with industry averages for your chosen industry.

The Exit Strategy Component

Your exit strategy component should at least include answers to the following questions:

6.12 How do you intend to get yourself (and your money) out of the business?

6.13 Will your children take over the business, or do you intend to sell it later?

6.14 Do you intend to grow the business to the point of an IPO?

6.15 How will investors get their money back?

The Critical Risks and Assumptions Component

Your critical risks and assumptions component should answer at least the following questions:

6.16 What will you do if your market does not develop as quickly as you predicted? What if your market develops too quickly?

6.17 What will you do if your competitors underprice or make your product obsolete?

6.18 What will you do if there is an unfavorable industry-wide trend?

6.19 What will happen if trained workers are not available as predicted?

6.20 What will you do if there is an erratic supply of products or raw materials?

The Appendix Component

Supplemental information and documents often are included in an appendix. Here are a few examples of some documents that can be included:

Résumés of owners and principal managers

Advertising samples and brochures

An organization chart

Floor plans

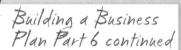
Building a Business Plan Part 6 continued

As you have discovered, writing a business plan involves a long series of interrelated steps. As with any project involving a number of complex steps and calculations, your business plan should be reviewed carefully and revised before you present it to potential investors, lenders, and suppliers.

Remember, there is one more component you need to prepare after your business plan is completed: The executive summary should be written last, but because of its importance, it appears after the introduction.

The Executive Summary Component

In the executive summary, give a one- to two-page overview of your entire business plan. This is the most important part of the business plan and is of special interest to busy bankers, investors, and other interested parties. Remember, this section is a summary; more detailed information is provided in the remainder of your business plan.

Make sure that the executive summary captures the reader's attention instantly in the first sentence by using a key selling point or benefit of the business.

Review of Business Plan Activities

Your executive summary should include answers to at least the following:

6.21 *Company information.* What product or service do you provide? What is your competitive advantage? When will the company be formed? What are your company objectives? What is the background of you and your management team?

6.22 *Market opportunity.* What is the expected size and growth rate of your market, your expected market share, and any relevant market trends?

Once again, review your answers to all the questions in the preceding parts to make sure that they are all consistent throughout the entire business plan.

Although many would-be entrepreneurs are excited about the prospects of opening their own business, remember that it takes a lot of hard work, time, and in most cases a substantial amount of money. While the business plan provides an enormous amount of information about your business, it is only the first step. Once it is completed, it is now your responsibility to implement the plan. Good luck in your business venture.

The information contained in "Building a Business Plan" will also assist you in completing the online Interactive *Business Plan*.

NOTES

CHAPTER 1

1   Jason Garcia, "Disney to Open Family-suites Hotel in Spring 2012," *Orlando Sentinel,* December 16, 2010, www.orlandosentinel.com; Brooks Barnes, "Disney Ends Strong Year with Quarter That's Soft," *New York Times,* November 12, 2010, p. B3; Ryan Tracy, "The Business of Magic," *Newsweek,* November 3, 2010, www.newsweek.com; James T. Areddy, "Disney to Build Shanghai Theme Park," *Wall Street Journal,* November 7, 2010, www.wsj.com; *The Walt Disney Company Fact Book 2009,* http://corporate.disney.go.com.

2   The Horatio Alger Web site at www.horatioalger.org (accessed January 10, 2011).

3   Ibid.

4   The National Basketball Association Web site at www.nba.com (accessed January 3, 2011).

5   Idy Fernandez, "Julie Stav," *Hispanic*, June-July, 2005, page 24.

6   The Walmart Corporate Web site at www.walmartstores.com (accessed January 3, 2011).

7   The General Mills Web site at www.general mills.com (accessed January 2, 2011).

8   The Bureau of Economic Analysis Web site at www.bea.gov (accessed January 3, 2011).

9   Ibid.

10 The Bureau of Labor Statistics Web site at www.bls.gov (accessed January 10, 2011).

11 The Bureau of Economic Analysis Web site at www.bea.gov (accessed January 10, 2011).

12 The Bureau of Labor Statistics Web site at www.bls.gov (accessed January 10, 2011).

13 The Treasury Direct Web site at www.treasurydirect.gov (accessed January 10, 2011).

14 The Investopedia Web site at www.investopedia.com (accessed January 11, 2011).

15 The Bureau of Labor Statistics Web site at www.bls.gov (accessed January 10, 2011).

16 Bill Weir, "Made in China: Your Job, Your Future, Your Fortune," ABC News Web site at www.abcnews.com (accessed September 20, 2005).

17 The Environmental Protection Agency Web site at www.epa.gov (accessed January 11, 2011).

18 The Nederlander Organization Company Web site at www.nederlanderconcerts.com (accessed January 20, 2011); "Nederlander Organization Company Overview," *Business Week,* August 20, 2010, www.businessweek.com; Hannah Heineman, "Moving Forward on Capital Improvement Projects," *Santa Monica Mirror,* July 28, 2010, www.smmirror.com; Steve Knopper, "Tour Biz Strong in Weak Economy," *Rolling Stone,* October 2, 2008, 11–12; Ray Waddell, "Nederlander/Viejas Deal Offers Touring Opportunities," *Billboard,* January 10, 2008, wwwbillboard.com; Interviews with Nederlander employees and the video "Entertainment Means Profits for Nederlander Concerts."

CHAPTER 2

1   Mike Ramsey, "Technology that Breaks the Car Industry Mold," *Wall Street Journal,* January 6, 2011, www.wsj.com; Shin Hyon-bee, "Hyundai Motor to Test-Run Hydrogen Fuel-Cell Car in 2011," *The Korea Herald,* December 19, 2010, www.koreaherald.com; Mike Ramsay, "Tesla Expects $60 Million in Revenue from Toyota RAV4," *Wall Street Journal,* December 16, 2010, www.wsj.com; Yoshio Takahashi, "Toyota's Prius to Become Top Japan Seller— Ever," *Wall Street Journal,* December 7, 2010, www.wsj.com; Bill Vlasic, "G.M. to Hire 1,000 to Engineer More Electric Cars," *New York Times,* December 1, 2010, www.nytimes.com; Takashi Ebuchi, Koji Nishimura, and Satoshi Kubo, "Nissan's Leaf Set to Give Hybrids a Run for Their Money," *Asahi Shimbun,* December 18, 2010, www.asahi.com/english.

2   The Wikipedia Web site at http://en.wikipedia.org/wiki/John_Rigas (accessed March 6, 2011).

3   The Wikipedia Web site at http://en.wikipedia.org/wiki/TAP_Pharmaceuticals (accessed March 6, 2011).

4   The United States Department of Justice Web site at www.justice.gov/opa/pr/2005/April/05_tax_210.htm (accessed March 2, 2011).

5   Frontlines (Washington, DC: U.S. Agency for International Development, September 2005), 16.

6   Deere & Company Corporate Governance—Code of Ethics Web site at www.deere.co m/en_US/ir/corporategovernance/ethics.html (accessed March 6, 2011).

7   U.S. Securities and Exchange Commission Web site at www.sec.gov/litigation/litreleases/2009/lr211129.htm and www.businessinsider.com/dennis-kozlowski-mansion-auction-pictures-2010-11 (accessed March 1, 2011).

8   The Politico Web site at www.politico.com/news/stories/0310/3410/34105.html and *The New York Times,* www.nytimes.com/2011/02/11/opinion/11fri3.html (accessed March 1, 2011).

9   The General Mills Web site at www.generalmills.com/en/Responsibility/Community_Engagement/Giving.aspx (accessed March 6, 2011).

10 The Michael and Susan Dell Foundation Web site at www.msdf.org/Grants/default.aspx (accessed March 12, 2011).

11 IBM *Press Release,* February 24, 2011 accessed at www-03.ibm.com/press/us/en/pressrelease/33834.wss (accessed March 8, 2011).

12 GE *Press Release,* January 19, 2011, www.genewscenter.com/content/detail.aspx? (accessed March 8, 2011).

13 Charles Schwab Foundation Web site at www.aboutschwab.com/about/facts/schwab-foundation.html (accessed March 9, 2011).

14 ExxonMobil Web site at www.exxonmobil.com/Corporate/community_women.aspx (accessed March 9, 2011).

15 AT&T Web site at www.att.com/gen/corporate-citizenship?pid=17884 (accessed March 8, 2011).

16 Wall Street Reform and Consumer Protection Act of 2010, www.govtrack.us/congress/bill.xpd?bill=h111-4173 (accessed March 9, 2011).

17 www.sholfieldhonda.com (accessed May 13, 2010); Adam Knapp, "Scholfield Honda Trying to Turn Green Movement into Good Business," *Wichita Business Journal,* http://wichita.bizjournals.com, March 7, 2008, and information provided through interviews with Scholfield Honda personnel and in the video "Scholfield Honda."

CHAPTER 3

1   Laurie Burkitt, "Selling Health Food to China," *Wall Street Journal,* December 13, 2010, www.wsj.com: Szu Ping Chan, "PepsiCo Tragets Health Conscious in $3.8bn Wimm-Bill-Dann Deal," *The Telegraph (UK),* December 2, 2010, www.telegraph.co.uk; Greg Farrell and Louise Lucas, "Russia at the Top of PepsiCo's Table," *Financial Times,* December 2, 2010, www.ft.com; www.pepsico.com

2   The White House, Office of the Press Secretary, Press Release, August 6, 2002.

3   The Census Bureau Web site at www.census.gov/foreign-trade/Press-Release/current_press_release/ (accessed March 7, 2011).

4   This section draws heavily from the *World Economic Outlook*, October 2010, International Monetary Fund Web site at imf.org/external/pubs/ft/weo/2010/02/index.htm (accessed March 7, 2011).

5   The Census Bureau Web site at www.census.gov/foreign-trade/statistics/highlights/top/top1012yr.html (accessed March 7, 2011).

6   World Trade Organization Web site at www.wto.org/english/news_e/press10_e/pr598__e.htm (accessed April 19, 2010).

7   Office of the United States Trade Representative Web site at www.ustr.gov/trade-agreements/free-trade-agreements/north-american-free-trade-agreement (accessed March 14, 2011).

8 U.S. CAFTA-DR Free Trade Agreement: How U.S. Companies Can Benefit, Export.Gov Web site at www.export.gov/FTA/cafta-dr/index.asp, (accessed April 19, 2010), and U.S. Department of Agriculture, International Agricultural Trade Report, issued October 25, 2010, usda.gov (accessed March 10, 2011).

9 ASEANSTATS Web site at aseansec.org/stat/SummaryTable.pdf, (accessed March 15, 2011) and Office of the U.S. Trade Representative, www.ustr.gov/ (accessed March 14, 2011).

10 William M. Pride and O.C. Ferrell, *Marketing*, 2008 Edition (Boston, MA: Houghton Mifflin, 2008), 194.

11 The World Bank *Annual Report* 2010, The World Bank Web site at http://web.worldbank.org/ (accessed March 14, 2011).

12 www.evogear.com (accessed May 13, 2010), and information provided through interviews with Evo personnel and in the video "Evo: The Global Environment."

13 Bob Driehaus, "A Cincinnati Ice Cream Maker Aims Big," *The New York Times,* September 12, 2010, N29; company Web site www.graeters.com (accessed September 2, 2010); Alexander Coolridge, "Winburn: Where Is Cincinnati Jobs Retention Plan?" Cincinnati.com, August 18, 2010, http://news.cincinnati.com; Lucy May, "Graeter's Northern Kentucky Franchisee Puts Stores on the Block," *Business Courier,* August 6, 2010, http://cincinnati.bizjournals.com; Ken Hoffman, "Graeter's Ice Cream Is Worthy Diet Buster," *The Houston Chronicle,* April 15, 2009, www.chron.com; Melissa Davis Haller, "The Big Chill," *Cincinnati Magazine,* February 2009, www.cincinnatimagazine.com; and interviews with company staff and the video, "Let's Go Get a Graeter's!"

CHAPTER 4

1 Dan Eaton, "Raising Cane's Ohio Rising," *Columbus Business Journal*, December 24, 2010, www.bizjournals.com/columbus; Richard N. Velotta, "Giving Back Boosts Raising Cane's Franchise," *Las Vegas Sun,* November 19, 2010, www.lasvegassun.com; "Raising Cane's: SCORE Client Opens 100th Restaurant," SCORE Success Stories, n.d., www.score.org; www.raisingcanes.com.

2 The Raising Cane Company Web site at www.raisingcanes.com (accessed February 23, 2011).

3 Ibid.

4 The Ivy Planning Group Web site at www.ivygroupllc.com (accessed February 10, 2011).

5 The Procter & Gamble Web site at www.pg.com (accessed February 10, 2011).

6 Ibid.

7 The Reader's Digest Association Web site at www.rd.com (accessed February 23, 2011).

8 The All Business Web site at www.allbusiness.com (accessed February 10, 2011).

9 The Hispanic PR Wire Web site at www.hispanicprwire.com (accessed March 16, 2010).

10 The Internal Revenue Service Web site at www.irs.gov (accessed February 10, 2011).

11 The Walmart Corporate Web site at www.walmartstores.com (accessed February 13, 2011).

12 "Update 2—GM IPO Filing Next Week—Sources," the Reuters Web site at www.reuters.com (accessed August 12, 2010).

13 The Walmart Corporate Web site at www.walmartstores.com (accessed February 13, 2011).

14 The Oracle Corporation Web site at www.oracle.com (accessed February 14, 2011).

15 Chris Crum, "Google Buys SayNow, Adds to Google Voice Team," the Web Pro News. Web site at www.webpronews.com (accessed January 25, 2011).

16 The Annie's Homegrown Web site at www.annies.com (accessed February 26, 2011); Lauren McKay, "From Organic Goods to Sustainable Ones," *Customer Relationship Management*, April 2010, 14; Tara Siegel Bernard, "Winning a Place on Grocery Store Shelves Annie's Homegrown Finds Some Room as Market for Organic Food Grows," *Wall Street Journal* at www.wsj.com, accessed March 29, 2005; "Leading Us All Into Temptation in a Healthy Way," *Organic Style,* May 2005; and information though interview with company personnel and in the video "Annie's Homegrown."

CHAPTER 5

1 Diane Mastrull, "Small Businesses Get Uptick, Hope It Lasts," *Philadelphia Inquirer,* January 3, 2011, www.philly.com; "Big Business Pipeline for Small Business," *Reuters,* September 10, 2010, http://blogs.reuters.com/small-business; Elizabeth Olson, "A Guiding Hand from Big Business to Small," *New York Times,* July 1, 2009, www.nytimes.com.

2 The SBA Web site, www.sba.gov/content/summary-size-standards-industry (accessed March 15, 2011).

3 U.S. Small Business Administration, Office of Advocacy, *Frequently Asked Questions*, updated January 2011, www.sba.gov/advo (accessed March 15, 2011).

4 ibid.

5 Ibid.

6 U.S. Small Business Administration, Office of Advocacy, *Quarterly Indicators*, Second Quarter, www.sba.gov/advo (accessed March 17, 2011).

7 Thomas A. Garrett, "Entrepreneurs Thrive in America," *Bridges,* Federal Reserve Bank of St. Louis, Spring 2005, 2.

8 U.S. Small Business Administration, Office of Advocacy, *Frequently Asked Questions*, updated January 2011, www.sba.gov/advo (accessed March 15, 2011).

9 The SBA Web site at sba.gov/about-offices-content/2/3106/success-stories/4140 (accessed March 15, 2011).

10 Small Business Administration, Office of Advocacy, *Frequently Asked Questions*, www.sba.gov/sites/default/files/files/sbfaq.pdf (accessed March 15, 2011).

11 SBA Press Release, "Computer Simulation Company from Florida Is National Small Business of the Year," May 25, 2010, www.sba.gov/news (accessed March 15, 2011).

12 U.S. Small Business Administration, Office of Advocacy, *Frequently Asked Questions*, September 2009, www.sba.gov/advo (accessed March 15, 2011).

13 U.S. Small Business Administration, Office of Advocacy, *News Release*, Number 10-03 ADVO, March 3, 2010, www.sba.gov/advo/press/10-03.html (accessed March 15, 2011).

14 Timothy S. Hatten, "*Small Business Management: Entrepreneurship and Beyond*," 4th ed., Copyright © 2009 by Houghton Mifflin Company, p. 238. Reprinted with permission.

15 SCORE Web site at www.score.org/media_fact_sheet.html#TOP (accessed March 15, 2011).

16 SCORE Web site at www.score.org/history.html (accessed March 17, 2011).

17 SBA Press Release, *Fact Sheet*, September 11, 2008, 2.

18 U.S. Small Business Administration, *News Release*, Release Number 10-33, May 26, 2010, www.sba.gov/news (accessed March 15, 2011).

19 Ibid.

20 SBA Press Release, "President Obama Proclaims National Small Business Week," May 21, 2010, www.sba.gov/news (accessed March 17, 2011).

21 SBA Press Release Number 10-414, *News Release*, May 14, 2010, www.sba.gov/news (accessed June 7, 2010).

22 Cindy Elmore, "Putting the Power into the Hands Small Business Owners," *Marketwise*, Federal Reserve Bank of Richmond, Issue II, 2005, 13.

23 U.S. Small Business Administration, www.sba.gov/managing/marketing/intlsales.html (accessed March 15, 2011).

24 U.S. Commercial Service Web site at www.trade.gov/cf/ (accessed March 17, 2011).

25 SBA Press Release at www.mass.gov/export/pdf/sba_2010_exp_oftheyear.pdf (accessed March 17, 2011).

26 Bob Driehaus, "A Cincinnati Ice Cream Maker Aims Big," *The New York Times,* September 12, 2010, N29; company Web site www.graeters.com (accessed September 2, 2010); Alexander Coolridge, "Winburn: Where Is Cincinnati Jobs Retention Plan?" *Cincinnati.com,* August 18, 2010, http://news.cincinnati.com; Lucy May, "Graeter's Northern Kentucky Franchisee Puts Stores on the Block," *Business Courier,* August 6, 2010, http://cincinnati.bizjournals.com; Ken Hoffman, "Graeter's Ice Cream Is Worthy Diet Buster," *The Houston Chronicle,* April 15, 2009, www.chron.com; Melissa Davis Haller, "The Big Chill," *Cincinnati Magazine,* February 2009, www.cincinnatimagazine.com; and interviews with company staff and the video, "Graeter's."

CHAPTER 6

1 John Kell, "S&P Lifts Heinz Outlook on Improved Financial Profile," *Wall Street Journal,* January 12, 2011, www.wsj.com; "Overseas Growth Helps Lift Revenue at Heinz," *New York Times,* September 2, 2010, p. B2; Inder Sidhu, "Profiles in Doing Both: How Tuning and Transforming Make Heinz Healthier," *Forbes*, November 30, 2010, http://blogs.forbes.com; Karlene Lukovitz, "ACSI Finds Customer Satisfaction Index Dips," *Media Post,* November 16, 2010, www.mediapost.com; Richard M. Smith, "'You Have to Take a Risk,'" *Newsweek*, April 9, 2010, www.newsweek.com; www.heinz.com.

2 "Lilly Aims at China's Growing Pharmaceutical Market," Seekingalpha.com, December 14, 2009, http://seekingalpha.com/article/178009-lilly-aims-at-chinas-growing-pharmaceutical-market?source=feed.

3 "Mission Statement," Starbucks, www.starbucks.com/about-us/company-information/mission-statement (accessed January 20, 2011); The Facebook Web site at www.facebook.com/facebook#!/facebook?v=info (accessed January 20, 2011).

4 "Responsibility," Starbucks, www.starbucks.com/responsibility (accessed September 5, 2011).

5   "Walmart Makes Organizational Moves to Raise Efficiency," *Reuters,* January 29, 2010.

6. Han Tianyang and Xiao Gong, "Volkswagen Planning New Guangzhou Assembly Plant," *China Daily*, February 1, 2010, www.chinadaily.com.cn/bizchina/2010-02/01/content_9406566.htm.

7   Lisa Biank Fasig, "Go-To-Market Plan Gets P&G There Faster, More Efficiently," Business Courier, February 12, 2007, www.bizjournals.com/cincinnati/stories/2007/02/12/story3.html (accessed January 20, 2011).

8   The Fast Company Web site at www.fastcompany.com; The General Electric Web site at www.ge.com/company/leadership/ceo.html (accessed January 20, 2011).

9   "Monster.com," Quancast, www.quantcast.com/monster.com (accessed January 20, 2011).

10 David Welch, David Kiley and Moon Ihlwan, "Korean Management Practices at Hyundai USA," BusinessWeek, March 21, 2008, http://kwikiblog.blogspot.com/2008/03/korean-management-practices-athyundai.html (accessed January 20, 2011).

11 http://flatworldknowledge.com/pub/1.0/principles-management/28990#ftn.fwk-carpenter-fn01-006 (accessed January 20, 2011); "The Google Culture," Google, www.google.com/intl/en/corporate/culture.html (accessed January 20, 2011).

12 Andrew J. Dubrin, *Leadership: Research Findings, Practice and Skills*, 6th ed. (Mason, OH: South-Western/Cengage Learning, 2010).

13 "Entrepreneurial Leadership," www.1000ventures.com/business_guide/crosscuttings/leadership_entrepreneurial.html (accessed February 24, 2010).

14 Ricky Griffin, *Management*, 10th ed. (Mason, OH: South-Western Cengage Learning, 2011), 273.

15 Claire Cain Miller, "Tailoring Its Approach, Starbucks Rebounds," *New York Times*, January 20, 2010.

16 Micheline Maynard and Hiroku Tabuchi, "Rapid Growth Has Its Perils, Toyota Learns," *New York Times*, January 27, 2010.

17 "Total Quality Management: A Continuous Improvement Process," www.foundation.phccweb.org/Library/Articles/TQM.pdf (accessed January 20, 2011).

18 Based on information on the company Web site www.llbean.com (accessed January 20, 2011); company news release; "L.L. Bean Installs a Solar Hot Water System to Its Flagship Store in Freeport," www.llbean.com, June 15, 2010; interviews with L.L. Bean employees; and the video, "L.L. Bean Relies on Its Core Values and Effective Leadership."

CHAPTER 7

1   Dina Bass, "Microsoft Is Said to Pay Nokia More than $1 Billion in Deal," *Bloomberg BusinessWeek*, March 7, 2011, www.businessweek.com; Christopher Lawton, "Nokia to Sell Qt Business," *Wall Street Journal*, March 7, 2011, www.wsj.com; Matt Rosoff, "Nokia Has Big Company Blues," *San Francisco Chronicle*, February 21, 2011, www.sfgate.com; Rick Wartzman, "For Nokia, One Good Call, One Bad," *Bloomberg BusinessWeek*, February 21, 2011, www.businessweek.com; Rosie Baker, "Nokia to Partner with Microsoft under New Structure," *Marketing Week*, February 11, 2011, www.marketingweek.co.uk; www.nokia.com.

2   Geoff Colvin, "How Top Companies Breed Stars," *Fortune*, September 20, 2007, http://money.cnn.com/magazines/fortune/fortune_archive/2007/10/01/100351829/index.htm.

3   Avon Expects Savings and Benefits Approaching $900 Million From Original Restructuring, Product Line Simplification and Strategic Sourcing Programs—Higher Than Anticipated," Avon, news release, February 19, 2009, http://media.avoncompany.com/index.php?s=10922&item=22955.

4   "Company Overview," Martha Stewart Living Omnimedia, Inc., http://phx.corporate-ir.net/phoenix.zhtml?c=96022&p=irol-homeprofile (accessed January 24, 2011).

5   Rob Goffee and Gareth Jones, "The Character of a Corporation: How Your Company's Culture Can Make or Break Your Business," *Jones Harper Business*, December 2003, 182.

6   Based on information from www.numitea.com (accessed January 24, 2011), and information provided through interviews with Numi personnel and in the video "Turbulent Times: Numi's New Manager."

CHAPTER 8

1   Stuart Smith, "Is Unilever's Sustainability Drive a Hostage to Fortune?" *Marketing Week*, December 9, 2010, www.marketingweek.co.uk; Julia Finch, "Unilever Unveils Ambitious Long Term Sustainability Program," *The Guardian (UK)*, November 15, 2010, www.guardian.co.uk; Paul Sonne, "New Products Lift Unilever Results," *Wall Street Journal*, April 29, 2010, www.wsj.com;

Jeroen Molenaar, "Unilever to Boost Indonesia Spending Amid P&G Threat," *BusinessWeek*, June 23, 2010, www.businessweek.com; www.unilever.com.

2   The Bureau of Labor Statistics Web site at www.bls.gov (accessed March 16, 2011).

3   Ibid.

4   John Engler, "Forging a Second American Century," *Forbes*, May 28, 2009, Web site at www.forbes.com.

5   Thomas D. Kuczmarski, "Remanufacturing America's Factory Sector," *Bloomberg BusinessWeek*, September 9, 2009, Web site at www.businessweek.com.

6   The Bureau of Labor Statistics Web site at www.bls.gov (accessed March 16, 2011).

7   Robert Kreitner, *Management* 11th edition, (Boston, MA: Houghton Mifflin, 2009), 474.

8   The 3M Corporation Web site at www.3m.com (accessed March 20, 2011).

9   The Berry Plastics Corporation Web site at www.berryplastics.com (accessed March 20, 2011).

10 The ATT – Supplier Diversity Web site at www.attsuppliers.com/sd (accessed March 24, 2011).

11 The National Institute for Standards and Technology Web site at www.nist.gov (accessed March 17, 2011).

12 The iSixsigma Web site at www.isixsigma.com (accessed April 30, 2010).

13 The International Organization of Standardization (ISO) Web site at www.iso.org (accessed March 25, 2011).

14 Ibid.

15 "International Comparisons of Manufacturing Productivity and Unit Labor Cost Trends, 2009," December 21, 2010, The Bureau of Labor Statistics Web site at www.bls.gov (accessed March 26, 2011).

16 Ibid.

17 Ibid.

18 The Illumina, Inc., Web site at www.illumina.com (accessed March 25, 2011).

19 The Dell Computer Corporation Web site at www.dell.com (accessed March 27, 2011).

20 The Burton Snowboard Company Web site at www.burton.com (accessed March 27, 2011); Mike Lewis, "Jake Burton on Taking the Helm," *Transworld Business*, May 4, 2010, wwwbusiness.transworld.net; "Laurent Potdevin Resigns as Burton CEO," *ESPN.com*, May 3, 2010, www.sports.espn.go.com); Bruce Edwards, "Burton Moving Factory to Austria," *Rutland Herald*, March 17, 2010, www.rutlandherald.com; interviews with company staff; and the video "Burton Snowboards, High Quality Standards."

21 The Graeter's Corporate Web site at www.graeters.com (accessed March 278, 2011); Bob Driehaus, "A Cincinnati Ice Cream Maker Aims Big," *The New York Times*, September 12, 2010, N29; Alexander Coolridge, "Winburn: Where is Cincinnati Jobs Retention Plan?" Cincinnati.com, August 18, 2010, http://news.cincinnati.com; Lucy May, "Graeter's Northern Kentucky Franchisee Puts Stores on the Block," *Business Courier*, August 6, 2010, www.cincinnati.bizjournals.com; Ken Hoffman, "Graeter's Ice Cream Is Worthy Diet Buster," *The Houston Chronicle*, April 15, 2009, www.chron.com; Melissa Davis Haller, "The Big Chill," *Cincinnati Magazine*, February 2009, www.cincinnatimagazine.com; and interviews with company staff and the video, "Graeter's Leadership and Management Efforts Enhance the Firm's Performance."

CHAPTER 9

1   Jenalia Moreno, "More to Luv?" *Houston Chronicle*, January 22, 2011, www.chron.com; William Taylor, "Hire for Attitude, Train for Skill," *Fast Company*, February 1, 2011, www.fastcompany.com; Terry Maxon, "Southwest Airlines to Resume Hiring Pilots, Flight Attendants," *Dallas Morning News*, November 9, 2010, http://aviationblog.dallasnews.com; www.southwest.com.

2   Nick Bunkley, "Ford Profit Comes as Toyota Hits a Bump," *New York Times*, January 28, 2010.

3   U.S. Department of Labor, Bureau of Labor Statistics, www.bls.gov (accessed January 24, 2011).

4   Barbara Frankel, "The DiversityInc Top 10 Global Diversity Companies List," *DiversityInc Magazine*, May 18, 2009.

5   The BLR Web site at http://hr.blr.com/about/about.aspx (accessed January 24, 2011).

6   The Procter & Gamble Web site at www.pg.com (accessed January 24, 2011).

7   Nanette Byrnes, "Start Search," *BusinessWeek*, October 10, 2005, 74–76.

8   U.S. Department of Labor, Bureau of Labor Statistics, *News Release*, December 8, 2010, www.bls.gov.

9   Milton Moskowitz, Robert Levering, and Christopher Tkaczyk, "100 Top Companies to Work For," *Fortune*, February 8, 2010 issue, http://money.cnn.com/magazines/fortune/bestcompanies/2010/.

10 Cynthia D. Fisher, Lyle F. Schoenfeldt, and James B. Shaw, *Human Resource Management* (Boston, MA: Houghton Mifflin, 2006), 464.

11 Ibid., 465.

12 The Whirlpool Web site at www.whirlpool.com (accessed January 24, 2011); information provided through interviews with Whirlpool personnel and in the video "Meeting the Challenge of Diversity: Whirlpool."

CHAPTER 10

1 Milton Moskowitz, Robert Levering, and Christopher Tkaczyk, "100 Best Companies to Work For," *Fortune,* February 7, 2011, p. 93; Richard Waters, "Google Tries New Angle on Hiring," *Financial Times,* February 6, 2011, www.ft.com; Claire Cain Miller and Miguel Helft, "Google Shake-up Is Effort to Revive Start-up Spark," *New York Times,* January 20, 2011, www.nytimes.com; Alexei Oreskovic, "Wanted: More than 2,000, in Google Hiring Spree," *Reuters,* November 19, 2010, www.reuters.com; www.google.com.

2 http://money.cnn.com

3 Milton Moskowitz, Robert Levering, and Christopher Tkaczyk, "100 Top Companies to Work For," *Fortune,* February 8, 2010 issue, http://money.cnn .com/magazines/fortune/bestcompanies/2010/.

4 Gary M. Stern, "Companies Switch Their Tack on Corporate Retreats," *Investor's Business Daily,* March 12, 2010, www.investors.com/NewsAndAnalysis/Article. aspx?id=527154&p=2.

5 Douglas McGregor, *The Human Side of Enterprise* (New York: McGraw-Hill, 1960).

6 William Ouchi, *Theory Z* (Reading, MA: Addison-Wesley, 1981).

7 Ricky W. Griffin, *Fundamentals of Management,* 6th ed. (Mason, OH; South-Western/Cengage Learning, 2012), 303–305.

8 Milton Moskowitz, Robert Levering, and Christopher Tkaczyk.

9 The Apple Store Web site at http://store.apple.com/us_smb_78313/browse/ home/campaigns/corporate_gifting (accessed January 25, 2011).

10 S. C. Johnson & Son, Press Release, September 22, 2009.

11 "Companies Find Benefits in Flex-Time," *American Public Media,* May 21, 2008, http://marketplace.publicradio.org/display/web/2008/05/21/flex_time/.

12 "In Hard Times, Re-Commit to Flex Time," Sylvia Ann Hewlett, *Harvard Business Review,* October 12, 2009.

13 The Starbucks Career Center Web site at www.starbucks.com/career-center (accessed January 25, 2011).

14 Victoria Stagg Elliott, "Job-sharing Can Boost Work-Life Balance, Cut Practice Expenses," *American Medical News,* February 8, 2010, www.ama-assn.org/ amednews/2010/02/08/bica0208.htm.

15 "100 Best Companies to Work For 2011," *Fortune,* http://money.cnn.com/ magazines/fortune/bestcompanies/2011/benefits/telecommuting.html (accessed August 31, 2011).

16 Arif Mohamed, "Bosses Split Over Productivity of Teleworkers," *Computer Weekly,* March 29, 2005, 55.

17 "100 Best Companies to Work For 2011," *Fortune;* The Cisco Web site at www .cisco.com/en/US/products/index.html (accessed January 25, 2011); "Cisco Study Finds Telecommuting Significantly Increases Employee Productivity, Work-Life Flexibility and Job Satisfaction," *Cisco, News Release,* June 25, 2009, http://newsroom.cisco.com/dlls/2009/prod_062609.html.

18 The W. L. Gore & Associates Web site at www.gore.com (accessed January 25, 2011).

19 "A Brief Overview of Employee Ownership in the U.S.," www.nceo.org, January 2009.

20 Ricky W. Griffin, *Fundamentals of Management* (Mason, OH; South-Western/ Cengage Learning, 2012), 396.

21 Richard L. Daft, *Management* (Mason, OH: South-Western/Cengage Learning, 2012), 510.

22 Christine Tierney, "Quality Panel to Review Toyota," *The Detroit News,* April 30, 2010, www.detroitnews.com/article/20100430/AUTO01/4300359/1148/ Quality-panel-to-review-Toyota.

23 Bill Fischer and Andy Boynton, "Virtuoso Teams," *Harvard Business Review,* July–August 2005, 116–123.

24 "Dow Wins Four 2010 Responsible Care® Energy Efficiency Awards," *Dow, Press Release,* May 5, 2010, http://news.dow.com/dow_news/ corporate/2010/20100505c.htm.

25 Linda Webb, "Microsoft's New Ergonomic Keyboard More Comfortable," *Cleveland Plain Dealer,* November 7, 2005, E4.

26 "Governance," Mozilla, www.mozilla.org/about/governance.html (accessed January 25, 2011).

27 Company Web site www.llbean.com (accessed January 25, 2011); Tom Tobin, "L.L. Bean Set for Splashy First Day," *Democrat and Chronicle.com,* June 27, 2010, www.democratandchronicle.com; Michael Arndt, "Customer Service Champs: L.L. Bean Follows Its Shoppers to the Web," *Bloomberg BusinessWeek,* February 18, 2010, www.businessweek.com; interviews with L.L. Bean employees and the video, "At L.L. Bean, Everyone Is Family."

28 Bob Driehaus, "A Cincinnati Ice Cream Maker Aims Big," *The New York Times,* September 12, 2010, N29; company Web site www.graeters.com (accessed September 2, 2010); Alexander Coolridge, "Winburn: Where Is Cincinnati Jobs Retention Plan?" *Cincinnati.com,* August 18, 2010, http://news.cincinnati .com; Lucy May, "Graeter's Northern Kentucky Franchisee Puts Stores on the Block," *Business Courier,* August 6, 2010, http://cincinnati.bizjournals. com; Ken Hoffman, "Graeter's Ice Cream Is Worthy Diet Buster," *The Houston Chronicle,* April 15, 2009, www.chron.com; Melissa Davis Haller, "The Big Chill," *Cincinnati Magazine,* February 2009, www.cincinnatimagazine.com; and interviews with company staff and the video, "Graeter's: Where Tenure Is a Proud Number."

CHAPTER 11

1 Bret Thorn, "Breakfast Pizza Heats Up Mornings," *Nation's Restaurant News,* January 14, 2011, www.nrn.com; Alicia Kelso, "Big Three Gear Up for the Big Game," *PizzaMarketplace,* January 26, 2011, www.pizzamarketplace.com; Tracy Stapp, "Domino's Pizza Turnaround Pays Off," *Entrepreneur,* March 4, 2010, www.entrepreneur.com; Steve Capp, "Domino's 'Pizza Turnaround' Represents About-Face in Marketing and Product," *Direct Marketing News,* March 1, 2010, www.dm.news.com; Rupal Parekh, "Pizza Chain Sees a Gutsy Move Pay Off as Foes Become Fans and Store Profits Reach an All-Time Industry Mark," *Advertising Age,* October 18, 2010, www.adage.com.

2 "Definition of Marketing," Marketing Power (American Marketing Association), www.marketingpower.com/AboutAMA/Pages/DefinitionofMarketing.aspx (accessed January 19, 2011)

3 The Sears Rewards Web site at www.shopyourwayrewards.com (accessed January 19, 2011)

4 V. Kumar, *Customer Lifetime Value* (Hanover, MA: now Publishers, 2008), 5.

5 Rajkumar Venkatesan and V. Kumar, "A Customer Lifetime Value Framework for Customer Selection and Resource Selection and Resource Allocation Strategy," *Journal of Marketing 68* (October 2004), 106–125).

6 Sears, press release, January 19, 2010, www.searsmedia.com/tools/press/ content.jsp?id_2010-01-19-0005167078; Elaine Wong, "Why Sears Is Rebranding Kenmore," *Brandweek,* February 24, 2010, www.brandweek.com/ bw/content_display/esearch/e3ie17592c1aa7a468849873c7d6a2fdc82.

7 "Nissan Announces U.S. Pricing on 2010 Cube," *PR Newswire,* January 28, 2010.

8 Paula Andruss, "New OfficeMax Catalog Courts Women Consumers," *Deliver Magazine,* June 29, 2009.

9 "Nissan Announces Nissan LEAF Purchase Process; Gives First Glimpse at Marketing Campaign," Nissan, news release, February 11, 2010, www .nissannews.com.

10 Brooks Barnes, "Movie Studios See a Threat in Growth of Redbox," *The New York Times,* September 6, 2009.

11 Michael Liedtke, "Newspaper Circulation May Be Worse Than It Looks," *The Seattle Times,* November 22, 2009.

12 Kevin Kelleher, "66,207,986 Bottles of Beer on the Wall," *Business 2.0 via CNN,* February 25, 2004, www.cnn.com.

13 Ellen Byron, "New Penney: Chain Goes for 'Missing Middle,'" *Wall Street Journal,* February 14, 2005, http://online.wsj.com/.

14 Catherine Arnold, "Self-examination: Researchers Reveal State of MR in Survey," *Marketing News,* February 1, 2005, 55, 56.

15 William M. Pride and O. C. Ferrell, *Foundations of Marketing* (Mason, OH: South-Western/Cengage Learning, 2011), 128.

16 The E*Trade Company Web site www.etrade.com (accessed January 19, 2011); Whitney Kisling, "E*Trade Gains Most Since December on Return to Profit," *Bloomberg BusinessWeek,* July 23, 2010, www.businessweek.com; Matt Ackerman, "E*Trade to Target Long-Term Investors," *American Banker,* January 29, 2010, www.americanbanker.com; interviews with company employees and the video "E*Trade Tries to Build Long-Term Customer Relationships."

CHAPTER 12

1 Greg Lamm, "Amazon's Kindle Notched Nearly Half of eReader Sales in 2010," *TechFlash,* March 13, 2011, www.techflash.com; Brett Arends, "Move Over, Apple! My Tablet Cost $200," *Wall Street Journal,* March 9, 2011, www.wsj.com; Jeff Bertolucci, "Will Amazon's Kindle Be Free by November?" *PC World,* February 28, 2011, www.pcworld.com.

2 Joshua Topolsky, "Apple iPad Review," *Engadget,* April 3, 2010, www.engadget .com/2010/04/03/apple-ipad-review/; Vladislav Savov, "Apple Sells 1,000,000 iPads in Revolution's First Month," *Engadget,* May 3, 2010, www.engadget .com/2010/05/03/apple-sells-1-000-000-ipads-in-revolutionsfirst-month?icid_ sphere_blogsmith_inpage_engadget/.

3 The Apple Web site at www.apple.com (accessed January 19, 2011).

4 "GM Ending Hummer: Controversial Brand to Be Discontinued," *Huffington Post*, April 26, 2010, www.huffingtonpost.com/2010/02/24/gm-endinghummer-controve_n_475464.html.

5 "All Brands," Procter & Gamble, www.pg.com/en_US/brands/all_brands.shtml (accessed January 19, 2011).

6 "Product Descriptions," The Coca-Cola Company, www.virtualvender.coca-cola.com/ft/index.jsp; "Our Brands," PepsiCo, www.pepsico.com/Company/Our-Brands.html (accessed January 19, 2011).

7 Ben Rooney, "8 Names You Know, R.I.P.," *CNN Money*, December 20, 2009, http://money.cnn.com/galleries/2009/news/0912/gallery.brands_we_lost/8.html.

8 Nadira A. Hira, "Fahrenheit 212—The Innovator's Paradise," December 16, 2009, *Fortune*, http://money.cnn.com/2009/12/15/news/companies/fahrenheit_212.fortune/index.htm; www.fahrenheit-212.com (accessed January 19, 2011).

9 Joseph Peña, "Aptera Secures Financing, Introduces New 2e Electric Car," *San Diego News Network*, April 14, 2010, www.sdnn.com/sandiego/2010-04-14/business-real-estate/aptera-secures-financingintroduces-new-2e-electric-car.

10 "Market Update," www.plma.com/StoreBrands/sbt10.html (accessed January 19, 2011).

11 Nick Bunkley, "Toyota's Sales Fall as GM and Ford Gain," *The New York Times*, February 2, 2010, www.nytimes.com/2010/02/03/business/03auto.html.

12 "Coca-Cola Buys Glaceau, Maker of Vitaminwater, for $4.1 Billion," *The Star*, May 28, 2007, http://thestar.com.my/news/story.asp?file_/2007/5/28/apworld/20070528105438&sec_apworld.

13 The Amazon Web site at www.amazon.com (accessed January 19, 2011).

14 Kenneth Hein, "BK Boxers Leads Pack of Worst Line Extensions," *BrandWeek*, December 15, 2008, www.brandweek.com/bw/content_display/esearch/e3ie36ce5eb50d8af6302e69db2d0b6b.

15 Bruce Horovitz, "Earthbound Farm, Naked Juice to Use 100% Recycled Plastic," *USA Today*, July 9, 2009, www.usatoday.com/money/industries/environment/2009-07-08-recycled-plastic-food-packaging_N.htm?loc_interstitialskip.

16 Steve Everly, "Showdown for INK CARTRIDGE MAKERS, REGULATORS," Buffalonews.com, August 21, 2010, www.buffalonews.com/business/blogs/moneysmart/article30457.ece (accessed March 23, 2011).

17 Janet Adamy, "Corporate News: Starbucks—Coffee Empire Seeks to Seem Less Expensive in Recession," *The Wall Street Journal*, February 9, 2009, B3.

18 Jim Zemlin, "Linux Can Compete with the iPad on Price, But Where's the Magic?" *The Linux Foundation*, January 28, 2010, www.linux-foundation.org/weblogs/jzemlin/2010/01/28/linux-can-compete-with-the-ipad-on-pricebut-where%e2%80%99s-the-magic/.

19 Dominic Haber, "Abercrombie & Fitch Plans Further Price Cuts After 1Q Loss," TopNews.com, May 17, 2009, http://topnews.us/content/25241-abercrombiefitch-plans-further-price-cuts-after-1q-loss.

20 The Verizon Web site at www.verizon.com (accessed March 23, 2011).

21 Based on information in www.bludot.com (accessed March 23, 2011); "Stuff," www.bludot.com (accessed March 23, 2011) and originally published in *Minnesota Monthly*; Carl Alviani, "Taking the Middle Ground: Massive Design for the Masses?" *Core 77*, http://core77.com/reactor/07.05_mlddleground.asp (accessed March 23, 2011); Todd Wasserman, "Guerilla Marketing: The Technology Revolution," *Ad Week*, January 11, 2010, www.adweek.com; interviews with company personnel and the film, "Blu Dot."

CHAPTER 13

1 Karen Talley, "Macy's 4Q Profit Up 50% on Lower Charges, Better Sales," *Wall Street Journal*, February 22, 2011, www.wsj.com; Natalie Zmuda, "Retailers on Quest to Rekindle the Personal Touch of a Bygone Era," *Advertising Age*, February 14, 2011, www.adage.com; Janet Cho, "My Macy's Tailors Merchandise to Northeast Ohio Tastes," *Cleveland Plain Dealer*, November 2, 2010, www.cleveland.com; www.macys.com.

2 "Gasoline Stations (NAICS 447)," U.S. Bureau of the Census, www.census.gov/econ/census/snapshots/SNAP44.htm

3 Stacy Mitchell, "Death of the Category Killers," The Institute for Local Self-Reliance, June 23, 2009, www.newrules.org/retail/news/death-category-killers (accessed September 1, 2011).

4 The Direct Selling Association Web site at www.dsa.org (accessed March 23, 2011).

5 Maris Halkias, "J.C.Penney's Big Catalog Soon to Be But a Memory," TheSeattleTimes.com, November 27, 2009, http://seattletimes.newsource.com/html/businesstechnology/2010365217_jcpenneycatalog27.html

6 "FAQ," The National Do Not Call Registry, www.donotcall.gov/faq/faqdefault.aspx (accessed March 23, 2011); "Additional Report to Congress," Federal Trade Commission, December 2009, www.ftc.gov/os/2010/01/100104dnc additionalreport.pdf (accessed March 23, 2011); "Federal Register," Federal Trade Commission, September 10, 2010, www.ftc.gov/os/fedreg/2010/august/100831telemarketing.pdf (accessed March 23, 2011).

7 The Netflix Web site at www.netflix.com (accessed March 23, 2011).

8 Zoom Systems, www.zoomsystems.com/ (accessed March 23, 2011).

9 Sandra O'Loughlin, "Out with the Old: Malls versus Centers," *Brandweek*, May 9 2005, p. 30.

10 Corinne Kator, "Warehouse Giants," November 2006, www.mmh.com.

11 eMarketer, Total Ad Spending in the United States, 2009–2015 (in Billions), http://totalaccess.emarketer.com/EssentialMetrics.aspx?mid=25&m=Total+Ad+Spending&gid=221&g=United+States (accessed March 23, 2011).

12 "The Impact of Direct-to-Consumer Drug Advertising on Seniors' Health," States News Service, October 10, 2005.

13 Paul Sloan, "The Sales Force that Rocks," July 1, 2005, http://cnnmoney.com.

14 Terence Shimp, *Advertising, Promotion, and Other Aspects of Integrated Marketing Communications* (Mason, OH: South-Western/Cengage Learning 2010), pp. 454–459.

15 "Consumers Use over $3.5 Billion in Coupons," Grocery Coupon Blog, July 8, 2011, http://grocery-coupon-blog.selectcouponprogram.com/2011/07/08/consumers-use-over-3-5-billion-in-coupons/ (accessed September 1, 2011).

16 Mya Frazier, James Tenser, and Tricia Despres, "Retail Lesson: Small Programs Best," March 20, 2008, pp. S2–S3.

17 "Berry & Homer Wraps Bus Leading Lance Armstrong and Tour of Hope Team on Cross-Country Trek," *Business Wire*, October 10, 2005, www.businesswire.com/news/home/20051010005762/en/Berry-Homer-Wraps-Bus-Leading-Lance-Armstrong.

18 Company Web site www.llbean.com (accessed July 20, 2010); "Photobrand 25 Ranks ESPN, GE, and Dunkin' Donuts as New England's Most Powerful Brands for 2010," *PR Newswire*, June 1, 2010, www.prnewswire.com; Michael Arndt, "Customer Service Champs: L.L. Bean Follows Its Shoppers to the Web," *Bloomberg BusinessWeek*, February 18, 2010, www.businessweek.com; interviews with L.L. Bean employees and the video, "L.L. Bean Employs a Variety of Promotion Methods to Communicate with Customers."

19 Bob Driehaus, "A Cincinnati Ice Cream Maker Aims Big," The *New York Times*, September 12, 2010, N29; company Web site www.graeters.com (accessed September 2, 2010); Alexander Coolridge, "Winburn: Where Is Cincinnati Jobs Retention Plan?" Cincinnati.com, August 18, 2010, http://news.cincinnati.com; Lucy May, "Graeter's Northern Kentucky Franchisee Puts Stores on the Block," *Business Courier*, August 6, 2010, http://cincinnati.bizjournals.com; Ken Hoffman, "Graeter's Ice Cream Is Worthy Diet Buster," *The Houston Chronicle*, April 15, 2009, www.chron.com; Melissa Davis Haller, "The Big Chill," *Cincinnati Magazine*, February 2009, www.cincinnatimagazine.com; and interviews with company staff and the video, "Graeter's Is Synonymous with Ice Cream."

CHAPTER 14

1 Leslie Josephs, "Selling Candy with a Conscience," *Wall Street Journal*, December 24, 2010, www.wsj.com; Yana Polikarpov, "Mars Sprinkles M&M's with Disney Characters," *BrandWeek*, May 1, 2009, www.brandweek.com; Jessie Scanlon, "How Mars Built a Business," *BusinessWeek*, December 28, 2009, www.businessweek.com; www.mars.com; www.mymms.com.

2 Bradley Mitchell, "What is (Wireless/Computer) Networking," the About.com Web site at www.about.com (accessed April 13, 2011).

3 Bradley Mitchell, "Lan – Local Area Network," the About.com Web site at www.about.com (accessed April 13, 2011).

4 Shar Van Boskirk, Christine Spivey Overby, and Jennifer Joseph McGann, "U.S. Interactive Marketing Forecast 2009 to 2014," July 6, 2009, The Forrester Web Site at www.forrester.com (accessed April 14, 2011).

5 The Internet World Stats Web site at www.internetworldstats.com (accessed April 14, 2011).

6 Ibid.

7 Ibid.

8 The Computer Industry Almanac Web site at www.c-i-a.com (accessed April 14, 2011).

9 "2011 Identity Fraud Survey Report, Consumer Version," The Javelin Strategy and Research Web site at www.idsafety.net (accessed April 15, 2011).

10 The E*Trade corporate Web site at www.etrade.com (accessed April 15, 2011); Whitney Kisling, "E*Trade Gains Most Since December on Return to Profit," *Bloomberg BusinessWeek*, July 23, 2010, www.businessweek.com; Matt Ackerman, "E*Trade to Target Long-Tem Investors," *American Banker*, January 29, 2010, www.americanbanker.com; and interviews with company employees and the video "E*Trade Uses e-Business to Meet Customer Needs."

CHAPTER 15

1. "No Surprises as Fraud Rockets in 2010," *The Mirror (U.K.),* January 11, 2011, http://blogs.mirror.co.uk; "KPMG Experiences Modest Revenue Improvement," *Accounting Today,* December 16, 2010, www.accountingtoday.com; Kyle Stock, "KPMG's Bruce Pfau: The Best and the Brightest," *Fins Finance,* April 12, 2010, www.fins.com/finance.
2. The Investopedia Web site at www.investopedia.com (accessed April 3, 2011).
3. "Financial Reporting in a Changing World," The International Accounting Standards Board, May 8, 2009, http://ifrs.org.
4. "System Failure Corporate America Has Lost Its Way," *Fortune Magazine,* June 24, 2002, www.money.cnn.com.
5. "Summary of the Provisions of the Sarbanes-Oxley Act of 2002," June 22, 2006, the AICPA Web site at www.aicpa.org.
6. *Occupational Outlook Handbook 2010-2011,* The U.S. Bureau of Labor Statistics Web site at www.bls.gov (accessed April 4, 2011).
7. The American Institute of Certified Public Accountants Web site at www.aicpa.org (accessed April 5, 2011).
8. Based on information found at The Little Guys Electronics Web site at http://thelittleguys.com (accessed April 2, 2011); Alan Wolf, "The Little Guys Get New Home, Amended Name," *TWICE,* April 19, 2010, 6, 22; Audrey Gray, "Perfecting a Soft Sell," *Dealerscope,* March 2009, 82; and information from interviews with company staff and the video, "The Little Guys."

CHAPTER 16

1. Chrissie Thompson, "GM to Pay Dividend to Holders of B Shares of Stock," *Detroit Free Press,* January 27, 2011, www.freep.com; Sharon Terlep and Josh Mitchell, "GM Drops Request for Loans," *Wall Street Journal,* January 28, 2011, www.wsj.com; Tom Walsh, "Game Isn't Won Yet for General Motors," *Detroit Free Press,* January 9, 2011, www.freep.com.
2. The 3M Corporation Web site at www.3m.com (accessed March 20, 2011).
3. The *Advertising Age* Web site at www.adagee.com (accessed June 20, 2010).
4. "Blockbuster Takeover Bid by Dish Wins Judge's OK," Yahoo News, April 7, 2011, http://news.yahoo.com.
5. U.S. Census Bureau, *Statistical Abstract of the United States, 2011* (Washington, D.C.: U.S. Government Printing Office, 2011), p. 740.
6. Matthew Boyle, "The Fed's Commercial Paper Chase," *Bloomberg BusinessWeek,* October 7, 2008, www.businessweek.com.
7. The Yahoo! Finance Web site at www.finance.yahoo.com (accessed April 21, 2011).
8. "Sunoco's SunCoke Energy files for $100 million IPO," Renaissance Capital, March 24, 2011, www.renaissancecapital.com.
9. The General Electric Web site at www.ge.com (accessed April 21, 2011).
10. The Advanced Micro Device Web site at www.amd.com (accessed April 21, 2011).
11. *Mergent Transportation Manual,* (New York: Mergent, Inc., 2009), 64.
12. The Nederlander Web site at www.nederlanderconcerts.com (accessed April 21, 2011); Nederlander Organization company overview, *BusinessWeek,* http:www.businessweek.com (accessed August 20, 2010); Hannah Heineman, "Moving Forward on Capital Improvement Projects," *Santa Monica Mirror,* July 29, 2010, wwwsmmirror.com; Steve Knopper, "Tour Biz Strong in Weak Economy," *Rolling Stone,* October 2, 2008, 11–12; Ray Waddell, "Nederlander/Viejas Deal Offers Touring Opportunities," *Billboard,* January 10, 2008, www.billboard.com; interviews with Nederlander employees and the video "Financial Planning and Budgets Equal Profits for Nederlander Concerts."
13. Randy A. Simes, "Bond Hill to Celebrate Dedication of $11M Graeter's Production Facility," UrbanCincy.com, www.urbancincy.com, September 28, 2010; Bob Driehaus, "A Cincinnati Ice Cream Maker Aims Big," *The New York Times,* September 12, 2010, p. N29; company website, www.graeters.com, accessed September 2, 2010; Alexander Coolridge, "Winburn: Where Is Cincinnati Jobs Retention Plan?" Cincinnati.com, http://news.cincinnati.com, August 18, 2010; Lucy May, "Graeter's Northern Kentucky Franchisee Puts Stores on the Block," *Business Courier,* http://cincinnat.bizjournals.com, August 6, 2010; Ken Hoffman, "Graeter's Ice Cream Is Worthy Diet Buster," *The Houston Chronicle,* www.chron.com, April 15, 2009; Melissa Davis Haller, "The Big Chill," *Cincinnati Magazine,* www.cincinnatimagazine.com, February 2009; and interviews with company staff and the video, "Graeter's."

ANSWER KEY

CHAPTER 1

1. g	2. c	3. j	4. e	5. d	6. b
7. f	8. a	9. h	10. i	11. F	12. F
13. T	14. F	15. T	16. T	17. F	18. T
19. F	20. T	21. a	22. c	23. d	24. e
25. d	26. b	27. d	28. c	29. d	30. e

CHAPTER 2

1. j	2. g	3. e	4. k	5. a	6. l
7. d	8. i	9. f	10. b	11. T	12. F
13. F	14. T	15. F	16. T	17. T	18. F
19. T	20. F	21. b	22. e	23. d	24. a
25. d	26. c	27. e	28. c	29. b	30. d

CHAPTER 3

1. i	2. d	3. g	4. j	5. h	6. l
7. e	8. f	9. a	10. c	11. F	12. T
13. T	14. F	15. T	16. F	17. F	18. T
19. F	20. T	21. c	22. d	23. c	24. c
25. a	26. c	27. e	28. c	29. b	30. c

CHAPTER 4

1. j	2. i	3. k	4, f	5. l	6. h
7. b	8. d	9. c	10. a	11. F	12. F
13. T	14. F	15. T	16. F	17. T	18. F
19. T	20. T	21. d	22. d	23. c	24. e
25. e	26. c	27. b	28. a	29. d	30. d

CHAPTER 5

1. i	2. e	3. k	4. a	5. d	6. f
7. b	8. g	9. j	10. l	11. T	12. F
13. F	14. T	15. F	16. F	17. F	18. F
19. F	20. T	21. b	22. e	23. a	24. d
25. c	26. d	27. e	28. e	29. b	30. c

CHAPTER 6

1. g	2. i	3. j	4. b	5. f	6. c
7. d	8. k	9. e	10. l	11. F	12. F
13. T	14. F	15. T	16. F	17. F	18. F
19. T	20. T	21. b	22. e	23. b	24. a
25. d	26. b	27. b	28. e	29. c	30. a

CHAPTER 7

1. c	2. j	3. f	4. e	5. b	6. k
7. h	8. d	9. g	10. l	11. T	12. F
13. T	14. T	15. F	16. T	17. F	18. F
19. F	20. T	21. d	22. d	23. e	24. b
25. a	26. c	27. d	28. b	29. a	30. d

CHAPTER 8

1. e	2. a	3. g	4. f	5. l	6. b
7. k	8. j	9. d	10. i	11. f	12. t
13. f	14. f	15. t	16. f	17. f	18. t
19. f	20. t	21. b	22. b	23. a	24. d
25. e	26. d	27. c	28. d	29. e	30. c

CHAPTER 9

1. h	2. e	3. i	4. k	5. b	6. c
7. j	8. f	9. a	10. d	11. T	12. F
13. T	14. T	15. F	16. T	17. F	18. F
19. T	20. F	21. d	22. a	23. a	24. a
25. d	26. d	27. b	28. a	29. a	30. a

CHAPTER 10

1. g	2. k	3. d	4. e	5. j	6. c
7. h	8. b	9. f	10. i	11. T	12. F
13. T	14. F	15. F	16. F	17. T	18. T
19. F	20. T	21. b	22. c	23. a	24. a
25. e	26. a	27. c	28. b	29. c	30. a

CHAPTER 11

1. f	2. g	3. c	4. e	5. b	6. i
7. k	8. a	9. l	10. j	11. T	12. F
13. F	14. T	15. T	16. T	17. F	18. F
19. T	20. T	21. a	22. b	23. b	24. a
25. c	26. c	27. c	28. e	29. e	30. b

CHAPTER 12

1. b	2. c	3. a	4. e	5. g	6. f
7. j	8. i	9. h	10. l	11. F	12. F
13. F	14. T	15. T	16. F	17. T	18. T
19. T	20. F	21. d	22. b	23. c	24. b
25. c	26. d	27. a	28. c	29. d	30. c

CHAPTER 13

1. b	2. a	3. c	4. f	5. e	6. g
7. j	8. d	9. l	10. k	11. F	12. T
13. F	14. T	15. F	16. F	17. T	18. T
19. T	20. F	21. b	22. b	23. c	24. c
25. d	26. c	27. c	28. b	29. b	30. c

CHAPTER 14

1. h	2. c	3. k	4. a	5. d	6. f
7. b	8. j	9. i	10. l	11. T	12. T
13. F	14. T	15. F	16. F	17. T	18. F
19. T	20. F	21. b	22. c	23. e	24. b
25. c	26. d	27. b	28. a	29. d	30. a

CHAPTER 15

1. a	2. g	3. j	4. k	5. b	6. h
7. c	8. l	9. i	10. e	11. F	12. F
13. T	14. F	15. T	16. T	17. T	18. F
19. T	20. T	21. c	22. a	23. c	24. e
25. d	26. c	27. b	28. c	29. a	30. b

CHAPTER 16

1. a	2. e	3. g	4. d	5. l	6. h
7. b	8. j	9. k	10. c	11. T	12. F
13. F	14. F	15. T	16. T	17. T	18. T
19. F	20. F	21. a	22. b	23. e	24. a
25. d	26. e	27. b	28. c	29. e	30. d

GLOSSARY

A

absolute advantage the ability to produce a specific product more efficiently than any other nation

accessory equipment standardized equipment used in a firm's production or office activities

accountability the obligation of a worker to accomplish an assigned job or task

accounting equation the basis for the accounting process:
assets = liabilities + owners' equity

accounting the process of systematically collecting, analyzing, and reporting financial information

accounts receivable turnover a financial ratio calculated by dividing net sales by accounts receivable

acid-test ratio a financial ratio calculated by adding cash, marketable securities, and receivables and dividing the total by current liabilities

ad hoc committee a committee created for a specific short-term purpose

administrative manager a manager who is not associated with any specific functional area but who provides overall administrative guidance and leadership

advertising agency an independent firm that plans, produces, and places advertising for its clients

advertising a paid nonpersonal message communicated to a select audience through a mass medium

affirmative action program a plan designed to increase the number of minority employees at all levels within an organization

agent a middleman that expedites exchanges, represents a buyer or a seller, and often is hired permanently on a commission basis

alien corporation a corporation chartered by a foreign government and conducting business in the United States

analytic skills the ability to identify problems correctly, generate reasonable alternatives, and select the "best" alternatives to solve problems

analytical process a process in operations management in which raw materials are broken into different component parts

annual report a report distributed to stockholders and other interested parties that describes a firm's operating activities and its financial condition

assets the resources that a business owns

audit an examination of a company's financial statements and the accounting practices that produced them

authority the power, within an organization, to accomplish an assigned job or task

autocratic leadership task-oriented leadership style in which workers are told what to do and how to accomplish it; workers have no say in the decision-making process

automatic vending the use of machines to dispense products

automation the total or near-total use of machines to do work

B

balance of payments the total flow of money into a country minus the total flow of money out of that country over some period of time

balance of trade the total value of a nation's exports minus the total value of its imports over some period of time

balance sheet (or statement of financial position) a summary of the dollar amounts of a firm's assets, liabilities, and owners' equity accounts at the end of a specific accounting period

banker's acceptance a written order for a bank to pay a third party a stated amount of money on a specific date

barter a system of exchange in which goods or services are traded directly for other goods or services without using money

behavior modification a systematic program of reinforcement to encourage desirable behavior

benchmarking a process used to evaluate the products, processes, or management practices of another organization that is superior in some way in order to improve quality

bill of lading document issued by a transport carrier to an exporter to prove that merchandise has been shipped

board of directors the top governing body of a corporation, the members of which are elected by the stockholders

bond indenture a legal document that details all the conditions relating to a bond issue

brand equity marketing and financial value associated with a brand's strength in a market

brand extension using an existing brand to brand a new product in a different product category

brand loyalty extent to which a customer is favorable toward buying a specific brand

brand mark the part of a brand that is a symbol or distinctive design

brand name the part of a brand that can be spoken

brand a name, term, symbol, design, or any combination of these that identifies a seller's products as distinct from those of other sellers

breakeven quantity the number of units that must be sold for the total revenue (from all units sold) to equal the total cost (of all units sold)

broker a middleman that specializes in a particular commodity, represents either a buyer or a seller, and is likely to be hired on a temporary basis

budget a financial statement that projects income, expenditures, or both over a specified future period

bundle pricing packaging together two or more complementary products and selling them for a single price

business buying behavior the purchasing of products by producers, resellers, governmental units, and institutions

business cycle the recurrence of periods of growth and recession in a nation's economic activity

business ethics the application of moral standards to business situations

business model represents a group of common characteristics and methods of doing business to generate sales revenues and reduce expenses

business plan a carefully constructed guide for the person starting a business

business product a product bought for resale, for making other products, or for use in a firm's operations

business service an intangible product that an organization uses in its operations

business the organized effort of individuals to produce and sell, for a profit, the products and services that satisfy society's needs

business-to-business (or B2B) model a model used by firms that conduct business with other businesses

business-to-consumer (or B2C) model a model used by firms that focus on conducting business with individual consumers

buying allowance a temporary price reduction to resellers for purchasing specified quantities of a product

buying behavior the decisions and actions of people involved in buying and using products

C

capacity the amount of products or services that an organization can produce in a given time

capital budget a financial statement that estimates a firm's expenditures for major assets and its long-term financing needs

capital-intensive technology a process in which machines and equipment do most of the work

capitalism an economic system in which individuals own and operate the majority of businesses that provide goods and services

captioned photograph a picture accompanied by a brief explanation

captive pricing pricing the basic product in a product line low, but pricing related items at a higher level

carrier a firm that offers transportation services

cash budget a financial statement that estimates cash receipts and cash expenditures over a specified period

cash flow the movement of money into and out of an organization

catalog marketing a type of marketing in which an organization provides a catalog from which customers make selections and place orders by mail, telephone, or the Internet

category killer a very large specialty store that concentrates on a single product line and competes on the basis of low prices and product availability

caveat emptor a Latin phrase meaning "let the buyer beware"

centralized organization an organization that systematically works to concentrate authority at the upper levels of the organization

certificate of deposit (CD) a document stating that the bank will pay the depositor a guaranteed interest rate on money left on deposit for a specified period of time

certified management accountant (CMA) an accountant who has met the requirements for education and experience, passed a rigorous exam, and is certified by the Institute of Management Accountants

certified public accountant (CPA) an individual who has met state requirements for accounting education and experience and has passed a rigorous accounting examination prepared by the AICPA

chain of command the line of authority that extends from the highest to the lowest levels of an organization

chain retailer a company that operates more than one retail outlet

check a written order for a bank or other financial institution to pay a stated dollar amount to the business or person indicated on the face of the check

chief financial officer (CFO) a high-level corporate executive who manages a firm's finances and reports directly to the company's chief executive officer or president

closed corporation a corporation whose stock is owned by relatively few people and is not sold to the general public

cloud computing a type of computer usage in which services stored on the Internet are provided to users on a temporary basis

code of ethics a guide to acceptable and ethical behavior as defined by the organization

collaborative learning system a work environment that allows problem solving participation by all team members

collateral real estate or property pledged as security for a loan

command economy an economic system in which the government decides what goods and services will be produced, how they will be produced, for whom available goods and services will be produced, and who owns and controls the major factors of production

commercial paper a short-term promissory note issued by a large corporation

commission a payment that is a percentage of sales revenue

common stock stock owned by individuals or firms who may vote on corporate matters but whose claims on profits and assets are subordinate to the claims of others

common stock stock whose owners may vote on corporate matters but whose claims on profits and assets are subordinate to the claims of others

communication skills the ability to speak, listen, and write effectively

community shopping center a planned shopping center that includes one or two department stores and some specialty stores, along with convenience stores

comparable worth a concept that seeks equal compensation for jobs requiring about the same level of education, training, and skills

comparative advantage the ability to produce a specific product more efficiently than any other product

comparison discounting setting a price at a specific level and comparing it with a higher price

compensation system the policies and strategies that determine employee compensation

compensation the payment employees receive in return for their labor

competition rivalry among businesses for sales to potential customers

component part an item that becomes part of a physical product and is either a finished item ready for assembly or a product that needs little processing before assembly

computer network a group of two or more computers linked together that allows users to share data and information

computer virus a software code designed to disrupt normal computer operations

computer-aided design (CAD) the use of computers to aid in the development of products

computer-aided manufacturing (CAM) the use of computers to plan and control manufacturing processes

computer-integrated manufacturing (CIM) a computer system that not only helps to design products but also controls the machinery needed to produce the finished product

conceptual skills the ability to think in abstract terms

consumer buying behavior the purchasing of products for personal or household use, not for business purposes

consumer price index (CPI) a monthly index that measures the changes in prices of a fixed basket of goods purchased by a typical consumer in an urban area

consumer product a product purchased to satisfy personal and family needs

consumer products goods and services purchased by individuals for personal consumption

consumer sales promotion method a sales promotion method designed to attract consumers to particular retail stores and to motivate them to purchase certain new or established products

consumerism all activities undertaken to protect the rights of consumers

contingency plan a plan that outlines alternative courses of action that may be taken if an organization's other plans are disrupted or become ineffective

continuous process a manufacturing process in which a firm produces the same product(s) over a long period of time

controlling the process of evaluating and regulating ongoing activities to ensure that goals are achieved

convenience product a relatively inexpensive, frequently purchased item for which buyers want to exert only minimal effort

convenience store a small food store that sells a limited variety of products but remains open well beyond normal business hours

convertible bond a bond that can be exchanged, at the owner's option, for a specified number of shares of the corporation's common stock

cookie a small piece of software sent by a Web site that tracks an individual's Internet use

cooperative advertising an arrangement whereby a manufacturer agrees to pay a certain amount of a retailer's media cost for advertising the manufacturer's products

core competencies approaches and processes that a company performs well that may give it an advantage over its competitors

corporate bond a corporation's written pledge that it will repay a specified amount of money with interest

corporate culture the inner rites, rituals, heroes, and values of a firm

corporate officers the chairman of the board, president, executive vice presidents, corporate secretary, treasurer, and any other top executive appointed by the board of directors

corporation an artificial person created by law with most of the legal rights of a real person, including the rights to start and operate a business, to buy or sell property, to borrow money, to sue or be sued, and to enter into binding contracts

cost of goods sold the dollar amount equal to beginning inventory *plus* net purchases *less* ending inventory

countertrade an international barter transaction

coupon reduces the retail price of a particular item by a stated amount at the time of purchase

creative selling selling products to new customers and increasing sales to present customers

cross-functional team a team of individuals with varying specialties, expertise, and skills that are brought together to achieve a common task

cross-functional team a team of individuals with varying specialties, expertise, and skills that are brought together to achieve a common task

cultural (or workplace) diversity differences among people in a workforce owing to race, ethnicity, and gender

cultural (workplace) diversity differences among people in a workforce owing to race, ethnicity, and gender

currency devaluation the reduction of the value of a nation's currency relative to the currencies of other countries

current assets assets that can be converted quickly into cash or that will be used in one year or less

current liabilities debts that will be repaid in one year or less

current ratio a financial ratio computed by dividing current assets by current liabilities

customary pricing pricing on the basis of tradition

customer lifetime value a measure of a customer's worth (sales minus costs) to a business over one's lifetime

customer relationship management (CRM) using information about customers to create marketing strategies that develop and sustain desirable customer relationships

D

data mining the practice of searching through data records looking for useful information

data processing the transformation of data into a form that is useful for a specific purpose

data numerical or verbal descriptions that usually result from some sort of measurement

database a single collection of data and information stored in one place that can be used by people throughout an organization to make decisions

debenture bond a bond backed only by the reputation of the issuing corporation

debit card a card that electronically subtracts the amount of a customer's purchase from her or his bank account at the moment the purchase is made

debt capital borrowed money obtained through loans of various types

debt-to-owners'-equity ratio a financial ratio calculated by dividing total liabilities by owners' equity

decentralized organization an organization in which management consciously attempts to spread authority widely in the lower levels of the organization

decision making the act of choosing one alternative from a set of alternatives

decision-support system (DSS) a type of computer program that provides relevant data and information to help a firm's employees make decisions

deflation a general decrease in the level of prices

delegation assigning part of a manager's work and power to other workers

demand the quantity of a product that buyers are willing to purchase at each of various prices

demand the quantity of a product that buyers are willing to purchase at each of various prices

department store a retail store that (1) employs 25 or more persons and (2) sells at least home furnishings, appliances, family apparel, and household linens and dry goods, each in a different part of the store

departmentalization by customer grouping activities according to the needs of various customer populations

departmentalization by function grouping jobs that relate to the same organizational activity

departmentalization by location grouping activities according to the defined geographic area in which they are performed

departmentalization by product grouping activities related to a particular product or service

departmentalization the process of grouping jobs into manageable units

depreciation the process of apportioning the cost of a fixed asset over the period during which it will be used

depression a severe recession that lasts longer than a typical recession

design planning the development of a plan for converting an idea into an actual product or service

direct marketing the use of the telephone, Internet, and nonpersonal media to introduce products to customers, who then can purchase them via mail, telephone, or the Internet

direct selling the marketing of products to customers through face-to-face sales presentations at home or in the workplace

directing the combined processes of leading and motivating

direct-response marketing a type of marketing in which a retailer advertises a product and makes it available through mail, telephone, or online orders

discount store a self-service general-merchandise outlet that sells products at lower-than-usual prices

discount a deduction from the price of an item

discretionary income disposable income *less* savings and expenditures on food, clothing, and housing

disposable income personal income *less* all additional personal taxes

distribution channel (or marketing channel) a sequence of marketing organizations that directs a product from the producer to the ultimate user

dividend a distribution of earnings to the stockholders of a corporation

domestic corporation a corporation in the state in which it is incorporated

domestic system a method of manufacturing in which an entrepreneur distributes raw materials to various homes, where families process them into finished goods to be offered for sale by the merchant entrepreneur

double-entry bookkeeping system a system in which each financial transaction is recorded as two separate accounting entries to maintain the balance shown in the accounting equation

draft issued by the exporter's bank, ordering the importer's bank to pay for the merchandise, thus guaranteeing payment once accepted by the importer's bank

dumping exportation of large quantities of a product at a price lower than that of the same product in the home market

E

earnings per share a financial ratio calculated by dividing net income after taxes by the number of shares of common stock outstanding

e-business (electronic business) the organized effort of individuals to produce and sell, for a profit, the products and services that satisfy society's needs through the facilities available on the Internet

e-business the organized effort of individuals to produce and sell through the Internet, for a profit, the products and services that satisfy society's needs

economic community an organization of nations formed to promote the free movement of resources and products among its members and to create common economic policies

economic model of social responsibility the view that society will benefit most when business is left alone to produce and market profitable products that society needs

economics the study of how wealth is created and distributed

economy the way in which people deal with the creation and distribution of wealth

electronic funds transfer (EFT) system a means of performing financial transactions through a computer terminal or telephone hookup

embargo a complete halt to trading with a particular nation or in a particular product

employee benefit a reward in addition to regular compensation that is provided indirectly to employees

employee ownership a situation in which employees own the company they work for by virtue of being stockholders

employee training the process of teaching operations and technical employees how to do their present jobs more effectively and efficiently

empowerment making employees more involved in their jobs by increasing their participation in decision making

entrepreneur a person who risks time, effort, and money to start and operate a business

entrepreneurial leadership personality-based leadership style in which the manager seeks to inspire workers with a vision of what can be accomplished to benefit all stakeholders

Equal Employment Opportunity Commission (EEOC) a government agency with the power to investigate complaints of employment discrimination and the power to sue firms that practice it

equity capital money received from the owners or from the sale of shares of ownership in a business

equity theory a theory of motivation based on the premise that people are motivated to obtain and preserve equitable treatment for themselves

esteem needs our need for respect, recognition, and a sense of our own accomplishment and worth

ethics the study of right and wrong and of the morality of the choices individuals make

everyday low prices (EDLPs) setting a low price for products on a consistent basis

exclusive distribution the use of only a single retail outlet for a product in a large geographic area

executive information system (EIS) a computer-based system that facilitates and supports the decision-making needs of top managers and senior executives by providing easy access to both internal and external information

expectancy theory a model of motivation based on the assumption that motivation depends on how much we want something and on how likely we think we are to get it

expert system a type of computer program that uses artificial intelligence to imitate a human's ability to think

Export-Import Bank of the United States an independent agency of the U.S. government whose function is to assist in financing the exports of American firms

exporting selling and shipping raw materials or products to other nations

express warranty a written explanation of the producer's responsibilities in the event that a product is found to be defective or otherwise unsatisfactory

external recruiting the attempt to attract job applicants from outside an organization

F

factor a firm that specializes in buying other firms' accounts receivable

factors of production resources used to produce goods and services

factory system a system of manufacturing in which all the materials, machinery, and workers required to manufacture a product are assembled in one place

family branding the strategy in which a firm uses the same brand for all or most of its products

feature article a piece (of up to 3,000 words) prepared by an organization for inclusion in a particular publication

federal deficit a shortfall created when the federal government spends more in a fiscal year than it receives

financial accounting generates financial statements and reports for interested people outside an organization

financial leverage the use of borrowed funds to increase the return on owners' equity

financial management all the activities concerned with obtaining money and using it effectively

financial manager a manager who is primarily responsible for an organization's financial resources

financial plan a plan for obtaining and using the money needed to implement an organization's goals

financial ratio a number that shows the relationship between two elements of a firm's financial statements

first-line manager a manager who coordinates and supervises the activities of operating employees

fiscal policy government influence on the amount of savings and expenditures; accomplished by altering the tax structure and by changing the levels of government spending

fixed assets assets that will be held or used for a period longer than one year

fixed cost a cost incurred no matter how many units of a product are produced or sold

flexible benefit plan compensation plan whereby an employee receives a predetermined amount of benefit dollars to spend on a package of benefits he or she has selected to meet individual needs

flexible manufacturing system (FMS) a single production system that combines electronic machines and computer-integrated manufacturing

flextime a system in which employees set their own work hours within employer-determined limits

foreign corporation a corporation in any state in which it does business except the one in which it is incorporated

foreign-exchange control a restriction on the amount of a particular foreign currency that can be purchased or sold

form utility utility created by converting production inputs into finished products

form utility utility created by people converting raw materials, finances, and information into finished products

franchise a license to operate an individually owned business as though it were part of a chain of outlets or stores

franchisee a person or organization purchasing a franchise

franchising the actual granting of a franchise

franchisor an individual or organization granting a franchise

free enterprise the system of business in which individuals are free to decide what to produce, how to produce it, and at what price to sell it

frequent-user incentive a program developed to reward customers who engage in repeat (frequent) purchases

full-service wholesaler a middleman that performs the entire range of wholesaler functions

functional middleman a middleman that helps in the transfer of ownership of products but does not take title to the products

G

General Agreement on Tariffs and Trade (GATT) an international organization of 153 nations dedicated to reducing or eliminating tariffs and other barriers to world trade

general partner a person who assumes full or shared responsibility for operating a business

generally accepted accounting principles (GAAPs) an accepted set of guidelines and practices for companies reporting financial information and for the accounting profession

general-merchandise wholesaler a middleman that deals in a wide variety of products

generic product (or brand) a product with no brand at all

goal an end result that an organization is expected to achieve over a one- to ten-year period

goal-setting theory a theory of motivation suggesting that employees are motivated to achieve goals that they and their managers establish together

grapevine the informal communications network within an organization

gross domestic product (GDP) the total dollar value of all goods and services produced by all people within the boundaries of a country during a one-year period

gross profit a firm's net sales *less* the cost of goods sold

gross sales the total dollar amount of all goods and services sold during the accounting period

groupware one of the latest types of software that facilitates the management of large projects among geographically dispersed employees as well as such group activities as problem solving and brainstorming

H

hard-core unemployed workers with little education or vocational training and a long history of unemployment

hostile takeover a situation in which the management and board of directors of a firm targeted for acquisition disapprove of the merger

hourly wage a specific amount of money paid for each hour of work

human resources management (HRM) all the activities involved in acquiring, maintaining, and developing an organization's human resources

human resources manager a person charged with managing an organization's human resources programs

human resources planning the development of strategies to meet a firm's future human resources needs

hygiene factors job factors that reduce dissatisfaction when present to an acceptable degree but that do not necessarily result in high levels of motivation

I

import duty (tariff) a tax levied on a particular foreign product entering a country

import quota a limit on the amount of a particular good that may be imported into a country during a given period of time

importing purchasing raw materials or products in other nations and bringing them into one's own country

incentive payment a payment in addition to wages, salary, or commissions

income statement a summary of a firm's revenues and expenses during a specified accounting period

independent retailer a firm that operates only one retail outlet

individual branding the strategy in which a firm uses a different brand for each of its products

inflation a general rise in the level of prices

informal group a group created by the members themselves to accomplish goals that may or may not be relevant to an organization

informal organization the pattern of behavior and interaction that stems from personal rather than official relationships

information society a society in which large groups of employees generate or depend on information to perform their jobs

information technology (IT) officer a manager at the executive level who is responsible for ensuring that a firm has the equipment necessary to provide the information the firm's employees and managers need to make effective decisions

information data presented in a form that is useful for a specific purpose

initial public offering (IPO) occurs when a corporation sells common stock to the general public for the first time

inspection the examination of the quality of work-in-process

institutional advertising advertising designed to enhance a firm's image or reputation

intangible assets assets that do not exist physically but that have a value based on the rights or privileges they confer on a firm

integrated marketing communications coordination of promotion efforts to ensure maximal informational and persuasive impact on customers

intensive distribution the use of all available outlets for a product

intermittent process a manufacturing process in which a firm's manufacturing machines and equipment are changed to produce different products

internal recruiting considering present employees as applicants for available positions

international business all business activities that involve exchanges across national boundaries

International Monetary Fund (IMF) an international bank with 186 member nations that makes short-term loans to developing countries experiencing balance-of-payment deficits

International Organization for Standardization (ISO) a network of national standards institutes and similar organizations from 160 different countries that is charged with developing standards for quality products and services that are traded throughout the globe

Internet a worldwide network of computers linked through telecommunications

interpersonal skills the ability to deal effectively with other people

intranet a smaller version of the Internet for use within a firm's computer network

inventory control the process of managing inventories in such a way as to minimize inventory costs, including both holding costs and potential stock-out costs

inventory management the process of managing inventories in such a way as to minimize inventory costs, including both holding costs and potential stock-out costs

inventory turnover a financial ratio calculated by dividing the cost of goods sold in one year by the average value of the inventory

investment banking firm an organization that assists corporations in raising funds, usually by helping to sell new issues of stocks, bonds, or other financial securities

invisible hand a term created by Adam Smith to describe how an individual's personal gain benefits others and a nation's economy

J

job analysis a systematic procedure for studying jobs to determine their various elements and requirements

job description a list of the elements that make up a particular job

job enlargement expanding a worker's assignments to include additional but similar tasks

job enrichment a motivation technique that provides employees with more variety and responsibility in their jobs

job evaluation the process of determining the relative worth of the various jobs within a firm

job redesign a type of job enrichment in which work is restructured to cultivate the worker–job match

job rotation the systematic shifting of employees from one job to another

job sharing an arrangement whereby two people share one full-time position

job specialization the separation of all organizational activities into distinct tasks and the assignment of different tasks to different people

job specification a list of the qualifications required to perform a particular job

joint venture an agreement between two or more groups to form a business entity in order to achieve a specific goal or to operate for a specific period of time

just-in-time inventory system a system designed to ensure that materials or supplies arrive at a facility just when they are needed so that storage and holding costs are minimized

K

knowledge management (KM) a firm's procedures for generating, using, and sharing the data and information

L

labeling the presentation of information on a product or its package

labor-intensive technology a process in which people must do most of the work

leadership the ability to influence others

leading the process of influencing people to work toward a common goal

lean manufacturing (sometimes referred to as lean production or just lean) a manufacturing approach that enhances efficiency, identifies and eliminates waste, and increases profits.

letter of credit a legal document issued by a bank or other financial institution guaranteeing to pay a seller a stated amount for a specified period of time

letter of credit issued by a bank on request of an importer stating that the bank will pay an amount of money to a stated beneficiary

liabilities a firm's debts and obligations

licensing a contractual agreement in which one firm permits another to produce and market its product and use its brand name in return for a royalty or other compensation

lifestyle shopping center an open-air-environment shopping center with upscale chain specialty stores

limited liability a feature of corporate ownership that limits each owner's financial liability to the amount of money that he or she has paid for the corporation's stock

limited partner a person who contributes capital to a business but has no management responsibility or liability for losses beyond the amount he or she invested in the partnership

limited-liability company (LLC) a form of business ownership that combines the benefits of a corporation and a partnership while avoiding some of the restrictions and disadvantages of those forms of ownership

limited-line wholesaler a middleman that stocks only a few product lines but carries numerous product items within each line

line extension development of a new product that is closely related to one or more products in the existing product line but designed specifically to meet somewhat different customer needs

line manager a position in which a person makes decisions and gives orders to subordinates to achieve the organization's goals

line of credit a loan that is approved before the money is actually needed

line structure an organizational structure in which the chain of command goes directly from person to person throughout the organization

line-and-staff structure an organizational structure that utilizes the chain of command from a line structure in combination with the assistance of staff managers

liquidity the ease with which an asset can be converted into cash

local-area network (LAN) a network that connects computers that are in close proximity to each other, such as an office building or a college campus

log-file records files that store a record of the Web sites visited

long-term financing money that will be used for longer than one year

long-term liabilities debts that need not be repaid for at least one year

lump-sum salary increase an entire pay raise taken in one lump sum

M

macroeconomics the study of the national economy and the global economy

major equipment large tools and machines used for production purposes

Malcolm Baldrige National Quality Award an award given by the U.S. president to organizations that apply and are judged to be outstanding in specific managerial tasks that lead to improved quality for both products and services

malware a general term that describes software designed to infiltrate a computer system without the user's consent

management by objectives (MBO) a motivation technique in which managers and employees collaborate in setting goals

management development the process of preparing managers and other professionals to assume increased responsibility in both present and future positions

management information system (MIS) a system that provides managers and employees with the information they need to perform their jobs as effectively as possible

management the process of coordinating people and other resources to achieve the goals of an organization

managerial accounting provides managers and employees with the information needed to make decisions about a firm's financing, investing, marketing, and operating activities

manufacturer (or producer) brand a brand that is owned by a manufacturer

market economy an economic system in which businesses and individuals decide what to produce and buy, and the market determines quantities sold and prices

market price the price at which the quantity demanded is exactly equal to the quantity supplied

market segment a group of individuals or organizations within a market that share one or more common characteristics

market segmentation the process of dividing a market into segments and directing a marketing mix at a particular segment or segments rather than at the total market

market a group of individuals or organizations, or both, that need products in a given category and that have the ability, willingness, and authority to purchase such products

marketing concept a business philosophy that a firm should provide goods and services that satisfy customers' needs through a coordinated set of activities that allow the firm to achieve its objectives

marketing information system a system for managing marketing information that is gathered continually from internal and external sources

marketing manager a manager who is responsible for facilitating the exchange of products between an organization and its customers or clients

marketing mix a combination of product, price, distribution, and promotion developed to satisfy a particular target market

marketing plan a written document that specifies an organization's resources, objectives, strategy, and implementation and control efforts to be used in marketing a specific product or product group

marketing research the process of systematically gathering, recording, and analyzing data concerning a particular marketing problem

marketing strategy a plan that will enable an organization to make the best use of its resources and advantages to meet its objectives

marketing the activity, set of institutions, and processes for creating, communicating, delivering, and exchanging offerings that have value for customers, clients, partners, and society at large

markup the amount a seller adds to the cost of a product to determine its basic selling price

Maslow's hierarchy of needs a sequence of human needs in the order of their importance

mass production a manufacturing process that lowers the cost required to produce a large number of identical or similar products over a long period of time

materials handling the actual physical handling of goods, in warehouses as well as during transportation

materials requirements planning (MRP) a computerized system that integrates production planning and inventory control

matrix structure an organizational structure that combines vertical and horizontal lines of authority, usually by superimposing product departmentalization on a functionally departmentalized organization

maturity date the date on which a corporation is to repay borrowed money

merchant middleman a middleman that actually takes title to products by buying them

merchant wholesaler a middleman that purchases goods in large quantities and then sells them to other wholesalers or retailers and to institutional, farm, government, professional, or industrial users

merger the purchase of one corporation by another

microeconomics the study of the decisions made by individuals and businesses

middle manager a manager who implements the strategy and major policies developed by top management

middleman (or marketing intermediary) a marketing organization that links a producer and user within a marketing channel

minority a racial, religious, political, national, or other group regarded as different from the larger group of which it is a part and that is often singled out for unfavorable treatment

mission a statement of the basic purpose that makes an organization different from others

missionary salesperson a salesperson—generally employed by a manufacturer—who visits retailers to persuade them to buy the manufacturer's products

mixed economy an economy that exhibits elements of both capitalism and socialism

monetary policies Federal Reserve decisions that determine the size of the supply of money in the nation and the level of interest rates

monopolistic competition a market situation in which there are many buyers along with a relatively large number of sellers who differentiate their products from the products of competitors

monopoly a market (or industry) with only one seller, and there are barriers to keep other firms from entering the industry

morale an employee's feelings about his or her job and superiors and about the firm itself

mortgage bond a corporate bond secured by various assets of the issuing firm

motivating the process of providing reasons for people to work in the best interests of an organization

motivation factors job factors that increase motivation, although their absence does not necessarily result in dissatisfaction

motivation the individual internal process that energizes, directs, and sustains behavior; the personal "force" that causes you or me to behave in a particular way

motivation–hygiene theory the idea that satisfaction and dissatisfaction are separate and distinct dimensions

multilateral development bank (MDB) an internationally supported bank that provides loans to developing countries to help them grow

multinational enterprise a firm that operates on a worldwide scale without ties to any specific nation or region

multiple-unit pricing the strategy of setting a single price for two or more units

N

National Alliance of Business (NAB) a joint business–government program to train the hard-core unemployed

national debt the total of all federal deficits

natural monopoly an industry requiring huge investments in capital and within which any duplication of facilities would be wasteful and thus not in the public interest

need a personal requirement

negotiated pricing establishing a final price through bargaining

neighborhood shopping center a planned shopping center consisting of several small convenience and specialty stores

net income occurs when revenues exceed expenses

net loss occurs when expenses exceed revenues

net sales the actual dollar amounts received by a firm for the goods and services it has sold after adjustment for returns, allowances, and discounts

network structure an organizational structure in which administration is the primary function, and most other functions are contracted out to other firms

news release a typed page of about 300 words provide by an organization to the media as a form of publicity

non-price competition competition based on factors other than price

nonstore retailing a type of retailing whereby consumers purchase products without visiting a store

nontariff barrier a nontax measure imposed by a government to favor domestic over foreign suppliers

not-for-profit corporation a corporation organized to provide a social, educational, religious, or other service rather than to earn a profit

O

objective a specific statement detailing what an organization intends to accomplish over a shorter period of time

odd-number pricing the strategy of setting prices using odd numbers that are slightly below whole-dollar amounts

off-price retailer a store that buys manufacturers' seconds, overruns, returns, and off-season merchandise for resale to consumers at deep discounts

oligopoly a market (or industry) in which there are few sellers

online retailing retailing that makes products available to buyers through computer connections

open corporation a corporation whose stock can be bought and sold by any individual

operating expenses all business costs other than the cost of goods sold

operational plan a type of plan designed to implement tactical plans

operations management all activities required to produce goods and services

operations manager a manager who manages the systems that convert resources into goods and services

order getter a salesperson who is responsible for selling a firm's products to new customers and increasing sales to present customers

order processing activities involved in receiving and filling customers' purchase orders

order taker a salesperson who handles repeat sales in ways that maintain positive relationships with customers

organization chart a diagram that represents the positions and relationships within an organization

organization a group of two or more people working together to achieve a common set of goals

organizational height the number of layers, or levels, of management in a firm

organizing the grouping of resources and activities to accomplish some end result in an efficient and effective manner

orientation the process of acquainting new employees with an organization

outsourcing the process of finding outside vendors and suppliers that provide professional help, parts, or materials at a lower cost

over-the-counter (OTC) market a network of dealers who buy and sell the stocks of corporations that are not listed on a securities exchange

owners' equity the difference between a firm's assets and its liabilities

P

packaging all the activities involved in developing and providing a container with graphics for a product

participative leadership leadership style in which all members of a team are involved in identifying essential goals and developing strategies to reach those goals

partnership a voluntary association of two or more persons to act as co-owners of a business for profit

part-time work permanent employment in which individuals work less than a standard work week

penetration pricing the strategy of setting a low price for a new product

perfect (or pure) competition the market situation in which there are many buyers and sellers of a product, and no single buyer or seller is powerful enough to affect the price of that product

performance appraisal the evaluation of employees' current and potential levels of performance to allow managers to make objective human resources decisions

periodic discounting temporary reduction of prices on a patterned or systematic basis

personal budget a specific plan for spending your income

personal income the income an individual receives from all sources *less* the Social Security taxes the individual must pay

personal selling personal communication aimed at informing customers and persuading them to buy a firm's products

physical distribution all those activities concerned with the efficient movement of products from the producer to the ultimate user

physiological needs the things we require for survival

piece-rate system a compensation system under which employees are paid a certain amount for each unit of output they produce

place utility utility created by making a product available at a location where customers wish to purchase it

plan an outline of the actions by which an organization intends to accomplish its goals and objectives

planning horizon the period during which an operational plan will be in effect

planning establishing organizational goals and deciding how to accomplish them

plant layout the arrangement of machinery, equipment, and personnel within a production facility

point-of-purchase display promotional material placed within a retail store

pollution the contamination of water, air, or land through the actions of people in an industrialized society

possession utility utility created by transferring title (or ownership) of a product to a buyer

preferred stock stock owned by individuals or firms who usually do not have voting rights but whose claims on dividends are paid before those of common-stock owners

preferred stock stock whose owners usually do not have voting rights but whose claims on dividends and assets are paid before those of common-stock owners

premium pricing pricing the highest-quality or most-versatile products higher than other models in the product line

premium a gift that a producer offers a customer in return for buying its product

press conference a meeting at which invited media personnel hear important news announcements and receive supplementary textual materials and photographs

price competition an emphasis on setting a price equal to or lower than competitors' prices to gain sales or market share

price leaders products priced below the usual markup, near cost, or below cost

price lining the strategy of selling goods only at certain predetermined prices that reflect definite price breaks

price skimming the strategy of charging the highest possible price for a product during the introduction stage of its life-cycle

price the amount of money a seller is willing to accept in exchange for a product at a given time and under given circumstances

primary market a market in which an investor purchases financial securities (via an investment bank) directly from the issuer of those securities

primary-demand advertising advertising whose purpose is to increase the demand for *all* brands of a product within a specific industry

prime interest rate the lowest rate charged by a bank for a short-term loan

private placement occurs when stock and other corporate securities are sold directly to insurance companies, pension funds, or large institutional investors

problem the discrepancy between an actual condition and a desired condition

problem-solving team a team of knowledgeable employees brought together to tackle a specific problem

process material a material that is used directly in the production of another product but is not readily identifiable in the finished product

producer price index (PPI) an index that measures prices that producers receive for their finished goods

product deletion the elimination of one or more products from a product line

product design the process of creating a set of specifications from which a product can be produced

product differentiation the process of developing and promoting differences between one's products and all similar products

product differentiation the process of developing and promoting differences between one's product and all similar products

product life-cycle a series of stages in which a product's sales revenue and profit increase, reach a peak, and then decline

product line a group of similar products that differ only in relatively minor characteristics

product line a group of similar products that differ only in relatively minor characteristics

product mix all the products a firm offers for sale

product modification the process of changing one or more of a product's characteristics

product everything one receives in an exchange, including all tangible and intangible attributes and expected benefits; it may be a good, a service, or an idea

productivity the average level of output per worker per hour

productivity the average level of output per worker per hour

profit what remains after all business expenses have been deducted from sales revenue

profit-sharing the distribution of a percentage of a firm's profit among its employees

promissory note a written pledge by a borrower to pay a certain sum of money to a creditor at a specified future date

promotion mix the particular combination of promotion methods a firm uses to reach a target market

promotion communication about an organization and its products that is intended to inform, persuade, or remind target-market members

proxy fight a technique used to gather enough stockholder votes to control a targeted company

proxy a legal form listing issues to be decided at a stockholders' meeting and enabling stockholders to transfer their voting rights to some other individual or individuals

public relations communication activities used to create and maintain favorable relationships between an organization and various public groups, both internal and external

publicity communication in news-story form about an organization, its products, or both

Q

purchasing all the activities involved in obtaining required materials, supplies, components, and parts from other firms

quality circle a team of employees who meet on company time to solve problems of product quality

quality control the process of ensuring that goods and services are produced in accordance with design specifications

R

random discounting temporary reduction of prices on an unsystematic basis

raw material a basic material that actually becomes part of a physical product; usually comes from mines, forests, oceans, or recycled solid wastes

rebate a return of part of the purchase price of a product

recession two or more consecutive three-month periods of decline in a country's GDP

recruiting the process of attracting qualified job applicants

reference pricing pricing a product at a moderate level and positioning it next to a more expensive model or brand

regional shopping center a planned shopping center containing large department stores, numerous specialty stores, restaurants, movie theaters, and sometimes even hotels

registered bond a bond registered in the owner's name by the issuing company

reinforcement theory a theory of motivation based on the premise that rewarded behavior is likely to be repeated, whereas punished behavior is less likely to recur

relationship marketing establishing long-term, mutually satisfying buyer–seller relationships

replacement chart a list of key personnel and their possible replacements within a firm

research and development (R&D) a set of activities intended to identify new ideas that have the potential to result in new goods and services

responsibility the duty to do a job or perform a task

retailer a middleman that buys from producers or other middlemen and sells to consumers

retained earnings the portion of a business's profits not distributed to stockholders

retained earnings the portion of a corporation's profits not distributed to stockholders

return on owners' (stockholders') equity a financial ratio calculated by dividing net income after taxes by owners' equity

return on sales (or profit margin) a financial ratio calculated by dividing net income after taxes by net sales

revenue stream a source of revenue flowing into a firm

revenues the dollar amounts earned by a firm from selling goods, providing services, or performing business activities

revolving credit agreement a guaranteed line of credit

risk-return ratio a ratio based on the principle that a high-risk decision should generate higher financial returns for a business and more conservative decisions often generate lower returns

robotics the use of programmable machines to perform a variety of tasks by manipulating materials and tools

S

safety needs the things we require for physical and emotional security

salary a specific amount of money paid for an employee's work during a set calendar period, regardless of the actual number of hours worked

sales forecast an estimate of the amount of a product that an organization expects to sell during a certain period of time based on a specified level of marketing effort

sales promotion the use of activities or materials as direct inducements to customers or salespersons

sales support personnel employees who aid in selling but are more involved in locating prospects, educating customers, building goodwill for the firm, and providing follow-up service

sample a free product given to customers to encourage trial and purchase

Sarbanes-Oxley Act of 2002 provides sweeping new legal protection for employees who report corporate misconduct

scheduling the process of ensuring that materials and other resources are at the right place at the right time

scientific management the application of scientific principles to management of work and workers

S-corporation a corporation that is taxed as though it were a partnership

secondary market a market for existing financial securities that are traded between investors

secondary-market pricing setting one price for the primary target market and a different price for another market

securities exchange a marketplace where member brokers meet to buy and sell securities

selection the process of gathering information about applicants for a position and then using that information to choose the most appropriate applicant

selective distribution the use of only a portion of the available outlets for a product in each geographic area

selective-demand (or brand) advertising advertising that is used to sell a particular brand of product

self-actualization needs the need to grow and develop and to become all that we are capable of being

self-managed teams groups of employees with the authority and skills to manage themselves

serial bonds bonds of a single issue that mature on different dates

Service Corps of Retired Executives (SCORE) a group of businesspeople who volunteer their services to small businesses through the SBA

service economy an economy in which more effort is devoted to the production of services than to the production of goods

service economy an economy in which more effort is devoted to the production of services than to the production of goods

shopping product an item for which buyers are willing to expend considerable effort on planning and making the purchase

short-term financing money that will be used for one year or less

sinking fund a sum of money to which deposits are made each year for the purpose of redeeming a bond issue

Six Sigma a disciplined approach that relies on statistical data and improved methods to eliminate defects for a firm's products and services

skills inventory a computerized data bank containing information on the skills and experience of all present employees

Small Business Administration (SBA) a governmental agency that assists, counsels, and protects the interests of small businesses in the United States

small business one that is independently owned and operated for profit and is not dominant in its field

small-business development centers (SBDCs) university-based groups that provide individual counseling and practical training to owners of small businesses

small-business institutes (SBIs) groups of senior and graduate students in business administration who provide management counseling to small businesses

small-business investment companies (SBICs) privately owned firms that provide venture capital to small enterprises that meet their investment standards

social audit a comprehensive report of what an organization has done and is doing with regard to social issues that affect it

social needs the human requirements for love and affection and a sense of belonging

social network site a Web site (often called a social site) that functions like an online community of Internet users where you can share your profile, messages, and photographs with family and friends

social responsibility the recognition that business activities have an impact on society and the consideration of that impact in business decision making

socioeconomic model of social responsibility the concept that business should emphasize not only profits but also the impact of its decisions on society

sole proprietorship a business that is owned (and usually operated) by one person

spamming the sending of massive amounts of unsolicited e-mails

span of management (or span of control) the number of workers who report directly to one manager

special-event pricing advertised sales or price cutting linked to a holiday, season, or event

specialization the separation of a manufacturing process into distinct tasks and the assignment of the different tasks to different individuals

specialty product an item that possesses one or more unique characteristics for which a significant group of buyers is willing to expend considerable purchasing effort

specialty-line wholesaler a middleman that carries a select group of products within a single line

speculative production the time lag between the actual production of goods and when the goods are sold

staff manager a position created to provide support, advice, and expertise within an organization

stakeholders all the different people or groups of people who are affected by the policies and decisions made by an organization

standard of living a loose, subjective measure of how well off an individual or a society is, mainly in terms of want satisfaction through goods and services

standing committee a relatively permanent committee charged with performing some recurring task

statement of cash flows a statement that illustrates how the company's operating, investing, and financing activities affect cash during an accounting period

statistic a measure that summarizes a particular characteristic of an entire group of numbers

stock the shares of ownership of a corporation

stockholder a person who owns a corporation's stock

store (or private) brand a brand that is owned by an individual wholesaler or retailer

strategic alliance a partnership formed to create competitive advantage on a worldwide basis

strategic plan an organization's broadest plan, developed as a guide for major policy setting and decision making

strategic planning process the establishment of an organization's major goals and objectives and the allocation of resources to achieve them

supermarket a large self-service store that sells primarily food and household products

superstore a large retail store that carries not only food and nonfood products ordinarily found in supermarkets but also additional product lines

supply an item that facilitates production and operations but does not become part of a finished product

supply the quantity of a product that producers are willing to sell at each of various prices

supply the quantity of a product that producers are willing to sell at each of various prices

supply-chain management long-term partnership among channel members working together to create a distribution system that reduces inefficiencies, costs, and redundancies while creating a competitive advantage and satisfying customers

sustainability meeting the needs of the present without compromising the ability of future generations to meet their own needs

SWOT analysis the identification and evaluation of a firm's strengths, weaknesses, opportunities, and threats

syndicate a temporary association of individuals or firms organized to perform a specific task that requires a large amount of capital

synthetic process a process in operations management in which raw materials or components are combined to create a finished product

T

tactical plan a smaller scale plan developed to implement a strategy

target market a group of individuals or organizations, or both, for which a firm develops and maintains a marketing mix suitable for the specific needs and preferences of that group

task force a committee established to investigate a major problem or pending decision

team two or more workers operating as a coordinated unit to accomplish a specific task or goal

technical salesperson a salesperson who assists a company's current customers in technical matters

technical skills specific skills needed to accomplish a specialized activity

telecommuting working at home all the time or for a portion of the work week

telemarketing the performance of marketing-related activities by telephone

television home shopping a form of selling in which products are presented to television viewers, who can buy them by calling a toll-free number and paying with a credit card

tender offer an offer to purchase the stock of a firm targeted for acquisition at a price just high enough to tempt stockholders to sell their shares

term-loan agreement a promissory note that requires a borrower to repay a loan in monthly, quarterly, semiannual, or annual installments

Theory X a concept of employee motivation generally consistent with Taylor's scientific management; assumes that employees dislike work and will function only in a highly controlled work environment

Theory Y a concept of employee motivation generally consistent with the ideas of the human relations movement; assumes that employees accept responsibility and work toward organizational goals, and by doing so they also achieve personal rewards

Theory Z the belief that some middle ground between type A and type J practices is best for American business

time utility utility created by making a product available when customers wish to purchase it

top manager an upper-level executive who guides and controls the overall fortunes of an organization

total cost the sum of the fixed costs and the variable costs attributed to a product

total quality management (TQM) the coordination of efforts directed at improving customer satisfaction, increasing employee participation, strengthening supplier partnerships, and facilitating an organizational atmosphere of continuous quality improvement

total revenue the total amount received from sales of a product

trade credit a type of short-term financing extended by a seller who does not require immediate payment after delivery of merchandise

trade deficit a negative balance of trade

trade name the complete and legal name of an organization

trade sales promotion method a sales promotion method designed to encourage wholesalers and retailers to stock and actively promote a manufacturer's product

trade salesperson a salesperson—generally employed by a food producer or processor—who assists customers in promoting products, especially in retail stores

trade show an industry-wide exhibit at which many sellers display their products

trademark a brand name or brand mark that is registered with the U.S. Patent and Trademark Office and thus is legally protected from use by anyone except its owner

trading company provides a link between buyers and sellers in different countries

traditional specialty store a store that carries a narrow product mix with deep product lines

transfer pricing prices charged in sales between an organization's units

transportation the shipment of products to customers

trustee an individual or an independent firm that acts as a bond owner's representative

U

undifferentiated approach directing a single marketing mix at the entire market for a particular product

unemployment rate the percentage of a nation's labor force unemployed at any time

unlimited liability a legal concept that holds a business owner personally responsible for all the debts of the business

unsecured financing financing that is not backed by collateral

utility the ability of a good or service to satisfy a human need

utility the ability of a good or service to satisfy a human need

V

variable cost a cost that depends on the number of units produced

venture capital money that is invested in small (and sometimes struggling) firms that have the potential to become very successful

virtual office allows employees to work at any place where they have access to computers, software, and other technology that enables them to perform their normal work activities

virtual team a team consisting of members who are geographically dispersed but communicate electronically

virtuoso team a team of exceptionally highly skilled and talented individuals brought together to produce significant change

W

wage survey a collection of data on prevailing wage rates within an industry or a geographic area

warehouse club a large-scale members-only establishment that combines features of cash-and-carry wholesaling with discount retailing

warehouse showroom a retail facility in a large, low-cost building with a large on-premises inventory and minimal service

warehousing the set of activities involved in receiving and storing goods and preparing them for reshipment

whistle-blowing informing the press or government officials about unethical practices within one's organization

wholesaler a middleman that sells products to other firms

wide-area network (WAN) a network that connects computers over a large geographic area, such as a city, a state, or even the world

working capital the difference between current assets and current liabilities

World Trade Organization (WTO) powerful successor to GATT that incorporates trade in goods, services, and ideas

World Wide Web (the Web) the Internet's multimedia environment of audio, visual, and text data

Z

zero-base budgeting a budgeting approach in which every expense in every budget must be justified

NAME INDEX

A

AAMCO Transmissions, 149
ABC television network, 3
Abercrombie & Fitch (A&F), 350
Academy of Management Executives, 246f
Accenture, 177f, 186, 268, 431
Accountancy Age, 443f
Accounting Today, 443f
Adelphia Communications Corp., 36, 39
Adidas, Inc., 340
Advanced Cast Stone, Inc., 216
Advanced Micro Devices (AMD), 490
Advertising Age, 85f, 285f, 316f, 320f, 321, 355f, 386f, 388
Advertising and Promotion (Belch and Belch), 387f
Affordable Care Act, 149
African Development Bank (AFDB), 91
Agency.com, 26
AIG, Inc., 138, 441
Air India, 87
AirTran Airlines, 242
Albert's Family Restaurants, 154
Allen, Kathleen R., 145f
Allman Brothers Band, 495
All Online Coupons, 393
Allstate Insurance, 169
Alrosa, 69
Alta Vista search engine, 421f
Amazon.com, 218, 228, 331, 344, 367, 375, 424, 430–431
Ambassador Roller Rink (MI), 369
American Airlines, 478
American Demographics, 342f
American Electric Power, 473
American Express, 5, 46, 132, 136f, 143f, 227, 490
American & Foreign Power Company, 490
American Greetings, Inc., 231
American Idol (television program), 425
American Institute of Certified Public Accountants (AICPA), 446f
American Marketing Association, 304
American National Standards Institute, 228
American Recovery and Reinvestment Act, 149
American Society for Training & Development, 269
America Online (AOL), 149, 329
Amway Products, 367, 376
Anderson, Keith E., 37
Anderson, Wayne, 37
Anderson's Ark and Associates, 37
Andron, Scott, 144f
Angwin, Julia, 320f
Anheuser-Busch, 318
AnnArbor.com, 108f, 203f
Annie's Homegrown, 128
Ante, Spencer E., 418f
Apple, Inc., 14, 39, 134, 139, 149, 175, 178, 189, 218, 231, 271, 285, 309, 331, 334–335, 350, 370, 418, 427
Aptera, Inc., 340

Archer, Leanna, 138
Archer Daniels Midland Company (ADM), 87
Arens, Christian, 387f
Arens, William F., 387f
Arguello, Carlos, 108
Ariel Investments, 170
Armstrong, Lance, 395
Armstrong, Waymon, 139
Arthur Andersen, 39
Ashby, Molly, 129
Asian Development Bank (ADB), 91
Associated Press, 121f
Association of Southeast Asian Nations, 83
Atlanta Journal-Constitution, 288f
AT&T, Inc., 38, 46, 50, 123, 132, 196, 224, 227, 288, 370, 386, 472
Aubree's Pizzeria and Tavern, 203
Audible.com, 344
Au Printemps (France), 374
Austin, Scott, 144f
Austin Entrepreneur Network, 203f
Avis Corporation, 151
Avon Products, 196, 198, 367–368, 376

B

Banco Galicia (Argentina), 488
Banker, The, 488f
Bank of America, 122, 132, 247, 448, 488
Banks, Dwayne, 147
Banks, Marilyn, 147
Barnes & Noble, 331
Barraso, Jose Manuel Durao, 82
Barron's magazine, 171
Bascaramurty, Dakshana, 309f
Baskin-Robbins, 154
Baskins, Ann, 37
Bates, Timothy, 152
Bath and Body Works, 375
Bayer, Inc., 47
Bazaarvoice, Inc., 203
Beacham, Ed, 369
Beacham's Clock Company (OR), 369
BearingPoint, Inc., 186
Bear Stearns, 138
Belch, George E., 387f
Belch, Michael, 387f
Bell, Alexander Graham, 46
Ben & Jerry's, 98, 307, 395, 402–403
Bentley, 332
Berdan, Stacie Nevadomski, 78f
Berggren, Eric, 342f
Berkshire Hathaway, 124, 475
Berry Plastics, 223
Best Buy, Inc., 10, 32, 107, 370, 373, 375, 466
Best Price Modern Wholesale stores (India), 122
Bethlehem Steel Company (PA), 273
BGT Partners (FL), 388
Bharti Enterprises (India), 121
Bill and Melinda Gates Foundation, 121
Bindrim, Kira, 418f

Birchall, Jonathan, 341f
BitTorrent.com, 428
Black & Decker, 214, 471
Black Enterprise, 109
Blake, Stacy, 246f
Blendtec, Inc., 316
Blink, David, 300, 497
Blockbuster Video, 315, 475
Blomstron, Robert L., 50f
Bloomberg Business Week, 175f
Bloomingdale's Department Stores, 367
Blu Dot, Inc., 363–364
BMW, 10, 344
Boeing, Inc., 88, 223, 226, 448
Bogle, John, 443
Bomey, Nathan, 108f
Bonobos, Inc., 285
Bookman Testing Services, Inc., 245
Booz & Co., 58f
Borders Books, 476–477
Borzacchiello, Maureen, 138
Bostic, Jim, 147
Boston Chicken, 152
Boston Globe, 46f
Boston Market, 164
Branson, Sir Richard, 135
Branson School of Entrepreneurship, 135
Bratt, Erik, 316f
Brin, Sergey, 177
Brinker International, 218
Bristol-Myers Squibb, 395
British Petroleum (BP), 58, 148, 230
Broadcast.com, 8
Brown, Floretta, 55
Bruce Miller Nurseries (TX), 471
Bulick, Beth Snyder, 388f
Burch, Sharon, 145
Burger King Corporation, 152–154
Burkitt, Laurie, 320f
Burlington Coat Factory, 375, 399
Burlington Northern Santa Fe Railway, 124
Burr, Barry B., 170f
Burrows, Peter, 39f, 418f
Burton's Snowboards, Inc., 236–237
Burt's Bees, 50
Busch Gardens Conservation Fund, 120–121
Bush, George W., 36, 40, 69
Business and Society: Concepts and Policy Issues (Davis, Frederick, and Blomstron), 50f
Business Periodicals Index (H.W. Wilson, Inc.), 401
Business Software Alliance, 377
BusinessWeek, 39f, 180f, 285f, 298, 413, 418f, 447f

C

California Milk Processor Board, 383
Callaway Golf, 471
Campbell's Soup Company, 179, 219, 346
Canadian Free Trade Agreement, 83
Cano, Karina Diaz, 250f

Canon, Inc., 231
Cap Gemini Ernst & Young, 186
Capital One Financial, 340
Career Builder, 5
Career One Stop, 5
Cargill Corn Milling North America, 226
Caribbean Basin Initiative (CBI), 84
Carl's Jr., 153
Carnival Cruise Lines, 4
Carpenter, Jake Burton, 236
Carter, Jimmy, 83
Casserly, Meghan, 175f
Caterine, Melinda J., 180f
Caterpillar, Inc., 78, 482
Cato Institute, 70
Cengage Learning, 342
Center for Trade Policy, Cato Institute, 70
Central American Free Trade Agreement (CAFTA), 83
Central European Free Trade Association, 77
Century 21 Real Estate, 153
Challenger, Gray & Christmas, 252
Challenger, John, 252
Character of a Corporation, The (Goffee and Jones), 202f
Charles Schwab Financial Services, 416
Charles Schwab Foundation, 46
Chase Bank, 479
Chevrolet Company, 353
Chevron, 215
Christakos, John, 364
Chrysler Group, 119, 192
Chu, Steven, 487
Church & Dwight, 458
Church's Chicken, 152
CIO Insight, 228f
Circle K Stores, 374
Cisco Systems, 288, 420
Citibank, 215
Citigroup, 132, 488
Civil Rights Act of 1964, 54
Clancy, Heather, 431f
Clarke, Richard T., 47
Clean Air Act, 59
Clean Water Act, 57
Clemson University, 136
clickz.com, 341f
Clinton, William J., 52, 83, 90
Clorox, Inc., 340, 458
Club Penguin children's Internet site, 3
CNet News, 486f
Coca-Cola Company, 49, 58, 150, 218, 257, 337, 340, 344, 434
Cohn, Michael, 443f
Coker, Ralph, 137f
Colgate-Palmolive, 49, 87, 458
Colorado Business, 203f
Columbia Gas, 147
Columbia Pictures Entertainment, 87
Colvin, Geoff, 196f
Committee for the Implementation of Textile Agreements, 74
Common Market of the Southern Cone (MERCOSUR), 84
Commonwealth of Independent States (former USSR), 81, 84
Compaq Computer Corp., 149
Computer Industry Almanac, 428
ComputerWeekly, 459f
ComputerWorld, 418f
ConAgra, 351
Condé Nast Publications, 338
Consolidated Edison, 485
Consorzio Foods, 129
Consumer Affairs, 6
Container Store, The, 429

Contemporary Advertising (Arens, Weigold, and Arens), 387f
Cool Whip, Inc., 346
Cooper, Cynthia, 43
Copley Pharmaceuticals, Inc., 36
Copycat Cupcakes Don't Cut It (McMath), 342f
Corcodikes, Nick, 250f
Corpus Christi Caller Times, 137f
Costco, Inc., 128, 373, 375
Council on Foreign Relations, 27
Cox, Taylor H., 246f
Cracker Barrel Old Country Stores, 10
Crain's Detroit Business, 418f
Crain's New York Business, 418f
Creative Display Solutions, 138
CRM Magazine, 85f
Cuban, Mark, 8
Curtin, Mary Liz, 369
Curves Fitness Centers, 151–152
Customer Relationship Magazine, 129
CVS Caremark, Inc., 373

D

Daft, Richard L., 246f
Daily Record, The, 6
Dairy Queen, 149, 151
Davis, Keith, 50f
Davis, Wendy, 320f
DeBalse, Colleen, 486f
De Beers, Inc., 344
Decker, Sam, 203f
Deepwater Horizon oil spill, 58
Deere & Company, 37
Dell Computer Corporation, 31, 202, 232, 341, 345, 368, 429
Dell Foundation, 45
Del Monte, 362
Deloitte Touche Tohmatsu, 78, 287, 399, 446–447, 459
Delphi Automotive Systems Corporation, 60
Demeter, Steve, 418
Demuth, Lee G., III, 341f
Denman, George, 403
Denny's Restaurants, 315
Deshpande, Abhijeet, 488f
Dingell, John, 37
Dinsmore, David, 252f
DirectTV, 357
Dish Network Corporation, 475
Disney, Roy, 3
Disney, Walt, 3
Disney Interactive Media Group, 3
Diversity-Business.com, 109
Dizzy Dean's Beef and Burgers, 152
DLA Piper Technology Leaders Forecast, 318f
Doctor's Associates, 152
Dodd-Frank Wall Street Reform and Consumer Protection Act, 473
Dodge Motor Company, 353
Dolan, Kerry A., 46f
Dollar General Stores, 367, 374
Domino's Pizza, 304
Domsic, Melissa, 108f
Donnelly, Tim, 355f
Dooney & Bourke, 311
Dow Chemical Company, 88, 196, 291
Dowling, Daisy Wademan, 144f
DPR Construction, 257
Drexel-Heritage furniture, 226
Dr Pepper/Seven-Up Companies, 150, 344
Drucker, Peter, 364
DuBois, Kathleen, 147
Dudley, Joe, 4–5, 9
Dun & Bradstreet (D&B), 137, 320, 458, 489
Dunkin' Donuts, 154, 180

Dunn, Andy, 285
Dunn, Patricia, 37
DuPont, Inc., 196
Duracell Batteries, 343
Durand, Douglas, 36

E

Eastman Kodak, 146, 249
eBay, 290, 386, 424, 428
Ebbers, Bernard, 473
Eco-Business, 488f
Economist, The, 170f
E-Consultancy, 376f
El-Badri, Abdalla Salem, 84
Eli Lilly & Co., Inc., 166, 193
Ellison, Larry, 122
eMarketer, 385f
Endeavor Personal Concierge, 355
Energizer, Inc., 338
Engineering & Computer Simulations, Inc., 140
Engle v. R. J. Reynolds, 36
English-Boswell, Chenille, 453
Enron, Inc., 39, 43, 441
Enterprise Development Group, 152
Entrepreneur magazine, 151
Environmental Leader, 39f
Equal Employment Opportunity Commission (EEOC), 55, 251, 263
Ernst & Young, 268, 446–447, 459
ESPN sports network, 3
Ethan Allen, 400
ETrade, 328
European Bank for Reconstruction and Development, 92
European Economic Area (EEA), 82
European Union (EU), 81–82
Evans, Dave, 341f
Evans, Teri, 26
EvoGear.com, 95–96
Export-Import Bank, 90–91
ExxonMobil, 46, 124, 192, 244, 249, 418

F

Facebook, 109, 124, 139–140, 167, 180, 208, 271, 304, 310, 316, 367, 376, 400, 403, 421, 429, 437, 459, 478, 486, 497
Fahrenheit 212, 340
Fallwell, Keren, 488f
Fannie Mae, 138, 441
Fantastic Foods, 129
Fast Company, 309f
Federal Communications Commission (FCC), 389
Federal Reserve, 20, 142
Federal Reserve Bank of St. Louis, 79f
Federal Reserve Bulletin, 413
Federal Trade Commission (FTC), 38–39, 154, 320, 377, 389
FedEx, Inc., 149, 271, 400
Ferrari, 290
Ferrell, O. C., 39f, 313f, 314f, 317f, 359f, 383f, 3913f
Fettig, Jeff, 268
Fidelity Investments, 416
Financial Times, 341f, 447f
Fine Living Channel, 402
First Business Bank (CA), 143
Fitzsimmons, Caitlin, 388f
Flannery, Matt, 111
Flavelle, Dana, 376f
Flinders, Karl, 459f
Flogging Molly, 495
Foden-Vencil, Kristian, 369f
Food Network, 159, 402

Foot Locker, 375
Foraker, John, 129
Forbes, Thom, 342f
Forbes magazine, 46f, 158, 175f, 320f
Ford, Gerald, 52
Ford, Henry, 25
Ford, Henry II, 56
Ford Motor Company, 8, 18, 23, 35, 139, 200, 226, 245, 309, 316, 353, 427, 476, 487
Forrester Research, 428
Fortune magazine, 41, 109, 196f, 249–250, 257, 274, 341f, 413, 447
Fotolog.com, 26
Foundation for Enterprise Development, 298
Foundations of Marketing (Pride and Ferrell), 359f
Fountain, Henry, 196f
Fox Business, 369f
Fox News Small Business Center, 137f
Freddie Mac, 138
Frederick, William C., 50f
Free Wave Technologies (CO), 282
French Connection, 376
Friedman, Thomas L., 69
Furman, Phyllis, 170f

G

Gabjhawala, Rekha, 153
Gallardo, Luis, 459f
Gallup Organization, 152
Gamble, James, 113
Gap, Inc., 8, 375, 393
Garfield, Bob, 320f
Gates Foundation, 121
Geico Insurance, 475
General Electric Company (GE), 45, 68, 114, 121, 146, 171, 196, 199, 213, 216, 227, 249, 274, 412, 418, 440, 472
General Mills, 12, 50, 56, 336, 340, 418
General Mills Foundation, 44
General Motors Company (GM), 23, 35, 87–88, 121–122, 141, 165, 336, 386, 469
Gerdes, Lindsey, 447f
Gerstein, Joseph, 36
Get Your Share (Stav), 8
Giant Food, 413
Gillette, 336
Girl Scouts of America, 121
Glader, Paul, 121f
Glad Products Company, 215
Globe and Mail, The (Canada), 309f
GNC (General Nutrition Centers), 149
Goffee, Rob, 202f
Gogoi, Pallavi, 78f
Goldman Sachs, 122
Gold Star Appliances, Inc., 478
Goodrich, Ben, 75
Google, Inc., 124, 130, 177, 196, 202, 228, 257, 271, 284, 418, 421–422, 428, 430–431
Goo Goo Dolls, 32
Goran, Leon, 185
Gorman, Leon, 298
Go-to-Market plan, 170
Gourmet magazine, 338
Government Accountability Office (GAO), 74
Graeter, Bob, 97–98, 160, 238, 300
Graeter, Charlie, 97
Graeter, Chip, 97, 160, 238, 300, 402
Graeter, Regina, 97
Graeter, Richard II, 160, 238, 300–301, 402, 497
Graeter's, 97–98, 160, 238, 300, 402–403, 497–498
Graffort, Cindy, 208
Grainger, Inc., 371
Grass, Martin L., 43
Graves, Todd, 104

Great Clips hair salons, 154
Graeter's, 160
GreenBiz.com, 196f
Greene, Susan D., 253f
Greener World Media, 288f
Green Grid, 420
Greenhouse, Steven, 447f
Greenpeace, 39
Gresham, Larry, 39f
Griffin, Ricky W., 200f, 246f, 411f
Griswold, Daniel T., 70
Grosnickle, Karolyn, 37
Groupon.com, 355
Group Swoop, 355
Gruma SA (Mexico), 87
Guitar Center, Inc., 391
Gunther, Marc, 341f

H

Häagen-Dazs, 98, 402
Haass, Richard, 27
Habitat for Humanity, 120
Halliburton, Inc., 39
Halvorsen, Elizabeth, 146
Hampp, Andrew, 316f
Hard Rock Cafe, 221
Harrington, Emily, 146
Harrods (UK), 374
Hart, Ariel, 288f
Hart, G. J., 275
Harvard Business Review Blog, 144f
Harvard Business School, 137
Harvard University, 138–140
Hasbro, Inc., 231
Hatten, Timothy, 144f
Healthcare Financial Management Association, 41
Heiferman, Scott, 26
Hendricks, Brian, 137
Herrera, Tilde, 196f
Hershey, Inc., 274, 340
Hertz Corporation, 151
Herzberg, Frederick, 276, 284
Hewlett-Packard Corp. (HP), 31, 37, 49, 113, 219, 227
Hickins, Michael, 320f
Hiebing, Inc. (WI), 388
Hi-Media Group, 26
Hird, Jake, 376f
Hispanic PR Wire, 116
History Channel, 402
Hitachi America, 50
H.J. Heinz Company, 105, 164, 343, 346
Hlar, Corbin, 431f
Hochberg, Fred P., 91
Holiday Inns, 151, 306
Home Depot, Inc., 132, 371, 373, 375, 399, 448
Homegrown Naturals, Inc., 129
Home Shopping Network (HSN), 377
Honda Motor Company, 23, 65, 170, 409
Honeywell, Inc., 227
Hoover, Inc., 425
Horatio Alger Award, 5
Horsford, Simon, 216f
Houston Community College, 167
H&R Block, 149
HR.BLR.COM, 247
HRWorld.com, 283f
Hsu, Tiffany, 196f, 486f
Hufbauer, Gary, 75
Huffington Post, 78f
Hulu.com, 400
Hurricane Katrina, 44
H.W. Wilson, Inc., 401

Hyatt Corporation, 176
Hyundai USA, 177

I

IBM, Inc., 45, 65, 132, 146, 227, 345, 420
Illumina, Inc., 231
Immelt, Jeffrey R., 170, 171
Inc. magazine, 147, 180f, 355f
Industrial Revolution, 307
Information Resources, Inc., 320
Infosys Technologies (India), 424
InfoWorld, 478f
Innovision Technologies, 135
Institute for International Economics, 75
Intel Corporation, 149
Inter-American Development Bank, 90–91
Intergovernmental Panel on Climate Change, 59
Internal Revenue Service (IRS), 119–120, 383
International Bank for Reconstruction and Development (IBRD), 91
International Development Association (IDA), 91
International Franchise Association, 154
International Monetary Fund (IMF), 76, 77f, 92
International Trade Loan program, SBA, 155
International Women's Day, 46
Inter RAO (Russia), 121
Iosebashvili, Ira, 121f
ISO (International Organization for Standardization), 227–228
i-traffic.com, 26
Ivey Planning Group, 108–109

J

J. Crew, 376
J. P. Morgan Chase, 122
Jackson, Lisa, 203f
Jackson Hewitt tax services, 320
Jaguar, 44
Javelin Strategy and Research, 430
JCPenney, 105, 319, 376
Jell-O Brand Gelatin, 345
Jha, Sanjay, 58
Jobs, Steve, 178
Johnson, Lyndon B., 56
Johnson, William, 164
Johnson & Johnson, Inc., 114, 386, 417, 434
Jones, Gareth, 202f
Jones, Huw, 443f
Journal of American Academy of Business, 341f
Journal of Marketing, 39f
JP Morgan Chase, 488
Junior Achievement, 138
JustFares.com, 95

K

Karisia safari firm (Kenya), 216
Kaufelt, Rob, 158
Kauffman, Raven, 137
Kazemi, Masoud Mir, 84
Kellogg's, 192, 214, 319, 346
Kelzer, Gregg, 418f
Kennedy, John F., 51, 80
Kepcher, Carolyn, 250f
KFC (Kentucky Fried Chicken), 151
Kiger, Patrick J., 309f
Kilduff, Angela, 355f
Kiley, David, 316f
Kimpton Hotels and Restaurants, 256–257
Kinsey, Matt, 285f
Kirby, Inc., 376
Kiva.org, 111

Kiviat, Barbara, 6, 309f
Kmart Corporation, 196
Kmart Stores, 114, 305, 374, 399
KnowThis.com, 321f
Koehn, Nancy F., 137
Kohl's Stores, 425
Kolesnik, Kris, 43
Kontzer, Tony, 228f
Korkki, Phyllis, 78f
Kosova, Weston, 39f
Kozlowski, Leo Dennis, 37
KPMG, 268, 440, 446–447, 459
Kraft Foods, 10, 129, 211, 319, 386, 444
Kroger Company, 97, 158, 160, 238, 373, 402–403
Krotz, Joanna L., 137f
Krummer, Robert, Jr., 143
Kuen, Leng, 488f
Kwe, Glenda, 6

L

LaFalce, John, 43
Lahontan Valley News (NV), 252f
LaMonica, Martin, 486f
Lamy, Pascal, 81
Lands' End, 367, 376
Lansing State Journal, 108f
La Prensa (Arguello), 108
Launching New Ventures: An Entrepreneurial Approach (Allen), 145f
Lauper, Cyndi, 32
Leahy, Jordan, 144
Leanna's Hair, Inc., 138
Learning Tree International, 268
Ledger, The (FL), 216f
LEGO Group, 85, 170
Lehman Brothers, 441–442
Leon & Lulu (MI), 369
Levering, Robert, 447f
Levi Srauss, 196
Lexis-Nexis, 320
Lexus, Inc., 343
Liebowitz, Matt, 478f
Limbach, James, 6
Lindblad Expeditions, 216
Lindquist, Lee, 65
LinkedIn, 180, 429, 459
Litow, Stanley S., 45
Little Guys, The, 466
Live Nation, 32
Liz Claiborne, Inc., 232
L.L. Bean, Inc., 139, 185, 298, 306, 347, 367, 400
Lockheed Martin, 44, 227
Lohr, Steve, 320f
L'Oréal, 386
Los Angeles Times, 137f, 196f, 486f
Louisiana State University, 104
Lowe's, Inc., 289, 373
Lublin, Joann S., 170f
Lufthansa AG, 87

M

MacMillan, Douglas, 418f
Mac OS X operating system, 420
Macy's, Inc., 367, 374, 399, 429
Mad Men (television program), 388
Madoff, Bernard, 37
Maggiano's Little Italy restaurants, 218
Maitland, Alison, 447f
Malcolm Baldrige National Quality Award, 226
Management (Daft), 246f
Management (Griffin), 200f, 411f
Management Review, 342f

Mancina, Saverio, 369f
Marathon Oil Corporation, 214
Marchionne, Sergio, 119
Marilyn's Gift Gallery and Sound Music World, 147
Marketing Concepts and Strategies (Pride and Ferrell), 313f, 314f, 317f, 383f, 391f
Marketing magazine, 375f
Marks, Richard, 37
Maroon 5, 32
Marriott International, 5, 147, 151, 345
Mars, Inc., 407
Marshall, Gary, 418f
Marshall, John, 113
Marshall Field's (IL), 374
Marshalls Stores, 375
Martel, Melanie C. L., 253f
Martha Stewart Living Omnimedia, 200
Marvel Entertainment, 3
Marx, Karl, 17
Marya, Radhika, 26
Mashable, 26
Maslow, Abraham, 274
Massachusetts Small Business Development Center, 155
Mattel, Inc., 21
Mattioli, Dana, 170f
Maxim Integrted Products, Inc., 222
Mayo, Elton, 274
Mayo Clinic, 165
Mayrhuber, Wolfgang, 87
McCarron, Suzanne, 46
McCormick, Chris, 185
McDaniel de Andrade, Dixie, 7
McDonald's Corporation, 13, 67, 139, 149, 152, 153, 180, 191, 196, 198, 223, 315
McGregor, Douglas, 277–278
McKay, Lauren, 85f
McMath, Robert, 342f
McMillion, Denver, 147
McNulty, Suzy, 287
Media Post, 320f
MediaShift, 431f
Medicare, 36
Mercedes-Benz, 227, 306, 314
Merck & Co., Inc., 47
Miami Herald, 144f
Michael and Susan Dell Foundation, 45
Michelin, Inc., 344
Michigan Office of Great Workplace Development, 283f
Microsoft Corporation, 24, 50, 55, 65, 114, 189, 271, 291, 329, 418–420, 430–431, 434, 458, 482
Midvale Steel Company (PA), 272
Mills, Karen, 139, 148–149
Milwaukee Public Schools (WI), 45
MindBodyFitness, 355
Minority Business Development Agency, 146
Mir Mine (Russia), 69
Mission Local (CA), 355f
Mission Minis, 355
MMR, 39f
M&M's candies, 407
Mobil33t iPhone app, 108
Modesto Academy of Music & Design, 148
Mom Corps of Miami, 7
Monahan, Jane, 488f
Money.CNN.com, 89f
Monster.com, 5, 249
Montgomery Ward catalog, 376
Monthly Labor Review, 413
Moorhead, Gregory, 246f
Morgan Stanley, 122
Morton Salt, 313

Moskowitz, Milton, 447f
Motorola, Inc., 58, 182, 226–227, 344, 409
Mozilla, Inc., 291, 421
Mulally, Alan, 487
Murray's Cheese, Inc., 158–159
MySpace, 208, 429

N

Nabisco, Inc., 338
Nacher, Thomas, 342f
Nader, Ralph, 52
Naked Juice, Inc., 347
Nanigan, Daniel J., 155
Nanmac Corporation, 155
Nardone, Paul, 129
NASA (National Aeronautics and Space Administration), 171
NASDAQ stock exchange, 37, 485
National Alliance of Business (NAB), 56
National Black McDonald's Operators Association, 152
National Center for Employee Ownership, 289
National Consumers' League, 52
National Export Initiative, 78
National Export Strategy (NES), 90–91
National Federation of Independent Business Foundation, 136f, 143f
National Franchise Mediation Program, 153
National Ice Cream Month, 403
National Small Business Person of the Year award, 139
National Small Business Week, 149
National Trade Data Bank, 96
National Trust for Historic Preservation, 46
National Whistle Blower Center, 43
Nederlander Concerts, 32–33, 495
Needleman, Sarah H., 6, 175f, 369f
Nestlé, 211, 226, 328–329, 340
Netflix video rentals, 315, 377
NetGrocer.com, 329
Newsweek, 39f
New United Motor Manufacturing, Inc. (NUMMI), 88
New York Daily News, 170f, 250f
New York Life Insurance, 214
New York Magazine, 26
New York Stock Exchange (NYSE), 469, 485
New York Times, 78f, 228f, 320f, 447f
New York Times Education Life Supplement, 196f
New York Yankees, 221
NFL football, 407
Nicole Miller, Inc., 319
Nielsen marketing research, 321, 421f
Nike, Inc., 189, 199, 311, 342, 343
Nisource, Inc., 147
Nissan Motor Company, 23, 35, 170, 311
Nixon, Richard, 37
Noise Control Act of 1972, 59–60
Nokia, 189
Nortel Networks Corporation, 38
North American Free Trade Agreement (NAFTA), 83, 96
Northrup Grumman Corporation, 227
Northwestern University, 144
Numi Organic Tea, 208
NYSE Euronext holding company, 485

O

Obama, Barack, 43, 78, 149, 473
Observer, The (UK), 216f
Occupational Outlook Handbook, 447
Office Depot, Inc., 375
OfficeMax, 313–314
Office of the U.S. Trade Representative, 83

Olay, 322
Old Navy, 393
Old School Forest Preserve (IL), 58
Olyai, Nikki, 135
O'Malley, Martin, 55
Oneida, Inc., 231
Open Pantry Stores, 374
Oprah Winfrey Show, 4, 402–403
Oracle Corporation, 122
Orbitz.com, 427
Oregon Public Broadcasting, 369f
Organizational Behavior (Griffin and
    Moorhead), 246f
Organization for Economic Cooperation and
    Development (OECD), 84
Organization of Petroleum Exporting
    Countries, 84
Ouchi, William, 278
Outback Steakhouse, Inc., 149
Oviedo, Dannielle, 208
Oxley, Michael J., 43

P

Pacific Rim, 84
Packard, Dave, 113
Page, Larry, 177
Pampered Chef Products, 376
Panasonic Corporation, 220
Parker Brothers, 334
Partners in Preservation Web site, 46f
Patagonia, 39
Patek Philippe, 371
Patel, Kumur, 355f
Paychex, Inc., 256
Pencil Makers Association, 73
Pensions & Investments, 170f
Pepperidge Farms, 13
PepsiCo, Inc., 50, 68, 128, 150, 153, 247, 337
Perkins, Tom, 203f
Pet Assure, Inc., 257
Petty, Herman, 152
Pfau, Bruce, 440
Pfizer, Inc., 132, 386
Philip Morris, Inc., 51, 88
Phillips, Bryce, 95–96
Phillips Petroleum, 44
Photobrand, 400
Pier 1 Imports, 68
Pixar Entertainment, 3
Pizza Hut, 219, 306, 342
Planters, 346
Plumb, Taryn, 46f
Polaroid, 139
Pollution Control Board of Kerala (India), 58
Polo Ralph Lauren, 343
Pomerantz, Carrie Schwab, 46
Porcino, Paul, 497
Portland Press Herald, 180f
Post-Industrial Society (Drucker), 364
Pottery Barn, 376
PricewaterhouseCoopers LLP, 37, 247, 446–447, 459
Pride, William M., 313f, 314f, 317f, 359f, 383f, 391f
Prior, Anna, 252f
Proactive skin care, 378
Procter, William, 113
Procter & Gamble Company (P&G), 38, 105,
    113, 139, 146, 170, 175, 192, 211, 249, 290,
    328–329, 336, 340–342, 345, 357, 370, 386,
    409, 458, 482
P&T Express (Vietnam), 121

Q

Quaker Oats, Inc., 257
Qualified Resources, Inc., 147

Questor Corporation, 85
Quicken accounting software, 420
QVC shopping network, 377
Qwest, Inc., 39

R

Rackspace.com, 430
RadioShack, 153
Rahim, Ahmed, 208
Rahim, Reem, 208
Raising Cane's restaurants, 104
Raitt, Bonnie, 495
Razor Gator, Inc., 344
Reader's Digest Association, 113–114, 320
Reagan, Ronald, 83
Reason Public Policy Institute, 287
Recorder app, 418
Redbox video rentals, 315
Red Cross, 5
Red Sox baseball team, 400
Reebok Company, 221
Reed, Kevin, 443f
Reed Business Information, 342f
Renaissance Capital, 484f
Restoration Hardware, 424
Reuters, 443f
Reynolds, Shelley, 107
Reynolds Signature Homes, 107
Richland Community Collge (TX), 226
Rigas, John J., 36
Rigas, Timothy J., 36
RIM (Research in Motion), 344
Rite Aid Corp., 43
Ritz-Carlton Hotels, 226
R.J. Reynolds, Inc., 51
Roebuck, Alvah, 117
Rolls-Royce, 311
Romanias, Chris, 153
Rooney, Jennifer, 388f
Roosevelt, Franklin D., 25, 48
Rosetta Stone language learning software, 378
Rostekhnologil (Russia), 121
Roundy's Supermarkets, 223
Royal Caribbean Cruise Lines, 4
Royal Crown Companies, 150–151
Royal Dutch/Shell Group, 114
Royer's Roundtop Café, 191
RoyOMartin Plywood, 252
Ruiz, Manny, 116

S

S. C. Johnson & Son, 41, 44
Safeway Stores, Inc., 208
SAIC, 121
Salon.com, 78f
Samsung, Inc., 189, 340
San Diego Union-Tribune, 316f
Sarah Coventry Products, 376
Sara Lee Corporation, 10
Sarbanes, Paul S., 43
SAS, Inc., 257, 274
Save the Children, Inc., 5
SayNow, 124
SBA Management Assistance Program, 145–146
Scannell, Stephen, 369
Scheer, David, 180f
Schmitt, Jeff, 175f
Schneider, Tehani, 6
Scholfield, Roger, 65
Schultz, Howard, 180–181
Schweitzer, Tamara, 180f
SC Johnson & Son Co., 257, 286
SCORE (Service Corps of Retired Executives),
    109, 146

SCORE Award for Outstanding Socially-
    Progressive Business, 104
Sears, Richard, 117
Sears, Roebuck & Co., 117, 141, 256, 305,
    309–310, 342, 356
Sears Holdings, Inc., 114, 196, 373, 380
Seattle Times, 250f
SeaWorld, 120
Securities and Exchange Commission (SEC), 43,
    443, 484
Security News Daily, 478f
Sephora Cosmetics, 378
Seton Hall University, 37
7-Eleven Stores, 165, 374, 399
Shafrir, Doree, 26
Shah, Premal, 111
Shanghai Disney, 3
Shea, Bill, 418f
Shearman, Sarah, 376f
Shell, Richard, 147
Shirouzu, Norihiko, 121f
Shutterfly.com, 344
Siegle, Lucy, 216f
Sierra Club, 65
Silicon Valley, 113
Singer Sewing Company, 151
Siyeza, Inc., 56
SkillView Technologies, Inc., 245
Skype, 309
Small Business Administration (SBA), 104, 133,
    139f, 150f, 155
Small Business Development Centers
    (SBDCs), 147
Small Business Institutes (SBIs), 147
Small Business Investment Companies
    (SBICs), 148
*Small Business Management: Entrepreneurship and
    Beyond* (Hatten), 144f
Small Business Saturday movement, 132
Small Business Training Network (SBTN), 146
Smartfood, 128
Smith, Adam, 13–14, 17, 192
Smith, Gary, 108–109
Smith, Janet, 108–109
Social Media Marketing Magazine, 459f
Sodexo, Inc., 286
Solera Capital LLC, 129
Sony Corporation, 10, 87, 114, 221, 345
South Florida Business Journal, 388f
Southwest Airlines, 165, 171–172, 215, 242
South-Western Publishing, 248
Space, 429
Spaly, Brian, 285
Speaker, Joe, 43
Springsteen, Bruce, 495
Sprint Nextel Communications, 425–426
SPSS, Inc., 319
Stahl, Jennifer, 287
Standard Chartered Bank (UK), 488
Standard & Poor's, 428, 458
Standard & Poor's Industry Surveys, 365
Stanford Business School, 285
Stanley Black & Decker, 471
Stanley Home Products, 376
Staples, Inc., 149
Starbucks Coffee, 49, 167, 180–181, 287, 340–341,
    367, 429
Star Online, The (Malaysia), 488f
StartUpPc, Inc., 138
Stav, Julie, 8
Strand, Cheryl, 136
Stross, Randall, 228f
Student magazine, 135
SUBWAY, 151–152, 154
Subway Corp., 131
SunCoke Energy, 484

Sunoco, Inc., 484
Superfund, 59
Supplemental Terrorist Activity Relief
    program, 148
Supplier Connection, 132
Sydney Morning Herald (Australia), 6

T

Takeda Pharmaceutical Company, Ltd. (Japan), 36
Taliman, Pam, 148
TAP Pharmaceutical Products, Inc., 36
Target Stores, Inc., 128, 373–374, 375, 453, 467
Taylor, Frederick W., 272, 277
Taylor, James, 495
TCBY Enterprises, 152
Tech Radar, 418f
Telephone Pionees of America, 46
Tesco, 211
Tesla Motors, Inc., 35
Texas A&M University, 283f
Texas A&M University-Corpus Christi, 137
Texas Instruments (TI), 41–42
Texas Roadhouse, 274–275
TGI Friday's, 164
Thomas, Gwen, 132
Thomas, Owen, 285f
Thomasville Furniture, Inc., 23
Thomsen, Linda Chatman, 43
Thornton, Beth, 147
Thorpe, Liz, 158
3M Company, 59–60, 218, 259, 335, 472
Thulasidas, V., 87
Thurm, Scott, 320f
Timber Industry Magazine, The, 488f
Time International, 216f
Time magazine, 6, 43, 140, 309f
Time Warner, Inc., 4, 386
Tire Rack, Inc., 344
T.J. Maxx, 375
Tkaczyk, Christopher, 447f
T-Mobile, 123
Tommy Hilfiger, 343
Toronto Star (Canada), 376f
Tour of Hope, 395
Town Talk (LA), 252f
Toyota Corporation, 18, 23, 35, 88, 170, 180, 231,
    290, 343, 353, 384
Trade Act of 2002, 69
Trade Promotion Coordinating Committee
    (TPCC), 90
Trammel, Angela, 151–152
Travel Channel, 402
Treaty of Asuncion, 84
Triangle Business Journal, 85f
Trism game, 418
Tupperware Products, 376
Turner, Jane, 43
Turner Broadcasting System, 321
21Vianet Group, 483
Twitter, 109, 124, 159, 180, 310, 341, 367, 400,
    429, 437, 459, 497
Tyco International, Ltc., 37
Tynan-Wood, Christina, 478f

U

Ultimate Job Hunter's Guidebook, The (Greene
    and Martel), 253f
Underwood, Carrie, 424

Unilever, 211, 328–329, 458
Union Bank, 50
Union Carbide, 87
Union Pacific Corporation, 491
United Airlines, 289
United Way, 44, 388
University of Central Florida, 137
University of Michigan, 108
*University of New Hampshire Technology
    Pipeline,* 6
University of Northern Iowa, 108
University of Wisconsin-Madison, 108
University of Wisconsin-Whitewater, 144
UPS (United Parcel Service), 78, 97, 121, 132, 177,
    379, 400, 402
Urban Outfitters, Inc., 364
U.S. Bureau of Labor Statistics, 7, 18, 217f, 229
U.S. Census Bureau, 55f, 56f, 71f, 105f, 106f,
    142, 374
U.S. Commercial Service, 155
U.S. Consumer Product Safety Commission, 51
U.S. Department of Commerce, 72f, 73, 78f, 89f,
    155, 217
U.S. Department of Energy, 487
U.S. Environmental Protection Agency (EPA), 27,
    57, 59, 142, 230
U.S. Food and Drug Administration (FDA), 36, 51,
    230, 389
U.S. Government Printing Office, 148
U.S. Navy, 179
U.S. Occupational Safety and Health
    Administration, 230
U.S. Office of Management and Budget, 140
U.S. Patent and Trademark Office, 342, 345
U.S. Steel Corp., 73
U.S. Supreme Court, 113
U.S. Uniform Partnership Act, 108
U.S. West, 321
U.S.Court of Appeals, 43
USDA Economic Research Service, 414f

V

Vanguard Mutual Funds, 443
VatorNews, 285f
VB Solutions, Inc., 138
Venture Beat, 285f
Verizon Communications, 38, 356–357, 370,
    386, 420
Village of Rochester Hills shopping
    center, 378
Virgin Group, 135
Vivendi, 50
Volkswagen AG, 114, 170
Volvo, 284, 344
Vroom, Victor, 280

W

W. L. Gore & Associates, 289
Wachovia Bank, 124
Walgreen's, Inc., 373
Wallace, DeWitt, 113
Wallace, Lila, 113
Wall Street Journal, 6, 26, 121f, 144f, 170f, 175f,
    250f, 252f, 320f, 369f, 413, 486f
Walmart Superstores, 11, 32, 44, 105, 121–122,
    169, 211, 357, 367, 369, 371, 373–374, 375,
    380, 471
Walsh, Daniel, 288f

Walt Disney Company, 3–4, 243, 316–317, 386,
    407, 420, 485
Walton, Sam, 11, 122
Watkins, Sherron S., 43
Wayne State University, 152
Wealth of Nations (Smith), 13, 192
Weather Channel, 400
Weight Watchers, 164, 331, 346
Weigold, Michael, 387f
Welburn, Craig, 152
Wells Fargo Bank, 124
Wendy's International, 152–153
Western Electric Company (IL), 274
West Virginia Small Business Development
    Centers (SBDC), 147
Wexler, David, 466
Wexler, Evie, 466
Whataburger, 223
What Were They Thinking? (McMath and
    Forbes), 342f
Whirlpool Corporation, 220, 268
White Hen Pantry, 374
Whole Foods, 208
Why Good Ideas Go Bust (Berggren and Nacher),
    342f
Willis, David, 6
Windows Internet Explorer, 421
Winston Churchill High School
    (MD), 138
WisBusiness, 144f
Withey, Annie, 128
Women's Business Enterprise National
    Council, 135
Working Mother, 109
World Bank, 91
WorldCom, Inc., 39, 43, 473
World Is Flat, The (Friedman), 69
World Monuments Fund, 46
World Trade Association (WTO), 73, 79f,
    80f, 81
Wrigley's gum, 369
Wuling Group, 121

X

Xerox Corporation, 139, 290, 345
XTO Energy, 124

Y

Yahoo!, Inc., 8, 50, 96, 130, 271, 421f,
    428, 467
Yankee Candle, 400
Yoplait yogurt, 84
Young Eagles, 44
YouTube, 109, 310, 316, 367,
    400, 459

Z

Zappos, Inc., 309
ZDNet, 431f
Zebco, Inc., 478
Zoom Systems, 378
Zuckerberg, Mark, 139–140. *See also*
    Facebook
Zwahlen, Cyndia, 137f
Zynga, Inc., 486

SUBJECT INDEX

A

absolute and comparative advantage, 69–70
acceptability, of pricing, 350
accessibility, of transportation, 381
accessory equipment, 333
accountability, 195
accounting information, 439–467
  accounting cycle, 447–448
  accounting equation, 448
  activity ratios, 460–461
  balance sheet, 449–452
  in business plan, 499
  company comparison from, 458
  debt-to-owner's-equity ratio, 461–462
  importance of, 441–444
  income statement, 452–455
  investment evaluation from, 457–458
  profitability ratios, 458–459
  short-term financial ratios from,
    459–460
  statement of cash flows, 455–456
  upgrading systems for, 497
  users of, 444–447
accounts payable, as current liabilities, 451
accounts receivable, 450, 482–483
accounts receivable turnover, 460–461
accumulated depreciation, 451
achievement, employee, 276–277
acid rain, 58
acid-test ratio, 460
activity ratios, 460–461
adaptations to products, 339
ad hoc committees, 203
adjourning teams, 292–293
administrative management, 174, 276, 411
advancement, employee, 276
advantage, absolute and comparative,
  69–70
advertising, 383–389
  advertising agencies, 388
  cooperative, 394
  developing campaigns, 385–388
  e-business model for, 428
  false and misleading, 38
  interactive marketing in, 428
  by purpose, 384–385
  sales orientation of, 308
  social and legal considerations in, 389
advisory authority, 198–199
aesthetic modifications to products, 338
affirmative action, 54–55, 263–264
African American markets, 319
African Development Bank (AFDB), 91
Age Discrimination in Employment Act, 263
agents
  in distribution channels, 369–370
  as wholesalers, 372–373
air pollution, 58–59
air transport, 382
alien corporations, 114

all-distance pricing, in telecommunications
  industry, 357
allocator, price as, 348
allowances
  buying, 394
  as discount, 359
  for doubtful accounts, 450
  sales, 452
"alternative" promotions, 400
"American Dream," 4
American Institute of Certified Public
  Accountants (AICPA), 446
Americans with Disabilities Act, 264
analytical processes, 214
analytic skills, of managers, 175
animation technology, 3
annual report, 448
antidumping duties, 73
applications for employment, 250–251
application software, 420
applied research, 218
approaching prospects for sales, 390
appropriation, advertising, 385–386
articles of partnership, 110–111
artificial intelligence (AI), 416
Asia, trade outlook and, 76
Asian Development Bank (ADB), 91
assembly line, 25, 222
assessment centers, employment, 253
assets, in accounting, 448, 450–451
Association of Southeast Asian Nations, 83
attrition, 245
auctions, online, 371
audience, target, 385
audited financial statements, 442–443, 457. See
  also accounting information
auditing, for ISO certification, 228
authority, 177, 195–196, 198–199
autocratic leadership style, 177
automated clearinghouses (ACHs), 478
automatic teller machines (ATMs), 377–378,
  478–479
automatic vending, 377
automation, 221, 231, 417
automobiles, eco-friendly, 35

B

balance of payments, 71, 74
balance of trade, 19, 70, 72
balance sheet, 449–452, 457
banker's acceptance, 479
banking
  bank credit statistic, 19
  drafts in, 86
  electronic, 478–479
  Equator Principles for, 488
  international, 479–480
  multilateral development banks, 91–92
  traditional, 477–478
bankruptcy, 119, 469, 476–477

bar charts, for presentations, 414–415
barter agreements, 24, 88
basic research, 218
basis, for market segmentation, 313
behavior modification, 285
benchmarking, 181
best practices, 181
better business bureaus, 389
bill of lading, 86
board of directors, corporate, 116
bond indenture, 490
bonds, corporate, 489–491
bookkeeping system, double-entry, 448
brainstorming, 179, 203, 292, 416
brand equity, 344, 367
brand extensions, 345–346
branding products, 342–346, 402
brand loyalty, 343–344, 402–403
brand marks, 342
brand names, 342
breakeven quantity, in pricing, 352
broadband access, 428
brokerage e-business model, 428
brokers, as wholesalers, 372–373
budgeting, 385–386, 475
building re-purposing, 369
bundle pricing, 356–357
business, introduction to, 2–33
  business cycle, 20–21
  changing nature of, 4–10
  competition, 21–24
  definition of, 10–12
  economic systems, 12–17
  measuring economic performance, 17–19
  in United States, 24–28
business analysis, of new products, 340
business application software, 419
business buying behavior, 322, 324
business cycle, 20–21, 140
business ethics. See ethics; social responsibility
business models, 426
business plans
  accounting information component, 499
  company and industry components, 161
  exit strategy component, 499
  human resources component, 301
  management team component, 239
  manufacturing component, 239
  marketing plan component, 403
  overview, 99–101
  for small businesses, 142–145
business products, 332, 358–359. See also goods
  and services; products
business reports, 414
business services, 333
business-to-business markets, 310
business-to-business (B2B) model, 427
business-to-consumer (B2C) model,
  427–428
buying allowances, 394
buying behavior, 305, 322–324, 409

"buy one, get one free" (BOGO) multiple-unit pricing, 356
buyouts, 245

C

cafeterias, company, 256
call centers, 185
Canada, trade outlook and, 76
Canadian Free Trade Agreement, 83
candy-printing technology, 407
capacity, 220–221, 223–224
capital, 13, 117, 142
capital budget, 475
capital-intensive technology, 221
capitalism, 13–15, 27
captioned photographs, for publicity, 395
captive pricing, 357
careers
    in accounting, 440, 445–447
    in advertising and marketing, 388
    career coaching, 250
    choosing, 5–6
    in financial management, 473–474
    "green," 196
    in international business, 78
    internships, 137, 144
    in management, 175
    nonspecialized paths for, 278
    in operations management, 213–214
    student business incubators, 108
    telecommuting during, 288
    Web cam interviews, 309
Caribbean Basin Institute (CBI), 84
carriers, in transportation, 381
carrying costs, 427
cash
    budget of, 475
    as current assets, 450
    discounts for, 359
cash flow
    financing for, 470–471
    problems in, 477
    in small business, 138
    statement of, 455–457
catalog selling, 367, 371, 376
category killers, 375
category management, 371
caveat emptor, 47
Central American Free Trade Agreement (CAFTA), 83
centralized government plans, in communism, 17
centralized organizations, 196
certificates of deposit (CDs), 477
certification, ISO, 228
certification, of products, 74
certified management accountants (CMA), 446
certified public accountants (CPA), 446
chain of command, 191–192, 198
chain retailers, 374
channels, distribution, 368–371
charts, organization, 191–192
checks, 477
chief financial officers (CFOs), 473
chief sustainability officer (CSO), 196
child-care services, 256
children, advertising to, 38
choice, consumer right to, 52
Civil Rights Acts, 263
classification of markets, 310
classroom training programs, 258
cleaning up short-term notes, 481
closed corporations, 113
closing sales, in personal selling, 391
cloud computing, 430–431
codes of ethics, 41–42

collaborative learning systems, 417
collaborative workplace culture, 171, 185, 271
collateral, 380, 480, 482
collective bargaining, 84
collective decision making, 278
command economies, 16–17
commercialization of new products, 341
commercial paper, 481–482
commissions, 255
committees and task forces, 203–204
common carriers, in transportation, 381–382
Common Market of the Southern Cone (MERCOSUR), 84
common stock, 115, 485
Commonwealth of Independent States (former USSR), 77, 81, 84
communal culture, 202
communications
    as advertising objective, 385
    ethical issues in, 38
    integrated marketing, 382–383
    in management, 175–176
    organizational height effect on, 197
    in small business, 134
    technology for, 416–417
communism, 16–17, 77
community shopping centers, 378
company policies, 276
comparable worth, 255
comparative advertising, 384
comparative and absolute advantage, 69–70
comparison discounting, 358
comparison of prices, 349
comparison other, in equity theory, 280
compensating balance, for loans, 481
compensation, 253–256
competition
    advertising and, 389
    in business environment, 27
    in concert business, 32
    consumer benefits from, 52
    penetration pricing to reduce, 354
    in premium products, 98
    in product categories, 402
    product life-cycle and, 334–336
    in small business, 141
    social responsibility and, 49
    types of, 21–24
competition-based pricing, 353
component parts, 333
computer-aided design (CAD), 231
computer-aided flexible manufacturing, 213
computer-aided manufacturing (CAM), 231
computer hardware, 420
computer-integrated manufacturing (CIM), 232
computer network, 420
computer viruses, 430
concentrated market segmentation approach, 312–313
concept testing new products, 340
conceptual skills, in management, 7
conceptual skills, of managers, 174
concierge services, 257
conferences, as training programs, 258
confidentiality, 430
conflicts of interest, 38
conglomerate mergers, 123–124
consensus leadership style, 177
consensus management, 238
consultative leadership style, 177
consumer buying behavior, 322–324
consumer confidence, 343
consumer markets, 310
consumer price index (CPI), 18–19
consumer products, 15, 332

consumers
    basic rights of, 51–52
    broadband access of, 428
    consumerism forces, 52–54
    households as, 15
    informed, 8
    mergers and acquisitions and, 123
    promotion methods for, 392
    reduced spending of, 3
    trade barrier effects on, 74–75
content, online, paying for, 358
contingency plans, 169–170
continual reinforcement, 279
continuity of business, 107, 112
continuous process manufacturing system, 232
continuous quality improvement, 181
contract carriers, in transportation, 381–382
controlling, as management function, 171–172
convenience, packaging for, 346
convenience products, 332, 370
convenience showrooms, 374
conversion process, in manufacturing, 214–216
convertible bonds, 490
cookies, to track Internet usage, 430
cooperative advertising, 394
cooperative partnerships, 371
copyrights, 24, 451
core competencies, 168
core time, in flextime systems, 286
corporate bonds, 489–491
corporate charter, 115
corporate raiders, 123
corporate retreats, 274
corporations
    advantages of, 116–117
    disadvantages of, 117–118
    forming, 114–115
    growth of, 122–125
    stock of, 113–114
    structure of, 116
corrective action, 51, 171
correlation analyses, in sales forecasts, 318
cost accounting, 445
cost-based pricing, 351–352
cost/benefit analysis, 415
cost of goods sold, 452–454
costs
    carrying, 427
    delivery, 359
    e-business to reduce, 425–426
    fixed, 352, 364
    flotation, 484
    holding, 225, 379
    insurance, 379
    outsourcing to reduce, 424
    shipping, 225, 306
    stock-out, 225, 379
    storage, 225, 379, 427
    total, 352
    transportation, 381
    variable, 352, 364
    See also price
countertrade, 88
coupons, 392–393, 403
coverage of market, 370–371
CPI (consumer price index), 18–19
credit, 20, 225, 478
credit-card theft, 377
credit unions, 256
cross-functional teams, 200–201, 290–291, 293
cultural diversity, 6, 245–247, 268
culture

collaborative, 171, 185, 271
corporate, 199, 208, 242
employee diversity, 245–247, 268
norms of, 39–40, 74
currency devaluation, 73–74
current assets, in accounting, 450–451
current liabilities, in accounting, 451
current ratio, 460
customary pricing, 357
customer-driven production, 232
customer lifetime value, 306
customer loyalty, 305, 393, 402
customer relationship management (CRM), 417
customer relationships, 303–329
buying behavior, 322–324
classification of markets, 310
departmentalization by, 194
managing, 305–306
marketing concept in, 307–310
marketing information, 318–322
marketing plan for, 316–317
marketing strategies for, 310–316
price and, 364
sales forecasting, 317–318
social networking for, 497
utility value for, 306–307
See also products
customer satisfaction, in quality management, 181
customer service, 218, 257, 298, 424
customer testimonials, 316
customization, 213

D

data
collecting, 412–413
information *versus,* 409–410
processing, 414
storing, 413
updating, 413
database marketing, 320, 382
databases, 410, 412
data mining, 430
"deal-a-day" Web sites, 355
debenture bonds, 490
debit card, 478
debt
long-term, 487–491
national, 3, 20–21
short-term, 480–483
debt capital, 476
debt-to-owner's-equity ratio, 461–462
decentralization, 196
deceptive and misleading advertising, 389
deceptive pricing practices, 358
decision-support systems (DSS), 416
decline stage, in product life-cycle, 335–336
definite price breaks, 357
deflation, 18
delegation, 195–196, 285
deleting products, 338
delivery costs, 359
demand, supply and, 22–23, 348–349
demand-based pricing, 353
democratic leadership style, 177
departmentalization, 193–195
department stores, 374
dependability, of transportation, 381
depreciation, accumulated, 451
depressions, 20, 25, 28, 48
design planning, for production, 219–221
desired behavior, 285
differential pricing, 354–356
differentiated market segmentation approach, 312–313

differentiation, 23, 350, 353
digital advertising agencies, 388
direct channel, 368, 370
directing, as management function, 171
direct investment, international business by, 87
direct marketing, 376–378
direct-response marketing, 376
direct selling, 376
direct-to-consumer prescription advertising, 389
discounts
on business products, 359
on car buying, 409
comparison, 358
"deal-a-day" Web sites for, 355
periodic, 355
purchase, 452
random, 356
sales, 452
discount stores, 374
discretionary income, in buying behavior, 323
discrimination, 54–55, 252, 263
displacement, by technology, 232
disposable income, in buying behavior, 323
dissatisfaction, employee, 276
distributing products, 366–382
channels for, 368–371
in marketing mix, 314–315
physical distribution, 379–382
retailers in, 373–379
supply chain management, 371
wholesalers in, 371–373
See also promoting products
distribution industries, 134
distributors, 372
diversity, cultural, 6, 245–247, 268
dividends, 115, 456, 484, 486
Dodd-Frank Wall Street Reform and Consumer Protection Act, 473
Doha round, of GATT negotiations, 81
domestic corporations, 114
domestic system of production, 24
do-not-call registry, 377
door-to-door selling, 376
door-to-door service, by trucks, 382
double taxation, of corporations, 118
downtown shopping districts, 379
drafts, bank, 86
dual-branded franchises, 152
dual-income families, 286
dual roles, in teams, 293
dumping, protective tariffs against, 73

E

early retirement, 245
earnings per share, 459
earnings statement, 452
Eastern Europe, trade outlook and, 76
e-book readers, 331
e-business, 422–432
future of, 428–432
for M&Ms, 407
models of, 426–428
overview, 25–26
profits from, 424–426
resources for, 422
satisfying needs with, 422–424
eco-friendly cars, 35
e-commerce, 169, 298, 400, 422
economic indicators, 18–19, 170
economic model of social responsibility, 49
economics, 27, 431–432
economies
capitalistic and command, 12–17
developing, 81

measuring performance of, 17–19
service, 26
stimulus programs for, 4
ecotourism, 216
EDI (electronic data interchange) technology, 371
education, salaries and, 5
efficiency, scientific management for, 272
e-learning, for training programs, 257
electronic banking, 478–479
electronic check conversion (ECC), 479
electronic couponing, 403
electronic data interchange (EDI) technology, 371
Electronic Funds Transfer Act, 479
electronic funds transfer (EFT) system, 478–479
electronic job boards, 440
electronic stock exchange, 485
"elevator pitch," 144
e-mail, 416–417, 429
embargos, 73
employee benefits, 7, 256–257
employee-centric approach, 284
employee participation, 181, 227
Employee Retirement Income Security Act, 263
employees, attracting and retaining, 241–269
benefits, 256–257
compensation, 253–256
cultural diversity, 245–247, 268
human resources management overview, 243–244
job analysis, 247–248
legislation on, 261–264
orientation, 253
performance appraisal, 258–261
planning for, 244–245
recruiting, 248–249, 418
selection, 249–253
in small business, 140
training and development, 257–258, 418
employees, motivating, 270–301
behavior modification, 285
employee ownership, 289
empowerment, 288–289, 298
equity theory, 280
expectation theory, 280–281
flextime, 286
goal-setting theory, 281–282
Hawthorne studies on, 274
Herzberg's motivation-hygiene theory, 276–277
Internet privacy of, 430
job enrichment, 284–285
job sharing, 287
management by objectives, 282–284
Maslow's hierarchy of needs, 274–275
motivation defined, 272
part-time work, 286–287
reinforcement theory, 278–280
scientific management, 272–273
teamwork, 289–294
telecommuting, 287–288
Theory X and Theory Y, 277–278
Theory Z, 278
employee stock ownership plans (ESOPs), 289
employee turnover, 208
employment agencies, 249
employment practices, 54–56
empowering employees, 288–289, 298
energy efficiency, 420, 431
English as a second language, 246–247
entrepreneurial leadership style, 177
entrepreneurship
in app development, 418
building re-use in, 369
business knowledge for, 8
corporate culture and, 203

entrepreneurship (*Cont.*)
  "deal-a-day" Web sites for promotion, 355
  as factor of production, 13
  Internet advertising agencies, 26
  motivation in, 285
  See also ownership of business; small businesses
environmental protection, 57–60, 185. *See also* green business practices; sustainability
epidemics, in contingency plans, 170
e-procurement hubs, 371
Equal Employment Opportunity Commission (EEOC), 263
Equal Pay Act, 262
Equator Principles, 488
equilibrium price, 23, 348–349
equipment, 333, 455
equipment breakdown, 224
equity capital, 476
equity financing sources, 483–487
equity theory of motivation, 280
esteem needs, of employees, 275
ethics, 34–66
  behavioral factors affecting, 38–40
  business ethics defined, 36
  of cloud computing, 431
  of ecotourism, 216
  encouraging, 40–44
  Equator Principles, 488
  financial information on foreign firms, 443
  Internet issues in, 429–430
  issues in, 36–38
  of job interviews, 252
  target marketing, 320
  See also social responsibility
Eurofactories, 87
Europe, trade outlook and, 76
European Bank for Reconstruction and Development, 92
European Commission, 443
European Economic Area (EEA), 82
European Union (EU), 81–82, 443
evaluating advertising effectiveness, 387–388
event sponsorships, 394
everyday low prices (EDLPs), 357
exclusive distribution, 370
executing advertising campaigns, 387
executive information systems (EIS), 416
exercise rooms, 256
exit strategy, 499
expansion periods, 21
expectation theory of motivation, 280–281
expenses, e-business to reduce, 425–426
expert systems, 416
export-import merchant, 85
exporting
  assistance for, 90
  entering international business by, 85–87
  overview, 70–71
  U.S. economy and, 77, 79
express warranty, 347
extensions to products, 338
external data sources, 413
external opportunities and threats, 168
external recruiting, 249
extinction, in behavior modification, 279

F

facilities planning, in production, 221–222
factoring accounts receivable, 482–483
factors of production, 13
factory system of manufacturing, 25
failure of products, 341
Fair Labor Standards Act, 262

fairness and honesty, 37. *See also* ethics
Fair Packaging and Labeling Act, 347
family branding, 345
family-owned businesses, 97
family packaging, 346
fast-food industry, franchising in, 151
feature articles, for publicity, 395
federal deficit, 21
federal income taxes, 455
Federal Trade Commission (FTC), 38–39, 154, 320, 358, 377, 389
feedback interviews, in performance appraisal, 260–261
female-dominated jobs, 255
field order takers, salespersons as, 390
financial accounting, 445
Financial Accounting Standards Board (FASB), 442
financial leverage, 487
financial management, 173, 468–500
  banking services for, 477–478
  credit transactions for, 478
  description of, 470–474
  electronic banking for, 478–479
  equity financing sources, 483–487
  international banking for, 479–480
  long-term debt sources, 487–491
  planning in, 474–477
  short-term debt sources, 480–483
financial managers, 411
financial plan, 474–476
financial ratios, 458–460
financial resources, 10–11, 165
financial security, of employees, 272
financial statements, 442–443, 448, 457. *See also* accounting information
financing, 90–92, 456
finished-goods inventory, 225
fires, in contingency plans, 170
firing employees, 245
first-line management, 173
fiscal policies, of Federal Reserve, 20
fixed assets, 451
fixed costs, 352, 364
fixed-position layout, for production, 223
flat organizations, 197–198
flexible employee benefit plans, 257
flexible manufacturing systems (FMS), 232
flextime, 286
floods, in contingency plans, 170
floor, price, 351
flotation costs, of IPOs, 484
FOB destination pricing, 359
FOB origin pricing, 359
focus, of conversion process, 215
following up, in personal selling, 391
follow-up, in production, 226
forecasting, 244–245, 317–318
foreclosures, of homes, 3, 20
foreign corporations, 114
foreign-exchange controls, 73
formal leadership, 177
forming effective teams, 292
form utility, 214, 306–307
401k retirement plans, 289, 300
fragmented culture, 202
franchising
  example of, 104, 497
  growth of, 151–155
  as limited monopolies, 24
  overview, 149–151
fraud, on Internet, 430
free enterprise system, 4
free-market economy, 14, 16
free shipping, 306
free trade, 67

freight charges, 359
freight forwarders, in transportation, 381
"French pot" method for manufacturing, 97
frequency, of transportation, 381
frequent-flier programs, 393
frequent-user incentives, 393–394
full-service wholesalers, 372
function, departmentalization by, 193
functional authority, 198–199
functional middlemen, 368–369, 372
functional modifications to products, 338
funds, sources of, 475–476. *See also* financial management

G

gain sharing, 255
GATT (General Agreement on Tariffs and Trade), 79–81
GDP (gross domestic product), 18–20, 75
general expenses, 455
general journal, 447–448
general ledger, 448
generally accepted accounting principles (GAAPs), 442, 457–458
general-merchandise wholesalers, 372
general partners, 109
generic brands, 343
generic products, 343
generic terms, in brand names, 345
geographic pricing strategies, 359
globalization, 67–101
  absolute and comparative advantage, 69–70
  accounting standards and, 442–443
  competition growth from, 27
  e-business and, 431–432
  entering international business, 84–89
  exporting and importing, 70–71, 90
  financing international business, 90–92
  productivity importance in, 17
  trade agreements, 79–84
  trade restrictions, 71–75
  U.S. competing in, 212–213
  world trade outlook, 76–79
goals and objectives in planning, 167–168
goal-setting theory of motivation, 281–282
goods and services, 210–239
  conversion process, 214–216
  innovations in, 218–219
  operations control, 224–229
  planning production of, 219–224
  production defined, 212–214
  service importance, 216–218
  technology for productivity, 229–232
  See also distributing products; promoting products
goodwill, 385, 451
government
  in Adam Smith's capitalism, 14–15
  on advertising, 389
  in command economies, 16–17
  consumerism legislation of, 53
  corporate regulation by, 118
  employment legislation of, 261–264
  environmental protection legislation of, 57
  ethical behavior encouraged by, 40–41
  information sources from, 413
  regulatory impact on productivity, 230
  services of, 16
  social responsibility legislation of, 48–49
government accounting, 445
governmental markets, 310
"grapevine," 204
graphs, for presentations, 414–415
Great Depression, 25, 28, 48
greed, accounting practices and, 442

"green" business practices
    career paths and, 196
    cloud computing, 431
    eco-friendly cars, 35, 65
    in information technology, 420
    in production, 211, 213
    for small business, 142
"greenwashing," 39
gross domestic product (GDP), 18–20, 75
gross profit, 454
gross sales, 452
groupware, 416
growth, employee, 276
growth stage, in product life-cycle, 335

H

hard-core unemployed, 55–56
Hawthorne studies of motivation, 274
hazardous wastes, 60
healthcare industry, 486
Herzberg's motivation-hygiene theory, 276–277,
    284
high-definition television, 219
Hispanic markets, 319
holding costs, 225, 379
holiday pay, 256
homes, foreclosures of, 3, 20
horizon, planning, 223
horizontal mergers, 123–124
hostile takeovers, 122–123
hourly wages, 255
households, in capitalism, 15
housing starts, 19
http (HyperText Transfer Protocol), 421
human factors, in motivating employees, 274
human relations movement, 274, 277
human resources, 10–11, 165, 221. See also
    employees
human resources management, 173, 243–244, 411
hygiene factors, 276

I

identity theft, 377, 478
imitation products, 339
immediate-response advertising, 384
implementation, development and, 218
implied control mechanisms, 278
import duties, 72
Import-Export Bank of the United States, 91
importing, 70–71, 79
incentive payments, 255
incentives, sales, 392–393
income, distribution of, 16. See also taxes
income statement, 452–455, 457
indenture, bond, 490
independent marketing intermediaries, 370
independent retailers, 373
in-depth interviews, for marketing research, 319
individual branding, 345
industrial markets, 310
Industrial Revolution, 25
industry associations, 384, 389
inflation, 18–19
informal leadership, 177
informal organization, 204
information resources, 406–438
    business need for, 10–11, 165–166
    consumer right to, 52
    e-business, 422–432
        future of, 428–432
        models of, 426–428
        profits from, 424–426
        resources for, 422
        satisfying needs with, 422–424

Internet to obtain, 420–422
    management information systems, 410–415
    marketing, 318–322
    productivity improvement with, 415–419
    risk reduction with, 408–410
information society, 420
information technology (IT), 410, 420
infringement on brands, 345
innovation
    corporate culture of, 203
    in goods and services, 213, 218–219
    matrix structure and, 201
    in products, 339
input-to-output ratio, 280
inside order takers, salespersons as, 390
inspection, 227
Institute of Management Accountants, 446
institutional advertising, 385
institutional investors, 487
institutional markets, 310
insurance, syndicates in, 122
insurance costs, 379
intangible assets, 451
integrated marketing communications, 382–383
integrated software, 419
intensive distribution, 370
interactive marketing, 428
Inter-American Development Bank (IDB), 91
interest expense, 455
interest rate, prime, 19
intermediaries, packaging for, 347. See also
    marketing intermediaries
intermittent process manufacturing systems, 232
internal data sources, 412
internal recruiting, 249
internal relationships, 175
International Accounting Standards Board
    (IASB), 442
international banking, 479–480
international business, 67–101
    absolute and comparative advantage, 69–70
    entering, 84–89
    exporting and importing, 70–71, 90
    financing, 90–92
    franchising for, 154
    restrictions to, 71–75
    trade agreements, 79–84
    world trade outlook, 76–79
International Development Association
    (IDA), 91
International Financial Reporting Standards
    Board (IFRS), 442
International Monetary Fund (IMF), 76, 92
Internet
    advertising on, 386–387
    e-commerce on, 400
    e-learning training programs on, 257
    information resources on, 420–422
    marketing collaboration on, 344
    marketing research on, 321
    price comparison on, 349
    social responsibility and, 49
    stockholders voting on, 115
    strategic planning affected by, 169
    See also e-business
internships, 137, 144
interpersonal relationships, 276
interpersonal skills, in management, 7
interpersonal skills, of managers, 175–176
interviews
    employment, 251–253
    for marketing research, 319
    on-campus, 440
    on Web cam, 309
intranets, 321, 420

introduction stage, in product life-cycle,
    334–335
invasion of privacy, 430
inventory
    business loans for, 477
    cash flow and, 466
    control of, 225–226
    as current assets, 450
    data updates on, 413
    inventory turnover ratio, 461
    loans secured by, 482
    management of, 379
    reducing, 371
investment banking firm, 484
investments
    cash flows from, 456
    evaluation of, 457–458
    informed investors, 8
    in partnerships, 112
"invisible hand," in capitalism, 13
involuntary layoffs, 245
involvement, sense of, 274
ISO 9000 and 14000, 227–228

J

Japan, trade outlook and, 76
job analysis, 247–248
jobbers, 372
job boards, electronic, 440
job descriptions, 247
job design, 192–193
job enlargement, 284
job enrichment, 284–285
job evaluation, 254
job redesign, 284
job rotation, 193
job-search Web sites, 6
job security, 276
job sharing, 287, 440
job specifications, 247
joint ventures, 87, 121–122
journalizing, in accounting cycle, 447
judgmental performance appraisal, 260
junk e-mail, 429
just-in-time inventory system (JIT), 225–226

K

Kennedy round, of GATT negotiations, 80
key industries, in socialism, 16
knowledge management (KM), 410

L

labeling products, 74, 347
labor, 13, 424. See also employees
laboratory testing services, for ISO
    certification, 228
labor-intensive technology, 221
Labor-Management Relations Act, 261–262
laissez-faire, 14, 300
LAN (local area network), 420–421
land, as factor of production, 13
landfills, 59
land pollution, 59–60
Latin America, trade outlook and, 76
lattice management structure, 289
lawsuits, consumer, 51
layoffs, 223–224, 245
leadership, 171, 176–178, 238
lean manufacturing, 231
legal issues, 389, 429–430. See also government
legal monopolies, 24
legislation. See government
letters of credit, 86, 479

liabilities
  in accounting, 448, 451–452
  in corporations, 116–117
  in partnerships, 112
  in sole proprietorships, 107
licensing, 24, 84–85, 104
life-cycle of products, 219, 333–336
lifestyle shopping centers, 378
lifetime employment, 278
lifetime value customers, 306
limited liability companies, 104, 119–120
limited liability partnerships (LLP), 112
limited-line retailers, 375
limited-line wholesalers, 372
limited monopolies, 24
limited partners, 109
line-and-staff structure for organizations, 198–199
line authority, 198
line managers, 198, 244
line of credit, 477
line of products versus product mix, 336–337
line structure for organizations, 198
linking, integrated software for, 419
liquidity, of assets, 450
load flexibility, of transportation, 381
loans
  business, 477–478, 481
  compensating balance for, 481
  for inventory, 477
  long-term, 478, 489
  secured by inventory, 482
  short-term, 477
  unsecured bank, 481
location, departmentalization by, 194
log-file records, for monitoring Internet
    usage, 430
long-term business loans, 478
long-term debt sources, 487–491
long-term financing sources, 471–472
long-term liabilities, in accounting, 451
losses, 11
low-wage workers, 213
lump-sum salary increases, 256

M

macroeconomics, 12
magnitude, of conversion process, 215
major equipment, 333
malpractice, 112
malware, on Internet, 430
management, 163–187
  accounting information for, 444
  corporate specialization in, 117
  of customer relationships, 305–306
  decision making in, 178–180
  definition, 165–166
  functions of, 166–172
  human resources, 243–244
  leadership versus, 176–178
  operations, 212
  partnership disagreements on, 112
  performance enhancement by, 238
  sales, 391
  skills for, 7–8, 174–176
  in small business, 138
  in sole proprietorships, 108
  span of, 197–198
  supply chain, 371
  total quality, 181–182
  types of, 172–174
  See also employees; financial management
management by objectives, 282–284
management development, 257
management information systems (MIS),
    410–415, 497

managerial accounting, 445
manufacturer brand, 342
manufacturer's agents, 373
manufacturing
  as businesses type, 10
  factory system of, 25
  "French pot" method for, 97
  wholesaler services to, 372
  See also goods and services
margins, target, 364
marketable securities, as current assets, 450
market capitalization, 113
market coverage, 370–371
market demand, 223
market economy, 14
marketing
  in business plans, 403
  direct, 376–378
  interactive, 428
  management of, 173, 220, 409, 411
  See also customer relationships
marketing communications, 382–383
marketing information systems, 318
marketing intermediaries
  agents as independent, 370
  discounts to, 359
  overview, 368
  resellers, 10
  retailers, 373–379
  wholesalers, 371–373
marketing mix, 310, 314–316
marketing research
  on car buying, 409
  description of, 318–320
  production affected by, 212
  surveys for, 401
market price, 23
market segmentation, 311–314
market share
  competition-based pricing for, 353
  line extensions for, 338
  penetration pricing for, 354
  pricing for, 23, 351
markup, 351, 364
Maslow's hierarchy of needs, 274–275
mass-media advertising, 382
mass production, 213–214
material resources, 10–11, 165
materials handling, 380
materials requirements planning (MRP), 225
matrix structure for organizations, 200–201
maturity date of corporate bonds, 490
maturity stage, in product life-cycle, 335–336
media plan, advertising, 386
Medicare, 37
mega-mergers, 123
members-only warehouse club stores, 375
mercenary culture, 202
merchandise inventory, as current assets, 450
merchant middlemen, 368
merchant wholesalers, 372
MERCOSUR (Common Market of the Southern
    Cone), 84
mergers and acquisitions, 122–124
merit pay, 255
message, advertising, 386
Mexico, trade outlook and, 76
microeconomics, 12
middle management, 172–173
middlemen, 359, 368–369. See also marketing
    intermediaries
minority groups, 54
minority-owned companies, 4, 146–148, 151
"missing middle" market segment, 319
mission, of organization, 167
missionary salespersons, 390

mix, promotion, 383
mixed economy, 14
mixed interviews, in performance appraisal, 261
"mobile" Web sites, 421
modifications to products, 337–338
monetary policies, of Federal Reserve, 20
monopolies, 24
monopolisitic competition, 23
morale, 201, 272
mortgage bonds, 490
mortgage lending, subprime, 76
mortgage payable, as long-term liability, 451
most-favored-nation status (MFN), 79
motivation, 136, 171, 276. See also employees
multilateral development banks, 91–92
multinational enterprises, 88–89. See also
    international business
multinational firms, 442
multiple distribution channels, 370
multiple-unit packaging, 346
multiple-unit pricing, 356
multisupplier online catalogs, 371

N

NASDAQ stock exchange, 37, 485
National Association of Colleges and Employers,
    445
national debt, 3, 20, 21
national do-not-call registry, 377
national income, 19
National Labor Relations Act, 261–262
national security, 74
National Trade Data Bank, 96
natural monopolies, 24
natural resources, 13
needs, 10–11, 274
negative reinforcement, 279
negligence, 112
negotiable instruments. See financial
    management
negotiated pricing, 355
neighborhood shopping centers, 378
net income, 455
net loss, 455
net sales, 453
networked culture, 202
networking, 6
network structure for organizations, 201
net worth, 449
new-product pricing, 354
news releases, for publicity, 395
New York Stock Exchange (NYSE), 469, 485
noise pollution, 60
nonfood products, sampling, 393
not-for-profit accounting, 445
nonparticipant roles, in teams, 293
non-price competition, 349
nonspecialized career paths, 278
nonstore selling, 376–378
nontariff barriers to trade, 73
non-union companies, 301
norming, in effective teams, 292
North American Free Trade Agreement (NAFTA),
    83, 96
notes payable, as current liabilities, 451
notes receivable, as current assets, 450
not-for-profit corporations, 5, 120–121

O

objections, in personal selling, 391
objective performance appraisal, 260
objectives
  management by, 282–284
  in planning, 167–168

Occupational Safety and Health Act (OSHA), 261, 263
odd-number pricing, 356
officers, corporate, 116
off-peak pricing, 355
off-price retailers, 375
off-shore oil drilling, 230
off-the-shelf materials, 364
oligopolistic competition, 23
one-store operators, 373
ongoing costs, of IPOs, 484
online content, paying for, 358
online information services, for marketing, 321
online "redlining," 320
online retailing, 376–377
online selling, 367
online shopping malls, 425
online videos, in marketing mix, 316
on-the-job coaching, 285
on-the-job training programs, 258
open-air configuration, at lifestyle shopping centers, 378
open corporations, 114
operating expenses, 455
operations
    cash flows from, 455–456
    control of, 224–229
    management of, 173, 212–214, 411
    plans for, 169–170
"opportunity," ethics affected by, 40
optimization, 168
order getters, salespersons as, 389
order processing, 379–380
order takers, salespersons as, 390
organizational height, 197
Organization for Economic Cooperation and Development (OECD), 84
Organization of Petroleum Exporting Countries, 84
organizations, business, 188–209
    committees and task forces in, 203–204
    corporate culture for, 201–203, 208
    decentralization in, 196
    definition, 190–192
    delegation in, 195–196
    departmentalization in, 193–195
    ethics and, 37–38
    informal, 204
    job design in, 192–193
    line-and-staff structure for, 198–199
    line structure for, 198
    management span in, 197–198
    matrix structure for, 200–201
    network structure for, 201
organizing, as management function, 170–171
orientation programs, for employees, 253
out-of-stock situations, 371
output quotas, 273
outside order takers, salespersons as, 390
outsourcing, 213, 422, 424
over-the-counter (OTC) stock market, 484–485
overtime, 255
owner's equity, 448–449, 452
ownership of business, 103–130
    corporations
        advantages, 116–117
        disadvantages, 117–118
        forming, 114–115
        growth of, 122–125
        stock of, 113–114
        structure of, 116
    by employees, 289
    joint ventures, 121–122
    limited liability companies, 119–120
    not-for-profit corporations, 120–121
    partnership, 108–112

S-corporations, 119
sole proprietorship, 105–108
syndicates, 122

P

Pacific Rim, trading in, 84
packaging, 346–347
pandemics, in contingency plans, 170
participative decision making, in Theory Z firms, 278
participative leadership style, 177
partnerships, 108–112
part-time work, 286–287
"party plan" selling, 376
passbook savings accounts, 477
pass-through taxation, 119
patents, 24, 133, 451
pay, 276. See also employees
pay-for-performance, 255
pay for time not worked, as employee benefit, 256
pay-per-view e-business model, 428
peak period, in economy, 20
peer-to-peer (P2P) business model, 428
penetration pricing, 354
pensions, 256
perfect competition, 21–23
performance
    appraisals of, 258–261
    of effective teams, 292
    measuring, 17–19, 300
    standards setting, 171
periodic discounting, 355
perishable products, 369
perpetual life, of corporations, 117
personal budget, 452
personal selling, 384, 389–391
personnel management, 243. See also employees
pharmaceutical industry, direct-to-consumer advertising of, 389
photographs, for publicity, 395
physical distribution, 379–382
physiological needs, of employees, 274
piece-rate system, 273–274
pie charts, for presentations, 414–415
piggyback transportation, 382
pipeline transport, 382
place utility, 306–307
planned shopping centers, 378
planning
    as management function, 167–170
    marketing, 316–317
    production, 219–224
plant layout, for production, 222
plastic packaging material, 347
platform, advertising, 385
point-of-purchase displays, 394
point-of-sale (POS) terminals, 479
"poison pills," to prevent acquisition, 123
pollution
    air, 58–59
    land, 59–60
    noise, 60
    overview, 56
    water, 57–58
    See also green business practices
Ponzi schemes, 37
"porcupine provisions," to prevent acquisition, 123
positive reinforcement, 279
possession utility, 306–307
power-grid improvements, 486
power outages, in contingency plans, 170
power-saving technology, 420, 431
PPI (producer price index), 19

preferred stock, 115, 485
"preferred" suppliers, 427
premium pricing, 350, 357
premiums, as product promotion, 393
premiums plus sticker prices, 353
prepaid expenses, as current assets, 450
prescription advertising, direct-to-consumer, 389
presenting information, 390–391, 414–415
press conferences, for publicity, 395
prestigious products, 370
price, 348–359
    of business products, 358–359
    buyer behavior and, 409
    competition factors in, 52, 349–350
    equilibrium or market, 23
    in marketing mix, 314–315
    methods of, 351–353
    objectives in, 350–351
    off-price retailers, 375
    in oligopolies, 23
    packaging for special, 346
    strategies for, 353–358
    supplier comparison of, 224
    supply and demand impact, 348–349
    trade barriers and, 75
price-conscious customers, 364
price leaders, 358
price lining, 357
primary-demand advertising, 384
primary market, initial public offering (IPO) for, 484
prime interest rate, 19, 481
privacy, 320, 430
private accountants, 446
private brand, 342–343
private carriers, in transportation, 381–382
private employment agencies, 249
private-equity firms, 129
private placements, 487
private warehouse, 380
problem-recognition stage, in buying decisions, 322
problem-solving approach, in performance appraisal, 261
problem-solving teams, 290
process layout, for production, 222
process materials, 333
producer markets, 310
producer price index (PPI), 19
producer-to-agent middleman-to-business user channel, 370
producer-to-agent-to-wholesaler-to-retailer-to-consumer channel, 369
producer-to-business user channel, 370
producer-to-consumer channel, 368
producer-to-retailer-to-consumer channel, 369
producer-to-wholesaler-to-retailer-to-consumer channel, 369
product demonstrations, 316, 391
product design, 220
product development, 340
product differentiation, 23
product extensions, 219
production, 13, 135, 222. See also goods and services; products
productivity
    globalization and, 17
    information resources to improve, 415–419
    management consultants on, 97
    matrix structure increases in, 201
    "soldiering" versus, 272
    technology for, 229–232, 371
    telecommuting and, 287
product layout, for production, 222
product life-cycle, 219, 333–336

product-line pricing, 357–358
product lines, 219–220
products, 330–365
  branding, 342–346
  classification of, 332–333
  departmentalization by, 193–194
  differentiation of, 350
  labeling, 347
  life-cycle of, 333–336
  in marketing mix, 314–315
  mix of, 336–342
    deleting products from, 338
    developing new products for, 339–341
    extensions to, 338
    failure of products in, 341
    line *versus*, 336–337
    modifications to, 337–338
  packaging, 346–347
  pricing, 348–359
    business products, 358–359
    competition factors in, 349–350
    methods of, 351–353
    objectives in, 350–351
    strategies for, 353–358
    supply and demand impact, 348–349
  sampling, 393
  speculative production of, 471
  See also distributing products; goods and
    services; price; promoting products
product testing, 74
professional development, 175
Professional Oversight Board (UK), 443
profitability ratios, 458–459
profit margin, 459
profits
  corporate, 19
  from customer relationship management, 305
  e-business, 424–426
  financial planning for, 495
  "giving away," 351
  gross, 454
  as household income, 15
  on income statement, 452
  overview, 11–12
  in partnerships, 111
  pricing to maximize, 350–351
  in sole proprietorships, 106
profit-sharing, 256, 282, 300
project managers, 200
promissory notes, 481
promoting products, 382–395
  advertising, 384–389
  "deal-a-day" Web sites for, 355
  example of, 400
  integrated marketing communications, 382–383
  in marketing mix, 314–315
  overview, 383–384
  packaging for, 346–347
  personal selling, 389–391
  public relations, 394–395
  sales promotion, 358, 392–394
  special-event pricing for, 358
  See also distributing products
promotion from within company, 249
proprietary accounting information, 444
prospecting for sales, 390
protective tariffs, 73
prototyping, 237, 340
proxy, to vote stock, 115, 123
psychological factors, in buying behavior, 323
psychological pricing, 356–357
public accountants, 446
public employment agencies, 249
publicity, 395
public relations, 384, 394–395
public utilities, 24

public warehouses, 380, 482
punishment, 279
purchase discounts, 452
purchasing, 224–225
pure competition, 21–23

Q
qualified individual with a disability, in ADA, 264
quality
  as brand builder, 402
  modifications to products for, 338
  price and, 350
  supplier comparison of, 225
quality circles, 227
quality control, 226–227
quantity discounts, 359
quick ratio, 460
quotas, 54–55, 73, 273

R
railroads, 382
random discounting, 356
rating scales, in performance appraisal, 260
raw materials, 333
raw-materials inventory, 225
reasonable accommodation for disabilities, in
    ADA, 264
rebates, 392–393
recessions
  in business cycle, 20–21
  financial management in, 472
  sales revenue in, 466
  small business affected by, 140, 149
  social responsibility and, 58
  trade outlook and, 76
recognition, employee, 272, 276–277
recovery periods, 21
recruiting employees, 248–249, 418
recycling packaging material, 347
"redlining," 320
reference interest rate, 481
references, for employment, 252
refinements to products, 219, 339
regional shopping centers, 379
registered corporate bonds, 490
registration of brands, 344–345
reinforcement theory of motivation, 278–280
reinvestment, 486
relationship marketing, 305
reliability of suppliers, 225, 228
reminder advertising, 384
renewable energy, 486
reordering inventory, 413
replacement chart, for HRM forecasting, 244
re-purposing buildings, 369
reputation, advertising to enhance, 384
research and development (R&D), 218, 340
resellers, 310, 392, 394
resource owners, households as, 15
responsibility, delegation of, 195
responsibility, employee, 276
restructuring, 198
résumés, 250
retailers
  cooperative advertising for, 394
  description of, 367, 369
  markup of, 351
  nonstore selling, 376–378
  packaging for, 347
  shopping centers, 378–379
  short-term financing needs of, 471
  as small businesses, 134
  store types, 373–375
  wholesaler services to, 372

retained earnings, 452, 486–487
retaliation, to trade barriers, 74
retirement, 245, 256, 289, 300
return on investment (ROI), pricing for, 351
return on owner's equity, 459
return on sales ratio, 459
returns, sales, 452
revenue stream, 424
revenue tariffs, 73
reverse discrimination, 55
revolving credit agreement, 477–478
risk
  as business plan component, 499
  default, 122
  profit as payment for, 12
  reducing, 408–410
  for small business, 142
risk-return ratio, 473
robotics, 231
role-playing, as training programs, 258
routing of materials, 226

S
safety, 51, 261, 263, 274
salaries, 255–256
salaries payable, as current liabilities, 451
sales agents, 373
sales force automation, 417
sales forces, agents *versus*, 369
sales forecasting, 317–318
sales managers, 391
sales promotion, 384, 392–394
sales revenue
  as advertising objective, 385
  commissions on, 255
  e-business, 424–425
  goods and services exchanged for, 15
  personal selling, 389–391
  profit relationship to, 11
  recession and, 466
  as source of funds, 475–476
  technology to assist, 417–418
samples, 393
Sarbanes-Oxley Act of 2002, 40–41, 443
satisfaction, employee, 274, 276
"satisficing," 180
savings accounts, 477
scam artists, 478
scandals, accounting, 441–442
scarcity, 12
scheduling, 226
scientific management, 272–273, 277
SCORE (Service Corps of Retired
    Executives), 109
S-corporations, 119
screening new products, 340
search engines, 33, 421
seasonal discounts, 359
seasonal products, 369
seasonal promotions, 358
secondary information, for marketing, 321
secondary market, for stock, 484–485
secondary-market pricing, 355
Securities and Exchange Commission (SEC), 43,
    443, 484
securities exchange, 485
segmentation of markets, 311–314
selection, of employees, 249–253
selective-demand advertising, 384–385
selective distribution, 370
self-actualization needs, of employees, 275
self-appraisal, in performance appraisal, 261
self-managed work teams, 290–291
selling expenses, 455
selling points, in advertising, 385